W9-ANB-746

2nd edition

ENCYCLOPEDIA OF
PHILOSOPHY

5

volume

2nd edition

ENCYCLOPEDIA OF

PHILOSOPHY

DONALD M. BORCHERT

Editor in Chief

MACMILLAN REFERENCE USA
An imprint of Thomson Gale, a part of The Thomson Corporation

Detroit • New York • San Francisco • San Diego • New Haven, Conn. • Waterville, Maine • London • Munich

Encyclopedia of Philosophy, Second Edition

Donald M. Borchert, Editor in Chief

© 2006 Thomson Gale, a part of the Thomson Corporation.

Thomson, Star Logo and Macmillan Reference USA are trademarks and Gale is a registered trademark used herein under license.

For more information, contact
Macmillan Reference USA
An imprint of Thomson Gale
27500 Drake Rd.
Farmington Hills, MI 48331-3535
Or you can visit our internet site at
http://www.gale.com

For permission to use material from this product, submit your request via Web at http://www.gale-edit.com/permissions, or you may download our Permissions Request form and submit your request by fax or mail to:

Permissions
Thomson Gale
27500 Drake Rd.
Farmington Hills, MI 48331-3535
Permissions Hotline:
248-699-8006 or 800-877-4253 ext. 8006
Fax: 248-699-8074 or 800-762-4058

Since this page cannot legibly accommodate all copyright notices, the acknowledgments constitute an extension of the copyright notice.

While every effort has been made to ensure the reliability of the information presented in this publication, Thomson Gale does not guarantee the accuracy of the data contained herein. Thomson Gale accepts no payment for listing; and inclusion in the publication of any organization, agency, institution, publication, service, or individual does not imply endorsement of the editors or publisher. Errors brought to the attention of the publisher and verified to the satisfaction of the publisher will be corrected in future editions.

LIBRARY OF CONGRESS CATALOGING-IN-PUBLICATION DATA

Encyclopedia of philosophy / Donald M. Borchert, editor in chief.—2nd ed.
    p. cm.
      Includes bibliographical references and index.
      ISBN 0-02-865780-2 (set hardcover : alk. paper)—
      ISBN 0-02-865781-0 (vol 1)—ISBN 0-02-865782-9 (vol 2)—
      ISBN 0-02-865783-7 (vol 3)—ISBN 0-02-865784-5 (vol 4)—
      ISBN 0-02-865785-3 (vol 5)—ISBN 0-02-865786-1 (vol 6)—
      ISBN 0-02-865787-X (vol 7)—ISBN 0-02-865788-8 (vol 8)—
      ISBN 0-02-865789-6 (vol 9)—ISBN 0-02-865790-X (vol 10)
      1. Philosophy–Encyclopedias. I. Borchert, Donald M., 1934-

B51.E53 2005
103–dc22

      2005018573

This title is also available as an e-book.
ISBN 0-02-866072-2
Contact your Thomson Gale representative for ordering information.

Printed in the United States of America
10 9 8 7 6 5 4 3 2 1

contents

volume 1

PREFACE TO 2ND EDITION

INTRODUCTION TO 1ST EDITION

LIST OF CONTRIBUTORS

LIST OF ARTICLES

ENCYCLOPEDIA OF
PHILOSOPHY

2nd edition

Abbagnano–Byzantine Philosophy

volume 2
Cabanis–Destutt de Tracy

volume 3
Determinables–Fuzzy Logic

volume 4
Gadamer–Just War Theory

volume 5
Kabbalah–Marxist Philosophy

volume 6
Masaryk–Nussbaum

volume 7
Oakeshott–Presupposition

volume 8
Price–Sextus Empiricus

volume 9
Shaftesbury–Zubiri

volume 10

APPENDIX: ADDITIONAL ARTICLES

THEMATIC OUTLINE

BIBLIOGRAPHIES

INDEX

KABBALAH

Kabbalah (literally "tradition") is used both as a general name for Jewish mysticism and as the specific designation for its major medieval variety. Mystical awareness is to be found in the biblical and rabbinic tradition and had literary expression in some of the prophetic writings, psalms, and apocalypses. More characteristically, however, what is referred to as Kabbalah is a type of occult theosophical formulation of the doctrines of the Jewish religion, particularly those concerned with creation, revelation, and redemption. This occult system structures and, in part, fossilizes individual intuitions of divine reality in terms of the culture in which it arose. Typically, the purpose of the complicated structuring of these formulated intuitions is to supply a focus in contemplation by which the Kabbalist can recover the untarnished brightness of direct mystical awareness.

Besides the sources of Kabbalah in the doctrines and literature of the Jewish tradition, a wide variety of other sources has been noted, which have introduced elements from the various cultures with which the Jewish people have come in contact in their dispersion. Among these influences should be included some Persian elements, both Parsi and Zoroastrian, and Neo-Platonic and Neo-

Pythagorean elements which entered during the Hellenistic period; Christian influences and Gnostic themes added at a somewhat later time; and borrowings from Muslim sectarianism after the emergence of Islam. This mixture of elements explains the difficulty that scholars have found in disentangling the sources of Kabbalah. It should be said, however, that the pursuit of sources has less relevance here than it may have for other subjects, because what is essential is not the materials out of which the Kabbalistic theosophical system was created, but rather the use that was made of the materials.

MAJOR DOCTRINES

CREATION. All Jewish mysticism has seen the need for reinterpretation of the literal account of creation given in the book of Genesis. As it stands, the account does not sufficiently emphasize the transcendence of God. God is too close to humankind and the world to be the Supreme Mystery that the mystical temper insists He must be. The reinterpretation has generally taken form as a demiurgic theory. In such a theory, God Himself, the Boundless, the Infinite, the Transcendent, did not perform the material act of creating the world. This was the work of a lesser spirit, or demiurge, who was brought into existence by God in order to do this specific job. As the conception of

God's transcendence developed, one demiurge seemed insufficient to express the sense of awesome distance between divinity and the material world. The remoteness of God from the world was heightened, therefore, by adding other intermediaries and thus forming a chain from God to matter whose links were of increasing materiality.

A second problem in the biblical account of creation concerns matter. If we accept God as infinite, all must be contained in Him. Where, then, is there a place for matter outside of God? This issue was finally resolved by a theory that combined the idea of God's voluntary self-contraction with the concept of emanation. In this account, God, prior to creation, was actually infinite. To make room for creation, however, He voluntarily contracted or limited Himself. Some excess of spiritual substance overflowed into the space from which God had removed Himself, and this excess, or emanation, provided both the demiurgic intermediaries described above and the matter out of which the world was created. Because all substance is thus ultimately an overflowing of God's substance, Kabbalah is a pantheistic doctrine. The completed series of emanations served the additional purpose of providing the road by which humanity's aspiring spirit might reach the heights of divinity; thus, it served both as the mechanism of creation and as the "itinerary of the mind to God" (to borrow an expression from St. Bonaventure).

REVELATION. After the first destruction of the Temple at Jerusalem, and even more after its second destruction, the Scriptures served as a focus for the religious devotion of the Jews. Their state was no more; their cultus was no more; all that was left to them was their belief in God and His Word. For the continuance of the Jewish religion, it came to seem necessary that not only the content of revelation, but even its physical form, should be considered sacrosanct and unchangeable. In all types of Judaism this regard for the letter of Scripture made necessary the development of exegetic techniques for raising the level of significance of much that is trivial in the Scriptures. For the mystics the problem was particularly difficult, because the level on which they had to interpret revelation to make it serve their purpose was highly symbolical. To make this reinterpretation possible, the Kabbalists developed letter and number symbolisms of great variety and complexity.

REDEMPTION. The Kabbalists maintained and even intensified the traditional Jewish view of redemption. In the Kabbalistic view salvation of the individual was little considered; it entered only as a means to the greater end of the salvation of humankind. This would come about through the agency of a Messiah of the Davidic line, who would lead the Jews in triumph to the Holy Land and inaugurate a reign of truth, justice, and mercy. The ideal of salvation is thus the establishment of an earthly paradise of human life, raised to its highest humanity. Other elements clouded this doctrine at various times in the history of mystical Messianism. For example, in the sixteenth century Isaac Luria introduced the idea that this regeneration could not take place until all preexisting souls had satisfactorily completed their earthly existence and that, since some souls were too weak to go unaided through life to perfection, other superior souls might coexist with them in one body to ensure their success. Although Luria's doctrine of transmigration found followers, it was exceptional rather than typical; in general, the Kabbalistic view of redemption was an extreme form of traditional Messianism. Attempts to calculate the exact date of the coming of the Messiah were widespread; the coincidence of various calculations in fixing on dates close to each other was sufficient to start a wave of Messianic movements and even to touch off a major explosion like the widespread impassioned support of Sabbatai Zevi, the so-called Messiah of Ismir (1626–1676).

HISTORICAL EXPRESSIONS

While a number of smaller groups, such as the Essenes of Palestine, the Therapeutae of whom Philo wrote, and the eighth-century Persian "Men of the Caves" whom the tenth-century Karaite historian Joseph ben Jacob al-Kirkisani described, maintained views similar in part to those that have been presented, these groups do not lie in the mainstream of Jewish mysticism. The main development is rather to be traced from the Jewish Gnosticism of the first millennium of the common era, with its concentration on the glory of God as manifested in His throne, supposedly located in the innermost of seven heavenly mansions, into the parallel forms of the medieval European developments of the Kabbalah—the practical, ethical, and sometimes magical mysticism of the German Jews and the speculative mysticism of the French and Spanish Jews. Thence the movement became enmeshed in the morbidity of seventeenth-century Messianism, before the two strains of mystical speculation and socioethical piety were reunited, in eastern Europe, in the still-flourishing movement of Hasidism.

The German pietist movement developed during the century between 1150 and 1250. Its chief formulators were Samuel the Hasid (fl. 1150), his son Judah the Hasid

(d. 1217), and a relative, Eleazar of Worms (fl. 1220). The chief literary expression of the movement is the *Book of the Pious* (Hebrew, *Sefer Hasidim*), a collection of the literary remains of the three founders, with special emphasis on Judah the Hasid, whose character and influence recall those of his Christian contemporary, St. Francis of Assisi, and, perhaps, remind one also of Paracelsus, who lived in the sixteenth century and who also combined genuine piety with magic. In addition to its concern with the doctrinal elements that have already been discussed as characteristic of all forms of Jewish mysticism, German Hasidism defined an ideal human type and a way of life-devoutness, rather than learning or traditionalism. The three chief elements in this devoutness were mental serenity, ascetic renunciation, and extreme altruism, leading to heights of devotion in which true fear of God and love of God became one. At these heights, the Hasid was thought to achieve a creative power of a magical nature.

In southern France, at the beginning of the thirteenth century, a more speculative Kabbalistic development began, under the sponsorship of Isaac the Blind (fl. 1200) and his disciples Ezra and Azariel. Their chief concern was the elaboration of emanation theory; they also suggested a doctrine of metempsychosis, although they did not develop it fully. In Spain, Abraham ben Samuel Abulafia (1240–c. 1292) combined this speculation with the development of number and letter symbolism and thus became one of the central figures in the development of Kabbalah. His disciple, Joseph ben Abraham Gikatilia (c. 1247–1305), presented both the techniques for symbolic interpretation and the doctrine of the ten emanations (Hebrew, *sephiroth*) in systematically interrelated form. About 1290 the Spanish Kabbalist Moses ben Shemtob de Leon (d. 1305) produced the work that, for many, represents the Kabbalah in its entirety: the lush compendium of esoteric doctrines in the form of a commentary on the Pentateuch known as *The Book of Splendor* (Hebrew, *Sefer Ha-Zohar*). From the time of its composition, this work has been the chief source of inspiration for later Jewish mystics and for Jewish mysticism. Of later Kabbalistic leaders, two in particular should be mentioned: Moses ben Jacob Cordovero (1522–1570), whose book, *A Garden of Pomegranates* (Hebrew, *Pardes Rimmonim*), is the most systematic and philosophical exposition of the doctrines of the Kabbalah up to his time; and his pupil, Isaac Luria (1534–1572), who left no written legacy, but whose disciples have made it clear that he developed the theosophic doctrines of creation and redemption far beyond his predecessors.

There are still Kabbalistic groups in existence, chiefly in Israel, but they are for the most part outgrowths of eighteenth-century Polish Hasidism, a movement akin to, though by no means identical with, earlier German pietism. Among major Jewish thinkers of the twentieth century, the chief rabbi of Jerusalem, Abraham Isaac Kook (1865–1935), approached most closely the spirit of the Kabbalah in his mystical awareness of the Messianic role of the Jewish people and in his Lurianic and Hasidic stress on the spark of holiness that is veiled by the material shell of things perceived by the senses. Martin Buber, whose reinterpretations of the Hasidic view of life are profound and suggestive, may also be named here and, among younger thinkers, Abraham Joshua Heschel, whose thought has clear kinship with Hasidic social ethics.

See also Bonaventure, St.; Buber, Martin; Cordovero, Moses ben Jacob; Creation and Conservation, Religious Doctrine of; Gnosticism; Jewish Philosophy; Mysticism, History of; Mysticism, Nature and Assessment of; Paracelsus; Philo Judaeus; Revelation.

Bibliography

TEXTS

Of the primary Kabbalistic literature, only the chief sections of the Zohar are available, in an English translation by Harry Sperling, Maurice Simon, and Paul P. Levertoff. 5 vols. (London: Soncino Press, 1931–1934). Other segments of the Zohar in inferior translations are included in S. L. MacGregor Mathers, *The Kabbalah Unveiled* (London, 1887). A theosophized version of *Sefer Yetzirah* is Knut Stenring, *The Book of Formation* (London, 1923). The Hebrew texts have not been critically edited.

Among recent writers of a mystical bent, the works of Martin Buber are readily available in English translations. None of Abraham Isaac Kook's works have been translated; however, there are good discussions of his life and thought in Jacob Agus, *Banner of Jerusalem* (New York: Bloch, 1946) and Isidore Epstein, *Abraham Kook, His Life and Works* (London, 1951). A. J. Heschel is best represented by *God in Search of Man: A Philosophy of Judaism.* (New York: Farrar Straus, 1955).

HISTORY OF KABBALAH

See Joshua Abelson, *Jewish Mysticism* (London, 1913); Christian D. Ginsburg, *The Kabbalah: Its Doctrine, Development, and Literature* (London, 1920); Adolph Franck, *The Kabbalah: or, the Religious Philosophy of the Hebrews* (New York: Kabbalah, 1926); Abba Hillel Silver, *A History of Messianic Speculation in Israel from the First through the Seventeenth Centuries* (Boston: Beacon Press, 1959); Gershom G. Scholem, *Major Trends in Jewish Mysticism* (New York: Schocken, 1946; and Joseph L. Blau,

The Story of Jewish Philosophy (New York: Random House, 1962).

J. L. Blau (1967)

KABBALAH [ADDENDUM]

Medieval Jewish philosophy contributed considerably to the mystical branch of Judaism known as Kabbalah. This movement is generally regarded as having its origins in twelfth and thirteenth-century Provence in the midrashically styled *Bahir* (*Book of Enlightenment*). Some, however, consider the much earlier *Sefer Yetsirah* (*Book of Formation*)—from the third through the seventh centuries—to be the earliest work of Kabbalah.

Chief among the philosophers who influenced concepts within Kabbalah were those who thrived in the Muslim cultures of Babylon (Iraq) and Spain. An example is Saadya Gaon (882—942), head of the Babylonian Yeshivah (religious academy) of Pumbedita. Although Saadya was a rationalist philosopher, he nevertheless published a detailed commentary on *Sefer Yetsirah*. In addition, he posited an intermediary between God and creation, known as the *kavod* or "glory." It is possible that this concept was influenced by the Karaite thinker, Benjamin al-Nahawandi (830–860), and that both were influenced by the Muslim *kalamic* (theological) view of the "creative word" of God. Contextually, the idea of the *kavod* is less likely to have been influenced by Christian ideas of the *logos*. The concept of an intermediary between God and creation influenced the seminal idea of the *sefirot* (emanations from the Divine), as developed in all major kabbalistic works.

Abraham ibn Ezra (1089–1164) was born in Muslim Tudela, northern Spain, but lived to see both his own birthplace and other major Spanish cities taken by Christian forces before he was thirty. At fifty he left Spain and traveled through northern Christian Europe, dying in a pogrom in London in 1164. Through his travels, he influenced kabbalistic thought in Ashkenazi and Christian domiciles at both a theoretical and practical level. For example, Ibn Ezra's complex attitude to the preexistence of "matter" impacted on circles in Provence, out of which the foundations for the *Bahir* emerged. The problem of "matter," which had not been widely discussed in works of popular Jewish biblical exegesis before Ibn Ezra, played a seminal part in kabbalistic thinking, both in relation to the *sefirot* and also in discussions about the origins and role of evil in the universe. This is particularly true of the sixteenth-century Lurianic Kabbalah of Sfat, northern Israel.

In some ways an even bolder innovation on Ibn Ezra's part was his emphasis on the importance of the *mitzvot* (religious commandments) that, when practiced correctly, could affect the deity. This theory influenced theurgical Kabbalah. It was instrumental in lending a psychological dimension to the practice of Kabbalah, in which human beings could be regarded as influencing the deity by means of the *sefirot*.

It is therefore not completely accurate to view Kabbalah solely as a movement (or series of movements) that emerges during certain tragic times of Jewish history. It is more accurate to see it as being embedded at the heart of the Jewish religion, with biblical and rabbinic antecedents. Kabbalah has also been compared to mystical traditions in other religions, notably Sufism, in which emphasis is placed on experience of the Divine. This approach has paralleled neuroscientific interest in the field of consciousness studies. Lastly, developments in the study of language and linguistics have led to emphasis on the importance of the "text" and letter mysticism in Kabbalah. Interest in Kabbalah may thus be summarized as historical, philosophical, psychological, linguistic, and experiential, but as being grounded in the same intellectual milieu as more conventional Jewish genres.

See also Chinese Philosophy: Buddhism; Consciousness; Experimentation and Instrumentation; Islamic Philosophy; Jewish Philosophy; Mysticism, History of; Philosophy of Language; Postmodernism; Sufism.

Bibliography

TRANSLATIONS INTO ENGLISH OF MAJOR KABBALISTIC WORKS

Kaplan, Aryeh. *The Bahir*. New York: Samuel Weiser, 1979.

Kaplan, Aryeh. *Sefer Yetzirah*. Rev. ed. York Beach, ME: Samuel Weiser, 1997.

Matt, Daniel. *The Zohar*. Vols. 1–2. Stanford, CA: Stanford University Press, 2004.

Tishby, Isaiah. *The Wisdom of the Zohar*. 3 vols. Translated by David Goldstein. Oxford: Oxford University Press, 1991 (1949).

SECONDARY SOURCES

Idel, Moshe. *Absorbing Perfections*. New Haven, CT: Yale University Press, 2002.

Idel, Moshe. *Kabbalah: New Perspectives*. New Haven, CT: Yale University Press, 1988.

Lancaster, Brian, L. *Approaches to Consciousness: The Marriage of Science and Mysticism*. Houndsmill, U.K.: Palgrave Macmillan, 2004.

Lancaster, Brian, L. *The Essence of Kabbalah*. London: Arcturus, 2005.

Lancaster, Irene. *Deconstructing the Bible*. London: Routledge Curzon, 2003.

Scholem, Gershom. *Major Trends in Jewish Mysticism*. New York: Schocken, 1961.

Scholem, Gershom. *On the Kabbalah and Its Symbolism*. New York: Schocken, 1965.

Wolfson, Elliot R. *Through a Speculum That Shines*. Princeton NJ: Princeton University Press, 1994.

Irene Lancaster (2005)

KAFKA, FRANZ
(1883–1924)

Franz Kafka, the German author, was the son of a Jewish businessman who had been a peddler in southern Bohemia. The family was German-speaking. Kafka studied law at the German University of Prague and at Munich and became an official of a workers' accident insurance company. He began writing in 1907 but by his own choice published little. About that time he contracted tuberculosis and for some years lived in various sanatoriums. His two engagements ended unhappily. In 1923 he moved to Berlin, where, living with a girl who was in charge of a Jewish orphanage, he achieved what happiness he was to know. He died of a tubercular infection of the larynx in a nursing home at Kierling, near Vienna.

The central experience of Kafka's life, it seems, was a manifold alienation—as a speaker of German in a Czech city, as a Jew among German and Czech Gentiles in a period of ardent nationalism, as a man full of doubts and an unquenched thirst for faith among conventional "liberal" Jews, as a born writer among people with business interests, as a sick man among the healthy, and as a timid and neurasthenic lover in exacting erotic relationships.

Kafka's narrative art is at once immensely original, prophetic, and fragmentary—hence the large number of mutually exclusive interpretations it has received. Several elements of his prose were the stock in trade of the minor literature of his day. His language is unemphatic and prosy and occasionally contains Prague-German provincialisms; some of the subjects of his stories belong to the horror literature of the turn of the twentieth century; he shared the modern interest in psychological motivation; and he often used the smaller prose genres cultivated by his contemporaries in Prague and Vienna. But the use Kafka made of these elements is startlingly original, and the compelling gnostic vision of the world that is fashioned from them has become one of the major literary and intellectual influences of our age. In Kafka's work the existentialists' conceptions of absurdity and dread are fully explored. Unlike the later existentialists, he did not derive a positive value from these modes of experience; the value of his writings lies in the intense lucidity of the exploration.

It is obvious from the very titles of many of Kafka's stories—*The Trial*, "The Judgment," "Before the Law," "The Penal Settlement"—that his work is informed by a strong legalistic strain, possibly derived from his Jewish heritage but then secularized. In the famous "Letter to His Father" (1919) he recounted a certain childhood episode that violated his sense of justice. Characteristically, its terror for him lay in his inability to connect the trivial "crime" with the monstrous punishment he received.

The novel *The Trial*, begun in 1914 and published by Kafka's friend Max Brod in 1925, at once challenges and refines our conventional ways of connecting causes and effects through the story of a young man, Josef K, who one day wakes up in his lodgings to find himself arrested without knowing what wrong he has done. He makes various attempts to justify himself against the enigmatic accusation and to influence a number of people who he believes may effect his acquittal. Although offered a chance of repudiating the jurisdiction of the court that is concerned with his case, he ends up by being marched off to his execution, to die "like a dog."

The question What has Josef K done? receives a number of detailed answers, the total effect of which is to undermine the reader's notion of guilt. Josef K has lived the unremarkable life of an average young man, a bank clerk. Since in his "ordinary" life he always based his relations with other people on asserting what he believed were his "rights" in this or that situation, it is consistent with his character that he should seek to justify himself before the Law. The only thing he knows about that Law (and the all but unattainable authority behind it) is that it is powerful, whereas he is weak. According to the "inescapable logic" of the world, he must therefore be outside the Law and thus, in some sense, guilty. With his every move the not wholly irrational sense of guilt drags more violently at his soul. At first, this sense is no more than an uneasy "They are sure to have something on me," but gradually it is magnified by all the actions, in themselves trivial, which constitute "normal" behavior in our world, coupled with Josef K's inability to live "outside the Law," which for Kafka amounted to consciousness itself. Simplifying the subtly involuted and complex texture of the novel, we may conclude that "minor guilt + situation of weakness + self-justification = major sense of guilt," which is tantamount to saying that Kafka's dialectical ingenuity is expended on making convincing the equation "[subjective] sense of guilt = [objective] guilt."

Similar dialectical devices are used in the second major work, the unfinished novel *The Castle* (1921–1922, published 1926). K, a land surveyor, has been called to a village that is governed by an authority that resides in a nearby castle. The village and its inhabitants are described only as they are related to K and to his attempts to justify his presence there. His commission, the authority on whose behalf he is to perform it, its relation to himself and to the villagers, the extent of its power, and the morality of its commands—all these are not so much vague as complexly contradictory. (Kafka was prophetically describing the anonymous, muffled workings of a totalitarian ministry as they affect the helpless victim, but since his style is that of an "objective" report, he allowed himself no expressions of pity.) Every assurance that K receives is thrown into doubt either by an oblique contradiction or by K's own unnerved (and, to the reader, unnerving) insistence on exploring its possible ambiguities.

Again, the novel elaborates a vicious circle. K uses the people he meets in order to wrest from them hints or indications about his task and status but because he lacks the assurance of a clearly defined status and task, he is an outsider and thus in a position of weakness. He is therefore bound to construe all these hints as hostile and thus distrust them. K does not have enough strength to break the spell that the Castle (like the court in *The Trial*) seems to be casting over him, for he looks to it as the place that, in justifying him, will give him strength. And, to keep alive K's torments of uncertainty, the Castle need do little more than send an occasional hint of a possible way of deliverance.

Leaving aside the various Freudian, Marxist, and Christian interpretations that Kafka's work has received, its fragmentary nature points to a fundamental hiatus. His heroes' desolate quests for justice, recognition, and acceptance by the world are meaningful to us because they invoke our sense of pity and justice, whereas the matter-of-fact ways in which these quests are presented invite us to accept cruelty and injustice as though they were necessary and self-evident modes of life. Thus, the meaningfulness of the quests is impaired. Kafka's writings are indeed prophetic intimations of the logic of the concentration camps; the monstrous insinuation inherent in his prophecies is that the exterminator is not wholly in the wrong, that his hold over his victim is something more than a matter of superior might, for the victim cooperates in his own destruction.

See also Alienation; Consciousness; Existentialism; Guilt; Metaphor.

Bibliography

WORKS BY KAFKA

Most of Kafka's writings were published posthumously and against his express wishes by his friend Max Brod. The complete edition is *Werke* (Frankfurt, 1952–). The "definitive" English edition, published in London, includes *The Trial*, translated by Willa Muir and Edwin Muir (1945); Kafka's *Diaries*, 2 vols., translated by J. Kresh, M. Greenberg, and H. Arendt (1948–1949); *America*, translated by Willa Muir and Edwin Muir (1949); *In the Penal Settlement: Tales and Short Prose Works*, translated by Willa Muir and Edwin Muir (1949); *The Castle*, translated by Willa Muir and Edwin Muir (1953); *Wedding Preparations in the Country and Other Posthumous Prose Writings*, translated by Ernst Kaiser and Eithne Wilkins (1954); and *Description of a Struggle and The Great Wall of China*, translated by Willa Muir and Edwin Muir and Tania Stern and James Stern (1960). See also Kafka's *Letters to Milena* (Jesenská), translated by Tania Stern and James Stern (London, 1953), and G. Janouch's *Conversations with Kafka* (New York, 1953).

WORKS ON KAFKA

Three biographical studies are available: Max Brod, *Franz Kafka: Eine Biographie* (Frankfurt, 1937), translated as *The Biography of Franz Kafka* (London: Secker and Warburg, 1947); K. Wagenbach, *Franz Kafka: Eine Biographie seiner Jugend, 1883–1912* (Bern: Francke, 1958); and P. Eisner, *Franz Kafka and Prague* (New York: Arts, 1950).

For critical works on Kafka see G. Anders, *Franz Kafka* (London: Bowes and Bowes, 1960); Ronald D. Gray, ed., *Kafka: A Collection of Critical Essays* (Englewood Cliffs, NJ: Prentice-Hall, 1962), which has important contributions by Albert Camus and E. Heller; and Heinz Politzer, *Franz Kafka: Parable and Paradox* (Ithaca, NY: Cornell University Press, 1962).

OTHER RECOMMENDED SOURCES

Biemel, Walter. "Franz Kafka: The Necessity for a Philosophical Interpretation of His Work." In *Explanation and Value in the Arts*, edited by Salim Kemal and Ivan Gaskell. New York: Cambridge University Press, 1993.

Cooper, Gabriele von Natzmer. *Kafka and Language: In the Stream of Thoughts and Life*. Riverside: Ariadne Press, 1991.

Heidsieck, Arnold. *The Intellectual Contexts of Kafka's Fiction: Philosophy, Law, Religion*. Columbia: Camden House, 1994.

Wade, Geoff. "Marxism and Modernist Aesthetics: Reading Kafka and Beckett." In *The Politics of Pleasure: Aesthetics and Cultural Theory*, edited by Stephen Regan. Buckingham; Philadelphia: Open University Press, 1992.

J. P. Stern (1967)
Bibliography updated by Desiree Matherly Martin (2005)

KAIBARA EKKEN
(1630–1714)

Kaibara Ekken, or Ekiken, a Japanese Confucianist influential in popularizing Confucian ethics among ordinary people, was born in Fukuoka. The son of a physician, he became a doctor himself, then left medicine to become a Zhu Xi neo-Confucianist. His teachers in Kyoto were Kinoshita Junan (1621–1698) and Yamazaki Ansai. At thirty-nine Kaibara returned to Fukuoka, where he spent the rest of his life in the service of the Kuroda fief. Blessed with an extraordinary capacity for work but little originality, he wrote on many subjects. He became an important botanist with the issuing of separate books on the vegetables, the flora, and the medicinal herbs of Japan. His books on education were pioneering works in pedagogy; *Onna daigaku* (The great learning for women), the standard book on women's ethics in the Tokugawa era, is attributed variously to him and to his well-educated wife. His books were a great success. Unlike most Confucianists, who wrote in Chinese, he wrote in Japanese; furthermore, his teaching was highly practical, applying Confucian morality to everyday life. His pedagogical ideas were not equalitarian (he assigned to women the role of mere submissiveness and obedience to their husbands), and his botanical studies were not at all scientific in the modern sense, but he played an important role in spreading education.

Kaibara's philosophical importance today rests on his *Taigiroku* (The great doubt), in which he aired his dissent with the official doctrine of the Zhu Xi school. Kaibara was also critical of the "ancient learning" school of Confucianism and its scholars Itō Jinsai and Ogyū Sorai, and of the Wang Yangming school, the rival of Zhu Xi. Kaibara disagreed with Zhu Xi Confucianism in his elevation of *ki,* the material force, over *ri,* the principle immanent in all things. For him *ki* is the "great limit" or the "ultimate" and is an all-pervading life force. Kaibara does not distinguish the original form of human nature from its acquired form; contrary to Zhu Xi, he is an optimist in his view of man and of the natural world. His cosmology is characterized by cosmic love that embraces all men, born as they are of heaven and earth. Man's indebtedness to nature is limitless, and for him the Confucian virtue of *jen,* "humaneness," comes close to being a religious benevolence, first toward nature and then toward men. His practical bent, however, makes it difficult to clarify his position, which seems to be one of eclectic doubt rather than critical inquiry. In administrative matters Kaibara opposed imitating Chinese ways; rather he was an ardent patriot, loyal in support of the emperor.

See also Chinese Philosophy; Itō Jinsai; Japanese Philosophy; Ogyū Sorai; Wang Yang-ming; Yamazaki Ansai; Zhu Xi (Chu Hsi).

Bibliography

Kaibara's works are available in Japanese in *Ekken zenshū* (Complete works of Kaibara Ekken), edited by Ekkenkai, 8 vols. (Tokyo, 1911). A secondary source in Japanese is Inoue Tadashi, *Kaibara Ekken* (Tokyo, 1963).

See also O. Graf, *Kaibara Ekiken* (Leiden: Brill, 1942); S. Atsuharu, "Kaibara E. and *Onna daigaku,*" in *Cultural Nippon* 7 (4) (1939): 43–56; and W. T. de Bary, Ryusaku Tsunoda, and Donald Keene, eds., *Sources of Japanese Tradition* (New York: Columbia University Press, 1958), pp. 374–377.

Gino K. Piovesana, S.J. (1967)

KALON

Kalon: the neuter of the Greek adjective *kalos,* beautiful, fine, also admirable, noble; accompanied by the definite article (*to kalon*), for example, *the* beautiful (or beauty). In Greek culture, what is *kalon* is typically the object of *erôs,* passionate or romantic love, and in (male-dominated) literature (and art), the term is predominantly applied to males around the age of puberty. Plato appropriates the *kalon* (along with the good and the just) as a key object for human striving and understanding in general, discovering in it, along with the good, one of the properties of the universe and of existence; *erôs* itself, in Plato, is transformed from a species of love into love or desire *tout court,* for whatever is truly desirable—and good (for the human agent). See especially his *Symposium, Phaedrus* (*Hippias Major,* possibly not by Plato, represents an unsuccessful attempt to define the *kalon*). The truly beautiful, or fine, is identical with the truly good, and also with the truly pleasant, as it is for Aristotle (*Eudemian Ethics* I.1, 1214a1–8). The Aristotelian good man acts "for the sake of the fine (*to kalon*)" (*Nicomachean Ethics* IV.2, 1122b6–7), an idea which is sometimes used as a basis for attributing to Aristotle a quasi-Kantian view of the ideal agent as acting *morally,* even—if occasion arises—*altruistically,* as opposed to acting out of a concern for his or her own good or pleasure. Against this, we need to take account of Aristotle's treatment of his good person as a *self-lover,* someone who seeks a disproportionate share of *the fine* for himself or herself (*NE* IX.8, 1169a35–b1), though he or she may willingly concede his or her share to a friend (*NE* IX.8, 1169a32–34). This is consistent with Aristotle's wanting to treat the fine (or the admirable) as itself part—the most important part—of the human good; and indeed, he ultimately seems to recognize only two objects of desire, the good and the pleasant (*NE* VIII.2, 1155b18–21; cf. e.g. *EE* VII.2, 1235b18–23). In this context *the pleasant* will include only those pleasures that are not *fine* and good. For this move we may compare Plato's *Gorgias* (474C–475D), where Socrates actually reduces *fine* to *good*, *pleasant*, or *both*. Later Greek philosophy trades on, while sometimes modifying, this complex of ideas, which also forms the basis for the analysis of beauty in literature or in the visual arts.

See also Aristotle; Beauty; Good, The; Plato; Pleasure; Socrates.

Bibliography

Aristotle. *Eudemian Ethics*. In *The Complete Works of Aristotle*, edited by Jonathan Barnes. Princeton, NJ: Princeton University Press, 1984.

Aristotle. *Nicomachean Ethics*. Translated by Christopher Rowe. In *Aristotle: Nicomachean Ethics*, edited by Sarah Broadie and Christopher Rowe. Oxford: Oxford University Press, 2002.

Plato. *Gorgias*. In *Plato, Complete Works*, edited by John M. Cooper. Indianapolis: Hackett, 1997.

Plato. *Hippias Major*. In *Plato, Complete Works*, edited by John M. Cooper. Indianapolis: Hackett, 1997.

Plato. *Lysis*. Translated by Christopher Rowe. In *Plato's Lysis*, edited by Terry Penner and Christopher Rowe. Cambridge Studies in the Dialogues of Plato. Cambridge, U.K.: Cambridge University Press, 2005.

Plato. *Phaedrus*. Translated by Christopher Rowe. Harmondsworth: Penguin Books, 2005.

Plato. *Symposium*. Translated by Christopher Rowe. In his *Plato: Symposium*. Warminster/Oxford: Aris & Phillips/ Oxbow Books, 1998.

Christopher Rowe (2005)

KAMES, LORD

See *Home, Henry*

KANT, IMMANUEL
(1724–1804)

Immanuel Kant, the propounder of the critical philosophy, was born at Königsberg in East Prussia; he was the son of a saddler and, according to his own account, the grandson of an emigrant from Scotland. He was educated at the local high school, the Collegium Fridericianum, and then at the University of Königsberg, where he had the good fortune to encounter a first-class teacher in the philosopher Martin Knutzen. After leaving the university, about 1746, Kant was employed for a few years as a tutor in a number of families in different parts of East Prussia. He kept up his studies during this period and in 1755 was able to take his master's degree at Königsberg and to begin teaching in the university as a *Privatdozent*. He taught a wide variety of subjects, including physics, mathematics, and physical geography as well as philosophy, but nevertheless remained poor for many years. It was not until 1770, when he was appointed to the chair of logic and metaphysics at Königsberg, that his financial stringencies were eased.

Kant's first book, *Gedanken von der wahren Schätzung der lebendigen Kräfte* (Thoughts on the True Estimation of Living Forces), was published as early as 1747 (Königsberg), and between 1754 and 1770 he produced an impressive stream of essays and treatises. His earlier works are primarily contributions to natural science or natural philosophy, the most notable being his *General History of Nature and Theory of the Heavens* of 1755; it was not until after 1760 that philosophical interests in the modern sense became dominant in his mind. Kant's publications had already won him a considerable reputation in German learned circles by the time he obtained his professorship. The ten years following his appointment form a period of literary silence during which Kant was engaged in preparing his magnum opus, the *Critique of Pure Reason*. The appearance of the *Critique* was eagerly awaited by Kant's friends and philosophical colleagues, but when it at last came out in 1781 the general reaction was more bewilderment than admiration. Kant tried to remove misunderstandings by restating the main argument in the *Prolegomena to Every Future Metaphysics* of 1783 and by rewriting some of the central sections of the *Critique* for a second edition in 1787. At the same time he continued, with most remarkable energy for a man of his years, the elaboration of the rest of his system. By 1790 the *Critique of Practical Reason* and the *Critique of Judgment* were in print, and of the major treatises only *Religion within the Bounds of Mere Reason* (1793) and *Metaphysic of Morals* (1797) had still to appear. Kant then enjoyed a tremendous reputation throughout Germany and was beginning to be known, though scarcely to be understood, in other European countries. In his declining years, however, he suffered the mortification of seeing some of the ablest young philosophers in his own country, among them Johann Gottlieb Fichte, Friedrich von Schelling, and J. S. Beck, proclaim that he had not really understood his own philosophy and

between mathematical ideas can always be observed *in concreto*, whereas the philosopher, having nothing to correspond to mathematical diagrams or symbolism, necessarily works on a more abstract level. The lesson of all this might seem to be that philosophical truths are incapable of strict demonstration, but Kant did not draw this conclusion in the case of natural theology, where he held to his attempted conceptual proof, though he inclined toward it in respect to "the primary grounds of morals." In general, Kant's tendency was to say that metaphysics must be an analytic activity that should follow a method that is fundamentally Newtonian: "It is far from the time for proceeding synthetically in metaphysics; only when analysis will have helped us to distinct concepts understood in their details will synthesis be able to subsume compounded cognitions under the simplest cognitions, as in mathematics" (*Critique of Practical Reason and Other Writings*, Beck translation, 1949, p. 275).

Kant viewed the prospects of attaining genuine metaphysical knowledge with increasing skepticism as the 1760s went on. In the enigmatic *Dreams of a Spirit-Seer* of 1766 he compared the thought constructions of metaphysics to the fantasies of Swedenborg, in a manner that is scarcely flattering to either. Metaphysical contentions are groundless, since metaphysical concepts such as spirit cannot be characterized in positive terms. To survive, metaphysics must change its nature and become a science of the limits of human knowledge. Kant's skepticism about metaphysics was increased by his discovery of the antinomies, which is often dated 1769 although something like the third antinomy is to be found in the *Nova Dilucidatio*. Astonishingly, however, in his inaugural dissertation in 1770 he reverted in some degree to the old dogmatic conception of the subject and argued for the possibility of genuine knowledge of an intelligible world. But the main interest of the dissertation lies in its account of sensory knowledge, which prepared the way for the fundamental criticisms of metaphysical pretensions in the *Critique of Pure Reason*.

THE INAUGURAL DISSERTATION

Kant's Latin dissertation, "On the Form and Principles of the Sensible and Intelligible Worlds," publicly defended on August 21, 1770, was his inaugural lecture as professor of logic and metaphysics at Königsberg. At least one of the themes of the dissertation, the status of the concept of space, represented a long-standing interest. As early as 1747 Kant had argued that the proposition that space has three dimensions is contingent; given a different law of the effects of different substances on one another, "an

extension with other properties and dimensions would have arisen. A science of all these possible kinds of space would undoubtedly be the highest enterprise which a finite understanding could undertake in the field of geometry" ("Living Forces," Handyside translation, in *Kant's Inaugural Dissertation and Early Writings on Space*, p. 12). Later, however, he regarded three-dimensionality as a necessary property of space, and used its necessity as a ground for rejecting Leibniz' account of the concept. In a short essay on space published in 1768 Kant had seemed to suggest that Newton's view of space as an absolute reality was the only alternative to Leibniz, but in the dissertation he rejected both theories and widened his treatment of the question so that it covered time as well as space. Despite this extension the dissertation is best viewed as directed mainly against Leibniz.

SPACE AND TIME. In general, Leibniz had followed the other great rationalists in interpreting perception as a confused form of thinking. Like Descartes, he had treated the deliverances of the senses as sometimes clear but never distinct. In the dissertation Kant developed two main arguments against this position. He maintained in the first place that it could not do justice to the special character of space and time, which are not, as Leibniz supposed, systems of relations abstracted from particular situations and confusedly apprehended, but rather unique individuals of which clear knowledge is presupposed in all perceptual description. The ideas of space and time are intuitive rather than conceptual in character; moreover, they are "pure" intuitions insofar as the essential nature of their referents is known in advance of experience and not as a result of it.

SPACE AND GEOMETRY. To reinforce this point Kant brought forward his second argument, that Leibniz' theory could not account for the apodictic character of geometry. There was, Kant supposed, an essential relation between geometry and space, for geometry "contemplates the relations of space" and "does not demonstrate its universal propositions by apprehending the object through a universal concept, as is done in matters of reason, but by submitting it to the eyes as a singular intuition, as is done in matters of sense" ("Dissertation," in *Kant's Inaugural Discussion and Early Writings on Space*, Sec. 15 C). But if space is what Leibniz said it was and if, as Kant added, "all properties of space are borrowed only from external relations through experience," then:

> geometrical axioms do not possess universality, but only that comparative universality which is acquired through induction and holds only so

widely as it is observed; nor do they possess necessity, except such as depends on fixed laws of nature; nor have they any precision save such as is matter of arbitrary convention; and we might hope, as in empirical matters, some day to discover a space endowed with other primary affections, and perhaps even a rectilinear figure enclosed by two straight lines. (Sec. 15 D)

Kant's own account of space at this stage was that it "*is not something objective and real*, neither substance, nor accident, nor relation, but [something] *subjective and ideal*; it is, as it were, a schema, issuing by a constant law from the nature of the mind, for the co-ordinating of all outer sensa whatever" (Sec. 15D). One major advantage of this subjectivist view, in Kant's eyes, was that it explains the possibility of applying geometry to the physical world. Space being a universal form of sensibility, "nothing whatsoever … can be given to the senses save in conformity with the primary axioms of space and the other consequences of its nature, as expounded by geometry" (Sec. 15 E).

APPEARANCE AND REALITY. Kant's view had another, more startling implication, namely that we cannot know things as they really are through sense perception. If space and time are contributed by the knowing mind, spatial and temporal objects will be altered in the very act of being apprehended. It follows that the world known through the senses—the world investigated by the physical sciences and familiar in everyday experience—can be no more than a phenomenal world. Kant was prepared to accept this conclusion in the dissertation, but he balanced it by saying that over and above this phenomenal world is another world of real objects, knowable not by the senses but by reason. Reason lacks intuitive powers—we cannot be acquainted with things as they are. But (and in this the contrast with the *Dreams* is at its strongest) reason possesses certain concepts of its own, among them "possibility, existence, necessity, substance, cause," by means of which it can arrive at a "symbolic cognition" of such things; that is, know some true propositions about them. The intellect, in its real as opposed to its logical use, can form the concept of a perfect being and use this both to measure the reality of other things and for moral purposes.

ACHIEVEMENTS. The doctrine of pure intellectual concepts in the dissertation is at best impressionistic and had to be completely rethought in the ten years that followed. But against this may be set Kant's positive achievements in the dissertation, seen from the point of view of his

future work. First, Kant had convinced himself that there is an absolute difference between sensing and thinking, and that sense experience need not be in any way confused. Second, he had worked out the main lines, though by no means all the details, of what was to be his mature theory of space and time. Third, he had revived the old antithesis of things real and things apparent, objects of the intellect and objects of the senses, to cope with the consequences of his views about space and time; in this way he was able to show (or so he thought) that physics gives us genuine knowledge, though only of appearances, and that the task of telling us about things as they really are is reserved for metaphysics. Fourth and last, he had recognized the existence of a special class of concepts, "given through the very nature of the intellect," and had seen that these have an important bearing on the question of the possibility of metaphysics.

What Kant had not done was to pose the problem of metaphysics with all its wider implications. As in the *Dreams*, he treated the question whether we have any knowledge of a world of pure spirit as one that is asked primarily for its theoretical interest. It was intellectual curiosity, that is to say, which at this stage prompted Kant to inquire whether physics and metaphysics could coexist, and, if they could, what should be said of their respective objects. He retained this curiosity when he wrote the *Critique of Pure Reason*, but it was not by then his only motive. For he had seen by 1781 that the question of the possibility of metaphysics was important not only to the academic philosopher, but because of its bearing on the universally interesting topics of God, freedom, and immortality, to the plain man as well; that it was a matter not just of intellectual, but also of moral, concern.

CRITIQUE OF PURE REASON: THEME AND PRELIMINARIES

Kant's principal task in the *Critique of Pure Reason* was to determine the cognitive powers of reason, to find out what it could and could not achieve in the way of knowledge. The term *reason* in the title was intended in its generic sense, to cover the intellect as a whole; Kant was not exclusively interested in the reason that he himself distinguished from and opposed to understanding. He was, however, particularly concerned with the capacities of "pure" reason, that is, with what reason could know when operating by itself and not in association with another faculty. Kant believed it important to answer this question for two reasons. He saw that there are spheres (mathematics, for instance) in which it is plausible to claim that pure reason is a source of important truths. He also saw that in another field, that of metaphysics, remarkable claims were advanced on reason's behalf: It was alleged that, by simply thinking, we could arrive at ultimate truth about the world, establishing thus a series of propositions whose certainty was unassailable and whose subject matter was of supreme importance. Kant, who had himself made this sort of claim in the dissertation, never doubted that what the metaphysician wants to say matters, but he did question his competence to say it. The fact that reason "precipitates itself into darkness and contradictions" once it enters this field struck him as deeply significant; the "intestine wars," the interminable disputes, of metaphysicians could only mean that their claims were pitched too high.

Nor was the scandal of metaphysics—the fact that nothing in metaphysics could be regarded as settled—of concern only to metaphysicians. By failing to make good his proofs, the metaphysician brought doubt on the acceptability of his conclusions, including such fundamental articles of belief as that God exists and that the will is free. In proposing a radical reexamination of the capacities of pure reason, Kant's ultimate motive was to safeguard such convictions by making clear that although they cannot be matters of knowledge, they can all the same be held to as matters of what he called pure rational faith.

TYPES OF JUDGMENT. In the preface to the *Critique*, Kant formulates his main question as "how much can understanding and reason know apart from all experience?" (A xvii). (The first edition is customarily referred to as A, the second edition as B.) In the introduction, he takes his first step toward an answer by substituting the formula "How are synthetic *a priori* judgments possible?" Two closely connected sets of distinctions lie behind these celebrated words. First, Kant distinguishes propositions that are a priori from all others; an a priori judgment "in being thought is thought as *necessary*" and is also thought "with strict universality, that is, in such a manner that no exception is allowed as possible" (B 3–4). A priori judgments have the twin characteristics of necessity and universality, neither of which can be found in conclusions from experience.

In holding that experience can present us with no more than contingent truths Kant echoes the views of many of his predecessors. But in his other distinction, between synthetic and analytic judgments, he shows greater originality. A judgment is analytic, he explains, if what is thought in the predicate-concept has already been thought in the subject-concept; a judgment is synthetic if

this condition does not obtain. Thus, "All bodies are extended" is analytic because our idea of a body is of something that is extended or occupies space; "All bodies have weight" is synthetic because the notion of weight is not comprised in the notion of body (we learn by experience that bodies have weight). In analytic judgments, again, the connection of subject and predicate is "thought through identity"; or, as Kant puts it elsewhere in the *Critique*, the highest principle of all analytic judgments is the principle of contradiction. It follows from this that every analytic judgment is a priori in that it is true or false without regard to experience; every analytic judgment is either necessarily true or necessarily false, and we establish its truth or falsity by reference only to definitions of the terms it contains and to the principle of contradiction. Synthetic judgments, by contrast, require for their authentication a different sort of reference, since in their case the connection of subject and predicate terms is "thought without identity." In the case of everyday judgments of fact, for example, we need to consult experience to see whether the connection asserted actually holds.

So far Kant's distinction is simply a more elaborate version of Hume's division of propositions into those that assert relations of ideas and those that express matters of fact and existence, a version inferior to Hume's in that it is formally tied to statements of the subject-predicate form. But at this point Kant gives the distinction a fresh twist by asserting that there are judgments that are both synthetic and a priori, thus cutting across the usual classifications. Nearly all the propositions of mathematics answer this description, according to Kant; he also thinks it obvious that "*natural science (physics) contains* a priori *synthetic judgments as principles.*" He gives two examples: "in all changes of the material world the quantity of matter remains unchanged; and … in all communication of motion action and reaction must always be equal" (B 17). The very existence of these judgments shows that reason has special cognitive powers of its own, and so lends plausibility to the claims of metaphysicians. But before accepting the claims of metaphysicians, Kant suggests, we need to ask ourselves how (under what conditions) it is possible to assert judgments of this type in the two fields concerned. Only when this question is answered can we decide whether metaphysicians can draw support from the example of mathematics and "pure" physics. This inquiry is what Kant is concerned with in the first half of the *Critique*.

ANALYTIC AND SYNTHETIC. The terms in which Kant states his problem seem at first sight clear, but the clarity diminishes on closer inspection. There is the criticism that he offers a dual account of the analytic-synthetic distinction, once in psychological and once in logical terms, and the criticism that reference to the principle of contradiction alone is inadequate for the logical formulation of the distinction (he should have referred to logical laws generally). Apart from these two matters, Kant's treatment is marred by a failure to offer any discussion of his key idea, "what is thought in a concept." This omission is the more remarkable because Kant in fact had views on the subject of definition, views that are hard to reconcile with his apparent assumption that every judgment is unequivocally analytic or synthetic. Elsewhere in the *Critique* he states that, according to the real meaning of "definition," an empirical concept "cannot be defined at all, but only made explicit" (B 755). He means that we cannot give the "real essence" (in Locke's terminology) of such a concept, but only its "nominal essence," or conventional signification, which is liable to change as knowledge increases or interests shift. If this is correct, it seems to be only by convention, or provisionally, that the judgment "All bodies are extended" is analytic and the judgment "All bodies have weight" synthetic.

Nor is Kant's other distinction, between a priori and a posteriori, as simple as he pretends. He tries to clarify it by explaining that the first class of judgments have the characteristics of necessity and universality, which serve as criteria that are "inseparable from one another." He fails to notice, however, that the necessity that belongs to synthetic a priori judgments must on his own account differ from that which characterizes analytic judgments. Analytic judgments are, or rather claim to be, logically necessary—to deny a true analytic judgment would be, if Kant is correct, to dispute the validity of the law of contradiction. But though no synthetic judgment can contravene the laws of logic, none can be true in virtue of these laws and of meanings alone. Accordingly, if any synthetic judgment is to be described as necessary, it must be necessary in some further sense.

Kant recognizes in practice that the synthetic a priori judgments he takes to be valid have their own special kind of necessity. In his own terminology, they are "transcendentally" necessary; necessary, that is to say, if we are to have the knowledge and experience we actually have. But he would have done better to acknowledge the ambiguity in his term *a priori* from the outset. It would also have been helpful had he given some elucidation of his statement that, when a judgment is thought with strict universality, "no exception is allowed as possible." He cannot mean that no exception is logically possible, or every a priori judgment would be analytic. But he does not, at

least at this early stage, make clear what other sort of possibility he has in mind.

TRANSCENDENTAL AESTHETIC

Kant's next step in the solution of the problem of how synthetic a priori judgments are possible is to examine the two types of case in which, in his view, we undoubtedly can make synthetic a priori judgments, and then to exhibit the bearing of his results on the possibility of metaphysical knowledge. In his short but important *Prolegomena to Every Future Metaphysics* he approaches these tasks directly. In the *Critique* itself his method is more roundabout, since he proposes there to delineate the entire cognitive powers of the mind and so to clarify the background against which synthetic a priori judgments are made. This leads him to undertake an inquiry first into the a priori elements involved in sensory knowledge (the "Transcendental Aesthetic") and then into the corresponding elements involved in thought (the "Transcendental Logic"). The sharp distinction between the senses and the intellect argued for in the dissertation is the obvious basis of this division.

A PRIORI INTUITIONS. It seems at first sight contradictory to say that there might be a priori elements involved in sensory knowledge. According to an old philosophical and psychological tradition, sensation is an essentially passive affair; the senses present us with data and we have no choice but to accept. Kant was quite ready to agree to this as a general account of sensation. But he was persuaded that there are some features of sensory experience that cannot be accepted as empirically given.

Kant identifies these features by a process similar to that in the dissertation: an examination of our ideas of space and time. These ideas, he argues, represent the form of experience rather than its matter; through them we structure the sensory given in the very act of sensing it. To establish this position Kant appeals to a variety of considerations.

First, he insists on the fundamental and ubiquitous character of space and time, as opposed to features like color and sound. Spatial predicates apply to whatever we know through the five senses, temporal predicates both to these and to the immediately experienced flow of our inner lives. Second, he argues that we cannot acquire the ideas of space and time by reflecting on what is empirically given. Some philosophers had said that we come by the idea of space by noticing such things as that one object is adjacent to another, and that we come by the idea of time by observing the way in which events succeed, are simultaneous with, or precede one another. Kant points out that the very description of such situations presupposes familiarity with space and time as such. For to know what is meant by saying that one thing is "next to" or "on top of" another we need to appreciate how the things in question are situated in a wider spatial framework, which in turn falls within a yet wider spatial system, until we come to the thought of space as a whole. Particular spaces are not instances of space, but limitations of it, and space is accordingly a special sort of particular. The same argument applies to time. Adding to these two points the fact that we know certain things to be necessarily true of space and time (space has only three dimensions, different times are not simultaneous but successive), Kant infers that the ideas of space and time are not only "intuitions," but "*a priori* intuitions."

MATHEMATICS. Kant finds confirmation for his view of space and time exactly as he had in the dissertation: in the thought that this view alone can explain the possibility of pure and applied mathematics. Pure geometry is possible because we are able to "construct," or show the real possibility of, its concepts in pure intuition. An experiment conducted in imagination shows at once that a triangle is a real spatial possibility, whereas a figure bounded by two straight lines is not. Applied geometry is possible because whatever is apprehended by the senses must necessarily accord with the forms of sensibility. Kant attempts at various points in his writings to extend his doctrine of the importance of pure intuition for mathematical thinking from geometry to the other parts of mathematics, but it cannot be said that he is ever convincing on this point. His reasons for saying that "seven and five are twelve" is a synthetic proposition were sharply and properly criticized by Gottlob Frege. His account of algebra (B 745, 762) is so sketchy as to be virtually unintelligible. Kant tries to say that in algebra there is a "symbolic construction" corresponding to the "ostensive construction" of the concepts of geometry, but it is not in the least clear what this has to do with the pure intuition of either space or time.

Some critics speak as if Kant's failure to produce a satisfactory philosophy of mathematics invalidated the whole "Aesthetic," and it is true that the central point of this part of his work is destroyed if his main contentions about mathematics are rejected. Kant's explanations fall to the ground if it turns out that there is no intrinsic connection between mathematics and space and time, or if it is held that mathematical propositions are analytic, not synthetic a priori. But it does not immediately follow that the whole Kantian doctrine of space and time must be rejected, for many of his arguments on this matter are independent of his philosophy of mathematics. Nor is it decisive against him that the treatment of space and time in modern physics is very different from his; he claims to be dealing with the space and time of immediate perception.

SIGNIFICANCE. Apart from the questions about truth, however, it is vital to appreciate the importance of the conclusions of the "Aesthetic" in the economy of the *Critique of Pure Reason* as a whole. The "transcendental ideality" of space and time carries with it, for Kant, the proposition that whatever we know through the senses (including "inner sense") is phenomenal; Kant's celebrated distinction between appearances and things-in-themselves has its origin, if not its justification, at this point. And the view that space and time are a priori forms of intuition is not only the model on which Kant constructed his theory of categories as concepts embodying the pure thought of an object in general; the view is carried over intact into the "Transcendental Analytic," and plays a crucial part there. To treat the theories of the "Aesthetic" as if they merely embodied a series of views that Kant had outgrown by the time he completed the *Critique*, as some commentators have proposed to do, is not in accord with Kant's own intentions. It is also to ignore a series of arguments that are of independent philosophical interest, and that demand careful notice from anyone writing on the philosophy of perception.

PURE CONCEPTS OF THE UNDERSTANDING

The main contentions of the aesthetic are to be found in the dissertation. Of the doctrine of pure intellectual concepts put forward in that inaugural lecture, on the other hand, almost nothing survives in the *Critique of Pure Reason*.

OBJECTIVE REFERENCE. In the dissertation Kant argues along two lines: First, that pure intellectual concepts are not derived from sense experience (they could not be described as "pure" if they were); and second, that they serve to give us information about things as they really are. Soon after writing this work, however, Kant realized that there was a fundamental difficulty in this position, a difficulty he stated at length in a letter to his friend Marcus Herz dated February 21, 1772. It was that of knowing how "pure" concepts could be said to determine an object of any kind. To elucidate the difficulty, Kant isolated two contrasting types of intelligence, *intellectus ectypus*, "which derives the data of its logical procedure from the sensuous intuition of things," and *intellectus archetypus*, "on whose intuition the things themselves are grounded." The concepts of the first type of intelligence, deriving as they do from objects, have a guaranteed relationship to objects. The concepts of the second type determine objects, because, in this sort of case, thinking itself brings objects into existence in the same way in which "the ideas in the Divine Mind are the archetypes of things." But the human intelligence, as described in the dissertation, answers to neither description, for some of its concepts are not empirically derived and yet none of its thinking is creative in the sense specified. The problem then arises, How can these concepts be said to have objective reference; how can we know that in using them we are thinking about anything actual? It is this problem that Kant professes to have solved in the *Critique of Pure Reason*. Roughly speaking, his solution is that pure concepts can be shown to determine an object if the object is phenomenal. By contrast, when an attempt is made to use them to specify characteristics of "things in general," there is no guarantee that anything significant is being said.

ANALYTIC AND DIALECTIC. The details of Kant's explanation of how pure concepts can be said to have objective reference is to be found in the lengthy section of the *Critique* labeled "Transcendental Logic" and divided into two main parts, "Transcendental Analytic" and "Transcendental Dialectic."

The first part contains an inventory of what at this point Kant calls pure concepts of the understanding, or categories, with an account of the function they perform in human knowledge and a series of arguments purporting to show that, in the absence of such pure concepts, objective knowledge would be impossible for human beings. In addition, the "Analytic" lists the principles that rest on these pure concepts and offers independent proofs of these principles. Transcendental analytic is said by Kant to be a "logic of truth," insofar as "no knowledge can contradict it without at once losing all content, that is, all relation to an object, and therefore all truth" (B 87). It deals, in short, with the proper use of a priori concepts, which is the use they have when they provide a framework for empirical inquiries.

Transcendental dialectic is introduced as if it were merely the negative counterpart of analytic—as if its sole purpose were to expose the illusions generated when dogmatic philosophers, unaware of the sensuous conditions under which alone we can make successful use of a priori concepts, attempt to apply them outside the sphere of possible experience. In fact a large part of the section

titled "Dialectic" is devoted to the exposure of metaphysical sophistries. But insofar as Kant recognizes in this part of his work the existence of a further set of intellectual operations involved in scientific inquiry, he seeks to show that the faculty of theoretical reason as well as that of the understanding has its appropriate pure employment.

JUDGMENT OR BELIEF. A good way to approach the central doctrines of the analytic is to see them as an intended answer to Hume. Kant's knowledge of Hume was limited—he had no firsthand acquaintance with the *Treatise of Human Nature*—but he grasped the importance of many of Hume's most challenging points. For instance, Hume had argued that "*belief is more properly an act of the sensitive, than of the cogitative part of our natures*" (*Treatise*, edited by L. A. Selby-Bigge, 1888, Book I, Part IV, Sec. 1, p. 183); in the last resort it is a matter of subjective conviction. It is one of Kant's main objects in the analytic to demonstrate that such a view cannot do justice to an all-important feature of what Hume calls belief and he calls judgment, namely, its claim to be true. When I judge that something is the case I do not merely commit myself to a certain assertion; there is a sense in which I commit all rational persons too, for I purport to state what holds objectively, that is to say for everyone. To make judgment primarily a matter of feeling, something private to an individual person, is to leave out what is most characteristic of it. Similarly, to explain thinking about matters of fact and existence in terms of the association of ideas, as Hume did, is to confuse the objective with the subjective, to put science on the level of idle reverie. Empirical thinking, to deserve its name, must proceed according to rules, and there is all the difference in the world between a rule, which cannot of its nature be private, and association, which is the connecting of ideas on a purely personal plane.

THE UNITY OF EXPERIENCE. There are many philosophers who would accept this criticism of Hume but would deny that empirical thinking involves not only rules, but rules that are a priori or necessary rules. To understand why Kant asserts that thinking must proceed according to necessary rules, we must explain his attitude to another of Hume's doctrines, the famous contention that "all our experimental conclusions proceed upon the supposition that the future will be conformable to the past" (*Enquiry concerning Human Understanding*, Sec. IV, Part II). Kant agrees with Hume that empirical knowledge involves connecting one part or element of experience with another; he agrees too that connection of this sort ("synthesis") proceeds on a principle that is neither propose to remedy the deficiency by producing "transcendental" systems of their own. There is reason to believe that the work on which Kant was engaged in the last years of his life was intended as a counterblast to such critics. But Kant was not able to complete it before his death, and all that remains of it are the fragments gathered together under the title *Opus Postumum*.

Kant's outer life was almost entirely uneventful. He never married. The one occasion on which he might have become politically prominent was in 1794 when, after the appearance of his book on religion, the Prussian king asked him not to publish further on a topic on which his views were causing alarm to the orthodox. But Kant duly promised, and no scandal ensued. For the rest, he fulfilled the duties of his professorship and took his turn as rector of the university; dined regularly with his friends; admired Jean-Jacques Rousseau and the French Revolution from afar; conversed eagerly with travelers who brought him news of a wider world he never saw himself. Never very robust in body, he carefully conserved his physical resources and was in good health until a relatively short time before his death. He was nearly eighty when he died.

CHARACTER OF KANT'S PHILOSOPHICAL WORK

Kant was the first of the major philosophers of modern times to spend his life as a professional teacher of the subject. He was required by university regulation to base his philosophy lectures on particular texts, and he used for this purpose not the works of such major thinkers as René Descartes and John Locke, but the handbooks of his professorial predecessors, notably Christian Wolff, Alexander Gottlieb Baumgarten, and G. F. Meier. Wolff and Baumgarten had dressed out the philosophy of Gottfried Wilhelm Leibniz in what they took to be decent academic garb, presenting Leibniz' thoughts in the form of a system and with an air of finality foreign to the original; Meier did the same for the doctrines of formal logic. Their example had a near-fatal effect on Kant, for he too thought that philosophy must be thorough if it is to be academically respectable—meaning, among other things, technical and schematic.

In the *Critique of Pure Reason* Kant set out his theories in what he later called progressive order, starting from what was logically first and working forward to familiar facts; in that work he also employed an elaborate terminology of his own and an apparatus of "parts," "divisions," and "books" whose titles are alarming and whose appropriateness to the subject matter is not immediately

obvious. It is not surprising that his first readers were unable to discover what the work as a whole was about. The *Critique of Practical Reason* and the *Critique of Judgment* were still more pedantic in form, since in them Kant persisted with much of the formal framework already used in the *Critique of Pure Reason*, in each case proceeding from a part labeled "Analytic" to another labeled "Dialectic," uncovering one or more "antinomies" in dealing with the dialectic, and ending with an untidy appendix irrelevantly titled "Doctrine of Method." The fact that Kant was already an old man when he composed these works doubtless explains his attachment to what some commentators have called his architectonic; it is a major obstacle to the proper grasp and unprejudiced evaluation of his ideas. Yet, as passages in his ethical writings in particular show, Kant was capable of expounding his thoughts with clarity, even with eloquence. He was not by nature a bad writer, but he accepted uncritically the scholastic manner cultivated by his fellow professors.

The first task in reading Kant is thus to cut through the formal academic dress in which he clothes his opinions. When this is done, what emerges is not a provincial pedant like Wolff or Baumgarten, but a person of remarkable intellectual and moral stature. Kant's knowledge of the major European philosophers was often no more than superficial, and his estimate of the work of some of his own contemporaries was certainly overgenerous. But he had, for all that, a sure sense of what was intellectually important at the time; he alone among the eighteenth-century philosophers at once appreciated the greatness of Isaac Newton and was fully aware of the challenge for ethics Newton's work presented once its seemingly deterministic implications were understood. To sum up Kant's mature philosophy in a single formula: He wished to insist on the authority of science and yet preserve the autonomy of morals. To achieve this result was a gigantic task, involving consideration of the whole question of the possibility of metaphysics as well as the construction of a theory of scientific knowledge and the elaboration of an ethical system.

Nor was Kant one to be content with mere generalities; he sought to work out his position in detail, with many specific arguments, as well as to state a general case. But the obscurities of his language combine with the extent of his intellectual ambitions to prevent the average reader from grasping precisely what Kant was after; individual points are picked up, but the shape of the whole is not discerned. Yet to be fair to Kant the reader must see the individual views in the wide setting in which Kant saw them himself. To estimate their philosophical value with-

probable. But he refuses principle from "Custom ly than Hume the conse- ical solution." If it were s "loose and separate" as d we be deprived of any ings, but we should have sort. For it is a necessary onsciousness that we be here and now to things mediate purview; if the lity, then neither is uni- lls in one place (A 113) earances" (the fact that connected in a single to the ability of the a single person with ation is one of mutual

explanation as he gave , in a passage in which the "Analytic" appear ersistent but nonethe- ve from saying that appearances must be sion that they must be universal and neces-

f knowledge, no m of knowledge ty of conscious- ntuitions, and by n of objects is al unchangeable endental apper- unity of apper- le appearances, another in one ese representa- unity of con- if the mind in d not become ion whereby it nowledge. The usness of the ne time a con- y unity of the rding to con- hich not only le but also in

so doing determine an object for their intuition, that is, the concept of something wherein they are necessarily interconnected. (A 107–108)

ROLE OF CATEGORIES. If the synthesis of appearances is to proceed in accordance with necessary laws, we must clearly operate not just with empirical but also with a priori concepts. But this must not be taken to mean that some items or features of fact can be known apart from all experience. For the role of an a priori concept is fundamentally different from that of its empirical counterpart. Categories are concepts of a higher order than empirical concepts; like the ideas of space and time, they have to do with the form of experience rather than its matter. Our possession of categories accordingly supplies no knowledge of particular things; categories are fertile only when brought to bear on empirical data. Thus, because we hold to the a priori concept of cause, we interrogate nature in a certain way; thanks to it, we refuse to believe that there could be an uncaused event. But the answers we get to our interrogation depend primarily not on the form of our questions, but on what turns up in experience. Those who accuse Kant of having believed in the material a priori have failed to understand his theory.

To summarize this part of Kant's argument: If we are to have knowledge (and it is Kant's assumption that we do), various conditions must be fulfilled. The different items that fall within our experience must be capable of being connected in a single consciousness; there can be no happenings that are genuinely loose and separate. But the connections thus demanded must be objective connections—they must hold not just for my consciousness, but for "consciousness in general," for everyone's. An objective connection for Kant is a connection determined by a rule, and a rule is of its nature something that claims intersubjective validity. Finally, if we are to establish the operation of empirical rules we must proceed in accordance with nonempirical rules of a higher order, rules that ensure that our different experiences are capable of connection within a single experience.

JUDGMENTS. In view of the close relation Kant sees between the making of judgments and the use of a priori concepts, it is perhaps not surprising that he tries to arrive at a full list of such concepts by scrutinizing the formal properties of judgments. In this connection he invokes the doctrines of general or formal logic, a science he believed had been brought to completion at a single stroke by Aristotle. Few scholars have been convinced by this section of his argument, for it seems clear that Kant adapted the list of judgment forms to suit his list of categories, rather than deriving the categories from the judgment forms. In any case, it is not obvious how formal logic, which is a logic of consistency, can supply a clue to the content of what professes to be a logic of truth.

IMAGINATION AND UNDERSTANDING. In the first part of the "Analytic" Kant has much to say not only about concepts, judgments, and the understanding but also about the imagination. For example, he remarks in a cryptic passage:

> Synthesis in general is the mere result of the power of imagination, a blind but indispensable function in the soul, without which we should have no knowledge whatsoever, but of which we are scarcely ever conscious. To bring this synthesis to concepts is a function which belongs to understanding, and it is through this function of the understanding that we first obtain knowledge properly so called. (B 103)

The contrasting and, in places, overlapping roles of understanding and imagination are among the most puzzling features of Kant's exposition. The reason why they are both introduced is related to the fact that, in the second edition of the *Critique of Pure Reason* in particular, Kant was concerned with two quite distinct questions. He first asked himself what conditions have to be fulfilled if any sort of discursive consciousness is to have objective knowledge; he then went on to put the question as it relates to the human discursive consciousness, which not only intuits data passively, but does so under the particular forms of space and time. When the first question is uppermost Kant tends to speak of the understanding; when the second is to the fore, he brings in the imagination as well. The passage quoted above, typical of many, suggests that it is the business of the imagination to connect, whereas that of the understanding is to make explicit the principles on which the connecting proceeds. But in one chapter, "Schematism of the Pure Concepts of Understanding," a more satisfying account of the relationship is offered.

SCHEMATA. The problem of the chapter on what Kant called "schematism" is the central problem of the analytic: How can concepts that do not originate in experience find application in experience? At first Kant speaks as if there were no comparable difficulty in the case of concepts originating in experience, although he later makes clear that there are schemata corresponding both to empirical and to mathematical concepts. To possess the concept triangle is to know its formal definition, to be able to frame intelligible sentences containing the word *triangle*, and so on; to possess the schema corresponding to the concept triangle is to be able to envisage the variety of things to which the word *triangle* applies. Thus for Kant a schema is not an image, but a capacity to form images or (perhaps) to construct models. Pure concepts of the understanding are such that they "can never be brought into any image whatsoever" (B 181); the thought they embody, springing from the pure intellect, cannot be pictured or imagined. Yet there must be some connection between the abstract idea and the experienced world to which that idea is expected to apply; it must be possible to specify the empirical circumstances in which pure concepts of the understanding can find application. Kant thinks that for the categories this requirement is met by the fact that we can find for each of them a "transcendental schema," which is, he explains, a "transcendental determination of time." Without such a schema the categories would be devoid of "sense and significance," except in a logical (verbal) way. With it, use of the categories is clearly restricted to the range of things that fall within time—meaning, for Kant, restricted to phenomena.

The meaning of this baffling doctrine can perhaps best be grasped through Kant's examples of schemata:

> The schema of substance is permanence of the real in time, that is, the representation of the real as a substrate of empirical determination of time in general. … The schema of cause… is the real upon which, whenever posited, something else always follows. It consists, therefore, in the succession of the manifold, in so far as that succession is subject to a rule. … The schema of necessity is existence of an object at all times. (B 183–184)

It emerges from these cryptic sentences that the transcendental schema is something like an empirical counterpart of the pure category. It is what the latter means when translated into phenomenal terms. In Kant's own words, the schema is "properly, only the phenomenon, or sensible concept, of an object in agreement with the category" (B 186). A category without its corresponding "sensible concept" would be a bare abstraction, virtually without significance. Insofar as he argues that schematization is the work of the imagination, Kant has found a genuine function for the imagination to perform.

ANALYTIC OF PRINCIPLES: PURE PHYSICS. In the first half of the "Analytic" Kant undertook to produce a "transcendental deduction," that is, a general proof of validity, of the categories. In the second half of the "Analytic" he

sition in the Kantian system, to do, is quite indefensible.

mmonly divided into two ly referred to as "precriti-y referred to as "critical." Kant's own description of n of "critical idealism," an the basis of a critique of critical period of Kant's though not exclusively, deas. Kant was educated arten version of Leibniz, independent Leibnizian ny years before he made an way of thinking. The Leibniz in Kant's early work he had also been re narrowly philosoph-Leibnizian, Christian rtant subsidiary influ-akened Kant from his but it seems likely that direction of empiricism

Kant had learned from his first metaphysical um Cognitionis Meta-sberg, 1755) he dis-causality, discussing an izian principle of suf-iples of identity and tage, as Crusius did, the real to the logical y idea of what he was ropositions asserting earer his mature view ntities (*Versuch, den n die Weltweisheit* pointed out that t from opposition in another are quite same predicate is But in none of his y raise the question causal principle, as

EXISTENCE. Kant's failure to press home his questions on causation is paralleled in his otherwise striking treatment of existence in another work published in 1763, "The Only Possible Ground of Proof of God's Existence." He began this work by declaring that even if the proposition that existence is no predicate or determination of anything seems "strange and contradictory," it is nevertheless indubitable and certain. "It is not a fully correct expression to say: 'A sea unicorn is an existent animal'; we should put it the other way round and say: 'To a certain existing sea animal there belong the predicates that I think of as collectively constituting a sea unicorn.'" On these grounds Kant rejected the Cartesian version of the Ontological Argument. But he held, even so, that an alternative conceptual proof of God's existence could be found: Nothing could be conceived as possible unless (as the point had already been put in the *Nova Dilucidatio*) "whatever of reality there is in every possible notion do exist, and indeed, absolutely necessarily. … Further, this complete reality must be united in a single being." There must, in other words, be a perfect being if there are to be any possibilities. Kant was to recall this proof in his derivation of the idea of the *ens realissimum* in the *Critique of Pure Reason*, but he then no longer believed that it had constitutive force. His treatment of attempts to produce causal proofs of God's existence in the *Critique* was also altogether more trenchant than in the precritical works, for though he saw there that the ordinary First Cause Argument was unsatisfactory, he regarded the Argument from Design as generally acceptable, even if not logically compulsive.

METAPHYSICAL PROPOSITIONS. Kant was more successful in another treatise written at the same period, "Untersuchungen über die Deutlichkeit der Grundsätze der natürlichen Theologie und der Moral" (On the Distinctness of the Principles of Natural Theology and Morals; 1764). The Berlin Academy had proposed the question, Are metaphysical truths generally, and the fundamental principles of natural theology and morals in particular, capable of proofs as distinct as those of geometry? If not, what is the true nature of their certainty? Kant answered by drawing a series of radical distinctions between argument in philosophy and argument in mathematics. The mathematician starts from definitions that are in effect arbitrary combinations of concepts; the philosopher must work toward definitions, not argue from them, since his business is to "analyze concepts which are given as confused." Mathematics contains few unanalyzable concepts and indemonstrable propositions; philosophy is full of them. Then too, the relationship gives a series of demonstrations of the synthetic a priori principles that rest on individual categories.

The categories are divided, for this and other purposes, into four groups: quantity, quality, relation, and modality. The four sets of corresponding principles are labeled axioms of intuition, anticipations of perception, analogies of experience, and postulates of empirical thought in general. Only one principle falls under each of the first two classes; the third contains a general principle and three more specific principles; the fourth contains three separate though closely connected principles. The first two classes are grouped together as "mathematical" principles; the third and fourth are described as "dynamical." Mathematical principles are said to be "immediately evident" and again to be "constitutive of their objects"; they apply directly to appearances. Dynamical principles are concerned with "the existence of such appearances and their relation to one another in respect of their existence." They are no less necessary than mathematical principles, but must be distinguished from them "in the nature of their evidence" and in that they are not "constitutive" but "regulative."

Behind this formidable façade some interesting ideas are hidden. In the first place, Kant makes stimulating though not altogether convincing remarks on the subject of proving principles of the understanding. The statement that every event has a cause carries strict necessity with it and therefore cannot be grounded on an inductive survey of empirical evidence. But equally it is not analytic, and so not open to straightforward conceptual proof. To be assured of its authenticity we consequently require a different type of argument altogether, which Kant calls a "transcendental" argument "from the possibility of experience." His idea is that only if the principles of the understanding are taken to be operative and in order can we have the type of experience we in fact have. Kant perhaps supposes that this type of proof is logically compulsive, but if so he overlooks the difficulty of setting up the original premise, of being sure that only if such-and-such were true should we have the experiences we have. But even with this defect his procedure has an immediate appeal, and is not without modern imitators.

AXIOMS OF INTUITION. The details of the particular arguments for the principles corresponding to the categories also deserve careful attention. The principle of axioms of intuition, that "all intuitions are extended magnitudes," is perhaps the most difficult to take seriously, since what it purports to prove has apparently already been dealt with in the "Aesthetic." Kant is once more ask-

ing questions about the application of mathematics to the world; in this section of the *Critique* the problem that apparently troubles him is how we know that inquiries about sizes or areas are always appropriate when we are dealing with things that occupy space. His solution is that they must be appropriate, since every such thing can be regarded as an aggregate of parts produced by the observer as he synthesizes his experiences. "I cannot represent to myself a line, however short, without drawing it in thought, that is, generating from a point all its parts one after another" (B 203).

ANTICIPATIONS OF PERCEPTION. Under the term "anticipations of perception" Kant is concerned with the question of the applicability of mathematics to sensations. What guarantee have we, he asks, that every sensation will turn out to have a determinate degree, in principle quantifiable? Might we not find, for instance, that an object is colored but with no precise depth of saturation, or a smell present in a room but with no specific magnitude? Kant attempts to rule out such possibilities by attention to the formal properties of sensations. We cannot anticipate the matter of sensation, but we can say in advance of experience that every sensation will have intensive magnitude, that is, a determinate degree, because it is possible to think of any given sensation as fading away until it is imperceptible, and conversely as being built up by continuous transitions on a scale from zero to the magnitude it has. Whatever may be the merits of this solution, there can be no doubt of the importance, and for that matter the novelty, of the question Kant asks here.

ANALOGIES OF EXPERIENCE. The section on the analogies of experience contains ideas as significant as any in Kant's writings.

The permanence of substance. The principle of the first analogy is that of the permanence of substance: "in all change of appearances substance is permanent; its quantum in nature is neither increased nor diminished." To believe in the permanence of substance is to believe that, whatever happens, nothing goes completely out of existence and nothing totally new is created: All change is transformation. Kant justifies the acceptance of this presupposition (which in his view, it should be remembered, applies only to things phenomenal) by arguing that without it we could not have a unitary temporal system. Coexistence and succession make sense only against a background that abides, and since time itself cannot be perceived, that background has got to be one of permanent things. This does not mean that we can determine a priori what form the permanent will take; empirical sci-entists are to pronounce on that question, and their answers may obviously change from time to time. All that Kant seeks to rule out is the possibility that there might be no permanent at all. His argument is defective at a vital point here, but presumably he is saying that if things could go completely out of existence, so that it would make no sense to ask what became of them, the establish-ment of connections between one part of experience and another would be impossible. Experience would be (or at least might be) full of unbridgeable gaps, with the result that no one set of happenings could be integrated with another, and the unity of time would be totally destroyed.

Causation. Kant carries his argument further in his discussion of the second and third analogies, in which he argues for the necessary operation of the concepts of cause and reciprocity (causal interaction). But just as the notion of substance he justifies is very different from that held by metaphysicians, so is the Kantian concept of cause different from that of, say, Leibniz; it seems at first sight much closer to Hume's idea of a cause as an invari-able antecedent. Causality for Kant as for Hume is a rela-tion between successive events; a cause is an event that regularly precedes its effect. But whereas Hume is content to treat the occurrence of regular sequences as an ulti-mate and entirely contingent fact, Kant believes that without the presumption of sequences that are regular (determined by a rule) there could be no knowledge of objective succession. His reason is that we have to distin-guish successions that happen only in ourselves, succes-sions merely in our apprehension, from those that occur in the objective world and are independent of us. We can do this only if an objective sequence is defined as a sequence happening according to a rule. The objective world is a world of events the occurrence of each of which determines the precise place in time of some other event. But though events are necessarily connected in this way, we must not conclude that causal connections can be established a priori; for Kant as for Hume causal proposi-tions are one and all synthetic and empirical. All we can know a priori is that there are such connections to be found, provided we have the skill or good fortune to dis-cover them.

POSTULATES OF EMPIRICAL THOUGHT.
One way of expressing Kant's attitude to substance and causality is to say that he thinks the principle of substance licenses us to ask the question, What became of that? Whenever some-thing happens, and that the principle of causality licenses the parallel question, What brought that about? If some-one tried to say that things might go out of existence alto-

gether, or happen for no reason at all, Kant would say that these were logical but not real possibilities. The contrast between real and logical possibility is explored by Kant in the section "The Postulates of Empirical Thought." This section contains an explanation of the notions of possi-bility, actuality, and necessity from the critical point of view. By "really possible" Kant means "that which agrees with the formal conditions of experience, that is, with the conditions of intuition and of concepts" (B 265). A two-sided figure enclosing a space is not really possible, though its concept is not self-contradictory, because such a figure does not accord with the formal conditions of intuition. Telepathy and precognition are not real possi-bilities; they "cannot be based on experience and its known laws" (B 270), presumably because their actuality would violate some principle of the understanding, although Kant fails to make the point clear. The notion of real possibility is for Kant intermediate between logical and empirical possibility. We need it and can use it only because the world we have to deal with is a world that is not independently existent, but has its being in essential relation to consciousness.

PHENOMENA AND THINGS-IN-THEMSELVES.
The distinction between phenomena and things-in-them-selves, insisted on in the "Aesthetic" to explain our having a priori knowledge of the properties of space and time, is invoked again in the "Analytic" to account for "pure physics." If the world we confronted were one of things-in-themselves, a priori knowledge of it, even of the very restricted sort for which Kant argues, would be quite impossible. The fact that we have such knowledge—that we possess the principles discussed above—is taken by Kant as proof that the objects of our knowledge are phe-nomena or appearances. He does not mean by this, how-ever, that they are private objects, at least insofar as they are spatial. The world we know in everyday and scientific experience is common to many observers; if not inde-pendent of consciousness as such, it is independent of particular consciousnesses. Parts of it are known only to particular experiencers—my inner life, for example, is accessible only to me—but that does not affect the gen-eral point.

Kant's acceptance of the distinction between phe-nomena and things-in-themselves has met with much criticism. Without the idea of the thing-in-itself, said his contemporary F. H. Jacobi, we cannot enter the world of the *Critique of Pure Reason*; with it we cannot remain inside. At the end of the "Analytic" Kant tries to defend himself against criticism of this sort by arguing that though he says that the objects of experience are phenomena and is prepared to admit that the obverse of a phenomenon is a noumenon or intelligible object, he is committed to noumena only in a negative sense. Having said that the categories, one of which is existence, apply only to phenomena, he cannot with consistency hold any other view. Nor is his position at this stage as devoid of logic as some have tried to make out. After all, to describe things as phenomena he does not need to assert that there actually are things of a different kind; he needs only the idea of such things. To talk about things as they might be in themselves is no more objectionable than to speak of an *intellectus archetypus*, as Kant did in the letter to Herz, or of an intuitive understanding, as he constantly does in both the *Critique of Pure Reason* and the *Critique of Judgment*.

THE ELIMINATION OF DOGMATIC METAPHYSICS

At the end of the section of the *Critique of Pure Reason* devoted to the transcendental analytic, there is a passage that can be taken as summarizing the second stage in Kant's emancipation from Leibnizian rationalism:

> The Transcendental Analytic leads to this important conclusion, that the most the understanding can achieve *a priori* is to anticipate the form of a possible experience in general. And since that which is not appearance cannot be an object of experience, the understanding can never transcend those limits of sensibility within which alone objects can be given to us. Its principles are merely rules for the exposition of appearances; and the proud name of an Ontology that presumptuously claims to supply, in systematic doctrinal form, synthetic *a priori* knowledge of things in general … must, therefore, give place to the modest title of a mere Analytic of pure understanding. (B 303)

Kant thus repudiates the possibility of knowledge through pure concepts of things as they really are; in 1770 he had still clung to it. Having disposed of ontology, Kant needed to consider, to complete the negative side of his work, the tenability of the remaining parts of metaphysics (rational psychology, rational cosmology, and natural theology in Baumgarten's classification), and this he did in the section titled "Transcendental Dialectic." To complete his own alternative to rationalism he needed to clarify the status of the propositions involved in "pure practical faith." His attempt to meet this requirement is made at the very end of the *Critique*, especially in the chapter "The Canon of Pure Reason" (B 823ff.).

REASON. Most of the conclusions of the "Dialectic" follow directly from those of the "Analytic," though there are new points of interest. As in the "Analytic," Kant's views are expressed inside a framework that is heavily scholastic. Kant claimed that human beings have an intellectual faculty in addition to the understanding. This additional faculty is reason, and it is equipped with a set of a priori concepts of its own, technically known as ideas of reason. An idea of reason can have no object corresponding to it in sense experience, for the ambition of reason is to arrive at absolute totality in the series of conditions for the empirically given, and in this way to grasp the unconditioned that falls outside experience altogether. However, this ambition can never be realized, and the only proper function for reason in its theoretical capacity is to regulate the operations of the understanding by encouraging it to pursue the search for conditions to the maximum extent that is empirically possible.

THE KNOWING SUBJECT. Kant's handling of the "psychological idea" at the beginning of the main part of the "Dialectic" is exceptionally brilliant. He maintains in the "Analytic" that what he there calls the "I think," or the unity of apperception, is the ultimate condition of experience, in the sense of being the logical subject of experience or the point to which all experience relates. All experience is experience for a subject; whatever thoughts or feelings I have I must be capable of recognizing as my thoughts or feelings. But the subject here referred to is not something substantial; it is merely a logical requirement, in that nothing follows about the nature of my soul or self from the fact that I say "I think." So far from being "an abiding and continuing intuition" (the sort of thing Hume vainly sought in the flow of his inner consciousness), for Kant the "representation 'I' … [is] simple, and in itself completely empty … we cannot even say that this is a concept, but only that it is a bare consciousness which accompanies all concepts. Through this I or he or it (the thing) which thinks, nothing further is represented than a transcendental subject of thoughts = *X*" (B 404). The same view is expressed in an earlier passage in the *Critique*, where Kant says that "in the synthetic original unity of apperception, I am conscious of, myself, not as I appear to myself, nor as I am in myself, but [I am conscious] only that I am. This *representation* is a *thought*, not an *intuition*" (B 157).

REFUTATION OF RATIONAL PSYCHOLOGY. These subtleties are unknown to the exponents of rational psychology, who develop the whole of their teaching around a "single text," which is "I think." From the fact that I am the subject of all my thoughts they infer that I am a think-ing substance; from the fact that the "I" of apperception is logically simple they conclude that I am, in substance, simple and not composite. The proposition that "in all the manifold of which I am conscious I am identical with myself" is taken by them as implying that I am possessed of continuing personal identity. Finally, my distinguish-ing my own existence as a thinking being from that of other things, including my own body, is put forward as proof that I am really distinct from such things and so could in principle exist in complete independence of them. None of these inferences is justified, for in each case a move is attempted from an analytically true prem-ise to a synthetic conclusion. As Kant remarks, "it would, indeed, be surprising if what in other cases requires so much labour to determine—namely, what, of all that is presented in intuition, is substance, and further, whether this substance can be simple …—should be thus given me directly, as if by revelation, in the poorest of all repre-sentations" (B 408).

MIND AND BODY. Kant presents the doctrines of rational psychology in his own idiosyncratic way, but anyone who reflects on the theories of Descartes will see that Kant was by no means attacking men of straw. Kant's treatment of the fourth paralogism, "of Ideality," is of spe-cial interest in this connection. Descartes inferred from his *cogito* argument that mind and body were separate in substance, which meant that the first could exist apart from the second. Bound up with this was the view that I am immediately aware of myself as a mind, but need to infer the existence of material things, which is in princi-ple open to doubt. A great many philosophers have sub-scribed to this opinion, but Kant thought he could show it to be definitively false. In order to say that my inner experiences come one before another I need to observe them against a permanent background, and this can only be a background of external objects, for there is nothing permanent in the flow of inner experience. As Kant put it in the second edition, in which he transposed the argu-ment to the discussion of existence in connection with the postulates of empirical thought), "*The mere, but empirically determined, consciousness of my own existence proves the existence of objects in space outside me*" (B 275). Kant is in no sense a behaviorist; he thinks that empirical self-knowledge is to be achieved through inner sense and declares in one passage that, for empirical purposes, dual-ism of soul and body must be taken as correct. Yet his commitment to "empirical realism" is quite unambigu-ous.

THE ANTINOMIES. Of the remaining parts of the "Dialectic," only the sections on the antinomies and on the existence of God can be discussed here. In the "Antin-omy of Pure Reason," Kant first sets out a series of pairs of metaphysical doctrines (which he says have to do with cosmology but which are in fact of wider interest). The two doctrines in each pair seem to contradict one another directly. He then produces for each pair what he regards as watertight proofs of both sides of the case, maintaining that if we adopt the dogmatic standpoint assumed with-out question by the parties to the dispute, we can prove, for example, both that the world has a beginning in time and that it has no beginning in time, both that "causality in accordance with laws of nature is not the only causal-ity" and that "everything in the world takes place solely in accordance with laws of nature." Thus Kant exhibits in systematic form the famous contradictions into which, as he notes, reason precipitates itself when it asks metaphys-ical questions. Kant is enormously impressed by the dis-covery of these contradictions, and it is regrettable only that he does not sufficiently discuss their formal charac-ter or illustrate them with genuine examples.

The only way to avoid these antinomies, in Kant's opinion, is to adopt his own (critical) point of view and recognize that the world that is the object of our knowl-edge is a world of appearances, existing only insofar as it is constructed; this solution enables us to dismiss both parties to the dispute in the case of the first two antino-mies, and to accept the contentions of both parties in the case of the other two. If the world exists only insofar as it is constructed, it is neither finite nor infinite but indefi-nitely extensible and so neither has nor lacks a limit in space and time. Equally, if the world is phenomenal we have at least the idea of a world that is not phenomenal; and natural causality can apply without restriction to the first without precluding the application of a different type of causality to the second. This is admittedly only an empty hypothesis so far as theoretical reason is con-cerned, but Kant argues that it can be converted into something more satisfactory if we take account of the activities of practical (moral) reason.

THE EXISTENCE OF GOD. The fourth antinomy is con-cerned with God's existence. Kant's full treatment of the subject is not in the section on the antinomies but in that headed "The Ideal of Pure Reason," the locus classicus for Kant's criticisms of speculative theology. These criticisms have proved as devastating as those he brought against rational psychology.

Speculative proofs. There are, Kant argues, only three ways of proving God's existence on the speculative plane. First, we can proceed entirely a priori and maintain that the very idea of God is such that God could not *not* exist; this is the method of the Ontological Argument. Second, we can move from the bare fact that the world exists to the position that God is its ultimate cause, as in the First Cause, or Cosmological, Argument. Finally, we can base our contention on the particular constitution of the world, as in the "physicotheological proof" (the Argument from Design).

Kant argues that all three types of proof are fallacious. The Ontological Argument fails because it treats existence as if it were a "real predicate," whereas "it is not a concept of something which could be added to the concept of a thing. It is merely the positing of a thing, or of certain determinations, as existing in themselves" (B 626). The First Cause Argument fails on several counts: because it uses the category of cause without realizing that only in the schematized form is the category significant; because it assumes that the only way to avoid an actually infinite causal series in the world is to posit a first cause; finally and most important, because it presupposes the validity of the Ontological Proof, in the step which identifies the "necessary being" or First Cause with God. The Argument from Design makes all these mistakes and some of its own, for even on its own terms it proves only the existence of an architect of the universe, not of a creator, and such an architect would possess remarkable but not infinite powers.

The moral proof. In spite of Kant's criticisms of the classical arguments for God's existence, he is neither an atheist nor even a believer in the principle of *credo quia impossibile.* He both believes in God and holds that the belief can be rationally justified. For although speculative theology is, broadly, a tissue of errors, moral theology is perfectly possible. But the moral proof of God's existence differs from the attempted speculative proofs in at least two significant respects. First, it begins neither from a concept nor from a fact about the world, but from an immediately experienced moral situation. The moral agent feels called upon to achieve certain results, in particular to bring about a state of affairs in which happiness is proportioned to virtue, and knows that he cannot do it by his own unaided efforts; insofar as he commits himself to action he shows his belief in a moral author of the universe. Affirmation of God's existence is intimately linked with practice; it is most definitely not the result of mere speculation. Again, a proof like the First Cause Argument claims universal validity; standing as it does on purely intellectual grounds it ought, if cogent, to persuade saint and sinner alike. But the moral proof as Kant states it would not even have meaning to a man who is unconscious of moral obligations; the very word *God*, removed from the moral context that gives it life, is almost or quite without significance. Accordingly Kant states that the result of this proof is not objective knowledge but a species of personal conviction, embodying not logical but moral certainty. He adds that "I must not even say '*It is* morally certain that there is a God …,' but '*I am* morally certain'" (B 857). In other words, the belief or faith Kant proposes as a replacement for discredited metaphysical knowledge can be neither strictly communicated nor learned from another. It is something that has to be achieved by every man for himself.

ETHICS

Kant perhaps intended originally to make the *Critique of Pure Reason* the vehicle of his entire philosophy, but it was clear before he completed it that some of his views, especially those on ethics, could be only touched on there. In the years immediately following its publication he displayed exceptional energy in defending and restating the theories he had already put forth and in extending his philosophy to cover topics he had hitherto not treated, or not treated in detail. By 1788 he had not only published the second, substantially revised edition of the *Critique of Pure Reason*, but had laid the foundations for his ethics in his short but influential *Groundwork of the Metaphysic of Morals* (1785) and had undertaken a more elaborate survey of moral concepts and assumptions in the *Critique of Practical Reason* (1788). He had also, in passing, written his essay *Metaphysical Foundations of Natural Science* (1786), intended as a first step toward a projected but never completed metaphysics of nature. Two years after the *Critique of Practical Reason* he produced yet another substantial work, the *Critique of Judgment*, in which he expressed his views on, among other topics, aesthetics and teleology.

MORAL ACTIONS. If he had published nothing else but the *Groundwork of the Metaphysic of Morals* Kant would be assured a place in the history of philosophy. Difficult as it is to interpret in some of its details, this work is written with an eloquence, depth of insight, and strength of feeling that make an immediate impact on the reader and put it among the classics of the subject. Kant says that his "sole aim" in the book is "to seek out and establish *the supreme principle of morality*." He wishes to delineate the basic features of the situation in which moral decisions are made, and so to clarify the special character of such decisions.

The situation as he sees it is roughly as follows. Man is a creature who is half sensual, half rational. Sensuous impulses are the determining factor in many of his actions, and the role of reason in these cases is that assigned to it by Hume; it is the slave or servant of the passions. But there is an identifiable class of actions in which reason plays a different part, leading rather than following. This is the class of moral actions. Such actions have the distinguishing feature that they are undertaken not for some ulterior end, but simply because of the principle they embody.

INTENTIONS AND MORAL JUDGMENTS. The moral worth of an action, as Kant puts it (*Grundlegung*, 2nd ed., p. 13), lies "not in the purpose to be attained by it, but in the maxim in accordance with which it is decided upon." Whether or not I attain my ends does not depend on me alone, and my actions cannot be pronounced good or bad according to the effects they actually bring about. But I can be praised or blamed for my intentions, and I can, if I choose, make sure that the maxim or subjective principle of my action accords with the requirements of morality. To do this I have only to ask myself the simple question whether I could will that the maxim should become a universal law, governing not merely this particular action of mine, but the actions of all agents similarly circumstanced. For it is a formal property of moral as of scientific judgments, recognized in practice even by the unsophisticated, that they hold without distinction of persons; the result is that an action can be permissible for me only if it is permissible for anyone in my situation.

PRACTICAL REASON. There are difficulties in this position of which Kant seems to have been unaware. In particular, he never asks how I am to decide what is the correct description, and hence the maxim, of my act or proposed act. Nor is it obvious how the theory shows the falsity of Hume's view that "reason alone can never be a motive to any action of the will"—how it can be shown, in Kant's language, that pure reason really is practical. The practical effectiveness of reason is manifested not in the capacity to reflect, which both Kant and Hume allow, but in the power to originate or inhibit action. Kant obviously thinks that the facts of temptation and resistance to temptation, which he sees as ubiquitous in the moral life, have a clear bearing on the question whether reason really has such a power. Recognition that I ought to follow a certain course of action, whether I want to or not, and that anything that is morally obligatory must also be

practically possible, is enough in his view to show that I am not necessarily at the mercy of my desires. In favorable cases, at any rate (Kant pays too little attention to the factors that diminish and sometimes demolish responsibility), I am free to resist my sensuous impulses and to determine my actions by rational considerations alone.

CONSEQUENCES OF THE MORAL LAW. Some commentators have seen Kant as an ethical intuitionist, but this view is clearly mistaken. His "practical reason" is not the faculty of insight into the content of the moral law; it is rather the capacity to act. In determining what the moral law commands, I have initially no other resources at my disposal than the reflection that it must be applied impartially. But in practice this criterion carries others with it. If the moral law applies without distinction of persons, Kant believes it follows that I must treat all human beings as equally entitled to rights under it, and that therefore I must regard them as ends in themselves and never as merely means to my own ends. Further, once I recognize that other people are morally in the same position as I am myself, and that we belong to the same moral community, I recognize both that I can legitimately pursue those of my purposes that do not conflict with the moral law and that I also have a duty to facilitate the like pursuit on the part of my fellows. So though Kant is a formalist in his view of moral reason (as in his view of the theoretical intellect), he sees his ethics as having practical consequences of the first importance. He sets these consequences out in his lectures on ethics and develops them in detail later in his 1797 *Metaphysic of Morals*. To judge him by the *Groundwork* alone, or even by the *Groundwork* and the *Critique of Practical Reason* taken together, is to do less than justice to the scope of his ethical reflection.

MORAL IMPERATIVES. Previous moral philosophies, Kant writes, whether they put their stress on moral sense or on moral reason, have all been vitiated by a failure to recognize the principle of the autonomy of the will. Utilitarianism, for instance, is a heteronomous ethical theory because, according to its supporters, the point of a moral action is to promote an end or purpose beyond the action, the greatest happiness of the greatest number. Kant is not unaware of the importance of ends and purposes in actions: In the *Critique of Practical Reason* he corrects the one-sidedness of the *Groundwork* by discoursing at length on the concept of "good" as well as on that of "duty." But he holds, even so, that consideration of ends cannot be of primary importance for the moral agent, since a moral action is one that is commanded for its own sake, not with a view to some purpose it is expected to bring about. The imperatives of morality command categorically, unlike those of skill or prudence, which have only hypothetical force. A rule of skill or a counsel of prudence bids us take certain steps if we wish to attain a certain end—good health or overall happiness, for example. There is no "if" about a command of morality; it bids me act in a certain way whether I want to or not, and without regard to any result the action may bring about. It represents a course of conduct as unconditionally necessary, not just necessary because it conduces to a certain end.

FREEDOM AND NECESSITY. The concepts of duty, the categorical imperative, the moral law, and the realm of ends (in which we are all at once subjects and lawgivers) are intended by Kant to illuminate the moral situation. But even when we know what that situation is, there are many features of it that remain mysterious. Morality as Kant expounds it involves autonomy of the will, and such autonomy clearly makes no sense except on the supposition of freedom. But how we can think of the will as free and at the same time regard ourselves as subject to the moral law, that is, as under obligation, has still to be explained. To throw light on this question, Kant invokes the concept of the two worlds, the sensible and the intelligible, to which he made appeal in the *Critique of Pure Reason.* Insofar as I exercise the faculty of reason I have to regard myself as belonging to the intelligible world; insofar as I exercise my "lower" faculties I am part of the world of nature, which is known through the senses. Were I a purely rational being, possessed of what Kant sometimes calls a "holy will," all my actions would be in perfect conformity with the principle of autonomy, and the notions of obligation and the moral law would have no meaning for me. They would similarly have no meaning if I were a purely sensuous being, for then everything I did would occur according to natural necessity, and there would be no sense in thinking that things ought to be otherwise. The peculiarities of the human moral situation arise from the fact that men are, or rather must think of themselves as being, at once intelligible and sensible. Because I regard myself as belonging to the intelligible order, I see myself as "under laws which, being independent of nature, are not empirical but have their ground in reason alone" (*Critique of Practical Reason,* p. 109). But I am also a natural being, and those laws therefore present themselves to me in the form of commands that I acknowledge as absolute because I recognize that the intelligible world is the ground of the sensible. We can thus see "how a categorical imperative is possible."

What we cannot see, if Kant is to be believed, is how freedom is possible. "All men think of themselves as having a free will. … Moreover, for *purposes of action* the footpath of freedom is the only one on which we can make use of reason in our conduct. Hence to argue freedom away is as impossible for the most abstruse philosophy as it is for the most ordinary human reason" (*Critique of Practical Reason,* p. 113–115). Yet freedom remains what it is in the *Critique of Pure Reason,* "only an idea whose objective reality is in itself questionable," and there is a prima facie clash between the claim to freedom and the knowledge that everything in nature is determined by natural necessity. Kant seeks to dissolve the antinomy of freedom and necessity by means of two expedients. First, he insists that the idea of freedom required for morals is not a theoretical but a practical idea. Freedom does not need to be established as a metaphysical fact; it is enough that we find it necessary to act on the assumption that freedom is real, since "every being who cannot act except under the idea of freedom is by this alone—from the practical point of view—really free" (p. 100). The status of the proposition that the will is free is identical with that of the proposition that there is a God. Both are postulates of practical reason—beliefs that we "inevitably" accept; but they are emphatically not items of knowledge in the strict sense of that term. Second, Kant sees no difficulty in our accepting the postulate of freedom, because there is no contradiction in thinking of the will as free. As an object of theoretical scrutiny I must regard myself as a phenomenon; as a moral agent possessed of a will I transfer myself to the intelligible world of noumena. I can be at once under necessity qua phenomenon and free qua noumenon. But the question of how I can be free leads to the extreme limits of practical philosophy. Freedom cannot be explained, for we lack all insight into the intelligible world; the most we can do is make clear why it cannot be explained. The critical philosophy purports to have performed this task.

EPISTEMOLOGY AND ETHICS. Kant advocates a form of nonnaturalist theory in ethics. But neither his ethics nor his theory of knowledge can be fully understood in isolation one from the other. The two together constitute an overall theory that is not so much a metaphysics as a substitute for a metaphysics: A theory that argues that human insight is strictly limited, but urges that, so far from being regrettable, this testifies to "the wise adaptation of man's cognitive faculties to his practical vocation" (*Critique of Practical Reason and Other Writings,* Beck translation, 1949, p. 247). If we knew more, we might indeed do as we ought, for "God and eternity in their awful majesty would stand unceasingly before our eyes," but we should not then do things as a matter of duty, but rather out of fear or hope. And thus the world would be poorer, for we should lose the opportunity to manifest "good will," the only thing in the world, "or even out of it, which can be taken as good without qualification."

THE CRITIQUE OF JUDGMENT

None of Kant's other writings is as forceful or original as the first two *Critiques* and the *Groundwork*. The *Critique of Judgment* contains some fresh ideas of remarkable power, but it constitutes a series of appendixes or addenda to Kant's earlier work rather than something wholly new. It should really be seen as three or four separate essays whose connecting link is the concept of purpose.

SYSTEM OF SCIENCE. The first essay, the introduction, begins with a pedantic discussion of the status of the power of judgment. It then takes up a problem aired in the appendix to the "Dialectic" in the *Critique of Pure Reason*—the problem of the special assumptions involved in the belief that we can construct a system of scientific laws. If we are to have such a system, Kant argues, we must proceed on the principle that nature is "formally purposive" in respect of empirical laws; that nature is such that we can make sense of it not merely in general, but also in detail. Kant's object is to show that this principle is not a constitutive principle of things, but simply a subjective maxim of judgment.

In the *Critique of Pure Reason* (B 670ff.) Kant argues for what he calls the regulative employment of the ideas of reason: the use of ideas to order empirical inquiries in such a way that we try at once to find greater and greater diversity of form in the material before us and to group different species and subspecies together under ever higher genera. In actual practice we assume that nature will display the unity-in-diversity required for this program to be carried out, but we cannot prove that it will do so as we can prove that whatever falls within experience will conform to the categories. Hence we are concerned not with objective rules, but only with maxims, defined in this connection as "subjective principles which are derived, not from the constitution of an object but from the interest of reason in respect of a certain possible perfection of the knowledge of the object" (B 694).

In the *Critique of Pure Reason* Kant ascribes these maxims to reason. In the *Critique of Judgment*, he assigns them to judgment, in effect the identical doctrine. The difference is accounted for by two facts. First, by the time Kant wrote the *Critique of Judgment*, the term *reason* suggested to him nothing but practical reason. Second, he had come to think that if the power of judgment is genuinely separate from understanding on the one hand and reason on the other it must have a priori principles of its own. A division within the power of judgment itself, into determinant and reflective activities, had helped to make this last point plausible, at least in the eyes of its author.

AESTHETICS. The "Critique of Aesthetic Judgment," the first major division of the *Critique of Judgment*, uses the term *aesthetic* in what has become its modern sense. The discussion is Kant's contribution to the controversies initiated by Lord Shaftesbury and Francis Hutcheson when they made both moral and aesthetic judgments matters of feeling; Kant rejects this view and also explains why he yet cannot approve of Baumgarten's attempt to "bring the critical treatment of the beautiful under rational principles, and so to raise its rules to the rank of a science" (B 35, note *a*). Kant needs to show, for the purposes of his general philosophy, that aesthetic judgments are essentially different from moral judgments on the one hand and scientific judgments on the other. This need apart, he had a long-standing independent interest in the subject; in 1764, thirty years before the *Critique of Judgment*, he published an essay on the beautiful and the sublime (*Beobachtung über das Gefühl des Schönen und Erhabenen*, Königsberg). Such an interest may seem surprising in view of the obvious limitations of Kant's own aesthetic experience; he had some feeling for literature, especially for satire, but little or no real knowledge of either painting or music. But what he has in mind in discussing the beautiful is the beauty of nature as much as anything, and his main interest is not in making aesthetic judgments, but in deciding on their logical status.

Judgments of taste, as Kant calls them, are peculiar in that they not only rest on feeling but also claim universal validity. That they rest on feeling seems to him obvious: When I ascribe beauty to an object or scene I do so not because I have observed some special character in it, but because contemplation of its form gives me immediate delight. But it is an entirely disinterested form of delight, quite different from that we feel concerning things that are agreeable, or even things that are good. When we take pleasure in something beautiful we are not desiring to possess it, or indeed taking up any attitude toward its existence. The fact that aesthetic delight is disinterested allows us to think of it as universally shared:

> Since the delight is not based on any inclination
> of the subject (or any other deliberate interest),
> but the Subject feels himself completely *free* in

respect to the liking which he accords to the object, he can find as reason for his delight no personal conditions to which his own subjective self might alone be party. Hence he must regard it as resting on what he may also presuppose in every other person; and therefore he must believe that he has reason for demanding a similar delight from every one. (*Critique of Judgment*, Meredith translation, Sec. 6)

Because they claim universal validity, judgments of taste appear to rest on concepts, but to think that they do is a mistake. The universality attaching to judgments of taste is not objective but subjective; to explain it we must refer to "nothing else than the mental state present in the free play of imagination and understanding (so far as these are in mutual accord, as is requisite for *cognition in general*)" (Sec. 9). As in the *Critique of Pure Reason*, Kant argues that both imagination and understanding are involved in the apprehension of any spatiotemporal object but that when we simply contemplate any such object aesthetically, no definite concept is adduced; and so the two faculties are in free play. It is the harmony between the faculties in any act of aesthetic contemplation that Kant takes to be universally communicable, and believes to be the basis for the pleasure we feel.

In addition to analyzing judgments about the beautiful, Kant devoted considerable attention in the *Critique of Judgment* to another concept which figured prominently in the aesthetics of his day, that of the sublime. Burke and others had given what was in effect a psychological description of the conditions in which we judge, say, the sight of a mountain range or a storm at sea to be sublime. Kant was all the more anxious to specify more exactly the meaning of such judgments and to establish their transcendental conditions because he was convinced that we here also have to do with a feeling that is held to be universally communicable. The feeling for the sublime, as he explained it, is connected not with the understanding, as is that for the beautiful, but with reason. To put his view somewhat crudely, we are at first abashed by the formlessness of some parts of nature, only to be elevated when we reflect on the utter inadequacy of these objects to measure up to our own ideas, and in particular to our moral ideas. Thus the sublime is not, as might at first sight be supposed, a quality which inheres in natural objects, but a feeling which the contemplation of natural objects provokes in us. It could have no existence for a being totally lacking in culture (a savage might feel fear on observing "thunderclouds piled up the vault of heaven," to use one of Kant's own examples, but could

not recognize their sublimity), yet it is not a mere product of culture or social convention. "Rather is it in human nature that its foundations are laid, and, in fact, in that which, at once with common understanding, we may expect everyone to possess and may require of him, namely, a native capacity for the feeling for (practical) ideas, that is, for moral feeling" (Sec. 29).

TELEOLOGY. One of Kant's motives for wanting to avoid making beauty an objective characteristic was that he thought such a view would lend force to the Argument from Design, and so encourage the revival of speculative theology. If things could be said to possess beauty in the same sort of way in which they possess weight, it would be a short step to talking about the Great Artificer who made them to delight us. Arguments of the same general kind were still more vividly present to his mind when he came to write the second main section of the *Critique of Judgment*, the "Critique of Teleological Judgment." Indeed, he ended the book with a lengthy section that underlines yet again the shortcomings of "physicotheology" and points up the merits of "ethicotheology."

Before confronting theology directly, Kant embarked on a detailed and penetrating discussion of the nature and use of teleological concepts. The existence of organic bodies, he argues, is something for which we cannot account satisfactorily by the mechanical principles sanctioned by the physical sciences; to deal with organic bodies we must employ a distinct principle, the principle of teleology, which can do justice to the fact that "*an organized natural product is one in which every part is reciprocally both means and end*" (Sec. 66). Such a principle cannot be used for cognitive purposes in the strict sense; it can be employed only by reflective judgment to guide "our investigation of … [organic bodies] by a remote analogy with our own causality according to ends generally, and as a basis for reflection upon their supreme source" (Sec. 65). Teleology is a concept that occupies an uneasy intermediate position between natural science and theology. We cannot help using it to describe the world about us, yet we cannot assign to it full scientific status. Kant mitigates the austerities of this position by suggesting in his section "The Antinomy of Judgment" that in the end the mechanical and teleological principles stand on the same level, both belonging to reflective judgment. But it is hard to see how this can be made consistent with the doctrines of the *Critique of Pure Reason*, which ascribes constitutive force to the concepts of "pure physics," or even with the distinction in the *Critique of Judgment* itself between explaining something and merely "making an estimate" of it. We use the categories to explain, but can employ teleological concepts only for the purpose of making an estimate. Kant's underlying attitude to the whole question is revealed most clearly in the passage at the end of Sec. 68 of the *Critique of Judgment*, where he asks why teleology "does not … form a special part of theoretical natural science, but is relegated to theology by way of a propaedeutic or transition." He answers:

> This is done in order to keep the study of the mechanical aspect of nature in close adherence to what we are able so to subject to our observation or experiment that we could ourselves produce it like nature, or at least produce it according to similar laws. For we have complete insight only into what we can make and accomplish according to our conceptions. But to effect by means of art a presentation similar to organization, as an intrinsic end of nature, infinitely surpasses all our powers. (Meredith translation)

It would be interesting to know if Kant would say the same were he alive today.

OTHER PHILOSOPHICAL WRITINGS

After publishing the three *Critiques*—Kant was sixty-six when the *Critique of Judgment* appeared—he continued to publish essays and treatises on a wide variety of philosophical subjects. Most of these are in fact contributions to applied philosophy, for he took the view that scientific inquiries and practical activities alike stand in need of philosophical foundations. In many cases he attempts to supply these foundations by means of the principles established in his main works—hence the general shape of his philosophies of science and religion, and of his political philosophy. It would, however, be wrong to see these as no more than mechanical applications of general Kantian conclusions. For although Kant was deeply and indeed unduly devoted to system, he also had a wide and in some cases penetrating knowledge of many different branches of learning and human activity, and there are few philosophical topics that he touches without illuminating; in fact, Kant gave the names still in use to most of the branches of applied philosophy he took up.

PHILOSOPHY OF NATURE. In the preface to his *Metaphysical Foundations of Natural Science*, Kant argues that the very concept of scientific knowledge is such that we can use the term properly only when dealing with truths that are both apodictically certain and systematically connected. A discipline that is thoroughly and entirely empirical cannot comply with these requirements; hence

Kant pronounces chemistry to be no better than "systematic art or experimental doctrine." But the situation is different in physics. Although Kant was as firmly persuaded as any empiricist that detailed knowledge of the physical world could be arrived at only by observation and experiment, he was also sure that physics has an unshakable a priori basis that makes it worthy of the name of science. It owes this, in Kant's judgment, to the fact that its fundamental concepts are capable of mathematical expression, as those of chemistry are not, and to the close connection of these concepts with the categories, the basic concepts of rational thought.

The main object of the *Metaphysical Foundations* is to demonstrate the second of these points by means of an examination of the idea of matter. Starting from what professes to be an empirically derived definition of matter, "that which is capable of movement in space," Kant proceeds to a deduction of its main properties in the light of the table of categories. The result is, in effect, a rereading or reinterpretation of then-current physical theory in which all the main doctrines of Newton find their place, but which is distinctive in that the atomism professed by many physicists of the day is rejected in favor of a dynamical theory of matter resembling that of Leibniz. Kant argues in the *Critique of Pure Reason* that only mistaken metaphysics leads scientists to think they must accept the notions of absolutely homogeneous matter and absolutely empty space. In the *Metaphysical Foundations* he works out an alternative conception of matter in terms of moving forces, omnipresent but varying in degree, and puts it forward as both theoretically satisfactory and consistent with the empirical findings.

It is difficult not to see in these views the beginnings of *Naturphilosophie* as it was to be practiced by Schelling and G. W. F. Hegel, the more so if we read the *Metaphysical Foundations* in the light of Kant's further treatment of the subject in the notes published as *Opus Postumum*. But in 1786 at any rate Kant was still far from committing the extravagances of the speculative philosophers of nature. For one thing, he was both more knowledgeable about and more respectful of the actual achievements of physical scientists than were his romantic successors, doubtless because, unlike them, he was something of a physical scientist himself. For another, the lesson he drew from his 1786 inquiries was not how much physical knowledge we can arrive at by the use of pure reason, but how little. To establish the metaphysical foundations of natural science was a useful task, but it was in no sense a substitute for empirical investigation. Despite these differences from *Naturphilosophie*, it must be allowed that *Metaphysical*

Foundations testifies, in name as well as in content, to the extent of Kant's commitment to rationalism (his theory of science could scarcely be further from Hume's) and to the way in which he was at least tempted by the constructivism favored by some of his younger contemporaries.

PHILOSOPHY OF HISTORY. Although Kant was quite unaware of the problems about historical knowledge and explanation with which philosophers since Wilhelm Dilthey have dealt, he made an important and characteristic contribution to speculative philosophy of history in his essay "Idee zu einer allgemeinen Geschichte in Weltbürgerlicher Absicht" (Idea of a Universal History from a Cosmopolitan Point of View; *Berliner Monatsschrift*, November 1784, 386–410). Observing that the actions of men, when looked at individually, add up to nothing significant, he suggests that nature or providence may be pursuing through these actions a long-term plan of which the agents are unaware. To see what the plan may be we have to reflect on two points: First, that nature would scarcely have implanted capacities in human beings if she had not meant them to be developed, and second, that many human intellectual capacities (for example, the talent for invention) are such that they cannot be satisfactorily developed in the lifetime of a single individual.

The development of such capacities belongs to the history of the species as a whole. Kant suggests that the hidden plan of nature in history may well be to provide conditions in which such capacities are more and more developed, so that men move from barbarism to culture and thus convert "a social union originating in pathological needs into a moral whole." The mechanism of the process lies in what Kant calls the "unsocial sociability" of human beings—the fact that they need each other's society and help and are nevertheless by nature individualists and egotists—which ensures that men develop their talents to the maximum extent, if only to get the better of their fellows, and at the same time necessitates man's eventually arriving at a form of civil society that allows for peaceful rivalry under a strict rule of law. But such a "republican" constitution would be of no value unless it had its counterpart in the international sphere, for the struggles of individuals against one another are paralleled by the struggles of states. We must accordingly conclude that the final purpose of nature in history is to produce an international society consisting of a league of nations, in which war is outlawed and the way is finally clear for peaceful competition between individuals and nations.

The difficulty with this as with other lines of Kant's thought is to understand its relation to empirical inquiries. From what Kant says it seems clear that he intended "philosophical" history to be an alternative to history of the everyday kind, not a substitute for it. Nor did he pretend to be writing philosophical history himself; his essay merely puts forward the idea of or offers a "clue" to, such a history, leaving it to nature to produce someone really capable of making sense of the historical facts as Johannes Kepler and Newton made sense of physical facts. It is difficult to see, even so, how Kant could have possessed the idea of history as meaningful without knowing the facts, or alternatively how he could know that the idea throws light on the facts when it was discovered without any reference to them.

PHILOSOPHY OF LAW AND POLITICS. Kant's views about law and politics, like his philosophy of history, are obviously tied up with his ethics. Kant holds that legal obligations are a subspecies of moral obligation; thus the rational will, and neither force nor the commands of God, is the basis of the law. His standpoint in philosophy of law is thus broadly liberal, though his attitude on many particular legal issues is far from liberal as the term is now understood. He holds, for instance, that if one of the partners to a marriage runs away or takes another partner, "the other is entitled, at any time, and incontestably, to bring such a one back to the former relation, as if that person were a thing" (*Metaphysic of Morals*, Sec. 25). He is notorious as a strong supporter of the retributive theory of punishment and an uncompromising advocate of the death penalty for murder. The explanation of his harshness in these matters is to be found in his legalistic approach to ethics, which leaves little room for sympathy or forgiveness.

In politics also Kant combines a fundamentally liberal attitude with specific views that are conservative, if not reactionary. Following Rousseau, he attempts to explain political authority partly in terms of the general will and partly in terms of the original contract. Insofar as he insists on the contract, which he interprets not as a historical fact but as a regulative idea, he is advocating a version of political liberalism which lays particular emphasis on the rule of law; insofar as he grounds supreme political authority in the will of the people as a whole, he is obviously flirting with more radical doctrines—from whose consequences he is quick to draw back. An admirer of the French Revolution, he nevertheless denies that the subjects of the most ill-governed states have any right of rebellion against their rulers. And though the mixed constitution he favors is one in which citizens can make their voices heard through their representatives, he is for confining the franchise to persons who possess "independence or self-sufficiency," thus excluding from "active" citizenship (according to Sec. 46 of the *Metaphysic of Morals*) apprentices, servants, woodcutters, plowmen, and, surprisingly, resident tutors, as well as "all women." The truth is, however, that Kant's political theorizing was done in a vacuum; in his day there was no real chance for a Prussian professor of philosophy to influence political events.

PHILOSOPHY OF RELIGION. In the sphere of religion the views of a professor of philosophy could be influential, and Kant's views on this subject were certainly provocative. He treats religion as essentially, if not quite exclusively, a matter of purity of heart—thus dispensing with speculative theology altogether and assigning a meager importance to the institutional side of religion. To adopt the religious attitude, as Kant sees it, is to look on duties as if they were divine commands. But this, he explains, is only to insist on the unconditioned character, the ineluctability, of moral obligation; it is a way of representing morality, not a way of going beyond it. Knowledge of the supersensible, as Kant thought he had shown in the *Critique of Pure Reason*, is impossible; and although moral practice carries with it belief in God and a future life, the whole meaning and force of that belief is to be found in a persistence in moral endeavor and a determination to repair moral shortcomings. The pure religion of morality needs no dogma apart from these two fundamental articles of belief, which are accessible immediately to the simplest intelligence. Still less has it any need of the external trappings of religion—priests, ceremonies, and the like—although the body of believers must think of themselves as belonging to a church, universal but invisible, and the practices of visible churches sometimes serve to stimulate or strengthen moral effort, in a way which is useful but not indispensable.

The religion of morality is on this account a religion of all good men. Despite this, Kant took a particular interest in Christianity, which he saw as at least approximating true religion though corrupted by the presence of extraneous elements derived from Judaism. His book *Religion within the Bounds of Mere Reason* (1793) is in effect a commentary on and a reinterpretation of Christian doctrine and practice, written with the object of making this conclusion clear. In this reinterpretation the doctrine of original sin is transformed into a doctrine of the radical evil in human nature, which is the positive source of moral failing; and that of the Incarnation is replaced by an account of the triumph of the good prin-

ciple over the bad, the part of the historical Jesus being taken by an idea of reason, that of man in his moral perfection. Kant sets aside the historical elements in Christianity as having no importance in themselves: Whatever is true in the religion must be derivable from moral reason. To think of the uttering of religious formulas or the performance of formal services to God as having a value of their own is to fall into the grossest superstition. It is perhaps scarcely surprising that these sentiments, whose attraction for youth can be seen in Hegel's *Jugendschriften*, should have struck the Prussian authorities as subversive and led the orthodox King Frederick William II to demand that Kant refrain from further pronouncements on religion. Though Kant, in his letter acceding to this demand, protested that he had no thought of criticizing Christianity in writing his book, it is hard to take his protest quite seriously, for he had certainly meant to suggest that many of the beliefs and actions of practicing Christians were without value, if not positively immoral. Indeed, the originality and continuing interest of his work on religion connect directly with that fact.

THE *OPUS POSTUMUM*. In the last years of his life—from about 1795 on—Kant was engaged in the composition of what would have been a substantial philosophical work; the preparatory notes for it have been published as *Opus Postumum*. Its original title was "Transition from Metaphysical Foundations of Natural Science to Physics," and in its original form its object was to carry further the process, begun in 1786 in the *Metaphysical Foundations of Natural Science*, of finding an a priori basis for physics. No longer content with the formal structure for which he had argued earlier, Kant thought he had to show that some of the particular laws of nature could be known in advance of experience. The broadest types of physical possibility were determined by the constitution of the human mind; it was this, for example, which explained the presence in nature of just so many fundamental forces, and even of an omnipresent ether.

These speculations about the foundations of physics led Kant to epistemological considerations of a wider kind. The whole subject of the relation of the form of experience to its matter, with the question how far the form shapes the matter, arose in his mind anew, doubtless because of the criticisms directed against the formalist position of the *Critique of Pure Reason* by self-professed disciples such as Fichte. In 1799 Kant dissociated himself publicly from the views expressed in Fichte's *Wissenschaftslehre*, according to which the subject of knowledge "posits" the objective world and so, in a way, creates nature. Yet the evidence of the *Opus Postumum* is that at this time, or shortly thereafter, Kant was toying with similar ideas and was even using some of the same vocabulary. It is perhaps fortunate for Kant's reputation that he was not able to get his final philosophical thoughts into publishable form.

See also Aesthetic Judgment; Appearance and Reality; Aristotle; Baumgarten, Alexander Gottlieb; Beck, Jakob Sigismund; Burke, Edmund; Causation; Cosmological Argument for the Existence of God; Crusius, Christian August; Descartes, René; Determinism and Freedom; Dilthey, Wilhelm; Ethics, History of; Fichte, Johann Gottlieb; Geometry; Hegel, Georg Wilhelm Friedrich; History and Historiography of Philosophy; Hume, David; Intuition; Jacobi, Friedrich Heinrich; Kepler, Johannes; Knutzen, Martin; Leibniz, Gottfried Wilhelm; Locke, John; Logic, History of; Meier, Georg Friedrich; Newton, Isaac; Ontological Argument for the Existence of God; Perception; Propositions; Reason; Rousseau, Jean-Jacques; Schelling, Friedrich Wilhelm Joseph von; Space; Teleology; Time; Wolff, Christian.

Bibliography

WORKS BY KANT

Collected Works

Gesammelte Schriften. 23 vols., edited under the supervision of the Berlin Academy of Sciences. Berlin: Reimer, 1902–1955. The standard collected edition of Kant's writings; contains his correspondence and hitherto unpublished notes (including those for the *Opus Postumum*) as well as everything he published. Further volumes covering Kant's lectures are in preparation.

Kants Werke. 10 vols, edited by Ernst Cassirer. Berlin: Cassirer, 1912–1922. Contains the published works, with full indications of the contents of the original editions.

Philosophische Bibliothek series. Leipzig and Hamburg, 1904–. Separately bound editions of all the treatises listed below under the head "Main Treatises," with useful introductions; also includes *Kleinere Schriften zur Geschichtsphilosophie, Ethik, und Politik.*

Main Treatises

Allgemeine Naturgeschichte und Theorie des Himmels. Königsberg and Leipzig, 1755. English translation by W. Hastie in *Kant's Cosmogony* (Glasgow, 1900).

Der einzig mögliche Beweisgrund zu einer Demonstration des Daseins Gottes. Königsberg, 1763. No serviceable translation.

Träume eines Geistersehers, erläutert durch Träume der Metaphysik. Königsberg, 1766. Translated by E. F. Goerwitz into English as *Dreams of Spirit-Seer* (New York, 1900).

De Mundi Sensibilis atque Intelligibilis Forma et Principiis Dissertatio. Königsberg, 1770. Translated into English in Handyside's *Kant's Inaugural Dissertation and Early Writings on Space* (Chicago: Open Court, 1929).

Kritik der reinen Vernunft. Riga, 1781; 2nd ed., Riga, 1787. The first edition is customarily referred to as A, the second edition as B. The most useful modern edition is by Raymond Schmidt (Leipzig, 1926). There are English translations by Francis Heywood (London, 1838); J. M. D. Meiklejohn (London, 1854), F. Max Müller (2 vols., London, 1881), and N. Kemp Smith (London Macmillan, 1929). Kemp Smith's version is the fullest and most reliable.

Prolegomena zu einer jeden künftigen Metaphysik die als Wissenschaft auftreten können. Riga, 1783. English translations are available by John Richardson (*Prolegomena to Future Metaphysics,* in *Metaphysical Works of the Celebrated Immanual Kant,* London, 1836), J. P. Mahaffy and J. H. Bernard (*The Prolegomena,* London, 1872), E. B. Bax (*Kant's Prolegomena and Metaphysical Foundations of Natural Science,* London, 1883), Paul Carus (*Prolegomena to Any Future Metaphysics,* Chicago, 1902), L. W. Beck (same title as Carus's, New York: Liberal Arts Press, 1951), and P. G. Lucas (same title as Carus's, Manchester, U.K., 1953). The Beck and Lucas translations are much the best.

Grundlegung zur Metaphysik der Sitten. Riga, 1785; 2nd ed., Riga, 1786. Translated into English by T. K. Abbott as *Fundamental Principles of the Metaphysic of Morals* (in *Kant's Critique of Practical Reason and Other Works on the Theory of Ethics,* London, 1873), by L. W. Beck as *Foundations of the Metaphysics of Morals* (in *Critique of Practical Reason and Other Writings in Moral Philosophy,* Chicago: University of Chicago Press, 1949), by H. J. Paton (from the 2nd edition) as *The Moral Law, or Kant's Groundwork of the Metaphysic of Morals* (London: Hutchinson, 1948). All three versions are good; Paton's is the most elegant. Quotations in the text of this article are from Paton's translation; the citations to page numbers in the 2nd edition are taken from Paton's marginal notation.

Metaphysische Anfangsgründe der Naturwissenschaft. Riga, 1786. Translated into English by E. B. Bax (in *Kant's Prolegomena and Metaphysical Foundations of Natural Science,* London, 1883).

Kritik der praktischen Vernunft. Riga, 1788. Translated into English by T. K. Abbott, and also by L. W. Beck, as *Critique of Practical Reason* in the books cited for the *Grundlegung zur Metaphysik der Sitten.* The Beck translation is accurate but somewhat clumsy; it has been published separately (New York, 1956).

Kritik der Urteilskraft. Berlin and Liebau, 1790. Translated into English by J. H. Bernard as *Kritik of Judgement* (London, 1892; later reprinted as *Critique of Judgement*). Also translated by J. C. Meredith in two parts, *Critique of Aesthetic Judgement* (Oxford, 1911) and *Critique of Teleological Judgement* (Oxford, 1928), which were reissued together as *The Critique of Judgement* (Oxford: Clarendon Press, 1952). Both the Bernard and the Meredith versions are of poor quality; Meredith's is slightly the better. Kant wrote an introduction to the *Kritik* that he discarded; it is available as *Erste Einleitung in die Kritik der Urteilskraft,* Vol. V, *Kants Werke* (Berlin, 1922), and in English translation by H. Kabir as *Immanuel Kant on Philosophy in General* (Calcutta: Calcutta University Press, 1935).

Die Religion innerhalb der Grenzen der blossen Vernunft. First part published separately, Berlin, 1792; published complete at Königsberg, 1793. Translated into English by John Richardson as *Religion within the Sphere of Naked Reason* (in

Essays and Treatises, London, 1798), by J. W. Semple as *Religion within the Boundary of Pure Reason* (Edinburgh, 1838), T. M. Greene and H. H. Hudson as *Religion within the Limits of Reason Alone* (Chicago: Open Court, 1934; 2nd ed., with new matter by J. R. Silber, New York: Harper, 1960). The 1960 edition (Greene-Hudson-Silber) is the best.

Zum ewigen Frieden: ein philosophischer Entwurf. Königsberg, 1795. The two best English translations are L. W. Beck's *Perpetual Peace* (in *Critique of Practical Reason and Other Writings in Moral Philosophy*, Chicago, 1949; separately bound, New York, 1957) and C. J. Friedrich's *Inevitable Peace* (New Haven, CT, 1948).

Metaphysik der Sitten, Part I, *Metaphysische Anfangsgründe der Rechtslehre*; Part II, *Metaphysische Anfangsgründe der Tugendlehre*. Separately bound, Königsberg, 1797. Part I translated into English by W. Hastie as *Kant's Philosophy of Law* (Edinburgh, 1887). Part II translated into English by James Ellington as *Metaphysical Principles of Virtue* (Indianapolis, 1964) and by Mary Gregor as *The Doctrine of Virtue* (New York: Harper and Row, 1964).

Anthropologie in pragmatischer Hinsicht. Königsberg, 1798. No English translation.

Eine Vorlesung über Ethik, edited from student's notes by P. Menzer. Berlin, 1924. Translated into English by Louis Infield as *Lectures on Ethics* (London: Methuen, 1930).

Kant on History. Indianapolis, 1963. Translations by L. W. Beck, R. E. Anchor, and E L. Fackenheim; contains Kant's minor essays on philosophy of history.

WORKS ON KANT

Life

The main sources for Kant's life, apart from his letters, are three memoirs published in Königsberg in 1804: L. E. Borowski's *Darstellung des Lebens und Characters Immanuel Kants*; R. B. Jachmann's *Immanuel Kant, geschildert in Briefen an einen Freund*; and E. A. C. Wasianski's *Immanuel Kant in seinen letzten Lebensjahren*. Wasianski's memoir is extensively used in Thomas De Quincey's "The Last Days of Kant" (*Works*, Vol. XII). See also Ernst Cassirer's *Kants Leben und Lehre* (Berlin, 1921), and for a useful short life Karl Vorländer's *Immanuel Kants Leben* (Leipzig, 1911).

Commentaries

Rudolf Eisler's *Kantlexicon* (Berlin, 1930) and Heinrich Ratke's *Systematisches Handlexicon zu Kants Kritik der reinen Vernunft* (Leipzig, 1929) are valuable aids to the Kantian student. The periodical *Kantstudien* has published many important contributions to Kantian scholarship and discussion.

For commentaries on the *Critique of Pure Reason*, see Hans Vaihinger, *Kommentar zur Kritik der reinen Vernunft*, 2 vols. (Stuttgart: Spemann, 1881–1892), which covers the opening sections only; N. Kemp Smith, *A Commentary to Kant's Critique of Pure Reason* (London: Macmillan, 1918; rev. ed., 1923), which is strongly influenced by Vaihinger's "patchwork" theory; H. J. Paton, *Kant's Metaphysic of Experience*, 2 vols. (London: Allen and Unwin, 1936), which covers the first half only and is sharply critical of Kemp Smith; A. C. Ewing, *A Short Commentary on Kant's Critique of Pure Reason* (London: Methuen, 1938). T. D. Weldon, *Kant's Critique of Pure Reason* (Oxford, 1945; 2nd ed., Oxford: Clarendon Press, 1958).

On the theory of knowledge see also H. A. Prichard, *Kant's Theory of Knowledge* (Oxford: Clarendon Press, 1909); A. C. Ewing, *Kant's Treatment of Causality* (London: K. Paul, Trench, Trubner, 1924); W. H. Walsh, *Reason and Experience* (Oxford: Clarendon Press, 1947); Graham Bird, *Kant's Theory of Knowledge* (London: Routledge and Paul, 1962); R. P Wolff, *Kant's Theory of Mental Activity* (Cambridge, MA: Harvard University Press, 1963).

For commentaries on the *Critique of Practical Reason* and other works on ethics, see L. W. Beck, *A Commentary on Kant's Critique of Practical Reason* (Chicago, 1960), a good source; H. J. Paton, *The Categorical Imperative* (London: Hutchinson, 1947), a detailed commentary on the *Grundlegung*; W. D. Ross, *Kant's Ethical Theory* (Oxford, 1954); A. R. C. Duncan, *Practical Reason and Morality* (Edinburgh, 1957); M. J. Gregor, *Laws of Freedom* (Oxford: Blackwell, 1963), which expounds the *Metaphysic of Morals*; P A. Schilpp, *Kant's Pre-Critical Ethics* (Evanston, IL: Northwestern University, 1938), A. E. Teale, *Kantian Ethics* (London: Oxford University Press, 1951).

For commentaries on the *Critique of Judgment*, see Konrad Marc-Wogau, *Vier Studien zu Kants Kritik der Urteilskraft* (Uppsala, Sweden, 1938); H. W. Cassirer, *A Commentary on Kant's Critique of Judgment* (London: Methuen, 1938).

Commentaries on other aspects of Kant's thought are also available. On the precritical writings, see Giorgio Tonelli, *Elementi metafisici e metodologici in Kant precritico* (Turin, 1959). On Kant's philosophy of religion, see C. C. J. Webb, *Kant's Philosophy of Religion* (Oxford: Clarendon Press, 1926) and F. E. England, *Kant's Conception of God* (London: Allen and Unwin, 1929). On Kant's philosophy of history, see Klaus Weyand, *Kants Geschichtsphilosophie* (Cologne: Cologne University Press, 1964). On Kant as a scientist, see Erich Adickes, *Kant als Naturforscher*, 2 vols. (Berlin, 1924–1925). On the *Opus Postumum*, see Erich Adickes, *Kants Opus Postumum dargestellt und beurteilt* (Berlin, 1920).

General Studies

S. Körner, *Kant* (Harmondsworth, U.K., 1955) is the best general introduction; see also G. J. Warnock's chapter in *A Critical History of Western Philosophy*, edited by D. J. O'Connor (New York: Free Press of Glencoe, 1964).

Edward Caird, *The Critical Philosophy of Kant*, 2 vols. (Glasgow, 1889), criticizes Kant from the Hegelian position. Martin Heidegger, *Kant und das Problem der Metaphysik* (Bonn: Cohen, 1929) examines Kant as an "ontologist." H. J. de Vleeschauwer, *La déduction transcendentale dans l'oeuvre de Kant*, 3 vols. (Antwerp, 1934–1937), presents an exhaustive survey of Kant's writings on the problem; de Vleeschauwer offers a one-volume summary in *L'évolution de la pensée kantienne* (Paris, 1939), which has been translated into English by A. R. C. Duncan as *The Development of Kantian Thought* (London: Nelson, 1962). Gottfried Martin, *Immanuel Kant, Ontologie und Wissenschaftstheorie* (Cologne, 1951), translated into English by P. G. Lucas as *Kant's Metaphysics and Theory of Science* (Manchester, U.K.: Manchester University Press, 1955), is influenced but not dominated by Heidegger. Richard Kroner, *Kants Weltanschauung* (Tübingen, 1914), translated into English by J. E. Smith as *Kant's Weltanschauung* (Chicago: University of Chicago Press, 1956), stresses Kant's emphasis on the practical. R. Daval, *La métaphysique de*

Kant (Paris: Presses Universitaires de France, 1951), presents "schematism" as the key idea in Kant's thought.

RECENT TRANSLATIONS

The Cambridge Edition of the Works of Immanuel Kant: Lectures on Metaphysics. Edited and translated by Karl Ameriks and Steve Naragon. Cambridge, U.K.: Cambridge University Press, 1997.

Critique of Pure Reason. Edited and translated by Paul Guyer and Allen W. Wood. Cambridge, U.K.: Cambridge University Press, 1998.

Ethical Philosophy. Translated by James W. Ellington. Indianapolis: Hackett, 1983.

Immanuel Kant: Critique of Judgment. Translated by Werner S. Pluhar. Indianpolis: Hackett, 1987.

Immanuel Kant: Critique of Pure Reason: Unified Edition (with all variants from the 1781 and 1787 editions). Edited and translated by Werner S. Pluhar. Indianapolis: Hackett, 1996.

The Metaphysics of Morals. Edited and translated by Mary Gregor. Cambridge, U.K.: Cambridge University Press, 1996.

Opus Postumum/Immanuel Kant. Edited by Eckart Forster. Translated by Eckhart Forster and Michael Rosen. Cambridge, U.K.: Cambridge University Press, 1993.

Perpetual Peace and Other Essays on Politics, History, and Morals. Translated by Ted Humphrey. Indianapolis: Hackett, 1983.

Prolegomena to Any Future Metaphysics: That Will Be Able to Come Forward as Science with Selections from the Critique of Pure Reason. Rev. ed. Edited and translated by Gary Hatfield. Cambridge, U.K.: Cambridge University Press, 2004.

RECENT SECONDARY LITERATURE

Allison, Henry E. *Kant's Theory of Freedom.* New York: Cambridge University Press, 1990.

Ameriks, Karl. *Kant and the Fate of Autonomy: Problems in the Appropriation of the Critical Philosophy.* New York: Cambridge University Press, 2000.

Ameriks, Karl. *Kant's Theory of Mind: An Analysis of the Paralogisms of Pure Reason.* 2nd ed. New York: Oxford University Press, 2000.

Beck, Lewis White. *Early German Philosophy; Kant and His Predecessors.* Cambridge, MA: Belknap Press of Harvard University Press, 1969.

Cohen, Ted, and Paul Guyer, eds. *Essays in Kant's Aesthetics.* Chicago: University of Chicago Press, 1982.

Di Giovanni, George. *Freedom and Religion in Kant and His Immediate Successors: The Vocation of Humankind, 1774–1800.* New York: Cambridge University Press, 2005.

Findlay, John N. *Kant and the Transcendental Object: A Hermeneutic Study.* New York: Oxford University Press, 1981.

Forster, Eckhart, ed. *Kant's Transcendental Deductions: The Three Critiques and the Opus Postumum.* Stanford, CA: Stanford University Press, 1989.

Friedman, Michael. *Kant and the Exact Sciences.* Cambridge, MA: Harvard University Press, 1992.

Guyer, Paul, ed. *The Cambridge Companion to Kant.* New York: Cambridge University Press, 1992.

Guyer, Paul. *Kant and the Claims of Knowledge.* New York: Cambridge University Press, 1987.

Guyer, Paul. *Kant and the Claims of Taste.* 2nd ed. New York: Cambridge University Press, 1997.

Guyer, Paul, ed. *Kant and the Experience of Freedom: Essays on Aesthetics and Morality.* New York: Cambridge University Press, 1993.

Guyer, Paul. *Kant on Freedom, Law, and Happiness.* New York: Cambridge University Press, 2000.

Henrich, Dieter. *Aesthetic Judgment and the Moral Image of the World: Studies in Kant.* Stanford, CA: Stanford University Press, 1992.

Keller, Pierre. *Kant and the Demands of Self-Consciousness.* Cambridge, U.K.: Cambridge University Press, 1998.

Kitcher, Patricia. *Kant's Critique of Pure Reason: Critical Essays.* Lanham: Rowman & Littlefield, 1998.

Kuehn, Manfred. *Kant: A Biography.* New York: Cambridge University Press, 2001.

Longuenesse, Beatrice. *Kant and the Capacity to Judge: Sensibility and Discursivity in the Transcendental Analytic of the Critique of Pure Reason.* Translated by Charles T. Wolfe. Princeton, NJ: Princeton University Press, 1998.

Neiman, Susan. *The Unity of Reason: Rereading Kant.* New York: Oxford University Press, 1994.

Stratton-Lake, Philip. *Kant, Duty, and Moral Worth.* London; New York: Routledge, 2000.

Van Cleve, James. *Problems from Kant.* New York: Oxford University Press, 1999.

Walker, Ralph C. S. *Kant.* New York: Routledge, 1999.

Walker, Ralph C. S. *Kant: The Arguments of the Philosophers.* Boston: Routledge & Kegan Paul, 1978.

Watkins, Eric. *Kant and the Metaphysics of Causality.* New York: Cambridge University Press, 2005.

Wood, Allen W. *Kant.* Malden, MA: Blackwell, 2005.

Wood, Allen W. *Self and Nature in Kant's Philosophy.* Ithaca, NY: Cornell University Press, 1984.

Yovel, Yirmiahu. *Kant and the Philosophy of History.* Princeton, NJ: Princeton University Press, 1980.

W. H. Walsh (1967)
Bibliography updated by Tamra Frei (2005)

KANT, IMMANUEL [ADDENDUM]

Immanuel Kant's philosophy continues to exercise significant influence on philosophical developments and generates an ever-growing body of scholarly literature. Work on Kant has progressed in two main directions. Central doctrines of the *Critique of Pure Reason* have been reconstructed, examined, and revised in the light of current philosophical concerns and standards; and the focus of scholarship has widened to include aspects and parts of Kant's work hitherto neglected, especially in the areas of ethics, aesthetics, philosophy of history, political philosophy, anthropology, and philosophy of science.

THE CRITIQUE OF PURE REASON

Further advances in interpreting the first *Critique* have occurred in three related areas: the nature and validity of Kant's overall argumentative procedure, with special emphasis on the deduction of the categories; the meaning and function of transcendental idealism and the associated distinction between things in themselves and appearances; and the role of mental activity in Kant's theory of experience.

The deduction of the categories, in which Kant sought to identify and justify the basic concepts underlying all experience and its objects, has become the center of major interpretive efforts. Stimulated by the neo-Kantian analytic metaphysics of Peter F. Strawson, philosophers have attempted to distill a type of argument from Kant's text that refutes skeptical doubts about the reality of the external world and other minds by showing how the skeptical challenge tacitly and unavoidably assumes the truth of the very assumptions it sets out to deny, namely, the reality of external objects and other minds.

While the force of such *transcendental arguments* remains controversial, the analytic–reconstructive approach to the deduction of the categories has also resulted in more textually based interpretations that reflect the whole spectrum of Kant scholarship. Readings of the deduction start either from the assumption of experience and proceed from there analytically to the necessary conditions of experience (the categories and the principles based on them), or take as their starting point some conception of self-consciousness or self-knowledge, either understood in Cartesian purity (a priori unity of apperception) or in phenomenological embeddedness (empirical self-consciousness), and argue from there to the synthetic conditions for the very possibility of such self-awareness. A key insight shared by many interpreters is the mutual requirement of object-knowledge and self-knowledge in Kant.

In interpretations of Kant's transcendental idealism, a major alternative has opened up between those scholars who see things-in-themselves and appearances as different aspects of one and the same things (*two-aspect view*) and those who regard the two as so many different sets of objects (*two-object view*). On the former view appearances are genuine objects. On the latter view they are representations. While the textual evidence is not conclusive for either view, the two-aspect theory has found many adherents because of its ontological economy and its avoidance of a phenomenalist reduction of things to representations.

The central role of human subjectivity in the deduction of the categories and in the defense of transcendental idealism has led to a renewed interest in Kant's philosophy of mind. Kant's theory of subjectivity is more and more seen as an integral part of his theoretical philosophy. Special areas of interest are the essential role of imagination in perception and experience, the distinction between inner sense and apperception, the relation between subjective or psychological and objective or logical grounds of knowledge, and the functional unity of sensibility and understanding. While no one advocates the derivation of the logical from the psychological in the manner of a reductive psychologism, the exact function of specifically psychological considerations in transcendental philosophy remains controversial. There is a minimal consensus that the self involved in the grounding of experience is distinct from the transcendent, noumenal self of the metaphysics of the soul, so forcefully rejected by Kant in the Transcendental Dialectic of the first *Critique*, and equally to be distinguished from the empirical self known through inner experience. Interpreters typically stress the formal and functional rather than the material and substantial sense of this *third*, transcendental self in Kant.

OTHER WORKS

Important new work on other parts of Kant's philosophy has occurred in three main areas: his practical philosophy, especially ethics; the *Critique of Judgment*, especially its aesthetics; and his philosophy of science. Scholarship on Kant's ethics has widened beyond the limited concern with the principle of morality (categorical imperative) to include other aspects of Kant's ethics as well as the position of Kant's moral theory within his social philosophy in its entirety and within the wider architectonic of the critical philosophy. A main inspiration of the work on Kant's ethics has been the neo-Kantian political philosophy of John Rawls, who sought to extract from Kant's formal approach to morality procedural guidelines for the ideal construction of the principles of social conduct. Increased attention has been paid to Kant's account of agency, the possible grounding of the categorical imperative in a generic conception of practical rationality, and the key features of Kant's moral psychology—including the theory of motivation, the role of moral judgment, and the function of subjective principles of action (maxims).

The move beyond the confines of Kant's foundational writings in moral philosophy has extended not only to his philosophy of law and theory of moral duties contained in the *Metaphysics of Morals* but also to his work in the philosophy of religion, political philosophy, philosophy of history, and anthropology to be found in a number of his smaller works, often written in a more popular vein. The picture of Kant's practical philosophy that emerges from these reconstructions, revisions, and rediscoveries is that of a highly complex theory that is sensitive to the social dimension of human existence and well being able to respond to the charges and challenges posed by utilitarianism and communitarianism as well as virtue ethics.

In work on the *Critique of Judgment*, the standard emphasis on Kant's theory of aesthetic judgments has been widened considerably in recognition of the role of the third *Critique* as a synthesis of theoretical and practical philosophy in a comprehensive philosophy of human cultural development. A main focus of the scholarship on Kant's philosophy of science has been the *Opus postumum* and its attempts to specify the transition from an a priori theory of material nature to physics proper.

See also Cartesianism; Communitarianism; Neo-Kantianism; Psychologism; Rawls, John; Strawson, Peter Frederick; Utilitarianism.

Bibliography

WORKS BY KANT

The Cambridge Edition of the Works of Immanuel Kant, general editors Paul Guyer and Allen W. Wood. 15 vols. This set is the first comprehensive edition of Kant's published works, literary remains, correspondence, and lecture transcripts in English. The individual volumes of this edition are as follows: *Theoretical Philosophy 1755–1770*, translated and edited by Michael Walford with Ralf Meerbote. Cambridge, U.K.: Cambridge University Press, 1992. *Lectures on Logic*, translated and edited by Michael Young. Cambridge, U.K.: Cambridge University Press, 1992. *Opus postumum.* Translated by Eckart Förster and M. Rosen; edited by Eckart Förster. Cambridge, U.K.: Cambridge University Press, 1993. *Practical Philosophy*, translated and edited by Mary J. Gregor. Cambridge, U.K.: Cambridge University Press, 1996. *Religion and Rational Theology*, translated and edited by Allen W. Wood and George di Giovanni. Cambridge, U.K.: Cambridge University Press, 1996. *Lectures on Ethics*, translated by Peter Heath, edited by Peter Heath and Jerome B. Schneewind. Cambridge, U.K.: Cambridge University Press, 1997.

Lectures on Metaphysics, translated and edited by Karl Ameriks and Steve Narragon. Cambridge, U.K.: Cambridge University Press, 1997. *Critique of Pure Reason*, translated and edited by Paul Guyer and Allen W. Wood. Cambridge, U.K.: Cambridge University Press, 1998. *Correspondence*, translated and edited by Arnulf Zweig. Cambridge, U.K.: Cambridge University Press, 1999. *Critique of the Power of Judgment*, translated by Paul Guyer and E. Matthews, edited by Paul Guyer. Cambridge, U.K.: Cambridge University Press, 2000. *Theoretical Philosophy after 1781*, translated by Henry E. Allison, M. Friedman, G. Hatfield, and Peter Heath, edited by Henry E. Allison with Peter Heath. Cambridge, U.K.: Cambridge University Press, 2002. *Notes and Fragments*, edited by Paul Guyer. Cambridge, U.K.: Cambridge University Press, 2005. *Anthropology, History, and Education*, translated and edited by Günter Zöller and Robert Louden. Cambridge, U.K.: Cambridge University Press, 2006. *Natural Science*, translated and edited by Eric Watkins. Cambridge, U.K.: Cambridge University Press, forthcoming. *Lectures on Anthropology*, translated and edited by Robert Louden. Cambridge, U.K.: Cambridge University Press, forthcoming.

WORKS ON KANT

Allison, Henry E. *Kant's Theory of Freedom*. Cambridge, U.K.: Cambridge University Press, 1990.

Allison, Henry E. *Kant's Theory of Taste: A Reading of the Critique of Aesthetic Judgment*. Cambridge, U.K.: Cambridge University Press, 2001.

Allison, Henry E. *Kant's Transcendental Idealism. An Interpretation and Defense*. New Haven, CT: Yale University Press, 1983. Rev. ed., 2004.

Ameriks, Karl. *Kant's Theory of Mind. An Analysis of the Paralogisms of Pure Reason*. Oxford: Clarendon Press, 1982. Rev. ed. New York: Oxford University Press, 2000.

Förster, Eckart. *Kant's Final Synthesis. An Essay on the Opus postumum*. Cambridge, MA: Harvard University Press, 2000.

Friedman, Michael. *Kant and the Exact Sciences*. Cambridge, MA: Harvard University Press, 1992.

Guyer, Paul, ed. *The Cambridge Companion to Kant*. Cambridge, U.K.: Cambridge University Press, 1992.

Guyer, Paul, ed. *The Cambridge Companion to Kant and Modern Philosophy*. Cambridge, U.K.: Cambridge University Press, 2006.

Guyer, Paul. *Kant and the Claims of Taste*. Cambridge, MA: Harvard University Press 1979.

Henrich, Dieter. *The Unity of Reason*. Cambridge, MA: Harvard University Press, 1994.

Jacobs, Brian, and Patrick Kain. *Essays on Kant's Anthropology*. Cambridge, U.K.: Cambridge University Press, 2003.

Korsgaard, Christine M. *Creating the Kingdom of Ends*. Cambridge, U.K.: Cambridge University Press, 1996.

Kuehn, Manfred. *Kant. A Biography*. Cambridge, U.K.: Cambridge University Press, 2001.

Longuenesse, Béatrice. *Kant and the Capacity to Judge. Sensibility and Discursivity in the Transcendental Analytic of the Critique of Pure Reason*. Princeton, NJ: Princeton University Press, 1997.

O'Neill, Onora. *Constructions of Reason*. Cambridge, U.K.: Cambridge University Press, 1989.

Strawson, Peter F. *The Bounds of Sense: An Essay on Kant's Critique of Pure Reason*. London: Methuen, 1966.

Timmons, Mark, ed. *Kant's Metaphysics of Morals. Interpretative Essays*. Oxford: Oxford University Press, 2002.

Van Cleve, James. *Problems from Kant*. New York: Oxford University Press, 1999.

Watkins, Eric, ed. *Kant and the Sciences*. New York: Oxford University Press, 2001.

Wood, Allen W. *Kant's Ethical Thought*. Cambridge, U.K.: Cambridge University Press, 1999.

Günter Zöller (2005)

KANTIAN ETHICS

Ethical theories may be said to be "Kantian" if they take their inspiration or focus from themes in the ethical theory of Immanuel Kant, while attempting something other than interpretation, development, or defense of Kant's own ethical theory. This is not a hard and fast distinction: What appears the right way to defend some thesis of Kant's to one may appear to another to be a complete departure from the crucial components of Kant's critical ethics. Moreover, some, like scholars Onora O'Neill (1975), Marcia Baron (1996), and Barbara Herman (1993), may see their work as exploring and defending the essential elements of Kant's moral theory, rather than developing an alternative theory inspired by him, even though they do not accept the metaphysical picture Kant thought crucial to his account. Many defenders of Kant's own account see the austere picture sometimes drawn of his ethics—as based on a rigoristic and formalistic obligation to *duty*—as mistaken, and argue that Kant's conception of what people are like as moral agents, and of what morality requires of people, is far richer and more satisfying than is often supposed. Still, it is useful to see Kantian theorists as holding that Kant had some crucial or seminal ethical matters right, while at the same time committing himself to claims or views that are from their perspective unacceptable. Thus, Kantian ethicists may be understood as attempting to rework cherished Kantian insights within the bounds of an overall more acceptable framework.

METAPHYSICS

For many Kantian theorists, the point of departure from Kant is Kant's metaphysics and the role his metaphysical commitments play in his ethical theory. Kant struggled for a solution to the problem of how moral agents could be held responsible for their actions in a world governed by natural laws of cause and effect. If every event has a cause, which is itself caused, how could one see human action as anything but determined by the causes antecedent to it? And if human action is caused by natural law, in what sense can individuals see themselves as morally responsible?

Kant's solution to the problem drew on the metaphysical view developed in his *Critique of Pure Reason*, where he distinguished two worlds, one the world of sense—natural, physical, and empirical—and the other rational or "intelligible." The empirical world is governed by natural law, and effects do follow causes in ways determined by natural law. However, human beings are not merely natural but rational, and as members of the rational order are capable of "spontaneity": of producing effects based on determinations of reason, not causes. Because we have these two-fold natures, people occupy both worlds at once, and their actions are simultaneously subject to natural law and (as rational agents) to moral law.

Many Kantian ethicists find the proposal that people are citizens of some nonnatural world of reason implausible and unattractive. They aim to reconstruct the crucial elements of Kant's ethical theory without Kant's reliance on these metaphysical speculations. Most Kantian ethics are intended to develop Kantian ethical ideas while drawing on people's understanding of themselves as simply members of the natural world.

UNIVERSALIZABILITY

The strain in Kant's ethics that has found broadest employment is his idea that a practical principle (or "maxim") suitable for morally worthy action must be one which can hold universally, or, as Kant puts it, can be willed as a universal law; this is the first formulation of his "Categorical Imperative." Kant thought that when one acts immorally, one makes an exception of oneself, or makes exceptions for "just this one time," from laws one would will that everyone obey. Morality is thus best understood as the apprehension of principles that are universalizable in their scope and application.

This element of Kant's thought has echoes in numerous later thinkers. Marcus Singer (1961), for example, focuses on the general logic of what he calls the "generalization principle": What is right for one person must be right for anyone in the same or similar circumstances. One accepts the force of the question, "What would happen if everyone did that?" and Singer's theory is a study in the conditions of its legitimate application. Singer maintains that this principle is presupposed by any genuine moral judgment, and is the key to the moral principles that ground any plausible moral theory. However, Singer departs from Kant both in the metaphysical commitments previously described, and in his departure from considering what one could *will* to be universal, to assessing the desirability of the consequences of a principle with universal application.

Alan Gewirth's moral theory takes on the principle of generic consistency as its supreme moral principle. Like Kant, Gewirth (1978) begins with the premise that people are agents who act for ends; unlike Kant, Gewirth holds that, as agents, one must see the ends one is acting to realize as good. One sees them as good, however, only in light of certain properties, or "generic features," of those ends. For example, one might have the end of getting adequate nutrition in virtue of its natural role in healthy life and agency. But then, Gewirth argues, consistency requires that one sees anything else with those "generic features" as good as well; thus, to be consistent, one must see as good adequate nutrition for anyone. Moreover, people are committed to seeing as good not only their capacity for action but also the freedom and well-being that make it possible, and consistency requires that they see these as good for others as well. They must thus see themselves as having claims against others that they respect their "generic rights": rights to freedom and well-being. But the principle of universalizability requires that, if people see themselves as having claims against others, they must likewise see others as having the same claims against *them*. Thus, as in Kant, the bare idea of agency, coupled with the rational requirement of universalizability, leads to the fundamental moral principle, in this case the principle of generic consistency, "Act in accord with the generic rights of your recipients as well as of yourself" (Gewirth 1978, p. 135).

For many theorists drawing on elements of Kant's view (Singer is an example), the Kantian approach is attractive as a way to oppose consequentialism in ethics. However, not all consequentialists agree. R. M. Hare (1981) argues that the focus on universalizability can be taken to ground a form of consequentialism. Hare argues that Kant's insights into the logical properties of moral terms lead, not to Kant's own ethical conclusions, but to a form of utilitarianism. This is because people must recognize that moral principles are *prescriptions* of a certain sort, namely universal prescriptions. But such prescriptions are in turn best understood as a sort of *preference*, and when one considers one's preferences as being constrained by the requirement that they hold universally, one sees that one's prescriptions must take the familiar consequentialist form of maximizing utility.

RESPECT FOR PERSONS

The second formulation of Kant's categorical imperative stipulates that persons are not to treat other persons as means only, but always at the same time as ends. Kant is often thought to have identified something crucial to a proper understanding of morality in this principle, and this way of understanding our obligations of respect for other persons has been widely influential.

Alan Donagan's work begins with some of the essential elements recognized in the notion of universalizability, but develops them in a direction more congruent with

this feature of Kant's theory. Donagan (1977) sees Kant as an exemplar of a moral theory based on a common core that reaches back to the Stoics, the Hebrews, and the Christian tradition. This core is based on the thought that morality is addressed to rational creatures as such, in virtue of their rationality, and that its precepts, or moral law, must somehow be accessible to moral agents in virtue of that rationality. In Donagan's view, what emerges from scrutiny of this common core is the requirement that every human being be treated with the respect due a rational creature. This is closely related to Kant's second formulation of the categorical imperative, which Donagan finds superior to the "universal law" formulation of that imperative. Thus Donagan is an example of a Kantian theorist who takes Kant's starting point in a shared capacity for rationality and ends with a focus on respect for human nature.

Others similarly have found this element of Kant's work central to their own ethical conceptions. Thomas Hill (1991) interprets the metaphysically hoary elements of Kant's theory as an examination of what it is for a deliberating agent to choose how to act, what ends to pursue, and so on. From this perspective, one's "autonomy"—one's capacity to see oneself as capable of more than simply the pursuit of self-interest or satisfaction of preferences—is crucial, as it presupposes that one's status as a rational agent must be essential in one's deliberating about how to act.

However, David Cummiskey (1996) argues that the focus on respect for persons as valuable in virtue of their status as rational agents can ground a consequentialist approach as well. Cummiskey maintains that Kant's attention to the value of persons as ends-in-themselves is appropriate, but is incapable of justifying the sorts of claims often made against consequentialist accounts, which by their nature require that value be maximized. Rather, Cummiskey argues, Kant's view that rational agents are ends in themselves is itself a view with a form of value at its core, and there is nothing in the balance of Kant's theory to block the inference that such value ought to be maximized as a matter of moral obligation.

CONSTRUCTIVISM

Without question the greatest single influence in Kantian ethics has been the work of John Rawls (1971, 1999). Rawls's best-known work is in political theory, not ethics, and it draws more from Kant's *method* than from the content of Kant's views. Rawls took Kant's singular contribution to moral theory to be the notion that moral truth is not constituted independently of human reasoning and rationality—independent of individuals in such a way that moral truth can be treated as an object of investigation, as scientific truth is; instead, moral truth is something that instead people constitute or bring into being ("construct") through the very process of deliberating about it. In Kant's own theory, this idea is represented in the argument that people understand moral obligation by way of reflection on what principles could be willed as universal law. This approach brings to the foreground the *procedures* by which individuals deliberate about and attempt to determine fundamental moral principles. Rawls's political theory consists in large part of the characterization of such a procedure to arrive at principles of justice, which, he argues, are best understood not as something individuals discover, but as something they would arrive at on deliberation under certain carefully crafted conditions. The conditions Rawls specifies for this deliberation are also intended to capture important features of Kant's conception of what people are like as moral and political agents, in particular the distinction between individual persons, deserving of the sort of respect Rawls believes his theory of justice provides.

Rawls's influence can be seen not only in political theory, but in a resurgence of interest in Kantian foundations for moral and political theorizing generally. Christine Korsgaard (1996) has adapted the constructivist approach in developing her Kantian ethical theory. On her view people recognize that, as reasoning agents, they need reasons to act, and as they assess where such reasons can come from—as they consider possible "sources of normativity"—they realize in the end that they must come from their own rational natures. People take their reasons, Korsgaard argues, from their "identities," and fundamental to any and all of these identities is their moral identity—their identity as agents acting on reasons. Reasons, Korsgaard argues, are inherently public, in the sense that they must be shareable among agents, so the enterprise of reflecting on how to act itself gives rise to the principles governing one's conduct.

See also Categorical Imperative; Constructivism, Moral; Deontological Ethics; Kant, Immanuel; Rationalism in Ethics.

Bibliography

Baron, Marcia, *Kantian Ethics Almost without Apology*. Ithaca, NY: Cornell University Press, 1995.

Cummiskey, David, *Kantian Consequentialism*. New York: Oxford University Press, 1996.

Donagan, Alan. *The Theory of Morality*. Chicago: University of Chicago Press, 1977.

Gewirth, Alan. *Reason and Morality*. Chicago: University of Chicago Press, 1978.

Hare, R. M. *Moral Thinking*. Oxford: Clarendon Press, 1981.

Herman, Barbara. *The Practice of Moral Judgment*. Cambridge, MA: Harvard University Press, 1993.

Hill, Thomas. *Autonomy and Self-Respect*. Cambridge, U.K.: Cambridge University Press, 1991.

Hill, Thomas. *Dignity and Practical Reason in Kant's Moral Theory*. Ithaca, NY: Cornell University Press, 1992.

Kant, Immanuel, *Critique of Pure Reason*. Translated by Norman Kemp Smith. New York: St. Martin's Press, 1965.

Kant, Immanuel. *Groundwork for the Metaphysics of Morals*. Translated by Allen W. Wood. New Haven, CT: Yale University Press, 2002.

Korsgaard, Christine. *Creating the Kingdom of Ends*. New York: Cambridge University Press, 1996.

Korsgaard, Christine. *The Sources of Normativity*. New York: Cambridge University Press, 1996.

O'Neill, Onora. *Acting on Principle*. New York: Columbia University Press, 1975.

Rawls, John. *Collected Papers*. Edited by Samuel Freeman. Cambridge, MA: Harvard University Press, 1999.

Rawls, John. *A Theory of Justice*. Cambridge, MA: Harvard University Press, 1971, 1999.

Singer, Marcus George. *Generalization in Ethics*. New York: Atheneum Press, 1961.

Mark LeBar (2005)

KANTIANISM

See *Neo-Kantianism*

KAPLAN, DAVID
(1933–)

An American philosopher and logician, David Benjamin Kaplan was born in Los Angeles in 1933 and has spent his career mainly at the University of California, Los Angeles: first as an undergraduate student (AB in Philosophy, 1956; AB in Mathematics, 1957); then as graduate student (PhD in Philosophy, 1964), where he wrote the last dissertation Rudolf Carnap supervised; later as a faculty member, where he became Hans Reichenbach Professor of Scientific Philosophy in 1994.

Kaplan is best known for his work in formal semantics, particularly on the semantics of demonstratives and other indexicals: expressions such as *this, that purple Mercedes convertible, I, you, here, now,* and *actually.* In *Demonstratives,* Kaplan developed a theoretical framework in which sentences express propositions relative to contexts. The content of an expression (relative to a context *C*) is what it contributes to the propositions expressed (relative to C) by sentences that contain it. The content of an expression determines an intension: a function from circumstances of evaluation to extensions (truth-values for sentences, individuals for singular terms, sets of individuals for predicates). Circumstances include at least possible worlds and perhaps also times. The character of an expression determines a function from contexts to contents.

In this framework, indexicals have variable contents but stable characters. For example, relative to a context c whose agent is McX, I has a content x (which determines a function that maps every circumstance onto McX himself); whereas, relative to a context c^* whose agent is Wyman, I has a different content y (which determines a function that maps every circumstance onto Wyman himself). But, relative to either context, I has the same character (which determines a function that maps c onto x and c^* onto y). Kaplan proposed that the character of an expression is its linguistic meaning and that it is an expression's character that is responsible for its cognitive value: The difference in cognitive value between "His pants are on fire!" and "My pants are on fire!," for example, lies in the difference between the characters of the indexicals *his* and *my*.

Indexicals are directly referential: For any context C, the content o of an indexical relative to C is the entity that the function determined by o maps every circumstance onto. For example, relative to c, whose agent is McX, the content of I is McX himself. Because indexicals are directly referential, a sentence that contains an indexical expresses a singular proposition (relative to a context C): a proposition that contains the entity that is the content of that indexical (relative to C). For example, relative to c, whose agent is McX, "I'm right" expresses a proposition that contains McX himself. This proposition can be represented as the ordered pair ⟨McX, the property being right⟩.

One surprising feature of this framework is that it allows one to distinguish logical truth and necessity. For example, "I am here now" is a logical truth in something like the following sense: Relative to any context C, it expresses a proposition that is true relative to the circumstance of C (at least provided that the agent of C is located at the time and place of C at the circumstance of C). But, at least relative to most contexts, the proposition expressed by "I am here now" is not necessary: It is not true relative to every circumstance (likewise for "I exist" and "ϕ if and only if actually ϕ").

Kaplan's philosophical thought has moved from Fregeanism to Russellianism. In his 1964 dissertation,

Foundations of Intensional Logic, Kaplan developed a Carnapian model-theoretic semantics for Alonzo Church's Fregean logic of sense and denotation. In "*Quantifying In*" (1968–1969), Kaplan developed a Fregean account of belief ascriptions and of belief, one that allows quantification into belief ascriptions (as in "There is an x such that Ralph believes that x is a spy") under certain circumstances. By *Dthat* (1978) Kaplan had turned away from his early Fregeanism toward a Russellian view on which "John is suspicious," for example, expresses a singular proposition, one that contains John himself and that can be represented as the ordered pair ⟨John, the property being suspicious⟩.

Kaplan went on to become a major proponent of the previously moribund theory of singular propositions. His Russellianism reached its apogee in *Demonstratives* (1989a), where he argued that indexicals are directly referential and, hence, that sentences containing indexicals express singular propositions. Although, in his 1989 *Afterthoughts*, Kaplan admitted to feeling "a resurgence of atavistic Fregeanism," he continued to treat indexicals as directly referential.

After *Demonstratives* and *Afterthoughts*, Kaplan has worked on a number of further topics. In *Words*, he argued that the relation between a word and its occurrences should be thought of as the relation, not between a type and its tokens, but rather between a perduring entity and its temporal parts. He also suggested that it is a word itself that is responsible for its cognitive value: The difference in cognitive value between "Hesperus equals Hesperus" and "Hesperus equals Phosphorus," for example, lies in the difference between the words *Hesperus* and *Phosphorus*. In work on expressives (expressions such as *ouch* and *oops*), Kaplan suggested that one should shift from a semantics that pairs expressions with entities (*meanings*) to a semantics that pairs expressions with rules for their correct use. Kaplan also suggested that characters might best be understood, not as entities, but rather as such rules.

See also Logic, History of; Philosophy of Language.

Bibliography

PRIMARY WORKS

"Quantifying In." *Synthese* 19 (1–2) (1968–1969): 178–214.

"Dthat." In *Syntax and Semantics*. Vol. 9, edited by Peter Cole. New York: Academic, 1978.

"Demonstratives: An Essay on The Semantics, Logic, Metaphysics, and Epistemology of Demonstratives and Other Indexicals" [1977]. In *Themes from Kaplan*, edited by

Joseph Almog, John Perry, and Howard Wettstein. Oxford: Oxford University Press, 1989a.

"Afterthoughts." In *Themes from Kaplan*, edited by Joseph Almog, John Perry, and Howard Wettstein. Oxford: Oxford University Press, 1989b.

"Words." *Supplement to the Aristotelian Society* 64 (1990): 93–119.

Ben Caplan (2005)

KAREEV, NIKOLAI IVANOVICH
(1850–1931)

Nikolai Ivanovich Kareev, the Russian historian and philosopher, was educated at Moscow University, where he took his doctorate in history (1884). During the late 1870s and early 1880s he spent several years studying abroad. Kareev taught modern European history, first at Warsaw University and then at St. Petersburg University. He became a corresponding member of the St. Petersburg Academy of Sciences in 1910 and an honorary member of the Soviet Academy of Sciences in 1929. His main historical studies were devoted to eighteenth-century France, especially the Revolution of 1789.

Although a moderate in politics, Kareev was deeply influenced by such radical Russian thinkers as Aleksandr Herzen, Dimitrii Pisarev, Pëtr Lavrov, and N. K. Mikhailovskii. Like Lavrov and Mikhailovskii, Kareev was a "semipositivist," but he was less influenced by either G. W. F. Hegel or Karl Marx than Lavrov had been. His views of history echo Herzen's "philosophy of chance." "History," Kareev declared, "is not a straight line, not a regular design traced out on a mathematical plane, but a living fabric of irregular and sinuous lines, which are intertwined in the most varied and unexpected ways" (*Osnovnye voprosy* [Fundamental problems], Part I, p. 153).

Kareev's position in ethics, which he called ethical individualism, was even more Kantian than that of Lavrov's early works. He defended individual autonomy against three dominant anti-individualist tendencies: that which breaks down the self into a series of psychic events (David Hume); that which turns the individual into an expression of the *Zeitgeist* or *Volksgeist* (Hegel); and that which reduces the individual to a product of socioeconomic relations (Marx). From the point of view of the "human dignity and worth of the individual person," Kareev insisted, "external [sociopolitical] freedom is a necessary condition for the spiritual growth and happiness of all the members of society" (*Mysli*, 2nd ed., 1896, p. 135).

Kareev rejected the "utilitarian attitude toward the person, which treats her as an object," adding that the "principle of individuality" guarantees the individual's right "not to be an instrument or means for another" or reduced to the status of an organ of a "social organism" (ibid., p. 138). In attributing absolute value to individuals as such, Kareev said, we take account of both their natural rights and—as Lavrov had stressed—their present potentiality for future moral and intellectual growth. In the name of this absolute value, Kareev condemned not only political assassination and capital punishment but also euthanasia. On this point he came close not only to Immanuel Kant but also to Lev Tolstoy, whose philosophy of history, like those of Hegel and Marx, he had criticized perceptively and in detail.

See also Ethics, History of; Hegel, Georg Wilhelm Friedrich; Herzen, Aleksandr Ivanovich; Kant, Immanuel; Lavrov, Pëtr Lavrovich; Marx, Karl; Mikhailovskii, Nikolai Konstantinovich; Philosophy of History; Pisarev, Dmitri Ivanovich; Russian Philosophy; Tolstoy, Lev (Leo) Nikolaevich.

Bibliography

WORKS BY KAREEV

"K voprosu o svobode voli s tochki zreniya teorii istoricheskovo protsessa" (On the question of freedom of the will from the standpoint of the theory of the historical process) appeared in *Voprosy filosofii i psikhologii* 1 (4) (1889–1890): 113–142. It was reprinted in *Istoriko-filosofskiye i sotsiologicheskiye etyudy* (Studies in sociology and the philosophy of history; St. Petersburg, 1895; 2nd ed., St. Petersburg, 1899), pp. 279–304. *Mysli ob osnovakh Nravstvennosti* (Thoughts on the foundations of morality) was published in St. Petersburg in 1895; 2nd ed., St. Petersburg, 1896.

Osnovnye voprosy filosofii istorii (Fundamental problems in the philosophy of history). Moscow: L. F. Panteleev, 1883.

Filosofiia kul'turnoi i sotsial'noi istorii novago vremeni (The philosophy of modern cultural and social history). St. Petersburg: M. M. Stasiulevich, 1893.

Obshchii khod vsemirnoi istorii: ocherki glavneishikh istoricheskikh epokh (The general course of world history: Essays on main historical epochs). St. Petersburg: Brokgauz-Efron, 1903.

Osnovy russkoi sotsiologii (Foundations of Russian sociology). St. Petersburg: Izdatel'stvo Ivana Limbakha, 1996.

WORKS ON KAREEV

Pogodin, S. *"Russkaia shkola" istorikov: N. I. Kareev, I. V. Luchitskii, M. M. Kovalevskii* (The "Russian school" of historians: N. I. Kareev, I. V. Luchitskii, M. M. Kovalevskii).

St. Petersburg: Sankt-Peterburgskii gosudarstvennyi tekhnicheskii universitet, 1997, pp. 139–202.

Zenkovsky, V. V. *Istoriya Russkoi filosofii*. 2 vols. Paris, 1948 and 1950. Translated by G. L. Kline as *A History of Russian Philosophy*, 2 vols. (London and New York, 1953), pp. 374–375.

Zolotarev, V. P. *Istoricheskaia kontseptsiia N. I. Kareeva: soderzhanie i evoliutsiia* (N. I. Kareev's conception of history: Its content and evolution). Leningrad: Izdatel'stvo Leningradskogo universiteta, 1988.

George L. Kline (1967)
Bibliography updated by Vladimir Marchenkov (2005)

KAREYEV, NICHOLAS IVANOVICH

See *Kareev, Nikolai Ivanovich*

KARMA

Karma (Sanskrit, *karman*; literally, "deed," "action") is an adjunct in Indian religious thought to the doctrine of Reincarnation. In one form or another, it is part of the beliefs of Buddhism, Jainism, and Hinduism. The actions of a living being are regarded as having a special class of causal effects that determine his future spiritual condition, both in this life and in succeeding ones. These effects are known as the "fruits" of the action. Good deeds lead to progress toward liberation (*mokṣa,* nirvana); bad ones, to regress from this goal. Usually caste status, disease, prosperity, and so forth are thought to be the consequences of actions in previous lives. Thus, karma is an ethically oriented causal law; and although some Hindus regard karma as the work of God, the concept does not necessitate this interpretation, and the award of deserts is as often regarded as an automatic process in nature.

The archaic notion of karma seems to have been that action as such binds men to the world (and thereby to suffering and ignorance); hence, liberation must involve suspension of all activity. Thus, in Jainism, which represents a very ancient strand in Indian religion, even a good action, although inducing an influx of meritorious karma, ties the person to matter. Indeed, karma, as the force determining rebirth, is itself regarded as a subtle form of matter. Also—and hence the emphasis on "noninjury" (*ahiṃsā*)—especially evil effects follow from a person's destroying life, even microorganisms. Such ideas lay behind the heroically quietistic Jain ideal of suicide by self-starvation. Moreover, the concept of karma in Vedic literature had the meaning of ritual act, so that combined with the need to refrain from activity there runs through much Indian ascetic thought the notion that even religious acts, although they may bring heavenly rewards, bind men to the cosmos and to rebirth: heaven is part of the cosmos and itself must be transcended.

These ideas presented a number of problems to speculative and religious thinkers: (1) How can liberation ever be achieved if even the effort to be inactive, and inactivity itself, may be forms of binding action? (2) How can the ordinary man, involved in his worldly duties and concerns, have any hope of escaping rebirth? (3) By what mechanism does karma operate on future births? (4) Why, if karma is what keeps empirical life going, does the saint (*jīvanmukta*), who has attained serenity and release in this life, keep on living? (5) How can there be any human initiative or free will if our present state is inexorably determined by past karma?

Various answers to these questions were given, among them the following: (1) The Jains hold that karmic matter can be annihilated by austerities, so that gradually it can be totally removed from an individual. On the other hand, Buddhism transformed the notion of karma by holding that motives, rather than the acts themselves, are what count and that karma needs craving (*taṇhā*) as a necessary condition of its effectiveness. Hence, by removing craving through the purification of one's motives, one can find release from rebirth. For the Hindu theologian Śankara, the power of karma depends on ignorance, so that the contemplative knowledge that the Self is the sole reality brings liberation from the continuing effects of karma.

(2) On the one hand, the ordinary man can hope to become a recluse, monk, or holy man in a future life. On the other hand, theistic ideas introduced grace as a countervailing means of liberation. Thus, in the *Bhagavad Gītā* it is stressed that a man, in performing his duties without regard to their fruits and in sole reliance upon the Lord, can escape the bonds of karma. Likewise, in Mahāyāna Buddhism the theory of the transfer of merit involves the belief that the otherwise unworthy individual can be given merit by a bodhisattva (Buddha-to-be) out of the latter's infinite store, acquired through many lives of heroic self-sacrifice on behalf of living beings; thereby the individual qualifies for rebirth in paradise (where the conditions for attaining nirvana are peculiarly favorable). Thus the operation of karma is short-circuited by grace and faith.

(3) It is commonly held that karma is *adṛṣṭa*, an invisible force, so that the need to postulate an observable

mechanism is evaded. However, among some schools the doctrine that the soul is all-pervasive (and not localized) helps to explain the concept of karmic action-at-a-distance. Traditional medical writings (first or second century) affirm that a person's characteristics are not derived solely from his parents (in this, there is an incipient conflict between modern genetics and the theory of karma).

(4) It is generally held that there is a limited continuance of karmic effects, like the running on of a potter's wheel after the potter has stopped turning it—but when the saint's death occurs, there will be no further rebirth for him.

(5) Various positions are adopted concerning the question of free will. The Buddha, for instance, was clearly impressed by the principle that knowledge of causes gives one the opportunity to determine the future, so that a proper understanding of karma and its causality should in no way involve fatalistic conclusions. He attacked Makkhali Gosāla, a contemporary teacher, for holding a fatalistic predestinationism, allied to extreme asceticism (which was in no sense a cause of final release, but merely symptomatic of one's progress). The Jains held that theoretically, in its pure state, the life monad or soul is capable of any kind of effort: Because of this "omnipotence" it never needs to be subservient to karma.

Although some schools argued that, since the effects of karma are morally regulated, one must presuppose a conscious regulator, namely God, atheistic and agnostic proponents of karma theory held that the difficulties of belief in God are as great as, or greater than, those inherent in assuming the automatic operation of karma. Moreover, belief in God generally involves the notion that unworthy people can short-circuit karma through calling on God in faith, and this cuts against the concepts of moral responsibility and self-help.

See also Indian Philosophy; Reincarnation; Responsibility, Moral and Legal.

Bibliography

Dasgupta, S. N. *A History of Indian Philosophy.* Cambridge, U.K.: Cambridge University Press, 1922. Vol. I, Ch. 4.

Paranjoti, Violet. *Saiva Siddhānta,* 2nd ed. London: Luzac, 1954. Pp. 38ff.

Parrinder, Geoffrey. *Upanishads, Gītā and Bible.* London, 1962. Ch. 9.

Tucci, Giuseppe. *Storia della filosofia indiana.* Bari, Italy, 1957. Part II, Ch. 10.

Zimmer, Heinrich. *Philosophies of India.* Edited by Joseph Campbell. New York: Meridian, 1956. Ch. 4, Sec. 7.

Ninian Smart (1967)

KARSAVIN, LEV PLATONOVICH
(1882–1952)

Russian historian-medievalist and religious philosopher Lev Platonovich Karsavin was born in St. Petersburg, the son of a ballet dancer and master, and the brother of the famous ballerina Tamara Karsavina. He graduated from the Department of History of Petersburg University in 1906 and stayed there as a teacher, doing studies in medieval spirituality and culture. Being a disciple of the prominent medievalist Ivan Grews, he soon started to develop his own approach, which can be considered in retrospect as an early prototype of the method of the French Annales school. His first big monograph (1912) was devoted to the early history of the Franciscan Order and the heretical sects of the Waldenses and Cathars. His next monograph, *Foundations of Medieval Spirituality in the Twelfth and Thirteenth Centuries, Mainly in Italy* (1915), is an important theoretical work of a type close to future studies in historical and cultural anthropology. Here Karsavin developed a methodology for historical studies based on the formation of general concepts like "an average religious person," "basic religious fund," and so forth, and tried to perform a reconstruction of the personality of the medieval individual in all its dimensions. The long-forgotten historical work of Karsavin, which includes also *Introduction to History: The Theory of History* (1920) and *Philosophy of History* (1923), was rediscovered in the 1970s and 1980s (chiefly in influential works by Aron Gurevich) and won recognition as a pioneering effort.

During the period of the Russian Revolution (1917–1922) Karsavin's thought shifted gradually to philosophy. This transition was stimulated by his interest in methodological and philosophical problems of history and Christian doctrine. Like a medieval scholastic thinker, he came to general metaphysical problems from reflection on Christian dogmas. In the same period, important changes in his life took place. Karsavin was opposed to the Bolshevik regime, not politically (he even considered the Bolsheviks to be the only force capable of ruling Russia), but ideologically and spiritually. Having a provocative style, he demonstrated his Christian convictions much more than he had before the revolution, lectured in a theological institute, and became the target of a vicious campaign in the official press. In the summer of 1922 he was arrested and then expelled to Germany together with a large group of noncommunist public figures, including leading religious philosophers (Nikolai

Berdyaev, Sergey Bulgakov, Nikolai Lossky, Semen Frank). In exile, he lived in Berlin (1922–1926), then in Clamart, next to Paris (1926–1928), and finally settled in Lithuania, where he was invited to hold the chair of general history at Kaunas University. Between 1925 and 1929 he took an active part in the Eurasian movement, becoming the leading theoretician of its left wing characterized by pro-Soviet views. During the twenties he wrote all his principal philosophical works, creating an original system of religious metaphysics.

Karsavin's system is the last big system of the so-called metaphysics of All-Unity. This philosophical school founded by Vladimir Solov'ëv took the central place in Russian religious philosophy and included leading figures of the Russian religious-philosophical renaissance of the twentieth century. By definition, its systems are based on the fundamental concept of All-Unity that represents a specific transrational principle of inner form describing perfect unity of a manifold such that any part of this manifold is identical to the whole of it. Karsavin gives this concept a new treatment, describing All-Unity as a sophisticated hierarchical system, structured vertically (into components or "moments" of higher and lower order, the latter being subsystems of the former) and horizontally (into a variety of moments of the same order). Vertical connections in this structure are described by the notion of *contractio* borrowed from Nicolas of Cusa, while horizontal ones are characterized by means of *conglomeratio et exglomeratio centri* found in Giordano Bruno and meaning that any two moments of the same order are connected not in a direct (i.e., causal) way, but only via the center of the whole system.

Drawing upon ancient doctrines and using their concepts in a constructivist and systematic way close to the theory of systems, this treatment is both archaizing and modernist. In Karsavin's system, the principle of All-Unity is subordinate to another fundamental principle, that of Tri-Unity, modeled on the Holy Trinity as it is presented in Christian dogma. Karsavin follows here the paradigm of dynamic ontology: Like many metaphysical doctrines, from Plotinus to Hegel, he treats being as a process governed by a triadic principle of development, where All-Unity represents the static aspect of Tri-Unity, its "stopping and rest."

Three ontological notions are identical in Karsavin's system: (perfect) Tri-Unity, God, and (perfect) Person. This trilateral identification also serves as the definition of Person. Human being is interpreted as an imperfect person that strives to perfection, that is, to God; all kinds of collective units, social and religious groups, nations,

and classes are also considered as imperfect, embryonic persons and called *symphonic persons*. Karsavin's personalistic turn was new for the metaphysics of All-Unity, which, starting with the Greeks, had traditionally developed in an impersonal symbolist vein. The personalistic trend is further enhanced in Karsavin's description of the world process. The three stages of ontological dynamics are primal unity, disjoining, reunification; the central stage is interpreted as nonbeing or death. In the act of creation God endows with being the reality that he creates, thus depriving himself of being (kenosis) and voluntarily choosing sacrificial death. This voluntary passing of one's own being to somebody, identical to voluntary sacrificial death for somebody, is the definition of (perfect) love—whence it follows that the creature, striving to God, advances to pass, in its turn, its own being to God and thereby ascends to its own sacrificial death out of love.

Thus Karsavin's philosophy presents itself as an ontological drama of death, sacrifice, and love. These principles of his thought turned out to be perfectly realized in the final years of his life. When in 1944 it was clear that the Soviet Union was about to recapture Lithuania, Karsavin refused to leave and move to the West. In 1946 he was dismissed from the university for his deliberately defiant attitude toward Soviet authorities. In 1949 he was arrested and sent to a concentration camp in Abez, near the polar circle. In the gulag he wrote about ten texts of spiritual poetry and metaphysics and until his final days (he died there from tuberculosis) was a spiritual guide and teacher for his fellow prisoners. After the fall of communism, all of Karsavin's principal works were republished in Russia and have been actively studied.

See also Philosophy of History; Philosophy of Religion; Russian Philosophy.

Bibliography

WORKS BY KARSAVIN

Vostok, Zapad i russkaia ideia. St. Petersburg: Academia, 1922. 2nd ed., Moscow, 1991.

Noctes Peropolitanae. St. Petersburg: A. S. Kagan, 1922.

O nachalakh. Berlin: Obelisk, 1925.

O lichnosti. Kaunas, Lithuania: 1929.

"Poema o smerti." *Eranus* 2 (1931): 231–310.

Religiosno-filosofskie sochineniia. Podgotovka tekstov, predislovie, kommentarii Sergey Horujy. Moscow: Renaissance, 1992.

Malye sochineniia. Podgotovka tekstov, predislovie, kommentarii Sergey Horujy. St. Peterburg: Aletheia, 1994.

WORKS ON KARSAVIN

Wetter, Gustav A. "L. P. Karsawins Ontologie der Dreieinheit." *Orientalia Christiana Periodica* 9 (1943): 366–405.

Wetter, Gustav A. "Zum Zeitproblem in der Philosophie des Ostens: Die Theorie der 'Allzeitlichkeit' bei L.P.Karsawin." *Scholastik* 3 (1949): 345–366.

While there are no English-language works devotedly solely to Karsavin, the following two English-language works contain sections on Karsavin: Zenkovsky, V. V., *A History of Russian Philosophy*, vol. 2 (London: Routledge & Kegan Paul Ltd., 1953); Meerson, Michael Aksionov, *The Trinity of Love in Modern Russian Theology* (Franciscan Press: 1998).

Sergey Horujy (2005)

KATHARSIS

Katharsis is a beneficial transformation of painful emotions through absorbed contemplation of a powerfully moving work of art. The root meaning of "katharsis" in Greek is cleansing. The word can indicate the removal of impurities from, hence the amelioration of, any kind of substance. Before Aristotle, some philosophers had spoken (metaphorically) of psychological katharsis. Aristotle's student Aristoxenus claimed that Pythagoreans "achieved katharsis of the body through medicine, katharsis of the soul through music" (frag. 26). Plato sometimes employs the terminology of "katharsis" for philosophically extricating the soul or intellect from bodily concerns (e.g., *Phaedo* 67c; compare *Sophist* 226d–231b). But Aristotle was the first person to apply the term "katharsis" to the experience of tragedy.

The last clause of Aristotle's definition of tragedy in *Poetics* 6 describes tragedy as "accomplishing through pity and fear the *katharsis* of such emotions." No further reference to katharsis as the effect of tragedy occurs in the *Poetics*. Controversy over the "katharsis" clause remains acute, with no solution commanding great confidence. At issue are questions like the following: Did Aristotle mean occurrent emotions or underlying dispositions? Are pity and fear the only emotions involved? Is emotion the object or only the agency of katharsis? Does the term "katharsis" carry medical and/or religious overtones? Are the minds of tragedy's spectators purged, purified, clarified, or refined?

Our best aid to interpreting tragic katharsis is the account of musical katharsis in Aristotle's *Politics* 8.6–7, where Aristotle posits both pathological and normal cases of the phenomenon. As pity and fear are specifically cited in this context and further elucidation is promised in a discussion of poetry, there is a clear link with the *Poetics*. While *Politics* 8, focusing on educational needs, distinguishes various uses of music, it adopts a fundamentally character-centered view of music's capacity to "change the soul" through the passions (1340a4–b19). Though Aristotle regards both tragedy and music as mimetic (representational and expressive) art forms that arouse intense emotional states in their audiences, in his general moral psychology, ethical judgment, while cognitive, is influenced by feeling (*Nicomachean Ethics* 2.2–5, *Rhetoric* 2.1–11). Hence, we should not drive a wedge between the emotional and cognitive implications of katharsis.

Aristotle partially compares the mental effects of musical katharsis to both medical and ritual katharsis, but he nonetheless keeps musical katharsis independent of those spheres. *Politics* 8 encourages a model of tragic katharsis that integrates cognitive, affective, and ethical reactions into the special pleasure of tragedy. Since these reactions stem from emotional engagement with a mimetic plot structure (*Poetics* 14), and since all experience of mimesis is guided by cognitive awareness (*Poetics* 4), Aristotle's larger theory of tragedy supports the view that katharsis operates together with cognition and pleasure. Even so, katharsis should be viewed not as tragic pleasure per se but as a beneficial transformation of painful emotions, through the absorbed contemplation of a powerfully moving artwork, into a key component of a satisfyingly unified experience.

Because katharsis requires an uninhibited flow of emotion, it may bring a sense of "relief" (*Politics* 1342a14) and reduce any excess. But the popular modern association of katharsis with mere draining of blocked emotion oversimplifies Aristotle's perspective. The combined evidence of the *Poetics* and *Politics* suggests that Aristotle addressed Plato's concerns about emotional responses to art (*Republic* 606) by maintaining that such heightened emotion could channel an ethically valuable alignment of feeling and understanding. If so, it is plausible that his concept of katharsis had application to several art forms, perhaps including comedy.

See also Aristotle; Emotion; Plato; Pythagoras and Pythagoreanism; Tragedy.

Bibliography

Aristotle. *Nicomachean Ethics.* Translated by Christopher Rowe. Oxford, U.K.: Oxford University Press, 2002.

Aristotle. *On Rhetoric.* Translated by George A. Kennedy. New York: Oxford University Press, 1991.

Aristotle. *Poetics.* Translated by Stephen Halliwell. Cambridge, MA: Harvard University Press, 1995.

Aristotle. *Politics. Books VII and VIII.* Translated by Richard Kraut. Oxford: Clarendon Press, 1997.

Halliwell, Stephen. *Aristotle's Poetics.* London: Duckworth, 1986.

Halliwell, Stephen. "La psychologie morale de la catharsis: Un essai de reconstruction." *Études philosophiques* 4 (2003): 499–517.

Lear, Jonathan. "*Katharsis.*" *Phronesis* 33 (1988): 297–326.

Plato. *Complete Works*, edited by J. M. Cooper. Indianapolis: Hackett, 1997.

Stephen Halliwell (2005)

KAUFMANN, WALTER ARNOLD
(1921–1980)

Walter Kaufmann was born in Freiburg, Germany, on July 1, 1921. He emigrated to the United States in 1939, as conditions in Germany became ominous for those of Jewish descent (Kaufmann's father—although not his mother—had converted to Protestantism, with the consequence that Kaufmann had been raised in that faith; but he converted to Judaism in 1933, in an early display of the sensitivity to religious questions that became one of the central features of his intellectual life). He attended Williams College, from which he graduated in 1941, and then went to Harvard, from which he received an MA degree in Philosophy in 1942. After military service in Europe during the Second World War (in capacities that took advantage of his equal facility in German and in English), he returned to Harvard, receiving his PhD in 1947. He joined the Philosophy Department at Princeton University in the fall of that year, which remained his academic base until his untimely death on September 4, 1980, at the age of only 59, from a mysterious illness he apparently contracted while traveling in Egypt and Africa.

Kaufmann played a major role in the introduction of existential philosophy (of Jean-Paul Sartre in particular) and the rehabilitation of G.W.F. Hegel and Friedrich Nietzsche (who had come to be all too closely associated with the Germany of the kaiser and of Adolf Hitler) in the English-speaking world in the decades following the Second World War. As one of the few members of major philosophy departments in those years who had a strong interest in developments in post-Kantian European philosophy, and as a prolific translator as well as interpreter of the writings of some of the most important figures in that tradition, he emerged as its most prominent, visible, and articulate champion, during the very decades in which the new Britain-based import of analytic philosophy became dominant in the philosophy departments at most major American universities. Much of Kaufmann's career was spent in often heated conflict as an advocate of the continental tradition (as it came to be called) against the newly dominant analytical paradigm that he regarded as a disaster for philosophy, and also as an advocate of those within that tradition (Hegel, Nietzsche, Sartre, and Martin Buber in particular) against the influence and popularity of others within it of whom he had a very low opinion (such as Karl Marx and Martin Heidegger).

Because Kaufmann had a Jewish identity and made no secret of it (even though he also made much of his rejection of Jewish theology), he was ideally positioned to be able to reject the charge of anti-Semitism that had contributed to the widespread hostility to Nietzsche before, during, and after the war years, and to defuse the imputation to Nietzsche of other proto-Nazi sentiments along with it. His association of Nietzsche with Sartrean existentialism was another of his strategies in pursuit of this objective; for, unlike Heidegger, Sartre's anti-Nazi credentials were impeccable, and Sartre himself sought to portray his existentialism as a kind of radical humanism. Kaufmann further presented Nietzsche as a kindred spirit of the heroes of the Enlightenment, and even of Emersonian individualism and later American pragmatism. This interpretation of Nietzsche found a ready reception in a wide and growing audience in the years following the publication of Kaufmann's classic *Nietzsche: Philosopher, Psychologist, Antichrist* in 1950, which remains one of the best general introductions to Nietzsche's thought written for English-speaking readers.

Moreover, while Kaufmann never published another book-length study of Nietzsche, he exerted an even greater influence upon the reception of Nietzsche in the English-speaking world through his much-needed new translations of (and introductions and notes to) most of Nietzsche's major works over a period of two decades, beginning with his phenomenally popular anthology *The Portable Nietzsche* in 1954, culminating with Nietzsche's *The Gay Science* in 1974, and including the controversial collection of selections from Nietzsche's notebooks from the 1880s published after his death under the title *The Will to Power*, thereby giving that volume a prominence and appearance of legitimacy that many feel it does not deserve. And by passing over the various works Nietzsche published between *The Birth of Tragedy* and *Thus Spoke Zarathustra*, Kaufmann influenced what English-speaking readers ever since have come to regard as Nietzsche's most important works.

Kaufmann simultaneously attempted to renew interest in Hegel, in a manner intended to liberate Hegel from the moribund tradition of interpretation that had flourished in Britain and America under the banner of idealism in the late nineteenth and early twentieth centuries. Kaufmann's Hegel was closer to existentialism than he was to that metaphysical idealism, as he tried to show in his *Hegel: A Reinterpretation* (1966); and his Hegel championed a political philosophy that was a major, but sadly forgotten and neglected, alternative to the options upon which attention was focusing in both analytical and Marxist circles at that time. So Kaufmann first published a study of *Hegel's Political Philosophy* (1970), and then a volume of his own essays in this area reflecting his own mix of Hegelian and Nietzschean elements, *Without Guilt and Justice* (1973). He aspired to be taken seriously as a moral, social, and political philosopher; but the failure of these volumes to attract significant attention led him to turn his efforts in other directions.

Kaufmann had followed his early study of Nietzsche and anthology of Nietzsche's writings with two very popular volumes attempting to do the same thing for existential philosophy—his anthology *Existentialism from Dostoevsky to Sartre* (1956), which was everyone's introduction to existentialism for many years, and his collection of essays *From Shakespeare to Existentialism* (1959), which sought to situate existentialism in intimate if not entirely harmonious relation to an intellectual tradition that included the greatest contributions to Western literature and thought. The relationship between existential and tragic thought, literature, and experience held a particular fascination for him, which he explored in his *Tragedy and Philosophy* (1968).

These interests led Kaufmann to attempt to position himself in relation to traditional forms of philosophical and religious thought, first in his combative early *Critique of Religion and Philosophy* (1958), and then in his impassioned attempt to formulate and articulate his own post-traditional secularly religious credo *The Faith of A Heretic* (1960). His attempts to come to terms with religion continued in two volumes published in 1976, a volume of essays on *Existentialism, Religion, and Death*, and a book intended for a wider audience and marking the beginning of his attempt to integrate philosophy and photography, *Religions in Four Dimensions: Existential and Aesthetic, Historical and Comparative*.

This experiment continued in a trilogy published three years later (1979), under the general title *Man's Lot*.

In this three-volume study of the human condition—*Life at the Limits*, *Time Is an Artist*, and *What Is Man?*—Kaufmann revealed himself as a truly gifted photographer with a powerful ability to employ that gift in the service of his attempt to plumb the heights and depths of human reality. That trilogy was followed by another, *Discovering the Mind* (1980–1981), with which his life abruptly ended, and the third volume of which was published following his death.

In each of these three last volumes Kaufmann considered the contributions of three major figures to this discovery: J.W. Von Goethe, Immanuel Kant, and Hegel; Nietzsche, Heidegger, and Buber; and Sigmund Freud, Alfred Adler and Carl Jung. This, he believed, was the real philosophy of mind; and it was his hope, through these volumes, to enrich philosophical thinking with respect to the mind by connecting it with this tradition—as he had sought to enrich philosophical thinking with respect to the human condition in the previous trilogy, and to enrich moral, social, and political thought by an infusion into them of Hegelian and Nietzschean ways of thinking.

Kaufmann found it at first frustrating and then deeply distressing that he was not taken seriously by the new analytic-philosophical establishment of his day, other than (by some) as Nietzsche's best translator and most appealing reinterpreter. This made him increasingly estranged from and critical of that establishment and philosophical orientation, and may have prompted his involvement in his last years with the EST human potential movement and his willingness to be associated with the Moon Unification Church's International Conference on the Unity of Sciences in the 1970s.

His later work itself was of a character that could hardly have been more at odds with the aims and paradigms of analytic-philosophical inquiry. Yet he considered himself to be true to the real heart and soul of the Socratic philosophical tradition, and to be its advocate and defender in a time in which he felt academic philosophy had lost its way. He welcomed the opportunity to enter the fray of popular debate as a public intellectual who was more than willing to continue Nietzsche's effort to fight the good fight of disillusioned enlightenment that was neither religious, scientistic, nor historically optimistic. He thought that philosophy could and should make a difference in human life, and that that difference should be in the direction of an uncompromisingly secular, post-metaphysical, strongly individualistic, but intensely interpersonal, existential humanism. Had he lived to develop and make a case for that vision of authentic humanity, he might well have attained the recognition in the philosophical community that escaped him.

See also Continental Philosophy.

Bibliography

WORKS BY KAUFMANN

Nietzsche: Philosopher, Psychologist, Antichrist. Princeton, NJ: Princeton University Press, 1950.

Critique of Religion and Philosophy. Princeton, NJ: Princeton University Press, 1958

From Shakespeare to Existentialism. Boston: Beacon Press, 1959.

The Faith of A Heretic. Garden City, NY: Doubleday, 1961.

Cain and Other Poems. Garden City, NY: Doubleday, 1962.

Hegel: A Reinterpretation. Notre Dame, IN: University of Notre Dame Press, 1966.

Hegel: Texts and Commentary. Notre Dame, IN: University of Notre Dame Press, 1966.

Tragedy and Philosophy. Garden City, NY: Doubleday, 1968.

Hegel's Political Philosophy. New York: Atherton Press, 1970.

Without Guilt and Justice: from Decidophobia to Autonomy. New York: P. H. Wyden, 1973.

Existentialism, Religion, and Death: Thirteen Essays. New York: New American Library, 1976.

Religions in Four Dimensions: Existential and Aesthetic, Historical and Comparative. New York: Reader's Digest Press, 1976.

The Future of the Humanities. New York: Reader's Digest Press, 1977.

Man's Lot. New York: Reader's Digest Press, 1979.

Discovering the Mind. New York: McGraw-Hill, 1980–1981.

Richard Schacht (2005)

KAUTSKY, KARL
(1854–1939)

Karl Kautsky was, with the exception of Karl Marx and Friedrich Engels, the leading theorist of orthodox Marxism before World War I. Born in Prague of Czech and German parentage, Kautsky studied at Vienna and showed much interest in social Darwinism and socialism. As an evolutionist and materialist, he found Marx's combination of dialectical materialism and economic determinism irresistible, and he worked with Engels himself during the 1880s. From 1883 to 1917 Kautsky was the editor of *Die neue Zeit,* the official organ of the German Social Democratic Party and the most influential socialist journal of the day. He edited and published the literary remains of Marx after Engels's death. In 1891 Kautsky wrote the famous first, or theoretical, part of the *Erfurter Programm,* the official policy statement of the German party. This document established that the greatest socialist party in history should be orthodox Marxist.

Kautsky, more than any other theorist of repute, accepted Marx's method and conclusions as he found them. The natural laws of economic development resulted in certain inevitable contradictions in capitalism that must necessarily lead to its destruction and replacement by socialism. This would occur, Marx and Kautsky held, because competition and technical improvements, together with the availability of surplus labor, would lead to the concentration of capital and the progressive immiserization of the proletariat, as well as the polarization of society into a few monopolists opposed by vast masses of starving workers. Recurrent depressions and economic catastrophes would finally destroy capitalism. Such crises would be caused mainly by the inability of the workers to purchase the products of their labor. The united proletariat, trained by its socialist leaders, would see that only social ownership of the means of production could end the contradiction between capitalism's ability to produce wealth and its inability to distribute that wealth through private ownership. Like Marx and Engels, Kautsky held that religion, philosophy, and ethics are reflections of the substructure of class interest and position and that the state is the puppet of the dominant social class.

Kautsky, the "defender of the faith," fought attempts of fellow socialists to make basic alterations in their Marxian heritage. He led the German Social Democratic Party in its struggle against Eduard Bernstein and the revisonists, who believed that the facts of European capitalism no longer supported his orthodox views and that parliamentary action and pragmatic flexibility could bring extensive and permanent reform. Kautsky was able to maintain the preeminence of orthodox Marxism in party theory, although the revisionists increasingly dominated party tactics and action. In the early years of the twentieth century, Kautsky and the orthodox centrists had increasingly to contend with the radical left wing of the party under Rosa Luxemburg and Karl Liebknecht. This group held strictly to Marx's economic teachings but rejected orthodox political tactics in favor of more immediately revolutionary doctrines. They hoped for more radical positions on questions before parliament and for greater encouragement of spontaneous revolutionary and general strike activity. Kautsky did not believe that the contradictions of capitalism or the class consciousness of the workers were advanced enough for such tactics. He did join the Left in parliament on various crucial questions, notably in its refusal to sanction the continuance of World War I as a war of conquest.

During the Weimar Republic, Kautsky lost his preeminent position as the reformists dominated the party and Leninism captured the Left. He was attacked by V. I. Lenin and Leon Trotsky for his castigation of their dictatorial and terroristic methods and their conquest of Georgia, then an independent socialist-controlled state. Forced into exile by the Nazis, Kautsky died in Amsterdam.

See also Darwinism; Dialectical Materialism; Engels, Friedrich; Lenin, Vladimir Il'ich; Marxist Philosophy; Marx, Karl; Socialism.

Bibliography

WORKS BY KAUTSKY

Das Erfurter Programm. Stuttgart, 1899.

The Social Revolution. London: Twentieth Century Press, 1909.

Bernstein und das sozialdemokratische Programm. Stuttgart, 1919.

Ethik und materialistische Geschichtsauffassung. Berlin, 1922.

Die Materialistische Geschichtsauffassung. Berlin, 1927. Translated by Raymond Meyer with John H. Kautsky as *The Materialist Conception of History.* New Haven, CT: Yale University Press, 1988.

Die Geschichte des Sozialismus. Berlin, 1947.

WORKS ON KAUTSKY

Lenin, Nikolai. *The Proletarian Revolution and Kautsky the Renegade.* London: British Socialist Party, 1920.

Renner, Karl. *Karl Kautsky.* Berlin, 1925.

Salvadori, Massimo L. *Karl Kautsky and the Socialist Revolution 1880–1938.* Translated by J. Rothschild. London: New Left Books, 1979.

Steenson, Gary P. *Karl Kautsky 1854–1938: Marxism in the Classical Years.* Pittsburgh: University of Pittsburgh Press, 1978.

Trotsky, Leon. *The Defense of Terrorism: A Reply to Kautsky.* New York, 1921.

John Weiss (1967)
Bibliography updated by Philip Reed (2005)

KAVELIN, KONSTANTIN DMITRIEVICH
(1818–1885)

Konstantin Dmitrievich Kavelin, the Russian historian and philosopher, was educated at Moscow University, where he was later professor of history. Kavelin also taught at St. Petersburg University and was for a time tutor to the royal family. In addition to numerous historical works, he wrote essays in psychology, sociology, and ethics. During the 1870s he carried on an active polemic with Vladimir Solov'ëv, defending a positivist (or "semi-positivist") position against Solov'ëv's criticisms. In politics Kavelin was a moderate liberal; in religion he remained devoutly Russian Orthodox.

Kavelin's main work in ethical theory, *Zadachi etiki* (Tasks [or problems] of ethics), appeared in 1844. In it he criticized the then fashionable one-sided "objectivism," which, he charged, blurred the distinction between inner intention and outward behavior, leading to the conclusion that intentions may be "unlawful" or volitions "criminal." From the neo-Kantian viewpoint that Kavelin adopted in this book, such a conclusion is absurd. Intentions and volitions, he insisted, are to be judged only "by their relationship to consciousness, to the understanding and inner conviction of the person in whom they occur" (*Sobranie sochinenii* [Collected works], Vol. III, col. 907).

When utilitarians equate virtue with utility and vice with social harm they are taking an "outsider's" view of moral experience, the view of a spectator rather than that of a moral agent. In fact, moral virtue may or may not be useful; this depends on the particular social system involved, and the latter is a nonmoral factor. Hence, social utility cannot provide a sound criterion of morality.

It is human individuality as a unique locus of value, Kavelin asserted, which provides such a criterion. However, this assertion raised serious problems for Kavelin's "scientific ethics," since, as he admitted, concrete individuality systematically eludes the abstract generalities of science. In the end, the "scientific ethics" that Kavelin had been laboring to construct coincided with Christian ethics—the "last word in ethical wisdom" and "an incontrovertible truth of individual spiritual life" (*Sobranie sochinenii* [Collected works], Vol. III, Cols. 940–941).

Kavelin's attempt to provide a scientific foundation for ethics, like the attempts of other nineteenth-century thinkers, must be judged a failure. However, Kavelin eloquently restated ideas derived from Vissarion Belinskii, Aleksandr Herzen, and the Russian Populists concerning the individual person and his sense of freedom and the role of convictions in morality. His was a genuine, if modest, philosophical contribution.

See also Belinskii, Vissarion Grigor'evich; Ethics, History of; Herzen, Aleksandr Ivanovich; Metaethics; Neo-Kantianism; Philosophy of History; Russian Philosophy; Solov'ëv (Solovyov), Vladimir Sergeevich; Utilitarianism.

Bibliography

Vol. III of Kavelin's four-volume *Sobraniye sochinenii* (Collected works; St. Petersburg: Stasiulevicha, 1898–1900) contains Kavelin's philosophical works, including *Zadachi etiki*, cols. 897–1018.

For literature on Kavelin, see V. V. Zenkovsky, *Istoriia Russkoi filosofii*. 2 vols. (Paris: YMCA Press, 1948–1950). Translated by George L. Kline as *A History of Russian Philosophy* (New York: Columbia University Press, 1953), pp. 345–348.

See also V. I. Prilenskii, *Opyt issledovaniia mirovozzreniia rannikh russkikh liberalov* (A study of early Russian liberals' world view). Moscow: Rossiiskaia akademiia nauk, Institut filosofii, 1995, pp. 149–-205.

George L. Kline (1967)
Bibliography updated by Vladimir Marchenkov (2005)

KELSEN, HANS
(1881–1973)

Born in Prague on October 11, 1881, Hans Kelsen grew up in Vienna. He studied law at the University of Vienna and completed, in 1911, the *Habilitation* (major dissertation required for the *venia legendi* or state license to hold university lectures). After military service in World War I, he worked up a number of drafts of what became the Austrian Federal Constitution of October 1920. Here Kelsen's most distinctive contribution was centralized constitutional review, an entirely new institutional practice. During the 1920s, Kelsen served as professor of law at the University of Vienna and also as Constitutional Court judge. Ousted from the latter position in 1930 by Austria's right-of-center Christian-Social Party, Kelsen took up a professorship in Cologne. Ousted from this position in the spring of 1933, on the basis of the notorious Nazi statute for the "Restoration of the Professional Civil Service" (authorizing the dismissal of those seen as politically unreliable and also those of Jewish ancestry), Kelsen spent the period from 1933 to 1940 in Geneva. He left in May 1940 for the United States, where he eventually secured a position at the University of California at Berkeley. He died in Berkeley on April 19, 1973.

Kelsen's juridico-philosophical work breaks down into three phases, although there is no bright line between the first two. Kelsen's first phase, critical constructivism, runs from 1911 to approximately 1920. His primary concern is to show that naturalism in legal science is mistaken, and he goes on to construct the basic concepts of the law in non-naturalistic terms. Kelsen's second phase, his classical or Neoneo-Kantian period, picks up at the end of the first phase and runs up to 1960. It is marked by two major developments.

The first of these is Kelsen's attempt to provide a foundation for the concepts he constructed in the first phase. His "purity postulate" precludes any appeal either to natural law or moral theory on the one hand, or to empirical data on the other. What remains? Kelsen answers with a transcendental argument, proceeding in standard Neoneo-Kantian fashion from the *Faktum der Wissenschaft* (here, the fact of legal science) to the necessity of the basic norm *qua* normative category. Without the normative category, legal science would not be possible, but since legal science is given, it must be the case that the normative category is presupposed.

A rather different development in the early years of the second phase is represented by Kelsen's adoption of the *Stufenbaulehre* (doctrine of hierarchical structure) from his gifted Vienna colleague, Adolf Julius Merkl. This doctrine calls for ever-greater concretization as the law moves from the general norms of the constitution, at the apex of the hierarchy, to individual legal acts of law—implementation at its base. Accommodating norms that represent every species of law (constitutional rule, statutory provision, administrative regulation, official's legal act), the doctrine gives the lie to later nineteenth-century *Gesetzespositivismus* (statutory positivism), which held that the statute alone was characteristic of the modern legal system. In a juridico-philosophical vein, the doctrine of hierarchical structure marks the introduction, into Kelsen's theory, of empowering norms, which, as he argues at a later point, represent the most fundamental normative modality.

In his third and last phase, beginning in 1960, Kelsen throws overboard the Neoneo-Kantian edifice of the classical phase and defends a will theory of law—a remarkable development in the case of a philosopher who, for literally half a century, had criticized the will theory as well-nigh wrong-headed. Kelsen's skepticism in this last phase is reflected, for example, in his rejection of any role for logic in the law.

Kelsen's significance stems not least of all from his work on the philosophically difficult concept of normativity. A "strong normativity thesis," defended as an interpretation of Kelsen by Joseph Raz, speaks to the classical question in legal philosophy, namely, whether—and, if so, how—the obligation to obey the law is to be justified. A "weak normativity thesis," which reflects Kelsen's abiding interest in preserving the autonomy of the law and, by the same token, the "purity" of legal science, looks to normativity in the name of noncausal change as Kelsen's juridico-philosophical alternative to naturalism.

See also Constructivism and Conventionalism; Legal Positivism; Natural Law; Neo-Kantianism; Philosophy of Law, History of.

Bibliography

Ebenstein, William. *The Pure Theory of Law*. Madison: University of Wisconsin Press, 1945.

Raz, Joseph., "Kelsen's Theory of the Basic Norm." In *Normativity and Norms: Critical Perspectives on Kelsenian Themes*, edited by Stanley L. Paulson and Bonnie Litschewski Paulson, pp. 47–67. Oxford: Clarendon Press, 1998.

WORKS BY KELSEN

Die philosophischen Grundlagen der Naturrechtslehre und des Rechtspositivismus. Charlottenburg, Germany: Rolf Heise, 1928. Translated by Wolfgang Herbert Kraus under the titleas "Natural Law Doctrine and Legal Positivism" as an appendix to Kelsen, *General Theory of Law and State*, 389–446.

Reine Rechtslehre. 1st ed. Leipzig, Germany: Deuticke, 1934. Translated by Bonnie Litschewski Paulson and Stanley L. Paulson as *Introduction to the Problems of Legal Theory*. Oxford: Clarendon Press, 1992.

General Theory of Law and State. Translated by Anders Wedberg. Cambridge, MA: Harvard University Press, 1945.

Reine Rechtslehre. 2nd ed. Vienna: Deuticke, 1960. Translated by Max Knight as *The Pure Theory of Law*. Berkeley: University of California Press, 1967.

Essays in Legal and Moral Philosophy, edited by Ota Weinberger; translated by Peter Heath. Dordrecht, Netherlands: Reidel, 1973.

Allgemeine Theorie der Normen, edited by Kurt Ringhofer and Robert Walter. Vienna: Manz, 1979. Translated by Michael Hartney as *General Theory of Norms*. Oxford: Clarendon Press, 1991.

Stanley L. Paulson (2005)

KEPLER, JOHANNES
(1571–1630)

Johannes Kepler, the founder of modern astronomy, was born in Weil der Stadt, near Stuttgart. During his life he was a student of theology, teacher of mathematics and astronomy, assistant to Tycho Brahe, imperial mathematicus to the emperors Rudolf II and Matthias, and astrologer to the duke of Wallenstein. His principal scientific discoveries were the three planetary laws named after him, the principle of continuity in geometry, and the Keplerian telescope. He was also responsible for decisive advances in the theory of optics and in work that led to the development of the infinitesimal calculus, and incidentally he coined a number of terms whose paternity has been forgotten, including *satellite* (for the moons of Jupiter), *dioptrics*, *focus* (of a conic section), and *camera obscura*.

SIGNIFICANCE OF KEPLER'S LAWS

Kepler's three laws of planetary motion postulate that the planets travel in elliptical orbits, one focus of each ellipse being occupied by the sun; that the radius vector connecting sun and planet sweeps over equal areas in equal times; and that the squares of the periods of revolution of any two planets are in the same ratio as the cubes of their mean distances from the sun.

The promulgation of the three laws was in several respects a turning point in the history of thought. They were the first "laws of nature" in the modern sense: precise, verifiable statements, expressed in mathematical terms, about universal relations governing particular phenomena. They put an end to the Aristotelian dogma of uniform motion in perfect circles, which had bedeviled cosmology for two millennia, and substituted for the Ptolemaic universe—a fictitious clockwork of wheels turning on wheels—a vision of material bodies not unlike Earth freely floating in space, moved by physical forces acting on them. Kepler's laws severed the ties between astronomy and theology and replaced the moving spirits of medieval cosmology by physical causation.

What has come to be called the Copernican revolution was in fact mainly the work of Kepler and Galileo Galilei. Kepler's laws and Galileo's studies on the motion of projectiles were the basic ingredients of the Newtonian synthesis. Nicolas Copernicus's *De Revolutionibus* was published in 1543, nearly thirty years before Kepler was born. Its first edition of a thousand copies never sold out, and it had altogether four reprintings in 400 years. By way of comparison, Christopher Clavius's textbook *The Treatise on the Sphere* had nineteen reprintings within fifty years; Copernicus's book had one. This curiosity is mentioned because it illustrates the fact that the Copernican theory attracted very little attention on the continent of Europe for more than fifty years—that is, for the next two generations. *De Revolutionibus* was an unreadable book describing an unworkable system. It revived the Pythagorean idea of a heliocentric universe, first proposed by Aristarchus of Samos in the third century BCE, but it adhered to the dogma of circular motion. As a result, Copernicus was forced to let the planets run on no less than forty-eight epicycles and eccentrics. He was in fact, as Kepler remarked, "interpreting Ptolemy rather than nature."

Kepler was the first astronomer to raise his voice in public in favor of the Copernican system. His *Mysterium*

Cosmographicum, published in 1597, fifty-four years after Copernicus's death, initiated the controversy; Galileo only entered the scene fifteen years later. At that time Kepler—aged twenty-six—knew little of astronomy. He had started as a theologian, but a chance opportunity made him accept the post of teacher of mathematics and astronomy at the provincial school of Gratz in Styria. Three years later, however, he became assistant to Tycho Brahe, whose observational data, of a hitherto unparalleled richness and precision, provided the empirical foundation for Kepler's efforts to determine the orbit of Mars. It took Kepler eight years of nerve-racking labor to succeed. The result was his magnum opus, published in 1609, which contains the first and second laws (the third came nine years later). It bears a provocative title:

A NEW ASTRONOMY *Based on Causation*
or A PHYSICS OF THE SKY
derived from Investigations of the
MOTIONS OF THE STAR MARS
Founded on Observations of
THE NOBLE TYCHO BRAHE.

The title is indeed symbolic of the work's revolutionary intent and achievement. Astronomy before Kepler had been a purely descriptive geometry of the skies, divorced from physical reality. Since the observed motions of the planets did not conform to the demands of circularity and uniformity, an increasing number of auxiliary wheels had to be added to the fictitious clockwork to save the phenomena. These wheels were thought to be somehow connected with the eight crystal spheres of medieval cosmology, which were kept in motion by a hierarchy of angels, but any pretense to regard them as a physically workable model had to be abandoned. The situation was summed up in a famous remark by Alfonso X of Castile, called the Wise, when he was initiated into the Ptolemaic system: "If the Lord Almighty had consulted me before embarking on the Creation, I should have recommended something simpler."

Copernicus upset the cosmic hierarchy by placing the sun in its center, but his universe was still cluttered (in John Milton's words) "with centric and eccentric scribbled o'er, Cycle and epicycle, orb in orb." It was Kepler who, by banishing epicycles and eccentrics "to the lumber-room" (as he wrote), finally demolished the very scaffolding, as it were, on which the medieval universe rested and replaced its hierarchy of spirit forces with the interplay of physical forces. The tortuous way in which he achieved this may serve as a cautionary tale to scientists and philosophers and represents a significant episode in the history of thought.

MYSTICISM AND EMPIRICISM

In Kepler all the contradictions of his age seem to have become incarnate—the age of transition from the medieval to the "new philosophy," as the scientific revolution was called by its founders. One half of his divided personality belonged to the past; he was a mystic, given to theological speculation, astrology, and number lore. However, he was also an empiricist with a scrupulous respect for observational data, who unhesitatingly threw out his earlier theory of planetary motions, the product of five years of dogged labor, because certain observed positions of Mars deviated from those that the theory demanded by a paltry eight-minute arc. He later wrote that Ptolemy and Copernicus had been able to shrug away such minor blemishes in their theories because their observations were accurate only within a margin of ten minutes, anyway, but those who, "by divine kindness," were in possession of the accurate observations of Brahe could no longer do so. "If I had believed that we could ignore those eight minutes," he wrote in the *Astronomia Nova* (II, Ch. 19), "I would have patched up my hypothesis accordingly. But since it was not permissible to ignore them, those eight minutes point the road to a complete reformation of astronomy."

This newfound respect for hard, obstinate facts was to transform what used to be called "natural philosophy" into the "exact" (or "experimental") sciences and to determine, to a large extent, the climate of European thought during the next three centuries. It provided Kepler with the necessary discipline and put a restraint on his exuberant fantasy, but the primary motivation of his researches was mysticism of a Pythagorean brand. Throughout his life he was obsessed by certain mystic convictions, each of which had the power of an idée fixe. The first was the belief that the solar system was patterned on the perfect, or "Pythagorean," solids (Saturn's orbit circumscribed a cube into which was inscribed the orbit of Jupiter; into this was inscribed the tetrahedron that circumscribed the orbit of Mars; and so on down to the octahedron inscribed into the orbit of Mercury). The second was the equally Pythagorean belief that the planetary motions were governed by musical harmonies (the book containing the third law is called *Harmonice Mundi*). Fortunately, both lent themselves to mathematical juggling almost ad lib, until they fitted the data. Far from interfering with his reasoning powers, these irrational obsessions were harnessed to his rational pursuits and provided the drive for his tireless labors. From a subjective point of view, Kepler's fundamental discoveries were in fact merely by-products of his chimerical quest. Toward the end of his life he proudly mentioned in retrospect some of his minor achievements, but there is no mention whatsoever of his epoch-making first and second laws.

EMERGENCE OF THE CONCEPT OF FORCE

The apparent paradox of a mystically inspired prejudice acting as a spur to scientific achievement is most clearly exemplified in the circumstances that led Kepler to introduce into astronomy the concept of physical forces. As has already been stated, he started his career as a student of theology (at the Lutheran University of Tübingen). The reason the concept of a heliocentric universe attracted the young theologian was later stated by him repeatedly. Thus, in the "Preface to the Reader" of his *Mysterium Cosmographicum* he explained that he had often defended the opinions of Copernicus in the discussions of the candidates at the seminary and had also written "a careful disputation on the first motion which consists in the rotation of the earth around the sun *for physical, or if you prefer, metaphysical reasons.*" (The last phrase is emphasized because it is repeated verbatim in various passages in Kepler's works.)

He then proceeded to explain the nature of these "metaphysical reasons." They were originally based on a supposed analogy between the stationary sun, the stars, and interstellar space, on the one hand, and God the Father, the Son, and the Holy Ghost, on the other. In his first book the young Kepler promised the reader to pursue this analogy in his future cosmographical work; twenty-five years later, when he was over fifty, he reaffirmed his belief in it. "It is by no means permissible to treat this analogy as an empty comparison; it must be considered by its Platonic form and archetypal quality as one of the primary causes" (*Mysterium Cosmographicum*, note to 2nd ed.).

He stuck to this belief to the end of his life, as he stuck to the Pythagorean solids and the harmony of the spheres. But gradually his cherished analogy underwent a significant change. The fixed stars were replaced by the moving stars—the planets. The sun in the center of the planets, "himself at rest and yet the source of motion," continued to represent God the Father, and "even as the Father creates through the Holy Ghost" so the sun "distributes his motive force through a medium which contains the moving bodies" (letter to Maestlin, March 10, 1595).

Thus, the Holy Ghost no longer merely fills the space between the motionless sun and the fixed stars. It has become an active agent, a *vis motrix* that drives the plan-ets. Nobody before had suspected the existence of such a force emanating from the sun. Astronomy had been concerned not with the causes of the heavenly motions but with their description. The passages just quoted are the first intimation of the forthcoming synthesis of cosmology and physics. Once he conceived the idea, derived from his analogy, that the sun was the source of the power that makes the planets go round, Kepler hit upon a question no one else had asked before him: Why do the planets closer to the sun go round faster than those farther away? His first answer to it, in the *Mysterium Cosmographicum*, was that there exists only one "moving soul" in the center of all the orbits—that is, the sun—which drives the planets "the more vigorously" the closer they are, but by the time it reaches the outer planets the force is quasi exhausted "because of the long distance and the weakening of the force which it entails."

Twenty-five years later, in the notes to the second edition, he commented that if we substitute for the word *soul* the word *force*, "then we get just the principle which underlies my physics of the skies." He continued to explain that he had once firmly believed the motive force was a soul; yet as he reflected that the force diminishes in proportion to distance, just as light diminishes in proportion to distance, he came to the conclusion "that this force must be something substantial—'substantial' not in the literal sense but … in the same manner as we say that light is something substantial, meaning by this an unsubstantial entity emanating from a substantial body."

The twenty-five years that separate these two quotations mark the transition from *anima motrix* to *vis motrix*, from a universe animated by purposeful intelligences to one moved by inanimate, "blind" forces devoid of purpose. For the rest of his life Kepler struggled with this new concept emerging from the womb of animism (its very name, *virtus*, or *vis*, betrays its origin) without ever coming to terms with it. At first he was not aware of the difficulties inherent in it. In a letter to a friend, which he wrote when the *Astronomia Nova* was nearing completion, he outlined his program:

> My aim is to show that the heavenly machine is not a kind of divine, live being, but a kind of clockwork (and he who believes that a clock has a soul, attributes the maker's glory to the work), insofar as nearly all the manifold motions are caused by a most simple, magnetic, and material force, just as all motions of the clock are caused by a simple weight. And I also show how these physical causes are to be given numerical and

geometrical expression. (Letter to Herwart, February 10, 1605)

Kepler had defined the essence of the scientific revolution. But it turned out to be easier to talk about a "most simple, magnetic, material force" than to form a concrete idea of its working. Kepler's efforts to visualize the nature of the "moving force" emanating from the sun are not only of exceptional interest from the historian's point of view; they also illuminate the philosophical difficulties that were inherent in the concept of "force" from its very beginning. Since no English translation of the *Astronomia Nova* was published by the time this article was written, a few quotations may be found in order. First, Kepler compared the "moving force" of the sun with the light emitted by it:

> Though the light of the sun cannot itself be the moving force … it may perhaps represent a kind of vehicle, or tool, that the moving force uses. But the following considerations seem to contradict this. First, the light is arrested in regions that lie in shade. If, then, the moving force were to use light as a vehicle, darkness would bring the planets to a standstill. …
>
> This kind of force, just like the kind of force that is light, … can be regarded not as something that expands into the space between its source and the movable body but as something that the movable body receives out of the space it occupies. … It is propagated through the universe … but it is nowhere received except where there is a movable body, such as a planet. The answer to this is: although the moving force has no substance, it is aimed at substance, i.e., at the planet-body to be moved. …
>
> Who, I ask, will pretend that light has substance? Yet nevertheless it acts and is acted upon in space, it is refracted and reflected, and it has quality, so that it may be dense or sparse and can be regarded as a plane where it is received by something capable of being lit up. For, as I said in my *Optics*, the same thing applies to light as to our moving force: it has no present existence in the space between the source and the object it lights up, although it has passed through that space in the past; it "is" not, it "was," so to speak. (*Astronomia Nova*, III, Ch. 33)

Thus, Kepler's gropings brought him closer to the modern concept of the field than to the Newtonian concept of force, and the modern scientist grappling with the paradoxes of quantum theory will find here an echo of his own perplexities. This may be the reason Kepler, having hit on the concept of universal gravity, subsequently discarded it—as Galileo and René Descartes were to discard it.

GRAVITY AND ANIMISM

The most precise pre-Newtonian formulations of gravity are to be found in the preface to the *Astronomia Nova*. Kepler started by refuting the Aristotelian doctrine according to which all "earthy" matter is heavy because it is its nature to strive toward the center of the world—that is, Earth. But all "fiery" matter strives by its nature toward the periphery of the universe and is therefore light. Kepler explained that there is no such thing as lightness, but, rather, the

> matter that is less dense, either by nature or through heat, is relatively lighter … and therefore less attracted [to the earth] than heavier matter. … Supposing the earth *were* in the center of the world, heavy bodies would be attracted to it, not because it is in the center, but because it is a material body. It follows that regardless of where we place the earth, heavenly bodies will always seek it. …
>
> Gravity is the mutual bodily tendency between cognate [i.e., material] bodies toward unity or contact (of which kind the magnetic force also is), so that the earth draws a stone much more than the stone draws the earth. …
>
> If the earth and the moon were not kept in their respective orbits by a spiritual or some equivalent force, the earth would ascend toward the moon 1/54 of the distance, and the moon would descend the remaining 53 parts of the interval, and thus they would unite. But this calculation presupposes that both bodies are of the same density.
>
> If the earth ceased to attract the waters of the sea, the seas would rise and flow into the moon. …
>
> If the attractive force of the moon reaches down to the earth, it follows that the attractive force of the earth, all the more, extends to the moon and even farther. …
>
> If two stones were placed anywhere in space near to each other, and outside the reach of force of a third cognate body, then they would come together, after the manner of magnetic bodies, at an intermediate point, each approaching the other in proportion to the other's mass.

In the same passage is to be found the first approximation to a correct theory of the tides, which Kepler explained as "a motion of the waters toward the regions where the moon stands in the zenith." In a work written at the same time—"Somnium—A Dream of the Moon" (an early exercise in science fiction)—he furthermore postulated that the sun's attraction, too, influences the tides—that is, that the gravitational force of the sun reaches as far as Earth.

But here we are faced with another paradox. In the preface to the *Astronomia Nova*, Kepler, as we have seen, had grasped the essence of gravity and even the idea that its force is proportionate to its mass; yet in the text of *Somnium*, and all subsequent works, he seems to have completely forgotten it. The force that emanates from the sun in the Keplerian universe is not a force of attraction but a tangential force, a kind of vortex or "raging current which tears all the planets, and perhaps all the celestial ether, from West to East."

To the question of what made Kepler drop gravity no answer is found anywhere in his profuse writings. Everything points to some unconscious psychological blockage, and we may gather hints about its nature in the writings of the other pioneers of the scientific revolution. Kepler's suggestion that the tides were caused by the moon's attraction Galileo indignantly rejected as an "occult fancy" (*Dialogue concerning the Two Chief World Systems*). Descartes was equally repelled by the idea of a nonmechanical force acting at a distance and, like Kepler, substituted for it vortices in the ether. As for Isaac Newton, his attitude is summed up in his famous third letter to Richard Bentley, in which he said it is inconceivable that "inanimate brute matter" should, without some mediating material substance, act upon other bodies.

> That gravity should be innate, inherent, and essential to matter, so that one body may act upon another, at a distance through a vacuum, without the mediation of anything else, by and through which their action and force may be conveyed from one to another, is to me so great an absurdity, that I believe no man who has in philosophical matters a competent faculty of thinking, can ever fall into it.

Kepler, Galileo, and Descartes did not fall into the philosophical abyss; their thinking was much too "modern"—that is, mechanistic—for that. The notion of a "force" that acts without an intermediary agent and pulls at immense stellar objects with ubiquitous ghost fingers appeared to them mystical and unscientific, a lapse into that Aristotelian animism from which they had just broken loose. Universal gravity, *gravitatio mundi*, smacked of the *anima mundi* of the ancients. Newton overcame the obstacle and made the concept of gravity respectable by invoking a ubiquitous ether, whose attributes were equally paradoxical, and by refusing to speculate on the manner in which gravity worked (his *hypothesis non fingo* refers to this problem, and to this problem only, though it is often quoted out of context). But above all, he provided a precise mathematical formula for the mysterious agency to which gravity referred. That formula Newton deduced from the laws of Kepler, who had intuitively glimpsed universal gravity and shied away from it. In such crooked ways does the tree of science grow.

SYNTHESIS OF ASTRONOMY AND PHYSICS

In the Aristotelian cosmos, physical forces operated only among the four elements in the sublunary sphere; the motions of the celestial bodies, made of a fifth element, were due to spiritual agencies and governed by the demands of geometrical perfection. Kepler and Galileo broke down this dualism by postulating that physical causality permeates the entire universe. Kepler's "physics of the sky" we know to have been all wrong. He had no notion of inertial momentum, and he had dropped gravity. In Kepler's universe the sun exerted a tangential force (diminishing in direct ratio with increasing distance), which the "lazy" planets resisted, and the eccentricity of the orbits was accounted for by magnetic forces. (Since the planets' magnetic poles always pointed in the same direction, they would be drawn closer to the sun in the aphelion and repelled in the perihelion.)

But though the model was wrong in every detail, his basic assumption, that there were several antagonistic forces acting on the planets, guided him in the right direction. A single force, as previously assumed—the Prime Mover and the allied hierarchy of angels—would never produce elliptical orbits and periodic changes of velocity. These could only be the result of some tug of war going on in the sky, and this dynamic concept, supported by a series of wild ad hoc hypotheses, led him in the end, after countless detours, to his three laws.

Kepler's determination of the orbit of Mars became the unifying link between two hitherto separate universes of discourse, celestial geometry and earthly physics. His was the first serious attempt to explain the mechanism of the solar system in terms of physical forces. Once the example was set, astronomy and physics could never again be divorced.

See also Aristotelianism; Copernicus, Nicolas; Descartes, René; Force; Galileo Galilei; Geometry; Laws of Nature; Mass; Matter; Milton, John; Nature, Philosophical Ideas of; Newton, Isaac; Philosophy of Physics; Pythagoras and Pythagoreanism; Scientific Revolutions.

Bibliography

WORKS BY KEPLER

Joannis Kepleri Astronomi Opera Omnia. 8 vols., edited by C. Frisch. Frankfurt and Erlangen: Heyder and Zimmer, 1858–1871.

Johannes Kepler, Gesammelte Werke, edited by W. van Dyck, Max Caspar, and Franz Hammer. Munich: C.H. Beck, 1938–.

"Somnium, Sive Astronomia Lunaris" (Somnium—A Dream of the Moon). Translated by Patricia Frueh Kirkwood, in John Lear, *Kepler's Dream.* Berkeley: University of California Press, 1965.

WORKS ON KEPLER

Barker, Peter. "Constructing Copernicus." *Perspectives on Science* 10(2) (2002): 208–227.

Caspar, Max. *Johannes Kepler.* Stuttgart: Kohlhammer, 1948. Translated by C. D. Hellman. New York, 1962 (paperbound).

Chen Morris, Raz D. "Optics, Imagination, and the Construction of Scientific Observation in Kepler's New Science." *Monist* 84(4) (2001): 453–486.

Dear, Peter. *Revolutionizing the Sciences: European Knowledge and its Ambitions, 1500–1700.* Princeton, NJ: Princeton University Press, 2001.

Diederich, Werner. "The Structure of the Copernican Revolution." *Dialogos* 36(77) (2001): 7–24.

Franklin, Allan, and Colin Howson. "Newton and Kepler, a Bayesian Approach." *Studies in History and Philosophy of Science* 16 (1985): 379–385.

Holton, Gerald. *Thematic Origins of Scientific Thought: Kepler to Einstein, Revised Edition.* Cambridge, MA: Harvard University Press, 1988.

Jarine, N. *The Birth of History and Philosophy of Science: Kepler's 'A Defence of Tycho Against Ursus', with Essays on Its Provenance and Significance.* New York: Cambridge University Press, 1984.

Kiikeri, Mika. "Interrogative Reasoning and Discovery: A New Perspective on Kepler's Inquiry." *Philosophica* 63(1) (1999): 51–87.

Kleiner, Scott A. "A New Look at Kepler and Abductive Argument." *Studies in History and Philosophy of Science* 14 (1983): 279–314.

Koestler, A. "Kepler and the Psychology of Discovery." In *The Logic of Personal Knowledge, Essays Presented to Michael Polanyi,* edited by Marjorie Grene. London: Routledge and Paul, 1961.

Koestler, A. *The Sleepwalkers.* London: Hutchinson, 1959.

Kozhamthadam, Job. *The Discovery of Kepler's Laws: The Interaction of Science, Philosophy, and Religion.* Notre Dame: University of Notre Dame Press, 1994.

Kozhamthadam, Job. "Kepler and the Sacredness of Natural Science." *Philosophy in Science* 7 (1997): 9–36.

Martens, Rhonda. "Kepler's Solution to the Problem of a Realist Celestial Mechanics." *Studies in History and Philosophy of Science* 30a(3) (1999): 377–394.

Phalet, A. "On the Logic of Kepler's Evolving Models" In *Logic of Discovery and Logic of Discourse,* edited by Jaakko Hintikka. New York: Plenum Press, 1985.

A. Koestler (1967)
Bibliography updated by Tamra Frei (2005)

KEYNES, JOHN MAYNARD
(1883–1946)

The English economist John Maynard Keynes, the son of a distinguished Cambridge logician and economist, was one of the most brilliant and influential men of the twentieth century. His role as the architect and chief negotiator of Britain's external economic policies in two world wars was only one side of his public life. During his own lifetime, his economic views, contained primarily in two great works, *A Treatise on Money* (London, 1930) and *The General Theory of Employment, Interest and Money* (London, 1936), revolutionized the economic practice, and to a lesser extent, the economic theory, of Western governments.

Keynes wrote only one philosophical work, *A Treatise on Probability* (London, 1921), but it is a philosophical classic. The following account of the book's leading ideas adheres to its own main divisions.

PHILOSOPHY OF PROBABILITY

Keynes's philosophy of probability is contained chiefly in Parts I and II. For Keynes, only a proposition can be probable or improbable. A proposition has probability only in relation to some other proposition(s) taken as premise(s). Hence a proposition may have different probabilities on different premises. Nevertheless, the probability that p does have, given q (which Keynes writes as p/q, is perfectly objective. Some probabilities are known to us indirectly—for example, as a result of applying the theorems of the probability calculus; but first, of course, some probabilities must be known directly. Where a probability is known to us directly, it is known to us in the way that the validity of a syllogistic argument is known, whatever that way is. The probability relation is not an empirical one. If it is true that $p/q > r/s$, or that $p/q > 1/3$, or that $r/s = 1/2$, then it is true a priori, and not in virtue of any matter of fact. In particular, the truth of such statements is independent of the factual truth of p, q, r, and s. Finally, $p/q = 0$ if p is inconsistent with q, and $p/q = 1$ if q entails p.

Keynes's fundamental thesis, of which the above statements are developments, is that there are inferences in which the premises do not entail the conclusion but are nevertheless, just by themselves, objectively more or less good reason for believing it. This thesis seems to require the existence of different degrees of implication. Such degrees are Keynes's probabilities. Thus, for Keynes the study of probability coincides exactly with the study of inference, demonstrative and nondemonstrative. He developed, though somewhat obscurely, a general theory of inference in Chapter X. However, from the axioms and definitions from which he derived the accepted theorems of the probability calculus, he also derived many theorems of demonstrative inference, for example, "if $a/h = 0$ then $ab/h = 0$."

It would be hard to exaggerate the importance of Keynes's fundamental thesis. Classical probability theory of the eighteenth and nineteenth centuries must have presupposed some such thesis. Recent theory on degrees of confirmation presupposes it. To Keynes, as to Pierre Simon de Laplace and Rudolf Carnap, this thesis appeared to be necessary as a means of avoiding skepticism about induction. But David Hume would presumably have rejected it outright, and it is by no means free from difficulty.

There are two negative theses that distinguish Keynes's philosophy of probability from most earlier or later formulations. One is that probabilities simply do not have a numerical value, except in certain exceptional circumstances, and never in normal inductive contexts. The other is that there are noncomparable probabilities, that is, probabilities that are neither equal to nor greater nor less than one another. For obvious reasons, these theses have contributed to the neglect of Keynes by statistical writers.

INDUCTION

In Part III, Keynes discussed induction. The most important arguments of those that are rational but not conclusive belong to the class of inductions whose conclusions are universal generalizations and whose premises are about instances of the generalization.

Keynes, like John Stuart Mill, regarded all scientific induction as essentially eliminative induction. His account of the circumstances in which we regard an inductive argument as strong is, in essentials (although not otherwise), a development in detail of Mill's method of agreement.

The mere number of confirmations of a hypothesis in itself is of no evidential weight. The important thing is the variety of the instances, in respects other than those that constitute the instances' confirming ones. We regard inductions as being of greatest weight when the evidence approaches the ideal case in which the confirming instances are known to be not all alike in every respect. Various ways in which our evidence can fall short of this ideal are discussed in Chapter XIX. Keynes thought that the extent to which the evidence, by its variety, eliminates alternative hypotheses is the only important factor—not only when our hypothesis is empirical, but when it is, for instance, mathematical or metaphysical.

Keynes very clearly distinguished between the task of analyzing those inductive arguments that we regard as strong and the task of justifying the fact that we regard them as strong.

The latter task, he appears to have assumed, requires a proof of the proposition that relative to instantial evidence, the probability of a universal hypothesis can approach certainty as a limit. It will do so, he purported to prove, if (and one must assume only if) the probability of the instantial evidence supposing the hypothesis to be false can be made small in comparison with the probability of the hypothesis prior to the instantial evidence (its "a priori" probability). To reduce the former probability is the object of "varying the circumstances." The required disparity between the two probabilities will exist, Keynes argued, if (and one must assume only if), inter alia, the hypothesis has finite a priori probability. This requires that it be a member of a finite disjunction of exhaustive alternatives.

When the universal hypothesis is an empirical one, this amounts to the assumption that there exists in nature the materials for only a finite number of generalizations linking empirical properties. In other words, the number of the logically independent properties of empirical objects, which a priori might have been constantly conjoined, is finite. This is the famous principle of limited independent variety (Chapter XX). Hence, the fact that the probability of any empirical universal generalization should approach certainty as a limit requires the assumption of this principle. Or rather, Keynes thought, all that is required for this principle is finite a priori probability, since experience can and does noncircularly support the principle, provided it does have this initial probability.

It does so, Keynes appears to have argued, because we have a direct apprehension of the truth of the principle, just as, he thought, we have an apprehension (not independent of experience, yet not inductively inferred) of the truth of the statement, "Color cannot exist without extension."

STATISTICAL INFERENCE

The main subject of Part V is those inductive inferences whose premises include a statement of the frequency of a property B in an observed series of A's, and whose conclusions concern B's frequency in the population of A's as a whole, or in a further series of A's, or the probability of the next A being a B.

The theory of statistical inference had been dominated by two methods of making such inferences, both due to Laplace. One is the "rule of succession," according to which the probability of the next A being B is

$$\frac{m+1}{m+n+2}$$

if m out of $m + n$ observed A's have been B. The other is the "inversion" of the great-numbers theorem of Bernoulli. This theorem permits us—under an important restriction—to infer what frequency of B is most probable among observed A's, given its frequency among A's as a whole. Laplace purported to supply a theorem that would guide our inferences in the reverse, inductive direction, that is, from observed A's to A's as a whole.

Keynes regarded both methods as "mathematical charlatanry." His many criticisms of them cannot be weighed here. Apart from these criticisms, however, he considered it absurd to imagine that we could have exact measures of the probability of statistical conclusions. Statistical induction is subject to all the difficulties that beset inductions with universal conclusions, and to others beside. Moreover, the only evidence taken into account by all methods like Laplace's is numerical. The vital requirement of variety in the instances is neglected. In statistical contexts, the variety of the positive "instances" takes the form of the stability of the observed frequency when the observed series is considered as divided into subseries according to many different principles of division.

Keynes did think that, under a number of extremely stringent conditions, an inversion of Bernoulli's theorem is legitimate. But even to license these inductive inferences, as Keynes interpreted them, the principle of limited independent variety is required.

Bibliography

Keynes's only philosophical work is *A Treatise on Probability* (London: Macmillan, 1921). On Keynes's life, see R. F. Harrod, *The Life of John Maynard Keynes* (London: Macmillan, 1951).

Valuable critical material on Keynes's theories of probability and induction may be found in the following: Jean Nicod, *Foundations of Geometry and Induction* (London: Kegan Paul Trench and Trubner, 1930); F. P. Ramsey, *Foundations of Mathematics* (London: Kegan Paul Trench and Trubner, 1931); G. H. von Wright, *The Logical Problem of Induction* (Helsingfors, 1941); G. H. von Wright, *A Treatise on Induction and Probability* (London: Routledge and Kegan Paul, 1951); Bertrand Russell, *Human Knowledge, Its Scope and Limits* (London: Allen and Unwin, 1948); and Arthur Pap, *An Introduction to the Philosophy of Science* (New York: Free Press of Glencoe, 1962). Joan Robinson, *Economic Philosophy* (London: Watts, 1962), Ch. 4, is a highly readable brief account of Keynes's place in economic theory.

For another facet of Keynes's many-sided career, see *Essays and Sketches in Biography* (New York, 1956), a varied collection of Keynes's writings on economists, politicians, acquaintances, and himself.

OTHER RECOMMENDED WORKS

Davis, John Bryan. *Keynes's Philosophical Development*. New York: Cambridge University Press, 1994.

Keynes, John Maynard. *The Collected Writings of John Maynard Keynes*. London: Macmillan; New York: St. Martin's Press, for the Royal Economic Society, 1971–1989.

Keynes, John Maynard. *The John Maynard Keynes Papers, King's College, Cambridge*. Cambridge, U.K.: Chadwyck-Healey, 1993.

Moggridge, D. E. *Maynard Keynes: An Economist's Biography*. New York: Routledge, 1992.

O'Donnell, R. M. *Keynes: Philosophy, Economics, and Politics: The Philosophical Foundations of Keynes's Thought and Their Influence on His Economics and Politics*. New York: St. Martin's, 1989.

Skidelsky, Robert Jacob Alexander. *John Maynard Keynes: Vol. 1, Hopes Betrayed 1883–1920: A Biography*. London: Macmillan, 1983.

Wittgenstein, Ludwig. *Letters to Russell, Keynes, and Moore*. Oxford: Basil Blackwell, 1974.

D. Stove (1967)
Bibliography updated by Michael J. Farmer (2005)

KEYSERLING, HERMANN ALEXANDER, GRAF VON
(1880–1946)

Hermann Alexander, Graf von Keyserling, a German philosopher of life and man, was born in Könno, Estonia. He studied geology and other natural sciences at the universities of Dorpat, Geneva, Heidelberg, and Vienna. In 1902 Keyserling received his doctorate at Vienna, where, under the influence of Houston Stewart Chamberlain, he turned to philosophy. He spent the next few years in Paris, interrupting his stay, however, by several trips to England. In 1908, after two years in Berlin, Keyserling returned to Estonia to take over his ancestral estate at

Rayküll. He traveled frequently and in 1911 and 1912 took a trip around the world. The loss of his property after the Russian Revolution led to Keyserling's immigration to Germany. In 1920 he founded the School of Wisdom in Darmstadt. Further journeys to North and South America followed. The last years of his life were spent in the Austrian Tyrol.

Keyserling was not a systematic philosopher; instead, he presented brilliant observations, suggestive generalizations, and in vague outline, an image of man. To measure his work by traditional philosophy is to reject his view of the philosophic enterprise. Keyserling wanted to replace the traditional philosopher with the sage, to replace critical examination with immediate appreciation, and to replace the university with his School of Wisdom. He held that, instead of criticizing another position, one should try to empathize with it. His own *Travel Diary* furnishes an example of this approach. Keyserling reduced philosophy to an exercise with the thoughts of other ages and cultures in the hope that such play would lead the reader to an awareness of the spirit that underlies these thoughts. Truth, in the sense of adequacy to fact, was of little concern to Keyserling; intuitive appreciation alone counted. Keyserling used the word *polyphonic* to distinguish his thinking from "homophonic," traditional philosophy. Polyphonic thinking has no definite point of view and presents no definite theses. It is essentially rootless, an exercise with possibilities, designed to reveal a meaning that escapes all philosophic systems.

Keyserling's approach to philosophy bears witness to his understanding of man. Following Arthur Schopenhauer, Friedrich Nietzsche, Wilhelm Dilthey, Henri Bergson, and Eastern thought, he asserted the rights of life in the face of the modern overemphasis on the intellect. His insistence on the protean nature of man anticipated the existentialists' claim that existence precedes essence. Keyserling asked us to intuit, amid cultural and natural diversity, the spirit that finds only inadequate expression in each definite form. Those matters that are truly important cannot be thought clearly but can only be intuited. Critical philosophy was renounced; the philosopher had become an artist. The success of Keyserling's works, particularly of the *Travel Diary,* was symptomatic of the spiritual situation following World War I. Keyserling lent expression to the feeling that many of the traditional answers had become meaningless. But instead of deploring this spiritual homelessness, Keyserling made it a necessary condition of the full life: Ideally, man is a traveler.

See also Bergson, Henri; Chamberlain, Houston Stewart; Dilthey, Wilhelm; Essence and Existence; Nietzsche, Friedrich; Schopenhauer, Arthur.

Bibliography

WORKS BY KEYSERLING

Unsterblichkeit. Munich: J. F. Lehmanns, 1907. Translated as *Immortality.* London: Oxford University Press, 1938.

Das Reisetagebuch eines Philosophen, 2 vols. Darmstadt: O. Reichl, 1920. Translated as *The Travel Diary of a Philosopher,* 2 vols. New York: Harcourt, Brace, 1925.

Schöpferische Erkenntnis. Darmstadt: O. Reichl, 1922. Translated as *Creative Understanding.* New York: Harper, 1929.

Wiedergeburt. Darmstadt: O. Reichl, 1927. Translated as *The Recovery of Truth.* New York: Harper, 1929.

Das Buch vom Ursprung. Baden-Baden: Roland, 1947.

Reise durch die Zeit. Vaduz, Liechtenstein, 1948.

Kritik des Denkens. Innsbruck: Palme, 1948.

Die Gesammelten Werke. Darmstadt, 1956–.

WORKS ON KEYSERLING

Feldkeller, Paul. *Graf Keyserlings Erkenntnisweg zum Übersinnlichen.* Darmstadt: O. Reichl, 1922.

Noack, Hermann. "Sinn und Geist." *Zeitschrift für philosophische Forschung* (1953): 592–597.

Parks, Mercedes G. *Introduction to Keyserling.* London: J. Cape, 1934.

Röhr, Rudolf. *Graf Keyserlings magische Geschichtsphilosophie.* Leipzig: S. Hirzel, 1939.

Karsten Harries (1967)

KHOMIAKOV, ALEKSEI STEPANOVICH
(1804–1860)

Aleksei Stepanovich Khomiakov (1804–1860), was a Russian philosopher, theologian, poet, and writer, a founder of Slavophilism. Born into a wealthy Muscovite family of landed nobility, Khomiakov was educated in Moscow University. In his youth he took part in the Russo-Turkish War of 1828–1829. In his mature years, he preferred to live as a "private" gentleman in Moscow and on the family. He traveled abroad on two occasions: in 1825–1826 to Paris to study painting, and in 1847 to Germany and England. In the Russian social order he preferred the niche of an independent writer, poet, and playwright. Before his death, he revived The Society of the Lovers of Russian Literature (first founded at the beginning of the nineteenth century) at Moscow University, and served as its head. He died when he contracted cholera while treating peasants on his estate.

Khomiakov was a man of encyclopedic knowledge and diverse talents who brought his polemical style to bear on discussion in several fields in the humanities. Perhaps of greatest significance is his contribution to the philosophy of history. In his *Semiramida*, a three-volume work in the genre of universal history that he began writing in 1837 and continued writing to the end of his life, Khomiakov's goal is to explore the prehistory of nations. His conclusion is that culture as a whole is an expression of a higher spiritual principle—that is, religion. The vista of universal history represents the action upon humanity of cultural-religious archetypes, combined with ideas of freedom and necessity. There initially existed, according to Khomiakov, two types of nations: "conquering nations" and "agricultural nations":

> In accordance with their original character, conquering nations permanently preserve the sense of personal pride and contempt not only for those who are conquered but also for all those who are foreign … When they are victorious, they repress those they have enslaved and do not mix with them; when they are defeated, they stubbornly resist the influence of the victors and preserve in their souls instincts engendered in them by epochs of former glory … [By contrast] agricultural nations are closer to universally human principles. They have not been affected by the proud magic of victory … Because of this they are more receptive to all things that are foreign. They do not experience aristocratic contempt for other nations; instead, they feel sympathy for all that is human. (1900)

Universal history, Khomiakov believes, unfolds according to the laws of the conflict between two opposite spiritual principles. Khomiakov calls the "agricultural" principle "Iranism," and its opposite "Kushitism." The spiritual history of humanity is viewed as the battle between Iranism and Kushitism. Such a conception was not entirely novel: Friedrich Schlegel had divided humanity into two opposed races—the Cainites and the Sethites—and in Hegel's *Philosophy of History* the Iranian "principle of light" is opposed to the Egyptian "principle of mystery." What was new was that Khomiakov did not base this antinomy on the principle of "good-bad"; instead, he viewed Iranism and Kushitism as two equally necessary forces in history.

Further, Kushitism consists in analysis and rationalism, whereas Iranism tends toward a synthetic and integral reception of the world. Therefore, these two types of national psychology are equally natural. Based on neces-

sity, Kushitism engenders the state as a community based on convention. All of the civilizations of Kushitism were remarkable for being based on powerful state structures: Egypt, Babylon, China, Southern India. In contrast, Iranism proclaims the natural union of people and therefore rarely takes the form of a powerful political state. Thus, Khomiakov affirms that the historical process tends toward "the inevitable triumph of the Kushite principle" and to a "gradual decline of Iranism." "Iranism … has always been reestablished," writes Khomiakov, "by the particular efforts of great minds, whereas Kushitism has crept into the historical process by the unceasing action of time and of the national masses." If it happens that in Iranism there is an admixture of Kushitism, the latter is inevitably victorious (we find this, for example, in the history of ancient Greece and ancient Rome): Spiritual freedom must be absolute, and any concession to necessity leads to the death of freedom. The appearance of Christianity was the critical point of history: Christ represented a heroic effort to oppose the Kushitism of the world. But Christ's victory did not signify the victory of Iranism: Kushitism "closed itself up into the logic of the philosophical schools" (1900). And Hegelianism, which Khomiakov rejected, became the triumph of Kushitism in the nineteenth century. The Slavs belong to the Iranian type; that is what defines their place in history.

In Khomiakov's opinion, humans possesses the ability to strive toward being, toward God; but to preserve this striving, a special state is necessary: "true faith," where the diversity of a person's spiritual powers are gathered into a living, ordered wholeness. From this point of view, faith—which is simultaneously knowledge and life ("life-knowledge")—plays a special role in one's life.

Khomiakov's central conception is *sobornost'* ("catholicity," integrity, inner fullness), which characterizes not only the Christian church but also the nature of humans, society, and the processes of cognition and creativity. *Sobornost* is the organizing metaphysical principle of all being; by the power of love it gathers diversity into a "free organic unity" (in this it is distinct from "collectivity"). It was Khomiakov who introduced the principle of *sobornost* into the Russian thought of the nineteenth century. He defines *sobornost* as "a free and organic unity, whose vital principle is the Divine grace of mutual love." (1900) The foundation of *sobornost* is *grace*, a notion Khomiakov derives from Metropolita Ilarion's eleventh-century "Sermon on Law and Grace." Khomiakov also insists that divine grace is likewise the foundation of the real church, which can only be known from within, through one's lived experience.

Khomiakov based his theological conception on personal *experience*; and therefore affiliation with the church essentially became a prerequisite for knowing reality in general. Thus, Khomiakov extends the doctrine of *sobornost* beyond theology to the entire domain of Russian culture. Khomiakov wrote that "Christianity—even with all its purity, with all its elevatedness over all human individuals—takes different forms for the Slav, for the Roman, and for the German" (1900). It often happens that the aggregate of national beliefs and convictions is reflected neither in "verbal monuments" nor in "monuments of stone," and can be understood "only by looking at the entire life of a people, at its total historical development." Khomiakov elaborated this broad conception in his theological works, which, for reasons of censorship, in his lifetime could only be published abroad.

Despite their apparently paradoxical nature, Khomiakov's theological ideas were expressed at times with astonishing simplicity: "The Church is one, for two Churches do not exist"; "For there is one God and one Church, and there is no conflict or disharmony in her"; "The Church is not an institution"; "To assert that the Church is an authority is blasphemy." One does not "belong" to the church the way one belongs to an organization. In the church, people live the way they live at home, in the bosom of their family, "humbly conscious of their weakness and subordinating the latter to the unanimous decision of the conscience of all in sobornost" (1900). And only this life in the church gives people freedom, which is the greatest good. In his letter "To the Serbians" (written just before his death), Khomiakov expressed his view on "the meaning and virtue of faith" as follows:

> They are in great error, those who think that it [faith] is limited to the mere fulfillment of rituals or even to the relations of man to God. No: faith permeates the entire being of a man and all of his relations to his neighbor. As if with invisible threads and roots, faith grasps and is intertwined into all of a man's feelings, convictions, and aspirations. Faith is like a better air, transforming the earthly principle in a man; or it is like a most perfect light, illuminating all the moral notions of a man and all of his opinions of other people and of the inner laws connecting him with them. Thus, faith is also a supreme social principle ... (1900)

Taking as his point of departure artistic intuition and "life-knowledge," which he strove to reconcile with scientific knowledge, Khomiakov attempted to unite two apparently incompatible sources: early patristics and ideas of Western romanticism and Western nature-philosophy. The organic principle of the interpretation of spiritual phenomena is evident not only in his ecclesiology, but also in his secular philosophy, as well as in his political and economic essays. The organic principle served as the foundation of his preference for gradual social development and conservatism. With the help of this principle Khomiakov sought to harmonize the Slavophile worldview with philosophical romanticism, bringing together such distinct categories as "the integrity of spirit," "the fullness of perception," and "the "organic character of social development" (1900). This principle was also the source of his doctrine of *sobornost* and of the view of the church as the regulator of the entire life of the Orthodox Christian.

In Khomiakov's social philosophy the opposition between *sobornost* and collectivity appears as the antithesis between *obshchina* (organic peasant community) and *druzhina* (organized "commune"), between "true brotherhood" and "conventional agreement." In Khomiakov's opinion, Russian history and Orthodox spirituality have manifested instances of true brotherhood, exhibited in the Russian peasant *obshchina*, which Khomiakov clearly idealizes, seeing in it the closest approximation to the social ideal. Petrine reforms, Khomiakov believes, led to the assimilation of "alien" principles by the Russian nobility and this, in turn, resulted in a split between the educated society and common people. Thus, in Khomiakov's opinion, genuine folk culture in Russia could be created only by returning to original folk principles. Khomiakov devoted to this subject numerous articles that provoked a polemic both in Russia and in Europe in the 1840s. Russian thought began to assimilate Khomiakov's heritage only many years after his death; his true stature became clear only at the end of the nineteenth century, when his major works were published (although not fully), and a Russian religious philosophy began to take shape.

See also Philosophy of History.

Bibliography

WORKS BY KHOMIAKOV

Polnoye sobranie sochinenii [Complete works]. 8 vols., edited by P. I. Bartenev and D. A. Khomyakov. Moscow, 1900–1911.

Stikhotvoreniia i dramy [Poems and plays], edited by B. F. Yegorov. Leningrad, 1969.

Sochineniia [Works]. 2 vols. Moscow, 1994.

On Spiritual Unity: A Slavophile Reader. Translated and edited by Boris Jakim and Robert Bird. Hudson, NY: Lindisfarne, 1998. This volume includes a translation of Khomiakov's

"The Church Is One," translations of three essays with "Remarks by an Orthodox Christian concerning the Western Communions," and the third and fifth letters to William Palmer. This volume also contains an extensive bibliography of works by and about Khomiakov, as well as about the Slavophiles in general.

WORKS ABOUT KHOMIAKOV

Berdiaev, N. A. *A. S. Khomiakov*. Moscow, 1912. Excerpts from Chapters 3, 4, and 8 of this work have been translated in Jakim and Bird, *On Spiritual Unity*. Hudson, NY: Lindisfarne, 1998.

Gratieux, A. *A. S. Khomiakov et le movement slavophile*. 2 vols. Paris, 1939. Translated from the French as *A. S. Khomiakov and the Slavophile Movement*. 2 vols. Belmont, MA: 1982.

Zenkovsky, V. V. *Istoriia russkoi filosofii*. 2 vols. Paris, 1948–1950. Translated by George L. Kline as *A History of Russian Philosophy*. 2 vols. (New York: Columbia University Press, 1953). See volume one of Kline, 180–205.

Christoff, P. K. *An Introduction to Nineteenth-Century Russian Slavophilism: A Study in Ideas*. Vol. 1, *A. S. Xomjakov*. Paris: Mouton, 1961.

O'Leary, P. P. *The Triune Church: A Study in the Ecclesiology of A. S. Khomiakov*. Freiburg: Universitätsverlag Freiburg Schweiz, 1982.

Khomiakovskii sbornik [Collection of essays on Khomiakov]. Vol. 1. Tomsk, 1998.

Koshelev, V. *Aleksei Stepanovich Khomiakov: Zhizneopisanie v dokumentakh, rassuzhdeniiakh i razyskaniiakh* [Aleksei Stepanovich Khomiakov: Biography in the form of documents, reflections, and inquiries]. Moscow: Novoe Literaturnoe Obozrenie, 2000.

Viacheslav Koshelev (2005)
Translated by Boris Jakim (2005)

KIERKEGAARD, SØREN AABYE

(1813–1855)

Søren Aabye Kierkegaard, the Danish philosopher and religious thinker, frequently considered the first important existentialist, was the youngest son of Mikaël Pederson Kierkegaard and Anne Sørensdatter Lund, born when his father was fifty-six years old and his mother was forty-four. His early childhood was spent in the close company of his father, who insisted on high standards of performance in Latin and Greek, inculcated an anxiety-ridden pietist devotion of a deeply emotional kind, and awakened his son's imagination by continually acting out stories and scenes. Kierkegaard thus felt early the demand that life should be at once intellectually satisfying, dramatic, and an arena for devotion. Confronted with the Hegelian system at the University of Copenhagen, he reacted strongly against it. It could not supply what he needed—"a truth which is true *for me*, to find *the idea for which I can live and die*" (*Journal,* August 1, 1835). Nor could contemporary Danish Lutheranism provide this. He ceased to practice his religion and embarked on a life of pleasure, spending heavily on food, drink, and clothes.

The melancholy that originated in his childhood continued to haunt him, however, and was increased by his father's confiding in him his own sense of guilt for having somehow sinned deeply against God. For Kierkegaard, the question of how a man can be rescued from despair was consequently intensified. He resolved to return to his studies and become a pastor. He finished his thesis *On the Concept of Irony* (1841) and preached his first sermon. He became engaged to the seventeen-year-old Regine Olsen. But as he became aware of the uniqueness of the vocation that he felt within himself, he found himself unable either to share his life with anyone else or to live out the conventional role of a Lutheran pastor. For him, breaking off his engagement was a decisive step in implementing his vocation. (This cosmic view of the breach does not appear to have been shared by his young fiancée, whose natural hurt pride and rejected affection led to her marriage to Fritz Schlegel, afterward governor of the Danish West Indies.) From then on Kierkegaard lived a withdrawn life as an author, although he did involve himself in two major public controversies. The first followed his denunciation of the low standards of the popular Copenhagen satirical paper *The Corsair*. *The Corsair* in turn caricatured Kierkegaard unmercifully. The second sprang from his contempt for the established Danish Lutheran Church, and especially for its primate, Bishop Mynster, who died in early 1854. When Mynster's about-to-be-appointed successor, Professor Hans Martensen, declared that Mynster had been "a witness to the truth," Kierkegaard delivered a series of bitter attacks on the church in the name of the incompatibility he saw between established ecclesiastical conformism and the inward and personal character of Christian faith. He died shortly after refusing to receive the sacrament from a pastor. "Pastors are royal officials; royal officials have nothing to do with Christianity."

Kierkegaard's biography is necessarily more relevant to his thought than is the case with most philosophers, for he himself saw philosophical inquiry neither as the construction of systems nor as the analysis of concepts, but as the expression of an individual existence. The epitaph that he composed for himself was simply, "That individual." From his own point of view, any verdict on his thought can only be the expression of the critic's own existence, not a critical assessment which could stand or fall according to some objective, impersonal standard. Hence all attempts at an objective evaluation of his thought were condemned by him in advance. He predicted and feared that he would fall into the hands of the professors. Moreover, the initial difficulty created by Kierkegaard's subjectivism is compounded by his style and manner of composition. Although he attacked G. W. F. Hegel, he inherited a large part of Hegel's vocabulary. Passages of great and glittering brilliance tend to alternate with paragraphs of turgid jargon. Both types of writing often prove inimical to clarity of expression. A great many of his books were written for highly specific purposes, and there is no clear thread of development in them. One device of Kierkegaard's must be given special mention: He issued several of his books under pseudonyms and used different pseudonyms so that he could, under one name, ostensibly attack his own work already published under some other name. His reason for doing this was precisely to avoid giving the appearance of attempting to construct a single, consistent, systematic edifice of thought. Systematic thought, especially the Hegelian system, was one of his principal targets.

THE SYSTEM, THE INDIVIDUAL, AND CHOICE

In Hegel's philosophical system, or rather in his successive construction of systems, the linked development of freedom and of reason is a logical one. Out of the most basic and abstract of concepts, Being and Nothing, there is developed first the concept of Becoming and the various phases of Becoming in which the Absolute Idea realizes itself during the course of human history. Each phase of history is the expression of a conceptual scheme, in which the gradual articulation of the concepts leads to a realization of their inadequacies and contradictions, so that the scheme is replaced by another higher and more adequate one, until finally Absolute Knowledge emerges and the whole historical process is comprehended as a single logical unfolding. It is this comprehension itself that is the culmination of the process, and this point was effectively reached for Hegel in his own philosophy. Thus, in *The Science of Logic* he was able to write that he was setting out not merely his own thoughts, but the thoughts of God—the idea of God being simply an anticipation of the Hegelian conception of the Absolute.

In the Hegelian view, both moral and religious development are simply phases in this total process. In *The Phenomenology of Mind,* Hegel described the moral individualism of the eighteenth century, for example, in terms of a logical progress from the hedonistic project of a universal pursuit of private pleasure, through the romantic idealization of "the noble soul," to the Kantian scheme of duty and the categorical imperative, trying to show how each was brought into being by the contradiction developed by its predecessor. In terms of the Hegelian view, an individual is essentially a representative of his age. His personal and religious views must give expression to his role in the total moral and religious development of humankind—a role that is imposed upon him by his place in the historical scheme. He can at best express, but not transcend, his age.

For Kierkegaard, Hegel dissolved the concreteness of individual existence into abstractions characteristic of the realm of concepts. Any particular conceptual scheme represents not an actuality but a possibility. Whether a given individual realizes this possibility, and so endows it with existence, depends upon the individual and not upon the concepts. What the individual does depends not upon what he understands, but upon what he wills. Kierkegaard invokes both Aristotle and Immanuel Kant in support of his contention that Hegel illegitimately assimilated concepts to individual existence; he praises in particular the manner of Kant's refutation of the Ontological Argument. But Kierkegaard, in his doctrine of the primacy of the will, is, in fact, more reminiscent of Quintus Septimius Florens Tertullian or Blaise Pascal.

Kierkegaard buttressed his doctrine of the will with his view of the ultimacy of undetermined choice. He maintained that the individual constitutes himself as the individual he is through his choice of one mode of existence rather than another. Christianity is not a phase in the total development of man's religious and moral ideas; it is a matter of choosing to accept or to reject God's Word. But choice is not restricted to this supreme decision; it is the core of all human existence. The Hegelian view that human existence develops logically within and through conceptual schemes is not merely an intellectual error. It is an attempt to disguise the true facts, to cast off the responsibility for choice, and to find an alibi for one's choices. Moreover, speculative system building falsifies human existence in another way, for it suggests that although those who lived prior to the construction of the system may have had to make do with a partial and inadequate view of reality, the arrival of the final system provides an absolute viewpoint. But according to Kierkegaard, such a viewpoint must be an illusion. Human existence is irremediably finite; its standpoint is incorrigibly partial and limited. To suppose otherwise is to yield to a temptation to pride; it is to attempt to put oneself in the place of God.

This conclusion is only a special case of Kierkegaard's general doctrine that his intellectual opponents are guilty fundamentally not of fallacies and mistakes, but of moral inadequacy. That Kierkegaard should have thought this not only reflects his unfortunate personality; it was a necessary consequence of his doctrine of choice. Another necessary consequence was his mode of authorship. On his own grounds, he cannot hope to produce pure intellectual conviction in his readers; all that he can do is to confront them with choices. Hence he should not try to present a single position. This explains Kierkegaard's method of expounding incompatible points of view in different books and using different pseudonyms for works with different standpoints. The author must conceal himself; his approach must be indirect. As an individual, he must testify to his chosen truth. Yet, as an author he cannot conceal the act of choice. From these views, it is apparent that Kierkegaard used a special concept of choice.

The essence of the Kierkegaardian concept of choice is that it is criterionless. On Kierkegaard's view, if criteria determine what I choose, it is not I who make the choice; hence the choice must be undetermined. Suppose, however, that I do invoke criteria in order to make my choice. Then all that has happened is that I have chosen the criteria. And if in turn I try to justify my selection of criteria by an appeal to logically cogent considerations, then I have in turn chosen the criteria in the light of which these considerations appear logically cogent. First principles at least must be chosen without the aid of criteria, simply in virtue of the fact that they are first. Thus, logical principles, or relationships between concepts, can in no sense determine a person's intellectual positions; for it is his choices that determine the authority such principles have for him. Is man then not even limited by such principles as those that enjoin consistency and prohibit contradiction? Apparently not. For even paradox challenges the intellect in such a way as to be a possible object of choice. The paradoxes that Kierkegaard has in mind at this point in his argument are those posed by the demands of ethics and religion. He is prepared to concede that in fields such as mathematics the ordinary procedures of reason are legitimate. But there are no objective standards where human existence is involved.

THE AESTHETIC AND THE ETHICAL

In *Either/Or: A Fragment of Life* (1843), the doctrine of choice is put to work in relation to a distinction between two ways of life, the ethical and the aesthetic. The aesthetic point of view is that of a sophisticated and roman-

tic hedonism. The enemies of the aesthetic standpoint are not only pain but also, and above all, boredom. As Kierkegaard wrote of the protagonist of aestheticism in *Purify Your Hearts!*, "See him in his season of pleasure: did he not crave for one pleasure after another, variety his watchword?" The protagonist tried to realize every possibility, and no possibility furnishes him with more than a momentary actuality. "Every mood, every thought, good or bad, cheerful or sad, you pursue to its utmost limit, yet in such a way that this comes to pass *in abstracto* rather than *in concreto*; in such a way that the pursuit itself is little more than a mood...." But just because boredom is always to be guarded against, so its threat is perpetual. In the end, the search for novelty leads to the threshold of despair.

By contrast, the ethical constitutes the sphere of duty, of universal rules, of unconditional demands and tasks. For the man in the ethical stage "the chief thing is, not whether one can count on one's fingers how many duties one has, but that a man has once felt the intensity of duty in such a way that the consciousness of it is for him the assurance of the eternal validity of his being" (*Either/Or*, II, p. 223). It is important to note how intensity of feeling enters into Kierkegaard's definition of the ethical stage. He thought that what his own age most notably lacked was passion; hence one must not be deceived by the Kantian overtones of his discussions of duty. Kierkegaard's categorical imperative is felt rather than reasoned. He is an heir of such romantics as the Schlegel brothers in his attitude toward feeling, just as he is the heir of Hegel in his mode of argument. Kierkegaard is a constant reminder of the fact that those who most loudly proclaim their own uniqueness are most likely to have derived their ideas from authors whom they consciously reject.

In *Either/Or* the argument between the ethical and the aesthetic is presented by two rival characters: an older man puts the case for the ethical, a younger for the aesthetic. The reader, as we should expect, is allegedly left to make his own choice. But is he? The description of the two alternatives seems heavily weighted in favor of the ethical. The difficulty is that Kierkegaard wished *both* to maintain that there could be no objective criterion for the decision between the two alternatives, *and* to show that the ethical was superior to the aesthetic. Indeed, one difference between the ethical and the aesthetic is that in the ethical stage the role of choice is acknowledged. Kierkegaard frames this criticism of the man who adheres to the aesthetic: "He has not chosen himself; like Narcissus he has fallen in love with himself. Such a situation has certainly ended not infrequently in suicide." Remarks like this suggest that in fact Kierkegaard thinks that the aesthetic fails on its own terms; but if he were to admit this, his concept of interested choice would no longer apply at this critical point. In one passage Kierkegaard asserts that if one chooses with sufficient passion, the passion will correct whatever was wrong with the choice. Here his inconsistency is explicit. According to his doctrine of choice, there can be no criterion of "correct" or "incorrect," but according to the values of his submerged romanticism, the criterion of both choice and truth is intensity of feeling.

This inconsistency is not resolved; rather it is canonized in the thesis that truth is subjectivity. On the one hand Kierkegaard wants to define truth in terms of the way in which it is apprehended; on the other he wants to define it in terms of what it is that is apprehended. When inconsistency results, he is all too apt to christen this inconsistency "paradox" and treat its appearance as the crowning glory of his argument.

Kierkegaard is not consistent, however, even in his treatment of inconsistency. For he sometimes seems to imply that if the ethical is forced to its limits, contradiction results, and one is therefore forced to pass from the ethical to the religious. "As soon as sin enters the discussion, ethics fails … for repentance is the supreme expression of ethics, but as such contains the most profound ethical contradiction" (*Fear and Trembling*, p. 147, footnote). What is this but Hegelianism of the purest kind?

Kierkegaard describes the transition from the ethical to the religious differently at different periods. In *Either/Or* the ethical sometimes seems to include the religious. By the time the *Concluding Unscientific Postscript* (1846) was written, the religious seems to have absorbed the ethical. In *Fear and Trembling* (1843), the passage from the ethical to the religious is even more striking than that from the aesthetic to the ethical. One of the heroes of this transition is Abraham. In demanding from Abraham the sacrifice of Isaac, God demands something that, from the standpoint of the ethical, is absolutely forbidden, a transgression of duty. Abraham must make the leap to faith, accept the absurd. He must concur in a "suspension of the ethical." At such a point the individual has to make a criterionless choice. General and universal rules cannot aid him here; it is as an individual that he has to choose. According to Kierkegaard, however, there are certain key experiences on the margins of the ethical and the religious through which one may come to censure oneself as an individual. One such experience is the despair that Kierkegaard describes in *The Sickness unto Death*; another is the generalized fear and anxiety that is characterized in

The Concept of Dread (1844). Despair and dread point in the same direction. The experience of each forces the individual to realize that he confronts a void and that he is, in fact, responsible for his own sick and sinful condition. In the state of despair he is brought to recognize that what he despairs of are not the contingent facts (such as the loss of a loved one) that he claims to be the objects of his despair; the individual despairs of himself, and to despair of oneself is to see oneself confronting an emptiness that cannot be filled by aesthetic pleasure or ethical rule-following. Moreover, it is in order to become conscious that one has brought oneself to this point. In analyzing despair, we recognize guilt; so too with dread. Kierkegaard contrasts the fear that has a specific and identifiable object with the dread that is objectless; or rather he identifies the fear that is a fear of nothing in particular as a fear of Nothing. (The reification of negatives into noun phrases is typically Hegelian.) In the experience of dread I become conscious of my bad will as something for which I am responsible, and yet which I did not originate. Original sin is seen as a doctrine deduced from the analysis of experience.

In these works of Kierkegaard it is plain that the existentialist philosophy of choice is in some danger of being submerged in the romantic philosophy of feeling. But the testimony of feeling serves as a propaedeutic to the encounter with Christianity.

CHRISTIANITY

Kierkegaard regarded his own central task as the explanation of what is involved in being a Christian. Apart from Christianity, the only religions he discusses are those of the Greeks and the Jews, and those only as a foil to Christianity. At first sight, Kierkegaard's doctrines of choice and of truth stand in an uneasy relationship to his allegiance to Christianity. For surely Christianity has always claimed to be objectively true, independently of anyone's subjective commitment, and Kierkegaard recognized this. "Not only does it [Christian revelation] express something which man has not given to himself, but something which would never have entered any man's mind even as a wisp or an idea, or under any other name one likes to give to it" (*Journal*, 1839).

If what we believe depends on the believer's own ultimate choice of rational criteria, then surely all beliefs have an equal moment, or rather equal lack of moment, for claiming objective truth. Kierkegaard, however, tried to evade this conclusion and continued to argue both that ultimate choice is criterionless and that one choice can be more correct than another.

Unfortunately, Kierkegaard never considered the issues raised by religions other than Christianity; for it would clarify our view of his position considerably if we could know what he would have said about an account of Islam or Buddhism that was logically parallel to his account of Christianity, in that it made their claims rest on a doctrine of ultimate choice. But the choices that Kierkegaard discusses are always those that might arise for an educated Dane of the nineteenth century. The foil to Christianity is not another religion, but secular philosophy.

This particular contrast is most fully elucidated in the *Philosophical Fragments* (1844), in which Kierkegaard begins from the paradox posed by Socrates in Plato's *Meno*. How can one come to know anything? For either one already knows what one is to come to know, or one does not. But in the former case, since one already knows, one cannot come to know; and in the latter case, how can one possibly recognize what one discovers as being the object of one's quest for knowledge? Plato's answer to this paradox is that in coming to know, we do not discover truths of which we had hitherto been totally ignorant, but truths of which we were once aware (when the soul pre-existed the body), but which we had forgotten. These truths lie dormant within us, and to teach is to elicit such truths. So Socrates makes the slave boy in the *Meno* aware that he knows geometrical truths which he did not know that he knew.

Suppose, however, Kierkegaard asks, that the truth is not within us already. It will then be the case that we are strangers to the truth, to whom the truth must be brought from outside. It will follow that the moment at which we learn the truth and the teacher from whom we learn the truth will not stand in a merely accidental relationship to us. On the Socratic view, one may learn geometry from this teacher or that, but the question of the truth of a geometric theorem is independent of the question from whom we learned it. Not so, on Kierkegaard's view. There are two possible conceptions of the truth that we must choose between, and the Socratic view represents only one alternative. It is important to note that in the *Philosophical Fragments* (1844) Kierkegaard does not say, as he says elsewhere, that one view of the truth is appropriate in matters of geometrical truth, but another is appropriate in matters concerning moral and religious truth. He speaks of two alternative views of the truth, which apparently cover every kind of subject matter, although for the rest of the book he discusses only religion.

Following Kierkegaard's preferred view of the truth, if the truth is not within us, it must be brought to us by a teacher. The teacher must transform us from beings who do not know the truth to beings who are acquainted with it. It is impossible to conceive any greater transformation, and only God could bring it about. But how could God become the teacher of man? If He appeared as He is, the effect on man would be to overawe him so that he could not possibly learn what God has to teach. (Kierkegaard cites the story of the prince in the fairy tale who could not appear to the swine girl as a prince because she would not have come to love him for himself.) Thus, Kierkegaard argues that if God is to be the teacher of man, He must appear in the form of a man, and more specifically, in the form of a servant. From the standpoint of human reason, the idea that God should come as a teacher in human form is an impossible paradox that reason cannot hope to comprehend within its own categories. But according to Kierkegaard, it is in encountering this paradox that reason becomes aware of the objective character of what it encounters.

To be a Christian is thus to subordinate one's reason to the authority of a revelation that is given in paradoxical form. The Christian lives before God by faith alone. His awareness of God is always an awareness of his own infinite distance from God. Christianity initially manifests itself in outward forms, and Kierkegaard reproaches Martin Luther for having tried to reduce Christianity to a pure inwardness—a project that has ended in its opposite, the replacement of inwardness by an ecclesiastical worldliness. Nonetheless, an inward suffering before God is the heart of Christianity.

As previously mentioned, Kierkegaard saw his own age as lacking in passion. The Greeks and the medieval monastics had true passion. The modern age lacks it, and because of this, it lacks a capacity for paradox, which is the passion of thought.

CRITICISMS OF KIERKEGAARD

Kierkegaard used Friedrich Trendelenburg's exposition of Aristotle's logic to criticize Hegel. But he never took the question of the nature of contradiction seriously, and hence he never explained the difference, if any, between paradox (in his sense of the word) and mere inconsistency. But without such a clarification, the notion is fatally unclear. The lack of clarity is increased by Kierkegaard's failure at times to distinguish between philosophy, as such, and Hegelianism. Kierkegaard sometimes seems to have thought that any philosophy that claims objectivity must consist solely of tautologies (*Papirer* III, B, 177).

His doctrine of choice raises at least two fundamental questions: Are there criterionless choices? And is it by such choices that we either can or do arrive at our criteria of true belief? Actual cases of criterionless choice usually seem in some way to be special cases. Either they are trivial, random selections (as of a ticket in a lottery) or they arise from conflicts of duties in which each alternative seems equally weighted. But none of these are choices of criteria. Such choices arise precisely at the point at which we are not presented with objective criteria. How do we arrive at such criteria? They appear to be internally connected with the subject matter of the relevant beliefs and judgment. Therefore we cannot choose our ultimate criteria in mathematics or physics. But what about morals and religion? Can one choose to consider the gratuitous infliction of pain a morally neutral activity? We are strongly inclined to say that an affirmative answer would indicate that the word *morally* had not been understood. But what is certain is that Kierkegaard's fundamental positions must remain doubtful until some series of questions such as this has been systematically considered. Kierkegaard himself never tried to ask them.

See also Absolute, The; Aristotle; Being; Existentialism; Hegel, Georg Wilhelm Friedrich; Hegelianism; Kant, Immanuel; Luther, Martin; Ontological Argument for the Existence of God; Pascal, Blaise; Schlegel, Friedrich von; Tertullian, Quintus Septimius Florens.

Bibliography

WORKS BY KIERKEGAARD

Texts
Papirer, 20 vols. Edited by P. A. Heiberg, V. Kuhr, and E. Torsting. Copenhagen: Gyldendal, 1909–1948.
Samlede Vaerker, 2nd ed., 14 vols. Edited by A. B. Drachmann, J. L. Heiberg, and H. O. Lange. Copenhagen, 1920–1931.

Texts in English Translation
The following listing is in order of original date of publication.
Either/Or, 2 vols. Vol. I, translated by D. F. Swenson and L. M. Swenson. Princeton, NJ, 1941. Vol. II, translated by W. Lowrie. Princeton, NJ, 1944.
Fear and Trembling. Translated by R. Payne. London: Oxford University Press, 1939. Also translated by W. Lowrie. Princeton, NJ: Princeton University Press, 1941.
Repetition: An Essay in Experimental Psychology. Translated by W. Lowrie. Princeton, NJ: Princeton University Press, 1941.
Philosophical Fragments: Or, A Fragment of Philosophy. Translated by D. F. Swenson. Princeton, NJ: Princeton University Press, 1936.
The Concept of Dread. Translated by W. Lowrie. Princeton, NJ: Princeton University Press, 1944.
Stages on Life's Way. Translated by W. Lowrie. Princeton, NJ, 1940.
Concluding Unscientific Postscript. Translated by D. F. Swenson and W. Lowrie. Princeton, NJ: Princeton University Press, 1941.
The Sickness unto Death. Translated by W. Lowrie. Princeton, NJ: Princeton University Press, 1941.
The Point of View. Translated by W. Lowrie. Princeton, NJ: Princeton University Press, 1941.
Training in Christianity. Translated by W. Lowrie. Princeton, NJ: Princeton University Press, 1944.
Purify Your Hearts! Translated by A. S. Aldworth and W. S. Fine. London: C. W. Daniel, 1937.
For Self-Examination. Translated by W. Lowrie. Princeton, NJ: Princeton University Press, 1941.
The Present Age. Translated by A. Dru and W. Lowrie. London: Oxford University Press, 1940.
Christian Discourses. Translated by W. Lowrie. London: Oxford University Press, 1939.
Works of Love. Translated by D. F. Swenson. Princeton, NJ: Princeton University Press, 1946.
The Attack upon "Christendom." Translated by W. Lowrie. Princeton, NJ: Princeton University Press, 1944.
The Journals of Søren Kierkegaard: A Selection. Edited and translated by A. Dru. Oxford: Oxford University Press, 1938.

WORKS ON KIERKEGAARD

Anthologies, Biography, and Critical Studies
Bretall, R. *A Kierkegaard Anthology.* Princeton, NJ: Princeton University Press, 1946.
Geismar, E. O. *Lectures on the Religious Thought of Søren Kierkegaard.* Minneapolis: Augsburg, 1937.
Hohlenberg, J. E. *Søren Kierkegaard.* London, 1954.
Jolivet, R. *Introduction to Kierkegaard.* London, 1950.
Lowrie, W. *Kierkegaard.* New York: Oxford University Press, 1938.
Lowrie, W. *A Short Life of Kierkegaard.* Princeton, NJ: Princeton University Press, 1942.
Swenson, D. F. *Something about Kierkegaard.* Minneapolis: Augsburg, 1941.
Wahl, J. *Études Kierkegaardiennes.* Paris, 1938.

Additional Background
Barrett, W. *Irrational Man.* Garden City, NY: Doubleday, 1958.
Blackham, H. J. *Six Existentialist Thinkers.* New York, 1952.
Collins, J. *The Existentialists: A Critical Study.* Chicago: Regnery, 1952.
Grene, M. *Introduction to Existentialism.* Chicago: University of Chicago Press, 1959.
Shestov, L. *Athènes et Jérusalem.* Paris: J. Vrin, 1938.

Alasdair MacIntyre (1967)

KIERKEGAARD, SØREN AABYE [ADDENDUM]

Søren Aabye Kierkegaard has been the subject of sharply rising scholarly interest since the mid-twentieth century.

In addition to several important works devoted to reexamining Kierkegaard's relation to G. W. F. Hegel, and numerous specialized treatments of key themes and problems in the authorship, newer studies have explored the significance of Kierkegaard's thought from literary, political, and historical viewpoints.

Niels Thulstrup (1967) traces the development of Kierkegaard's critical engagement with Hegel from 1835 to the conclusion of the pseudonymous authorship in 1846. Thulstrup carefully delineates the main sources of Kierkegaard's knowledge of Hegelian philosophy. This is an invaluable service, considering that much of what Kierkegaard knew about the German philosopher was actually gleaned from secondary sources. Of special interest are the Danish Hegelians, Johan Ludvig Heiberg and Hans Lassen Martensen, and the anti-Hegelians, Frederik Christian Sibbern and Poul Martin Møller. Thulstrup also examines the influence of important German writers such as Johann Erdmann, Johann Gottlieb Fichte, Friedrich von Schelling, Adolf Trendelenburg, Marheinecke, and Werder. The notable tendency in this work to read Hegel through a Kierkegaardian lens leads the author to conclude that the two "have nothing in common as thinkers." This conclusion, however, has been challenged by other commentators who claim to find deeper parallels in their thought.

Several such parallels are noted by Mark C. Taylor (1980). Taylor points out, for instance, that both thinkers see the spiritlessness of modernity as the chief obstacle to selfhood and that both attempt to recover spirit through a process of "aesthetic education." For Hegel, however, spiritlessness represents a form of self-alienation that can be overcome only by a reconciliation of self and other, a mediation of the individual's personal and social life; while for Kierkegaard, the threat to spirit lies in the modern tendency to objectify and systematize, to dissolve the distinction between the individual and "the crowd." Taylor argues that Kierkegaard's exclusive emphasis on the individual is ultimately self-negating, since the self is never merely the self but bears a necessary and internal relation to the other. Hegel's relational conception of selfhood is thus shown to be more adequate and more comprehensive than Kierkegaard's, which "necessarily passes over into its opposite—Hegelian spirit" (p. 272). There remains a genuine question, however, about whether Kierkegaard's critique of "the crowd" precludes the possibility of a genuine human community in which individual responsibility is preserved.

Stephen N. Dunning (1985) goes even further than Taylor, suggesting that a relational conception of selfhood is implicit in the dialectical structure of Kierkegaard's writings. Dunning argues that the solitude of the self is "always a moment in a development that embraces interpersonal relations that can be contradictory (the aesthetic stage), reciprocal (the ethical stage), or paradoxically both incommunicable and reciprocal (the religious stage)" (pp. 248–49). According to this reading the *Postscript* describes a religious dialectic that culminates in a paradoxical unity of the self as both "other to itself (in sin) and restored to itself by God" (p. 249), and at the same time related to the entire community of Christians by a deep bond of sympathy. In this way, the theory of stages confirms the Hegelian insight that the solitary self is incomprehensible apart from the relational structures that give it meaning. It has been noted, however, that the formal similarities between Kierkegaardian and Hegelian dialectic may mask important conceptual differences noted by Thulstrup and Taylor.

Three studies of Kierkegaard's moral and religious philosophy deserve special mention. The first is Gregor Malantschuk's excellent study (1968). Working mainly from the journals, Malantschuk shows that the authorship is governed by a qualitative dialectic, which is aimed at illuminating the subjective dimensions of human existence, while the later polemical writings make use of a quantitative dialectic, which invokes the visible degradation of Christ as a judgment on Christendom. The dialectical method is thus seen to be the golden thread that runs through all of Kierkegaard's writings and places the individual works in the larger context of his avowed purpose as a religious author.

C. Stephen Evans's study of the *Fragments* and *Postscript* (1983) is widely recognized as one of the best general introductions to the Climacus writings available in any language. Though the book is written for the "ordinary" reader rather than the specialist—there is no critical engagement with the secondary literature—students and scholars alike have found it immensely useful for its coherent presentation of the main themes in Kierkegaard's religious philosophy, including his complex use of irony and humor in connection with the theory of indirect communication. The clarity of Evans's exposition is unsurpassed, even by his 1992 book, which returns to many of the issues addressed in the earlier work.

M. Jamie Ferreira (1991) explores one of the most difficult conceptual problems in the authorship: the nature of religious conversion. Challenging volitionalist and antivolitionalist accounts of the Kierkegaardian leap, Ferreira reconceptualizes the transition to faith as a "reorienting, transforming, shift in perspective" (p. 57).

Central to this account is the concept of surrender, which is explicated in terms of the imaginative activities of suspension and engagement. Based on this analysis, Ferreira offers a compelling refutation of the popular but mistaken assumption that Kierkegaard viewed ethical and religious choice as criterionless and hence immune to critical appraisal. Her analysis suggests rather that the more wholeheartedly one chooses, the more likely one is to discover whether one has made the wrong choice. On this reading passionate engagement is not meant to guarantee that one will continue in a choice no matter what, but it does ensure that one will experience more fully what is implied by a choice. In this way passionate engagement is seen to facilitate the possibility of critical appraisal.

Louis Mackey (1971) uses the tools of literary criticism to explore the complex relation between the literary and philosophical dimensions of Kierkegaard's authorship. Mackey argues that even the most philosophical of Kierkegaard's books, the *Fragments* and *Postscript*, call into question the very nature of the philosophical enterprise. His use of literary devices, intended to create a poetic indirection, always leave the reader somewhere between assertion and irony. Mackey goes on to make a more general point about the relation between philosophy and poetry, observing that "all humane philosophy is a poetic and for that reason an indirect communication" (p. 295). Indeed, the philosophers of Western tradition have in this sense, he claims, "always been poetic philosophers" (p. 295). This theme is developed further in Mackey (1986), which attempts to situate Kierkegaard in relation to current trends in deconstructionist thought and literary practice.

Bruce Kirmmse (1990) traces the political, economic, and social history of Denmark from 1780 to 1850, giving us a detailed picture of the cultural milieu in which Kierkegaard lived and wrote. Focusing on the boundaries between the public and the private, between politics and religion, Kirmmse lays a foundation for understanding the connection between Kierkegaard's critique of society and his attack on the established church. The exposition is facilitated by a discussion of Kierkegaard's important religious writings, which are frequently overlooked in major surveys of his thought. Until recently Kierkegaard's social and political views had received scant attention in the secondary literature. Other notable discussions can be found in chapters 8 and 9 of Alastair Hannay (1982) and in Merold Westphal (1987).

See also Fichte, Johann Gottlieb; Hegel, Georg Wilhelm Friedrich; Schelling, Friedrich Wilhelm Joseph von.

Bibliography

Adorno, T. *Kierkegaard: Construction of the Aesthetic.* Minneapolis: University of Minneapolis Press, 1989.

Collins, J. *The Mind of Kierkegaard.* Chicago: Regnery, 1953.

Dunning, S. N. *Kierkegaard's Dialectic of Inwardness: A Structural Analysis of the Theory of Stages.* Princeton, NJ: Princeton University Press, 1985.

Evans, C. S. *Kierkegaard's "Fragments" and "Postscript": The Religious Philosophy of Johannes Climacus.* Atlantic Highlands, NJ: Humanities Press, 1983.

Evans, C. S. *Passionate Reason: Making Sense of Kierkegaard's Philosophical Fragments.* Bloomington: Indiana University Press, 1992.

Ferreira, M. J. *Transforming Vision: Imagination and Will in Kierkegaardian Faith.* Oxford: Clarendon Press, 1991.

Hannay, A. *Kierkegaard.* London: Routledge and Kegan Paul, 1982.

Kirmmse, B. H. *Kierkegaard in Golden-Age Denmark.* Bloomington: Indiana University Press, 1990. Contains an extensive scholarly bibliography.

Mackey, L. *Kierkegaard: A Kind of Poet.* Philadelphia: University of Pennsylvania Press, 1971.

Mackey, L. *Points of View: Readings of Kierkegaard.* Tallahassee: Florida State University Press, 1986.

Malantschuk, G. *Dialektik og Eksistens hos Søren Kierkegaard* (1968). Translated by H. V. Hong and E. H. Hong as *Kierkegaard's Thought.* Princeton, NJ: Princeton University Press, 1971.

Taylor, M. C. *Journeys to Selfhood: Hegel and Kierkegaard.* Berkeley: University of California Press, 1980.

Taylor, M. C. *Kierkegaard's Pseudonymous Authorship: A Study of Time and the Self.* Princeton, NJ: Princeton University Press, 1975.

Thulstrup, N. *Kierkegaards forhold til Hegel.* Copenhagen: Gyldendal, 1967. Translated by G. L. Stengren as *Kierkegaard's Relation to Hegel.* Princeton, NJ: Princeton University Press, 1980.

Westphal, K. *Becoming a Self: A Reading of Kierkegaard's "Concluding Unscientific Postscript."* West Lafayette, IN: Purdue University Press, 1996.

Westphal, K. *Kierkegaard's Critique of Reason and Society.* Macon, GA: Mercer University Press, 1987.

Steven M. Emmanuel (1996)
Bibliography updated by Thomas Nenon (2005)

KILVINGTON, RICHARD
(c. 1302–1361)

Richard Kilvington, Master of Arts (c. 1325) and Doctor of Theology (c. 1335) at Oxford, was a member of Richard de Bury's household, later becoming archdeacon and finally dean of Saint Paul's Cathedral in London. Along with Thomas Bradwardine, Kilvington formed the first academic generation of the school known as the "Oxford Calculators." All of Kilvington's philosophical works—*Sophismata* and *Quaestiones super De generatione et corruptione* (written before 1325), *Quaestiones super Physicam* (c. 1326) and *Quaestiones super libros Ethicorum* (before 1332)—and his theological questions on Lombard's *Sentences* (c. 1334) stem from lectures at Oxford. In his *Physics*, Kilvington found an original way to apply the Euclidean theory of ratios to a new formula relating speeds, forces, and resistances in motions. Because the new rule avoided a serious weakness in Aristotle's theory of motion, nearly everyone adopted it, including the most famous Oxford Calculator, Thomas Bradwardine, in his renowned treatise on velocities in motions, written in 1328.

Following William of Ockham, Kilvington refuted the Aristotelian prohibition against *metabasis* and was convinced that mathematics is useful in all branches of scientific inquiry. He made broad use of the most popular fourteenth-century calculative techniques to solve physical, ethical, and theological problems. Four types of measurement are present in his works: by limits, that is, by the first and last instants of continuous processes, and by the intrinsic and extrinsic limits of capacities of passive and active potencies; by latitude or degree of forms, to measure intensive changes; by a calculus of compounding ratios, to determine speed of motion; and by one to one correspondence, to compare different infinities. Having adopted Ockham's position of ontological minimalism, Kilvington claimed that absolutes—that is, substances and qualities—are the only subjects that change and therefore all other terms, such as "motion," "time," "latitude," or "degree," are modes of speech. Accordingly, he contrasted things that are really distinct with things that are merely distinct rationally or in imagination. Because imaginable means possible—that is, not self-contradictory—in physics Kilvington discussed *secundum imaginationem* (according to imagination) counterfactual cases, such as the rectilinear motion of the earth or motion in a vacuum, and pondered questions that would never arise from direct observation, because the structure of nature can only be uncovered by highly abstract analysis.

Like many Oxford Calculators, Kilvington refrained from including God in the speculations of natural science. However, like almost everyone in the fourteenth-century, he distinguished between God's absolute power (*potentia Dei absoluta*) and ordained power (*potentia Dei ordinata*). The laws of nature reflect God's ordained power. Thanks to his absolute power and will, a presently active power, God might intervene to change or contradict the order of things that he had established. Therefore, it is possible for the past to have been otherwise, because all past events are contingent. Kilvington's teaching on logic, natural philosophy, and theology was markedly influential both in England and elsewhere in Europe. He inspired both the next generation of Oxford Calculators and important Parisian masters such as Nicolas Oresme.

See also Bradwardine, Thomas; Buridan, John; Oresme, Nicholas; William of Ockham.

Bibliography

WORKS BY KILVINGTON

The Sophismata of Richard Kilvington, edited by Norman Kretzmann and Barbara E. Kretzmann. Oxford: Oxford University Press, 1990.

The Sophismata of Richard Kilvington. Introduction, translation, and commentary by Norman Kretzmann and Barbara E. Kretzmann. Cambridge, U.K.: Cambridge University Press, 1990.

WORKS ON KILVINGTON

Jung-Palczewska, Elżbieta. "Works by Richard Kilvington." *Archives d'Histoire Doctrinale et Littéraire du Moyen Age* 67 (2000): 181–223.

Katz, Bernard D. "On a *Sophisma* of Richard Kilvington and a Problem of Analysis." *Medieval Philosophy and Theology* 5 (1996): 31–38.

Elżbieta Jung (2005)

KILWARDBY, ROBERT
(c. 1210–1279)

Robert Kilwardby was an English Dominican. He was a master of arts at the University of Paris between 1237 and 1245 and a student and master of theology at Blackfriars, Oxford, between 1248 and 1261. He then became prior provincial of the English Dominicans and in 1273 he was consecrated archbishop of Canterbury. In 1278 he entered the papal service as cardinal-bishop of Porto and Santa Rufina; he died in Viterbo in 1279.

Kilwardby had a profound influence on thirteenth- and fourteenth-century Scholasticism. In general he tried to promote the philosophical views of Augustine in a time when Aristotle's influence was becoming more and more important. As archbishop of Canterbury he even tried to suppress Aristotelian views by condemning thirty errors in philosophy in the so-called Oxford condemnation of 1277.

His most important and long-lasting influence, however, was in logic. During his Paris years he commented on the whole *Organon* of Aristotle, wrote two *Sophismata*

(*Sophismata grammaticalia* and *Sophismata logicalia*) and also several books on grammar. His commentary on *Priscianus minor* is the most important. During this incredibly productive time of his life he also wrote a commentary on Porphyry's *Isagoge*, and perhaps the earliest commentary on Aristotle's *Nicomachean Ethics*.

Very few of these works have been studied, and most of them still remain in manuscripts. The logical work that in recent years has received most attention is his commentary on Aristotle's *Prior Analytics*. As an exposition of Aristotle's theory of the syllogism, the commentary maintains an extraordinarily high degree of fidelity to Aristotle's text. As part of his overall project of constructing faithful interpretations of Aristotle, Kilwardby aims in his commentary to produce an accurate interpretation of Aristotle's modal syllogistic. The commentary is significant because it appears to be the origin, in the Latin world, of a tradition in which Aristotle's essentialist metaphysics is deployed in the interpretation of his syllogistic.

Kilwardby's work makes use of a number of technical concepts in a very disciplined way. These include notions of a *per se* term and a *per se* necessity and two concepts of *simpliciter* predication. The analysis of these concepts requires both the notion of an essential property and the notion of a necessary proposition. For example, a term is *per se* provided that it is necessary that, whatever it is, it is essentially that. *Per se* terms are contrasted with *per accidens* terms like *walking* for which nothing that is walking is essentially walking. Hence, a sentence like "Every *B* is necessarily *A*" expresses a *per se* necessity provided that (i) "*B*" is a *per se* term and (ii) "*A*" is a *per se* term and (iii) "Every *B* is *A*" is a necessary proposition.

The most important works from Kilwardby's tenure in Oxford are the *De ortu scientiarum* (1250), which is a classification of the sciences and was intended to be an introduction to philosophy, and his questions on the *Sentences* of Peter Lombard from around 1256. The *Sentence*-commentary is influenced by Richard Rufus of Cornwall. Kilwardby also produced smaller but very interesting treatises on relation, on time, and on imagination during this period.

See also Aristotelianism; Augustinianism; Logic, History of: Medieval (European) Logic; Rufus, Richard.

Bibliography

PRIMARY WORKS

De natura relationis (On relation, c. 1256–1261), edited by L. Schmücker, Brixen: L. Schmücker, 1980. A late work on relations.

De ortu scientiarum (On the origin of science, c. 1250), edited by A. G. Judy. Auctores Britannici Medii Aevi 4, London: British Academy, 1976. Kilwardby on natural philosophy.

De spiritu fantastico (On imagination, c. 1256–1261). *On Time and Imagination: De tempore, De spiritu fantastico*, edited by P. O. Lewry. Auctores Britannici Medii Aevi 9. Oxford: Oxford University Press for the British Academy, 1987. A late work on imagination.

De tempore (On time, c. 1256–1261). *On Time and Imagination: De tempore, De spiritu fantastico*, edited by P. O. Lewry. Auctores Britannici Medii Aevi 9. Oxford: Oxford University Press for the British Academy, 1987. A late work on time.

In donati artem maiorem III (Commentary on Donatus, c. 1237–1245), edited by L. Schmücker. Brixen: Typographia A. Weger Fund, 1984. Commentary on the grammatical work of Donatus.

In libros Priorum Analyticorum expositio (Exposition on the books of the *Prior Analytics*, c. 1240). Printed under the name Aegidius Romanus, Venice 1516. Reprinted Frankfurt 1968. Commentary on the *Prior Analytics*.

Notule libri prisciani de accidentibus (Commentary on *De accidentibus*, c. 1237–1245), edited by P. O. Lewry, "Thirteenth-Century Teaching on Speech and Accentuation: Robert Kilwardby's Commentary on *De accidentibus* of Pseudo-Priscian." *Medieval Studies* 50 (1988): 96–185. Commentary on Priscian.

Quaestiones in librum [primum/secundum/tertium/quartum] Sententiarum (Questions of the [first/second/third/fourth] book of the *Sentences*) [c. 1256]. *primum*, edited by J. Schneider; *secundum*, edited by G. Leibold; *tertium*, part 1, *Christologie* (Christology), edited by E. Gössmann, and part 2, *Tugendlehre* [Virtue], edited by G. Leibold; *quartum*, edited by R. Schenk. Veröffentlichungen der Kommission für die Herausgabe ungedruckter Texte aus der mittelalterlichen Geisteswelt. Munich: Verlag der Bayerischen Akademie der Wissenschaften, *primum*, 1986; *secundum*, 1992; *tertium*, 1982 (part 1), 1985 (part 2); *quartum*, 1993. Questions on the *Sentences* of Peter Lombard.

SECONDARY WORKS

Braakhuis, H. A. G. "Kilwardby verus Bacon? The Contribution to the Discussion on Univocal Signification of Beings and Non-Beings found in a Sophism attributed to Robert Kilwardby." In *Medieval Semantics and Metaphysics*, edited by E. P. Bos, 111–142. Artistarium supplementa 2, Nijmegen: Ingenium, 1985. An introduction to Kilwardby's theory of meaning.

Celano, A. J. "Robert Kilwardby and the Limits of Moral Science." In *Philosophy and the God of Abraham*, edited by R. James Long, 31–40. Toronto: Pontifical Institute of Mediaeval Studies, 1991. Study of Kilwardby's moral philosophy.

Ebbesen, S. "Albert (the Great?)'s Companion to the Organon." In *Albert der Grosse. Seine Zeit, sein Werk, seine Wirkung*, edited by A. Zimmerman, 89–103. Berlin: Walter de Gruyter, 1981. Ebbesen shows that Albert the Great copies Kilwardby's *Prior Analytics* commentary.

Gál, G. "Robert Kilwardby's Questions on the Metaphysics and Physics of Aristotle." *Franciscan Studies* 13 (1953): 7–28. On the attribution of a set of questions on metaphysics and physics.

Lagerlund, Henrik. *Modal Syllogistics in the Middle Ages.* Leiden: Brill, 2000. Chapter 2 contains a detailed study on Kilwardby's modal syllogistics.

Lewry, P. Osmund. "The Oxford Condemnation of 1277 in Grammar and Logic." In *English Logic and Semantics from the End of the Twelfth Century to the Time of Ockham and Burleigh*, edited by H. A. G. Braakhuis and L. M. de Rijk, 235–278. Artistarium supplementa 1, Nijmegen: Ingenium, 1981. An account of the implications for logic of the 1277 condemnation.

Lewry, P. Osmund. "Robert Kilwardby on Imagination: the Reconciliation of Aristotle and Augustine." *Medioevo* 9 (1983):1–42. Discussion of Kilwardby's view of the soul.

Lewry, P. Osmund. "Robert Kilwarby's Commentary on the Ethica nova and Vetus." In *L'homme et son univers au moyen-âge*, edited by C. Wedin, 799–807. Philosophes médiévaux 27, Louvain-la-Neuve: Editions de l'Institut Superieur de Philosophie, 1986. A summary of Kilwardby's views on ethics.

Lewry, P. Osmund. "Robert Kilwardby's Writings on the Logica Vetus Studied with Regards to Their Teaching and Method." Ph.D. diss. University of Oxford, 1978. Still the standard text for a discussion of Kilwardby's logic.

Henrik Lagerlund (2005)

KIM, JAEGWON
(1934–)

Jaegwon Kim is a Korean American philosopher born in Taegu (Korea) and educated at Seoul National University, Dartmouth College, and Princeton University. He has taught at Cornell University, University of Michigan, and Brown University, among other institutions. Kim's decisive contributions to philosophy range mainly over many central topics in the philosophy of mind and metaphysics but extend to philosophy of science and epistemology as well. Kim's most influential views in metaphysics and his early stance about the mind were defended in essays published from the early 1970s to the early 1990s and collected in the book *Supervenience and Mind* (1993). His later views on the mind are defended in two books: *Mind in a Physical World* (1998) and *Physicalism, or Something Near Enough* (2005).

In metaphysics, Kim's most crucial influence has been in event theory and the nature of dependence relations, including causation and supervenience. Kim's *property exemplification* account of events is regarded, together with Donald Davidson's account, as one of the two main contenders in the field. According to Kim (1993, essays 1 and 3) an event is not a basic component of ontology; it is a complex entity constituted by a property P (or a relation) exemplified by an object O (or n-tuple of objects) at a time t. If events are the *relata* of

causal relations and causal relations require nomological connections (two widespread assumptions that Kim supports), Kim's fine-grained account of events has the advantage of indicating, in a causal relation, which feature of the *cause event* (its constitutive property) is nomologically connected with which feature of the *effect event* (its constitutive property).

Kim argues that just as causation (about which he is a regularist and a realist) constitutes the diachronic connection among phenomena, there are other metaphysically significant cementing relations that are noncausal (1993, essay 2). One of those relations is particularly important: supervenience, a synchronic dependence relation that connects properties in a given *supervenient* level with properties of a more basic level so that the most basic ones fully determine the supervenient ones. Kim is widely regarded as the leading theorist on supervenience, having carefully distinguished between several types of supervenience relations (e.g., weak, strong, and global) their consequences for reduction and for naturalist ontologies, having applied the notion to a general ontological stance he calls the *layered view of reality* and having used the concept to analyze perennial issues in the mind-body problem (1993, essays 4 to 10).

In the philosophy of mind Kim's work can be divided in three phases. In the early 1980s he defended a nonreductive naturalist/physicalist model of mental causation called supervenient causation. Given two mental properties M and M^* that supervene, respectively, upon physical properties P and P^*, if P causes P^*, M superveniently causes M^*. And if M supervenes on P and P causes P^*, M superveniently causes P^*. Supervenient causation is not outright causation but Kim claimed it was sufficient to endow mental properties with causal efficacy since these properties supervene on properties involved directly in causal processes. Supervenience plays here the double role of articulating the naturalist commitment and accounting for an acceptable (yet somewhat deflationary) approach to mental causation. The model is nonreductive because despite the causal powers of mental properties being reduced to those of their bases, the properties themselves are not reduced since supervenience does not imply identity.

In the late 1980s Kim produced several famous attacks against different forms of nonreductive physicalism (1993, essays 13 to 17; 1998, chapters 2 and 3). Against Davidson's anomalism, Kim argues that the view implies that the fact that an event falls under a mental kind is a causally irrelevant fact. Against functionalism, he claims that its multiple realizability thesis implies *local* reductions and as such does not have the intended nonreductive force. More generally, he develops an argument against all forms of nonreductive physicalism called the causal/explanatory exclusion argument. For a physicalist every physical event has to have a complete physical cause. Kim shows by analyzing and ruling out scenarios that go from partial causes to causal overdetermination that within that framework, we cannot attribute a causal role to the mental unless it is identified with the physical, turning nonreducible mental properties into epiphenomena. Since he also defends the principle that without causal efficacy an entity cannot be real, every form of nonreductive physicalism turns into an eliminativist view. It soon became evident to Kim as much as to his critics that his supervenient causation model is also an easy target of the exclusion argument. Additionally, Kim has lost faith on the explanatory power of the supervenience relation in general, and in particular as a tool for analyzing mental causation. If supervenience is only a superficial relation of property covariation between the mental and the physical and it is itself in need of explanation, it cannot articulate a deep explanatory relation between the mental and the physical.

With this background Kim developed in the 1990s an approach to the mental that can be called functional reductionism (1998, 2005). The proposal consists of grounding the mind-body supervenience relation on the realization relation proposed by functionalism. Mental properties are second-order properties defined over a set of first-order properties that satisfy a given causal/functional condition and thus are eligible as realizers of such second-order properties. Given a mental property M we attempt to construct a functionalization of it in which M is characterized in terms of its typical causes and effects. This functionalization of a property is, Kim argues, sufficient for reduction (under a non-Nagelian, functional account of reduction). Reductive functionalization explains why there are the dependence relations there are and provides ontological simplification by identifying the second-order property with an exhaustive disjunction of all its realizers or else, according to Kim, we may decide to recognize only second-order *concepts* or *predicates* but not second-order properties. Still, Kim thinks that the qualitative properties of experience, unlike the rest of mental states, cannot be functionalized. Since, according to Kim, they are not reducible through type identification with neural-biological properties either, we have to accept them as a *mental residue* that prevents us from embracing a fully generalized physicalism.

Within philosophy of science, Kim's most significant contribution is a sophisticated view of what he calls the *metaphysics of explanation* that combines explanatory realism and pluralism (1989, 1994). According to realism, explanations are grounded in structural, *world-cementing* objective relations between the events referred to by the *explanandum* and the *explanans*. According to pluralism there are, in addition to causal explanations, explanations tied to noncausal, structural dependence relations (such as supervenience). This view can be seen to accord well with Kim's views regarding causal realism and the importance of noncausal relations, and explicitly includes the claim that pluralist realism explains via unification the cognitive value of explanations. In epistemology, Kim has produced an influential critique of Willard Van Orman Quine's naturalized epistemology (1993, essay 12). While defending epistemological naturalism in the sense that epistemic properties supervene upon factual, nonepistemic properties, he criticizes Quine's purely nomological, nonnormative approach to studying how evidence relates to beliefs. The gist of Kim's argument is that the very concept of knowledge disappears if we abandon the normative notion of justification.

See also Davidson, Donald; Epistemology; Metaphysics; Ontology; Philosophy of Mind; Philosophy of Science, Problems in; Quine, Willard Van Orman.

Bibliography

WORKS BY KIM

"Psychophysical Supervenience as a Mind-Body Theory." *Cognition and Brain Theory* 5 (1982): 129–147.

"Explanatory Realism, Causal Realism and Explanatory Exclusion." *Midwest Studies in Philosophy* 12 (1988): 225–239.

Supervenience and Mind. Cambridge, U.K.: Cambridge University Press, 1993.

"Explanatory Knowledge and Metaphysical Dependence." *Philosophical Issues* 5 (1994): 51–69.

Mind in a Physical World. Cambridge, MA: MIT Press, 1998.

Physicalism, or Something Near Enough. Princeton, NJ: Princeton University Press, 2005.

WORKS BY OTHERS

Block, Ned. "Antireductionism Slaps Back." *Philosophical Perspectives* 11 (1997): 107–132.

Fodor, Jerry. "Special Sciences: Still Autonomous After All These Years." *Philosophical Perspectives* 11 (1997): 149–163.

Horgan, Terence. "Kim on Mental Causation and Causal Exclusion." *Philosophical Perspectives* 11 (1997): 165–184.

Loewer, Barry. "Comments on Jaegwon Kim's *Mind in a Physical World*." *Philosophy and Phenomenological Research* 65 (2002): 655–662.

Sabatés, Marcelo. "*Mind* in a Physical World?" *Philosophy and Phenomenological Research* 65 (2002): 663–670

Marcelo H. Sabatés (2005)

KINDĪ, ABŪ-YŪSUF YAʿQŪB IBN ISḤĀQ AL-

See *al-Kindī, Abū-Yūsuf Yaʿqūb ibn Isḥāq*

KING, MARTIN LUTHER
(1929–1968)

Martin Luther King Jr. was born in 1929 in Atlanta, Georgia. He attended Morehouse College, Crozer Theological Seminary, and Boston University, where he earned a doctorate in philosophical theology. In 1964, he was awarded the Nobel Peace Prize. He was assassinated in Memphis, Tennessee, in 1968.

King first gained international attention when, after completing his doctoral studies and becoming pastor of the Dexter Avenue Baptist Church in Montgomery, Alabama, he led the fight to desegregate public transportation in Montgomery. His strategy was nonviolent passive resistance. The faith that underlay that strategy was that white Americans could be persuaded by black suffering and moral argument to agree on the injustice of laws requiring the segregation of the races. The essentials of that faith are eloquently summarized in his frequently reprinted "Letter from Birmingham City Jail," and in his arguably most famous speech, "I Have a Dream." In that letter and speech King stressed his vision of the "beloved community," his vision of the "color-blind society," his conviction that injustice could be cured if exposed to the light of human conscience, and his conviction that every person has a duty to love one's enemies, and to avoid violence.

However, even in these works, King was not as optimistic or as completely reliant on white conscience as many have apparently thought him to be. For example, as his essay on civil disobedience reveals, his strategy of civil disobedience was designed not only to appeal to white conscience, but also to bring economic pressure on merchants. It is therefore a mistake to identify his theory with that of John Rawls, although Rawls himself stated that the two theories are similar.

King's more pessimistic or at least realistic views emerged more clearly in later speeches. Probably he was influenced by nationalists like Malcolm X and Stokely Carmichael (later known as Kwame Ture.) Certainly he admitted that he had started seeing his dream turning into a "nightmare," and that most Americans were "unconscious racists." Like Frederick Douglass before him, King concluded that moral suasion alone would not succeed in moving the white political establishment to implement the needed reforms, and that black people and their allies should therefore seek political power, though unlike Douglass he never advocated violence. In King's mature philosophy this new turn coincided with a greater emphasis on the poverty of many black Americans, and the relation of their plight to America's behavior in the international arena. King believed that the injustice of that behavior was being then revealed dramatically by the war in Vietnam and his criticisms of that war, together with his evidently growing sympathies for socialism lost him many allies. King's last speech, "I See the Promised Land," seems to contain premonitions of his assassination on the next day.

Unfortunately, as scholars of King's philosophy have noted, conservatives of the late twentieth and early twenty-first centuries have skillfully misused King's vision of a future color-blind society, especially his longing for a nation in which his four little children "will not be judged by the color of their skin but by the content of their character," to oppose color-conscious means like affirmative action for achieving such a nation.

See also Civil Disobedience; Justice; Pacifism; Racism; Rawls, John; Rights; Violence.

Bibliography

WORKS BY MARTIN LUTHER KING
Stride toward Freedom. New York: Harper and Row, 1958.
Strength to Love. New York: Harper and Row, 1963.
Why We Can't Wait. New York: Harper and Row, 1963.
Where Do We Go from Here: Chaos or Community? New York: Harper and Row, 1967.
The Trumpet of Conscience. New York: Harper and Row, 1968.
A Testament of Hope, edited by James Melvin Washington. New York: Harper and Row, 1986. An anthology of sermons and essays.

WORKS ABOUT MARTIN LUTHER KING
Ansbro, John J. *Martin Luther King, Jr.: The Making of a Mind*. New York: Orbis, 1982.
Cone, James H. *Martin and Malcolm and America: A Dream or a Nightmare*. New York: Orbis Books 1991.
Dyson, Michael Eric. *I May Not Get There with You: The True Martin Luther King Jr.* New York: Touchstone Books, 2000.
Garrow, David J. *Bearing the Cross: Martin Luther King Jr. and the Southern Christian Leadership Conference*. New York: Random House, 1986.
Lewis, David L. *King: A Critical Biography*. Baltimore, MD: Penguin, 1970.
Lincoln, C. Eric, ed. *Martin Luther King Jr.: A Profile*. New York: Hill and Wang, 1984.

Moses, Greg. *Revolution of Conscience: Martin Luther King, Jr., and the Philosophy of Nonviolence.* Foreword by Leonard Harris. New York: Guilford Press, 1997.

Bernard Boxill (2005)

KIREEVSKII, IVAN VASIL'EVICH
(1806–1856)

Ivan Vasil'evich Kireevskii, Russian literary critic and religious philosopher, was born in Moscow in a family of the old nobility related to the important poet Vasilii Zhukovskii (1783–1852). Kireevskii's father died in 1812 after contracting typhus in a hospital he founded for wounded soldiers. After his father's death, the young boy's education was largely guided by Zhukovskii, who did much for the development of Kireevskii's literary talent. Zhukovskii repeatedly affirmed, with total sincerity, that his young relative could become a fine writer. In 1823 Kireevskii became a member of the *Obshchestvo liubomudrov* (Society of the lovers of wisdom), organized by Dmitrii Venevitinov and Prince Vladimir Odoevskii for the study of German philosophy, especially Schelling. To complete his education, Kireevskii went abroad in 1830. In Germany he attended the lectures of Hegel, Schelling, and Schleiermacher. When he returned to Russia, he began to publish the journal *Evropeets* (The European, 1832), which was soon prohibited by the government. The orientation of the journal was somewhat "pro-Western": Kireevskii had set himself the task of synthesizing Western-European and Russian thought.

Kireevskii's further evolution was closely connected with Slavophilism. In 1845, for a period of time he was the editor of the Slavophile journal *Moskovitianin* (The Muscovite); and later he expounded his religio-philosophical ideas in the collection of articles *Moskovsii Sbornik* (Moscow collection, 1852), published by the Slavophile circle. In the final years of his life, Kireevskii was working on a course of philosophy in which his intent was to clearly display the distinguishing characteristics of the Russian philosophical tradition. The course was not completed. Kireevskii's collected works were first published in 1861, in two volumes.

The central idea of Kireevskii's philosophy was the integrity of the spirit: A human being can remain a person as long as he preserves in himself the unity of his "mind and heart," the "integrity" of his consciousness, of his "inner organization." Meanwhile, Kireevskii's epistemological theories were closely connected with his socio-historical views. Only by attaining a harmonious "integral thinking" can the person and society avoid the two extremes: the ignorance that separates a nation from the "living communion of minds" and "abstract logical thinking" (rationalism) that fragments the integrity of the spirit into its separate elements (Kireevskii 1984, pp. 221–222).

Kireevskii tended to associate what he perceived as the limitations of Western society primarily with the one-sidedness of rationalism. He viewed Hegel as the final and supreme peak of Western rationalistic thought, continuing the tradition of Aristotle. In assessing various attempts to overcome rationalism in Europe (Schelling), Kireevskii considered that their failure was predetermined: Philosophy depends on the "character of the dominant faith," but in the Catholic-Protestant West the two dominant Christian faiths are, according to the Slavophile assessment, profoundly rationalistic. Kireevskii's own allegiance was to Orthodox theism, and he viewed the future "new" philosophy as a harmony of reason and Orthodox faith based on feeling.

Kireevskii thought that Western culture had already passed the highest point of its development and exhausted its potential. In his article "On the Nature of European Culture and on its Relationship to Russian Culture," Kireevskii writes that contemporary Western man "fragments his life into separate strivings or tendencies"; in "one corner of his heart there lives the religious sense; in another corner, separately, there live the powers of the intelligence and exertions related to everyday occupations; in a third corner there lives the desire for sensuous pleasures; in a fourth there lives moral feeling related to family life; and in a fifth there lives the desire for personal gain" (Kireevskii 1984, pp. 203, 229). That is, the souls of contemporary Westerners is mosaiclike, fragmented.

According to Kireevskii, such a transformation of human consciousness into a "calculating machine" will lead, in the final analysis, to the triumph of the lower desires, the instincts, where people will shut themselves up in their physical persons and desire only material comfort. It is precisely for this reason that Kireevskii began to seek the sources of a "new" and "young" philosophy, which was destined to supplant rationalism, overcome the fragmentedness of man's being, and lead to the "integral spirit." Kireevskii turned his glance toward the Russo-Slavic culture, in which, in his opinion, Orthodoxy was the principle that unified all spheres of life, combining spirit, reason, conscience, will, and feeling into a "thinking that believes." This thesis of Kireevskii's was, not without justification, called "epistemological utopianism" by Vasilii Zenkovsky, the well-known historian of Russian philosophy.

Kireevskii attempted to answer the question of why the European and Russian cultures were separated as it were by an invisible wall. In doing so, he defined the sources of the European culture of his day. He identified three such principles or "elements": (1) the influence of the Christian religion; (2) the spirit of the barbarian nations that destroyed the Roman Empire; and (3) the remnants of the ancient world, of classical scholarship. Kireevskii analyzed these principles of Western civilization and arrived at the conclusion that the development of Russia lacked the classical heritage of the ancient world.

This "lack of the classical world" (Kireevskii 1984, p. 72) was, in his opinion, the reason why the influence of the Orthodox Church on Russia was not as strong as the influence of the Roman Catholic Church on the Western European countries, the Roman Church having experienced the enormous influence of the Roman government and Roman law on its organization. As a result, the Christian church in Russia could not become a force that would unite spiritually and politically fragmented Russia, which because of this fragmentation fell subject to the Tatar Yoke for several centuries. On the one hand, without a spiritual center (the kind of center that the Vatican was for fragmented Europe), Russia could be unified not spiritually but only materially (in other words, not in a spiritual but in a material *sobornost*), and this material unification took many centuries. On the other hand, the peculiar character of the development of Russia led to a situation where the Russo-Slavic world found itself separated and protected from Europe's deadening rationalism, the external and formal character of Europe's juridical law (inherited from Rome), and the coercive character of European governmental power, which was formed as a result of military conquests; moreover, in these circumstances, the Church in Russia had preserved its "purity," remaining independent of the governmental authority and secular goals.

Eastern Christianity, leading (as Kireevskii believed) from discursive rationalistic thinking to a free moral intuitive understanding, was assimilated by Russia in a form undistorted by the classical heritage. According to Kireevskii, the purity and undistorted character of its Christian principles are what give Russian culture a right to claim that it has a special role to play in the history of humankind. The "seed" (which is how he figuratively referred to the religious idea) has fallen onto a special "soil"—the Slavic national soul, which is characterized

"both by dignity and by humility, attesting to equilibrium of spirit" (Kireevskii 1984, p. 224). But the main thing is that the Slavic "soil" is characterized by an original native principle of the organization of social life—the *obshchina* (or Russian commune). Not the personal right to property (as in the West) but the communal ownership of land is the foundation of the "relations of social life" in Russian society, for which individualism is a foreign principle. This is precisely why Kireevskii believed that the "new" philosophy and culture, so indispensable for humankind, could arise in his country. He associated the birth of this new thinking not with the construction of systems but with a radical transformation of the social consciousness, with the "education of society" as a result of common efforts rooted in *sobornost*. In this way, society will experience the infusion of a new philosophy that will overcome rationalism. This new philosophy will reorient humankind's spiritual life and produce in both society and in the individual an inner integrity of consciousness, a harmony of the social life.

By no means did this opposition between the Western fragmentedness and individualism and the Russian integrity and sobornost lead Kireevskii to reject the Western tradition. He dreamt of "integrity"; and here his ideal was the synthesis of what he considered the best features of the spiritual life of the West and of the East in such a manner that the "Russian principles," without nullifying European culture, would bestow upon the latter "higher meaning and definitive development" (Kireevskii 1984, p. 238). In the light of this, for Kireevskii the task of an original Russian philosophy would be the reworking of contemporary Western philosophy in the spirit of the teachings of Eastern patristics.

Kireevskii's views influenced a number of twentieth-century Russian philosophers, including Nikolai Berdiaev, Sergei Bulgakov, and Dmitrii Merezhkovskii. Kireevskii's central ideas—for example, about Orthodoxy as the foundation of Russian culture; the "conciliar" (*soborny*) nature of knowledge; and the fundamental difference between the European and Russian cultural traditions—have had a great impact and become the subject of close study by philosophers both in Russia and in Europe and North America.

See also Aristotle; Berdyaev, Nikolai Aleksandrovich; Bulgakov, Sergei Nikolaevich; Hegel, Georg Wilhelm Friedrich; Rationalism; Russian Philosophy; Schelling, Friedrich Wilhelm Joseph von; Schleiermacher, Friedrich Daniel Ernst; Zen'kovskii, Vasilii Vasil'evich.

Bibliography

WORKS BY KIREEVSKII

Izbrannye stat'i [Selected articles], edited by V. Kotelnikov, Moscow: Sovremennik, 1984.

On Spiritual Unity: A Slavophile Reader. Translated and edited by Boris Jakim and Robert Bird. Hudson, NY: Lindisfarne, 1998.

"On the Nature of European Culture and Its Relation to the Culture of Russia." In *Russian Intellectual History: An Anthology*, edited by Marc Raeff. Atlantic Highlands, NJ: Humanities Press, 1978.

Polnoe Sobranie Sochinenii [Complete works]. Edited by Mikhail Gershenzon. 2 vols. Moscow, 1911.

WORKS ABOUT KIREEVSKII

Christoff, P. K. *An Introduction to Nineteenth-Century Russian Slavophilism: A Study in Ideas.* Vol. 2, *I. V. Kireevskij.* The Hague: Mouton, 1972.

Gleason, Abbott. *European and Muscovite: Ivan Kireevsky and the Origin of Slavophilism.* Cambridge, MA: Harvard University Press, 1972.

Zenkovsky, V. V. *Istoriia russkoi filosofii.* 2 vols. Paris, 1948–1950. Translated by George L. Kline as *A History of Russian Philosophy.* 2 vols. (New York: Columbia University Press, 1953). See volume 1, 207–227.

Olga Volkogonova (2005)
Translated by Boris Jakim

KITCHER, PATRICIA
(1948–)

Patricia Kitcher is widely known for her work on Kant and on philosophy of psychology. Born Patricia Williams, she attended Wellesley College and then graduate school in philosophy at Princeton where she studied with George Pitcher. Kitcher's interest in cognition manifested early and has continued to shape and inform her work throughout her career. Her doctoral dissertation defended a psychological continuity criterion for personal identity but extended the scope of the psychological criterion beyond that traditionally posited to include broader and more abstract cognitive characteristics, such as cognitive approach or cognitive style. Since then her work has ranged widely from traditional philosophy of psychology, to Freud, and ultimately to her greatest philosophical passion: Kant scholarship.

In her early work Kitcher wrote a number of papers in philosophy of psychology, philosophy of mind, and philosophy of science. She argued for the viability of intentional psychology and the autonomy of functionalist psychology from neurophysiology. Later work predominantly concentrated on analysis of problems stemming from the interpretation of Kant's first *Critique*.

Kitcher has written numerous articles on the forms of intuition, Kant's epistemology, self-consciousness, and on how transcendental arguments work.

Kitcher has written two books that also pursue psychological themes. *Kant's Transcendental Psychology* was a radical departure from most Kant exegesis. The book makes two main claims about the *Critique of Pure Reason.* First, contra Peter Frederick Strawson, Kitcher argues that to understand synthetic a priori knowledge, it is essential to consider transcendental psychology. Second, she explicates a Kantian argument for the necessity of an integrated thinking subject, which serves as a reply to David Hume's denial of the unity of the self. An expanded and amended version of this position is being fleshed out more fully in a book she is currently writing, *Kant's Thinker*, which also explores the question of how we are to understand the faculties, and how the *Critique* contributes to debates about conscious and unconscious ideas.

In *Freud's Dream* Kitcher argued that Freud was the first cognitive scientist: Psychoanalysis should be thought of as an exercise in interdisciplinary theory construction, and as such, it illuminates the pitfalls to which such interdisciplinary approaches are subject. (Kitcher jokes that her arguments managed to alienate all readers: Freudians, because she exposes the mistaken foundation of psychoanalysis, and anti-Freudians, because she portrays his program as scientifically legitimate.)

Around the turn of the new century, Kitcher's interests turned toward Kantian ethics. Her works from this period provide an account of Kantian *maxims* and an interpretation of Kant's argument for the Formulation of the Universal Law for the Categorical Imperative, a task that has led many other Kant experts to throw up their hands in perplexity.

Kitcher's prodigious published contributions to philosophy are matched by her contributions to the philosophical community. She has served as department chair in three different universities, on numerous academic committees (including being a founding chair of the UC committee on the status of women), as president of the Society for Philosophy and Psychology, as president of the North American Kant Society, and on the editorial board of *Journal of Philosophy*. Her philosophical integrity, her fiery lectures, and her incisive comments on student papers make her an inspiring teacher and mentor.

Patricia Kitcher has held faculty positions at the University of Vermont, the University of Minnesota, and University of California, San Diego, and a visiting position at

University of Michigan. In 1998 she went to Columbia University where she became the Mark van Doren Professor of the Humanities and chair of the philosophy department. She lives in New York City with her husband, Philip, also a philosopher, with whom she has two sons, Andrew and Charles.

See also Ethics; Hume, David; Kant, Immanuel; Philosophy of Mind; Philosophy of Science, Problems of.

Selected Bibliography

WORKS

"The Crucial Relation in Personal Identity." *Canadian Journal of Philosophy* 7 (1) (1978): 131–145.

"Kant on Self-Identity." *Philosophical Review* 91 (1) (1982): 41–72.

"Kant's Paralogisms." *Philosophical Review* 91 (4) (1982): 515–547.

"In Defense of Intentional Psychology." *Journal of Philosophy* 81 (2) (1984): 89–106.

"Narrow Taxonomy and Wide Functionalism." *Philosophy of Science* 52 (1) (1985): 78–97.

"Discovering the Forms of Intuition." *Philosophical Review* 96 (1987): 205–248.

Kant's Transcendental Psychology. New York: Oxford University Press, 1990.

Freud's Dream: A Complete Interdisciplinary Science of Mind. Cambridge, MA: Bradford Books/M.I.T. Press, 1992.

"Revisiting Kant's Epistemology: Skepticism, Apriority, and Psychologism." *Noûs* 29 (3) (1995): 285–315.

"Kant on Self-Consciousness." *Philosophical Review* 108 (1999): 345–386.

"On Interpreting Kant's Thinker as Wittgenstein's 'I'." *Philosophy and Phenomenological Research* 61 (2000): 33–63.

"Kant's Argument for the Categorical Imperative." *Noûs* 38 (4) (2004) 555–584.

Adina L. Roskies (2005)

KLAGES, LUDWIG

(1872–1956)

Ludwig Klages, a German psychologist and philosopher, was the leading figure in the field of characterology. Born in Hanover, Klages studied chemistry, physics, and philosophy at Munich, receiving his doctorate in chemistry in 1900. As a member of the Stefan George circle, he collaborated with George in the editing of the *Blättern für die Kunst.* In 1905 Klages founded at the University of Munich a *Seminar für Ausdruckskunde,* which soon became Germany's main center of characterological psychology. In 1919 the seminar was moved to Kilchberg, near Zürich, where Klages remained until his death.

Klages was the principal representative in psychology of the vitalist movement that swept Germany from 1895 to 1915. His most important work was directed toward the formulation of a science of character that would reestablish the undifferentiated union of the life forms that had been ruptured by the emergence of ego in the human species. To this end he explored some of the more bizarre pseudo sciences, such as graphology, and attempted to use their insights as the bases for auxiliary disciplines in his study of character types.

In addition to the literary influences of the romantic poets, of Johann Wolfgang von Goethe, and of Stefan George, Klages was also influenced by the physiologist E. G. Carus and the psychologist Theodore Lipps and, most important, by the philosopher Friedrich Nietzsche. All of these strands of thought converged in Klages to make of him a major spokesman of a generation of intellectuals consciously dedicated to the repudiation of reason in the name of instinct, and of civilization in the name of life. In short, his work was similar in content and general effect to that of Ernst Jünger, Oswald Spengler, and Martin Heidegger in providing—however unintentionally—an intellectual basis for Nazism.

According to Klages, Nietzsche had perceived correctly that man was distinguished from the rest of animal nature only by his ability to clothe in images the reality given by the senses. But Nietzsche had been wrong, Klages maintained, to regard this image-making ability as necessarily acting in the service of vital forces. In fact, he argued, man's ability to conceive a world in the imagination and to present this imagined world as a project or possible attainment against lived experience was unnatural and, in the end, profoundly hostile to life itself. Human life, for Klages, differed from animal life in general by virtue of the emergence in man of spirit (*Geist*); man's capacity to think and to will provided the source of his estrangement from the world and the cause of his peculiar psychic illnesses.

Animal life is possessed of both body (*Leib*) and soul (*Seele*), whose functions constitute "genuine processes." "The Body finds expression in the process of sensation and in the impulse towards movement, the Soul in the process of contemplation and in the impulse to formation (that is, to the magical *or* mechanical realization of images) … ." The processes of body and soul express the "eternal" life force, which is characterized by spontaneous creativity and flows beneath individual duration. In man, however, spirit appears, characterized by the "act of apprehension and the act of willing," which are in turn the origin of ego, utterly lacking in animals and impelling man to the "unnatural" desire for immortality "or, more briefly, the urge to self-preservation."

This unnatural urge to self-preservation in man creates the tensions of human life. Man is a field whereon animal consciousness and human consciousness vie for supremacy. The former promotes the impulse to return to nature, expressed in the quest for "eternal life," while the latter promotes the life-destructive impulse to transcend the animal condition, reflected in science, religion, philosophy, and even art. The different quanta of soul and spirit present within an individual account for differences in character. Characterology, which is the study of these differences, constructs a typology of attitudes and structural forms as manifested in different egos. Most men live in the middle range of a spectrum of characterological types that runs from an almost total repression of spirit, as in primitive peoples, to an almost total repression of bodily forces, as in the asceticism of the redemptive religions. But in the science of character, Klages hoped, the true nature of the struggle between life and spirit raging in the individual would be clarified, the disastrous consequences of the triumph of spirit over life would be revealed, and science, art, and religion would be turned upon the spirit, destroy it, and lead to the dissolution of the individual ego in the undifferentiated nature out of which it had unnaturally emerged.

See also Carus, Carl Gustav; Goethe, Johann Wolfgang von; Heidegger, Martin; Jünger, Ernst; Lipps, Theodor; Nietzsche, Friedrich; Psychology; Spengler, Oswald; Vitalism.

Bibliography

Works by Klages include *Prinzipien der Charakterologie* (Leipzig, 1910), of which the 4th and subsequent editions are titled *Grundlagen der Charakterkunde* (11th ed., Bonn, 1951). *The Science of Character*, a translation of the 5th and 6th editions of this work, was prepared by W. H. Johnson (London: Allen and Unwin, 1929). Other writings are *Handschrift und Charakter* (Leipzig, 1917); *Die psychologischen Errungenschaften Nietzsches* (Leipzig: J. A. Barth, 1926); *Der Geist als Widersacher der Seele,* 3 vols. (Leipzig: J. A. Barth, 1929–1932); *Graphologie* (Heidelberg, 1931); *Geist und Leben* (Berlin, 1935); *Ursprünge der Seelenforschung* (Leipzig: P. Reclam, 1942) and *Die Sprache als Quelle der Seelen-Kunde* (Zürich, 1948).

For works on Klages see Max Bense, *Anti-Klages* (Berlin, 1937); K. Haeberlein, *Einführung in die Forschungsergebnisse von Klages* (Kampen, 1934); Herbert Hönel, ed., *Ludwig Klages: Erforscher und Künder. Festschrift zum 75. Geburtstage* (Linz: Österreichischer, 1947); Hans Kasdorff, *Um Seele und Geist: Ein Wegweiser zum Hauptwerk von Ludwig Klages* (Munich, 1954); Hans Prinzhorn, ed., *Die Wissenschaft am Scheidewege von Leben und Geist: Ludwig Klages zum 60.*

Geburtstag (Leipzig, 1932); Ernest Sellière, *De la déesse nature à la déesse vie* (Paris, 1931); and Jean Toulemonde, *La caractérologie* (Paris: Payot, 1951).

Hayden V. White (1967)

KLEIST, HEINRICH VON
(1777–1811)

Heinrich von Kleist, a German dramatist, poet, and novelist, was born in Frankfurt on the Oder. Following a family tradition, Kleist entered the Prussian military service at fourteen, but he left, dissatisfied, in 1799. Uncertain what profession to adopt, Kleist prepared himself for the university by studying privately philosophy, mathematics, and classical languages. An intensive study of Immanuel Kant, or perhaps of Johann Gottlieb Fichte, led to a spiritual crisis in March 1801. The relativity of all knowledge seemed to Kleist to render life, especially a life dedicated to the pursuit of knowledge, pointless. In disgust he discontinued his studies and journeyed to Paris and Switzerland. His decision to pursue a literary career led to a second crisis: Afraid that he had no talent, he burned his tragedy *Robert Guiskard* in 1803. A period of restless activity followed. In 1805 he obtained a minor civil service position in Königsberg, which relieved him of his immediate worries. His two comedies, *Amphitryon* and *Der zerbrochene Krug,* were written at this time. Eager to aid the anti-Napoleonic cause he left Königsberg for Berlin, where in 1807 he was seized as a spy and sent to prison in France. After his sister had obtained his release, Kleist made an attempt to establish himself in Dresden from 1807 to 1809. With Adam Müller he founded the literary magazine *Phöbus*, which, however, soon failed. Attempts to help the patriotic cause with his literary efforts (*Hermannsschlacht*, 1808) met with little response. He returned to Berlin, where for a time he published the *Abendblätter*. When this project also failed, partly because of political pressure, Kleist was left without means. On November 21, 1811, Kleist committed suicide with Henriette Vogel near Berlin.

Kleist's reading of Kant taught him that all attempts to penetrate the veil of phenomena were futile, that the world possesses no higher meaning. In his first play, *Die Familie Schroffenstein* (1803), love, the only value, is destroyed by the force of illusion and circumstance—a theme that was to recur in such stories as *Die Verlobung in St. Domingo* and *Das Erdbeben in Chile*. Like G. W. F. Hegel, Kleist saw life as essentially tragic, but unlike Hegel, he saw tragedy in absurdity, in the indifference of the world to man's demands for love and meaning.

Kleist's heroes confront this absurdity with demonic defiance. Thus Michael Kohlhaas, in the novella of the same name (1810), becomes inhuman in his pursuit of justice; and the heroines of Kleist's plays *Penthesilea* (1808) and *Das Käthchen von Heilbronn* (1810) become inhuman in their pursuit of love—one by being totally aggressive, the other by being totally submissive. In his last play, *Der Prinz von Homburg* (1810), Kleist attempted to oppose the order provided by the state to the uncertainties of the human situation. The prince disobeys orders, wins a battle, and yet is condemned to death. At first incapable of understanding this judgment and driven only by his fear of death, he regains control of himself when made judge of his own actions, and freely accepts the verdict.

See also Fichte, Johann Gottlieb; Hegel, Georg Wilhelm Friedrich; Kant, Immanuel; Love.

Bibliography

WORKS BY KLEIST

Werke, 5 vols. Edited by E. Schmidt. Leipzig, 1905; 2nd ed., 7 vols., edited by G. Minde-Pouet, Leipzig: Bibliographisches institut, 1936–.

Werke, 2 vols. Edited by H. Sembdner. Munich, 1961.

The Marquise of O, and Other Stories. Translated by Martin Greenberg. New York: Criterion, 1960.

TRANSLATIONS OF PLAYS

"The Feud of the Schroffensteins." Translated by M. J. and L. M. Price. *Poet Lore* (Boston) 27 (5) (1916): 457–576.

The Prince of Homburg. Translated by C. E. Passage. New York: Liberal Arts Press, 1956.

Katie of Heilbronn. Translated by A. H. Hughes. Hartford, CT: Trinity College, 1960.

The Broken Pitcher. Translated by B. Q. Morgan. Chapel Hill: University of North Carolina Press, 1961.

WORKS ON KLEIST

Blankenagel, J. C. *The Dramas of Heinrich von Kleist.* Chapel Hill: University of North Carolina Press, 1931.

Blöcker, Günter. *Heinrich von Kleist oder Das absolute Ich.* Berlin: Argon, 1960.

Cassirer, Ernst. *Idee und Gestalt.* Berlin: Cassirer, 1921.

Fricke, Gerhard. *Gefühl und Schicksal bei Heinrich von Kleist.* Berlin, 1929.

March, Richard. *Heinrich von Kleist.* Cambridge, U.K.: Bowes and Bowes, 1954.

Muth, Ludwig. *Kleist und Kant.* Cologne, 1954.

Silz, W. *Heinrich von Kleist.* Philadelphia: University of Pennsylvania Press, 1962.

Stahl, E. L. *Heinrich von Kleist's Dramas.* Oxford: Blackwell, 1948.

Witkop, Philipp. *Heinrich von Kleist.* Leipzig: Haessel, 1922.

Karsten Harries (1967)

KNOWLEDGE, A PRIORI

The prominence of the a priori within traditional epistemology is largely due to the influence of Immanuel Kant's *Critique of Pure Reason* (1965), where he introduces a conceptual framework that involves three distinctions: the epistemic distinction between a priori and empirical (or a posteriori) knowledge; the metaphysical distinction between necessary and contingent propositions; and the semantic distinction between analytic and synthetic propositions. Within this framework, Kant poses four questions:

1. What is a priori knowledge?

2. Is there a priori knowledge?

3. What is the relationship between the a priori and the necessary?

4. Is there synthetic a priori knowledge?

These questions remain at the center of the contemporary debate.

Kant maintains that a priori knowledge is "independent of experience," contrasting it with a posteriori knowledge, which has its "sources" in experience (1965, p. 43). He offers two criteria for a priori knowledge, necessity and strict universality, which he claims are inseparable from one another. Invoking the first, he argues that mathematical knowledge is a priori. Kant's claim that necessity is a criterion of the a priori entails:

(K1) All knowledge of necessary propositions is a priori.

He also appears to endorse

(K2) All propositions known a priori are necessary.

Kant maintains that all propositions of the form "All A are B" are either analytic or synthetic: analytic if the predicate is contained in the subject; synthetic if it is not. Utilizing this distinction, he argues that

(K3) All knowledge of analytic propositions is a priori; and

(K4) Some propositions known a priori are synthetic.

In support of (K4), Kant claims that the predicate terms of "7 + 5 = 12" and "The straight line between two points is the shortest" are not contained in their respective subjects.

THE CONCEPT

Kant provides the core of the traditional conception of the a priori. When he speaks of the source of knowledge, he does not mean the source of the belief in question, but the source of its justification. Hence, according to Kant,

> (APK) S knows a priori that p if and only if S's belief that p is justified a priori and the other conditions on knowledge are satisfied; and

> (APJ) S's belief that p is justified a priori if and only if S's justification for the belief that p does not depend on experience.

(APJ) has been criticized from two directions. First, some maintain that it is not sufficiently informative; it tells one what a priori justification is not, but not what it is. Hence, Laurence BonJour (1985) rejects (APJ) in favor of

> (AP1) S's belief that p is justified a priori just in case S intuitively "sees" or apprehends that p is necessarily true.

Alvin Plantinga (1993) and BonJour (1998) offer variants of (AP1). Second, others maintain that the sense of *dependence* relevant to a priori justification requires articulation and offer two competing accounts. Albert Casullo (2003) endorses

> (AP2) S's belief that p is justified a priori if and only if S's belief that p is nonexperientially justified (i.e., justified by some nonexperiential source).

Hilary Putnam (1983) and Philip Kitcher (1983) favor

> (AP3) S's belief that p is justified a priori if and only if S's belief that p is nonexperientially justified and cannot be defeated by experience.

(AP1) and (AP3) face serious objections.

The term *see* is used metaphorically in (AP1). Let us assume that it shares with the literal use of *see* one basic feature: "S sees that p" entails "S believes that p." Hence, (AP1) has the consequence that if S's belief that p is justified a priori then S believes that p is necessarily true. This consequence faces two problems. Suppose that Sam is a mathematician who believes some generally accepted theorem T on the basis of a valid proof. Presumably, Sam's belief is justified. But suppose that Sam is also a serious student of philosophy who has come to doubt the cogency of the distinction between necessary and contingent propositions and, as a consequence, refrains from modal beliefs. It is implausible to maintain that Sam's belief that T is not justified a priori merely because of his

views about a controversial metaphysical thesis. (AP1) is also threatened with a regress. It entails that if S's belief that p is justified a priori then S believes that necessarily p. Must S's belief that necessarily p be justified? If not, it is hard to see why it is a necessary condition of having an a priori justified belief that p. If so, then presumably it is justified a priori. But for S's belief that necessarily p to be justified a priori, S must believe that necessarily necessarily p, and the same question arises with respect to the latter belief. Must it be justified or not? Hence, (AP1) must either maintain that having an unjustified belief that necessarily p is a necessary condition of having a justified belief that p, or face an infinite regress of justified modal beliefs.

(AP3) is also open to serious objection. Saul Kripke (1980) and Kitcher (1983) maintain that an adequate conception of a priori knowledge should allow for the possibility that a person knows empirically some proposition that he or she can know a priori. (AP3) precludes this possibility. Assume that

> (A) S knows empirically that p and S can know a priori that p.

From the left conjunct of (A), it follows that

> (1) S's belief that p is justified$_k$ empirically,

where "justified$_k$" abbreviates "justified to the degree minimally sufficient for knowledge." Consider now the empirical sources that have been alleged to justify mathematical propositions empirically: counting objects, reading a textbook, consulting a mathematician, and computer results. (Tyler Burge [1993] discusses the relationship between testimony and a priori knowledge.) Each of these sources is fallible in an important respect. The justification each confers on a belief that p is defeasible by an empirically justified overriding defeater; that is, by an empirically justified belief that not-p. If S's belief that p is justified by counting a collection of objects and arriving at a particular result, then it is possible that S recounts the collection and arrives at a different result. If S's belief that p is justified by a textbook (or mathematician or computer result) that states that p, then it is possible that S encounters a different textbook (or mathematician or computer result) that states that not-p. In each case, the latter result is an empirically justified overriding defeater for S's original justification. Hence, given the fallible character of empirical justification, it follows that

> (2) S's empirical justification for the belief that p is defeasible by an empirically justified belief that not-p.

(2), however, entails that

(3)   S's belief that not-p is justifiable$_d$ empirically,

where "justifiable$_d$" abbreviates "justifiable to the degree minimally sufficient to defeat S's justified$_k$ belief that p." Furthermore, the conjunction of (AP3) and the right conjunct of (A) entails

(4)   It is not the case that S's nonexperiential justification$_k$ for the belief that p is defeasible by S's empirically justified belief that not-p.

(4), however, entails that

(5)   It is not the case that S's belief that not-p is justifiable$_d$ empirically.

The conjunction of (3) and (5) is a contradiction. Hence, (AP3) is incompatible with (A). (AP2), however, is compatible with (A) since the conjunction of (AP2) and the right conjunct of (A) does not entail (4).

SUPPORTING ARGUMENTS

Kant offers the most influential traditional argument for the existence of a priori knowledge. He holds that necessity is a criterion of the a priori: "[I]f we have a proposition which in being thought is thought as *necessary*, it is an a priori judgment" (1965, p. 43). He then argues that "mathematical propositions, strictly so called, are always judgments a priori, not empirical; because they carry with them necessity, which cannot be derived from experience" (p. 52). Kant's argument can be presented as follows:

(K1)   All knowledge of necessary propositions is a priori.

(K2)   Mathematical propositions are necessary.

(K3)   Therefore, knowledge of mathematical propositions is a priori.

Premise (K1) is ambiguous. There are two ways of reading it:

(K1T)   All knowledge of the truth value of necessary propositions is a priori; or

(K1G)   All knowledge of the general modal status of necessary propositions is a priori.

Kant supports (K1) with the observation that "[e]xperience teaches us that a thing is so and so, but not that it cannot be otherwise" (1965, p. 52). This observation supports (K1G) but not (K1T), since Kant allows that experience can provide evidence that something is the case, but denies that it can provide evidence that something

must be the case. The conclusion of the argument, however, is that knowledge of the truth value of mathematical propositions, such as that $7 + 5 = 12$, is a priori.

Kant's argument can now be articulated as follows:

(K1G)   All knowledge of the general modal status of necessary propositions is a priori.

(K2)   Mathematical propositions are necessary.

(K3T)   Therefore, knowledge of the truth value of mathematical propositions is a priori.

The argument involves this assumption:

(KA)   If the general modal status of p is knowable only a priori, then the truth value of p is knowable only a priori.

(KA), however, is false. If one can know only a priori that a proposition is necessary, then one can know only a priori that a proposition is contingent. The evidence relevant to determining the latter is the same as that relevant to determining the former. For example, if I determine that "$2 + 2 = 4$" is necessary by trying to conceive of its falsehood and failing, I determine that "Kant is a philosopher" is contingent by trying to conceive of its falsehood and succeeding. However, if my knowledge that "Kant is a philosopher" is contingent is a priori, it does not follow that my knowledge that "Kant is a philosopher" is true is a priori. Clearly, it is a posteriori.

Roderick Chisholm (1977) suggests the following reformulation of Kant's argument:

(K1G)   All knowledge of the general modal status of necessary propositions is a priori.

(K2)   Mathematical propositions are necessary.

(K3G)   Therefore, knowledge of the general modal status of mathematical propositions is a priori.

This argument faces a different problem. Why accept Kant's claim that experience can teach one only what is the case? A good deal of one's ordinary practical knowledge and the bulk of one's scientific knowledge provide clear counterexamples to the claim. My knowledge that my pen will fall if I drop it does not provide information about what is the case for the antecedent is contrary to fact. Scientific laws are not mere descriptions of the actual world. They support counterfactual conditionals and, hence, provide information beyond what is true of the actual world. In the absence of further support, Kant's claim should be rejected.

A second strategy for defending the existence of a priori knowledge is offered by proponents of logical empiricism, such as Alfred Jules Ayer (1952) and Carl Hempel (1972), who reject John Stuart Mill's contention that knowledge of basic mathematical propositions, such as that $2 \times 5 = 10$, is based on induction from observed cases. Both draw attention to the fact that if one is justified in believing that some general proposition is true on the basis of experience, then contrary experiences should justify one in believing that the proposition is false. But no experiences would justify one in believing that a mathematical proposition, such as that $2 \times 5 = 10$, is false. Suppose, for example, that I count what appear to be five pairs of shoes and arrive at the result that there are only nine shoes. Ayer contends that

> [o]ne would say that I was wrong in supposing that there were five pairs of objects to start with, or that one of the objects had been taken away while I was counting, or that two of them had coalesced, or that I had counted wrongly. One would adopt as an explanation whatever empirical hypothesis fitted in best with the accredited facts. The one explanation which would in no circumstances be adopted is that ten is not always the product of two and five. (1952, pp. 75–76)

Since Ayer maintains that one would not regard any experiences as evidence that a mathematical proposition is false, he concludes that no experiences provide evidence that they are true.

Ayer's argument can be stated as follows:

(A1) No experiences provide evidence that mathematical propositions are false.

(A2) If no experiences provide evidence that mathematical propositions are false, then no experiences provide evidence that they are true.

(A3) Therefore, no experiences provide evidence that mathematical propositions are true.

Ayer's defense of (A1) is weak in several respects. First, it does not take into account the number of apparent confirming instances of the proposition in question. Second, it involves only a single disconfirming instance of the proposition. Third, the hypotheses that are invoked to explain away the apparent disconfirming instance are not subjected to an independent empirical test. In a situation where there is a strong background of supporting evidence for an inductive generalization and an isolated disconfirming instance, it is reasonable to discount the disconfirming instance as apparent and to explain it away on whatever empirical grounds are most plausible.

The case against premise (A1) can be considerably strengthened by revising Ayer's scenario as follows: Increase the number of disconfirming instances of the proposition so that it is large relative to the number of confirming instances; and subject the hypotheses invoked to explain away the apparent disconfirming instances to independent tests that fail to support them. Let us now suppose that one has experienced a large number of apparent disconfirming instances of the proposition that $2 \times 5 = 10$ and, furthermore, that empirical investigations of the hypotheses invoked to explain away these disconfirming instances produce little, if any, support for the hypotheses. Given these revisions, Ayer can continue to endorse premise (A1) only at the expense of holding empirical beliefs that are at odds with the available evidence.

OPPOSING ARGUMENTS

Radical empiricism is the view that denies the existence of a priori knowledge. Its most famous proponents are John Stuart Mill and Willard Van Orman Quine. One common strategy that radical empiricists employ in arguing against the existence of a priori knowledge is to consider the most prominent examples of propositions alleged to be knowable only a priori and to maintain that such propositions are known empirically. Since mathematical knowledge has received the most attention, this entry will focus on it.

Mill's (1973) account of mathematical knowledge is a version of inductive empiricism. Inductive empiricism with respect to a domain of knowledge involves two theses. First, some propositions within that domain are epistemically more basic than the others, in the sense that the nonbasic propositions derive their justification from the basic propositions via inference. Second, the basic propositions are known by a process of inductive inference from observed cases. Mill's focus is on the basic propositions of arithmetic and geometry, the axioms and definitions of each domain. His primary thesis is that they are known by induction from observed cases.

Mill's position faces formidable objections, such as those offered by Gottlob Frege (1974). Let us assume, however, that these objections can be deflected and that Mill offers a plausible inductive empiricist account of mathematical knowledge to assess how this concession bears on the existence of a priori knowledge. If Mill is right, then all epistemically basic propositions of arithmetic and geometry are justified on the basis of observation and inductive generalization. It follows that Kant's claim that mathematical knowledge cannot be derived from experience is wrong. It does not follow, however, that the claim that such knowledge is a priori is wrong. From the fact that mathematical knowledge is or can be derived from experience, it does not immediately follow that such knowledge is not or cannot be derived from some nonexperiential source. Mill is aware of the gap in his argument and attempts to close it with the following observations:

> They cannot, however, but allow that the truth of the axiom, Two straight lines cannot inclose a space, even if evident independently of experience, is also evident from experience. … Where then is the necessity for assuming that our recognition of these truths has a different origin from the rest of our knowledge, when its existence is perfectly accounted for by supposing its origin to be the same? … The burden of proof lies on the advocates of the contrary opinion: it is for them to point out some fact, inconsistent with the supposition that this part of our knowledge of nature is derived from the same sources as every other part. (1973, pp. 231–232)

Mill moves from the premise that inductive empiricism provides an account of knowledge of mathematical axioms to the stronger conclusion that knowledge of such axioms is not a priori by appealing to a version of the explanatory simplicity principle: If a putative source of knowledge is not necessary to explain knowledge of the propositions within some domain, then it is not a source of knowledge of the propositions within that domain. Mill's argument can be articulated as follows:

(M1) Inductive empiricism provides an account of mathematical knowledge based on inductive generalization from observed cases.

(M2) φ is a source of knowledge for some domain D only if φ is necessary to explain knowledge of some propositions within D.

(M3) Therefore, mathematical knowledge is not a priori.

The burden of the argument is carried by (M2), the explanatory simplicity principle.

Casullo (forthcoming) maintains that the explanatory simplicity principle conflicts with a familiar fact of one's epistemic life. The justification of some of one's beliefs is overdetermined by different sources. There are some beliefs for which one has more than one justifica-

tion, each of those justifications derives from a different source, and each, in the absence of the others, is sufficient to justify the belief in question. For example, I have misplaced my wallet again and wonder where I might have left it. I suddenly recall having left it on the kitchen table when I came in from the garage last night. My recollection justifies my belief that my wallet is on the kitchen table. However, just to be sure, I walk out to the kitchen to check. To my relief, I see my wallet on the table. My seeing my wallet on the table also justifies my belief that my wallet is on the table. So here my justification is overdetermined by different sources. If the justification of my belief is overdetermined by two different sources, it follows that my belief is justified by two different sources. Hence, in the absence of an argument against the possibility of epistemic overdetermination, Mill's appeal to the explanatory simplicity principle simply begs the question.

Quine rejects inductive empiricism. He rejects the idea that there are basic mathematical propositions that, taken in isolation, are directly justified by observation and inductive generalization. Quine's account of mathematical knowledge is a version of holistic empiricism. Mathematical propositions are components of scientific theories. They are not tested directly against observation, but only indirectly via their observational consequences. Moreover, they do not have observational consequences in isolation, but only in conjunction with the other propositions of the theory. Hence, according to holistic empiricism, entire scientific theories, including their mathematical components, are indirectly confirmed or disconfirmed by experience via their observational consequences.

The main concern in this entry is not to assess the cogency of Quine's account of mathematical knowledge, but to determine whether it provides an argument against the existence of a priori knowledge. The argument of Quine's classic paper "Two Dogmas of Empiricism" (1963) remains controversial (for further discussion, see Boghossian 1996). The stated target of his attack is a conception of analyticity inspired by Frege: A statement is analytic if it can be turned into a logical truth by replacing synonyms with synonyms. Quine's contentions can be summarized as follows:

(1) Definition presupposes synonymy rather than explaining it.

(2) Interchangeability *salva veritate* is not a sufficient condition of cognitive synonymy in an extensional language.

(3) Semantic rules do not explain "Statement S is analytic for language L," with variable "S" and "L."

(4) The verification theory of meaning provides an account of statement synonymy that presupposes reductionism, but reductionism fails.

(5) Any statement can be held to be true come what may. No statement is immune to revision.

Quine's contentions appear to be directed at the concept of synonymy and the doctrine of reductionism. They are not explicitly directed at a priori knowledge. Hence, if "Two Dogmas" does indeed present a challenge to the existence of a priori knowledge, then some additional premise is necessary that connects those contentions to the a priori.

According to the traditional reading of his argument, Quine's contentions constitute an extended attack on the cogency of the analytic-synthetic distinction. Quine's ultimate goal is to undermine the central claim of the logical empiricist tradition:

(LE) All a priori knowledge is of analytic truths.

On this reading, (LE) provides the connection between his contentions and the rejection of the a priori. Let us grant that Quine's goal is to undermine (LE) and that he successfully challenges the cogency of the analytic-synthetic distinction. Does it follow that there is no a priori knowledge? No. (LE) is a thesis about the nature of the propositions alleged to be known a priori. If Quine is right, then (LE) itself is incoherent. But from the fact that a thesis about the nature of propositions known a priori is incoherent, it does not follow that there is no a priori knowledge.

An alternative response is to take (LE) as a conceptual claim; that is, to take it as claiming that the concept of a priori knowledge involves the concept of analytic truth. On this reading, the incoherence of the concept of analytic truth entails the incoherence of the concept of a priori knowledge. This response, however, rests on a false conceptual claim. The concept of a priori knowledge does not explicitly involve the concept of analytic truth. One might argue that it implicitly involves the concept of analytic truth by maintaining that all a priori knowledge is of necessary truths; and endorsing some version of the so-called linguistic theory of necessary truth. There are, however, two problems with this argument. First, the concept of a priori knowledge does not involve, either explicitly or implicitly, the concept of necessary truth.

Second, there is no plausible analysis of the concept of necessary truth in terms of the concept of analytic truth.

Some champions of "Two Dogmas" propose an alternative connection between Quine's contentions and the rejection of the a priori. Putnam (1983) maintains that Quine's contentions are directed toward two different targets. The initial contentions are directed toward the semantic concept of analyticity. Contention (5), however, is directed toward the concept of a statement that is confirmed no matter what, which is not a semantic concept. The concept of a statement that is confirmed no matter what is an epistemic concept. It is a concept of apriority. Kitcher endorses Putnam's reading of Quine's argument, "If we can know a priori that *p* then no experience could deprive us of our warrant to believe that *p*" (1983, p. 80). But, according to Quine, no statement is immune from revision. Hence, the Putnam-Kitcher version of Quine's argument can be stated as follows:

(Q1) No statement is immune to revision in light of recalcitrant experience.

(Q2) If S's belief that p is justified a priori, then S's belief that p is not rationally revisable in light of any experiential evidence.

(Q3) Therefore, no knowledge is a priori.

The argument fails. Premise (Q2) is open to the objection presented against (AP3) in the first section.

THE EXPLANATORY CHALLENGE

A more recent challenge to the a priori derives from Quine's influential "Epistemology Naturalized" (1969). Epistemic naturalism comes in many different forms. The most radical form advocates the replacement of philosophical investigations into the nature of human knowledge with scientific investigations. More moderate forms advocate that philosophical theories concerning human knowledge cohere with scientific theories. Paul Benacerraf (1973), for example, argues that the truth conditions for mathematical statements make reference to abstract entities and that knowing a statement requires that one be causally related to the entities referred to by its truth conditions. Since abstract entities cannot stand in causal relations, one cannot know mathematical statements. The argument raises a more general challenge to the possibility of a priori knowledge since proponents of the a priori (apriorists) generally hold that most, if not all, a priori knowledge, is of necessary truths; and that the truth conditions of necessary truths make reference to abstract entities. Although some reject the argument on the grounds that its epistemic premise appears to presuppose the generally rejected causal theory of knowledge, others, such as Hartry Field (1989), maintain that it points to a deeper problem. In the absence of an explanation of how it is possible to have knowledge of abstract entities, a priori knowledge remains mysterious.

The explanatory challenge goes beyond a commitment to epistemic naturalism. It derives support from broader epistemological considerations. To appreciate the full import of the challenge, two issues regarding the existence of a priori knowledge must be distinguished. Apriorists typically maintain that one knows certain logical, mathematical, and conceptual truths and that such knowledge is a priori. Radical skeptics deny that one has knowledge of the truths in question. Radical empiricists, however, are not radical skeptics. They do not deny that one knows the truths in question. Radical empiricists only deny that one's knowledge of these truths is a priori. Therefore, the primary dispute between apriorists and radical empiricists is over the source of the knowledge in question. They offer two competing theories of the source of the knowledge in question, and each maintains that its theory offers the better explanation of the knowledge in question. Therefore, to support their primary contention, apriorists must provide supporting evidence for the claim that there exist nonexperiential sources of justification and that such sources explain how one knows the truths in question.

BonJour (1998) and Ernest Sosa (2000) offer philosophical supporting evidence, a mix of phenomenological and a priori considerations. Casullo (2003) argues that a more promising approach is to supplement the philosophical evidence with evidence based on empirical investigations. Before empirical evidence can be enlisted to support the case for the a priori, however, additional philosophical work is necessary. The first step is to provide (1) a generally accepted phenomenological description of the cognitive states that noninferentially justify beliefs a priori, (2) the type of beliefs they justify, and (3) the conditions under which they justify the beliefs in question. Apriorists typically defend the claim that there are nonexperiential sources of justification by reflecting on their own cognitive situations and identifying phenomenologically distinct states, which they claim justify certain beliefs a priori. A cursory survey of the descriptions of these states offered by different theorists reveals wide variation. George Bealer (1996) and Sosa (1996) both maintain that the cognitive states that justify a priori are aptly described as *seemings*, but they offer different phenomenological descriptions of seemings. Plantinga

(1993) and BonJour (1998) maintain that the states in question are more aptly described as *seeings*, but they offer different phenomenological descriptions of seeings. Bealer agrees with BonJour that the cognitive states that justify a priori are irreducible, but disagrees with him over the character of the states. On the contrary, Sosa agrees with Plantinga that the states are reducible to more familiar cognitive states, but disagrees with him over the character of the reducing states.

There is also wide variation among apriorists over the scope of beliefs justified a priori. Within the context of arguing against radical empiricism, the focus is on stock examples such as elementary logical or mathematical propositions and some familiar examples of alleged synthetic a priori truths. Few apriorists, however, believe that a priori justification is limited to those cases. Consequently, they must provide a more complete specification of the range of beliefs alleged to be justified by such cognitive states. One issue requires particular attention. The examples of a priori knowledge typically cited by apriorists are necessary truths. But here it is important to distinguish between knowledge of the truth value and knowledge of the general modal status of necessary propositions. A critical question now emerges: What is the target of a priori justification? Is it the general modal status of a proposition, its truth value, or both? If it is both, two further questions arise. Are beliefs about the truth value of a necessary proposition and beliefs about its general modal status justified by the same cognitive state or different cognitive states? Are some beliefs about the truth value of contingent propositions justified a priori?

Once the philosophical work is complete, the project of providing empirical supporting evidence for the a priori can be pursued. This involves providing (1) evidence that the cognitive states identified at the phenomenological level are associated with processes of a single type or relevantly similar types; (2) evidence that the associated processes play a role in producing or sustaining the beliefs they are alleged to justify; (3) evidence that the associated processes are truth-conducive; and (4) an explanation of how the associated processes produce the beliefs they are alleged to justify. The third area of empirical investigation offers the prospect of supporting the claim that there are nonexperiential sources of justification. Many prominent apriorists, including Bealer, BonJour, Plantinga, and Sosa, maintain that truth conduciveness is a necessary condition for epistemic justification. Moreover, even those who deny this concede that evidence that a source of beliefs is error conducive defeats whatever justification that the source confers on the beliefs that it justifies. The claim that a source of beliefs is truth conducive or, more minimally, that it is not error conducive is a contingent empirical claim that can be supported only by empirical investigation.

The fourth area of empirical investigation offers the prospect of addressing the explanatory challenge. First, causal-perceptual models appear to be of limited utility in explaining how nonexperiential sources of justification provide cognitive access to necessary truths. Empirical investigation into human cognition offers the prospect of uncovering alternative models of cognitive access that can be utilized in the case of nonexperiential sources. Second, investigation of the specific cognitive processes associated with the cognitive states alleged to justify a priori may provide a better understanding of how the processes in question produce true beliefs about their subject matter. This understanding, in turn, is the key to providing a noncausal explanation of how the states in question provide cognitive access to the subject matter of the beliefs they produce. Third, although apriorists deny that epistemology is a chapter of science, they acknowledge that both epistemology and science contribute to the overall understanding of human knowledge. Establishing that the cognitive processes invoked by their epistemological theory are underwritten by their scientific commitments strengthens the apriorist's overall theory by demonstrating the coherence of its components.

See also Analyticity; A Priori and A Posteriori; Ayer, Alfred Jules; Chisholm, Roderick; Field, Hartry; Frege, Gottlob; Hempel, Carl Gustav; Kant, Immanuel; Knowledge and Modality; Kripke, Saul; Mathematics, Foundations of; Mill, John Stuart; Plantinga, Alvin; Putnam, Hilary; Quine, Willard Van Orman; Sosa, Ernest.

Bibliography

Ayer, A. J. *Language, Truth and Logic.* New York: Dover, 1952.

Bealer, George. "A Priori Knowledge and the Scope of Philosophy." *Philosophical Studies* 81 (1996): 121–142.

Benacerraf, Paul. "Mathematical Truth." *Journal of Philosophy* 70 (1973): 661–679.

Boghossian, Paul A. "Analyticity Reconsidered." *Noûs* 30 (1996): 360–391.

BonJour, Laurence. *In Defense of Pure Reason.* New York: Cambridge University Press, 1998.

BonJour, Laurence. *The Structure of Empirical Knowledge.* Cambridge, MA: Harvard University Press, 1985.

Burge, Tyler. "Content Preservation." *Philosophical Review* 102 (1993): 457–488.

Casullo, Albert. *A Priori Justification.* New York: Oxford University Press, 2003.

Casullo, Albert. "Epistemic Overdetermination and A Priori Justification." *Philosophical Perspectives* 19 (2005): 41–58.

Chisholm, Roderick M. *Theory of Knowledge.* 2nd ed. Englewood Cliffs, NJ: Prentice-Hall, 1977.

Field, Hartry. *Realism, Mathematics, and Modality.* Oxford, U.K.: Blackwell, 1989.

Frege, Gottlob. *The Foundations of Arithmetic.* 2nd ed. Translated by J. L. Austin. Evanston, IL: Northwestern University Press, 1974.

Hempel, Carl. "On the Nature of Mathematical Truth." In *Necessary Truth,* edited by R. C. Sleigh. Englewood Cliffs, NJ: Prentice-Hall, 1972.

Kant, Immanuel. *Critique of Pure Reason.* Translated by Norman Kemp Smith. New York: St Martin's Press, 1965.

Kitcher, Philip. *The Nature of Mathematical Knowledge.* New York: Oxford University Press, 1983.

Kripke, Saul. *Naming and Necessity.* Cambridge, MA: Harvard University Press, 1980.

Mill, John Stuart. *A System of Logic,* edited by J. M. Robson. Toronto, Canada: University of Toronto Press, 1973.

Plantinga, Alvin. *Warrant and Proper Function.* New York: Oxford University Press, 1993.

Putnam, Hilary. "'Two Dogmas' Revisited." In *Realism and Reason: Philosophical Papers.* Vol. 3. New York: Cambridge University Press, 1983.

Quine, W. V. O. "Epistemology Naturalized." In *Ontological Relativity and Other Essays.* New York: Columbia University Press, 1969.

Quine, W. V. O. "Two Dogmas of Empiricism." In *From a Logical Point of View.* 2nd ed. New York: Harper and Row, 1963.

Sosa, Ernest. "Modal and Other A Priori Epistemology: How Can We Know What Is Possible and What Impossible?" *Southern Journal of Philosophy* 38 (Supplement) (2000): 1–16.

Sosa, Ernest. "Rational Intuition: Bealer on its Nature and Epistemic Status." *Philosophical Studies* 81 (1996): 151–162.

Albert Casullo (2005)

KNOWLEDGE, THE PRIORITY OF

One fairly specific understanding of the priority of knowledge is the idea that instead of trying to explain knowledge in terms of belief plus truth, justification, and something, we should explain belief in terms of knowledge. This is to reverse the usual explanatory priority of knowledge and belief. This fairly specific idea generalizes in two directions. (1) Perhaps we should explain other notions in terms of knowledge as well. Some possibilities include assertion, justification or evidence, mental content, and intentional action. (2) Perhaps we could explain other relatively internal states like intentions, attempts, and appearances in terms of their more obviously external counterparts: intentional action and perception.

That knowledge is prior to belief has historically been a minority opinion. The idea that a belief, and the mind more generally, is what it is regardless of any actual connection to the external world is still widely accepted. Accepting the priority of knowledge constitutes a rejection of the picture of the mind as a self-contained, inner realm.

UNDERSTANDING BELIEF

Bernard Williams (1973) tries to explain the impossibility of believing at will in terms of the idea that belief aims at the truth. Suppose you are anxious about tomorrow's weather but have no access to a weather forecast or any other evidence. If you want to reduce your anxiety, then you might, if it was in your power to do so, simply decide to believe that it will be sunny tomorrow. But if you knew that this attempted belief was based not on evidence or any apparent connection to the facts, but on a decision, then it would be hard for you to see your attempted belief as aiming at the truth. It would also be hard for you to see it as a belief. So, perhaps, it could not be a belief.

Let us agree that in this particular case seeing your attempted belief as the result of a decision seriously casts doubt on the possibility of its being a belief. Is this best explained by the idea that belief aims at the truth? Since you have no evidence about the weather, the problem cannot be that you have reason to think the attempted belief will fail to achieve this aim. On the contrary, you have every reason to think it is at least possible that it will achieve this aim. So what keeps you from aiming at it?

If you merely guess that a flipped coin will come up heads, then you probably do not believe that it will. Guesses are not beliefs. But guessing aims at the truth. In guessing you are trying to get it right, and if you succeed, this is as good as a guess can get. When you see your attempted belief as the result of a decision, you may still be hoping, trying, or aiming to get things right. But you know believing is not epistemically justified for you in that instance. Whatever practical reasons you may have for believing that p, you have no evidence that p. It is seeing your state as unjustified while remaining in it that seriously casts doubt on the possibility of its being a belief. To understand belief, we need a connection between belief and justification, not just between belief and truth.

Suppose that someone has an unjustified, true belief. If belief aims at the truth, then this belief has achieved its aim. Perhaps justification is a good guide or a means to the truth. But if truth is the aim, and this belief has achieved that aim by other means, then epistemic justifi-

cation or lack thereof is irrelevant to the evaluation of this belief. So if belief merely aimed at the truth, then it would not be automatically subject to evaluation from the epistemic point of view. If belief aims at knowledge, however, instead of mere truth, then it is clear why it is subject to this kind of evaluation. Unjustified beliefs may be true, but they cannot constitute knowledge.

Perhaps this does not capture what is meant in saying that belief aims at the truth. When you believe that p, you do not merely hope or try to get things right. In some sense it seems to you as though you already have gotten things right. We do not want to say that if you believe that p, you believe that your belief that p is true. This leads to an infinite number of beliefs. You do not need beliefs about beliefs to have beliefs about the world. But if you do have a view about your views, it must cohere with those views, where coherence involves more than just logical consistency. You can think that your belief that p is true, but you cannot think that your belief that p is false. You cannot assert, "I believe that p, but not p," and you cannot believe it either. This "cannot" is probably a normative "cannot," rather than an expression of logical impossibility.

What goes for error goes for ignorance as well. There is something wrong with assertions of the form "p, but I do not believe that p." Whatever is wrong with these assertions, they would be just as bad in the privacy of your own mind. If you think about Moore-paradoxical statements from the normative perspective, then the same kind of incoherence that is involved in the standard cases also seems to infect the following: p, but I have no reason to believe that p; I believe that p, but I should not believe it; and p, but I am completely unreliable about these things. The belief that p not only conflicts with the belief that you are wrong or that you do not believe that p. It also rules out the belief that you are unjustified or not in a position to know. These first-person facts about belief can be explained by the idea that belief aims at knowledge, but not by the idea that belief aims at truth.

The idea that belief aims at knowledge is a normative claim. From the point of view of belief there is something wrong with false beliefs, but there is also something wrong with unjustified beliefs. There is something wrong with accidentally true beliefs, even when they are justified. But from the point of view of belief, there is nothing wrong with knowledge. For a belief, knowledge is as good as it gets.

ASSERTION AND EVIDENCE

Moore's Paradox tells us not only about the nature of belief but also about the nature of assertion. Peter Unger

(1975) and Timothy Williamson (2000) are both defenders of the priority of knowledge. Both agree that when you assert that p, you not only represent p as being true—you not only represent yourself as believing that p—you also represent yourself as knowing that p. Propositions of the form "p, but I do not know that p" are unassertable because they violate the rule of assertion: assert only what you know. Unlike Williamson, Unger is a radical skeptic. When he tells you not to assert what you do not know, he is basically telling you to keep quiet. The consequences you draw from the priority of knowledge will depend on your general views about knowledge. But the basic idea does not discriminate against skeptics.

Unger and Williamson also agree that there is an important connection between knowledge and justification, though they articulate the connection in different ways. Unger's general idea is that if you are justified in believing that p, then you must know something. More specifically, he believes that if your reason for believing that p is that q, then you must know that q. According to Williamson evidence is knowledge. If your body of evidence consists of a set of propositions, then you must know each member of this set. Both of these views open up the possibility of merely apparent evidence. This is not a problem for Unger, since he thinks that all evidence is merely apparent.

Is there a problem for Williamson? Suppose you have a justified, false belief that p; you infer that q on the basis of this belief; and you think that p is your evidence that q. If evidence is knowledge, then you are simply mistaken in thinking that p is your evidence that q. You may even be mistaken in thinking that you have evidence that q. This can seem problematic if you think that evidence is such that, if you have some, then you are at least in a position to know that you have some; and if you do not have any, then you are in a position to know that you do not have any; and if p is or is not evidence for you to believe that q, then you are in a position to know whether or not this is so.

According to Williamson evidence is not this kind of thing, but neither is anything else. In Williamson's terminology a condition is "luminous" just in case one is in a position to know that the condition obtains, if it does. For example, you could easily be sleeping in a cold room without being able to tell that the room is cold. So the condition of one's being in a cold room is not luminous. But you might have thought that, if you feel cold, seem to see a red wall, or believe that there is life on Mars, then you are in a position to know that you feel cold, seem to see a red wall, or believe that there is life on Mars. In other words you might have thought that these conditions are luminous.

Williamson has a general argument designed to show that there are no nontrivial luminous conditions. Not even the condition that one feels cold is luminous. There is always a potential gap between the facts and your ability to know the facts, even when the facts are about your own present state of mind. So the idea that evidence would not be luminous if only knowledge were or could be evidence is no objection to the view. Evidence would not be luminous regardless what it was. If we do have some other form of privileged access to evidence or the justification of our own beliefs, and if our having that access is incompatible with the idea that evidence is knowledge, then it must be shown.

MENTAL CONTENT

Gilbert Harman (1999) believes that the basic mental notions are knowledge and intentional action. Belief and intention are generalizations of these that allow for error and failure. Harman therefore clearly endorses the priority of knowledge. He also believes that the content of a concept is determined by its functional or conceptual role: its typical or normal connections to perception, its role in practical and theoretical reasoning, and its connection to intentional action. Finally, he accepts content externalism: the view that it is possible for intrinsic duplicates to differ in the contents of their thoughts.

The first two of Harman's views explain why he holds the third. My concept of water is typically caused by perceptions of and hearing about water, and the concept is causally involved in my intentional interactions with water. Suppose that I have an intrinsic duplicate on Hilary Putnam's (1975) Twin Earth. On Twin Earth there is something that looks, smells, tastes, and feels like water but is not water. Call it XYZ. When I interact with water, my twin interacts with XYZ. This difference in our interactions does not influence our intrinsic natures. But it does influence the contents of our thoughts. Unlike me, my twin never perceives or interacts with water. Even if you dragged my twin into my kitchen, he would not intentionally interact with water, nor would he perceive that the water was running. My concept differs in content from my duplicate's concept because the functional roles of the concepts are different. The functional roles of the concepts are different because these roles must be understood in terms of knowledge, perception, and intentional action.

Harman is not the only philosopher to combine the priority of knowledge with a conceptual role account of content. Christopher Peacocke (1999) has a sophisticated version of this view. According to Peacocke epistemically individuated concepts can be individuated, at least in part, in terms of the conditions under which certain judgments involving those concepts would constitute knowledge. Furthermore, every concept is either epistemically individuated, or individuated in part in terms of its relations to epistemically individuated concepts. If epistemically individuated concepts do in fact play this central role in our system of concepts, then the priority of knowledge may provide an explanation of this fact.

The conceptual role theory of content is or is a descendant of the idea that the content of a thought or concept is determined by what Wilfrid Sellars (1956) calls its place in a space of reasons. John McDowell (1996) argues, among other things, that if you take this idea seriously, then thinking of the space of reasons broadly enough to encompass not only beliefs but also knowledge is not an optional extra. There is no purely internal space of reasons. To understand how experience can be part of the logical space of reasons, and so how our thoughts can have any content at all, we need to understand how a subject can be open to the way things manifestly are, where this involves knowing about what is going on around you.

Setting aside conceptual roles, the priority of knowledge may provide an adequacy condition for the theory of content. Suppose there was a kind of content or a kind of representation that could not distinguish a situation in which water is wet from a situation in which something that merely looks, smells, feels, and tastes like water is wet. A picture in the head, qualitatively conceived, may be such a representation. Accepting this kind of representation or content could never constitute knowledge, since there would not be the right kind of distinction between justification and knowledge. If one of your beliefs about barns constitutes knowledge, then it matters whether or not there are fake barns in your neighborhood. If believing something about barns were a matter of accepting one of these phony propositions that cannot distinguish between real and fake barns, then it would not matter whether the barns were real or fake. According to the priority of knowledge, if these representations are not even candidates for knowledge, then they are not to be believed.

CONTACT

What justifies this preoccupation with knowledge? Each account of something in terms of knowledge must of course be judged on its own merits, but is there anything special about knowledge that holds them all together? A true belief will match or accurately represent the world, but knowledge seems to involve a kind of contact with the world. The recognition of the importance of this kind of contact is one of the underlying ideas that unifies these various approaches.

Edmund L. Gettier (1963) shows that justified, true belief alone is not sufficient for knowledge. If a justified, true belief is inferred from a false premise, then it will not constitute knowledge, even if that premise was justified. Not all cases of justified, true belief without knowledge involve inference from a false belief. Alvin I. Goldman (1992) imagines a case in which you look at a barn that is surrounded by realistic barn facades and form the justified, true belief that it is a barn. You do not know even though you are right because you just got lucky. Though you do get lucky, and it is just an accident, we cannot deny that your belief about the barn is causally connected to the barn. If we were trying to understand knowledge in terms of being in contact with the world, then we would need to specify the right kind of contact. But if you are using the notion of knowledge to explain other things, then it is easy to say what kind of contact you have in mind: you are connected in the right way to p if you know that p.

The presence or absence of this kind of contact matters in a variety of areas in philosophy. For example, as Unger argues, a factive propositional attitude either entails knowledge or the absence of knowledge. If you are happy that it is raining, or you notice that it is raining, then it follows that it is raining. These propositional attitudes are factive. Moreover, if you are in one of these mental states, then it also follows that you know that it is raining. By contrast, if you forget that it is raining, then it still follows that it is raining. Forgetting that p is just as factive as being surprised or embarrassed that p, but if you forget or are unaware that p, then it does not follow that you know that p. It follows that you do not know that p. Not all factive attitudes entail knowledge. But they do not leave the question of knowledge open. As Robert Gordon (1969) points out the propositional emotions, even the nonfactive ones, do not leave open the question of knowledge either. If you fear, hope, or are worried that p, then it does not follow that p. But it does follow that you do not know whether or not that p.

What matters in all these cases is genuine contact with the world, rather than merely a match between what is inside and what is outside the mind. You might be happy when it rains without being happy that it rains. You need the right kind of connection between the rain and the happiness for the happiness to be about the rain.

If the disturbing sight of the rain leads to your taking certain kinds of medication, then the rain, and your knowledge thereof, may cause the happiness, but you will not necessarily be happy that it is raining. The rain is causally related to the happiness, but not in the right way. What is the right way? It looks like the happiness has to be connected to the rain in the same way that a belief has to be connected to a fact for the belief to constitute knowledge.

Whenever something interesting requires contact between the mind and the world, a causal theory of that thing will at least look plausible. But any such theory will be faced with deviant causal chains: cases where there is a causal connection, but not the right kind of causal connection. You might intend to run over your uncle, and this may lead you to back your car out of your driveway to drive to his house. But if, unknown to you, your uncle is napping behind the wheels of your car, you will run him over; your intention to run him over will cause you to run him over; but you will not, in this case, run him over on purpose. Your intention to A is causally related to your A-ing, but not in the right way, so you do not intentionally A. This is a deviant causal chain.

Here is one thing to notice about the case. You correctly believe that backing out of your driveway will lead to running over your uncle. Given your plan, the belief, we may say, is justified. But the belief does not constitute knowledge. If it is just an accident that your belief is true, and you act on that belief, then it will just be an accident that your attempts are successful, if they are successful at all. To get intentional action, your means-ends beliefs must constitute knowledge. This is one suggestion for ruling out causal deviance in action theory. If this is right, then it not only follows that we can explain particular actions in terms of particular states of knowledge. It at least suggests that we understand intentional action, one kind of contact between the mind and the world, in terms of knowledge. Unless we also have to understand knowledge in terms of action, it looks as though knowledge is the more fundamental notion.

See also Belief.

Bibliography

Adler, Jonathan E. *Belief's Own Ethics*. Cambridge: Massachusetts Institute of Technology Press, 2002.

Burge, Tyler. "Individualism and the Mental." In *Midwest Studies in Philosophy*. Vol. 4, edited by Peter A. French, Theodore E. Uehling, and Howard K. Wettstein. Minneapolis: University of Minnesota Press, 1979.

Gettier, Edmund L. "Is Justified True Belief Knowledge?" *Analysis* 23 (1963): 121–123.

Gibbons, John. "Knowledge in Action." *Philosophy and Phenomenological Research* 62 (2001): 579–600.

Goldman, Alvin I. "Discrimination and Perceptual Knowledge." In *Liaisons: Philosophy Meets the Cognitive and Social Sciences*. Cambridge: Massachusetts Institute of Technology Press, 1992.

Gordon, Robert. "Emotions and Knowledge." *Journal of Philosophy* 66 (1969): 408–413.

Griffiths, A. Phillips, ed. *Knowledge and Belief*. London: Oxford University Press, 1967.

Harman, Gilbert. "(Nonsolisistic) Conceptual Role Semantics." In *Reasoning, Meaning, and Mind*. Oxford, U.K.: Clarendon Press, 1999.

McDowell, John. "Knowledge and the Internal." In *Meaning, Knowledge, and Reality*. Cambridge, MA: Harvard University Press, 1998.

McDowell, John. *Mind and World*. Cambridge, MA: Harvard University Press, 1996.

Moore, G. E. *Commonplace Book, 1919–1953*, edited by Casimir Lewy. London: Allen and Unwin, 1962.

Peacocke, Christopher. *Being Known*. Oxford, U.K.: Clarendon Press, 1999.

Putnam, Hilary. "The Meaning of 'Meaning.'" In *Mind, Language, and Reality*. Cambridge, U.K.: Cambridge University Press, 1975.

Sellars, Wilfrid. "Empiricism and the Philosophy of Mind." In *Minnesota Studies in the Philosophy of Science*. Vol. 1, edited by Herbert Feigl and Michael Scriven. Minneapolis: University of Minnesota Press, 1956.

Shoemaker, Sydney. "Moore's Paradox and Self-Knowledge." In *The First-Person Perspective and Other Essays*. Cambridge, U.K.: Cambridge University Press, 1996.

Sorensen, Roy A. *Blindspots*. Oxford, U.K.: Clarendon Press, 1988.

Unger, Peter. *Ignorance: A Case for Scepticism*. Oxford, U.K.: Clarendon Press, 1975.

Velleman, J. David. "On the Aim of Belief." In *The Possibility of Practical Reason*. Oxford, U.K.: Clarendon Press, 2000.

Williams, Bernard. "Deciding to Believe." In *Problems of the Self: Philosophical Papers, 1956–1972*. Cambridge, U.K.: Cambridge University Press, 1973.

Williamson, Timothy. *Knowledge and Its Limits*. Oxford, U.K.: Oxford University Press, 2000.

John Gibbons (2005)

KNOWLEDGE, SOCIOLOGY OF

See *Sociology of Knowledge*

KNOWLEDGE, SPECIAL SORTS OF

See *Knowledge, A Priori; Knowledge and Modality; Moral Epistemology*

KNOWLEDGE, SPECIAL SOURCES OF

See *Inference to the Best Explanation; Introspection; Intuition; Memory; Perception; Perception, Contemporary Views; Testimony*

KNOWLEDGE, THEORY OF

See *Epistemology; Epistemology, History of*

KNOWLEDGE AND BELIEF

The nature of knowledge has been a central problem in philosophy from the earliest times. One of Plato's most brilliant dialogues, the *Theaetetus*, is an attempt to arrive at a satisfactory definition of the concept, and Plato's dualistic ontology—a real world of eternal Forms contrasted with a less real world of changing sensible particulars—rests on epistemological foundations.

The problem of knowledge occupies an important place in most major philosophical systems. If philosophy is conceived as an ontological undertaking, as an endeavor to describe the ultimate nature of reality or to say what there really is, it requires a preliminary investigation of the scope and validity of knowledge. Only that can reasonably be said to exist which can be known to exist. If, on the other hand, philosophy is conceived as a critical inquiry, as a second-order discipline concerned with the claims of various concrete forms of intellectual activity, it must consider the extent to which these activities issue in knowledge.

In modern philosophy in the widest sense of the phrase—that is, philosophy since the Renaissance—theory of knowledge has usually been the primary field of philosophical investigation. René Descartes and John Locke, David Hume and Immanuel Kant, were all, in the first instance, epistemologists. Epistemological considerations played an important part in the work of Arthur Schopenhauer, but they were less central in G. W. F. Hegel and Friedrich Nietzsche, who were more occupied with the nature of the human mind in general and with the institutions within which it is exercised than with its more narrowly cognitive aspects. With Søren Kierkegaard and his existentialist descendants the focus of interest was man's will rather than his intellect. Anglo-Saxon philosophy, however, has remained epistemological. J. S. Mill, Bertrand Russell, and the analytic philosophers of the

twentieth century continued to work in the area marked out by Locke and Hume. Even the British Hegelians of the late nineteenth century, the school of Thomas Hill Green and F. H. Bradley, were led into far-reaching epistemological studies by the character of the native tradition they were seeking to overthrow.

Belief has had less attention from philosophers. It has generally been taken to be a more or less unproblematic inner state, accessible to introspection. But there has been disagreement about whether it is active or passive, Descartes having contended that assent is a matter of will, Hume that it is an emotional condition in which one finds oneself. Alexander Bain urged that belief should be interpreted in terms of the tendencies to action with which it is associated, and Charles Sanders Peirce took the view that it is an unobstructed habit of action that, like health, comes to our notice only when we have lost it. Faith, especially religious faith, and probability, the logic of rational belief, have been thoroughly examined, but belief itself has received surprisingly cursory treatment.

THE DEFINITION OF KNOWLEDGE

According to the most widely accepted definition, knowledge is justified true belief. That it is a kind of belief is supported by the fact that both knowledge and belief can have the same objects (thus, half an hour ago I believed I had left my raincoat in the garage; now I know that I have) and that what is true of someone who believes something to be the case is also true, among other things, of one who knows it. One who comes to know what he formerly believed does not lose the conviction he formerly had.

It is obvious and generally admitted that we can have knowledge only of what is true. If I admit that *p* is false, I must admit that I did not know it and that no one else did, although I may have thought and said so. It is urged, on the ground that beliefs that merely happen to be true cannot be regarded as knowledge, that knowledge must be justified. I may draw a true conclusion by invalid means from false premises or believe a truth on the strength of a dream or the misremembered testimony of a notorious liar. In such cases as these I do not really know the things I believe, although what I believe is true. There are, however, objections to all three parts of the definition of knowledge as justified true belief.

TRUTH. It has been suggested that the requirement that what is known be true is excessively stringent. Complete certainty of a statement's truth is not to be had; the best we can achieve is very strong grounds for thinking it true.

Thus, if knowledge entails truth, we can never attain knowledge or, at any rate, never know that we have done so. This objection is misconceived. If I firmly believe that something is true on what I take to be sufficient grounds, I am right to say that I know it. It may be that the grounds are, in fact, insufficient and that what I claim to know is false. In that case my claim is mistaken, but it does not follow that I was wrong to make it in the sense that I had no justification for doing so.

It has also been argued, with a view to showing that knowledge and belief are quite distinct and unrelated, that whereas beliefs can be true or false, knowledge is neither. This argument exploits the fact that we speak of a belief but not of a knowledge, only of a piece or item of knowledge. Furthermore, since all items or pieces of knowledge are by definition true, we never need to speak of them as true items or pieces in order to distinguish them from false ones.

BELIEF. It is often objected that knowledge cannot be a kind of belief, even though they can have the same objects, because they exclude each other. If I know that p, it would be wrong for me to say that I believe it, since this would suggest that I do *not* know it. If, knowing p, I am asked "Do you believe that p?," I should reply "No, 1 know it." This is hardly a serious argument. I should mislead people if I described my wife as the woman I live with, and I might say, "No, she's my wife," if I were asked whether she is the woman I live with. Nevertheless, my wife is the woman I live with. What is true is that I do not *merely* live with her. Likewise, if I know that p, I do not merely believe it, but I do believe it all the same. It is often wrong or misleading in certain circumstances to say something that is unquestionably true. The boy who, having taken two jam tarts, answers the question "How many have you had?" by saying "One" has told the truth but not the whole truth.

A more powerful argument against the definition of knowledge in terms of belief is that people can, it seems, know something to be the case and yet refuse, or be unable to bring themselves, to believe it. A woman told by wholly reliable witnesses with a wealth of circumstantial detail that her husband has been killed in an accident might be in this position. One way of getting around this objection is to say that she believes both that her husband is dead and that he is not. It is possible and not uncommon to believe something and its contradictory. It is not possible both to believe something and to not believe it at the same time, and what she will say is, "I don't believe it," although what she means is that she believes it is false.

Another possibility is to say that although she has conclusive grounds for believing that her husband is dead, she does not, in fact, believe it and does not know it either. To have conclusive grounds is one thing; to recognize that they are conclusive is another.

It should be noted that where knowledge and belief overlap, the kind of knowledge involved is propositional knowledge, or what Gilbert Ryle called "knowing that." There is also "knowing how" (to skate, tie a reef knot, do long division), where there are no propositions to be true or false and where knowledge can vary in degree. The two kinds of knowledge are connected in that both are the outcome of learning. Belief is always propositional or believing that; there is no believing how that serves as a defective version of knowing how to do something.

JUSTIFICATION. We often express unreasonable hunches or intuitions by saying, "I know," and if they turn out, to our gratified amazement, to be correct, we rejoice by saying, "I knew it." Does this show that true belief can be knowledge even without justification? The emphasis we put on the verb when we use it in such a case suggests that it is an abnormal or marginal use. It is generally accepted that lucky guesses should not count as knowledge.

An important difficulty arises from the requirement that true belief must be justified if it is to be knowledge. What is it for a belief to be justified? One obvious answer is that my belief in q is justified if there is some other belief p that entails or supports it. It is clearly not enough that this further belief p should merely exist. It must also be a belief of mine; I must know it to be true, and I must know that it justifies q. But if this is a definition of justification, the original definition of knowledge is rendered circular and generates a regress. It has the consequence that before any belief can be justified, an infinite series of justifications must already have taken place.

How can such a regress be halted? A natural step is to ask whether all justification has to be of this propositional or inferential kind. As Russell has observed, we can define derivative knowledge in this way but must add an account of intuitive or uninferred knowledge. Philosophers have fastened on two forms of intuitive knowledge that, by standing as the uninferred first premises of all inference, can terminate the regress of justification. First, there are self-evident necessary truths, and, second, there are basic contingent statements, immediately justified by the experiences they report and not dependent on the support of any further statable items of knowledge.

In the first group are the axioms of logic and mathematics, such as the law of excluded middle and the principle of the commutativity of addition ($a + b = b + a$), and statements that correspond to familiar verbal definitions, such as that kittens are young cats. Some philosophers hold that such intuitive, necessary truths record the results of intellectual intuition, the direct inspection of the relations of timeless universals; others, that their truth is essentially verbal in character, that one must accept them in order to be regarded as understanding the ordinary meaning of the words they contain. To accept an intuitive, necessary truth is to be ready to draw inferences in accordance with it. If I understand and accept the truth of "If (if p, then q), then (if not-q, then not-p)," I must regard the deduction of "If he's not over twenty-one, he's not eligible" from "If he's eligible, he's over twenty-one" as valid. By applying such rules of inference to intuitive necessary premises, further demonstrative necessary truths are arrived at.

Intuitive contingent truths have been held to be those that describe the immediate objects of perceptual or introspective experience—for example, "There is a green patch in the middle of my visual field" or "There appears to me to be a green flag here" and "I am in pain" or "I want to go to sleep." Basic statements like these are said to be incorrigible in the sense that they are wholly certified by the experiences they report and are logically immune from falsification by the results of any further experience. There may be no green flag here, but whatever may happen, there does now appear to be one. I may find it impossible to go to sleep once I get into bed, but I still want to go to sleep now. A statement is incorrigible if its truth follows from the fact that it is believed by the person to whom it refers. Thus, although I can make such a statement falsely, I must know that the statement is false when I do so. I cannot be honestly mistaken about my pains or the contents of my visual field.

It has sometimes been denied that there are any contingent, empirical statements that are basic and incorrigible in this sense. Coherence theories of knowledge have been propounded by the absolute idealists of the late nineteenth century and by C. S. Peirce, Karl R. Popper, and W. V. Quine in more empiricist forms in which beliefs are seen as justifying one another but none as in any sense self-justifying. To overcome the apparent circularity of the doctrine, it has been argued that some beliefs are relatively basic in that they can be accepted as true by some kind of convention or posited for the time being but that the element of dogmatism involved is only provisional and is open to revision.

PLATO'S *THEAETETUS*. Several of the points raised concerning truth, belief, and justification were first made in the *Theaetetus*, that most modern in spirit of Plato's dialogues. In it three definitions of knowledge are examined, and in the end all are rejected. The three are that knowledge is (1) perception or sensation, (2) true belief, and (3) true belief *meta logou*, translated by John Burnet as "accompanied by a rational account of itself or ground." Against the view that knowledge is true belief Plato made the point that lawyers can persuade juries to accept beliefs that are, in fact, true by using rhetorical devices but cannot be said to provide them with knowledge by doing so. Against the third definition, which, in effect, takes knowledge to be justified true belief, he pointed out that it is circular and regressive.

There is an obvious objection to the definition of knowledge as perception. Perception itself must be defined in terms of knowledge—namely, as the acquisition of knowledge about the external world by means of the senses. Plato's meaning here is perhaps better rendered by understanding his first definition to equate knowledge and sensation. Certainly this makes more plausible Plato's identification of this definition with Protagoras's thesis that man is the measure of all things (or that the truth for each man is simply what appears to him to be the case). In fact, Protagoras's thesis would be more accurately interpreted as the view that knowledge and belief are one and the same. This contention has obviously contradictory implications, as Plato pointed out. We all believe some beliefs of others to be truer than our own, and most people believe that Protagoras's theory is false. Something like that theory persists, however, in the view, to which we shall later return, that the foundations of empirical knowledge consist of incorrigible statements about immediate experience. According to this view, what we believe about our current sensations or experiences, whatever we may choose to say about them, is true. If it is also correct that such sensations are self-intimating, in the sense that they cannot occur without our knowing them to occur, it follows that every sensation is an item of knowledge though not that every item of knowledge is a sensation.

In his discussion of knowledge as true belief Plato raised the problem of false belief. How can we believe falsely that X is Y since if the belief is false, there is no X that is Y to form a belief, true or false, about? A false belief, it seems, is no belief at all. A perhaps oversimple solution to the problem is that we can know a thing X well enough to be able to identify it as a subject of discourse without knowing everything about it (whether, for instance, it is Y or not-Y). This draws attention to the point that the objects of knowledge are not always propositional, that not all knowledge is knowledge that. In addition to the knowledge how emphasized by Ryle, there is knowledge with a direct object, or knowledge of, claimed in such remarks as "I know Jones" or "I know Paris."

A claim to know a person can be intended and understood in two main ways. In saying that I know Jones, I may mean that I have met him and that I could not recognize him (and, usually, that we have had enough to do with one another for him to remember me). On the other hand, I may mean that I know what his character is like, what sort of things he is likely to do. According to the first interpretation, very little knowing that is involved, although I should be expected to be capable of giving some description of Jones's appearance; according to the second, some knowledge that relating to his character is implied, but none about his past history, health, occupation, and so on is.

A claim to know a place is ordinarily a claim to knowledge how, to an ability to find one's way about in it. It is not enough simply to have been there. Among other individual objects of knowledge are games, languages, and works of art. The last of these kinds of knowledge can be treated in much the same way as knowledge of persons; the others, as cases of knowing how, as claims to the possession of a skill. In general, knowledge of can be reduced to varying mixtures of knowing how and knowing that, though by no single recipe. It never involves a claim to knowledge that of all the facts involving the individual in question. A further point against Plato is that I can know enough about an individual or a thing to be able to refer significantly and successfully to him or it without being in a position to say that I know him or it *simpliciter*. I know enough about Samarqand to refer to it as a city in Uzbekistan and to ascribe to it a degree of beauty, historical interest, and size, but I do not know Samarqand at all, for I have never been there and could not find my way about in it.

IS KNOWLEDGE DEFINABLE? The English philosopher John Cook Wilson (1849–1915), closely followed in this by his disciple H. A. Prichard (1871–1947), strenuously maintained that the concept of knowledge is primitive and indefinable. Against such idealist logicians as F. H. Bradley and Bernard Bosanquet, they argued that judgment is not a genus of which knowledge, belief, and opinion are species. A judgment, said Wilson, is the conclusion of an inference, but some knowledge must be uninferred. Nor is knowledge a kind or species of thinking or a species of belief, for belief rests on knowledge in that it requires that there should be both some known evidence for it and the knowledge that this evidence is insufficient. No doubt, belief usually does rest on evidence or what is taken to be evidence, but it is not, as Wilson supposed, necessary that it should do so. I may believe a woman to be married because I take her to be wearing a wedding ring. The fact that it is not a wedding ring that she is wearing does not in the least imply that I do not really believe what I infer from my mistake.

According to Prichard, knowledge is completely sui generis and cannot, as he put it, "be explained." We cannot, he said, derive knowledge from what is not knowledge. This observation, if it is relevant at all, is simply a dogmatic assertion of the indefinability of knowledge. We can certainly define some things in terms of what they are not; for instance, not all cats are kittens, and not all young things are kittens, but a kitten is by definition a young cat. Knowledge and belief, Prichard held, are utterly distinct and cannot be mistaken for each other. We know directly and infallibly whether our state of mind is one of knowledge or belief. If so, knowledge and belief could not be related as genus and species, although they could still be different species of the same genus, another possibility that Prichard ruled out. His view that the two cannot be mistaken for each other seems clearly mistaken. We often claim with complete sincerity to know things that turn out to be false in the end. In so doing, we have taken a belief, mistakenly, to be knowledge.

Is the opposite possibility ever realized? Do we ever take to be mere belief something that, in fact, we really know? Is there a difference between knowing something and knowing that we know it? Benedict de Spinoza held that there is not. "He who has a true idea, knows at that same time that he has a true idea, nor can he doubt concerning the truth of the thing" (*Ethics*, Part 2, Proposition 43). As Spinoza expressed it, the doctrine is plainly false. I can perfectly well have very little confidence in a belief that is really true if, for example, it has been communicated to me by a notoriously unreliable informant. In other words, I can have a belief that is really true without knowing that it is true. But can I know that something is the case without knowing that I know it? I can certainly have a justified true belief without knowing that that is what it is, for I may not realize that the grounds I have for believing it really do justify it. The question deserves a more thorough investigation than it can be given here.

RATIONALIST THEORY OF KNOWLEDGE. Plato's distinction between knowledge and belief has had a greater influence on the subsequent course of philosophy than his penetrating but unsuccessful attempts to find a definition of the concept. His essential point was that knowledge and belief are not only distinct attitudes but that they also have distinct and proprietary objects. Knowledge can be only of what is eternal and unchanging, of Forms, Ideas or universals; belief has for its objects the changing sensible particulars that make up the temporal world. Plato's reflections on mathematics seem to have led him to this conclusion. The propositions of geometry are preeminently objects of knowledge in that they can be established as conclusively true, once and for all, by demonstrative reasoning. Our beliefs about matters of temporal fact, on the other hand, are much more liable to illusion and error. The sensible objects of perceptual belief are infected with contradiction; they undergo change and have contrary properties at different times. But the objects of mathematical knowledge are wholly different. The circles and triangles studied by geometers are exact and perfect; they are ideals that the circular and triangular things we perceive with the senses approximate but always fall short of.

There are three ways in which a circular concrete thing may not be really circular. It may be circular at one time and elliptical at another; it may be other things (for example, green, cold, and sweet) as well as circular; and as concrete and sensible, it may not be strictly or perfectly circular. From these facts Plato concluded that such a thing is not wholly real in the way that the ideal circle of the geometer is. The ideal circle is a genuine object of knowledge, and only such wholly knowable things can be wholly real. From the distinction between knowledge and belief, then, Plato derived a distinction between two sorts of object, each sort constituting a separate world of its own—the abstract world of eternal Forms, which is the knowable reality, and the concrete world of changing particulars, which is only appearance, not nonexistent but not wholly real either, and of which one can have not knowledge but only belief.

Plato's arguments for the unknowability and unreality of concrete, sensible things are not very persuasive. If this once circular mat is now elliptical, it does not follow that it was not really circular before. If this circular object is also green and cold, that does not in any way detract from its circularity. Finally, even if it is not perfectly circular, it may be quite definitely green. In general, there would seem to be many propositions that are known by some people but only believed by others; a mathematician will know the truth of a proposition he has proved, whereas another person will simply believe it on his authority. Some things I now know I used only to believe—for instance, that I should be writing this here today; some things I now only believe I once used to know—for instance, where I bought my raincoat. These considerations show that the objects of knowledge and belief are not wholly mutually exclusive. But it may still be true that there are some things that can be only believed, whereas others can be both believed and known.

At the center of Plato's thinking about this subject is a principle that defines one important sense of the word *rationalism*—the principle that only necessary truths, established by a priori reasoning, can really be known. Something like this principle was accepted by Aristotle, although he rejected Plato's doctrine that Forms or universals occupied a separate abstract world of their own beyond time and space. Aristotle agreed that only the form of things could be known and that the matter that individuated or particularized them was beyond the reach of knowledge. For him true knowledge was to be attained by a process of intuitive induction that discerned the necessary connections between the forms present in concrete things. A science or ordered body of knowledge must consist of propositions deduced from self-evident first principles of this kind.

Descartes's rationalism was inspired by the reflection that ordinary claims to knowledge often prove mistaken. True knowledge, he insisted, must be objectively certain and impossible to doubt. His methodical endeavors to doubt everything were brought up short by the celebrated "I think, therefore I exist." I cannot doubt that I doubt, for in the act of doubting it I prove it to be true; if I doubt, I think; and if I think, I exist. What, he then inquired, is so special about *cogito* and *sum*? What makes them so indubitably certain? His unhelpful conclusion is that they are clearly and distinctly perceived to be true. What he meant by this weakly formulated criterion of certainty can best be discovered by seeing what, in practice, he took it to certify. It appears that two sorts of proposition are clearly and distinctly perceived to be true: (1) necessary truths whose denial is self-evidently contradictory and (2) the immediate deliverances of sensation and introspection about one's own current mental state. Premises of both kinds figure in his first proof of God's existence:

Every event must have an adequate cause.
I have a clear and distinct idea of God.
God alone is an adequate cause for my idea of him.
Therefore, God exists.

In fact, *cogito*, I think, is not a clear instance of either, let alone both, of these two kinds of knowable, and even if it were, it would not follow from its being, on one hand, necessary and immediate and, on the other, certain that anything else that was necessary and immediate was also certain. Descartes's primary certainty was perhaps first thought of on a Thursday, but it does not follow that anything first thought of on a Thursday either by him or by anyone else is certain, too. It is not a necessary truth that I think or exist, for I might not be awake and might never have existed. If this is the case, the facts in question could not, of course, have been expressed in the first person singular.

Locke, despite his justly recognized position as a founding father of empiricism, reached much the same rationalist conclusion as Descartes, although by a very different route. He defined knowledge as "the perception of the agreement or disagreement of two ideas" (*Essay concerning Human Understanding*, Book 4, Ch. 1, Sec. 2). He went on to distinguish three kinds of knowledge: (1) intuitive knowledge of such things as the fact that red is not green and the fact of one's own existence; (2) demonstrative knowledge, which includes mathematics, morality, and the existence of God; and (3) sensitive knowledge, which is concerned with "the particular existence of finite beings without us." The third type of knowledge does not conform to his general definition, as he admitted. To become aware of a finite being outside us, we have to infer the existence of something that is not an idea from the ideas of sensation we take it to cause, and in part, to resemble. Locke's definition, as he understood it, restricts knowledge to the domain of a priori necessary truths. In intuition and demonstration there is a direct or indirect awareness of the connection between ideas present to the mind. But in the third case a connection is asserted between an idea of sensation and a physical thing that is not and cannot be directly present to the mind.

Locke did not introduce a special category to accommodate our knowledge of the ideas we passively experience but remitted them in passing to the category of intuitive knowledge. This sort of knowledge is quite unlike his exemplary cases of intuition, being contingent and empirical where the exemplary cases are necessary and a priori, and he might well have introduced a special category of reflective knowledge to accommodate it. It would comprise assertions of the connection of particular ideas, whereas intuition and demonstration would cover the connections of abstract, general ideas. Thus, although Locke's official definition of knowledge confines its application to necessary truths, it could, with a little modification, have been extended to cover a person's awareness of the present contents of his mind. But it could not, by any contortions, have been made to cover sensitive knowledge of real existence, that empirical knowledge par excellence which it was Locke's avowed purpose to justify and explain.

CERTAINTY. The indestructible vitality of the rationalist theory that necessary truths alone or necessary truths and reports of immediate experience are really knowledge was proved by its wide acceptance among empirically minded philosophers of the twentieth century—for example, Russell, C. I. Lewis, and A. J. Ayer. In support of it a powerful battery of arguments was produced, designed to show that despite the subjective certainty we feel in many kinds of belief, they cannot count as knowledge because they are not objectively certain.

Russell contended that all the sources of what we ordinarily regard as common knowledge of fact are in some degree untrustworthy. Perception is tainted by illusions, hallucinations, and dreams. Memory is notoriously fallible. Testimony, which plays such a large part in building up the social fabric of belief, presupposes an inference to other minds that is inevitably shaky and conjectural. Induction never certifies its conclusions, imparting at best only a measure of probability to them. Even introspection, if it is held to convey information about the self as a continuing personality, goes beyond what is directly present to the mind. Only what is directly present to it—currently occurring thoughts and feelings—is the object of certain, infallible, and indubitable belief.

Lewis generalized Russell's position by distinguishing expressive judgments that report current states of mind from all other empirical propositions on the ground that they alone are wholly nonpredictive and have no implications about future observable happenings by whose failure to occur they might be refuted. Ayer, at one time, went even further. He held that all contingent, empirical propositions whatsoever, including reports of immediate experience, are uncertain on the ground that every such proposition involves the application of a general predicative term to its subject and thus makes a comparison with previous and perhaps faultily remembered instances of the term's application.

This kind of fallibilism about empirical belief was doggedly resisted by G. E. Moore and, after him, by Ludwig Wittgenstein, J. L. Austin, and Norman Malcolm. Moore's main point was that the word *certain* is learned and thus acquires its meaning from such situations as that in which a man holds up his hand and makes the perceptual judgment "I know for certain that this is a hand." Some rather subtler arguments are sketched in his book *Philosophical Papers*. Their general upshot is that the rationalists and fallibilists have been working with an unconsidered and excessively stringent concept of certainty. They have simply taken it for granted that for a belief to be certain, it must be impossible to doubt it. Russell, for example, began his search for certain knowledge with the question "Is there any knowledge in the world which is so certain that no reasonable man could doubt it?"

There are at least four senses in which it may be held that a belief cannot be doubted. The first is psychological; a man cannot doubt a belief if he cannot, in fact, bring himself to suspend judgment about it. This kind of certainty will vary from person to person and is of no direct philosophical interest. The second sense is logical. Here "doubt" is taken to mean "suppose false" and "can" to mean "can without logical inconsistency." This yields the strict rationalist view, since only necessary truths cannot be supposed false without inconsistency. A third sense identifies certainty with incorrigibility. According to it, a belief cannot be doubted if its truth follows from the fact that it is believed. Anyone who doubts an incorrigible belief shows that he does not understand the words that express it. The favorite examples of incorrigible beliefs are reports of immediate experience, such as "I am in pain" or "It seems to me now that there is a table here." But the notion would also apply to the more elementary and intuitive kind of necessary truth, such as the law of contradiction. Finally, there is the concept of certainty that, say Moore and his adherents, we actually employ in common speech where it means what cannot reasonably be doubted or supposed false. That people make all sorts of mistakes is not, according to this view, a reason for doubting the truth of a particular proposition. What is required to justify doubt is that propositions just like this, made in circumstances just like these and resting on just this kind of evidence, have in the past turned out to be mistaken. In this sense of certainty many beliefs based on perception, memory, testimony, and induction are objectively certain and thus properly regarded as items of knowledge. This view has the merit of allowing that many propositions that are, in fact, necessary truths are or once were less than certain, and it does not require the theory that there are any incorrigible propositions to be accepted. A further point in its favor is that such surprising theses as the one that no factual belief is certain can surprise us and escape triviality only if they are taken in this sense.

SOME MODERN VIEWS. In the mid-twentieth century, philosophical discussions of knowledge were much concerned with three distinctions drawn by Russell, Ryle, and Austin that must be briefly mentioned.

Acquaintance and description. In Russell's early writings he drew a distinction between knowledge of things and knowledge of truths, between knowledge of and knowledge that, a distinction marked in French by the verbs *connaître* and *savoir*. Within each kind he also discerned a distinction between an immediate and a derived form. Immediate knowledge of truths is conveyed in intuitive statements—for example, basic judgments of perception and the axioms of logic and mathematics; derivative knowledge of truths, in demonstrable necessary propositions and inferred empirical statements. Parallel to this on the side of knowledge of things is the distinction between knowledge by acquaintance and knowledge by description.

Acquaintance, as Russell defined it, is the converse of presentation; it is the direct and infallible apprehension of some sort of object. But objects of description, unlike those of acquaintance, can fail to exist. Russell held that we are acquainted with present and past particulars and also with universals. This doctrine has led to a good deal of confusion. Certainly we do know things, persons, and places by acquaintance, but to do so is generally to know that something is true of them and is at least to know how to recognize them. The words with which we refer to things we are not acquainted with can be defined or explained in terms of those connected with objects of acquaintance. But this produces understanding rather than knowledge, understanding of singular terms (whether what they purport to refer to exists or not) and of general terms (whether or not there is anything they apply to). Russell's principle of acquaintance ("Every proposition which we can understand must be composed wholly of constituents with which we are acquainted") is really a version of the empiricist theory of meaning. Asserted without qualification, it is highly unplausible. We are not acquainted with anything corresponding to the "if" that occurs in the verbal expression of a hypothetical proposition although we understand the word. In general, to become acquainted with things is to acquire some intuitive knowledge of truths in which they figure, particular objects of acquaintance being the subjects of such truths and universal objects of acquaintance their predicates. In other words, knowledge of things cannot be separated from and regarded as prior to knowledge of truths in the way Russell supposed.

Knowing how and knowing that. Ryle's distinction between knowing how and knowing that has already been mentioned. There is a parallel distinction between remembering how and remembering that (there is also memory *of* past events). Ryle is anxious to correct the intellectualist bias of theorists of knowledge and to draw attention to the dispositional nature of all kinds of knowledge and belief; we speak, after all, of the knowledge and beliefs of those who are fast asleep. He tends to suggest that knowing that is a special, verbal form of knowing how, that it consists in having learned how to answer certain questions and now being ready to answer them.

Performative and descriptive verbs. John Austin's work on performative utterances has interested many philosophers in that class of verbs that are used in the first person present to do things rather than to describe what is being done. Examples of such performative verbs are "promise," "swear," "take thee, *X*, to be my wedded wife," and "name this ship *Y*." A verb ϕ is performative if it follows that I ϕ from the fact that I say, "I ϕ." Austin appears to have thought, wrongly, that "know" is a verb of this kind and that its function is to guarantee or authorize the acceptance of the piece of information that followed it. It is true that to prefix "I know" to a statement of fact does not add much to its content. But *p* and "I know that *p*" are not equivalent, since the former may be true when the latter is false. Austin was right in denying that knowledge is a state of assurance stronger than the most assured belief, though it is not clear that anyone ever supposed that it was. But the correctness of this denial, although it entails that it is not some describable psychological feature of the knower's state of mind that differentiates knowledge from belief, does not entail that the difference is not at all describable and lies, rather, in some nondescriptive function that the word performs.

THE NATURE OF BELIEF

Most philosophers who have in any way adverted to the nature of belief have assumed that belief is an inner state of mind, directly accessible to introspection and distinct from, though causally related to, the believer's behavior. In *The Emotions and the Will* (1859) the Scottish philosopher Alexander Bain proposed that belief should be defined in terms of behavior: "Belief has no meaning except in reference to our actions … no mere conception that does not directly or indirectly implicate our voluntary exertions can ever amount to the state in question." In support of Bain's theory is the fact that not only can others check our claims to believe by considering whether

we behave appropriately but we ourselves may also take the results of such a test to overrule claims to believe that we have sincerely made.

Careful statements of the opposing doctrines were given by H. H. Price and R. B. Braithwaite. Price's mentalist definition of belief equates it with entertainment of a proposition together with assent. To entertain a proposition is to understand and attend to its meaning; when it occurs by itself, it is neutral and uncommitted as regards the proposition's truth or falsehood. Price breaks assent down into a volitional and an emotional part. He describes the volitional element as a mental act of preferring a proposition to any incompatible alternatives that have occurred to one; the emotional element is a feeling of conviction or assurance and may vary in degree. Braithwaite identifies belief in a proposition with its entertainment together with a dispositional readiness to act as if it were true. "Being ready to act as if *p* were true" has at first sight a suggestion of circularity, for it seems to mean being ready to act as if one believed *p*. But this can be avoided. I act as if *p* were true if I act in a way that would satisfy my desires if *p* were in fact true.

Against both theories it should be said that "entertainment" is dispensable if the normal sense of "believe" is in question, for we attend consciously to the propositions we believe only at rare intervals. As regards Price, what is to be understood by an act of preferring as opposed to an emotion of preference? It looks very like the silent assertion of the proposition itself, an inner rehearsal of a piece of outward verbal behavior. Second, feelings of conviction do not always attend even the beliefs we consciously entertain. Unless our confident beliefs are actually challenged, our state would seem to be one of easy and unemotional taking for granted.

Against the view of Bain and Braithwaite it has been urged by Mill, Franz Brentano, and Russell that if a belief has behavioral effects different from mere entertainment, it must differ in its intrinsic mental character. This is a misunderstanding. For a behaviorist there is a difference in the dispositions of one who believes and of one who merely entertains a proposition. A more serious difficulty is presented by beliefs that have negligible practical consequences, such as those about remote historical or astronomical events. But even here there is a disposition to verbal behavior, and, again, a disposition can exist without being actualized. There is also the difficulty that my claims about what I believe become, according to this theory, inductive conjectures about what I should do if certain circumstances arose. One reply is that not all inductive conjectures are conjectural to that degree. I need not, for example, feel very hesitant about what would happen if this iron table were dropped on that china teapot. Braithwaite adds that his theory has the merit of making possible rather precise measurements of subjective probability or degree of belief. The numerical probability I attach to a belief can be regarded as the least favorable odds I should accept on its turning out to be correct. Thus, unless I accept an odds-on bet, I do not believe something more than I believe its denial.

There is an interesting and extreme opposition in the history of philosophy between Descartes, who held that assent is a matter of will that can be freely given or withheld, and Hume, who represented us as largely passive in belief, which he conceived as a feeling that we find ourselves with and must put up with whether we like it or not, much as we find ourselves equipped with desires and aversions. Descartes's activism is shown first in his proposal that the philosopher should undertake a course of methodical doubt, suspending judgment about all the beliefs he has hitherto taken for granted. It reaches its fullest development in his attempt to solve the theological problem of error or intellectual evil, to reconcile the fact, on which his whole philosophy depends, that many of our beliefs are false with the goodness of God. The solution he offered is that God has fitted us out with limited intellects, appropriate to our earthly needs, but in his own image, with unrestricted freedom of will. When we make mistakes it is because we have culpably given free assent to propositions beyond the effective reach of our limited intellects.

In Descartes's favor is the fact that we do assess beliefs as more or less reasonable, a practice whose theory is logic and methodology. And the ethics of belief has not always been confined to distinguishing logically reasonable beliefs from others. It has often been held that some beliefs—in the existence of God, for example—are morally obligatory, and some beliefs are often recommended as prudent or useful. Hume himself propounded rules for judging causes and effects whose acceptance, he maintained, will enable us to advance science and avoid superstition. On Hume's side is the fact that it seems no more possible to resolve to believe something one actually does not believe than it is to increase one's height or eradicate one's distaste for endives by a simple effort of will. What one can do is to fortify or undermine one's belief in a proposition indirectly by voluntarily concentrating one's attention on the evidence for or against it.

It is quite commonly said that belief must rest on evidence and sometimes, especially by those who hold knowledge to be indefinable, that it must rest on knowledge. It is certainly usual for belief to rest on something the believer regards as evidence, whether or not it is true and whether or not it lends any support to the belief in question. But a wildly dogmatic or superstitious belief, maintained in the teeth of all the evidence, is still a belief, however unreasonable it may be.

FAITH. There is some point to the malicious definition of faith as firm belief in something for which there is no evidence, for faith does involve a measure of risk, a voluntary decision to repose more confidence in a proposition, person, or institution than the statable grounds for doing so would, if neutrally considered, justify. Locke defined faith as resting on authoritative testimony, "the assent to any proposition, not thus made out by the deductions of reason, but upon the credit of the proposer." This applies well enough to the religious faith of traditional Christianity, but it is too narrow to cover the general use of the concept. It is often said that science rests on faith in the uniformity and intelligibility of nature as much as religion does on an undemonstrable conviction that the world is under the direction of a wise and benevolent intelligence. Certainly, science would be wholly sterilized if men were not prepared to consider adventurous and unjustified hypotheses. But it is not obvious that these adventurous conjectures have to be believed by their propounders. The austere maxim of W. K. Clifford—"It is wrong, everywhere and for anyone, to believe anything upon insufficient evidence"—is not strictly incompatible with intellectual enterprise. Yet even Popper, who of all theorists of knowledge is most insistent on the conjectural and fallible nature of science, admits that "our guesses are guided by the unscientific, the metaphysical (though biologically explicable) faith in laws, in regularities which we can uncover."

See also A Priori and A Posteriori; Evans, Gareth; Kant, Immanuel; Knowledge, A Priori; Kripke, Saul; Meaning; Plantinga, Alvin; Propositions; Putnam, Hilary; Reference.

Bibliography

CLASSIC DISCUSSIONS

Bain, Alexander. *The Emotions and the Will.* London: J.W. Parker, 1859.

Descartes, René. *Meditations.*

Locke, John. *Essay concerning Human Understanding.* Book 4.

Plato. *Republic.* Books 5–7.

Plato. *Theaetetus.*

MODERN ACCOUNTS

Armstrong, D. M. *Belief, Truth, and Knowledge*. Cambridge, U.K.: Cambridge University Press, 1973.

Audi, Robert. *Epistemology: A Contemporary Introduction to the Theory of Knowledge*. 2nd ed. New York: Routledge, 2003.

Austin, John. "Other Minds." In his *Philosophical Papers*. London: Oxford University Press, 1962.

Ayer, A. J. *The Foundations of Empirical Knowledge*. London: Macmillan, 1940.

Ayer, A. J. *The Problem of Knowledge*. London: Macmillan, 1956. Chs. 1–2.

BonJour, Lawrence. *The Structure of Empirical Knowledge*. Cambridge, MA: Harvard University Press, 1985.

Brewer, Bill. *Perception and Reason*. Oxford: Clarendon Press, 2002.

Chisholm, Roderick. *The Foundations of Knowing*. Minneapolis: University of Minnesota Press, 1982.

Chisholm, Roderick M. *Perceiving: A Philosophical Study*. Ithaca, NY: Cornell University Press, 1957. Part I.

Dretske, Fred. *Seeing and Knowing*. London: Routledge and Kegan Paul, 1969.

Foley, Richard. *Working without a Net*. New York: Oxford University Press, 1993.

Goldman, Alvin. *Epistemology and Cognition*. Cambridge, MA: Harvard University Press, 1986.

Harman, Gil. *Thought*. Princeton, NJ: Princeton University Press, 1973.

Hintikka, Jaakko. *Knowledge and Belief*. Ithaca, NY: Cornell University Press, 1962.

Klein, Peter. *Certainty: A Refutation of Scepticism*. Minneapolis: University of Minnesota Press, 1981.

Lehrer, Keith. *Theory of Knowledge*. Boulder, CO: Westview Press, 1990.

Lewis, C. I. *Mind and the World-Order*. New York: Scribners, 1929. Ch. 9.

Malcolm, Norman. *Knowledge and Certainty*. Englewood Cliffs, NJ: Prentice Hall, 1963.

Moore, G. E. *Philosophical Papers*. London: Allen and Unwin, 1959.

Plantinga, Alvin. *Warrant and Proper Function*. Oxford: Oxford University Press, 1993.

Popper, Karl R. *Conjectures and Refutations*. London: Routledge, 1963. See the introduction.

Prichard, H. A. *Knowledge and Perception*. Oxford: Clarendon Press, 1950.

Russell, Bertrand. *Problems of Philosophy*. London: Williams and Norgate, 1912. Chs. 5, 13.

Ryle, Gilbert. *The Concept of Mind*. London: Hutchinson, 1949. Ch. 2.

Sosa, Ernest. *Knowledge in Perspective: Selected Essays in Epistemology*. Cambridge, U.K.: Cambridge University Press, 1991.

Wilson, John Cook. *Statement and Inference*. Oxford: Clarendon Press, 1926. Part 1, Chs. 2, 4; Part II, Chs. 1–3.

Woozley, A. D. *Theory of Knowledge: An Introduction*. London: Hutchinson, 1949. Ch. 8.

Anthony Quinton (1967)
Bibliography updated by Benjamin Fiedor (2005)

KNOWLEDGE AND MODALITY

The prominence of the modalities (i.e., necessity and contingency) in epistemological discussions is due to the influence of Immanuel Kant (1965), who maintained that:

(1) All knowledge of necessary propositions is a priori; and

(2) All propositions known a priori are necessary.

Saul Kripke (1971, 1980) renewed interest in Kant's account of the relationship between the a priori and the necessary by arguing that some necessary propositions are known a posteriori and some contingent propositions are known a priori. A cogent assessment of the controversy requires some preliminary clarification.

The distinction between necessary and contingent propositions is metaphysical. A necessarily true (false) proposition is one that is true (false) and cannot be false (true). The distinction between a priori and a posteriori knowledge is epistemic. S knows a priori that p just in case: (a) S knows that p; and (b) S's justification for believing that p does not depend on experience. Condition (b) is controversial. On the traditional reading, (b) is equivalent to (c): S's belief that p is nonexperientially justified. Hilary Putnam (1983) and Philip Kitcher (1983), however, argue that (b) is equivalent to (d): S's belief that p is nonexperientially justified and cannot be defeated by experience. Albert Casullo (2003) rejects the Putnam-Kitcher reading on the grounds that it yields an analysis of a priori knowledge that excludes the possibility that someone knows a posteriori a proposition that can be known a priori.

The expression "knowledge of necessary propositions" in (1) is ambiguous. The following definitions remove the ambiguity:

(A) S knows the *general modal status* of p just in case S knows that p is a necessary proposition (i.e., either necessarily true or necessarily false) or S knows that p is a contingent proposition (i.e., either contingently true or contingently false);

(B) S knows the *truth value* of p just in case S knows that p is true or S knows that p is false (assuming truth is always bivalent);

(C) S knows the *specific modal status* of p just in case S knows that p is necessarily true or S knows that p is necessarily false or S knows that p is contingently true or S knows that p is contingently false.

(A) and (B) are logically independent. One can know that Goldbach's Conjecture is a necessary proposition but not know whether it is true or false. Alternatively, one can know that some mathematical proposition is true but not know whether it is a necessary proposition or a contingent proposition. (C), however, is not independent of (A) and (B). One cannot know the specific modal status of a proposition unless one knows both its general modal status and its truth value.

(1) is crucial for Kant, because it is the leading premise of his only argument in support of the existence of a priori knowledge:

(1) All knowledge of necessary propositions is a priori.

(3) Mathematical propositions, such as that $7 + 5 = 12$, are necessary.

(4) Therefore, knowledge of mathematical propositions, such as that $7 + 5 = 12$, is a priori.

(1), however, is ambiguous. There are two ways of reading it:

(1T) All knowledge of the *truth value* of necessary propositions is a priori, or

(1G) All knowledge of the *general modal status* of necessary propositions is a priori.

The argument is valid only if (1) is read as (1T). Kant, however, supports (1) with the observation that although experience teaches that something is so and so, it does not teach us that it cannot be otherwise. Taken at face value, this observation states that experience teaches us that a proposition is true and that experience does not teach us that it is necessary. This supports (1G), not (1T).

Kripke rejects (1) by offering examples of necessary truths that are alleged to be known a posteriori. First, he maintains that if P is an identity statement between names, such as "Hesperus = Phosphorus," or a statement asserting that an object has an essential property, such as "This table is made of wood," then one knows a priori that:

(5) If P then necessarily P.

Second, he argues that because one knows by empirical investigation that Hesperus = Phosphorus and that this table is made of wood, one knows a posteriori that:

(6) P.

Kripke concludes that one knows by *modus ponens* that:

(7) Necessarily P.

(7) is known a posteriori because it is based on (6), which is known a posteriori.

How do Kripke's examples bear on (1)? Once again, a distinction must be made between (1G) and (1T). Kripke's examples, if cogent, establish that (1T) is false: They establish that one knows a posteriori that some necessary propositions are true. They do not, however, establish that (1G) is false: They do not establish that one knows a posteriori that some necessary propositions are necessary. It may appear that Kripke's conclusion that one has a posteriori knowledge that necessarily P entails that (1G) is false. Here a distinction must be made between (1G) and:

(1S) All knowledge of the *specific modal status* of necessary propositions is a priori.

Kripke's examples establish that (1S) is false: They establish that one knows a posteriori that some necessary propositions are necessarily true. Because knowledge of the specific modal status of a proposition is the conjunction of knowledge of its general modal status and knowledge of its truth value, it follows from the fact that one's knowledge of the truth value of P is a posteriori that one's knowledge of its specific modal status is also a posteriori. However, from the fact that one's knowledge of the specific modal status of P is a posteriori, it does not follow that one's knowledge of its general modal status is also a posteriori.

(1G) has not gone unchallenged. Kitcher (1983) argues that even if knowledge of the general modal status of propositions is justified by nonexperiential evidence, such as the results of abstract reasoning or thought experiments, it does not follow that such knowledge is a priori because the nonexperiential justification in question can be defeated by experience. Casullo (2003) rejects (1G) on the grounds that the Kantian contention that experience can provide knowledge of only the actual world overlooks the fact that much practical and scientific knowledge involves counterfactual conditionals, which provide information that goes beyond what is true of the actual world.

Kripke also argues that some contingent truths are known a priori. His examples are based on the observation that a definite description can be employed to fix the reference—as opposed to give the meaning—of a term. Consider someone who employs the definition description "the length of S at t_0" to fix the reference of the expression "one meter." Kripke maintains that this person knows, without further empirical investigation, that S is one meter long at t_0. Yet the statement is contingent because "one meter" rigidly designates the length that is in fact the length of S at t_0 but, under different conditions, S would have had a different length at t_0. In reply, Alvin Plantinga (1974) and Keith Donnellan (1979) contend that, without empirical investigation, the reference fixer knows that the sentence "S is one meter long at t_0" expresses a truth, though not the truth that it expresses. Gareth Evans (1979) disputes this contention.

Bibliography

Casullo, Albert. *A Priori Justification*. New York: Oxford University Press, 2003.

Donnellan, Keith S. "The Contingent *A Priori* and Rigid Designators." In *Contemporary Perspectives on the Philosophy of Language*, edited by P. French et al. Minneapolis: University of Minnesota Press, 1979.

Evans, Gareth. "Reference and Contingency." *Monist* 62 (1979): 161–189.

Kant, Immanuel. *Critique of Pure Reason*. Translated by Norman Kemp Smith. New York: St. Martin's Press, 1965.

Kitcher, Philip. *The Nature of Mathematical Knowledge*. New York: Oxford University Press, 1983.

Kripke, Saul. "Identity and Necessity." In *Identity and Individuation*, edited by M. K. Munitz. New York: New York University Press, 1971.

Kripke, Saul. *Naming and Necessity*. Cambridge, MA: Harvard University Press, 1980.

Plantinga, Alvin. *The Nature of Necessity*. Oxford: Oxford University Press, 1974.

Putnam, Hilary. "'Two Dogmas' Revisited." In *Realism and Reason: Philosophical Papers*. Vol. 3. Cambridge, U.K.: Cambridge University Press, 1983.

Albert Casullo (1996, 2005)

KNOWLEDGE AND TRUTH, THE VALUE OF

Questions concerning the value of knowledge and truth range from those that suggest complete skepticism about such value to those that reflect more discriminating concerns about the precise nature of the value in question and the comparative judgment that one of the two is more valuable than the other.

THE COMPARATIVE QUESTION AND THE PRAGMATIC ACCOUNT

The history of epistemology has its conceptual roots in the dialogues of Plato, and the question of the value of knowledge and truth arises there as well. In Plato's *Meno*, Socrates and Meno discuss a number of issues, including the issue of the nature and value of knowledge. Socrates

raises the question of the value of knowledge, and Meno answers by proposing a pragmatic theory: knowledge is valuable because it gets us what we want. Socrates immediately proposes a counterexample, to the effect that true opinion would work just as well: If you want to get to Larissa, hiring a guide who has a true opinion of how to get there will have the same practical results as hiring a guide who knows the way. Meno then voices a philosophically deep perplexity, wondering aloud why knowledge should be more prized than true opinion and whether there is any difference between the two. Meno thus questions two assumptions, the first being the assumption that knowledge is more valuable than true opinion, and the second that knowledge is something more than true opinion.

Socrates's counterexample suggests another: If you want to get to Larissa, it matters not whether your guide has true opinion or merely empirically adequate views on the matter. To see the counterexample, we need to understand that an empirically adequate theory is one that "saves the appearances," in other words, one that would never be refuted by any sensory experience. The simplest way to see that such a theory is not the same thing as a true theory is to consider skeptical scenarios such as René Descartes's evil demon world. The denizens of such a world will have roughly the same views as we do, and their views will be as empirically adequate as ours. Since the demon is so skillful at carrying out his intentions, however, their views will be false even if ours are true. In such a world, there are no guides with true opinions about how to get to Larissa. Instead, the best one could hope for is a guide who has an empirically adequate view of the matter. Yet, if we compare the two situations, the one in the actual world where the hired guide has a true opinion, and the one in the demon world where the hired guide has only an empirically adequate opinion, no suffering accrues to the traveler in the demon world that does not also accrue to the traveler in the actual world, and no benefits are experienced by the traveler in the demon world that are not also experienced by the traveler in the actual world. That is to say, their experiences are indistinguishable, leaving us to wonder what practical advantage truth has over empirical adequacy.

SKEPTICISM ABOUT THE VALUE OF KNOWLEDGE AND TRUTH

Besides this Platonic threat to the value of knowledge and truth, there are other threats. One arises from the specter of skepticism. If we grant that there is no adequate answer to the skeptic, we might have the experience of philosophical sour grapes, denying the value of what we cannot have.

More respectable threats to the value of knowledge and truth come from positions that question the ordinary thinking that knowledge and truth contribute to well-being. Pyrrhonian skepticism maintains that such ordinary thinking is mistaken, and that the path to happiness requires abandoning a search for knowledge and truth, ridding oneself of beliefs and instead "acquiescing to the appearances." Arguments for skepticism play an important role in this process insofar as they can play a role in eliminating the dogmatism purportedly inherent in belief, but the Pyrrhonian appeal to skepticism is not simply that of philosophical sour grapes: it is motivated instead by a conception of what human well-being involves and requires.

There is no question that the Pyrrhonian school was sensitive to a real threat to human happiness, for dogmatism has caused immense suffering (for one monumental example, think of the suffering caused by religious wars). It is philosophical overkill, however, to move from such obvious points to skepticism and a denigration of the value of knowledge and truth. For one thing, dogmatism is compatible with a full appreciation of the rights of other human beings and so need not lead to massive human rights violations. Moreover, even if dogmatism has practical consequences that are troubling, a defender of the value of knowledge and truth has a counterargument here. The typical epistemological approach involves abstracting away from the causal consequences of holding the beliefs in question, concerning itself more with intrinsic features of cognition, the kind reflected in talk of inquiry for its own sake. When we engage in inquiry for its own sake, successful results will partake of a kind of success that is independent of any causal contribution to well-being or other practical concerns. When epistemologists reflect on the nature of successful cognition and the extent to which an organism achieves it, the predominant approach has been to reflect on a kind of success that abstracts from the consequences of cognition, whether those consequences are practical, moral, religious, political, or social.

Given such an abstraction, a defender of the value of knowledge and truth can argue that even if Pyrrhonism is correct as a general approach to cognition, it fails to show that, from the abstract point of view of what is involved in inquiry for its own sake, knowledge and truth are not valuable. One of the factors to be considered in evaluating the plausibility of any view regarding the all-things-considered value of knowledge and truth is the perspectival value of these things, such as the value they (appear to) have from the perspective of inquiry for its own sake.

Moreover, the argument for Pyrrhonism as the best view of the all-things-considered value of knowledge and belief is weak. To the extent that dogmatism itself has untoward consequences, the proper remedy is a sense of human fallibility, and only a highly questionable theory in which knowledge must be infallible could view skepticism as the only antidote to dogmatism.

Another threat arose in the latter half of the twentieth century, from those whom Bernard Williams in his last major philosophical work (2002) labeled "deniers" of the value of truth. Some of these deniers claim, in postmodernist spirit, that the ideals of truth and objectivity in inquiry are pretensions in service of other, baser motives. Problems for such denials of the value of truth arise when attempts are made to delineate accurately the nature of the pretensions in question and the lessons to be learned about the human condition from such investigation. Some, such as Richard Rorty (1989), have sought to espouse views while at the same time denying their accuracy, but such a position is not intellectually stable. The instability of the view is masked by the false dilemma involved in always capitalizing terms like "Truth" and "Reality" to gain purchase for the view that these concepts always and everywhere posit a metaphysical space hidden behind the pale of language or experience, yielding the claim that inquiry should aim at something weaker than truth, such as widest possible agreement (see Rorty 1998). As Williams points out, however, it makes little sense to value the number of converts to a view unless convincing them of the view has something to do with convincing them that the view is true. Put more generally, among the regulating ideas concerning truth is that there is an obvious logical equivalence between *p* and *it is true that p*, so that to assert a claim is to represent that claim as being true, and no philosophical sleight of hand involving capitalization of terms or scare-quotes, to which such deniers are prone, undermines this central point about truth. The deniers may have useful and important critiques of pretensions to objectivity, but it is a fundamental principle of inquiry that claims and arguments that are self-refuting should be avoided.

THE NATURE OF THE VALUE IN QUESTION

So there are three primary questions regarding the value of knowledge and truth. The first is whether knowledge and truth are valuable, all things considered. The second question is whether they are valuable from the abstract point of view of what is involved in inquiry for its own sake. And the third question pertains to the issue of explanation, asking whether it is really knowledge that is valuable from this purely cognitive point of view, or something else instead.

The first question is a very large one, but a proper answer to it depends on answers to the second two questions, for if knowledge and truth do not pass scrutiny when considered from the purely cognitive point of view, then they have little to be said in their favor from an all-things-considered point of view. Furthermore, a negative answer to the third question would threaten the significance of a positive answer to the second question.

THE VALUE OF TRUTH. The major concerns involved in the third question are whether knowledge is more valuable than its parts and whether truth has anything to be said on its behalf over mere empirical adequacy. From a purely cognitive point of view, as William James (1956) noted, human beings are motivated by two primary concerns, a concern for not being duped and a concern for not missing out on something important. The first concern is relevant to the issue regarding whether truth has anything to be said on its behalf over mere empirical adequacy. If we adopt the literary device of a narrator commenting on various scenarios, we find something of an answer to this question. If one of the scenarios is the evil demon world and the other the actual world (as we suppose it to be), with the narrator being the very same person in each of these scenarios, the narrative will almost certainly treat the evil demon scenario as disturbing in comparison to the actual scenario, precisely because the narrator is being duped in the former but not in the latter. The most straightforward explanation of this response is that we find getting to the truth intrinsically valuable in virtue of our concern for not being duped.

The second concern above, the concern for not missing out on something important, raises a further problem, the problem of whether all truth is intrinsically valuable or only the important truths (see Ernest Sosa 2003). It is certainly true that we view some truths as simply unimportant, but that fact need not be taken to undermine the intrinsic value of truth, for it may be that our practical needs, goals, and interests interact with the intrinsic value of truth so that some truths are simply unimportant, all things considered, even though truth is still intrinsically valuable from a purely cognitive point of view, or from the point of view of inquiry for its own sake.

THE VALUE OF KNOWLEDGE. The value of truth raises the question of whether knowledge is more valuable than the sum of its parts; an affirmative answer to this question faces serious obstacles. Note first the variety of ways in which one might defend the value of knowledge. After seeing the above defense of the value of truth, an obvious response would be to argue that knowledge is intrinsically valuable, valuable independently of any value possessed by its parts, and more valuable intrinsically than any collection of its parts. It is instructive to note that such a maneuver is not as promising here as it is in the case of truth. On the one hand, when asked, "Why, from a purely cognitive point of view, do you value truth?" we are hard pressed to say anything informative at all, and this difficulty is an indication that we do not value truth on the basis of our valuing something else, but rather that we value it intrinsically. On the other hand, when asked, "Why, from a purely cognitive point of view, do you value knowledge?" we are inclined to answer. Our answer might be that we want to be correct, but not merely by accident, as happens when one has merely a true belief. The inclination to answer in ways such as this suggests that we value knowledge in a way that is different from the way in which we value truth, that even if truth is intrinsically valuable, knowledge is valuable because of the features that distinguish it from true belief.

What are these features? The traditional view is that knowledge is true belief that is justified, but the literature deriving from Edmund Gettier's seminal paper of 1963 shows that no fallibilist view about justification can accept this account of knowledge. Fallibilism about justification is the view that justified false beliefs are possible, perhaps clarified in terms of the claim that no matter how good our evidence is for what we believe, we might still be wrong. Given this view, it turns out to be unavoidable that there could be cases of justified true belief that are not cases of knowledge. Hence another condition—a fourth condition—must be added.

Justification and knowledge. We should expect to find the value of knowledge, then, by examining the value of the additional elements of knowledge—justification and whatever fourth condition is needed. The standard conception of justification makes it difficult to use in a defense of the value of knowledge, however. The standard conception of justification is teleological: holding justified beliefs is the proper means to adopt when one's goal is to get to the truth (and avoid error). If we think of means to a goal in terms of that which makes achieving the goal likely, the standard conception of justification amounts to the idea that justification is a property of a

ENCYCLOPEDIA OF PHILOSOPHY
2nd edition

belief in virtue of which that belief is objectively likely to be true.

A theory will need to say something different from the simple claim that justification is to be understood in terms of objective likelihood of truth, however, if it is to have any hope of providing a basis for explaining the value of knowledge over the value of its parts. Recall that the task is to explain the value of knowledge over that of true belief, so if an appeal to justification is to aid in this task, the theory of justification provided must support the idea that justified true belief is more valuable than mere true belief. It is not enough simply that justification is a valuable property for a belief to have, for that result would only show that justified belief is more valuable than unjustified belief, not that justified true belief is more valuable than true belief. Another way to put this point is as follows: It is necessary for justification to be valuable for it to play a role in explaining the value of knowledge, but its having such value is not by itself sufficient for it to play such a role.

The reason the value of justification is not sufficient is because of the swamping problem, as explained by Linda Zagzebski (1996), Richard Swinburne (2001), and Jonathan Kvanvig (2003). To see the problem, consider the following analogy. Suppose one wants to visit a nearby bookstore with a good philosophy section while visiting an unfamiliar city, and one searches the Internet to find a store. Two sites are generated, one titled "Bookstores with a good philosophy section" and another titled "Bookstores likely to have a good philosophy section." Presumably, one will be more interested in the first than in the second, but the relevant point to note in our context is something different. Suppose one takes the time to construct the intersection of the two lists, resulting in a list of bookstores that both have and are likely to have a good philosophy section.

The point of the analogy is that it may be true that the first list is analogous to true belief, the second to justified belief, and the third to justified true belief. The swamping problem occurs in the bookstore example because the third list is no more valuable than the first when one's interests are simply to visit a bookstore with a good philosophy section. The swamping problem in epistemology is simply that the value of justification is swamped by the value of truth when justification is conceived solely in terms of objective likelihood of truth, for the same reasons that a list of bookstores that both have and are likely to have a good philosophy section is no more valuable than a list of bookstores that have a good philosophy section.

There are two ways to develop a theory of justification that addresses the swamping problem and thereby provides an account of justification that is helpful in an attempt to explain the value of knowledge. The first is to deny that the means-ends relationship needs to be one of objective likelihood. According to this approach, sometimes the means we adopt are nothing more than wishes or hopes or prayers for achieving the goals we have, but they are means to the goal in question nonetheless. For examples of such, think of the plight of the hopeless suitor, flailing away in the dark trying to find some way of winning the heart of his beloved. He knows he has no clue how to succeed and he knows that everything he tries may not even increase his chances of success. Even if his efforts are not successful, however, they still constitute the means he has adopted to achieve the goal in question.

Just so, justification may be a means to the goal of having true beliefs without being conceived to yield objective likelihood of having such. According to such subjective approaches, there is value in pursuing the truth by whatever means or methods are best by one's own lights, in full knowledge that these means or methods might having nothing more in their favor than hopes and wishes. Moreover, the value added by this property is not obviously swamped by the value of truth in the way that the property proposed by objective likelihood theorists is swamped, just as we value honesty and sincerity even when restricting our considerations to accurate reports. So one way of developing a theory of justification useful in the project of explaining the value of knowledge is to develop a subjective theory of justification.

The other way is to add further elements to the objective approaches so that the swamping problem is eliminated. One way to do so appeals to virtue epistemology, according to which knowledge is the product of the application of one's intellectual virtues (see Greco 2003, Riggs 2002, and Sosa 2003). On a standard account of the intellectual virtues, a virtue is a stable trait of character that makes the beliefs it produces likely to be true. In this way, standard virtue theories adopt objective likelihood accounts of justification. They do not stop, however, with the idea that justification is simply objective likelihood of truth. They add that this objective likelihood of truth must also arise from the display of some laudable intellectual character. The true beliefs that result are not merely likely to be true, they also constitute *accomplishments* of the believer, so that having the true belief is something for which the believer is responsible. As a result, the cognizer deserves credit for having a true belief, and this credit is valuable in a way not explained by the likelihood that the belief is true. For this reason, virtue approaches to justification have some hope of avoiding the swamping problem of providing an account of justification that is useful in the project of explaining the value of justification in terms greater than the value of its parts.

The fourth condition for knowledge. Were knowledge nothing more than justified true belief, these approaches to justification would give significant hope to the idea that knowledge is more valuable than its parts. Knowledge, however, is more than justified true belief; it is justified true belief where the connection between justification and truth is, in an appropriate way, nonaccidental. Various theories have been proposed regarding the appropriate kind of nonaccidentality that is required for knowledge, with the two most popular being the defeasibility theory and the relevant alternatives theory. There are serious worries that any approach to the fourth condition undermines the idea that knowledge is more valuable than its parts, and we can use these two theories to illustrate the difficulties.

The fundamental problem faced by all theories of the fourth condition is an insensitivity to the problem of the value of knowledge. In the *Meno*, Meno's response to Socrates's counterexample was to question why we prize knowledge more than true opinion and, indeed, whether there is any difference between the two. Meno's response reveals an important constraint on a theory of knowledge. To the extent that the theory focuses on the nature of knowledge at the expense of being able to account for the value of knowledge, it is suspect; and to the extent that a theory focuses on the issue of the value of knowledge at the expense of being able to account for the nature of knowledge, it is suspect as well.

The two major approaches to the fourth condition cited above provide excellent illustrations of how to err in each of these directions. Take first the relevant alternatives theory. On a relevant alternatives approach, the difference between knowledge and justified true belief is determined by whether one would be immune from error in alternatives to the actual situation. In perceptual cases, for example, suppose the surrounding area is littered with fake barns, but one happens to be looking at the only real barn in the area. Then in alternatives to the actual situation, one is not immune from error, for had one been looking at a fake barn, one would still have believed of it that it is a (real) barn.

This theory handles the fake barn case quite well, but it also risks implying global skepticism, if we consider the alternative situation in which Descartes's evil demon is operative. In order to avoid this skeptical consequence, this approach introduces the qualifier "relevant," and holds that the evil demon scenario is not a relevant alternative to the actual situation. The pressing issue for this approach is to specify what makes a situation relevant, and here relevant alternatives theorists have had little to say. The most simplistic version of the view would simply rely on our intuitive understanding of the concept of relevance, claiming that no more precise theoretical specification is needed.

Such a theory is well suited to addressing the issue of the value of knowledge. Immunity from error is itself a good thing, and it would be hard to argue that one should prefer such immunity in *irrelevant* alternatives to immunity in *relevant* alternatives. Whether this value could withstand the scrutiny needed to provide a full and complete answer to the question of the value of knowledge would remain to be seen, but the theory provides some hope of such. It provides such hope by identifying a property with obvious evaluative dimensions, and in this way follows the strategy of addressing questions regarding the value of knowledge by identifying evaluative features of knowledge not present in mere true belief or even in justified true belief.

What this theory gains through the use of the concept of relevance in addressing the problem of the value of knowledge, however, it sacrifices in addressing the problem of the nature of knowledge. For without some clarification of the concept of relevance, this approach is a nonstarter for addressing the problem of the nature of knowledge. It is important to recognize explicitly the significance of the intuitive concept of relevance, however. For the evaluative nature of this concept gives one precisely what one would wish for when focusing on the question of the value of knowledge. It is unfortunate that the simplistic version of this approach has no similar hope of adequately addressing questions regarding the nature of knowledge.

The defeasibility approach begins from a starting point that appears attractive in the search for a solution to the problem of the value of knowledge as well. The starting point for such theories is that what distinguishes knowledge from mere justified true belief is the absence of defeaters—information that, if acquired, would undermine the justification in question. In the fake barn case above, the further (unknown) information is that the landscape is littered with fake barns that cannot be distinguished from real ones.

This starting point is attractive from the point of view of the problem of the value of knowledge, for it cites a valuable property for a belief to have. It is valuable to have a belief whose justification cannot be undermined by learning any new information. The problem is that this starting point is inadequate, and to the credit of defeasibility theorists, they move beyond the simple relevant alternatives theory above by providing detailed and sophisticated accounts of precisely what unknown information undermines knowledge.

These accounts thus provide the detail needed in a serious effort to uncover the nature of knowledge, but the details of these accounts are completely insensitive to questions regarding the value of knowledge. The standard approach to developing the needed detail is to assemble a stable of examples, some of which involve knowledge and some of which do not, and attempt to find some distinguishing feature of the defeaters in cases of knowledge to use in refining the initial insight of the defeasibility theory. The result of this strategy is an approach that has little hope of providing a defeasibility condition that tracks any difference in value, and thus provides little hope in the attempt to explain the value of knowledge over that of its parts.

For example, consider one of the ways in which the simple defeasibility account is inadequate. Testimony by reliable persons often provides a defeater for what we would otherwise be justified in believing. Suppose we have visual evidence that a friend, Tom, left the library at 11 p.m. Our justification can be defeated if Tom's mother says that Tom has an identical twin that we did not know about who was in the library while Tom was at home fixing his mother's dishwasher. Whether it undermines our knowledge, however, depends on other factors such as who she reports this information to and what they know about her. It will not undermine our knowledge, for instance, if she fabricates the testimony to the police who are checking out a crime that occurred in the library, and the police have a large file of made-up stories from this woman in defense of Tom, who has a long criminal record, especially if the file contains precisely this concocted story, which the police have already checked in prior cases, discovering that Tom is an only child.

The simple defeasibility approach was attractive in the search for an explanation of the value of knowledge because it is valuable to have opinions that no further learning can undermine. Once we see cases such as the above, however, the defeasibility approach loses this attractive feature, for one can have knowledge even when further learning would rationally undermine one's opinion. In such cases, it is true that even more learning would restore one's original opinion, but there is little comfort to be found there, for the same will be true of any true belief, since if one knows all there is to know about a given claim, one will believe it if and only if it is true.

Defeasibility theories have had considerable difficulty in finding a condition that properly distinguishes when defeaters undermine knowledge and when they do not. The problem created by such approaches for the problem of the value of knowledge, however, is the tortured and ad hoc way in which various complex conditions are proposed to do the job. In light of the labyrinthine complexity that such accounts of knowledge display, no optimism is justified that such conditions will track any value difference between satisfying those complex conditions and not satisfying them. It appears that the most warranted conclusion to draw is that the task of distinguishing cases of knowledge from cases of nonknowledge has been revealed to be so difficult that epistemologists make progress on the question of the nature of knowledge only by proposing conditions that undermine any explanation of the value of knowledge by appeal to those conditions.

CONCLUSION

So the idea that truth is valuable on intrinsic grounds from a purely cognitive point of view may be defensible, but the same kind of defense of the value of knowledge is implausible. Instead, the more plausible approach tries to show that knowledge is valuable in virtue of its parts, but attempts along these lines founder on the admission that knowledge can be fallible. Such a result is compatible with truth and knowledge being valuable both from a purely cognitive point of view and from an all-things-considered point of view, but then knowledge will not have the type of value it is ordinarily assumed to have.

See also Truth.

Bibliography

Craig, Edward. *Knowledge and the State of Nature: An Essay in Conceptual Synthesis*. Oxford: Oxford University Press, 1990.

Fogelin, Robert. *Pyrrhonian Reflections on Knowledge and Justification*. Oxford: Oxford University Press, 1994.

Gettier, Edmund. "Is Justified True Belief Knowledge?" *Analysis* 23 (1963): 121–123.

Greco, John. "Knowledge as Credit for True Belief." In *Intellectual Virtue: Perspectives from Ethics and Epistemology*, edited by Michael DePaul and Linda Zagzebski. Oxford: Oxford University Press, 2003.

James, William. "The Will to Believe." In his *The Will to Believe and Other Essays in Popular Philosophy*. New York: Dover Publications, 1956.

Kvanvig, Jonathan. *The Value of Knowledge and the Pursuit of Understanding*. New York: Cambridge University Press, 2003.

Riggs, Wayne D. "Beyond Truth and Falsehood: The Real Value of Knowing that P." *Philosophical Studies*107 (2002): 87–108.

Rorty, Richard. *Contingency, Irony, and Solidarity*. Cambridge, U.K.: Cambridge University Press, 1989.

Rorty, Richard. *Truth and Progress*. Vol. 3 of *Philosophical Papers*. Cambridge, U.K.: Cambridge University Press, 1998.

Sosa, Ernest. "The Place of Truth in Epistemology." In *Intellectual Virtue: Perspectives from Ethics and Epistemology*, edited by Michael DePaul and Linda Zagzebski. New York: Oxford University Press, 2003.

Swinburne, Richard. *Epistemic Justification*. Oxford: Oxford University Press, 2001.

Williams, Bernard. *Truth and Truthfulness*. Princeton, NJ: Princeton University Press, 2002.

Zagzebski, Linda Trinkaus. *Virtues of the Mind: An Inquiry into the Nature of Virtue and the Ethical Foundation of Knowledge*. New York: Cambridge University Press, 1996.

Jonathan L. Kvanvig (2005)

KNOWLEDGE AND VAGUENESS

When anthropologists painstakingly identified the taxon of the skeleton that later became known as "Lucy's child,"

> There was no eureka. There was no grand turning point. The evidence kept dribbling in, and through hard labor and some dogged thinking we *did* solve the puzzle, not through revelation but through a sort of absorption, just below the level of explicit consciousness. It was as if the truth had slowly seeped through our pores, until we had come know it without knowing that we did. So when the final, indisputable confirmation came, we hardly noticed the event. What had once been a mystery had become—in hindsight, mind you—obvious from the start (Johanson and James Shreeve 1989, p. 203).

Instead of there being a clear point at which the anthropologists knew that the specimen was *Homo habilis*, there was stratification: The researchers began from obvious ignorance, inched up to being borderline knowers, and eventually emerged as clear knowers.

The vagueness of knowledge has substantial implications. When skeptics took over Plato's Academy, they tried to prove that there can be no knowledge. Such a proof would ensure that everything is a clear negative case of "knowledge." *Knowledge* would be a perfectly precise term; a skeptic should think twice before complaining about the vagueness of knowledge! Typically, borderline cases are flanked by clear cases (Figure 1), so

FIGURE 1

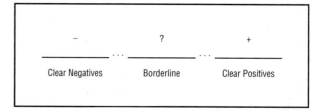

the vagueness of "know" positively invites the inference that there is at least some knowledge.

The vagueness of knowledge also affects principles of epistemic logic such as the "KK thesis": If you know, then you know you know. If the KK thesis were true, the anthropologists would have known that they knew from the moment they knew the taxon of Lucy's child.

Given a naturalistic perspective on knowers, the vagueness of "know" should be expected. Human perceptual capacities and memory trail off in the patterns made famous by evolutionary iconography (Figure 2).

1. THE SORITES PARADOX

Only a vague term (e.g., *human*) can serve as the inductive predicate of a sorites argument:

Base Step: There are now humans.

Induction Step: If there were humans n years ago, then there were humans $n - 1$ years ago.

Conclusion: There were humans five billion years ago.

Because the earth is only 4.6 billion years old, the conclusion is false. The base step is clearly true and the argument is classically valid. Therefore, people naturally suspect the induction step. However, they are unable to specify a value for n at which the generalization is false.

If vagueness is merely a kind of ignorance, there is no need to find a counterexample to the induction step. One can know a generalization is false even if one cannot pinpoint where it breaks down. Consider an anthropologist who doubts that all of the skeletal fragments in a bag belong to a single individual but cannot identify any pair of fragments as belonging to distinct specimens. When the anthropologist weighs the bag and learns there are more than enough fragments to constitute one skeleton, that is all that is needed to refute the generalization that all of the fragments come from a single individual.

In common usage, a borderline case is often simply one that cannot be settled at a given stage of inquiry. When an archeologist sorts stones, a few are obviously tools and most others are clearly just rocks. There will be another

FIGURE 2

group of stones whose status cannot be determined by unaided observation. These borderline cases are put under a field microscope. The three-way sorting begins afresh. Borderline cases that survive this second stage of inquiry may eventually wind up under an electron microscope.

Philosophers focus on the minority of borderline cases in which there is no prospect of resolution. How many years did the Middle Ages last? Is Israel a new state or an ancient state? Philosophers are at sea with these questions, and because people are unsure what would count as correctly answering these questions, their ignorance cannot be relativized to a set of resources.

Epistemicists insist there remains a crucial resemblance between these absolute borderline cases and relative borderline cases; they take all vagueness to be a form of ignorance. Epistemicists solve the sorites paradox by claiming that there is a hidden counterexample to the induction step. After all, they know the base step is true and the conclusion is false; classical logic then licenses the deduction that the induction step is false.

In classical logic, denying the induction step of the above sorites argument is equivalent to asserting there is a number n such that n years ago there was at least one human being but the year before that there were no human beings. So belief that there is a counterexample to the induction step is equivalent to the belief that there was a first human!

Incredulous anthropologists counter that nature does not draw a sharp line between humans and nonhumans. Speakers have not made up for the absence of sharp boundary by supplying an artificial one. Consequently, anyone who searches for the exact year humans appear on the evolutionary timeline is conceptually confused.

2. INFINITE REGRESSES

David Sanford (1975a) points out that if finite sequences do not need beginnings or endings, there are neglected solutions to infinite regress problems. Consider the infinite regress of justification: A belief can only be justified by another justified belief. Justification cannot be achieved by reasoning in a circle. Nor can chains of justification be infinitely long. The skeptic concludes that no beliefs are justified. The foundationalist responds by conferring axiomatic status on some beliefs; axioms justify other beliefs without needing justification from other beliefs. The vagueness of "justified" suggests another solution to this infinite regress: Admit that the chain of justification is finite but deny it must terminate in an axiomatic belief.

Compare justification to motherhood. Each woman must have a mother. Her family tree cannot go back infinitely and cannot circle back on itself. Is one to conclude that some woman lacks a mother? Sanford instead appeals to the vagueness of "mother." As one moves down her ancestral line, what counts as a mother eventually becomes less and less clear. After passing through a stretch of borderline cases, one arrives at ancestors who clearly lack a gender and therefore are clear nonmothers. Sanford says that an insistence that finite sequences have terminal points is an incarnation of the sorites paradox.

3. THE LOGICAL PREDICAMENT

Because the sorites argument is classically valid, David Sanford must espouse a deviant logic. Supplemental logics (modal logic, deontic logic, etc.) merely add theorems to the standard stock; they cannot subtract the sorites from the list of valid arguments. So Sanford must target classical logic, weakening it just enough to stop its validation of the sorites—without causing too much collateral damage. In standard fuzzy logic, almost all classical theorems are rejected—except for the special case in which the truth-values equal full truth or full falsehood (Machina 1976). Sanford (1975b) accepts degrees of truth but prefers to keep all classical theorems by rejecting the truth-functionality of the logical connectives. Other deviant logicians reject some classical inference rules. For instance, intuitionists closely associate proof with truth and so try to derail the sorites paradox by rejecting the validity of double-negation (Putnam 1983). Supervaluationists either reject inference rules such as contraposition and reductio ad absurdum or reject core semantic principles such as Tarski's convention T (McGee and McLaughlin 1995).

These changes occur at the center of the human web of belief and so reverberate widely. Because knowledge implies truth, new questions are raised by the fuzzy logician's talk of degrees of truth. For instance, can one know a proposition that has a degree of truth less than one? The fuzzy logician wants to explain human ignorance of typical borderline cases and so is committed to saying that people are ignorant of propositions that are as close to being false as to being true. But what about propositions that are nearly true? Fuzzy logicians say that many propositions that appear to be clear truths merely have a high degree of truth. So if knowledge implies full truth, people know less than they seem to know.

4. THE CREDIBILITY GAP

Knowledge does seem to imply full truth because knowledge implies belief and one can only believe what one considers to be fully true. "It is not fully true that the Black Skull is an australopithecine but I believe it is an australopithecine" is as hard on the ear as G. E. Moore's paradoxical sentence "It is raining but I do not believe it" (Moore 1942, 543).

This credibility gap hinders efforts to moderate epistemicism. Intuitively, people's wishy-washy attitude toward borderline cases seems like a reaction to the vagueness of these cases. But a subjectivist may reverse the relationship and say that the wishy-washy attitudes are what make propositions vague. If indeterminacy is a *projection* of human ambivalence, then people may hope to avoid the metaphysical burden of epistemicism. The epistemicist would be right in basing vagueness in the subject's limitations but wrong in postulating sharp thresholds.

Crispin Wright (2001) says that *x* is a borderline case of F-ness if two parties can disagree about whether *x* is F without either party being guilty of a cognitive shortcoming. Each party knows all the relevant facts, each is a competent speaker, and each has reasoned well. Wright compares this faultless stalemate with the cultural variation that makes relativism popular among ethnographers.

Critics of Wright object that anyone who takes a position on a borderline statement is guilty of a cognitive shortcoming; they ought to be agnostic. If one thinks that same-sex civil unions are borderline cases of marriages, then one cannot believe that they are marriages.

Stephen Schiffer (1998) has suggested that people have a special attitude toward cases that they take to be borderline. "Vague partial belief" differs from the belief humans extend to precise propositions. It also differs from the degrees of belief that people associate with probability theory. The probability calculus instructs people to assign a higher probability to a disjunction than either of its contingent disjuncts. But when the disjuncts

are borderline cases, Schiffer only assigns the disjunction as much vague partial belief as he assigns the strongest disjunct.

This result (which echoes the fuzzy logician's rule for calculating disjunctions) grates against the observation that hedging a claim can make it more assertible. One can know that Blaise Pascal died at thirty-nine but not be sure whether this counts as dying as a young man. However, one can confidently say that *either* Pascal died as a young man or as a man in middle age.

Supervaluationists have a simple explanation of why people do not believe borderline statements: they lack truth-values. Belief aims at truth, thus people cannot believe a statement that they believe to be borderline. However, this explanation overgeneralizes, for it does seem possible to have weak propositional attitudes (guessing, doubting, and suspecting) toward statements that one acknowledges to be borderline.

Supervaluationists also have trouble explaining why one can make a statement more credible by adding an *epistemic* hedge. If one believes linguistic indecision prevents "ten is a small number" from having a truth-value, then one cannot believe it may be true. Yet if ten clearly is a borderline case of a small number, then it is appropriate to shrug one's shoulders and conclude "ten might be a small number and ten might not be a small number." Indeed, prefixing any statement that is clearly borderline with "maybe" seems to make it clearly true.

Supervaluationists use truth-value gaps and the principle that knowledge implies truth to explain why humans are absolutely ignorant of borderline statements. God cannot know when a fetus becomes a human being because there is nothing to know.

Supervaluationists pride themselves on the modesty of their revision of classical logic. The workhorse of their adjustment is the notion of super-truth: A statement is super-true if and only if it comes out true under all admissible precisifications of the statement. For instance, "Either the specimen is a *Homo erectus* or an archaic *Homo Sapien*" is super-true because it comes out true regardless of how one precisifies *Homo erectus* and *archaic Homo sapien*.

Any statement that has the form of a classical tautology will be super-true even if it contains vague terms. So supervaluationists claim to preserve all the theorems of classical logic.

But can one believe a statement by virtue of its super-truth? Truth under all *disambiguations* is not enough. Suppose a person says "bachelors are mammals" and it is not clear whether that person is referring to unmarried men or to college graduates or to just any young male mammal. One knows the statement expresses a truth but does not know which truth it expresses. Ambiguous statements are not objects of knowledge.

But vague statements are objects of knowledge. People know "the number of men is either an even number or an odd number" even though the vagueness of "man" makes it impossible to count the number of men. Supervaluationists have trouble accepting asymmetries between vagueness and ambiguity. They characterize vagueness in semantic terms rather than epistemic terms, so supervaluationism looks more like a logic of ambiguity (Lewis 1982).

5. HIGHER ORDER VAGUENESS

In *Purity and Danger* Mary Douglas conjectures that the bearers of taboos are borderline cases (moles, eels, twilight, and so on). She interprets rituals of purification as attempts to reclassify doubtful cases (as when hermaphrodites are declared men through a rite of passage). Assessment of Douglas's hypothesis is hindered by the vagueness of "borderline case."

Borderline cases of "borderline case" are normal with vague terms. In addition to there being borderline cases of "human," there are borderline cases of "borderline human." So in addition to first order vagueness there is second order vagueness, third order vagueness, and so on, apparently ad infinitum.

Higher order vagueness is a problem for deviant logicians because they employ classical logic and set theory in the metalanguages they use to describe vague terms. This classical medium forces them to represent the transition from clear to borderline cases as a sharp threshold. For instance, supervaluationist semantics implies that there is a first point at which "*x* is a human" is true. So instead of having the epistemicist's sharp threshold between truth and falsehood, the supervaluationist has a sharp threshold between truth and absence of truth. Similarly, the fuzzy logician has sharp thresholds between each degree of truth, and can only approximate vagueness by using a large quantity of discrete microtransitions. The fuzzy logician's representation of vagueness is like a dot matrix printer's representation of gray—a black and white affair when examined close up.

What originally bothered philosophers were *sharp thresholds*, not sharp thresholds *between truth and falsehood*. Thus epistemicists advertise themselves as just self-consciously biting a bullet that others gnaw absentmindedly.

6. EXPLAINING THE IGNORANCE

Recent epistemicists are careful to endorse the principle that inquiry into borderline cases is futile. That is why they stress that borderline statements are unknowable. But if these statements have truth-values, why can't they be known? One response is to challenge the presumption in favor of knowability—to portray ignorance as a natural state in need of no explanation.

However, Timothy Williamson (1994) directly answers the question of why borderline statements cannot be known. He traces the unknowability of borderline statements to the knower's need for a margin for error. When at a stadium, one can know there are about ten thousand people. But one cannot know there are exactly ten thousand, for a person cannot reliably discriminate between there being ten thousand and there being ten thousand and one. Given that "human" has the sort of precise threshold epistemicists allege, anyone who happened to correctly believe that humans originated *n* years ago, would have to be right by luck. For all this person knows, the origin could have been a year earlier.

Williamson believes that thresholds for vague predicates are determined by the psychology, social conditions, and environment of the speech community. These conditions are too complicated to allow humans to ascertain the threshold for vague terms.

The margin for error principle yields different limits for different kinds of knowers. For much of the history of *Homo sapiens* there were other hominids who had different cognitive capacities. Williamson's theory does not preclude these hominids from knowing the threshold of some vague terms. Some of what is chaotic to humans may be predictable to these homonids. Williamson is committed to the relativity of all borderline cases. Supervaluationists claim an advantage over Williamson insofar as they neatly model absolute borderline cases.

Roy Sorensen (2001) has speculated that an epistemicist can match the neatness of the supervaluationists by using truth-maker gaps instead of truth-value gaps. A truth-maker is what makes a proposition true. For instance, "Humans and chimpanzees had a common ancestor seven million years ago" is made true by a Miocene primate who had as descendants both Noam Chomsky and Nim Chimpsky. One learns the truth-value of propositions only by becoming appropriately related to their truth-makers. Propositions that lack truth-makers have truth-values that are not anchored to any piece of reality. This objective indeterminacy makes the propositions absolutely unknowable.

7. VAGUENESS AND EPISTEMIC LOGIC

If the relationship between knowledge and borderline cases is orderly, epistemicists can offer a logic of vagueness as a branch of epistemic logic. For instance, Timothy Williamson elaborates his "logic of clarity" in a way that makes it isomorphic to supervaluationism. The basic idea is that a statement is definitely true if it comes out true "under all sharp interpretations of the language indiscriminable from the right one" (Williamson 1999, p. 128). This mirrors the supervaluationist's principle that a statement is definitely true if it comes out true under all admissible completions of the language.

Epistemicists are divided on how closely vagueness is bound up with borderline cases. Everybody agrees that a vague term need not have actual borderline cases. Possible borderline cases are sufficient. But what about borderline cases that are merely epistemically possible? Perhaps the mere threat of an objective borderline case can be enough to make a predicate vague (Sorensen 2001). After all, if the threat cannot be exposed as false, then there will be irremediable linguistic ignorance without borderline cases. One would be able to embed the predicate in a sorites argument and bedevil people with doubts about termination points.

See also Agnosticism; Classical Foundationalism; Contextualism; Doubt; Laws of Thought; Relevant Alternatives.

Bibliography

Johanson, Donald, and James Shreeve. *Lucy's Child*. New York: Avon Books, 1989.

Lewis, David. "Logic for Equivocators." *Noûs* 16 (1982): 431–441.

Machina, Kenton. "Truth, Belief and Vagueness." *Journal of Philosophical Logic* 5 (1976): 47–78. Reprinted in *Vagueness: A Reader*, edited by Rosanna Keefe and Peter Smith, 174–203. Cambridge, MA: MIT Press.

McGee, Vann, and Brian McLaughlin. "Distinctions Without a Difference." *Southern Journal of Philosophy* 33 (Supplement) (1995): 203–251.

Moore, G. E. "A Reply to My Critics" in *The Philosophy of G. E. Moore*, edited by P. A. Schlipp. Evantston, IL: Northwestern University, 1942.

Putnam, Hilary. "Vagueness and Alternative Logic." In his *Realism and Reason*. Cambridge, U.K.: Cambridge University Press, 1983.

Sanford, David. "Borderline Logic." *American Philosophical Quarterly* 12/1 (1975b): 29–39.

Sanford, David. "Infinity and Vagueness." *Philosophical Review* 84 (1975b): 520–535.

Schiffer, Stephen. "Two Issues of Vagueness." *Monist* 81 (2) (1998): 193–214.

Sorensen, Roy. *Vagueness and Contradiction*. Oxford: Clarendon Press, 2001.

Sorensen, Roy. "The Vagueness of Knowledge." *Canadian Journal of Philosophy* 17 (4) (1987): 767–804.

Williamson, Timothy. "On the Structure of Higher-Order Vagueness." *Mind* 108 (1999): 127–143.

Williamson, Timothy. *Vagueness*. London: Routledge, 1994.

Wright, Crispin. "On Being in a Quandary." *Mind* 110 (437) (2001): 45–98.

Roy Sorensen (2005)

KNOWLEDGE ARGUMENT

The definitive statement of the knowledge argument was formulated by Frank Jackson in a paper titled "Epiphenomenal Qualia" that appeared in the *Philosophical Quarterly* in 1982. Arguments in the same spirit had appeared earlier (Broad 1925, Robinson 1982), but Jackson's argument is most often compared with Thomas Nagel's argument in "What Is It Like to Be a Bat?" (1974). Jackson, however, takes pains to distinguish his argument from Nagel's. This entry will follow standard practice in focusing on Jackson's argument, though it also describes the main points of alleged similarity and dissimilarity between these two arguments.

The knowledge argument targets physicalism about the mind, which claims that, as Jackson puts it in a follow-up article, "the actual world … is entirely physical" (1986, p. 281). The argument provided one of the chief sources of doubt about physicalism in the late twentieth century, and continues to shape discussion of the mind-body problem into the twenty-first. It is unclear whether the argument converted many to dualism; still, most readers found the argument's core thought experiment highly compelling. Physicalists thus faced the challenge of identifying an error in the argument. The potency of the knowledge argument is clear because while all materialists reject its conclusion, there is little agreement among them as to how, precisely, its reasoning is flawed.

THE ARGUMENT

Jackson's original argument is disarmingly brief. He invites the reader to imagine the following scenario: Mary, a brilliant neuroscientist, has spent her entire life in a room in which the only visible colors are black and white. Partly through the use of a black-and-white television monitor, Mary comes to know all of the physical facts about color vision. These facts include the nature of causal interactions between the surface reflectance properties of objects, wavelengths of light, and retinal stimulation. Jackson then asks: "What will happen when Mary is released from her black and white room or is given a color television monitor? Will she *learn* anything or not?" He answers: "It seems just obvious that she will learn something about the world and our visual experience of it" (Jackson 1982, p. 130). He thinks that when Mary finally leaves the room and, for the first time, gazes upon an object that is red (and that she knows to be red), she learns *what it's like* to see red. Jackson concludes that, because physicalism requires that all facts are physical facts, physicalism is false.

Jackson's conclusion is a dualism of properties, rather than of substances; and this is all that his argument warrants. For a difference in properties—between the property *instantiating neurophysiological state N*, and the property *instantiating qualitative state Q*, say—suffices for a difference in corresponding facts.

A formalization of the argument will be useful.

(1) While in the black-and-white room, Mary knows all of the physical facts about color experience.

(2) Mary learns something about color experience upon her release.

(3) If Mary learns something about color experience upon her release, she does not know all of the facts about color experience while in the room.

(4) Mary does not know all of the facts about color experience while in the room (from 2 and 3).

(5) There are facts about color experience that are not physical facts (from 1 and 4).

(6) If physicalism is true, then all facts are physical facts.

Therefore,

(7) Physicalism is false (from 5 and 6).

As mentioned above, Jackson distinguishes this argument from Nagel's 1974 argument. Nagel had argued that no amount of physical information about bats—including knowledge of their neurophysiological, behavioral, and evolutionary features—could allow us to grasp the experiential aspect of using echolocation; that is, to know what it's like to be a bat. According to Jackson, these arguments differ in two ways. First, he claims that his argument concerns knowledge of a general property of experience, what it's like to see red, whereas Nagel's argument concerns knowledge of a property specific to an individual; that is, what it's like to be a (particular) bat. But to some, this difference has seemed at most a quirk of exposition: for Nagel's argument does draw into question whether we can know a general property of experience, namely, what it's like to use echolocation. However, oth-

ers—including Jackson himself—have claimed that whereas Jackson's argument specifically targets the contrast between the phenomenal and the physical, Nagel's argument instead targets the contrast between the subjective and the objective.

The second point of contrast that Jackson draws is this: Nagel's argument simply shows that humans cannot imagine what it's like to use echolocation, and this limit to our imaginative powers is irrelevant to the issue of physicalism. Whether Nagel's argument rests on this issue about imaginability, or whether it would remain intact when using an experience that is within the normal course of human experience (as Jackson's does), is largely a question of interpretation. But the point about imaginability brings out an important and sometimes overlooked feature of Jackson's argument: that nothing in the argument excludes the possibility that Mary, perhaps through an exercise of imagination or as the result of taking a hallucinogen, undergoes an experience while in the room that is, in fact, a *seeing red* experience. Jackson's point remains so long as Mary is unable to determine that the experience is a *seeing red* experience as opposed to, say, a *seeing green* experience. This brings out the epistemic character of the argument. Jackson's argument requires only that Mary cannot *deduce* that a certain experience is the sort of experience her subjects undergo when seeing a ripe tomato (say). Upon leaving the room, Mary has the opportunity to *correlate* these, by gazing at a tomato herself. (She could, of course, correlate them while inside the room, by scanning her own brain while she is undergoing the *seeing red* experience. In the context of the argument, having the opportunity to make this correlation is tantamount to leaving the room.)

OBJECTIONS TO THE ARGUMENT

This entry now turns to the four most influential types of objection to the argument. The first is simply to deny the conjunction of premises (1) and (2). On this view, Mary does not know all of the physical facts unless she knows what it's like to see red. Daniel Dennett (1991) takes this approach, arguing that we cannot truly conceive knowing all of the relevant physical facts. This limitation explains why it seems that Mary learns something upon her release; but, Dennett maintains, if (1) is true, then (2) is false. In response, defenders of the knowledge argument have pointed out that the argument requires only that we understand the basic kind of knowledge that Mary has while in the room, not that we can mentally rehearse each bit of information she possesses. Because we do have a grasp of the sort of physical facts she knows, our powers of conceiving are strong enough to evaluate the possibility that (1) and (2) are true simultaneously.

The next two objections deny premise (3). Churchland (1985) describes what Mary gains upon her release as a kind of *knowledge by acquaintance* of what it's like to see red; that is, as nonpropositional knowledge of this fact. Using this analysis of the case, he argues that a parallel argument would condemn dualism as well, because Mary would lack such knowledge by acquaintance even if she had exhaustive propositional knowledge about the nonphysical. Jackson (1986) responds that these are not on a par, for one could know all of the physical facts about seeing red without knowing what it's like, but one could not know all of the facts (physical and nonphysical) about seeing red without knowing what it's like. This may seem question-begging, but it has seemed highly intuitive to many philosophers, and hence this second avenue of objection has attracted relatively few proponents. (But see Earl Conee 1994 for a more developed version of the acquaintance analysis.)

Another objection that denies premise (3) claims that what Mary gains upon leaving the room is an ability, rather than knowledge of a fact. This objection originated in Laurence Nemirow's review of Nagel's argument (1980), and is defended by David Lewis (1988). On this *ability* approach to defusing the argument, when she finally sees something red, Mary learns how to remember, recognize, and/or imagine a *seeing red* experience. The fact that experience is required for such abilities carries no antiphysicalist consequences; after all, exhaustive propositional knowledge does not generally guarantee that one possesses the relevant ability. If it did, professional baseball teams would be staffed by physicists, who can master all of the relevant facts about how to hit a curve ball.

While the ability approach remains influential, it does face difficult challenges. One challenge is to specify an ability that is gained when, and only when, Mary learns what it's like to see red. At the moment of her grasping this, she is not yet able to remember what it's like, for the moment has not passed; and if she has a poor imagination, experience may not enable her to imagine what it's like. (For responses along these lines, see Conee 1994 and Torin Alter 1998.) Arguably, the best candidate for what Mary gains is the ability to recognize *seeing red* experiences. But the ability analysis may be mistaken even if this recognitional ability is perfectly correlated with knowing what it's like to see red. For, as Brie Gertler (1999) argues, it seems plausible that Mary is able to recognize a *seeing red* experience *because* she knows what it's like, where *because* is used in an explanatory sense. If knowing what it's like explains the recognitional ability, then it does not reduce to that ability.

The fourth and most widely accepted type of objection to the knowledge argument rejects premise (6). It claims that our ways of representing reality may be more fine-grained than the reality we represent, and what Mary gains is simply a new way to represent a portion of reality that was already known to her. (There are two competing ways to use *fact* in this context. One is to read *fact* as inheriting the fineness of grain that our representations possess; it is this reading that has been used in saying that this objection targets premise (6). The second reading uses *fact* as less fine-grained than our representations. On that reading, the current objection would instead reject premise (3), claiming that Mary didn't learn any new facts but only encountered old facts under a new guise or mode of presentation. The difference here is purely verbal, and this entry will continue to use *fact* in the former sense.)

This sort of objection was present in earlier papers (including Terence Horgan 1984 and Michael Tye 1986), but is usually associated with Brian Loar, who provided a nuanced version of it in 1990. Loar argues that a single property may be the referent of distinct concepts. In particular, a property that Mary knew as *instantiating neurophysiological state N* may be identical to the property *instantiating qualitative state Q*, even if knowledge that a state falls under the former concept does not generate knowledge that it falls under the latter. Thus, Mary's ignorance can be attributed to a distinction in concepts that does not imply any distinction in properties.

More generally, this line of response to the knowledge argument construes the change in Mary as purely epistemic, and denies that her epistemic advance, upon leaving the room, reflects any grasp of a hitherto unknown ontological feature of the world. As such, it represents a more general, highly influential position about the mind-body problem: The apparent disparity between physical and phenomenal features of the world (called *the explanatory gap* after Joseph Levine "1983") is purely epistemic, and not ontological.

This position belongs to a more general outlook known as *a posteriori physicalism*. According to *a posteriori* physicalists, antiphysicalist arguments that are based on thought experiments show, at most, that physicalism is not an a priori truth; but as Saul Kripke (1980) demonstrated, some identities are *a posteriori* (yet necessarily true). Strikingly, Kripke himself rejects *a posteriori* physicalism and claims that the distinctive way in which phenomenal concepts operate rules out the possibility of *a posteriori* identities between phenomenal and physical (or functional) properties. In a paper co-written with David Chalmers, Jackson also objects to *a posteriori* physicalism. According to Chalmers and Jackson (2001), the approach used by *a posteriori* physicalists presumes that there is a deep schism between concepts and ontology, a schism that would undercut the justification for uncontroversial identity statements.

Despite his continuing opposition to *a posteriori* physicalism, Jackson now rejects the knowledge argument (Jackson 2003). He contends that phenomenal knowledge is deducible, in principle, from physical knowledge, even if we may be unable to perform the deduction. Jackson's turnabout is based on his acceptance of representationalism, which claims that the phenomenal character of a state is exhausted by its representational content. For instance, suppose that one of Mary's subjects, Joe, gazes at a ripe tomato. Representationalists maintain that the visual phenomenal quality of Joe's experience is fully captured by the fact that his state represents *there is something round and red before me*. (Specific representational contents will be much more detailed, of course.) Because Mary can, in principle, know the representational contents of Joe's states before her release, she can in principle know all that there is to know about what it is like to see red.

OVERALL ASSESSMENT

The knowledge argument is an argument against physicalism. Yet its importance stems as much from the richness and variety of the responses inspired by its provocative reasoning as from its conclusion. Discussion of the argument has profoundly affected debate on a range of issues, including: differences between propositional knowledge and ability, the relation between identity and deducibility, and the special features of phenomenal knowledge. While the majority of philosophers ultimately reject the argument, a vocal minority accepts it as sound.

See also Functionalism; Mind-Body Problem; Physicalism; Qualia.

Bibliography

Alter, Torin. "A Limited Defense of the Knowledge Argument." *Philosophical Studies* 90 (1998): 35–56.

Broad, C. D. *Mind and its Place in Nature.* London: Routledge and Kegan Paul, 1925.

Chalmers, David, and Frank Jackson. "Conceptual Analysis and Reductive Explanation." *Philosophical Review* 110 (2001): 315–360.

Churchland, Paul. "Reduction, Qualia, and the Direct Introspection of Brain States." *Journal of Philosophy* 82 (1985): 8–28.

Conee, Earl. "Phenomenal Knowledge." *Australasian Journal of Philosophy* 72 (1994): 136–150.

Dennett, Daniel. *Consciousness Explained.* Boston: Little, Brown, 1991.

Gertler, Brie. "A Defense of the Knowledge Argument." *Philosophical Studies* 93 (1999): 317–336.

Horgan, Terence. "Jackson on Physical Information and Qualia." *Philosophical Quarterly* 34 (1984): 147–52.

Jackson, Frank. "Epiphenomenal Qualia." *Philosophical Quarterly* 32 (1982): 127–136.

Jackson, Frank. "Mind and Illusion." In *Minds and Persons*, edited by Anthony O'Hear. Cambridge, U.K.: Cambridge University Press, 2003.

Jackson, Frank. "What Mary Didn't Know." *Journal of Philosophy* 83 (1986): 291–295.

Kripke, Saul. *Naming and Necessity.* Cambridge, MA: Harvard University Press, 1980.

Levine, Joseph. "Materialism and Qualia: The Explanatory Gap." *Pacific Philosophical Quarterly* 64 (1983): 354–361.

Lewis, David. "What Experience Teaches." *Proceedings of the Russellian Society* 13 (1988): 29–57. Reprinted in Ludlow et al., *There's Something About Mary.*

Loar, Brian. "Phenomenal States." In *Philosophical Perspectives*, vol. 4: *Action Theory and Philosophy of Mind*, edited by James Tomberlin. Atascadero, CA: Ridgeview Press, 1990.

Ludlow, Peter, Yujin Nagasawa, and Daniel Stoljar, eds. *There's Something About Mary: Essays on Phenomenal Consciousness and Frank Jackson's Knowledge Argument.* Cambridge, MA: MIT Press, 2004.

Nagel, Thomas. "What Is It Like to Be a Bat?" *Philosophical Review* 83 (1974): 435–50. Reprinted in his *Mortal Questions* (Cambridge, U.K.: Cambridge University Press, 1979).

Nemirow, Laurence. "Review of Thomas Nagel's *Mortal Questions*" *Philosophical Review* 89 (1980): 473–477.

Robinson, Howard. *Matter and Sense: A Critique of Contemporary Materialism.* Cambridge, U.K.: Cambridge University Press, 1982.

Tye, M. "The Subjective Qualities of Experience." *Mind* 95 (1986): 1–17.

Brie Gertler (2005)

KNOWLEDGE IN INDIAN PHILOSOPHY

Almost all the philosophical texts in classical India were written in Sanskrit. How does one say *knowledge* in Sanskrit? And what do the Sanskrit terms that may be translated by the English word *knowledge* mean exactly? There are no simple answers to these questions.

In Western philosophy truth and falsity are usually ascribed to statements, propositions, or beliefs. In the Indian tradition truth and falsity are ascribed to a cognition or an awareness (the most common term is *jñāna*, but there are a relatively large number of synonyms, or quasi synonyms, such as *vijñāna*, *buddhi*, *dhī* and *citta*). The word *jñāna* is derived from the root *jñā*, which is etymologically related to the English word *know*. Nevertheless, the rendering of *jñāna* as knowledge is generally avoided because *jñāna* can be true or false, whereas false knowledge or wrong knowledge seems like a contradiction in terms (at least in English). Furthermore, *jñāna* is a particular and momentary event, whereas *knowledge* often refers to a general and lasting acquaintance with facts. Furthermore, knowledge is, or may be, an abstract entity that is shared by many persons; *jñāna* is always individual and belongs to a single person. Finally, *knowledge*, unlike *jñāna*, is a collective term and can only be used in the singular. A person has many *jñānas*, but not many *knowledges*.

The different ontologies of the various traditions of Indian philosophy necessitate different notions of *jñāna*. According to some Brahminical schools, *jñāna* is a momentary property of the eternal individual soul (*ātman*). The relationship between *jñāna* and *soul* is the relationship between quality and substance. It is the same relation that occurs between a color and the material substance like a pot in which it inheres. In contrast, the Buddhists reject the idea of substance in general and of a permanent soul or self in particular. According to them an awareness (*jñāna*) is a primitive (nonderivative) element of existence (*dharma*) that depends only on its causes and conditions (e.g., sense, object, and previous mental factors), not on any substrate such as a permanent soul. The Sāṃkhya and Yoga are unique in the Brahminical tradition in claiming that the cognitive and psychological processes occur in the realm of matter and have no direct contact with the conscious soul, which is distinct from them and completely passive (for more details, see Chakravarti 1975, pp. 171–196). Finally, according to the materialists (Cārvāka or Lokāyata), an awareness, or consciousness, arises from the combination of the material elements earth, water, fire, and wind when they evolve into body, sense, and object, just as the power of intoxication arises when certain substances ferment (Namai 1976, Franco 1997, pp. 98–99).

Knowledge in general as referring to an organized body of knowledge, or even a science, is usually called *veda* or *vidyā* (words that are cognate with Latin *videre* and the English *to wit*). When the word *veda* is mentioned without further qualification, it always refers to the four collections of texts known as Ṛgveda, Yajurveda, Sāmaveda, and Atharvaveda. These contain *the* knowledge, the knowledge par excellence. The Vedas are the primary scriptures of Brah-

manism and Hinduism. According to Brahminical orthodoxy they are neither of human nor Godly origin, for they are eternal and infallible. The text of the Vedas was revealed (not created) by omniscient Gods such as Brahma, or directly heard by inspired seers (Rishis) of old. Various enumerations and classifications of systematic knowledge, or sciences, have been transmitted; perhaps the most common ones refer to fourteen or eighteen locations of knowledge (*vidyāshtāna*): the four Vedas and the six auxiliary sciences to the Vedic texts (the sciences of articulation or phonology, prosody, grammar, etymology, astronomy/astrology, and ritual/ceremony), religious and social law (*dharmaśāstra*), collections of ancient myths (*purāṇa*), hermeneutics (*mīmāṃsā*), and dialectics (*tarka*); the eighteenfold enumeration adds medicine (*āyurveda*), archery or the science of weapons in general (*dhanurveda*), and *arthaśāstra*, which includes politics and economy.

These lists do not exhaust all the sciences known in ancient India, but they point to an attempt at an exhaustive classification of human cultural practices (Pollock 1985, p. 502). Sheldon Pollock, who examined the notion of *śāstra* in classical India, points out that virtually every human activity had been codified into a science (or a theory, as he renders the word *śāstra*), for instance, cookery, erotics (*kāmaśāstra*), thievery (*cauraśāstra*), agriculture, mathematics, logic, ascetic renunciation, and spiritual liberation. As a rule (there are notable exceptions), the various sciences have not been discovered by their practitioners. Rather, all practice is said to be derived from previously existing knowledge. Science itself is primordial; it is not accumulative, and can only decrease with time.

In Buddhist texts (both in India and Tibet) one encounters a list of five places or locations of knowledge (*vidyāsthānas*) that are to be cultivated by the Bodhisattva on his way to enlightenment. The first of these, the inner science or the own science (*adhyātmavidyā*), is specific to Buddhists, the other four—the science of logical reasons, grammar, medicine, and arts and crafts—are external and considered common to Buddhist and non-Buddhists (Seyfort Ruegg 1995, pp. 9–10). However, the status of the science of reasons, that is, philosophy/dialectics/logic, was ambiguous. Although its position following the inner science clearly implies that it is an external (or non-Buddhist) science, it was sometimes considered to be part of the Buddhist teachings. The science of logical reasons could be assimilated either to *tarka*, dialectics, which have nothing particularly Buddhist about them, or it could be understood as the science of the means of knowledge (*pramāṇa*), as expounded by Dharmakirti (seventh century) and his followers that was closely associated to the understanding and interpretation of the Buddhist teachings (Seyfort Ruegg 1995, p. 105). Deliberation and reasoning on the Buddha's teaching were widely perceived to be necessary steps before meditation. Traditionally, the study of the Buddhist scriptures was divided into three steps: listening to the Buddha's words, reflecting on them, and meditating on them.

However, another term that is often used to convey the idea of knowledge is *kala*, sometimes translated by "art and craft," refers to both "knowledge that" and "knowledge how." There are long lists of the various *kalās* (also called *śilpas*), some of them enumerating sixty-four, some seventy-eight, some more than ninety types. A typical list would include the knowledges of writing, calculation, sculpting, painting, dancing, singing, playing on musical instruments, gambling, speaking courteously, various games, preparing drinks, preparing perfumes, composing poems in various meters, divination, poisons and antidotes, the movement of heavenly bodies, training horses and elephants, archery, and various forms of fighting.

However, these terms for knowledge are not extensively treated in Indian philosophical texts, and except for the four Vedas, do not play an important role in Indian theories of knowledge. For Indian philosophers are not so much concerned with the nature of knowledge as such, but with the means of knowledge (*pramāṇa*).

PRAMĀṆA

To the question "how can one know something?" all Indian philosophers would answer unanimously: by having a means of knowledge. This answer may sound almost tautological and no two significant philosophers would understand the term in exactly the same manner. Nevertheless, the term *pramāṇa* played a crucial role in structuring the Indian epistemologies. It is around this concept, its definitions, and its varieties that Indian philosophy developed in its most dynamic period (roughly from the fifth to the twelfth century). The most important means of knowledge are sense perception (*pratyakṣa*), inference (*anumāna*), and verbal communication (*śabda*), under which sacred writings such as the Vedas or the teaching of the Buddha are subsumed.

What are the means of knowledge (*pramāṇa*)?

The number of means of knowledge that are accepted by the different schools of thought varies strongly. Madhyamaka Buddhists like Nāgārjuna, skeptics like Jayarāśi (Franco 1994), and monists of the Advaita-Vedānta tradition like Śrīharṣa, all of whom deny the possibility of knowledge, obviously accept no means of knowledge to be

reliable (Matilal 1977). All other schools admit that sense perception is a means of knowledge. The materialist school (Lokāyata) is distinguished from other schools by its claim that only sense perception is valid. The Vaiśeṣikas and the Buddhists after Dignāga (fifth century) admit two means of knowledge, namely, perception and inference. The Sāṃkhyas admit verbal communication by a trustworthy person (*āptavacana*) besides these two; Buddhist philosophers before Dignāga, for example, Vasubandhu, also admit verbal communication to be a means of knowledge. Philosophers of the Nyāya tradition, with the notable exception of Bhāsarvajña (ninth century), also admit analogy (*upamāna*) as a fourth means of knowledge. The same position was held by certain Buddhists (Franco 2001). The Prābhākara Mīmāṃsakas accept five means of knowledge: the previously mentioned four and presumption (*arthāpatti*). The Bhāṭṭa Mīmāṃsakas and Advaita-Vedāntins admit six means of knowledge: the previously mentioned five and absence (*abhāva*) or nonperception (*anupalabdhi*). In nonphilosophical texts one also encounters inclusion (*sambhava*) and tradition (*aitihya*) as means of knowledge. Since inference and verbal communication are dealt with in separate entries, this entry will focus mainly on a discussion of perception.

PERCEPTION AND SENSES

Perception here refers primarily to sense perception. Indeed, the Sanskrit word that is usually rendered by *perception* is *pratyakṣa*; it contains the semantic element—*akṣa*—which means "eye." However, in some cases such as mental perception of feelings or the extrasensory perception of Yogis, the senses play no role in its arising. Perception is usually said to arise from sense and object. In this connection one has to emphasize the distinction between sense (or sense-faculty) and sense organ. The senses are not identical with the bodily organs to which they are associated. It is an extremely common mistake in Western publications to refer to the senses of seeing, hearing, smelling, touching, and tasting as eyes, ears, nose, skin, and tongue. Indian philosophers, however, clearly distinguish between them.

Thus, according to Nyāya the sense of sight is not the eye, but an invisible ray of light that rests on the pupil of the eye and goes out to reach the object. The sense of hearing is not the ear, but a part of space-ether (*ākāśa*) that is enclosed in the ear. The sense of taste is not the tongue, but a watery substance in the form of half-moon that is spread at the front of the tongue. The sense of smell is a substance made of earth and is found inside the nose; its base is usually called *nāsā*—a cognate of nose—

but sometimes also *tripuñika*, that is, "the three cavities," or "the triple cavity," which seems to indicate that its base is the root of the nose. The sense of touch, which is sometimes interpreted as a sense of temperature, is also found inside and throughout the body, not only on the skin.

Already in the early philosophy of nature, the senses were considered to be material. Each sense—except for the auditory—was composed of the four material elements (earth, water, fire, and wind). Their special ability to grasp a certain elemental quality was explained as being due to their composition. The gustatory sense consists mainly of water, and it possesses the quality to be grasped, namely, flavor (*VS* 8.16–17). Although the element earth also possesses flavor, this quality is not predominant in it. The elemental constitution of the senses is based on the principle that "similar perceives similar." The Nyāya, Vaiśeṣika, and the Mīmāṃsā accepted the so-called accumulation theory of qualities in elements.

Except for hearing, the senses are made of special invisible atoms. Therefore, they cannot perceive themselves and can only be inferred: From the fact that one has a visual awareness, one infers that one has a sense of sight. According to the Buddhists the senses are made of a special subtle and transparent matter (*bhūtaprasāda*); the transparency of this matter is used to explain both its invisibility and its receptivity to other forms. Unlike normal matter, the subtle matter of which the senses are made does not obstruct other matter. When Indian philosophers write about the senses, they think above all about sight. The sense of sight is often used as a model for all other senses; hearing is treated cursorily, the other senses are hardly ever discussed.

PERCEPTION AND CONTACT

There was a strong debate that lasted for centuries between Buddhists and Naiyāyikas on the question of whether the sense and the object must be in contact to produce sense perception. The debate concerned only the senses of seeing and hearing (for everyone agreed that the other senses must be in contact with their objects). The Naiyāyikas and the Mīmāṃsakas maintained that all senses must be in contact with their objects to perceive them. In response to the Buddhist objection that sight perceives objects at a distance and objects that are larger in size than the sense itself, the Naiyāyikas postulated an invisible ray of light that goes from the eye and enters in contact with the object. This ray of light has a broad tip so that it can be in contact with large objects. It is in this context that certain optical theories were developed (Preisendanz 1989).

PERCEPTION AND THE CRITERION OF TRUTH

For a general discussion of truth and error, notably of false inferences, see the entry "Truth and Falsity in Indian Philosophy." The problem of truth is addressed here only in respect to perception. The earliest discussion on the criterion of truth can be found in a short passage of an anonymous Mīmāṃsā commentary that is now lost except in quotations and references in later sources that refer to its author simply as "The Commentator" (*vṛttikāra*) (Frauwallner 1968, pp. 107–111). It may seem odd that a Mīmāṃsā commentary that deals with Vedic exegesis should contain digressions on perception and related epistemological problems. Indeed, the rationale for the treatment of perception in Mīmāṃsā writings was originally a negative one: the rejection of sense perception as a means for the apprehension of the *dharma*, understood here as Vedic injunctions (*MS* 1.1.4).

According to the Commentator, "true perception is the arising of awareness when the senses of a man are in contact with precisely that which the awareness has for its object" (*ŚBh* 26.3–4). In other words, when the internal object that appears in the awareness and the external object that is in contact with the senses are identical, the resulting awareness is perception. This is, however, only a general definition. How can one know whether a specific awareness has arisen when the senses are in contact with the same object that appears in the awareness, or whether they were in contact with a different object? One may have an awareness of silver, but how is one to know whether the senses are in contact with silver, or with a glittering conch shell that produces an illusion of silver? The Commentator answers that a sublating awareness (*bādhaka-jñāna*) arises in respect to a false awareness and asserts its falsity, "That was not silver, the awareness was false." However, the problem with sublation (*bādhā*) as a criterion of truth is that the sublating awareness arises later, sometimes much later, than the false awareness. How does one know when an awareness is true or false at the time it arises? At that moment there is no difference whatsoever between true and false awarenesses, for the person who mistakes a conch shell for a piece of silver also thinks, "My sense of sight is in contact with silver."

The Commentator suggests that when the causal complex that produces the awareness is disturbed, the awareness is false; otherwise it is true. For instance, when the mind is disturbed by hunger, when the sense of sight is disturbed by an illness, or when the external object is too subtle, the awareness is false; when the causal complex is not disturbed, the awareness that arises from it is true. By this assertion the Commentator makes the true awarenesses the normal ones, those people usually have, and errors are considered to be an exception. In other words, there is nothing inherently wrong in the cognitive process itself. However, the assertion that a true awareness is produced by undisturbed causes tells one what happens, but not when it happens. That a particular awareness has arisen from undisturbed causes remains to be proved for every single case. The Commentator maintains that if one earnestly searches and does not find any fault with the causal complex, then, because there is no proof to the contrary, we should think (*manyemahi*) that the awareness is true.

Later Mīmāṃsakas like Kumārila (seventh century) had to deal with problems that the Commentator had left open. For instance, in certain cases one is not in a position to rectify an erroneous awareness (*ŚV, Vṛttikāragrantha* 23). A certain illness of the eye distorts vision in such a way that one sees a double moon. In such cases the mistaken person learns in his or her communication with other people that there is only one moon in the sky. Kumārila also had to deal also with errors that are immanent to the cognitive process. Such errors would render all everyday awarenesses, even those that are usually considered true, essentially erroneous. For instance, according to the Buddhists, every empirical awareness involves a conceptual construction. Empirical awarenesses have wholes (*avayavin*) and universals (*jāti*) as their objects, but these have no correspondence in reality. Even a simple awareness such as "this is a cow" contains at least two parts. The part *this* refers to some concrete individual, the part *cow* to a universal "bovinity" that, at least according to the Indian realists, is a single eternal entity present in all cows and is responsible for the fact that a great number of different individuals are all called cow.

The Buddhists have adduced powerful arguments against the existence of such universals. For instance, the universal bovinity cannot be present entirely in one individual cow, because if this were the case, it would not be able to reside in other cows. Nor can it be partly present in one cow, because it has no parts. Thus, all empirical awarenesses are false because they involve conceptual constructions, and conceptual constructions are faulty because they involve incoherent notions such as that of a universal. Kumārila's response to such objections was to refuse a philosophical engagement. No matter what arguments the Buddhists may raise: If everybody invariably has the awareness in respect to a certain individual, "this is a cow," then such awareness cannot be sublated, for it is more powerful than the other awareness that has found fault in it.

The concept of sublation may seem to presuppose a coherence theory of truth, in which truth is defined by relations between statements (or in the Indian case, between awarenesses), not in terms of relations between statements and reality, as is the case in a correspondence theory of truth. However, in general Indian philosophers always seem to presuppose a correspondence theory of truth. Even though only an awareness can sublate, or assert the falsity of another awareness, this is possible only because the sublating awareness corresponds to reality and the sublated awareness does not. The direct relationship between the two awarenesses remained problematic, and in the final analysis unexplained. To the question of how an awareness that arises later can apprehend the inexistence of an object of an earlier awareness Jayanta, a Nyāya philosopher of the ninth century, simply replies, "What [can] we do, since this is the way the awareness arises?" (*NM* I 171.12)

The correspondence theory of truth is clearly presupposed by the Nyāya criterion of truth called efficiency of activity (*pravṛttisāmarthya*). The Naiyāyikas argued in favor of a pragmatic principle of confirmation. When one has an awareness of water, one goes toward the perceived water, and if this endeavor is efficient, that is, if one obtains water, then the awareness is true. Otherwise it is false (*NBh*, Introduction). The discussions of the efficiency of activity seem to presuppose a difference in the reliability of the senses. The awareness that has to be confirmed is usually a visual one, and the confirming awareness is of touch or taste (as in the case of water). The expression "efficiency of activity" is often interchangeable with the expression "obtainment of an object/purpose" (*arthaprāpti*). The Naiyāyikas argue that when the awareness is true the object is obtained, and when it is false the object is not obtained.

Another similar but different criterion of truth is used by Dharmakirti and his followers. Dharmakirti argues that the production of efficient action (*arthakriyākāritva*) indicates whether an awareness is valid or not. The difference between this and the Nyāya criterion is that the former is not used to prove that the object of the awareness is real. According to Dharmakirti a false awareness can nevertheless be valid. Although all awarenesses that involve conceptual constructions are false, some such awarenesses (notably inferential awarenesses that always involve universals) lead to successful activity. Dharmakirti likens their case to someone who mistakes diamond rays for the diamond itself (*PV*, 3.57). Although such a person acts on a false awareness, he or she is nevertheless successful in obtaining the diamond. Another important aspect that distinguishes the Buddhist criterion from that of the Nyāya is that the object seen and the object obtained can never be the same. According to the Buddhists everything is momentary. Thus, the water seen and the water obtained are not the same water. Another difference between the two criteria is due to the rejection of the substance. The Buddhists denied that there is a certain substance such as water that has properties such a color and flavor. Thus, the seen water and the tasted water are in fact entirely different kinds of atoms that are only loosely connected by a causal relationship (*PVSV* 70.14f)

The preceding discussion treats the realistic schools. The topic of the criterion of truth in idealistic and illusionistic schools, which consider all empirical awarenesses to be false, arises from a different set of problems and specific metaphysical doctrines. For instance, certain Buddhist Yogācāras consider only those awarenesses to be true that have a correspondence in an unconscious awareness called *ālayavijñāna*. Vedāntins like Śaṅkara (700?–750?) consider empirical awarenesses to be provisionally true until one attains the realization of the identity between ātman and brahman. Everyday awarenesses are like a dream. As long as the dream lasts, the awarenesses of the dream are considered true; when one wakes up they are realized to have been false. These positions, however, are usually ignored in the philosophical debates in classical India.

A SKEPTICAL RESPONSE TO THE CRITERION OF TRUTH

Jayarāśi Bhaṭṭa (fl. c. 800), a skeptic philosopher loosely affiliated to the materialist Lokāyata school, raised a devastating critique of the various criteria of truth. The production by undisturbed causes, he says, cannot be used as a criterion, because it cannot be known whether the causes are undisturbed. The senses do not apprehend themselves, and therefore, cannot apprehend whether their functioning is disturbed or not. Nor can their proper functioning be inferred, because there is no inferential sign on which the inference can rest. If the correct awareness itself is considered to be such a sign, then the argument results in mutual dependence. The awareness is correct because the causes are undisturbed, and the causes are undisturbed because the awareness is correct.

Also, the absence of sublation cannot be used as a criterion of truth. At most one can say that those awarenesses that are sublated are false, but not that those that are not sublated are true. It is possible that sublations do not arise because some causal factor is missing. A person may have an illusion of water in respect to sun rays and not go toward the place of the sun rays. Thus, the causal factor that could produce the sublation (the proximity) is absent and the sublation does not arise. Besides, one may simply die before the sublation is produced. It is impossible to know at any given moment which awarenesses are true and which are going to be sublated in the future. Jayarāśi's argument bears an obvious similarity to Karl Popper's assertion that the scientific doctrines one holds to be true are only those that are not yet refuted, but they are liable to be so in the future. Of course, the basic concerns of Jayarāśi and Popper are entirely different.

The efficiency of activity based on an awareness also cannot be used as a criterion of an awareness' truth because the claim of efficiency also has to be confirmed: it has to be apprehended and its apprehension has to be ascertained as nonerroneous by another efficiency of activity. It is not true that an awareness will give satisfaction if and only if it is true. To repeat James's example, the pragmatist claims that if one believes that there are tigers in India, and one goes to India and finds tigers there, then, to use the Nyāya terms, the activity is efficient and the awareness is true. However, as critics of pragmatism point out, one may go to Syria, find some tigers there and think that one is in India, or one may go to India and mistake some big cats for tigers, or one can even go to India find tigers and mistake them for cats. Thus, a confirming awareness must be confirmed in its turn, and this would lead to an infinite regress. The arguments against Nyāya apply to the Buddhist criterion of production of efficient action, except that the Buddhist faces some additional difficulties due to the doctrine of momentariness and the rejection of universals.

VERBAL COMMUNICATION

The two main questions with which Indian philosophers who deal with verbal communication are concerned are: (1) What is the process by which one understands the meaning of words? (2) How does one know that words, once understood, are truthful? Concerning the first question see the entry "Philosophy of Language in India." This entry will focus only on the second question.

The veracity of words is crucial to Indian philosophers because knowledge derived from the sacred writings depends on it. Clearly, most religious doctrines could not be established by other means of knowledge such as perception or inference. Furthermore, when one is faced with a plurality of religious traditions, the question invariably arises as to which tradition can be trusted, for all of them cannot be true. Thus, each tradition had to adduce some arguments to justify the teachings it considered to be true. According to the Nyāya-Vaiśeṣika the

Veda was revealed to normal human beings by the Rishis who have direct knowledge of it, and consequently the truthfulness of the Veda, at least as known to one, depends on the truthfulness of the Rishis. Vātsyāyana (fifth century) enumerates three characteristics that must be present if one is to be considered a trustworthy or authoritative person: One has to have direct knowledge of things, compassion toward living beings, and the desire to teach things as they are.

There are basically two ways to prove the validity of a statement made by a reliable person. Either the reliability of the person making the statement is established, or the truthfulness of the statement is directly perceived or inferred. Ideally, the statement should be directly confirmed, but in the case of the Veda this is not always possible, for the truthfulness of a Vedic statement is often beyond the realm of examination by normal human beings, for example, statements concerning heaven. Vātsyāyana's proof is based on the assumption that the different parts of the Veda have the same authors. The statements of the Āyurveda and magical spells (*mantra*), which according to Vātsyāyana form a part of the Veda, have visible results. When certain spells that are intended to remove poison are uttered, the poison is actually removed. Furthermore, certain parts of the Veda proper also have visible results, for example, "One desirous of a village should perform a sacrifice" (*grāmakāmo yajeta*). Vātsyāyana's inference of the validity of the Veda runs as follows: From the parts of the Veda that have visible results one infers the trustworthiness of its authors (qualified by the three characteristics mentioned earlier), and because these are the same trustworthy authors as those of the rest of the Veda, the validity of the latter can be inferred.

The proof of reliability of a person was further developed by Dharmakirti, who was concerned with the trustworthiness of the Buddha. It was clear to Dharmakirti, who was conscious of the problem of induction, that the argument as it appears in *Nyāyabhāṣya* and *Nyāyavārttika* is not valid: Just because someone is trustworthy in matter x (e.g., medicine) does not necessarily mean he or she is trustworthy in matter y (e.g., rituals and sacrifices). Consequently, Dharmakirti modifies the argument in two points. First, he does not simply draw an inference from trustworthiness in any part x to trustworthiness in any part y; he allows such an inference only when one moves from the main part of a teaching to its secondary part. Second, the logical reason used in Dharmakirti's inference is not just the sameness of the author, but includes the motivations of the speaker in his reasoning,

for example, one should consider whether the speaker may have a motivation to lie.

More specifically the proof runs as follows: The main part of the Buddha's teaching are the four noble truths. These truths can be established independently of the Buddha's authority through perception and inference. Once the four noble truths are established, one can conclude that the Buddha was knowledgeable at least in matters of salvation. From such knowledge one infers that the Buddha has practiced various means for salvation for a long time (i.e., during many lives). However, he need not have practiced for such a long time had he been interested only in his own salvation. Therefore, his efforts were for the sake of other people. His engagement for the benefit of other (in fact, all) living beings in this manner presupposes compassion. Furthermore, the Buddha does not lie, because he has nothing to gain by lying. Therefore, the Buddha is trustworthy. Consequently, one can infer the truth in secondary matters in his teachings that are not open to an examination by normal human beings. As an example for such a domain Dharmakirti mentions the law of karma. Later Tibetan commentators also mention certain monastic rules that cannot be established independently of the Buddha's word (Tillemans 1993).

Interestingly, the reliability of the Gods must also be established. The Śaiva commentator Sadyajyotis (ninth century) says: Why is the word of Śiva authoritative? Because he is a pure, infallible, gracious lord endowed with knowledge that extends to everything. And his words whose objects are seen can be perceived as fruitful. Therefore, it can be inferred that his words whose objects are not seen are fruitful in exactly the same manner (Franco 1997, pp. 41–42).

THE OTHER PRAMĀṆAS

It is unfortunate that the other means of knowledge receive little attention in the Indian tradition. The Naiyāyikas and the Mīmāṃsakas have accepted analogy or comparison (*upamāna*) as a separate means of knowledge, but discussions about it remain rudimentary. It is defined as "proof of what has to be proved from similarity to something well known" (*NS* 1.1.6). The stock example for the use of analogy is: Someone does not know what a gayal is and is told "a gayal is like a cow." He or she then goes to the forest and is able to recognize a gayal on seeing it. Another example concerns the recognition of something from its name. For instance, knowing that the herb called bean leaf is like a bean, a person who finds this herb realizes that this is the thing to which the name applies. The Naiyāyikas were not unanimous as to what exactly constitutes the means of knowledge in this case. The older Naiyāyikas argued that the statement of the instructing person is the means of knowledge; the later Naiyāyikas maintained that it is the cognition of similarity that brings about the understanding. Means of knowledge, by definition, must lead to an awareness of an object previously unknown, for if the object is already known, its awareness will be nothing but recollection, and, except for the Jainas, no school of thought accepted memory as a means of knowledge.

There was some uncertainty as to what exactly is new about the object of the awareness resulting from comparison. To repeat the stock example, when one recognizes that a certain animal is a gayal, it is not the animal as such that is the object of the comparison, because it is apprehended by sense perception. It is also not that there is a similarity between the cow and the gayal, because the similarity was already conveyed by verbal communication. Nor can the resulting awareness consist in the conclusion that the particular animal observed for the first time is a gayal, because in this case comparison would not be different from inference. Indeed, some Mīmāṃsakas who professed this opinion were criticized by the Naiyāyikas for reducing comparison to inference (Bhatt 1962, pp. 290ff). The Naiyāyikas (NBh 1.1.6) as well as some Buddhists of the Kushana period (Franco 2001, pp. 11–12) maintained that the result of comparison is the awareness of the designation, that is, that the animal seen in the forest is called gayal. Nevertheless, it remained controversial what distinguishes analogy from inference on the one hand and from verbal testimony on the other, and different opinions were put forward on this issue. The Buddhists, the Vaiśeṣikas, and the Sāṃkhyas did not consider analogy to be a separate means of knowledge (Bhatt 1962, pp. 289–307).

Another potentially interesting means of knowledge that remained underdeveloped is arthāpatti. There is no agreed translation for this means of knowledge, and it is rendered by presumption, supposition, implication, negative implication, circumstantial evidence, and so on. The two most common examples for arthāpatti are: (1) Knowing that someone is alive and not finding him or her at home, one concludes that he or she is outside. (2) One is told that fat Devadatta does not eat during the day, and one concludes that he eats at night. The two examples are distinguished as presumption based on something seen (dṛṣṭārthāpatti) and presumption based on something heard (śrutārthāpatti). In later texts one distinguishes six types of presumption according to the six means of knowledge on which a presumption can be based.

The examples mentioned in this connection seem construed and artificial and are not taken from an actual philosophical discourse or from everyday life. For instance, presumption based on inference is illustrated as follows: One knows by inference that the sun moves (its movement cannot be perceived, but is inferred because it changes its place in the sky). However, things that move usually possess limbs such as legs. Thus, a conflict between two means of knowledge arises, and this conflict is resolved by the presumption that the sun has a moving power. Conflict or apparent contradiction (anupapatti) between two means of knowledge is the essential ingredient of arthāpatti, and the resulting presumption resolves the conflict. The contradiction must be apparent. If the contradiction is real, for example, two awarenesses about the same object, one perceiving it as silver and the other as mother-of-pearl, the way of resolving it is by rejecting one of the alternatives as false, not by making a new supposition. Among the important philosophical schools, only the Mīmāṃsā and Vedānta accepted presumption as an independent means of knowledge (Bhatt 1962, pp. 313–340).

The Bhāṭṭa Mīmāṃsakas accepted absence (abhāva) as a sixth means of knowledge. A discussion as to how mere absence or nonexistence can be an object of valid cognition appears already in NS 2.2.7–12. An objector argues that a negating cognition cannot be valid because it cannot refer to an object in reality. The objection is rebuked by reference to common experience. When some pieces of cloth are marked and some are unmarked, one can be told "Fetch the unmarked pieces," and one is able to do so. The Naiyāyikas, however, just like the Vaiśeṣikas, the Sāṃkhyas, the Buddhists, and the Prābhākara Mīmāṃsakas, considered absence or nonperception to be included in inference. Praśastapāda identified absence with inference from absence of effect to absence of cause.

CIRCULARITY OF PRAMĀṆAS

A general objection to the pramāṇas as such has been raised from the earliest times. If everything is established by means of knowledge, how are the means of knowledge themselves established? If they are established by other means of knowledge, these other means also have to be established by yet other means of knowledge and thus an infinite regress results. If the means of knowledge were to establish one another, a circularity would result. If one claims that the means of knowledge need not be established, the initial position that everything has to be established by means of knowledge has been abandoned. Some claimed that the means of knowledge establish both their objects and themselves, just as a lamp illuminates itself and its surroundings. However, it remained unclear how this metaphor should actually apply to the *pramāṇas*, and some, like Nāgārjuna (*VV*, verses 30ff) even argued that actually a lamp cannot illuminate itself.

See also Atomic Theory in Indian Philosophy; Causation in Indian Philosophy; Liberation in Indian Philosophy; Logic, History of: Logic and Inference in Indian Philosophy; Meditation in Indian Philosophy; Mind and Mental States in Buddhist Philosophy; Philosophy of Language in India; Self in Indian Philosophy; Truth and Falsity in Indian Philosophy; Universal Properties in Indian Philosophical Traditions.

Bibliography

PRIMARY SOURCES

NBh: Nyāyabhāṣya of Vātsyāyāna in Taranatha Nyayatarkatirtha and Amarendramohan Tarkatirtha (ed.). *Nyāyadarśanam with Vātsyāyana's Bhāṣya, Uddyotakara's Vārttika, Vācaspati Miśra's Tātparyaṭīkā and Viśvanātha's Vṛtti.* Calcutta, India: 1936, 1944.

NM: Nyāyamañjarī in V. K. S. Varadacharya (ed.) *Nyāyamañjarī of Jayanta Bhaṭṭa with Ṭippaṇi—Nyāyasaurabha by the Editor,* Mysore: Prācyavidyāsaṁśodhanālayaḥ, Maisūruviśvavidyālayaḥ, 1969–1983.

NV: Nyāyavārttika of Uddyotakara. See *NBh*.

NS: Nyāyasūtra in Ruben, Walter, *Die Nyāyasūtra's. Text, Übersetzung, Erläuterung und Glossar.* Leipzig, Germany: 1928.

PV: Pramāṇavārttika of Dharmakīrti. Ed. Y Miyasaka. *Acta Indologica,* Vol. 2. Narita, Japan: Naritasan Shinshoji, 1971–1972.

PVSV: Prāmāṇavārttikasvavṛtti in R. Gnoli (ed.), *The Pramāṇavārttikam of Dharmakīrti.* Rome, Italy: 1960.

MS: Mīmāṃsāsūtra in Frauwallner 1968.

VV: Vigrahavyāvatanī of Nāgārjuna in K. Bhattacharya E.H. Johnston and A. Kunst, *The Dialectical Method of Nāgārjuna.* Delhi, India: 1978.

VS: Vaiśeṣikasūtra in Muni Jambuvijayaji (ed.), *Vaiśeṣikasūtra of Kaṇāda with the Commentary of Candrānanda.* Baroda, India: Oriental Institute, 1961.

ŚBh: Śābarabhāṣya in Frauwallner 1968.

ŚV: Ślokavārttika of Kumārila in Svāmī Dvārikadāsa Śāstrī (ed.), *Ślokavārttika of Śrī Kumārila Bhaṭṭa. With the Commentary Nyāyaratnākara of Śrī Pārthasārathi Miśra.* Varanasi, India: Tara Publications, 1978.

SECONDARY SOURCES

Bhatt, Govardhan P. *Epistemology of the Bhāṭṭa School of Pūrvamīmāṃsā.* Varanasi, India: Chowkhamba Sanskrit Series Office, 1962.

Chakravarty, Pulinbihari. *Origin and Development of Sāṃkhya System of Thought.* 2nd ed. Delhi, India: 1975.

Franco, Eli. *Perception, Knowledge, and Disbelief: A Study of Jayarāśi's Scepticism.* 2nd ed. Delhi, India: 1994.

Franco, Eli. *Dharmakīrti on Compassion and Rebirth.* Vienna, Austria: Arbeitskreis für Tibetische und Buddhistische Studien, Universität Wien, 1997.

Franco, Eli. "Fragments of a Buddhist *Pramāṇa*-Theory from the Kuṣāṇa Period." *Bukkyō Dendō Kyōkai Fellowship Newsletter* 4 (2001): 2–12.

Frauwallner, Erich. *Materialien zur Ältesten Erkenntnislehre der Karmamīṃāṃsā.* Vienna, Austria: Graz, Köln, Böhlau in Kommission, 1968.

Matilal, Bimal Krishna. *The Logical Illumination of Indian Mysticism: An Inaugural Lecture Delivered before the University of Oxford on 5 May 1977.* Oxford, U.K.: Clarendon Press, 1977.

Namai, Mamoru. "A Survey of Bārhaspatya Philosophy." *Indological Review* (Kyoto) 2 (1976): 29–74.

Pollock, Sheldon. "The Theory of Practice and the Practice of Theory." *Journal of the American Oriental Society* 105 (3) (1985): 499–519.

Preisendanz, Karin. "On *Ātmendriyamanorthasannikarṣa* and the Nyāya-Vaiśeṣika Theory of Vision." *Berliner Indologische Studien* 4–5 (1989): 141–213.

Seyfort Ruegg, David. *Ordre spirituel et ordre temporel dans la pensée bouddhisque de l'Inde et du Tibet: quatre conférences au collège de France.* Paris: Collège de France, Institut de civilisation indienne, Diffusion De Boccard, 1995.

Tillemans, Tom J. F. *Persons of Authority.* Stuttgart, Germany: F. Steiner, 1993.

Eli Franco (2005)

KNUTZEN, MARTIN
(1713–1751)

Martin Knutzen, the German Wolffian philosopher, studied at the University of Königsberg and became an extraordinary professor there in 1734. Because he was a Wolffian, even though an unorthodox one, he never attained a full professorship in that Pietist-dominated school. However, because he was also a Pietist, Knutzen could never attain such a position in other German universities where Wolffians held the power of appointment.

Knutzen disagreed with Christian Wolff on several significant points. His *Commentatio Philosophica de commercio Mentis et Corporis* (Philosophical Commentary on the Relation between Mind and Body; Königsberg, 1735) was an attempt to reconcile Wolff's theory of preestablished harmony with the Pietist doctrine of physical influence. He extended the problem beyond Wolff, from the relation of soul and body to the interrelations of simple substances in general. In this and in a panpsychistic metaphysics, he was closer to Gottfried Wilhelm Leibniz than to Wolff. Knutzen, in his cosmological work *Vernünftige Gedanken von den Cometen* (Rational thought concerning comets; Königsberg, 1744), was one of the first philosophers in Germany to accept, at least partially, the Newtonian theory of gravitational attraction. His theological work was derivative and of little significance.

Knutzen's reputation is due more to his having been the teacher of Immanuel Kant than to his own significance. His influence on Kant has been much overrated. Recent research has shown that his influence was confined to the solution given by Kant in his first essay, *Gedanken von den wahren Schätzung der lebendigen Kräfte* (Thoughts on the true estimation of living forces; Königsberg, 1747), to the problem of the interrelation of substances, and to Kant's acceptance of Newtonian attraction. On the second point, Kant was also strongly influenced by the Berlin circle around Pierre-Louis Moreau de Maupertuis, even though Maupertuis himself was reluctant to accept attraction; and in accepting attraction as a real force and in trying to give a metaphysical explanation for it, Kant went beyond the Berlin circle, Knutzen, and Isaac Newton himself in his published statements.

Both Kant's "Wolffianism" and his "Pietism" have been attributed by some historians to Knutzen's influence; but although Kant received a Pietist education, he was never either a Pietist or a Wolffian. Kant always opposed Wolff's doctrines, and any Pietist influence came through the general philosophical influence of C. A. Crusius. Even an alleged influence of Knutzen's theology on Kant's religious philosophy has been disproven.

See also Wolff, Christian.

Bibliography

ADDITIONAL WORKS BY KNUTZEN
Dissertatio metaphysica de Aeternitate Mundi Impossibili. Königsberg, 1733.
Philosophischer Beweis von der Wahrheit der christlichen Religion. Königsberg, 1740.
Commentatio Philosophica de Humanae Mentis Individua Natura sive Immortalitate. Königsberg, 1741.

WORKS ON KNUTZEN
Biéma, M. van. *Martin Knutzen, La critique de l'harmonie préétablie.* Paris, 1908.
Bohatec, J. *Die Religionsphilosophie Kants.* Hamburg, 1938.
Erdmann, Benno. *Martin Knutzen und seine Zeit.* Leipzig: L. Voss, 1876.
Tonelli, Giorgio. *Elementi metodologici e metafisici in Kant dal 1745 al 1768.* Vol. 1. Turin, 1959. Chs. 1 and 2.
Watkins, Eric. "The Development of Physical Influx in Early Eighteenth-Century Germany: Gottsched, Knutzen, and Crusius." *Review of Metaphysics* 49 (2) (1995): 295–339.
Watkins, Eric. "Forces and Causes in Kant's Early Pre-Critical Writings." *Studies in History and Philosophy of Science* 34a (1) (2003): 5–27.

Giorgio Tonelli (1967)
Bibliography updated by Tamra Frei (2005)

KOCHEN-SPECKER THEOREM

See *Quantum Mechanics*

KOFFKA, KURT
(1886–1941)

Kurt Koffka, one of the three founders of the Gestalt movement in psychology, was born in Berlin. In 1903 he went to the university there to study philosophy, and he is said to have had a special interest in Immanuel Kant and Friedrich Nietzsche at that time. In 1904 he moved to Edinburgh, and in the next few years his interest in psychology became increasingly strong. Soon after receiving his doctorate at Berlin in 1908, he moved to Würzburg, where he served as an assistant to Oswald Külpe and Karl Marbe. In 1910–1911 he taught at the Academy at Frankfurt am Main, and it was during this period, as a result of the joint deliberations of Max Wertheimer, Wolfgang Köhler, and himself, that the central notions of Gestalt theory began to emerge. In 1911 Koffka became a lecturer at the University of Giessen, and from 1919 to about 1927 he was assistant professor.

The early 1920s saw the founding of *Psychologische Forschung,* a periodical in which several of the original articles on Gestalt theory were originally published, and of which Koffka was for many years the editor. During this decade he traveled extensively: A visit to Oxford for the International Congress of Psychology in 1923 resulted in much wider recognition of Gestalt theory than had hitherto been possible, and in succeeding years he was visiting professor at Cornell, Chicago, and Wisconsin. In 1927 he took up permanent residence in the United States, having accepted a professorship at Smith College, Northampton, Massachusetts. In 1932, at the invitation of the USSR State Institute, he joined an expedition to Uzbekistan to carry out ethno-psychological research, but at an early stage he was forced to return because of illness. He remained intellectually active until his death. He is said to have been a person of considerable kindness and charm, with wide interests that included music, art, and travel. His friendship with Wertheimer and Köhler was lifelong.

To separate Koffka's distinctive contributions from those of Wertheimer and Köhler is not easy, since each was influenced considerably by the other two. Koffka's *The Growth of the Mind* was an attempt to apply Gestalt principles to child psychology, while *Principles of Gestalt Psy-*

chology was a comprehensive account of a wide range of psychological work up to 1935, with detailed theoretical discussion. One of his central claims was that it is possible to take seriously the advances of science while still finding a place for the concepts of meaning and value; indeed, scientific inquiries themselves suffer if one does not do so. An aggressive materialism or behaviorism was quite foreign to him, but the alternative to this for Koffka was a new approach, using the concept of Gestalt, rather than a return to vitalism or Cartesian dualism. In an interesting passage in *Principles of Gestalt Psychology* he called attention to the difference in intellectual climate between Germany and America. The more abstract and speculative ideas, in which many German scholars were interested, had to be kept in the background when Gestalt theory was presented to the Americans, whose "high regard for science, accurate and earthbound" was accompanied by "an aversion, sometimes bordering on contempt, for metaphysics that tries to escape from the welter of mere facts into a loftier realm of ideas and ideals" (p. 18).

Philosophically interesting contributions found in *Principles of Gestalt Psychology* include the distinction between the geographical and behavioral environments, a discussion of the criteria by means of which "things" in the behavioral environment are distinguished from "not-things," and an attempt to reinstate the concept of ego. The behavioral environment is, in effect, the perceived world, the world of commonsense experience, whereas the geographical environment is the world as studied by the physical scientist. There are features in the geographical environment (such as infrared rays) that in ordinary circumstances are not present in the behavioral environment, whereas there are features in the behavioral environment (for example, the fact that two lines are grouped together when someone looks at them) that have no direct counterpart in the geographical environment. Examples of "things" are sticks, stones, clouds, and some types of fog; marginal cases are waves, words, and noises, while "a fog that makes our ocean liner reduce speed and sound its piercing horn is not thing-like at all, as little as the mist from which we emerge when we climb a mountain" (ibid., p. 70). The three characteristics of things are "shaped boundedness, dynamic properties, and constancy." As for the ego, "it has a very definite place in that [the behavioral] world, and well-defined, if variable boundaries.... 'In front,' 'to the left and right,' 'behind,' and 'above and below' are characteristics of space which it possesses with regard to an object which serves as the origin of the system of spatial co-ordinates" (ibid., p. 322).

In this case science itself is seriously impoverished if the concept of the ego is simply ignored. The study (sometimes called phenomenology) of how the world appears at the commonsense level is logically independent, according to Koffka's view, of any new discovery in physics about what is "really" happening.

Many of the problems that Koffka raised are of current philosophical interest, and as a psychologist he ranks among the greatest of his generation.

See also Dualism in the Philosophy of Mind; Gestalt Theory; Kant, Immanuel; Köhler, Wolfgang; Külpe, Oswald; Nietzsche, Friedrich; Vitalism.

Bibliography

WORKS BY KOFFKA

Besides numerous articles published in journals, Koffka's works include *Principles of Gestalt Psychology* (New York: Harcourt Brace, 1935); *The Growth of the Mind*, translated by R. M. Ogden (London: Routledge and Kegan Paul, 1924); "Mental Development," in *Psychologies of 1925*, edited by Carl Murchison (Worcester, MA: Clark University, 1928), pp. 129–143; and "Some Problems of Space Perception," in *Psychologies of 1930*, edited by Carl Murchison (Worcester, MA: Clark University, 1930), pp. 161–187. See also "Perception: an Introduction to the *Gestalt-theorie*." *Psychological Bulletin* 19 (1922): 531–585; "Problems in the Psychology of Art," in *Art: a Bryn Mawr Symposium* (Bryn Mawr, PA: Bryn Mawr College, 1940).

SECONDARY WORKS

For discussions of Koffka's work, see G. W. Hartmann, *Gestalt Psychology; A Survey of Facts and Principles* (New York: Ronald Press, 1935). See bibliography to the Gestalt Theory entry for works discussing Gestalt psychology as a whole.

ADDITIONAL SOURCES

Arnheim, R. "The Two Faces of Gestalt Psychology." *American Psychologist* 41 (1986): 820–824.

Ash, Mitchell G. *Gestalt Psychology in German Culture 1890–1967: Holism and the Quest for Objectivity*. Cambridge, U.K.: Cambridge University Press, 1995.

Harrower, Molly. *Kurt Koffka, an Unwitting Self-Portait*. Gainesville: University Presses of Florida, 1983.

Petermann, Bruno. *The Gestalt Theory and the Problem of Configuration*. Translated by Meyer Fortes. New York: Harcourt Brace, 1932.

Smith, Barry, ed. *Foundations of Gestalt Theory*. Munich: Philosophia, 1988.

T. R. Miles (1967)
Bibliography updated by Alyssa Ney (2005)

KÖHLER, WOLFGANG
(1887–1967)

Wolfgang Köhler, the German Gestalt psychologist, was born in Tallinn, Estonia. He studied first at the University of Tübingen and then at Bonn. He next studied physics under Max Planck and psychology under Carl Stumpf at the University of Berlin, and received his PhD from that school in 1909 for investigations on hearing. In 1911 he became Privatdozent at Frankfurt. Max Wertheimer came to Frankfurt in 1912, and in the same year Köhler and Kurt Koffka served as the subjects for Wertheimer's famous experiments on stroboscopic motion that are widely regarded as the beginning of Gestalt psychology.

In 1913 Köhler became director of the anthropoid experiment station operated by the Prussian Academy of Sciences at Tenerife in the Canary Islands, and he remained there, throughout World War I, until 1920. The pioneering studies in the psychology of chimpanzees that he carried out there were published in several papers and in the monograph *Intelligenzprüfungen an Anthropoiden* (*The Mentality of Apes,* 1917).

Köhler's next major work, *Die physischen Gestalten in Ruhe und im stationären Zustand* (Physical Gestalten in rest and in the stationary state), was published at Brunswick in 1920. It is primarily a work in physics and reveals Köhler's indebtedness to Planck, but its major themes played important roles in his more strictly psychological writings.

In 1921, with Wertheimer, Koffka, Kurt Goldstein, and Hans Gruhle, Köhler founded the journal *Psychologische Forschung,* which served as the leading organ of the Gestalt psychologists until Köhler was forced to suspend publication because of the difficulties of editing it from the United States. In 1922 Köhler succeeded Stumpf as director of the Psychological Institute and professor of philosophy at the University of Berlin. He held a visiting professorship at Clark University in the academic year 1925–1926 and returned to America for another visit in 1929. In the same year his *Gestalt Psychology* was published in English.

Köhler was the only leading member of the Gestalt school who was not Jewish, but he was strongly opposed to the Nazis. He published a letter against them in a Berlin newspaper after they took power and a bit later left Germany. Köhler gave the William James Lectures at Harvard in 1934 and published them as *The Place of Value in a World of Fact* in 1938. In 1935 he was appointed professor of psychology at Swarthmore College. His Page-Barbour Lectures given at the University of Virginia in 1938 were published in an expanded version in 1940 as *Dynamics in Psychology.* Köhler became professor emeritus at Swarthmore in 1957. In 1959 the school awarded him an honorary doctorate and he became visiting research professor at Dartmouth, a position he retained until his death.

Köhler is correctly thought of primarily as a psychologist. Nevertheless, throughout his career he never hesitated to interpret the results and methodology of the physical sciences and to apply his interpretations to the delineation of the proper task of psychology and to the elucidation of its problems. He admitted a debt to the phenomenology of Edmund Husserl, and his own work was broadly in the phenomenological stream. Both phenomenology and physics influenced his vocabulary, his methods of research, and his theoretical conclusions. Köhler was an ardent controversialist, and he engaged in a continuing polemical defense of the Gestalt theory. He believed that the theory offered a new resolution of the controversy between those who believe in innate ideas or tendencies and those who stress the importance of ideas acquired by learning. He thought that his Gestalt physics could resolve the biological controversy between mechanism and vitalism. He claimed to have dissolved the philosophical controversies between idealism and realism and between monism and dualism, and he advocated a form of epiphenomenalism or even an identity theory of mind and body. Köhler believed that by phenomenological analysis he could demonstrate both the existence and something of the nature of value, and that value, or "requiredness," was more general than moral philosophers and aestheticians believed; thus, he held, the psychologist's investigation of value was of prime importance to the philosopher.

Köhler, then, not only advanced psychological theories and views about the proper subject matter of this science but also presented well-reasoned opinions on speculative problems in biology, physiology, physics, and chemistry, and suggested possibly fruitful lines of research for these sciences to undertake. He also presented theories belonging to such central philosophical disciplines as epistemology, metaphysics, and value theory. This entry will discuss some of the philosophically interesting issues raised by Köhler in the physical sciences and psychology, as well as some of his general philosophical positions. It will not attempt to discuss his contributions to Gestalt psychology proper, except for his discussion of isomorphism.

PHYSICS AND PHYSIOLOGY

Köhler discussed physical concepts and discoveries for at least three main purposes: to demonstrate the existence of physical structures analogous to perceptual gestalten; to provide a physicochemical theory of perception and other mental functions; and to delineate the proper task of psychology by comparing its present status with the status of physics at various times in its history.

PHYSICAL GESTALTEN. Köhler, like the other Gestalt psychologists, claimed that a central subject of psychology is the investigation of certain kinds of structures in which "the whole is more than the sum of its parts." An analysis of these gestalten would explain many puzzling facts of vision, touch, hearing, memory, and understanding. The existence of such structures was denied on the ground that the whole can never be more than the sum of its parts. Köhler sought to show that there are a variety of recognized physical systems in which the whole is more than the sum of its parts. Machines are structures whose movements are strictly determined. From a knowledge of the parts of a machine and their interrelationships, we can know the motions of the whole. Thus a machine, according to Köhler, is no more than the sum of its parts. But in many physical systems it is the state of the whole that determines the state of the parts. Examples of such systems are the distribution of an electrical charge over the surface of a conductor, which varies with the shape of the conductor; the distribution of a current of electricity or fluid in a network of wires or pipes; the distribution of particles of a fluid body whose only constraint is the walls of the container; and a planetary system. The common characteristic of these systems is that the parts interact dynamically rather than mechanically. And in these systems, he claimed, the whole is greater than the parts.

These physical systems all exhibit another characteristic, which Köhler thinks is strikingly analogous to a characteristic of phenomenal gestalten. When the physical systems are disturbed, the interaction of their parts tends more or less rapidly to restore the systems to a state of equilibrium. They are thus dynamically self-regulating systems. Phenomenal gestalten are also dynamically self-regulating. The parts of the gestalten interact with one another to produce, or reproduce, systematic wholes within the perceptual field. Köhler recognizes, following Wertheimer, a set of five factors involved in the recognition of gestalten. If any of these factors are present, then we tend to perceive a gestalt, unless inhibiting factors are also present or the factors are so present as to cancel out one another. The five factors are (1) *proximity*: Objects that appear close together are more likely to be classed as part of the same gestalt than those which are far apart; (2) *similarity*: Objects that resemble each other tend to be classed as belonging together; (3) "*common destiny*": If objects move or change together, they tend to be perceived as part of the same thing or as belonging together; (4) "*good gestalt*": Forms that are not quite regular tend to be perceived as more regular than they are; (5) *closure*: Forms that are in some way incomplete tend to be perceived as complete—for example, a circle with a small arc missing will be perceived as a full circle.

The resemblance between dynamically self-regulating physical systems and phenomenal gestalten suggested to Köhler that it might be more fruitful to attempt to understand mental phenomena by means of a dynamic rather than a mechanical model, and in fact this model continued to serve Köhler throughout his career as a fruitful explanatory hypothesis in psychology. He was particularly successful in applying it to problems of perception, of memory, and of intelligence or insight—of coming to understand a situation or a problem.

Despite Köhler's apparent success in applying the two notions that in certain physical and phenomenal structures the whole is greater than the sum of its parts and that psychological phenomena should be interpreted dynamically rather than mechanically, they have been widely criticized. Both notions, it is said, are enormously vague. It is not surprising that they seem to "work," for by their very vagueness they can be made to fit almost any body of facts. Surely in some generally accepted sense of "whole" and "part" almost any whole can be shown to be greater than the sum of its parts. But it is not clear that Köhler was applying the two terms univocally in the phenomenal cases he adduced as examples, and it is even less clear that he was using them in the same sense when speaking of the parts of phenomenal gestalten and of the parts of physical systems. Similarly, although the dynamic model may have aided Köhler in the design of new experiments and the interpretation of many phenomenal facts, it has been claimed that, outside of a certain limited range of cases, the apparent use of a dynamic model can mean no more than a recognition that phenomena change. The substance of the theory is probably Wertheimer's set of dynamic factors, which had in large part been anticipated by earlier psychologists, and there seems no reason to connect them with any specific physical theory.

ISOMORPHISM. Probably the most central concept in all of Köhler's thought is isomorphism, or similarity of form. He used this notion for two major and several minor purposes. The two major functions combine into a theory of knowledge that is partly conceptual and partly physicochemical and physiological. Köhler distinguished between (1) phenomena, or percepts; (2) their cortical correlates, or brain-states; and (3) nature, or the physical world. He was perfectly willing to believe that percepts and brain-states may eventually be shown to be identical and in this sense does not exclude the possibility of a metaphysical monism. He holds, in opposition to both phenomenalists and new realists, that the phenomenal world and the physical world are not identical, and thus is an epistemological dualist. (These points are discussed below.) It is the theory of isomorphism that serves as the connecting link among these three elements. Percepts, it is claimed, are related to one another within the phenomenal field as their cortical correlates are related to one another in the cortex and as the corresponding physical objects are related to one another in physical space. The structural relations within any of the three realms are reproduced in the others. If a man-percept appears in phenomenal space atop a horse-percept, then in physical space there is a man atop a horse, and in the brain there are two brain processes dynamically related to each other in the cortical correlative of the relation "on top of."

What concerns us here is the isomorphy between the phenomenal world and brain-states. In this connection Köhler formulated the principle of isomorphism for spatial relations (it can be formulated for any type of phenomenal ordering) as: *"Experienced order in space is always structurally identical with a functional order in the distribution of underlying brain processes"* (*Gestalt Psychology,* Mentor edition, New York, 1959, p. 39). The parts of the visual field are not independent of one another; they exhibit structural relationships. If, for example, there is in my visual field a white square on a black ground, then in my brain there are processes corresponding to the white square, the black ground, and the boundary between the two. The topological relations between the brain processes are functionally identical with the corresponding visual relations. Metrical relationships are not preserved, but such relationships as betweenness are. In memory, these relationships are preserved in memory-traces. Thus it is form or structure rather than exact pictorial images that are preserved.

Köhler holds that the physiological processes in the brain that are involved in perception and memory are very probably electrochemical in nature. In the case of the white square, the brain process corresponding to the square-percept contains a higher concentration of ions than the brain process corresponding to the black ground. The two processes are functionally connected at a boundary corresponding to the edge of the square. There is a potential difference across this boundary; an electric flow of ions therefore takes place, and the square is perceived. Changes in the solution leave memory traces, which are subject to alteration in the course of time. These traces are superimposed on one another and thus functionally mirror the order of time of the percepts themselves.

The theory of isomorphism, both in its conceptual outline and in its physiological accompaniment, has been only inadequately outlined here. The physiological element, despite the important role it plays in Köhler's claim that functionally an identity theory of mind and body is at least feasible, is a matter for empirical investigation. Much of what Köhler says sounds rather plausible, but there are difficulties in stating the theory with the proper degree of precision. Although he speaks of a cortical retina, Köhler does not mean that perception involves the reproduction of a (two-dimensional or three-dimensional) image of the object within the cortex. This would be complete isomorphism. On the other hand, almost any set of relationships can represent any other by some form of correspondence, and the correspondences, if any, actually involved in perception might be very complex or in some other way not what we would intuitively grasp as a correspondence.

There are other issues involved that can only be raised and not explored here. Suppose it were established that when a certain macroscopic brain-state is observed in people, they generally claim to perceive a certain object. For instance, take any of the reversible figures that appear to an observer now in one way and now in another, such as a Maltese cross, composed of alternating black and white rays, which can be seen in two different ways. In one way of looking at it certain parts appear as the figure and the others as ground, while in the other way what was ground appears as figure and what was figure appears as ground. According to Köhler, each way of seeing the figure corresponds to a different electrochemical state in the brain. Now suppose that one person's descriptions of the cross fail to correspond, in either a regular or irregular manner, to the descriptions that we have generally found associated with his brain-states. We may wish to claim that he is misdescribing what he is seeing. But how we choose to regard the situation is not merely a matter of fact; it involves at least one conceptual matter, a choice between conflicting criteria of what the person is seeing—the person's description (which is, of course, the only criterion we now have) and our knowledge of his brain-states. And empirical investigation alone cannot settle this conflict.

The same point applies to another example, in which a further factor becomes apparent. There is experimental evidence that when people see two parallel lines close to each other, one of which extends beyond the other at each end, they claim to see shadowy lines connecting the ends of the two lines to complete a trapezoid. Köhler suggests that the shadowy lines are caused by potential barriers in the cortex created by the cortical correlates of the lines actually drawn. Again, if it could be shown that such potential barriers are present in a person's brain although he claims not to see such lines, we might put it down to misdescription. But surely here we are inclined to take him at his word. In the first case we can describe what it means to see the cross in one way rather than another. But in this case we can only point out where the shadowy lines ought to be seen. The achieving aspect of perception is perhaps more obvious here. It is not simply a matter of what is seen but also of how we learn to describe what we see. In most descriptions it is clear what the standards of an accurate description are, and we can understand a proposal for a change in standards. In the present case it is not even clear what the standards are, if there are any. It is this element of conventional standards, which Köhler has omitted from his discussion, that makes his problems of the relationship among percepts, objects, and brain-states not merely a matter of physiological and psychological experimentation but of conceptual analysis.

Isomorphism and language. Köhler developed an interesting linguistic theory as a corollary of his theory of isomorphism. This corollary, except for Köhler's added complexity, resembles the picture theory of meaning advanced by Ludwig Wittgenstein in his *Tractatus Logico-Philosophicus* and seems to have been developed out of similar considerations. If the only way one thing can represent another is by having the same form, then the only way language can represent a situation is through a common form. Since, according to the theory of isomorphism, a phenomenal event has a physiological correlate possessing a similar form, then language represents both the event and the physiological correlate indifferently. A statement ostensibly about an observed phenomenon can be interpreted as a statement about brain-states and vice versa: ". . . language . . . is the peripheral outcome of antecedent physiological processes, among others of those upon which my experience depends. According to our general hypothesis, the concrete order of this experience pictures the dynamic order of such processes. Thus, if to me my words represent a description of my experi-

ences, they are at the same time objective representations of the processes that underlie these experiences. Consequently, it does not matter very much whether my words are taken as messages about experience or about these physiological facts. For, so far as the order of events is concerned, the message is the same in both cases" (*Gestalt Psychology,* p. 40).

PHYSICS AND PSYCHOLOGY. The third way in which Köhler has used physics is to elucidate what he regards as the proper program for psychology. Physics, in his view, is an old, established discipline whose techniques have been developed and refined over a long period of time. Quantitative methods and pointer readings are appropriate in physics because there are thoroughgoing and widely accepted theories that give meaning to the numbers arrived at. Even in the early days of physics, in the time of Galileo Galilei, many of the problems could be investigated quantitatively, because the phenomena investigated had long been known from everyday life and this knowledge provided the necessary qualitative meaning. Where everyday life did not supply the necessary qualitative background, as in the study of electricity, physics had to proceed by qualitative investigations before quantitative ones could be undertaken profitably. The problems of psychology, Köhler claims, are more often like those of electricity than those of Galilean mechanics. In general, in psychology the necessary meaning-giving theory is absent. Intelligence quotients are notoriously hard to interpret. The difficulty in assessing their significance arises out of a lack of any clear notion of what intelligence consists in. Psychology should first try to develop a theory of intelligence before it tries to measure intelligence. Until a satisfactory theory is arrived at, it can hardly be determined whether or not intelligence quotients do measure intelligence and how well they do it.

GESTALT PSYCHOLOGY

CRITIQUE OF BEHAVIORISM. Köhler's attempt to show that qualitative methods are the most appropriate in the present state of psychology arose in the context of his repudiation of behaviorism. His phenomenological view of the nature of the subject matter of psychology was radically different from the notion that psychology is the study of behavior, with its related stimulus-response physiological theory. The behaviorists, according to Köhler, have taken too much to heart one epistemological teaching but ignored its wider context. They seek to limit psychology to the observation of the response of human beings in scientifically controlled situations because they have become aware of the truth that one person cannot directly observe another person's experience. However, the behaviorist cannot avoid the study of direct experience by limiting himself to the observation of human reactions in controlled situations, for the only evidence he has of such reactions is his own experience. The behaviorist seeks to be objective, but he confuses two pairs of meanings of the terms *subjective* and *objective*. In one sense, observations of another person's reactions are no less subjective than my hearing his statements about what he is experiencing: Both are part of my experience. But in the primary sense *subjective* and *objective* refer to differently characterized phenomena within my experience. In this sense there is no reason why I cannot examine both subjective and objective experience; in the first sense I cannot help but investigate subjective phenomena.

CRITIQUE OF INTROSPECTIONISM.

Whereas Köhler criticized behaviorism for misunderstanding the nature of direct experience, he criticized introspectionism for distorting the facts of experience to fit a preconceived theory. By "introspectionism" Köhler does not mean the gathering of information from an inspection of one's own experience in general; he has criticized the behaviorists for their refusal to accept information so gathered as unscientific. When he attacks introspectionism, Köhler has in mind certain characteristic theories and procedures of the psychologists of his own and the previous generation who relied on introspection. Philosophers and psychologists long believed, under the influence of geometrical optics, that, for example, a round penny must appear elliptical in most positions or that a white surface under a very low degree of illumination must appear gray, and a darker gray than a black surface under a very high degree of illumination. Experimentation has shown, however, that a "naive" observer tends to describe the penny as round no matter what shape strikes the retina and the white surface as white in almost any circumstances. The naive observer, it was held, could not be seeing what he claimed to be seeing. Introspectionists devised elaborate techniques by which a "trained" observer could be made to claim to see what by the laws of optics he should be seeing. In essence, these techniques consisted in excluding from the visual field of the observer all of the surroundings of the object to be observed. In this way, the introspectionists claimed, all the factors of learning are excluded and the object is seen as it "really" appears, before the process of education has distorted our pristine perceptions.

Köhler rightly points out that by employing this technique of exclusion in the interests of a theory, all

other factors that might explain why the round penny looks round have been barred. The Gestalt theory offers an alternative explanation of this fact that does not involve the notion of an elaborate hoax played upon the naive observer, an explanation that cannot even be tested by the exclusionary techniques of introspectionism. The defects of introspectionism were further evidenced, Köhler claims, by the fact that introspective psychology had degenerated into an investigation of minute and trivial facts of interest only to specialists.

ASSOCIATIONISM AND ATOMISM.

Köhler criticized both the introspectionists and the behaviorists for their psychological atomism or, as he also called it, their mosaic theory. Closely related to psychological atomism is the theory of associationism, which Köhler likewise regarded as inadequate. Psychological atomism is the view that what we perceive is a mosaic of bits and pieces, each independent and essentially unconnected with any other. The parts of the visual and other sensory fields thus lack any sort of relatedness. Yet we do recognize this brown patch and that white patch as belonging together and both as being parts of a dog, rather than one belonging with the ground underneath the dog and the other to the wall behind the dog.

Psychological atomism, according to Köhler, is a theory about the nature of the objects of perception. The theory of association is a theory as to how the experience of order arises out of the unordered psychological atoms postulated by psychological atomism. I have seen white patches associated with dogs in the past, and thus I come to expect that when I see a white patch of a particular kind in the future, it will belong to a dog.

Köhler's answer to psychological atomism is that we do not experience the parts of the visual field, for example, as separate from and unrelated to one another, but that we experience relationships among its parts. Certain wholes separate themselves from other parts of the field, and these wholes are composed of parts related to each other by means of the Wertheimer factors mentioned earlier. If we are in fact led to see things as belonging together by the very structure of experience, then the theory of association is unnecessary. Köhler went on to show that it is also inadequate, in that it cannot fully explain all that it was intended to explain.

Many of Köhler's criticisms of atomism and associationism as psychological theories are justified. But he apparently thought that in arguing against psychological atomism he was also arguing against any epistemological atomism as well. Part of his theory of isomorphism is the claim that the world as experienced contains experienced relationships among its constituents and that the observer does not add this structure to the world. But here, as earlier, conceptual matters are involved: It is not only a matter of experienced relationships but also of learning what it is to experience a relationship. We must learn the established criteria of what is to count as a relationship before we can know that what we are experiencing is a relationship.

Köhler also believed that the theory of associationism led to a hidden limitation in methods of investigation. According to the associationist, he holds, organization arises out of previous association, whereas, in his view, association depends on previous organization. Sensory gestalten, melodies, and meaningful sentences are organized wholes, and their parts are readily associated. Totally unrelated visual or auditory objects or nonsense syllables, on the other hand, have first to be organized into some kind of order before they can be recognized or be later remembered as having been associated. Köhler does not deny the facts of association but, rather, that association is a fundamental explanatory category. If it were recognized that order is more easily found than made, then it would be seen that organization should play a role in the design of experiments. As it is, far too many experiments fail. For instance, in experiments designed to test an animal's intelligence the apparatus may be too complex for the animal to grasp the relations of the parts and thus be beyond his capacity, whereas by a slight revision the apparatus could serve adequately in carrying out the experiments.

PHILOSOPHICAL PROBLEMS

EPISTEMOLOGY. Köhler's epistemological views are difficult to organize and apparently are not altogether consistent. Probably the most careful and accurate presentation of his views is found in *The Place of Value in a World of Fact*. His theory is, as he claims, a form of epistemological dualism, here couched in the form of a refutation of both phenomenalism and the new realism and aimed at showing that the body-mind problem is a pseudo problem. Köhler's theory, both in content and in terminology, is strikingly similar to that developed by Bertrand Russell in *The Analysis of Matter* and *The Outline of Philosophy*.

The body-mind problem, Köhler claims, concerns the location of percepts. Physiology tells us that they are in our interior, in our brains, yet they appear to be outside ourselves. The resolution is that percepts are inside our bodies in one sense and outside our bodies in quite a different sense. We should distinguish between the body as a physical organism and the body as a percept. Percepts depend on processes within the physical organism; without such processes they would not take place. They appear as located outside the body, which is itself a percept. This perceptual body has a definite place in perceptual space, and other percepts have a definite relation to it within perceptual space. There is no more need to wonder why a perceptual dog appears outside of my perceptual body than to wonder why it appears outside of a perceptual house. Relationships in perceptual space say nothing about the location of percepts in physical space.

In some way what Köhler was saying has been recognized at least since Immanuel Kant's distinction between phenomena and noumena, and Köhler's position seems open to much the same objections as Kant's. What is needed is an account of the relationships between physical space and perceptual space, or between physical object and percept, and this is not what Köhler has given. In physical space percepts are inside the observer's body; in perceptual space they are outside. Here is a radical disparity between spatial relations in the phenomenal and the transphenomenal realms. But Köhler wants to hold that relationships in the phenomenal and the physical worlds are isomorphic. The phenomenal house is between two phenomenal trees; the physical house is likewise between two physical trees. Phenomenal relationships are thus supposed to give us knowledge of physical relationships. And our knowledge of phenomenal relations is the only basis for any knowledge we may have of physical relations. But how do we get from percepts in the physical world to physical objects? And how can we avoid solipsism? Köhler claims that two scientists do not observe the same galvanometer. It is self-evident for him that neither can observe the other's phenomenal world. But physically the percept of each is different, for each is in his own brain. Köhler has not shown how we get from the two percepts to a common physical object.

That Kant spoke of things-in-themselves and Köhler of a physical world, or of nature, should not mask the fundamental similarities of their views. Despite Köhler's belief that the phenomenal world itself gives evidence of a nonphenomenal world, his physical world stands in exactly the same position as Kant's things-in-themselves. They are both unknowable.

CAUSATION. With his emphasis on experienced relationships between the parts of perceived entities, it is not surprising that Köhler denies David Hume's claim that we do not experience causal relations. Causation is only a special case of a general characteristic of experienced phenomena that Köhler terms *requiredness,* other cases of which are discussed in the section on value. In any of various ways one experience "demands" another for its completion. What Köhler calls insight is the coming to see what is demanded, what is needed to complete a set of factors. Men, and animals to a more limited degree, can have insight into, among other things, what caused a particular event or what will be the probable outcome of a particular line of action. The insight is the experiencing of a causal relation between cause and effect. Köhler concedes that the Humean theory of regular sequence accounts for our practice in various situations of subjecting causal theories to experimental testing after they have occurred to us, but it cannot by itself account for our first recognition of a cause.

Köhler has been criticized by defenders of the regularity theory for confusing psychological issues with logical ones. It may well be the case that in human (as well as in purely physical) situations we frequently arrive at the true answer to a causal problem without any elaborate examination of classes of sequences. From this, however, it does not follow that causation is a "simple" relation like, for example, coexistence that can be given in a single experience. Granting that I may truly judge that A_1 is the cause of B_1 without having performed elaborate controlled experiments, Hume's regularity theory has nevertheless been vindicated as an analysis of the concept of causation if I am prepared to admit that A_1 was not really the cause of B_1 were I to discover that other instances of A are or were not followed by instances of B.

VALUE. Köhler's epistemological views are developed most fully in *The Place of Value in a World of Fact.* This volume is a contribution to the discussion of axiology that played such a prominent role in American philosophy during the 1920s and 1930s. The argument of the work is long, digressive, and difficult to summarize. The views on isomorphism and on epistemology mentioned above form an integral part of the argument. At the cost of oversimplifying Köhler's views to the point of distortion, it can be said that he holds that we can have direct perceptual knowledge of value. Value is an objective fact of the phenomenal, and hence also of the physical, world. Both phenomenal gestalten and physical gestalten spontaneously change in a certain direction. Melodies and visual shapes require completion in certain ways. Very often when we are attempting to remember something, the context in our mind shows us not only the sort of thing we seek to remember but also whether we are getting close to remembering it. Whatever the proper inter-

pretation of these phenomena may be, Köhler believes that they all demonstrate the factor that he terms *requiredness* and that in the case of memory, the requiredness is a characteristic of something outside the present phenomenal situation. Valuation, an assessment of what ought to be, is not a unique phenomenon but another special case of the recognition of requiredness. Köhler does not directly undertake an analysis of valuation but only of requiredness in general. He hoped that his analysis would be of use to philosophers in their own analyses of ethical and aesthetic requiredness.

MECHANISM AND VITALISM. Toward the end of *The Place of Value in a World of Fact,* Köhler returns to two topics that had engaged him earlier, the dispute between mechanism and vitalism and the question of the precise metaphysical classification of his own theory. In the first case, as in many other situations, Köhler argues that the apparent alternatives are not exhaustive. Mechanists, in their treatment of living processes, take the same shortsighted view that they take of the nature of physical processes mentioned earlier. Mechanical systems are not the only kind of physical systems; there are also the dynamically self-regulating systems. The premise that man must be a machine because physics finds only mechanical systems in the world is thus undermined. On the other hand, one does not have to hold to vitalism just because men are obviously different from machines. Living organisms, including man, can quite easily be physical systems without being machines. And in fact, Köhler held, living organisms can be explained quite satisfactorily as dynamically self-regulating systems without postulating some mysterious nonphysical vital force.

BODY-MIND PROBLEM. Köhler seems to advocate an epistemological dualism. He was not, however, a dualist in the sense in which the term is used in connection with the body-mind problem. Other psychologists have labeled him a physicalist, and he did not totally reject the terms *materialist* and *monist* as used to describe his metaphysical views. He found the label "materialist" misleading because he accepted the modern physicists' account of the world, and this account is very different from any traditional account of matter as composed of solid impenetrable particles. He believed that eventually it may be shown that phenomenal colors are identical with chemical states in the brain and that in this way the physicists' account of reality would be complete. In this sense he did not reject the possibility that monism is true, but in the meantime phenomenal qualities appear so different from any physical correlates that the possibility of the falsehood of monism likewise cannot be ruled out. There is some similarity between Köhler's views on this subject and the theory of J. J. C. Smart and U. T. Place that sensations and brain processes are identical. Like Smart and Place, Köhler argues that the undeniable phenomenological differences between colors and chemical states of the brain do not rule out the possibility that, in an important sense, they may nevertheless be identical. However, unlike Smart and Place, Köhler does not claim that such an identity has in fact been established.

See also Atomism; Behaviorism; Causation: Philosophy of Science; Epistemology; Galileo Galilei; Gestalt Theory; Hume, David; Husserl, Edmund; Introspection; Kant, Immanuel; Koffka, Kurt; Mind-Body Problem; Planck, Max; Realism; Psychology; Russell, Bertrand Arthur William; Smart, John Jamieson Carswell; Stumpf, Karl; Value and Valuation; Vitalism; Wittgenstein, Ludwig Josef Johann.

Bibliography

WORKS BY KÖHLER

"Über unbemerkte Empfindungen und Urteilstäuschungen." *Zeitschrift für Psychologie* 63 (1913): 51–80.

Intelligenzprüfungen an Anthropoiden. Berlin, 1917. Revised 2nd ed. as *Intelligenzprüfungen an Menschenaffen.* Berlin: Springer, 1921. Translated from the 2nd ed. by Ella Winter as *The Mentality of Apes.* London: Routledge and Kegan Paul, 1925.

Die physischen Gestalten in Ruhe und im stationären Zustand. Brunswick, Germany, 1920; 2nd ed., Erlangen: Philosophische Akademie, 1924.

"An Aspect of Gestalt Psychology." In *Psychologies of 1925,* edited by Carl Murchison. Worcester, MA: Clark University Press, 1925. Ch. 8.

"Gestaltprobleme und Anfänge einer Gestalttheorie." *Jahresbericht über das gesamte Physiologie und experimental Pharmakologie* 3 (1925): 512–539.

"Komplextheorie und Gestalttheorie." *Psychologische Forschung* 6 (1925): 358–416.

Gestalt Psychology. New York: Liveright, 1929. German edition published as *Psychologische Probleme,* Berlin, 1933.

"Some Tasks of Gestalt Psychology." In *Psychologies of 1930,* edited by Carl Murchison. Worcester, MA: Clark University Press, 1930. Ch. 8.

"Zur Psychophysik des Vergleichs und des Raumes." *Psychologische Forschung* 18 (1933): 343–360.

The Place of Value in a World of Fact. New York: Liveright, 1938.

Dynamics in Psychology. New York: Liveright, 1940.

"On the Nature of Associations." *Proceedings of the American Philosophical Society* 84 (1941): 489–502.

"Figural After-Effects: An Investigation of Visual Processes." *Proceedings of the American Philosophical Society* 88 (1944): 269–357.

"Gestalt Psychology Today." *American Psychologist* 14 (1959): 727–734.

The Task of Gestalt Psychology. Princeton, NJ: Princeton University Press, 1969.

The Selected Papers of Wolfgang Koehler. Edited by Mary Henle. New York: Liveright, 1971.

In Anthologies

Ellis, W. D. *A Source Book of Gestalt Psychology.* London: Kegan Paul, 1938. Contains translation of portions of *Die physikalischen Gestalten in Ruhe und im stationären Zustand.*

Henle, Mary. *Documents of Gestalt Psychology.* Berkeley: University of California Press, 1961. Contains Köhler's presidential address to the American Psychological Association (1959) and other later papers.

WORKS ON KÖHLER

Arnheim, R. "The Two Faces of Gestalt Psychology." *American Psychologist* 41 (1986): 820–824.

Ash, Mitchell G. *Gestalt Psychology in German Culture 1890–1967: Holism and the Quest for Objectivity.* Cambridge, U.K.: Cambridge University Press, 1995.

Ayer, A. J. *The Foundations of Empirical Knowledge,* 113–135. London, 1947.

Ayer, A. J. *Language, Truth and Logic,* 2nd ed., 56–59. New York, 1946.

Boring, E. G. "The Gestalt Psychology and the Gestalt Movement." *American Journal of Psychology* 42 (1930): 308–315.

Driesch, Hans. "Physische Gestalten und Organismen." *Annalen der Philosophie* 5 (1925).

Grelling, Kurt, and Paul Oppenheim. "Der Gestaltbegriff in Lichte der neuen Logik." *Erkenntnis* 7 (1938): 211–225.

Hamlyn, D. W. "Psychological Explanation and the Gestalt Hypothesis." *Mind* 60 (1951).

Hamlyn, D. W. *The Psychology of Perception.* London: Routledge and Paul, 1957.

Hartmann, George W. *Gestalt Psychology: A Survey of Facts and Principles.* New York: Ronald Press, 1935.

Henle, Mary. "One Man against the Nazis: Wolfgang Köhler." *American Psychologist* 33 (1978): 939–944.

Hobart, R. E. "Hume without Scepticism." *Mind* 39 (1930).

Katz, David. *Gestalt Psychology: Its Nature and Significance.* Translated by Robert Tyson. New York: Ronald Press, 1950.

Ley, Ronald. *A Whisper of Espionage: Wolfgang Kohler and the Apes of Tenerife.* Garden City Park, NY: Avery, 1990.

Müller, G. E. *Komplextheorie und Gestalttheorie.* Göttingen: Vandenhoeck and Ruprecht, 1923.

Nagel, Ernest. *The Structure of Science,* 380–397. New York: Harcourt Brace, 1961.

Petermann, Bruno. *Die Wertheimer-Koffka-Köhlersche Gestalttheorie.* Leipzig: Barth, 1929. Translated by Meyer Fortes as *The Gestalt Theory and the Problem of Configuration.* London: K. Paul, Trench, Trubner, 1932.

Reiser, O. L. "The Logic of Gestalt Psychology." *Psychological Review* 38 (1931): 359–368.

Rignano, Eugenio. "The Psychological Theory of Form." *Psychological Review* 35 (1928): 118–135.

Sherrill, R., Jr. "Natural Wholes: Wolfgang Kohler and Gestalt Theory." In *Portraits of Pioneers in Psychology,* Vol. 1, edited by G. A. Kimble, M. Wertheimer, and C. White, 257–273.

Washington, DC: American Psychological Association; Hillsdale, NJ: L. Erlbaum Associates, 1991.

Smith, Barry, ed. *Foundations of Gestalt Theory.* Munich: Philosophia, 1988.

Philip W. Cummings (1967)
Bibliography updated by Alyssa Ney (2005)

KOREAN PHILOSOPHY

Scholars hold diverse opinions on the identity and origin of Korean philosophy. Although some trace the origin back to antiquity when the mythical figure Dangun supposedly founded the country in 2333 BCE, there is little historical evidence to support it. It is more plausible to estimate that philosophy began in Korea during the Three Kingdom era (second century CE) when people unfettered themselves from myths, legends, and shamanist beliefs of the tribes, and began to think in more general and philosophical terms. During this period Buddhism, a systematic and conceptually advanced religion, was introduced into the Three Kingdoms (Shilla, Baekje, and Koguryo), all of which embraced it to serve as a social and spiritual foundation for a trans-tribal ethical system. After its introduction, Korean Buddhism went through diverse phases of changes and developments, sometimes as a result of adaptations to changing social and political environments and sometimes as a result of theoretical debates. Neo-Confucianism and Western thought that were later introduced to Korea underwent similar turns and twists.

Korean philosophy, largely formed on the basis of external thought and influences, is notable not for the uniqueness of thoughts per se, but for the special manner in which it internalized the established and widely disseminated thought systems of Asia and the West and developed them into identifiably Korean forms. Korea's geographical and historical circumstances exposed the country to sudden and often torrential influxes of mature and powerful foreign culture and thought systems. Thus, the development of Korean philosophy has consisted in selecting an appropriate trend of thought carefully and reinterpreting it to meet the challenges of the society.

Because Korean philosophy had to concentrate on the selected trend, its characteristic is fundamentalist in that there was a tendency to select a specific trend or interpretation and adhere to it as the only source of truth to the exclusion of other trends. Because Korean philosophy attempted to synthesize diverse thought within the selected trend in order to meet the challenges of the society, the ability to weave divergent thoughts into a coherent whole was crucial. Even today when Western philosophy prevails, the two characteristics of fundamentalism and integrationism are still valid as a description of Korean Philosophy.

THE BEGINNING OF PHILOSOPHICAL THINKING—THE INTRODUCTION OF BUDDHISM AND THE DEVELOPMENT OF KOREAN BUDDHIST PHILOSOPHY

As the Three Kingdoms expanded to constitute sovereign states, politics began to separate from religion. Tribal federations were gradually transformed into monarchies, and the mythologies of clans and the associated religious rituals that had so far dominated the spiritual world of people were no longer adequate to serve as the basis of a state. This created a need for a unified belief system that would reconcile diverse native religious thought and practice, and provide a political rationale for the monarch-centered sovereign state. Such an ideology was also needed to counteract the aristocrats who resented the increasing concentration of political power in the monarch. The introduction of Buddhism from China at this time filled just this need, and it was welcomed by the royal authority.

From its inception Buddhism was allied with the royal authority, so it was advocated not only as a higher, more sophisticated religion, but also as a theoretical ground for strengthening the sovereignty. For example, the Buddhist notion of cause and effect, together with its karmic associations, were helpful in promoting the belief that their king was not a ruler arbitrarily chosen by Heaven, and that his status was a necessary consequence of the good deeds done in his past lives. Buddhist doctrines were also invoked to justify the authority and legitimacy of the royal rule. For that reason the Three Kingdoms endorsed at first the School of Precepts (the Vinaya School), which stressed the importance of rule abidance, in order to solidify the ethical norms and regulations of the newly established nations. As the number of Buddhist monks increased, their mission extended beyond the performance of ceremonies and rituals; they started to study the Buddhist doctrines and texts from a scholarly point of view.

Koguryo, in the north of the Korean peninsula, adopted a branch of Buddhism that interpreted Buddhism in terms of the Daoist concept of nothingness, a concept that was familiar in the local shamanist beliefs. It was succeeded by the Three Treatise School (the Madhyamika School), which upheld the doctrine of emptiness

(*Sunyata*) with the motto "What can be said, cannot be real." Whereas Buddhism, with an emphasis on nothingness or emptiness, was popular in Koguryo, a different perspective on Buddhism was embraced in Shilla. It was called the Consciousness-Only School (the Yogacara School). As the name suggests, their main claim was that the external world is nothing more than the objectification of inner cognitive activities and that only consciousness and cognition exist. It was popularized by Shilla monk Woncheuk (613–696), who studied and practiced his theory in China. His theory was influential not only within Shilla, but also in Tibet.

After the seventh century, more monks returned after studying abroad and brought with them Buddhist doctrines of numerous schools, adding diversity to the early Korean Buddhism. It also improved the quality of Buddhist studies, but at the same time it caused deep confusion. All the teachings were from one Buddha. So how could one make sense of all these diverse interpretations, some of them in conflict with others? The perplexity was especially acute in Shilla, which had an alliance with Tang China and sent many monks there to study Buddhist doctrines. This created fierce debates and disputes among the monks, each group arguing that what it had learned was the exclusive truth. Through this process, conflicting theoretical stances adjusted themselves to accommodate each other, which led to the unique characteristic of Korean Buddhism called *integrationism*.

Shilla monk Wonhyo (617–686) was the first Buddhist scholar who established his own unique theory. He meticulously analyzed three core concepts of Buddhism—mind (*citra*), enlightenment (*bodhi*), and ignorance (*avidyā*)—and attempted to illuminate their mutual relationship. According to Wonhyo, Buddha's mind and people's minds are one and the same and people born with the mind of Buddha lost track of the true facet of human existence because they are blinded by ignorance (i.e., self-centeredness and greed). Thus, being in the state of Buddha's mind (enlightenment) is nothing above and beyond being in the state of freedom from ignorance and thus returning to the original state of the human mind. On this basis, he argued that the Three Treatise School's method that tried to reach Buddha's mind by removing ignorance and the Consciousness-Only School's converse method of removing ignorance by reaching Buddha's mind were just two different paths to the same goal. This illustrates the way in which Wonhyo attempted to harmonize doctrinal differences among diverse schools. Because of Wonhyo's influence, the Buddhist schools in Korea henceforth sought in a single-minded way to reach an all-encompassing interpretation of Buddhism.

Whereas Wonhyo laid the philosophical foundation of Korean Buddhism, Uisang (625–702) focused his work on unifying numerous Buddhist schools active in all parts of the nation. Upon his return from Tang China shortly after Shilla absorbed and consolidated the other two kingdoms into the United Shilla (676), Uisang reorganized the Buddhist temples with divergent doctrinal allegiances by embracing the Flower Garland School (the Avatamsaka School). On the basis of the claim that particulars and universals, many and the one, were all different aspects of dharma (the principle, law, or a universal norm that orders both the natural world and human conduct), he advocated the holistic view that all things in the universe, causally interconnected under dharma, represented the same supreme mind. This holistic doctrine of the Flower Garland School provided a spiritual background for the harmony that must exist between individuals and the state, and between individuals and the universe. Thus it helped support the political consolidation of the Unified Shilla dynasty.

THE ACCEPTANCE OF ZEN BUDDHISM AND ITS DEVELOPMENT

In the eighth century the Unified Shilla made great strides in doctrinal studies, particularly in the areas of the Flower Garland and Consciousness-Only Schools. During the latter half of the eighth century, however, the role of king shrank to that of a protector of his own clan, and powerful clans in the provinces rose to supersede the royal authority. Accordingly, the Flower Garland School that provided the spiritual basis for unification was succeeded by Zen Buddhism backed by regional aristocrats. Zen Buddhism emphasized that enlightenment was attained not through laborious doctrinal studies, but through discovering the Buddha mind within oneself. Even though Korean Zen Buddhism prospered as diverse branches of Chinese Zen Buddhism were introduced, the philosophical message was no different from what had been taught by Flower Garland School or Wonhyo—that ignorance is the beginning of enlightenment and that everything is dependent on one's mind. It should be noted, however, that practice-oriented characteristics of Zen Buddhism paved the way for Korean Buddhism to become a popular religion without being trapped in theoretical intricacies.

In 936 the Koryo dynasty emerged, leaving behind the chaotic ruins of the Shilla dynasty. While the Koryo dynasty was developing into a state, it exploited Confucianism for practical purposes. Confucianism was introduced into Korea around the second century BCE and Koreans were familiar with its major teachings for more than 1,000 years. Although Confucian education was gradually strengthened mainly for the purpose of building a bureaucratic system, Koryo Confucianism at this time had yet to reach a level of philosophical significance. Spiritually, the primary concern of Koryo was integrating diversified schools of thought, and it was still Buddhism that undertook the role. Thus, one can witness the strong integrationist tendency in Buddhism throughout the Koryo dynasty.

Chinul (1158–1210) invigorated and established Zen Buddhism as a strong tradition in Koryo by providing it a firm philosophical basis. Thinking that Zen Buddhism of his time had dwindled in popularity mainly because of its inherent subjectivity and excessive aversion to doctrinal studies, he argued that both the doctrinal component and the meditative component must be incorporated into a correct version of Buddhism. This led to the creation of his own unique program of "sudden awakening and gradual cultivation." According to this program, one can clear oneself of secular concerns and arrive at Buddha's mind only if one comes to be enlightened by meditative insights and at the same time carries out self-cultivation to verify whether what one has understood by enlightenment corresponds to the general truth of Buddhism. This unique theory within the meditation camp became one of the most representative views of Korean Buddhism, influential up to the early twenty-first century.

After Chinul, there emerged a variety of Buddhist philosophies such as purely meditative Buddhism, a Confucian Buddhism, and so on. Still the unique characteristic of Korean Buddhism lies in the fact that it has constantly sought a synthesis of two major traditions of Buddhism, doctrinal tradition and Zen tradition, and it is often argued that Korean Buddhism has been most successful at that. With the formation of the Chosun dynasty, however, Buddhism came to be regarded as something to be overcome and was by and large excluded from ideological pursuits.

THE ACCEPTANCE OF NEO-CONFUCIANISM

Although it is hard to trace exactly when Confucianism was first introduced to Korea, it is estimated that its introduction accompanied the import of the Chinese writing system roughly around the second century BCE. Koreans began to accept Confucianism as the Three Kingdoms transformed themselves into ancient states and this created a need for Confucian bureaucrats who were versed in the Chinese writing system well enough to fulfill practical purposes of composing diplomatic documents. Each of the Three Kingdoms had Confucian educational institutions, which produced Confucian scholars and students. From the fact that Confucian virtues such as loyalty and filial piety were prized in the Three Kingdoms, it can be inferred that Confucianism was held in high esteem, even though the scholarship was not up to the level of philosophical analysis.

Confucianism during the Koryo period, as in the Shilla period, was chiefly used as a useful political and practical complement to Buddhism. After the eleventh century, however, as the sovereignty and its administrative structure became stabilized, Confucianism began to distinguish itself from Buddhism. Confucianism that had been only an object of a practical interest began to be the object of serious theoretical research as well. Koryo's Confucian scholars, represented by Choi Chung (984–1068) and his twelve disciples, considerably advanced the level of Confucian studies as they participated in public administration from the time of King Seong (who ruled from 981 to 997) to King Mun (1046–1083). The private Confucian educational institution Choi founded taught major Confucian Classics. Still, because the program of study was largely oriented toward preparing students for national examinations, it seems that more time was spent on literary exercises than on philosophical investigations.

The later Koryo period was an important time for Confucianism in Korea: This was when Korean Confucian scholars started distancing themselves from Buddhism. Scholars returning from Yuan China brought home with them the Confucianism that was already Yuan's political ideology, and this transformed Koryo's Confucianism in a novel way. The Neo-Confucian master Zhu Xi's writings were introduced in 1289 and numerous Confucian scholars from then on gradually extended the understanding of Confucianism and Neo-Confucianism. A truly novel phenomenon occurring was that these scholars began to mount an attack on Buddhism with philosophical arguments. Yi Saek (1328–1396), one of the last scholars to return from Yuan China, exerted an extensive influence on later Korean Confucians. Even though his own understanding of Neo-Confucianism remained still at a comparatively naive stage in that it simple-mindedly identified Confucian benevolence with Buddhist compassion, and Confucian repose with Buddhist calmness, Yi Saek produced prominent and influential disciples.

They were trained at the national Confucian educational institution, called Sungkeunguan, which was founded by the government in 1289. They became major figures during the transition period from Koryo to Chosun, which succeeded the Koryo dynasty in 1392. With philosophical explanations of why Buddhism was fundamentally a heresy, they decisively broke with the previous generations of scholars who were largely tolerant of Buddhism. They also played a crucial role in constructing, for the new state, an ideological framework based on Confucianism.

The Chosun dynasty, which replaced the Buddhist Koryo dynasty, adopted Confucian ideology, custom, and order as the political and social foundation of the new state. Those who framed the political philosophical framework for the new dynasty were a group of scholars led by Chung Dojeon. Chung had a leading role in laying the foundation of Chosun's Neo-Confucianism and enabled Confucian ideology to prevail. Because his interpretation of Neo-Confucianism was constructed with a deliberate intention to buttress the new society with a philosophical basis, his philosophy went beyond the personal realm of self-cultivation and moral improvement.

What Chung stressed the most as he propounded Neo-Confucianism was the criticism of Buddhism. He methodically compared the Buddhist worldview with that of Neo-Confucianism, arguing that whereas the basis of the Buddhist worldview was nihilism based on emptiness (*Sunyata*), a robust realism based on *li* and *qi* was the foundation of Neo-Confucianism. *Li* and *qi* are the two most important concepts in Neo-Confucianism. In Zhu Xi's philosophical system, *li*, which is similar to the Platonic idea or the Aristotelian notion of form, is an abstract being. *Li*, like the Buddhist dharma, is often appealed to in the explanation of universal truths governing the natural world and human conduct. *Qi*, on the other hand, corresponds roughly to matter in Western philosophy and it is often invoked to explain the changes in spatiotemporal objects including human bodies and minds. However, *qi* differs from matter as conceived in the West in two important respects. First, Neo-Confucianism locates mind in the domain of *qi*, whereas the Western tradition has tended to regard mind to be distinct from matter. Second, *qi* was construed to be animate, whereas matter is usually construed to be inert and inanimate.

Chung, following the Neo-Confucian tradition, explained the generation and decay of man and nature in terms of *qi* and, on its basis, attacked the Buddhist theory that argued for the illusory nature of the world, the unre-ality of things, and the transmigration and eternity of the soul. He also attacked the Buddhist doctrine of Karma by claiming that people's differences were not because of what they had done in the past, but because of the *qi* that each person possessed from birth. Chung distinguished Neo-Confucianism from Buddhism in the domain of morality as well. He contended that although the Buddhist notion of compassion had some similarities with the Confucian notion of benevolence, they fundamentally differed in that compassion required treating all beings with indiscriminate equality, whereas benevolence allowed for unequal treatments based on the type of relationship between the benefactor and the recipient. Confucian benevolence, thus construed, served as the fundamental value to sustain the order of the new hierarchical society. Chung's denunciation of Buddhism as a heresy successfully derailed the attempts to revive Buddhism during the early Chosun period and paved the way for other scholars of the upcoming generations to develop and systematize Korean Neo-Confucianism.

The groundwork laid by Chung, however, did not lead immediately to fruitful Confucian research. During the first years of Chosun, a period marked by intense conflicts among the major political factions, Neo-Confucianism as a national ideology lost its initial momentum and was bogged down in exegetical studies. It was during the years of King Sung (1457–1494) that Neo-Confucian scholars returned to hold positions of great influence in the government. Neo-Confucianism began to serve as a practical guide to governance, going beyond its role as a mere ideology. Cho Kwangjo (1482–1519) was the scholar who was most influential in this transition. He claimed that the ruler's moral cultivation was especially important because his moral commitments would exert great influence on the whole nation. Cho urged the view that an ideal Confucian state could be realized through the internalization of Confucian moral values on a national scale and he subsequently led a movement to actualize the view. Views like these were commonly held by the Confucian literati of the time, and it led Neo-Confucians to delve into the nature of human mind and explore the ground and the method of moral practice.

THE THEORETICAL DEVELOPMENT OF NEO-CONFUCIANISM

Although Neo-Confucianism during the early Chosun period put more emphasis on the practical side, the theoretical side was not completely ignored. For example, the concept of *qi* was exploited to explicate problems such as man and nature, life and death, and the existence of souls and spirits. The scholar who added depth to the philosophy of *qi* was Seo Kyeongdeok (1489–1546). Seo, classified as a *qi*-philosopher during the early to middle Chosun period, constructed a highly complex and sophisticated theory of cosmology and human nature on the basis of *qi*.

Drawing on the views of Chinese *qi* philosophers during the Song dynasty, in particular Zhang Hengqi and Shao Kangjie, Seo attempted to explain the macroscopic movements and changes in nature in terms of the diverse phases of *qi* and transitions between them. For example, he discriminated between *qi* as a root of everything (pre-celestial *qi*) and *qi* as a changing phenomenon (post-celestial *qi*). Pre-celestial *qi* is the ultimate basis of existing entities, whose movement and change determine variance in post-celestial phenomena. The phenomenal world, which is generated through *qi*'s movements and changes, disappears as *qi* disperses, yet the dispersed *qi* returns again to the pre-celestial realm, which in turn becomes a causal basis of the regeneration of another phenomenal world. Seo associated this cosmology with the principle of Great Change as manifested in the Book of Changes, and applied his theory to the problems of life and death, and even to the question of life after death. His theory of *qi* enabled people to overcome the Daoist concept of nothingness and the Buddhist notion of eternity of the soul; most importantly, it helped the Neo-Confucianism of the Chosun dynasty to gain a unique perspective on man and nature.

The philosophers who completed the framework of Neo-Confucian moral philosophy were Yi Hwang (1501–1570) and Yi I (1536–1584). Yi Hwang, better known by his pen name Toegye, researched in depth the Chinese Neo-Confucian master Zhu Xi, whom he regarded as the ultimate source and authority for Neo-Confucianism. In contrast to Seo before him, he argued that *li* was the ultimate and essential being that determined the movement of *qi*. What particularly concerned Toegye, however, was not the ontology of *li* and *qi* per se, but their roles in grounding morality. He believed that if *li* did not act upon the external world, there would be no ontological ground for morality. In other words, he thought that moral intuition or wisdom would be useless if all human emotions are vulnerable to physical intemperance and overindulgence. It seemed obvious to Toegye, however, that humans had an intellectual control over the mind. From this, he concluded that there must be a domain of emotions that are distinctively moral, and that these must be distinguished from mundane nonmoral emotions. He went on to construct the unique view

that everyday nonmoral emotions were manifestations of *qi*, whereas moral emotions were manifestations of *li*. In placing morality within the domain of emotions, Toegye put a greater emphasis on the cultivation of the emotions rather than on purely rational and intellectual training.

Another philosopher who elevated the Chosun dynasty's Neo-Confucianism to another level of sophistication was Yi I (1536–1584), better known by his pen name Yulgok. While revering Toegye's scholarship, he thought that Toegye's dualistic interpretation of Zhu Xi's philosophy had a fundamental problem. Placing a higher value on the aforementioned metaphysical system devised by Seo, Yulgok claimed that although *li* and *qi* were differentiated conceptually, they were not two independent beings. Applying this view to morality, Yulgok maintained that there was no separate source or domain of moral emotions; everyday emotions that conformed to the moral standard were themselves moral emotions. All the emotions including moral emotions were manifestations of *qi*, but they were regulated by *li*. A moral action was not a natural emanation from a separate moral emotion, but the outcome of the recognition of the universal norms and a personal decision to make that recognition bear on the mundane emotions. Because Yulgok considered reason, rather than emotion, to play a central role in living a moral life, he concluded that the enhancement of our rational capacity for right judgments should be emphasized over emotional enrichment.

Weighing between emotion and reason, and between *qi* and *li*, the philosophies of Toegye and Yulgok manifested subtle but significant differences in all respects, leading to two lineages of Neo-Confucianism during the Chosun period. One was *li*-centered and the other *qi*-centered. As the two schools contended for the title of Neo-Confucian orthodoxy, the Chosun dynasty's Neo-Confucianism became increasingly more dogmatic and doctrinaire, leading scholars to the rigid position that all social and individual conduct should conform to the Confucian code of behavior. Leaving behind the metaphysical basis of a moral mind, the debate now moved to another issue over how to apply abstract morality to the real world. Thus, the theory of rites and rituals came to replace the theory of mind, and formed the mainstream philosophy of the seventeenth-century Chosun dynasty.

As the Chosun dynasty's Neo-Confucianism became increasingly more doctrinaire and ritualistic, the chasm between theory and reality, and between philosophy and social development, widened. Scholars, convinced that a blind adherence to Zhu Xi's texts had led them into a dead end, began to search for a breakthrough outside Zhu

Xi. Two trends are notable as consequences of this movement; one was the acceptance of the Chinese Yangming philosophy that recognized the significance of the individual will and freedom. The other was the emergence of exegetical studies that focused on a positivistic interpretation of Confucian Classics free from political ideologies. Scholars involved in these studies hoped to overcome Zhu Xi's philosophy by an appeal to a superior authority (i.e., revered ancient Confucian Classics). The rejection of Zhu Xi's philosophy was significant and it exerted a strong influence on later philosophers, particularly on those belonging to the Practical Study School.

Meanwhile, the scholars from the Yulgok's lineage went on to articulate their philosophical system. In their attempt to refine Yulgok's philosophy, a discordance within his system was discovered, which led to the biggest philosophical debate of the eighteenth century and subsequently caused a split of the school into the *Ho* line and the *Rak* line (*Ho* and *Rak* are names of the regions where their advocates resided). The *Ho-Rak* debate was over the question whether there existed a nature common to both humans and other creatures in the world. The debate that initially started between two scholars gradually widened and came to involve almost all the scholars of the Yulgok school. The debate evolved to cover a wide range of topics such as the relationship between mind and nature, the distinction between the sage and the commoner, and the sameness or difference between human nature and animal nature. In debating over whether there was a general nature common to all things in nature, they came to address the relationship between *li* and *qi* and consequently it provided an opportunity to rethink the status and meaning of *li*. This in turn gave rise to a wide spectrum of thoughts such as the *qi*-only theory and the *li*-only theory.

THE RISE OF MODERN THOUGHT— THE INTRODUCTION AND RECEPTION OF WESTERN THOUGHT AND PRACTICAL STUDY

As Korea opened its door to Western thought in the eighteenth century, a notable change in the trend of Korean philosophy took place, and this was the emergence of the Practical Study School. From the early eighteenth century on, the inadequacy of Neo-Confucianism as a political ideology became increasingly more evident. In order to go beyond the limit of Neo-Confucianism and to go along with new social environments, a group of scholars turned their attention from morality and self-cultivation to more practical questions such as economy and the land

system. This trend came to be called Practical Study. Scholars belonging to this movement tried to attain new philosophical insights by blending traditional Neo-Confucianism with newly introduced Western thought, especially Catholicism and Western sciences.

Yi Ik (1681–1763), deeply impressed by the astronomy and the solar calendar brought to Korea by the Christian missionaries, took an active part in introducing Western thought to Korea. He created an atmosphere that enabled his disciples to play leading roles in spreading and promoting Western thought. On the issue of accepting the Catholic doctrine, however, they diverged into a receptive group called the Accept-West Party and a critical group called the Reject-West Party. The latter criticized the fundamental premises of Catholicism including the theory of anima from a Neo-Confucian perspective on the nature of mind. They claimed that Catholicism and Confucianism differed in fundamental assumptions and could not be harmonized with each other.

The Accept-West Party maintained a more open attitude toward Western thought. Among the more influential members of this group was Chong Yakyong (1762–1836), better known by the pen name Dasan, who constructed a comprehensive and influential theory of the Practical Study School, incorporating Catholic theories in his philosophical system. Through a novel reinterpretation of Confucian Classics, not only did he attempt to recover the practical spirit of early Confucianism, but he also tried to synthesize Confucianism and Catholicism. For example, he argued that God in Christianity and Heaven in ancient Confucianism were one and the same; according to him, Heaven in the Confucian tradition was essentially a subject with volitions, desires, and perceptions, and also an agent who used those faculties to rule the universe. Thus, the Confucian Heaven was not to be explicated in terms of metaphysical and abstract principles such as *li* or yin and yang. According to him, then, the term *high-emperor* as employed by ancient Confucians portrayed the meaning of Heaven in the most adequate way, and Heaven, thus construed, was no different from the Christian God.

Dasan also drew on Christian ideas in his explications of morality. Criticizing the Neo-Confucian view that morality was a part of inherent human nature, he maintained that human nature was so constituted as to follow self-regarding desires and preferences and thus it was fundamentally egotistic and hedonistic. He advocated, on this basis, the Christian idea that moral perfection was possible only through recognizing God's will and acting accordingly. Then he attempted to graft Confucianism onto Christianity by adopting the Confucian theory of cultivation as a way of internalizing God's orders. However, such attempts by Dasan and other Accept-West Party scholars caused, among the mainstream scholars who were still committed to Neo-Confucianism as their philosophical idea, a deep sense of insecurity. This played a part in bringing about an official oppression of the Catholic church later, which started in 1785 and lasted on and off for eighty years.

Unlike Yi Ik's disciples who attempted to overcome the limits of Neo-Confucianism by adopting Catholicism, other mainstream scholars in powerful positions embraced Western sciences to improve their Neo-Confucian system. They were called Study-North Scholars, and Hong Daeyong (1731–1783) and Choi Hangi (1803–1877) were the leading figures. Hong, keenly interested in Western sciences, turned his attention from a value-laden Confucian worldview to a morally neutral, positivistic, and scientific worldview. Believing that human existence was on the same level as the existence of any other natural beings, he attempted to explicate everything in terms of qi's movement. Hong's notion of qi was similar to today's concept of matter, more so than that of any other qi-scholars. Qi was, for Hong, a concept suited to cosmology and useful in explaining natural phenomena; he explained the rotation of the earth, tides, and climatic changes by using the concepts such as shrouding qi, flowing qi, and great qi. Thus, in Hong's theory, the dynamic transformations of qi were more salient than the ultimate nature of qi itself. The significance of Hong's philosophy of qi was that it went beyond the Confucian moralist view of the natural world and gave Korean philosophy a modern naturalistic outlook by combining traditional philosophy with the newly introduced Western sciences.

In the case of Choi Hangi, the influence of Western science is even more evident. In Choi's theory, the traditional concept of qi played a critical mediating role in assimilating Western scientific theories into his own system. Choi believed that human conduct and natural phenomena were all manifestations of qi, and therefore that both Confucian ethics and Western science could be proven to be truths on the same level. Rejecting the Neo-Confucian perspective on morality, he claimed that ethical norms were based on, and derivable from, laws of nature. His qi-centered theory not only encompassed existing Confucianism, Buddhism, and Daoism, but could also be harmonized with Western scientific theories.

Two main characteristics of qi in Choi's theory were quantifiability and perceivability. Because everything was a manifestation of qi and qi was perceivable, one could accumulate knowledge only through empirical investigations. According to Choi, the knowledge thus obtained should be able to reach, through verifications and repeated corrections, a level where the fundamental principles common to humans and the natural world could be discovered and natural phenomena scientifically understood. He was also convinced that qi could be quantified by numbers. Because the numerical system could reveal changes of qi in an objective and general way, scientific studies such as menology (calendar studies), calculus, and physics could reveal the nature of the world most accurately. He even thought that the movement of qi could be proven mathematically. What is especially notable in Choi's theory is that Choi had unfettered himself completely from the value-centered, intuition-dependent philosophy of Neo-Confucianism and paved a way to a modern naturalistic way of thinking.

Dasan's Catholic Confucianism, Hong Daeyong's scientific Neo-Confucianism, and Choi Hangi's empirical epistemology were just a few representative attempts, during the eighteenth and nineteenth centuries, to embrace the newly introduced Western thought within traditional philosophy. They had the potential for launching a vital and original philosophical movement. With the fall of the Chosun dynasty, however, these philosophical endeavors did not lead to the formation of modern Korean philosophy. They remained only as one dead-end strand in the history of Korean philosophy.

MODERN KOREAN PHILOSOPHY

The period from the end of the nineteenth century to the beginning of the twentieth century was a critical turning point for Korea and for Korean philosophy. The Japanese colonialism backed by Western culture and technology began to encroach on Korea. Korea was forced to sign an unequal treaty with Japan in 1876. That provoked other imperialistic countries to coerce similar forms of agreements with Korea. As a result, Korea was defenseless against the tidal influx of Western culture, new languages, and new modes of thinking. Although Korean intellectuals at the time attempted to save Korea from colonization by westernizing Korea itself, it was too little and too late as Korea was annexed by Japan in 1910.

A notable phenomenon that followed was the shift of Korea's and Japan's roles in the transfer of cultures. Traditionally China was the dominant cultural force in the region, and Korea used to import Chinese culture and incorporate it into its own, and then export the outcome to Japan. By the turn of the century, this pattern of cultural exchanges underwent a dramatic change; the West replaced China and Japan became the conduit of the Western culture to Korea. Even though Korea had earlier contact with Western religion and science, it was only after the Japanese colonization that Korea made its first encounter with Western philosophy. The word *chulhak* was also first introduced to Korea. The word, made up of two Chinese characters, was coined in Japan as a translation of the term *philosophy*, and it is now the standard term for philosophy in the Asian countries in which Chinese characters are used for academic purposes, including China, Korea, and Japan.

That Western philosophy was introduced to Korea through Japanese colonialism, combined with the prevalent picture of Western power and wealth, defined the early perception of Western philosophy in Korea. Philosophy was regarded as something indigenous to the West and completely alien to Korea, having nothing in common with the traditional thought of Korea. In the minds of Korean intellectuals at the turn of the century, the historical dominance of Confucianism was the main reason for Korea's falling behind in the process of modernization. Traditional ways of thinking and Confucianism, in particular, were what had to be overcome, whereas Western culture and philosophy were to be welcomed and assimilated. The introduction of a neologism, *chulhak*, to signify Western philosophy might have reinforced this frame of mind. For example, *Philosophy*, the first academic journal of philosophy published in 1933, contained no article on traditional Korean thought. It took many years to recognize the common features between Western philosophy and Asian thought and to apply the term *chulhak* to both.

Western philosophy was mostly German philosophy. Japan and Germany were allies and the Western philosophy in Japan was for the most part German philosophy. In consequence, Western philosophy introduced to Korea via Japan was also mostly German. Even though Bertrand Russell and John Dewey visited China and Japan respectively in 1910 and 1919 and that these visits aroused the interest of philosophers in Korea, their impact was limited. The dominance of German philosophy in Korea lasted for some time even after Korea's liberation from Japan in 1945, and this continued during the post-World War II years when the influence of German philosophy was diminishing in the rest of the world. Scholars specializing in German philosophy filled the philosophy faculties of the major universities, and they determined the

overall shape and course of the profession until philosophers of a new generation began replacing them.

Writings of Korean philosophers in the early twentieth century were oriented toward practice. Korean philosophers, like any other Korean intellectual at the time, thought of themselves as pioneers of modernization and westernization. Philosophy was supposed to enlighten people and build a new way of thinking. The tendency to highlight the importance of doing philosophy with practical minds, rather than to introduce Western philosophy for its own sake, was manifest in the first issue of the above-mentioned journal, *Philosophy*. The articles published in the first issue included *One Question concerning the Starting Point of Philosophizing*, *What Is Philosophy?: On the Eternity of Philosophy*, *The Idea of an Ethical Evaluation*, and *The Structure of Concrete Existence*. In these articles, the nature of philosophy was defined with an emphasis on its relevance to practice. However, as the Japanese control over academia became ever more strict and rigid, emphases on practice grew weaker.

Korea was liberated from Japan in 1945. However, the country was divided into two Koreas with conflicting ideologies. This led, in 1950, to a calamitous national tragedy, the Korean War (1950–1953). This series of major events left significant marks on the contour of philosophy in Korea. Marxism, which was experimented with and advocated by a scant few philosophers during the Japanese colonial period, blossomed in the midst of the ideological conflicts that followed the liberation. Even though Marxism was soon officially suppressed in South Korea and many influential Marxist philosophers fled to the more hospitable North, Marxism left an indelible impression. Along with Marxism, existentialism emerged as a major player in Korean philosophy. This was mainly due to the Korean War; in particular, French existentialism, born in the ruins and despair of World War II (1939–1945), strongly resonated with Koreans with similar experiences during the Korean war.

A long-standing bias toward German philosophy began to change in the early 1950s. The Korean Philosophical Association was formed in 1953, and its official journal was founded. More important was that Korea started having direct contacts with Western philosophies. Philosophers came to visit Korea from the United States, Great Britain, and Germany. Students went to various parts of the world for studies. By having direct contacts, Korean philosophers gained firsthand access to Western philosophy, helping them to overcome the distortions inflicted by Japanese translations and interpretations.

Another outcome of this direct and broad exposure to Western philosophy has been the revival of interest in traditional philosophy. Ever-expanding contacts with diverse cultures and philosophies made Korean philosophers rethink the roots and identity of Korean thought. Traditional Korean philosophy, which had been ignored as useless and retrogressive during the Japanese colonial period, began to receive fresh scrutiny and assessment. In the late 1950s, Korean traditional thought came to be accommodated under the umbrella of philosophy.

As a result of interaction with diverse parts of the world, different trends of philosophy are evenly reflected in Korean philosophy today. Anglo-American analytic philosophy is one of the strongest trends. German philosophy is still going strong even though it is not as prominent as it once was. Many philosophers in Korea specialize in traditional Korean philosophy and other Asian philosophies. The world of philosophy in Korea is a melting pot. A large variety of traditions and trends are actively and vigorously represented—from phenomenology and existentialism to analytic philosophy, Buddhism, and Confucianism. Now philosophers pursuing diverse perspectives are starting to hold dialogues with each other. It is exciting to wait and see whether and how the world of philosophy in Korea will continue its tradition of integrationism and what the outcome will be.

See also Buddhism; Chinese Philosophy: Overview; Chinese Philosophy: Daosim; Confucius; Japanese Philosophy; Zhu Xi (Chu Hsi).

Bibliography

Buswell Jr., Robert E. *The Formation of the Ch'an Ideology in China and Korea.* Princeton NJ: Princeton University Press, 1989.

Chung, Edward. *The Korean Neo-Confucianism of Yi Toegye and Yi Yulgok—An Reappraisal of the "Four-Seven Thesis" and its Practical Implication for Self-Cultivation.* New York: SUNY Press, 1995.

Haboush, Jahyun Kim, and Wm. Theodore de Bary, eds. *The Rise of Neo-Confucianism in Korea.* New York: Columbia University, 1985.

Kalton, Michael. *The Four-Seven Debate—An Annotation of Translation of the Most Famous Controversy in Korean Neo-Confucianism.* New York: SUNY Press, 1994.

Keel, Hee-Sung. *Chinul, the Founder of the Korean Son Tradition.* Seoul: Pojinjae, 1984.

Kendall, Laurel, and Griffin Dix, eds. *Religion and Ritual in Korean Society.* Berkeley, CA.: Institute of East Asian Studies, 1987.

The Korean National Commission for UNESCO. *Main Currents of Korean Thought.* Seoul: Si-sa-young-o-sa Publishers, 1978.

Lancaster, Lewis. *Buddhism in Chosŏn.* Berkeley, CA.: Institute of East Asian Studies, 1996.

Lancaster, Lewis. *Buddhism in Koryŏ: A Royal Religion.* Berkeley, CA: Institute of East Asian Studies, 1996.

Lee, Peter H. *Sourcebook of Korean Civilization.* Vols. 1 and 2. New York: Columbia University Press, 1993.

Lee, Peter H. *Sources of Korean Tradition.* New York: Columbia University Press, 1997.

Park, Sung Bae. *Buddhist Faith and Sudden Enlightenment.* Albany, NY: SUNY Press, 1983.

Setton, Mark. *Chong Yag-yong—Korea's Challenge to Orthodox Neo-Confucianism.* New York: SUNY Press, 1997.

Shim, Jae-ryong. *Korean Buddhism: Tradition and Transformation.* Seoul: Jimoondang, 1999.

Namjin Huh and Kihyeon Kim (2005)

KORN, ALEJANDRO
(1860–1936)

Alejandro Korn, an Argentine metaphysician and ethical philosopher, was born in San Vicente. He took his doctorate in medicine and directed a hospital for the mentally ill. In 1906 he joined the faculty of philosophy and letters at Buenos Aires. Although he wrote little, he had immense personal influence on Argentine philosophy. His philosophical writing came late in his life: *La libertad creadora* (La Plata, 1930), his major work, is a compilation of five essays dating from 1918 to 1930.

Korn is sometimes called a positivist, a label suggested by his scientific training, his empiricism, the skeptical note in his metaphysics, and his ethical relativism. However, his "Incipit Vita Nova" (1918) set the stage for his own criticism of positivism. In this essay, he maintained that despite the scientific and technological progress of preceding decades, contemporary man is dissatisfied and disillusioned. The cause is the impairment of ethics by the spread of the positivistic doctrine that man is a machine without liberty; the remedy is a libertarian philosophy that subordinates science to ethics. Korn's sources were not Auguste Comte or Herbert Spencer, but Henri Bergson, Arthur Schopenhauer, and Immanuel Kant.

Korn's methodology rests on an experiential intuition whose objects are concrete particulars of ordinary experience. This common intuition is not passive and its content is not simple. Reason supplies concepts that are merely formal and symbolic but that penetrate intuition; the latter always has discursive elements. There is also a more intimate intuition or vision, which has intellectual, mystical, and aesthetic forms corresponding to metaphysics, religion, and art. Intuition as vision suggests profound convictions and has an important place in the spiritual life of man, but it carries no assurance of truth. For comparative certainty we must turn to the two disciplines of ordinary intuition: science, which has a measurable object in the external world of fact, and axiology, which has an unmeasurable object in the internal world of evaluation. The third great intellectual enterprise, metaphysics, attempts to describe reality through concepts that transcend all possible experience. Metaphysical systems are dialectical poems. We cannot live without metaphysics, but we cannot convert it into a science; it should contain sincere convictions, free from dogmatism.

The external world of science, of the not-self, known through sensations, is spatial, measurable, and governed by strict causal law. The internal world of axiology, of the self, constituted of emotions, volitions, and judgments, is nonspatial, immeasurable, purposive, and free. These are the two halves of one encompassing domain of consciousness, which comprises all that we know and, it seems, all that is real. Common to both halves of consciousness are three further characters: activity or perpetual becoming, which shows that stable things and rigid names are false; relativity, which expresses the fact that every particular act has its reason in another; and time. Most significant in distinguishing the subjective from the objective order is freedom: economic freedom, or mastery of the external world, and ethical freedom, or mastery of self.

The search for an ultimate reality beyond consciousness led Korn to deny monistic realism, dualistic realism, and solipsism, and to affirm a type of absolute idealism. Experienced things, space, and time depend on consciousness, evidently because they involve organizing concepts or forms. A thing lying beyond consciousness and implied as cause of the experienced thing is denied: causality is a creature of our thought. The known object thus depends on consciousness and has its being there. But that does not entail the dependence of objects on my self. The self, or subjective order, is only a part of consciousness; it is not the source of the known world. The further definition of this idealism is through the theory of the *acción consciente*: consciousness as an everlasting, dynamic, and creative process, unknown in itself but manifested as aspiration toward absolute liberty.

This ontological goal is the key to Korn's theory of values. A value is the created object of an affirmative valuation, and valuation is the reaction of the human will to an event. Values therefore are subjective. There are instinctive, erotic, vital, economic, social, religious, ethical, logical, and aesthetic values, none of which can be reduced to any other. Values achieve unity through their common source in human personality and through their common goal in the liberty of man. Creative liberty is the recurring motif of Korn's philosophy.

See also Bergson, Henri; Comte, Auguste; Idealism; Intuition; Kant, Immanuel; Latin American Philosophy; Metaphysics; Positivism; Schopenhauer, Arthur.

Bibliography
Obras, 3 vols. La Plata: Tomás Palumbo, 1933–1940.
"Influencias filosóficas en la evolución nacional." *Revista de la universidad de Buenos Aires* (1912). Reprinted in *Obras*, Vol. III.
Apuntes filosóficos. Buenos Aires, 1935.

Arthur Berndtson (1967)

KOTARBIŃSKI, TADEUSZ
(1886–1981)

Tadeusz Kotarbiński, a Polish philosopher and logician, was born in Warsaw in 1886. He studied philosophy and the classics at the University of Lvov, where he obtained his doctorate in 1912. He began teaching at the University of Warsaw in 1918 and soon became perhaps the most influential philosophy teacher in Poland. His enlightened views, integrity, public spirit, and social zeal frequently brought him into conflict with established opinions and with the government, both before and after World War II. Admired by many and respected by all, Kotarbiński commanded a unique position of moral and intellectual prestige in his country. He was a member of the Polish Academy of Science and of the International Institute of Philosophy, and he was for a long time chairman of both bodies. He held an honorary doctorate from the Université Libre in Brussels and was a corresponding fellow of the British Academy and an honorary member of the Academy of Sciences of the U.S.S.R. and of other foreign scientific organizations.

CONCRETISM

Kotarbiński began his philosophical career as a minimalist. He advocated the abandonment of such terms as *philosophy* and *philosopher* because of their ambiguity and vagueness. The miscellaneous collection of subjects traditionally known as philosophy lacks any factual or logical coherence. These various subjects should be reconstructed as specialized fields of study and thus acquire some recognized criteria of professional competence. "The philosopher" should mean "the teacher of philosophy," and "philosophy" should be used restrictively to denote moral philosophy and logic in the broad sense, which comprises formal logic, the philosophy of language, the methodology of science, and the theory of knowledge. Kotarbiński himself chose logic in this broad sense as the chief subject of his own concern. He wished to transform logic into a science as exact as mathematical logic and he applied himself to the construction of the conceptual apparatus necessary for this task. However, the results of this analytical work, accomplished between 1920 and 1935, exceeded the original design and produced a system known as reism or concretism. Kotarbiński regarded it as a program rather than a set doctrine and for linguistic reasons prefered *concretism* to *reism*.

Concretism arose from the puzzle about how qualities can belong to or inhere in the things of which they are characteristics. Kotarbiński believed that the puzzle can be resolved if we recognize that whereas things may be hard or soft, black or white, and so forth, nothing is hardness or softness, blackness or whiteness. Thus, the insight underlying concretism can be expressed in the proposition "only concrete individual objects exist." The expression "*a* exists" has the same meaning as "something is an *a*" (ex $a =_{Df} (\exists x) x$ is a) and the meaning of *is* can be explicated as follows:

$$(a,b) :: a \epsilon b. \equiv \therefore (\exists x). x \epsilon a \therefore (x) : x \epsilon a. \supset . x \epsilon b \therefore (x,y) : x \epsilon a. y \epsilon a. \supset . x \epsilon y.$$

This theorem is an early formulation of the single axiom of Leśniewski's ontology and should be read as an implicit definition of the functor "is" in expressions of the type "*a* is *b*," in which "is" has its main existential meaning.

SEMANTIC REISM.
Concretism is both a metaphysical and a semantic doctrine; as metaphysics its basic characteristic is materialism and as semantics it is nominalism. Nominalism is an essential part of concretism, but materialism is not. For instance, Franz Brentano, although a concretist, was a Cartesian dualist.

If the dyadic functor "is" in expressions of the type "*a* is *b*" has the meaning defined above, then only genuine, empty or nonempty, shared or unshared names are admissible values for *a*. This should be clear in view of the fact that if *a* is *b*, then for some *x*, *x* is *a*, that is, *a* exists (therefore, if an empty name is substituted for *a*, "*a* is *b*" always becomes a false sentence). Semantic reism is a set of linguistic and logical rules that allow us to test the meaningfulness and truth of the expressions of language *L* as determined by their syntactic structure and semantic function.

According to semantic reism, names of concrete objects only, either corporeal or sentient, are genuine names. The names of properties, relations, events, facts, propositions, or classes are objectless and apparent names. Literally understood, sentences involving such fictitious names and implying the existence of properties, relations, events, facts, propositions, or classes are grammatically meaningful expressions, but reistically they are nonsense in disguise or falsehood. Only if, by a suitable transformation, such sentences can be reduced to equivalent expressions involving no apparent names can they become reistically meaningful and either true or false. For instance, in its literal meaning the sentence "the relation *being part of* is transitive" is either false or nonsensical. But if it is regarded as a shorthand statement of the fact that for all *x*, *y*, and *z*, if *x* is part of *y* and *y* is part of *z*, then *x* is part of *z*, the expanded version of this abbreviated sentence expresses a genuine and true proposition.

ONTOLOGICAL REISM.
Nominalism is the view that the only admissible values for bound variables are entities of the lowest type as understood in the simplified theory of types. To apply this assumption outside logic and mathematics we need operational rules specifying the entities of the lowest type, that is, the referents of genuine names. For this purpose semantic reism must be supplemented by ontological reism; in other words, one's metaphysical commitments must be explicitly stated.

The basic proposition of ontological reism states that every object is a thing. *Object* is the most general ontological term, synonymous with *something*, the name of an arbitrarily chosen thing and thus extensionally equivalent to *thing*. *Thing* is a defined term and means a physical or a sentient body, in the nonexclusive meaning of *or*. *Physical* means spatial, temporal, and resistant, and *sentient* is defined by the Socratic definition as a term appropriately qualifying such bodies as animals or human beings (and probably also plants). Kotarbiński described ontological reism as somatism rather than as materialism, because for a reist "matter" is an apparent, quasi name, unless it is defined as a metatheoretical concept, in terms of which we speak about material or physical objects identified by the attributes of spatiality, temporality, and resistance and not by material substance. But somatism entails pansomatism, the proposition that every soul or mind (sentient entity) is a body. Therefore, a concretist who accepts pansomatism and asserts that there are only bodies in the universe is a materialist in the sense that he subscribes, speaking loosely, to the identity theory of mind and body. He leaves it to science to discover how it came about that there are sentient as well as physical bodies in the world.

In the theory of knowledge concretism implies the abandonment of the epistemological dualism of the theory of representative perception and the adherence to some form of sensational realism. Since there are no mental images or elements or sense data distinct from the object perceived, a concretist believes that all that is known is apprehended directly and that the so-called perceptual content is part of the physical object.

IMITATIONISM. If reality consists exclusively of bodies, and if the soul or mind is identical with part or the entire organism of a human individual, assertions about mental states and processes are not semantically well-formed sentences; they are objectionable on ontological grounds and consequently false. To be reistically acceptable they must be regarded as assertions of special sorts about persons, reducible, when fully stated, to descriptions of human individuals acting upon their environment and being affected by the external world. This view of the nature of psychological statements, together with the procedure by means of which they can be reduced to statements about persons doing and undergoing things, Kotarbiński called "imitationism." This name is intended to indicate that we come to understand the experiences of other people by imitating their behavior and, in general, that psychological knowledge is acquired not from introspection but by imitation or self-imitation.

Imitationism assumes that every singular psychological statement is a substitution of the schema "A experiences this: P," where A is a proper-name variable and P is a variable admitting all kinds of enunciations referring to the physical environment of the person whose name is substituted for A. The first part of the schema is the announcement by the experiencing person, EP, or the observer, O, of what its second part expresses by describing the environment in the same way that EP describes or would describe it. If EP and O are two different persons, the announcement refers to the imitation of EP by O and mentions the respect in which EP will be imitated. If EP and O are the same person, imitation becomes self-imitation and the description of the environment, including EP's own body, is self-description.

PRACTICAL PHILOSOPHY

Kotarbiński had a lasting interest in practical philosophy. He saw its main task as the formulation of precepts and recommendations concerning the three questions of how to achieve happiness, how to live a good life, and how to act effectively. It is the second and third set of questions to which he devoted most attention. He was a staunch defender of the autonomy of ethics and approached its problems deontologically. Inspired both by a theoretical interest and by the desire to help his fellow men, he produced a general theory of efficient action known as praxeology. Although he had some predecessors, in particular A. A. Bogdanov (1873–1928) and Georges Hostelet (1875–1960), he accomplished pioneer work and opened a new field of study.

See also Brentano, Franz; Cartesianism; Logic, History of: Modern Logic: From Frege to Gödel; Materialism; Nominalism, Modern.

Bibliography

WORKS BY KOTARBIŃSKI

Wybór Pism (Selected works). 2 vols. Warsaw: Panstwowe Wydawn, 1957–1958. Includes all important essays and articles published between 1913 and 1954.

Elementy Teorii Poznania, Logiki Formalnej i Metodologii Nauk (Elements of the theory of knowledge, formal logic and methodology of science). Lvov, 1929; 2nd ed., Wrocław, Warsaw, and Kraków: Ossolinskich, 1961.

Kurs Logiki dla Prawników (A course of logic for lawyers). Warsaw: Gebethner and Wolff, 1951; 6th ed., 1963.

Traktat o Dobrej Robocie (Treatise on good work). Lodz: Zaklad im Ossolinskich we Wroclawiu, 1955; 2nd ed., Wrocław and Warsaw, 1958. Translated as *Praxiology: An Introduction to the Sciences of Efficient Action*. Oxford and Warsaw: Pergamon Press, 1965.

"The Fundamental Ideas of Pansomatism." *Mind* 64 (1955): 488–500.

Wyklady z Dziejów Logiki (Lectures on the history of logic). Lodz: Zaklad Narodowy im Ossolinskich we Wroclawiu, 1957. Translated as *Leçons sur l'histoire de la logique*. Paris: Presses Universitaires de France, 1964.

"Filozof" (The philosopher). *Studia Filozoficzne* (1) (1957): 4–16.

"Essai de réduire la connaissance psychologique à l'extraspection." In *Atti del XII Congresso Internazionale di Filosofia (Venezia, 12–18 Settembre 1958)—Proceedings of the XIIth International Congress of Philosophy*, 12 vols. Florence, 1958–1961. Vol. V (Florence, 1960), pp. 295–299.

"Zasady Etyki Niezależnej" (Principles of autonomous ethics). *Studia Filozoficzne* (1/4) (1958): 3–13.

"Fazy Rozwojowe Konkretyzmu" (The Stages of the development of concretism). *Studia Filozoficzne* (4/7) (1958): 3–13.

"La Philosophie dans la Pologne contemporaine." In *Philosophy in the Mid-Century: A Survey*. 4 vols., edited by Raymond Klibansky. Florence: Nuova Italia, 1958–1959. Vol. I, *Logic and the Philosophy of Science* (Florence, 1958), pp. 224–235.

"Psychological Propositions." In *Scientific Psychology: Principles and Approaches*, edited by Benjamin B. Wolman and Ernest Nagel, 44–49. New York, 1965.

WORKS ON KOTARBIŃSKI

Ajdukiewicz, Kazimierz. Review of Kotarbiński's *Elementy Teorii Poznania, Logiki Formalnej i Metodologii Nauk*. *Przegląd Filozoficzny* 33 (1930): 140–160. Reprinted in *Język i Poznanie*. 2 vols. Warsaw: Panstwowe Wydawn, 1960, 1965, Vol. I, pp. 79–101. Available in Polish only.

Ajdukiewicz, Kazimierz. "Der logistische Antiirrationalismus in Polen." *Erkenntnis* 5 (1935): 151–161.

Grzegorczyk, Andrzej. "O Pewnych Formalnych Konsekwencjach Reizmu" (On certain formal implications of reism). In *Fragmenty Filozoficzne, Seria Druga*, 7–14. Warsaw: Panstwowe Wydawn, 1959. Available in Polish only.

Jordan, Z. A. *The Development of Mathematical Logic and Logical Positivism in Poland between the Two Wars*. London, 1945.

Jordan, Z. A. *Philosophy and Ideology: The Development of Philosophy and Marxism-Leninism in Poland since the Second World War*, 34–38, 195–197. Dordrecht, Netherlands: Reidel, 1963.

Jordan Z. A. "Próba Analizy Teorii Zdań Psychologicznych Prof. T. Kotarbińskiego" (An analysis of Professor Kotarbiński's theory of psychological statements). *Psychometria* 2 (1935): 347–375. Available in Polish only.

Lejewski, Czeslaw. "On Leśniewski's Ontology." *Ratio* 1 (1958): 150–176.

Rand, R. "Kotarbińskis Philosophie auf Grund seines Hauptwerkes: 'Elemente der Erkenntnistheorie, der Logik und der Methodologie der Wissenschaften.'" *Erkenntnis* 7 (1937–1938): 92–120.

Z. A. Jordan (1967)

KOZLOV, ALEKSEI ALEKSANDROVICH

(1831–1901)

Aleksei Aleksandrovich Kozlov, the Russian personalist philosopher, was the first major Russian exponent of a pluralistic idealism derived from Gottfried Wilhelm Leibniz. In his youth Kozlov studied the social sciences and was attracted to the ideas of Ludwig Feuerbach and François Marie Charles Fourier. His socialist views led to a short prison term in 1866 and the loss of his teaching position in a Moscow secondary school. He began to study philosophy seriously only in the 1870s, when, after an initial interest in materialism, he came successively under the influence of Arthur Schopenhauer, Eduard von Hartmann, and Immanuel Kant. In 1876 he became professor of philosophy at Kiev University, where he published the first Russian philosophical journal, *Filosofskii trekhmesiachnik* (Philosophical quarterly), and began to formulate his own mature position under the influence of Leibniz and his followers—notably Gustav Teichmüller. When illness forced Kozlov to retire in 1887, he moved to St. Petersburg and expounded his views systematically in a private journal, *Svoe slovo* (A personal word), published occasionally from 1888 to 1898.

In Kozlov's metaphysics, which he called panpsychism, there is a plurality of conscious spiritual substances, or monads. Each is an agent whose being consists not only in its substantiality, but also in its (psychic) activities and the contents of these activities. (Thus, Parmenides erred by considering substance alone, Johann Gottlieb Fichte by considering activity alone, and other philosophers erred similarly.) Together, these spiritual substances form a closed totality which is grounded in a Supreme Substance, God, and within which these substances (unlike Leibniz's monads) interact. The human body is a collection of less conscious spiritual substances with which our ego interacts until death. Kozlov suggested that after death the ego is reincarnated by interacting with other spiritual substances to form a new body.

The "material" aspect of the body, as of all supposed "material" entities, is produced by thought in our interaction with other spiritual substances, and is symbolic of these substances. Space and time (to which Kozlov devoted much attention) are likewise products of the thinking subject. Neither is objectively real, but each is symbolic of reality: Space is symbolic of the fact that real substances exist in connection, and time of the fact that within this connection there is variety and activity. Thus sense perception, which purports to show us objects in space and time, does not penetrate to the essentially timeless and spiritual reality. Kozlov developed an intuitivist epistemology, in which knowledge is based upon "primitive consciousness"—primarily consciousness of one's own ego. Primitive consciousness, however, being simple and immediate, is nonconceptual and ineffable. Knowledge, on the other hand, is complex and mediated; the mind constructs it by relating the elements of primitive consciousness. Thus we are directly conscious of God. Acquiring conceptual knowledge of God, however, is a difficult intellectual enterprise.

Kozlov did not develop his views fully in other areas, but his metaphysics and epistemology influenced many Russian philosophers, including his son, Sergei A. Askol'dov, and Nikolai Losskii.

See also Losskii, Nikolai Onufrievich.

Bibliography

ADDITIONAL WORKS BY KOZLOV

Filosofskie etiudy (Philosophical studies). 2 vols. St. Petersburg, 1876–1880.

Filosofiia kak nauka (Philosophy as a science). Kiev, 1877.

WORKS ON KOZLOV

Askol'dov, S. A. *A. A. Kozlov*. Moscow, 1912.

Lossky, N. O. "Kozlov: ego panpsikhizm" (Kozlov: His Panpsychism). *Voprosy filosofii i psikhologii* (Questions of philosophy and psychology) (58) (1901): 198–202.

Zenkovsky, V. V. *Istoriia Russkoi Filosofii*. 2 vols. Paris: YMCA Press, 1948–1950. Translated by George L. Kline as *A History of Russian Philosophy*. 2 vols. New York: Columbia University Press, 1953.

James P. Scanlan (1967)
Bibliography updated by Vladimir Marchenkov (2005)

KRAUSE, KARL CHRISTIAN FRIEDRICH

(1781–1832)

Karl Christian Friedrich Krause, a German pantheistic philosopher, was born at Eisenberg in Thuringia. He studied at Jena, where he came under the influence of Johann Gottlieb Fichte and Friedrich Schelling. In 1812 he became Privatdozent, but his many efforts to secure a professorship were all unsuccessful. For a time he taught music in Dresden. In 1805 he joined the Freemasons, to further his ideal of a world society. His internationalist leanings were responsible for his failure to be appointed professor in Göttingen, and in Munich his chances were spoiled by the opposition of Schelling. Just as he finally obtained a position, Krause died of a heart attack.

Like several of his contemporaries, Krause claimed to be developing the true Kantian position. His orientation, however, was mystical and spiritualistic. The obscurity of his style is awesome; he expressed himself in an artificial and often unfathomable vocabulary which included such monstrous neologisms as *Or-om-wesenlebverhaltheit* and *Vereinselbganzweseninnesein*—words that are untranslatable into German, let alone into English. He called his system the theory of essence (*Wesenlehre*) and presented an elaborate set of categories, including Unity, Selfhood, Propositionality (*Satzheit*), "Graspness" (*Fassheit*), Unification-in-propositionality (*Satzheitvereinheit*), and so forth. The system was intended to mediate between pantheism and theism; hence Krause called his position "Panentheism," to suggest the idea that God or Absolute Being is one with the world, though not exhausted by it. From this central doctrine Krause derived a theory of man and of history. He regarded all men as part of a spiritual whole, an ideal League of Humanity (*Menschheitsbund*), the actualization of which is the goal of history.

Like Fichte, Krause took self-consciousness as his starting point in the belief that it provides a key to the essence of all things. The ego discovers itself to be both mind and body, enduring and changing; it is an organic, self-sustaining whole. According to Krause, this is the clue to the nature of other beings and of God. Considering its own finitude and that of other beings it encounters, the ego is led to the idea of an absolute, unconditioned principle upon which it and all other creatures and organizations are dependent. This principle is God, or Essence, whose nature is grasped in a spiritual intuition (*geistigen Schauen*), an immediately certain vision that is the foundation for all subsequent knowledge. God is primordial being (*Orwesen*), the being without contrareity; he is the unity of all that exists. Though he contains the world, he is nevertheless other than and superior to it. The distinction between God and the world is that of whole and part. Krause expressed this by speaking of God as *in himself* Contrabeing (*Gegenwesen*) and Unified Being (*Vereinwesen*), while *as himself,* or qua Primordial Being, he is absolute identity.

The existence of the world follows from an inner opposition in God's actuality (*Wesenheit*). Reason and Nature are two subordinate beings distinguished from, and yet lying within, God. Humanity is a synthesis of these. Humanity and the world, along with numerous basic human institutions, are organisms through which the divine life expresses itself. Thus, every being or group of beings is godlike in essence. Mind and body are integrated in the particular unified being that is man, reflecting the compresence of Reason and Nature in all things. Nature composes all individuals into a single whole. It is a mistake to view nature as a blind, mechanical system without consciousness; for its infinite perpetual activity, which is a pure self-determination, is free. Nature is a divine work of art; at the same time it is itself the artist, fashioning itself. The recognition of this divine character gives meaning and value to life.

Individual human minds together constitute the realm of Reason throughout which mind is organically distributed. But mind does not exist only in man and his institutions. Nature and Reason interpenetrate so fully that even animals are a unification of the two. Among animals, however, the career of each is fixed inexorably, according to the hierarchy of living forms. Man is the supreme unification of Reason and Nature, for he possesses the highest sort of mind joined to the highest sort of body. The individual souls that make up humanity are eternal, uncreated, immortal. Their number can neither be increased nor diminished. Humanity is thus complete at every moment.

What men should strive for is the imitation of the divine life in their own inner lives and in their social organizations. God is good, and men should participate in this goodness. The inner union with God (*Gottesinnigkeit*), or fervor for the divine, is the foundation of ethics, and ethics is the heart of religion. But individuals cannot achieve the moral life alone, since they are what they are only as parts of the whole. The community and its various institutions are thus indispensable.

Ideally, the community is governed by Right, which Krause defined as the organic whole of all of the internal and external conditions necessary for the completion of life that are dependent on freedom. This supernational law is grounded in the nature of the divine; it expresses the right of Humanity, not simply the right of individual human beings. The rights of individuals, groups, and nations can be recognized, but only as subordinate to the right of Humanity as a whole. Humanity is divided into a series of social organisms. There are, Krause speculated, human inhabitants in many cosmic systems. These human beings are subdivided into nations, races, communities, families, and so forth. There is an aesthetic community, a scientific community, a religious community, and a moral community. Each community has rights, although the right of Humanity takes precedence.

Men are all citizens of the universe, which is an infinite divine government. Because he revered the individual as a partial embodiment of the divine, Krause argued against the death penalty and maintained that punishment can be justified only as educative and reformatory. Only a republican form of government, he believed, is entirely compatible with the ideal of justice.

According to Krause's philosophy of history, the development of humanity is the temporal unfolding of a moral ideal. History follows a three-stage pattern, which is mirrored in every individual life as well. The development is not, however, purely progressive. There are two orders, one "ascending" and one "descending," so that the divine life may be presented again and again in the infinitely repeated epochs of history. The three steps in the ascending order are Wholeness, Selfhood, and Whollyunified-selfhood. In the stage of Wholeness, each individual or higher organism exists germinally in the larger whole to which it belongs. In Selfhood, it enters into a free opposition to that whole and strives to develop its unique character. Evil appears as the individual organism tears itself loose from the harmony of the whole. Finally, the organism achieves a loving reunion with other beings (man, for example, becomes reunited with Nature, Reason, Humanity, and God), and with this rediscovery of harmony, all evil is negated. Afterward, however, the historical path leads downward, to a final involution that is both the ending of a career and the birth of a new life. Since the transition is gradual, an older age may survive for a time in a newer age. Each development, nevertheless, exhibits genuine, unforeseeable novelty.

Following this order, the individual man enters the world, proceeds through the stages of embryonic life, boyhood, and youth, and becomes increasingly independent, until he finally achieves the maturity of manhood, from which point he descends in a reverse series. Every human institution and organization pursues the same course of evolution, reflecting the basic laws of the divine organic life. In history, the first stage is marked by polytheism, slavery, caste systems, despotic governments, and a state of war between peoples. In the second period, the age of growth, men recognize the divine as an infinite being standing above all that is finite. This is monotheism, which Krause accuses of fostering theocracy, religious censorship of science and art, and contempt for the world. Finally, in the third stage (to which Krause's own philosophy is supposed to inspire men), humanity comes of age, the finite is reunited with the infinite, and world citizenship, philanthropy, and tolerance become the rule. According to Krause, the transition to this stage began with Benedict de Spinoza's discovery of the nature of being, and his own system was to be the development of that theory. He envisaged humanity as arriving at an organic completeness that represents the maturity of the race, and with visionary eloquence he depicted the unification of all humankind, as all men and all associations of men enter into a common life.

Krause's philosophy, while not very influential in Germany, found considerable support in Spain, where, for a time, "Krausism" flourished. This was largely due to the efforts of Julian Sanz del Rio, the minister of culture, who visited Germany and Belgium in 1844 and came into contact with a number of Krause's disciples, notably Heinrich Ahrens in Brussels and Hermann von Leonhardi in Heidelberg.

See also Consciousness; Fichte, Johann Gottlieb; Pantheism; Philosophy of History; Reason; Schelling, Friedrich Wilhelm Joseph von; Spinoza, Benedict (Baruch) de.

Bibliography

Krause's most important work is *Das Urbild der Menschheit* (Dresden, 1812), translated into Spanish by Sanz del Rio as *El ideal de la humanidad* (Madrid, 1860). Included among his other works are *System der Sittenlehre* (Leipzig, 1810);

Vorlesungen über das System der Philosophie (Göttingen, 1828); and the short *Abriss des Systems der Rechtsphilosophie* (Göttingen, 1828).

For Krause's influence in Spain, see Sanz del Rio, *K. C. F. Krause: lecciones sobre el sistema de la filosofia analitica* (Madrid, 1850) and Juan Lopez Morillas, *El Krausismo español* (Mexico City, 1956). See also Hans Flasche, "Studie zu K. C. F. Krauses Philosophie in Spanien," in *Deutsche Vierteljarsschrift für Literaturwissenschaft und Geistesgeschichte* 14 (1936): 382–397. Flasche mentions the "left" and "right" wing of Krausism in Spain and, to account for Krause's success in Spain, tries to show (with a tenuous argument) the compatibility of Krause's views with Catholicism. Sharply critical of Krause is Eduard von Hartmann, "Krause's Aesthetik," in *Zeitschrift für Philosophie und philosophische Kritik* 86 (1) (1885): 112–130. Sympathetic accounts of Krause are to be found in Paul Hohfeld, *Die Krause'sche Philosophie* (Jena: H. Costenoble, 1879) and Rudolf Eucken, *Zur Erinnerung an K. Ch. Krause* (Leipzig, 1881). (Hohfeld edited a number of Krause's works, and Eucken studied with a student of Krause.) Clay Macauley, *K. C. F. Krause, Heroic Pioneer for Thought and Life* (Berkeley, CA, 1925) is a eulogistic pamphlet.

Arnulf Zweig (1967)

KRIPKE, SAUL

(1940–)

Saul Kripke is an American logician and philosopher born in New York in 1940. After earning a BA from Harvard University in 1962, he held positions at Harvard, Rockefeller, Princeton, New York Universities, and elsewhere.

MODAL LOGIC

Saul Kripke has worked in many branches of logic (higher recursion theory, set theory, models of arithmetic, and relevance logic), but the work best known to philosophers, and much cited in the literature of linguistic semantics, computer science, and other disciplines, is his development of Kripke models for modal and related logics. At the level of sentential logic such a model consists of a set X (of "states of the world," often misleadingly called "worlds"), a binary relation R (of "relative possibility") thereon, plus an assignment to each atomic formula p of the set of those x in X at which p is true. The assignment extends to all formulas, taking "Necessarily A" to be true at x if A is true at every y with xRy.

Kripke was the first to publish proofs of completeness theorems to the effect that truth at all x in all models with R reflexive (and transitive) (and symmetric) coincides with provability in the modal logic **T** (respectively **S4**) (respectively **S5**), and he obtained similar results for other modal logics. Announced in "Semantic Considerations on Modal Logic" (1963), and presented in detail in a subsequent series of technical papers, Kripke's work covers modal and intuitionistic sentential and predicate logic, and includes besides completeness theorems results on decidability and undecidability.

SEMANTIC PARADOXES

Also well known is Kripke's work on semantic paradoxes in "Outline of a Theory of Truth" (1975). A truth-predicate in a language L permitting quotation or equivalent means of self-reference would be a predicate T such that the following biconditional holds with any sentence of L in the blanks:

"T('___')" is true if and only if "___" is true.

The liar paradox shows there cannot be a truth-predicate in L if L has no truth-value gaps. Given a partial interpretation I of a predicate U (under which U is declared true of some items, declared false of others, or not declared either of the rest), any treatment of truth-value gaps, such as Stephen Cole Kleene's three-valued or Bas van Fraassen's supervaluational approach, will dictate which sentences containing U are to be declared true, declared false, or not declared either. If U is being thought of as "is true," this amounts to dictating a new partial interpretation I^* of U. For a fixed point, or partial interpretation having $I = I^*$, the biconditional displayed earlier holds.

Kripke's work, besides more purely philosophical contributions, shows how to obtain a minimal fixed point (contained in any other, and explicating an intuitive notion of *groundedness*), a maximal intrinsic fixed point (not declaring true anything declared false by any other fixed point), and many others, for any reasonable treatments of gaps.

WITTGENSTEIN AND SKEPTICISM

Turning from logic to philosophy of language and its applications to analytic metaphysics, Kripke has written two much-discussed books that are almost entirely independent of each other. In *Wittgenstein on Rules and Private Language* (1982) he advances as noteworthy, though not as sound, an argument inspired by his reading of Ludwig Wittgenstein's *Philosophical Investigations* (1953/1993) that is not unqualifiedly attributed to Wittgenstein. On Kripke's reading the target of the argument is any theory (such as that of the *Tractatus Logico-Philosophicus*) that conceives of meaning as given by conditions for truth, conceived as correspondence with facts. Kripke compares Wittgenstein as he reads him to David Hume (more specifically, to a version of Hume that takes seriously his protestations that he is only a mitigated, not an extreme skeptic). So read, Wittgenstein's attack on correspondence theories of meaning consists, like Hume's attack on rationalist theories of inference, of two phases.

First there is a "skeptical paradox." Consider an ascription of meaning, say that according to which by "plus" I mean *plus*, so that 125 is the right answer to the question "what is 68 plus 57?" as I mean it. To what fact does this correspond? Not the record of how I have worked sums in the past. (Perhaps I have never worked this one before, and many rules are compatible with all the ones I have worked so far.) Not my ability to state general rules for doing sums, since this only raises the question what fact corresponds to my meaning what I do by the words in these rules. Not my behavioral dispositions (nor anything in the structure or functioning of my brain causally underlying them) since what answer I am *disposed* to give is one question, and what answer would be the *right* one for me to give is another question; and I am disposed to give wrong answers fairly often even for medium-sized numbers, and to give no answer at all for really big ones. Further considerations rule out also introspectable feelings accompanying calculation. No candidates seem to remain, so it seems that there is *no* fact to which an ascription of meaning corresponds. The conclusion is that *if* meaning consists in conditions for truth and truth of correspondence with facts, *then* ascriptions of meaning like "What I mean by 'plus' is *plus*" are neither true nor meaningful, and no one ever means anything by anything.

Second, there is a "skeptical solution," defying short summary. This solution identifies the meaningfulness of a sentence with the possession *not* of truth-conditions but of a potential for use within a speech community. The aspects of use—of usage and utility—that are emphasized are on the one hand the conditions under which assertion of a sentence is warranted, and on the other hand the applications warranted when a sentence is accepted.

One objection, anticipated by Kripke, is that Wittgenstein does accept talk of "truth" and "facts" in a deflated sense, in which sense to say, "It is true or a fact that by 'plus' I mean *plus*," amounts to no more than saying, "By 'plus' I mean *plus*," which on Kripke's reading Wittgenstein never denies. So a straightforward statement of Wittgenstein's view as the thesis that there are no "facts" corresponding to meaning ascriptions will not do. But as Kripke notes, one of the tasks of a reading of Wittgenstein is precisely to explain why he does *not* state his view in straightforward philosophical theses. Other objections to Kripke's interpretation, which has Wittgenstein opposing one theory of meaning to another, have been advanced by those who interpret Wittgenstein as a "therapist" who aims to treat philosophical questions not by developing philosophical theories (of meaning or of anything else) to answer these questions, but by developing methods to cure one of wanting to ask such questions. But such a reading may be less utterly irreconcilable with the reading of Wittgenstein as skeptic than its proponents generally recognize, since after all historical skepticism was itself a form of psychotherapy, aiming to achieve philosophic *ataraxia* by cultivating indifference to unanswerable questions.

REFERENCE AND METAPHYSICS

Kripke's most famous work is *Naming and Necessity* (1980), which consists of a transcription (with addenda and a preface written a decade later) of lectures given at Princeton in 1970. Only a rough, brief treatment will be possible here, leaving entirely to one side the influential ancillary papers "Speaker's Reference and Semantic Reference" and "A Puzzle about Belief," related work of Keith Donnellan (on proper names) and Hilary Putnam (on natural kind terms), and Kripke's provocative discussion of several side topics (among them the contingent *a priori* and the identity theory in philosophy of mind).

Kripke maintains the following doctrines about naming, illustrating them with examples, many of which have become famous. The reference of a proper name (e.g. "Phosphorus," "Feynman," "Newton") is *not* determined by some associated definite description (or cluster of descriptions, which is to say, description of the form "the object of which *most* of the following is true …"). The description a speaker associates with a name may be incorrect. (The speaker may describe Isaac Newton as "the man who was hit on the head by an apple and thereby struck with the idea of a force of gravity.") Even if correct, it may fail to be uniquely identifying. (The speaker may be able to describe Richard Feynman [1918–1988] only as "a famous physicist," which does not distinguish him from Murray Gell-Man [1929–].) Even if correct and uniquely identifying, it may be so only contingently, so that in speaking of certain counterfactual situations the description may denote something else or nothing at all. (Phosphorus, though it *is* the brightest object regularly visible in the eastern sky before sunrise, might have only been second brightest, in which case "the brightest …" would have denoted something else; while if it had been tied for brightest, "*the* brightest …" would denote nothing.) By contrast, names designate rigidly, continuing to designate the same thing even when discussing counterfactual hypotheses. (If I say, "If there had been a brighter object, Phosphorus would have been only second brightest," I am still speaking of *Phosphorus*.)

A better picture than the description theory of how a name comes to denote its bearer would be this: The first user of the proper name or "initial baptist" may fix its reference by some description (possibly involving demonstratives and requiring supplementation by ostension, for example, "that bright object over there by the eastern horizon"). The second user may use the name with the intention of referring to whatever the first user was referring to, while perhaps ignorant of the original description. And so on in a historical chain. (Some commentators say causal chain, but it is important to note that there need not be any causal connection between initial baptist and thing named, which may be a mathematical object.) Kripke also offers an analogous picture of how a natural kind term comes to denote the kind of things it does.

Kripke also maintains the following doctrines about necessity, partly as corollaries to the above doctrines about naming. A true identity linking proper names (e.g., "Hesperus is Phosphorus") is necessary (as a consequence of rigidity, since even in a counterfactual situation each name will continue to denote the bearer it actually denotes, and therefore the two will continue to denote the *same* object, if they actually do so). But such an identity is not *a priori* (the identity of the heavenly body spotted at dawn and called "Phosphorus" with the one seen at dusk and dubbed "Hesperus" being an empirical astronomical discovery). Therefore, the metaphysical notion of necessity, "what could not have been otherwise," must be distinguished from epistemological notions like "what can be known *a priori* to be so."

There are other examples of metaphysical necessities, many involving natural kind terms: the facts of identity of heat with random molecular motion, of water with H_2O, of gold with the element of atomic number 79, and more; that a given object (e.g., a table) is composed of the material it is composed of (wood rather than ice); that a given person or organism has the ancestry he, she, or it does (e.g., that Elizabeth II is the daughter of George VI, and if he had had no daughter, she would never have been born). This is so even though in none of these examples does one have *a priori* knowledge. (There would be no internal logical contradiction in a tabloid press article claiming Elizabeth II to be the daughter of Harry Truman.) Historically, from Immanuel Kant to Gottlob Frege to Rudolf Carnap and beyond, necessity had tended to dwindle to aprioricity, which in turn had tended to dwindle to analyticity; Kripke's sharp reversal of this trend is perhaps his most important single contribution to philosophy.

See also Liar Paradox, The; Modal Logic; Philosophy of Language; Philosophy of Mind; Putnam, Hilary.

Bibliography

Wittgenstein, Ludwig. *Philosophical Investigations* (1953). Translated by G. E. M. Anscombe. Malden, MA: Blackwell, 1993.

WORKS BY KRIPKE

"Semantic Considerations on Modal Logic." *Acta Philosophica Fennica* 16 (1963): 83–94.
"Outline of a Theory of Truth." *Journal of Philosophy* 72 (1975): 690–716.
"Speaker's Reference and Semantic Reference." *Midwest Studies in Philosophy* 2 (1977): 255–276.
"A Puzzle about Belief." In *Meaning and Use: Papers Presented at the Second Jerusalem Philosophical Encounter, April 1976,* edited by Avishai Margalit. Dordrecht, Netherlands: Reidel, 1979.
Naming and Necessity. Cambridge, MA: Harvard University Press, 1980.
Wittgenstein on Rules and Private Language: An Elementary Exposition. Cambridge, MA: Harvard University Press, 1982.

John P. Burgess (1996, 2005)

KRISTEVA, JULIA
(1941–)

Julia Kristeva was born on June 24, 1941, in Sliven, Bulgaria. She was educated by French nuns, studied literature, and worked as a journalist before going to Paris in 1966 to do graduate work with Lucien Goldmann and Roland Barthes. While in Paris she finished her doctorate, was appointed to the faculty of the Department of Texts and Documents at the University of Paris VI (Denis Diderot) and began psychoanalytic training. Currently, Kristeva is Director of the Department of Science of Texts and Documents at the University of Paris VII, where she teaches in the Department of Literature and Humanities.

In her early writing, Kristeva is concerned with bringing the speaking body back into phenomenology and linguistics. In order to counteract what she sees as the necrophilia of phenomenology and structural linguistics, which study a dead or silent body, Kristeva develops a new science that she calls *semanalysis*. She describes semanalysis as a combination of semiology (or Semiotics) from Ferdinand de Saussure, and psychoanalysis from Sigmund Freud. Unlike traditional linguistics, semanalysis addresses an element that is heterogeneous to language, the unconscious. The introduction of the unconscious into the science of signs, however, challenges the possibility of science, meaning, and reason. This is why Kristeva maintains that certain nineteenth-century poets whose work discharged unconscious drive force and emphasized the semiotic element of signification began a revolution in poetic language.

With semanalysis, Kristeva attempts to bring the speaking body, complete with drives, back into language. She does this both by putting language back into the body and by putting the body into language. She argues that the logic of signification is already present in the material body. In *Revolution in Poetic Language* she suggests that negation and identification—the two primary logical operations of language—are already operating within the body prior to the onset of signification: Expelling waste from the body prefigures negation and incorporating food into the body prefigures identification. The second way in which Kristeva brings the speaking body back to language is by maintaining that bodily drives make their way into language. One of Kristeva's major contributions to philosophy of language is her distinction between two heterogeneous elements in signification: the semiotic and the symbolic. Within Kristeva's writings, *semiotic* (*le sémiotique*) becomes a technical term that she distinguishes from *semiotics* (*la sémiotique*). The semiotic elements within the signifying process are the drives as they discharge within language. This drive discharge is associated with rhythm and tone. The semiotic has meaning but not does refer to anything. The symbolic, on the other hand, is the element of language that allows for referential meaning. The symbolic is associated with syntax or grammar and with the ability to take a position or make a judgment that syntax engenders.

Kristeva describes the relation between the semiotic and the symbolic as a dialectic oscillation. Without the symbolic there is only delirium, whereas without the semiotic, language would be completely empty, if not impossible. There would be no reason for people to speak if it were not for the semiotic drive force. The oscillation between the semiotic and the symbolic is both productive and necessary. The oscillation between rejection and stasis already existing within the material body produces the oscillation between semiotic and symbolic in the speaking subject.

In *The Powers and Limits of Psychoanalysis*, Kristeva revisits the theme of revolution so prominent in her earlier work. In *Revolution in Poetic Language* Kristeva identifies the possibility of revolution in language—a revolution she deems *analogous* to social revolution—with (maternal) semiotic forces in avante-garde literature. In *Powers of Horror* this semiotic force of drives is not only associated with the maternal but more particularly with the abject or revolting aspects of the maternal. Here, the revolting becomes revolutionary through the return of the repressed (maternal) within (paternal) symbolic systems. Two decades later, in *The Sense and Non-Sense of Revolt*, Kristeva asks if revolt is possible today. In this book, volume one of *The Powers and Limits of Psychoanalysis*, she claims that within postindustrial and post-Communist democracies we are confronted with a new political and social economy governed by the spectacle within which it becomes increasingly difficult to think of the possibility of revolt. The two main reasons are that within media culture, the status of power and the status of the individual have changed. Kristeva argues that in contemporary culture there is a power vacuum that results in the inability to locate the agent or agency of power and authority or to assign responsibility. In a no-fault society, who or what can people revolt against?

In addition to the power vacuum, Kristeva identifies the impossibility of revolt with the changing status of the individual. The human being as a person with rights is becoming nothing more than an ensemble of organs that can be bought and sold or otherwise exchanged, what she calls the *patrimonial individual*. And, how can an ensemble of organs revolt? Not only is there no one or nothing to revolt against, but also there is no one to revolt. And without the possibility of revolt, especially the psychic revolt necessary for creativity, people are left with new maladies of the soul that make life seem meaningless.

In her *Female Genius* trilogy, Kristeva suggests that women with their attention to the sensory realm may provide an antidote for the meaninglessness that results from contemporary forms of nihilism. She argues that the genius of extraordinary women such as Hannah Arendt, Melanie Klein, and Colette help all women to see what is extraordinary in their own ordinary lives. Conversely, Kristeva maintains that the genius of everyday life is women's genius, particularly the genius of mothers; in creating new human beings, mothers are singular innovators, reinventing the child anew all the time. Kristeva maintains that mothers may represent a safeguard against the automation of human beings.

See also Aesthetics, History of; Arendt, Hannah; Barthes, Roland; Feminism and Continental Philosophy; Feminism and the History of Philosophy; Feminist Aesthetics and Criticism; Feminist Philosophy; Freud, Sigmund; Language and Thought; Modernism and Postmodernism; Philosophy of Language; Psychoanalysis; Structuralism and Post-structuralism; Unconscious; Women in the History of Philosophy.

Bibliography

WORKS BY KRISTEVA

La révolution du langage poétique: L'avant-garde à la fin du XIXe siècle, Lautréamont et Mallarmé. Paris: Éditions du Seiul, 1974. Translated by Margaret Waller as *Revolution in Poetic Language* (New York: Columbia University Press, 1984).

Pouvoirs de l'horreur. Paris: Éditions du Seiul, 1980. Translated by Leon Roudiez as *Powers of Horror* (New York: Columbia University Press, 1982).

Histoires d'amour. Paris: Éditions Denoêl, 1983. Translated by Leon Roudiez as *Tales of Love* (New York: Columbia University Press, 1987).

Soleil noir: Dépression et mélancolie. Paris: Gallimard, 1987. Translated by Leon Roudiez as *Black Sun: Depression and Melancholy* (New York: Columbia University Press, 1989).

Étrangers à nous-memes. Paris: Fayard, 1989. Translated by Leon Roudiez as *Strangers to Ourselves* (New York: Columbia University Press, 1991).

Les nouvelles maladies de l'ame. Paris: Fayard, 1993. Translated by Ross Guberman as *New Maladies of the Soul* (New York: Columbia University Press, 1995).

Sens et non-sens de la révolte: Pouvoirs et limites de la psychanalyse I. Paris: Fayard, 1996. Translated by Jeanine Hermane as *The Sense and Non-Sense of Revolt* (New York: Columbia University Press, 2000).

La révolte intime: Pouvoirs et limites de la psychanalyse II. Paris: Fayard, 1997. Translated by Jeanine Herman as *Intimate Revolt: The Powers and Limits of Psychoanalysis, Volume II* (New York: Columbia University Press, 2002).

Le génie féminin, Tome premier, Hannah Arendt. Paris: Librairie Arthème Fayard, 1999. Translated by Ross Guberman as *Feminine Genius, Volume One, Hannah Arendt* (New York: Columbia University Press, 2001).

Le génie féminin, Tome II, Melanie Klein. Paris: Librairie Arthème Fayard, 2000. Translated by Ross Guberman as *Feminine Genius, Volume Two, Melanie Klein* (New York: Columbia University Press, 2001).

The Portable Kristeva. 2nd ed. Edited by Kelly Oliver. New York: Columbia University Press, 2002.

WORKS ABOUT KRISTEVA

Beardsworth, Sarah. *Julia Kristeva: Psychoanalysis and Modernity.* Albany, NY: SUNY Press, 2004.

Lechte, John, and Maria Margaroni. *Julia Kristeva: Live Theory.* London: Continuum Press, 2004.

McAfee, Noelle. *Julia Kristeva.* New York: Routledge, 2004.

Oliver, Kelly, ed. *Ethics, Politics and Difference in Kristeva's Writing.* New York: Routledge Press, 1993.

Oliver, Kelly. *Reading Kristeva: Unraveling the Doublebind.* Bloomington: Indiana University Press, 1993.

Kelly Oliver (2005)

KROPOTKIN, PËTR ALEKSEEVICH
(1842–1921)

Pëtr Alekseevich Kropotkin, the geographer and libertarian philosopher, was the principal exponent of the theories of anarchist-communism. He was born of a line of Russian princes who claimed descent from Riurik, the reputed founder of the Russian Empire. His father was a general, and he himself seemed destined for a military career. He was educated in the Corps of Pages and served as personal attendant to Tsar Alexander II. When the time came for him to choose a career, Kropotkin applied for a commission in the Mounted Cossacks of the Amur and went to Siberia because he felt his chance of serving humanity was greater there than in Russia. He had already come under the influence of liberal ideas through reading the clandestinely distributed writings of Aleksandr Herzen.

In Siberia Kropotkin carried out an investigation of the Russian penal system, which aroused in him a revulsion against the effects of autocratic government. During the early 1860s he led a series of expeditions into the untraveled regions of Siberia and, on the basis of his observations, developed an original and influential theory concerning the structure of the mountains of Asia. He also made important discoveries regarding the glacial ages and the great desiccation of east Asia, which resulted in the onset of barbarian wanderings.

In the solitude of the Siberian wastes, Kropotkin's thoughts turned more and more toward social protest. In 1865 the exiled poet M. L. Mikhailov introduced him to the writings of the French anarchist Pierre-Joseph Proudhon, and in 1866 Kropotkin resigned his commission in protest against the execution of a group of Polish prisoners who had tried to escape.

For some years he devoted himself to science, and in 1871 he was exploring the eskers of Finland when he was offered the secretaryship of the Russian Geographical Society. It was the moment of decision. Kropotkin was already feeling the urge to "go to the people" that affected many of the conscience-stricken Russian noblemen of the

1870s, and he decided to abandon science. In 1872 he visited Switzerland to make contact with exiled Russian liberals and revolutionaries. After listening to many radical views, he went to the Jura, where the watchmakers were fervent disciples of Mikhail Bakunin. "When I came away from the mountains, after a week's stay with the watchmakers, my views upon socialism were settled; I was an anarchist" (*Memoirs of a Revolutionist*).

In Russia Kropotkin joined the underground circle led by Nikolai Chaikovskii. In 1874 he was arrested and imprisoned in the Peter and Paul Fortress. Two years later he made a sensational escape and returned to western Europe, where he became an active worker in the rising anarchist movement. In 1879 he founded *Le révolté*, the most important anarchist paper to appear since the end of Proudhon's journalistic career in 1850, and in 1881 he took part in the London International Anarchist Congress, which founded the celebrated but short-lived "Black International." In 1882 he was arrested by the French authorities and was tried at Lyons along with a number of French anarchists. He was sentenced to five years imprisonment for alleged membership in the International Workingmen's Association. The sentence aroused wide international protest, and Kropotkin was released early in 1886. He went to England, where he lived until he returned to Russia after the 1917 revolution.

Kropotkin's career in western Europe was sharply altered by his arrival in England. On the Continent, from 1876 to 1886, he had been a revolutionary agitator, conspiring, lecturing, pamphleteering, and taking part in radical demonstrations. His writings were mainly periodical pieces for *Le révolté*. At first they were topical, but by 1880 Kropotkin was already developing the theory of anarchist-communism in a series of articles later incorporated in two books—*Paroles d'un révolté* (Paris, 1885) and *La conquête du pain* (Paris, 1892).

ANARCHIST-COMMUNISM

The doctrine of anarchist-communism differed from the collectivism preached by Bakunin and his followers in the 1860s in that it considered the need of the consumer rather than the achievement of the producer as the measure for distribution. In the vision of the anarchist-communist, the free-distribution warehouse would replace the earlier systems evolved by Proudhon and retained by the collectivists, which determined the worker's due either by hours of labor or quantity of production. Also, the anarchist-communists laid particular stress on the commune (in the sense of locality), rather than the industrial association, as the unit of social organization. In other respects—their rejection of the state, their stress on federalism, their emphasis on direct rather than parliamentary action, their denunciation of political forms—they did not differ profoundly from other schools of anarchism.

SOURCES. Although he became its leading exponent, Kropotkin did not originate anarchist-communism. The form of distribution embodied in the theory dates back at least as early as Thomas More's *Utopia* (1515–1516), and it appeared in a modified form in François Marie Charles Fourier's Phalansterian communities. The geographer Élisée Reclus, a former Phalansterian, appears to have brought the idea with him when he came to anarchism; it was first developed in writing by François Dumartheray, a Geneva artisan who helped Kropotkin in the founding of *Le révolté*. But Kropotkin developed the theory and, in *La conquête du pain*, he tried to show how it would work. This benign vision of an anarchist future reflects not only the optimism of Kropotkin's views, but also the benevolence of his character. For, although he always paid homage to the ideas of violent revolution, he did so against his nature; as Lev Tolstoy shrewdly remarked, "His arguments in favour of violence do not seem to me the expression of his opinions, but only of his faith to the banner under which he has served all his life."

ANARCHISM AND SCIENCE

When he reached England, Kropotkin moved into a world where he was respected by people in all walks of life. His achievements as a geographer were remembered; he was honored by learned societies; his articles were published in scientific journals; and his books were welcomed by respectable publishers. He did not abandon his ideals, but his role changed from that of agitator to that of writer and libertarian philosopher.

The most important books Kropotkin wrote during this period were his autobiography, *Memoirs of a Revolutionist* (New York, 1899), and *Mutual Aid: A Factor of Evolution* (London, 1902). *Mutual Aid*, together with *Modern Science and Anarchism* (London, 1912), shows Kropotkin attempting to base anarchist theory on a scientific foundation. These books reveal him as a devoted evolutionist, to the extent that he explains revolutions as part of the natural process by which man, as a social animal, evolves. He sees revolutions arising obscurely in the consciousness of the people and punctuating the slow tenor of progress by sudden mutations in social organization, while he views anarchism as a backward trend toward a natural order that has been perverted by the emergence of authoritarian institutions. Man is naturally social, he suggests; therefore he does not need government, which itself perpetuates the unequal conditions that breed crime and violence. In their sociality, human beings resemble the more successful species of animals that depend for their survival on cooperation among their members. This idea is the core of *Mutual Aid*, which is an attempt, based largely on the arguments of K. F. Kessler, to reform evolutionary theory by demonstrating that the neo-Darwinians wrongly stressed competition as a factor in evolution, to the exclusion of cooperation. In biological terms, his point was well taken; the appearance of *Mutual Aid* led to modifications in evolutionary theory. But Kropotkin never convincingly welded his ideal of mutual aid to his anarchistic love of freedom, since he ignored the extent to which customs restrict liberty in most societies in which nongovernmental cooperation dominates the pattern of life.

Kropotkin's departure to Russia in 1917 led to tragic disappointment. He found himself out of touch with Russian realities and isolated during the events that led to the October Revolution. He retired to the village of Dmitrov outside Moscow, where he spent his last years writing. He denounced the Bolshevik dictatorship and the terror it imposed. When he died in 1921, his funeral was the last great demonstration against communist rule.

ETHICS

Kropotkin's last years were spent on the uncompleted *Etika* (*Ethics*), which was published posthumously in Moscow in 1922. In part a history of ethical theories, this book seeks to present ethics as a science. In developing his naturalistic viewpoint, Kropotkin shows the emergence of morality among animals as an outgrowth of mutual aid and demonstrates its extension into human society, where it acquires a disinterestedness that goes beyond mere equality. He sees morality as the extension of human good will beyond equity and justice. The historical parts of *Ethics* are admirable, but the work is incomplete; Kropotkin's own ethical system is barely worked out.

See also Anarchism; Bakunin, Mikhail Aleksandrovich; Communism; Evolutionary Ethics; Evolutionary Theory; Fourier, François Marie Charles; Herzen, Aleksandr Ivanovich; Libertarianism; More, Thomas; Proudhon, Pierre-Joseph; Russian Philosophy; Tolstoy, Lev (Leo) Nikolaevich.

Bibliography

WORKS BY KROPOTKIN

Anarchism: A Collection of Revolutionary Writings. Edited by Roger N. Baldwin. Mineola, NY: Dover Publications, 2002.

The Conquest of Bread. New York: New York University Press, 1972.

The Great French Revolution. Montreal: Black Rose Books, 1989.

Kropotkin's Revolutionary Pamphlets: A Collection of Writings. New York: B. Blom, 1968.

Russian Literature: Ideals and Realities. Montreal and New York: Black Rose Books, 1991.

Works. Vols. 7–11 edited by George Woodcock. Montreal and New York: Black Rose Books, 1992–1995.

WORKS ON KROPOTKIN

Cahm, Caroline. *Kropotkin and the Rise of Revolutionary Anarchism, 1872–1886.* Cambridge, U.K., and New York: Cambridge University Press, 1989.

Marshall, Peter. *Demanding the Impossible: A History of Anarchism.* London: HarperCollins, 1992.

Morland, David. *Demanding the Impossible? Human Nature and Politics in Nineteenth-Century Social Anarchism.* London and Washington, DC: Cassell, 1997.

Morris, Brian. *Kropotkin: The Politics of Community.* Amherst and New York: Humanity Books, 2004.

Woodcock, George, and Ivan Avakumovic. *Peter Kropotkin: From Prince to Rebel.* Montreal: Black Rose Books, 1990.

George Woodcock (1967)
Bibliography updated by Vladimir Marchenkov (2005)

KRUEGER, FELIX
(1874–1948)

Felix Krueger, a German philosopher and psychologist, was born in Poznán and received his doctorate in 1897 from the University of Munich, where he studied under Hans Cornelius and Theodor Lipps. After working as an assistant at the Physiological Institute in Kiel he became a *Privatdozent* at Leipzig under Wilhelm Wundt. From 1906 to 1908 Krueger held a professorship at Buenos Aires, where he organized the development of scientific psychology in Argentina and left lasting traces of his views and activities. After returning to Leipzig he was called to Halle to succeed Hermann Ebbinghaus. In 1912–1913 Krueger was an exchange professor at Columbia University. In 1917, after three years of military service, he returned to Leipzig as Wundt's successor. At Leipzig Krueger founded the second Leipzig school of psychology, whose basic principles were designated as a genetic psychology of wholeness and structure (*genetische Ganzheits- und Strukturpsychologie*). In 1928 he received an honorary doctorate from Wittenberg College, Springfield, Ohio. In

1935 Krueger was appointed rector of Leipzig University. He immediately became involved in political conflicts and was removed from the rectorship and for some time forbidden to lecture; in 1935 he retired prematurely from academic life. Krueger edited two series of psychological works, "Neue psychologische Studien" and "Arbeiten zur Entwicklungspsychologie," from 1914 and 1926, respectively. Early in 1945 he moved to Switzerland.

Krueger's first work, a philosophical one, was *Der Begriff des absolut Wertvollen als Grundbegriff der Moralphilosophie* (The concept of the absolutely valuable as the basic concept of moral philosophy; Leipzig, 1898). In this work he presented a critique of Immanuel Kant running counter to that of Neo-Kantianism. He tried to show that there was a material vein in the formal ethics of Kant himself, and he stressed that ethical responsibility is moored in the person, in his "energy of evaluation" (*Energie des Wertens*) and in his attitude toward values (*Werthaltung*), which Krueger understood as the "core structure" of personality or character.

After this work Krueger turned to empirical and experimental psychology, in which he became known particularly for his new theory of consonance and dissonance based on the influence of the different tones and for experiments in phonetics and the psychology of speech. In connection with this work he began to develop, as early as 1900, a theory of psychological wholeness, arising from the exhibition of emotional and physiognomic experiencing, which he characterized as a quality of complexes (*Komplexqualität*) parallel to Christian von Ehrenfels's Gestalt qualities (*Gestaltqualität*). Together with his English friend and student (who was, nevertheless, older than he), Charles Spearman, Krueger introduced into psychology the calculus of correlation including the first reflections on factor analysis.

In 1915, in *Über Entwicklungspsychologie, ihre historische und sachliche Notwendigkeit* (On developmental psychology, its historical and factual necessity) Krueger developed a theory of cultural origins departing from Wundt's psychology of peoples and carried it further in *Zur Entwicklungspsychologie des Rechts* (The developmental psychology of law; "Arbeiten zur Entwicklungspsychologie," No. 7, Munich, 1926). In 1918 and (in English) in 1927, Krueger presented sketches for a theory of the emotions, which he defined as the *Komplexqualitäten* of one's total experience, that is, as supersummative qualities not to be confused or identified with gestalt.

These various strands, including his old moral philosophy, were united by Krueger in 1923 in a theory of structure, which was both critically related to and opposed to the thought of Wilhelm Dilthey. Krueger defined structure as the new scientific conception of the mind, as "the organismic construct of psychophysical wholeness," that is, as the basis of events in experience in the form of disposition, attitude and readiness, inclination, habit, and capability. The existence and individuality of personal structure can be demonstrated particularly in experiences of personal significance and "depth," but also in the subjective predispositions or preconstellations of perception, thought, memory, etc. Structure is the bearer of development and of personal identity. Besides personal structure there are social and "objective" intellectual structures. Formally, the structure of the experienced gestalt, which exists in becoming, can be compared to the "actual genesis" (or microgenesis) of the gestalt. The development of man, like that of animals, arises from qualitatively complex, pregestalt experience and is only gradually differentiated into an articulated gestalt and into rational clarification. Krueger's last work, *Die Lehre von dem Ganzen* (The doctrine of the whole; Bern, 1948), began with psychology but culminated in cosmology.

There are four main points in Krueger's philosophical psychology: holism (opposition to associationism, emotionism (or emphasis on feeling and emotion), social evolutionism, and antiphenomenalism (structural personalism). Krueger's genetic *Ganzheitspsychologie* was carried on by many of his outstanding students. Shortly after his death it was characterized as a "re-establishment of the science of the mind" in the full sense of the word, as opposing both mere introspectionism and mere behaviorism. It is the radical rejection of atomism, mechanism, sensationalism, and phenomenalism (psychologism) of traditional psychology, whose loss of credit among academic psychologists is largely due to Krueger. The slogans and basic ideas of *Ganzheitspsychologie* have also stimulated and fertilized related fields, particularly aesthetics and education.

See also Dilthey, Wilhelm; Ehrenfels, Christian Freiherr von; Emotion; Gestalt Theory; Holism and Individualism in History and Social Science; Kant, Immanuel; Latin American Philosophy; Lipps, Theodor; Neo-Kantianism; Personalism; Psychology; Wundt, Wilhelm.

Bibliography

WORKS BY KRUEGER

In English

"Consonance and Dissonance." *Journal of Philosophy, Psychology and Scientific Method* 10 (1913).

"Magical Factors in the First Development of Human Labor." *American Journal of Psychology* 24 (1913).

"The Essence of Feeling." In *Feelings and Emotions.* Worcester, MA: Clark University Press, 1928.

In German

Zur Philosophie und Psychologie der Ganzheit. Edited by E. Heuss. Berlin and Heidelberg: Springer, 1953. Writings by Krueger dating from 1918 to 1940, with a complete bibliography.

WORKS ON KRUEGER

Buss, Onko. *Die Ganzheitspsychologie Felix Kruegers.* Munich, 1934.

Odebrecht, Rudolf. *Gefühl und Gestalt: Die Ideengehalt der Psychologie Felix Kruegers.* Berlin: Junker und Dünnhaupt, 1929.

Wellek, Albert. *Das Problem des seelischen Seins: Die Strukturtheorie Felix Kruegers,* 2nd ed. Meisenheim and Vienna, 1953.

Wellek, Albert. *Die Widerherstellung der Seelwissenschaft im Lebenswerk Felix Kruegers.* Hamburg, 1950.

Albert Wellek (1967)
Translated by Tessa Byck

KUHN, THOMAS
(1922–1996)

Educated at Harvard University (SB, 1943; PhD in physics, 1949), Thomas Kuhn taught at Harvard (1951–1956), University of California, Berkeley (1956–1964), Princeton University (1964–1979), and Massachusetts Institute of Technology (1979–1991). His book *The Structure of Scientific Revolutions*, first published in 1962 (2nd. ed., 1970), continues to stimulate discussion among historians and philosophers of science even as its concepts of "paradigm" and "paradigm shift" have been adopted by a great diversity of writers, often at some remove from their source in Kuhn's book.

CONCEPTUAL SCHEMES, PARADIGMS, AND NORMAL SCIENCE

At Harvard Kuhn became the protégé of its president, James B. Conant, to whom he dedicated the first edition of *Structure of Scientific Revolutions*. Conant's concept of "conceptual scheme," applied especially to the chemical revolution's phlogiston and oxygen theories, reappeared in Kuhn's first book, *The Copernican Revolution: Planetary Astronomy in the Development of Western Thought* (1957), and was one of the principal sources of Kuhn's all-important paradigm concept. His evolving understanding of that concept also reflected a pivotal experience in 1947, in which he suddenly appreciated that

Aristotle could not properly be understood from the perspective of post-Galilean physics, but only from within Aristotle's own context of problems, concepts, and assumptions. Kuhn's early conviction that such systems of scientific thought can only be understood holistically and that a scientist's appreciation for a radically new system comes in a flash of insight underlay his notions of the incommensurability of paradigms and of the gestalt switch that marks the transition from one paradigm to another.

Kuhn announced his central problem as "the nature of science and the reasons for its special success" (1970, p. v). He forged his concept of "paradigms"—glossed here as "universally recognized scientific achievements that for a time provide model problems and solutions to a community of practitioners" (p. viii)—in part as a way to understand why there is less disagreement among natural scientists over fundamentals than there is among social scientists and psychologists. Kuhn rejected the view that scientific knowledge grows incrementally through the accumulation of individual facts, laws, and theories. He linked his rejection of demarcationist issues—what distinguishes good science from error or superstition—to his insistence that superseded conceptual systems like Aristotelian dynamics and phlogistic chemistry were, in their context, no less scientific than currently accepted science.

Kuhn applied the term "normal science" to "research firmly based upon one or more past scientific achievements, achievements that some particular scientific community acknowledges for a time as supplying the foundation for its further practice" (1970, p. 10). Paradigm-defining works like Aristotle's *Physics*, Isaac Newton's *Principia*, and Antoine Lavoisier's *Chemistry* were "sufficiently unprecedented to attract an enduring group of adherents away from competing modes of scientific activity" and "sufficiently open-ended to leave all sorts of problems for the redefined group of practitioners to resolve" (p. 10). Subsequent scientists (and students of science) study such works as "concrete models," whereby they become "committed to the same rules and standards for scientific practice" (p. 11). Strong commitment and broad consensus characterize the practitioners of Kuhnian normal science. The paradigm that defines that practice limits the questions worth asking and the experiments worth performing as it specifies the entities the world is composed of and the relevance of putative facts.

For Kuhn, most scientists are engaged in "mopping-up operations" resembling "an attempt to force nature into the preformed and relatively inflexible box that the paradigm supplies" (p. 24). Kuhn likened normal science to "puzzle-solving": a solution must be assumed to exist for any problem worth addressing, and one knows ahead of time the general form the solution will take. Kuhn insisted that paradigms guide research not via rules and definitions but as models (later called "exemplars") of proper scientific practice. He associated his understanding with Michael Polanyi's concept of tacit knowledge and Ludwig Wittgenstein's notion that one can employ words without having reduced their meaning to some putative essence.

In the context of his discussion of anomalies and the emergence of scientific discoveries, Kuhn began to employ the terms "paradigm" and "paradigm change" in a broader sense closer to his and Conant's earlier "conceptual scheme," whereby his central example was the chemical revolution associated with Lavoisier's oxygen theory. Kuhn here insisted that unanticipated discoveries of new sorts of phenomena typically occur in response to the perception of anomaly with regard to the expectations of normal science. Kuhn likened scientists' response to anomalies to subjects in an experiment with playing cards who are asked to identify—among normal cards—black hearts and red spades, and who typically try unconsciously to assimilate those anomalies to the expected categories: "In science, as in the playing card experiment, novelty emerges only with difficulty, manifested by resistance, against a background provided by expectation" (1970, p. 64).

ANOMALIES, CRISES, AND PARADIGM SHIFTS

The point is of crucial importance. Anomalies enable scientists to isolate weaknesses within the dominant paradigm and to devise a solution that ultimately induces the scientific community to embrace a new and more effective paradigm. These are the "paradigm shifts" associated with the Copernican, Newtonian, and chemical revolutions. In Kuhn's view awareness of serious anomaly—always with regard to internal, technical issues, not to any of various external factors—leads to a period of crisis characterized by "the proliferation of competing articulations, the willingness to try anything, the expression of explicit discontent, the recourse to philosophy and to debate over fundamentals" (1970, p. 91)—that is, by what he termed "extraordinary science."

Although Kuhn recognized that "every problem that normal science sees as a puzzle can be seen, from another viewpoint, as a counterinstance and thus as a source of crisis" (p. 79), he offered no satisfactory explanation for

why only some unsolved problems are perceived as anomalies, and why only some anomalies lead to crises. In his view no fundamental changes to a paradigm can come from the resources of normal science itself. The transition from one paradigm to another constitutes "a reconstruction of the field from new fundamentals, a reconstruction that changes some of the field's most elementary theoretical generalizations as well as many of its paradigm methods and applications" (p. 85). Kuhn likened such a paradigm shift to "a change in visual gestalt" (p. 84) and defined the associated "scientific revolutions" as "those non-cumulative developmental episodes in which an older paradigm is replaced in whole or in part by an incompatible new one" (p. 92).

INCOMMENSURABILITY AND RELATIVISM

In elaborating parallels between scientific and political revolutions, Kuhn introduced a number of ideas that would prove controversial. He argued that because they recognize no common higher authority, "the parties to a revolutionary conflict must finally resort to the techniques of mass persuasion, often including force" (1970, p. 93).

> Like the choice between competing political institutions, that between competing paradigms proves to be a choice between incompatible modes of community life. Because it has that character, the choice is not and cannot be determined merely by the evaluative procedures characteristic of normal science, for these depend in part upon a particular paradigm…. As in political revolutions, so in paradigm choice—there is no standard higher than the assent of the relevant community. (p. 94)

Such assertions led many to accuse Kuhn of making science a matter of might makes right, of mob psychology, where the techniques of political persuasion replace those of evidence and rational argument.

Because different paradigms make different ontological claims, define different problems as significant, and employ different standards of what properly belongs to science, "the normal-scientific tradition that emerges from a scientific revolution is not only incompatible but often actually incommensurable with that which has gone before" (1970, p. 103). Hence defenders of opposing paradigms, absent a shared set of values, "will inevitably talk through each other when debating the relative merits of their respective paradigms" (p. 109). Although Kuhn resisted the charge of relativism, his position clearly relativizes scientific knowledge to the paradigm-dependent standards enforced by particular scientific communities, not to ostensibly objective experimental tests.

That implicit relativism was reinforced by Kuhn's insistence that scientists working within different paradigms see the world in profoundly different ways, that they effectively live in different worlds. Again, analogies—gestalt switches and experiments with inverting lenses and anomalous playing cards—were invoked to enhance the claim's plausibility. The transformation of vision that students undergo as they learn to read bubble-chamber photographs parallels "the shifts in scientific perception that accompany paradigm change" (1970, p. 117). The sudden and unstructured gestalt switch that accompanies a paradigm shift thrusts scientists into a world "incommensurable" with the one they had inhabited before. Kuhn's insistence that such transformations of vision are not reducible to a reinterpretation of individual stable data derived from his rejection of the possibility of a neutral observation language for science. In speaking of the "flashes of intuition through which a new paradigm is born" (p. 123), Kuhn transformed the gestalt switch from a metaphor to an operative element in the dynamics of scientific change. And in shifting the locus of conceptual change from the ostensibly objective externalities of experiment and argument to the psychological internality of a holistically unanalyzable gestalt switch, he seemed to many to undercut the epistemological legitimacy of science. Kuhn likened a revolutionary paradigm shift to a conversion experience that cannot be forced by logic and neutral experience. "Persuasion" and "conversion" are the terms that dominate Kuhn's discussion of paradigm shift.

Although he appealed to the greater problem-solving ability of postrevolution theories, Kuhn had no paradigm-independent way to define scientific progress and no way at all to address the question of the truth value of particular scientific claims. He sought to make this stance acceptable by appealing to an analogy between the historical development of science and Charles Darwin's rejection of the goal-directedness of evolution. The process by which one paradigm wins out over its competitors "is the selection by conflict within the scientific community of the fittest way to practice future science. … Successive stages in that developmental process are marked by an increase in articulation and specialization. And the entire process may have occurred, as we now suppose biological evolution did, without benefit of a set goal, a permanent fixed scientific truth, of which each

stage in the development of scientific knowledge is a better exemplar" (1970, pp. 172–173). But goal-directedness is not the same thing as correspondence to the physical world, and although this may be a viable way to account for the history of science, it does not address the underlying epistemological question concerning the truth-likeness of scientific theories. In asking why scientific communities are able to reach consensus at all, Kuhn failed to assign a principal role to inputs from the physical world as he increasingly appealed to the sociology of scientific communities.

SCIENTIFIC AND LINGUISTIC COMMUNITIES

In the postscript appended to the second edition of *Structure of Scientific Revolutions*, Kuhn defended his original claims while effectively abandoning the term "paradigm." One important amplification was his appeal to the analogy between members of scientific and linguistic communities, whereby he urged "that men who hold incommensurable viewpoints be thought of as members of different language communities and that their communication problems be analyzed as problems of translation" (1970, p. 175). Like the acceptance of a new paradigm, Kuhn saw the transition accompanying translation into a new language as a qualitatively discontinuous conversion experience: "The conversion experience that I have likened to a gestalt switch remains, therefore, at the heart of the revolutionary process" (p. 204).

See also Aristotle; Galileo Galilei; Lavoisier, Antoine; Newton, Isaac; Paradigm-Case Argument; Philosophy of Science, Problems of; Wittgenstein, Ludwig Josef Johann.

Bibliography

WORKS BY KUHN

The Copernican Revolution: Planetary Astronomy in the Development of Western Thought. Cambridge, MA: Harvard University Press, 1957. Rev. ed., 1979.

The Structure of Scientific Revolutions. 1962. 2nd ed. with postscript. Chicago: University of Chicago Press, 1970. 3rd ed. with index, 1996.

The Essential Tension: Selected Studies in Scientific Tradition and Change. Chicago: University of Chicago Press, 1977.

The Road since Structure: Philosophical Essays, 1970–1993, with an Autobiographical Interview, edited by James Conant and John Haugeland. Chicago: University of Chicago Press, 2000. Contains a complete bibliography of Kuhn's publications.

WORKS ABOUT KUHN

Barnes, Barry. *T. S. Kuhn and Social Science*. New York: Columbia University Press, 1982.

Buchwald, Jed Z., and George E. Smith. "Thomas S. Kuhn, 1922–1996." *Philosophy of Science* 64 (1997): 361–376.

Caneva, Kenneth L. "Possible Kuhns in the History of Science: Anomalies of Incommensurable Paradigms." *Studies in History and Philosophy of Science* 31 (1) (March 2000): 87–124.

Gutting, Gary, ed. *Paradigms and Revolutions: Appraisals and Applications of Thomas Kuhn's Philosophy of Science*. Notre Dame, IN: University of Notre Dame Press, 1980.

Hoyningen-Huene, Paul. *Reconstructing Scientific Revolutions: Thomas S. Kuhn's Philosophy of Science*. Translated by Alexander T. Levine. Chicago: University of Chicago Press, 1993.

Lakatos, Imre, and Alan Musgrave, eds. *Criticism and the Growth of Knowledge*. Cambridge, U.K.: Cambridge University Press, 1970.

Nickles, Thomas, ed. *Thomas Kuhn*. Cambridge, U.K.: Cambridge University Press, 2003. Contains a short bibliography of important studies on Kuhn and his influence.

Kenneth L. Caneva (2005)

KÜLPE, OSWALD
(1862–1915)

A German psychologist, philosopher, and historian of philosophy, Oswald Külpe was born in Kandava, Latvia. After teaching history, Külpe entered the University of Leipzig in 1881, intending to continue in history. However, the lectures of Wilhelm Wundt stimulated his interest in philosophy and psychology, and after further studies in Berlin, Göttingen, and Dorpat (Russia), he returned to Wundt's seminar in 1886, receiving his doctorate the following year. In 1894 he was appointed extraordinary professor at Leipzig but left to accept a full professorship at Würzburg, where he founded a psychological laboratory. Külpe returned to Leipzig in 1896, and he subsequently held academic positions at Bonn and Munich. Primarily because of his work in organizing experimental laboratories, Külpe is regarded as a pioneer of experimental psychology in Germany. He died in Munich during World War I of influenza contracted while visiting wounded German soldiers.

PSYCHOLOGY AND EPISTEMOLOGY

Külpe's philosophical position, a form of critical realism, was closely related to his work in psychology. He came to regard the positivistic attempts of Ernst Mach and Richard Avenarius to reduce mental processes to sensa-tions as incapable of accounting for the findings of intro-spective experiments. In one series of experiments, Külpe presented cards with nonsense syllables of varying colors and arrangements to subjects who were asked to report either the color, pattern, or number of items seen. Each person abstracted the features he had been instructed to report, remaining unconscious of the other features of the cards. Külpe concluded that the process of abstraction depends not only on the material presented to sensation but also on the subject's apprehension. This was taken to prove that sensations—as well as physical phenomena—must be distinguished from their apprehension. Thus he questioned the equation of "being" with "being per-ceived," even at the level of sensation.

Külpe abandoned the sensationalist psychology of contents in favor of a psychology recognizing both con-tents and acts of mind. Abstraction, he maintained, is a mental act or function that cannot be directly observed, but its occurrence is undeniable, even though it is discov-erable only retrospectively. There exist both thought con-tents (*Gedanken*) and thought processes (*Denken*). The latter include the impalpable acts of thinking, meaning, and judging, which are not merely relations among con-tents but activities of the ego that transform the actuali-ties (*Wirklichkeiten*) of consciousness into realities (*Realitäten*).

Külpe's position was thus hostile to both naive real-ism and idealism. Against the former, he argued that thought, although it does not produce the object of knowledge, is nevertheless genuinely spontaneous and creative in contributing to the realization of the object. His argument against idealism held that the facts of con-scious experience require the existence of independent objects. When a scientist studies the maturation of an egg, for example, he assumes that this process takes place while no consciousness is directed upon it. Such continu-ity of development implies the object's independence of its being thought, a presupposition of every science.

Külpe used the word *awareness* (*Bewusstheit*) to indi-cate that the meanings of abstract words can be discov-ered in consciousness even when only the words themselves are perceivable entities. This thesis is an appli-cation of the theory that there exist impalpable (*unan-schaulich*) or imageless contents of consciousness, a theory for which Külpe's "Würzburg school" of psychol-ogy was noted. Meanings can be experienced and objecti-fied even without words or other signs. Although we cannot analyze precisely how these contents are given, retrospective acts make the world of meanings accessible to us. Külpe's indebtedness to Edmund Husserl and Franz

Brentano is evident. Mental acts provide knowledge of meanings, and the act of meaning (*das Meinen*) may be directed even to such objects as God, the soul, electrons, or atoms, which could not possibly be actualized in consciousness. The capacity for imageless thought is essential if thought is to relate itself to something independent of it. When one wants to imagine a certain structure, the particular image one has in mind is only representative of the structure; the image points beyond itself or is the occasion for such an intentional act.

AESTHETICS

In aesthetics, Külpe attempted to support Gustav Fechner's results concerning the golden section. Like Wundt, he maintained that the aesthetic pleasure produced by ideally proportioned objects results from mental economy. When the ratio of a whole to its larger part is the same as that of the larger to the smaller part, the perception involves the least effort combined with the greatest possible diversity.

Külpe attempted to further the development of experimental aesthetics by such methods as asking people to record their reactions to glimpses of slides showing works of art. His findings indicated no sympathetic empathy on the part of his subjects, thus opposing the contention of Theodor Lipps that such empathy (*Einfühlung*) is the basic condition of all aesthetic enjoyment. In the reports of his subjects Külpe found that form, orderliness, symmetry, and harmony were related to attractiveness. However, he recognized the limited validity of his findings, admitting that aesthetically inexperienced people might respond differently than his subjects. This reluctance to claim more for a theory than was warranted by experimental findings was characteristic of Külpe's work in psychology.

See also Aesthetics, History of; Avenarius, Richard; Brentano, Franz; Critical Realism; Fechner, Gustav Theodor; Husserl, Edmund; Idealism; Lipps, Theodor; Mach, Ernst; Psychology; Wundt, Wilhelm.

Bibliography

WORKS BY KÜLPE

Grundriss der Psychologie auf experimenteller Grundlage dargestellt. Leipzig: Engelmann, 1893. Translated by E. B. Titchener as *Outlines of Psychology, Based upon the Results of Experimental Investigation.* New York: Macmillan, 1895.

Einleitung in die Philosophie. Leipzig, 1895. Translated by W. B. Pillsbury and E. B. Titchener as *Introduction to Philosophy.* London, 1910.

Die Philosophie der Gegenwart in Deutschland. Leipzig: Teubner, 1902. Translated by M. L. Patrick and G. T. W. Patrick as *The Philosophy of the Present in Germany.* London: G. Allen, 1913.

Immanuel Kant. Leipzig, 1907.

Die Realisierung. Vol. I, Leipzig, 1912; Vols. II and III, edited by August Messer, Leipzig, 1920 and 1923.

Ethik und der Krieg. Leipzig: Hirzel, 1915. Külpe's defense of Germany's position in World War I.

Grundlagen der Aesthetik. Edited by S. Behn. Leipzig, 1921.

WORKS ON KÜLPE

Messer, August. *Der Kritische Realismus.* Karlsruhe, 1923.

Ogden, R. M. "Oswald Külpe and the Würzburg School." *American Journal of Psychology* 61 (1951): 4–19.

Arnulf Zweig (1967)

KUMAZAWA BANZAN
(1619–1691)

Kumazawa Banzan, a Japanese Confucianist of the Wang Yangming school, was born in Kyoto and died at Koga, Shimoda prefecture. Both he and his father were masterless samurai. Deciding to become a scholar, Kumazawa went to Nakae Tōju (1608–1648); in 1642 Nakae taught him the doctrine of Wang Yangming (in Japanese, Ōyōmei)—"innate knowledge" and cultivation of the mind. Kumazawa entered the service of Lord Ikeda Mitsumasa of Okayama, but his ideas, contrasting with the officially established doctrine, Zhu Xi neo-Confucianism, aroused suspicion. However, his character and practical ability were recognized, and Ikeda put him in charge of the fief. For seven years (1649–1656) he successfully brought forth administrative reforms that transformed Okayama into a model fief. Paramount among his accomplishments was his role in organizing the Okayama college. Yet the extreme nature of these reforms, even in monasteries, angered many. Moreover, there were rebellious samurai among his pupils. He decided to retire to the studious life of a teacher in Kyoto, but slander of his teaching forced him to move in 1667; he did pass eight quiet years (1679–1687) at Yadasan near Kōriyama. On the official request of the Tokugawa government, he presented a plan of reform (possibly in his *Daigaku wakumon*). Thereupon his enemies, especially Hayashi, the defender of Zhu Xi Confucianism, succeeded in having him confined at Koga.

Kumazawa is typical of the early Tokugawa nonconformists, who were beset by adversities that multiplied with success. His politico-economic ideas, which were indeed very bold for his times, were the real reason for his difficulties. They are expressed in *Daigaku wakumon* (Some questions concerning the great learning), which is not a commentary on the Confucian classic "The Great Learning" but rather a tract on many subjects concerning how to rule the realm according to the Confucian precept of *jinsei,* or "benevolent rule." Both his unconventional proposals and his pragmatic attitude toward doctrine are striking.

See also Chinese Philosophy; Hayashi Razan; Japanese Philosophy; Nakae Tōju; Wang Yang-ming; Zhu Xi (Chu Hsi).

Bibliography

For a guide to primary sources, see the bibliography to the Japanese Philosophy entry. See also M. Fisher, "Kumazawa B., His Life and Ideas," *Transactions of the Asiatic Society of Japan,* 2nd series, 16 (1938): 221–259; 259–356. W. T. de Bary, ed., *Sources of Japanese Tradition* (New York: Columbia University Press, 1958), pp. 384–392.

Gino K. Piovesana, S.J. (1967)

KUNG-SUN LUNG

See *Gongsun Long*

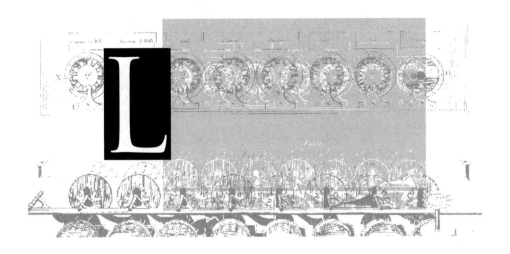

LAAS, ERNST

(1837–1885)

Ernst Laas, the German philosopher, was born in Förstenwalde. From 1872 on, he was professor in Strasbourg. His first important book, *Kants Analogien der Erfahrung* (Berlin, 1876), was a critical study both of Immanuel Kant and of "the foundations of theoretical philosophy"; but in his main work, *Idealismus und Positivismus* (3 vols., Berlin, 1879–1884), he launched a general attack on idealism, including Aristotle, René Descartes, Gottfried Wilhelm Leibniz, and especially Plato as its founder, as well as Kant. His purpose was to provide a remedy for the "discontinuity of philosophy"; that is, its failure to make progress over the centuries and its want of any clear standards. The remedy lay first of all in a new critical approach to the history of philosophy, which in the past had usually been at best merely scholarly and accurate. This new analysis revealed a basic dualism throughout the history of philosophy between the outlooks of Plato and Protagoras; and this revelation, in turn, permitted a revision of the judgment rendered in favor of Plato that had ever since benefited his followers at the expense of their opponents, such as the British empiricists. Laas referred specifically to J. S. Mill and cited approvingly a review of his own book on Kant that had compared it to Mill's *Examination of Sir William Hamilton's Philosophy.*

By "positivism" Laas meant, as was usual in Germany at the time, the tradition of Protagoras and the British empiricists, not the doctrine of Auguste Comte, whom Laas mentioned rarely and with little sympathy. Laas's position might more accurately, especially in English usage, be called neo-empiricism. It proposed to limit knowledge to the data of sense experience, thereby denying both a consciousness independent of the content of perception (insisting on the correlation of subject and object) and objects independent of the process of perception (asserting the instant changeability of objects of perception). At the same time Laas avoided the conclusions drawn by some empiricists, such as George Berkeley, by rejecting any version of subjective idealism (which would assert the superiority or exclusive reality of the perceiver vis-à-vis the objects of perception or sensation) even more vehemently than he rejected the objective idealism originated by Plato. He identified this idealistic tradition in logic with conceptual realism, in epistemology with a priori deductive rationalism, and in metaphysics with both spontaneous human creativity and superhuman teleology. He associated idealism with a mathematically inspired desire to attain to the knowledge of absolutes and with the doctrines of innate ideas and final causes.

However, in his anxiety to escape from the "monstrous" notions of subjective idealism, as well as from "skepticism," "frivolity," and the "banal philosophy of common sense," Laas came close to a neo-Kantian position in postulating an ideal or total consciousness. Recognizing, with Mill, that the sum total of actual objects of sensation is insufficient to construct an intelligible world, he asserted that the world consists of the sum total of possible contents of perception, which would be vouchsafed to an ideal consciousness and which it is the task of philosophy to construct. Since facts (objects) exist independently of consciousness (although not of perception), including this ideal consciousness, Laas claimed in this way to have saved the possibility of scientific investigation of the physical world from "skepticism," even though that world is relative and variable.

Just as he quite openly sided even with idealism (particularly with Kant, whom he often cited sympathetically) rather than with epistemological skepticism, Laas also seeks to defend his ethical doctrine (mainly in Vol. II of *Idealismus und Positivismus*) against any imputation of relying on egoism. Here again, however, his main concern was to overcome what he saw as the Platonic tradition of asceticism founded on a set of absolute and transcendental ideals. For this he proposed to substitute a "positive" ethics for this world, based on its values as revealed by "enlightened self-interest." Laas acknowledged the founders of this ethical doctrine to be Epicurus, Claude-Adrien Helvétius, and Jeremy Bentham, but he diverged from them on the crucial point of egoism. He denied the identification of self-interest with egoism and held, rather, that self-interest dictates the performance of duties and the fulfillment of demands and expectations imposed on the individual by his environment. In this way, ethical values are the consequences of a particular social order. They acquire validity when they are judged, in the long run and by a considerable number of people, to be worthwhile. Laas characteristically listed as ethically desirable values security of employment, social harmony, the laws and institutions of the state, and cultural progress. These ethical teachings were the most influential part of his philosophy, affecting, in particular, the ideas of Theobald Ziegler and Friedrich Jodl.

See also Aristotle; Bentham, Jeremy; Berkeley, George; Comte, Auguste; Descartes, René; Empiricism; Epicurus; Ethical Egoism; Ethics, History of; Helvétius, Claude-Adrien; Idealism; Innate Ideas; Jodl, Friedrich; Kant, Immanuel; Leibniz, Gottfried Wilhelm; Mill, John Stuart; Plato; Positivism; Protagoras of Abdera; Realism; Teleology.

Bibliography

In addition to the works cited in text, see Laas's *Literarischer Nachlass,* edited by B. Kerry (Vienna: Deutschen Worte, 1887).

For material on Laas, see Nikolaus Koch, *Das Verhältniss der Erkenntnistheorie von Ernst Laas zu Kant* (Würzburg, 1940) and Ludwig Salamonowicz, *Die Ethik des Positivismus nach Ernst Laas* (Berlin: H. Lücker, 1935).

W. M. Simon (1967)

LABERTHONNIÈRE, LUCIEN
(1860–1932)

Lucien Laberthonnière, the French philosopher of religion and a leading figure in the modernist movement in the Roman Catholic Church, was born at Chazelet (Indre). He studied for the priesthood and was ordained as an Oratorian in 1886. He then taught in various institutions, mainly in the college at Juilly, where he became rector in 1900. Laberthonnière was influenced by philosophies of life and action; he mentions Maine de Biran and Étienne Boutroux as the two philosophers who had most impressed him. Maurice Blondel's philosophy of action was another important formative factor, although Laberthonnière later found it moving too far toward intellectualism. He himself not only advocated a pragmatic point of view but also had an intense distaste for intellectualism and speculative philosophy. In particular, he had no sympathy for the attempted Thomist synthesis of faith and reason, believing that the task is not to conciliate these two but to choose between them. His teachings brought him into conflict with ecclesiastical authorities, and his principal writings were put on the Index in 1906. In 1913 he was prohibited from further publication.

Laberthonnière was not concerned with merely speculative philosophy that is constructed apart from life. He believed that the purpose of all philosophy is to give sense to life, and this motivation underlies even metaphysics, whether or not the metaphysician is aware of it. In the long run, the test of a philosophy must be its viability or its aptness for life, and the criterion of philosophical truth is a pragmatic one. We mistake the character of philosophy if we think of it as a theoretical enterprise resulting in a system of propositions linked together by abstract logical principles. A philosophical doctrine has a moral as well as an intellectual character, so that a worthwhile philosophy has to be worked out by living. The test of its truth is whether it can be illuminating when brought to bear on the problems of life.

Although Laberthonnière apparently held that all philosophy has a pragmatic or existential motivation, even if this remains unconscious, he also believed that some philosophies have been much more successful than others in relating to life. The theme of one of his principal writings, *Le réalisme chrétien et l'idéalisme grec* (Paris, 1904), is the contrast between two supposedly extreme cases, Greek philosophy and Christian thought. Greek philosophy was concerned with abstract essences, conceived God as static and immutable, and proposed the life of pure contemplation as its ideal for man. In contrast to such idealism or intellectualism, Christianity is presented as a realism. Its concern is with the concrete life of action, and God himself is conceived as active, the living God of the Bible. Hence, the truth of Christianity cannot be reached by intellectual contemplation, as if it were something external to us. Such truth as Christianity teaches is concrete and intrinsic to life, so that we grasp it only in living and in re-creating this truth in ourselves. These ideas about religious truth had already found expression in Laberthonnière's *Essais de philosophie religieuse* (Paris, 1903), where it is maintained that the doctrines of religion are to be understood not as general truths of the same kind as scientific truths but as concrete truths that must be brought into experience and realized if we are to understand them and know their value.

Although these views lean strongly toward pragmatism, Laberthonnière did not think that religion could be reduced to a purely practical affair or that it could be adequately explicated in naturalistic terms. It is significant that in spite of the harsh treatment that he received from the Roman Catholic Church, he remained devoted to it and believed his philosophical views to be compatible with its teaching. If he went far toward abolishing the traditional distinction between the natural and the supernatural, this is not to be understood as the reduction of the latter to the former. Rather, it was Laberthonnière's conviction that the natural is itself already permeated by divine grace. Thus, we should look for God not in some upper or outer realm but in the immediate world, where he is active, and especially in the depth of human life itself.

See also Blondel, Maurice; Idealism; Maine de Biran; Modernism; Pragmatism; Realism; Thomism.

Bibliography

In addition to the writings mentioned above, Laberthonnière published *Positivisme et catholicisme* (Paris, 1911). His other work, including an important study of Descartes, appeared posthumously in *Oeuvres*, 2 vols. (Paris, 1948–1955).

See also M.-M. d'Hendecourt, "Laberthonnière," in *Revue de métaphysique et de morale* 63 (1961).

John Macquarrie (1967)

LABRIOLA, ANTONIO
(1843–1904)

Antonio Labriola, professor of philosophy in Rome from 1874 to 1904, was the first Italian Marxist philosopher. He wrote little, but that little was widely publicized by two disciples, Georges Sorel and Benedetto Croce; he exercised his extensive influence through lectures and discussions. Trained as a Hegelian in Naples, he became a Herbartian, more interested in Johan Friedrich Herbart's ethics and pedagogy than in his metaphysics. He discovered Marxism around 1890 and began a correspondence with Friedrich Engels that lasted until the latter's death and was published in *Lettere a Engels* (Rome, 1949). This discovery of Marxism was a decisive event in Italian intellectual life, for from it dates the introduction of Marxist theory into Italy's academic culture, where it still occupies a prominent place.

Labriola's articles on Marxism, published in Italy by Croce and in France by Sorel, were first collected in French, as *Essais sur la conception matérialiste de l'histoire* (Paris, 1897). Their publication established Labriola's international reputation as an expositor of Marxism. He wrote Sorel ten letters on the subject, published as *Discorrendo di socialismo e di filosofia* (Rome, 1897). These books were the first exposition of Marxism as an independent philosophy to be made by an academic philosopher. They have been widely used in later efforts to combat all varieties of philosophical revisionism, whether from neo-Kantian or positivist sources. The "return to Labriola," as recommended by Antonio Gramsci and as undertaken in Italy since 1950, has meant going back to the original innocence of a supposedly pure and independent Marxist philosophy, for Labriola claimed not to be an original thinker, and even less to be interested in developing or criticizing Marxism. He wanted to be simply an expositor and systematizer of a philosophy implicit in Karl Marx's work.

The philosophy he found in Marx's work closely resembled the Hegelian views that Labriola had defended in controversies with neo-Kantians before he had heard of Marx. For example, he held that scientific socialism is not subjective criticism applied to things, but the statement of the self-criticism that is in things themselves. The only criticism of society is society itself, for there is an objective dialectic immanent in history, which progresses by contradictions. Socialism was no longer an aspiration or project (a view soon to be revived by neo-Kantian revisionists); it was the inevitable result of current contradictions in capitalist society. Labriola stressed the "scientific, objective" status of these assertions, in contrast to mere philosophies of history, which he dismissed as ideology. Historical materialism was no philosophy, but simply a method of research, a guiding thread like the Darwinian hypothesis.

Labriola, Croce, and Sorel were nicknamed the Holy Trinity of Latin Marxism, but the Roman professor came to feel that his spiritual sons were "going too far" in their development and criticism of the doctrine. They lacked that inflexible orthodoxy of which Labriola is the first eminent example in the Marxist tradition, and they touched off the revisionist controversy. That dispute broke out simultaneously in several countries, although Croce gave priority to his own and Sorel's writings. At all events, Eduard Bernstein in Germany, Sorel in France, Croce and Saverio Merlino in Italy, T. G. Masaryk in Prague, and the Fabians in England drew freely on each other's work, and Labriola found himself being quoted by and confounded with the "heretics." In a celebrated dispute, he broke publicly with Croce and Sorel, saying that revisionism was an international conspiracy organized by "scientific police-spies"—perhaps the first appearance of a philosophical terminology that was to become familiar later. Labriola never wrote on Marxism again. His earlier minor works, which include a *Socrate,* have been published by Croce (Bari, 1909) but are of small importance.

See also Continental Philosophy; Croce, Benedetto; Engels, Friedrich; Gramsci, Antonio; Herbart, Johann Friedrich; Historical Materialism; Marx, Karl; Marxist Philosophy; Masaryk, Tomáš Garrigue; Neo-Kantianism; Sorel, Georges.

Bibliography

WORKS BY LABRIOLA

Essays on the Materialistic Conception of History. Translated by C. H. Kerr. Chicago: Kerr, 1904.

Socialism and Philosophy. Translated by E. Untermann. Chicago: Kerr, 1907.

Opere, 3 vols. Edited by L. Dal Pane. Milan: Feltrinelli, 1959.

WORKS ON LABRIOLA

Bellamy, Richard. "Antonio Labriola." In *Modern Italian Social Theory: Ideology and Politics from Pareto to the Present.* Stanford, CA: Stanford University Press, 1987.

Bruzzo, S. *Il pensiero di Antonio Labriola.* Bari, 1942.

Dal Pane, L. *Antonio Labriola: la vita e il pensiero.* Rome, 1935.

Diambrini Palazzi, S. *Il pensiero filosofico di Antonio Labriola.* Bologna: Zanichelli, 1923.

Kolakowski, Leszek. "Antonio Labriola: An Attempt at an Open Orthodoxy." In *Main Currents of Marxism,* Vol. 2. Translated by P. S. Falla. Oxford: Oxford University Press, 1982.

Plekhanov, G. "The Materialist Conception of History." *Novoye Slovo* (September 1897). Also published separately. New York: International, 1940. Originally written as a review of Labriola's *Essays.*

Neil McInnes (1967)
Bibliography updated by Philip Reed (2005)

LA BRUYÈRE, JEAN DE
(1645–1696)

Jean de La Bruyère, the French author and moralist, was born in Paris, the son of a city official. After some legal training he apparently fell on hard times, but through the influence of Jacques Bénigne Bossuet he was appointed tutor to the grandson of the great Condé in 1684. After his tutorial functions were ended, he stayed on as librarian. The family seems to have been unpleasant; his colleagues, uncongenial; and the humiliations inflicted on him in this aristocratic society left a lasting mark. Elected to the Academy in 1693 after several unsuccessful attempts, he led a lonely and somewhat frustrated life, never marrying, making few friends, but showing passionate loyalty to those who, like Bossuet, won his respect.

La Bruyère's one famous work, the *Caractères,* reflects his personal experiences. Ostensibly modeled on the Greek *Characters* of Theophrastus, which La Bruyère translated and published in the same volume, the *Caractères* owes more to the quite different genre of La Rochefoucauld's *Maximes* and to the work of such contemporary moralists as Blaise Pascal and the Chevalier Antoine Gombault de Méré. Fifteen chapters somewhat arbitrarily group together epigrams (although La Bruyère explicitly disclaimed any intention of producing anything so authoritative as maxims), extended pen portraits (readily, and often wrongly, identified with living people) and brief moral essays, all arranged to cover, with considerable overlapping, the main characteristics and activities of contemporary society, from literary criticism to money lending, from sex to sermons. The last chapter, which, La Bruyère implausibly claimed, constituted the purpose and culmination of the previous fifteen, is devoted to a defense of religion against the freethinkers. It combines in an agreeable rather than a compelling manner the stock arguments for God's existence from his visible effects in nature with others reminiscent of Pascal and drawn from human psychology. The length of the book more than doubled in the course of nine editions from 1688 to 1696, and it came to include more and more of the concrete and detailed description, based on acute observation and couched in brilliant style, which makes La Bruyère at once a distinctive and a distinguished author.

In La Bruyère's time the splendors of Louis XIV's reign had come to demand too high a price, both economically and morally, of those obliged to maintain it. La Bruyère, a bourgeois himself, soured by personal experience of aristocratic arrogance and temperamentally allergic to worldly frivolity, was unsparing in his criticism of the court, where methodical hypocrisy marked the lives of those enslaved by self-interest and the desire for royal favor.

Like Bossuet, his hero and patron, La Bruyère felt able to combine vehement attacks on social abuses, due certainly in fact (if not in theory) to royal absolutism as currently practiced, with fulsome eulogy of Louis himself, going so far as to assimilate respect for the prince to fear of God. A convinced Christian, he had a genuine social conscience, as is illustrated by his famous remarks about the pitiful condition of the peasants. He contrasted the elegant heartlessness of the nobles with the rough kindliness of the people, with whom, in the last analysis, he would wish to be classed. He was, however, neither egalitarian nor republican, but believed that inequality founded on order is divinely instituted; and it was on moral and religious grounds, not in the name of equality, that he dissociated himself from a society he regarded as irremediably corrupt.

In common with other moralists of the age, La Bruyère was fascinated by the discrepancy between appearance and reality in human behavior. He recorded how skill in playing the social game usurps the name and place of virtue, how fashion makes mock of convictions (a happily married couple finds it socially expedient to simulate infidelity), and how self-interest is the one constant motive of those who disguise it so ingeniously. He was, however, gloomy rather than hopeless about human nature, and did not despair of the potential goodness of men as yet uncontaminated by society. He also believed in the possibility of satisfactory human relationships, speaking with attractive warmth of love and friendship.

Moderate as well as modest, La Bruyère was saved by common sense from the clever cynicism that is purely destructive, and his work is characterized by a positive and humane quality underlying the bitterest criticism. Although the *Caractères* falls short of absolute greatness, it reflects with exceptional accuracy the wane of the *grand siècle*.

See also Appearance and Reality; Bossuet, Jacques Bénigne; Continental Philosophy; La Rochefoucauld, Duc François de; Moral Epistemology; Pascal, Blaise; Theophrastus.

Bibliography

La Bruyère's *Les caractères*, edited by G. Servois, appeared in 3 vols. (Paris, 1865–1882) and was also issued by Bibliothèque de la Pléiade (Paris, 1934). It was translated by H. van Laun as *The Characters* (Oxford, 1963).

Works on La Bruyère are A. Adam, *Histoire de la littérature française au XVIIe siècle* (Paris, 1956), Vol. V, Ch. 6; M. Lange, *La Bruyère critique des conditions et des institutions sociales* (Paris, 1909); P. Richard, *La Bruyère et ses Caractères* (Amiens, 1946); F. Tavera, *L'idéal moral et l'idée religieuse dans les Caractères* (Paris: Mellottée, 1941); Edward C. Knox, *Jean de la Bruyère* (New York: Twayne Publishers, 1973).

A. J. Krailsheimer (1967)
Bibliography updated by Tamra Frei (2005)

LACAN, JACQUES
(1901–1981)

Jacques Lacan is undoubtedly the most philosophical of psychoanalytic authors. He developed his psychoanalytic theory of subjectivity—as a ferocious critique of the modern metaphysical tradition—in direct dialogue with a number of major philosophical figures: Descartes, Kant, Heidegger, and many others.

Lacan never had any formal philosophical training. After studying medicine and psychiatry, he got involved in the surrealist movement in the early 1930s. Along with Sartre and Bataille, he participated in Alexandre Kojève's famous seminars on Hegel's *Phenomenology of Spirit* at the Ecole des Hautes Etudes en Sciences Sociales. Lacan joined the Société Psychanalytique de Paris in 1936. Both his theories—specifically his critique of ego psychology, which he carried out under the label of a "return to Freud"—and his practice of short psychoanalytic sessions caused discord within the French and the international psychoanalytic movement in the fifties. As a result of this rift, Lacan and his followers founded the Société française de psychanalyse in 1956 and later the Ecole freudienne in

1963. In the beginning of the fifties, Lacan also started to give seminars in Paris that not only attracted psychoanalysts but also a great number of philosophers such as Jean Hyppolite and Paul Ricoeur. In this way, psychoanalysis became a central force within French philosophical thinking of the second half of the twentieth century.

Lacan's theory of the mirror stage is his first original contribution to psychoanalytic thinking. This theory was first formulated at a conference in Marienbad in 1936. Although it is a reformulation of Freud's theory of narcissism, it has important consequences for the philosophical reflection on the status of the subject. Indeed, according to Lacan, the ego is an effect of an identification with an image (paradigmatically the mirror image) that represents an ideal of unity and completeness and that is not the ego itself: "*Je est un autre.*" The ego is thus characterised by an alienation that cannot be undone. It gains access to itself only through the image of the other. In the mirror stage—and in all "imaginary" relations that function according to the same logic—the ego misrecognizes its difference from the image/ideal with which it identifies itself and of which it believes that it expresses its very essence.

Lacan's work of the 1930s and 1940s mainly consists of a detailed exploration of the characteristics and the dynamics of the mirror stage and the realm of the imaginary that is characterized by it. In this context, he specifically focuses on typical forms of human aggression. Human aggression is not primarily an effect of the frustration of vital needs. Indeed, since the ego structurally misrecognizes its difference from the image/ideal of the other with which it identifies itself, the latter also inevitably appears as an usurper that provokes aggressiveness. S/he indeed appears in the process at a place that seems to be rightfully mine. I desire what s/he desires because, on the basis of the identification, I am what s/he is. As a consequence, this desire is intrinsically conflictual. Lacan often refers in this context to Saint Augustine, who describes a scene in which a well-fed infant expresses uncontrollable anger at the sight of his baby brother being breastfed. This is a clear illustration of one of the meanings of Lacan's famous dictum that "desire is the desire of the other."

This intrinsic link between the mirror stage and human aggression explains why Lacan thinks of the former as an impasse that has to be overcome. The emergence of structuralism in the early fifties, and more particularly the publication of Levi-Strauss's *The Elementary Structures of Kinship* in 1949, allowed Lacan to explain once and for all how overcoming this impasse is possible. He now claimed that the symbolic order—the order of language and of the law—precedes and dominates the imaginary that is structured by it. Hence, the identification with the mirror image is only possible on the basis of a symbolic point of reference: "Look, that image in the mirror, that is little Jimmy."

Whereas in the thirties and forties Lacan mainly studied the dynamics of imaginary relations, during the fifties he focused on the relation between human beings and the symbolic order that he calls "the Other." Lacan turns to Hegel's idea that "the word is the murder of the thing." Entry into the symbolic order implies a loss of immediacy that desire tries to undo. This desire is essentially dependent on the symbolic order through which it takes shape. Humans desire in accordance with the symbolic systems in which they are born. Lacan shows, for instance, how the inability to write of one of his patients was linked to his youth in a Muslim country. When he was small, his father was accused of theft and, according to Islamic law, the hands of a thief should be cut off. This illustrates the second meaning of Lacan's dictum, "Desire is the desire of the Other." Here "the Other" indeed refers to the symbolic system—in the case of Lacan's patient: Islamic law—in which the subject participates without realizing its impact.

In the early 1960s, Lacan shifted his attention from the imaginary and the symbolic to the Real and the object a. Language consists, according to Lacan, of differentially determined signifiers whose meaning is completely dependent on the context in which they are used. Because there is no ultimate context that would end the production of meaning once and for all, the loss of immediacy can never be overcome or "sublated" in an ultimate synthesis. Something is irremediably lost and cannot be recuperated into the order of meaning (the imaginary and the symbolic). This is what Lacan calls the Real. This notion is intrinsically linked to Lacan's theory of the object a that is the cause (and not the telos) of desire. Examples of objects a include Freudian part-objects such as breast and feces as well as the voice and the gaze, which are paradigmatic examples of the object a, according to Lacan. The object a is a (dis)incarnation of the lack that causes desire: it gives the lack a bodily determination, on the one hand; at the same time, however, these objects cannot be grasped in the phenomenal world (when we reach for the gaze, we touch … the eye). In this way, they refer to the infinite character of human desire.

From the early 1960s onward, Lacan became more and more interested in topological figures like Borommean knots or rings. He believed that they could be used to articulate the fundamental structures of human subjectivity. Lacan died in 1981 in Paris.

See also Psychoanalysis.

Bibliography

WORKS BY JACQUES LACAN

Ecrits: A Selection. Translated by Bruce Fink. New York and London: Norton, 2004.

The Ethics of Psychoanalysis. Translated by Dennis Porter. New York and London: Norton, 1997.

The Four Fundamental Concepts of Psychoanalysis (The Seminar of Jacques Lacan, Book 11). Translated by A. Sheridan. New York and London: Norton, 1998.

On Feminine Sexuality, the Limits of Love and Knowledge: The Seminar of Jacques Lacan, Book XX, Encore. Translated by Bruce Fink. New York and London: Norton, 1999.

WORKS ON JACQUES LACAN

Borch-Jacobsen, M. *Lacan: The Absolute Master*. Palo Alto: Stanford University Press, 1991.

Fink, Bruce. *Lacan to the Letter: Reading* Ecrits *Closely*. Minneapolis: University of Minnesota Press, 2004.

Rabaté, J. M. *The Cambridge Companion to Lacan*. Cambridge University Press, 2003.

Van Haute, Philippe. *Against Adaptation: Jacques Lacan's "Subversion" of the Subject. A Comment*. New York: Other Press, 2002.

Philippe van Haute (2005)

LACHELIER, JULES
(1832–1918)

Jules Lachelier, the French idealist, was born at Fontainebleau and studied at the École Normale Supérieure in Paris. He received his *docteur ès lettres* in 1871 and held various professorial and administrative positions in the French educational system until his retirement from the post of *inspecteur général* in 1900. Lachelier joined with his teacher Jean Gaspard Félix Ravaisson-Mollien in founding the neospiritualist movement in French philosophy, a movement opposed to what seemed to be the naive acceptance of science and the scientific attitude in all phases of life. Among those who have acknowledged Lachelier's influence are Émile Boutroux, Victor Brochard, Jules Lagneau, and Henri Bergson.

Lachelier advanced a number of skeptical arguments that tend to reduce objects to phenomena, phenomena to sensations, and, more generally, to resolve the external world into thought. Nevertheless, he retained the conviction that we live in a common, objective world. Accordingly, his philosophy is directed toward the conclusion that the objectivity of our knowledge and experience is derived from mind. He summarized his idealistic philosophy as the discovery of "a thought which does not think, suspended from a thought which thinks itself."

To avoid the pitfalls of both the empiricism and the spiritualism of his day, Lachelier attempted to provide a basis for induction in a philosophy of nature. His procedure consisted of a Kantian reflection upon the necessary conditions for the existence of the world as we know it. He began by observing that, if knowledge is to be possible, sensations must exhibit the same unities that are found in phenomena. By eliminating competing hypotheses, he found that the unifying element within any phenomenon, as well as the unifying element among phenomena, is established by the necessary relations operative in them and is expressed by the law of efficient causes. The necessity of this law cannot be discovered in sensations alone, in phenomena as such, or in their mere juxtaposition; nor can it be isolated in any locus from which mind is separated. It must be regarded, rather, as a kind of unconscious but logical thought diffused throughout nature. The mechanical linkages among events in nature reflect the logical relations in thought. Lachelier concluded that the unity of thought and the formal unity of nature are inverses of each other.

Given a series of phenomena, the law of efficient cause is sufficient to account for their organization in a mechanically interrelated series. But the questions remain: Why do whole phenomena occur? How are several series of mechanically ordered individual phenomenal objects coordinated into groups in order to form complex and recurrent phenomena? The question of recurrence involves the problem of induction and indicates that some principle—in addition to the law of efficient causes—must be found to explain the recurrence of phenomena. If we are neither to stretch the principle of efficient causes beyond reasonable bounds nor to supplement it with some occult principle ex machina, then we must suppose that the whole phenomenon—complex yet persistent—contains the reasons for its unity and recurrence. Lachelier, like Immanuel Kant, recognized a whole to be an end when the whole contained the reason for the organization of its parts. (A whole of this kind is illustrated in a stable chemical compound or in a living organism.)

Thus, in view of the fact that we indisputably are aware of phenomena which are harmonious and recurring complexes or wholes of this sort, Lachelier arrived at a second principle: The law of final causes. By its operation, sensa are grouped into perceptions of which we are actually aware, and thus they provide content and reality for the necessary but empty form of the universal mechanism. This law is to the matter of phenomena what the law of efficient causes is to their form. In these terms the distinction is drawn between the abstract existence of mechanical nature and the concrete existence of teleologically unified but contingent individuals. Since all actual objects are complex, they all presuppose the operation of the law of final causes. This law is, then, prior to the law of efficient causes in respect to actual existence.

These two laws are not on the same logical footing. Lachelier regards the law of efficient causes as proved. The proof is of the Kantian type. Given coherent experiences, this law, which is logic projected into phenomena, expresses the condition under which they cohere and are intelligible. The law of final causes, however, is not reached in the same way. Presumably, simple phenomena might remain logically ordered while being grouped in different ways. Their actual grouping into the harmonious and persistent unities that we experience is the consequence of a law which operates more like an act of will than like a formal or logical requirement. Thus, the law of final causes is said to be regulative only.

The twin laws of efficient and final causes provide the foundation for induction. Induction is thereby "founded" in the sense that it is partly proved or derived from the conditions for experience and partly justified as expressing a teleology of nature. The practice of induction, therefore, may be expected to be partly the logical deduction of events from previous events, and partly a "divining" that natural phenomena will cooperate with each other in a given way under given circumstances.

This foundation, however, is not ultimate. It does not explain why these two laws alone are the ordering principles of our existent world. Lachelier, in considering this point, observed that some organisms realize to a higher degree than others that harmony toward which nature moves. In fact, the law of final causes entails a whole hierarchy of beings that increase in order and harmony. The more complexly unified organisms in nature are not the chance products of accidentally unified simpler organisms. Rather, the simpler organisms, implicit in the more complex ones, are separated from them by a kind of "division and refraction."

The human being can free himself in thought from the particular mechanical conditions of phenomena. He has the capacity to separate some perceptions from others and, using them as symbols, to represent general properties of things. In his ability to abstract and gener-

alize, the human being, although distinguished from all other things by this capacity, can be said to be in contact with the whole universe. The universe can be discovered again in thought but under a new condition, freedom. In addition, man is free because he can select the means and ends of his activity by reference to ideas. Hence, through man, the realm of final causes and the freedom that is its condition penetrate the organic and mechanical realms. Furthermore, without freedom it would be impossible to conceive of either mechanism or finality. Thus, the laws of efficient and final causality, upon which induction is founded, are themselves founded upon freedom—and freedom is the essential property of thought.

The process of founding induction within a philosophy of nature, therefore, consists partly in a demonstration and partly in a discovery of regulative rules. Finally, the process terminates in a metaphysics that affirms the basic reality of thought. This metaphysics is intended to found the philosophy of nature in the sense of providing a reason for belief in the unity of its laws and in its idealistic source. Lachelier's metaphysics of freedom is further developed in his article "Psychologie et métaphysique" (1885) and is given a religious dimension in "Le pari de Pascal" (1901).

See also Bergson, Henri; Continental Philosophy; Idealism; Induction; Kant, Immanuel; Ravaisson-Mollien, Jean Gaspard Félix.

Bibliography

WORKS BY LACHELIER

Oeuvres de Jules Lachelier. 2 vols. Paris: Alcan, 1933.

Lachelier, la nature, l'esprit, Dieu. Edited by Louis Millet. Paris, 1955.

The Philosophy of Jules Lachelier. Edited by Edward G. Ballard. The Hague: Nijhoff, 1960. Contains an introduction and translations by Ballard of "Du fondement de l'induction," "Psychologie et métaphysique," "Le pari de Pascal," and several short writings.

WORKS ON LACHELIER

Devivaise, C. "La philosophic religieuse de Jules Lachelier." *Revue des sciences philosophiques et théologiques* (1939): 435–464.

Mauchaussat, Gaston. *L'idéalisme de Lachelier.* Paris: Presses Universitaires de France, 1961.

Millet, Louis. *Le symbolisme dans la philosophie de Jules Lachelier.* Paris, 1959. Contains a comprehensive bibliography of Lachelier's writings and of the commentaries.

Noël, Georges. "La philosophie de M. Lachelier." *Revue de métaphysique et de morale* (1898): 230–259.

Séailles, Gabriel. *La philosophie de Jules Lachelier.* Paris, 1921.

Edward G. Ballard (1967)

LAKATOS, IMRE
(1922–1974)

LIFE

Imre Lakatos did important work in the 1960s and 1970s in the philosophy both of mathematics and science. He was born Imré Lipsitz in Debrecen Hungary, and by the time he left for England after the Hungarian Uprising in 1956, he had already lived a complex, charged, and controversial life. A convinced and influential Marxist, he had been unofficial leader of a group of young Jews in hiding from the Nazis after the invasion in 1944. As a high ranking official in the Ministry of Education after the war, he was involved in significant and controversial education reform before being arrested by the secret police in 1953 and held for three years under appalling conditions, sometimes in solitary confinement, in Recsk—the worst of the Gulag-style camps in Hungary.

He studied mathematics, physics, and philosophy at the University of Debrecen, graduating in 1944. He obtained a first PhD (with highest honors) from the Eötvös Collegium in 1947—this for a thesis on the sociology of science that he later insisted was worthless. After leaving Hungary in 1956, he obtained a Rockefeller Foundation grant to study for a second PhD at the University of Cambridge. From 1959 onward he regularly attended Karl Popper's seminar at the London School of Economics (LSE). Popper became the most important influence on him; amongst other things, Popper's Open Society views reinforced the decline of his faith in Marxism that had begun in 1956. Lakatos accepted a lectureship in logic at LSE in 1960 and was promoted to a personal chair (in Logic, with special reference to the philosophy of mathematics) in 1970. He was only fifty-one years old and still teaching at LSE at the sadly early time of his death from a heart attack in 1974.

PHILOSOPHY OF MATHEMATICS

Lakatos's Cambridge PhD thesis became the basis for his *Proofs and Refutations*. This work, published initially in the form of journal articles in 1963–1964 and in book form only posthumously in 1976, constitutes his major contribution to the philosophy of mathematics. A dialogue between a group of frighteningly bright students and their teacher, it reconstructs the process by which Euler's famous conjecture about polyhedra (that they all satisfy the formula: number of vertices plus number of faces minus the number of edges equals two) was proved and, in the process, heavily modified and transformed.

Lakatos's claim was that although the eventual proof of the theorem in mathematics may be cast as a straightforward deduction, the process by which the proof is found is a more exciting process, involving counterexamples, reformulations, counterexamples to the reformulations, and careful analysis of failed proofs leading to further modifications of the theorem. Any number of interesting claims about both the history and philosophy of mathematics are thrown in to the mix—sometimes in the main text, sometimes in one of the voluminous footnotes. The work is a literary tour de force.

The extent to which *Proofs and Refutations* represents a distinctive epistemological view that might challenge more traditional accounts in the philosophy of mathematics, such as logicism or formalism, is a controversial one. Lakatos sometimes described himself as extending Popper's fallibilist-falsificationist view of science into the field of mathematics, and there are even hints of Lakatos's Hegelian past in some of the claims about the autonomous development of mathematics. An alternative view, however, is that the main significance of his work is to cast light simply, though importantly, on the development of mathematics—on how mathematical truth is arrived at—and that it has nothing distinctive to say about the epistemological status of mathematical truths once they have been arrived at. But even if this alternative view is correct, there is a good of undoubtedly epistemological significance in some of the particular issues raised (for example, what he calls the problem of translation highlighting issues about how the formal systems, within which effectively infallible proof can be achieved, relate to the informal mathematics said to be captured by those formal systems).

PHILOSOPHY OF SCIENCE

As indicated, Lakatos thought of himself for some years as extending Popperianism, developed as an account of natural science, into the seemingly unlikely field of mathematics. However, he eventually began to discern faults in Popper's philosophy of natural science. Most significantly, in comparing Popper's views with those of Thomas Kuhn, Lakatos came to realize that Popper's view on the way that evidence impacts on scientific theories is seriously awry.

Lakatos claimed that science is best viewed as consisting not of single, isolated theories but rather of broader research programs. A hard core of principles characterizes such a program, but this needs to be supplemented by an evolving protective belt of more specific and auxiliary assumptions in order to come into contact with experiment. When the latest theory produced by a program proves to be inconsistent with some empirical result, then the standard response of the program's proponents will be to retain the hard core and look to modify some element of the protective belt. This is a process much closer to Kuhn's idea of adverse experimental results being treated as anomalies than to the standard Popperian idea of falsification. However, while Popper used his framework to defend the idea that theory-change in science is a rational process, Lakatos believed that to accept Kuhn's account of paradigms and paradigm shifts was in effect to abandon the view that the development of science is rational. Kuhn's view, he (in)famously claimed, makes theory-change a matter of mob psychology. He was therefore led to make the important distinction between progressive and degenerating programs. The latest Newtonian theory was inconsistent with observations of Uranus's orbit; Newtonians reacted not by giving up the basic theory but by postulating a new planet.

Philip Gosse (1810–1888) realized that claim that God created the world essentially as it now is in 4004 BC is inconsistent with what Darwinians believed to be the fossil record; Gosse reacted not by surrendering the basic creationist theory (hard core), but by postulating that the alleged fossils were parts of God's initial creation. The first was a great scientific success; the second bears the clear hallmark of pseudoscience. Why? Lakatos's answer is that the Newtonian shift was progressive: It not only solved the anomaly of Uranus but made extra predictions (of the existence of a new and hitherto unsuspected planet) that could be tested empirically and were indeed confirmed (by the discovery of Neptune). Gosse's shift is degenerating: All it does is reconcile the basic creationist theory with observation but permits no independent test. The development of science consists of the replacement of degenerating programs by progressive ones. There are many other interesting aspects of the methodology, particularly concerning the role of heuristic principles, and of whether it does satisfactorily save the rationality of science.

See also Epistemology; Hegel, Georg Wilhelm Friedrich; Kuhn, Thomas; Logic, History of: Precursors of Modern Logic: Euler; Marx, Karl; Newton, Isaac; Philosophy of Science; Popper, Karl Raimund.

Bibliography

WORKS BY LAKATOS

With Alan Musgrave, eds. *Criticism and the Growth of Knowledge.* Cambridge, U.K.: Cambridge University Press, 1970.

Proofs and Refutations. The Logic of Mathematical Discovery, edited by John Worrall and E.G. Zahar. Cambridge, U.K.: Cambridge University Press, 1976.

The Methodology of Scientific Research Programmes and Mathematics, Science and Epistemology. Philosophical Papers. Vols. 1 and 2, edited by John Worrall and Gregory Currie. Cambridge, U.K.: Cambridge University Press, 1978.

With Paul Feyerabend. *For and Against Method: Including Lakatos's Lectures on Scientific Method and the Lakatos-Feyerabend Correspondence,* edited and with an introduction by Matteo Motterlini. Chicago, IL: University of Chicago Press. 1999.

WORKS BY OTHERS

Kampis, George, Ladislav Kvasz, and Michael Stölzner, eds. *Appraising Lakatos: Mathematics, Methodology and the Man.* Dordrecht, Netherlands: Kluwer, 2002.

Larvor, Brendon. *Lakatos: An Introduction.* London: Routledge, 1998.

John Worrall (2005)

LALANDE, ANDRÉ
(1867–1964)

André Lalande, the French philosopher, was born in Dijon and entered the École Normale Supérieure in 1885. He took his doctorate in 1899 and taught in *lycées* until he was appointed first to a lectureship and then, in 1904, to a chair of philosophy at the University of Paris.

Lalande was a rationalist whose whole life was devoted to the cause of international communication and the dissemination of knowledge. His constant preoccupation after 1902 was the launching, and subsequent reediting, of the *Vocabulaire technique et critique de la philosophie,* which aimed at the concise definition and standardization of philosophical terminology. His own philosophical work corresponds to this recognition and promotion of an interdependent humanity.

In his thesis of 1899, *L'idée directrice de la dissolution opposée à celle de l'évolution,* Lalande challenged Herbert Spencer's thesis that progress is evolutionary and differentiating, and held that, on the contrary, dissolution—or, as he later called it, involution—is more widespread and significant. Involution, or movement from the heterogeneous to the homogeneous, is observable in nature as entropy, or increase of randomness. In human life, however, this movement toward uniformity is fruitful and is served by reason, which, in scientific investigation, leads to the progressive subsumption of more and more classes of phenomena under fewer general laws.

Lalande disapproved of an imposed uniformity, which represents merely the transference from the individual to the group of evolutionary, divisive drives. True reason ensures that although people feel differently, they shall think in the same way and thus understand each other even when they do not resemble each other. Lalande's concern was for the individual, whose uniqueness is sacrificed to function in a rigidly specialized and differentiated society. The application of reason to life in the technological field liberates the individual from his functional role, and the application of reason in the cultural field enables men to afford, and to benefit from, the diversity that is their birthright.

In *La raison et les normes* Lalande restated his involutionist case in the light of recent philosophies of "being-in-the-world." He took cognizance, for example, of the argument that geometrical, objective space is derived from the neuromotor "spaces" of man facing his tasks, but for Lalande the superiority of a common space amenable to conceptualization remained unimpaired. Similarly, he preferred chronological time to the "real" time of naive emotional experience. Lalande reaffirmed his universalist conception of rationality against more recent phenomenological thinking.

See also Continental Philosophy; Rationalism.

Bibliography

WORKS BY LALANDE

Lectures sur la philosophic des sciences. Paris, 1893; and Paris: Hachette, 1907.

L'idée directrice de la dissolution opposée à celle de l'évolution. Paris, 1899; revised and reissued as *Les illusions évolutionnistes.* Paris, 1930.

Quid de Mathematica vel Rationali vel Naturali Senserit Baconus Verulamius. Paris, 1899. Latin thesis.

Précis raisonné de morale pratique. Paris: Hachette, 1907.

Les théories de l'induction et de l'expérimentation. Paris: Boivin, 1929.

La raison et les normes. Paris, 1948.

Vocabulaire technique et critique de la philosophic, 8th ed. Paris: Presses Universitaires de France, 1960.

WORKS ON LALANDE

Lavelle, L. *La philosophic française entre les deux guerres.* Paris, 1942.

Smith, Colin. *Contemporary French Philosophy.* New York: Barnes and Noble, 1964.

Colin Smith (1967)

LAMARCK, CHEVALIER DE
(1744–1829)

Jean Baptiste Pierre Antoine de Monet, Chevalier de Lamarck, the French biologist and formulator of the first comprehensive theory of evolution, was born at Bazentin-le-Petit, a village in northeastern France. As a youth he studied briefly for the priesthood, but later withdrew to follow the family tradition of army service. While in Paris recovering from an injury and intermittently studying medicine, he met Jean-Jacques Rousseau, through whom he became interested in botany. This interest led to investigations that culminated in the publication of a large work on the flora of France, which brought Lamarck immediate fame and election to the Academy of Sciences. From 1783 to 1793 he held a small post at the Jardin du Roi, which was reorganized and expanded along lines proposed by Lamarck to include a museum of natural history and twelve professorial chairs. The last of these, for the study of invertebrates, went almost by default to Lamarck himself. Hence, at the age of fifty he began his indefatigable labors as a zoologist. These labors led to his conclusion, at some time between 1794 and 1802, that a transmutation of animal species had taken place. He expounded his views in a succession of important works: *Système des animaux sans vertèbres* (Paris, 1801), *Rechêrches sur l'organisation des corps vivans* (Paris, 1802), *Philosophie zoologique* (2 vols., Paris, 1809–1830, translated by H. Elliot as *Zoological Philosophy,* London, 1914), and *Histoire naturelle des animaux sans vertèbres,* (7 vols., Paris, 1815–1822). The significance of Lamarck's contribution was scarcely appreciated by his contemporaries. When he died at the age of eighty-five, blind and poor, he had become a forgotten man. His body was buried in a pauper's grave whose exact location is unknown.

SYSTEM OF NATURE

Lamarck aspired to produce a large-scale "system of nature" set in a deistic framework. He held that nature, "the immense totality of different beings," is neither eternal nor self-explanatory. It is the creation of a "Supreme Author" who brought matter into being and instituted the world order by means of laws that govern whatever happens. Within nature, change is universal. But nature in toto is unchangeable and "should be regarded as a whole constituted by its parts, for a purpose which its Author alone knows." This whole, however, is as distinct from the Creator as a watch is from the watchmaker. Hence, nature has productive powers of its own that the sciences can properly interpret in mechanical and materialistic terms. The system that Lamarck originally planned was to have included sections on physics, chemistry, meteorology, geology, and biology. Some of his writings did, in fact, discuss all these topics, but what appeared can hardly be said to form a unified scheme. His attention was increasingly occupied by his reflections on living things, the science of which he named biology in 1802.

EVOLUTION

Lamarck effected a breakthrough to an evolutionary conception of nature by bringing together several lines of thought. His geological studies convinced him that Earth had endured for an immense span of time, during which it had undergone many changes of a gradual sort, especially in its surface features. His observation of fossils supported the conclusion that animal life had existed for a large part of geological time and had also undergone gradual changes. Hence, species must be mutable, and their apparent stability is due to man's limited time perspective. Furthermore, organisms are simply physical bodies whose parts are highly organized. Thus, Lamarck was opposed to vitalism. "Every fact or phenomenon observed in a living body," he held, "is ... a physical fact or phenomenon, and a product of organization" (*Histoire naturelle des animaux sans vertèbres,* Vol. I, p. 53). Accordingly, he accepted the conclusion that a "spontaneous generation" of organisms had occurred. Animals and plants represent two independent lines stemming from two distinct types of spontaneous generation that utilized chemical materials differently. These materials are wholly inanimate and display none of the characteristic properties observed in the organisms they constitute.

PERFECTING POWER IN NATURE

The history of living things on Earth reveals a steady increase in the complexity of their organization, a process by which they have also been perfected. "Nature has produced all the species of animals in succession, beginning with the most imperfect or simplest, and ending her work with the most perfect." Man is the being who exemplifies the highest excellence of bodily organization, and he thereby provides "the standard for judging the perfection or degradation of other animal organizations." Lamarck's thought at this point was influenced by the idea of the "great chain of being," the infinitely graded series of forms from highest to lowest, which was a doctrine congenial to eighteenth-century deism. Since, in his evolutionary approach, the series came into existence from the bottom, Lamarck attributed it to a perfecting power inherent in nature. The postulating of this perfecting power is the feature of Lamarck's evolutionism that separates it most sharply from that of Charles Darwin.

CAUSES OF THE POWER OF EVOLUTION

If the environment were unchanging, the perfecting power of nature would produce a simple, linear sequence of organisms. But the environment is ceaselessly changing, and, as a result, evolution is "deflected" from a linear path into the "branching" pattern actually found among plants and animals. The mechanism by which the branching pattern is formed consists of a group of causal factors often mistakenly supposed to be the whole of Lamarck's theory, instead of just a part of it.

The causal factors are specified in several "laws"—two in *Philosophie zoologique* and four in *Histoire naturelle des animaux*—whose purport can be summarized as follows. The organs and habits by which animals maintain their adaptation to the environment are controlled by bodily fluids that are constantly in motion. Animals whose structure is so elementary that they have no faculty of feeling are acted on mechanically by environmental changes. New motions of the internal fluids are set up, and these give rise to adaptive alterations in the organs and habits. The case is different with animals whose structure is complicated enough to enable them to feel wants or needs (*besoins*). When the environment of these animals changes, new needs are felt, and each need, "exciting their inner feeling (*sentiment intérieur*), forthwith sets the fluids in motion and forces them toward the point of the body where an action may satisfy the want experienced" (ibid., p. 185). If a suitable organ already exists at that point, it is immediately incited to action. If not, the felt need gradually causes the organ to be generated, "provided the need be pressing and continuous." Everything thus acquired by an individual animal during its lifetime is preserved by heredity (*génération*) and transmitted to that individual's progeny. The operation of these causal factors, superimposed on the general perfecting tendency of nature, accounts for all that has happened in evolution.

MAN

Man's place in this theory was a topic that Lamarck understandably treated with caution. He stressed man's "extreme superiority" over other living things because of his possession of reason, although anatomically he differs only in degree from monkeys and apes. Is it not plausible to suppose that the differences have been "gradually acquired" over a long period of time? "What a subject for reflection," Lamarck commented, "for those who have the courage to enter into it!" He himself dared in a short section of *Philosophie zoologique* to outline a hypothetical explanation of how apelike beings might "at length be transformed" into manlike beings, able to walk upright, to use tools, and to develop "the marvelous faculty of speaking." Throughout the process, changed habits would produce new wants and new capacities, until true human beings appeared. "Such are the reflections which might be aroused, if man were distinguished from animals only by his organization, and if his origin were not different from theirs." At this point Lamarck's courage apparently gave out.

ASSESSMENT

Despite the comprehensiveness of his outlook, Lamarck failed to formulate a unified theory of evolution. Therefore, he had to conclude that the diversification of plants and simple animals was due to mechanical factors alone, whereas in the case of complex animals an important psychological and teleological factor was operative. He held that no species had ever been totally extinguished, in spite of what the fossil evidence indicated, because he believed that the plan of the Supreme Author of the universe would not allow such wastage. His acceptance of the perfecting tendency obliged him to affirm that there are really two animal series: the grand one from simple to complex, and the particular, branching series that have deviated from it. Above all, his theory demanded not only that modifications acquired by parents during their lifetime should affect their offspring, but also that they should affect the same parts in the offspring as in the parents and should become a permanent hereditary feature in that line of descent, regardless of later modifying factors. Modern genetic research has shown strong, although perhaps not conclusive, reasons for believing that such an "inheritance of acquired characteristics" cannot occur. None of these difficulties, however, can detract from the greatness of Lamarck's contribution. "He first did the eminent service," Darwin remarked, "of arousing attention to the probability of all change in the organic world being the result of law, and not of miraculous interposition."

See also Darwin, Charles Robert; Darwinism; Evolutionary Theory; Laws of Nature; Rousseau, Jean-Jacques; Vitalism.

Bibliography

Cannon, H. G. *Lamarck and Modern Genetics.* Springfield, IL: Thomas, 1960.

Gillispie, C. C. "The Formation of Lamarck's Evolutionary Theory." *Archives internationale d'histoire des sciences* 35 (1956): 323–338.

Gillispie, C. C. "Lamarck and Darwin in the History of Science." *American Scientist* 46 (1958): 388–409.

Landrieu, Marcel. *Lamarck.* Paris: Société Zoologique de France, 1909.

Packard, A. S. *Lamarck, the Founder of Evolution.* New York: n.p., 1901.

Russell, E. S. *Form and Function.* Cambridge, U.K.: Murray, 1916. Ch. 13.

Wilkie, J. S. "Buffon, Lamarck and Darwin." In *Darwin's Biological Work,* edited by P. R. Bell, 262–307. Cambridge, U.K.: Cambridge University Press, 1959.

T. A. Goudge (1967)

LAMBERT, JOHANN HEINRICH
(1728–1777)

Johann Heinrich Lambert, the German mathematician, physicist, astronomer, and philosopher, was born in Mulhouse, Alsace. He taught himself mathematics, philosophy, and Asian languages; after 1748 he served as tutor in a Swiss family, traveling about Europe with his pupils for several years. He became a member of the Munich Academy in 1759 and of the Berlin Academy in 1764. In 1765 he was appointed by Frederick II as Prussian surveyor of public works. He did research in heat, light, and color and was the founder of the science of photometry. In mathematics Lambert demonstrated that π is an irrational number, and he introduced the conception of hyperbolic functions into trigonometry. In his *Kosmologische Briefe über die Einrichtung des Weltbaues* (Cosmological letters on the structure of the universe; Augsburg, 1761), Lambert proposed a cosmogonic hypothesis based on Isaac Newton's theory of gravitation; it was similar to the nebular hypothesis proposed earlier by Immanuel Kant in his *Allgemeine Naturgeschichte und Theorie des Himmels* (Königsberg and Leipzig, 1755) but unknown to Lambert.

Lambert's *Neues Organon, oder Gedanken über die Erforschung und Bezeichnung des Wahren und dessen Unterscheidung von Irrtum und Schein* (New organon, or thoughts on the investigation and indication of truth and of the distinction between error and appearance; 2 vols., Leipzig, 1764) was an attempt to reform Wolffian logic. It was strongly influenced by the logical treatises of the Pietist philosophers A. F. Hoffmann and C. F. Crusius, and like their work it widened the field of logic to cover psychological and methodological questions. Although Lambert believed that metaphysics should follow a mathematical method, he assumed, like the Pietists and John

Locke, a multiplicity of elementary notions. The a priori sciences (pure theoretical and practical philosophy) should be constructed by combining these elementary notions mathematically. The final section of the *Neues Organon* discusses appearance and gives a theory of experimental and probable knowledge. It contains rules for distinguishing false (or subjective) appearance from true (or objective) appearance, the latter arising from true perception of the phenomenal world. As a blend of Leibnizian, Wolffian, Lockean, and Pietist elements the *Neues Organon* was neither more original nor more influential in its time than several Pietist treatises on logic or J. B. Basedow's *Philalethie.*

The lesser-known *Anlage zur Architektonik, oder Theorie des Einfachen und Ersten in der philosophischen und mathematischen Erkentniss* (Foundation of architectonic, or theory of the simple and primary elements in philosophical and mathematical knowledge; 2 vols., Riga, 1771) was a much more important work. In this work Lambert, dissatisfied with classical German and particularly Wolffian metaphysics, proposed a far-reaching reform through an analysis of the sources, genesis, and development of the basic concepts and axioms of metaphysics and their interrelations. Reacting also against sensationalism, skepticism, and the new schools of commonsense and popular philosophy, Lambert wished to save metaphysics by presenting it in a phenomenalistic manner (as J. N. Tetens and Kant were to do later).

Following Locke, Lambert assumed a certain set of concepts as given and then examined them. Once the analysis was completed, Lambert held, it would be possible to change from an empirical to a rationalistic procedure—the a priori deductive construction, modeled on the procedures of mathematics, of a body of general sciences that are true both logically and metaphysically. The deduced propositions of these sciences would then be applied to experience in the manner of applied mathematics. The joining of such propositions with rules abstracted from observation and experiments would give a foundation for truth in each of the particular sciences.

There were thus two main aspects to Lambert's philosophy, the analytic and the constructive. The former was the predominating interest in the *Anlage zur Architektonik.* This work consists largely of detailed discussions of, and subtle distinctions between, many of the most common simple notions and axioms and elementary interrelations discussed in traditional metaphysics. This refined analysis, too detailed even to be sampled here, exerted a great influence on Teten's mature work and on the making of Kant's *Kritik der reinen Vernunft.* Kant had

earlier been much impressed by the *Neues Organon,* and acknowledged to Lambert in correspondence his interest in Lambert's analyses.

The second, constructive, aspect of Lambert's philosophy was an attempt to develop a mathematical logic (or "intensional calculus") for deducing propositions by an easy and exact method from the simple notions and axioms, once they have been established analytically.

See also Crusius, Christian August; Kant, Immanuel; Locke, John; Logic, History of; Metaphysics; Newton, Isaac; Tetens, Johann Nicolaus.

Bibliography

ADDITIONAL WORKS BY LAMBERT

Deutscher gelehrter Briefwechsel. 5 vols. Edited by Johann Bernoulli. Berlin, 1781–1787. Correspondence.

Logische und philosophische Abhandlungen. 2 vols. Edited by Johann Bernoulli. Berlin and Dessau, 1782.

Abhandlungen vom Criterium Veritatis. Edited by K. Bopp. Berlin: Reuther and Reichard, 1915.

Über die Methode, die Metaphysik, Theologie und Moral richtiger zu beweisen. Edited by K. Bopp. Berlin: Reuther and Reichard, 1918.

WORKS ON LAMBERT

Arndt, H. W. *Der Moglichkeitsbegriff bei Chr. Wolff und J. H. Lambert.* Göttingen, 1959. A mimeographed thesis.

Baensch, O. *J. H. Lambert und seine Stellung zu Kant.* Tübingen, 1902.

Eisenring, M. E. *Johann Heinrich Lambert und die wissenschaftliche Philosophie der Gegenwart.* Zürich, 1942.

Huber, D. *J. H. Lambert nach seinem Leben und Wirken.* Basel, 1829.

Krienelke, K. *J. H. Lamberts Philosophie der Mathematik.* Berlin, 1909.

Lepsius, Johann. *J. H. Lambert.* Munich, 1881.

Zimmermann, R. *Lambert der Vorgänger Kants.* Vienna, 1879.

Giorgio Tonelli (1967)

LAMENNAIS, HUGUES FÉLICITÉ ROBERT DE
(1782–1854)

Hugues Félicité Robert de Lamennais, the French ecclesiastic and philosopher, was born in Saint-Malo, Brittany, and died in Paris. Lamennais received the tonsure in 1809 but was not ordained a priest until 1816. His early works in defense of ultramontanism won him the approval of Rome, but it was not long before his inability to compromise in the interest of expediency led to his condemnation. Although never excommunicated, he voluntarily relinquished all sacerdotal functions and died after refusing the last rites.

ULTRAMONTANISM

Lamennais's first influential work, *De la tradition de l'église sur l'institution des évêques* (Paris, 1814), written in collaboration with his brother Jean, was an attack on Gallicanism. Directly inspired by Vicomte de Bonald, it propounded three theses—the supremacy of the Church of Rome, papal infallibility in matters of doctrine, and the basic authority of tradition. It did not, however, grant the pope any sovereign rights in temporal matters. Lamennais's second work, the *Essai sur l'indifférence en matière de religion* (1817–1823) was welcomed enthusiastically in Catholic circles and received the approval of Leo XII. It took as its premises that no beliefs are without influence on the welfare of society and that religious beliefs are of primary importance in this respect. Hence, no man has the right to be neutral in religious disputes. Neutrality may arise from false notions of religion's place in life, from a failure to distinguish between orthodoxy and heresy, or from ignorance, lack of serious purpose, or simple sloth. Since no one can rightly maintain two antithetical ideas, there can be only one religious truth, one mouthpiece for it, and one tradition.

TRADITIONALISM

The traditionalism involved in this led to Lamennais's denial of the individual's rational powers, a denial that he clung to consistently. Our senses, feelings, and reason may lead to the truth, but only accidentally. Certitude can be acquired only by the common reason, that of the human race. One must therefore fuse his opinions with those of his fellow men and find the solution to his problems in faith, authority, and common sense. Trust in one's own insight is madness, as is eccentricity of behavior. But if one asks whence comes the authority of the general reason, the answer is, from God. God has entrusted it to the church, which speaks through the pope. No individual philosopher, even though he be a Descartes, can substitute his method for that based on revelation.

THE CONDEMNATION

So extreme a form of ultramontanism may have been logical, granted its premises, but it was politically inexpedient. Its anti-Gallicanism alone would have aroused resentment, but it was coupled with violent attacks on the French university system, the Charter, and certain personalities, such as Comte Denis de Frayssinous. Lamennais paid little attention to his critics, turned from them

to the Vatican, and was shocked to receive in 1832 the encyclical *Mirari Vos*, which, without mentioning him by name, nevertheless condemned his ultramontanism on the ground that it disrupted the existing harmony between church and state. At the same time, it condemned freedom of conscience and opinion, which could lead only to freedom to err. Lamennais submitted but restricted his submission to questions of religion. During this period he also published his *Paroles d'un croyant* (1834), a series of prose poems that preached fraternity, freedom of association, and confidence in God and in prayer. This work was condemned outright in the encyclical *Singulari Nos* (1834).

PHILOSOPHY

In substituting "the Christianity of the human race" for that of the Vatican, Lamennais retained his traditionalism but abandoned his ultramontanism. His point of view was expressed in a three-volume work, the *Esquisse d'une philosophie* (1840), of which he published a fourth volume in 1846. It began with a theology, continued through a philosophical anthropology, aesthetics, and philosophy of science, and was to have been completed with a social philosophy. Lamennais's theology was Trinitarian and made the three persons of the Deity power, intelligence, and love, all interfused. Each realm of being reflected this triune nature, which was undemonstrable but demanded by the very nature of human thought. The work as a whole developed this thesis.

Lamennais's philosophy was Christian traditionalism minus ecclesiasticism, but with a philosophy of nature added. No man, he held, can assent to his own deductions if they are not in harmony with those of the whole human race, and the opinions of the human race will be found in tradition. The inconsistencies of tradition were never dwelt upon. His *Esquisse*, because of its Christian overtones, had no popularity in republican circles and, as for his Catholic associates, they felt little if any need for it.

See also Bonald, Louis Gabriel Ambroise, Vicomte de; Continental Philosophy; Traditionalism.

Bibliography

WORKS BY LAMENNAIS

De la tradition de l'église sur l'institution des évêques. 3 vols. Liège and Paris, 1814.

Essai sur l'indifférence en matière de religion. 4 vols. Paris, 1817–1823.

Défense de l'essai sur l'indifférence. Paris, 1821.

Paroles d'un croyant. Paris, 1834.

Oeuvres complètes. 12 vols. Paris: n.p., 1836–1837. Not complete.

Oeuvres choisies et philosophiques. 10 vols. Paris, 1837–1841.

Esquisse d'une philosophie. 4 vols. Paris, 1840–1846.

Amschaspands et Darvands. Paris, 1843.

WORKS ON LAMENNAIS

Duine, F. *La mennais.* Évreux, 1922. The most authoritative work, based in part on previously unpublished material.

Gibson, William. *The Abbé de Lamennais and the Liberal Catholic Movement in France.* London and New York: Longmans, Green, 1896.

Janet, Paul. *La philosophie de Lamennais.* Paris: Alcan, 1890.

Mourre, M. *Lamennais, ou l'hérésie des temps modernes.* Paris: Amiot-Dumont, 1955.

Spuller, Eugène. *Lamennais: étude d'histoire politique et religieuse.* Paris, 1892.

George Boas (1967)

LA METTRIE, JULIEN OFFRAY DE
(1709–1751)

Julien Offray de La Mettrie, the French physician and philosopher, was born in Saint-Malo, Brittany. After attending the Collège d'Harcourt, he studied medicine at the University of Paris, finally obtaining his doctor's degree from the Faculty of Rheims in 1733. He next went to Leiden to complete his training under the celebrated Dr. Hermann Boerhaave, whose iatromechanist doctrines were to have a decisive influence on his orientation in the philosophical, no less than in the medical, domain. Back in Saint-Malo as a practicing physician, La Mettrie undertook to popularize Boerhaave's teachings by translating into French a number of the latter's principal works. His marriage in 1739 to Marie-Louise Droneau proved unhappy and led before long to a separation. From 1743 to 1745 La Mettrie, as surgeon to the *Gardes Françaises* regiment, participated in several campaigns of the War of the Austrian Succession. The publication in 1745 of his first philosophical work, the *Histoire naturelle de l'âme*, brought him under severe official censure for his materialist views. This circumstance, along with an imprudent satire he wrote on the foibles of his medical colleagues, caused La Mettrie to exile himself to Holland. It was there that he published in 1747 *L'homme machine*, his best known and most influential book, whose atheistic and materialistic contents aroused even the liberal-minded Dutch to angry protest.

La Mettrie was fortunate enough, at this crucial moment, to find a protector in Frederick the Great, who invited him to Berlin. In Prussia he was appointed a member of the Royal Academy of Sciences, as well as "physician ordinary" and "reader" to the king. Profiting from the security of his position, he brought out, among other writings, *L'homme plante* (1748), *Le système d'Epicure* (1750), and *Discours sur le bonheur* (1750), each of which attested, in its own way, to the sort of scandalizing unorthodoxy of thought for which their author had already acquired a unique reputation. His numerous enemies, powerless to suppress either him or his ideas, contented themselves with a plethora of refutations that were too often irrelevant in substance or abusive in tone; in particular, they drew a portrait of La Mettrie himself as a monster of depravity. But apart from his theoretical advocacy and personal pursuit of a frankly hedonistic ideal and his delight in provoking or shocking those of a stiffly bourgeois or pious outlook, La Mettrie's character was actually far from deserving the ignominy heaped upon it. He died in 1751 of what was regarded by his contemporaries, somewhat unkindly, as the effects of overeating—a diagnosis exploited by his foes to prove both the practical dangers of materialism and the providential punishment reserved for atheists. Frederick II composed the eulogy that was read before the Berlin Academy. Besides his philosophical works, La Mettrie wrote several medical treatises of only minor value, a series of polemical and ironical pamphlets aimed at his critics, and three mordant, informative satires on what he considered to be the incompetence and "malpractice" of the doctors of the period, the best being his *Machiavel en médecine* (1748–1750).

"THE HISTORY OF THE SOUL"

In the *Histoire naturelle de l'âme*, directed against the metaphysical dualism of René Descartes, Nicolas Malebranche, Gottfried Wilhelm Leibniz, and their followers, La Mettrie contended that the soul owes its being to those specific organic forms, produced by a *force motrice* inhering in matter, on which the mental faculties and operations remain dependent. The "history of the soul" thus becomes an aspect of the body's history and falls under the authority, not of the metaphysician or theologian, but of the natural scientist. In this claim we have the fundamental attitude of La Mettrie, from which his originality as a philosopher would spring. His method of inquiry consisted in moving regularly from the empirical sphere of scientific facts and theories to that of philosophy proper—the latter being regarded, at least with respect to epistemological and psychological problems, as the logical extension of such branches of knowledge as anatomy, physiology, chemistry, medicine, and the like. La Mettrie was perhaps the first "medical" philosopher in the complete and true sense—a designation suggesting at once the strengths and weaknesses peculiar to his thought.

In the *Histoire de l'âme*, La Mettrie sought to substantiate his naturalistic conception of the soul by means of two types of evidence, profusely cited, which tend to complement each other. Drawing, on the one hand, from the common fund of Lockean sensationalism (to which he gave, incidentally, a materialist meaning), La Mettrie argued that the contents of the mind—hence the mind itself—have no reality independently of the natural world in which sense impressions originate or of the sense organs by which these are transmitted. Utilizing, on the other hand, the technical data offered by the medical sciences of his time, he affirmed that the sensitive and intellectual activities of what is conventionally called the soul depend essentially on the structure and functions of the central nervous system, in general, and of the brain, in particular. Establishing a natural continuity from the external world through the sensory apparatus to the brain itself, La Mettrie identified the soul with a physically conditioned process in a way that allowed him to explain the various faculties of the soul, such as memory, reflection, imagination, the emotions, judgment, volition, solely in terms of their related organic causes.

However, a special feature of the *Histoire de l'âme* was its exposition of materialism within the conceptual framework of Aristotelian metaphysics. La Mettrie speculated that it is by virtue of the appropriate "material forms" and "substantial forms" that matter, actively organized by an intrinsic *force motrice*, realizes its potential attributes of a "vegetative soul" and a "sensitive soul"; each of these, in turn, he makes the "directing principle" of the biological or psychological functions coming under its sway. In presenting his empirico-physiological theory of mind under Scholastic auspices, La Mettrie intended, no doubt, to lend it some measure of metaphysical support, but probably more important was his wish to disarm the censorship by insisting—as he did throughout—on his theory's conformity with the prevailing orthodox tradition in Western philosophy. His strategy did not succeed very well, however, for the Aristotelianism on which he grafted his opinions served only to render them obscure and confused, yet apparently not quite obscure enough to prevent the authorities from recognizing and suppressing his "heretical" defense of materialism.

MAN A MACHINE

The thesis of *L'homme machine*, in asserting and illustrating the material dependence of the states of the soul uniformly on the corresponding states of the body, remains similar to that of the *Histoire de l'âme*, but its mode of expression and exact meaning are appreciably different. Composed in a lively, unmethodical, popular fashion, its exposition of materialism is effected not only without any metaphysical substructure but in a definitely antimetaphysical spirit. Its naturalistic view of man, consequently, is offered mainly as a general heuristic hypothesis necessary in the positive study of behavior, without the need being felt, beyond such a standpoint, to make mental processes reductively identical with their physiological causes. Concurrently La Mettrie proposed an experimental-inductive method, as opposed to the then prevalent apriorist ones, in the search for the principles of psychology. Discussing the organic basis of both vital and psychic events, he insisted on the mechanistic character of the causation involved. This important point was not brought out clearly in *Histoire de l'âme* because of the attempted materialization of the pseudo-Scholastic "souls" and "faculties."

In *L'homme machine* no essential distinction remained between the conscious and voluntary, as against the merely vital, involuntary, or instinctual activities of the "human machine"; the two types of activity are presumed explainable by the relative complexity of the mechanical structures responsible for their production. Thus La Mettrie could claim that his man-machine theory was the extension to its logical and empirical limits of the Cartesian animal-automaton doctrine. However, he must be credited with conceiving of the "living machine" in a manner that goes beyond the inadequacies of Descartes's passive and inert notion of mechanism. The organic machine that sustains the sensitive and mental life of the individual is defined by La Mettrie as a purposively self-moving and self-sufficient system, consisting of dynamically interrelated parts. It was typical of his empirical procedure that he found proof of the autonomous energy and internal finality of the organism in the physiological data of irritability. Following the pioneering researches of Albrecht von Haller, La Mettrie was among the first to understand the radical value of the capacity for irritability, and he succeeded in interpreting it with particular relevance for his thesis of psychophysical automatism.

Among the subsidiary themes of *L'homme machine*, the declaration of atheism was a new and significant development. On the one hand, it served a polemical and propagandist aim against the religious enemies of La Mettrie's philosophical position. On the other hand, it was a logical outcome of the universal naturalism in which the man-machine theory was appropriately framed; the traditional belief in an Intelligent Creator was replaced by the concept of an active, self-creating nature.

In epistemology, La Mettrie's characteristic approach was to offer picturable analogies between mind and brain, suggesting (however crudely) the model of a "thinking machine" into which sense perceptions feed ideas in the form of coded symbols that are, in turn, stored, classed, compared, and combined by the cerebral apparatus in order to engender all the known varieties of thought. This mechanical ordering and manipulation by the brain of its symbolically represented contents prompted La Mettrie to consider that the fundamental faculty of the mind is "imagination."

Another feature of *L'homme machine* is its persistent tendency to assimilate human to animal nature with the aid of evidence drawn from the spheres of comparative anatomy and experimental psychology. The doctrine of free will, of course, becomes meaningless in the light of physiological necessity. The moral aspect of behavior is regarded as no less determined than its other aspects, although it should be noted that the man-machine theory, despite its context of universal determinism, leads to the affirmation of a hierarchy of individual values and capabilities, inasmuch as no two "machines" could ever be identical or equal. The problem of the moral or intellectual perfectibility of man, within the compass of La Mettrie's materialism, becomes primarily a medical problem, for its solution depends on the possibility of perfecting the state of the organism.

DISCOURSE ON HAPPINESS

In the *Discours sur le bonheur*, intended as a refutation of Senecan Stoicism, La Mettrie viewed the *summum bonum* of happiness in a manner no less individualistic than hedonistic. In consistence with his materialist premises, he described happiness as the optimum state of pleasurable well-being of the "man-machine." Underlying his entire treatment of the subject is the assumption that happiness was destined by nature as a benefit to be enjoyed by each and every person, regardless of moral, intellectual, or social preconditions of any sort; that is, the goal of happiness is divorced basically from such traditional considerations as vice and virtue, ignorance and knowledge, social status and responsibility. La Mettrie obviously conceived of the problem of happiness, seen from the perspective of medical ethics, as similar to—

indeed, as a special instance of—the more comprehensive problem of health. Accordingly, he diagnosed the greatest threat to felicity to be "remorse," a morbid and "unnatural" symptom, which he proposed, ever faithful to the Hippocratic oath, to alleviate in all and sundry, including even conscience-ridden criminals; he remarked that the practical control of social behavior was a political matter and no business of his.

The *Discours sur le bonheur* was misinterpreted as a cynical inducement to vice and crime and, more than any of his works, gave to the author an enduring reputation for immoralism among philosophes and antiphilosophes alike.

MINOR WORKS

Among La Mettrie's minor works, perhaps the most curious is the *Système d'Epicure*. Its concern with ontogenesis and the origin of species represented a broadening of La Mettrie's materialism into an area of biological speculation which, at the time, was just beginning to excite interest. But his description of the "evolutionary" process, in which monstrous and unviable productions are supposed to have been eliminated in favor of the well-constituted types now extant, did little more than revive Lucretian memories.

In *L'homme plante*, La Mettrie's purpose was to stress the various parallelisms of structure and function between two such seemingly disparate things as the human organism and vegetable life. Reflecting his strong taste for analogical reasoning, it is an extreme confirmation of the "chain-of-being" idea, which it interprets in the sense of a uniform destiny for man and for all other living forms, excluding the possibility of a spiritual transcendence of nature.

Les animaux plus que machines is mainly a polemical piece directed against the school of animistic biology. By elaborating a mock defense of the opinion that a "soul" governs the animal economy, La Mettrie managed to expose, with the support of much physiological evidence, the absurdity and uselessness of such a hypothesis. The inference is that it would be equally ridiculous to claim that the operations of the human machine presuppose the agency of a "soul."

La Mettrie's philosophy, and in particular the man-machine doctrine central to it, has, owing to its very character, grown somewhat obsolete, together with the scientific documentation to which it was so intimately linked. The specific features of his mechanistic theory of mind might, in relation to what is now known or still unknown about neural processes, seem naive, crude, superficial, and pretentious. Nevertheless, his was the first naturalistic rationale for, and technical application of, a consistently physiological method in psychology. And while his philosophic contribution remains circumscribed by the biomedical standpoint that shaped his thinking, the man-machine hypothesis may be said, within its proper limits, to have retained a basic validity and vitality. Despite La Mettrie's bad name in his own age, and the many attempts to suppress, disfigure, or discredit his ideas, he exerted (surreptitiously, on the whole) a considerable influence in the eighteenth-century milieu. Among those indebted to the man-machine conception and to the naturalistic overtones and consequences that accompanied its formulation, the most important were Denis Diderot, Baron d'Holbach, and Pierre-Jean Georges Cabanis. Long neglected after his death, La Mettrie has been recognized since the latter part of the nineteenth century as one of the major forerunners of modern materialism. His nonreductive form of materialism may be regarded as an early version of a theory that is widely advocated at the present time by, among others, Ernest Nagel and various American naturalists; and his view that human beings can be fruitfully considered as a certain type of machine has obvious similarities to the principles underlying the science of cybernetics.

See also Animal Mind; Aristotelianism; Atheism; Cabanis, Pierre-Jean Georges; Continental Philosophy; Descartes, René; Diderot, Denis; Happiness; Holbach, Paul-Henri Thiry, Baron d'; Leibniz, Gottfried Wilhelm; Malebranche, Nicolas; Materialism; Mind-Body Problem; Nagel, Ernest; Naturalism; Stoicism.

Bibliography

WORKS BY LA METTRIE

Oeuvres philosophiques. 3 vols. Berlin and Paris, 1796.

L'homme machine. Translated as *Man a Machine.* London: G. Smith, 1750. A later translation is *Man a Machine; including Frederick the Great's "Eulogy" … and extracts from "The Natural History of the Soul."* Translated with philosophical and historical notes by Gertrude C. Bussey. Chicago: Open Court, 1912.

WORKS ON LA METTRIE

Bergmann, Ernst. *Die Satiren des Herrn Maschine.* Leipzig, 1913. On La Mettrie's activities as a satirist.

Boissier, Raymond. *La Mettrie, médecin, pamphlétaire, et philosophe.* Paris, 1931. Mainly on the medical background of La Mettrie's thought.

Campbell, Blair. "La Mettrie: The Robot and the Automaton." *Journal of the History of Ideas* 31 (1970): 555–572.

Lange, F. A. *History of Materialism.* London: K. Paul, Trench, Trubner, 1925. Bk. I, Sec. IV, Ch. 2 has a good discussion of La Mettrie.

Lemée, Pierre. *Julien Offray de La Mettrie, médecin, philosophe, polémiste: sa vie, son oeuvre.* Mortain, France, 1954. Best biographical account.

Perkins, Jean. "Diderot and La Mettrie." *Studies on Voltaire and the 18th Century* 10 (1959): 49–100.

Pflug, Günther. "Lamettrie und die biologische Theorien des 18. Jahrhunderts." *Deutsche Vierteljahrsschrift für Literaturwissenschaft und Geistesgeschichte* 27 (1953): 509–527.

Poritzky, J. E. *Julien Offray de La Mettrie, sein Leben und seine Werke.* Berlin, 1900. Best general treatment of La Mettrie's philosophy.

Thomson, Ann. "La Mettrie, Machines, and the Denial of Liberty." *Graduate Faculty Philosophy Journal* 22(1) (2000): 71–86.

Thomson, Ann. *Materialism and Society in the Mid-Eighteenth Century: La Mettrie's Discours Préliminaire.* Genève: Droz, 1981.

Vartanian, Aram. *La Mettrie's L'Homme Machine: A Study in the Origins of an Idea.* Princeton, NJ: Princeton University Press, 1960. Critical edition with introductory monograph and notes.

Vartanian, Aram. "Trembley's Polyp, La Mettrie, and Eighteenth-Century French Materialism." *Journal of the History of Ideas* 11 (1950): 259–286.

Wright, John P., and Paul Potter, eds. *Psyche and Soma: Physicians and Metaphysicians on the Mind -Body Problem from Antiquity to Enlightenment.* Oxford: Clarendon Press, 2000.

Aram Vartanian (1967)
Bibliography updated by Tamra Frei (2005)

LA MOTHE LE VAYER, FRANÇOIS DE
(1588–1672)

François de La Mothe Le Vayer, a French skeptical philosopher, was born in Paris, the son of a government official. He acquired his father's post when the latter died in 1625. His wife was the daughter of a Scottish intellectual, Adam Blackwood. During his early years La Mothe Le Vayer traveled widely in Europe. In 1639 he was elected to the Académie française and in 1647 was appointed preceptor to the Duke of Orléans. He was a prominent figure in avant-garde circles in Paris—in the group around Michel Eyquem de Montaigne's adopted daughter, Mademoiselle De Gournay; in the group of *libertins érudits* with Gabriel Naudé (1600–1653), Guy Patin (1601–1672), and Pierre Gassendi; in the scientific group around Marin Mersenne; and in the literary world of Molière (1622–1673; who jested at La Mothe Le Vayer in

Le Mariage forcé and other plays) and Savinien de Cyrano de Bergerac. His many writings on skepticism began with *Dialogues d'Oratius Tubero* (1630), followed by the *Discours chrétien de l'immortalité de l'âme* (1637, the year of René Descartes's *Discours de la méthode*), *De la Vertu des payens* (1642, published with Cardinal de Richelieu [1585–1642]as the sponsor), and a long series of skeptical essays on history and culture throughout the rest of his life.

Although his views are based primarily on those of Sextus Empiricus (whom he calls "le divin Sexte" and the author of "notre décalogue") and Montaigne, La Mothe Le Vayer's skepticism represents perhaps the most extreme type of antirationalism in the seventeenth century. He continually offers a wealth of evidence to show the variations in human moral behavior, the diversity of people's religious beliefs and practices, the vanity of scientific study, and the virtues of skepticism. He rarely develops his case theoretically by means of systematic arguments. Instead, he usually offers only illustrative materials, followed by a fideistic message that man can find truth only through faith, not through the use of his reason and senses.

In *Petit Traité sceptique sur cette façon de parler, n'avoir pas le sens commun* (1647) La Mothe Le Vayer contends that man does not understand the nature of even the most obvious things. All of one's information is relative to one's faculties. Even if there are any instruments for finding the truth about things, one, unfortunately, is unable to discover them. One's senses are unreliable, and one lacks any guaranteed criterion for distinguishing veridical experiences from others. Indubitable truths can be known only in heaven, not here and not through any human science.

These views are further developed in his *Discours pour montrer que les doutes de la philosophie sceptique sont de grande usage dans les sciences* (1669), where it is claimed, as the title shows, that the great service of Pyrrhonian skepticism for the sciences is that it can eliminate any serious concern with scientific research and that such research is a form of blasphemy. He asserts, without offering any real arguments, that logic is unreliable and physics only a problematical subject about which there are conflicting opinions. Nature is the free manifestation of God's will. Therefore, any attempt to restrict God's achievement to what man can measure and understand is an attempt to limit God's freedom and is hence blasphemous. When the scientists realize how uncertain their disciplines are, they should give them up and adopt skepticism, "the inestimable antidote against the presumptuous knowledge of the learned ones."

This complete skepticism should undermine the dogmatist's confidence and pride and lead him or her to the true faith: Christianity. In *La prose chagrine* (1661) La Mothe Le Vayer proclaims that of all the ancient philosophies, "there is no other that agrees so easily with Christianity as skepticism, respectful towards Heaven and submissive to the Faith." Had not St. Paul preached that skepticism was the way to salvation? The true Christian skeptic leaves his or her doubts at the foot of the altar and lives by faith.

La Mothe Le Vayer's anti-intellectual and destructive attack on human rational knowledge (presented almost obliviously to the scientific revolution going on around him, and especially to the achievements of Descartes) and his appeal to faith, although not introducing much that was new to skeptical argumentation, carried the Montaignian position to an absurd extreme. He denied any and all value to intellectual activities and left only blind faith. As a result, many commentators from Antoine Arnauld on have assumed that he was a pure libertine, undermining all bases for religion, and have classified him, partly on the basis of his risqué work *Hexaméron rustique* (1670), as an *incrédule volupteux* (sensual nonbeliever). His views, however, are compatible with his having been either a sincere Christian skeptic or a secret atheist undermining confidence in all views and beliefs—a genuine fideist or an irreligious doubter. His philosophical influence seems to have been more through personal contact than through any serious presentation of philosophical skepticism. As a representative of the skeptical view, he was still important in Pierre Bayle's time, but was forgotten for the most part thereafter.

See also Continental Philosophy; Descartes, René; Fideism; Gassendi, Pierre; Mersenne, Marin; Montaigne, Michel Eyquem de; Sextus Empiricus; Skepticism.

Bibliography

WORKS BY LA MOTHE LE VAYER
Oeuvres. 15 vols. Paris: L. Billaine, 1669.

WORKS ABOUT LA MOTHE LE VAYER
Bayle, Pierre. "Vayer." In *Dictionnaire historique et critique*, 2 vols. Rotterdam, Netherlands: Reinier Leers, 1697.

Charles-Daubert, Françoise. *Les Libertins érudits en France au XVIIe siècle.* Paris: Presses Universitaires de France, 1998.

Giocanti, Sylvia. "La Mothe Le Vayer: Modes de diversion sceptique." In *Libertinage et philosophie au XVIIe siècle.* Saint-Étienne, France: Publications de l'Université de Saint-Étienne, 1996.

Paganini, Gianni. "'Pyrrhonism tout pur' ou 'circoncis'? La dynamique du scepticisme chez La Mothe Le Vayer." In *Libertinage et philosophie au XVIIe siècle*, edited by Antony McKenna and Pierre-François Moreau. Saint-Étienne, France: Publications de l'Université de Saint-Étienne, 1996.

Pintard, René. *Le libertinage érudit dans la première moitié du XVIIe siècle.* 2 vols. Paris: Boivin, 1943.

Popkin, Richard H. *The History of Scepticism: From Savonarola to Bayle.* Rev. ed. New York: Oxford University Press, 2003.

Richard Popkin (1967, 2005)

LANDGREBE, LUDWIG
(1902–1992)

One of the most faithful followers of Edmund Husserl's phenomenology and phenomenological philosophy, Ludwig Landgrebe is equally known for his own contributions to these fields. What characterizes Landgrebe's work is his combination of philosophical issues and arguments with the precise delimitation of principles (or essential structures) whose rejection involves a contradiction. For example, he maintains that if one negates awareness, one nevertheless presupposes an awareness of this negation. (Landgrebe prefers the term "awareness" to "consciousness" due to the many traditional meanings associated with the latter.) As an assistant to Husserl, Landgrebe edited a number of Husserl's texts, including the classic *Experience and Judgment.* As a professor of philosophy at the university of Cologne, he formed a following of phenomenologists among whom are such notables as Klaus Held, Ulrich Klaesges, and Donn Welton. Landgrebe attracted students and audiences by his vast scholarship and personal modesty, both of which were seamlessly coupled with conceptual and logical clarity. While at home in all the modern speculative metaphysics, from Descartes through Kant, German Idealism, Nietzsche, and twentieth-century French thought, Landgrebe did not engage in speculative philosophy. When asked at DePaul University (Chicago) during a discussion of Husserl's understanding of the "subject" what its proper phenomenological status is, Landgrebe replied: "If I were to speculate, I would say that it is a monad with a window." He lectured widely in Latin America, the United States, and Eastern and Western Europe.

For Landgrebe, phenomenological philosophy is an effort to combine as clearly as possible an exposition of a given philosophical position, an analysis of the prejudgments or principles without which such a position could not be maintained, and an examination of the adequacy of the principles necessary to account for it within the context of the phenomena encountered in human awareness. For example, Kant proposes to account for all knowledge on the basis of a priori structures in the manner of a transcendental deduction that explicates the empirical domain; but he does not, on Landgrebe's view, account for the mode of awareness required to secure access to the a priori domain at issue in this deduction. Such awareness is required, according to Landgrebe, if the a priori, or any other epistemological, ontological, or even metaphysical conditions are to be evidentially legitimated. This does not mean that Landgrebe avoids treating such conditions in terms of their conceptual meanings; however, he maintains that anyone positing such conditions will also have to show the manner in which they are accessible to awareness, because failing this, the one positing them is placed in the untenable position of positing conditions that she is unaware of. Only the interrogation of such awareness will be able to decipher what is essential in each condition. Thus Landgrebe's analyses and investigations are designed to articulate the awareness implicit in the most fundamental experiences that open up what is essential in the experienced, lived world.

THEMES OF LANDGREBE'S WORK

Landgrebe's work has three major themes: philosophical anthropology, the basic structures of awareness, and history.

THE FIRST THEME. The first theme, according to Landgrebe, is called for by modern philosophical, cultural, and historical relativity. Within the latter, two claims are preeminent: (1) that different cultures, historical periods, and societies offer various, even clashing, interpretations of human beings; and (2) that modern scientific and technological thinking offers the means to "make" the human into something "new" or even radically different from what it has been previously. Landgrebe points out that these various views and proposed transformations of the human assume a tacit "essence" as far as awareness is concerned, which allows the difference inseparable from the different views and transformations to be directed toward something that appears to awareness as an invariant. Without the latter, no sense could be made of the claim that what "humans" are depends on cultural, historical, social, and even technical definitions and constructs. All these are different from one another. Yet simple differences would allow only the claim that at different times and in different places there were descriptively different creatures, which could only result in a catalogue of the various differing depictions. But even those who claim that there are radical differences in cultures, societies, and histories, still insist in using the phrase "different humans"—and it is this phrase that implicates the appearance of an invariant across all differences.

THE SECOND THEME. Landgrebe's second theme maintains that neither empiricism, with its emphasis on the contingency of facts, nor rationalism, with its stress on conceptuality and universal necessity, is adequate to account for concrete human awareness. The former, with its succession of impressions, cannot account for the continuity and unity of experience. The latter, as is obvious from Kant, can account for neither the unity of experience without positing the "I think" accompanying all representations, nor for the individuality wherein such representations could be attributed as "mine." In terms of philosophical anthropology, empiricism reduces the human to a *factum brutum,* whereas rationalism treats the factual human as an instance of a universal concept.

Landgrebe holds that this fails to account for the distinguishability of individual subjects from one another. To confront this issue, Landgrebe's investigation begins with the life-world and our direct experiential "opening" to it. Movement, in correlation to the things of the environment, is an epistemic requirement needed to form primal perspectivity, time awareness, and special formations. From the movement of the eyes that trace out the contours of things, to traveling around the planet, the focus and maintenance of the identity of anything is formed by body movements (kinaesthetic processes), movements that, for Landgrebe, manifest the body side of the transcendental subject. Moreover, various higher-level linguistic structures are formed at the level of movement, such as "if-then" implications: "If I want to see the other side, then I shall have to walk around the thing." Access to time and space is equally provided by bodily activities: "If I want to see the other side, I will have to be there and then." Activities also reveal the fundamental human "intentionality" and purposive understanding, including the instrumental selectivity of proper and unfitting factors leading to the fulfillment of purposes.

For Landgrebe, activities form habits and the primacy of the practical "I can" or "I cannot" perform something. They comprise singular "habits" (though not in the Humean sense of the association of ideas) that distinguish one individual from another. Such distinctions arise as activities oriented to common tasks wherein we begin to recognize our "otherness" on the grounds of what we can and cannot do, and not on the basis of the initial encounter with others as subjects or minds inside of bodies. Intersubjectivity is primarily formed at the level of bodily abilities such that we recognize ourselves and others on the basis of activities. The latter, in turn, are not arbitrary, but emerge in correlation to things that make "objective" demands on such activities. This means that the world is neither in doubt nor our construct. As "Euclidean beings," we must move around and not through things.

This claim must not be confused with any kind of realism or naturalism. According to Landgrebe, the natural presence of the world still requires an explication of the processes of awareness that are structurally distinct from the composition of things. Hence, metaphysical speculations might suggest that a special-temporal object is actually a flow of energies, or a slowly changing substance, but for awareness the thing is an X that is maintained as constant and given through the formation of movements and perspectives, of expectations of the next side and the unification of the previous side as sides of the same X. The X suggests the possibility of an indefinite ability to explore the given thing, an ability that is proper to it. One can see it from more perspectives, take it apart, and thus open up the "inner horizon" of the explored X. This complex process comprises the phenomena through which the real thing is experienced.

This level of primal awareness also opens up the "outer horizon" such that the thing is in a room, the room is in a house, the house is in the field, the field is in a region, and so on. The opening up of the external horizon is equally founded on the "I can," which is able to go on exploring and hence comprising an open space-time horizon which, while implicit in the initial awareness of the thing, opens up possibilities for exploration of the world. One may be aware that in one's own region there are hills, and more hills, but the horizon does not close; it is possible that beyond the hills there are deserts, lakes, flatlands, forests, cities, and strangers who "do things differently."

This horizon extends into indefinite possibilities that the ego can concretize by going from its region to that region "then" and discovering whether its intentional orientation toward the "that and then" region, say, as a possible desert, is concretized or disappointed. The ego expected a desert and there appeared a lake. Without such a horizon of possibilities and expectations there would be no mistakes. Empiricism and rationalism fail at this juncture. It needs to be said that at the level of movement the formation of horizons belonging to awareness involves a shift from direct perceptual fulfillment to an open world-horizon whose possibilities can only be partially concretized in direct awareness. Hence, on the one hand, in this awareness there is a "consciousness" that suggests perceptual fulfillability, whereas on the other hand, this same awareness is experienced as a transcendental condition for the experience of the world as a totality, albeit one completely accessible to a singular subject in her engagements with the world. This state of affairs leads Landgrebe to his next step: historical awareness.

THE THIRD THEME. Historical awareness, Landgrebe's third theme, manifests itself as a horizon of the past achievements of others and their appropriation by the current inhabitants of the life world, including the manner that they may vary such achievements. At this level, Landgrebe raises the question concerning our experience of the historical past and rejects Hegelian dialectics, Marxian materialism, and empirical research. None can "travel to the past," except symbolically, and none can account for such would be symbolic understanding. Apart from that, such metaphysical "accounts" of history assume a continuous theoretical time without, however, offering any justification for its continuity. In this sense, we cannot think of history as a succession of events "in time" ruled by causes, or a deduction from the "eternity" of the "laws of dialectics" (either Hegelian or Marxian). Rather, history is an active engagement of making and building, of concrete projects based on what we can do and what others have done. What they have done is present to us such that we too could have acted and performed similar tasks, but we no longer do them in this way. We have acquired different abilities and hence have no necessary continuity with our predecessors.

The discontinuity does not imply that we are not open to the understanding of how they made things, what purposes are present in their buildings, implements, and comportment. We may learn some abilities from what they did, but also vary them in order to perform our own tasks. As was the case with the horizon of awareness, history comprises a horizon of what others have accomplished, thus extending our own horizon of possibility for transforming and varying our own abilities. This means that the historical others extend my perception and abilities, thus forming a "poli-centric" field of understanding. Our own perceptions would be limited without the others from whom we "borrow" perceptions and abilities and thus recognize our limitations and possibilities—all of which, indeed, are open to the future. This view prevents speaking of a singular historical aim. Some tasks are com-

pleted and discontinued, the accomplishments abandoned; others are taken up in part after the builders and makers have long since disappeared, and still others are postponed for the future. The historical horizon of possibilities cannot be concretized in a totality; hence this openness precludes any claim that history has a singular purpose.

For Landgrebe there is another level of historical awareness: the transcendental. This type of awareness comprises a way to access the modes of perception that others assumed in their understanding of the world. Thus, whereas we may not have any knowledge of Aristotle's psychological, social, political, and personal life, we can say, from his writings, that Aristotle regarded the world as composed of substances. Each substance could be regarded under specific categories accessible to him as well as to us. In this sense, historical awareness of others is not regarded psychologically or internally, but as a mode of awareness that comprises a transcendental orientation toward the world accessible to anyone. Even when we disagree with Aristotle or Plato, we also must be aware of the way Plato or Aristotle regarded the world. This type of awareness is already intersubjective and is a condition for the claim that our own awareness is limited and in turn extended through others. We can "borrow" Aristotle's mode of awareness and enhance our own. This illustrates the sense in which for Landgrebe we comprise a field of poli-centric awareness that has historical depth prior to specific temporal locations. From this vantage point Landgrebe avoids various theoretical dilemmas. If a social philosophy claims that all social life, including theoretical thinking, is a result of material conditions, then previous historical views would not be accessible to us, because we do not live under those conditions. In turn, the view that all theories are based on given material conditions is itself a specific theory that reflects current material conditions; as such, it would follow that such a theory cannot make a universal claim. The same holds for theories of history that are premised on the notion that history is a contingent fact and all necessary truths, even in logic, are a result of "historical development." A contingent fact cannot be posited as a ground of necessity, because its "sense" as such a fact excludes "necessity."

CONCLUSION

Finally, beyond advancing the above theoretical issues, Landgrebe also engaged in the controversies surrounding the issue of whether there is one life world that is presumed as a ground of various societies and cultures, or whether such societies and cultures comprise distinct and, at times, incompatible life worlds. For Landgrebe this controversy reveals a most fundamental issue of awareness. If there were one life world, and we were completely immersed in it, then we would not be able to recognize our immersion in it. If there were more than one, we would then either belong to one or another and thus would interpret the other in terms of our own; hence, we would fail to recognize the distinction between them. If we can achieve access to both, then we cannot belong to either and must have an awareness of both and their differences. This awareness is taken for granted in all such comparative studies, and makes its appearance with Landgrebe's question: For whom are such life worlds given? This opens the discussion of transcendental awareness in its own right, apart from this or that (however radically different) content of such awareness. And it belongs to Landgrebe's enduring merit as a phenomenologist that this discussion can only be enriched by the consideration of his seminal researches into these three major themes of his work.

See also Husserl, Edmund; Phenomenology.

Bibliography

WORKS BY LANDGREBE

Philosophie der Gegenwart. Frankfurt: Ullstein Buecher, 1961.

Der Weg der Phänomenologie. Guetersloh, Germany: Guetersloher Verlagshaus, 1963.

Major Problems in Contemporary European Philosophy, from Dilthey to Heidegger. Translated by Kurt F. Reinhardt. New York: F. Ungar, 1966.

Phänomenologie und Geschichte. Darmstadt, Germany: Wissenschaftliche Buchgesellschaft, 1968.

Perspektiven transcendentalphänomenologisches Forschung; für Ludwig Landgrebe zum 70. Geburtstag von seinen Kölner Schülern. Hrsg. von Ulrich Klaesges und Klaus Held. The Hauge: M. Nijhoff, 1972.

Phaenomenologie Heute; Festschrift fuer Ludwig Landgrebe. Herausgeber Walter Biemel. The Hauge: M. Nijhoff, 1972.

Experience and Judgment: Investigations in a Genealogy of Logic. Translated by James S. Churchill and Karl Ameriks. Evanston, IL: Northwestern University Press, 1973.

The Phenomenology of Edmund Husserl: Six Essays, edited and translated by Donn Welton. Ithaca, NY: Cornell University Press, 1981.

Faktizität und Individuation: Studien zu den Grundlagen der Phänomenologie. Hamburg: Meiner, 1982.

Algis Mickunas (2005)
Burt Hopkins (2005)

LANGE, FRIEDRICH ALBERT
(1828–1875)

The German philosopher, historian, and sociologist Friedrich Albert Lange was born at Wald near Solingen. He studied at Duisberg, in Zürich, where he attended the lectures of a disciple of Johann Gottfried Herbart, and at Bonn. After receiving a degree at Bonn, he taught high school in Cologne, and in 1851 he became a university instructor at Bonn. His dissertation concerned the relation between theories of education and various worldviews. From 1858 to 1861 he taught school in Duisberg but resigned because of a government order forbidding teachers to participate in political agitation. Lange remained in Duisberg as a newspaper editor and secretary of the chamber of commerce. His socialist sympathies were not incompatible with a genius for finance. In 1866 he returned to Switzerland and in 1870 became professor of inductive logic at Zürich. He was appointed to a professorship at Marburg in 1873 and remained there until his death. The philosophical poems of Friedrich Schiller, on which he sometimes lectured, were said to be his final comfort.

Lange's importance in philosophy rests mainly on his brilliantly written *History of Materialism and Critique of Its Present Significance* (1866). This work gave support to the opponents of materialism and helped to stimulate the revival of interest in Immanuel Kant that led to the neo-Kantian schools of the last decades of the century. Less important philosophically, but a prominent part of Lange's versatile career, was his concern with social questions, as in *Die Arbeiterfrage* (1865), and his work for constitutional reform in the direction of democratic socialism.

Lange argued that materialistic theories of reality are just as guilty of transcending the proper limits of human knowledge as are the speculative systems of idealism. He appealed to Kant's arguments, rejecting the possibility of any metaphysical knowledge that pretends to take us beyond the sphere of experience. In his view, the attempt to comprehend the world as a whole is doomed to failure. But this criticism applied as much to the materialistic rejection of unobservable spiritual or mental agencies as to their defense. According to Lange, metaphysical theories belong to the realm of art and religion, a field governed by poetizing (*dichten*). This activity is not an illegitimate one, however. It is an essential human need, expressive of men's yearnings for an ideal realm. But religion and the speculative systems of metaphysics do not yield scientific knowledge or any substitute for it.

Lange saw materialism both as a demand for mechanistic explanations of natural phenomena and as a naive realism and dogmatic metaphysics. The first demand he considered valid, but the second, he held, had been refuted by Kant and by the development of physiological psychology. The demand that natural occurrences be explained in terms of material causes is a useful, even indispensable, postulate of scientific method. In attempting to explain human behavior, for instance, it is unreasonable to think of consciousness as intervening somewhere in the series of physical events from stimulus to brain, nerve, and muscular response. Mental processes are not members of this series.

While the only valid categories for science are those that, like space, time, and causality, render nature mechanistically intelligible, these categories have no proper role beyond that of organizing our sense experience. Along with the basic concepts of physics—matter, atom, force, physical object—they are the products of human invention. The Kantian theory of the a priori had shown this, while discoveries in the physiology of sensation proved that our knowledge is sifted through human sense organs. The scientist is not a passive recipient of data; the laws that he discovers are constructions whose objectivity is only an objectivity for us. Though the world which science presents is the cognitive realm valid for all men, there is also the individual's world of ideals. To confuse the two worlds is wrong, because each has its significance.

Lange's physiological interpretation of the categories was rejected by his neo-Kantian successors at Marburg, Hermann Cohen and Paul Natorp. His influence was very strong, however, on Hans Vaihinger, whose pragmatism owes much to Lange's concept of categories as no more than maxims of scientific method. Lange's rejection of all metaphysics placed him also in the positivistic tradition, and it is no surprise that he referred to Auguste Comte as "the noble Comte." Though Lange was critical of Ludwig Feuerbach, whom he regarded as only half emancipated from G. W. F. Hegel, his own sympathetic but noncognitivist view of religion and ideals is akin to the humanism of Feuerbach.

See also A Priori and A Posteriori; Cohen, Hermann; Comte, Auguste; Continental Philosophy; Feuerbach, Ludwig Andreas; Hegel, Georg Wilhelm Friedrich; Herbart, Johann Gottfried; Humanism; Kant, Immanuel; Materialism; Natorp, Paul; Neo-Kantianism; Schiller, Friedrich; Vaihinger, Hans.

Bibliography

WORKS BY LANGE

Die Arbeiterfrage. Winterthur, Switzerland, 1865.

Geschichte des Materialismus und Kritik seiner Bedeutung in der Gegenwart. 2 vols. Iserlohn and Leipzig, 1866. The edition published at Leipzig in 1902 has an introduction and critical appendix by Hermann Cohen. English translation by E. C. Thomas, 3 vols. London, 1877–1879, reprinted with an important introduction by Bertrand Russell, 1 vol. Edinburgh, 1925.

J. S. Mill's Ansichten über die Social Frage. Duisburg, Germany, 1866.

Logische Studien. Edited by H. Cohen. Iserlohn and Leipzig, 1877.

WORKS ON LANGE

Ellissen, O. A. *Friedrich Albert Lange.* Leipzig: Baedeker, 1891. Contains letters of interest.

Vaihinger, Hans. *Hartmann, Dühring, und Lange.* Iserlohn: Baedecker, 1876.

Vaihinger, Hans. *Die Philosophie des Als-Ob.* Berlin: Reuther & Reichard, 1911. Translated by C. K. Ogden as *The Philosophy of "As if."* New York: Harcourt Brace, 1924.

Arnulf Zweig (1967)

LANGER, SUSANNE K.
(1895–1985)

Susanne Langer was an American philosopher whose work remains significant because of her distinctive views on the philosophy of art, as expressed in her books *Philosophy in a New Key* (1942) and *Feeling and Form* (1953). Though now relatively neglected, various aspects of her views remain of interest, as shown by the following considerations concerning her most characteristic doctrines.

Langer rejects positivist views of meaning and thinking according to which only literal, scientific language has any objective significance—a view the consequence of which is that any other apparent kinds of meaning are mere subjective expressions of feeling (1957, ch. 4). Instead she argues that there is another kind of objective thinking that has a different kind of symbolic form. In place of the discursive, sequential structure of linguistic statements it uses a *presentational* symbolic mode, which communicates by showing rather than saying, as do images or pictures. Such presentational modes have their origin in low-level kinds of sensory experience, which provide the basis for the often metaphorical and imagistic experiences that underlie conscious thought (1957, chs. 4, 6).

As applied to the arts, Langer claims that all of the arts are to be explained in terms of such presentational symbolic forms. For example, pictures are able to communicate their content by showing or presenting—rather than by linguistically stating—their message (1957, ch. 4); while music, dance, and other art forms similarly present rather than state their meaningful content (1957, ch. 8; 1953).

But if such presentational forms do not communicate or express objective factual information, as do discursive linguistic forms, then what do they express? Langer's answer is that they express *feeling*—not the mere subjective feelings that the positivists rejected, but instead objective forms or structures of feeling that cannot be identified either with the betrayal of the personal feelings of an artist who creates an artwork, nor with the arousal of feelings in the audience who experience that work. For example, she says of music that it "is 'significant form,' and its significance is that of a symbol ... which by virtue of its dynamic structure can express the forms of vital experience ... Feeling, life, motion and emotion constitute its import" (1953, p. 32). Thus artistic symbolic forms communicate, in virtue of their structure, the same forms of feeling that occur in sentient life generally.

The above views, that art involves nondiscursive symbolic forms that primarily communicate feeling, have been much criticized (e.g., see Davies 1994, ch. 3 for incisive music-related criticisms). However, there remain other, more neglected aspects of Langer's theory that are harder to dismiss, such as her view that art involves what she calls "semblance" (1953, ch. 4), a seeming or illusory quality that is both experienced as such—"The 'otherness' that gives even a bona fide product like a building or a vase some aura of illusion" (1953, p. 46)—and which also implies the objective unreality or virtuality of those forms themselves. This quality of semblance enables Langer to distinguish between, for instance, the *actual* spatial qualities of a sculpture or building when considered purely as a physical object, and its *seeming* spatial qualities, which in part constitute, on her view, the perceptually experienced symbolic artwork itself.

To be sure, such an account seems to imply that artworks are relative to perception in some way (Khatchadourian 1978), hence raising questions about their objective status that Langer does not answer, but many would view her general insistence on the objectivity and cultural independence of the symbolic forms of artworks as being too strong in any case. Independently of such issues of objectivity and semblance versus reality, Langer's resulting analyses are sometimes of interest in their own right, such as her account of the ways in which sculptures are able to organize the spaces in which they occur—unlike paintings, whose spatial worlds are self-contained; this is an account that connects with other significant differences between sculptural and pictorial forms (Hopkins 2004).

In terms of the general classification of theories of art, Langer's theory is an unusual combination of a formalist and an expression theory in that her view is that all artworks express feeling in virtue of their specific symbolic form. Probably one reason for her current neglect is that she in turn neglects issues of artistic intention and individual expression that generally are thought to be at least relevant, if not central, issues in the philosophy of art. Nevertheless, whatever her theoretical flaws may be, Langer remains an engaging and insightful writer whose previous wide popularity is not hard to understand.

See also Aesthetics, History of.

Bibliography

WORKS BY LANGER

Philosophy in a New Key: A Study in the Symbolism of Reason, Rite and Art. Cambridge, MA: Harvard University Press, 1942. 3rd ed., 1957.
Feeling and Form: A Theory of Art. New York: Scribner, 1953.

WORKS ON LANGER

Davies, Stephen. *Musical Meaning and Expression.* Ithaca, NY: Cornell University Press, 1994.
Hopkins, Robert. "Painting, Sculpture, Sight and Touch." *British Journal of Aesthetics* 44 (2004): 149–166.
Khatchadourian, Haig. "Movement and Action in the Performing Arts." *Journal of Aesthetics and Art Criticism* 37 (1978): 25–36.

John Dilworth (2005)

LANGUAGE

What is a "language"? Is it an internal component of a speaker's mind, or is it wholly dependent on our external behavior? Is it a matter of social practice, or are languages to be viewed as independently existing abstract objects? Arguments have been offered in favor of each of these conceptions.

Adherents to these different positions can agree that linguistic theories provide the most precise way of characterizing particular languages. A theory, or grammar, supplies a set of rules describing the semantic properties of the basic expressions and their permissible syntactic combinations into meaningful wholes. The disagreements that arise concern the interpretation of linguistic theories and the nature of the linguistic objects and properties they describe.

Platonists, for instance, argue that languages are purely formal, or abstract entities, whose natures are fully specified by formal theories. For the Platonist, linguistics is a branch of mathematics. In contrast, mentalists see linguistics as a branch of cognitive psychology and take linguistic theories to be about the psychological states or processes of linguistically competent speakers. For others, linguistic theories can be seen as systematizing a vast range of facts about the behavior of an individual or community of speakers, with the rules describing regularities in individual or social practice.

For Platonists, such as J. Katz and S. Soames, languages with their properties of meaning and structure exist independently of speakers. A firm distinction is drawn between languages and linguistic competence: Theories of the former are not to be confused with theories of the latter. The formal properties of a language, on which its identity depends, owes nothing to its users. Speakers of those languages may be blind to some of its properties of meaning or structure, although these may be deduced from the theory. Moreover, languages with just these formal properties exist whether anyone speaks them or not. They may be defined, according to D. Lewis, as sets of expression meaning-pairs, with the set of human (or natural) languages making up a very small portion of the set of all possible languages. The task for Platonists is to explain what makes one rather than another of these abstract entities the language of a given individual or population. To explain this the Platonist must define an *actual-language relation* between speakers, or populations, and particular abstract objects (see Schiffer for discussion). This may depend, as Lewis thinks, on facts about the conventions that exist among a population of speakers. Or it may be based upon psychological facts about speakers' competence such as the claim that speakers have internalized a grammar that somehow generates either the set, or a subset, of the sentences described by the formal theory.

Mentalists, such as Noam Chomsky and Jerry A. Fodor, insist to the contrary that the best account of speakers' actual languages should fit the facts about the meanings and structures individuals actually give to expressions: Theories of language should be tailored to the contours of linguistic competence. Thus for Chomsky, a theory of language is a theory of a speaker's knowledge of language. The formal entities described by Platonists are just projections of the linguistic properties

that speakers give to the expressions they produce and respond to. For mentalists, language is not in the world. The world contains only marks and sounds. Language is in the mind of speakers and consists in the assignments of meaning and structure given to particular marks and sounds.

For Chomsky, a grammar is a theory of the speaker's linguistic competence: An internalized system of rules or principles a person uses to map sounds to meanings. This is a body of tacit knowledge that the speaker puts to use in the production and comprehension of speech. It contains a largely innate, and species-specific, component common to all human language users. The workings of this component are described by universal grammar. Linguistic competence is just one of the factors affecting linguistic performance. Memory, attention, and other cognitive factors contribute to the actual production of speech. For Fodor, by contrast, the rules of grammar describe the actual psycholinguistic mechanisms at work in our production and comprehension of language. Language is just one of the perceptual modules, or sensory input systems, that serve our central cognitive processing.

In contrast to the Platonist and mentalist construals of language, behaviorists insist that grammars are merely theoretical representations of a speaker's practical abilities: The ability to use expressions in particular ways. For Willard Van Orman Quine, a language is a set of dispositions to verbal behavior. Quine argues that the only evidence for linguistic theory is linguistic behavior, and that many grammars will serve equally well to generate the set of sentences a speaker is disposed to produce and respond to. Thus grammars and the sentence structures they describe are construed as artifacts of theory. Chomsky denies that behavior provides the only evidence for testing theories of grammar. Psycholinguistic evidence and language acquisition are also relevant. He also argues that we could not have learned to produce and respond to so many novel sentences just on the basis of observed behavior. The data are too impoverished to support such inductive inferences: Sentences alike in surface structure differ in underlying levels of structure, and speakers respond to them differently. Chomsky concludes that speakers must bring their own internally generated representations of structure to bear on the evidence. Predictions of the sentences they find acceptable and unacceptable, and the interpretations they can and cannot allow, will be based on the fewest linguistic generalizations that fit the pattern of elicited data, and explain any gaps in the data. Claims about a speaker's grammar are thus based on inference to the best explanation about the principles by which she generates structural descriptions (SDs) for the utterances she hears. A speaker's language is an internally generated set of structures.

Donald Davidson, like Quine, accepts that all facts about meaning must be exhibited in behavior. But unlike Quine, he holds that the assignments of meaning depend on facts about what the speaker believes and intends. Thus linguistic meaning cannot be reduced to behavior. The notions of belief and meaning are settled together by a total theory for interpreting what a speaker says and does.

Finally, is language an essentially social phenomenon? Michael Anthony Eardley Dummett argues that a language is a shared social practice upon which the possibility for communication among speakers depends. Lewis, although a Platonist, also argues that facts about the conventional regularities maintained by populations relate them to particular languages. Chomsky and Davidson, on the other hand, conclude that the fundamental notion of language is that of an individual's language, or idiolect. Differences in grammar and vocabulary between speakers ensure that no two speakers have exactly the same language: They can still communicate because there is often overlap in idiolects, and they can work out what others are saying. Chomsky distinguishes between E-languages, which are ill-assorted, externally described, and extensionally characterized social practices, and I-languages, which are the intensionally characterized, internalized grammars of individuals that assign SDs to expressions. For Chomsky, the former notion is ill-defined, so only the latter is of use in the scientific study of language. He argues that a language L cannot be identified apart from its structure, and the structure of L is the structure assigned to it by its speaker(s). He thus casts doubt on behaviorism. Many languages will share the same sounds: Whether a string of sounds is a sentence depends on how different speakers perceive those sounds. Relative to one structural assignment, the sound string may be grammatical, relative to another it may not. Quine's and Lewis's idea of a set of well-formed strings, which can be generated by different grammars, becomes problematic; instead we have a set of structures that speakers assign to sounds and signs. We might reconstruct the notion as follows: An E-language is a set of grammatical strings, where a "string" is grammatical if it has at least one structural description (SD), which is permitted by the I-language of some set of speakers in the sense that it conflicts with no principles of universal grammar (UG).

In the case of meaning, Tyler Burge has argued that word meaning depends on the social norms operating in the speaker's community; while Hilary Putnam stresses that the meaning and reference of natural terms are settled by a group of experts to whom ordinary speakers defer in their use of these terms. These social factors are compatible with the claim that the primary notion of language is that of an idiolect, as they concern vocabulary items only. Each of these different conceptions of language may coexist, all of them serving a different philosophical or scientific interest.

See also Behaviorism; Chomsky, Noam; Davidson, Donald; Dummett, Michael Anthony Eardley; Fodor, Jerry A.; Inference to the Best Explanation; Lewis, David; Meaning; Philosophy of Language; Putnam, Hilary; Quine, Willard Van Orman; Reference.

Bibliography

Burge, T. "Wherein Is Language Social." In *Reflections on Chomsky,* edited by A. George. Cambridge, MA: Blackwell, 1990.

Chomsky, N. *Knowledge of Language: Its Nature, Origin, and Use.* New York: Praeger, 1986.

Davidson, D. "Radical Interpretation." In his *Inquiries into Truth and Interpretation.* New York: Oxford University Press, 1984.

Dummett, M. "Language and Communication." In *Reflections on Chomsky,* edited by A. George. Cambridge, MA: Blackwell, 1990.

Fodor, J. "Some Notes on What Linguistics Is About." In *The Philosophy of Linguistics,* edited by J. Katz. New York: Oxford University Press, 1985.

Katz, J., ed. *The Philosophy of Linguistics.* New York: Oxford University Press, 1985.

Lewis, D. "Languages and Language." In his *Philosophical Papers,* Vol. 1. New York: Oxford University Press, 1983.

Putnam, H. "The Meaning of Meaning." In his *Philosophical Papers,* Vol. 2. New York: Cambridge University Press, 1975.

Quine, W. V. O. "Methodological Reflections on Current Linguistic Theory." In *Semantics of Natural Language,* edited by D. Davidson and G. Harman. Dordrecht: Reidel, 1972.

Schiffer, S. "Actual-Language Relations." In *Philosophical Perspectives,* edited by J. Tomberlin. Atascadero, CA, 1973.

Soames, S. "Semantics and Psychology." In *The Philosophy of Linguistics,* edited by J. Katz. New York: Oxford University Press, 1985.

Barry C. Smith (1996)

LANGUAGE, ARTIFICIAL AND NATURAL

See Artificial and Natural Languages

LANGUAGE, PRIVATE

See *Private Language Problem*

LANGUAGE, RELIGIOUS

See *Religious Language*

LANGUAGE AND THOUGHT

Should questions about "thought"—about intentionality, beliefs, and concept possession, for example—be approached directly or, instead, indirectly via the philosophy of "language"? There are two slightly different ways in which questions about language and meaning might seem to offer illumination of issues concerning thought. One way relates to language that is explicitly about thoughts, as when someone says, "Bruce believes that boomerangs seldom come back." The idea that a philosophical investigation of thought should proceed via a study of the logical properties of language that is about thoughts is a particular case of a more general view that philosophy of language enjoys a certain priority over metaphysics.

The other way relates to the use of language to express thoughts, and this provides the topic for the present entry. Suppose that Bruce believes that boomerangs seldom come back, and expresses this thought in the English sentence: "Boomerangs seldom come back." Which takes priority, the meaning of the English sentence or the content of Bruce's thought?

A claim of priority is the converse of a claim of one-way dependence: X enjoys priority over Y if Y depends on X but X does not depend on Y. Thus, a question of the relative priority of X and Y has four possible answers: X has priority; Y has priority; X and Y are mutually dependent; X and Y are independent. But the question of the relative priority of thought and language is still unclear, until the relevant kind of priority has been specified. It is useful to distinguish three kinds of priority question: ontological, epistemological, and analytical (see Avramides 1989 for a similar distinction).

To say that thought enjoys *ontological priority* over language is to say that language is ontologically dependent on thought, while thought is not so dependent on language. That is, there can be thought without language, but there cannot be language without thought. To say that

thought enjoys *epistemological priority* over language is to say that the route to knowledge about language (specifically, about linguistic meaning) goes via knowledge about thought (specifically, about the contents of thought), while knowledge about thought can be had without going via knowledge about language.

Donald Davidson denies both these priority claims. As for ontological priority, he argues (1975) that there cannot be thought without language: In order to have thoughts (specifically, beliefs), a creature must be a member of a language community, and an interpreter of the speech of others. As for epistemological priority, Davidson argues (1974) that it is not possible to find out in detail what a person believes without interpreting the person's speech.

Analytical priority is priority in the order of philosophical analysis or elucidation. To say that X is analytically prior to Y is to say that key notions in the study of Y can be analyzed or elucidated in terms of key notions in the study of X, while the analysis or elucidation of the X notions does not have to advert to the Y notions. On the question of the relative analytical priority of thought and language, there are, then, four positions to consider: two priority views, and two no-priority views.

PRIORITY FOR THOUGHT

A philosophical account of the content of thoughts—of intentionality—can be given without essential appeal to language, and the notion of linguistic meaning can then be analyzed or elucidated in terms of the thoughts that language is used to express. The analytical program of Paul Grice was aimed at an analysis of linguistic meaning in terms of the beliefs and intentions of language users, though Grice did not offer any account of the intentionality of mental states themselves (Grice 1989; see also Schiffer 1972). There are many proposals for explaining the intentionality of mental states without appeal to linguistic meaning, and these might be coupled with an elucidation of linguistic meaning in terms of mental notions. It is widely reckoned, however, that the Gricean analytical program cannot be carried through (Schiffer 1987).

PRIORITY FOR LANGUAGE

An account of linguistic meaning can be given without bringing in the intentionality of thoughts, and what a person's thoughts are about can then be analyzed in terms of the use of language. This view can be found in Michael Dummett's work (1973, 1991, 1993). If a theorist attempts to give a substantive account of linguistic meaning in accordance with this view, then the resources that can be invoked are seriously limited, since the account cannot presume upon everyday psychological notions such as belief and intention. Because of this, it would not be surprising to find hints of behaviorism in work that is influenced by this view.

NO PRIORITY—INTERDEPENDENCE

There is no way of giving an account of either intentionality or linguistic meaning without bringing in the other member of the pair. The two notions have to be explained together. This is Davidson's view (Davidson 1984). He thus maintains an ontological, epistemological, and analytical no-priority position. While the three no-priority claims go together quite naturally, it is important to note that they are separable claims and that the analytical no-priority claim is not entailed by the ontological and epistemological no-priority claims.

NO PRIORITY—INDEPENDENCE

The notions of intentionality for mental states and of linguistic meaning are unrelated. This view might be defended if a language is considered as an abstract entity, composed of a set of expressions together with a function that assigns a value to each expression (a proposition to each sentence, for example). On such a conception, meaning is a purely formal notion. But for the notion of linguistic meaning as it applies to a public language in use, this fourth view is implausible.

See also Behaviorism; Davidson, Donald; Dummett, Michael Anthony Eardley; Grice, Herbert Paul; Intentionality; Language; Meaning; Philosophy of Language.

Bibliography

Avramides, A. *Meaning and Mind: An Examination of a Gricean Account of Language.* Cambridge, MA: MIT Press, 1989.

Davidson, D. "Belief and the Basis of Meaning." *Synthese* 27 (1974): 309–323.

Davidson, D. *Inquiries into Truth and Interpretation.* Oxford: Clarendon Press, 1984.

Davidson, D. "Thought and Talk." In *Mind and Language,* edited by S. Guttenplan. Oxford: Clarendon Press, 1975.

Dummett, M. *Frege: Philosophy of Language.* London: Duckworth, 1973.

Dummett, M. *The Logical Basis of Metaphysics.* Cambridge, MA: Harvard University Press, 1991.

Dummett, M. *The Seas of Language.* Oxford: Clarendon Press, 1993.

Dummett, M. *Truth and Other Enigmas.* London: Duckworth, 1978.

Grice, H. P. *Studies in the Way of Words.* Cambridge, MA: Harvard University Press, 1989.

Schiffer, S. *Meaning* (1972). Oxford, 1988.

Schiffer, S. *The Remnants of Meaning.* Cambridge, MA: MIT Press, 1987.

Sellars, W. S., and R. M. Chisholm. "Intentionality and the Mental." In *Minnesota Studies in the Philosophy of Science,* edited by H. Feigl, M. Scriven, and G. Maxwell, Vol. 2: *Concepts, Theories, and the Mind-Body Problem.* Minneapolis: University of Minnesota Press, 1958.

Martin Davies (1996)

LANGUAGE OF THOUGHT

Simply stated, the language-of-thought thesis (LOT) holds that thinking (i.e., cognition) is carried out in a languagelike medium, where the thoughts that constitute thinking are themselves sentencelike states of the thinker. Since the demise of philosophical behaviorism in the early 1960s the LOT thesis has enjoyed considerable support as a central tenet of a more encompassing representationalist theory of mind (RTM). Proponents of RTM, led by Jerry Fodor, have mounted a sustained defense of LOT.

RTM offers an account of propositional attitudes—beliefs, desires, doubts, and so on—according to which propositional attitudes relate the possessor of the attitude to a mental representation (cf. Fodor 1981). Mental representations have both semantic and physically realized formal properties: They are semantically evaluable (e.g., as being true or false, as being about or referring to certain entities or properties); they stand in inferential relations to other mental representations; and, like words, pictures, and other representations, they also have certain formal properties (e.g., shape, size, etc.) in virtue of being physical, presumably neural, entities. Mental representations, and hence propositional attitudes, have their causal roles in thinking and behavior in virtue of their formal properties. Propositional attitudes inherit semantic properties from the mental representations that are one of their relata. RTM is silent as to what kind or sort of representation these mental representations are (cf. Fodor 1987, pp. 136–138).

LOT supplements RTM with a specific proposal or hypothesis about the character of mental representations: Like sentences of a language, they are structured entities, and their structures provide the basis for the particular semantic and causal properties that propositional attitudes exhibit. More specifically, they are syntactically structured entities, composed of atomic constituents (concepts) that refer to or denote things and properties in the world. The semantic properties of a mental representation, including both truth conditions and inferential relations, are determined by the representation's syntactic structure together with the semantic properties of its atomic constituents. Mental representations, in other words, have a combinatorial semantics. The causal properties of a representation are similarly determined by the representation's syntactic structure together with the formal properties of its atomic constituents.

Three sorts of arguments have been advanced in support of LOT. The first makes much of the apparent semantic parallels between thoughts and sentences. Both beliefs and declarative sentences, for example, are typically meaningful, truth valued, and intentional (in the sense of being about something). Both stand in various inferential relations to other beliefs and assertions. One obvious explanation of these parallels is that thought has a languagelike character, individual thoughts a sentencelike structure. A second sort of argument focuses on the productivity and systematicity of thought. Thought, like language, is productive in the sense that there are indefinitely many, indefinitely complex thoughts. Whatever can be said can also be thought. Thought, like language, is also systematic in the sense that you can think one thought (e.g., that the child bit the monkey) if and only if one can also think certain other systematically related thoughts (that the monkey bit the child). Again, one obvious explanation is that thought has a languagelike character, individual thoughts a sentencelike structure. A third sort of argument claims that much cognitive scientific theorizing seems committed to LOT. Specifically, our best theories of rational choice, perception, and learning seem committed to the claim, not simply that cognition is a matter of the creation and manipulation of mental representations, but also that these representations are sentential in character. It is claimed, for example, that our best theories of learning are a species of hypothesis testing. But such a procedure, it is argued, presupposes the existence of a language, that is, a language of thought in which the hypothesis being tested is formulated.

Proponents of LOT readily concede that these arguments are not decisive. Each is an instance of inference to the best explanation, and as such each is vulnerable to refutation by some alternative explanation that does not appeal to a language of thought.

Critics of LOT find the foregoing sorts of arguments unpersuasive for any of a number of reasons. Either they believe that there are equally good explanations that do not appeal to a language of thought, or they deny the phenomena that LOT is said to explain, or they hold that the proposed explanations either rest on false presuppositions or are so sketchy and incomplete as not to merit the name, or they believe that these explanations have entailments so implausible as to impugn the explanatory premise that there exists a language of thought. Thus, for example, the argument from learning discussed above apparently entails that to learn a language one must already know a language. Many critics find in this entailment a reductio of LOT. Proponents such as Fodor, by contrast, have courageously embraced this entailment, arguing that all concepts, including, for example, our concept of a Boeing 747, are innate. Whatever the specific merits and defects of the arguments and counterarguments, it seems fair to say that the existence of a language of thought remains an open empirical question.

See also Behaviorism; Fodor, Jerry A.; Inference to the Best Explanation; Mental Representation; Philosophy of Mind; Propositional Attitudes: Issues in the Philosophy of Mind and Psychology.

Bibliography

DEFENDING LOT

Field, H. "Mental Representations." *Erkenntnis* 13 (1978): 9–61.

Fodor, J. *The Language of Thought.* New York: Crowell, 1975.

Fodor, J. *Representations.* Cambridge, MA: MIT Press, 1981.

Fodor, J. "Why There Still Has to Be a Language of Thought." In *Psychosemantics.* Cambridge, MA: MIT Press, 1987.

CRITICIZING LOT

Churchland, P. M., and P. S. Churchland. "Stalking the Wild Epistemic Engine." *Noûs* 17 (1983): 5–18.

Dennett, D. C. "Brain Writing and Mind Reading." In *Brainstorms.* Montgomery, VT: Bradford Books, 1978.

Dennett, D. C. "A Cure for the Common Code." In *Brainstorms.* Montgomery, VT: Bradford Books, 1978.

Loar, B. "Must Beliefs Be Sentences?" In *Proceedings of the PSA, 1982,* edited by P. Asquith and T. Nickles. East Lansing, MI: Philosophy of Science Association, 1983.

Schiffer, S. *Remnants of Meaning.* Cambridge, MA: MIT Press, 1987.

ADDITIONAL SOURCES

Aydede, M. "Language of Thought: The Connectionist Contribution." *Minds and Machines* 7 (1997): 57–101.

Barsalou, L. "Perceptual Symbol Systems." *Behavioral and Brain Sciences* 22 (1999): 507–569.

Cowie, F. *What's Within? Nativism Reconsidered.* Oxford: Oxford University Press, 1998.

Devitt, Michael. *Coming to Our Senses: A Naturalistic Program for Semantic Localism.* Cambridge, U.K.: Cambridge University Press, 1996.

Fodor, J. *Concepts: Where Cognitive Science Went Wrong.* Oxford: Oxford University Press, 1998.

Fodor, J. "Doing without What's Within: Fiona Cowie's Critique of Nativism." *Mind* 110 (2001): 99–148.

Knowles, J. "The Language of Thought and Natural Language Understanding." *Analysis* 58 (1998): 264–272.

Kosslyn, S. *Image and Brain.* Cambridge, MA: MIT Press, 1994.

Laurence, S., and E. Margolis. "Radical Concept Nativism." *Cognition* 86 (2002): 22–55.

Laurence, S., and E. Margolis. "Regress Arguments against the Language of Thought." *Analysis* 57 (1997): 60–66.

Leeds, S. "Perception, Transparency, and the Language of Thought." *Noûs* 36 (2002): 104–129.

Prinz, J. *Furnishing the Mind: Concepts and Their Perceptual Basis.* Cambridge, MA: MIT Press, 2002.

Rey, G. *Contemporary Philosophy of Mind: A Contentiously Classical Approach.* Oxford: Blackwell, 1997.

Vinueza, A. "Sensations and the Language of Thought." *Philosophical Psychology* 13 (2000): 373–392.

Robert J. Matthews (1996)
Bibliography updated by Alyssa Ney (2005)

LAO TZU

See *Laozi*

LAOZI

(sixth century BCE)

Laozi, according to the *Records of History* by Sima Qian, is believed to have been an elder contemporary of Confucius (551–479 BCE) and the author of the *Laozi* (*Daode jing* or *Tao-te-ching*), a work roughly five thousand characters long. This and other traditional accounts of Laozi and the date of his work have been seriously challenged, and various hypotheses about the authorship of the work and its date have been proposed. Nevertheless, three incomplete Guodian bamboo versions of the *Laozi* excavated in 1993 prove that the text was in circulation in the fourth century BCE and may have been composed still earlier.

Laozi is believed to be the first person in Chinese intellectual history to develop a brief theory on the source and grounds of the universe, represented by the concept of Dao (also commonly called Tao in Western writings).

DAO: SOURCE AND GROUNDS

Dao literally means "the way" and was often extended to cover the political or moral principles by which different schools expounded their ideas. Laozi attributed to this term a totally new meaning: "Dao produced the One, One produced the Two, Two produced the Three, and Three produced the ten thousand things" (chapter 42). Here, the One, Two, and Three do not indicate anything specific, just a general cosmological formula: from Nothing to Being, one to multitude, and simple to complex. This formula has been compared to the Big Bang theory of modern astrophysics. Dao is the primordial root of all beings and creatures, and all beings and creatures in turn depend on it. As the ultimate source and grounds of the universe, Dao would be termed a metaphysical, as opposed to an empirical, concept in European philosophy. But in Chinese philosophy there is no dichotomy between the metaphysical and the physical, the ontological and the axiological, the descriptive and the prescriptive, and so on. Dao runs through the whole universe and human life; it is both transcendent and immanent. As the model for human behavior and the object of ultimate concern for human beings, Dao is similar to God, but has nothing to do with will, feelings, or purpose. Dao runs through and embodies "ten thousands things," and *de* (power or virtue) is in each being. It can be said that Dao is a quasi-metaphysical concept, and de is its manifestation in all beings.

ZIRAN: THE CORE VALUE

The second key concept in Laozi's philosophy is *ziran*, or naturalness. Laozi advocates that "Man models himself on the earth, the earth models itself on heaven, heaven models itself on the Dao, and the Dao models itself on *ziran*" (chapter 25). The true meaning and message of this statement is that humans should practice the principle of naturalness, which involves allowing things to unfold without external coercion or, in the case of individual humans, without striving for things such as wealth and power. This permits actualizing natural harmony in human life and with one's surroundings. The word *ziran* comprises two parts: self (*zi*) and so (*ran*). Its basic meaning is "self-so." It may be rendered as naturalness to show its adjectival meaning and grammatical function as a noun.

One should not confuse ziran with Nature or the natural world. Ziran is used to indicate Nature in modern Chinese, but in classical contexts words such as *tian* (heaven), *di* (earth), and *wanwu* (ten thousand things) denoted the natural world. Some scholars relate ziran with Thomas Hobbes's (1588–1679) "state of nature," which is a hypothetical term for scientific argument and suggests that everyone is at war with everyone. Instead, Laozi's ziran is the ideal condition of human societies, namely natural harmony, and represents the highest principle and core value in his philosophy; it is embodied and promoted by Dao. Natural harmony and order are valuable and desirable compared with humanly contrived order, which depresses human nature and arouses resistance and even inevitably leads to chaos. Human nature can only flourish within societies that have natural order, hence ziran is also the optimal condition of individuals. Laozi contends that "the sage should foster the *ziran* of the ten thousand things and dare not take action" (chapter 64). This leads us to the next fundamental concept: *wuwei*.

WUWEI: PRINCIPLED METHOD

Wuwei also comprises two parts: no (*wu*) and action (*wei*). Superficially, it means "no action at all," but in fact wuwei only negates some kinds of actions, not all. Obviously, "fostering the *ziran* of ten thousand things" is not the kind of action wuwei would exclude. The agent of wuwei in Laozi's theory is mainly the sage, the ideal model of rulers, who fosters potential in others instead of directly ordering, forcing, interfering, and interrupting. So there is a social and political message in Laozi that is absent in the Inner Chapters of the *Zhuangzi*. Laozi's wuwei implies two aspects: Its negative expression suggests preventing certain societal actions, such as oppression, confrontation, and strife, while its positive meaning advocates an alternative, sophisticated manner of behavior for better results of natural development and harmony in societies, such as fostering, assisting, and being patient. In his famous proclamation about "doing nothing yet leaving nothing undone," Laozi clearly reveals the positive objective of wuwei. "Doing nothing" is a means of realizing the end of "leaving nothing undone." Wuwei actually purports to be both a superior approach to and the consummate realization of human activity. It derives from comprehensive humanistic perspectives and considerations, not from fashions or trends of governance aimed at achieving immediate benefits.

Humans make two kinds of mistakes: One is not making enough effort, the other is overdoing. The former mistake is easy to remedy because it does not waste too many resources or shake morale. Correcting the second is more difficult, as in the case of environmental degradation. Here is an additional sense in which wuwei is reasonable and significant.

REVERSION: PARADOXICAL THINKING

Another distinctive feature of Laozi's philosophy is his dialectical or paradoxical thinking, which emerges through doctrines dealing with the unity and transformation of pairs of contradictions. One doctrine concerns the interdependence of opposite things and concepts. For example, "Calamity is that upon which happiness depends; happiness is that in which calamity is latent." Another is the reversibility of opposite sides, such as the "correct can become the perverse, and good may become evil." According to Laozi, all things are in motion and they are changing and proceeding toward their reverse. Thus, humility produces greatness, and ambitions bring about failure. Obverse and reverse sides often exchange positions. Things in both human societies and the natural world can work out to be the very opposite of our expectation and intention.

To sum up, wuwei is the methodological principle for fostering ziran, the core value in Laozi's system. Dao, as the ultimate source and grounds of the universe, is the quasi-metaphysical and axiological foundation for both wuwei and ziran, while the theory of dialectics supports ziran and wuwei from the perspective of human experience.

See also Chinese Philosophy: Daoism.

Bibliography

Chan, Wing-tsit. "The Natural Way of Lao Tze." In *A Source Book in Chinese Philosophy*, 136–176. Princeton, NJ: Princeton University Press, 1963. This includes a translation of the received version of the *Laozi*.

Graham, A. C. *Disputers of the Tao: Philosophical Argument in Ancient China*. La Salle, IL: Open Court, 1989.

Hansen, Chad. *A Daoist Theory of Chinese Thought: A Philosophical Interpretation*. New York: Oxford University Press, 1992.

Henricks, Robert G. *Lao Tzu's Tao Te Ching: A Translation of the Startling New Documents Found at Guodian*. New York: Columbia University Press, 2000. This is the translation of the bamboo versions excavated in 1993.

LaFargue, Michael. *Tao and Method: A Reasoned Approach to the Tao Te Ching*. Albany: State University of New York Press, 1994.

Laozi. *Tao Te Ching*. Translated by D. C. Lau. Hong Kong: Chinese University Press, 1989. This is the translation of silk versions excavated in 1973.

Liu, Xiaogan. "Naturalness (tzu-jan), the Core Value in Taoism: Its Ancient Meaning and Significance Today." In *Lao-tzu and the Tao-te-ching*, edited by Livia Kohn and Michael LaFargue, 211–228. Albany: State University of New York Press, 1998.

Liu, Xiaogan. "Non-action and the Environment Today: A Conceptual and Applied Study of Laozi's Philosophy." In *Daoism and Ecology: Ways within a Cosmic Landscape*, edited by N. J. Girardot, James Miller, and Liu Xiaogan, 315–340. Cambridge, MA: Center for the Study of World Religions, Harvard Divinity School, 2001.

Slingerland, Edward. *Effortless Action: Wu-wei as Conceptual Metaphor and Spiritual Ideal in Early China*. New York: Oxford University Press, 2003.

Xiaogan Liu (2005)

LA PEYRÈRE, ISAAC
(1596–1676)

Isaac La Peyrère, or Pereira, was born in Bordeaux, France, a Calvinist of Portuguese New Christian, or converted Jewish, background. He became the Prince of Condé's secretary. Apparently he was friendly with leading Parisian avant-garde intellectuals such as Pierre Gassendi, François de La Mothe Le Vayer, Hugo Grotius, Guy Patin (1601–1672), and Ménage. La Peyrère's first book, *Du rappel des juifs* (1643), deals with the conversion of the Jews, their potential return to Palestine, and the beginning of the Messianic Age. In 1644 he went to Denmark and gathered there the material for his *Relation de l'Islande* (1663) and *Relation du Groenland* (1647), both written as letters to La Mothe Le Vayer. His most famous works, the *Prae-Adamitae* and the *Systema Theologicum ex Prae-Adamitarum Hypothesi*, apparently written by 1643, were published in Amsterdam in 1655. Queen Christina of Sweden (1626–1689), whom he had recently met in Belgium, offered to pay the publishing expenses, so he took his manuscript to Amsterdam to get a printer. Five editions of these works were published almost immediately, and the book appeared not only in Latin but in English and Dutch. Among the early readers of his book was the young Spinoza. La Peyrère argued that the only consistent interpretation of certain biblical passages, and of the anthropological and historical evidence about the Chinese, Mexicans, Eskimos, and other peoples, is that there were men before Adam and that the Bible deals only with Jewish history and not world history. The effect of this work was like that of a bombshell to the seventeenth-century intellectual world. It appeared at almost the same time as Archbishop James Ussher's (1581–1656) proof, on the basis of biblical data, that the world was created in 4004 BCE. La Peyrère was immediately attacked and refuted on all sides. His book was burned in Paris, and he himself was arrested and kept in prison in Belgium for six months until he retracted his views and became a Catholic. He then went to Rome and begged the pope's forgiveness, publishing a formal retraction of his views. In 1659 he entered a religious order near Paris, where he remained until his death. Despite his official retractions, it is believed that he continued to hold to his pre-Adamite views. For example, Pierre Bayle cites a letter in which La Peyrère's religious superior is supposed to have said that "he was always writing books that … would be burned as soon as the good man died. La Peyrère was the best man in the world, the sweetest, who tranquilly believed very little."

La Peyrère's revolutionary work on the pre-Adamite theory had tremendous influence on seventeenth- and eighteenth-century thought. In raising the possibility that biblical data might only apply to Jewish history, he introduced a radical new conception of human development and led people to speculate on the relative merits of various cultures and religions. Further anthropological and geological studies, as well as investigations into comparative religion, soon led to the abandonment of biblical chronology and history as the framework for understanding all human history and led also to the beginning of higher criticism of the Bible by writers like Spinoza and Richard Simon and to the Enlightenment critiques of traditional religion. Pre-Adamism was a radical hypothesis in the Enlightenment that accounted for the variety of human beings.

Most writers for at least a century after La Peyrère seem to have been directly or indirectly aware of his pre-Adamite hypothesis and its extraordinary implications. In the nineteenth century La Peyrère's pre-Adamite hypothesis was developed into a racist view and finally into the ideology of British Israelites and of the Aryan Nation in the United States.

See also Bayle, Pierre; Continental Philosophy; Deism; Enlightenment; Gassendi, Pierre; Grotius, Hugo; La Mothe Le Vayer, François de; Philosophy of History; Simon, Richard; Spinoza, Benedict (Baruch) de.

Bibliography

WORKS BY LA PEYRÈRE

Du rappel des juifs. 1643.

Relation de Groenland. Paris: A. Covrbe, 1647.

Prae-Adamitae. Amsterdam, 1655. Translated as *Men Before Adam.* London, 1956.

Relation de l'islande. Paris: Iolly, 1663.

WORKS ABOUT LA PEYRÈRE

Allen, D. C. *The Legend of Noah: Renaissance Rationalism in Art, Science, and Letters.* Urbana: University of Illinois Press, 1963.

Bayle, Pierre. "Peyrère, Isaac La." In *Dictionnaire historique et critique.* Rotterdam, Netherlands: Reinier Leers, 1695–1697.

Katz, David S., and Richard H. Popkin. *The Messianic Revolution: Radical Religious Politics to the End of the Second Millennium.* New York: Hill and Wang, 1998. See especially chapter 7.

McKee, David R. "Isaac La Peyrère, a Precursor of Eighteenth-Century Critical Deists." *PMLA* 59 (1944): 456–485.

Popkin, Richard H. *Isaac La Peyrère (1596–1676): His Life, Work and Influence.* Leiden, Netherlands: Brill, 1987.

Richard Popkin (1967, 2005)

LAPLACE, PIERRE SIMON DE

(1749–1827)

Pierre Simon de Laplace, the French astronomer and mathematician famous for his celestial mechanics and theory of probability, was born in Normandy. Upon coming to Paris, he attracted the attention of Jean Le Rond d'Alembert, who found him employment in the École Militaire. Here he taught mathematics to trainee artillery officers, among whom was Napoleon Bonaparte. When the revolutionary government established the École Polytechnique, Laplace was one of its founding professors. He served with distinction on many of the great committees of the French Academy of Sciences and of the government. He helped devise the meter, standardized weights and measures, and worked out an ingenious system of sampling to provide an economical and efficient census. The elegance of his mathematical work has yet to be rivaled, and his power of analysis is matched only by that of Isaac Newton and Joseph-Louis Lagrange. His philosophical opinions, especially those in his *Exposition du système du monde (The System of the World)* and *Essai philosophique sur les probabilités (A Philosophical Essay on Probabilities)*, have a bluntness and clarity of expression that ensured their popularity.

Laplace's adult life was passed in conditions of civil strife and sometimes of chaos, but despite his revolutionary affiliations, the restoration of the Bourbons brought him neither poverty nor disgrace; he died honored by all, a newly created marquis. Against this background of political confusion, he came to believe that the theory of probability, properly and widely applied, would reduce most of the problems of society (like the attainment of justice) to something manageable; with the help of probability theory, he believed, a man of delicate intuition and wide experience could find practical solutions to most social difficulties.

Laplace's scientific work had a strong element of tidiness about it. It consisted largely of the final polishing of the Newtonian enterprise, knitting up its loose ends. Using the improved calculus devised by his colleagues, particularly Lagrange, he removed all known errors from, and explained all known anomalies in, the Newtonian cosmology and physics. It seemed to Laplace that there was no phenomenon that the improved and polished Newtonian physics was incapable of handling. He came to regard the enormous explanatory power of the system as practically a demonstration of its truth. New observations would only confirm it further, he thought, and their consequences were as certain as if they had already been observed.

What had produced this remarkable confidence was a series of complete successes. Newton had never been convinced of the stability of the solar system, which he suggested might need divine correction from time to time. Laplace showed, in effect, that every known secular variation, such as the changing speeds of Saturn and Jupiter, was cyclic and that the system was indeed entirely stable and required no divine maintenance. (It was this triumph that occasioned his celebrated reply to Napoleon's query about the absence of God from the theory; Laplace said that he had no need of that hypothesis.) He also completed the theory of the tides and solved another of Newton's famous problems, the deduction from first principles of the velocity of sound in air. Laplace added a very accurately estimated correction for the heating effect produced by rapidity of the oscillation, which was too short to allow the heat of compression to be dissipated.

DETERMINISM AND PROBABILITY

Not only was Laplace confident of the Newtonian theory, but he was also greatly struck by its determinist nature. Where one could gather accurate information about initial conditions, later states of a mechanical system could be deduced with both precision and certainty. The only obstacle to complete knowledge of the world was ignorance of initial conditions. Laplace's confidence in Newtonian theory is exemplified in the introduction to his *Philosophical Essay on Probabilities,* in which he envisaged a superhuman intelligence capable of grasping both the position at any time of every particle in the universe and all the forces acting upon it. For such an intelligence "nothing would be uncertain and the future, as the past, would be present to its eyes. The human mind offers, in the perfection which it has been able to give to astronomy, a feeble idea of this intelligence" (*Philosophical Essay,* p. 4).

But this ideal is difficult to attain, since we are frequently ignorant of initial conditions. The way to cope with the actual world, Laplace thought, is to use the theory of probability. The superhuman intelligence would have no need of a theory of probability. Laplace would have regarded as ridiculous the idea that there could be systems that would react to stimuli in only more or less probable ways. He said, "The curve described by a simple molecule of air or vapor is regulated in a manner just as certain as the planetary orbits; the only difference between them is that which comes from our ignorance" (*Philosophical Essay*, p. 6). He then defined a measure of probability as follows:

> The theory of chance consists in reducing all the events of the same kind to a certain number of cases equally possible … and in determining the number of cases favorable to the event whose probability is sought. The ratio of this number to that of all the cases possible is the measure of this probability, which is thus simply a fraction whose numerator is the number of favorable cases and whose denominator is the number of all the cases possible. (*Philosophical Essay*, p. 6)

This is the definition of probability known today as the proportion of alternatives. Then as now, it involves the very tricky notion of equipossible cases. Laplace deals with this notion by glossing equipossible cases as those that "we may be equally undecided about in regard to their existence" (*Philosophical Essay*, p. 6).

This account does have its difficulties. Equal indecision is not at all easy to determine and may, in the end, hinge upon states of mind quite irrelevant to a sound estimate of probabilities. Throughout his study of probability Laplace refers to such subjective factors as honesty, good judgment, and absence of prejudice, which are required in using probability theory. However, he does give a much sounder criterion for its practice; it encourages one to reckon as equally possible those kinds of events instances of which we have no special reason to believe will occur. Equality of ignorance then becomes his criterion for equality of possibility. Laplace is quite happy about this, since he believed—perhaps rightly—that the proper occasion for the recourse to probability is ignorance of the initial conditions, the relevant theory, or both. Actual estimates of probability are made statistically. In his practical examples he appears to depend on a further distinction, which also seems correct. It is the distinction between the meaning of the statement of probability for a certain kind of event (that is, ratio of number of favorable to equipossible kinds of events) and the usual estimate of this probability, which is the relative frequency of actual events of the kind under consideration among all appropriate cases.

APPLICATIONS OF PROBABILITY

Laplace made several practical applications of probability theory. In science he applied it to the problem of sampling for the census and to the theory of errors; to both of these studies he made valuable contributions. He also believed that probability theory would have great utility in the moral sciences. He studied the optimum size for a jury to give the least doubtful verdict and the voting procedures of assemblies both on candidates for office and on propositions. He discussed the advantages and disadvantages of voting by ranking in order of merit and of voting by the knockout majority system. In this study and in his reflections on what it is reasonable to risk and in what kind of game, one gets the occasional glimpse of Laplace's basic moral principle, "Only bet on a reasonably sure thing."

PHILOSOPHY OF SCIENCE

In his philosophy of science and in his views on the nature of scientific method, Laplace expressed himself somewhat along the same lines as Newton, but more liberally. He saw quite clearly that science is not the accumulation of isolated and particular items of information. "It is by comparing phenomena together, and by endeavouring to trace their connection with each other, that he [man] has succeeded in discovering these laws, the existence of which may be perceived even in the most complicated of their effects" (*System*, Vol. I, p. 205). In searching for connections we do not need to shun hypotheses. Laplace said of hypotheses what Newton should have said, considering the use he made of them: that if we refuse to attribute them to reality and regard them merely as the means of connecting phenomena in order to discover the laws (which we correct according to further observations), they can lead us to the real causes or at least enable us to infer from observed phenomena those which given conditions ought to produce.

In fact, it is by excluding on the basis of decisive experiments all those hypotheses that are false that "we should arrive … at the true one." Ideally, Laplace sees scientific method as the formulation of generalizations of connection between phenomena, proceeding inductively from phenomena to laws (which are the ratios connecting particular phenomena), and from these to forces. When these forces reveal some general principle, that principle is verified by direct experience, if possible, or by examination of its agreement or disagreement with known phenomena.

Testing consists both of trying to formulate a deductive system based upon the highest hypotheses and designed to explain the phenomena, "even in their smallest details," and of seeing whether the theory agrees with as varied and as numerous phenomena as are relevant to it. If a theory passes these tests, it "acquires the highest degree of certainty and of perfection that it is able to obtain."

Laplace saw that our confidence in predictions had to be based upon confidence in some principle of the uniformity of nature. The sources of his confidence in some principle of uniformity were twofold. First, there is the condition of the absence of interference. If there is no reason why a change should occur, a change will not occur—a principle deeply embedded in Newtonian science. As Laplace put it, "Being assured that nothing will interfere between these causes and their effects, we venture to extend our views into futurity, and contemplate the series of events which time alone can develop" (*System,* Vol. I, p. 206). Second, simplicity was to be regarded as a mark of future reliability. The principle of induction, said Laplace, is that "the simplest ratios are the most common." He said, too, "We judge by induction that if various events, movements for example, appear constantly and have been long connected by a simple ratio, they will continue to be subjected to it" (*Philosophical Essay,* p. 178). The theory of probability supplies a connection between the two sources of confidence, for, said Laplace, we conclude from the fact that a simple ratio is found among quantities in nature "that the ratio is due, not to hazard, but to a regular cause." Thus, if no other causes intervene, we may expect a likeness of effects, in fact, a uniformity of nature.

Summing up scientific method, Laplace said, "Induction, analogy, hypotheses founded upon facts and rectified continually by new observations, a happy tact given by nature and strengthened by numerous comparisons of its indications with experience, such are the principal means for arriving at truth" (*Philosophical Essay,* p. 176).

See also Alembert, Jean Le Rond d'; Determinism, A Historical Survey; Induction; Newton, Isaac; Probability; Scientific Method.

Bibliography

WORKS BY LAPLACE

Oeuvres complètes. 14 vols. Paris: Gauthier-Villars, 1878–1914.

Exposition du système du monde. Paris, 1798. Translated by J. Pond as *The System of the World.* London: R. Phillips, 1809. Contains two important conjectures: that the planets might have been formed by the condensation of a large, diffuse solar atmosphere as it contracted, and the hypothesis, since confirmed, that the nebulae are clouds of stars and that the Milky Way is our view of that nebula of which our sun is a star.

Traité de la mécanique céleste, 5 vols. Paris: Chez J.B.M. Duprat, 1799–1825. Translated by N. Bowditch as *Mécanique Céleste,* 4 vols. Boston: Hillard, Gray, Little, and Wilkins, 1829–1839.

Théorie analytique des probabilités. Paris: Courcier, 1812.

Essai philosophique sur les probabilités. Paris: Courcier, 1814. Translated by F. W. Truscott and F. L. Emory as *A Philosophical Essay on Probabilities.* New York: Wiley, 1902; New York: Dover, 1951. A semipopular introduction to the *Théorie analytique.*

WORKS ON LAPLACE

Andoyer, H. *L'oeuvre scientifique de Laplace.* Paris: Payot, 1922.

Whittaker, Sir E. "Laplace." *Mathematical Gazette* 33 (303) (1949): 1–12.

R. Harré (1967)

LAPSHIN, IVAN IVANOVICH
(1870–1952)

Ivan Ivanovich Lapshin, the Russian neo-Kantian philosopher, was born in Moscow and studied at the University of St. Petersburg under the leading Russian neo-Kantian, Aleksandr Vvedenskii. Lapshin pursued his studies abroad for some years after 1893, concentrating particularly on Kantianism in English philosophy. With the publication in 1906 of his dissertation and chief philosophical work, *Zakony myshleniia i formy poznaniia* (The laws of thought and the forms of cognition), he received his doctorate from the University of St. Petersburg and in 1913 was made professor of philosophy at that institution. Along with many other noted Russian scholars Lapshin was exiled from the Soviet Union in 1922; he settled in Prague, where he lived until his death. His many writings cover a broad range of topics in philosophy, psychology, literature, music, and art, and include Russian translations of works by William James.

In his chief work Lapshin developed an antimetaphysical position on Kantian grounds, arguing specifically that the "laws of thought" derive their necessity solely from their connection with the forms through which sensory objects are cognized and that, therefore, it cannot be known whether these laws apply beyond the bounds of possible experience. According to Lapshin the law of contradiction, for example, can be understood only in reference to space and time (which, contrary to Immanuel Kant, he held to be categories of the understanding rather than forms of sensibility); and since the categories of space and time do not necessarily apply to transempirical objects, neither does the law of contradiction. Consequently nothing can legitimately be affirmed of "things in themselves," not even their existence.

Lapshin devoted little attention to problems of ethics and did not accept Kant's transition to a noumenal realm and to religious faith via the dictates of moral consciousness. In general he regarded metaphysics and religion as entirely without epistemological foundation and as obstacles to the progress and vitality of human thought.

Much of Lapshin's later philosophical work was concerned with questions of the psychology of creativity and with the epistemological basis of our knowledge of other minds. His two-volume study of creativity in philosophy (1922) was complemented by a number of other writings on creativity in literature and the arts.

As early as 1910 Lapshin had published a historical account of the problem of other selves, and in 1923 he presented his resolution of the problem in the article *Oproverzhenie solipsizma* (A refutation of solipsism). He argued that our sense of the immediate giveness of other selves is an illusion based on the projection of subjective impressions; other selves are hypothetical constructs, which can be called "immanently real" but cannot be shown to have transcendent reality.

See also James, William; Kantian Ethics; Kant, Immanuel; Neo-Kantianism; Russian Philosophy; Solipsism.

Bibliography

WORKS BY LAPSHIN

Zakony myshleniia i formy poznaniia. St. Petersburg, 1906.

Problema chuzhovo "ia" v noveishei filosofii (The problem of other selves in modern philosophy). St. Petersburg: Senatskaia, 1910.

Filosofiia izobreteniia i izobretenie filosofii (Philosophy of invention and the invention of philosophy). 2 vols. Petrograd, 1922; 2nd ed., Prague, 1924.

"Oproverzhenie solipsizma" (A refutation of solipsism). In *Trudy russkikh uchonykh za granitsei.* No. 1. Prague, 1923. A German translation is available: *Von der Ueberwindung des Solipsismus* Melbourne: D. Jakovenko, 1969.

Spor o svobode voli v sovremennoi filosofii (The debate on the freedom of the will in contemporary philosophy). Prague: Russkii svobodnyi universitet, 1941.

WORKS ON LAPSHIN

Losskii, N. O. *History of Russian Philosophy.* New York: International Universities Press, 1951.

Zen'kovskii, V. V. *Istoriia Russkoi Filosofii.* 2 vols. Paris: YMCA Press, 1948–1950. Translated by George L. Kline as *A History of Russian Philosophy.* 2 vols. New York: Columbia University Press, 1953.

James P. Scanlan (1967)
Bibliography updated by Vladimir Marchenkov (2005)

LA ROCHEFOUCAULD, DUC FRANÇOIS DE
(1613–1680)

Duc François de La Rochefoucauld, the French epigrammatist and moral critic, was born in Paris; he was known as the prince de Marcillac until he succeeded his father in 1650. An incurable love of adventure and imprudent women brought him into early conflict with Cardinal Richelieu, who imprisoned him briefly in the Bastille in 1637. Contempt for Jules Mazarin, whose treatment he bitterly resented, led La Rochefoucauld to join the faction of the Cardinal de Retz when the Fronde broke out in 1648, but before the end of hostilities he had gone over to Condé's side and was seriously wounded in 1652.

In 1656 he was permitted to return from exile to Paris, where he lived until his death, which occurred after many crippling years of gout. During this period, he became a leading figure in salon society, where his closest friends were Mme. de Lafayette and Mme. de Sévigné, as well as in the Port Royal circle, which included Antoine Arnauld and Mme. de Sablé.

Shortly after his return to Paris he began his *Mémoires*, first Books III–VI (covering the Fronde), then Book II (on the years from 1642 to 1649), and finally Book I (on the years from 1624 to 1642). A grossly inaccurate pirated Dutch edition, which appeared in 1662, caused a great scandal, but the authentic text was not published until the nineteenth century. These *Mémoires*, although less ample and distinguished than those by Retz on the same events, are indispensable to an understanding of the *Maximes*, since they show the inconsistency, dishonesty, and superficiality characteristic of the aristocratic *Frondeurs*.

The *Maximes* were begun as a joint enterprise with Mme. de Sablé and Jacques Esprit (of the Port Royal Circle) and reflect a popular salon pastime, but after the appearance of a pirated Dutch edition in 1664, successive authorized editions followed from 1665 to 1678, considerably altering the scope and nature of the work. The contributions of La Rochefoucauld's friends, as well as maxims too closely resembling such models as Seneca and Montaigne, were deleted, and the original brief moral reflections that occupied a page or so were cut up into the present highly condensed epigrammatic form of a few lines.

The *Maximes* deal with human nature from a strictly human standpoint, all references to God and religion having been systematically removed. They give a lucid and penetrating analysis of the manifold forms taken by self-interest, which, according to La Rochefoucauld, is the fundamental motive behind human behavior. He also claims that "reason is most often the dupe of the heart," so that human nature is a mass of capricious and unpredictable passions of physiological origin, and what commonly passes for virtue, when it is not pure accident, is really disguised, or unrecognized, vice. He shows little confidence in the Cartesian program of passions controlled by reason and will, and no confidence whatsoever in any concept of natural virtue such as that held by admirers of the virtuous pagans of antiquity. The *Maximes* stress the importance of self-analysis and being honest with oneself; without these qualities love and friendship are a hollow sham, and even with them they may be no more than exercises in egoism.

The predominantly pessimistic outlook reflected in the *Maximes* is partly relieved by the brilliance of the style and the subtlety of the analysis, and also partly by various qualified admissions that true friendship and genuine integrity (*honnêteté*), although rare, may occasionally be encountered. The growing pressure of conformism in a highly artificial society, the author's own experience of pointless heroism and shabby motives in the *Fronde*, and above all his proud and melancholy temperament serve to explain the harsh verdict of the *Maximes*. For all their abiding interest these epigrams remain the direct product and reflection of the age in which they were written. Some brief essays, portraits, and numerous letters constitute the rest of La Rochefoucauld's work.

See also Arnauld, Antoine; Continental Philosophy; Montaigne, Michel Eyquem de; Self-Interest; Seneca, Lucius Annaeus; Virtue and Vice.

Bibliography

La Rochefoucauld's writings may be found in his *Oeuvres complètes*, Bibliothèque de la Pléiade (Paris, 1957). More recent editions of the *Maximes* include an edition edited by J. Vallier (Lausanne, 1962) and the English translations of C. Fitzgibbon (London: Allan Wingate, 1957) and L. W. Tancock (Harmondsworth: Penguin, 1959).

For literature on La Rochefoucauld, see E. Magne, *Le vrai visage de La Rochefoucauld* (Paris, 1923). There is also an excellent chapter on him in A. Adam, *Histoire de la littérature française au XVIIe siècle*, Vol. 4, Ch. 2 (Paris, 1954). See also Susan R. Baker, "The Works of La Rochefoucauld in Relation to Machiavellian Ideas of Morals and Politics," *Journal of the History of Ideas* (44[1983]: 207–218); Henry C. Clark, "La Rochefoucauld and the Social Bases of Aristocratic Ethics," *History of European Ideas* (8[1987]: 61–76); Peter M. Fine, *Vauvenargues and La Rochefoucauld* (Manchester, U.K.: Manchester University Press, 1974); J. E. Parsons, Jr., "On La Rochefoucauld: Preliminary Reflections," *Interpretation* (2 [1971]: 126–142); Tilo Schabert, "The Para-Moral Principles of Early Modern Society: Contextual Reflections upon the Maxims of La Rochefoucauld," *History of European Ideas* (7[1986]: 67–84).

A. J. Krailsheimer (1967)
Bibliography updated by Tamra Frei (2005)

LAROMIGUIÈRE, PIERRE
(1756–1837)

Pierre Laromiguière, the French professor of philosophy, was born at Livignac in the district of Rouergue. As a young man, he was ordained a priest and exercised his ecclesiastical duties for a short period before becoming professor of philosophy successively at Carcassonne, Tarbes, Toulouse, and the Sorbonne. He was a close student of Étienne Bonnot de Condillac and an associate of the Idéologues but departed from the teachings of both in certain particulars. Excessively shy, he refused to propose his candidacy to the French Academy, though twice urged to do so, and confined his public appearances to the classroom. He died in Paris, one of the most esteemed and beloved of teachers. Among his more famous pupils were Victor Cousin and Théodore Jouffroy.

Laromiguière's disagreement with the school of Condillac arose over the question of the mind's passivity. He argued that if all our ideas were modifications of sensory material impressed upon us by external causes, it would be impossible to account for attention, comparison, and reason. These, he held, were essentially active. There is a fundamental distinction to be made, he said, between seeing and looking, listening and hearing, and the difference cannot be explained if the soul is a passive recipient of sensory stimuli. Activity was indefinable for Laromiguière, since it had no anterior ideas from which it could be derived. He seemed to believe that anyone hearing the term would grasp its meaning.

The three activities of the understanding were attention, comparison, and reasoning; and the three activities of the will corresponding to them were desire, preference, and freedom—the latter being the power to act or not to act. Laromiguière's insistence on the soul's activity was most welcome to his contemporaries, for it restored to men the autonomy that, they felt, Condillac had destroyed. While disagreeing with Condillac on this point, Laromiguière agreed with his predecessor that the primary business of philosophy was the analysis of ideas. In his best known and extremely popular work, *Leçons de philosophie*, which ran through six editions between 1815 and 1844, he assigned to metaphysics the single task of discovering the origin of all our ideas.

Laromiguière was particularly admired for the perfection of his literary style, the fame of which was acknowledged even by Hippolyte-Adolphe Taine.

See also Condillac, Étienne Bonnot de; Cousin, Victor; French Philosophy; Ideas; Jouffroy, Théodore Simon; Taine, Hippolyte-Adolphe.

Bibliography

WORKS BY LAROMIGUIÈRE

Projet d'éléments de métaphysique. Toulouse, 1793.

Sur les paradoxes de Condillac. Paris, 1805.

Leçons de philosophie sur les principes de l'intelligence. Paris, 1815–1818.

WORKS ON LAROMIGUIÈRE

Boas, George. *French Philosophies of the Romantic Period,* 33–42. Baltimore: Johns Hopkins Press, 1925.

Janet, Paul. "Laromiguière, la liberté de penser." *Revue philosophique et littéraire* 1 (1848): 253–263, 358–368.

Picavet, François. *Les idéologues,* 520–548, 552–567. Paris: Alcan, 1891. Second section referred to deals with Laromiguière's influence.

Taine, Hippolyte. *Les philosophes classiques du XIXe siècle en France.* Paris: Hachette, 1868. Ch. 1.

George Boas (1967)

LAROUI, ABDULLAH
(1935–)

A Moroccan intellectual born in 1935, Abdullah Laroui taught at Mohammed V University in Rabat and was one of a distinguished group of Moroccan thinkers such as M. A. Lahbabi and M. A. al-Jabri. His work involves a variety of theoretical and disciplinary perspectives, including history (his main professional discipline), sociology, philosophy, and literature. He has produced histories of the Maghreb (North Africa) and of the Arab world in general, and his writings on modernity and strike at the heart of many key issues that are important for Arab culture in the postcolonial world. He raised in particular the questions how history should be written and how to understand the cultural life of a group of people through understanding their histroy. This comes out as a much more complicated issue than might initially appear to be the case, and Laroui uses the conceptual machinery of both Ibn Khaldun and Machiavelli to try to position Arabi history within an appropriate theoretical context.

One of Laroyi's major achievement is in laying out the ambiguous nature of some of the key concepts of Arab culture in the contemporary world, including modernity, the state, authenticity, continuity, rationality, and tradition. He argues that the Arab world cannot adopt wholeheartedly the Western concept of the state since this is essentially a secular notion and pays little regard to the past, while for Arabs the link with Islam and their history is a crucial aspect of political legitimacy. In any case, the state is only a part of the whole Islamic *umma*, or community, and there is a notion of an Arab *umma* in which the state exists, and that produces a nexus of relationships for the concept of the state, that makes little sense of the Western notion. As with his predecessor Ibn Khaldun, Laroui has an approach to understanding society that makes it important to develop and clearly specify a theoretical perspective and put a particular social structure with in its historical and cultural context. In this way it is possible to say something both true and interesting about Arab ideology, while using the conceptual tools imported directly from outside the region is unlikely to be helpful.

Laroui's thought has moved from his earlier Marxism to produce a more nuanced approach to the philosophy of history and the understanding of culture. He is part of a significant movement in the modern Arab world that tries to define Arab culture and its unique features, while at the same time making use of theories from outside the region where they can shed light on the issue.

See also Ibn Khaldūn; Islamic Philosophy; Machiavelli, Niccolò; Marxist Philosophy; Philosophy of History.

Bibliography

Laroui, Abdullah. *Crisis of the Arab Intellectual: Traditionalism vs. Historicism.* Translated by D. Cammell. Berkeley: University of California Press, 1976.

Hasan Hanafi (2005)
Oliver Leaman (2005)

LASSALLE, FERDINAND
(1825–1864)

Ferdinand Lassalle, the German socialist, was born Ferdinand Lasal in Breslau, Silesia, of a middle-class Jewish family. The young Lassalle—he gallicized his name—was a poor and rebellious student. Quite early he indicated his persistent, but never conflicting, longings both to relieve the oppressed and to achieve aristocratic status. These two desires illuminate the paradoxical nature of a man who championed the causes of oppressed workers and oppressed noblewomen with equal vigor. He corresponded regularly with Karl Marx, defended the honor of the Countess von Hatzfeldt in a lengthy and celebrated lawsuit, sought the acclaim of Berlin society, founded the Allgemeiner Deutscher Arbeiterverein (the first political party for German workers), dressed fastidiously, and died at the age of thirty-nine, from wounds suffered in a duel with Count von Racowitza.

Lassalle attended the universities of Berlin and Breslau, falling under the influence of Hegelian philosophy at the latter. But, although he had philosophic pretensions and sought the acclaim of philosophers, he preferred a life of action to one of theory; and his fame rests chiefly on his founding the Allgemeiner Deutscher Arbeiterverein in 1863, to which German Social Democrats still trace their origin.

Lassalle referred to his exposure to G. W. F. Hegel as his "second birth." He avidly consumed Hegel's works, as well as those of young Hegelians like David Friedrich Strauss and Ludwig Feuerbach. Hegel's reference to the ancient Ionian philosopher Heraclitus of Ephesus as his forerunner led Lassalle to study Heraclitus; and he sought to demonstrate that Heraclitus had forecast Hegelian ideas. Lassalle also aspired unashamedly to the fame that a major philological and philosophical work would provide for him in German society. He began his research while not yet twenty, but did not complete it until fifteen years later. Berlin academicians hailed the publication in 1858 of *Die Philosophie Herakleitos des Dunkeln von Ephesos,* but later critics have found grave defects in the work, most notably Lassalle's preoccupation with Hegel rather than Heraclitus.

Hegelian ideas dominated Lassalle's historical and economic thought as well. His historical and economic theories, although not carefully formulated, emerge most clearly from the works of his last years, when he was organizing the Arbeiterverein, especially *Das System der erworbenen Rechte* (Leipzig, 1861); *Arbeiter-Programm* (Berlin, 1862); *Über Verfassungswesen; Die indirekte Steuer und die Lage der arbeitende Klassen* (1863; reprinted Berlin, 1874); and *Herr Bastiat-Schulze von Delitzsch, der ökonomische Julian, oder Kapital und Arbeit* (Berlin, 1864). He shared with Marx the belief that revolutions are not "created" by revolutionaries, but occur as the result of a historical process. Men called revolutionaries are in fact merely the midwives to a new age produced in the womb of time. Lassalle described this process in Hegelian terms. A new social order, when it appeared, would rise on the wings of Hegelian ideas. The bourgeois idea of freedom had destroyed feudal solidarity in 1789. The bourgeoisie had liberated itself by reducing the state to the role of "nightwatchman." The proletariat would in turn liberate itself through association, at first within a political party that would demand and obtain universal suffrage from the state. Having achieved universal suffrage, the proletariat would use the power of the state to form great workers' associations or cooperatives. These would in turn liberate the worker from the cruel "iron law of wages" and achieve freedom for him.

Lassalle worked arduously at organizing the workers into a national political party. He did not intend to overthrow the state, but to use it. The idea of freedom would find eventual embodiment through the state. All previous conflicts would be synthesized in this final stage of history. Thus Lassalle accepted the Prussian state and perhaps even the Prussian monarchy. His position on the latter, as well as on private property, is ambiguous. Lassalle wrote and agitated under Prussian censorship and was constantly being tried for treasonable activity. His published works and public statements are therefore not always consistent with his private correspondence and conversations.

Lassalle's relationship with Marx waxed warm and cool. Lassalle undoubtedly admired Marx and sought the latter's approval, whereas Marx disapproved of much that Lassalle wrote and did. Marx regarded Lassalle as a friend, an informant, a creditor, a publishing agent, and an immature, pompous plagiarist. They broke off their correspondence before Lassalle's death.

See also Feuerbach, Ludwig Andreas; Hegel, Georg Wilhelm Friedrich; Hegelianism; Heraclitus of Ephesus; Marx, Karl; Socialism; Strauss, David Friedrich.

Bibliography

COLLECTED WORKS OF LASSALLE

Gesammelten Reden und Schriften. 12 vols. Edited by Eduard Bernstein. Berlin, 1919–1920.

Nachgelassene Briefe und Schriften. 6 vols. Edited by Gustav Mayer. Stuttgart: Deutsche Verlagsanstalt, 1921–1925.

WORKS ON LASSALLE

Baron, S. *Die politische Theorie Ferdinand Lassalles.* Leipzig: Hirschfeld, 1923.

Bernstein, Eduard. "Ferdinand Lassalle und seine Bedeutung in der Geschichte der Sozialdemokratie." In Ferdinand Lassalle, *Reden und Schriften,* Vol. I. Berlin, 1892.

Brandes, Georg. *Ferdinand Lassalle.* Berlin, 1877. Translated by Eden and Cedar Paul. London: W. Heinemann, 1911.

Footman, David. *The Primrose Path, a Life of Ferdinand Lassalle.* London: Cresset Press, 1946. A good biography.

Knapp, Vincent J. "Ferdinand Lassalle on the State and Society: A Legacy to Welfare Statism." *Australian Journal of Politics and History*17 (3) (1971): 377–385.

Lewis, Vivian. "Ferdinand Lassalle, 1825–1864." *History Today* 15 (1) (1965): 58–64.

Oncken, Hermann. *Lassalle.* Stuttgart: Frommanns, 1904. An excellent biography.

Schirokauer, Arno. *Lassalle, die Macht der Illusion, die Illusion der Macht.* Leipzig: P. List, 1928. Translated as *Lassalle, the Power of Illusion and the Illusion of Power.* London: Allen and Unwin, 1931. A good biography.

Thier, Erich. *Rodbertus, Lassalle, Adolph Wagner.* Jena, Germany, 1930.

Sterling Fishman (1967)
Bibliography updated by Philip Reed (2005)

LATIN AMERICAN PHILOSOPHY

Latin American philosophy covers primarily the philosophy produced in the parts of the Americas that belonged to the Spanish and Portuguese empires after 1492. The Maya, Toltec, Aztec, and Inca civilizations engaged in some philosophical speculation in the form of religious myths and cosmological accounts prior to the arrival of the Europeans, but most of the records of these efforts were destroyed during the conquest. As happened with almost everything else in the wake of colonization, Iberians took control over the development of philosophy and scholastic philosophy became the most influential philosophical trend in the New World.

The encounter posed new challenges to European thought and initiated new developments in both Europe and Latin America. In Iberia, new issues, primarily concerned with the rights of conquered peoples and just war, took center stage, and the greatest Iberian philosophers of the times, Francisco de Vitoria (c. 1492–1546) and Francisco Suárez (1548–1617) addressed them. In the colonies, some attention was given to pre-Columbian worldviews, but these slowly receded into the background, making way for the concerns, first, of the Iberians living in the colonies and, then, of *criollos*—that is, native-born authors.

The colonial roots of Latin American philosophy helped set the stage for the emphasis on sociopolitical issues, such as human rights and social justice, which have been so central to the philosophical development in the region. In addition to addressing standard philosophical questions concerning the nature of being, knowledge,

and value, Latin American philosophers have demonstrated a strong commitment to more concrete issues involving educational policy, political organization, and social reform. In contrast to their Anglo-American colleagues, many Latin American philosophers have developed their ideas not in technical articles and systematic treatises intended for specialized audiences, but in newspaper articles, essays, and even fiction, meant to be read by a broad public. This is consonant with the view that philosophy should be a tool for social change and has led some historians to speak of two trends in Latin American philosophy: academic and Latin Americanist. The first is inspired by European philosophy and is practiced in universities; the second is more autochthonous and extends beyond the boundaries of academia. Most authors cited in this entry belong to the first trend. Some of the best known thinkers who belong to the second are Eugenio María Hostos (Puerto Rico, 1839–1903), Justo Sierra (Mexico, 1848–1912), José Martí (Cuba, 1853–1895), José Enrique Rodó (Uruguay, 1871–1917), Jorge Luis Borges (Argentina, 1899–1986), Octavio Paz (Mexico, 1914–1998), Carlos Fuentes (Mexico, b. 1928), Mario Vargas Llosa (Peru, b. 1936), and Luis Castro Leiva (Venezuela, 1943–1999).

MAJOR PERIODS OF LATIN AMERICAN PHILOSOPHY

Four major periods in the history of Latin American philosophy stand out: colonial, independentist, positivist, and contemporary.

COLONIAL PERIOD (C. 1550–1750)

Latin American philosophy begins within the scholastic fold provided by the Iberian clergy sent by the Spanish and Portuguese Crowns to convert the indigenous inhabitants of the territories they had conquered. The main philosophical centers during the early colonial period were Mexico and Peru, the two places in which major empires had flourished and the Europeans found the gold and silver they coveted. The texts studied were those of medieval scholastics and of their Iberian commentators, and the issues addressed concerned logic, natural philosophy (physics), and metaphysics. The first author to publish systematic treatises on these topics was Alonso de la Vera Cruz (1504–1584), but it was Antonio Rubio's (1548–1615) *Logica mexicana* (*Mexican Logic*, 1603) that first gained prominence in the New World and Europe.

Although scholasticism was central to, and many thinkers continued to write within, this tradition, others were guided by humanist ideas. In particular, they were concerned with the political and legal questions raised by the process of colonization. Arguably, the most important of these thinkers was Bartolomé de las Casas (1474–1566), a Dominican friar from Spain who became the leading champion of the rights of the Indians. His long life was devoted to arguing before the Spanish Crown that the indigenous groups of New Spain were not barbarians "in the strict sense"; they were no less human than Spaniards and so just as deserving of the same basic human rights.

Las Casas first brought up what became known in Spain as "the Indian Question." As early as 1515, he began to petition the Crown to enact laws that would eliminate the notorious *encomiendas*. This system gave Spanish settlers custody of groups of indigenous peoples who were then exploited in mining and agriculture. In 1550 an important debate took place in Valladolid, Spain, between the humanist Juan Ginés de Sepúlveda (1490–1573), a leading ideologue of the *Conquista*, and Las Casas. Las Casas argued that it was unjust to wage war against the indigenous peoples and to enslave them.

Las Casas's defense of the Indians reflects the influence of several sources. The thought of Aristotle (384–322 BCE), known as "the Philosopher" among scholastics, is behind several distinctions upon which Las Casas based his defense. Other sources included canon and Roman law, and such Christian thinkers as Augustine (354–430) and Thomas Aquinas (c. 1225–1274). Las Casas was scholastically trained and the scholastic method informs the structure and content of his rebuttal of Sepúlveda.

The debate between Las Casas and Sepúlveda raised questions concerning the natures of humanity and justice, issues that continue to shape Latin American philosophy to this day. Social injustice did not have only one face. Women also suffered oppression, although for most of the thinkers of the colonial period, this went unnoticed. Aristotle had claimed that women were inferior to men, and most of his scholastic followers did not question this view. But there were isolated voices that cried out against the claim that women were not fit for intellectual activity. One of the most eloquent and powerful of these voices was that of the nun Sor Juana Inés de la Cruz (Mexico, 1651–1695). A recurring theme in her writings is the image of a human being as a microcosm, and reflects the influence of neoplatonic philosophy upon her thought. Much of her writings, whether in prose or poetic form, displays a concern with the unjust position of women in colonial society.

INDEPENDENTIST PERIOD (C. 1750–1850)

A more complete break with scholasticism was attempted during the independentist period. This phase of Latin American thought receives its name from the political rationale articulated in the eighteenth century to gain independence from Spain and Portugal. The intellectuals engaged in this enterprise were men of action who used ideas for practical ends. The strong influence of Utilitarianism is reflected in their emphasis on progress and the attempt to employ ideas as tools for social change. Another source that shaped the period came from the liberal views of the French *philosophes*, who made reason a measure of legitimacy in social and political matters.

Most leading figures from this period were not philosophers in the strict sense. Simón Bolívar (Venezuela, 1783–1830), José Joaquin Fernández de Lizardi (Mexico, 1776–1827), Mariano Moreno (Argentina, 1778–1811), and José Cecilio del Valle (Honduras, 1780–1834) can be most accurately characterized as independence leaders rather than as philosophers. Instead of devoting their lives to developing systems of thought, they were more interested in concrete political and military action that would lead to the independence of the Iberian colonies.

Bolívar, known as the Liberator, successfully led northern South America to independence from Spain and was the founding father of five republics (Colombia, Venezuela, Ecuador, Peru, and Bolivia). Monumental deeds such as these are a central part of his legacy. Yet, his writings also helped to change the political structures in America and drew attention to the dangers confronting the newly liberated regions. In his *Carta de Jamaica* (*Jamaica Letter*, 1815), a call to independence from Spain, he complains of both a state of permanent infancy experienced by the nations of Spanish America and their dependence upon Europe. The problem of dependence is an enduring one in the Latin American philosophical tradition, shaping one of the most widespread strands of Latin American thought, the philosophy of liberation. In the *Carta*, Bolívar also touches upon the question of identity, another central theme of the tradition, prompted by the merging of indigenous and European populations and cultures.

Bolívar influenced thinkers of the contemporary period, such as the father of the Cuban revolution, José Martí (1853–1895), as well as the Mexican philosophers Samuel Ramos (1897–1959) and Leopoldo Zea (1912–2004). All of these thinkers devote considerable attention to the issues of liberation and cultural identity.

POSITIVISM (C. 1850–1910)

Once political independence had been achieved, a somewhat more stable period of philosophical activity, known as positivism, began. With the exception of scholasticism, positivism has been the most widespread and deeply rooted current in Latin American thought to date. The depth of its impact can be explained in historical terms: It took shape just in time to address the need for nation building in the region. Positivism was in part a response to the social, financial, and political needs of the newly liberated countries of Latin America.

The European father of positivism was the French philosopher Auguste Comte (1793–1857), who attempted to develop a rigorous and systematic understanding of human beings in both their individual and social dimensions. He emphasized experience over theoretical speculation and empirical science over metaphysics. The value of knowledge rests on its practical applications: Knowledge is a servant of action and should lead to the solution of concrete problems. This practical dimension was one of the most captivating aspects of Comte's thought for Latin Americans, for they wished to overcome anarchy, eradicate poverty and disease, and place their own countries on the path of progress.

Practical considerations, however, were not the only cause of positivism's success. Cultural and theoretical reasons also played a role. Since the colonial period, Latin American philosophy had been nurtured by scholasticism and, consequently, important practical issues had been neglected. Conceptual and terminological vagueness, excessive speculation, as well as unfounded and archaic dogmatism were predominant characteristics of much of the philosophy of the region. Positivists, by contrast, emphasized principles based on experience and logical rigor, and offered the assurance of progress, insisting that their claims rested on solid empirical evidence. With positivism, the leaders of the newly liberated republics thought they would finally leave not only the political legacy of the colonization behind, but the philosophical one as well.

The movement benefited greatly from the increasing prestige of science, because it proposed to limit its methods to those used by natural scientists. It was widely believed by those who favored this perspective that a new era had begun in which scientific study would make it possible to identify the causes of social evils and to eliminate them, just as medicine had begun to do with endemic diseases.

Comte's law of the three stages captured the attention of many Latin American intellectuals. According to this law, humanity passes through a theological, a metaphysical, and a scientific or positive stage. In the theological stage, the interpretation of reality is founded on prejudice and superstition. In the metaphysical, it is characterized by speculation, and facts are either ignored or not given adequate attention. Finally, in the positive stage, superstition and speculation are replaced by the establishment of facts, and knowledge is founded on experience.

Latin American thinkers applied Comte's law to the history of their own countries. An example of this application is found in the *Oración cívica* (*Civic Oration*, 1867) delivered by the Mexican Gabino Barreda in Guanajuato. With this text in mind, President Benito Juárez named Barreda member of a committee to draft a law, approved on December 2, 1867, that gave birth to public education in Mexico. The fact that another renowned teacher, Justo Sierra (1848–1912), succeeded to Barreda's position and continued to apply positivist principles to educational policy explains the strength that this perspective had in Mexico until the fall of the dictator Porfirio Díaz in 1911. Positivism was the official philosophy in Mexico during the twenty-seven-year dictatorship, and the government was guided by Comte's slogan "Order and Progress."

The chaos and backwardness that prevailed in some Latin American countries as the power vacuums left in the wake of colonial rule were filled by *caudillos* and other nondemocratic political leaders and structures helps to explain in part why positivist teachings captivated the minds of so many intellectuals and politicians. For example, the influence of positivism can be observed in the work of the Argentine thinker and statesman Domingo Faustino Sarmiento (1811–1888). His account of civilization in *Facundo, o civilización y barbarie* (*Facundo, or Civilization and Barbarism*, 1845) is shaped by positivist principles.

Each country of Latin America had its own particular way of appropriating positivism. Latin American positivism was shaped not only by Comte, but also by the social Darwinism expounded by the English philosopher Herbert Spencer (1820–1903). Comte had a stronger impact in Brazil, Mexico, and Chile, whereas Spencer was more influential in Argentina, Uruguay, and Cuba. In some cases, preference was given to one over the other for purely political reasons. In Cuba, for example, Enrique José Varona (1849–1933) rejected Comte's ideas because they did not favor the emancipation of Cuba from Spanish rule, and he adopted instead Spencer's notion of lib-

ENCYCLOPEDIA OF PHILOSOPHY
2nd edition

erty. In spite of these and many other national differences, one can speak of Latin American positivism as a unified, yet evolving movement in which the influence of Comte was greater toward the beginning of the period and that of Spencer predominated toward the end.

Juan Bautista Alberdi (Argentina, 1812–1884) and Andrés Bello (Venezuela, 1781–1865) were also influenced by positivism. Positivism's legacy in Argentina remained strong because it was never involved in any political movement, so it never came to be associated with dictatorships as, for example, was the case in Mexico. Furthermore, in Argentina positivism had an effective role in the development of educational institutions and, through the work of José Ingenieros (1877–1925), acquired renown in scientific and philosophical circles.

As in Argentina, positivism played a role in the development of Brazilian education. Nisia Floresta (1809–1885), one of the founders of the positivist movement in Brazil, was director of a school in Rio de Janeiro and, upon moving to Paris, established a close friendship with Comte. Furthermore, in Brazil, positivism was associated with the founding of the Republic in 1889, and the positivist motto, "Ordem e Progresso" (Order and progress), is inscribed on the Brazilian flag. Brazil was one of the last countries of Latin America to abolish slavery (1888) in part due to the positivist movement in Brazil. An understanding of Brazil's history in the eighteenth century is impossible without an appreciation of the role that positivist thinkers such as Raimundo Teixeira Mendes (1855–1927), Miguel Lemos (1854–1917), and Luis Pereira Barreto (1840–1923) played in the founding of the Republic.

CONTEMPORARY PERIOD (C. 1910–PRESENT)

The period following positivism is known as the contemporary period, and it can be broken down into three phases: the foundational stage, the period of normalcy, and the period of maturity.

FOUNDATIONAL STAGE (C. 1910–1940). This phase begins with the decline of positivism. The generation of thinkers who first rejected the central tenets of positivism became known as "the founders," a label coined by Francisco Romero (Argentina, 1891–1962). It included: Deústua, Alejandro Korn (Argentina, 1860–1936), Enrique Molina (Chile, 1871–1964), Carlos Vaz Ferreira (Uruguay, 1872–1958), Raimundo de Farias Brito (Brazil, 1862–1917), José Vasconcelos (Mexico, 1882–1959), and Antonio Caso (Mexico, 1883–1946), among others.

The general decline of positivism stems from several factors, and the national context must be taken into consideration insofar as the predominance of any particular cause varies from country to country. Still there were causes common to all Latin America. The first of these was the disappointment that Latin American intellectuals experienced when reality did not measure up to positivism's promises and aspirations. Immediate and assured results were envisioned and anxiously awaited, but progress was slow and uncertain. To uphold general principles and criteria for the study of social problems is one thing, but it is quite a different matter to develop effective, scientifically based procedures that can be applied in order to solve concrete problems. Stark reality shattered many illusions. The ideal of a scientific knowledge of society began to crumble in the face of difficulties, and the initial naive optimism gave way to corroding pessimism.

In addition, many thinkers began to discover fundamental theoretical shortcomings in positivism. The indiscriminate application of the principle of causality led positivists to deny freedom to human beings. Theoretical objections to determinism acquired momentum in the moral realm. No one can be held accountable for an act if it is determined, the critics of positivism claimed: positivism seemed to lead to an ethical dead end.

In particular, positivism seemed to spell disaster for aesthetic creation. If humans are not free, how can they be aesthetic agents? A mechanical explanation of the creative process factored out the very meaning of artistic creation, something that many Latin Americans found unacceptable. Deústua in particular responds by developing an aesthetic theory in his influential *Estética* (*Aesthetics*, 1923), in which aesthetic value is conceived as the source of all value. This "value of all values" as he calls it, is the product of free activity whose essential function consists in the creation and contemplation of an ideal aside from any practical intent. In contrast to the essentially instrumental character of other values, aesthetic value constitutes its own end, generating a completely disinterested activity, the creation of beauty.

Political considerations also factored into the general disenchantment with positivism. As already mentioned, in some countries such as Mexico, positivism was associated with a dictatorship that had been overthrown; in others such as Cuba, Comtian positivism was believed to support the colonial status quo against the possibility of independence to which many Cubans aspired. For countries that had suffered first under Spanish oppression and then under a succession of dictators, setting freedom aside seemed too high a price to pay for the promise of progress. Indeed, freedom had become the battle flag, so if positivism could not make room for freedom, then positivism must be abandoned.

In 1909 a group of young intellectuals in Mexico, who later acquired well-deserved renown in the field of philosophy and literature, founded the "Ateneo de la Juventud" (Atheneum of youth). They studied the philosophical classics, especially Plato and Kant, and contemporary philosophers who had rejected positivism in Europe, such as Henri Bergson (1859–1941) and Benedetto Croce (1866–1952). The influence of Friedrich Nietzsche (1844–1900) and Arthur Schopenhauer (1788–1860), whose thought was a counterweight to the narrow, scientific emphasis of positivism, was also felt. Following these studies, lectures were given in which positivist doctrine was roundly criticized and new ideas were proposed.

Vasconcelos is one of the most influential figures of this generation. He was not only an accomplished philosopher, but, like so many other Latin American intellectuals, also a devoted educator and political activist. Much of his work focuses upon the meaning of Mexican culture in particular and the destiny of Latin America in general. In two of his most popular works, *La raza cósmica* (*The Cosmic Race*, 1925) and *Indología* (*Indology*, 1926), he claims that the future will be constituted by the cosmic race, a synthesis of the four basic races of the world that will emerge in the region of the Amazon basin and fulfill "the divine mission of America." He contrasts this to the ethnic egoism and nationalism that dominates in Anglo-Saxon culture and claims that the new race of which he speaks will be characterized by a universalist spirit based on love.

Two other key figures are Caso in Mexico and Korn in Argentina. They are particularly important because they functioned as influential teachers and mentors of the generation that followed them. The first developed a moral theory based on the principle that there are two basic attitudes toward existence: One is based on the notion of existence as economy, where action is dictated by maximum advantage with minimum effort; the other is guided by disinterest, where action is dictated by maximum effort with least concern for advantage. The first is a positivist morality, the second is a morality based on love. In a somewhat similar vein, Korn developed a philosophy of creative freedom inspired by Kant. Although the physical realm operates according to necessary laws, subjects can formulate ideals and act according to them, thus resisting the tyranny of nature.

Crucial influences in the overcoming of positivism and its legacy were vitalism and intuitionism, especially the versions imported from French philosophers such as Émile Boutroux (1845–1921) and Bergson. Vitalism was a metaphysical position that conceived reality in terms of life. Intuitionism was an epistemic view in which knowledge, particularly about values, is based on intuition. Representative of this move away from positivism's narrow approach was the work of Vaz Ferreira. In books such as *Conocimiento y acción* (*Knowledge and Action*, 1907), *Lógica viva* (*Vital Logic*, 1910), and *Fermentario* (*Fermentary*, 1938), he attacks the narrow, purely rational concept of knowledge that excludes the dynamic vitality of reality. He also pioneered the discussion of feminist issues in *Sobre feminismo* (*On Feminism*, written between 1914 and 1922, but first published in 1933).

An important force in the transition from positivism to vitalism was the Spanish philosopher José Ortega y Gasset (1883–1955). But there were also others, who belonged to what has come to be called the Generation of 98. The year 1898 marked the end of Spain's colonial empire, yet it also signaled the opening of a promising, new intellectual movement. The famous generation of 1898 gave Spain some of its most brilliant intellectuals, including two of its greatest philosophers, Ortega and Miguel de Unamuno (1864–1936).

Many thinkers in Spain, a country located at the geographical margins of Europe, struggled to be recognized as European, but Unamuno was more interested in developing the notion of *hispanidad* (Hispanicity) and to the *hispanización* (Hispanization) of Europe. The notion of *hispanidad* came to serve as an important bridge between the philosophy of Spain and Latin America. Interest in analyzing the meaning of *hispanidad* has continued into the twenty-first century, with philosophers in the United States developing arguments concerning rights for Hispanics and debating the very meaning of the term "Hispanic."

Like Unamuno, Ortega also made the intellectual, political, and social situation of Spain central to his philosophy. He developed what has become known as a "philosophy of circumstance," well captured in the famous lines: "*Yo soy yo y mis circunstancias y si no las salvo a ellas no me salvo yo*" (I am myself and my circumstances, and if I don't save them, I cannot save myself). The idea is that the self is not an entity apart from its context. Integral to this view is the notion that all knowledge is perspectival—that is, it is the expression of a view from a particular perspective. Ortega's perspectivism came to play a critical role in the work of several Latin American philosophers.

THE FORGERS. The thought of the generation that followed the founders was shaped by ideas imported from Spain, France, and Germany, and Ortega is generally credited with having introduced them, particularly German philosophy, into Latin America. The extraordinary impact of Max Scheler (1874–1928) and Nicolai Hartmann (1882–1950) can be explained only through Ortega's influence. This group of philosophers has been characterized by Francisco Miró Quesada (Peru, b. 1918), as "the generation of forgers" because of the major role they played in setting the parameters for the subsequent development of Latin American philosophy. A major figure of this generation was Samuel Ramos (Mexico, 1897–1959). He focused upon Mexican culture, thereby inspiring interest in what is culturally unique to Latin American nations. Ramos' book, *El perfil del hombre y la cultura en México* (Profile of man and culture in Mexico, 1934), was the first attempt at interpreting Mexican culture. Francisco Romero was also an important thinker who developed an elaborate philosophical anthropology in his *Teoría del hombre* (Theory of man, 1952). He sought to frame a view of human beings in terms of universal notions such as intentionality and spirituality, rather than the culturally specific parameters used by Ramos.

Throughout the history of Latin American thought there has been a tension between philosophers who focus on the universal human condition and those who emphasize particular cultural circumstances. In Mexico, for example, many philosophers have discussed the impact of the colonization on the development of culture in Mexico. And in *Siete ensayos de interpretación de la realidad peruana* (Seven interpretative essays on Peruvian reality, 1928), the Peruvian Carlos Mariátegui (1894–1930) proposed an interpretation of Marxism that emphasized the particular conditions that characterized the Peruvian situation. This particularist tendency grew in part as result of a historical event that brought the Spanish and Latin American philosophical traditions into even closer contact with one another and heralded yet another stage in the latter.

The historical circumstances of Spain in the twentieth century were complicated, and part of the influence that Spanish thinkers came to have upon the development of philosophy in several Latin American countries can be attributed to the political upheaval caused by the Spanish Civil War (1936–1939) and the ensuing dictatorship of Francisco Franco (1939–1975). Many of the most important Spanish philosophers of this period were driven into exile during the years of Franco's oppressive dictatorship and several of them settled in Latin America.

THE "TRANSTERRADOS" AND THE PERIOD OF NORMALCY (C. 1940–1960). During the late 1930s and 1940s, due to the upheavals created by the Spanish Civil War, a significant group of thinkers from Spain arrived in Latin America. These philosophers became known as the *transterrados* (trans-landed). Seeking refuge from Franco's dictatorship, they settled in various countries of Latin America. Among them were Joaquín Xirau (1895–1946), Eduardo Nicol (1907–1986), José Ferrater Mora (1912–1991), José Gaos (1900–1969), Luis Recaséns Siches (1903–1977), and Juan D. García Bacca (1901–1992). Their presence helped to break some of the national barriers that had existed in Latin America before their arrival. The conception of *hispanidad* that they inherited from Unamuno and the need to establish themselves in their adopted land helped the process; they went from country to country, spreading ideas and contributing to an ever broadening philosophical dialogue. Their influence showed itself most strongly when the generation born around 1910 reached maturity.

Gaos was one of the most influential *transterrados*. He was a student of Ortega and became the teacher of one of Mexico's most important philosophers, Leopoldo Zea. Gaos encouraged Zea to study the history of Mexican thought, and this resulted in one of Zea's most important books, *El positivismo en México* (Positivism in Mexico, 1943). Through Gaos, Ortega had a strong influence on Zea's views. Following Ortega's insights that in order to understand ourselves, we must understand our circumstance, and that all knowledge is perspectival, Zea turned to the meaning of the Latin American circumstance for the development of the philosophy of the region.

Zea's philosophy was also influenced by Ramos's work. The latter's existential, psychoanalytic approach to the problem of cultural identity was transformed by Zea into a critique of philosophy and the articulation of a *mestizo* (mixed) consciousness. The term *mestizo* points to issues associated with race and culture, opening a philosophical discussion concerning the identity of persons who share Spanish and indigenous heritage. The source of this line of questioning can be traced back to the events following the colonization, when the Spaniards began to mix with the indigenous people to create what has come to be known as a *mestizo* race and culture. Zea's notion of *mestizaje* had a strong influence on the Argentine philosopher Arturo Andrés Roig (b.1922) and the Peruvian Miró Quesada. The relation between these thinkers constitutes an example of a growing philosophical Pan-Americanism. During this period, philosophers from different countries in Latin America began to respond to each other and to interact critically with one another.

PERIOD OF MATURITY (C. 1960–PRESENT). This Pan-American trend continues to the present and has been further supported by the activities of various organizations founded to facilitate meetings and publications. From 1960 to the present, the level of philosophical activity in several Latin American countries has improved significantly. This is due, in part, to the institutionalization of philosophy. The number of national philosophical societies and of centers, institutes, faculties, and departments that have as their exclusive end the teaching and investigation of philosophy has increased substantially as have the number of philosophy journals. All of this activity has begun to awaken interest outside of Latin America, and indeed to give rise to a diversification of philosophical trends within Latin America itself. Three trends in particular illustrate the current situation of Latin America: philosophical analysis, liberation philosophy, and discussions of identity.

Philosophical analysis. Analytic philosophy is characterized by a preoccupation with language, a strong interest in logic, a positive attitude toward science, and a general mistrust of metaphysics. Its founders are G. E. Moore (1873–1958), Bertrand Russell (1872–1970), Ludwig Wittgenstein (1889–1951), and the members of the Vienna Circle. Analytical philosophy is often contrasted to Continental philosophy, which has its roots in France and Germany and is based on the thought of such figures as Hegel, Nietzsche, Jean-Paul Sartre (1905–1980), and Martin Heidegger (1889–1976). Continental philosophy was disseminated earlier and more widely than analytic philosophy in Latin America. Even in the early twenty-first century, authentic Latin American philosophy is often taken to be concerned exclusively with issues of Latin American cultural identity and liberation, and so to have little in common with the analytic tradition. Yet, this is a misconception.

The groundwork for the favorable reception of analysis in Latin America can be traced back to positivism. In the 1920s, key texts from the analytic tradition, such as G. E. Moore's *Ethics* and Bertrand Russell's *The Problems of Philosophy*, were translated into Spanish.

While marginalized from its inception, philosophical analysis has provided a robust methodological alternative to Ortega's perspectivism and Continental philosophy.

The fruits of the interest in analytic philosophy became evident in the 1940s, when Vicente Ferreira da Silva (1916–1963) published a manual of mathematical logic in Brazil, and Miró Quesada published one in Peru. Miró Quesada has maintained a balanced view of philosophy throughout his career. His works, *Despertar y proyecto del filosofar latinoamericano* (The awakening and project of Latin American philosophy, 1974) and *El problema de la filosofía latinoamericana* (The problem of Latin American philosophy, 1976), testify to his view that philosophy must combine both solid philosophical analysis and a historical approach that takes into account the particular circumstances of Latin America.

In Buenos Aires, Hans A. Lindemann, who had connections to the Vienna Circle, brought attention to philosophical analysis in Argentina, as the work of Gregorio Klimovsky (b. 1922) and Julio Rey Pastor (1888–1962) illustrates. In *El punto de partida del filosofar* (Philosophizing's point of departure, 1945), Risieri Frondizi (Argentina, 1910–1983) offered a serious critique of logical positivism while displaying the influence of philosophical analysis.

In the 1960s, philosophical analysis was integrated into many philosophy departments throughout Latin America. Argentina continued to be a center of this kind of philosophy. Mario Bunge's (Argentina, b. 1919) *Causalidad* (Causality, 1961) and Tomás Moro Simpson's *Formas lógicas, realidad y significado* (Logical forms, reality and meaning, 1964) are examples of philosophical analysis in Argentina. In 1972 Eduardo Rabossi (b. 1930), who has published extensively on human rights, founded the *Sociedad Argentina de Análisis Filosófico* (SADAF), which, as its name indicates, is committed to the advancement of the analytic tradition and publishes the journal *Análisis Filosófico*.

The influence of philosophical analysis is also evident in Brazil, particularly in *Manuscrito*, a journal published by the Center of Logic, Epistemology and Philosophy of Science at Campinas. In Mexico, Alejandro Rossi (b. 1932), Fernando Salmerón (1925–1997), and Luis Villoro (b. 1922) founded *Crítica* in 1967, a journal devoted to discussions from an analytic perspective. And the Instituto de Investigaciones Filosóficas of Mexico has been actively engaged in supporting the work of analytic philosophy.

While we can speak of a period of stability in the development of philosophical analysis in Latin America, there has been widespread political instability in many countries of the region. As a result, many outstanding analytic philosophers had to leave Latin America. Bunge was a professor of philosophy at the University of Buenos Aires from 1957 to 1963, but has worked at McGill University in Montreal since 1966. Hector-Neri Castañeda (Guatemala, 1924–1991) worked in the United States for most of his career, and Ernest Sosa (b. 1940) and Jorge Gracia (b. 1942) came to the United States from Cuba. Apart from contributions in the history of philosophy, metaphysics, and hermeneutics, Gracia has published in many areas of Latin American philosophy, including the impact of philosophical analysis in Latin America. Sosa works primarily in epistemology and metaphysics and was recently elected president of the Eastern Division of the American Philosophical Association; he is active in the promotion of analytic philosophy in Latin America.

Philosophical analysis is generally recognized as an important philosophical current in Latin America and analytic philosophers have the support of several institutes and journals, but there is some animosity in some quarters against this philosophical approach. Indeed, some Latin American philosophers have explicitly accused analytic philosophers of turning a blind eye to social injustice and the pressing political and economic issues that plague the region.

The philosophy of liberation. One current within the Latin American philosophical tradition that puts social concerns at the center is the philosophy of liberation. For this movement, the fundamental task of philosophy consists in the social and national liberation from the unjust relations, such as that of dominator-dominated, which have traditionally characterized Latin American philosophy. The philosophy of liberation is rooted in the political discourse of marginalized and exploited segments of society.

This current grew out of liberation theology, which in turn began in Peru and Brazil. Its origins can be traced to the 1970s in Argentina, to a group of thinkers that included Arturo Andrés Roig (b. 1922), Horacio Cerutti Guldberg (b. 1950), and Enrique Dussel (b. 1934). Because of the political turmoil during this period, many of these philosophers were forced into exile, thus disrupting the continuity of the movement and leading to the creation of various distinct strands of the philosophy of liberation. In spite of differences, however, they share a common concern with what it means to do philosophy from the periphery—that is, from the condition of dependence that these thinkers claim characterizes Latin American culture. The philosophy of liberation has been influenced by Marxist and Catholic ideas and is one of the most active philosophical currents in Latin America.

Identity. The problem of identity in Latin American philosophy has two dimensions: the identity of Latin American thought and cultural identity. In dealing with these aspects of the problem, philosophers tend to favor either what may be called a national approach or a continental—in a purely geographical sense—approach. Mariátegui, for example, addressed Peru's reality, applying Marxist principles in order to solve the problems facing Peruvians, *not* Latin Americans in general. In contrast, the Cuban thinker José Martí addressed issues of *nuestra América* (our America), emphasizing what is common to all the nations that comprise the region. Both thinkers prepared the way for the exploration of what it means to speak of Latin America and of Latin American philosophy.

The question of the existence and character of Latin American philosophy was first explicitly raised by Zea and Frondizi in the 1940s, although related questions had been alluded to even earlier by Alberdi. According to Alberdi, a Latin American philosophy must have a social and political character intimately related to the most vital needs of the continent. Because he conceives philosophy as an instrument for social, political, and economic change, Alberdi rejects metaphysics and other "pure and abstract" philosophical fields.

Zea's work extended the discussion of the meaning of Latin American philosophy. His culturalist perspective, according to which philosophy is intimately related to the culture and history from which it emerges, has won many adherents. Supporters find in this approach to defining philosophy a way of opening space for contributions that do not fall under the umbrella of the European and Anglo-American philosophical traditions under whose shadows they tend to remain marginalized. Abelardo Villegas (Mexico, 1934–2001), Ricaurte Soler (Panama, 1932–1994), and Guillermo Francovich (Peru, 1911–1990) are just three of the many philosophers who have adopted Zea's view. In Venezuela, Ernesto Mayz Vallenilla (b. 1925) has addressed some of these issues both in his work and in his capacity as public educator.

The problem facing philosophers as they grapple with the issue of the identity of Latin American nations, peoples, and intellectual traditions has become even more complicated as these discussions have entered the United States. Philosophers concerned with the place of Hispanics or Latinos in the United States explore questions related to what happens to the identity of Mexicans, Cubans, Colombians, and other Latin Americans who immigrate to the United States. Is there a term that can capture the identity of this diverse group? If so, which term? Or should we give up on the enterprise altogether? These questions take on particular relevance in light of the discussion of group rights. Latin American thinkers working in the United States on such issues include Ofelia Schutte (Cuba, b. 1945) and Gracia.

Latin American philosophy has a rich and variegated history. Latin American philosophers have a tradition of concern for the specific social and political problems that plague the population of the Americas. But they remain engaged with the universal concerns that have characterized philosophy since its inception—problems of truth, goodness, and justice, among others—that are not the product of any particular political structure, social context, or geographical location.

See also Aristotle; Augustine, St.; Bergson, Henri; Caso, Antonio; Comte, Auguste; Continental Philosophy; Croce, Benedetto; Farias Brito, Raimundo de; Hartmann, Nicolai; Hegel, Georg Wilhelm Friedrich; Heidegger, Martin; Identity; Ingenieros, José; Kant, Immanuel; Korn, Alejandro; Liberation Theology; Logical Positivism; Molina Garmendia, Enrique; Moore, George Edward; Neoplatonism; Nietzsche, Friedrich; Ortega y Gasset, José; Plato; Positivism; Romero, Francisco; Russell, Bertrand Arthur William; Sartre, Jean-Paul; Scheler, Max; Schopenhauer, Arthur; Sosa, Ernest; Spencer, Herbert; Suárez, Francisco; Thomas Aquinas, St.; Unamuno y Jugo, Miguel de; Utilitarianism; Varona y Pera, Enrique José; Vasconcelos, José; Vaz Ferreira, Carlos; Vitalism; Vitoria, Francisco de; Wittgenstein, Ludwig Josef Johann.

Bibliography

Ardao, Arturo. "Assimilation and Transformation of Positivism in Latin America." *Journal of the History of Ideas* 24 (1963): 515–522.

Beuchot, Mauricio. *The History of Philosophy in Colonial Mexico.* Translated by Elizabeth Millán. Foreword by Jorge J. E. Gracia. Washington, DC: The Catholic University of America Press, 1998.

Crawford, William Rex. *A Century of Latin American Thought.* 3rd ed. New York: Praeger, 1966.

Cruz Costa, João. *A History of Ideas in Brazil: The Development of Philosophy in Brazil and the Evolution of National History.* Berkeley: University of California Press, 1965.

Dascal, Marcelo, ed. *Cultural Relativism and Philosophy: North and Latin American Perspectives.* Leiden, Netherlands: E. J. Brill, 1991.

Davis, Harold Eugene. *Latin American Social Thought: The History of Its Development since Independence, with Selected Readings.* Washington, DC: University Press of Washington, 1963.

Davis, Harold Eugene. *Latin American Thought: A Historical Introduction.* New York: Free Press, 1972.

Duran, Manuel, and William Kluback, eds. *Reason in Exile: Essays on Catalan Philosophers.* New York: Peter Lang, 1994.

Dussel, Enrique D. *Philosophy of Liberation.* Translated by Aquilina Martínez and Christine Morkovsky. New York: Orbis Books, 1985.

Fernández Retamar, Roberto. *Calibán and Other Essays.* Translated by Edward Baker. Minneapolis: University of Minnesota Press, 1980.

Ferrater Mora, José. *La filosofía en América.* Vol. 1, Actas del IX Congreso Interamericano de Filosofía. Caracas: Sociedad Venezolana de Filosofía, 1979.

Frondizi, Risieri. "Is There an Ibero-American Philosophy?" *Philosophy and Phenomenological Research* 9 (1948–1949): 345–355.

Frondizi, Risieri. "On the Unity of the Philosophies of the Two Americas." *Review of Metaphysics* 4 (1951): 617–622.

Gaos, José, ed. *Antología del pensamiento de lengua española en la edad contemporánea.* Mexico City: Séneca, 1945.

Gaos, José. *En torno a la filosofía mexicana.* With an introduction by Leopoldo Zea. Mexico City: Alianza, 1980.

Gómez Martínez, José, ed. *Proyecto Ensayo Hispánico.* Available from www.ensayistas.org/.

Gómez Robledo, Antonio. *La filosofía en el Brasil.* Mexico: Imprenta Universitaria, 1946.

Gracia, Jorge J. E. *Filosofía hispánica: Concepto, origen y foco historiográfico.* Pamplona: Universidad de Navarra, 1998.

Gracia, Jorge J. E. *Hispanic/Latino Identity: A Philosophical Perspective.* Oxford: Blackwell, 2000.

Gracia, Jorge J. E., ed. *Latin American Philosophy Today.* Double issue of *Philosophical Forum* 20 (1-2) (1988–1989).

Gracia, Jorge J. E., and Mireya Camurati, eds. *Philosophy and Literature in Latin America: A Critical Assessment of the Current Situation.* Albany: State University of New York Press, 1989.

Gracia, Jorge J. E., and Iván Jaksić, eds. *Filosofía e identidad cultural en América Latina.* Caracas, Venezuela: Monte Avila, 1988.

Gracia, Jorge J. E., and Elizabeth Millán-Zaibert, eds. *Latin American Philosophy for the 21st Century: The Human Condition, Values, and the Search for Identity.* New York: Prometheus, 2004.

Gracia, Jorge J. E., and Eduardo Rabossi, Enrique Villanueva, and Marcelo Dascal, eds. *Philosophical Analysis in Latin America.* Dordrecht, Netherlands: Kluwer, 1984. More extensive Spanish edition: *El análisis filosófico en América Latina.* Mexico City: Fondo de Cultura Económica, 1985.

Hanke, Lewis. *Aristotle and the American Indians: A Study in Race Prejudice in the Mondern World.* Chicago: Henry Regnery, 1959.

Jaksi?, Iván. *Academic Rebels in Chile: The Role of Philosophy in Higher Education and Politics.* Albany, NY: State University of New York Press, 1989.

León-Portilla, Miguel. *Time and Reality in the Thought of the Maya.* 2nd ed. Norman: University of Oklahoma Press, 1988.

Liss, S. B. *Marxist Thought in Latin America*. Berkeley: University of California Press, 1984.

Löwy, M., ed. *Marxism in Latin America from 1909 to the Present: An Anthology*. Translated by M. Pearlman. Atlantic Highlands, NJ: Humanities Press, 1990.

Martí, Oscar R. "Is There a Latin American Philosophy?" *Metaphilosophy* 1 (1983): 46–52.

Mayz Vallenilla, Ernesto. *El problema de América*. Caracas, Venezuela: Ediciones de la Universidad Simón Bolívar, 1992.

Mendieta, Eduardo, ed. *Latin American Philosophy: Currents, Issues, Debates*. Bloomington: Indiana University Press, 2003.

Millán-Zaibert, Elizabeth, and Arleen Salles, eds. *The Role of History in Latin American Philosophy*. Albany, NY: State University of New York Press, 2005.

Miró Quesada, Francisco. "The Impact of Metaphysics on Latin American Ideology." *Journal of the History of Ideas* 29 (1963): 539–552.

Nuccetelli, Susana, and Gary Seay, eds. *Latin American Philosophy: An Introduction with Readings*. Upper Saddle River, NJ: Prentice Hall, 2004.

Nuccetelli, Susana. *Latin American Thought: Philosophical Problems and Arguments*. Boulder, CO: Westview Press, 2002.

Redmond, W. *Bibliography of the Philosophy in the Iberian Colonies of America*. The Hague: Nijhoff, 1972.

Rodó, José Enrique. *Ariel*. Translated by Margaret Sayers Peden. Foreword by James Symington. Prologue by Carlos Fuentes. Austin: University of Texas Press, 1988.

Roig, Arturo Andrés. "Nuestra América frente al panamericanismo y el hispanismo: la lectura de Leopoldo Zea." In *América Latina. Historia y destino. Homenaje a Leopodo Zea*, edited by Horacio Cerutti-Guldberg. Mexico City: UNAM, 1992: 279–284.

Roig, Arturo Andrés. *Teoría y crítica del pensamiento latinoamericano*. Mexico City: Fondo de Cultura Económica, 1981.

Romero, Francisco. *Sobre la filosofía en America*. Buenos Aires: Raigal, 1952.

Sáenz, Mario, ed. *Latin American Perspectives on Globalization: Ethics, Politics, and Alternative Visions*. Lanham, MD: Rowman & Littlefield, 2002.

Sánchez Reulet, A., ed. *Contemporary Latin American Philosophy: A Selection with an Introduction and Notes* Translated by W. R. Trask. Albuquerque: University of New Mexico Press, 1954.

Sasso, Javier. *La filosofía latinoamericana y las construcciones de su historia*. Caracas, Venezuela: Monte Ávila, 1998.

Schutte, Ofelia. *Cultural Identity and Social Liberation in Latin American Thought*. New York: State University of New York Press, 1993.

Stabb, Martin S. *The Dissenting Voice: The New Essay of Spanish America, 1960–1985*. Austin: University of Texas Press, 1995.

Stabb, Martin S. *In Quest of Identity: Patterns in the Spanish American Essay of Ideas, 1890–1960*. Chapel Hill: University of North Carolina Press, 1967.

Woodward, R. L., ed. *Positivism in Latin America: 1850–1900: Are Order and Progress Reconcilable?* Lexington, MA: Heath, 1971.

Zea, Leopoldo. *The Latin-American Mind*. Translated by James H. Abbott and Lowell Dunham. Norman: University of Oklahoma Press, 1963.

Zea, Leopoldo. *El pensamiento latinoamericano*. Barcelona: Ariel, 1976.

Zea, Leopoldo. *Positivism in Mexico*. Austin: University of Texas Press, 1974.

Zea, Leopoldo. *The Role of the Americas in History*. Savage, MD: Rowman & Littlefield Publishers, 1992.

Jorge J. E. Gracia (2005)
Elizabeth Millán-Zaibert (2005)

LAVATER, JOHANN KASPAR
(1741–1801)

Johann Kaspar Lavater, the German-Swiss poet, physiognomist, and theologian, was born in Zürich. He studied at the gymnasium there under the literary critics Johann Jakob Bodmer and Johann Jakob Breitinger. Later, in northern Germany, he attended the lectures of the Protestant pastor Johann Jakob Spalding, who, influenced by the Earl of Shaftesbury and the English moralists, sought to reconcile reason and sentiment and stressed the moral and religious conscience. While in northern Germany Lavater also met Johann Georg Sulzer, Moses Mendelssohn (whom he later tried to convert to Christianity), the dramatist Friedrich Gottlieb Klopstock, and other persons of note. Returning to Zürich in 1764, he held various posts in churches there from 1769 on. He traveled widely in Germany, was acquainted with many culturally important people, and was one of the most sought-after and famous persons of that time. As a poet, he published a volume of religious verse, *Christlicher Lieder* (1771), and two epic poems in the manner of Klopstock, *Jesus Messias* (1780) and *Joseph von Arimathia* (1794). Because of his opposition to the Zürich government, Lavater was forced to move to Basel in 1796. He returned, only to be wounded during the French capture of Zürich in 1799. He died of this wound in 1801.

Lavater is chiefly known as a physiognomist. His theories were expounded in two main works, *Von der Physiognomik* (Leipzig, 1772) and *Physiognomische Fragmente zur Beförderung der Menschenkenntnis und Menschenliebe* (Physiognomic fragments for furthering the knowledge and love of man; 4 vols., Winterthur, Switzerland, 1775–1778). Johann Gottfried Herder and Lavater's close and longtime friend Johann Wolfgang von Goethe both collaborated on the latter work. Lavater claimed independence from traditional physiognomy dating from the time of Aristotle, but his independence was chiefly a matter of superficial knowledge of the tradition. He supported the classical view that the human body is influenced in shape by the character of the person, and vice versa; but his criteria were inconsistent and confused. There were two main reasons for his unprecedented success: First, his lively and simple manner of exposition that followed the pattern of the "popular philosopher"; and second, the psychology of character at the base of his theory.

Lavater stressed "feeling" and such spiritual qualities as inspiration and creative genius, which were being widely discussed in the eighteenth century. The native language of genius, and of virtue and wisdom, could become known only by studying the human form. Man is the measure of truth. That which harmonizes in form with a man, and is a part of him, is what exists for him. There is no absolute truth, but only a subjective experiencing. Therefore feeling should be cultivated, as it is in the genius. Lavater's psychology of genius, which gave emotions a place beside reason, was an important link between Pietism and sentimentalism on the one hand, and *Sturm und Drang* on the other. Lavater was severely criticized—notably by Georg Christoff Lichtenberg—but his handsomely printed volumes, with their illustrations, and his complimentary analyses of various influential contemporary figures were widely read.

As a writer of religious and devotional literature, Lavater was equally influential. His religious views were based on a belief in inner light, making his subjectivism a mystical and sentimental anthropomorphic theology. God is what satisfies the needs of man. The Bible is historically true but it is to be interpreted subjectively. Lavater was strongly convinced of the magical force of grace and prayer, and was strongly interested in miracles and prophecies. He was therefore drawn to spiritualism and mesmerism.

See also Aristotle; Goethe, Johann Wolfgang von; Herder, Johann Gottfried; Lichtenberg, Georg Christoph; Mendelssohn, Moses; Miracles; Pietism; Shaftesbury, Third Earl of (Anthony Ashley Cooper); Sulzer, Johann Georg.

Bibliography

ADDITIONAL WORKS BY LAVATER

Aussichten in die Ewigkeit in Briefen an Zimmermann. 2 parts. Zürich, 1768–1769; 2nd ed. and 3rd part, 1773; 4th part, 1778.

Geheimes Tagebuch von einem Beobachter seiner selbst. 2 vols. Leipzig, 1771–1773.

Pontius Pilatus oder die Menschen in allen Gestalten, oder die Bibel im Kleinen und der Mensch im Grossen. 4 parts. Zürich, 1782–1785.

Nathanael, oder die Göttlichkeit des Christenthums. Winterthur, Switzerland, 1786.

Ausgewählte Werke. Edited by E. Stähelin. 4 vols. Zürich: Zwingli, 1943.

WORKS ON LAVATER

Bracken, Ernst von. *Die Selbstbeobachtung bei Lavater, Beitrag zur Geschichte der Idee der Subjektivität im 18. Jahrhunderts.* Münster, 1932. Dissertation.

Forssmann, J. *Lavater und die religiösen Strömungen des 18. Jahrhunderts.* Riga, 1935.

Janentzky, Christian. *J. K. Lavater.* Frauenfeld, Switzerland, 1928.

Maier, Heinrich. *An der Grenze der Philosophie Melanchton, Lavater, D. F. Strauss.* Tübingen, 1909.

Muncker, Franz. *J. F. Lavater, Eine Skizze seines Lebens und Wirkens.* Stuttgart, 1883.

Vömel, Alexander. *J. K. Lavater 1741–1801. Ein Lebensbild.* Elberfeld, 1923.

Giorgio Tonelli (1967)

LAVELLE, LOUIS
(1883–1951)

Louis Lavelle, the French philosopher, was born in Saint-Martin-de-Villéréal, in southwestern France. He was professor of philosophy at the Sorbonne from 1932 to 1934 and at the Collège de France from 1941 until his death. In a time of reaction against speculative system-building, Lavelle boldly elaborated an extensive system combining elements of the French *philosophie de l'esprit* and existentialism. Convinced that the modern world needs basic security, Lavelle, like other existentialist thinkers, sought philosophical and moral certitude in the experience of the self, "pure inwardness," and "absolute existence." Unlike such philosophers as Jean-Paul Sartre, who "disintegrated" the human universe inherited from tradition, Lavelle, like Karl Jaspers and Karl Barth, attempted to "reintegrate" the basic experiences of humanity in a novel form. In his spiritualistic interpretation of the self Lavelle continued the French tradition of Nicolas Malebranche, Maine de Biran, Octave Hamelin, Henri Bergson, and Maurice Blondel.

METAPHYSICS OF PARTICIPATION

Metaphysics was for Lavelle "the science of spiritual inwardness." According to him, Immanuel Kant had shown that we cannot find true reality on the side of the object, or thing, because objects and the world they compose cannot have independent existence. The essence of things resides in their relation to a being for whom they are "objects." Consequently, in the search for true or absolute reality we must turn toward the act of consciousness, the "inwardness" of the human being. Thus Lavelle's central preoccupation was to discover and describe the fundamental relation between our innermost being and the Absolute.

Lavelle pointed out that there is a "primitive act" upon which our very being depends, as well as the being of the entire world. It is our primordial experience of being part of the world, in which act we find ourselves also "participating" in something that infinitely transcends us—the Act (Absolute Being, God). From a subtle dialectic description of this spiritual act of "participation" flow the broad lines of Lavelle's doctrine.

ONTOLOGY OF SPIRITUALISTIC EXISTENTIALISM

The originality of Lavelle's conception of the nature of beings in their relation to Being consists in his introducing a dynamic and "actualistic" content into the traditional themes of Aristotelian ontology. His approach yields a finalistic and optimistic view of the universe and human destiny.

All experiences of humankind emerge against the background of the limited individual being, participating in the Absolute Being. By their relation to participation, which is constant and eternal, individual beings establish their relation to the world, and through the notions of essence and existence they establish their spiritual identity. The Absolute Being is pure actuality, the infinite source of existential dynamism, and an endless reservoir of all possible forms or essences, from which individual beings receive their own limited existence. In spite of this direct and continuous dependence of the individual on his source, actualism is reconciled in Lavelle's thought with temporal progression, dynamism with formal immobility, and human freedom is safeguarded by the self-creativity of the individual. Indeed, from the human point of view, participation is a pursuit of an ideal that constantly moves ahead of our efforts. In this pursuit we create our spiritual self, and our experiences, moving onward, progressively acquire a unique form. Our effort in life is meant to discover this form, which has its prototype in the reservoir of Being and is our spiritual essence. The accomplishment of our essence at our death means the radical passage from limited existence into transfinite Being. Thus participation appears as the means of humanity's ultimate redemption, toward which everything occurring in the universe converges.

The world is the interval that separates pure Act (Being) from the limited act of participation (human existence). Matter, in limiting the spirit, offers the resistance necessary for the self to transcend itself. The world comprises three modes of reality: the world of things, that of ideas, and that of individual beings (consciousnesses). The material world plays the necessary role of separating beings; ideas give spiritual meaning to things. The world of individual consciousnesses is necessarily conscious because the essence of the Absolute Being from which they proceed is itself perfect inwardness; as such it is eternally fecund and intended to communicate the creative act to beings which, in turn, propagate it in self-creation.

ETHICS OF CONSENT

In Lavelle's moral philosophy an unusual meaning is given to existential themes, such as freedom, human destiny, and solitude. Lavelle had a constructive conception of man's vocation and of the ideal of life.

Freedom is the essence of man. But whereas the Absolute Act is synonymous with absolute freedom, man, the participating act, is limited by the "natural spontaneity" of the instinct. Consequently, the life of the spirit, which he proposed as the ideal of human life, is a fighting toward gradual liberation from the passivity peculiar to instinct. We become fully human by subordinating natural spontaneity to reflection and rational discipline. Human freedom originates in this process; and this conversion of spontaneity into freedom is the real vehicle of participation. The spiritual being, like the Leibnizian monad, is endowed with potentialities for the accomplishment of its preestablished essence. Our vocation is to seek to make our actual selves coincide with the "better part of ourselves," which represents these potentialities. This self-searching and self-controlling effort presupposes an "act of consent" to our vocation of the spirit. In opposition to other existentialist thinkers who glorify the "exceptional instant," Lavelle rehabilitated everyday existence, seeing even in the least significant instant an opportunity for consent to the self-creative effort and, thereby, an opportunity for participation in the Absolute.

Finally, the theme of solitude was reconciled with that of human communion insofar as the ideal of wisdom was seen to lie in the union between a certain asceticism and everyday life and love.

See also Absolute, The; Aristotelianism; Barth, Karl; Being; Bergson, Henri; Blondel, Maurice; Continental Philosophy; Essence and Existence; Existentialism; Freedom; Hamelin, Octave; Jaspers, Karl; Kant, Immanuel; Maine de Biran; Malebranche, Nicolas; Sartre, Jean-Paul; Self.

Bibliography

WORKS BY LAVELLE

La dialectique du monde sensible. Strasbourg: Commission des publications de la Faculté des lettres, 1921.

La perception visuelle de la profondeur. Strasbourg: Commission des publications de la Faculté des lettres, 1921.

La dialectique de l'éternel présent. 3 vols. Vol. 1: *De l'être*. Paris: Alcan, 1928; Vol. 2: *De l'acte*. Paris, 1937; Vol. 3: *Du temps et de l'éternité*. Paris: Aubier, Éditions Montaigne, 1945.

La conscience de soi. Paris: Grasset, 1933.

La présence totale. Paris, 1934.

De l'acte. Paris: Aubier 1937; Paris: Flammarion, 1992.

Les puissances du moi. Paris, 1939.

L'erreur de Narcisse. Paris: Grasset, 1939.

Le mal et la souffrance. Paris, 1940.

La parole et l'écriture. Paris: L'artisan du livre, 1942.

La philosophie française entre les deux guerres. Paris: Aubier, 1942.

Du temps et de l'éternité. Paris, 1945.

Introduction à l'ontologie. Paris: Presses Universitaires de France, 1947.

Science, ésthetique, métaphysique: chroniques philosophiques. Paris: Albin Michel, 1967.

Psychologie et spiritualité. Paris: Albin Michel, 1967.

Règles de la vie quotidienn. Paris: Arfuyen, 2004.

TRANSLATIONS

The Meaning of Holiness. New York: Pantheon Books, 1956.

The Dilemma of Narcissus. Larson: Burdett, NY, 1993.

The Act of Presence, Works of Louis Lavelle. Introduction and tranlation into English of selected texts of Louis Lavelle by Robert Jones, posted at http://association-lavelle.chez.tiscali.fr/Robert%20Jones.pdf.

WORKS ON LAVELLE

Ainval, Christiane d'. *Une doctrine de la présence spirituelle: La philosophie de Louis Lavelle*. Paris: Nauwelaerts, 1967.

Bourbon-Busset, Jacques de. *La raison ardente*. Paris: Gallimard, 2000.

Chretien, Jean-Louis, *L'arche de la parole*. Paris: PUF, 1999.

Delfgaauw, B. M. I. *Het Spiritualistiche Existentialisme van Louis Lavelle*. Amsterdam, 1947.

Ecole, Jean, *Métaphysique de l'être, doctrine de la connaissance et philosophie de la religion chez Louis Lavelle*. Gênes: L'Arcipelago, 1994.

Foulquié, P. *L'existentialisme*, 109–122. Paris, 1946.

Grasso, Pier G. *L. Lavelle*. Brescia: La Scuola, 1949.

Nobile, O. M. *La filosofia di Louis Lavelle*. Florence: Sansoni, 1943.

Reymond, Christiane, *Autrui dans la Dialectique de l'éternel présent de Louis Lavelle*. Paris: Presses universitaires de France, 1972.

True, G. *De Jean-Paul Sartre à Louis Lavelle, ou désagrégation et réintegration*. Paris, 1946.

Anna-Teresa Tymieniecka (1967)
Bibliography updated by Tamra Frei (2005)

LAVOISIER, ANTOINE
(1743–1794)

Antoine Lavoisier played the central role in what has come to be known as the chemical revolution. He is credited with establishing that oxygen is an element and water its compound with hydrogen, refining experimental methods in chemistry, reforming chemical nomenclature along systematic lines, defining *element* operationally, and denying phlogiston a place in chemical explanation.

EARLY LIFE AND WORK

Lavoisier was born into a wealthy family of lawyers in 1743, and in preparation for a legal career attended the Collège des Quatre Nations (or Collège Mazarin), earning a baccalaureate in law in 1763. He pursued scientific interests under the guidance of the geologist Jean-Étienne Guettard (1715–1786), a family friend, and attended Guillaume-François Rouelle's (1703–1770) popular and influential lectures on chemistry and mineralogy at the Jardin du Roi. From 1763 Lavoisier assisted Guettard on field trips for the first geological survey of France. His first chemical work was a study of gypsum and plaster of Paris, which was read to the Academy of Sciences in 1765, to which he was elected in 1768. That year Lavoisier also joined the Ferme Générale, a private company collecting indirect taxes in return for a fixed payment to the Crown. This investment would secure his fortune, but also prove his downfall. In 1771 he married Marie Anne Paulze, the fourteen-year-old daughter of a senior member of the Ferme. Marie became a significant collaborator: She learned English to translate important scientific papers, assisted in the laboratory, and trained in the visual arts, providing the engravings for Lavoisier's *Traité Elémentaire de Chimie* (1789).

Lavoisier was active outside of chemistry, especially in economic and farming reform. As an academician, he pursued many technological projects in the service of the state, helping to investigate water supply and storage, food purity, ballooning, bleaching, and ceramics and to develop the metric system. From 1776 he was in charge of the production and administration of gunpowder, working from a laboratory in the Royal Arsenal.

Lavoisier's contributions to chemistry began at a time when advancing experimental techniques made clearer the atmosphere's active role in chemical reactions, but phlogiston, the principle of inflammability, still provided the prevailing framework for understanding combustion and calcination (the formation of metal oxides). In 1772 Louis-Bernard Guyton de Morveau (1737–1816)

ENCYCLOPEDIA OF PHILOSOPHY
2nd edition

reported to the Academy of Sciences that metals increase their weight on calcination. This was in tension with the phlogistonists' view that combustion and calcination involved loss of phlogiston to the air. Guyton de Morveau argued that the light phlogiston must "buoy up" the metal, but Lavoisier saw calcination instead as fixation of air in the calx. In the long and carefully constructed series of experiments that followed, Lavoisier studied the combustion and calcination of metals and nonmetals, measured the volumes of air absorbed or evolved, and weighed and investigated the solid products and the residual air. By 1778, drawing also on the experimental work of others, he was convinced that a particular component of air was involved in combustion, the "purest part of air" or "eminently respirable air," which combines with carbon to form fixed air (carbon dioxide). Lavoisier also noted during the 1770s that air was absorbed in the formation of phosphoric, sulfuric, and nitric acids and of fixed air, which was weakly acidic in solution. In papers read to the Academy of Sciences between 1776 and 1779 he concluded first that the acids were a chemical genus, containing air combined with different principles, and later that "eminently respirable air" contains the principle of acidity, which he called *principe oxigine* (later to become *oxygène*). Water he identified as oxygen combined with "inflammable air" (which he renamed hydrogen). Oxygen the gas was not *itself* the principle of acidity, though: Lavoisier saw gases also as a chemical genus, their common constituent being caloric, the matter of heat. Thus in combustion, substances combine with the oxygen principle, releasing caloric from oxygen gas, which explained why heat was evolved in the process. Experiments on animal respiration convinced him that respiration is a slow version of combustion, and in 1785 he extended his theory of acidity, accounting for the solution of metals in acids as wet calcination.

CHEMICAL REVOLUTION

These three theories—of combustion, acidity, and the gaseous state—gave Lavoisier a framework comprehensive enough to deny phlogiston its explanatory role. In 1785 he read "Réflexions sur le Phlogistique," a direct attack on the theory, to the Academy of Sciences. In 1787 he published, with Guyton de Morveau and others, a new nomenclature for chemistry, replacing a jumble of uninformative traditional names with a system for naming compounds based on their composition, reflecting the latest discoveries. This is largely still in use in modern chemistry.

Lavoisier published his most influential work, *Traité Elémentaire de Chimie*, in 1789. This combined a clear presentation of his own theories of gases, of combustion and acidity in part I, with (in parts II and III) a summary of less controversial material on acids, bases, and salts and on experimental methods. In the preface, he introduced his empirical definition of *elementhood*: rejecting the traditional speculations about the "simple substances," he proposed to treat as simple any substance that had not yet been decomposed in the laboratory.

After 1789 political revolution in France intervened increasingly in Lavoisier's activities, curtailing his scientific researches, though at first he was sympathetic to its aims. Scientific and administrative institutions of the ancien régime, in which he had played a prominent (though liberal and reforming) role, were successively abolished: the Ferme Générale in 1791 and the Academy of Sciences in 1793. Members of the Ferme were arrested in November 1793, and on May 8, 1794, were convicted of adulterating tobacco and withholding taxes from the government. Lavoisier was executed that same day, just after his father-in-law.

Lavoisier's achievement raises important historiographical and philosophical questions about progress in science. Lavoisier himself, writing in 1773, foresaw a revolution in chemistry, and his name appears throughout Thomas S. Kuhn's *Structure of Scientific Revolutions* (1970). In this technical sense the defeat of the phlogiston theory has been called a scientific revolution because: (1) it involved wholesale revision to theoretical interpretations of empirical evidence and accepted views of the relative simplicity of whole classes of substances (e.g., metals and their calxes); and (2) it was accompanied by a major reform of chemical nomenclature that embedded the oxygen theory in the very language of chemistry. The importance of his empirical definition of *elementhood* is less clear. It was not original to him, and it applied only selectively to his own list of elements.

See also Chemistry, Philosophy of.

Bibliography

WORKS BY LAVOISIER

Traité Elémentaire de Chimie. 2 vols. Paris: Cuchet, 1789. Translated by Robert Kerr as *The Elements of Chemistry* (Edinburgh, Scotland: William Creech, 1790), reprinted as David Knight (ed.) *The Development of Chemistry*, Vol. 2 (New York: Routledge/Thoemmes Press, 1998).

WORKS ABOUT LAVOISIER

Donovan, Arthur. *Antoine Lavoisier: Science, Administration, and Revolution*. Cambridge, MA: Blackwell, 1993.

Hendry, Robin Findlay. "Lavoisier and Mendeleev on the Elements." In *Foundations of Chemistry* 7 (1) (2005): 31–48.

Holmes, Frederic Lawrence. *Antoine Lavoisier: The Next Crucial Year, or The Sources of His Quantitative Method in Chemistry*. Princeton, NJ: Princeton University Press, 1998.

Holmes, Frederic Lawrence. *Eighteenth-Century Chemistry as an Investigative Enterprise*. Berkeley: Office for History of Science and Technology, University of California at Berkeley, 1989.

Kitcher, Philip. *The Advancement of Science: Science without Legend, Objectivity without Illusions*. New York: Oxford University Press, 1993.

Kuhn, Thomas S. *The Structure of Scientific Revolutions*. 2nd ed. Chicago: University of Chicago Press, 1970.

Thagard, Paul. "The Conceptual Structure of the Chemical Revolution." In *Philosophy of Science* 57 (2) (1990): 183–209.

Robin Findlay Hendry (2005)

LAVROV, PËTR LAVROVICH

(1823–1900)

Pëtr Lavrovich Lavrov was a Russian philosopher and social thinker, a major theoretician of Russian Populism and the leading exponent of a distinctive form of positivism in nineteenth-century Russian philosophy (also elaborated by Nikolai Mikhailovskii). Lavrov was born in Melekhov, the son of a landed gentleman and retired artillery officer. He was sent to the Artillery School in St. Petersburg in 1837 and received his commission upon graduating in 1842. In 1844 he joined the faculty of the Artillery School, and for more than twenty years (during which he rose to the rank of colonel), he taught mathematics and the history of science at military institutions in St. Petersburg. At the same time Lavrov read widely in philosophy and gained a reputation as a writer—first for his poetry and after 1858 for his scholarly essays in philosophy. In the 1860s, the increasing liberalism of his social views aroused the suspicion of the tsarist authorities. Arrested in 1866, he was exiled to the provinces in the following year. In 1870 he fled to Paris, where he played an active role in the Commune of 1871. After sojourns in London and Zürich, he settled in Paris in 1877. A friend of Karl Marx and Friedrich Engels, Lavrov became the voice of Russian socialism abroad and a revered figure in the international socialist movement. He died in Paris.

Lavrov developed an early interest in socialism through reading François Marie Charles Fourier and other leading socialists; he was particularly attracted to the ideas of Pierre-Joseph Proudhon and Aleksandr Herzen. Philosophically, Lavrov's initial scientific orientation evolved in the direction of positivism rather than in the direction of the "materialism" that was prevalent in Russian radical circles of the day, among such thinkers as Nikolai Chernyshevskii and Dmitrii Pisarev. However, his positivistic philosophy was based more on German models than on Auguste Comte. Lavrov did not become acquainted with Comte's writings until the middle of the 1860s; by then his thinking had been given strong direction by a close study of Immanuel Kant, G. W. F. Hegel, the neo-Kantian Albert Lange, and "young Hegelians" such as Ludwig Feuerbach and Arnold Ruge.

In his first important philosophical writings, which consisted of several long essays written between 1858 and 1861, Lavrov criticized materialism as a metaphysical system that unnecessarily restricts science to matter in motion. Distinguishing between material phenomena, conscious phenomena, and historical phenomena, he maintained that phenomena of the last two classes cannot be dealt with by the methods of the natural sciences. The phenomena of consciousness, in particular, require a "subjective," introspective method, and furthermore, these phenomena must be regarded as scientifically primary, since every investigator must begin from the facts of his own consciousness. Calling this approach "anthropologism," Lavrov developed it into a neo-Kantian positivism that, while it rejected supernaturalistic metaphysics and religion, did not reject moral imperatives. It stressed the thought and action of the free individual who finds in his own consciousness an absolute sanction to strive toward the realization of moral ideals such as individual dignity and social justice. While material phenomena are governed by universal natural laws, man's conscious conviction that he is free is inescapable and thus may be taken as a foundation for practical philosophy. Moral ideals are ultimately grounded in man's striving for pleasure, but in the consciousness of the cultivated individual they present themselves as nonegoistic, universal imperatives.

In his best-known philosophical work, *Istoricheskie pis'ma* (Historical letters), first published serially in the magazine *Nedelia* (Week) in 1868 and 1869, Lavrov continued his attack upon materialistic reductionism by applying "anthropologism" to history. Arguing that man can view history only "subjectively" and teleologically, he defined the goal of history as the physical, moral, and intellectual development of the individual. On this basis he maintained that the "critically thinking individuals" who have already achieved such development have a moral obligation to extend the opportunity for development to the masses, whose toil has given the privileged few the leisure and the resources needed for self-cultivation. Lavrov asserted that in coming to understand the defects of existing social institutions and in actively striving to reform them, the "critically thinking individuals" both discharge their "debt to the people" and serve as the moving forces of history. He envisaged a future in which all social institutions will conform to man's natural needs and the coercive institutions of the state will be all but eliminated. *Istoricheskiye Pis'ma* had a great impact on the Russian revolutionary youth of the 1870s.

Lavrov was able to develop his socialist program more explicitly abroad, where he was free from tsarist censorship. From 1873 to 1876 he edited the journal *Vperyed!* (Forward!), the chief organ of Russian Populist socialism—a form of agrarian socialism, inspired by Herzen and Chernyshevskii, which stressed the Russian village commune and the possibility it afforded Russia of moving directly to a socialist order, thus bypassing the evils of capitalism. Lavrov's political theory was further elaborated in *Gosudarstvennyi element v budushchem obshchestve* (The state element in future society), published in London in 1876. Acknowledging the need for revolution, Lavrov at first stressed the value of preparatory education and propaganda. Later he came to condone revolutionary terrorism and was associated with the Russian extremist party, *Narodnaia volia* (The people's will).

In his later socialist views, which were closer to those of Marx, Lavrov gave more attention to class conflict and to the process of production, but he never adopted a fully Marxist view of history or social dynamics. His emphasis remained moralistic and individualistic, with its focus on the development and activity of the "critically thinking individual." The philosophical outlook reflected in Lavrov's *Istoricheskiye Pis'ma* remained fundamentally unchanged in his last major work, which consisted of two lengthy introductory volumes of an unfinished intellectual history titled *Opyt istorii mysly novogo vremeni* (Essay in the history of modern thought; Geneva, 1894).

See also Chernyshevskii, Nikolai Gavrilovich; Comte, Auguste; Engels, Friedrich; Feuerbach, Ludwig Andreas; Fourier, François Marie Charles; Hegel, Georg Wilhelm Friedrich; Herzen, Aleksandr Ivanovich; Kant, Immanuel; Lange, Friedrich Albert; Marx, Karl; Materialism; Mikhailovskii, Nikolai Konstantinovich; Pisarev, Dmitri Ivanovich; Positivism; Proudhon, Pierre-Joseph; Russian Philosophy; Socialism.

Bibliography

WORKS BY LAVROV

Sobranie sochinenii (Collected works). 11 numbers. Petrograd, 1917–1920.

Izbrannye sochineniia (Selected works). 4 vols. Moscow, 1934–1935.

Filosofiya i sotsiologiya. 2 vols. Moscow, 1965.

Historical Letters. Translated by James P. Scanlan. Berkeley, CA: University of California Press, 1967.

O religii (On religion). Moscow: Mysl, 1989.

WORKS ON LAVROV

Itenberg, B. S. *P. L. Lavrov v russkom revoliutsionnom dvizhenii* (P. L. Lavrov in Russian revolutionary movement). Moscow: Nauka, 1988.

Kazakov, A. P. *Teoriia progressa v russkoi sotsiologii kontsa XIX veka (P. L. Lavrov, N. K. Mikhailovskii, M. M. Kovalevskii)* (The theory of progress in late nineteenth-century Russian sociology [P. L. Lavrov, N. K. Mikhailovskii, M. M. Kovalevskii]). Leningrad: Izdatel'stvo leningradskogo universiteta, 1969.

Pomper, Philip. *Peter Lavrov and the Russian Revolutionary Movement.* Chicago: University of Chicago Press, 1970.

Semenkova, T. G. *Ekonomicheskie vzgliady P. L. Lavrova* (The economic views of P. L. Lavrov). Moscow: Vysshaia shkola, 1980.

Venturi, Franco. *Il populismo russo.* Rome, 1952. Translated into English by Frances Haskell as *Roots of Revolution.* New York, 1960.

Volodin, A. I. *Lavrov.* Moscow: Molodaia gvardiia, 1981.

Zenkovsky, V. V. *Istoriya Russkoy Filosofii.* 2 vols. Paris, 1948–1950. Translated into English by George L. Kline as *A History of Russian Philosophy.* 2 vols. New York and London, 1953.

James P. Scanlan (1967)
Bibliography updated by Vladimir Marchenkov (2005)

LAW, PHILOSOPHY OF

In addition to the detailed survey entries *Philosophy of Law, History of,* and *Philosophy of Law, Problems of,* the Encyclopedia includes the following entries in which legal theories and concepts are discussed: *Analytic Jurisprudence; Historical School of Jurisprudence; Justice; Legal Positivism; Legal Realism; Natural Law; Property; Punishment; Responsibility, Moral and Legal; Rights;* and *Sovereignty.* See "Philosophy of Law, History of," and "Philosophy of Law, Problems of," in the index for entries on philosophers and legal theorists who have concerned themselves especially with questions in the philosophy of law.

LAW, WILLIAM
(1686–1761)

William Law, the English devotional writer, controversialist, theologian, and mystic, was a fellow of Emmanuel College, Cambridge. As a nonjuror, he refused to take the oath to King George I and thus terminated his career at the university and in the church. For a time he was a tutor in the household of Edward Gibbon, grandfather of the historian. His later life was virtually without incident, and after years of retirement, he died in his native village of King's Cliffe, Northamptonshire.

Law is best known as a devotional writer and especially for his *A Serious Call to a Devout and Holy Life* (1728); but his importance in the history of thought lies elsewhere, in his resistance to latitudinarianism, his defense of morality, his attack on deism, and his mystical writings.

Law was a formidable controversialist, and in his *Three Letters to the Bishop of Bangor* (1717) he brought remorseless logic to bear on Benjamin Hoadly's lax view of the nature of the church. Bernard de Mandeville had contended in the *Fable of the Bees* that private vices are actually public benefits; Law subjected the work to rigorous examination and showed that the canons of morality cannot be understood in terms of such specious sophistries. His most serious and celebrated work was his attack on deism. In *Christianity as old as the Creation*, Matthew Tindal argued that reason is the only test of truth; insofar as Christianity is valid, it rests on rationalist principles that owe nothing to revelation. Law's *Case of Reason* was a closely argued refutation of the prevailing rationalism of the period. Human reason is not able, by itself, to encompass all knowledge, nor is it sufficient to test all truth. Those who exalt natural religion are exposed to the same criticism as those who accept revelation without question. The universe is less simple and the ways of God are more mysterious than the arrogance of rationalism admits. Law shared with George Berkeley and Joseph Butler the credit for terminating the active phase of the deistic controversy.

Law's later writings reflect the profound influence that mysticism (especially as expounded by Jakob Boehme) came to exercise over his thought. He reached the conclusion that real knowledge is "the communion of the knowing and the known." To convey his new insights, Law organized his teaching in the form of "myth." He believed that mysticism gives birth to symbols within which its truth can live. Law felt that he had penetrated to a deeper understanding of human nature and that it could best be interpreted through a grasp of the meaning of the myth of the Fall on the one hand and through an understanding of divine self-communication in love on the other ("Love is the first *Fiat* of God"). Law's mystical teaching about life was related to a restatement of orthodox Christianity. He expounded the atonement with great beauty and insight and believed that the Trinity was the most illuminating way to describe the self-unfolding of the Eternal.

Law's mystical writings were perplexing to thinkers of the eighteenth century (see John Wesley's letter to Law about mysticism), but his *Serious Call* exercised a profound influence at the time (especially on Samuel Johnson and John Wesley) and is still considered a classic work on the Christian life.

See also Berkeley, George; Boehme, Jakob; Butler, Joseph; Deism; Johnson, Samuel; Mandeville, Bernard; Mysticism, History of; Rationalism; Religion and Morality; Tindal, Matthew.

Bibliography

WORKS BY LAW

The Works of William Law. 9 vols. Edited by G. Moreton. London, 1892.

Selected Mystical Writings of William Law, edited by S. Hobhouse. London: C.W. Daniel, 1938.

WORKS ON LAW

Cragg, G. R. *Reason and Authority in the Eighteenth Century*. Cambridge, U.K.: Cambridge University Press, 1964.

Overton, J. H. *The Life and Opinions of the Rev. William Law*. London, 1881.

Talon, H. *William Law*. London: Rockliff, 1948.

Gerald R. Cragg (1967)

LAWS, SCIENTIFIC

On the standard picture there are three kinds of facts. Some facts cannot have been otherwise. These facts include the conceptual truths (e.g., the fact that Rebecca is taller than Abe if Abe is shorter than Rebecca) and the mathematical truths (e.g., that $2 + 1 = 3$). The remaining facts (i.e., the "contingent" ones) are divided between the other two classes: (1) the laws of nature (and their contingent logical consequences), such as the fact that all copper objects are electrically conductive, and (2) the "accidents," such as the fact that Jones has ten fingers and the fact (one can suppose it is a fact, though humanity may never discover it) that there never exists a solid gold cube larger than a cubic mile.

It is widely believed that one of science's chief goals is to discover the laws of nature. Philosophers have studied the role that the concept of natural law plays in scientific reasoning.

LAWS VERSUS ACCIDENTS: NECESSITY AND COUNTERFACTUALS

An accident just happens to obtain. A gold cube larger than a cubic mile could have formed, but the proper conditions for it to have done so happened never to arise. In contrast, it is no accident that an electrically insulating copper object never formed, since the natural laws prohibit such a thing. In short, events must conform to the laws of nature—the laws have a kind of necessity—whereas accidents are mere coincidences. The kind of necessity characteristic of laws (and their logical consequences) is usually called *nomic* or *physical* necessity to distinguish it from various stronger varieties of necessity (such as logical, conceptual, and metaphysical necessity) possessed by various facts that cannot have been otherwise.

Had Bill Gates wanted to build a large gold cube, then there would have been a gold cube exceeding one cubic mile. But even if Gates had wanted to build an electrically insulating copper object, all copper objects would still have been electrically conductive, since events are obliged to conform to the natural laws. In other words the laws govern not only what actually happens but also what would have happened under various circumstances that did not actually happen. The laws support *counterfactuals* (i.e., facts expressed by statements of the form "Had p been the case, then q would have been the case"). Consequently, scientists use the laws to ascertain, for example, the conditions that would have prevailed on Earth had Earth been ten times nearer to the Sun. The laws are preserved under this counterfactual supposition. In contrast, an accident would not still have held, had p been the case, for some p that is *nomically possible* (i.e., consistent with all the laws' logical consequences).

Counterfactuals are notoriously context sensitive. For example, when one is emphasizing how baseball pitching talent has declined over the years, one might correctly remark that were Babe Ruth playing in the major leagues today, he would hit an astounding 120 home runs in a single season. But in a different context, one might correctly remark that were the Babe playing today, he would hit only ten homers per season, since by now he would be an old man. Which facts are to be held fixed

under some counterfactual supposition, and which are allowed to vary, depends somewhat on one's interests in entertaining that supposition. But it appears that in any context, the laws would still have held under every nomic possibility. This idea is sometimes called *nomic preservation*.

LAWS VERSUS ACCIDENTS: EXPLANATION AND INDUCTION

Laws have an explanatory power that accidents lack. For example, a certain powder burns with yellow flames, not another color, because the powder is a sodium salt and it is a law that all sodium salts, when ignited, burn with yellow flames. The powder had to burn with yellow flames considering that it was a sodium salt. This "had-to-ness" reflects the law's necessity. In contrast, that a couple has two children is not explained by the fact that all the families on the couple's block have two children, since this fact is accidental. Were a childless couple to move onto the block, this couple would not encounter an irresistible opposing force.

One believes that it would be mere coincidence if all U.S. presidents elected in years ending in 0 died in office. Hence, one's discovery that Warren Harding (elected in 1920) died in office fails to justify raising one's confidence that whoever was elected in 1840 died in office. A candidate law is confirmed differently: That one sample of a given chemical substance melts at 383 degrees (in standard conditions) is evidence, for every unexamined sample of that substance, that its melting point is 383 degrees (under standard conditions). This difference in inductive role between laws and accidents seems related to the fact that laws, unlike accidents, express similarities among things that reflect their belonging to the same *natural kind*. The electron, the emerald, and the electromagnetic force are all natural kinds, whereas the families on a block and the gold cubes do not form natural kinds (though gold objects, cubical and otherwise, constitute a natural kind).

DIFFICULTIES DISTINGUISHING LAWS FROM ACCIDENTS

The previous discussion is the standard view of the scientifically relevant differences between laws and accidents. Insofar as the same claims play all these special roles, scientific reasoning apparently recognizes an important distinction here, which philosophers label as the difference between accidents and laws. (Obviously, this distinction involves what laws do rather than which facts happen to be called "laws"; Archimedes' principle of buoyancy, the axioms of quantum mechanics, and Maxwell's equations are all laws of physics.) However, it is notoriously difficult to capture the laws' special roles precisely.

For example, suppose one tries to distinguish laws from accidents on the grounds that laws support counterfactuals differently from accidents. That a car's maximum speed on a dry, flat road is a certain function of its gas pedal's distance from the floor is not a law (since it reflects accidental features of the car's engine). Nevertheless, this function supports counterfactuals regarding the car's maximum speed had the pedal been depressed to one-half inch from the floor, though not had certain changes been made to the engine. Indeed, all gold cubes would still have been smaller than a cubic mile even if Jones had been wearing a different shirt today. Of course, there are some nomic possibilities under which the gold-cubes generalization would not still have held. But circularity threatens if one uses the concept of nomic possibility to delimit the range of counterfactual suppositions under which a fact must be preserved for that fact to qualify as a logical consequence of the laws.

Likewise, a car's pedal-speed function, despite being accidental, can apparently be confirmed inductively. Moreover, when coupled with the road's condition and the pedal's position, it can explain the car's maximum speed. So although a fact's lawhood apparently makes a difference to science, it is difficult to identify exactly what difference it makes. This problem's stubbornness has led some philosophers to suggest that it is a mistake to distinguish laws sharply from accidents. There are merely various facts, each having a range of counterfactual suppositions under which it is preserved.

ARE THERE LAWS OUTSIDE OF FUNDAMENTAL PHYSICS?

Some so-called laws are plainly accidents—if they are true at all. Kepler's first law of planetary motion (that planets trace elliptical orbits) presupposes that the planets' masses happen to be negligible compared to the Sun's (since otherwise, the planets would be disturbed by their mutual gravitational influences) and that no body collides with a planet, knocking it out of its orbit. Some philosophers believe that the fundamental laws of microphysics (whatever they turn out to be) are the only genuine natural laws. This opinion is sometimes prompted by the fact that all events are ultimately nothing but the outcome of microphysical processes governed by the fundamental laws.

However, along with the laws of fundamental physics there might seem to be additional laws holding inde-pendent of the universe's microphysical details. The second law of thermodynamics, according to which the entropy of a closed system is likely to increase, seems not to reflect any peculiarities of the fundamental forces governing the universe's ultimate constituents; even if gravity had been twice as strong as it actually is, for example, the perfume molecules from a recently opened bottle would be more likely to spread quickly throughout the room than to remain in the bottle. Likewise, the principle of natural selection, according to which fitter traits are more likely to increase their prevalence in a closed population, seems like it would still hold whatever the laws of fundamental physics might have been.

Additionally, the second law of thermodynamics appears to require that certain initial microconditions be rare—for example, that the perfume molecules within recently opened bottles not usually be arranged so that whenever one molecule threatens to escape from the bottle, another happens to come along and knock it back inside. That the perfume molecules in recently opened bottles are indeed not so coordinated would seem to be an accident rather than a nomic necessity. Accordingly, perhaps the second law is not a law at all.

The principle of natural selection is perhaps also not a law, but a conceptual truth. That a trait is "fitter" in a given environment may simply mean that it is more likely to become increasingly common in subsequent generations. Nevertheless, both the second law of thermodynamics and the principle of natural selection appear to undergo inductive confirmation, to support counterfactuals, and to explain events in the manner of natural laws.

LAWS OF INEXACT SCIENCES: THE PROBLEM OF CETERIS PARIBUS

A "special" or "inexact" science (such as anatomy, ballistics, ecology, economics, marketing, or psychology) might appear to seek (or perhaps even to have already found) facts that in these sciences play the various roles characteristic of laws. However, there are three main obstacles to regarding Boyle's law (that the product of a gas's pressure P and its volume V is constant) as a law of gases, to regarding Gresham's law (that agents hoard sound money and spend currency of more dubious value) as a law of economics, or to regarding the area law (that larger islands have greater biodiversity) as a law of island biogeography. Each of these obstacles has persuaded some philosophers to deny that inexact sciences have laws.

First, any such "law" comes with a *ceteris paribus* qualification. Though *ceteris paribus* means roughly "all other things being equal," a given qualification may be better captured as the idea that the specified correlation holds "normally," "in the ideal case," "in the absence of disturbing factors," or as long as certain other factors have certain values. The law is "hedged" in some way. For example, the gas in a container departs significantly from Boyle's law when its temperature is changed, some of the gas escapes, or the pressure is high. These circumstances are ruled out by the *ceteris paribus* proviso to Boyle's law. But what exactly does "PV is constant, *ceteris paribus*" mean?

If it means that PV is constant unless it is not, then the "law" is a trivial, noncontingent truth rather than an interesting discovery. If instead *ceteris paribus* is shorthand for a list of every factor allowed by fundamental microphysics and able to cause a gas's PV to vary, then Robert Boyle could not have discovered his law, since he did not know some of these factors (e.g., gas molecules adhering to the container's walls or attracting one another). Alternatively, some philosophers contend that Boyle's law describes only fictitious "ideal gases" that lack any interfering factors. But then it is unclear how observations of actual gases could confirm Boyle's law or how knowledge of Boyle's law could justify scientists in using it to predict the behavior of actual gases. Boyle had neither the concept of an ideal gas nor an account of what makes a gas ideal (e.g., that it consists of molecules without mutual attraction and occupying no finite volume). Such an account is not part of Boyle's law. Rather, the extent to which an actual gas has constant PV is explained by the extent to which it resembles an ideal gas.

Apparently then, *ceteris paribus* in Boyle's law refers only to the disturbing factors of which Boyle was aware (high pressure, changes to the gas's temperature, and so forth). There may be no complete list of these factors. Obviously (to shift examples), Gresham's law does not apply if the society is wiped out, if its members believe that hoarding the sounder currency causes illness, and so forth. Part of understanding Gresham's law is knowing how to recognize whether some factor qualifies as disturbing. One can catch on to which factors these are without having to read a complete list of them. (Nonexperts may even [in an attenuated sense] understand the *ceteris paribus* proviso without being able to tell themselves whether some factor qualifies as disturbing, just as they understand other technical terms: by virtue of knowing who the relevant experts are to whom they should defer.)

LAWS OF INEXACT SCIENCES: THE PROBLEM OF TRUTH

However, societal events are ultimately nothing but the outcomes of microphysical processes. Certain sequences of microevents permitted by the fundamental laws of physics involve a society's members hoarding the weaker currency and spending the sounder. In one such sequence each member of the society happens whenever he or she spends money to forget momentarily which currency is sounder, because as chance would have it, some neuron in each agent's brain behaves at that moment in a manner that the fundamental microlaws deem extremely unlikely, but nevertheless possible. The *ceteris paribus* proviso to Gresham's law does not rule out this freakish sequence of events, since economists surely do not need to grasp the subtleties of fundamental microphysics to understand the proviso to Gresham's law.

In other words, not all exceptions to a macrolevel "law" can be specified in the vocabulary of the macroscience. For example, it might require physics (or at least neurology) to specify certain circumstance in which an agent would depart from a psychological "law." The *ceteris paribus* proviso fails to cover those exceptions.

This is the second obstacle to regarding inexact sciences as having genuine laws: The alleged laws are false or, if true, merely accidentally so. Perhaps, however, one should relax the requirement that genuine laws be exceptionless in favor of holding that a law be sufficiently accurate for the relevant purposes. The proviso to Boyle's law neglects to mention a host of petty influences that make the PV of actual gases vary somewhat. Still, Boyle's law with its proviso (which rules out the major interfering factors—the ones that scientists cannot afford to neglect) is often enough close enough to the truth for various purposes in chemistry, theoretical and practical. Fully understanding Boyle's law requires knowing the range of purposes for which it can safely be applied. Likewise, the freakish sequence of neural events mentioned earlier is too rare to make Gresham's law unreliable for the purposes of economics.

The limited range of a special science's interests influence which facts qualify as laws of that science. Consider another example: The human aorta carries all the body's oxygenated blood from the heart to the systemic circulation. This reference to "the human aorta" (a generic), rather than to all or to most human aortas, apparently indicates that one is dealing here with a policy of drawing influences that, although fallible, is sufficiently reliable for certain purposes—in this case for forming expectations about medical patients in the absence of more specific information regarding them. In human medicine this fact about the human aorta apparently functions as a law in connection with counterfactuals, explanations, and inductions. However, this aorta fact is merely an accident of natural history; it might not have held had evolutionary history taken a different path. Still, medicine does not treat evolutionary history as a variable. A physician might say that the shooting victim would not have survived even if he or she had been brought to the hospital sooner, since the bullet punctured his or her aorta and the human aorta carries all the body's oxygenated blood from the heart to the systemic circulation. (This aorta fact would still have held had the victim been brought to the hospital sooner.) But it would not be medically relevant to point out that the victim might have survived had evolutionary history taken a different course. Accordingly, that the human aorta carries all the body's oxygenated blood to the systemic circulation may be a law of human physiology even if it is an accident of physics.

LAWS OF INEXACT SCIENCES: THE PROBLEM OF NECESSITY

But (to shift examples) even if the law that larger islands have greater biodiversity (all other things—such as their distance from the mainland—being equal) is sufficiently reliable for the purposes of island biogeography, what makes this fact an island-biogeographical law? What makes it necessary? This is the third obstacle to inexact sciences having genuine laws of their own—that is, to their being autonomous.

Recall *nomic preservation*: that the laws would still have held under any counterfactual supposition that is logically consistent with every law. There appears to be no set of truths that is closed under logical consequence and that contains accidents (except the set of all truths) where every member of the set would still have been true under every counterfactual supposition that is logically consistent with every member of the set. Accordingly, it has been suggested that a truth n is a nomic necessity exactly when n belongs to a stable set, where a set is stable exactly when it includes every logical consequence of its members, it does not contain every truth, and its members are not only true but also all preserved under as broad a range of counterfactual suppositions as they could all logically possibly be—namely, under every supposition that is logically consistent with every member. On this view necessity involves possessing maximal invariance under counterfactual perturbations. No necessity is possessed by an accident, even one (such as a car's pedal-speed

function) that would still have held under many counterfactual suppositions. (The set consisting of a car's pedal-speed function, with its logical consequences, is unstable since its members would not all still have held under engine alterations with which the pedal-speed function is logically consistent.) Stability allows one to draw a sharp distinction between laws and accidents. It also gives one a way to escape the circle involved in specifying the nomic necessities as the truths that would still have held under every nomic possibility.

This conception of nomic necessity can easily be relativized to particular sciences. Perhaps the area law belongs to a set of claims that are all sufficiently reliable for the purposes of island biogeography, where the set does not contain all such claims and where its members would all still have been sufficiently reliable under any counterfactual supposition that is not only consistent with all of them being reliable but also relevant to island biogeography. In that case the set's members are collectively as resilient under counterfactual suppositions relevant to island biogeography as they collectively could be. Therefore, they possess nomic necessity for island biogeography.

On this view a special science's laws need not include every detail of the fundamental microphysical laws. For example, biological species would still have been distributed according to the laws of island biogeography (if there are any such laws) even if creatures were made of a continuous rigid substance rather than molecules, contrary to microphysical laws. Whether a given special science is autonomous remains for scientific research to discover. Whether the fundamental microphysical laws are privileged among the natural laws (e.g., in having greater generality or being strictly true) remains philosophically controversial.

See also Causation: Philosophy of Science; Laws of Nature; Metaphysics; Theories and Theoretical Terms.

Bibliography

Armstrong, David A. *What Is a Law of Nature?* New York: Cambridge University Press, 1983.

Beatty, John. "The Evolutionary Contingency Thesis." In *Concepts, Theories, and Rationality in the Biological Sciences*, edited by Gereon Wolters and James G. Lennox. Pittsburgh, PA: University of Pittsburgh Press, 1995.

Carlson, Gregory N., and Francis Jeffry Pelletier, eds. *The Generic Book*. Chicago: University of Chicago Press, 1995.

Carroll, John W. *Laws of Nature*. New York: Cambridge University Press, 1994.

Carroll, John W., ed. *Readings on Laws of Nature*. Pittsburgh: University of Pittsburgh Press, 2004.

Cartwright, Nancy. *The Dappled World: A Study of the Boundaries of Science*. New York: Cambridge University Press, 1999.

Cartwright, Nancy. *How the Laws of Physics Lie*. New York: Oxford University Press, 1983.

Dretske, Fred. "Laws of Nature." *Philosophy of Science* 44 (1977): 248–268.

Earman, John, and John Roberts. "Ceteris Paribus, There Is No Problem of Provisos." *Synthese* 118 (1999): 439–478.

Earman, John, Clark Glymour, and Sandra Mitchell. *Ceteris Paribus Laws*. Dordrecht, Netherlands: Kluwer Academic, 2002.

Fodor, Jerry A. "Special Sciences, or the Disunity of Science as a Working Hypothesis." *Synthese* 28 (2) (1974): 97–115.

Gardner, Patrick L. *The Nature of Historical Explanation*. London: Oxford University Press, 1952.

Goodman, Nelson. *Fact, Fiction, and Forecast*, 4th ed. Cambridge, MA: Harvard University Press, 1983.

Hempel, Carl G. *Aspects of Scientific Explanation and Other Essays in the Philosophy of Science*. New York: Free Press, 1965.

Kincaid, Harold. *Philosophical Foundations of the Social Sciences: Analyzing Controversies in Social Research*. New York: Cambridge University Press, 1996.

Lange, Marc. *Natural Laws in Scientific Practice*. New York: Oxford University Press, 2000.

Lewis, David K. *Counterfactuals*. Cambridge, MA: Harvard University Press, 1973.

Lewis, David K. *Philosophical Papers*. Vol. 2. New York: Oxford University Press, 1986.

Loewer, Barry. "Humean Supervenience." *Philosophical Topics* 24 (1996) 101–127.

Mill, John Stuart. *A System of Logic*. 8th ed. New York: Harper, 1893.

Scriven, Michael. "Truisms as the Ground for Historical Explanations." In *Theories of History*, edited by Patrick L. Gardner. London: George Allen and Unwin, 1959.

Sklar, Lawrence. *Physics and Chance: Philosophical Issues in the Foundations of Statistical Mechanics*. New York: Cambridge University Press, 1993.

Sober, Elliott. *Philosophy of Biology*. 2nd ed. Boulder, CO: Westview Press, 2000.

Van Fraassen, Bas C. *Laws and Symmetry*. New York: Oxford University Press, 1989.

Woodward, James. "Explanation and Invariance in the Special Sciences." *British Journal for the Philosophy of Science* 51 (2) (2000): 197–254.

Marc Lange (2005)

LAWS OF NATURE

The "laws of nature" are the general ways of working of the physical and mental world. Many natural scientists have as one of their great aims the uncovering of these laws. The topic of laws of nature has been the subject of vigorous discussion in contemporary philosophy. Three broad tendencies have emerged, with a number of important variations within these tendencies.

THE REGULARITY OR HUMEAN VIEW

Since the work of David Hume, at least, there have been many philosophers, particularly those in the empiricist tradition, who have tried to analyze both causes and laws (which they tend not to distinguish very clearly) in terms of mere regular successions or other regularities in the behavior of things. Laws tell us that, given a phenomenon of a certain sort, then a further phenomenon of a certain sort must occur in a certain relation to the first phenomenon. Particularly since the rise of quantum physics, this may be modified by saying that there must be a certain probability that the further phenomenon will occur. Regularity theorists see this "must" as mere universality: This is what always happens.

A great many difficulties have been raised against this position (for a fairly full listing see Armstrong 1983, pt. 1). The most important of these are as follows.

1. The intuitive difference between merely accidental uniformities and nomic (lawlike) uniformities. The traditional example is the contrast between the accidental uniformity that every sphere of gold has a diameter of less than one mile and the nomic uniformity that every sphere of uranium 235 has a diameter of less than one mile, because that diameter would ensure "critical mass" and the explosion of the sphere.

2. Laws of nature "sustain counterfactuals." If it is a law that arsenic is poisonous, then if, contrary to the facts, you had drunk arsenic, you would have been very sick. But from the fact that no human being of Neanderthal race ever spoke English, it by no means follows that if, contrary to fact, some of them had lived in an English-speaking society, they would not have spoken English. The uniformity that Neanderthals spoke no English does not sustain counterfactuals.

3. A regularity theorist cannot give a satisfactory solution to the problem of induction. If laws are mere regularities, what rational grounds have we for believing that observed uniformities will continue to hold in the future and for the unobserved generally?

4. A regularity theorist is likely to identify merely probabilistic laws with actually occurring frequencies. This identification is difficult, because

such laws do not actually rule out distributions with the "wrong" frequencies. All that probabilistic laws do is to make such frequencies improbable; they do not make them nomically impossible.

5. Science admits certain laws that may well have no positive instances falling under them. The most famous example is Isaac Newton's first law of motion. An uninstantiated law would have to be a vacuous uniformity, but there are far too many such uniformities all to be laws.

Those who continue to work in the regularity tradition try to meet these and other difficulties largely by distinguishing "good" uniformities that deserve to be called laws and "bad" ones that do not. There are two main approaches, the epistemic and the systematic.

Epistemic theorists emphasize the nature of the evidence that we have for claiming that certain uniformities obtain. References and criticism may be found in W. A. Suchting (1974), G. Molnar (1974), Fred Dretske (1977), and David M. Armstrong (1983). Brian Skyrms's (1980) resiliency account is a sophisticated epistemic approach. His basic idea is that we give assent to a generalization, and count it lawlike, only if we find it to hold under a wide variety of circumstances and conditions. For criticism of Skyrms, see Michael Tooley (1987) and J. Carroll (1990).

The systematic approach has been championed by David Lewis, explicitly basing himself on a suggestion made by F. P. Ramsey. Lewis says that "contingent generalization is a *law of nature* if and only if it appears as a theorem (or axiom) in each of the true deductive systems that achieves the best combination of simplicity and strength" (1973, p. 73). Further discussion may be found in Lewis (1986). He himself finds that his greatest difficulties are associated with probabilistic laws. For criticism of Lewis see Armstrong (1983), Tooley (1987), and Carroll (1990).

STRONG LAWS

One who judges that no regularity theory of laws can succeed may wish to argue that laws are something stronger than mere uniformities or statistical distributions. Laws may be called strong if their existence entails the existence of the corresponding uniformities and so on but the reverse entailment fails to hold.

Traditional theories of strong laws tended to see these laws as holding necessarily. Given all the antecedent conditions, the consequent is entailed. In the days when Euclidean geometry was unchallenged, geometrical models were attractive. As with geometrical theorems, this necessity was thought to be discoverable, at least potentially, a priori. Granted that laws might in practice be discovered by experience, just as the Pythagorean theorem might be discovered by measuring and adding areas, it was still thought that a sufficiently powerful intellect might spell out the necessity involved without the aid of experience. This approach seems to have been abandoned by contemporary philosophers (though there are hints in Martin 1993). It now seems agreed, in general, and in agreement with regularity theorists, that the laws of nature can be discovered only a posteriori.

Upholders of strong laws do, however, differ among themselves whether these laws are contingent or necessary. The contingency view (also held by regularity theorists) is represented by Dretske (1977), Tooley (1977, 1987) and Armstrong (1983). These three evolved their rather similar views independently and almost simultaneously. Laws are argued to be dyadic relations of necessitation holding contingently between universals, schematically N(F,G). Such a relation entails the regularity that all Fs are Gs, but the regularity does not entail N(F,G). Dretske presents the central idea with particular clarity; Tooley and Armstrong develop the theory more fully. Tooley argues that the possibility of certain sorts of uninstantiated laws demands uninstantiated universals, leading him to what he calls a factual Platonism about universals. Armstrong, however, tries to get along with instantiated universals only.

The theory appears to be able to handle probabilistic laws (see Armstrong 1983, chap. 9; Tooley 1987, chap. 4). The connection between universals envisaged by the theory may be thought of as involving connections of differing strength holding between antecedent and consequent universals. The greatest strength, one (exactly one, not one minus an infinitesimal), represents the probability involved in an old-style deterministic law. The consequent universal must be instantiated if the antecedent universal is. Numbers between nought and one give the lesser probability of the consequent being instantiated under these conditions. This probability is an objective one. The antecedent universal, if instantiated, bestows an objective propensity, as some say, for the instantiation of the consequent.

An obvious cost of this sort of theory is that it must postulate universals. This is a stumbling block to many. But by far the most important criticism of this account has been developed by Bas van Fraassen (1989, chap. 5; see also the discussion-review of this book by him, Earman, Cartwright, and Armstrong 1993). He poses two difficulties: the identification problem and the inference problem. The first is the problem of identifying in a non-circular way the nature of the necessitation relation supposed to hold between the universals involved in the law. The second is the problem, given a concrete account of this relation, of understanding why it is legitimate to infer from the fact that the universals are so related to the existence of corresponding uniformities or frequencies in the world. Van Fraassen argues that solving the one problem makes it impossible to solve the other. A clear account of the relation makes the inference problematic; a clearly valid inference makes the relation no more than something that validates the inference.

The view that laws of nature are necessities discovered a posteriori is developed by Sydney Shoemaker (1984) and Chris Swoyer (1982). They build on Saul Kripke's (1980) arguments for a posteriori knowledge of necessity, and Kripke hints that laws of nature may have this status. Their view depends upon taking a different view of properties from that found in Dretske, Tooley, and Armstrong. For the latter, properties are conceived of as "categorical" or self-contained entities. But for Shoemaker and Swoyer, properties, either singly or in combination, are nothing apart from the laws they enter into. They might be described as pure powers or dispositions to produce law-governed consequences.

On this view, therefore, if it is a law that property F ensures possession of property G, then it is the very essence of F so to ensure G, and so the law is necessary. That there are things having property F is contingent, but that F ensures G is necessary. It seems, then, that the dispute between contingent strong laws and necessary ones depends on the true theory of properties. See Richard Swinburne's (1983) critical comments on Shoemaker.

The view of properties just discussed might be called dispositionalism as opposed to categoricalism. There are theorists who favor a view of properties that gives them both a categorical and a dispositional (or power) side; see Evan Fales (1990) and C. B. Martin (1993). It is to be noted that both in pure dispositionalism and this mixed theory there is a strong tendency to regard laws as not fundamental but rather analyzable in terms of causal relations holding between individual events and particulars (singular causation). These causal relations, and so their laws, are determined by the nature of the dispositions or powers that particulars have.

ELIMINATIVISM ABOUT LAWS

The regularity theory of laws is a deflationary theory. It holds that there is less to being a law than one might naturally think. It also faces a number of serious difficulties. One response, rather typical of our age, is to meet the difficulties, not by proposing a strengthened theory of laws, but by taking the deflation further and arguing that there are no such things as laws. This is the position taken by van Fraassen in *Laws and Symmetry* (1989). A natural comparison is with eliminative materialism, which denies the existence of the mind in favor of the brain.

Van Fraassen begins with a systematic criticism, first of Lewis's version of the regularity theory, and then of various strong views. The rejection of laws he links to his "constructive empiricism," according to which the aim of science is not truth in general but only empirical adequacy, defined as truth with respect to what is observed. Beyond the observable, all that can usefully be done is the constructing of models that are in a deep way adequate to the phenomena and that may be true but about which we can have no special reason to think them true. In these constructions considerations of symmetry play an energizing role.

A certain skepticism about laws is also to be found in Nancy Cartwright's *How the Laws of Physics Lie* (1983). Her skepticism concerns the fundamental as opposed to more messy phenomenological laws. The former may explain better, but the latter are truer to the facts! The distinction she is concerned with is one made by physicists, and the "phenomenological" laws go far beyond van Fraassen's observables. Cartwright accepts these laws because the entities they deal with, though perhaps unobserved, appear to exist and to act as causes. In *Nature's Capacities and Their Measurement* (1989), she argues that the world is a world of singular causes, individual entities interacting with each other. The nature of these interactions is determined by the capacities of these entities. Her capacities seem close to the dispositions and powers that contemporary necessitarians identify with properties.

See also Armstrong, David M.; Cartwright, Nancy; Descartes, René; Dretske, Fred; Earman, John; Eliminative Materialism, Eliminativism; Empiricism; Geometry; Hobbes, Thomas; Hume, David; Induction; Kripke, Saul; Lewis, David; Locke, John; Newton, Isaac; Probability and Chance; Ramsey, Frank Plumpton; Shoemaker, Sydney; Van Fraassen, Bas.

Bibliography

Armstrong, D. M. *What Is a Law of Nature?* Cambridge, U.K.: Cambridge University Press, 1983.

Carroll, J. "The Humean Tradition." *Philosophical Review* 99 (1990): 261–276.

Carroll, J. *Laws of Nature.* Cambridge, U.K.: Cambridge University Press, 1994. Contains a useful set of references.

Cartwright, N. *How the Laws of Physics Lie.* Oxford: Clarendon Press, 1983.

Cartwright, N. *Nature's Capacities and Their Measurement.* Oxford Clarendon Press, 1989.

Dretske, F. "Laws of Nature." *Philosophy of Science* 44 (1977): 248–268.

Fales, E. *Causation and Universals.* London: Routledge, 1990.

Kripke, S. *Naming and Necessity.* Cambridge, MA: Harvard University Press, 1980.

Lewis, D. *Counterfactuals.* Cambridge, MA: Harvard University Press, 1973.

Lewis, D. *Philosophical Papers,* Vol. 2. New York: Oxford University Press, 1986.

Martin, C. B. "Power for Realists." In *Ontology, Causality, and Mind,* edited by J. Bacon, K. Campbell, and L. Reinhardt. Cambridge, U.K.: Cambridge University Press, 1993.

Molnar, G. "Kneale's Argument Revisited." In *Philosophical Problems of Causation,* edited by T. Beauchamp. Encino, CA: Dickenson, 1974.

Shoemaker, S. "Causality and Properties." In *Identity, Cause, and Mind.* Cambridge, U.K.: Cambridge University Press, 1984.

Skyrms, B. *Causal Necessity.* New Haven, CT: Yale University Press, 1980.

Suchting, W. A. "Regularity and Law." In *Boston Studies in the Philosophy of Science,* edited by R. S. Cohen and M. W. Wartofsky. Dordrecht: Reidel, 1974.

Swinburne, R. "Reply to Shoemaker." In *Aspects of Inductive Logic,* edited by L. J. Cohen and M. Hesse. Oxford, 1983. See also Shoemaker's paper in the same volume.

Swoyer, C. "The Nature of Natural Laws." *Australasian Journal of Philosophy* 60 (1982): 203–223.

Tooley, M. *Causation: A Realist Approach.* Oxford: Clarendon Press, 1987.

Tooley, M. "The Nature of Laws." *Canadian Journal of Philosophy* 7 (1977): 667–698.

van Fraassen, B. *Laws and Symmetry.* Oxford: Oxford University Press, 1989.

van Fraassen, B., J. Earman, D. M. Armstrong, and N. Cartwright. "A Book Symposium on Laws and Symmetry." *Philosophy and Phenomenological Research* 53 (1993): 411–444.

David M. Armstrong (1996)

LAWS OF NATURE [ADDENDUM]

Since David M. Armstrong's entry was first published in 1996, the philosophical debates he identifies have evolved in minor ways. There is still the central debate between the Humeans (the regularity theorists) and the anti-Humeans (the proponents of strong laws), and there are still those who choose to deny that there are any laws, to be eliminativists, rather than engage in the central debate.

This addendum indicates how the literature has shifted focus to questions surrounding supervenience and whether laws govern. It also engages in a fuller discussion of the relationship between laws of nature and epistemological issues, including the role of laws in inductive inference and some skeptical challenges for both Humeans and anti-Humeans.

SUPERVENIENCE

The persevering Humean theory of laws is the systematic approach made popular by David Lewis and described briefly by Armstrong. (Versions of this account are also defended in Earman [1984] and in Loewer [1996].) A feature of this view prized by its supporters is its consistency with Humean supervenience, a thesis formulated various ways (see Earman and Roberts, 2005, Part I) but that basically maintains that the most fundamental nonmodal features of a universe fix everything else about it, including what its laws of nature are. Some anti-Humeans, the ones who think that laws are metaphysical necessities (e.g., Bigelow, Ellis, and Lierse 1992) accept that the laws do supervene for the mere reason that metaphysical necessities hold no matter what. But most anti-Humeans, the ones who believe that it is a contingent matter of fact whether something is a law, think that what the laws are does not supervene.

Michael Tooley (1977) asks one to suppose that there are exactly ten different kinds of fundamental particles. So, there are fifty-five possible kinds of two-particle interactions. Suppose also that fifty-four of these kinds of interactions have been studied and fifty-four laws have been proposed and thoroughly tested. It just so happens that there are no interactions between the last two kinds of particles ever. These final two kinds of particles are arbitrarily labeled as X and Y particles. What is interesting about this example is that it seems that many different X-Y interaction laws are consistent with all the events that take place: There might be a law that, when X and Y particles interact, the particles are destroyed; but instead there might be a law that, when X and Y particles interact, the particles bond.

Tooley's example presents a problem for Humeans. Consider what a certain, simple, regularity account would say about the seeming possibility that it is a law in the ten-particle world that when X and Y particles interact they bond. The account holds that P is a law of nature if and only if P is a true, contingent, universal generalization. It implies the absurdity that both of the X-Y regularities mentioned earlier are laws. This is absurd because such annihilation and bonding events are incompatible. The account fails to pick out the bonding regularity as the law because the concepts invoked do not differentiate between bonding and annihilation. Because the two X-Y regularities are both true, contingent, universal generalizations, they both get counted as laws. Prima facie, Lewis's more sophisticated account is faced with the same problem. Not only do the two key X-Y regularities not differ regarding their truth, their contingency, or their logical form, they also do not differ regarding their simplicity or their strength. So, arguably, either these two regularities would both belong to all the true deductive systems with a best combination of simplicity and strength or else neither of them would.

Eliminativists may acknowledge the intuitiveness of Tooley's example but may see that as reason to think there are no laws. There is also a certain nonstandard way of being Humean that sidesteps the issue in something of a similar fashion. Barry Ward, in "Humeanism without Humean Supervenience: A Projectivist Account of Laws and Possibilities" (2002), maintains that lawhood sentences are not fact-stating, that they serve a different role, one of projecting some noncognitive attitude.

DO LAWS GOVERN?

The standard approach for Humeans is to somehow deny that Tooley's example and other cases to the same effect (see Carroll 1994, pp. 57–85) are genuinely possible. They hold that the intuition that the lawfulness of each of the two X-Y interaction principles is consistent with the events of the ten-particle world is somehow misleading or ill founded. Helen Beebee, in "The Non-governing Conception of Laws of Nature" (2000), suggests that the source of the intuition is a certain veneration of a conception of laws that holds that laws govern the course of history (also see Loewer 1996, pp. 115–117). The idea is that, if one comes to the debate with the governing conception in mind, one is likely to find nonsupervenience examples convincing, but using this conception to reject Humean analyses of lawhood is to beg the question because it is a conception Humeans reject. Having their own conception of laws not as governing but as summarizing, Humeans insist that at most one of the two X-Y interaction laws is consistent with the events of the ten-particle world. Anti-Humeans are sometimes accused of relying on a nonscientific or even theistic or legalistic conception of what it is to be a law, though the anti-Humeans themselves will insist, on the contrary, that it is their conception that is the scientific conception and that it needs no theistic or legalistic underpinning. Nevertheless, one idiosyncratic anti-Humean, John Foster, in *The*

Divine Lawmaker: Lectures on Induction, Laws of Nature, and the Existence of God (2004), provides fuel for the Humean fire by arguing that lawful regularities ultimately must be explained in terms of the agency of God.

LAWS AND INDUCTION

In "The New Riddle of Induction" (1983) Nelson Goodman argues that the difference between laws of nature and accidental uniformities is linked with the problem of induction via the concept of lawlikeness. Lawlikeness is whatever additional characteristic a universal generalization needs, aside from truth, to be a law. Goodman claims that, if a true generalization is accidentally true (and so not lawlike), then an instance of the generalization does not confirm the generalization.

There are examples that threaten Goodman's contention. Suppose a brand new die will be thrown twice and then destroyed. Also suppose that one is interested in whether it will come up six both times it is tossed. It is thrown the first time and it does land six. Notice that this single instance has increased dramatically the probability that all tosses of this die will land six. Before the first toss, that probability was one out of thirty-six. Now that the first toss has landed six, that probability has gone up to one-sixth. So, apparently, Goodman's claim is mistaken; observation of one instance of the generalization that every toss of this die will land six has provided confirmation even though the generalization is not lawlike.

One natural response to this kind of example maintains that probability raising is not the notion of confirmation that Goodman had in mind. The temptation is to hold instead that a generalization is lawlike if observed instances confirm that the generalization also holds for unexamined cases. (Notice that, in the die example, the first roll landing six does not raise the probability that the second roll will land six.) But this alternative is not right either. Maybe you know that Sam sorts his coins by putting nickels in one pocket, dimes in another, and so on; he is fanatical that way. You do not know, however, which pocket he keeps his nickels in. Sam shows you one of the coins from his left-front pocket and you see that it is a nickel. Evidently this instance of the generalization that all the coins in Sam's left-front pocket are nickels has confirmed that all the coins in this pocket are nickels. Given your background knowledge, you seem perfectly justified in believing that the generalization is true even though it is not lawlike. You also have reason to believe that the other coins in his left-front pocket, the ones you have not examined, are nickels.

Followers of Goodman have their work cut out for them. The biggest obstacle involves background beliefs, as is evidenced by the two examples just given where prior knowledge that the die would only be tossed twice and prior knowledge of Sam's fanatical coin sorting played a major role. Here is the basic problem: The confirmation of a generalization or its unexamined instances is sensitive to the background assumptions in place. So much so, that with assumptions of the right sort, just about anything can be confirmed irrespective of its lawlikeness. Elliot Sober's "Confirmation and Law-likeness" (1988) presents a series of difficult cases and concludes by expressing this concern about background assumptions. Marc Lange's *Natural Laws in Scientific Practice* (2000, pp. 111–142) takes up the challenge, in part, by further refining the relevant notion of confirmation, characterizing what he takes to be an intuitive notion of inductive confirmation, and arguing that only those generalizations that are not believed not to be lawlike can be inductively confirmed.

A SKEPTICAL CHALLENGE FOR HUMEANS

Sometimes the idea that laws have a special role to play in induction serves as the starting point for an anti-Humean criticism of Humean analyses. Fred I. Dretske (1977, pp. 261–262) and Armstrong (1983, pp. 52–59) adopt a view according to which induction involves an inference to the best explanation (also see Foster 2004). On its simplest construal, the view describes a pattern that begins with an observation of instances of a generalization, includes an inference to the corresponding law (this is the inference to the best explanation), and concludes with an inference to the regularity itself or to some conclusion about its unexamined instances. The complaint lodged against Humeans is that, on their view of what laws are, laws are not suited to explain their instances and so cannot sustain the required inference to the best explanation. After all, if laws are summaries of their instances, then they cannot explain their instances. Does the fact that all Fs are Gs explain why this F is a G? It is hard to see how it could; that this F is G is part of what makes it true that all Fs are Gs.

A SKEPTICAL CHALLENGE FOR ANTI-HUMEANS

Sometimes very different skeptical considerations are used by Humeans against the anti-Humeans. Prompted by examples like Tooley's, it can seem that the events of the actual world fail to determine what the laws are. Scientists and philosophers believe it is a law that all signals have speeds less than the speed of light, but if the course of our actual history is consistent with this generalization not being a law, with it being a remarkable coincidence, then can anyone really know that it is a law of nature?

John Earman and John Roberts formalize this kind of reasoning in "Contact with the Nomic: A Challenge for Deniers of Humean Supervenience about Laws of Nature (Part II): The Epistemological Argument for Humean Supervenience" (2005). Let T be a theory that posits at least one law. Label one of the laws L and reformulate the theory as the conjunction that L is a law of nature and X. (So, X is the rest of the theory aside from the part that posits L as a law.) Let T* be the theory that L is true, not a law of nature, and X. So, T and T* cannot both be true; they differ on whether L is a law, though they agree on L's truth. Then, the argument is straightforward:

(1) If Humean supervenience is false, then no empirical evidence can favor T or T* over the other

(2) If no empirical evidence can favor T or T* over the other, then one cannot be epistemically justified in believing that T is true

(3) If Humean supervenience is false, one cannot be epistemically justified in believing that T is true

Earman and Roberts make no assumptions about T other than that it takes something to be a law. So, if Earman and Roberts's argument is sound and Humean supervenience is false, then no one is justified in believing that any proposition is a law. It is only a short step from there to the conclusion that no one knows what any of the laws are. As Earman and Roberts deny skepticism about laws, they ultimately see this as an argument for Humean supervenience.

In response, the anti-Humean will appeal to the history of philosophy, citing instances of epistemological questions that have befuddled metaphysical issues. George Berkeley's idealism is a dramatic example. Faced with René Descartes's skeptical investigations, Berkeley advanced the untenable metaphysical position according to which material objects are nothing more than collections of ideas. So, Humeans have to make it clear that they are not making a mistake parallel to the one made by Berkeley. Also, it is important to remember that, in some sense, it could be that nobody knows what the laws are; it is obvious that there are a great many ways that our world could be such that scientists will not discover every fact, and so our world could be such that no one will discover any of the laws.

Nevertheless, Humeans and anti-Humeans alike are right to balk at a conclusion to the effect that we can never know what the laws are. If a philosophical position on lawhood, be it the identification of laws with regularities or the denial of Humean supervenience or something else, has the consequence that no one ever knows anything to be a law, then the defender of that position should be concerned. Part of the motivation for engaging in a philosophical investigation of laws is the seeming truism that science has as one of its aims to uncover the laws. If it should turn out that science is bound not to result in knowledge of the laws, then philosophy would have led us to at least a disturbing take on the nature of the world.

See also Armstrong, David M.; Berkeley, George; Descartes, René; Dretske, Fred; Earman, John; Goodman, Nelson; Hume, David; Induction; Lewis, David; Natural Law; Supervenience.

Bibliography

Armstrong, David M. *What Is a Law of Nature?*. New York: Cambridge University Press, 1983.

Beebee, Helen. "The Non-governing Conception of Laws of Nature." *Philosophy and Phenomenological Research* 61 (2000): 571–594.

Bigelow, John, Brian Ellis, and Caroline Lierse. "The World as One of a Kind: Natural Necessity and Laws of Nature." *British Journal for the Philosophy of Science* 43 (1992): 371–388.

Carroll, John W. *Laws of Nature*. New York: Cambridge University Press, 1994.

Carroll, John W., ed. *Readings on Laws of Nature*. Pittsburgh, PA: Pittsburgh University Press, 2004.

Dretske, Fred I. "Laws of Nature." *Philosophy of Science* 44 (1977): 248–268.

Earman, John. "Laws of Nature: The Empiricist Challenge." In *D. M. Armstrong*, edited by Radu J. Bogdan. Dordrecht, Netherlands: D. Reidel, 1984.

Earman, John, and John Roberts. "Contact with the Nomic: A Challenge for Deniers of Humean Supervenience about Laws of Nature (Part I) Humean Supervenience." *Philosophy and Phenomenological Research* 71 (2005).

Earman, John, and John Roberts. "Contact with the Nomic: A Challenge for Deniers of Humean Supervenience about Laws of Nature (Part II): The Epistemological Argument for Humean Supervenience." *Philosophy and Phenomenological Research* 71 (2005).

Foster, John. *The Divine Lawmaker: Lectures on Induction, Laws of Nature, and the Existence of God*. Oxford, U.K.: Clarendon Press, 2004.

Goodman, Nelson. "The New Riddle of Induction." In *Fact, Fiction, and Forecast*. 4th ed., 59–83. Cambridge, MA: Harvard University Press, 1983.

Lange, Marc. *Natural Laws in Scientific Practice*. New York: Oxford University Press, 2000.

Loewer, Barry. "Humean Supervenience." *Philosophical Topics* 24 (1996): 101–127.

Sober, Elliott. "Confirmation and Law-likeness." *Philosophical Review* 97 (1988): 93–98.

Tooley, Michael. "The Nature of Laws." *Canadian Journal of Philosophy* 7 (4) (1977): 667–698.

Ward, Barry. "Humeanism without Humean Supervenience: A Projectivist Account of Laws and Possibilities." *Philosophical Studies* 107 (2002): 191–218.

John W. Carroll (2005)

LAWS OF THOUGHT

The term "laws of thought" traditionally covered the principles of identity, of contradiction, of excluded middle, and occasionally the principle of sufficient reason. Whereas these principles were frequently discussed from the time of the Greeks until the beginning of the twentieth century, the term has become obsolete, for at least two good reasons. One is the great and confusing variety of meanings with which it has been used, the other is the now generally acknowledged fact that no viable system of logic can be constructed in which the principles of identity, contradiction, and excluded middle would be the only axioms. Typical discussions of these principles are to be found, for example, in Friedrich Ueberweg's *System der Logik* and in H. W. B. Joseph's *Introduction to Logic*. In the following discussion the principle of sufficient reason, which, unlike the others, cannot be interpreted as a principle of formal logic, will not be dealt with.

The three laws of thought have in the main been conceived of as descriptive, prescriptive, or formal. As *descriptive* laws, they have been regarded as descriptive (*a*) of the nature of "being as such," (*b*) of the subject matter common to all sciences, or (*c*) of the activity of thinking or reasoning. As *prescriptive* laws, they have been conceived of as expressing absolute or conventional standards of correct thinking or reasoning. As *formal* laws, they have been held to be propositions which are true in virtue of their form and independently of their content, true *in* all possible worlds, or true *of* any objects whatsoever, whether these objects exist or not. Distinctions between these conceptions are often blurred, since they depend on implicit and often unclear assumptions about the relations between factual, normative, and metaphysical propositions: It is, for example, rarely investigated either to what extent various kinds of rules depend for their satisfiability on what is the case or to what extent logic is or can be free from metaphysical presuppositions or implications.

All these very different conceptions of the laws of thought are compatible with their traditional formulations, which lack the precision now achievable by means of the axiomatization and formalization of theories. Examples of typical, traditional formulations are: For the law of identity, *A* is *A*; everything is what it is; every subject is its own predicate. For the law of contradiction, *A* is not not-*A*; judgments contradictorily opposed to each other cannot both be true. For the law of excluded middle, everything is either *A* or not-*A*; judgments opposed as contradictories cannot both be false, nor can they admit the truth of a third or middle judgment, but one or the other must be true, and the truth of the one follows from the falsehood of the other. An obvious ambiguity concerning the law of identity is connected with the question whether *is* is to be taken as expressing equality or as the copula between subject and predicate, and, in the latter case, whether or not it implies the existence of the subject. Again, the term *not* admits of different interpretations according to different metaphysical and logical assumptions about negation.

DESCRIPTIVE INTERPRETATIONS

METAPHYSICAL INTERPRETATION. For Aristotle, who discussed the laws of thought in his logical and metaphysical works, they are primarily descriptive of being as such and only secondarily standards of correct thinking. It is thus a metaphysical or ontological impossibility that "the same can and cannot belong to the same in the same reference" (*Metaphysics* III, 2, 2), from which it follows as a rule of correct thought and speech that it is incorrect to assert that "the same is and is not" (*Metaphysics* IV, 6, 12). Aristotle produced seven "proofs" to demonstrate the indispensability of the law of contradiction. With a similar intention, formal logicians are nowadays wont to show that its negation implies any proposition whatever (and thus also the law of contradiction itself) by some such reasoning as the following: (1) To assume that the law of contradiction is false is to assume for some proposition *p* that *p* and not-*p* are both true. (2) From the truth of *p* it follows that "*p* or *x*" is also true, where *x* is an arbitrary proposition and "or" is used in the nonexclusive sense of "and/or." (3) From the truth of "*p* or *x*" and the truth of not-*p* the truth of *x* follows. But *x* is an arbitrary proposition for which, for example, the law of contradiction may be chosen.

Aristotle's defense of the law of contradiction as descriptive of "being as such" includes implicitly a defense of the metaphysical principle of identity against Heraclitus, who held it possible for the same thing to be and not to be and who explained the concept of becoming as implying the falsehood of the principle that everything is what it is. Before Aristotle this metaphysical principle had been defended by Parmenides.

Aristotle's arguments for the truth of the principle of excluded middle are again metaphysical. They are connected with his rejection of the Platonic doctrine that attempts to mediate between Heraclitus and Parmenides. The changing sensible and material objects, which in Plato's phrase "tumble about between being and nonbeing," are placed by Plato between the eternal Forms, which fully and truly exist, and that which does not exist at all, that is, they are "a third" between being and nonbeing. The metaphysical principle of excluded middle, as understood by Aristotle, excludes any such third. This principle has sometimes been taken to imply fatalism: Since of any two contradictory statements one must be true, of any two contradictory statements about the future one must be true, so that, it is argued, the future is wholly determined. In a famous passage about "the sea fight tomorrow" Aristotle refutes this argument: It is, he points out, necessary that the sea fight will or will not take place tomorrow. But it is not true that it will *necessarily* take place tomorrow or *necessarily* not take place tomorrow. Indeed the logical necessity of a disjunction "*p* or not-*p*" does not imply that either *p* or not-*p* is a necessary proposition.

METAPHYSICAL REFUTATION. Heraclitus, Parmenides, Plato, and Aristotle conceived of the laws of thought as controversial metaphysical principles, and just as Aristotle attempted their justification on metaphysical grounds, so did G. W. F. Hegel, Karl Marx, and Friedrich Engels attempt their refutation on metaphysical grounds. Hegel's attack was based on his distinction between abstract understanding, which petrifies and thus misdescribes the ever-changing "dialectical" process that is reality, and reason, which apprehends its true nature. Hegel objected to the principle that *A* is *A* or, what for him amounts to the same thing, that *A* cannot at the same time be *A* and not-*A* because "no mind thinks or forms conceptions or speaks in accordance with this law, and … no existence of any kind whatever conforms to it" (*Die Encyclopädie der philosophischen Wissenschaften*). For Hegel contradiction is not a relation that holds merely between propositions but one which is also exemplified in the real world, for example, in such phenomena as the polarity of magnetism, the antithesis between organic and inorganic matter, and even the complementarity of complementary colors. With such an interpretation it becomes possible for him to assert that "contradiction is the very moving principle of the world" and that "it is ridiculous to say that contradiction is unthinkable." Aristotle's metaphysics corresponds to a logic in which the metaphysical principles of identity, contradiction, and excluded middle have their logical counterpart in corresponding laws of reasoning. The counterpart of Hegel's rejection of these metaphysical principles is not any traditional logical theory but a "dialectical" logic, or dialectics.

The Hegelian point of view was adopted by Marx and Engels with the difference that they conceived reality not as ideal but as material. Engels, unlike Hegel, did not even acknowledge the law of identity as valid for the abstractions of mathematics. His arguments, based on the alleged structure of the differential and integral calculus, seem—at least today—confused. He held, for example, that under certain circumstances straight lines and curves are literally identical.

EMPIRICAL INTERPRETATION. From the conception of the laws of thought as descriptive of "being as such," whatever this may mean precisely, we must distinguish the conception of them as empirical generalizations of very high order. This view was most clearly expressed by John Stuart Mill in his *System of Logic* (London, 1843). Thus, he regarded the principle of contradiction as one "of our first empirical generalizations from experience" and as "originally founded on our distinction between belief and disbelief as two different mutually exclusive states" (*System of Logic*, Book II, Ch. 7). He similarly argued that the empirical character of the law of excluded middle follows from, among other things, the fact that it requires for its truth a large qualification, namely "that the predicate in any affirmative categorical proposition must be capable of being meaningfully attributed to the subject, since between the true and the false there is the third possibility of the meaningless" (Book II, ch. 7). Mill's view must not be taken to imply that the laws of thought are psychological laws, describing the processes of thought—a view which rests on a confusion between thinking and correct thinking.

PRESCRIPTIVE INTERPRETATIONS

REGULATIVE INTERPRETATION. Another interpretation of the laws of thought regards them as in some sense prescriptive—based on some absolute authority, by analogy with moral laws, or based on conventions admitting of possible alternatives, by analogy with municipal laws. Traces of the former view are, for example, still found in J. N. Keynes's *Formal Logic*, one of the last valuable treatises on traditional formal logic. According to the preface

of this work, logic deals with the laws regulating the processes of formal reasoning purely as "regulative and authoritative" and as affording criteria for the discrimination between valid and invalid reasoning.

CONVENTIONALIST INTERPRETATION. Versions of the conception that all logical principles are based on conventions have rarely been worked out with sufficient care. According to A. J. Ayer's *Language, Truth and Logic* (1936; 2nd ed., 1946) every logical principle is based on conventions. Thus "not (p and not-p)" is logically necessary because the use of "and" and "not" is governed by certain linguistic conventions, which are neither true nor false. Yet given these conventions the proposition "not (p and not-p)," that is, the law of contradiction, is necessarily true. Ayer and those who have held similar views never consider the question whether, and to what extent, linguistic conventions depend on some nonconventional framework which restricts one's freedom to formulate, accept, or reject them. Can one, for example, by adopting suitable conventions for the use of "or" and "not" really think or speak in contravention of the principle that under the usual conventions is expressed by "not (p and not-p)"?

Conventionalism is most plausible when it explains the necessity of alternative systems of definitions and of alternative systems of logic as being based on conventions, in the sense of rules whose acceptance is not obligatory. In the case of the law of contradiction no alternative is conceivable, so that the "convention" on which it is based would have to be obligatory in a sense in which the other conventions are not. However, an admission of "conventions obligatory for all thinkers" would bring conventionalism much nearer to views of logic which, at least prima facie, it seems to reject.

FORMAL INTERPRETATIONS

LEIBNIZ AND KANT. According to Gottfried Wilhelm Leibniz there are two kinds of truths, truths of fact and truths of reason, truths of reason being true in all possible worlds and therefore descriptive of facts in such a way that not even God can change them. Leibniz regarded as a necessary and sufficient condition for a truth's being a truth of reason, and thus logically necessary, that its analysis should reveal it to depend wholly on propositions whose negation involves a contradiction, that is, on identical propositions (see, for example, *Monadology*, Secs. 31–35). He even held, in the second letter to Samuel Clarke, that the law of contradiction is "by itself sufficient" for the demonstration of "the whole of arithmetic and geometry." Although the thesis that all logical, as well as all mathematical, truths are demonstrable by means of the law of contradiction alone is, from the point of view of contemporary knowledge, mistaken or at least obscurely expressed, the characterization of logical truths as true in all possible worlds is still the root of the Bolzano-Tarski definition of logical validity.

Although Immanuel Kant opposed the Leibnizian doctrine that the truths of mathematics are logical truths, he adhered to the principle of contradiction as the supreme principle of all logical truths or, more precisely, as the "general and wholly sufficient principle of all analytical knowledge." Since the truth of such knowledge in no way depends on whether or not the objects which are referred to exist, the principle of contradiction is a necessary but not a sufficient condition of factual knowledge. What is true of possible objects must be true of all actual ones—what is true in all possible worlds must be true of the actual one. But since the converse statement is false, the principles of formal logic cannot be an "organon" of any particular science, that is, a means for attaining knowledge of its subject matter. (See *Kritik der reinen Vernunft*, 2nd ed., introduction to Part II of "Transcendentale Elementarlehre.")

CONTEMPORARY LOGIC. In contemporary logical theory the conception of "true in every possible world" or "true of any objects whatever" has been sharpened into the conception of valid statement forms and valid statements which are well formed in accordance with the precisely formulated syntactical rules of elementary logic—propositional calculus, quantification theory, and theory of identity. A distinction is made between the logical particles, or constants, on the one hand and nonlogical constants and variables on the other. The logical constants are (1) "$\neg$," "$\vee$," "$\wedge$," and other connectives, whose intended interpretations are, respectively, "not," "or," "and," and so on, conceived as connecting true or false propositions so as to form other true or false propositions in such a way that the truth or falsehood of any compound statement depends only on the truth or falsehood of the component statements; (2) the quantifiers "$\forall$" and "$\exists$," the intended interpretation of which is such that "$\forall x\, Px$" and "$\exists x\, Px$" mean, respectively, that for a well-demarcated domain of individuals, which may be finite or infinite, every element x has the predicate P, and that there exists an individual x which possesses P (in addition to such monadic predicates as Px, such dyadic predicates as Pxy and polyadic predicates are also admitted, so that, for example, $\forall x\, \exists y\, Pxy$, $\forall x\, \forall y\, Pxy$, and so

on, are also admitted); and (3) the sign "$=$" with the intended interpretation as identity of individuals.

The nonlogical constants are (*a*) names of specific individuals, such as "Socrates" or, indeterminately, "x_0," (*b*) names of specific predicates, such as "green" or, indeterminately, "P_0," where two predicate names which are truly asserted of the same individuals of the given domain are regarded as naming the same predicate, (*c*) names of specific statements, such as "Socrates is mortal" or, indeterminately, "p_0." The variables are individual variables such as "x," predicate variables such as "P," and statement variables such as "p." Variables are either free (or, more precisely, free for substitution by names of corresponding constants) or bound by a quantifier so that, for example, "Px" contains a free individual variable and a free predicate variables, whereas $\forall x\, Px$ contains only a free predicate variable.

A well-formed formula of elementary logic that contains free variables is a statement form. A statement form is valid if—with the intended interpretation of the logical constants—every substitution instance of it is valid in every nonempty domain, provided that every individual, predicate, and statement variable is replaced by the same individual, predicate, and statement constant wherever it occurs in the statement form. Clearly the laws of thought are valid statement forms in, for example, the following formulations: Principle of identity: $x = x$. Principle of contradiction: $\neg(p \wedge \neg p)$, $\forall x\, \neg\, (Px \wedge \neg Px)$. Principle of excluded middle: $p \vee \neg p$, $(\forall x\, Px) \vee (\exists x\, \neg Px)$. It is equally clear that many other well-formed formulas such as $\neg\neg p \vee \neg p$ are valid. Valid statement forms that contain only statement variables have been called tautologies by Wittgenstein.

The great precision and clarity given to the conception of the laws of thought as principles of formal logic has, however, not lifted them out of the range of philosophical controversy. Thus, intuitionist philosophers of mathematics argue that the principle of excluded middle is valid only for finite domains and that the extension of its validity to the nonfinite domain of arithmetic is based on the mistaken notion of an actually infinite domain of natural numbers, a notion that unjustifiably assimilates the number sequence to a finite class of objects. Similarly, they deny the validity of other classically valid statement forms, such as $\neg\neg p \rightarrow \neg p$.

The results of modern mathematical logic have deprived the laws of thought of their privileged status as the supreme principles of all logical truths. But since these results do not imply that there is only one true logic, the choice between classical elementary logic, intuitionist logic, and perhaps some other logical theories still depends, at least at the present time, on extralogical, philosophical arguments.

See also Bolzano, Bernard; Determinism, a Historical Survey; Mathematics, Foundations of; Semantics.

Bibliography

Alston, William P. "The Role of Reason in the Regulation of Belief." In *Rationality in the Calvinian Tradition*, edited by N. Wolterstorff et al. Lanham, MD: University Press of America, 1983.

Aristotle. *Metaphysics.*

Ayer, A. J. *Language, Truth and Logic.* London: Gollancz, 1936; 2nd ed., 1946.

Engels, Friedrich. *Herrn Eugen Dührings Umwälzung der Wissenschaft.* Leipzig, 1878. Translated by E. Burns as *Herr Eugen Dühring's Revolution in Science.* London, 1934.

Georg, Rolf. "Bolzano and the Problem of Psychologism." In *Husserl's Logical Investigations Reconsidered*, edited by Denis Fisette. Dordrecht: Kluwer, 2003.

Goddard, L. "Laws of Thought." *Australasian Journal of Philosophy* 37 (1959): 28–40.

Hacker, P. M. S. "Frege and the Later Wittgenstein." In *German Philosophy since Kant*, edited by Anthony O'Hear. New York: Cambridge University Press, 1999.

Hahn, Hans. *Logik, Mathematik und Naturerkennen.* Vienna, 1933. Partially translated by Arthur Pap as "Logic, Mathematics and Knowledge of Nature" in *Logical Positivism*, edited by A. J. Ayer, 147–161. Glencoe, IL: Free Press, 1959.

Halperin, Thoedore. "Boole's Abandoned Propositional Logic." *History and Philosophy of Logic* 5 (1984): 39–48.

Hegel, G. W. F. *Die Encyclopädie der philosophischen Wissenschaften.* Heidelberg, 1817. Partially translated by W. Wallace as *The Logic of Hegel*, Oxford: Clarendon Press, 1874, and *Hegel's Philosophy of Mind*, Oxford: Clarendon Press, 1894.

Husserl, Edmund. *Logische Untersuchungen.* 2 vols. Halle, 1900–1901. Chs. 4 and 5.

Jeffrey, Richard. *The Logic of Decision.* New York: McGraw-Hill, 1965.

Joseph, H. W. B. *Introduction to Logic.* Oxford: Clarendon Press, 1906; 2nd ed., 1925.

Kant, Immanuel. *Kritik der reinen Vernunft.* 2nd ed. Riga, 1787.

Katz, Jerrold. "Analyticity, Necessity, and the Epistemology of Semantics." *Philosophy and Phenomenological Research* 56 (1997): 1–28.

Keynes, J. N. *Studies and Exercises in Formal Logic.* London and New York, 1884.

Kornblith, Hilary. "The Laws of Thought." *Philosophy and Phenomenological Research* 52 (1992): 895–911.

Leibniz, G. W. *Monadology*, in *The Monadology and Other Writings.* Translated by Robert Latta. Oxford, 1898.

Musgrave, A. "George Boole and Psychologism." *Sciencia* 107 (1972): 593–608.

Nagel, Ernest. "Logic without Ontology." In *Naturalism and the Human Spirit*, edited by Y. H. Krikorian. New York: Columbia University Press, 1944. Reprinted in Nagel's *Logic without Metaphysics.* Glencoe, IL: Free Press, 1956.

Russell, Bertrand. *The Problems of Philosophy.* London: Williams and Norgate, 1912.

Slater, B. H. "Wittgenstein's Later Logic." *Philosophy* 54 (1979): 199–209.

Sober, Elliot. "Psychologism." *Journal for the Theory of Social Behavior* 8 (1978): 165–191.

Ueberweg, Friedrich. *System der Logik.* Bonn, 1857. Translated by T. M. Lindsay as *System of Logic.* London: Longmans Green, 1871.

Wittgenstein, Ludwig. *Tractatus Logico-Philosophicus.* London: Routledge, 1922.

Woods, John, and Douglas Walton. "Laws of Thought and Epistemic Proofs." *Idealistic Studies* 9 (1979): 55–65.

S. Körner (1967)
Bibliography updated by Benjamin Fiedor (2005)

LEBENPHILOSOPHIE

See *Philosophical Anthropology*

LE CLERC, JEAN
(1657–1736)

Although Jean Le Clerc, the philosopher and Arminian theologian, was not a major figure, he had a considerable influence on eighteenth-century French philosophy. He championed rational religion, which was later widely accepted, and was also the first disciple of John Locke, whose work he introduced to Continental audiences. Through his learned reviews, the *Bibliothèque universelle et historique* (1686–1693), the *Bibliothèque choisie* (1703–1713), and the *Bibliothèque ancienne et moderne* (1714–1727), he stated and defended Locke's views.

Raised in Geneva during a period of strife over the Calvinist dogma of predestination, Le Clerc was a confirmed rationalist when he left the Geneva Academy. He believed that the fundamentals of Christianity (God's existence and the divinity of Scripture) are capable of demonstration. Scripture must be rationally interpreted; one cannot believe what conflicts with rational truths, and doctrines over which rational men disagree are not essentials of faith. For this doctrine, Le Clerc was expelled from Geneva in 1683.

He went first to England and then settled permanently in Holland, a haven for political and religious exiles. He found a spiritual home in the rationalistic Remonstrant Church and soon became professor of Hebrew, philosophy, and belles-lettres at the Remonstrant College at Amsterdam. At this time Le Clerc met John Locke, then in exile, and acquired a systematic philosophy. In 1688, two years before the English publication of the *Essay concerning Human Understanding,* he printed a long French summary in his *Bibliothèque universelle.* He also helped popularize many other English writers and published a long review of George Berkeley's *New Theory of Vision* in the *Bibliothèque choisie* (1711).

Le Clerc's philosophy was purely Lockean. He rejected innate ideas, used the notion of abstract ideas, and continued the critique of the idea of substance. He opposed René Descartes, Nicolas Malebranche, Benedict de Spinoza, and Gottfried Wilhelm Leibniz because their theories claim knowledge beyond human ideas. However, whereas Locke was indifferent to the rise of radical skepticism, Le Clerc was quite critical of it. He vigorously asserted the reality of human knowledge, although restricting its scope, and tried to refute each of the leading skeptics (Sextus Empiricus, Michel Eyquem de Montaigne, Pierre-Daniel Huet, and Pierre Bayle). He became involved in an acrimonious dispute with Bayle, who argued that the conflict between fundamental Christian doctrines and the principles of reason must be considered as a basis for skepticism regarding reason. To Le Clerc, Bayle's view led to irreligion or fanaticism. He insisted that reason is the criterion of truth and that faith and reason are compatible.

See also Arminius and Arminianism; Bayle, Pierre; Berkeley, George; Descartes, René; Determinism, A Historical Survey; Huet, Pierre-Daniel; Innate Ideas; Leibniz, Gottfried Wilhelm; Locke, John; Malebranche, Nicolas; Montaigne, Michel Eyquem de; Rationalism; Sextus Empiricus; Skepticism, History of; Spinoza, Benedict (Baruch) de.

Bibliography

WORKS BY LE CLERC

Logica, sive Ars Ratiocinandi. Amsterdam, 1694.

Ontologia, sive de Ente in Genere & Pneumatologia. Amsterdam, 1694.

Physica, sive de Rebus Corporeus libri quinque. Amsterdam, 1696.

Vita et Opera ad Annum 1711. Amsterdam, 1711. This work includes the philosophical texts listed separately above.

WORKS ON LE CLERC

Barnes, Annie. *Jean Le Clerc et la république des lettres.* Paris: E. Droz, 1938. Contains details on Le Clerc's often stormy career.

Colie, Rosalie. *Light and Enlightenment, a Study of the Cambridge Platonists and Dutch Arminians.* Cambridge,

U.K.: Cambridge University Press, 1957. Contains a discussion of Le Clerc's thought.

Haag, Eugene, and Émile Haag. *La France protestante.* Paris: J. Cherbuliez, 1846. This work and the Barnes mentioned above contain bibliographies of Le Clerc's diverse works on philosophy, theology, history, philology, and biblical criticism.

Phillip D. Cummins (1967)

LE CLERC, JEAN [ADDENDUM]

Although embroiled in many intellectual controversies throughout his career, Jean Le Clerc's repeated disputes with Pierre Bayle were of greatest significance. Bayle had argued that Christianity strengthens Pyrrhonian skepticism in that a number of axioms of logic and metaphysics are contradicted by Christian dogmas. Therefore, even self-evidence (*évidence*) is not an infallible criterion of truth, since these axioms are self-evident, yet false. In the same vein, Bayle argued that one cannot conceive how an omnipotent and omnibenevolent God could allow human suffering either here or in the afterlife. Le Clerc replied that God's justice demands that those who freely choose to sin be punished, but conceded that the torments of hell might not be eternal.

Similarly, when Le Clerc championed the notion of plastic natures—insentient, immaterial substances causally responsible for the organization of animal bodies—Bayle argued that the hypothesis undermined the most compelling argument for God's existence by severing the conceptual connection between complex effects and conscious design.

Underlying their debates were two fundamentally different conceptions of the relation between faith and reason. For Le Clerc, Bayle's insistence on the irrationality of Christianity constituted a thinly veiled attack on religion itself, whereas Bayle saw Le Clerc's demand that scripture be interpreted according to rational principles as ultimately leading to deism or atheism.

See also Atheism; Bayle, Pierre; Deism; Faith; Pyrrho; Reason.

Bibliography

Golden, Samuel A. *Jean LeClerc.* New York: Twayne, 1972. Study of Le Clerc's career as editor of a number of highly successful learned journals.

Rosa, Susan E. "Ralph Cudworth in the *République des Lettres*: The Controversy about Plastick Nature and the Reputation of Pierre Bayle." *Studies in Eighteenth-Century Culture* 23 (1994): 147–160.

Todd Ryan (2005)

LEGAL POSITIVISM

In many discussions of the nature of law the terms "legal positivism" and "natural law" are assumed to be the names of rival theories. In fact, each of these designations stands for a number of different and logically distinct doctrines, with the unfortunate result that in many disputes between "positivism" and "natural law" the precise point of conflict is unclear and the classification of a legal theorist as a "positivist" may afford very little indication of the nature of his theory. Thus, what is called the imperative theory of law, that is, the view that laws are commands, is usually treated as a central tenet of legal positivism; but although Jeremy Bentham and John Austin held this view, Hans Kelsen (usually regarded as the most uncompromising of modern legal positivists) held neither this view nor its corollary, that international law is not really law but a mere species of morality. Similarly, "legal positivism" is sometimes used as a designation for a thesis concerning the nature of moral judgments, including those made about the justice or injustice or the goodness or badness of human laws. This is the thesis (sometimes termed "noncognitivism") that such judgments cannot be established by reasoning but are merely expressions of human feelings or choices or "prescriptions." Kelsen held this view of moral judgments but Bentham and Austin did not. Bentham and Austin were both utilitarians who considered that moral judgments could be rationally established by the application of the test of utility, which according to Austin was also an "index" of God's commands.

A variety of other doctrines about law, besides those mentioned above, have been described as "positivist." These include the doctrine that although law and morals may often overlap or be causally related, there is no necessary or conceptual connection between them; the doctrine that judicial decisions are or should be deducible by logical means from legal rules and involve no choice or creative activity on the part of the judge; and the doctrine that there is an absolute moral obligation to obey the law, however morally iniquitous it may be.

The etymology of the word *positivism* and cognate expressions offers little guidance to its use in the philosophy of law. Since at least the fourteenth century, the expression "positive law" has been used to refer to laws laid down or made by human beings in contrast to natural or divine law, which is regarded as something discovered and not made by man. But the expression "positive law" has also long been used to refer to any law brought into being by a command or act of will and so includes the law of God as well as human legislation. More recently, the use of the expression "legal positivism" has been colored by the philosophical sense of "positivism" introduced by Auguste Comte. In this sense a "positivist" doctrine is one according to which nothing can be truthfully (or in later versions, meaningfully) said to exist unless it is in principle observable by human beings.

More important for legal theory than the etymology of the word is the identification and classification of the principal issues in relation to which philosophers of law or legal theorists have advanced views commonly styled positivist. Five such issues may be distinguished, and the discussion of these constitutes the remainder of this entry.

POSITIVISM AS A THEORY OF A FORM OF LEGAL STUDY

Bentham, Austin, and Kelsen, while differing as noted above on certain points, agreed that there is an important branch of legal study distinguished by two features: that it is not concerned with any ideal law or legal system but only with actual or existent law and legal systems; and that its concern with law is morally, politically, and evaluatively neutral. The object of this form of legal study is the clarification of the meaning of law, the identification of the characteristic structure of a legal system, and the analysis of pervasive and fundamental legal notions, such as right, duty, ownership, or legal personality. Bentham, Austin, and Kelsen were all concerned to distinguish such an "analytical" jurisprudence, as this form of legal study is now called, from critical or evaluative studies of the law, and they have stressed the importance of this distinction. However, none of these theorists—though the contrary is sometimes suggested—considered that analytical jurisprudence excluded critical or evaluative studies of the law or rendered them unimportant.

It should be observed that belief in the importance of analytical studies of the law does not strictly entail belief in other forms of legal positivism, though in fact it has usually been associated with one or more of these other forms. It is also true that not all morally or evaluatively neutral studies of the law need take an analytical form. Many sociological descriptions of the operation of law and society, and many sociological theories of the causal connection between law and other social phenomena are also evaluatively neutral, at least in intention. Hence, some of these, too, have at times been regarded as forms of positivism.

POSITIVISM IN THE DEFINITION OF LAW

The definition of law as the command of the "sovereign" is no doubt the most prominent example of a form of positivism. But the expression "positivist" is also used in a wider sense to include any doctrine according to which law is defined as the expression of human will or as man-made, even if it does not take the form of a command. Thus, both the doctrines known in American jurisprudence by the loose title of "legal realism," according to which only decisions of courts and the predictions of such decisions are law, and those theories of international law which insist that it is composed exclusively of rules originating in custom or in agreements between states are usually described as positivist. It is to be noted, however, that both Bentham and Austin, who defined law as the command of a sovereign, extended the notion of a command to include both customary law and judge-made law. For this purpose they invoked the idea of a "tacit," or "indirect," command resting on the principle that whatever the sovereign permits he commands.

POSITIVISM AS A THEORY OF THE JUDICIAL PROCESS

Sometimes the term "legal positivism" is used to refer to the view that correct legal decisions are uniquely determined by preexisting legal rules and that the courts either do or should reach their decisions solely by logical deduction from a conjunction of a statement of the relevant legal rules and a statement of the facts of the case. This is sometimes referred to as the "automatic" or "slot-machine" conception of the judicial process; but it is doubtful whether any Anglo American writer who is usually classified as a positivist would subscribe to any such view. It is true, however, that Bentham and Austin thought that the area of choice allowed to judges by a system of case law was excessive and led to great uncertainty, and they claimed that this could and should be drastically reduced by classification and codification of the law in clear and detailed terms. But they were both well aware of the fact of judicial legislation and creative activity, and as noted above, they sought to reconcile this fact with their definition of law as the command of the sovereign by using the idea of a tacit command. The doctrine that a judge should not exercise choice in his decision of cases but should merely be the mouthpiece of previously exist-

ing law is to be found in the works of eighteenth-century writers not usually classed as positivists, such as Baron de Montesquieu's *L'esprit des lois*. They looked upon this doctrine as a corollary of the doctrine of the separation of powers and as a protection of the individual against arbitrary decisions, uncertainty, and privilege.

POSITIVISM AS A THEORY OF LAWS AND MORALS

It seems that all writers classed as positivists have subscribed to the view that unless the law itself provides to the contrary, the fact that a legal rule is morally iniquitous or unjust does not entail that it is invalid or not law. This view may also be expressed as the claim that no reference to justice or other moral values enters into the definition of law. "The existence of law is one thing: its merit or demerit another" (Austin). "Legal norms may have any kind of content" (Kelsen). Such a denial of a necessary or definitional connection between law or legal validity and morality is perhaps the principal point of conflict between legal positivism and theories of natural law. For nearly all variants of the latter refuse to recognize as law or legally valid rules that violate certain fundamental moral principles. It is, however, important to remember that this denial of a necessary connection between law and morals is compatible with the recognition of many other important connections between them. Thus few, if any, positivists have denied that the development of the law has in fact been influenced by morality or that moral considerations should be taken into account by legislators and also by judges in choosing between competing interpretations or conflicting claims as to what the law is.

POSITIVISM AND THE OBLIGATION TO OBEY LAW

If positivism has become a pejorative term, it is very largely because it has been identified by some critics with the claim that where a legal system is in operation, there is an unconditional moral obligation to obey the law, however unjust or iniquitous it may be. This claim may be based either on the view that there is a moral obligation to obey law as such or on the belief that the actual existence of a legal system, however oppressive or unjust, provides large numbers of human beings with a minimum of peace, order, and security and that these are values that no individual is morally justified in jeopardizing by resistance to the law. The German legal theorist K. M. Bergbohm, perhaps the best-known legal positivist in continental Europe in the nineteenth century, held this view; but though he in fact also subscribed to other forms of legal positivism described above, this view is logically quite independent of them. Utilitarian positivists, such as Bentham and Austin, held that resistance to law might be justified in extreme cases, but before this step was taken, careful calculations in terms of utility were necessary to ascertain that a balance of good over evil was likely to result. They criticized the doctrine of natural law and natural rights not because they believed that there was an unconditional obligation to obey the law, but because in their view these doctrines presented standing temptations for men to revolt without making such calculations of the consequences.

See also Austin, John; Bentham, Jeremy; Comte, Auguste; Kelsen, Hans; Natural Law; Noncognitivism; Philosophy of Law, History of; Philosophy of Law, Problems of; Positivism.

Bibliography

WORKS BY LEGAL POSITIVISTS

Austin, John. *Essay on the Uses of the Study of Jurisprudence.* London, 1863.

Austin, John. *Lectures on Jurisprudence, or the Philosophy of Positive Law.* London, 1863.

Austin, John. *The Province of Jurisprudence Defined.* London, 1832.

Bentham, Jeremy. *A Fragment on Government.* London: T. Payne, P. Elmsly, and E. Brooke, 1776.

Bentham, Jeremy. *Introduction to the Principles of Morals and Legislation.* London, 1789.

Bentham, Jeremy. *The Limits of Jurisprudence Defined.* New York: Columbia University Press, 1945.

Bentham, Jeremy. *The Theory of Legislation,* 2 vols. London: K. Paul, Trench, Trubner, 1931.

Bergbohm, K. M. *Jurisprudenz und Rechtsphilosophie.* Leipzig: Duncker and Humblot, 1892.

Kelsen, Hans. *The General Theory of Law and State.* Cambridge, MA: Harvard University Press, 1945.

WORKS ON LEGAL POSITIVISM

Fuller, Lon. "Positivism and Fidelity to Law." *Harvard Law Review* 71 (1958): 630–672.

Gray, J. C. *The Nature and Sources of Law.* New York, 1909.

Hart, H. L. A. *The Concept of Law.* Oxford: Clarendon Press, 1961.

Holmes, O. W. "The Path of the Law." In his *Collected Legal Papers.* Boston, 1920.

Morison, W. L. "Some Myths about Positivism." *Yale Law Journal* 68 (1958): 217–222.

Pound, Roscoe. "Mechanical Jurisprudence." *Columbia Law Review* 8 (1908): 605ff.

Roguin, E. *La science juridique pure.* Paris: Sousanne, 1923.

Ross, Alf. *On Law and Justice.* London: Stevens, 1958.

Stone, J. *The Province and Function of Law.* London: Stevens, 1947.

Numerous articles critical of various forms of legal positivism may be found in the *Natural Law Forum,* published since 1955 by the Notre Dame Law School.

H. L. A. Hart (1967)

LEGAL POSITIVISM: ANGLO-AMERICAN LEGAL POSITIVISM SINCE H. L. A. HART

HART'S POSITIVISM AND DWORKIN'S INITIAL OBJECTIONS

Herbert Lionel Adolphus Hart's version of legal positivism, developed in *The Concept of Law* and refined in the Postscript to the second edition, has been the centerpiece in the development of contemporary legal positivism as well as the focal point of the strongest and most interesting objections to it in the philosophy of law. Hart's own argument builds on the work of positivists who preceded him. In particular, Hart seeks to address and correct the main shortcomings he identifies in the theories of law offered by John Austin and Hans Kelsen. Both Austin and Kelsen thought that laws are a distinguishable subset of norms, identifiable by their possession of an intrinsic and necessary property. In other words, they saw the fundamental project of jurisprudence as determining what it is to be *a law*. For Austin, laws are orders or commands backed by a threat of sanction issued by a sovereign. The threat of sanction distinguishes a command from a plea or a request while the fact of issuance by a sovereign distinguishes legal commands from all other commands. A sovereign, properly so called, is a person who has secured the habit of obedience from the vast majority of the populace and who is not in the habit of obeying anyone. Like Austin, Kelsen holds that sanctions are both intrinsic to law and necessary for their existence. Unlike Austin, however, he argues that although sanctions are imposed on citizens, legal norms are directives to officials to impose sanctions against citizens in the event that they behave in ways identified as sanctionable by the law.

One of Hart's most important claims is that laws are irreducibly of at least two sorts: (1) power-conferring, or secondary, rules; and (2) primary rules that impose obligations to act or to forbear from acting. Power-conferring rules are not themselves reducible to rules that impose obligations because the failure to comply with a power-conferring rule renders one's action a nullity in law and is neither the basis of liability nor a liability itself. An act nullified is one that does not have the legal effect a successful exercise of the legal power would have produced. A failure to exercise a power according to the required formula is not a failure to comply with an obligation to act or to forbear from doing so. Nullification, in turn, is no sanction. In one fell swoop, then, Hart undermines both the claim that legal rules are of one type and that what is distinctive of the type is the presence of sanctions.

Power-conferring, or secondary, rules are themselves of two kinds: private and public. Private secondary rules empower those governed by law to alter the normative relations among themselves (e.g., as in transferring private property through contracts, marital agreements, and wills) and a legal power to call upon the state's resources to enforce those relations. Public power-conferring rules create and regulate the offices to which legal authority attaches, and their existence is implicated in the very idea of private power-conferring rules as well. For Hart, the most important secondary rule is what he terms the rule of recognition. This rule sets forth the conditions that must be satisfied in order for a norm to constitute part of the community's law and in so doing constitutes an identity condition of a legal system. Beyond that, the rule of recognition both confers a power and imposes a duty on certain officials to evaluate conduct in the light of the norms that satisfy the criteria of law it sets forth.

It is important to Hart's account that rules are expressed in general terms. Such terms possess a core of settled meaning and a penumbra of disputed meaning. This maps on to the distinction between those cases in which no competent speaker of a language can legitimately deny that a rule applies (the core of a rule) and those cases in which reasonable, competent speakers of a language can legitimately disagree (the penumbra). In cases falling within the core of a rule, the law settles the matter and a judge is under a duty to apply the law to the facts at hand. In cases falling within the penumbra of a rule, there is no settled law on the matter and a judge must exercise discretion. The scope of judicial duty is fixed by settled meaning or practice. Where either meaning or practice runs out, judicial discretion—a rationally constrained power, not a license—enters. Some contend that Hart believed that the function of law is to guide conduct by reasons, but this is not his view. Whereas the heart's natural function is to pump blood, the law has no such function. Instead, it can serve any number of human ends and purposes—some laudatory and others evil. Hart's view is that whatever business law does, it goes

about it by regulating conduct through rules that are reasons. That is its mode of operation, not its function.

For Hart, law is to be understood in terms of its structure—in the union of primary and secondary rules—not in terms of its having a natural function. Thus, Hart's positivism can be identified with the following tenets: laws are rules; legal rules are of two irreducible types—power conferring and duty imposing. Wherever there is law, there is a rule of recognition that sets out the criteria for the laws of a community. That rule is part of the identity conditions of a legal system. All rules are expressed in general terms, and the set of norms that satisfy the criteria of legality are finite. Thus, there will be gaps in meaning and in settled or controlling law. Discretion is inevitable.

Beyond his particular disagreements with them, Hart's positivism shares with its predecessors a view about the relationship between law and morality. This is the view that there is no necessary connection between law and morality—the so-called separability thesis. Most commentators take the separability thesis to be the sine qua non of legal positivism, but some recent work on legal positivism has raised doubts about the centrality of this claim to the field. Still, there is no denying that Hart was committed to it.

For our purposes, the important features of Hart's positivism are its commitment to judicial discretion and the rule of recognition. The set of binding legal standards in any community is determined by the criteria of legality in that community. Those criteria are set forth in a rule of recognition whose existence and content is fixed by the critical, reflective attitude (the internal point of view) of officials—in particular, judges. The set of standards or rules that satisfy these criteria is finite and thus, in principle, there will be disputes that are not resolved by available legal resources. Judges will be required, therefore, to exercise discretion: a legal power to rely on nonlegal standards, some of which will be moral standards, to resolve legal disputes. This is the so-called discretion thesis.

DWORKIN'S FIRST OBJECTIONS

Discretion is inevitable where settled law runs out. It is this feature of Hart's account that Ronald Dworkin exploits and which forms the basis of his first and most famous objections to Hart's account. Cases in which the *law runs out* are *hard cases*. Because discretion is a constrained power, judges must decide hard cases by appealing to rationally defensible standards. *Ex hypothesi*, such standards are not part of the law, but they must be principles or other standards that constitute good reasons or justifications for the decisions a judge reaches at law. Dworkin notes that judges do not act as if the standards to which they appeal in deciding hard cases are optional for them. If we allow, instead, that the moral principles to which judges appeal in deciding hard cases are sometimes legal, binding because they are law, and law because they express an appropriate dimension of morality, one must abandon not only the discretion thesis but the other basic tenets of positivism as well—such is the nature of the relations among them.

First, if the moral *principles* to which judges appeal in hard cases are even sometimes law, then it cannot be true that all laws are *rules*. Second, if these principles are law, then they are not law in virtue of their satisfying the rule of recognition. They have no institutional source in that sense. This suggests that their legality depends on their content, in particular, on their moral value or worth. But if they are binding in virtue of the fact that they express an appropriate aspect of fairness or justice, then the separability thesis—which appears to reject the claim that legality can depend on morality—must be abandoned. So, too, must the rule of recognition, for it is not true that wherever there is law, there is a Master Rule that determines fully a community's binding legal standards.

EXCLUSIVE AND INCLUSIVE LEGAL POSITIVISM

Positivists have adopted one of two approaches to Dworkin's objections. Common to both is a willingness to grant one of Dworkin's main premises, namely, that at least in some cases the moral standards judges apply are binding on them, not optional. These approaches differ with respect to the second premise: In virtue of their being binding on officials, are those standards part of the community's law?

Those who reject the second premise are exclusive legal positivists (exclusivists); those willing to accept both premises are inclusive legal positivists (inclusivists, incorporationists, or soft positivists). Though he does not employ these labels, Joseph Raz (1939–) is most often cited as the leading positivist of the first sort whereas Jules Coleman (1947–) is usually cited as the most prominent advocate of the latter approach. Both approaches reject Dworkin's claim that the binding nature of moral principles undermines positivism, but for importantly different reasons.

Raz emphasizes a significant distinction between a norm being binding on an official (e.g., a judge) and its being binding in virtue of its being the law of his com-

munity. Laws of jurisdiction A may, under certain conditions, make laws of jurisdiction B binding on officials in jurisdiction A. That is not enough to make the laws of jurisdiction B laws of jurisdiction A. Understood in this way, Raz's argument is that Dworkin has not made the case that moral principles are part of the law. In fact, however, Raz advances the much stronger claim that if moral principles are binding on officials, they can only bind in the way that norms of other jurisdictions do. This stronger argument relies only on general considerations regarding the relationship between the concepts of law and authority and from no distinctive commitments of legal positivism. Instead, Raz begins with a putative conceptual truth about law: that it necessarily claims to be a legitimate authority. As long as governance by law is not an incoherent idea, then law must be the sort of thing of which the claim to authority could be true—even if, as a factual matter, it always turns out to be false. This feature of the claim to authority constrains the kind of thing law can be, but the exact constraints it imposes depends on what the claim to being a legitimate authority entails.

On Raz's account, an authority mediates between persons and reasons in such a way that in accepting an authority, an agent is (with rare exceptions) precluded from appealing directly to the reasons that would justify the authority's directives. If one appeals to what Raz calls the *dependent reasons* in order to identify what the law is or to determine its content, then one vitiates the law's claim to authority. Since the dependent reasons on which law relies and which justify laws are moral reasons, it follows that morality itself cannot be a condition or ground of law. Instead, all law must have what Raz calls a social source. Thus, the claim to authority in conjunction with Raz's theory of authority entails what has come to be called the sources thesis. Some positivists, most notably John Gardner (1965–), advance the view that the core of legal positivism is the sources thesis but note that the thesis itself derives from no claim of legal positivism at all. It derives, instead, from the conjunction of a conceptual claim about law and a theoretical and quite general, if controversial, theory of the meaning of authority.

The inclusivist grants both of Dworkin's premises: that moral standards can sometimes be legally binding and that they can sometimes be part of the community's law. His strategy is to show that none of Dworkin's objections to legal positivism are entailed by accepting these two premises.

Coleman argues that it cannot be Dworkin's view that all moral principles are law merely in virtue of their content or moral merits. That would make all of morality part of the law everywhere and always. Put another way, there must be some institutional or social fact that makes some moral principles part of the law in the jurisdictions in which they are law. But then it would have to be that fact that makes them law, not their individual merits. Coleman then argues that there is no reason in principle why the relevant social or institutional fact that renders moral principles law could not be agreement among officials to count those moral principles as law. Nothing in legal positivism, in any case, precludes that.

THE NEXT PHASE

It is important to draw a distinction that is rarely explicitly made but which is central to understanding the various current disputes among positivists and between positivists and their critics. This is the distinction between the grounds, or sources of law, on the one hand, and the grounds of the grounds of law, on the other. The grounds, sources, or criteria of law refer to the *test* for legality within a community. Both the sources thesis and inclusivism are claims about possible constraints on the grounds of law. The sources thesis claims that all such grounds must be social sources; the inclusivist denies that. Dworkin's argument in "The Model of Rules" is that morality can be a ground of law, which is incompatible with the sources thesis and thus with exclusive legal positivism but not with inclusivism.

The fact that inclusivism shares with Dworkin the view that morality can be a source of law has led Dworkin to chide inclusivists, especially Coleman, for having an underdeveloped version of his view. The criticism cuts no ice, however. The core of legal positivism is not a claim about the grounds of law; it is a claim about the grounds of the grounds of law. And on this score, both exclusivists and inclusivists agree that only social facts—facts about individual behavior and attitude—can be the grounds of the grounds of law. What distinguishes positivists from one another is what they take this claim about the grounds of the grounds of law to allow. Inclusivists believe that commitment to social facts at this level does not impose any constraints on potential grounds of law. They hold, moreover, that nothing about the nature of law or authority does either. In contrast, exclusivists hold that facts about the nature of law, in particular its role in our practical lives, imposes constraints on potential grounds of law. Thus, exclusivists accept the sources thesis whereas inclusivists do not. That does not render the inclusivist a proto-Dworkinian.

The sources thesis is said to follow from the conjunction of the claim that law necessarily claims authority in conjunction with a particular account of what that claim requires. In order to escape this implication, the inclusivist might reject the conceptual and/or the theoretical claim, reject the alleged relationship between them, or accept both but deny that they entail the sources thesis. Coleman, for one, rejects both of the premises of the argument, but he is willing to accept them because, he argues, they do not in fact entail the sources thesis.

Roughly, his argument is this: Whereas appealing to the dependent reasons that purport to justify an authoritative directive in order to determine the directive or its content undermines the directive's claim to authority, it does not follow that every moral principle offered as a condition of legality for norms must be among the dependent reasons that justify the particular directive in question. For instance, a clause making *equal protection of the law* a condition of legality for every putative legal rule need not be a reason that justifies any particular law—one outlawing murder, for example. There is nothing in the logic of law that precludes reasons *R1* through *R5* being the grounds that justify a law *L*, but reasons *R6* through *R9* being the conditions of the legality of *L*. The mere fact of appealing to moral premises as the conditions of law does not mean that one is appealing to the reasons that would be offered to justify the law.

As Raz characterizes it, the theory of authority claims that one cannot appeal to moral principles to identify the law or to determine its content. This is an epistemic constraint on identifying law and determining its content. But inclusivism is a theory about the grounds of law: the conditions that make law *determinate*—what makes it the law. Inclusivism is, in a broad sense, an ontological or metaphysical theory that may well be untouched by the epistemic constraints that are said to fall out of the appropriate theory of authority.

DWORKIN AND THE POSITIVISTS REDUX

Dworkin has not been persuaded by either the inclusivist or the exclusivist strategies, but he has focused primarily on the inclusivist strategy. Recall that Coleman responds to Dworkin's objections to Hart by noting that moral facts cannot be law merely in virtue of their being moral facts, for that would render all moral facts legal facts. Instead, the positivist need not deny that moral facts can be legal facts; he need only argue that moral facts are legal facts in virtue of certain legally significant social facts about them—typically acceptance among officials of their status as part of the law. Any such account of the way in which social facts make moral facts part of the law is going to be a form of legal positivism.

Dworkin has responded in two ways: one positive, the other critical. On the one hand, he has developed an argument, expounded primarily in *Law's Empire*, designed to show how certain kinds of moral facts, not just social facts, turn other moral facts into law. This is his *theory of constructive interpretation*. On the other hand, he has offered a variety of interesting and important objections to the inclusivist claim that moral facts can be grounds of law and, ultimately, to the claim that they can be grounds of law in virtue of certain social facts or practices.

The point of departure for some of these objections is the idea that morality is inherently controversial, and this fact about it is incompatible with the claim that it can be a condition of legality. At one point, Dworkin argued that positivism holds that the function of law is to guide conduct, in part by resolving disputes and disagreements about what one ought to do. This is one reason for his oft-repeated view that legal positivists identify law with plain or hard fact—the sort of thing one could determine with near certitude by looking it up in a book. Morality is too controversial for its inclusion in law to serve this function. This objection has no force. Presumably, one role of morality in our lives is to guide conduct. If morality is capable of guiding conduct, therefore, it is capable of guiding conduct whether it is part of the law or not. Beyond that, nothing in legal positivism would suggest that legal disputes must be resolved in a way that is essentially uncontroversial.

A more serious version of the objection maintains that the essentially controversial nature of morality means that judges applying the criteria of legality that includes morality will often disagree, and this level of disagreement is incompatible with the positivist claim that at the foundation of law resides a social rule, namely, the rule of recognition. A social rule has two dimensions: shared, convergent behavior and a shared critical, reflective attitude toward that behavior. One consequence of allowing that morality might be a condition of legality is widespread disagreement among officials that is incompatible with the requisite agreement necessary for the criteria of law to be determined by a social rule among officials.

Note that the key here is the connection between the grounds of law and the grounds of the grounds of law. If morality can be a condition of legality (a ground of law), as inclusivists claim, then the foundation of law (the grounds of the grounds of law)—the rule of recogni-

tion—cannot be a social rule. The claim that the grounds of the grounds of law are social facts precludes moral facts from being among the grounds of law. Positivism cannot have it both ways. The problem with this objection is that it treats disagreement about whether the grounds of law are satisfied as if it entailed disagreement about what the grounds of law are. You and I can disagree about whether someone is intelligent while agreeing that we should only hire intelligent people for our company. Disagreement about whether the conditions of legality are satisfied is perfectly compatible with agreement about what those conditions are. If any sort of agreement is required in order for there to be a rule of recognition, it is agreement of the second sort.

At one point, Dworkin responded that all disagreements about whether a rule applies could be formulated as disagreements about what the rule is, thereby raising doubts about whether the distinction Coleman points to between agreement about the criteria and agreement about its applications is helpful. Dworkin's response has proven unpersuasive because it identifies a rule with the set of its instances, which cannot be a plausible understanding of what it is to be a rule. Dworkin eventually adopted a more interesting line of attack, which begins by reflecting on a more general philosophical concern regarding the sort of agreement that is necessary in order for disagreements to make sense; that is, for individuals actually to be disagreeing with one another rather than merely talking past one another. He associates legal positivism with the view that judges and other officials must agree on the grounds of law in order for their disagreements about what satisfies those grounds to be meaningful.

If he has diagnosed the commitments of legal positivism correctly, Dworkin may have identified a powerful objection to it since it appears as if legal positivism cannot explain the possibility of disagreement about what the grounds of law are. Yet such disagreement is a significant feature of legal practice. At bottom, Dworkin has a picture of legal positivism that is very likely warranted by Hart's formulations and much of the positivist literature that has followed. In this picture, legal positivism represents a certain architectural rendering of law and of legal practice. Law is a closed normative system whose boundaries are determined by the scope of agreement. It has a set of initial premises (we can think of these as rules of recognition) whose existence depends on agreement about what they assert or prescribe. Once these rules are in place, we can have a practice called law. These rules make the practice possible and are both inside and outside the practice. They are part of the law, but not, as it were, in the mix. If anything, they are like Carnapian *meaning postulates*. They are not subject to revision from within the practice; they are immune in that sense. If the practice fails to achieve the aims we have for it, we can change the ground rules and have a new practice. But we do not have a practice that changes from within. We can disagree about what falls within the practice, but we cannot disagree about what the rules are that constitute the practice itself.

Dworkin's most interesting objections to legal positivism can be recast as trying to shed doubt on this *architecture* of the law. For Dworkin, the fluidity of the boundaries between law and other normative systems, between what is inside and outside law, his deep anti-Archimedianism, are all different ways of getting at the same problem. Dworkin is Willard Van Orman Quine to legal positivism's Rudolph Carnap.

As Coleman and others have argued, the heart of legal positivism is the claim that the grounds of the grounds of law are social facts—facts about behavior and attitudes. It is not obvious that this claim entails either of Dworkin's objections to positivism, namely, the claim that positivism cannot account for disagreement about the grounds of law or the related claim that positivism imposes a Carnapian architecture on legal practice. In fact, the Quinean picture of legal practice is completely compatible with positivism.

ANOTHER PICTURE

If, for the sake of simplicity, we use the term *rule of recognition* to refer to the grounds of law, then positivism can hold that the rule of recognition is at the *center* of law, not at the foundation of law. Thus, the rule of recognition is in the mix, subject to revision and even abandonment on the same grounds as are other rules and standards within law. There is a distinction worth emphasizing between the *existence* conditions of a rule and its *revisability* conditions. The rule of recognition's special status, moreover, is not a function of it being at the foundation of law but of its inferential importance. Much of the rest of the law of particular communities makes sense inferentially in virtue of the rule of recognition. As the importance of various grounds of law to inferences that warrant other settled areas of the law diminishes, the likelihood of revising that *ground of law* increases.

Nor is there a distinctive problem in understanding disagreement among participants about the grounds of law, for the rule of recognition is not rigidly fixed by agreement. The complexity of any particular legal prac-

tice is likely to mean that there will be different and quite varied views about which putative grounds of law are more or less central to the practice in place.

More importantly, the claim that the content of the rule of recognition is fixed by social facts does not entail that the content of the rule, or its proper formulation, is transparent or otherwise available to officials—that is, those whose conduct is regulated by it. No more so must the content of the rule be transparent than must the rule governing the use of personal pronouns be accessible to ordinary speakers of a language whose speech it governs. If transparency of the rule to officials is required to coordinate their behavior—and it is an empirical question whether in fact it is—sharing the rule in the sense Dworkin attributes to positivism is no more than an efficiency condition of law and not a theoretical commitment of legal positivism. There is nothing in the idea that law rests ultimately on social facts that is itself incompatible with disagreement about the grounds of law. Still less does the claim that law is created by social facts alone entail the architectural view of law that renders the grounds of law immune to revision from within.

Positivism need not necessarily be understood in the way sketched here. Rather, the above sketch is designed to suggest only that the social facts thesis does not render positivism vulnerable to the charge that it cannot explain disagreement about the grounds of law. Nor does the social facts thesis leave positivism vulnerable to the charge that it pictures law as *shut off* from or *bounded* by other normative systems (other legal systems and other schemes of regulating conduct) in the way the architectural picture of a definite inside and outside of law suggests. Whether this line of argument on behalf of positivism proves ultimately persuasive remains very much an open question.

See also Austin, John; Carnap, Rudolf; Dworkin, Ronald; Epistemology; Hart, Herbert Lionel Adolphus; Kelsen, Hans; Legal Positivism; Quine, Willard Van Orman.

Bibliography

Bratman, Michael. *Faces of Intention*. Cambridge, U.K.: Cambridge University Press, 1999.

Campbell, Tom D., ed. *Legal Positivism*. Aldershot, U.K.: Ashgate Publishing, 1999.

Coleman, Jules. "Constraints on the Criteria of Legality." *Legal Theory* 6 (2) (2000): 171–183.

Coleman, Jules. "Incorporationism, Conventionality, and the Practical Difference Thesis." In *Hart's Postscript*. Edited by Jules Coleman, 99–148. Oxford: Oxford University Press, 2001.

Coleman, Jules. "Negative and Positive Positivism." In *Markets, Morals, and the Law*. Cambridge, U.K.: Cambridge University Press, 1988.

Coleman, Jules. *The Practice of Principle*. Oxford: Oxford University Press, 2001.

Coleman, Jules. "Second Thoughts and Other First Impressions." In *Analyzing Law: New Essays in Legal Theory*. Edited by Brian Bix, 257–322. Oxford: Oxford University Press, 1998.

Coleman, Jules, and Brian Leiter. "Legal Positivism." In *A Companion to Philosophy of Law and Legal Theory*. Edited by Dennis Patterson, 241–260. Oxford: Blackwell, 1996.

Dworkin, Ronald. *Law's Empire*. Cambridge, MA: Harvard University Press, 1986.

Dworkin, Ronald. "Objectivity and Truth: You'd Better Believe It." *Philosophy and Public Affairs* 25 (1996): 87–139.

Dworkin, Ronald. "The Model of Rules I," in *Taking Rights Seriously*, 14–45. Cambridge, MA: Harvard University Press, 1997.

Dworkin, Ronald. "The Model of Rules II," in *Taking Rights Seriously*, 46–80. Cambridge, MA: Harvard University Press, 1997.

Finnis, John. "On the Incoherence of Legal Positivism." *Notre Dame Law Review*. 75 (2000): 1597–1611.

Finnis, John. "The Truth in Legal Positivism." In *The Autonomy of Law: Essays on Legal Positivism*. Edited by Robert P. George, 195–214. Oxford: Clarendon Press, 1996.

Gardner, John. "Legal Positivism: 5 ½ Myths." *American Journal of Jurisprudence* 46 (2000): 199–227.

George, Robert P., ed. *The Autonomy of Law: Essays on Legal Positivism*. Oxford: Clarendon Press, 1996.

Green, Leslie. "Legal Positivism." *Stanford Encyclopedia of Philosophy*, 2003. Available from http://plato.stanford.edu/entries/legal-positivism.

Green, Leslie. "Positivism and Conventionalism." *Canadian Journal of Jurisprudence* 12 (1999): 35–52.

Hart, H. L. A. *The Concept of Law*. Edited by Penelope A. Bulloch and Joseph Raz. Oxford: Clarendon Press, 1994.

Himma, Kenneth Einar. "H. L. A. Hart and the Practical Difference Thesis." *Legal Theory* 6 (1) (2000): 1–43.

Himma, Kenneth Einar. "Inclusive Legal Positivism." In *The Oxford Handbook of Jurisprudence and Legal Philosophy*. Edited by Jules Coleman and Scott Shapiro, 125–65. Oxford: Oxford University Press, 2001.

Kramer, Matthew. *In Defense of Legal Positivism*. Oxford: Clarendon Press, 1999.

Leiter, Brian. "Legal Realism, Hard Positivism, and the Limits of Conceptual Analysis." In *Hart's Postscript*. Edited by Jules Coleman, 355–370. Oxford: Oxford University Press, 2001.

Leiter, Brian, ed. *Objectivity in Law and Morals*. Cambridge, U.K.: Cambridge University Press, 2001.

Lyons, David. "Principles, Positivism, and Legal Theory." *Yale Law Journal* 87 (1997): 415–435.

Marmor, Andrei. "Exclusive Legal Positivism." In *The Oxford Handbook of Jurisprudence and Legal Philosophy*. Edited by Jules Coleman and Scott Shapiro, 104–124. Oxford: Oxford University Press, 2001.

Marmor, Andrei, ed. *Law and Interpretation*. Oxford: Oxford University Press, 1995.

Perry, Stephen. "Varieties of Legal Positivism." *Canadian Journal of Law and Jurisprudence* 9 (1996): 361–381.

Postema, Gerald. "Coordination and Convention at the Foundation of Law." *Journal of Legal Studies* 11 (1982): 165–203.

Raz, Joseph. *The Authority of Law: Essays on Law and Morality*. Oxford: Clarendon Press, 1979.

Raz, Joseph. *Ethics in the Public Domain*. Oxford: Clarendon Press, 1995.

Shapiro, Scott J. "Law, Morality, and the Guidance of Conduct." *Legal Theory* 6 (2) (2000): 127–170.

Shapiro, Scott J. "Laws, Plans, and Practical Reason." *Legal Theory* 8 (2002): 387–441.

Shapiro, Scott J. "On Hart's Way Out." In *Hart's Postscript*. Edited by Jules Coleman, 149–192. Oxford: Oxford University Press, 2001.

Soper, Philip. "Legal Theory and the Obligation of a Judge: The Hart/Dworkin Dispute." *Michigan Law Review* 75 (1977): 473–519.

Soper, Philip. *A Theory of Law*. Cambridge, MA: Harvard University Press, 1984.

Waldron, Jeremy. "Normative or Ethical Positivism." In *Hart's Postscript*. Edited by Jules Coleman, 410–434. Oxford: Oxford University Press, 2001.

Waluchow, W. J. "Authority and the Practical Difference Thesis: A Defense of Inclusive Legal Positivism." *Legal Theory* 6 (1) (2000): 45–81.

Waluchow, W. J. *Inclusive Legal Positivism*. Oxford: Clarendon Press, 1994.

Zipursky, Benjamin C. "The Model of Social Facts." In *Hart's Postscript*. Edited by Jules Coleman, 219–270. Oxford: Oxford University Press, 2001.

Jules L. Coleman (2005)

LEGAL REALISM

Beginning about 1920, an iconoclastic group of American legal writers, led by K. N. Llewellyn, Walter Wheeler Cook, Jerome Frank, Herman Oliphant, and Underhill Moore, denounced the established legal tradition as formalistic and conservative. That tradition, they charged, wrongly saw the law as a complete and autonomous system of logically consistent principles, concepts, and rules. To apply the law was to unfold the ineluctable implications of those rules. The judge's techniques were socially neutral, his or her private views irrelevant; judging was more like finding than making, a matter of necessity rather than choice. The realists, by contrast, saw legal certainty as rarely attainable and perhaps even undesirable in a changing society. In their view the paramount concern of the law was not logical consistency but socially desirable consequences. Law was an instrument of government, and jurisprudence should focus less on legal concepts than on social facts.

BASIS OF LEGAL REALISM

According to the realists, legal decisions were not compelled; choice was necessary at every step. Just as lawmakers built their ideological preferences into a statute, judges built theirs into their formulation of "the facts" of a case. Legal concepts represented nothing more than tentative decisions to consider diverse cases identical with respect to a given concern. Unless readjusted continually, such concepts could be rendered irrelevant by changing circumstances and purposes.

Realism meant opposition to illusion or pretense, sometimes to abstractions or appearances. Judges had always made law, but now, the realists insisted, they must know and say that they did. They must acknowledge their responsibility instead of attributing their choices, through tortured technicalities, to the compulsions of legal doctrine. (Oliver Wendell Holmes, the favorite judge of the realists, had said that law becomes more civilized as it becomes more self-conscious.) If the judges' latent motives and official reasons were reconciled, their judgments would be not only more honest but more informed. Moreover, assumptions about the nature of law could then be considered in the light of scientific knowledge of the actual workings of legal institutions, and assumptions about social policy could be seen in the light of scientific knowledge about society. The realists took the possibility of such scientific knowledge for granted. They further assumed that society had its own mechanisms for effecting changes and that, in general, the law should reflect social change, not shape it. Yet the realists avoided the conservative conclusions that usually accompany this view, for being, above all, reformers, they believed that the constant flux of modern society required a legal system flexible enough to match its pace.

Like other iconoclasts, the realists saw rationalization and self-deception beneath traditional claims to objectivity. They "saw through" appearances, theories, and justifications to underlying motivations or functions. They sought complete candor. The natural sciences provided their model; John Dewey, their philosophical vocabulary. They also drew on the tradition of sociological jurisprudence, which in both Europe and America had already prescribed the study of society as the proper way to discover social preferences beneath the neutral forms of the law.

These ideas were more influential in America because of the unique power of American judges to declare statutes unconstitutional. Moreover, the differences among the states in their approach to identical legal problems frustrated belief in inexorable solutions. Thus,

Holmes had asserted since the 1870s that "the true grounds of decision are considerations of policy and of social advantage." John Chipman Gray saw the sources of law brought to life only in the crucial act of judicial interpretation; he believed that since courts have the last word, "all law is judge-made law." At the turn of the twentieth century Roscoe Pound attacked "mechanical jurisprudence," distinguished "law in action" from "law in books," and conceived of a sociological jurisprudence that would increase legal sensitivity to social needs and to the social effects of legal rules.

The realists were distinctive, however, in their preoccupation with the processes of judicial decision, with how law is made. They put forward a theory of precedent starting from Llewellyn's assertion that "a case stands not for one thing, but for a wide variety of things." Following Dewey, for whom a judgment was always somebody judging something, they stressed the crucial position of the judge who decided whether a case was "the same" as a previous case—that is, which similarities between them should be considered important. Skeptical of principles abstracted from a particular factual context, the realists found support in the common-law tradition that principles should evolve from rather than precede the disposition of particular cases. They trusted the judge's trained reaction to the entire set of facts before him—his "intuition of experience" (Oliphant), which depended on "knowing how" rather than "knowing that"—much more than they trusted the justification he supplied in his opinion. They therefore wanted precedents to be based on what a court actually did in response to a particular set of facts, not on its language. But emphasizing particularity means getting less direction from previous cases, for facts vary enormously. The more that precedent presupposes factual similarity between cases, the fewer its applications; future judges are freer. No two cases are identical, and if any distinction distinguishes, no precedents are possible. Logically, it is always open to a judge to decide either way, to see a previous case as a precedent or not. Some realists therefore concluded that every decision was a "free" moral decision. This conclusion, shorn of the analysis of the logic of precedent behind it and interpreted simply as giving judges greater discretionary power than the traditional view allowed them, was seen by most of the legal community as the essential message of legal realism.

RISE OF LEGAL REALISM

Grant Gilmore has related the realist's view of precedent to the remarkable increase, starting around 1890, in the amount of litigation and in the proportion of cases reported, an increase that threatened to inundate a system depending on "a comfortable number of precedents, but not too many." According to Gilmore, the realists responded to this crisis by allowing fewer cases to count as precedents. In this way, Gilmore has noted, legal realism was part of the major social developments of 1880–1930, notably the rise of urbanism and modern industrialism and technology; during this period realism was not confined to the law. The search for fact, for concreteness, for the truth behind appearances, can be found everywhere—in literature, in painting, in social criticism. Consider, for example, the salient characteristics of a movement quite unrelated to legal theory—progressive education. For both progressive education and legal realism, pursuing "reality" meant going from theoretical formulas to what worked in practice, from books to life, from text to context, from passively and mechanically transmitting a received tradition to actively and flexibly responding to each pupil or case. Both progressive education and legal realism flourished in the 1930s during the New Deal. Both can be seen as to some extent a response to sheer numbers, to universal education and the increase in litigation, respectively.

INFLUENCE OF LEGAL REALISM

Throughout the law the realists contributed to greater candor about the social bases of decision. They also suggested specific improvements in practical areas of the law—for example, Charles E. Clark on covenants' running with the land, Cook on conflict of laws, Arthur Corbin on contracts, Leon Green on torts, and Llewellyn on sales. On the other hand, they underestimated the role of generalization and of justification in the law. Dewey had distinguished clearly between the "logic of inquiry" and the "logic of exposition," between an argument's source and its persuasiveness. Yet the realists often pointed to a judge's psychological processes or social background as if they were demonstrating the irrelevance of her justifications or the speciousness of her claim to be applying rules.

Realism is especially inadequate if taken to be the comprehensive explanation or theory of the nature of law suggested by the definitional form of certain central realist slogans. Thus, realists constantly endorsed Holmes's statement that "the prophecies of what the courts will do in fact ... are what I mean by the law." This remark can be accepted as a paradoxical emphasis on the individual discretion inherent in applying "open-textured" concepts to particular circumstances; accordingly, the exercise of individual discretion becomes part of any adequate concept of law. But Holmes's remark cannot be accepted if it is read as an assertion that the best understanding of legal reality derives from equating law with prediction. A predictive viewpoint obscures the role of legal rules as guides to conduct. As H. L. A. Hart said, "legal rules function as such in social life: they are *used* as rules not as descriptions of habits or predictions" (*The Concept of Law,* Oxford, 1961, pp. 134–135). If the normative character of legal rules were not generally accepted, our concept of law would be entirely different.

However, it may be that attempts, like that of the realists, to jolt accepted habits of thought must rely on paradox and exaggeration. Pierre-Joseph Proudhon said, "Property is theft," knowing full well the immediate sense in which "property" is not "theft" at all. In jurisprudence the very distortion frequently produces the insight; we often learn more from a caricature than from a photograph.

See also Dewey, John; Hart, Herbert Lionel Adolphus; Philosophy of Law, History of; Philosophy of Law, Problems of; Proudhon, Pierre-Joseph; Realism.

Bibliography

Fisher, William W., III, Morton J. Horwitz, and Thomas A. Reed. *American Legal Realism.* New York: Oxford University Press, 1993.

Frank, Jerome. *Law and the Modern Mind,* 2nd ed. New York: Coward-McCann, 1949.

Fuller, Lon. "American Legal Realism." *University of Pennsylvania Law Review* 82 (1934): 429–462.

Gilmore, Grant. "Legal Realism: Its Cause and Cure." *Yale Law Journal* 70 (1961): 1037–1048.

Horwitz, Morton J. *The Transformation of American Law, 1870–1960: The Crisis of Legal Orthodoxy.* New York: Oxford University Press, 1992.

Kalman, Laura. *Legal Realism at Yale: 1927–1960.* Chapel Hill: University of North Carolina Press, 1986.

Llewellyn, K. N. *Jurisprudence.* Chicago: University of Chicago Press, 1962.

Martin, Michael. *Legal Realism: American and Scandinavian.* New York: Lang, 1997.

Purcell, Edward A., Jr. "American Jurisprudence between the Wars: Legal Realism and the Crisis of Democratic Theory." In *American Law and the Constitutional Order,* edited by Lawrence Friedman and Harry Scheiber. Cambridge, MA: Harvard University Press, 1978.

Twining, William. *Karl Llewellyn and the Realist Movement.* London: Weidenfeld and Nicholson, 1973.

Yosal Rogat (1967)
Bibliography updated by Philip Reed (2005)

LEGAL RESPONSIBILITY

See *Punishment; Responsibility, Moral and Legal*

LEHRER, KEITH

(1936–)

Keith Lehrer was born January 10, 1936, in Minneapolis, Minnesota. He attended the University of Minnesota from 1953 to 1957, earning his BA in Philosophy magna cum laude. His teachers at Minnesota included Alan Donagan, John Hospers, Michael Scriven, Mary Shaw, May Brodbeck, Herbert Feigel, and Wilfred Sellers. Lehrer went on earn his AM in 1959 and his PhD in 1960, both in philosophy, at Brown University, where his teachers included Roderick Chisholm, John Ladd, John Lenz, Stephan K(rner, Vincent Thomas, Wesley Salmon, and Richard Taylor. Chisholm supervised Lehrer's master's thesis on epistemology, and Taylor supervised Lehrer's doctoral dissertation on free will. Chisholm's and Taylor's continuing support were not due to Lehrer's agreement with their positions: Lehrer was then and continues to be a coherence theorist in epistemology, whereas Chisholm was a foundationalist, and Lehrer has always endorsed compatibilism, whereas Taylor was a libertarian.

Lehrer is best known for his work on free will, theory of knowledge, rational consensus, and the philosophy of Thomas Reid. His earliest philosophical works clearly reflect the ordinary language and common sense approaches to philosophy that he learned first from Hospers at Minnesota, and then through the influence of Reid, partly gained indirectly from Reid's influence on both Chisholm and Taylor. Lehrer's first published article (1960) was a common sense defense of the claim that humans can know they have free will simply through introspection.

Despite his lifelong commitment to compatibilism, many of Lehrer's earliest works were critical of various analyses of freedom intended to defend that view—particularly hypothetical analyses of freedom (e.g., that S is free to do X just in case S would do X if S tries to do X). Lehrer's argument against such analyses is that the conditional might apply to S, but S might lack some advantage necessary for exemplifying the antecedent of the conditional. So, for example, it could be true that S would do X if S tried to do X, but because of some phobia or other disadvantage, S could never actually try to do X. One may thus have control over external circumstances, but not have control over oneself, and such a disadvantage leaves one unfree.

His own first defenses of the compatibility of freedom and determinism were based upon a possible worlds analysis of freedom. His work in the late twentieth and early twenty-first centuries analyzes freedom in terms of a power preference that is a preference for having the preference structure one has concerning an action. To insure freedom, one must have that power preference because one prefers to have it. The preference for the preference structure must be the primary explanation of one's having it.

Lehrer is one of the best known proponents of a coherence theory of knowledge. On Lehrer's view, coherence consists in a cognitive system that is able to meet critical objections to the acceptance of a target proposition. Although his first analyses included a standard belief condition, Lehrer later argues that acceptance rather than belief should constitute the relevant condition, partly because the former involves a decision one makes. One's epistemic mission is to accept what is true and not to accept what is false. One cannot decide what to believe at a given moment; but one can decide what to accept in the pursuit of one's epistemic mission.

The ability of a background system to meet critical objections to the accepting of something one accepts provides personal justification. Lehrer first construed this background system as consisting only in states of acceptance designed to pursue the subject's epistemic mission; he expanded this view of the background system, which he later calls the "evaluation system," to include preferences and reasonings.

Much of Lehrer's earliest work in epistemology critiqued various attempts to solve the Gettier problem. The Gettier problem shows that one can have convincing justification of a true belief and yet not have knowledge because some part of the justification is false, where if that part were removed or replaced by the truth, one would no longer qualify as justified. Where such problems in justification exist, the justification is "defeated," and defeasibility theorists seek to solve the Gettier problem by formulating and explicating as a necessary condition the stipulation that one who knows has undefeated justification for what one knows. Defeasibility remains a central concern in Lehrer's most recent work in epistemology, *Theory of Knowledge* (2000), according to which knowledge is the product of true belief that is personally justified on the basis of coherence with the evaluation system, where such justification is undefeated. Undefeated justification, according to Lehrer, is a kind of justification that cannot be refuted by pointing out errors in the evaluation system (2000).

Lehrer has also offered a number of criticisms of recent "naturalistic" or externalist approaches to knowledge and justification, on the general ground that reliable cognitive mechanisms or ways of believing that track truth without cognitive self-evaluation are insufficient for knowledge. Lehrer's development of this element of his epistemology derives from his interest in the philosophy of Thomas Reid. Lehrer noted within Reid's system a metaprinciple according to which our faculties and the principles thereof are trustworthy. Lehrer applies this same principle to allow the knower to meet critical and skeptical objections, while also immunizing his own analysis of knowledge—despite its requirement for cognitive self-evaluation—against the KK-regress (namely, that one's knowing requires knowing that one knows, that one knows that one knows one knows, and so on ad infinitum) (1990, 2000).

The theory of rational consensus, which Lehrer developed with Carl Wagner (1981), was an attempt to incorporate a social component into the theory of rationality—another echo of Reid's common sense approach to philosophy. Social rationality, in Lehrer's and Wagner's theory, results from the evaluations people make of others, expressed mathematically as weights. They argue that under plausible conditions of evaluation social convergence would yield rational consensus. Lehrer went on to unify his work on justification and preference in *Self Trust* (1997), in which he sought to explain the trustworthiness of the self in terms of rationality, theoretical and practical as well as personal and social. In this and in his epistemology, Lehrer claims that complete explanation will contain a loop of the sort Lehrer first found in Reid's philosophy. There is a fundamental choice, according to Lehrer, between starting with unexplained first principles or, instead, maximizing explanation by including a principle of trustworthiness, which explains both why people are justified in accepting everything else that they accept and also why people are justified in accepting the principle itself. The effectiveness of the explanation depends on the wider system of explanation as well, and not simply on the "keystone principle" of self-trust.

See also Chisholm, Roderick; Coherentism; Determinism and Freedom; Epistemology; Epistemology, History of; Freedom; Reid, Thomas; Salmon, Wesley; Self; Sellars, Wilfrid.

Bibliography

Bogdan, Radu, ed. *Keith Lehrer*. Dordrecht, Netherlands: D. Reidel, 1980. Several essays by various authors on various aspects of Lehrer's philosophy, with a single essay in reply as well as a 101-page self-profile by Lehrer himself.

Brandl, Johannes, et al., eds. *Metamind, Knowledge, and Coherence: Essays on the Philosophy of Keith Lehrer*. Amsterdam: Rodopi, 1991. Several essays by various authors on various aspects of Lehrer's philosophy, each with a reply by Lehrer.

Lehrer, Keith. "Can We Know that We Have Free Will by Introspection?" *The Journal of Philosophy* 57 (1960): 145–157. A defense of freedom on the ground that human possession of freedom is entirely obvious from introspection.

Lehrer, Keith. *Metamind*. Oxford: Clarendon Press, 1990. A study of ways in which people's epistemic and preference assessments can also apply at metalevels, and to themselves.

Lehrer, Keith. *Self Trust: A Study of Reason, Knowledge and Autonomy*. Oxford: Clarendon Press, 1997. Brings together into one theoretical presentation most of Lehrer's views about knowledge, justification, rationality, and preference.

Lehrer, Keith. *Theory of Knowledge*. 2nd ed. Boulder, CO: Westview Press, 2000. Explicates and critiques several different conceptions of knowledge and justification, and argues for Lehrer's own version of the coherence theory.

Lehrer, Keith, and Carl Wagner. *Rational Consensus in Science and Society*. Dordrecht, Netherlands: D. Reidel, 1981. Argues that rational consensus can be reached by assigning weights to others' evaluations.

Olsson, Erik J., ed. *The Epistemology of Keith Lehrer*. Dordrecht, Netherlands: Kluwer, 2003. Essays by various authors with a reply by Lehrer.

Nicholas D. Smith (2005)

LEIBNIZ, GOTTFRIED WILHELM
(1646–1716)

The German polymath Gottfried Wilhelm Leibniz made significant contributions to philosophy, logic, mathematics, physics, jurisprudence, politics, the mechanical arts, and history. He worked as a diplomat, an engineer, an attorney, and a political advisor. He corresponded with queens and emperors and with the most eminent intellectuals of the age. Yet his reputation as a philosopher depends largely on texts that were unpublished at the time of his death, including some never intended for publication. Besides well-known works such as the *Discourse on Metaphysics*, *First Truths*, *New Essays*, and *Monadology*, there are thousands of pages of other texts, many of which are still unpublished. Interpreting these vast writings is a daunting task, best approached by attending closely to the historical and cultural context in which he was working and by taking into consideration as many texts as possible. Against the background of Leibniz's long, complicated life, it is possible to trace the development of his philosophical views, from his earliest essays in Leipzig in the 1660s to his last letters written in Hanover fifty years later.

The sheer volume of Leibniz's writings, combined with the fact that some are published and some are not, can sometimes make citing Leibniz seem complicated. The standard edition of his works is *Gottfried Wilhelm Leibniz: Sämtliche Schriften und Briefe*, which was published by the Akademie Verlag in 1923. To simplify citations in this text, it is abbreviated throughout simply as "A," followed by series, volume, and page number (see "A" in the Abbreviations section of the Bibliography at the end of this essay for full publication information). When an English-language translation exists, it follows a colon at the end of the German-language information. In addition to the abbreviation for that primary work, other prominent texts on Leibniz's life and works have also been abbreviated in the in-text citations that appear throughout this essay—a list of those abbreviations and full publication information for every one of them is provided in the Abbreviations section at the very beginning of the Bibliography.

It should be noted that, in regard to Leibniz's philosophical texts, as of mid-2005, only those written up to June 1690 had been published; for texts written after that date that are referenced in this essay, the best available edition has been cited. Finally, works by Leibniz that are divided into short sections have been cited by section number instead of by page number.

LIFE

Leibniz was born in the Lutheran city of Leipzig on July 1, 1646 to Friedrich Leibniz (1597–1652), professor of moral philosophy at the University of Leipzig and the son of a noblewoman and his third wife, Catharina Schmuck (1621–1664), the daughter of a celebrated jurist. An orphan, Schmuck was raised by Johann Hopner, professor of theology, as well as by Quirinus Schacher, professor of law. Upon Friedrich's death in 1652, Schmuck committed herself to the education of her son and his sister, Anna Catharina (1648–1672). As a very young boy, Leibniz was given access to his father's library where by his own account he taught himself Latin and read poetry, history, theology, and some Aristotelian philosophy.

On graduating from the Nicolai School, Leibniz entered the University of Leipzig in April 1661, aged fourteen. He studied ancient languages and literature and heard lectures in mathematics (mainly Euclid) and philosophy. Although the new mechanical philosophy of René Descartes, Thomas Hobbes, and Pierre Gassendi had not been embraced by the professors in Leipzig, there was a diverse intellectual culture available there. Johann Adam Scherzer (1628–1683), professor of philosophy, Hebrew, and theology, published on a wide range of topics, including Kabbalistic theology while Jakob Thomasius (1622–1684) promoted an eclectic mixture of Platonism, Aristotelianism, and other prominent historical schools. Thomasius was an unusually careful historian of philosophy, keen to distinguish between the true and false proposals of the various philosophical *sects*. As the father of Christian Thomasius, who (with Christian Wolff) is often credited as founding the German enlightenment, Jakob Thomasius occupies an important place in the development of German philosophy. Thomasius supervised Leibniz's bachelor's thesis titled *Disputatio metaphysica de principio individui* (Metaphysical Disputation on the Principle of Individuation), which Leibniz defended and published in 1663. The thesis argues for a monadic account of substantial individuation, a position that prefigures his mature views.

Leibniz spent the summer of 1663 at the University of Jena studying under Erhard Weigel (1625–1699), professor of mathematics. Weigel was more progressive than the professors at Leipzig and included mechanical physics within his eclectic mixture, combining Euclid, Aristotle, and the *new philosophers* in an attempt to construct the true philosophy. He returned to Leipzig in October 1663 and received his bachelor of law degree in 1665 under professors Schacher and Bartholomäus Schwendendörffer. In 1666, he published *Dissertatio de arte combinatoria* (Dissertation on the Combinatorial Arts). It contains his first thoughts on the universal characteristic and related logical issues. He planned to pursue legal studies at Leipzig but was refused admission (probably because of his age) and went instead to the University of Altdorf, near Nuremberg, where he quickly earned a doctorate. His dissertation *Disputatio de casibus perplexis in jure* (Disputation on Difficult Cases in Law, 1668) was so well written and defended that the Altdorf faculty immediately offered him a professorship.

Leibniz declined the Altdorf professorship and chose, instead, a life of public service. In Mainz, he impressed Baron Johann Christian von Boineburg (1622–1672), a pious Catholic, distinguished diplomat, and minister to the archbishop of Mainz, Elector Johann Philipp von Schönborn (1605–1673). Boineburg became Leibniz's patron and employed him as an assistant, attorney, librarian, and foreign advisor. In this last capacity, Leibniz produced a lengthy work supporting Schönborn's candidate for the Polish throne. The Catholic Boineburg encouraged the Lutheran Leibniz to pursue ecumenical and conciliatory projects, and he began a project, *Demonstrationes Catholicae* (*Catholic Demonstrations*), aimed at devising a metaphysics consistent with Catholic and Lutheran doctrines. He worked on the *Catholic Demonstrations* between 1668–1671 and returned to it in 1679. Although never completed, it contains his earliest essays on central metaphysical topics.

Besides pursuing peace in politics and religion, the young Leibniz was committed to philosophical peace. In an effort to offer a conciliatory method in philosophy, he prepared a new edition of Marius Nizolius' (1498–1576) 1553 work, *De veris principiis, et vera ratione philosophandi contra pseudophilosophos* (On true principles, and the true method of philosophizing against the false philosophers). Also, between 1669 and 1671, he composed a series of notes titled *Elementa juris naturalis* (*Elements of Natural Law*), in which he discusses theology, metaphysics, and ethics. These notes cover a wide range of topics, including divine and human justice, knowledge, and universal harmony. At this time he began a correspondence with the Duke of Brunswick Johann Friedrich (1652–1679), presenting his views about the souls or *vital principles* in nature, to which he attached important theological essays on the immortality of the soul and the resurrection of the body.

In 1671 Leibniz published two related works that constitute his first extended account of the laws of motion and their metaphysical foundations. The first, the *Hypothesis physica nova* (*New Physical Hypothesis*), subtitled *Theoria motus concreti* (*Theory of Concrete Motion*), he dedicated to the Royal Society of London; the second, the *Theoria motus abstracti* (*Theory of Abstract Motion*), he dedicated to the French Academy of Sciences. Together these works, which employ the Hobbesian notion of *conatus* along with the indivisibles of authors such as Bonaventura Cavalieri (c. 1598–1647), propose a physical system, including a creation story and laws of collision, which relies on the notion of momentary minds. Thus, by 1671 he had already begun to think of minds as the only source of motion and activity in the world; minds in nonhuman substances are momentary while human minds persist and have memory. This attempt to combine an original account of mind with a Hobbesian notion of *conatus* reveals his conciliatory tendencies as well as his capacity to engage in contemporary discussions in physics.

In 1671 Leibniz and Boineburg devised an elaborate plan to divert a pending European war. With secret papers in hand, Leibniz traveled to Paris in March 1672 to meet with a representative of King Louis XIV but arrived too late. Despite this failed diplomatic undertaking, he remained in Paris, at first to promote other political plans of his mentor and then, upon Boineburg's sudden death at the end of 1672, to pursue philosophical peace. He stayed in Paris until 1676 and struggled to stay longer, arguing that the pursuit of science in the service of humanity could be better achieved there than in Hanover, where the Duke of Brunswick had recently employed him.

Leibniz's four years in Paris were enormously productive. In the fall of 1672, he met the Dutch mathematician Christiaan Huygens (1629–1695) who immediately recognized the young man's talent and guided his mathematical studies. Although his education had not acquainted him with recent developments in mathematics, he devoted himself to study and by the fall of 1675 had laid the foundations of his calculus. During his lifetime he suffered from accusations that he had stolen the insights that led to his discovery of the differential and integral calculus from Isaac Newton. But twentieth-century historians of science exonerated him from these charges, showing that he arrived at the calculus independently of Newton.

In early 1673 Leibniz traveled briefly to England on a political mission and met mathematicians and natural philosophers, including Robert Hooke (1635–1703), Robert Boyle, and Henry Oldenburg (1619–1677), secretary of the Royal Society. Back in Paris, he finished a lengthy dialogue, *Confessio Philosophi* (*Philosopher's Confession*), in which he discusses the problem of evil, a topic that would engage him until his death. He also wrote an essay "De vera methodo philosophiae et theologiae ac de natura corporis" ("On the True Method in Philosophy and Theology and on the Nature of Body," in which he restates his fundamental methodological concerns and insists that neither mechanical physics nor mathematics speaks directly to what is most important, namely, the good of the soul and the truths of theology. In 1675 he designed and demonstrated a calculating machine and befriended the young mathematician Ehrenfried Walther von Tschirnhaus, who introduced him to the philosophy of Benedict (Baruch) de Spinoza. At the same time he began work on a group of notes, given the title *De Summa Rerum* (*On the Greatest of Things*), in which he discusses a diverse group of theological and metaphysical topics.

Partly due to prejudices against his religion and nationality, Leibniz failed to attain appropriate employment in Paris, and in 1676 he reluctantly accepted an offer from Johann Friedrich to serve as librarian and adviser at the court of Hanover. In October he traveled from Paris to London and Holland before proceeding to Hanover where he took up residency in December. During his journey he composed a dialogue, *Pacidius Philalethi Prima de Motu Philosophia* (Pacidius to Philalethes: A First Philosophy of Motion), which concerns the problem of the continuum and offers an account of motion. In London he met with Oldenburg again and also John Collins (1624–1683), mathematician and librarian of the Royal Society, who showed him some of Newton's papers. In Holland he met with prominent Dutch mathematicians and scientists, including the microscopists Jan Swammerdam (1637–1680) and Antoni van Leeuwenhoek (1632–1723). He talked at length with Spinoza and possibly saw a draft of Spinoza's *Ethics*

Settled in Hanover Leibniz continued to work in logic, metaphysics, theology, and mathematics. He met visiting scholars and theologians (including Nicolaus Steno [1631–1686]) and wrote a dialogue on free will, *Dialogue entre Poliandre and Théophile*. He took notes on Spinoza's *Ethics*, then newly published, corresponded with Nicolas Malebranche on metaphysics, and returned to the *Catholic Demonstrations* and his work on the universal characteristic. He studied chemistry and made detailed proposals to Johann Friedrich about administrative matters, including the expansion of mining in the Harz mountains. Besides technical tasks involved with the mines, he was much occupied in 1678–1679 with logical topics. He composed a series of highly original notes, given the title *Calculus Universalis* (*Universal Calculus*, in which he tries to formulate a logical calculus. Underlying this work is again his interest in methodology as a means of leading people to the truth and thereby effecting peace. Inspired by the multivolume *Encyclopedia* by Johann Heinrich Alsted (1588–1638), he planned his own encyclopedia project. Also during this time he made a breakthrough in his work on dynamics, defending the notion of force as against the Cartesian principle of conserved motion.

The sudden death of Johann Friedrich and the succession of his brother, Ernst August (1629–1698), in 1680, marked the end of this period of intense productivity. Leibniz remained on good terms with the duke and developed a close friendship with the duke's wife, Sophie, Duchess of Brunswick (1613–1714), with whom he cor-

responded on political, theological, and philosophical topics. The new duke, who would later become elector, encouraged Leibniz's technical and political schemes but was less receptive to academic matters and left the philosopher much less time to develop his own projects. Leibniz was assigned the burdensome task of compiling a history of the House of Brunswick, with the aim of establishing descent from the wealthy Italian house of Este. This project occupied him until his death (by which time, for all his efforts, he had only reached the year 1005).

Between 1680 and 1686 Leibniz worked primarily on logic and on the Harz mining project designing windmills and other equipment. When Leipzig professor Otto Mencke (1644–1707) began publishing a scholarly journal the *Acta Eruditorum*, with the aim of introducing new ideas to German scholars, Leibniz applauded the project and became a frequent contributor on scientific topics. During this time he began another attempt to formulate a logical calculus and renewed his work on the reconciliation of Protestantism and Catholicism. In that context he began a correspondence with Landgrave Ernst von Hessen-Rheinfels (1623–1699), a Catholic eager to promote religious peace.

Caught in a snowstorm for a few days in the Harz mountains in early 1686, Leibniz took advantage of the free time to compose one of his most famous works, the *Discours de métaphysique* (*Discourse on Metaphysics*). It represents his first attempt to summarize the main ideas of his philosophy. He asked Landgrave Ernst to send a synopsis to Antoine Arnauld, and thus began one of the most interesting philosophical correspondences of the seventeenth, or any other, century. Arnauld's criticisms forced Leibniz to explain and expand upon some of his most fundamental ideas.

Leibniz was disappointed when the duke abandoned the Harz mining project but immediately began planning a trip to research the history of the House of Brunswick. In October 1687 he set out on an extended tour of the southern German states, Austria, and Italy. His official duty was to research family history; his personal desire, encouraged by Landgrave Ernst, was to promote religious and political peace. He visited public archives and personal libraries and talked with politicians, monks, and cardinals. During his residence in Vienna, he met the Austrian emperor, to whom he recommended, among other things, the reorganization of the economy, the formation of a general research library, and the establishment of an insurance fund; he worked on proposals for an Imperial College of History; for reforming the coinage of Austria, Brunswick, and Saxony; and for lighting the streets of the city. And he wrote an important paper on motion later published in the *Acta Eruditorum.*

Leibniz spent a year in Italy traveling as far south as Naples and meeting with prominent intellectuals along the way. In Rome (April—November 1689), he made contact with leading Italian scientists, Jesuits (including Claudio Grimaldi [1638–1712], who had lived in China and with whom Leibniz corresponded), and Jansenists. Visits to the Physical-Mathematical Academy led to a treatise on dynamics, *Dynamica de potentia et legibus naturae corporeae* (Dynamics: Concerning the force and laws of natural bodies), which has two parts, one on abstract and the other on concrete dynamics. In Modena he arranged a marriage between the House of Modena and one of Duke Friedrich's daughters. In Venice he met the scientist and Jesuit Michel Angelo Fardella (1650–1708), with whom he later corresponded on philosophical topics.

Before leaving Italy Leibniz wrote a long (last) letter to Arnauld in which he develops further details of his metaphysics. At about the same time, he composed one of his most well-known texts, *Primae Veritates* (*First Truths*). Written on Italian paper, the paper (given the title *Principia Logico-Metaphysica* by the academy editors) dates from the time during—or soon after—his trip to Italy. The four-page essay is a neat summary of his most fundamental philosophical principles, which are outlined in a form interestingly different from previous presentations. Leaving Venice in March 1690, he traveled through Vienna, Prague, Leipzig, and other cities before returning to Hanover. In Vienna he wrote an important paper on motion and gravity titled *De causa gravitatis, et defensio sententiae auctoris de veris naturae legibus contra cartesianos* (On the cause of gravity), which was published in the *Acta Eruditorum* in May. When he arrived back in June 1690, he had been away for more than two and a half years.

Upon his return Leibniz felt the need to justify his lengthy and relatively expensive trip and so committed a good deal of time to his history of the House of Brunswick. In 1690 he became director of the ducal library in Wolfenbüttel, a position that he held for the rest of his life. During the early 1690s he maintained his close relationship with Sophie, by this time Electress of Hanover, published often (especially on mathematical and dynamical topics) in the German *Acta Eruditorum* and the French *Journal des Sçavans*, continued old correspondences, and began new ones (for example, with Johann Bernoulli [1667–1748]). His relations with members of the Royal Society, which had never been unprob-

lematic, took an unfortunate turn when he was accused of using Newton's work as the basis for his own calculus. In March 1693 he wrote directly to Newton about the topic.

In the 1690s Leibniz exchanged several letters with Paul Pellisson-Fontanier (1624–1693), which were then shared with interested parties, including Sophie and her Catholic sister, Marie de Brinon. These letters addressed differences between Catholic and Protestant theology and the possibility of unification among the churches. The well-known physician, Kabbalist, and Quaker sympathizer, Francis Mercury van Helmont (1614–1698) visited Hanover and spent several days lecturing Leibniz and Sophie about his views. Becoming more and more fascinated with reports from Jesuits in China about the science and mathematics of that culture, Leibniz published *Novissima Sinica* (Latest news from China) in 1697, which is an edition of letters and reports from the Jesuit's mission there. For Leibniz the reports from China supported his assumption that there is an underlying truth that all people seek and that could be glimpsed, regardless of religion.

At each stage of his life, Leibniz worked on many diverse projects and wrote thousands of notes on philosophy, mathematics, science, and theology. As an intellect he was in constant motion. It is therefore striking that he published so little. After the texts of 1670–1671, he did not publish a general account of his views until 1695 when his *Système nouveau de la nature et des la communication de substances, aussi bien que de l'union qu'il y a entre l'âme et le corps* (New system of nature), a relatively brief account of a part of his metaphysics, appeared in the French *Journal des Savants*. This led to discussions with prominent Cartesians and others, including Simon Foucher and Basnage de Beauval (1692–1708).

In 1695 Leibniz was promoted to privy counselor of justice, a high-ranking position at court. However, he was not entirely content, complaining that he had little time for new ideas and projects and that, apart from Electress Sophie, there was no one with whom he could discuss intellectual matters. Ernst August died in early 1698 and was succeeded by his eldest son, Georg Ludwig (1660–1727) (later George I of England). Georg Ludwig had little patience either for Leibniz's slow progress on the history of the House of Brunswick or for his other *invisible* projects, and Leibniz received less financial support and freedom of movement. But his friendship with Sophie continued, and his relations with her daughter, Sophie Charlotte, Electress of Brandenburg (and soon to be Queen of Prussia) also became close. Sophie Charlotte often asked Leibniz to act on her behalf, and she supported him in his successful attempt to set up the Berlin Society of Sciences in 1700. As founding president, he wrote its charter.

At this point Leibniz was ready to publish further details of his system of *preestablished harmony*. One of the most important accounts, *De Ipsa Natura* (On Nature Itself), appeared in *Acta Eruditorum* in 1698 and contains his first use of the term *monad*. These publications led to important intellectual exchanges with Pierre Bayle, Burchard de Volder (1643–1709), Lady Damaris Masham (1658–1708), Bernoulli, Bernard le Bovier de Fontenelle, Bartholomew des Bosses (1668-1728), Wolff (who became a kind of disciple), and others.

In the final years of the seventeenth century, Leibniz engaged again in controversy over the invention of the calculus. He was also drawn into secret diplomacy with the English court over the royal succession. Sophie Charlotte and he frequently conversed and exchanged letters about political and philosophical matters. After her sudden death in 1705, he wrote a memorial on topics they had discussed, which subsequently became his *Essais de Théodicée* (*Theodicy*), dedicated to her. Published in 1710, the *Theodicy* is the longest and most prominent publication of his life. In it he attempts to reconcile the goodness of God, the freedom of human kind, and the origin of evil. Its central claim, that this is the best of all possible worlds, was subsequently ridiculed by François-Marie Arouet de Voltaire in *Candide*.

By 1705 Georg Ludwig had lost all patience with Leibniz and forbade him to leave Hanover without permission until the history of the House of Brunswick was complete. Besides visits to nearby Wolfenbüttel, he spent much of his time over the next few years on the history and political relations among the courts in England, Hanover, and Brandenburg. But despite these duties, he began a study of John Locke's *Essay concerning Human Understanding* and wrote essays, some of which he published, on philosophy. As a result of his critical respect for Locke, he composed a lengthy dialogue between a Lockean and a Leibnizian but chose not to publish this text, *Nouveaux essays sur l'entendement humain* (New Essays on Human Understanding) because Locke died in 1704, around the time the work was finished.

In his last years Leibniz continued as librarian of Wolfenbüttel, political adviser, and historian. In 1711 he met Russian Czar Peter the Great (1672–1725) who wanted to engage him on legal and scientific matters. In 1713 Leibniz traveled to Vienna where the Austrian emperor appointed him imperial privy counselor and agreed to create a Society of Sciences. From Vienna he counseled friends in Hanover and Wolfenbüttel though dislike for him at court had increased. When Georg Ludwig became King George I of England in 1714, Leibniz returned to Hanover in hopes of seeing his employer. They missed one another, but the king left instructions insisting that the history of the House of Brunswick be finished. Despite these pressures and encroaching ill health, he began new correspondences—with Nicolas Remond in Paris and Samuel Clarke, an English Newtonian. He also wrote *Principes de la nature et de la grace, fondés en raison* (The Principles of nature and grace, based on reason); the *Discours sur la théologie naturelle des Chinois* (Discourse on the natural theology of the Chinese), in which he shows the connections between Chinese thought and his own *true* philosophy; and the *Monadology*, perhaps his most famous work, providing a summary of the basic tenets of his later philosophy.

Leibniz suffered from gout and by 1714 was severely affected. In the last months of his life, he developed sores on his right leg. Distrusting physicians he refused to see a doctor when he suffered an attack of kidney stones. Working constantly he died in bed on 14 November 1716. By this time he was so out of favor with the court that only a handful of people attended his funeral. Because few of his works were published during his lifetime, it was only in the later part of the eighteenth-century that the extent of his genius began to be understood and acknowledged. It would be left to twentieth-century scholars to uncover the extraordinary breadth of his contributions in physics, mathematics, logic, theology, and philosophy.

PHILOSOPHICAL CORPUS

Among the writings of great early modern thinkers, Leibniz's are unusually problematic. Descartes, Galileo, Spinoza, Hobbes, Malebranche all produced brilliant explications of their philosophies. But there is no single exposition of Leibniz's metaphysics replete with extended arguments and details. He published little during his lifetime and no published text (e.g., *A New System of Nature*, the *Theodicy*) provides a thorough-going account of his philosophy. Although there are a number of identifiable *main* texts, it remains unclear how to treat them since they differ noticeably from each other and were written over many years.

Leibniz wrote more pages—in Latin, French, and German—than most scholars can read in a lifetime. Stored in Hanover after his death, his papers were unorganized, unedited, and undated. The main part of his philosophical corpus has not been available in a standard edition. The early editions of his philosophical work—a late eighteenth-century edition by L. Dutens and a late nineteenth-century collection by C. I. Gerhardt—are incomplete and sometimes inaccurate. The Prussian Academy of Science (now the German Academy of Science) began to publish the standard edition of his papers in 1923, but it has taken decades to cover even the main works in philosophy. The publication of the remainder is expected to take until 2050. It is surely difficult to acquire a broad understanding of his writings when only a small selection is available.

Leibniz's philosophical writings pose additional problems. First, many of them are hastily written personal notes, often both incomplete and undated. As he himself wrote about his papers: "Instead of treasure … you will only find ashes; instead of elaborate works, a few sheets of paper and some poorly expressed vestiges of hasty reflections, which were only saved for the sake of my memory" (A VI i 533). Second, even in the publications and letters sent to the great philosophers of Europe, he had specific methodological reasons for not being forthright about his views: His goal was to avoid preaching in an attempt to engage his reader. By such means he hoped to nudge the wayward soul toward the truth. In a frank moment in 1676 he writes: "A metaphysics should be written with accurate definitions and demonstrations, but nothing should be demonstrated in it apart from that which does not clash too much with received opinions. For in that way this metaphysics can be accepted; and once it has been approved then, if people examine it more deeply later, they themselves will draw the necessary consequences" (A VI iii 573–574: Pk 93). Finally, given his astonishing erudition, it is difficult to reconstruct the conceptual framework of his writings. Not only did he use major parts of the history of philosophy without citation or explanation, he thought that it was a *good thing* to combine ideas taken from the great philosophical systems. One of the main reasons that it is so difficult for us to recognize the borrowed doctrines and transformed assumptions in his writings is that he made such abundant use of the entire history of philosophy as it was conceived in the seventeenth century.

Due to the difficulties posed by Leibniz's writings, texts such as the *Discourse on Metaphysics, First Truths, New System, New Essays,* and *Monadology*—all of which suited twentieth-century philosophical tastes—became his canonical writings. As important as these writings are, they do not represent the extraordinary range and quirky diversity of his ideas. He is rarely explicit about the precise relations among his ideas, but he is clear about the fact that they are tightly connected. At the end of his life, he insists: "My principles are such that they can hardly be torn apart … whoever knows one well knows them all" (G II 412: L 599).

In an attempt to reveal the breadth of Leibniz's philosophical system and the connections among core doctrines, this article cites a diverse group of texts selected from all the main periods of his life. He borrowed ideas from the whole history of philosophy, and so before considering some of his philosophical ideas, we will situate them in their proper historical context.

METHODOLOGY AND INTELLECTUAL HARMONY

The early Renaissance philosopher Giovanni Pico della Mirandola, formulates in his *On the Dignity of Man* (1486) one of the defining statements of the conciliatory methodology of many humanist thinkers. Pico recommends that the seeker of truth study all the masters of philosophy. Once the truths in each philosophical tradition are discovered, they will be combined into a comprehensive philosophy. One of the main points of Pico's project is to show that *a concord* can be forged between the philosophies of Plato and Aristotle. For intellectual conciliators such as Pico, the doctrines of the prominent philosophical traditions, despite their apparent differences, can be made to form a coherent philosophical system.

In the aftermath of the Thirty Years War, whose battles were fought mostly on German soil, this methodology of peace was extremely attractive, especially to German thinkers, many of whom had witnessed the devastation and horrors of the war firsthand. As a young man Leibniz committed himself to his own form of conciliatory eclecticism. Like Pico he thought that the fundamental truths were (mostly) those offered by the illustrious ancient thinkers. Some of his basic metaphysical beliefs were taken directly from the Aristotelian, Platonist, and mechanical philosophies: that a substance is something wholly self-sufficient, that each creature is an emanation of God's essence, and that all corporeal features are to be explained mechanically. But he also went beyond Pico in his commitment to a philosophy that is consistent with specific Christian doctrines, such as those of the Eucharist and the resurrection of the body. His grand philosophical system is the result of the clever interweaving of ancient and modern assumptions.

In 1671 Leibniz published an edition of a text by the sixteenth-century humanist Mario Nizolio (1488–1567). He wrote a lengthy introduction to Nizolio's 1553 book

On the True Principles and the True Method of Philosophy, Against the Pseudo-philosophers. Both Nizolio's text and Leibniz's introduction discuss the proper way of philosophizing. It is significant that Leibniz attached to his introduction a slightly revised version of his April 1669 letter to Jakob Thomasius. The letter thereby became the young man's first published text on a contemporary metaphysical topic. Instead of being yet another philosopher "lusting for novelty," Leibniz seeks to find the "interconnections among doctrines" (A VI ii 426). He presents what he calls a "reformed philosophy," a philosophy that combines the "rule" of the new mechanical physics and the metaphysics of Aristotle (A VI II 434: L 94). He focuses on corporeal substances and reforms Aristotle's notions of substantial form and matter so that they accommodate the mechanical physics. By demoting the mechanical notion of matter as extended stuff to Aristotelian prime matter, he cleverly constructs a theory of substance that has the structure of the Aristotelian notion and yet is consistent with mechanical explanations in physics. He happily concludes that by such means, the mechanical philosophy "can be reconciled with Aristotle's" (A VI ii 435: L 95). The details of his views about substance would change over the years, but the basic structure of this theory of substance, developed as a synthesis of Aristotelianism and mechanism, would remain the same.

In his *New Essays*, written in response to Locke in the early years of the eighteenth century, Leibniz reflects on the methodology that produced his philosophy: "This system appears to unite Plato with Democritus, Aristotle with Descartes, the scholastics with the moderns, theology and morality with reason. It seems to take the best from all quarters and then goes further than anyone has done before" (A VI vi 71–73). His concern with intellectual harmony emerges also in his concern to engage his readers and interlocutors so as to enlist them in his march toward truth. In a letter of March 1678, he explains:

> I am concerned, as are all who wish to hold a middle ground, not to seem too much inclined toward either of the two opposed adversaries. Whenever I discuss matters with the Cartesians ... I extol Aristotle where he deserves it and undertake a defense of the ancient philosophy, because I see that many Cartesians read their one master only ... and thus unwisely impose limits on their own ability. ... I think that the two philosophies should be combined and that where the old leaves off, the new should begin." (A II i 402: L 190)

For Leibniz the true metaphysics will be consistent with Christian doctrine and constructed from the underlying truths in the great philosophical systems. An underappreciated aspect of his brilliance is his ability to gather ideas from different philosophical sources and make them his own.

GOD AND CREATION

Like other prominent thinkers of the seventeenth century, Leibniz believed in a perfectly good Supreme Being who created and maintained the world and whose existence could be proven. He sometimes employed versions of the cosmological argument for God's existence. For example, in the *Monadology* (1714), he argues for God a posteriori based on the harmonized diversity of the world and the fact that there are contingent beings whose "final or sufficient reason" must be in a "necessary being" (§39, §45). But his favorite argument is an original version of the ontological argument, which is critical of Descartes's version and based on the mere possibility of God: "Since nothing can prevent the possibility of what is without limits, without negation, and consequently without contradiction, this by itself is sufficient for us to know the existence of God a priori" (§45).

Like many of his contemporaries, Leibniz owed a number of his assumptions about God as creator of the world to an ancient (mostly Platonist) tradition. From prominent professors at the University of Leipzig, he acquired a solid education in Platonism. The version of this ancient philosophical "sect" taught in Leipzig was one inspired by the third-century Platonist, Plotinus (c. 204–270) and by Jewish Kabbalism. Many of his most fundamental assumptions about knowledge, mind, plenitude, the nature of creation, and the relations among substances are rooted in this tradition. Two assumptions that he embraced as a young man are as follows:

GOD AND EMANATION. There is an ultimately good, perfectly self-sufficient, and thoroughly unified Supreme Being on which everything else depends and which itself depends on nothing. God's mind contains a number of Ideas or attributes (say, the Idea of Justice), which are the perfect essences of things (these are roughly based on Plato's theory of Ideas) and which are used as models for created things. The Idea or attribute of God is emanated to a creature in such a way that neither God nor God's attribute is depleted in any way while the creature acquires the attribute, though in an inferior manner. The emanative process is continual so that a creature instantiates a divine attribute if and only if God emanates the attribute to the creature. For many Platonists, a corollary of this causal theory of emanation is that every product of the Supreme Being contains all the attributes (and hence the essence) of God though the product instantiates each of those attributes in a manner inferior to the way in which they exist in the Supreme Being. Justice as conceived by God is perfect; justice as instantiated by Socrates is not. Leibniz summarizes the position in §14 of the *Discourse on Metaphysics*: "It is evident that created substances depend upon God, who preserves them and who even produces them continually by a kind of emanation."

PLENITUDE AND SYMPATHY. The divine essence is emanated not just to each creature but to the whole of creation. The principle of plenitude develops from the idea that the more of the divine essence in the world—and hence of being and goodness—the better. Although the principle of plenitude suggests that there will be as much diverse being as possible (the more being, the better the world), this diversity of being must also be properly unified (the more unity, the better the world). One of the results of this unity among the parts of the world is a cosmic sympathy. Here the idea is that each part of the world is *in sympathy* with all the others. In other words, the principle of plenitude was supposed to imply that God fills creation with as much being as possible and unifies those diverse beings as much as possible. Such a diverse and unified world was supposed to engender wonder, delight, and awe in human observers. In the *Monadology*, he agrees with the ancient philosopher Hippocrates who claimed that all things are in sympathy with one another: everything "is affected by anything that happens in the universe, to such an extent that he who sees all can read in each thing what happens everywhere, and even what has happened or what will happen, by observing in the present what is remote in time as well as in space" (§61).

These ancient Platonist assumptions about emanation, plenitude, and sympathy inform much of Leibniz's thinking about the world. They inspire his theory of universal harmony, many of his views about mind, his account of knowledge, his solution to the problem of evil, and his views about the mirroring and expressing of substance. In this section, we consider the core doctrines closely related to these Platonist assumptions. As we will see, Leibniz remains committed to these doctrines throughout his philosophical career.

UNIVERSAL HARMONY. Leibniz first articulates the doctrine of universal harmony in a series of notes titled *Elements of Natural Law*, written between 1668 and 1671. As he summarizes the idea for Arnauld in 1671: "I define … harmony as diversity compensated by identity" (A II i 173–174: L 150). By the time he wrote the *Discourse on Metaphysics* in 1686, he had come to formulate the doctrine in terms of hypotheses though the underlying idea is still the same. In §6 of the *Discourse*, he explains: "God has chosen the most perfect world, that is, the one which is at the same time the simplest in hypotheses and the richest in phenomena." According to Leibniz, the single, unified, and perfect Supreme Being freely chooses to emanate the divine attributes to creatures; God remains transcendent while all creatures become an imperfect instantiation of God's attributes. Because God emanates the divine essence to all its products, he describes God as the reason (*ratio*) of the world and the one (*unum*) in it.

Universal harmony entails that God relates to the world and to each creature in it in two ways. God is the multiplicity in the world insofar as the divine essence is variously manifested in the vast diversity of creatures and in the diversity of the perceptions of each creature, but God is also the unity insofar as each created thing is a unified instantiation of the divine essence (although a manifestation of the essence far inferior to that of God) and therefore related to and reflective of all the others. The world is full of various perceptions of the world or *phenomena* because the world contains an infinity of different expressions of the divine essence. Leibniz's notion of universal harmony forms the basis for his mature theory of pre-established harmony.

PLENITUDE, DIFFERENCE, AND PRINCIPLE OF THE IDENTITY OF INDISCERNIBLES. From 1676 on Leibniz is increasingly explicit about the significance of the principle of plenitude. In a series of notes written in Paris titled *On the Greatest of Things*, he writes: "I take as a principle … that the greatest amount of essence that can exist does exist" (A VI iii 472: Pk 21). He never wavers from this commitment to plenitude. In *On the Ultimate Origination of Things* of 1697, he explains that God is the *reason*, or source, of things and argues that "there is a certain urge for existence or (so to speak) a straining toward existence in possible things or in the possibility of essence itself; in a word essence in and of itself strives for existence" (G VIII 303: AG 150). For Leibniz, the world is not just very full, it is as full of being as it can possibly be, consistent with harmony. As for his contemporaries Spinoza and Anne Conway, infinity is for Leibniz a mark of the fullness of being. Whereas Spinoza assigns God or nature an infinity of attributes, both Conway and Leibniz make each portion of the world infinitely full. In 1676 he claims that every part of the world, regardless of how small, "contains an infinity of creatures," which is itself a kind of "world" (A VI iii 474: Pk 25). He emphasizes the same point later in *First Truths* (1689): "Every particle of the universe contains a world of an infinity of creatures" (VI iv [B] 1647–1648: AG 34). For Leibniz there is an aesthetic aspect to this elaborate harmony among the infinity of creatures. As he puts the point in the *Monadology*:

> the author of nature has been able to practice this divine and infinitely marvelous art, because each portion of matter is not only divisible to infinity, as the ancients have recognized, but is also actually subdivided without end, each part divided into parts …; otherwise, it would be impossible for each portion of matter to express the whole universe" (§65).

Nor is Leibniz content merely to fill the world with being. He argues that in order to contribute to the world's diversity, each created thing must be essentially distinct from every other. One of his most famous principles, the principle of the identity of indiscernibles, demands that no two substances are exactly alike. He writes in *Discourse*: "It is not true that two substances can resemble each other completely and differ only in number" (§9). Although he is not explicit about the importance of the principle until the late 1680s and then formulates it in a variety of ways, the basic idea is straightforward enough: There is always more than a mere numerical difference between substances. Two eggs might seem perfectly similar but they will not differ merely numerically; there will always be something true of one egg that is not true of the other. In *First Truths* he argues: "In nature, there cannot be two individual things that differ in number alone. For it certainly must be possible to explain why they are different, and that explanation must derive from some difference they contain" (A VI iv [B] 1645: AG 32). As he puts it in the *Monadology*: "It is also necessary that each monad be different from each other. For there are never two beings in nature that are perfectly alike, two beings in which it is not possible to discover an internal difference" (§9).

What the principle of the identity of indiscernibles claims is fairly clear; why he wanted to make such a claim is less so. His commitment to the principle of plenitude and theory of emanation offers insight into his underlying motivation. For Leibniz, as for many theists, the goodness of the world is a function of the diversity of beings as well as the order among them. Given that each creature contains the divine essence, the world will be better if it is as full of diverse emanations of the divine

nature as is consistent with unity and harmony. His principle of the identity of indiscernibles pushes this intuition to its logical extreme: By demanding that no two substances (that is, no two emanations of the divine essence) be the same, he thereby increases the amount of diversity in the world. The principle of the identity of indiscernibles is a neat way of insisting on difference of the required sort.

MIRRORS AND EXPRESSIONS. The image of the mind as a mirror is a permanent fixture of Leibniz's mature thought. He first develops this idea in the *Elements of Natural Law* (1668–1671). Consider the following passage: "Since every mind is like a mirror, there will be one mirror in our mind, another in other minds. Thus, if there are many mirrors, that is, many minds recognizing our goods, there will be a greater light, the mirrors blending the light not only in the [individual] eye but also among each other. The gathered splendor produces glory" (A VI i 464: L 137). By such means, he goes beyond the plenitude and sympathy of his Platonist predecessors. He does not just maximize creatures and the assumed sympathetic relations among them, he heightens their connections by making each substance a mirror of all the others because each mind is (unconsciously) aware of all the others.

In the notes written in Paris in 1676, he develops his growing commitment to plenitude in a number of directions. For Leibniz, in *On the Greatest of Things*, each mind eternally mirrors the entirety of the world, and each does so from its own perspective. That is, consistent with the principle of the identity of indiscernibles, no two substances mirror the world from the same perspective. To elucidate his point he offers an analogy that he will use for the rest of his philosophical career: In the same way that travelers approaching a town from different directions see the town from different perspectives, so each mind approaches the world from a different perspective. For Leibniz it is important that each mind has a unique view of the world for "in this way a wonderful variety arises" (A VI iii 524: Pk 85). As he summarizes the point in *On the Greatest of Things* in 1676: "A most perfect being is one that contains the most. Such a being is capable of ideas and thoughts, for this multiplies the varieties of things, like a mirror" (A VI iii 475: Pk 29).

Forty years later Leibniz sets out the same claims, employing the same analogies, in the *Monadology*: "This interconnection or accommodation of all created things to each other, and each to all the others, brings it about that each simple substance has relations that express all the others, and consequently, that each simple substance is a perpetual, living mirror of the universe" (§56).

> Just as the same city viewed from different directions appears entirely different and, as it were, multiplied perspectively, in just the same way it happens that, because of the infinite multitude of simple substances, there are, as it were, just as many different universes, which are, nevertheless, only perspectives on a single one, corresponding to the different points of view of each monad. … And this is the way of obtaining as much variety as possible, but with the greatest order possible, that is, it is the way of obtaining as much perfection as possible. (§57–58)

As these quotations suggest, there are close connections between the mirroring activity of minds and Leibniz's mature doctrine of expression. In various texts and in various ways, he claims that each substance expresses God, each substance expresses the world, and each substance expresses every other substance. After years of analysis of the texts, scholars have remained unclear about the implications and interconnections of these claims and about how exactly the doctrine of expression relates to the idea of minds as mirrors. The 1676 Paris notes, *On the Greatest of Things*, help solve some of the most recalcitrant problems by revealing the underlying motivation behind the doctrine. Each substance is an emanation of God's essence, and in this sense each shares the same essence. Each emanation will differ from every other by *expressing* the divine essence differently: "The essence of all things is the same," and they differ "only in the manner of their expression" (A VI iii 573: Pk 95). To explain his point he compares the essence of God to a number that can be expressed in an infinity of ways, each of which is a more or less clear expression of the essence. For the number 6, whether the expression is 3+3, 3×2, or 4+2, each is an expression of the same thing although "no one can doubt that the one expression differs from the other" (A VI iii 518: Pk 77). In the same way that the number 6 may be thought to contain its full essence, so God contains perfectly the divine essence. Whether the expression of 6 is 2+4, 3×2, 36−32+2, or any of the other infinite means of expressing it, each is a more or less clear expression of the same thing. Similarly, each substance—whether a human, roach, or chimpanzee—is a more or less clear expression of the divine essence. Leibniz concludes: "So do things differ from each other and from God" (A VI iii 519: Pk 77).

The arithmetical analogy makes it easier to see how expression works. Each substance expresses God insofar as it expresses the divine essence; each expresses the world insofar as the world just is the totality of expressions of God; and finally, each substance expresses every other insofar as each is a more or less clear expression of the same thing. The *Discourse on Metaphysics* employs expression to great effect: "Every substance is like a complete world and like a mirror of God or of the whole universe, which each one expresses in its own way, somewhat as the same city is variously represented depending upon the different positions from which it is viewed" (§9). He goes on to add that substances are "different expressions of the same universal cause, namely, God," where "the expressions vary in perfection" (§15).

Nor should we worry that creatures have become "little Gods." Although in the *Monadology* Leibniz is happy to describe human minds as "images of the divinity itself" (§83), he always distinguishes between the perfection of God and the limitations of creatures. In the *Monadology*, he insists that "what is limited in us is limitless" in God (§30), and argues: "God alone is the primitive unity or the first simple substance; all created or derivative monads are products, and are generated, so to speak, by continual fulgurations of the divinity from moment to moment, limited by the receptivity of the creature, to which it is essential to be limited" (§47).

GOD, MIND, AND KNOWLEDGE

The Platonism of Leibniz's professors bequeathed to him central concerns relating to mind. In the *Phaedo* Plato argues that it is "the divine-like" nature of the soul that guarantees its self-sufficiency, vitality, and unity. Because the soul remains "always the same as itself," it is immortal. The body, because it is never the "same as itself," is mortal (80a–e). Subsequent Platonists had to explain how the soul and the body could be causally related. Among the explanatory alternatives, the fifteenth-century Platonist Marsilio Ficino offered a version of one that influenced Leibniz strongly. In his *Platonic Theology*, Ficino uses the causal theory of emanation to bind the body to the soul. According to Ficino, the soul, which is "always alive," emanates its "vivifying" and "indivisible power" to its body so that it "causes life to be diffused" and thereby creates a harmony of components. As the unifying power of God is to the world, so is the soul to the body (Book II, chapter 3).

Besides a Platonist account of the soul and its relation to the body, the young Leibniz also took up a Platonist epistemology according to which the only true objects of knowledge (as opposed to opinion) are the eternal and immutable Ideas. Many Platonists placed the

Ideas within the soul, where they remain, waiting to become objects of conscious thought. Although Platonists differed about the precise role played by the senses in the acquisition of knowledge, most agreed that the process of coming to know the Ideas was one of removing oneself from the mutable world of the senses and letting one's understanding (*intellectus*) grasp the immutable Ideas within. For some Platonists cosmic sympathy aids in this pursuit of knowledge; the same Ideas that are implanted in souls are also evident in the harmony among creatures in the world. Theists often reinterpreted Plato's realm of Ideas as the mind of God and the Ideas as paradigms employed by God in creation. Acquisition of knowledge of these Ideas is a necessary step toward knowledge of God, to be achieved both by turning away from the world to the immutable ideas within and by attending to the connections among all things.

In some notes written during his stay in Venice in 1690, Leibniz summarizes this Platonist stance: "Each thing is so connected to the whole universe, and one mode of each thing contains such order and consideration with respect to the individual modes of other things, that in any given thing, indeed in each and every mode of any given thing, God clearly and distinctly sees the universe as implied and inscribed." Due to this connection among things:

> "when I perceive one thing or one mode of a thing, I always perceive the whole universe confusedly; and the more perfectly I perceive one thing, the better I come to know many properties of other things from it. And from this perfect consonance of things there also arises the greatest harmony and beauty of the universe, which exhibits to us the power and wisdom of the Highest Maker." (AG 103)

MIND AND ACTIVITY. From the beginning of his philosophical career, Leibniz associates activity with mind. Whether he calls these principles of activity souls, minds, substantial forms, or monads, the idea is always that the only sources of activity in the world are divine-like principles that have the power to generate unity, self-sufficiency, and vitality. In a note of 1671, he argues: "Just as God thinks things … because they follow from his nature, so does Mind. … Mind and God do not differ except that one is finite and the other infinite" (A VI ii 287–288). In the *Monadology*, he notes: "that souls, in general, are living mirrors or images of the universe of creatures, but that minds are also images of the divinity itself, or of the author of nature, capable of knowing the system of the universe … each mind being like a little divinity in its own realm" (§83).

For a short period in 1670–1671, Leibniz distinguished between the momentary minds in nature and conscious minds. His published treatises the *New Physical Hypothesis* and *Theory of Abstract Motion* of 1671 employ momentary minds as the cause of the motion in bodies to great effect. By 1676 his commitment to the plenitude has led him to make all minds eternal: "Every mind is of endless duration" and "is indissolubly implanted in matter. …There are innumerable minds everywhere" which "do not perish" (A VI iii 476–477: Pk 31). In *On the Greatest of Things* minds act constantly and constitute self-sufficient beings that are eternal and indestructible by anything but God. Human minds are created by God and then exist eternally. Nonhuman minds exist from the beginning of the world to its end. Despite appearances to the contrary, Fido the dog does not die but shrinks down to *an invisible core* of substance from which it activates another substance, and so on for all of eternity. This remained Leibniz's view: "There is never total generation nor, strictly speaking, perfect death, death consisting in the separation of the soul. And what we call *generations* are developments and growths, as what we call deaths are enfoldings and diminutions" (*Monadology* §73).

MARKS AND TRACES. The eternity of all mind-like active things is not an obviously plausible theory. Leibniz endorsed it because the eternity of minds adds significantly to the plenitude and harmony of the world. While developing his opinions about plenitude in *On the Greatest of Things*, he hit upon the idea that each mind-like creature eternally perceives the entirety of the world. Each mind "senses all the endeavors" of all the other minds in the whole history of the world; "no endeavor in the universe is lost; they are stored up in the mind, not destroyed" (A VI iii 393: Pk 47). He came to believe that plenitude requires that each moment in the eternity of the world contain its whole history: past, present, and future. Minds not only sense all the present activities of all the minds in the world, they also retain a memory or *trace* of them: "It is not credible that the effect of all perceptions should vanish" (A VI iii 510: Pk 61). Each mind "retains the effect of what precedes it" and also "has a quality of such a kind as to bring this [state or effect] about" (A VI iii 491: Pk 51).

Thus, in 1676 Leibniz develops a version of his doctrine of marks and traces according to which each mind at every moment includes an effect or trace of all it has done as well as a quality or mark of all it will do. In §8 of the *Discourse*, he offers the soul of Alexander as an example: "There are vestiges of everything that has happened to him and marks of everything that will happen to him and even traces of everything that happens in the universe, even though God alone would recognize them all" (A VI iv [B] 1534: AG 41). By making minds eternal, allowing them to sense all endeavors, and assigning them traces of all that has gone before and marks of all that will occur, he makes each mind a mirror of the entire course of the world at every moment in time. Each mind reflects or mirrors the entire world at every moment of the mind's eternal existence. In *Discourse* §15, he summarizes the point in terms of expression: Each substance is of "infinite extension insofar as it expresses everything" (A VI iv [B] 1646). By such means he agrees with Plato "who taught that our soul expresses God, the universe, and all essences" (*Discourse*, §27).

GOD AND KNOWLEDGE. Throughout his life Leibniz was keen to acquire information about the world and to contribute to the sciences of his time. He studied history, designed machines, proposed lighting systems, created insurance programs, and contributed to the development of modern physics. Underlying all these enterprises, however, was his commitment to a Platonist epistemology according to which the divine Ideas are instantiated in the creatures in the world and exist in human minds innately. He summarizes this view in §28 of the *Discourse*: "The essence of our soul is a certain expression, imitation or image of the divine essence ... and of all the ideas comprised in it."

From the very beginning of Leibniz's philosophical reflections on universal harmony, he recognizes its epistemological significance. In *Elements of Natural Law* (1668–1671), he presents for the first time the main steps that must be taken to acquire knowledge of fundamental truths. Since the goal of human life is to recognize the beauty and harmony in things, and harmony consists in *consonance* beneath apparent *dissonance*, we must learn to see beyond the dissonance. Once we abstract from the confusion of things and begin to recognize the underlying order of the world, the journey to this ultimate knowledge has begun. The first objects of knowledge are our innate Ideas, each of which is also an Idea in God's mind and so also instantiated in the world. By grasping one of these Ideas in the right way, we begin the process of knowing God and the ultimate nature of things. The goal of life is to recognize that everything is an emanation of God and hence a proper object of love. In a 1671 letter to Arnauld, he concludes this part of the project: "I show

that it is the same thing to love others and to love God, the seat of universal harmony" (A II i 173–174: L 150).

In the *Philosopher's Confession* (1672–1673), Leibniz clarifies and expands upon the relation between universal harmony and knowledge: "The nature of mind is to think; therefore, the harmony of the mind will consist in thinking about harmony; and the greatest harmony of the mind or happiness will consist in the concentration of universal harmony, i.e., of God, in the mind" (A VI iii 116–117). The goal of life is to intuit the essence of God, which is evident in the "universal harmony" of the world. The means to this goal is to grasp "the eternal and immutable ... Ideas" (A VI iii 120). The journey to knowledge begins when one "withdraws from the senses and draws back into his own mind." After a sincere "struggle toward the truth," "a stroke of light" may appear "as a split in the darkness" (A VI iii 120–121). Through the proper approach to the world, it is possible to be "admitted to God, i.e., universal harmony," to grasp it "in a single stroke of vision," and thereby to have "delight without end" (A VI iii 139). However, because minds are mostly "deformed" and exist "in shadow," many fail to recognize the "wondrous" interconnections among things (A VI i 464–465).

Leibniz remained committed to this form of innatism throughout his life. Thirty years after the *Elements of Natural Law*, he criticized the empiricism of Locke's *Essay concerning Human Understanding* in his own *New Essays*, noting that innate ideas distinguish us from beasts. According to Leibniz: "This is how ideas and truths are innate in us, as natural inclinations, dispositions, habits, or potentialities." Agreeing with Plato, he maintains: "The soul contains from the beginning the source of several notions and doctrines, which external objects awaken on certain occasions." Endorsing Paul's approach to knowledge, he quotes Paul's Letter to the Romans (2:15): "The law of God is written in our hearts" (A VI vi 49–52: AG 292–294).

Universal harmony increases the possibility for knowledge; the mirroring of minds increases it still more. For Leibniz *the wisdom of God* requires that creatures mirror one another and thereby add to the beauty and harmony of the world. He was motivated to convert the world into a harmony of mirroring substances at least partly in order to maximize the likelihood of such reflective awareness. The mirroring of minds increases variety and harmony because each mind encompasses the whole of existence. In *On the Greatest of Things*, each mind perceives the entire world at every moment of its eternal existence: "It seems to me that every mind is omniscient in a confused way, that any mind perceives simultaneously whatever happens in the entire world" (A VI iii 524: Pk 85). In developing these views about plenitude and harmony, he reasons that it is good to maximize the number of diverse creatures in the world; it is even better to maximize the perception of that infinity of good things by making each creature mirror every other; but it is best to maximize the harmony among creatures by making all minds connected to all others at all moments in the eternity of the world.

Leibniz is rarely as explicit about the close relation between emanation and knowledge as he is in *On the True Mystical Theology*, a German text written (probably) in the final years of the seventeenth century. He begins with the metaphysics of universal harmony and its related epistemology: "Every perfection flows immediately from God. Only the inner light that God himself kindles in us has the power to give us a right knowledge of God." But it is not easy to acquire this knowledge: "The divine perfections are concealed in all things, but very few know how to discover them there. Hence there are many who are learned without being illumined, because they believe not God or the light but only their earthly teachers or their external senses and so remain in the contemplation of imperfections." Each created thing or "self-being" is from God and is therefore "a single self-sufficient" and "indestructible thing."

This separateness from God makes it difficult to recognize the divinity within us, but in our connectedness to God, it becomes easy: "God is the easiest and the hardest being to know." We can find "the essential truth" by seeking out the attributes of God: "The knowledge of God is the beginning of wisdom, the divine attributes are the primary truths for the right order of knowledge." Once we acquire knowledge of an attribute of God, which is present within us as an innate idea, we begin to approach "the essential light," which is "the eternal Word of God, in which is all wisdom, all light, indeed the original of all beings and the origin of truths. Without the radiation of this light no ones achieves true faith, and without true faith no one attains blessedness." He summarizes: In each mind "there lies an infinity, a footprint or reflection of the omniscience and omnipresence of God." Were we to acquire this "right knowledge of God," we would thereby attain "all wisdom, all light, indeed the original of all beings and the origin of all truth" (Guhrauer, 411–412: L 367–369).

LOGIC, TRUTH, AND PEACE

Biographers have claimed that as a boy Leibniz became dissatisfied with the categories of Aristotelian logic. Whatever truth there is in this, the youthful Leibniz joined the growing debate about the possibility of a universal language and a formal system for determining truth. For many seventeenth-century philosophers, the hope was to construct "an alphabet of human thought" that would form the basis for a universal language and a means of identifying truths. Leibniz intended to find a way to assign letters or numbers to the elements of thought so as to produce, "through the analysis of words" a means of judging the truth of all statements in the language. In *Dissertation On the Combinatorial Art* (1666), a young Leibniz begins work on this project, which he calls "the universal characteristic."

Although scholars have often treated Leibniz's account of logic and truth independently of his views about God and emanation, the two parts of his philosophy are closely related. The divine Ideas are the source of all truths, and human minds contain these Ideas innately, so the analysis of truth will involve these Ideas. Opening one of the main sections of *Dissertation On the Combinatorial Art*, he explains: "To begin at the top, Metaphysics treats being and the affections of being" (VI i 170: L 76). In 1671 he observes that although we are "conquerors of the world," we cannot have real knowledge until the mind has clarity about itself (A VI i 459). Leibniz's account of emanation and divine Ideas constitute a major part of the foundation for his program in logic because the ideas innate in us are also those emanated by God in the creations of the world. This connection persists in his thought until the very end; in the *Monadology* he observes that our mind contains "knowledge of eternal and necessary truths … thus in thinking of ourselves we think of being" and "of the immaterial and of God himself" (§29–30).

The relation between being and truth motivates other projects related to language. As with many of his contemporaries, Leibniz was fascinated with the evolution of languages since the "original language" of Eden. Many assumed that the language spoken by Adam and Eve made the truth more perspicuous and so attempted to recreate it. He went beyond most of his contemporaries in his fascination with the Chinese—both their language and culture. Like many of the Jesuit missionaries in China, he believed that the (apparently) extraordinary insights of the Chinese proved that the *elements of truth* were available to any who knew how to seek them and that the identification of such truths would promote universal communication and eventually universal peace.

GOD, EVIL, AND THE BEST

PHILOSOPHER'S CONFESSION. Written within a year of his arrival in Paris, the *Philosopher's Confession* is a dialogue in which Leibniz discusses at length and for the first time the problem of evil, a problem that, together with a group of related problems, would engage his attention for the next forty years. The problem is ancient: How can the evil in the world (say, the suffering of innocents) be reconciled with the existence of an infinitely powerful, just, and good Supreme Being? Already in 1672–1673, he has a solution, one that would remain an important part of his thinking: The goodness of God is sufficient reason to create a world that is the best possible, and (apparent) evil is a necessary part of such a world. His solution is embedded in his notion of universal harmony: The world is the best and most harmonious possible despite the fact that its enormous diversity includes events that often suggest otherwise.

In order to explain how this world is best, it was necessary to develop a more thorough-going account of creation. Leibniz did this in the *Philosopher's Confession.* The divine intellect contains an unspecified number of eternal and immutable Ideas that constitute the divine essence and that God wills to instantiate in the world. That is, the essence of God "contains" the "nature of the things themselves" (A VI iii 124). But the essence of God does not necessitate *this* nature of things. Rather, God selects among possible versions of the divine essence and then emanates the selected version so as to create and sustain the world. He refers to these versions as possible *series of things*; he will later call these possible worlds. Each individual created thing is an instantiation of the (selected) divine essence. Further, God has a sufficient reason for choosing each thing, and each thing has a sufficient reason for acting as it does. He summarizes his position: "The present state of things depends on the series of things. The series of things depends on the universal harmony. The universal harmony depends on those well -known eternal and immutable ideas themselves … contained in the divine intellect" (A VI iii 131). God is "the sufficient and complete reason" for the world (A VI iii 123). God understands this world to be most harmonious and thereby has sufficient reason to choose it.

Leibniz's *best possible world* solution to the problem of evil gives rise to further problems: One concerns (what scholars sometimes call) the *author of sin*; another concerns the status of human freedom. On Leibniz's account,

God causes evil, for God creates the best series of things, including many things that are, when considered in themselves, bad or sinful. In the *Philosopher's Confession* he responds to this problem by pointing out that God takes no delight in the existence of evil and hence is not properly thought to will it. In later works, he came to regard this response as inadequate. According to Leibniz, there is a sufficient reason for every thing that happens in the world. As we will see below, this principle plays an important role in his thinking about the world. When applied to the problem of human freedom, the principle commits him to determinism. For Leibniz, the will is never free of antecedent causes and in that sense it is always determined. But he is also a compatibilist in the sense that, just as God's perfect freedom does not involve lack of determination by the divine essence, so human freedom does not require undetermined choices. Freedom requires only spontaneity, or more exactly, the sort of spontaneity possessed by rational substances.

In both the *Elements of Natural Law* and *Philosopher's Confession,* Leibniz's approach to the problem of evil also has an epistemological aspect. The nature of universal harmony makes the acquisition of knowledge both more difficult and more *glorious.* Because there is a struggle, there will be some who fail. Yet the world is a better place because of the struggle to recognize the harmony among all things. When one sees an "unexpected" unity "where no one would suspect a connection" (A VI i 484–485), there is more delight and happiness. "The most confused discord fits into the order of the most exquisite harmony unexpectedly, as a painting is set off by shadow, as the harmony due to dissonances transforms the dissonances into consonance" (A VI iii 126). "Given that the whole is pleasing, it does not follow that each part is pleasing. … Only the whole is pleasing, only the whole is harmonious" (A VI iii 130). For Leibniz the beauty and goodness of the whole justifies the *apparent* ugliness and evil of some parts. In the end, the world is better because apparent disorder will "unexpectedly" reveal "the wonderful reason" behind this "greatest" of symmetries (A VI iii 122).

THEODICY. Leibniz's last extended treatment of the problem of evil restates many of the themes from the *Philosopher's Confession,* written almost forty years earlier. The *Theodicy* is a long, digressive work, devoted mainly to the topics listed in its subtitle: the goodness of God, human freedom, and the origin of evil. But the book also functions as a defense of the consistency of faith and reason. It is divided, rather arbitrarily, into three *essays,* preceded by an author's preface and a "Preliminary Dissertation on the Conformity of Faith with Reason," and succeeded by various appendices.

Much of the *Theodicy* consists of Leibniz's responses to other authors, Bayle in particular. His own metaphysical system is in the background. His idealism, for example, is barely mentioned at all. But the characteristic themes of his philosophical theology nevertheless dominate the text, and it is in the *Theodicy* that his most complete response to the problem of evil is found. That response is, at its core, the same as the response that he gave in the *Philosopher's Confession*: that this is the best, that is, the most harmonious of all possible worlds; that the evils within it are not to be judged apart from the entire series of things; that God's perfection requires that only the best possible world be created; that humans therefore cannot reasonably wish that things had been different; that happiness is to be sought through understanding the perfection of God, the creator of all things, and the perfection of all the things that God has created.

The problem of the author of sin, to which Leibniz had given only a weak response in the *Philosopher's Confession*, is in the *Theodicy* handled with much more verve and power. He distinguishes between God's antecedent and consequent will. God wills each possible thing antecedently in proportion to its perfection. But some possible things are not compossible with others, so not all God's antecedent willings can be realized. God's consequent, that is, final and decisive, will is the existence of that series of things that realizes as much perfection as possible. To this account is added an Augustinian idea of metaphysical evil as mere privation or limitation. Thus, God does not will evil at all, for God's willing is directed only toward the perfection in things, and imperfections are nothing at all, and so not even possible objects of will.

The *Theodicy* contains extensive discussion of freedom, including many objections to so-called *freedom of indifference*—the capacity to choose between alternatives that are equally advantageous (or disadvantageous). Leibniz's commitment to the principle of sufficient reason rules out any such capacity, even in the case of God—a conclusion that plays a significant role in some of the argument in his later correspondence with Clarke. He allies himself with Augustine and the Thomists in holding that everything is determined and with Aristotle in requiring as conditions of freedom only spontaneity and intelligence. The rejection of a contracausal account of freedom also reflects Lutheran doctrine, and one of the declared goals of the *Theodicy* is to provide an account of human freedom on which Catholics and Protestants can agree.

As in other writings Leibniz struggles in the *Theodicy* to give an account of contingency that avoids necessitarianism. Absolute or metaphysically necessary truths exclude any alternative; they rely on the principle of noncontradiction. This kind of necessity is incompatible with freedom, and not even God is free with respect to these truths. Thus, according to Leibniz, God was not free to create spaces with fewer or more dimensions than three, for such spaces are logically impossible. Physical and moral necessity, by contrast, resting on the principle of sufficient reason, is not incompatible with freedom. God is free in choosing to create the best possible world because there are other worlds that are possible in themselves (even though God, being perfect, would not in fact create them); rational creatures are free in the choices they make if there are other options (even though, given preceding causes, they will not in fact choose them). His compatibilist account of freedom appears here in its starkest form: Both divine and human freedom require only the bare logical possibility of some alternative course of action. God is perfectly free because perfectly rational; humans are imperfectly free because less than perfectly rational. Acting against or without reason is, for Leibniz, the paradigm case of unfreedom.

This compatibilism, even if acceptable, leaves little room for contingency, and scholars have long argued the question whether Leibniz manages to avoid the claim that everything that happens, happens necessarily. His standard answer, given many times in the *Theodicy*, is that it depends what sort of necessity is intended. Nothing happens by logical necessity except when the opposite involves a contradiction; everything happens by moral necessity, for unless this entire *series of things* were the uniquely best, God would lack a sufficient reason to create it. It is nevertheless hard to see how any other series of things is ever possible given the necessary existence and perfection of God. Here the tension between his Platonism and the voluntarism of the Christian tradition is at its greatest.

Leibniz himself seems never to have wavered from the underlying optimism of his account of *the best of all possible worlds*. He often notes that he knows no one as happy as he. He summarizes the source of his contentment in a letter to Queen Sophie Charlotte:

> But the consideration of the perfection of things, or, what is the same, of the supreme power, wisdom, and goodness of God, who does everything for the best, that is, with the greatest order, is sufficient to make all reasonable people content, and to convince them that contentment

should be greater to the extent that we are disposed to follow order or reason." (AG 192)

Leibniz's optimism, and his claim that this is the best of all possible worlds, was viciously satirized by Voltaire in *Candide*. But Voltaire's Dr. Pangloss, the representative of optimism, is a very unreliable guide to Leibniz, or even to the Leibnizianism of his disciple Wolff. Leibniz, from the *Philosopher's Confession* on, insists that the best possible world is not best in all of its parts. By the time of the *Theodicy*, he has a battery of arguments against the kinds of objections that Voltaire advances. But Voltaire's short and witty tale is a far better read than the long and, at times, tedious *Theodicy*, so it is not surprising that its *argument* is better liked.

SUBSTANCE, MATTER, AND NATURE

At the very end of his life, Leibniz explains that in order to understand the intellectual *discoveries* of others, it is often necessary "to detect the source of their invention" (G III 568). In presenting his views about God, creation, mind, activity, knowledge, and harmony, it is helpful to detect their Platonist sources. In order to understand his *discoveries* about the natural world, it will be necessary to detect the sources of his *invention*.

ARISTOTELIANISM AND MECHANISM. For most of his life Leibniz takes there to be two kinds of basic, natural entities, or substances. The first sort is a corporeal substance constituted of two *principles of nature*: one active, one passive. Corporeal substances are analogous to organisms: They are active, unified things with a material component or body and an organizing principle. The second kind of substance is variously called "mind, soul, spiritual substance," and "substantial form[s]." Although these are the active things in nature, which are tied to a material component of some sort, they are themselves also substances. Toward the end of his life, Leibniz began to call the ultimate components of nature monads. In the world of his monadology, there are only mind-like simple substances in various collections.

The Aristotelian philosophy offered the raw materials for Leibniz's account of substance; the new mechanical philosophy constituted the basis for his physics. Although he transformed those philosophies to suit his own philosophical and theological needs, he remained wedded to (what he considered to be) Aristotle's basic insights about the self-sufficiency of substances and to the mechanists' commitment to explain corporeal phenomena in terms of matter and motion.

For most Aristotelian philosophers, natural objects are constituted of two principles, matter and form, and natural events are explained in terms of the actualization of the potency of these two principles. When Leibniz began constructing his own philosophy in the mid-1660s, there was a new explanatory model available, one that had greatly diminished the power of the scholastic model. According to the mechanical philosophy (as it came to be called), nature is composed of matter—whether the extended stuff (*res extensa*) of Descartes, the atoms of Gassendi, or one of the many less popular accounts of corporeity—whose actions and movements cause and explain all the phenomena of nature. For the mechanist all physical phenomena are to be explained in terms of some kind of matter and motion. Although these thinkers disagreed about how to define the material component in nature, they all took it to be void of substantial forms.

Despite the genuine innovation of the new mechanical philosophy, it failed to solve adequately a number of important theological and metaphysical problems. By the middle of the seventeenth century, especially in the Protestant areas of northern Europe, a number of conciliators took it upon themselves to *reform* the Aristotelian philosophy rather than abandon it. Different reformers had different recipes for mixing the old with the new, but they all combined some part of the mechanical physics with Aristotelian metaphysics. Each claimed that, when properly understood, the Aristotelian philosophy could comfortably accommodate mechanical philosophy. Like these reformers, Leibniz also recognized very early on that the Aristotelian theory of substance could easily accommodate the new mechanical physics and thereby explain the phenomena.

The Aristotelian philosophy appealed to the young Leibniz for several reasons. At the heart of the Platonized Aristotelianism that his mentor, Jakob Thomasius, bequeathed to him stands the idea that nature is constituted of individual corporeal substances whose substantial forms act to compose a divinely arranged harmony. From the beginning of his philosophical career, Leibniz embraced the assumption that everything in the world acts to instantiate the good. Unlike those of his contemporaries who rejected final causation, he embraced the Aristotelian idea that nature moves toward the good. For Leibniz, an Aristotelian account of substance formed a secure foundation for such a rational, harmonious, and good world although it needed to be *reformed* to fit mechanical explanations in physics. He committed himself to the Aristotelian and mechanical philosophies as a youth and maintained this commitment until his death.

In the *Monadology* he writes: "Souls act according to the laws of final causes. … Bodies act according to the laws of efficient causes or of motions. And these two kingdoms, that of efficient causes and that of final causes, are in harmony with each other" (§79).

Leibniz had excellent metaphysical reasons to accept a major part of the Aristotelian philosophy. But he had other incentives as well. From the perspective of war-ravaged Germany, Aristotelianism must have seemed to Leibniz the safest bet as a philosophy of religious reconciliation. The doctrinal declarations of contemporary Catholics were framed in Aristotelian terms while Aristotelianism survived in Lutheran cities such as Leipzig. Aristotelian notions of substance thus presented themselves as ideal both for understanding the divinely arranged harmony in the world and for working toward religious and political harmony within it.

SUBSTANCE, SELF-SUFFICIENCY, AND THE REFORMATION OF THE MECHANICAL PHILOSOPHY. The young Leibniz intended to transform the Aristotelian notion of substance so that it would accommodate mechanical physics. For Leibniz, the mechanical physics of philosophers such as Descartes, Hobbes, Gassendi, and Galileo reduces to the following claims: There is some sort of matter or extended stuff (*res extensa*), which is (somehow) moved and whose arrangements both cause and explain the corporeal features of individual bodies; therefore, a body is organized *res extensa*, and all corporeal features are reducible to the arrangements of such extended stuff. Leibniz was *never* satisfied with the metaphysical foundations offered by leading proponents of the mechanical physics; the physical explanations of particular phenomena seemed adequate, but the metaphysical underpinnings of those explanations did not.

Leibniz's most fundamental assumption about the natural world is that it is composed of substances, each of which has its own source of activity by means of which it is constituted as a self-sufficient, unified thing. The material stuff of the mechanical philosophers did not have its own internal source of activity and so was neither self-sufficient nor properly unified; it therefore could not by itself constitute genuine substances. In his earliest comments about substances, Leibniz explains that because the corporeal substance of the mechanists "is not self-sufficient … an incorporeal principle must be added" (A VI i 490: L 110). This incorporeal principle is a substantial form or mind that organizes the matter and thereby makes it into a unified, self-sufficient thing. He corrects the mistakes of the mechanists by making substance active, allowing it to be both causally and explanatorily complete. He demotes the matter of mechanical physics to the status of the passive principle in substance and insists that the active mind or substantial form organizes the passive principle so as to make a unity with it.

The result is an individual corporeal substance that can act as the cause and explanation of its own (at least) basic features. Although the details of his views about substance will continue to evolve over the course of his long philosophical career (e.g., he comes to conceive the passive principle as itself constituted of mind-like substances and eventually prefers to construct the world entirely out of monads), he never wavers from his commitment to the causal and explanatory autonomy of the fundamental entities of nature. It is this robust self-sufficiency that is his most profound debt to the metaphysics of Aristotle. And it is this robust self-sufficiency that inspired many of the core doctrines of his mature thought.

THE METAPHYSICS OF SUBSTANCE BEFORE 1680

For much of the twentieth century, scholars maintained that Leibniz developed his theory of substance in the 1680s. Except for a few scattered works—mostly those in logic and physics—his earlier texts were either neglected or dismissed as juvenilia. However, close attention to writings from the 1660s and 1670s reveals that Leibniz developed his theory of substance much earlier. In this section we consider the most important of the early texts.

ORIGINAL ASSUMPTIONS ABOUT SUBSTANCE, ACTIVITY, AND SELF-SUFFICIENCY. During the mid-1660s, Leibniz worked on a number of related projects in law, logic, and theology. Encouraged by the distinguished German statesmen Boineburg, he began composition of the *Catholic Demonstrations* in 1668. The work, as Leibniz conceived it then, was to consist of a series of philosophical prolegomena and four parts. The prolegomena were to contain the *elements of philosophy*, that is, the *first principles* of metaphysics, logic, mathematics, physics, and practical philosophy, while the four parts were to be demonstrations of the existence of God, the immortality of the soul, the Christian mysteries (e.g., the Eucharist), and the authority of the church and scripture. The work was designed to offer a metaphysics that would cohere with Catholic and Lutheran doctrine and thereby effect a reconciliation between the two churches. But another sort of reconciliation is promoted within the work, for when Leibniz began the *Catholic Demonstrations*, he was committed to a version of Aristotelian philosophy as he interpreted it and also to a mechanical account of the phenomena of nature.

The theological writings indicate exactly how his reconciliation of these two philosophies evolved in his attempt to explain the theological doctrines of the Eucharist, the immortality of the soul, and so on. He takes the Aristotelian notion of substantial form as the active principle of nature and combines it with the mechanical notion of passive extended stuff as the passive principle to create a coherent *reformed* Aristotelianism. At work in these theological essays are a number of philosophical assumptions. The most important of these are as follows (except for the Principle of Sufficient Reason, the names are not his):

- The *principle of substantial activity* assumes that a being is a substance if and only if it subsists per se, and a being subsists per se if and only if it has a principle of activity within its own nature.

- The *principle of sufficient reason* assumes that there is a complete or sufficient reason for everything.

- A *complete reason* for a state or feature *f*: (1) constitutes the necessary and sufficient condition for *f*; (2) is perspicuous in that, in those cases where one can understand it, one sees exactly why *f* as opposed to some other state of affairs came about; (3) is such that in those cases when a full account of it can be given, that account constitutes a complete explanation of *f*; and (4) does not require a reason of the same type.

- The *logical assumption* claims that, for any state or feature *f*, the logically necessary and sufficient conditions of *f* exist and in theory can be articulated.

- The *intelligibility assumption* claims that those conditions are in theory intelligible.

- The *substantial nature assumption* claims that every substance has a nature that contains the set of necessary and sufficient conditions or the complete reason for those features that strictly belong to it, and moreover, those conditions are in theory intelligible.

The precise status of these assumptions in the *Catholic Demonstrations* and related early texts is unclear. They constitute the underlying principles of Leibniz's discussions during this period. Although in the texts of 1668–1671 they may have the status of working hypotheses, they continue to inform and direct his thinking about metaphysical matters for years to come. Some of his most characteristic doctrines directly develop from these assumptions.

SUBSTANTIAL FORMS AND ACTIVITY. While developing his account of substances as the fundamental entities of nature in 1668–1671, Leibniz was also working on the *Elements of Natural Law*. As his views about universal harmony evolved, he integrated his Platonist assumptions about activity, emanation, and unity into the Aristotelian and mechanical assumptions about self-sufficiency, substantial forms, and matter. He assumes that substantial forms are divine-like and possess the kind of metaphysical powers described by Ficino. The idea here is that God continually emanates the divine essence to each individual mind and furnishes each mind with its own source of activity thereby generating unity and self-sufficiency. He suggests that each active thing acts constantly according to a *reason* given it by God: "Just as God thinks things … because they follow from his nature, so does Mind" (A VI ii 287–288). By being Godlike the active principles or substantial forms possess divine-like features, such as unity and self-sufficiency. They also act according to a divinely arranged *reason* (A VI i 534).

The principle of substantial activity reveals the close relation between substancehood and activity: Anything that possesses its own source of activity will be self-sufficient and hence substantial. In Paris, Leibniz develops this idea so that mind-like, active things are indestructible and the source of the individuality, unity, and identity of the corporeal substances of the world. No active creature is ever without a body or passive principle; only divine mind is "devoid of body" (A VI iii 100). God "arranged all things from the beginning" (A VI iii 477: Pk 31) so as to give each created substance a *rule* or set of instructions by means of which it acts (VI iii 483: Pk 39). As he summarizes his position:

> There are certainly many and important things to be said … about the principle of activity or what the scholastics called substantial form, from which a great light is thrown on Natural Theology and … the mysteries of faith. The result is that not only souls but all substances can be said to exist in a place only through the operation of their active principle, that souls can be destroyed by no power of body; and that every power of acting exists from the highest mind whose will is the final reason for all things, the cause being universal harmony; that God as creator can unite the body to the soul, and that in fact, every finite soul is embodied, even the angels are not excepted. (A VI iii 158)

In the pre-Paris period, minds are considered constantly active and therefore self-sufficient, unified things. In *On the Greatest of Things*, written during his final year in Paris, Leibniz develops and expands on the relations between activity, self-sufficiency, unity, and divisibility: "whatever acts cannot be destroyed" naturally, and yet "whatever is divided is destroyed" (A VI iii 392–393: Pk 45–47). Mind or substantial form acts as the "cement" in a corporeal substance and thereby guarantees that its passive principle will not be divided (A VI iii 474: Pk 27). Consistent with the theory of corporeal substance developed earlier, the mind-like substantial form acts constantly through its passive principle to create a single "unsplittable" thing, which Leibniz sometimes calls an "atom" (A VI iii 393: Pk 47). This atom or unified thing is a corporeal substance constituted of an active and a passive principle. Consistent with the substantial nature assumption, the nature of the substance acts as the necessary and sufficient condition of its features. In 1676, then, the activity of mind individuates the substance, unifies it, and makes it eternal. Throughout a substance's eternal existence, it is its active principle that will organize its passive principle so as to constitute its eternally self-sufficient nature.

In these early years the persistence of the substantial nature through various changes is especially important to Leibniz because of his concern for developing a metaphysics consistent with Christian doctrine. The doctrine of resurrection, for example, gives rise to the question: How can it be the same human substance that persists through the radical changes in a human life, then dies, and then is resurrected? He explains that the mind "is firmly planted in a flower of substance [that] subsists perpetually in all changes" and that can be "diffused" through a greater or less expanse of the original body (A VI iii 478–479: Pk 33). The mind-like principle of activity acts as the *cement* of the substance and forms the unity that persists through all substantial changes, including even bodily death and resurrection. In a letter to Johann Friedrich of 1671, he explains that in the same way that "God is diffused through everything," so mind is diffused through its body; just as the activities of God do not diminish the divine essence, so too the mind acts on its body "without being diminished" (II i 113).

It is clear from these texts of 1670–1676 that Leibniz believes he has hit upon an account of substance that comfortably accommodates the severe metaphysical demands of Christian doctrine, the physical explanations of the mechanists, and the Aristotelian commitment to the causal completeness and self-sufficiency of substance.

Although the details of his position are in flux and will shift over time, the basic structure of this account of substance will not vary until the development of the world of the monadology. For Leibniz, a corporeal substance is a self-sufficient and unified thing that results from a substantial form activating and organizing its passive principle. The substantial form acts constantly on its passive principle by *a set of instructions* given it by God. The passive principle is the substantial form's *instrument of acting*. The unity is what results from the constant activity of the active principle on the passive one, thereby forming an organized unified thing.

MATTER, EXTENSION, AND PASSIVITY. Within weeks of entering the University of Leipzig, at the age of fourteen, Leibniz had a major philosophical insight. He recalls walking in some woods near his home and "deliberating whether I should keep the substantial forms" or convert to mechanism. In the end he decided to accept the physical explanations of the mechanical philosophers as opposed to those of the scholastics and thereby "to apply" himself to mathematics (G III 606: L 655). The young Leibniz thus assumes that the passive principle in corporeal substances is material, like the *res extensa* of Descartes. For the next few years he maintains that the active principle or substantial form takes this passive extended stuff, organizes it into an individual body, and thereby creates a unified thing or corporeal substance.

In the theological essays of 1668–1671, he conceives the union between the active and passive principles as involving constant activity, where the mind-like substantial form cannot "act outside itself" except through its passive principle (A VI i 533–534). The unity here is analogous to that in organisms in the sense that if the activity involved in maintaining an organic unity stops, so does the unity. When the maintenance of the organization ceases (e.g., the heart stops, the liver no longer functions), the unity of the substantial form and matter does so as well (e.g., the entity dies, the formerly organized body becomes a heap of decaying flesh). The nature of organic unities also helps us to understand what he means when he says that the active principle cannot act outside itself except through the passive: In order to act externally, the source or cause of the organization has to act through the passive principle that it organizes.

In the 1670s Leibniz became dissatisfied with this account of passivity. There were several problems. First, the mechanical account of body could not easily accommodate important theological doctrines, such as the Eucharist and resurrection of the body. According to the

Lutheran account of the *mystery* of the Eucharist, the body of Christ and the body of the bread exist side by side. However, if the body of Christ is a collection of extended stuff, it is unclear how it can be distinct from and coextensive with the extended stuff that constitutes the matter of the bread. Leibiniz argues: "For if body and space are one and the same, how can we avoid the consequence that in different spaces or places there must be different bodies" (A VI iii 157–158). He concludes that the views of the mechanists, who believe that *the essence of body consists in extension*, are therefore incompatible with the miracle of the Eucharist. He also argues that since, according to Descartes and other mechanists, each body is constituted of extended stuff and since all extended stuff is essentially the same, it becomes enormously difficult to give any particular body (say, Christ's body) a stable identity. Leibniz concludes: "One cannot say…why it is called the body of Christ rather than bread, to which it is very similar" (A II i 170). Nor, to take the case of another Christian doctrine, can one say how to identify and individuate bodies at the time of the resurrection.

Another problem facing Leibniz's early account of the passive principle in corporeal substance is less overtly theological. According to the principle of plenitude as he interpreted the ancient doctrine, the world is as full of diverse being as possible. But according to the version of Platonism that Leibniz learned as a university student, matter is uniform, divisible, unreal stuff. In the *Phaedo*, Plato describes it as "as unintelligible, soluble and never consistently the same" (80e). Matter lacks all unity and activity; it contributes nothing positive to the world. It follows from these Platonist assumptions that the world would be made better by filling it with mind-like unified things and stripping it entirely of extended passive matter.

There has been much disagreement among scholars about when Leibniz does finally strip the world of extended stuff. Once we take seriously Leibniz's interest in Platonism and his concern to solve the theological problems posed by doctrines such as the Eucharist and resurrection of the body, it seems relatively clear that he abandons extended stuff while still in Paris although he remains undecided about what exactly to put in its place. In the Paris texts he asks as many questions as he answers: "Since mind is something that has a certain relation to some portion of matter, it must be stated why it extends itself to this portion and not to all adjacent portions; or why it is that some body, and not every body, belongs to it in the same way" (A VI iii 392: Pk 45). In 1676 he did

not have consistent answers to these questions; the texts are unclear about the precise nature of the passive principle in substances. However, one of the hypotheses that he entertained is that bodies are themselves unextended collections of mind-like substances whose only actions are perceptual states.

BODY AND FORCE. The young Leibniz embraced mechanical physics, according to which the features of bodies are to be explained in terms of the broadly geometrical properties of their parts—whether these are tiny indivisible atoms or infinitely divisible stuff—whose configurations shift and change through motion and whose motion changes through collision. When he published his *New Physical Hypothesis* and *Theory of Abstract Motion* in 1671, he agreed with the standard mechanical account of collision as the only means by which bodies naturally change motion. His *abstract* account of motion is offered in terms of the Hobbesian notion of conatus, defined here as "an indivisible, nonextended part of motion" and as "the beginning and end of motion" (A VI ii 264–265: L 139–140). In 1671 he agreed with Descartes that "all power in bodies depends on speed." If two bodies with unequal speeds collide, they will move together after the collision in the direction of the faster body with a speed that is the difference between the two (A VI ii 228). By the time he met Spinoza in the autumn of 1676, he had begun to question features of this mechanical account, and in particular, the law of the conservation of motion proposed by Descartes.

In the winter of 1677–1678, Leibniz takes some observations made by Huygens about impact and transforms them into a notion central to his thought. He decides that force or power of action must be conserved in collision between bodies rather than mere speed. By January 1678 he has hit upon the proper account of this force: mv^2 (mass times velocity squared). Given the importance of this insight, it is odd that he does not publish any part of his findings until 1686, and even then, in his *Brief Demonstration*, he merely criticizes Descartes's conservation principle and ONLY hints at his own account. Over the next few years, he will work out the details of his dynamics, especially in response to Newton's *Principia Mathematica* (1687).

Leibniz's discovery of mv^2 was enormously important and radically changed his account of the physical world. As he explains in the *Specimen of Dynamics* (1695), he was forced to recognize that in physics, purely geometrical notions were inadequate: "We must add to material mass a certain superior and so to speak formal principle.

Whether we call this principle form or entelechy or force does not matter so long as we remember that it can only be explained through the notion of force" (GM VI 241: AG 124–135). He notes the easy fit between an Aristotelian approach to substance (whose principle of activity is often described as *form or entelechy*) and the new notion of force. Leibniz had hit upon the basic features of his Aristotelian account of substance in the late 1660s. With the development of his dynamics, all he had to do was to redescribe the active principle in nature. The mind-like substantial forms in nature were now responsible for more than just the activity of creatures; they were also responsible for their force.

THE PRINCIPLE OF SUFFICIENT REASON. Leibniz is well known for his commitment to the principle of sufficient reason, which he often calls his *great principle*. As early as 1668 he assumes that God always has a reason for *choosing* one state of affairs rather than another and that this reason must be sufficient. In 1671 he calls the principle a *first* truth; and by way of demonstration, he adds: "Everything that is has all its requisites" since a state of affairs will not exist unless all its requisites "are given. … Consequently, everything that is has a sufficient reason" (A VI ii 483). Later in his career he articulates the principle in various ways, often in terms consistent with his account of truth. In the *Monadology*, for example, he presents it as the principle "by virtue of which we consider that we can find no true or existent fact, no true assertion, without there being a sufficient reason why it is thus and not otherwise, although most of the time these reasons cannot be known to us" (§32).

Leibniz's early commitment to the principle is matched by his early application of the principle to God as the sufficient reason of the world and to the natures of substances as the sufficient reason for their features. According to the substantial nature assumption, every substance has a nature that contains the set of necessary and sufficient conditions or the complete reason for its features. But a question arises about which features are covered here. If the nature of a substance is so complete as to contain the sufficient reason for all the features of the substance, then the principle of sufficient reason and the substantial nature assumption together bring us to the brink of two of his more startling metaphysical claims. The first is phenomenalism; the second preestablished harmony.

PREESTABLISHED HARMONY AND PHENOMENALISM. Although Leibniz does not use the term *preestablished harmony* until the 1690s (in the 1680s he calls it the

theory of *concomitance*), there is significant evidence that he adopted its constitutive tenets in the 1670s and perhaps as early as 1671. The doctrine of preestablished harmony holds that each substance acts out of its own nature (spontaneity), that no substance causally interacts with any other substance (world apartness), and yet that each substance in the world parallels the activities of all the other substances perfectly (parallelism). The theory is closely related to another component of his mature philosophy: phenomenalism. The phenomenalism of the mature Leibniz, what is sometimes called *well-founded phenomenalism*, includes at least the following two claims: Bodies are phenomenal objects and so our perceptions of them arise from our own internal nature; and our perceptions nonetheless correspond to (parallel) the activities of real (unextended and mind-like) substances and in that sense are *well founded*.

The *New System* of 1695 summarizes the doctrines: "We must say that God originally created the soul (and any other real unity) in such a way that everything must arise for it from its own depths, through a perfect *spontaneity* relative to itself, and yet with a perfect *conformity* relative to external things." Since our perceptions are "internal perceptions in the soul itself" they "must arise because of its own original constitution," which is "given to the soul from its creation," and "constitutes its individual character. … This is what makes every substance represent the whole universe" from its own point of view, and "makes the perceptions or expressions of external things occur in the soul at a given time, in virtue of its own laws, as if in a world apart, and as if there existed only God and itself." In the perfectly harmonious world chosen by God, "there will be a perfect agreement among all these substances, producing the same effect that would be noticed if they communicated" (G IV 484-85: AG 143-44).

There is much, though scattered, evidence in the texts of the 1670s that Leibniz adopted most of the claims constitutive of phenomenalism and preestablished harmony early on. Neither preestablished harmony nor phenomenalism came to him suddenly. Rather, their core claims emerged gradually out of his attempts to solve the theological and philosophical problems that most concerned him. As he reflected on problems in ethics, law, theology, physics, and metaphysics, he developed his account of universal harmony and substance in an attempt to solve those problems. Preestablished harmony and phenomenalism resulted from the convergence of these solutions. These elaborate metaphysical doctrines were the most elegant way to solve a diverse group of difficult problems, to capture the rationality and goodness of God, and to reconcile ancient and modern ideas.

Preestablished harmony may be seen to result from the combination of universal harmony, the self-sufficiency of substances, and the mirroring of substances. According to universal harmony, God emanates the divine essence to every creature. The unity of the world is due to the fact that all creatures express the same thing: its multiplicity to the fact that each creature expresses the divine essence in a different way. The substantial nature assumption may be taken to entail that the complete reason for all the features of a substance is contained in its nature, in which case the complete reason for its perceptual states is contained there as well. The conjunction of the substantial nature assumption and universal harmony suggests spontaneity: For each substance, the manner of its expression of the divine essence will be contained *in its nature*. Further, if we assume that the substantial nature of a substance contains the necessary and sufficient conditions for each and every feature of it, then it seems to follow that the cause of every feature of the substance is *contained* in its nature, which is consistent with world apartness and the idea that there is no causal interaction among substances.

Finally, the theory that each substance mirrors all the others resembles the tenet of parallelism. Indeed, the parallelism of well-founded phenomenalism and preestablished harmony seems to be an extension of the Platonist notion of sympathy: Each substance, in its manifestation of the divine essence, is in perfect sympathy—for Leibniz, in perfect coordination—with every other. The doctrine of marks and traces is itself an elaboration of this notion of sympathy; it is also closely related to the idea that each substance is a world apart. Preestablished harmony is fundamentally emanation and sympathy perfectly organized in the self-sufficient substantial natures of the created world.

In the *Discourse* Leibniz implies that preestablished harmony is the blending of just these assumptions, and he acknowledges its close relation to his phenomenalism: "It is very evident that created substances depend upon God" who "produces them continually by emanation." In order to manifest divine "glory," God creates various substances to "express the universe." It follows from this account of God's relation to the world that "each substance is like a world apart, independent of all other things, except for God" from "whom all individuals emanate continually." By acting on us, God arranges things so that "all our phenomena, that is, all the things that can ever happen to us, are only consequences of our

being" such that these phenomena are "in conformity with the world which is in us." It follows that "the perceptions or expressions of all substances mutually correspond" although each expression differs from every other. Finally, "if I were capable of considering distinctly everything that happens or appears to me at this time, I could see in it everything that will ever happen or appear to me" (A VI iv [B] 1549-51: §14).

Whether or not Leibniz commits himself to phenomenalism in the 1670s, he surely toys with the position. During his Paris period he often reduces the existence of bodies to the consistency of perceptions and concludes: "It does not follow that there exists anything but perception, and the cause of this perception and its consistency." The cause of perception is such that: "a reason can be given for everything and everything can be predicted" (A VI iii 511: Pk 63-65). From the perspective of conscious beings, in order to explain existence, it is unnecessary to resort to outside bodies; rather, we can reduce all existence to the consistency of perceptions, where the latter includes both the consistency of the perceptions within a mind and the coordination among minds: "We sense or perceive that we exist; when we say that bodies exist, we mean that there exist certain consistent perceptions, having a particular constant cause" (A VI iii 512: Pk 67).

In these and related texts of 1676, Leibniz seems to extend the substantial nature assumption to encompass all the features of substances, including their perceptual states. The suggestion is that God gives each substance a set of instructions or *rule* that makes each substantial nature the sufficient cause of all its features, including its perceptions. Thus, consistent with spontaneity and world-apartness, all the features of a substance are caused by its nature and there is no causal interaction among substances. Consistent with parallelism, "existence consists in" the coordinated perceiving of objects so that "several people perceive the same." It is "not necessary either that we act on them or that they act on us, but only that we perceive with such conformity" (VI iii 511: Pk 63). As a "perfect mind" God "arranged all things from the beginning" so as to make them "most harmonious" (A VI iii 474–476: Pk 25–29). For Leibniz in these texts of 1676, a major theme in this harmony is God's coordination of the perceptions among minds. Indeed: "Without sentient beings, nothing would exist. Without one primary sentient being, which is the same as the cause of all things, nothing would be perceived" (A VI iii 588: Pk 113). As he writes to Malebranche in 1679, "I have always been convinced ... that strictly speaking bodies do not act on us" (A II i 472-73: L 210).

THE METAPHYSICS OF SUBSTANCE, SECOND STAGE

Written during a snow storm in the Harz mountains in 1686, the *Discourse on Metaphysics* is the first general account of Leibniz's mature metaphysics. He sent a synopsis to Arnauld and thereby began the well-known correspondence between these two great seventeenth-century thinkers. Although not published during his lifetime, the *Discourse* and the correspondence with Arnauld, together with the terse summary of metaphysics contained in *First Truths*, have been favorites of twentieth-century Leibniz scholars. These texts have received a large amount scholarly attention, some of which is excellent. But we now know that many of their most important doctrines developed years earlier. For the most part, the *Discourse* and *First Truths* are summaries of doctrines extant in the 1670s, and what is new in them develops neatly from earlier views.

SUBSTANCES, SUBJECTS, AND TRUTH. In 1900 Bertrand Russell published a book in which he argued that Leibniz's metaphysics developed from his logic and theory of truth. For much of the twentieth century, scholars agreed with Russell that the theory of truth offers the key to Leibniz's philosophy and that the theory of substance developed out of that theory. With access to more of his writings and through attention to the sources of his ideas, it is clear that the core of his metaphysics—the account of substance and the theory of universal harmony—developed several years before the theory of truth. So, though the mature Leibniz sometimes puts the theory of truth front and center, it developed out of his views about the self-sufficiency, intelligibility, and explanatory completeness of substances; it was a consequence of those other views, not their source.

In 1676 Leibniz begins to emphasize subjects as the bearers of features. This is an important clarification of claims contained in the core metaphysics and constitutes a step toward the development of his conception of truth. One of his basic, Aristotelian assumptions is that substances are causally and explanatorily self-sufficient (at least with regard to their primary features). Another is that the relation between a feature and the substance to which it belongs is both logical and intelligible. These logical and intelligibility assumptions imply, for any feature of a substance, that the substance contains the logically necessary and sufficient conditions for that feature,

that these conditions are in theory intelligible, and therefore that the truth of the attribution of the feature to the substance is in theory discoverable in the nature of that substance. When he extends the substantial nature assumption to cover all features, he commits himself to a truth-conferring relation between a substance and its features; a feature is truly predicated of a substance if and only if the nature of the substance contains the complete reason of that feature.

As Leibniz began to refine his views about the relation between the attributes of God and their instantiation in the world in the spring of 1676, he took his first steps toward the development of the idea that truth is a matter of relations among concepts. In *On the Greatest of Things*, he notes the metaphysical significance of substances as subjects or bearers of predicates and of truth as grounded in the relation between substances and their states: "It is a wonderful fact that a subject is different from forms or attributes. This is necessary because nothing can be said about forms on account of their simplicity; therefore, there would be no true propositions unless forms were united to a subject" (A VI iii 514: Pk 69). Once he has hit upon the idea that a substance is a subject in which a modification of the divine attributes has been placed, and once he sees truth in terms of the relation between a subject and such attributes, the materials are in place for the concept containment theory of truth. That there is a close connection between his metaphysical views about self-sufficiency and his theory of truth is clear. in a text of 1676 we find one of his first attributions of completeness to substance: "A substance or complete Being is for me that which alone involves all things, or for the perfect understanding of which, no other thing needs to be understood" (A VI iii 400: Pk 109).

By the spring of 1676, the metaphysical underpinnings of the theory of truth are in place, including the claim that there is a hierarchy of subjects. First there is God, who is the subject of all simple attributes; then there are creatures, each of which is the subject of a partial expression of those attributes. According to Leibniz: "The essence of God consists in the fact that he is the subject of all compatible attributes" or forms while it is the nature of created "subjects" to be "conceived through forms" (A VI iii 514: Pk 69–71). Before creation the Supreme Being conceives the fully articulated essence for each individual substance. It follows that all true statements about the active things in the world will be statements about a substance as a subject and its relation to one of the predicates contained in its complete concept. In such a world all basic truths about the created world involve the inclusion of a predicate in the concept of a subject. For Leibniz, all the truths about an individual substance are contained in its nature.

Against this metaphysical background, it is unsurprising that, when Leibniz began working on logical matters in his early years in Hanover, he concluded that all truths were a matter of concept containment. For Leibniz, all there is in the world are divine attributes and their combinations. In a striking passage of 1676, he acknowledges this point: "There is the same variety in any kind of world, and this is nothing other than the same essence related in various ways, as if you were to look at the same town from various places, or, if you relate the essence of the number 6 to the number 3, it will be 3x2 or 3+3, but if you relate it to the number 4 it will be 6/4=3/2, or 6=4x3/2" (A VI iii 523: Pk 83). In a world in which everything is constituted of combinations of divine attributes, it is not difficult to think of truth in terms of concept containment.

In April 1679 Leibniz produced a series of papers titled *On the Universal Calculus* that treat a number of questions related to formal validity and in which he first proposes a concept containment account of truth. Underlying these discussions is the idea that an affirmative categorical proposition is true just in case the concept of its predicate is contained in the concept of its subject. He takes true propositions to signify "nothing other than some connection between predicate and subject" in the sense that "the predicate is said to be in the subject, or contained in the subject" (A VI iv [A] 197: L 236). In the complexities of the logical papers of the late 1670s, we can discern the development of the fascinating view that a theory of truth for categorical affirmative propositions will settle the truth conditions for all propositions.

SUBJECTS AND TRUTH IN THE *DISCOURSE ON METAPHYSICS*.

The *Discourse* of 1686 is also governed by the series of assumptions found in the early works about activity, self-sufficiency, identity, difference, and the nature of substance although some of the terminology has changed. The most original argument in the text concerns what scholars often call the *logical notion* of substance. This account is introduced in one of the most famous paragraphs in Leibniz's writings. He begins §8 of the *Discourse* with a summary: "To distinguish the actions of God from those of creatures we explain the notion of an individual substance." He then makes two new observations. First, he notes that "it is evident that all true predication has some basis in the nature of things and that, when a proposition is not an identity, that is, when

the predicate is not explicitly contained in the subject, it must be contained in it virtually." Second, he suggests that from this account of truth it follows that "it is the nature of an individual substance or a complete being ... to have a notion so complete that it is sufficient to contain and to allow us to deduce from it all the predicates of the subject to which this notion is attributed" (A VI iv [B] 1539–1540). That is, an individual substance has a complete concept that contains all the predicates that can truly be predicated of it.

From these observations about substance Leibniz drew support for his doctrine of marks and traces: There must be something within each substance in virtue of which every predicate is presently true of it and which also provides the basis for the deduction of all the predicates that will ever be true of it, that is, traces of all the features that it has possessed in the past and marks of all those that it will possess in the future. He then begins § 9 of the *Discourse* by noting that "from this" account of substance follow "several notable paradoxes." Among others he lists the indestructibility of substances and the identity of indiscernibles (A VI iv [B] 1541-42).

SUBJECTS AND TRUTH IN *FIRST TRUTHS*.

Roughly four years after the *Discourse*, Leibniz wrote a brief essay, usually titled *First Truths*, in which he presents many of his core ideas in terse logical fashion. Although we now know that *First Truths* was written either during or soon after his year-long stay in Italy (A VI iv [B] 1643), scholars in the early part of the twentieth century assigned the text an earlier date (around 1686), and this encouraged the belief that his metaphysics developed out of his theory of truth rather than the other way round. But even if the metaphysics of substance came first, it is nonetheless significant that he came to see the theory of truth as so fundamental.

In *First Truths* Leibniz begins with the account of truth, explaining that in true propositions, the predicate is "always in the subject." This *inclusion* means that all true propositions are identities, some of which are implicit and others explicit. That is, for some identities (for example, *A* is *AB*), the inclusion in the subject is explicit; for others (for example, Alexander defeated Darius) it is implicit, and a more thorough analysis of the concept *Alexander* is required. He goes on to claim that "a wonderful secret" about the difference between necessity and contingency lies hidden here. He believes that contingency is a matter of implicit inclusion; necessity a matter of explicit inclusion. All truths are a priori in the sense that the concept of the predicate is contained in the concept of the subject. But some of these truths are more explicit than others. Those that are not explicit are contingent. After presenting his theory of truth, he claims first that the principle of sufficient reason *directly follows* from it (A VI iv [B] 1645: AG 31). Having given an account of that principle, he runs through all the major tenets of his metaphysics as though they follow from these considerations. Consistent with the substantial nature assumption, he insists: "No created substance exerts a metaphysical action or influx on any other" because "what we call causes are only concurrent requisites" (VI iv [B] 1647: AG 33).

Leibniz's claim that all true predication involves the containment of the predicate in the subject threatens to collapse the distinction between necessary and contingent truths. His stock response to this threat was to distinguish, as in the *Discourse*, between explicit and virtual containment or, as in *First Truths*, between explicit and implicit inclusion. But many critics (including Arnauld) have not been convinced. What does it mean to say that a predicate is contained in a subject virtually or implicitly rather than explicitly? His principal answer to this question, probably developed in the late 1680s in part as a reaction to Arnauld's objections, relies upon a distinction between finite and infinite analysis. Necessary truths are those where the containment of the predicate in the subject is revealed after only finitely many steps of conceptual analysis; a corresponding analysis in the case of a contingent truth would require infinitely many steps and cannot be completed by any finite mind. Only God can see to the end of an infinite analysis. Though some scholars have suggested that this infinite-analysis account of contingency was later abandoned by him, it is to be found in the *Theodicy* (1710) and also in a letter to Louis Bourguet (1678–1742) written in the last year of his life.

Infinite analysis, though it provided Leibniz with a way of distinguishing necessary and contingent truths, raised difficulties for his project of developing the universal characteristic: If contingent truths required an infinite analysis to show that a predicate is contained in the concept of its subject, then even if conceptual connections could be represented numerically, the calculations required to demonstrate them could not be carried out, at least not by any finite mind. He seems largely to have given up on the project after 1690. In the *Monadology* he makes the distinction this way:

There are also two kinds of *truths*, those of *reasoning* and those of *fact*. The truths of reasoning are necessary and their opposite is impossible; the truths of fact are contingent, and their oppo-

site is possible. When a truth is necessary, its reason can be found by analysis, resolving it into simpler ideas and simpler truths until we reach the primitives." (§33)

First Truths derives another typical Leibnizian doctrine, that there are no purely relational properties, from the concept-containment account of truth: "*There are not purely extrinsic denominations.* ... For it is necessary that the notion of the subject denominated contain the notion of the predicate. And consequently, whenever the denomination of a thing is changed, there must be a variation in the thing itself." Here the metaphysical presuppositions that lie behind the notion of substance as self-sufficient extend, through the theory that truth consists in conceptual containment, to cover all predications whatsoever. Another Leibnizian doctrine follows immediately: "Every individual substance contains in its perfect notion the entire universe and everything that exists in it, past, present, and future. For there is no thing on which one cannot impose some true denomination from another thing, at the very least a denomination of comparison and relation." It is not surprising that presented with this text, Russell was inclined to see the theory of truth as the heart of Leibniz's mature philosophy. But even in that text, he remarks of the claim that there are no purely relational properties that: "I have shown the same thing in many other ways, all in harmony with one another" (VI iv [B] 1646: AG 32–33).

UNITY AND AGGREGATES. For Leibniz, one of the main goals of the *Discourse* and related texts is to tempt philosophers such as Arnauld away from Cartesianism and toward the metaphysics of (what he will soon call) preestablished harmony. It is not surprising, therefore, that he is keen to note the various weaknesses of the Cartesian account of corporeal substance. As a means to this goal, he is concerned to show that something whose essence consists merely of *res extensa* is inadequate as a substance. He develops an argument for his account of corporeal substances that has roots in his early views and that highlights a weakness in the Cartesian account of corporeal substance.

Leibniz's early assumption, captured in the principle of substantial activity, is that anything substantial will have its own principle of activity. He also believes that activity alone can generate self-sufficiency and unity. In 1676 he begins to connect self-sufficiency and completeness. He distinguishes substances or "complete things" from bodies or things "with figures." In order to have a "perfect understanding" of a substance, one must only understand the substance or "complete being" itself. But a "figure is not of this kind, for in order to understand from what a figure of such and such a kind has arisen, there must be a recourse to motion. Each complete being can be produced in only one way: that figures can be produced in various ways is enough to indicate that they are not complete beings" (A VI iii 400: Pk 115). In the 1680s he stresses that there will be something real in extension only if there are self-sufficient, unified things. He also begins to describe bodies as aggregates or collections of substances and to distinguish them from a real, single substance. He summarizes the point in 1690: "A BODY [*sic*] is not a substance but an aggregate of substances, since it is always further divisible, and any given part always has another part, to infinity." Therefore: "It is contradictory to hold that a body is a single substance, since it necessarily contains in itself an infinite multitude, or an infinity of bodies, each of which, in turn, contains an infinite number of substances." From this it follows that:

> Over and above a body or bodies, there must be substances, to which true unity belongs. For indeed, if there are many substances, then it is necessary that there be one true substance. Or, to put the same thing another way, if there are many created things it is necessary that there be some created thing that is truly one. For a plurality of things can neither be understood nor can exist unless one first understands the thing that is one, that to which the multitude necessarily reduces." (Foucher de Careil 319: AG 103)

Arnauld wonders what constitutes the difference between a corporeal substance or unity and an aggregate. in response leibniz insists in his letter of April 1687 that some individuals are fundamental but others are not. The latter are aggregates, which are divisible, destructible, and temporary. They admit of degrees in the sense that they can be more or less unified and more or less divisible (e.g., a pile of rocks is more divisible than a piece of marble). The former are substances, which have a substantial forms, each of which creates a *living unity*. There is no reality to an aggregate above and beyond the reality of the entities that make it up. He insists that the unity that bodies or aggregates have is *imaginary*; a perceiving mind may see them as though they were a single thing. He writes to Arnauld that aggregates "have their unity in our mind only, a unity founded on the relation or modes of true substances" (G II 97: AG 86). Aggregates are logical constructions from modes and states of the entities aggregated.

As scholars have long noted, neither the *Discourse* nor the correspondence with Arnauld contains a clear account of exactly how a substantial form confers unity and identity on its substance. But the underlying assumption here, consistent with Leibniz's original views about self-sufficiency and the unifying powers of mind-like things, is that a substantial form confers unity and identity on its substance by acting constantly in relation to its passive principle. In the 1680s he believed that the human soul acts on its body by *concomitance* where the idea is that the two act in perfect preestablished parallelism. He writes in 1690:

> Hence, since I am truly a single indivisible substance, unresolvable into many others, the permanent and constant subject of my actions and passions, it is necessary that there be a persisting individual substance over and above the organic body. This persisting individual substance is completely different from the nature of body, which, assuming that it is in a state of continual flux of parts, never remains permanent, but is perpetually changed." (Foucher de Careil 320: AG 104)

MIND-BODY UNION AND PREESTABLISHED HARMONY. There are reasons to believe that Leibniz understood the relation between mind and body in terms of preestablished harmony as early as the 1670s. But it is not until the texts of the 1690s that he put this account of union front and center. In *A New System of the Nature and Communication of Substances, and of the Union of the Soul and the Body*, published anonymously in the *Journal des Savants* in 1695, he offers his account as an improvement over that of Descartes. He explains that it was the problem of "the union of soul and body" that led him to reject Descartes's philosophy and to recognize the need to "rehabilitate the substantial forms" (G IV 482–483: AG 142–143).

Here we have yet another approach to the core metaphysics, cleverly constructed to engage his audience—many of whom would have been quite interested in Cartesianism of one sort or another—on one of the weakest elements in the Cartesian system. The rhetorical hook here is that Cartesian dualism cannot adequately account for the mind-body union whereas preestablished harmony can. In the *New System* Leibniz declares that the great benefit of his metaphysics is that it offers a neat account of the world while at the same time explaining mind-body interaction. Because "it is not possible for the soul or any other true substance to receive something from without," the mind acts out of its own "depths," but with perfect "spontaneity" and in perfect "conformity" to everything external to it, including the substances that make up its body. While each substance expresses the whole universe in its own way, the soul is related to the "organized mass that is its body" more "closely" than to other external things. Both the soul and the substances that constitute its body will express one another more closely than they do other "external" things. He concludes that this "hypothesis" displays "the marvelous idea of the harmony of the universe and the perfection of the works of God" (G IV 485–486: AG 143–144).

According to Leibniz the solution to the problem of the interaction between mind and body resides in the harmony constructed by God between the mind and its body. The mind wills to move its finger and the finger moves in perfect preestablished coordination. As he famously puts it, they are coordinated like two clocks constructed "from the start with so much skill and accuracy that one can be certain of their subsequent agreement." Their "sympathy" is guaranteed by the "divine artifice" that has given each substance its "very own law … from the beginning" (G IV 498–499: AG 148). In the *Monadology*, he writes: "According to this system, bodies act as if there were no souls (though this is impossible); and souls act as if there were no bodies; and both act as if each influenced the other" (G VI 621: §81).

METAPHYSICS OF SUBSTANCE, MONADOLOGY

Scholars generally agree that by the time of the *Monadology*, Leibniz holds that the created world is constituted entirely of mind-like monads and that extended things are phenomenal. But there has been a good deal of discussion about when Leibniz gave up the extended substances of his youth. Some scholars have claimed that when he began to construct his own philosophical ideas they were based on a version of mental monism while others have dated the commitment to phenomenalism to the *Discourse* and the correspondence with Arnauld. Until all the writings of the period 1690–1716 have been thoroughly edited and published, there is little chance of solving this mystery. But whenever the phenomenalism begins, there can be no doubt that the notion of corporeal substance plays a key role in the *Discourse* and correspondence. Whether the passivity in such substances is constituted of extended force or collections of mind-like substances, there are corporeal substances constituted of active and passive principles. At some point after 1700, he seems to have become less convinced that the basic entities of the world should be modeled on organisms conceived as combinations of substantial forms and passive principles. In the late 1690s, perhaps in response to criticisms leveled by Arnauld, he begins to emphasize the simplicity of substances, which he now sometimes calls monads, and to reduce everything in the world to these simple, mind-like monads and their perceptions. He writes to De Volder: "Considering the matter carefully, it must be said that there is nothing in the world except simple substances and in them, perception and appetite" (G II 270: L537).

MONADOLOGY. While he was in Vienna, Leibniz wrote this, the most famous of all his works, three years before his death. Written for a friend, he intended it as a summary of his philosophy. Although he did not publish it during his lifetime, generations of scholars have taken it to be the most complete and accurate account of his philosophy. He begins the work with a series of definitions: The monad is "a simple substance that enters into composites—simple, that is, without parts." Monads are the "true atoms" or "elements" of nature and can form aggregates. The activities of monads are of two sorts; they have perceptions and appetitions. "The passing state which involves and represents a multitude in the unity or in the simple substance is nothing other than what one calls perception"; "The action of the internal principle which brings about the change or passage from one perception to another can be called *appetition*" (§14, §15). Although there is a good deal of discussion among scholars about the notion of appetition, it seems closely related to the *reason* or rule of action of the early period. It is the internal feature of the substance that drives it forward, determining its next state on the basis of its present state.

The monad itself may be taken to be another version of his original notion of substance as what is fundamentally unified and self-sufficient. In a related text of 1714, he explains that the Greek term "*monas* signifies unity, or what is one" (G VI 598: AG 207). While there is no doubt that many of the terms and some of the details are new, much of the text merely explicates standard Leibnizian doctrines. We find the various assumptions whose inspiration was originally Platonist. Each monad is an emanation of God, offers a unique perspective on the world, mirrors the universe, and is an indestructible and eternally active thing. He writes: "[Human] minds are images of the divinity itself, or of the author of nature, capable of knowing the system of the universe … each mind being like a little divinity in its own realm" (§83). We find the commitment to the assumptions whose source was Aristotelian: The self-sufficiency of substance now makes them *windowless*, but they constitute the fundamental entities whose natures anchor the theory of truth, the notion of a complete substance, the expression theory, the perfect coordination and harmony among things. Because each simple substance has its own entelechy, they can act as "the sources of their internal actions" (§18). Because "every present state of a simple substance is a natural consequence of its preceding state, the present is pregnant with the future" (§22).

Thus, the *Monadology* fits neatly into the sometimes subtle but always interesting evolution of Leibniz's views about substance. From the late 1660s to the last years of his life, these fundamental entities constitute the basis for his account of nature. And regardless of the evolution of his ideas about substance, he persists in seeing them as a perfectly rational and divine ordained harmony.

SUMMARY

Few thinkers in the history of philosophy have written so much, thought so deeply, and contributed so profoundly to so many areas. The vastness of Leibniz's texts, the difficulty of his thought, and the quirkiness of some of his ideas make him both a difficult and delightful philosopher to study. As more and more of his works are published, there will be more gems to discover and more interconnections to discern. Not only does Leibniz offer profound philosophical insights, he is admirable as someone who thought deeply about the history of philosophy and the need for intellectual and political peace. As he wrote at the end of his life: "I have tried to uncover and unite the truth buried and scattered under the opinions of all the different Philosophical Sects, and I believe that I have added something of my own which takes a few steps forward. ... I flatter myself to have penetrated into the Harmony of these different realms" (G III 606: L 655).

See also Aristotle; Arnauld, Antoine; Augustine, St.; Bayle, Pierre; Boyle, Robert; Cartesianism; Clarke, Samuel; Conway, Anne; Descartes, René; Epistemology; Ficino, Marsilio; Fontenelle, Bernard Le Bovier de; Foucher, Simon; Galileo Galilei; Gassendi, Pierre; Hippocrates and the Hippocratic Corpus; Hobbes, Thomas; Kabbalah; Locke, John; Luther, Martin; Malebranche, Nicolas; Metaphysics; Newton, Isaac; Philosophy; Pico Della Mirandola, Count Giovanni; Plato; Russell, Bertrand Arthur William; Spinoza, Benedict (Baruch) de; Thomasius, Christian; Thomism; Tschirnhaus, Ehrenfried Walter von; Voltaire, François-Marie Arouet de; Wolff, Christian.

Bibliography

ABBREVIATIONS

A: Akademie der Wissenschaften, eds. *Gottfried Wilhelm Leibniz: Sämtliche Schriften und Briefe*. Berlin: Akademie Verlag, 1923–. (Capital roman numerals represent series number; lower case roman numerals represent volume number; arabic numerals represent page number).

AG: Ariew, Roger, and Daniel Garber, eds. *G. W. Leibniz: Philosophical Essays*. Indianapolis, IN: Hackett, 1989.

G: Gerhardt, C. I., ed. *Die Philosophischen Schriften von Leibniz*. 7 vols. Berlin: Wiedmann, 1875–1890. Reprinted, Hildesheim: Olms, 1965.

GM: Gerhardt, C. I., ed. *Mathematische Schriften*. 7 vols. Berlin: A. Asher/Halle: H. W. Schmidt, 1848–63. Reprinted, Hildesheim: Olms, 1962.

Guhrauer: Guhrauer, G. E., ed. *Leibniz' Deutsche Schriften*. 2 vols. Vol. I, 410. Berlin:1838–1840.

L: Loemker, Leroy E., ed. *G. W. Leibniz: Philosophical Papers and Letters*. 2nd ed. Dordrecht, Netherlands: Reidel, 1969.

Pk: Parkinson, G. H. R., ed. *G.W. Leibniz: De summa rerum: Metaphysical Papers 1675–76*. New Haven, CT: Yale University Press, 1992.

EDITIONS AND TRANSLATIONS

The standard of Leibniz's original texts is the Academy edition (A above). The projected completion date is 2050. For a discussion of the editorial project, see Christia Mercer on "Gottfried Wilhelm Leibniz: *Sämtliche Schriften und Briefe*, edited by Akademie der Wissenschaften, Berlin: Akademie Verlag, 1923–, Series VI, volume 4," in the *Times Literary Supplement* Oct. 18, 2002, 7–9.

Other than the Academy edition, the best editions of original texts are G and GM (above). Also helpful are:

Works

Opera Omnia. 6 vols., edited by Ludovici Dutens, Geneva: De Tournes, 1768. Reprinted, Hildesheim: Georg Olms, 1989.

Leibniz' Deutsche Schriften. 2 vols., edited by G. E. Guhrauer, Berlin: 1838–1840.

Nouvelles lettres et opuscules inédits de Leibniz, edited by Alexandre Foucher de Careil. Paris: Ladrange, 1857.

Textes inédits d'après des manuscrits de la Bibliothèque provinciale d'Hanovre. 2 vols., edited by Gaston Grua. Paris: Presses Universitaires de France, 1948.

Leibniz Korrespondiert mit China: Der Briefwechsel mit dem Jesuiten Missionaren (1689–1714), edited by Rita Widmaier, Frankfurt: Klostermann, 1990.

Standard English-language translations of texts are L and AG (above) and the following:

Translated Works

Selections, edited by P. P. Wiener, New York: Scribner's, 1951.

New Essays on Human Understanding, edited and translated by Peter Remnant and Johathan Bennett. Cambridge, U.K.: Cambridge University Press, 1981.

De Summa Rerum: Metaphysical Papers 1675–1676, edited by G. H. R. Parkinson. New Haven, CT: Yale University Press, 1992.

Writings on China, edited and translated by Daniel J. Cook and Henry Rosemont Jr. Chicago: Open Court, 1994.

G. W. Leibniz: Philosophical Texts. Edited and translated by R. S. Woolhouse and Richard Francks, Oxford: Oxford University Press, 1998.

The Labyrinth of the Continuum: Writings on the Continuum Problem, 1672–1676, edited and translated by Richard T. W. Arthur. New Haven, CT: Yale University Press, 2001.

Confessio Philosophi: Papers concerning the Problem of Evil: 1671–1678. In *The Yale Leibniz,* edited by R. C. Sleigh Jr. New Haven, CT: Yale University Press (forthcoming)

PROMINENT SECONDARY LITERATURE IN ENGLISH

Adams, Robert M. *Leibniz: Determinist, Theist, Idealist.* Oxford: Oxford University Press, 1994.

Aiton, Eric J. *Leibniz: A Biography.* Bristol, U.K.: Adam Hilger, 1985.

Broad, C. D. *Leibniz: An Introduction.* Cambridge, U.K.: Cambridge University Press, 1975.

Brown, Stuart, *Leibniz.* Sussex, U.K.: Harvester, 1984.

Brown, Stuart, ed. *The Young Leibniz and his Philosophy: 1646–1676.* Dordrecht, Netherlands: Kluwer Academic, 1999.

Coudert, Allison. *Leibniz and the Kabbalah.* Boston: Kluwer Academic, 1995.

Deleuze, Gilles. *The Fold: Leibniz and the Baroque.* Translated by Tom Conley. Minneapolis: University of Minnesota Press, 1993.

Garber, Daniel. "Leibniz and the Foundations of Physics: The Middle Years." In *The Natural Philosophy of Leibniz,* edited by D. Okruhlik and J. R. Brown, 27–130. Dordrecht, Netherlands: D. Reidel, 1985.

Hartz, Glenn. "Leibniz's Phenomenalisms." *The Philosophical Review* 101 (1992): 511–549.

Hartz, Glenn. "Why Corporeal Substances Keep Popping Up in Leibniz's Later Philosophy." *British Journal for the History of Philosophy* 6 (2) (1998): 192–207.

Ishiguro, H. *Leibniz's Philosophy of Logic and Language.* 2nd ed. Ithaca, NY: Cambridge University Press, 1990.

Jolley, Nicholas, ed. *The Cambridge Companion to Leibniz.* New York: Cambridge University Press, 1995.

Jolley, Nicholas. "Leibniz and Phenomenalism" *Studia Leibnitiana* 18 (1986): 38–51.

Jolley, Nicholas. *The Light of the Soul: Theories of Idea in Leibniz, Malebranche, and Descartes.* Oxford: Clarendon Press, 1990.

Kulstad, Mark, "Causation and Pre-established Harmony in the Early Development of Leibniz's Philosophy." In *Causation in Early Modern Philosophy: Cartesianism, Occasionalism, and Pre-established Harmony,* edited by Steven Nadler, 93–118. University Park, PA: Pennsylvania State University Press, 1993.

Kulstad, Mark. *Leibniz on Apperception, Consciousness, and Reflection.* Munich: Philosophia, 1991.

Leclerc, Ivor, ed. *The Philosophy of Leibniz and the Modern World.* Nashville, TN: Vanderbilt University Press, 1973.

Lodge, Paul, ed. *Leibniz and His Correspondents.* Cambridge, U.K.: Cambridge University Press, 2004.

Lodge, Paul. "Leibniz's Commitment to Pre-established Harmony in the Late 1670s and Early 1680s." *Archiv für Geschichte der Philosophie* 80 (3) (1998): 292–320.

Loemker, Leroy E. "Leibniz and the Herborn Encyclopedists." *Journal of the History of Ideas* 22 (1961): 323–338.

Loemker, Leroy E. "Leibniz's Conception of Philosophical Method." In *The Philosophy of Leibniz and the Modern World,* edited by Ivor Leclerc, 135–157. Nashville, TN: Vanderbilt University Press, 1973.

Loemker, Leroy E. *Struggle for Synthesis.* Cambridge, MA: Harvard University Press, 1972.

Mates, Benson, *The Philosophy of Leibniz: Metaphysics and Language.* Oxford: Oxford University Press, 1986.

McCullough, Lawrence B. *Leibniz on Individuals and Individuation.* Dordrecht, Netherlands: Kluwer Academic, 1996.

Mercer, Christia. *Leibniz's Metaphysics: Its Origins and Development.* New York: Cambridge University Press, 2001.

Mercer, Christia, with Robert C. Sleigh Jr. "Metaphysics: The Early Period to the *Discourse on Metaphysics.*" In *The Cambridge Companion to Leibniz,* edited by Nicholas Jolley, 67–123. New York: Cambridge University Press, 1995.

Mondadori, Fabrizio. "A Harmony of One's Own and Universal Harmony in Leibniz's Paris Writings." *Studia Leibnitiana Supplementa* 18 (1978): *Leibniz à Paris (1672–1676)* 151–168.

Mondadori, Fabrizio. "Mirrors of the Universe." In *Leibniz: Die Frage nach Subjektivitat,* edited by Renato Cristin, 83–106. Stuttgard: Franz Steiner Verlag, 1994.

Mondadori, Fabrizio, "On Some Disputed Questions in Leibniz's Metaphysics." *Studia Leibnitiana* 25 (2) (1993): 153–173.

Mondadori, Fabrizio, "Reference, Essentialism, and Modality in Leibniz's Metaphysics." *Studia Leibnitiana* 5 (1) (1973): 73–101.

Nadler, Steven, ed. *Causation in Early Modern Philosophy.* University Park: Pennsylvania State University Press, 1993.

Parkinson, G. H. R. *Logic and Reality in Leibniz's Metaphysics.* Oxford: Clarendon Press, 1965.

Rescher, Nicholas. *Leibniz: An Introduction to his Philosophy.* Totowa, NJ: Rowman and Littlefield, 1979.

Rescher, Nicholas. *Leibniz's Metaphysics of Nature.* Dordrecht, Netherlands: D. Reidel, 1981.

Riley, Patrick. *Leibniz' Universal Jurisprudence: Justice as the Charity of the Wise.* Cambridge, MA: Harvard University Press, 1996.

Russell, Bertrand. *A Critical Exposition of the Philosophy of Leibniz.* Northampton: John Dickens. 1967.

Rutherford, Donald. *Leibniz and the Rational Order of Nature.* New York: Cambridge University Press, 1995.

Sleigh, R. C. Jr. *Leibniz and Arnauld: A Commentary on Their Correspondence.* New Haven, CT: Yale University Press, 1990.

Wilson, Catherine. *Leibniz's Metaphysics: A Historical and Comparative Study.* Princeton, NJ: Princeton University Press, 1989.

Wilson, Catherine. *The Invisible World: Early Modern Philosophy and the Invention of the Microscope.* Princeton, NJ: Princeton University Press, 1995.

Woolhouse, Roger. *Descartes, Spinoza, Leibniz: The Concept of Substance in the Seventeenth Century Metaphysics.* London: Routledge, 1993.

Woolhouse, Roger, ed. *Leibniz's "New System" (1695).* Florence: Leo S. Olschki Editore, 1996.

For recent literature in other languages, see Christia Mercer's *Leibniz's Metaphysics* and issues of the *Leibniz Review.*

ADDITIONAL RESOURCES

Alsted, Johann Heinrich. *Encyclopaedia, septem tomis distincta.* Herborn: 1630.

Ficino, Marsilio. *Theologia Platonica, de immortalitate animorum.* Paris: 1559. Reprinted in 1995 in Hildesheim, Germany, by Georg Olms Verlag; p. 43. There is a translation of some of this material by Luc Deitz in *Cambridge Translations of Renaissance Philosophical Texts*, edited by Jill Kraye, pp. 30–36.

Ficino, Marsilio. *Platonic Theology.* 2 vols. Volume 1 edited by J. Hankins, translated by M. J. B. Allen. Cambridge, MA: Harvard University Press, 2002.

Locke, John. *Essay concerning Human Understanding.* London: 1690.

Newton, Isaac. *Principia mathematica philosophiae naturalis.* London: 1687.

Newton, Isaac. *The* Principia: *Mathematical Principles of Natural Philosophy.* Translated by I. Bernard Cohen and Anne Whitman. Berkeley: University of California Press, 1999.

Nizolio, Mario. *De Veris Principiis et Vera Ratione Philosophandi contra Pseudophilosophos.* Parma, Italy: 1553. There was an edition edited by G. W. Leibniz published in Frankfort in 1670.

Pico della Mirandola, Giovanni. *De Hominis Dignitate, Heptaplus, De Ente et Uno, e Scritti Vari*, edited by Eugenio Garin. Florence: Vallecchi,1942.

Pico della Mirandola, Giovanni. *On the Dignity of Man, On Being and One, Heptaplus*, Translated by Charles G. Wallis, Paul J. W. Miller, and Douglas Carmichael. Indianapolis, IN: Bobbs-Merrill, 1965.

Plato *Phaedo.* In *Plato, Complete Works*, edited by John M. Cooper. Indianapolis: Hackett, 1997.

Plotinus. *Enneads.* Translated by A. H. Armstrong. Cambridge, MA: Harvard University Press, 1990.

Spinoza, Benedictus de. *Ethica.* In *Opera.* Vol. 2, edited by Carl Gephardt, Heidelberg: C. Winter, 1925.

Voltaire, François-Marie Arouet de. *Candide.* 1759.

Christia Mercer (2005)

LENIN, VLADIMIR IL'ICH
(1870–1924)

Lenin was a Marxist revolutionary, Russian Communist political leader, and major contributor to the philosophy of dialectical materialism. Although his mentor Georgii Valentinovich Plekhanov is considered the father of Russian Marxism, Lenin's distinctive version of the doctrine (later dubbed *Marxism-Leninism*) was considered authoritative by the Soviet Communist leadership and had an immense impact on Russia and the world through most of the twentieth century.

LIFE

Lenin was born Vladimir Ilich Ulyanov into the family of a well-to-do school official in Simbirsk, Russia. He enrolled in the University of Kazan in 1887, the same year his elder brother Alexander was executed for involvement in a plot to kill Tsar Alexander III. Lenin was soon expelled from the university for taking part in student disturbances, but he gained admission to the University of St. Petersburg as an external student and in 1892 graduated with a degree in law. His activity in Marxist and other radical circles, beginning in 1888 in Kazan and Samara and continuing in St. Petersburg from 1893, led to his imprisonment in 1895, followed by banishment to eastern Siberia in 1897. Allowed to leave Siberia in 1900, he promptly fled to western Europe. For most of the next seventeen years he worked in various locations outside Russia, writing and conspiring with fellow Russian Marxists to promote the overthrow of the tsarist regime in their homeland.

From the time of the formation of the Russian Social Democratic Labor Party in 1898, Lenin worked tirelessly to gain control of the group and mold it into a militant Marxist revolutionary force. His ideas and aggressive political tactics brought him into bitter conflict with other leading Russian Marxists, including Plekhanov, but eventually his Bolshevik faction of the party became dominant (the Russian term *bol'shevik* means a member of the majority) and in continuing intraparty struggles he consolidated his position as both a theoretician and a leader. After the February Revolution of 1917 he was able, with the help of German military authorities, to travel to Petrograd, where in the October Revolution he led the Bolsheviks in seizing control of the Russian government. In power for six stormy years, marked by attempted assassination, civil war, famine, and the formation of the Union of Soviet Socialist Republics, Lenin suffered a series of strokes beginning in 1922 and died in January 1924.

PHILOSOPHICAL WRITINGS

Lenin's philosophical activity extended from his student days to the Bolshevik revolution, and throughout this period its character was determined by his dogmatic materialism and his devotion to the theory and practice of Marxist social reconstruction as he understood it. His writings are strongly polemical in style, exemplifying the Leninist concept of *partiinost* (partisanship, party spirit) in philosophy.

Lenin first studied the writings of Karl Marx and his colleague Friedrich Engels systematically in 1888 and

1889. One of his earliest works, *What the "Friends of the People" Are and How They Fight the Social-Democrats* (1894)—directed against the Russian Populists, such as Nikolai Mikhailovsky—shows Lenin's general acceptance of dialectical materialism, the materialist conception of history, and the characteristic concepts of Marxist socialism. The distinctively Leninist element already evident is the strong emphasis on action, on the need to combine theory with revolutionary practice. Lenin asserted that the objective, necessary character of the laws of social change in no way destroys the role of active individuals in history. Thus, unlike those Marxists who feared that Russia was not sufficiently developed for a socialist revolution, Lenin stressed the need for expeditiously organizing the revolution, focusing on the proletariat (not the peasantry) as the leading revolutionary class. This activist approach was carried further in subsequent writings, chiefly *What Is to Be Done?* (1902)—the first work in which he used the pseudonym *Lenin)*—and *One Step Forward, Two Steps Back* (1904). In both of these works Lenin elaborated the need for a clandestine, militant, centralized, highly disciplined party to unify and direct the proletariat.

Lenin's book *Materialism and Empirio-Criticism* (1909)—the principal philosophical work published during his lifetime—is directed against a group of Russian writers, including Alexander Bogdanov and Anatoly Lunacharsky, who attempted to supplement Marxism with the phenomenalistic positivism of Richard Avenarius and Ernst Mach. Characterizing their position as a form of subjective idealism (and thus as inimical to Marxism), Lenin defended dialectical materialism on the chief points at issue, particularly the status and character of matter and the nature of knowledge. Opposing the view that matter is a construct of sensations, Lenin argued that it is ontologically primary, existing independently of consciousness. Likewise, space and time are not subjective modes of ordering experience but objective forms of the existence of matter. Opposing the view that discoveries of modern science cast doubt on the objectivity of matter, Lenin distinguished between scientific conceptions of matter, which are provisional and relative because no constituent of a material thing can be regarded as indivisible or irreducible, and the philosophical conception, according to which matter is simply the objective reality known to our senses. The only property of matter to which philosophical materialism is committed, according to Lenin, is the property of existing objectively. In epistemology, Lenin opposed the so-called hieroglyph theory of Plekhanov, according to which sensations are signs of an external reality that they do not

necessarily resemble, and developed a strictly realist position, the copy theory, according to which sensations depict or mirror the real world. On this basis Lenin defended the possibility of objective truth, emphasizing practical experience as its test.

Dialectics, which Lenin had long considered the heart of Marxism, is treated most fully in *Philosophical Notebooks* (1933), a posthumous compilation of notebook entries and fragments dating chiefly from 1914 to 1916, including his extracts from, and comments on, a number of works by other thinkers, above all Georg Wilhelm Friedrich Hegel's *Science of Logic*. Lenin showed a high regard for the Hegelian dialectic, which he found thoroughly compatible with materialism, and he asserted that dialectics, logic, and the theory of knowledge are identical. In his conception of dialectics Lenin departed from Engels in laying the greatest stress not on the transition from quantity to quality but on the struggle of opposing (contradictory) forces or tendencies within every natural object and process; Lenin saw this struggle as the internal basis of all change, and thus as the core of dialectics.

Lenin's last major works are concerned mainly with economic and political aspects of the revolutionary transition from capitalism to communism. In *Imperialism, the Highest Stage of Capitalism* (1917) he argued that capitalism had reached its final, monopolistic phase and was ripe for overthrow, but that, because of the uneven development of capitalism in different countries, socialism would not triumph in all or most countries simultaneously, as Marx had expected. In *State and Revolution* (1918), directed against the supposed opportunism of Marxist rivals such as Plekhanov and Karl Kautsky, Lenin elaborated on the Marxist thesis that the state is an instrument of class domination. He laid special stress on a number of points not fully developed by Marx or Engels: One was the need for shattering the bourgeois state machinery and establishing a proletarian state or dictatorship of the proletariat, and another was the distinction between the lower phase of communism, in which people are rewarded in proportion to the work they perform and the state is still needed to repress remnants of the former exploiting classes, and the higher phase, in which rewards are proportional to peoples' needs and the state will wither away because all class antagonisms have been eliminated.

INFLUENCE

Throughout the twentieth-century Communist world (including China), Lenin was regarded as a philosophical luminary of the first magnitude. In the Soviet philosophical pantheon, he was considered the greatest thinker in history after Marx. Formal education in philosophy in Russia under Communist rule was structured on the premise that Lenin's pronouncements were beyond criticism; his writings were published in vast editions in all major and many minor languages, making him the most widely published philosophical thinker of the twentieth century. In one sense he was also the most influential: Although his conceptual contributions to the development of philosophy as an intellectual discipline were negligible, his ideas provided the impetus and the rationale for policies that materially and often tragically affected the lives of millions of people.

The attack on Stalinism begun by Nikita Khrushchev in 1956 did not immediately disturb the cult of Lenin, whose principles Joseph Stalin was said to have betrayed, not implemented. With the introduction of *perestroika* in the mid-1980s under Mikhail Gorbachev, however, significant responsibility for the flaws and evils of the Soviet system was traced back to Lenin himself; in particular, his theory of imperialism and his fixation on class antagonisms to the neglect of common human interests and moral values were criticized at the highest levels. When the Soviet Union collapsed at the end of 1991, the Communist Party lost political power and Lenin's philosophical authority all but evaporated in Russia and the former Soviet bloc. Thereafter, educational curricula in Russia and Eastern Europe were reworked to eliminate the vestiges of Marxism-Leninism, and the publication of Lenin's writings ceased.

See also Communism; Dialectical Materialism; Engels, Friedrich; Marxist Philosophy; Russian Philosophy.

Bibliography

Harding, Neil. *Lenin's Political Thought*. 2 vols. New York: St. Martin's, 1977–1981.

Kolakowski, Leszek. *Main Currents of Marxism: Its Rise, Growth, and Dissolution*. Vol. 2: *The Golden Age*. Translated by P. S. Falla. Oxford: Clarendon Press, 1978.

Lenin, Vladimir Ilich. *Collected Works*. 45 vols. Moscow: Progress Publishers, 1960–1970.

Reference Index to V. I. Lenin, Collected Works. 2 vols. Moscow: Progress Publishers, 1978–1980.

Scanlan, James P. *Marxism in the USSR: A Critical Survey of Current Soviet Thought*. Ithaca, NY: Cornell University Press, 1985.

Service, Robert. *Lenin: A Biography*. Cambridge, MA: Harvard University Press, 2000.

Service, Robert. *Lenin: A Political Life*. 3 vols. Bloomington: Indiana University Press, 1985–1995.

Wetter, Gustav A. *Dialectical Materialism: A Historical and Systematic Survey of Philosophy in the Soviet Union*. Translated by Peter Heath. London: Routledge and Kegan Paul, 1958.

Wolfe, Bertram D. *Three Who Made a Revolution: A Biographical History*. 4th rev. ed. New York: Dell, 1964.

James P. Scanlan (1967, 2005)

LEONARDO DA VINCI
(1452–1519)

Leonardo da Vinci, the Florentine artist, scientist, and inventor, was born at Vinci in Tuscany, the natural son of a notary, and died near Amboise, France. At his death he left a sizable collection of notebooks that were subsequently scattered in the various libraries of Europe. From 1881 on, many of these notebooks have been published. They consist of notes and jottings on various topics: mechanics, physics, anatomy, physiology, literature, and philosophy. They contain, moreover, plans and designs for machines that frequently have suggested Leonardo's "precursive genius." There are machines of war and of peace, flying machines based on the flight of birds, a parachute, a helicopter, tools and gadgets of all kinds. Leonardo's notebooks are also full of methodological notations on the procedures of scientific inquiry and philosophical considerations about the processes of nature. Undoubtedly many of the arguments that he discussed were taken from the philosophical literature of the time, especially from the writings of the Ockhamists; however, a coherent and complete philosophical scheme cannot be found in the notes, whose chronological order is extremely uncertain. Pierre Duhem held that Leonardo was mainly inspired by the doctrines of Nicholas of Cusa, but recent studies tend to emphasize his dependence on Marsilio Ficino. Leonardo lived in Florence for the first thirty years of his life and subsequently returned there many times.

Leonardo's *Treatise on Painting* (published 1651) reveals the artist and the scientist united in one personality. Painting, which he placed above all other arts, aims at representing the work of nature to the senses. Thus it extends to the surfaces, the colors, and the forms of natural objects, which science studies in their intrinsic forms. The beauty that painting seeks in things is the proportion of the things themselves, and proportion is also the object of the scientific consideration of nature. According to Leonardo, understanding nature means understanding the proportion that is found not only in numbers but also in sounds, weights, times, spaces, and any natural power whatever. Both art and science have the same object, the harmonious order of nature, which art represents to the senses and science expresses in its laws.

Leonardo held that the two pillars on which science stands are experience and mathematical calculation. As an "unlettered man" (as he called himself) he had contempt for those who, instead of learning from experience, claimed to learn from books (the commentators and followers of Aristotle). He contrasted his work as an inventor with their work of "trumpeting and reciting the work of others." "Wisdom is the daughter of experience," he said. Experience never deceives, and those who lament its deceitfulness should lament their own ignorance because they demand from experience what is beyond its limits. The judgment of experience can be mistaken; and the only way to avoid error is to subject every judgment to mathematical calculation and to use mathematics unrestrictedly to understand and demonstrate the reasons for the things that experience manifests. Mathematics is therefore, according to Leonardo, the basis of all certitude, since without recourse to mathematics it is impossible to put an end to the verbal disagreements of what he called the sophistic sciences—that is, the philosophical disputes about nature.

The privilege accorded to mathematics was most certainly a legacy from Platonism. Leonardo took from Plato's *Timaeus* and Ficino's commentary on it the doctrine that the elements of natural bodies are geometric forms; thus the efficacy of mathematics as an instrument of investigation was justified for him by the fact that nature itself is written in mathematical characters and that only those who know the language of mathematics can decipher it. This is the major contribution that ancient Platonism made to the formation of modern science. Nicolas Copernicus and Galileo Galilei shared this obviously metaphysical doctrine that, however, strongly contributed to launching science from its origins to its mathematical organization. It helped bring scientific consideration from the domain of quality (of natures or essences) to that of quantity by permitting consideration of the natural object as measurable; that is, in the extremes, by reducing the objectivity of nature to its measurability.

However, if the order of nature is a mathematical order, then it is a necessary order; and this necessity is, according to Leonardo, the only true "miracle" of nature: "O wondrous and awesome necessity! With your law you constrain all effects to result from their causes by the shortest path, and according to the highest and irrevocable law every natural action obeys you with the briefest operation." The phrases "by the shortest path" and "with the briefest operation" refer to another feature of the necessary order of nature: its simplicity. Nature follows the shortest or simplest path in its operations. It does not like useless loitering, and this also reveals the mathematical character of its structures. Necessity and simplicity of nature exclude the presence of arbitrary or miraculous forces, as well as the efficacy of magic and of those forces to which it appeals.

Guided by these criteria, Leonardo could arrive at and formulate important theorems and principles of statics and dynamics. The theorem of the composition of forces, the principle of inertia, and the principle of action and reaction are the most notable of these formulations, which, of course, he did not state in the precise form that they received later from René Descartes and Isaac Newton. Nevertheless, they demonstrate his genius for moving from the limited work of the inventor to the generalizations of the scientist.

See also Aesthetics, History of; Copernicus, Nicolas; Descartes, René; Duhem, Pierre Maurice Marie; Ficino, Marsilio; Galileo Galilei; Mathematics, Foundations of; Newton, Isaac; Nicholas of Cusa; Ockhamism; Plato; Platonism and the Platonic Tradition.

Bibliography

Leonardo's manuscripts have been published with photographic reproductions by Charles Ravaisson-Mollien, 6 vols. (Paris, 1881–1891). They have also been published in *Codex Atlanticus*, edited by G. Piumati (Milan, 1894–1904) and *I manoscritti e i disegni di Leonardo da Vinci*, published by the Reale Commissione Vinciana (Rome, 1923–1930). The best collection of selections is J. P. Richter, *The Literary Work of Leonardo da Vinci*, 2 vols. (London, 1883; 2nd ed., 1939). *Leonardo da Vinci on Painting: A Lost Book*, edited and translated from the *Codex Vaticanus Urbinas*, No. 1270, and from the *Codex Leicester* by Carlo Pedretti (Berkeley: University of California Press, 1964), includes a preface by Kenneth Clark and some material never published before.

Works on Leonardo include the following: Pierre Duhem, *Études sur Leonardo da Vinci*, 3 vols. (Paris, 1906–1913); E. Solmi, *Leonardo* (Florence, 1900); C. Luporini, *La mente di Leonardo* (Florence: Sansoni, 1953); Eugenio Garin, *Medioevo e Rinascimento* (Bari: Laterza, 1954), pp. 311ff., and *Cultura filosofica del Rinascimento italiano* (Florence: Sansoni, 1961), pp. 388ff.; I. B. Hart, *The World of Leonardo da Vinci* (London: Macdonald, 1961); James Beck, *Leonardo's Rules of Painting: An Unconventional Approach to Modern Art* (New York: Viking Press, 1979); and Boris Kouznetsov, "The Rationalism of Leonardo Da Vinci and the Dawn of Classical Science," *Diogenes* (69 [1970]: 1–11).

Nicola Abbagnano (1967)
Translated by Nino Langiulli
Bibliography updated by Tamra Frei (2005)

LEONT'EV, KONSTANTIN NIKOLAEVICH

(1831–1891)

Konstantin Nikolaevich Leont'ev was a Russian writer, philosopher, critic, and publicist. Like almost all important nineteenth-century Russian authors, Leont'ev came from a family of landowners. He was trained in medicine at the University of Moscow and served for three years as an army doctor in the Crimean war. After the war he took the post of family doctor on a country estate in the province of Nizhnii-Novgorod, married, and published his first novel, *Podlipki* (1861). In 1863 he entered the Russian diplomatic service and worked for eight years as a consular official on the island of Crete and the Balkans. After a cure from dysentery, he underwent a spiritual crisis and spent a year (1871–1872) in a Greek monastery on Mount Athos. Soon after he left the consular service, and he returned to Russia where he worked as a journalist in various cities and a censor of literature in Moscow. In 1887 he decided to renounce the secular world, was officially divorced from his wife, and retired to the Optyna Pustyn' cloister in the province of Tula. Shortly before his death he took monastic vows and died a monk in the Trinity-St. Sergius Monastery near Moscow.

Although Leont'ev can be considered one of the brilliant representatives of nineteenth-century Russian culture, on a par with Alexander Herzen, his work is not very well known. His novels and stories have hardly been translated and his philosophical and political views only scantily studied. The main reason for this seems to be his odd, maverick-like personality, which expressed itself in views so paradoxical and extreme that it is almost impossible to weld them together and to integrate them with the main ideas of his age.

Leont'ev was torn between an amoral aestheticism and the intense desire for saving his soul by the ascetic renunciation of the world. The protagonist of almost all his novels (among which, apart from *Podlipki*, *V svoem kraiu* [In my own land, 1864], and *Egipetskii golub'* [The Egyptian dove, 1881–1882]) is a narcissistic superhero (more or less identical with Leont'ev himself) who takes delight in all things beautiful and considers it his duty to lead a poetic life. "Ethics does not coincide with aesthetics: otherwise it is impossible to approve the beauty of Alcibiades, of a diamond, of a tiger." Which is better: "the bloody and spiritually exuberant age of the Renaissance, or contemporary Denmark, Holland, Switzerland— humble, prosperous, moderate?" (*Sobranie sochinenii*, Vol. I, p. 282; 414). However, the hero is dissatisfied with his actual self as he realizes his own limitations and the vanity of his sensuous experience and of the world he has enjoyed so much.

It is this latter attitude that made Leont'ev severely criticize contemporary writers such as Fëdor Dostoevsky, Lev Tolstoy, and Vladimir Solov'ëv. In the essay "*Nashi novye khristiane: F. M. Dostoevskii i graf Lev Tolstoi*" ("Our new Christians: F. M. Dostoevsky and Count Lev Tolstoy, 1882) he ridiculed the *rose-colored Christianity* of these authors. By promising paradise on earth (just like the utopian socialists), Leont'ev stated, they introduced heretical, humanistic elements into their religious views, making God a diluted God of love instead of a God of fear. However, in another essay he made a brilliant analysis of Tolstoy's novels, in particular praising *War and Peace*.

Leont'ev is best known for his aesthetic approach to history and his uncompromising criticism of his own age, which according to him, was dominated by equality and its unavoidable counterpart mediocrity. Just as such thinkers as de Maistre, Comte Joseph de Maistre, Thomas Carlyle, Friedrich Nietzsche, and John Stuart Mill, Leont'ev rejected the industrial revolution of the nineteenth century, which had led to democracies in which there was no place for great men and intense, *creative* contradictions. In his collection of essays *Vostok, Rossiia i slavianstvo* (The East, Russia, and Slavdom, 1885–1886), which included his main work "*Vizantizm i slavianstvo*" (Byzantinism and Slavdom, 1875) he developed a *biological* theory of the evolution of history. Each historical cycle comprises three periods: a period of childhood, or *primitive simplicity*; a second period of adulthood, characterized by differentiation and *flourishing complexity*; and a final period of old age, which through decline and disintegration leads to a *secondary simplicity*.

According to Leont'ev Europe was already in its third phase, the first being the period of the barbarian invasions, the second the High Middle Ages. As clear signs of the contemporary decay, he considered the disappearance of class distinctions and the dominance of bourgeois culture, the culture of the *average man*. Since the time of Peter the Great (1672–1725), this European *leveling interfusion* had infected Russia. Russia's salvation, he maintains, lies in reversing this process, which can only be done by defending its prime institutions, autocracy and orthodoxy, and promoting a situation in which "despotism, danger, strong passions, prejudices, superstitions, fanaticism …, in a word everything to which the nineteenth century is opposed" (*Sobranie sochinenii*, Vol. VIII, p. 98) could flourish. More extreme and reactionary than the older Slavophiles such as Aleksei Khomiakov and the brothers Ivan and Petr Kireevskii, Leont'ev had no scruples about supporting strict censorship and political repression in order to reverse the *pernicious* process of democratization. However, he with great insight foretold the excrescences of the "fixed equality" of communism, which "through a series of combinations with other principles must gradually lead, on the one hand, to a decreased mobility of capital and property, and, on the other, to a new juridical inequality, to new privileges, to restrictions on individual freedom, and to *compulsory* corporate groups, clearly defined by laws—probably even to new forms of personal slavery or serfdom." (Edie, Scanlan, Zeldin 1965, p. 278).

Leont'ev is often called the Russian Nietzsche. With his pessimistic view on the development of European culture and society, he can be seen as a forerunner of Oswald Spengler. In Russia interest in his work has grown considerably since the 1990s. Biographical data, his complete works, and criticism about him (in Russian) can be found on the web at http://knleontiev.narod.ru.

See also Carlyle, Thomas; Dostoevsky, Fëdor Mikhailovich; Khomiakov, Aleksei Stepanovich; Kireevskii, Ivan Vasil'evich; Maistre, Comte Joseph de; Mill, John Stuart; Nietzsche, Friedrich; Solov'ëv (Solovyov), Vladimir Sergeevich; Spengler, Oswald; Tolstoy, Lev Nikolaevich.

Bibliography

WORKS

Edie, James M., James P. Scanlan, and Mary-Barbara Zeldin, eds. *Russian Philosophy.* Vol. II. Chicago: Quadrangle Press, 1965.

Sobranie sochinenii (Collected works). 9 vols. Moscow: Sablina, 1912–1914. (Reprint of vols. 1–4, Würzburg, Germany: JAL, 1975).

Egyptian Dove: The Story of a Russian. Translated by George Reavey. New York: Weybright and Talley, 1969.

Zapiski otshel'nika (The notes of a hermit). Moscow: Russkaia kniga, 1992.

STUDIES

Berdyaev, N. *Leontiev.* Translated by George Reavey. London: Centenary Press, 1940.

Lukashevich, S. *Konstantin Leontev (1831–1891). A Study in Russian "Heroic Vitalism."* New York: Pageant Press, 1967.

Ivask, Yurii *Konstantin Leont'ev: Zhizn' i tvorchestvo* (Konstantin Leont'ev: life and works). Bern and Frankfurt, Germany: Herbert Lang, 1974.

Rzhevsky, Nicholas "Leontiev's Prickly Rose." *Slavic Review* 35 (1976): 258–268.

Willem G. Weststeijn (2005)

LEOPARDI, COUNT GIACOMO
(1798–1837)

Count Giacomo Leopardi, the Italian poet and prose writer, was one of five children born to Count Monaldo Leopardi and Marquise Adelaide Antici, in Recanati, near Ancona. His brief and anguished existence was plagued both by continuous illnesses (among them rachitis, which made him a hunchback) and the bigotry of his parents, who refused him financial support. A liberal and an agnostic, he yearned to leave the "bodiless, soulless, lifeless" ancestral abode where he had spent all his time devouring books; learning Latin, Greek, Hebrew, and a number of modern languages; and translating and writing critical essays on the classics, history, and astronomy. A fellow philologist, Pietro Giordani, opened to him the world beyond his "savage native town." Afterward, he traveled to Rome, Milan, Bologna, Pisa, Florence, and Naples, never venturing beyond the Alps because of his frail constitution, and even refusing the Dante Alighieri chair offered to him by the University of Bonn. Often he returned to Recanati, only to leave after a short stay. Nature and beauty offered him moments of precious calm, but these few instants could not dispel the physical and metaphysical oppression that, for Leopardi, seemed to weigh upon the world. Everywhere reality proved a bitter disillusionment. Several devoted publishers and friends offered him various jobs and forms of subsistence, but generally to little avail. The poet both expected and invoked death, which came to him in Naples in 1837, shortly after he had dictated his last poem.

THE *CANTI*

As Elme Marie Caro said, Leopardi wanted to be, deserved to be, and was a philosopher. He did not come to philosophy through poetry, or to poetry through philosophy; his poetry is his philosophy. While Leopardi's prose works (the magnificently cogent *Operette morali*, 1827; the diary called the *Zibaldone*, 1898–1900; and the copious correspondence, or *Epistolario*, published posthumously) reflect the melancholy meditations of a thinker concerned with universal sorrow, the most fulfilling expression of his thoughts is to be found in his poetry, the *Canti* (1831, 1835, 1845). The *Canti* complement and complete the *Operette*, because in expression and content they constitute an organic outgrowth of the nature and orientation of Leopardi's philosophy.

PESSIMISM

Leopardi's philosophy, which should not be viewed as a methodically pondered and presented system, has been labeled skeptical and pessimistic, a philosophy of despair. Indeed, it dwells upon the triumph of evil over good and of nature over man, the mystery and insignificance of our mortal existence, the anguish of our miseries, the extinction of youth, and the lure of death. As Arthur Schopenhauer recognized, "No one has treated these subjects more fundamentally and exhaustively in our day than Leopardi." Given the limited dissemination of Schopenhauer's *Die Welt als Wille und Vorstellung* (1819) at that time, it is unlikely that Leopardi read the work or that he met the author. It is certain, however, that Schopenhauer read Leopardi's poems; yet while he mentions them, he in no way indicates whether they influenced the development of his own thought.

Yet the similarities run deep. Leopardi characterized life—this life we love, not for itself but, erroneously, for its promise of happiness—under the rubrics of sorrow (*dolore*), or unhappiness (*infelicità*), and tedium (*noia*). By means of this perspective, he was able to discard many cherished notions. Assuming the hapless state of humanity, the notions of patriotism and heroism vanish as follies, as does the glory of genius, which the poet had once assiduously pursued and which later, like Eduard von Hartmann, he relegated to the category of illusions. As for love and beauty, they entice soul and senses cruelly, since their ephemerality brands them as colossal deceptions. Nature, which according to Leopardi is the mysterious principle of being, closely related to Hartmann's concept of the Unconscious as a neutral absolute, answers none of man's queries about the secret of things; it is undecipherable, mechanical, unreasoning and unreasonable, and at times brutally hostile toward men. Man, then, is nothing; if he is something, he is so by virtue of being his own greatest enemy. In the *Operette morali,* Schopenhauer's gloomy picture of life as a gory chase in which men scramble for spoils differs only moderately from Leopardi's description of Prometheus's and Momus's journey.

Death as nonbeing is therefore, like love during its moment of existence, a thing of beauty. Death as suicide, however, solves nothing because it constitutes not a negation of existence but rather, as Schopenhauer asserted, an act directed against the accidental portion of unhappiness that creeps into human existence. Moreover, the future holds no promise, and *progress* and *perfectibility* are empty words.

EVIL

Leopardian pessimism differs from Schopenhauer's on two questions: the principle of evil and the remedy of evil. Leopardi refused to consider the problem of the necessity of evil and, in any case, would not have ascribed evil to a principle, such as Will or the Unconscious, simply because he believed that evil is an empirical datum and does not require metaphysical or transcendental explanation. He felt the existence of evil and saw only gross arbitrariness in those who attempt to show why it must exist, or who make a transcendent dialectics of the universal law of suffering. Historical pessimism, which stems from the "restless creative mind" of men who boldly oppose unconquerable nature, and cosmic pessimism, through which evil, inherent in nature, subjugates man, are fundamentally interrelated in Leopardi's philosophy and preclude all thought of remedy. The individual's only recourse is stoic dignity—resignation, silence, and scorn. "Of what value is our life, except to despise it?" In this respect, Leopardi was a precursor of German pessimism.

Schopenhauer also upheld Stoic dignity, but for Leopardi dignity was less a remedy for suffering than an instinctive and protective reaction that neither alters suffering nor consoles the sufferer. Schopenhauer even found some consolation in the Buddhist ideal of nirvāṇa, which Leopardi could not. And while Schopenhauer could derive a sense of pride from his belief that the more developed the organism, the greater its misery, Leopardi, even when speaking of man's nobility, could not find in it any basic gratification. The degree to which both men felt a sense of compassion differed: Leopardi's pity, although less central to his ethics than *Mitleid* was to Schopenhauer's, was still less condescending and more sympathetic than Schopenhauer's.

Leopardi held to the inexorability of destiny and nature's blind subservience to it—subservience which fails to take into account man's struggle and misery. Everything, therefore, is deceit; the only truth lies in nothingness. For Leopardi, what counts is the philosophical negation of life, both in its effective pains and in its false felicities. Only in this way can one claim to demonstrate moral consistency—through the affirmation of a negative totality.

ILLUSIONS AND REALITY

Reason, then, in Leopardi is tantamount to negation. Illusions are merely dreams, substances insofar as they may be considered "essential ingredients" of living, "half-real things." Since all that is real comes to nothing, Leopardi inverted the concept of reality and asserted that only the illusory is real. In claiming this, he did not suggest that reality is a mere phenomenon concealing a noumenon. On the contrary: The reality of the world in which man lives and which has meaning for him is neither rational nor spiritual, but natural and imaginary; it is a reality that is necessarily maintained by what we call illusions. Beyond it lies complete negation. Hence Leopardi professed the opposite of the instinctive noumenalism of man's mind. The world is real in relation to the absence of those other substances that we seek under the heading of truth. Just as the world is arbitrary, so men's beliefs, desires, hopes, and "certainties" (justice, science, virtue, freedom, idealism) are merely groundless illusions. Leopardi despised theological, dogmatic, spiritualistic philosophies, along with any form of presumptuous optimism.

RELIGION

The philosophy outlined above precluded religious faith. Leopardi might assent to the Scriptures' theory of man's decadence, but he could not admit Christian Providence or the Resurrection. Yet although he is unhappy (*infelice*), the poet is not irreligious. His "atheism" bespeaks the combined awareness of the necessity and of the absence of God—in short, of the impossibility of hope. Escape into pleasure is self-deceiving ("pleasure is a subjective speculation and is unreal"), for we seek the idea of pleasure more than we seek pleasure itself; indeed, the latter does not exist. The resulting tedium closely approaches Martin Heidegger's *Angst*, which reflects the experience of nothingness.

VALUE OF LIFE

Because Leopardi is an artist and poet, the immensity of his despair loses its bitterness in a melancholy and fraternal contemplation of existence. Despair allows him to understand the value of human life, although in the long run life is a "useless misery." As a measure of exiguous man's infinite desires against the infinity of being, tedium itself (that is, enthusiasm, heroism, and desperation successively experienced and resulting in a sense of nothingness) seemed to him "the greatest sign of grandeur and nobility in human nature." He recognized illusion as a positive value, offsetting negation and "the infinite vanity of all things." This kind of deception is of value to man, since it constitutes his only justifiable pleasure. Despite it, or actually because of it, Leopardi called for brotherly solidarity and compassion, not out of love of God, but out of a desire to combat the cruelty of destiny and of nature.

What Leopardi finally did was to negate negation, thus creating what he called an ultraphilosophy. He developed a philosophy about philosophy (namely, that we should not philosophize) that rejects reason. For, wrote Leopardi, "As [Pierre] Bayle said, in metaphysics and morals reason cannot edify, only destroy." But by denying itself, reason in a sense vindicates its own power and worth. While exposing the pains and infirmities of existence, Leopardi makes us love the very objects of his despair. By glorifying illusion, art, in the pureness of its beauty (which supersedes the misery of all material things), becomes the most important postulate of ultraphilosophy. Art transfigures sorrow and, by not limiting its own strength and freedom, converts that sorrow into human greatness—a greatness that constitutes the triumph of free creative power and of infinite strength.

See also Beauty; Evil, The Problem of; Hartmann, Eduard von; Heidegger, Martin; Illusions; Life, Meaning and Value of; Pessimism and Optimism; Schopenhauer, Arthur.

Bibliography

WORKS BY LEOPARDI

The critical edition of Leopardi's collected works is *Tutte le opere,* edited by Francesco Flora, 5 vols. (Milan, 1937–1949). For English translations, see *Essays, Dialogues and Thoughts,* translated by James Thomson (New York, 1905?); *The Poems of Leopardi,* a translation of all the *Canti* by Geoffrey L. Bickersteth (Cambridge, U.K.: Cambridge University Press, 1923); *Translations from Leopardi* by R. C. Trevelyan (Cambridge, U.K.: Cambridge University Press, 1941); *Giacomo Leopardi: Poems,* translated and with an introduction by Jean-Pierre Barricelli (New York: Las Americas, 1963).

WORKS ON LEOPARDI

For literature on Leopardi, see Giovanni Amelotti, *Filosofia del Leopardi* (Genoa, 1937); Aristide Baragiola, *Giacomo Leopardi: filosofo, poeta e prosatore* (Strasbourg, 1876); Elme Marie Caro, *Le pessimisme au XIXe siècle* (Paris, 1880); Karl Vossler, *Leopardi* (Munich: Musarion, 1923); Giovanni Gentile, *Poesia e filosofia di Giacomo Leopardi* (Florence: Sansoni, 1939); Iris Origo, *Leopardi: A Biography* (London: Oxford University Press, H. Milford, 1935); J. H. Whitfield, *Giacomo Leopardi* (Oxford: Blackwell, 1954); and G. Singh, *Leopardi and the Theory of Poetry* (Lexington: University of Kentucky Press, 1964).

Jean-Pierre Barricelli (1967)

LEQUIER, (JOSEPH LOUIS) JULES
(1814–1862)

(Joseph Louis) Jules Lequier, or Léquyer, the French philosopher, was born at Quintin in Brittany. He was educated there and in Paris at the *collège* of St. Stanislas and the École Polytechnique. An intensely religious though extremely heterodox Roman Catholic, Lequier devoured the literatures of philosophy and theology, and although none of his own work was published during his lifetime, he wrote voluminously and also translated Sir Humphry Davy's autobiography. Jean Wahl has made interesting comparisons between certain aspects of the thought of Lequier and Søren Kierkegaard, although neither could actually have influenced the other. However, Lequier directly influenced Charles Renouvier, who always considered him his "master in philosophy," and through Renouvier he attracted the attention of William James. Renouvier later published Lequier's book, *La recherche d'une première vérité* (Paris, 1865).

Lequier's philosophy aimed at but never achieved systematic wholeness; its essential theses, however, may be restated in four interrelated doctrines. First, Cartesian methodological doubt must be genuine, not feigned, and unless it is employed in good faith, one is likely to err in doubting real evidence, just as, without methodological doubt one is likely to err in allowing unwarranted belief. Accordingly, doubt has no privileged status over belief. Ability to attain truth as well as falsehood must underlie the quest for truth, and freedom is thus a condition of the possibility of knowing truth as well as of being mistaken.

Second, freedom is a "double dilemma." Either causal necessity or freedom is a fundamental truth, and each doctrine must be asserted either necessarily or freely. If necessity is the true doctrine, my affirmation thereof is *eo ipso* necessary, but since neither doubt nor belief relative to evidence would function in that determination, doubt results. If necessity is true but I affirm freedom, then in addition to my inconsistency (for my affirmation is made necessarily), there is only a subjective foundation for knowledge and morality. Given the truth of determinism, erroneous as well as true judgments are necessary, and any supposed distinction between them is illusory. According to the hypothesis of freedom, if I freely affirm global necessity I am fundamentally inconsistent. Finally, if I affirm freedom under the same hypothesis, not only is my affirmation consistent with the hypothesis but I have a foundation for knowledge and morality. Under the

double dilemma, the only satisfactory alternative is freely to affirm freedom—Lequier's "first truth." Freedom is essentially the power to add some novel reality to the existing world. Causality must be explained through freedom and not vice versa.

Third, the data that are present to a given event of consciousness arise out of the past relative to that event; they are past actualities but present potentialities for the internal character of that event of consciousness out of which a determining decision is made. Human consciousness is a succession of self-creative events, each of which is given its ancestor selves as well as other data, and each of which is partially *causa sui*, a "dependent independence." Thus, the totality of causal conditions of any human experience does not make this experience necessary, but only possible, while internal decision makes it contingently actual. All choice-making contains some arbitrary element.

Fourth, in extending these doctrines to theology, and taking as axiomatic the concept that freedom, responsibility, and moral and religious values depend upon choice-decisions, Lequier holds that an omniscient God need not know future contingents, since, in relation to any divine experience, they are not yet existent. To be knowable is to be determinate, and if all were known "from eternity," then all would be eternally determinate, and time and choice-making would be illusions. Also, since contingents are unequivocally in part *causa sui*, they are not wholly dependent on divine power. Far from viewing divine power as absolute total control, Lequier insists that the only power worthy of God is the far greater one of creating self-creators. Real choice in the world is incompatible with all-embracing necessity, and it is neither metaphysically requisite nor religiously desirable that God be wholly immutable and eternal. God must have a temporal aspect in order to come to know contingents as they are realized; thus he remains always omniscient in knowing all there is to know. Lequier's theology is thus that of an eternal-temporal being, his omniscience and omnipotence being relative to the irreducible contingency and self-creativity in the world.

Lequier's philosophy bears various striking resemblances to themes in Samuel Alexander, Henri Bergson, Nikolai Berdyaev, Émile Boutroux, William James, Kierkegaard, C. S. Peirce, and A. N. Whitehead.

See also Alexander, Samuel; Berdyaev, Nikolai Aleksandrovich; Bergson, Henri; Boutroux, Émile; Cartesianism; Consciousness; Freedom; James, William;

Kierkegaard, Søren; Peirce, Charles Sanders; Renouvier, Charles Bernard; Whitehead, Alfred North.

Bibliography

For works by Lequier, see *Oeuvres complètes,* edited by Jean Grenier (Neuchâtel: Baconnière, 1952).

Literature on Lequier includes Émile Callot, *Propos sur Jules Lequier* (Paris: Rivière, 1962); Jean Grenier, *La philosophie de Jules Lequier* (Paris: Société d'édition "Les Belles lettres," 1936); Charles Hartshorne and William L. Reese, eds. *Philosophers Speak of God* (Chicago: University of Chicago Press, 1953), the only material by Lequier now available in English; Adolphe Lazareff, *Vie et connaissance* (Paris: Vrin, 1948); Xavier Tilliette, *Jules Lequier ou le tourment de la liberté* (Paris, 1964); and Jean Wahl, *Jules Lequier* (Paris, 1948), which contains an introduction and selections.

Harvey H. Brimmer II (1967)

LE ROY, ÉDOUARD

(1870–1954)

Édouard Le Roy, the French philosopher of science, ethics, and religion, was born in Paris and studied science at the École Normale Supérieure. He passed the *agrégation* examination in mathematics in 1895 and took a doctorate in science in 1898. Le Roy became a *lycée* teacher of mathematics in Paris but was soon drawn to philosophical problems through an interest in the philosophy of Henri Bergson. He succeeded Bergson, to whose thought his own was deeply indebted, as professor of philosophy at the Collège de France in 1921 and was elected to the French Academy in 1945.

In a series of articles titled "Science et philosophie" (*Revue de métaphysique et de morale* 7 [1899]: 375–425, 503–562, 706–731, and 8 [1900]: 37–72), Le Roy took a pragmatic view of the nature of scientific truth, a view more or less shared by his contemporaries Bergson, Jules Henri Poincaré, and E. Wilbois. Scientific laws and even scientific "facts," Le Roy maintained, are arbitrary constructs designed to meet our needs and to facilitate effective action in pursuit of those needs. Scientific reason, in other words, distorts reality in the interests of practical action. The scientific facts on which induction is based are artificially extracted from the continuous flow of happenings and experiences and built up into convenient (rather than "true") thought structures, which constitute "the grammar of discourse" and enable us to talk about, and deal with, what would otherwise be "the amorphous material of the given." Thus, in reacting against scientific mechanism, Le Roy presented an extreme view of mind as the creator of its own reality.

Le Roy took the same pragmatic view of discursive religious truth in *Dogme et critique* (Paris, 1906). His views were supported by the Catholic modernists and condemned as dangerous in a papal encyclical. Le Roy held that the validity of dogmas cannot be proved, nor do they profess to be provable; they depend upon a rigid and externally imposed authority; their expression and frame of reference is that of medieval philosophy; and they are alien to, and incompatible with, the body of modern knowledge. For these four reasons they are unacceptable to the modern mind as truths. Nevertheless, they possess a pragmatic value; they fulfill a purpose, in this case a moral one. "Although mysterious for the intelligence in search of explanatory theories," Le Roy held, "these dogmas lend themselves nonetheless to perfectly specific formulation as directives for action." Christianity is thus not a system of speculative philosophy, but a set of stated or implied injunctions, a way of life. For example, the belief in a personal God demands that our relation to him resemble our relation to a human person. The doctrine of the resurrection of Christ teaches that we should behave in relation to him as if he were alive today.

Le Roy's misgivings concerning religious dogmas arose because the dogmas seemed to him irreconcilable with a homogeneous system of rational knowledge. In a pragmatic and relativist conception of truth such incompatibility should not be significant. However, the criterion of truth, for Le Roy, was neither use nor coherence, but "life" itself, dynamic and self-developing. Scientific theory is useful distortion, religious teaching a source of moral action, and both are arbitrary in their choice of concepts and symbols. Genuine knowledge is a kind of self-identification with the object in its primitive reality, uncontaminated by the demands of practical need. Intuition, not discursive thought, is the instrument of such knowledge, and the criterion of truth is that one should have lived it; otherwise, according to Le Roy, one ought not to understand it. This, as L. Susan Stebbing rightly pointed out, altogether removes the criterion from rational criticism, since life is both truth and the criterion of truth.

Le Roy's philosophy culminated in moral and religious concerns, as is seen in Volume 2 of his posthumously published *Essai d'une philosophie première* (2 vols., Paris, 1956–1958). His position is similar to Bergson's in *Les deux sources de la morale et de la religion*. The élan vital that animates us takes the form of an "open," that is, indeterminate, moral demand. This generalized obligation is the essence of the self as a free and self-creating agent. Le Roy stated that "to believe is to perceive a spiritual exigency and to act under its inspiration." The open nature of the exigency "beyond any ideal capable of being formulated" places Le Roy's view in the same category as much recent morality of authenticity. The agent is constantly transcending the determinate in the direction of some necessarily unspecified self-fulfillment. Because morality implies precepts and precepts imply universalizability, the notion of a morality that cannot be formulated would seem to be self-defeating. In his conception of a moral quest Le Roy, in fact, seemed to presuppose the Christian values to which he subscribed.

See also Bergson, Henri; Laws, Scientific; Modernism; Philosophy of Science; Poincaré, Jules Henri; Religion; Stebbing, Lizzie Susan.

Bibliography

ADDITIONAL WORKS BY LE ROY

Une philosophic nouvelle: Henri Bergson. Paris: Alcan, 1912.
L'exigence idéaliste et le fait de l'évolution. Paris: Boivin, 1927.
Les origines humaines et l'évolution de l'intelligence. Paris: Boivin, 1928.
Le problème de Dieu. Paris, 1929.
La pensée intuitive. 2 vols. Paris: Boivin, 1929–1930.
Introduction à l'étude du problème religieux. Paris, 1944.
La pensée mathématique pure. Paris, 1960.

WORKS ON LE ROY

Gagnebin, S. *La philosophie de l'intuition. Essai sur les idées d'Édouard Le Roy.* Paris, 1912.
Olgiati, F. *Édouard Le Roy e il problema di Dio.* Milan, 1929.
Stebbing, L. Susan. *Pragmatism and French Voluntarism.* Cambridge, U.K.: Cambridge University Press, 1914.

Colin Smith (1967)

LE SENNE, RENÉ
(1882–1954)

René Le Senne, the French spiritualistic philosopher, was born in Elbeuf in Normandy. From 1903 to 1906 he was a pupil of Frédéric Rauh and Octave Hamelin at the École Normale Supérieure, where he passed the *agrégation* examination in philosophy in 1906. He obtained his doctorate in 1930 with a thesis titled *Le devoir* (Duty). After holding provincial teaching posts he was appointed to the Lycée Louis-le-Grand in Paris and, in 1942, to a chair of moral philosophy at the University of Paris. He distinguished himself as joint editor, with Louis Lavelle, of the series of works published in the collection "Philosophie

de l'esprit." In 1948 he was elected to the Académie des Sciences Morales et Politiques.

The conception of philosophy underlying the "Philosophie de l'esprit" was traced by Le Senne to the Cartesian tradition, which, he held, identified existence with the act of thought and regarded existence as dependent upon a transcendent and infinite being. This tradition, according to Le Senne, was threatened both by positivism, which discounts the self-creating principle that raises man above causally determined physical nature, and by an excessive modern subjectivism, which makes man the measure of all things. Against these threats to the French "psycho-metaphysical" tradition Le Senne and Lavelle launched their series, in what they conceived as a kind of philosophicomoral mission, a reassertion of metaphysical philosophy against antiphilosophy.

Like much of recent French thought, Le Senne's work evokes not so much René Descartes as Maine de Biran. The essence of the self is consciousness of action against the resistance and limitation of reality. This could be rendered: I will, or I strive, therefore I am. Thus, personality for Le Senne was "existence as it is formed by the double cogito: hindered by obstacles, elevating itself by and towards value." Man participates in absolute and transcendent value. Although value outruns him and is not wholly his creation, it is made determinate by him in a given, concrete situation.

Reality, then, is at once the organ of self-creation and an obstacle to it. In a sense it degrades value, yet it actualizes value by making it determinate. We are, moreover, called back to awareness of the value-creating source in which we participate. This is a spiritual flow, or upsurge (*essor*). "Some obstacle has to break the continuity of the upsurge before the self, concentrating upon it the body's energy, begins to will." The willing self owes its being and consciousness to the obstacles it encounters. We participate in a world of absolute value and a world of brute reality and create ourselves unceasingly through them.

See also Cartesianism; Descartes, René; Essence and Existence; French Philosophy; Hamelin, Octave; Lavelle, Louis; Maine de Biran; Positivism.

Bibliography

WORKS BY LE SENNE

Introduction à la philosophie. Paris, 1925.
Le devoir. Paris: Alcan, 1930.
Le mensonge et le caractère. Paris: Alcan, 1930.
Obstacle et valeur. Paris: Aubier, 1934.

Traité de morale générale. Paris: Presses Universitaires de France, 1942.

Traité de caractérologie. Paris: Presses Universitaires de France, 1945.

La destinée personnelle. Paris: Flammarion, 1951.

La découverte de Dieu. Paris, 1955.

WORKS ON LE SENNE

Paumen, J. *Le spiritualisme existentiel de René Le Senne.* Paris: Presses Universitaires de France, 1949.

Pirlot, J. *Destinée et valeur. La philosophie de René Le Senne.* Namur, Belgium: Secrétariat des Publications, Facultés Universitaires, 1953.

Vax, L. "Pensée souffrante et pensée triomphante chez René Le Senne." *Critique* 12 (1956): 142–152.

Colin Smith (1967)

LEŚNIEWSKI, STANISŁAW
(1886–1939)

Leśniewski, Stanisław (1886–1939) was one of the founders of the Warsaw School of logic, which flourished from 1919 to 1939. He was the author of a highly original system for the foundations of mathematics, and one of the most innovative and unorthodox logicians of the twentieth century.

LIFE AND INFLUENCE

Leśniewski was born in Serpukhov, Russia, and received his schooling in Irkutsk. After studying at German universities, including Leipzig and Munich, he moved in 1910 to Lwów where he studied philosophy with Kazimierz Twardowski and obtained his doctorate in 1912. Leśniewski published several papers before the First World War, which he spent in Moscow. His preoccupation with the logical antinomies, which began in 1911 when he read Jan Łukasiewicz's book *On the Principle of Contradiction in Aristotle,* shifted his interests permanently from philosophy of language to the logical foundations of mathematics. In 1919 he was appointed professor of the Philosophy of Mathematics at the University of Warsaw. From then until his early death from cancer he was at the center of developments in mathematical logic in Poland, first developing his systems, then from 1927 publishing his results. Leśniewski's notes, correspondence, and a monograph on the antinomies were destroyed in the 1944 Warsaw Uprising: After the war several of his surviving students worked to reconstruct the lost results.

Leśniewski's sole doctoral student Alfred Tarski—Leśniewski boasted proudly of having one hundred percent geniuses as doctoral students—inherited many of his teacher's attitudes, but Tarski's increasing willingness to embrace platonistic set theory for the sake of metamathematical results caused tensions between them. Other pupils such as Jerzy Słupecki, Bolesław Sobociński, Czesław Lejewski, and Henry Hiż remained closer to Leśniewski's views, but their influence was limited. Quine's concern with ontological commitment and the meaning of the quantifiers probably went back to discussions he had with Leśniewski in 1933 on the interpretation of higher-order quantification. Because of the inconvenience of his systems, his forbidding perfectionism, and the idiosyncrasy of his positions, Leśniewski's work remained outside the mainstream, but some aspects became widely influential outside Poland. These include: the object language/metalanguage distinction, exact canons of definition, the theory of semantic categories, and mereology.

FORMAL SYSTEMS

After learning about Russell's Paradox, Leśniewski set himself to produce an antinomy-free foundation for mathematics. Disconcerted by the inexactitudes of Russell's and Whitehead's *Principia mathematica,* he initially forswore logical symbolism and formulated his views in highly regimented Polish, but in 1920 Leon Chwistek persuaded him to formalize his work, which he did with unprecedented precision. The logical order of Leśniewski's three systems is the reverse of the chronological order of their discovery. Leśniewski diagnosed an ambiguity in the notion of class which he made responsible for Russell's Antinomy, and in 1916 developed the theory of concrete classes, later renamed *mereology.* Then he set about formalizing the underlying logic of names, predicates and higher-order functors, which he called *ontology,* axiomatizing it in 1920. Finally he formalized the theory of sentences, connectives, and quantification which underlay the other theories, calling the resulting system *prototothetic.* The axiomatization of protothetic was assisted by Tarski's 1923 discovery that conjunction could be defined in terms of material equivalence and universal quantification. Leśniewski and others improved the results through the 1920s, and he published accounts of protothetic in a series of German papers, and mereology in a Polish series.

MEREOLOGY

Mereology (from Greek *meros,* part), a formal theory of the part-whole relation and cognate concepts, is Leśniewski's nominalistically acceptable partial substitute for set theory. It understands classes as concrete wholes literally composed of their members. Classes (now usually called mereological sums or fusions) are identical when they have the same parts, so the same sum may be determined by different pluralities of members—for example a chess board is the sum of its squares, but also of its ranks or its files. Sums exist if their members do, and a sum need not be spatiotemporally connected. There is no null or empty sum. Mereology can be axiomatized in many ways using many different undefined constants, its axiom(s) being added to ontology. The following perspicuous four-axiom system uses the primitive notion pt( ), meaning *part of*, and understood to include the case of identity or improper part; the variables in this system are all nominal (intended singular variables being capitalized), and the ontological notion presupposed is the copula "ϵ" of singular inclusion:

M1 $\qquad \forall AB\, [\, A\, \epsilon\, \text{pt}(B) \rightarrow B\, \epsilon\, B\,]$

M2 $\forall ABC\, [\, ((A\, \epsilon\, \text{pt}(B)\, \&\, B\, \epsilon\, \text{pt}(C)) \rightarrow A\, \epsilon\, \text{pt}(C))\,]$

M3 $\forall Ab\, [\, A\, \epsilon\, \text{Sm}(b) \leftrightarrow (A\, \epsilon\, A\, \&\, \forall C\, [\, C\, \epsilon\, b \rightarrow C\, \epsilon\, \text{pt}(A)\,]$
$$\&$$
$\forall D\, [\, D\, \epsilon\, \text{pt}(A) \rightarrow \exists EF\, [\, E\, \epsilon\, b\, \&\, F\, \epsilon\, \text{pt}(E)\, \&\, F\, \epsilon\, \text{pt}(D)]\,]\,]\,)\,]$

M4 $\qquad \forall Ab\, [\, A\, \epsilon\, b \rightarrow \text{Sm}(b)\, \epsilon\, \text{Sm}(b)\,]$

These axioms say: (M1) that whatever has a part is an individual; (M2) that parthood is transitive; (M3) define the sum of all the *b*s as that unique individual *A* which overlaps all and only *b*s; and state (M4) that if there is at least one *b* then the sum of all *b*s exists and is unique. Mereology is consistent relative to protothetic. It is independent of this system whether or not there are atoms—that is, objects without proper parts.

Mereology was the first system rigorously formulated by Leśniewski and remains the most thoroughly investigated. Its principles are much weaker than those of set theory, although some of its assumptions, especially the general sum principle M4, have been questioned on philosophical grounds. Especially when based on standard predicate logic rather than Leśniewski's ontology, mereology has come into standard use in ontology and cognitive science.

ONTOLOGY

Mereology presupposes ontology, so called because Leśniewski took it to formulate several meanings of *be*. He intended it as a modernized term logic of the sort formulated by Ernst Schröder, and in its admittance of empty and plural terms it is closer to traditional logic than to Frege-Russell predicate logic, whose terms are all

singular. Like mereology, ontology can be based on many different primitives, but the most frequently used is the one chosen by Leśniewski, namely the singular inclusion functor "ϵ." The basic sentence-form "$A\, \epsilon\, b$," readable as "A is a b" but best read perhaps as "A is one of the bs" captures the distributive rather than collective sense of "class": "A is a member of the class of the bs" just means "A is one of the bs" and no individual called "the class of the bs" is assumed.

Leśniewski's original (1920) axiom, though not the shortest, remains the most perspicuous:

O1 $\quad \forall Ab\, [\, A\, \epsilon\, b \leftrightarrow (\, \exists C\, [\, C\, \epsilon\, A\,]\, \&\, \forall DE\, [\, (D\, \epsilon\, A\, \&\, E\, \epsilon\, A)$
$$\rightarrow D\, \epsilon\, E]\, \&$$
$$\forall F\, [\, F\, \epsilon\, A \rightarrow F\, \epsilon\, b]\,)\,]$$

This says that A is a b if and only if (1) there is at least one A, and (2) there is at most one A, and (3) every A is a b. This axiomatic equivalence, which constitutes a sort of implicit self-definition of "ϵ" mirrors the analysis of singular definite descriptions by Russell, as can be seen by reading "$A\epsilon\, b$" as "the A is a b." Existential import in ontology is located in the functor "ϵ." rather than the quantifiers: "$A\epsilon\, b$" is only true if an A exists.

The axiom is not ontology's only source of logical power. Leśniewski allows new constants to be defined, and as these are introduced, new semantic categories of expression and thereby new categories of bindable variable become available. Each category of expression is subject to a principle of extensionality, and so the system grows in logical strength, ascending as required to higher types of variable. Thus although the axiom binds only nominal variables, later theses allow variables for predicates and other higher-order functors to be bound. Because Leśniewski allows plural names, his first-order calculus is equivalent in logical strength to standard monadic second-order predicate calculus. There is no axiom of choice in ontology, but a directive can be formulated allowing choice principles to be stated for each higher logical type (semantic category). Like mereology, ontology is consistent relative to protothetic. Despite its expressive power, ontology is ontologically neutral in that no thesis stating the existence of an individual can be derived. It is thus true of the empty universe as well as others.

Ontology is in many ways Leśniewski's most innovative system, combining features of traditional, Schröderian, and Fregean logic with a potential expressive power equivalent to that of the simple theory of types. Nevertheless, apart from some exploitation for purposes of historical comparison, and some development by Lejewski and others, it has found few supporters.

PROTOTHETIC

The basis of Leśniewski's logic is protothetic, a bivalent propositional calculus to which may be added propositional functors of any order, and incorporating the theory of quantification. It is equivalent in potential to a system of propositional types. Leśniewski, following Peirce, took quantification as embodying cardinally unconstrained conjunction and disjunction, and as part of the basis of logic rather than attaching primarily to nominal variables. The quantifiers $\forall$ and $\exists$ bind variables of any category. Leśniewski experimented from 1921 onwards with different axiomatic and combinatorial bases for protothetic. He chose material equivalence as sole undefined connective because he formulated definitions as object-language equivalences, and he developed the calculus of equivalent statements. But an intuitive axiomatization of protethic using implication is:

P1 $\qquad \forall pq\,[\,p \to (q \to p)\,]$

P2 $\qquad \forall pqrf\,[\,f(r\,p) \to (f(r\,\forall s[s]) \to f(r\,q))\,]$

Quantifier apart, the first thesis is familiar from propositional calculus. The second exploits a variable f for functors taking two propositional arguments, with "$\forall s[s]$" a standard false sentence. Like ontology, protothetic derives much of its strength from the rules permitting the formulation of new definitions and extensionality principles for higher types. Each propositional type is finite in its extensions, starting from the basic types of sentences, which has just two extensions, the True and the False, so in principle the quantifiers can be replaced by computational principles running through the extensions for each type considered in a sentence. Leśniewski took great pains over protothetic but it remains the least discussed of his logical systems.

Though his published works covered mainly his own systems, with incidental but incisive criticism of such contemporaries as Russell and Whitehead, von Neumann and Zermelo, in his Warsaw lectures Leśniewski ranged more widely, finding single axioms for general and abelian group theory, developing Peano's axioms, investigating inductive definitions, comparing mereology with Whitehead's theory of events, and criticizing Łukasiewicz's many-valued logic.

PHILOSOPHICAL METALOGIC

Though an unprecedentedly exact formalizer, Leśniewski deplored all formalism. Having come to logic through regimented ordinary language, he understood his logical systems throughout as interpreted with a determinate intended meaning, and intended his theses as general truths. From his first paper Leśniewski scrupulously distinguished use from mention of expressions, and literally failed to understand writings where this distinction was not observed, notably *Principia*. By contrast he admired and extolled the great rigor of Frege's formal systems, notwithstanding their inconsistency. Leśniewski's strictures on quotation were inherited and made influential by Tarski.

Leśniewski criticized Twardowski's platonism and strove to make his logical systems compatible with nominalism. This meant treating systems not as abstract entities but as concrete collections of physical inscriptions, growing in time by the addition of new inscriptions called *theses*. Because the systems as they develop allow new expressions to be introduced via definitions, and new types of variable to become available for quantification, the regulation of their growth had to be precise but schematic. Leśniewski achieved this by formulating for each system regulatory directives allowing new theses to be introduced. These directives are self-adjusting in that what they allow expands as the system grows. Leśniewski considered faulty definition to be responsible for the logical antinomies, and by bringing definitions within the system as object-language equivalences—rather than metalinguistic abbreviations—kept them under tight control. The highly complex directives for adding definitions in protothetic and ontology are Leśniewski's proudest achievement. To formulate them and the other directives governing substitution, quantifier distribution, modus ponens, and extensionality required a sequence of more than fifty metalogical definitions called *terminological explanations*. In his everyday logical working however, Leśniewski used an unofficial system of natural deduction from assumptions, understood as delivering an outline which could, if necessary be transformed into a proof according to the directives. This he never formalized. The complexities of formulating general terminological explanations and directives for variable-binding operators were beyond even Leśniewski, and he had to rest content in his official system with a sole syncategorematic operator, the universal quantifier.

The formulation of the directives employed Leśniewski's notion of semantic categories, a systematic logical grammar inspired by Frege's practice and

Husserl's theory of *Bedeutungskategorien*, and intended as an ontologically parsimonious alternative to type theory. Though not codified by Leśniewski, the subsequent systematization by Ajdukiewicz and others has made this part of mainstream logic and linguistics. The basic category of protothetic was the sentence, to which ontology added the basic category of name. Mereology required no new categories or directives.

Leśniewski had definite ideas about the intellectual economy of logic. A system ought to have as few primitive notions, axioms, and directives as possible; the axioms ought to be as short as possible, logically independent, and organic—that is, not contain provable theses as subformulas. The search for ever shorter axioms was a general feature of the Warsaw School, which Leśniewski and his followers sometimes pursued at the expense of defending controversial aspects of the systems, such as their interpretation of quantification, their radical nominalism, and their thoroughgoing extensionalism.

Leśniewski's avowed metaphysical neutrality combined with his liberal use of quantifiers to bind nonnominal variables drew criticism from Quine. Leśniewski rejected Quine's accusation of platonism, and on reflection Quine came to regard Leśniewski's quantifiers as substitutional, committing not to corresponding entities, but to expressions to be substituted for variables bound by a quantifier. That Leśniewski cannot understand the quantifiers objectually is clear because a standard empty name "$\wedge$" can be substituted normally for bound variables: From the true "no $\wedge$ exists" one may validly infer "for some a, no a exists," so "for some" ($\exists$) cannot mean "there exists." In the light of its subsequent development, the substitutional interpretation fits Leśniewski no better than the objectual, because it would commit him to an infinity of platonic expression types. Comparison with standard accounts is complicated by Leśniewski's incriptional understanding of expressions and the import of his directives, which are conditional prescriptions rather than categorical descriptions. The directive "If A is the last thesis belonging to the system then a thesis B may be added if for some thesis C preceding A, B is a result of substitution from C into A" quantifies only over extant tokens. The question remains how expressions employed in a logical system (including the quantifiers) have their meanings. On this Leśniewski remains silent. How to theorize metalogically about meaning and truth within Leśniewski's strictures remains perhaps the biggest open question concerning his systems.

See also Logical Paradoxes; Łukasiewicz, Jan; Mereology; Syntactical and Semantic Categories; Tarski, Alfred; Twardowski, Kazimierz.

Bibliography

WORKS BY LEŚNIEWSKI
The only collected edition of Leśniewski's works is their English translation:

Leśniewski, Stanisław. *Collected Works*. 2 vols., edited by Stanisław J. Surma, Jan T. J. Srzednicki, and Dene I. Barnett, with an annotated bibliography by V. Frederick Rickey. Dordrecht, Netherlands: Kluwer, 1992. Rickey's bibliography lists the original Polish locations of these writings.

Srzednicki, Jan T. J., and Stachniak, Zbigniew, eds. *S. Leśniewski's Lecture Notes in Logic*. Dordrecht, Netherlands: Kluwer, 1988. Contains edited transcriptions of student notes from lecture courses Leśniewski gave in Warsaw.

WORKS ABOUT LEŚNIEWSKI
Luschei, Eugene C. *The Logical Systems of Leśniewski*. Amsterdam, Netherlands: North-Holland, 1962. The most comprehensive monograph on Leśniewski.

Miéville, Dénis. *Un développement des systèmes logiques de Stanislaw Lesniewski: Protothétique – Ontologie – Méréologie*. Berne, Switzerland: Lang, 1984. The nearest thing to an elementary introduction to Leśniewki.

Miéville, Dénis and Dénis Vernant, eds. *Stanislaw Lesniewski Aujourd'hui*. Grenoble, France: Université Pierre Mendès France, 1995. A collection of essays including an informative survey by Czesław Lejewski, "Remembering Stanislaw Lesniewski," pp. 25–66.

Srzednicki, Jan T. J., V. Frederick Rickey, and J. Czelakowski, eds. *Leśniewski's Systems: Ontology and Mereology*. Dordrecht, Netherlands: Kluwer 1984. Seminal commentaries and improvements by Lejewski, Słupecki, Robert E. Clay and others.

Srzednicki, Jan T. J., and Zbigniew Stachniak, eds. *Leśniewski's Systems: Prototothetic*. Dordrecht, Netherlands: Kluwer, 1998. A similar compilation of important commentaries and improvements in prototothetic.

Woleński, Jan. *Logic and Philosophy in the Lvov-Warsaw School*. Dordrecht, Netherlands: Kluwer, 1989. Definitive history, with a copious bibliography, situating Leśniewski in the context of the logical movement in Poland.

Peter Simons (2005)

LESSING, GOTTHOLD EPHRAIM
(1729–1781)

Gotthold Ephraim Lessing, the German dramatist and critic, was born at Kamenz in Saxony. The son of a scholarly Lutheran pastor, he was sent to study theology at Leipzig University. There, however, he absorbed the popular rationalism of the Enlightenment, whose leading contemporary exponent was the Leibnizian Christian Wolff, of Halle. Lessing was influenced in the same direction by his friends from Berlin, Christoph Friedrich Nicolai and Moses Mendelssohn, and by the writings of the English deists, many of which had been translated into German. Although literature, and especially the drama, became Lessing's supreme interest, he was to return to theology in the last decade of his life. He has no special claim to being ranked as a philosopher of originality and distinction, but with regard to the diffusion of certain ideas and attitudes among educated minds, his historical influence is preeminent. He was above all a critic, and his attitude may be described as one of "passionate detachment." His nonconformity made him appear to be perennially restless; he was never permanently satisfied to adopt the conventional opinions of society, always preferring to be in a "minority of one." The movement of his mind carried him beyond his parents' theological beliefs and the commonplace deism of his twenties until, through his invocation of Benedict de Spinoza, he eventually prepared the way for the romantic reaction against the Enlightenment.

LITERATURE AND ART

Lessing's approach to the drama was based on his conviction that it was urgently necessary to break the tyrannical dominance over German literature exerted by the established French classicism—a trend that was encouraged by Frederick II of Prussia. In Lessing's eyes, the effect of this French influence was the suppression of the native German genius. In a series of "literary letters" (*Briefe, die neueste Literatur betreffend*, Leipzig, 1759–1765), written in cooperation with Nicolai and Mendelssohn, Lessing exhorted German writers to turn their backs on the artificial perfections of Pierre Corneille and Jean Racine; he claimed that they should take as their stylistic model the bold naturalism of William Shakespeare, whom Voltaire had characteristically dismissed as a "drunken savage."

Lessing's best-known work of criticism is his *Laokoon, oder, über die Grenzen der Malerei und Poesie* (*Laocoön, or the Bounds of Painting and Poesie*, Berlin, 1766). Judged as constructive thinking about the nature of art, it is a disappointing work, although it is noteworthy in that it contains the first explicit statement of the concept of "art for art's sake." Moreover, its overt thesis—that painting works by forms and colors in space, while poetry belongs to a quite different category in that it sets out to describe successive moments in time—is not only inadequate, since it fails to take account of lyric poetry and indeed of all poetry that describes states of mind, but

also much less original than Lessing implied. But it is significant that the *Laokoon* takes the form of a critique of Lessing's German, English, and French predecessors; he could not write well without a target to attack. In the *Laokoon*, Lessing's main critique was directed against Johann Joachim Winckelmann and the latter's idealization of "noble simplicity and quiet grandeur." Lessing was prepared to acknowledge that this ideal may hold good for painting, which, he claimed, is exclusively concerned with the beauty of physical form. But he wholly denied its validity or relevance for judging poetry, which is concerned with action and passion. *Laokoon*, like much that Lessing wrote, has a subtle undercurrent of irony and polemic, the thrust of which, on the surface, is not apparent to the rapid reader. Although Lessing took as his text a famous piece of ancient sculpture, his essay is more an oblique sermon about literature than an aesthetic analysis of the visual arts by a critic with a real understanding of, or even sympathy for, his subject. Its essential thesis is a warning that Winckelmann's neoclassical ideals must not constrict the freedom of the poet, who, unlike the painter, is primarily concerned with passionate action.

Lessing's writings on art and literature do not constitute a serious analysis and critique of aesthetic experience. But his work was directed toward liberating the artist from all the limiting rules and conventions of artificial formality. Lessing was not in any sense a romantic writer, but because of his demand for the free expression of natural feelings and his retrospective interest in antiquity, he occupies an important place among the forces that made German romanticism possible. The significance of Lessing's role as a precursor of the romantic movement emerges even more prominently in his treatment of religious problems. He initiated the endeavor to discover within the immanent order of the world those values that had been derived by traditional Christianity from a transcendental view of the universe.

HISTORY AND THEOLOGY

Lessing inherited from his father strong scholarly and historical interests. By temperament antipathetic to all partisan historiography, he published a series of *Rettungen* (Vindications) in 1754, in which he defended historical figures to whom ecclesiastical historians, for dogmatic reasons, had not been quite fair. These essays are quite characteristic of Lessing's nature and cast of mind. Written with suppressed passion and permeated with a profound sense of engagement, they nevertheless remain uncommitted to any personal judgment either for or against the doctrinal beliefs of those whom he was vindicating. His neutrality toward Christianity never took the form of quasi-Gibbonian irony. He always wrote as one wholly sympathetic to Christian ethical ideals, but coolly reserved toward dogmatic formulas that breed unreasoning prejudice and the negation of humane values.

The turning point of Lessing's life occurred in 1769, when he became librarian for the duke of Brunswick at Wolfenbüttel. In 1773 he began to publish essays on historical theology based on the Wolfenbüttel manuscripts. Earlier, during a three-year residence in Hamburg from 1766 to 1769 as a theater critic, Lessing had met the deist Hermann Samuel Reimarus (1694–1768), whose daughter had lent him the manuscript of an unpublished book by her father titled *Apologie oder Schutzschrift für die vernünftigen Verehrer Gottes* (Apology for rational worshipers of God). In 1774, and from 1777 to 1778, Lessing printed extracts from this work as fragments from the writings of an anonymous and unidentifiable deist whose manuscripts had presumably been found in the Wolfenbüttel library ("Wolfenbüttler Fragmente eines Ungenannten," in *Beiträge zur Geschichte und Literatur*).

The last and most important fragment precipitated a violent controversy with a Hamburg pastor, Johann Melchior Goeze, and effectively initiated the long nineteenth-century quest for the Jesus of history behind the Christ of faith. Reimarus was a believer in natural religion, but he was skeptical about revelation. His objections to traditional Christianity presuppose that biblical inerrancy is essential to faith. Lessing sometimes wrote as if he shared this assumption and sometimes as if he did not, so that it is not possible to arrive at a strictly coherent view on this point.

In his more cynical moments, Lessing treated liberal theology, such as that represented by J. S. Semler of Halle, with hostile contempt, on the ground that it was deceptively credible; he preferred to "defend" orthodoxy as being so patently absurd that by defense it would be sooner ended. Strictly as a scholar, Lessing was Semler's inferior; nevertheless, Lessing's genuinely scholarly instinct, combined with his inner detachment from the entrenched positions of the contemporary theological schools, as well as from those of the Enlightenment, enabled him to begin the critical study of the sources of the Synoptic Gospels (a fundamental question on which Reimarus had naively said nothing) with his pioneer essay, *Neue Hypothese über die Evangelisten als bloss menschliche Geschichtsschreiber betrachtet* (New Hypothesis concerning the Evangelists Regarded as Merely Human Historian). This was written from 1777 to 1778 and first printed in 1784 in Lessing's *Theologische Nachlass*.

Prevented by the duke of Brunswick from indulging in theological controversies, Lessing put his theology into a play, *Nathan der Weise (Nathan the Wise, 1779)* which was a plea for religious indifferentism on the ground that what is required of man is not an assent to the propositions of a creed, but sincerity, brotherly love, and tolerance. It is not easy to discover precisely what Lessing's positive beliefs were, so little did he commit himself, either in published writings or even in private correspondence, to any positive avowal of convictions. But he certainly accepted the commonplace thesis of the Enlightenment that the quintessence of Christianity, hidden beneath the accretions of theology, consists in universal brotherhood and a basic moral code. Like many rationalists of his age, he passed for a time into Freemasonry, though he emerged disillusioned with what was for him evidently a pale substitute for Christianity. In one sense, it could be said that Lessing spent his life hoping that Christianity was true and arguing that it was not. But his basic attitude toward religious belief was neither one of affirmation nor of denial; it took the form of an impassioned question.

Lessing was the first modern writer explicitly to emphasize that even if conclusions about historical events were more certain than they are, any religious affirmation based upon them involves a transition to another plane of discourse, that of faith. He was torn between the idea of revelation as the communication of timeless propositional truths, and the untidiness and irrationality of history. "Accidental truths of history can never become the proof of necessary truths of reason" (*Über den Beweis des Geistes und der Kraft*, 1777). Events and truths belong to altogether different categories, and there is no logical connection between one and another. Lessing's statement of this antithesis presupposes on the one hand the epistemology of Gottfried Wilhelm Leibniz, with its sharp distinction between necessary truths of reason (mathematically certain and known a priori) and contingent truths (known by sense perception), and on the other hand the thesis of Spinoza's *Tractatus Theologico-Politicus*, that the truth of a historical narrative, however certain, cannot give us the knowledge of God, which should be derived from general ideas that are in themselves certain and known. Lessing's own way out of the dilemma was to conceive the role of religious belief in the historical process as a relative state in the advance of humanity toward maturity, a thesis that he argued at length in the tract *Die Erziehung des Menschengeschlechts* (The Education of the Human Race; Berlin, 1780). Lessing thus became the father both of the "post-Christian" consciousness expressed in nineteenth-century positivism, and of the liberal religion of thinkers such as Samuel Taylor Coleridge and Frederick Denison Maurice.

There is more relativism than skepticism in Lessing's view. He did not think that absolute truth is revealed; but even if it were, and even if he were capable of apprehending it, he would not have wished to apprehend it. Adapting an aphorism of Clement of Alexandria, Lessing declared:

> The worth of a man does not consist in the truth he possesses, or thinks he possesses, but in the pains he has taken to attain that truth. For his powers are extended not through possession but through the search for truth. In this alone his ever-growing perfection consists. Possession makes him lazy, indolent, and proud. If God held all truth in his right hand and in his left the everlasting striving after truth, so that I should always and everlastingly be mistaken and said to me, Choose, with humility I would pick on the left hand and say, Father grant me that; absolute truth is for thee alone. (*Eine Duplik*, K. Lachmann and F. Muncker, eds., Vol. XIII, p. 23)

THE MOVE TO IMMANENTISM

Several fragmentary notes found among Lessing's papers, and published in 1784 by his brother Karl in *Theologischen Nachlass*, disclose the extent of Leibniz's influence. Lessing's interest was always most deeply aroused by Leibniz's references to theology and ethics. One of these pieces, written by Lessing about 1753, "Das Christentum der Vernunft" (The Christianity of Reason), foreshadowed a section of *Die Erziehung* in its attempt at making a speculative restatement of the doctrine of the Trinity, with the help of Leibnizian ideas on the hierarchy of being and the harmony of the monads. But there is a strong admixture of Spinoza in Lessing's conception of this harmony; he did not think of it as something preestablished by a Creator who is a superobject behind and beyond phenomena, but rather as being itself God, so that the perfect continuum of existents, in which there can be no gap, is indistinguishable from the perfection of the divine being. Similarly, in the brief notes titled "Ueber die Wirklichkeit der Dinge ausser Gott" (On the Reality of Things outside God; written in 1763, published in 1795 in Karl Lessing's *Lessings Leben*), Lessing denied the thesis of traditional theism that the created world exists independently of its Creator, in the sense of being distinct from him. Lessing urged that nothing can be outside the divine mind, and that there need be no hesitation before the conclusion that, since ideas of contingent things are

themselves contingent, there is contingency even in God. These aphoristic fragments hardly amount to a coherent system. They show Lessing looking toward Spinoza, whom he had studied in his years at Breslau from 1760 to 1765, for a solution to some of the problems left unanswered by Leibniz.

Leibniz had formally asserted the freedom of the will, though it was doubted by Pierre Bayle and others whether Leibniz's libertarian assertions were in fact fully compatible with his philosophical principles. Lessing agreed with Spinoza that free will is a superfluity and an illusion. In 1776 Lessing published the *Philosophische Aufsätze* ("Philosophical Papers") of Karl Wilhelm Jerusalem, with the intention of making a protest against Johann Wolfgang von Goethe's *Werther*, with its description of Jerusalem's suicide. In a note to Jerusalem's third essay Lessing commented on his wisdom in recognizing that freedom is nothing but a cause of anxiety and fear, and that the recognition of necessity and destiny as beneficent is the only way to true happiness. "I thank my God," Lessing added, "that I am under necessity, that the best must be." The notion that the moralist has anything to fear from deterministic philosophies is just a mistake.

In 1785 at Breslau, Friedrich Heinrich Jacobi published his *Ueber die Lehre des Spinoza in Briefen an der Herrn Moses Mendelssohn* (Letters to Moses Mendelssohn on Spinoza's Doctrine), in which he disclosed that at Wolfenbüttel in July 1780, he had been told by Lessing, seven months before Lessing's death, that he could not believe the old transcendental metaphysic, and that he unreservedly accepted the pantheism of Spinoza— "There is no other philosophy." Jacobi was astonished to hear Lessing add that the determinism of Spinoza was no obstacle to him, and indeed that he had no desire for free will. Jacobi's revelations precipitated a furious controversy known as the *Pantheismusstreit*. The Enlightenment had derived from Bayle's *Dictionnaire historique et critique* such an unflattering picture of Spinoza that Jacobi's attribution of Spinozistic views to Lessing seemed like a shocking libel of a dead man. Moses Mendelssohn was moved to write an irate reply, in which he denied that Lessing was a pantheist and a determinist. Although not all of Jacobi's deductions were correct, the substantial accuracy of his account of what Lessing said is sufficiently vindicated by the fragments found among Lessing's papers. Lessing's final creed was a belief in an immanent destiny, with no room either for the concept of transcendence or for special revelation in any form; he believed in a determined pattern of cause and effect extending not only throughout the physical order of nature, but also to morality and "the realm of ends."

Lessing's legacy to posterity was therefore to give an impetus to the notion of historical inevitability, especially in *Die Erziehung des Menschengeschlechts* at the end of which he even toyed with speculations about the transmigration of souls—obviously because this concept seemed to him more compatible with his historical determinism than the traditional eschatology connected with the Christian ideas of freedom and of personality.

The strong influence of Lessing is manifested in the history of religious thought in the nineteenth century. It can be traced particularly in the work of Søren Kierkegaard, whose *Concluding Unscientific Postscript* took its starting point from Lessing's statement about the intellectually impossible leap from the contingent truths of history to the necessary truths of divine revelation. The other, more liberal, side of Lessing was reflected in Coleridge, whose work was even suspected of being a plagiarism of Lessing's. In the field of literature and art, Lessing's attack on French classicism opened the way for the romantic ideal of free self-expression and naturalism, while his final theological position of Spinozistic immanentism clearly foreshadowed Friedrich Daniel Ernst Schleiermacher's *Speeches on Religion* (*Reden über die Religion*, 1799). His consciousness of living in an age of humanist maturity anticipated the Hegelian and Comtian estimates of religion as a useful, though now surpassed, stage in the education of humanity toward something higher and truer. Probably Lessing did as much as anyone to encourage among the educated European minds of his time an attitude of critical doubt that would lead to passionate engagement, rather than impersonal remoteness.

See also Aesthetic Experience; Clement of Alexandria; Deism; Enlightenment; Jacobi, Friedrich Heinrich; Kierkegaard, Søren Aabye; Leibniz, Gottfried Wilhelm; Mendelssohn, Moses; Nicolai, Christian Friedrich; Pantheismusstreit; Positivism; Rationalism; Reimarus, Hermann Samuel; Schleiermacher, Friedrich Daniel Ernst; Spinoza, Benedict (Baruch) de; Coleridge, Samuel Taylor; Voltaire, François-Marie Arouet de; Winckelmann, Johann Joachim; Wolff, Christian.

Bibliography

WORKS BY LESSING

Selected Prose Works. Translated by E. C. Beasley and Helen Zimmern. London, 1879.

Gesammelte Werke. 23 vols., edited by Karl Lachmann and Franz Muncker. 1886–1924.

Werke, edited by Julius Petersen and W. von Olshausen. Berlin, 1925–1935.

Hamburgischen Dramaturgie, edited by G. Waterhouse. Cambridge, U.K., 1926.

Lessings Gesammelte Werke. 10 vols., edited by Paul Rilla. Berlin: Aufbau-Verlag, 1954–1958.

Laocoön. Translated by E. A. McCormick. New York, 1962.

WORKS ON LESSING

Aner, K. *Die Theologie der Lessingzeit*. Halle: Niemeyer, 1929.

Bernstein, J. M., ed. *Classic and Romantic German Aesthetics*. New York: Cambridge University Press, 2003.

Cassirer, Ernst. *Die Philosophie der Aufklärung*. Tübingen: Mohr, 1932. Translated by F. C. A. Koelln and J. P. Pettegrove as *The Philosophy of the Enlightenment*. Princeton, NJ: Princeton University Press, 1951.

Chadwick, Henry. *Lessing's Theological Writings*. Palo Alto, CA, 1956.

Goetschel, Willi. *Spinoza's Modernity: Mendelssohn, Lessing, and Heine*. Madison: University of Wisconsin Press, 2004.

Gombrich, E. H. "Lessing." *Proceedings of the British Academy* 43 (1957): 133–156.

Hazard, Paul. *La pensée européenne au 18 ème siècle. De Montesquieu à Lessing*. Paris, 1946. Translated by J. Lewis May as *European Thought in the 18th Century*. London, 1954.

O'Flaherty, James C. *The Quarrel of Reason with Itself: Essays on Hamann, Michaelis, Lessing, Nietzsche*. Columbia: Camden House, 1988.

Ritchie, Gisela F. "Contributors to the Genesis of Europe: Gotthold Ephraim Lessing and His Followers." *History of European Ideas* 19(1–3) (1994): 425–430.

Wessel, Leonard P. *G. Lessing's Theology, Reinterpretation: A Study in the Problematic Nature of the Enlightenment*. The Hague: Mouton, 1977.

Henry Chadwick (1967)
Bibliography updated by Tamra Frei (2005)

LEUCIPPUS AND DEMOCRITUS

Leucippus and Democritus were the earliest Greek atomists. The originator of the atomic theory, Leucippus (fifth century BCE), must be considered a speculative thinker of the first order, but to Democritus (c. 460–c. 370 BCE) must go the credit for working out the detailed application of the theory and supporting it with a subtle epistemology. Moreover, the range of Democritus's researches surpassed that of any earlier philosopher, and he appears to have been an original and, for his day, advanced ethical thinker.

We have very little biographical data for Leucippus. Epicurus is even reported to have said that there was no philosopher Leucippus, but the evidence of Aristotle decisively refutes this opinion (if, indeed, Epicurus did not merely intend to deny Leucippus's philosophical importance). Leucippus was probably born at Miletus; reports associating him with Elea or Abdera should be taken as reflecting views concerning his philosophical affiliations rather than as reliable evidence for his birthplace. He was presumably older than Democritus. His book *On Mind* may have been directed partly against Anaxagoras, and according to Theophrastus, Diogenes of Apollonia derived some of his theories from Leucippus. All this suggests that Leucippus was a slightly younger contemporary of Anaxagoras and that his main philosophical activity fell some time within the broad limits of 450–420 BCE.

Democritus was born at Abdera. He described himself in the *Little World-System* as a young man in the old age of Anaxagoras; Diogenes Laërtius says that he was forty years younger than Anaxagoras. On this evidence the date given for his birth by Apollodorus (in the 80th Olympiad, 460–456 BCE) is generally preferred to that suggested by Thrasylus (the third year of the 77th Olympiad, 470–469 BCE). He is variously reported to have lived between 90 and 109 years. To judge from the number of his writings, his literary activity extended over a considerable period, but we have no means of assigning different works to different times in his life. His statement that he wrote the *Little World-System* 730 years after the fall of Troy (Diogenes Laërtius, *Lives* IX, 41) is of little value since we cannot tell which of several possible chronologies for the Trojan War Democritus accepted.

Many stories, most of them apocryphal, relating to Democritus's life and character circulated in antiquity. There are the accounts of his saving the Abderites from a plague, of his dying by voluntarily abstaining from food, and of his reputation as the "Laughing Philosopher." The tradition that he traveled extensively is, however, more plausible and better grounded. The authenticity of the fragment (299) in which he claimed to be the most widely traveled of his contemporaries is disputed, and the genuineness of the five books dealing with foreign travel mentioned by Diogenes Laërtius (for example, *A Voyage round the Ocean*) has also been doubted. But evidence concerning his travels goes back to Theophrastus (see Aelian, *Varia Historia* IV, 20), and the reports that he visited such places as Egypt, Chaldea, and the Red Sea (see Diogenes Laërtius, *Lives* IX, 35) may well have a sound basis in fact.

All that has been preserved of the original writings of Leucippus and Democritus is a poor selection of isolated quotations, most of which derive from the ethical works of Democritus. For the atomic theory itself we rely on reports in Aristotle, Theophrastus, and later doxographers, who were often unsympathetic to the views of the atomists. In most of the principal texts referring to Leucippus, his doctrines are not clearly distinguished from those of Democritus, and the precise contribution of each philosopher is in question. Aristotle, however, undoubtedly treated Leucippus as the founder of atomism (*De Generatione et Corruptione* 325a23ff.), and we may reasonably attribute both the principles of the physical theory and a fairly complex cosmogony to him. Democritus evidently elaborated the atomic theory and was responsible for the detailed account of sensible qualities, besides going far beyond Leucippus both in the range of his scientific inquiries and in his interest in moral philosophy.

WRITINGS

Only two works are ascribed to Leucippus, *On Mind*, from which our sole surviving quotation comes, and the *Great World-System*, which may be attributed to Leucippus on the authority of Theophrastus (Diogenes Laërtius, *Lives* IX, 46), although Thrasylus later assigned it to Democritus.

Democritus, on the other hand, wrote some sixty-odd works, the titles of which provide valuable evidence of the scope of his interests. The main works were cataloged by Thrasylus into thirteen tetralogies. Two tetralogies are devoted to ethics and four to physics (including *Little World-System, On the Planets, On Nature, On the Nature of Man, On the Senses,* and *On Colors*). These were followed by nine works not arranged in tetralogies—for example, *Causes of Celestial Phenomena, Causes concerning Seeds, Plants and Fruits,* and three books of *Causes concerning Animals*. Three tetralogies are classified as mathematics, two deal with music and literature, and two consist of technical works, including treatises on medicine, agriculture, painting, and warfare. Nine other miscellaneous works, mostly concerning travel, are also mentioned by Diogenes Laërtius but are less certainly authentic as they were not included in Thrasylus's catalog.

Democritus's style is described by Cicero as elegant (*De Oratore* I, 11, 49) and lucid (*De Divinatione* II, 64, 133), and an anecdote recorded by Diogenes Laërtius (*Lives* IX, 40) implies that his works already had wide circulation by the time of Plato.

ENCYCLOPEDIA OF PHILOSOPHY
2nd edition

THE ATOMIC THEORY

The basic postulate of Greek atomism in its original form was that atoms and the void alone are real. The differences between physical objects, including both qualitative differences and what we think of as differences in substance, were all explained in terms of modifications in the shape, arrangement, and position of the atoms. Aristotle illustrates these three modes of difference with the examples A and N, AN and NA, and ⊐ and H.

This theory was already interpreted by Aristotle as an answer to the Eleatic denial of change and movement. Other post-Parmenidean philosophers had countered this denial in different ways, but both Empedocles and Anaxagoras had assumed a variety of elemental substances, on the one hand, the four "roots," on the other, an original mixture containing every kind of natural substance. In postulating a single elemental substance, Leucippus remained closer to Parmenides' own conception. In common with Parmenides' One Being the individual atoms are ungenerated, indestructible, unalterable, homogeneous, solid, and indivisible. Leucippus may be said to have postulated an infinite plurality of Eleatic ones, and he may even have been directly influenced by Melissus's argument (Fr. 8) that "if there were a plurality, they would have to be as the One is." Leucippus also agreed with the Eleatics that without void movement is impossible. Yet whereas the Eleatics denied the existence of the void, or "what is not," Leucippus maintained that not only "what is" (the atoms), but also "what is not" (the void), must be considered real. Leucippus thereby reinstated both plurality and change; the void is that which separates the atoms and that through which they move.

The atoms are infinite in number, dispersed through an infinite void. Their shapes are infinitely various, there being no reason that any atom should be of one shape rather than another. Democritus, at least, also allowed differences in the sizes of the atoms, but whether he thought any atom large enough to be visible seems doubtful. Late sources that report that atoms are unlimited in size as well as number (Diogenes Laërtius, *Lives* IX, 44) or which suggest the possibility of an atom the size of the world (Aëtius, *Placita* I, 12, 6) are difficult to credit in view of the testimony of Aristotle, who apparently believed that for both Leucippus and Democritus the atoms are all so small that they are invisible.

The atoms are in continuous motion. Aristotle, among others, objected that the atomists did not explain the origin of movement or say what kind of movement is natural to the atoms. However, they evidently assumed that the motion of the atoms is eternal, just as the atoms themselves are, and they perhaps drew no clear distinction between original and derived motion. Although Epicurus was later to suggest that atoms naturally fall vertically, the earlier atomists probably did not consider movement in any particular direction prior to movement in any other. Weight for them, it seems, was not a primary property of the atoms nor a cause of their interactions, although in a developed cosmos the atoms have "weight" corresponding to their size (and the weight of compound bodies varies according to the proportion of atoms and void they contain).

The movements of the atoms give rise to constant collisions whose effects are twofold. Sometimes, the atoms rebound from one another; alternatively, when the colliding atoms are hooked or barbed or their shapes otherwise correspond, they cohere and thus form compound bodies. Change of all sorts is accordingly interpreted in terms of the combining and separating of atoms, which themselves remain unaltered in substance. The compound bodies thus formed possess various sensible qualities—color, taste, temperature, and so on—and Democritus undertook a detailed exposition relating these qualities to specific atomic configurations.

COSMOGONY. Evidence concerning Leucippus's cosmogony comes mainly from Diogenes Laërtius (*Lives* IX, 31ff.). The process begins when a large group of atoms becomes isolated in a great void. There they conglomerate and form a whirl or vortex in which atoms of similar shape and size come together. In this vortex the finer atoms are squeezed out into the outer void, but the remainder tend toward the center, where they form a spherical mass. More atoms are drawn into this mass on contact with the whirl, and some of these are ignited by the speed of the revolution, thus forming the heavenly bodies. Earth is formed by atoms that cohere in the center of the mass. The cosmogonical process is not unique. The atomists argued that since atoms and the void are infinite, there are innumerable worlds. These worlds are not all alike, however; Democritus held that some worlds have no sun or moon and that some lack moisture and all forms of life (Hippolytus, *Refutatio* I, 13, 2f.).

Several features of this account are obscure, and two apparently conflicting criticisms were leveled against it in antiquity—first, that although the atomists asserted that the cosmogonical process came about by necessity, they did not explain what this necessity was (Diogenes Laërtius, *Lives* IX, 33); second, that they maintained that it occurred spontaneously (Aristotle clearly has the atomists in mind when he considered this view, *Physics* 196a24ff.).

But Aristotle's judgment should be taken as referring primarily to the atomists' exclusion of final causes; in Aristotelian terms the atomists held that the world arose spontaneously because they denied that it was intelligently planned. Leucippus explicitly stated that "nothing happens at random, but everything for a reason and by necessity" (Fr. 2), and throughout their cosmology the atomists not only excluded purpose or design but also assumed that every event is the product of a definite, theoretically determinable cause. Thus, they doubtless conceived the vortex to arise from certain mechanical interactions between the colliding atoms, although it is unlikely that they attempted to say precisely how this came about. Democritus illustrated his doctrine that like things tend to come together with examples drawn from both the inanimate and the animate sphere (Fr. 164). And like many of the pre-Socratics, the atomists constructed their cosmogony in part on an embryological model. The outer envelope of the world was likened to a membrane, and in both Leucippus's cosmogony and Democritus's embryology the process of differentiation apparently takes place from the outside (see Aristotle, *De Generatione Animalium* 740a13ff.).

ASTRONOMY AND BIOLOGY. Leucippus's astronomical theories are surprisingly retrograde. He accepted the old Ionian picture of a flat earth, tilted toward the south, and he believed that the sun is the most distant of the heavenly bodies. Democritus's theories were generally less crude, and he attempted rational explanations of a wide variety of obscure phenomena. He accepted Leucippus's account of Earth with only minor modifications (Aëtius, *Placita* III, 10, 5) but corrected his notion of the relative positions of the heavenly bodies, observing, for example, that the planets are not equidistant from Earth and placing Venus between the sun and moon. Among other topics on which some of Democritus's theories are recorded are the behavior of the magnet, the nourishment of the embryo, and the relative longevity of different types of plants. Of his biological doctrines the notion that the seed is drawn from the whole of the body (the pangenesis theory) was particularly influential (Aëtius, *Placita* V, 3, 6).

SOUL, KNOWLEDGE, AND SENSATION. Our evidence concerning the atomists' psychological and epistemological doctrines derives very largely from Democritus, although his theory of the soul was probably developed from ideas outlined by Leucippus. This theory was a materialist one in line with the principles of atomism. Democritus conceived of the soul as consisting of spherical atoms, this being the shape best adapted to penetrate and move things. Fire, too, is composed of spherical atoms, and he evidently subscribed to the common Greek belief in the connection between life and heat, now interpreted in terms of the similarity in the shapes of soul atoms and fire atoms. The soul atoms tend to be extruded from the body by the pressure of the surrounding air, but this process is counteracted by other soul atoms that enter the body with the air we breathe; life depends on this continuous replenishment.

Our main source for Democritus's theory of knowledge is Sextus Empiricus. Several of the fragments that he quotes appear to express an extreme skepticism—for instance, "We know nothing truly about anything" (Fr. 7). However, Fragment 11 shows that Democritus was no outright skeptic. There he distinguished between two modes of cognition; the senses provide what is called a "bastard" knowledge but contrasted with this is a "legitimate" knowledge, which operates on objects too fine for the senses to perceive. Clearly, "legitimate" knowledge relates to atoms and the void, which alone are real; the objects of sensation, on the other hand, exist "by convention" (Fr. 9). The doctrine enunciated in the fragments is that sense perception is not trustworthy, and Aristotle's repeated statement that the atomists found truth in appearance (*De Generatione et Corruptione* 315b9ff.) should be understood as an interpretative comment based on Aristotle's own conception of the distinction between sensibles and intelligibles. Yet although we must rely on reasoning to attain knowledge, Democritus acknowledged that the mind derives its data from the senses (Fr. 125). Not a pure intellectualist like Parmenides, a crude sensationalist like Protagoras, nor a complete skeptic as Gorgias made himself out to be, Democritus advocated critical reflection on the evidence of the senses as our best means of approaching the truth; yet since thought itself, like sensation, involves physical interactions between atoms, it, too, is subject to distortion, and even "legitimate" knowledge is at best, it seems, only opinion (Fr. 7).

Democritus's detailed accounts of the five senses were reported and criticized at length by Theophrastus (*De Sensibus* 49–82). According to Alexander (*In Librum de Sensu* 24, 14ff.), Leucippus already held that physical objects constantly emit images that effect vision on entering the eye. Democritus modified and complicated this doctrine by suggesting that images from both the object and the eye itself meet and imprint the air in front of the eye. Each of the other senses, too, is produced by contact between the organ and images deriving from the object, and thought was analogously explained as the contact between soul atoms and images coming from outside the body. But not content merely to assert in general terms that secondary qualities are due to differences in the shapes and sizes of the atoms, Democritus also proposed a detailed account relating specific tastes, colors, smells, and so on to specific shapes. Thus, an acid taste is composed of angular, small, thin atoms and a sweet taste of round, moderate-sized ones. Democritus's primary colors—black, white, red, and greenish yellow—were similarly associated with certain shapes and arrangements of atoms, and other colors were derived from combinations of these four. For all its crudities Democritus's theory may claim to be the first fully elaborated account of the physical basis of sensation.

MATHEMATICS. Democritus's interest in mathematics is apparent from the titles of fives works dealing with mathematical subjects, and we are told, for example, that he discovered the relation between the volumes of a pyramid and a prism with the same base and equal height. We have, however, little evidence on the part of his mathematical work that related directly to the atomic theory. The atoms are definitely conceived of as physically indivisible (on the grounds that they are solid and contain no void), but it is not clear whether they are absolute minima in the sense of being mathematically indivisible. Epicurus later distinguished between atomic bodies (which are physically indivisible but logically divisible) and the "minima in the atom." But Aristotle appears to have assumed that Leucippus and Democritus themselves drew no distinction between the limits of physical and mathematical divisibility (*De Generatione et Corruptione* 315b28ff.), and he considered that their atomic theory necessarily conflicted with the mathematical sciences (*De Caelo* 303a20ff.). Unless Aristotle has completely misrepresented the atomists, it would appear that Democritus was unaware of any inconsistency in holding both (1) that the atoms have different shapes and sizes and (2) that they are mathematically as well as physically indivisible. But it must be repeated that the evidence on which to convict or absolve Democritus of this gross confusion is scanty.

ETHICS. Although serious doubts have been raised concerning the transmission of the ethical fragments of Democritus, most scholars now consider that the majority of those accepted by Hermann Diels and Walther Kranz may be used as a basis from which to reconstruct his ethics. There remain, however, wide disagreements on the nature and value of his moral teaching. Alongside the fragments that convey traditional sentiments (for example, on the dangers of fame and wealth if not accompanied by intelligence) we find others that expound notions far in advance of the popular morality of the day, as, for instance, the doctrine that it is one's own consciousness of right and wrong, not fear of the law or public opinion, that should prevent one from doing anything shameful (Frs. 181, 264). And sayings such as Fragment 45 ("The wrongdoer is more unfortunate than he who is wronged") express views more commonly associated with Socrates than with Democritus.

The ethical ideal is termed "well-being" or "cheerfulness," which is to be gained through uprightness and a harmonious life. Although Democritus clearly implied that life without pleasure is not worth living and even said that pleasure is the mark of what is expedient (Fr. 188), it is the higher pleasures of the soul that we should cultivate, not those of the body. Sensual pleasures are condemned as short-lived. He repeatedly stressed that we should moderate our desires and ambitions, become self-sufficient, and be content, in the main, with simple pleasures. Yet Democritus was no quietist. Rather, he recognized that worthwhile objects are to be achieved only through effort (Frs. 157, 182).

One of the salient features of Democritus's ethics is his rejection of supernatural sanctions of behavior. In part, he seems to have rationalized belief in the gods as a mistaken inference from terrifying natural phenomena (Sextus, *Adversus Mathematicos* IX, 24), and yet he did not dismiss notions of the gods entirely, for he appears to have related certain such ideas to images, some beneficent, some harmful, that visit humans (Fr. 166). Religious sanctions are, however, rigorously excluded from his ethics. He refuted those who concocted fictions concerning the afterlife (Fr. 297), and he spoke with apparent irony of those who prayed to Zeus as "king of all" (Fr. 30). Equally, he castigated those who invented chance as an excuse for their own thoughtlessness or who failed to recognize that their misfortunes stemmed from their own incontinence (Frs. 119, 234). Throughout his ethics he may be said to have set high standards of personal integrity and social responsibility.

The question of the relation between Democritus's ethics and his physics has been much debated. In some respects, such as in the idea that excesses "cause great movements in the soul"—that is, presumably, in the soul atoms (Fr. 191)—his ethics reflect a psychology that is based on his physical theories. Whether we should expect other aspects of the atomic doctrine to be in evidence in the ethical fragments seems very doubtful. Democritus clearly did not feel (nor need he have felt) that the notion of necessity in his physics (the belief that every event has a definite cause to be sought in the interactions of the atoms) conflicted with his doctrine of moral responsibility in the sphere of human behavior. His denial of supernatural sanctions in his ethics parallels his rejection of teleology in his cosmology. And his ethics have in common with his epistemological theory that he argued against an unreflecting acceptance of the evidence of the senses concerning what is pleasant just as much as concerning the nature of reality as a whole.

SOCIOLOGY AND POLITICS. The only indication we have of Democritus's political leanings is the idealistic but otherwise rather inconclusive Fragment 251: "Poverty under democracy is as much to be preferred to so-called happiness under tyrants as freedom to slavery." It has, however, been conjectured that the account of the origin of civilization preserved in Diodorus (*Bibliotheca Historica* I, 8) owes much to Democritus. According to this, primitive peoples originally gathered in groups for the sake of mutual protection from wild animals, and subsequently language and the arts were also invented under the spur of human needs. It is very uncertain how far this reproduces Democritus's ideas, but there is some evidence in the fragments that he maintained a naturalistic theory of civilization and progress and excluded teleological explanations here, as he did elsewhere in his philosophy. Fragment 144 may be taken to suggest that he believed that the earliest arts (although not some of the later ones) were products of necessity, and in Fragment 154 he argued that humans learned many of their skills by copying the behavior of animals.

The theory founded by Leucippus and developed by Democritus was the most coherent and economical physical system of its day, and the history of its influence can be traced from the fourth century BCE to modern times. Although Plato mentioned neither Leucippus nor Democritus, the *Timaeus* is markedly indebted to their thought. Even Aristotle, who rejected atomism outright, conceded that of all his predecessors Democritus was the most notable physicist. Later, the Epicureans championed atomism against the continuum theory of the Stoics. Leucippus's theory, in origin primarily an answer to the Eleatic arguments against change, was the first clear formulation of the doctrine that matter exists in the form of discrete particles, and as such it may legitimately be considered the prototype of modern theories of the discontinuous structure of matter, even though the nature of

such theories, the problems they are intended to resolve, and the methods used to establish them all differ fundamentally from those of ancient atomism.

See also Alexander of Aphrodisias; Anaxagoras of Clazomenae; Aristotle; Atomism; Cosmology; Diodorus Cronus; Diogenes Laertius; Diogenes of Apollonia; Empedocles; Epicureanism and the Epicurean School; Epicurus; Gorgias of Leontini; Parmenides of Elea; Plato; Pre-Socratic Philosophy; Protagoras of Abdera; Quantum Mechanics; Sextus Empiricus; Stoicism; Theophrastus.

Bibliography

The extant fragments of Leucippus and Democritus and the principal reports and commentaries in ancient authors are collected in Hermann Diels's *Die Fragmente der Vorsokratiker*, Vol. II, 6th ed., with additions by Walther Kranz, ed. (Berlin, 1952). There is an English translation of the fragments in Kathleen Freeman, *Ancilla to the Pre-Socratic Philosophers* (Cambridge, MA: Harvard University Press, 1948).

More recent collections of texts are S. Luria, *Democritea* (Leningrad, 1970; original texts of fragments and testimonia with Russian translation and commentary) and C. C. W. Taylor, *The Atomists: Leucippus and Democritus. Fragments: A Text and Translation with a Commentary* (Toronto: University of Toronto Press, 1999; fragments in Greek with facing English translation, testimonia in translation, commentary).

A classic monograph on Leucippus and Democritus is Cyril Bailey, *The Greek Atomists and Epicurus* (Oxford, 1928). Lucid, brief expositions of their thought are found in G. S. Kirk, J. E. Raven and M. Schofield, *The Presocratic Philosophers*, 2nd ed. (Cambridge, U.K., 1983) and in R. D. McKirahan Jr., *Philosophy before Socrates* (Indianapolis and Cambridge, 1994). W. K. C. Guthrie, *A History of Greek Philosophy*, vol. 2 (Cambridge, U.K.: Cambridge University Press, 1965), contains a full discussion and extensive bibliography. Other significant general studies are E. Zeller, *Die Philosophie der Griechen*, 6th ed., revised and enlarged by W. Nestle (Leipzig, 1920), Part I, Sec. 2, pp. 1038–1194; Wilhelm Schmidt in Wilhelm Schmidt and Otto Stählin, eds., *Geschichte der griechischen Literatur* (Munich, 1948), Part I, Sec. 5, pp. 224–349; V. E. Alfieri, *Gli atomisti* (Bari, 1936) and *Atomos Idea*, 2nd ed. (Florence, 1979); J. Barnes, *The Presocratic Philosophers*, 2nd ed. (London and Boston: Routledge and K. Paul, 1982), Chapters 17, 19 (*b*), 20, 21 (*c*), 23 (*d*), 24 (*e*); P.-M. Morel, *Démocrite et la recherche des causes* (Paris, 1996); and J. Salem, *Démocrite: Grains de poussière dans un rayon de soleil* (Paris: CNRS-Éditions, 1996).

A full discussion of the chronological and biographical data on Democritus is contained in D. O'Brien, "Démocrite d'Abdère" in R. Goulet, ed., *Dictionnaire des Philosophes Antiques*, vol. 2, pp. 649–715 (Paris: CNRS-Éditions, 1994).

PHYSICS AND COSMOLOGY

Barnes, J. "Reason and Necessity in Leucippus." In *Proceedings of the First International Conference on Democritus,* edited by L. Benakis. Vol. 1, pp. 141–158. Xanthi, 1984.

Bury, R. G. "The Origin of Atomism." *Classical Review* 30 (1916): 1–4.

Dyroff, Adolf. *Demokritstudien.* Leipzig: Dieterich, 1899.

Fritz, Kurt von. *Philosophie und sprachlicher Ausdruck bei Demokrit, Plato und Aristoteles.* New York, n.d. [1939].

Furley, D. J. *Cosmic Problems.* Cambridge, U.K., and New York: Cambridge University Press, 1989. Chapters 7–9.

Furley, D. J. *The Greek Cosmologists.* Cambridge, U.K., and New York: Cambridge University Press, 1987. Chapters 9–13.

Furley, D. J. "Weight and Motion in Democritus' Theory." *Oxford Studies in Ancient Philosophy* 1 (1983): 193–209.

Hammer-Jensen, Ingeborg. "Demokrit und Platon." *Archiv für Geschichte der Philosophie,* n.s. 16 (1910): 92–105, 211–229.

Kersehensteiner, Jula. "Zu Leukippos A 1." *Hermes* 87 (1959): 441–448.

Löbl, R. *Demokrits Atomphysik.* Darmstadt: Wissenschaftliche Buchgesellschaft, 1987.

Löwenheim, Louis. *Die Wissenschaft Demokrits.* Berlin: Simion, 1914.

Makin, S. *Indifference Argument.* Oxford and Cambridge, MA: Blackwell, 1993.

McDiarmid, J. B. "Theophrastus *De Sensibus* 61–62: Democritus' Theory of Weight." *Classical Philology* 55 (1960): 28–30.

Mugler, Charles. "Sur Quelques Particularités de l'atomisme ancien." *Revue de philologie,* 3rd series 27 (1953): 141–174.

O'Brien, D. *Theories of Weight in the Ancient World.* Vol. 1: *Democritus: Weight and Size.* Paris: les Belles Letters; and Leiden: Brill, 1981.

Sambursky, Samuel. "Atomism versus Continuum Theory in Ancient Greece." *Scientia* 96 (1961): 376–381.

EPISTEMOLOGY

McDiarmid, J. B. "Theophrastus *De Sensibus* 66: Democritus' Explanation of Salinity." *American Journal of Philology* 80 (1959): 56–66.

McKim, R. "Democritus against Scepticism: All Sense-Impressions Are True." In Benakis op. cit., vol. 1, pp. 281–290.

Weiss, Helene. "Democritus' Theory of Cognition." *Classical Quarterly* 32 (1938): 47–56.

MATHEMATICS

Bodnár, I. M. "Atomic Independence and Indivisibility." *Oxford Studies in Ancient Philosophy* 16 (1998): 35–61.

Furley, D. J. *Two Studies in the Greek Atomists.* Princeton, NJ, 1977. Study 1, "Indivisible Magnitudes."

Makin, S. "The Indivisibility of the Atom." *Archiv für Geschichte der Philosophie* 71 (1989): 125–149.

Luria, Salomo. "Die Infinitesimaltheorie der antiken Atomisten." *Quellen und Studien zur Geschichte der Mathematik, Astronomie und Physik,* Part 2 (Studies) 2, Sec. 2 (Berlin, 1932–1933): 106–185.

Mau, Jürgen. *Zum Problem des Infinitesimalen bei den antiken Atomisten.* Berlin: Akademie-Verlag, 1954.

Philippson, Robert. "Democritea." *Hermes* 64 (1929): 175–183.

Vlastos, Gregory. "Minimal Parts in Epicurean Atomism." *Isis* 56 (1965): 121–147.

Zubov, V. P. "K Voprosu o Matematicheskom Atomisme Democrita." *Vestnik Drevnei Istorii* 4 (1951): 204–208.

ETHICS

Kahn, C. H. "Democritus and the Origins of Moral Psychology." *American Journal of Philology* 106 (1985): 1–31.

Langerbeck, Hermann. ΔΟΞΙΣ ΕΠΙΡΥΣΜΙΗ. *Neue Philologische Untersuchungen,* Vol. X. Berlin, 1935.

Laue, Heinrich. *De Democriti Fragmentis Ethicis.* Unpublished dissertation, University of Göttingen, 1921.

Laue, Heinrich. "Die Ethik des Demokritos." *Sokrates,* n.s. 11 (1923–1924): 23–28, 49–62.

Luria, Salomo. *Zur Frage der materialistischen Begründung der Ethik bei Demokrit.* Berlin: Akademie-Verlag, 1964.

McGibbon, Donal. "Pleasure as the 'Criterion' in Democritus." *Phronesis* 5 (1960): 75–77.

McGibbon, Donal. "The Religious Thought of Democritus." *Hermes* 93 (1965): 385–397.

Natorp, Paul. *Die Ethika des Demokritos.* Marburg: Elwert, 1893.

Philippson, Robert. "Demokrits Sittensprüche." *Hermes* 59 (1924): 369–419.

Stewart, Zeph. "Democritus and the Cynics." *Harvard Studies in Classical Philology* 63 (1958): 179–191.

Taylor, C. C. W. "Pleasure, Knowledge and Sensation in Democritus." *Phronesis* 12 (1967): 6–27.

Vlastos, Gregory. "Ethics and Physics in Democritus." *Philosophical Review* 54 (1945): 578–592; 55 (1946): 53–64.

Warren, J. *Epicurus and Democritean Ethics.* Cambridge, U.K., and New York: Cambridge University Press, 2002.

SOCIOLOGY AND POLITICS

Aalders, G. J. D. "The Political Faith of Democritus." *Mnemosyne,* 4th series, 3 (1950): 302–313.

Procopé, J. F. "Democritus on Politics and the Care of the Soul." *Classical Quarterly,* n.s. 39 (1989): 307–331 and 40 (1990): 21–45.

Vlastos, Gregory. "On the Pre-history in Diodorus." *American Journal of Philology* 67 (1946): 51–59.

G. E. R. Lloyd (1967)
Bibliography updated by C. C. W. Taylor (2005)

LEVINAS, EMMANUEL
(1906–1995)

Emmanuel Levinas was born in Kaunas, Lithuania, of Jewish parents. His education familiarized him with the Hebrew Bible and the Russian novelists. After having studied at the gymnasiums in Kaunas and Charkow, Ukraine, he traveled to Strasbourg, where he studied philosophy from 1924 to 1929. He spent the academic year of 1928–1929 in Freiburg, where he attended the last seminars given by Edmund Husserl and the lectures and seminars of Martin Heidegger. His dissertation, *La théorie de l'intuition dans la phénoménologie de Husserl,* was published in 1930. In 1930 Levinas settled in Paris, where he worked for the Alliance Israélite Universelle and its schools located throughout the Mediterranean. In 1947 he became the director of the École Normale Israélite Orientale, the training facility for teachers of those schools. In 1961 he was appointed professor of philosophy at the University of Poitiers and in 1967 at the University of Nanterre. In 1973 he moved to the Sorbonne, where he became an honorary professor in 1976. Levinas died on December 25, 1995, a few days before his 90th birthday.

WORKS

Until World War II most of Levinas's writing focused on introducing the phenomenology of Husserl and Heidegger into France. His early commentaries on their work were collected in *En découvrant l'existence avec Husserl et Heidegger* (1949). His first personal essay was the article "De l'évasion" (1935), whose central question was whether it is possible to evade the totalizing tendency of being. The search for an answer coincided with the beginning of his criticism of Heidegger's ontology. Levinas's first personal book, with the anti-Heideggerian title *De l'existence à l'existant* (*From Existence to Existents* or *From Being to Beings*), was published in 1947. In the same year he gave a lecture series under the title *Le temps et l'autre* (*Time and the Other*), in which some central thoughts of his later work are anticipated. A part of *De l'existence à l'existant* to which Levinas later refers with approval is its phenomenology of *il y a* ("there is"), that is, being in its most general and indeterminate or empty sense, preceding all determination, order, and structure. Levinas describes it as a formless and obscure night and a silent murmur, an anonymous and chaotic atmosphere or field of forces from which no being can escape. It threatens the existing entities by engulfing and suffocating them. As such, being is horrible, not because it would kill—death is not an evasion from it—but because of its depersonalizing character. All beings are caught in the anonymity of this primordial materiality—much different from the giving essence of *es gibt* as described by Heidegger.

The work that made Levinas famous is *Totalité et infini. Essai sur l'extériorité* (1961). As an attack on the entirety of Western philosophy, including Heidegger's ontology, this work tries to show why philosophy has not been faithful to the most important facts of human existence and how its basic perspective should be replaced by another one. The "totality" of the title stands for the absolutization of a panoramic perspective from which reality is understood as an all-encompassing universe. All kinds of relation, separation, exteriority, and alterity are then reduced to internal moments of one totality. Borrowing from Plato's *Sophist,* Levinas affirms that Western philosophy reduces the other (*to heteron*) to "the Same" (*tauton*). The resulting tautology is an egology because the totalization is operated by the consciousness of an ego that does not recognize any irreducible heteronomy.

The relative truth of the ego's autonomy is shown in a phenomenology of the way in which human beings inhabit the world. Levinas characterizes this "economy" (from *oikos* = house, and *nomos* = law) as vitality and enjoyment of the elements. Implicitly polemicizing against Heidegger's description of *Dasein*'s being-in-the-world, he focuses on the dimension of human eating, drinking, walking, swimming, dwelling, and laboring, a dimension more primordial than the handling of tools and much closer to the natural elements than scientific or technological objectification.

The infinite (*l'infini*), which Levinas contrasts with the totality, is another name for "the Other" insofar as this does not fit into the totality. In order to determine the relation between consciousness, the totality, and the infinite, Levinas refers to René Descartes's *Meditations on the First Philosophy,* in which Descartes insists on the fact that the idea of the infinite is original and cannot be deduced from any other idea. It surpasses the capacity of consciousness, which in it "thinks more than it can think" (see Levinas's *Collected Philosophical Papers,* p. 56). The relation between the ego and the infinite is one of transcendence: The infinite remains exterior to consciousness, although this is essentially related to its "height."

The concrete sense of the formal structure thus indicated is shown through a phenomenology of the human other, whose "epiphany" reveals an absolute command: As soon as I am confronted, I discover myself to be under an absolute obligation. The fact of the other's existence immediately reveals to me the basic ought of all ethics. On this level is and ought are inseparable. Instead of the other (*l'autre* or *autrui*), Levinas often uses the expressions "the face" (*le visage*) or "the speech" (*la parole,* also *le langage*) because the other's looking at me and speaking to me are the two most striking expressions of the other's infinity or "height." As the relation between an economically established ego and the infinite other, the intersubjective relation is asymmetrical: The other appears primarily not as equal to me but rather as "higher" and commanding me. I am responsible for the other's life, a responsibility that puts infinite demands on me, but I cannot order another to give his or her life for me.

In his second major work, *Autrement qu'être ou audelà de l'essence* (1974), Levinas continues his analyses of the relationship between the ego and the other but now emphasizes the basic structure of the ego, or rather of the "me" in the accusative, as put into question, accused, and unseated by the other. The relationship is described as nonchosen responsibility, substitution, obsession, being hostage, persecution. Subjectivity (the "me" of *me voici*) is determined as a nonchosen being-for-the-other and, thus, as basically nonidentical with itself, a passivity more or otherwise passive than the passivity that is opposed to activity. Subjectivity is primarily sensibility, being touched and affected by the other, vulnerability.

In the course of his analyses Levinas discovered that the other, me, and the transcendence that relates and separates them do not fit into the framework of phenomenology: Neither the other nor I (me) is phenomenon; transcendence does not have the structure of intentionality. Through phenomenology Levinas thus arrived at another level of thinking. He did not join Heidegger's call for a new ontology, however.

In *Autrement qu'être* Levinas gives a new description of the way being "is": *Esse* is *interesse*; being is an active and transitive "interestingness" (*intéressement*), which permeates all beings and weaves them together in a network of mutual interest. If ontology is the study of (this) being, it is not able to express the other, transcendence, and subjectivity. Transcendence surpasses being. Appealing to Plato, who characterized the good as *epekeina tès ousias*, Levinas points at transcendence, infinity, and otherness as "otherwise" and "beyond" the realm of being (or essence).

The other, subjectivity, and transcendence—but then also morality, affectivity, death, suffering, freedom, love, history, and many other (quasi-)phenomena—resist, not only phenomenology and ontology, but all kinds of objectification and thematization. As soon as they are treated in a reflective discourse, they are converted into a said (*dit*). The saying (*dire*), in which the "otherwise than being" (that which is not a phenomenon, a being, or a theme) addresses itself to an addressee, is lost in the text of the said. However, thematization and objectification are inevitable, especially in philosophy and science, but also in the practical dimensions of law, economy, and politics. The organization of justice cannot do without generalization and grouping of individuals into totalities. The transition from the asymmetrical relation between the other and me to the generalities of justice is founded in the fact that the other human who, here and now, obligates me infinitely somehow represents all other humans.

How does the intersubjective and asymmetric transcendence differ from the relationship to God? "Otherness," "infinity," and "beyond" do not apply to God in the same way as to the human other. God is neither an object nor a you; no human being can meet with God directly, but God has left a trace. The infinite responsibility of the one for the other refers to an election that precedes freedom. In coming from an immemorial, anachronical "past," responsibility indicates the "preoriginary" "illeity" of God. The *il* or *ille* of "the most high" is sharply distinguished from the chaotic anonymity of *il y a*; the dimensions of economy, morality, and justice separate the indeterminacy of being from the beyond-all-determinacy of God. However, as the practical and theoretical recognition of the relationship between God and humans, religion cannot be separated from ethics: The only way to venerate God is through devotion to human others.

Besides the two books summarized here, Levinas wrote many articles. Most of these were collected in *Humanisme de l'autre homme* (1972), *De Dieu qui vient à l'idée* (1982), *Hors sujet* (1987), and *Entre nous* (1991).

Like all other philosophers, Levinas has convictions that cannot be reduced to universally shared experiences, common sense, or purely rational principles. In addition to his philosophical work he wrote extensively on Jewish questions from an orthodox Jewish, and especially Talmudic, point of view. In his philosophical writings he quotes the Bible perhaps as often as William Shakespeare or Fëdor Dostoevsky, but these quotations are not meant to replace philosophical justification of his assertions. Phenomenological rigor and emphasis are typical of his method, even where he points beyond the dimensions of phenomena and conceptuality.

See also Consciousness in Phenomenology; Descartes, René; Dostoevsky, Fyodor Mikhailovich; Heidegger, Martin; Husserl, Edmund; Infinity in Theology and Metaphysics; Ontology; Phenomenology; Plato.

Bibliography

A complete bibliography of primary and secondary texts published between 1929 and 1989 is given in Roger Burggraeve, *Emmanuel Levinas; une bibliographie primaire et secondaire (1929–1985) avec complément 1985–1989.* Leuven: Peeters, 1990.

The most important philosophical books of Levinas are:

La théorie de l'intuition dans la phénoménologie de Husserl. Paris: Alcan, 1930; 2nd ed., 1963. Translated by A. Orianne as *The Theory of Intuition in Husserl's Phenomenology.* Evanston, IL: Northwestern University Press, 1973.

De l'existence à l'existant. Paris, 1947; 2nd ed., 1978. Translated by A. Lingis as *Existence and Existents.* The Hague: Nijhoff, 1978.

Le temps et l'autre. Montpellier, 1979 (2nd ed. of Levinas's contribution to *Le choix, le monde, l'existence* [Paris, 1948]). Translated by R. Cohen as *Time and the Other.* Pittsburgh: Duquesne University Press, 1987.

En découvrant l'existence avec Husserl et Heidegger. Paris, 1949; 2nd ed., Paris: Vrin, 1967. Partially translated by A. Lingis in *Collected Philosophical Papers* (v. infra).

Totalité et Infini. Essai sur l'extériorité. The Hague: Nijhoff, 1961. Translated by A. Lingis as *Totality and Infinity: An Essay on Exteriority.* Pittsburgh: Duquesne University Press, 1969.

Humanisme de l'autre homme. Montpellier: Fata Morgana, 1972.

Autrement qu'être ou au-delà de l'essence. The Hague: Nijhoff, 1974. Translated by A. Lingis as *Otherwise than Being or Beyond Essence.* The Hague: Nijhoff, 1981.

De Dieu qui vient à l'idée. Paris: Vrin, 1982.

Collected Philosophical Papers. Translated by A. Lingis. Boston: Nijhoff, 1987. Contains the English translation of twelve thematic essays from several volumes and journals.

Hors sujet. Montpellier, 1987.

Entre nous: Essais sur le penser-à-l'autre. Paris: Bernard Grasset, 1991.

SECONDARY LITERATURE

Bernasconi, R., and S. Critchley, eds. *Re-reading Levinas.* Bloomington: Indiana University Press, 1991.

Bernasconi, R., and D. Wood, eds. *The Provocation of Levinas: Rethinking the Other.* London: Routledge, 1988.

Chalier, C., and M. Abensour, eds. *Emmanuel Levinas.* Paris: Editions de l'Herne, 1991.

Cohen, R., ed. *Face to Face with Levinas.* Albany: State University of New York Press, 1986.

Greisch, J., and J. Rolland, eds. *Emmanuel Levinas. L'éthique comme philosophie première.* Paris, 1993.

Peperzak, A., ed. *Ethics as First Philosophy: The Significance of Emmanuel Levinas for Religion, Literature and Philosophy.* New York: Routledge, 1995.

Peperzak, A. *To the Other: An Introduction to the Philosophy of Emmanuel Levinas.* West Lafayette, IN: Purdue University Press, 1993.

Wyschogrod, E. *Emmanuel Levinas: The Problem of Ethical Metaphysics.* The Hague: Nijhoff, 1974.

Adriaan Peperzak (1996)

LÉVY-BRUHL, LUCIEN
(1857–1939)

Lucien Lévy-Bruhl, the French philosopher and social anthropologist, was educated at the University of Paris and the École Normale Supérieure. He occupied the chair of philosophy at the Lycée Louis-le-Grand from 1885 to 1895, when he became *maître de conférences* at the Sorbonne; in 1908 he was appointed titular professor. In 1916 he became editor of the *Revue philosophique.*

Lévy-Bruhl's early work was devoted to the history of philosophy, particularly that of Auguste Comte. While still under the influence of Comte and also of Émile Durkheim, he published *La morale et la science des moeurs* (Paris, 1903; translated by E. Lee as *Ethics and Moral Science,* London, 1905). It stressed the need for detailed empirical studies of the diverse moral attitudes and ideas of different societies as well as the adaptation of these ideas to the social structure of the group. He considered such a description and explanation as a preliminary to a possible applied science of morals, which would give men the same power to modify social life as physical technology gives them over natural phenomena.

Lévy-Bruhl did not develop this idea of a moral technology but devoted most of his life to investigating an extremely wide range of anthropological data derived from the reports of other observers. The interest of his work lies in the theoretical ideas that he applied to this material.

Lévy-Bruhl argued that the behavior of men in primitive societies must be understood in terms of Durkheim's concept of "collective representations," which are emotional and mystical rather than intellectual. The primitive man's world is dominated by occult powers, and his thought is "prelogical," following a law of participation and quite indifferent to what civilized man would regard as self-contradictions. For example, the members of a totemic group may regard themselves as actually identical with their totem, as belonging to a continuum of spiritual powers, rather than as existing as distinct individuals. Prelogical concepts imply no systematic unity but "welter, as it were, in an atmosphere of mystical possibilities" (*How Natives Think,* Ch. 3). Space, for instance, is conceived, not as a homogeneous whole, but in terms of the mystical ties binding each tribe to a particular region, the structure of the ties being understood in terms of the various occult forces to which the life of the tribe is subject.

Primitive man is similarly indifferent to conceptions of causality as understood in civilized cultures. For him there is no natural order within which perceptible phenomena are causally interconnected, but, equally, nothing happens by chance. Events are brought about directly, not through any mechanism of secondary causes; they are effected by the imperceptible denizens of an occult realm who have no definite spatiotemporal location and who may be felt as present in several places simultaneously.

Durkheim's followers have criticized Lévy-Bruhl for failing to bring out the connections between primitive collective representations and social structure. He has also been accused of overstressing the extent of prelogical elements in primitive thought. In attempting to reconcile the existence of fairly highly developed arts and crafts in primitive tribes with his denial that such tribes thought at all in terms of logical and causal connections, he held that such manual skills are not based on reasoning but "are guided by a kind of special sense or tact," refined by experience without benefit of reflection. Lévy-Bruhl's most serious philosophical shortcoming, perhaps, is his failure to see anything problematic about the nature of logic itself and the role it plays in civilized life. His identification of logical thought with the thought of Western civilization prevented him from perceiving many important continuities and analogies between primitive and civilized attitudes and practices.

See also Comte, Auguste; Durkheim, Émile; History and Historiography of Philosophy; Logic, History of; Philosophical Anthropology.

Bibliography

ADDITIONAL WORKS BY LÉVY-BRUHL

History of Modern Philosophy in France (1899). New York: B. Franklin, 1971.

La philosophie d'Auguste Comte. Paris: Alcan, 1900. Translated by K. de Braumont-Klein as *The Philosophy of Auguste Comte.* London: Sonnenschein, 1903.

Les fonctions mentales dans les sociétés inférieures. Paris: Alcan, 1910. Translated by L. A. Clare as *How Natives Think.* London: Allen and Unwin, 1926.

La mentalité primitive. Paris: Alcan, 1922. Translated by L. A. Clare as *Primitive Mentality.* New York: Macmillan, 1923.

L'ame primitive. Paris: Alcan, 1927. Translated by L. A. Clare as *The "Soul" of the Primitive.* London: Allen and Unwin, 1928.

La morale et la science des moeurs (1927). 16th ed. Paris: Presses Universitaires de France, 1971.

Le surnaturel et la nature dans la mentalité primitive. Paris: Alcan, 1931. Translated by L. A. Clare as *Primitives and the Supernatural.* London: Allen and Unwin, 1936.

La mythologie primitive. Le monde mythique des Australiens et des Papous. Paris: Alcan, 1935.

Les carnets de Lucien Lévy-Bruhl. Paris: Presses Universitaires de France, 1949.

The Notebooks on Primitive Mentality. Oxford: Blackwell, 1975.

WORKS ON LÉVY-BRUHL

Cailliet, Émile. *Mysticisme et "mentalité mystique." Étude d'un problème posé par les travaux de M. Lévy-Bruhl sur la mentalité primitive.* Paris, 1938.

Leroy, Olivier. *La raison primitive. Essai de réfutation de la théorie du prélogisme.* Paris: Geuthner, 1927.

Peter Winch (1967)

LEWIS, CLARENCE IRVING
(1883–1964)

Clarence Irving Lewis, the American epistemologist, logician, and moral philosopher, was born in Stoneham, Massachusetts, and educated at Harvard University (AB, 1906; PhD, 1910). He taught at the University of California from 1911 to 1920 and at Harvard from 1920 until his retirement in 1953; after 1930 he was the Edward Pierce professor of philosophy. He delivered the Carus Lectures in 1945 and the Woodbridge Lectures in 1954.

Lewis was a student and critic of modern extensional systems of logic and developed a modal logic based on the notion of strict implication. In epistemology and ethics, he was a pragmatic Kantian.

Lewis internalized within himself the great dialogue on knowledge and reality which began with René Descartes and continued with the British empiricists, Immanuel Kant and the German idealists, and the American pragmatists. It may be said that this tortuous development, both in its long history and in the intellectual life of Lewis, is the attempt of the modern mind to achieve consistency and adequacy in its conceptual foundations.

The basic commitments of any philosopher, whether formulated or not, concern the nature and modes of knowledge; they not only determine what is philosophically problematic for him but also determine how intelligibility can be achieved. Lewis modifies the classical certainty theory of knowledge, which maintains that knowing is an infallible state of mind. He contends that it does not make sense to talk about knowledge where there is no possibility of error. Knowing, according to him, is an assertive state of mind that is subject to appraisal as correct or incorrect by virtue of its relationship to what it is about, and also subject to appraisal as justified or unjustified in terms of its grounds or reasons. Thus the apprehension of a sensory given, or, in other words, the occurrence of an appearance, the classical paradigm of empirical knowledge, is not regarded by Lewis as knowledge, for there is no possibility of error. The apprehension of the appearance and its existence are indistinguishable.

Yet Lewis's departure from the tradition is not great. He, too, insists that at the foundation of our knowledge structure there must be certainty and that this is found in knowledge of sensory appearances. This certainty, however, does not reside in the apprehension of the given. Sensory appearances may be linguistically reported in "expressive" language, which denotes and signifies only appearances. Although there can be no error in the apprehension of a given appearance, it is possible to tell lies about it. Therefore, such reports are statements with truth-values. But still there is no knowledge, for no judgment is made in which the person could be in error. Knowledge is born at the level of what Lewis calls "terminating judgments," which are of the form "'S being given, if A then E,' where [in expressive language] 'A' represents some mode of action taken to be possible, 'E' some expected consequence in experience, and 'S' the sensory cue." For example, there being a red patch in my visual field, if I seem to turn my head to the left, the red patch moves to the right. Such a judgment is not merely the apprehension of a given, or the linguistic expression of such. It embodies a prediction that the red patch will be displaced to the right if the specified condition is fulfilled, which Lewis contends is conclusively verified by the occurrence of the mentioned appearances.

Thus Lewis locates certainty in verified terminating judgments, which are about sensory appearances. Furthermore, he claims that all knowledge about the world is grounded in and derived from such certainties. Although this is more sophisticated than the traditional empiricist's account, it comes to much the same subjectivistic conclusion, namely, that the direct objects of knowledge are subjective and private, and therefore falls heir to all the problems of modern subjectivism. Lewis's major works are devoted to the central and toughest of these problems: how to make intelligible, from within these epistemological commitments, empirical knowledge of the objective world; a priori knowledge, including mathematics, logic, and philosophy itself; and value claims and normative judgments.

EMPIRICAL KNOWLEDGE OF THE OBJECTIVE WORLD

The paradigm of empirical knowledge for Lewis is the verified terminating judgment. It alone can be conclusively verified. All other empirical judgments are nonterminating. They may be shown to be probable but cannot be established with certainty. The probability value they have is conferred upon them by the verification of terminating judgments that they entail. Therefore, a necessary condition for a nonterminating judgment to be confirmable in any degree, and thus meaningful, is for it to entail terminating judgments.

Any statement that purports to be about objects other than appearances, such as physical objects, is nonterminating, and insofar as it is confirmable and therefore meaningful, it entails terminating judgments, which are about appearances only. It would seem that the full meaning of such a statement would be expressible in the

terminating statements entailed by it and that, since these statements are about appearances only, the physical-object statement itself would really refer only to appearances. This would be phenomenalism.

Lewis resists this conclusion. He gives two arguments for realism. The first is that although a physical-object statement is intensionally equivalent to an inexhaustible set of terminating statements and the terms in the latter refer only to appearances, the terms in the physical-object statement genuinely denote physical objects. Thus we have two sets of statements, phenomenalistic and physical-object statements. For each physical-object statement there is a set (although inexhaustible) of phenomenalistic statements intensionally equivalent to it. By confirming the phenomenalistic set we confirm its equivalent physical-object statement with the same degree of probability. Yet the two are about radically different kinds of objects, and from knowledge of appearances we derive knowledge of physical objects.

This argument turns upon his theory of meaning. Lewis distinguishes four modes of the meaning of terms: (1) *denotation,* "the class of all actual things to which the term applies" (for example, the denotation of "man" is the class of all actual men, past, present, and future); (2) *comprehension,* "the classification of all possible or consistently thinkable things to which the term would be correctly applicable" (for example, the comprehension of "man" includes not only actual men but those who might have been but were not, like the present writer's sisters, since he has none); (3) *signification,* "that property in things the presence of which indicates that the term correctly applies, and the absence of which indicates that it does not apply" (for example, the property "rationality" is often regarded as included in the signification of "man"), and (4) *intension,* which consists of (*a*) linguistic intension or connotation, all other terms which must be applicable to anything to which the given term is applicable (for example, "animal" must be applicable to anything to which "man" is applicable); and (*b*) sense meaning, the criterion in mind, an imagined operation "by reference to which one is able to apply or refuse to apply the expression in question in the case of the presented, or imagined, things or situations" (for example, the sense meaning of "kilogon" is the imagined operation of counting the sides of a plane figure and the completion of the operation with the count of 1,000). Since he regards "propositions," statements with the assertive factor extracted (for example, "Mary's baking pies"), as terms, these modes of meaning apply to them as well. He further distinguishes between the "holophrastic" meaning of a statement, its meaning as a whole, and its "analytic" meaning, the meaning of its terms.

His argument is that although the holophrastic intensional meaning of a physical-object statement is the same as that of a set of phenomenalistic statements, the physical-object statement and its corresponding set of phenomenalistic statements are different in their analytic denotive meaning, the former denoting physical objects and the latter appearances.

Lewis rightly maintains that any two expressions that have the same intension have the same signification. Yet if a term denotes a physical object, it must signify a physical-object property. Therefore such a term could not have the same signification as a phenomenalistic term. Hence it seems that a physical-object statement could not have the same intension as a set of phenomenalistic statements.

Lewis senses this difficulty and seeks to avoid it by speaking of intension, in the form of sense meaning, as "that in mind which refers to signification." Appearances are said to signalize objective properties or states of affairs. Yet he gives no account of how this is possible for beings who can apprehend only appearances. How can appearances, as simple occurrences, be signs of anything other than other appearances? It would seem that the only way out of this subjectivistic trap is to regard appearances not as simple occurrences or objects of apprehension but as intentional in nature, as experiences of physical objects that embody truth claims about them which can be assessed as true or false on the basis of their consistency or lack of it with the claims of other experiences.

Lewis's second argument for realism turns upon the interpretation of "if ... then ..." in terminating judgments. He regards it as a contrary-to-fact conditional, that is, he claims that the truth of the conditional as a whole is independent of the truth-value of the antecedent and therefore may be significantly asserted when the antecedent is known to be false. Therefore, since it does not express a logical relation of entailment or a truth-functional relationship, it must express a real connection, perhaps causality, that holds between the facts or states of affairs located or referred to by the antecedent and the consequent of the conditional sentence. Belief in a real world, he maintains, is belief in such contrary-to-fact conditionals.

It is not clear how this is an argument for realism. Why must independent physical objects be assumed to account for the contrary-to-fact character of terminating judgments? Why couldn't the "real" connection hold between kinds of appearances?

Furthermore, if terminating judgments are to be interpreted in the manner of the contrary-to-fact conditional, does this not compromise their conclusive verifiability? It would seem to introduce an element of generality that would transcend any specific sequence of subjective experiences. In fact, Lewis himself, for other reasons, held that no terminating judgment of the form "S being given, if A then E" is strictly entailed by a physical-object statement. The most we can say, he concluded, is "If P [physical-object statement], then when presentation S is given and act A is performed, it is more or less highly probable that E will be observed to follow." Since the statement is inconclusive, it seems that he has given up the terminating character of "terminating" judgments.

Lewis has not, it seems, made a convincing case for realism from within his phenomenalistic foundations. Some have concluded that it is impossible to do so and that the only way out of phenomenalism is to abandon the subjectivistic starting point itself.

A PRIORI KNOWLEDGE

The a priori disciplines, namely, mathematics, logic, and philosophy, were the stronghold of classical rationalism. They were regarded as yielding knowledge, grounded in rational intuition, about the essential and necessary structure of the world. Empiricists, for the most part, claim that such knowledge is only intralinguistic, that it consists of analytic truths, which are said to be uninformative about the world.

Lewis subscribes to the view that all "a priori truth is definitive in nature and rises exclusively from the analysis of concepts." Unlike many empiricists, however, he is not content with merely characterizing a priori knowledge as analytic. For him, concepts, their logical relations, and their relation to the data of sense and the structure of the world are highly problematic. He regards concepts, logical relations, and a priori truths arising from them as the peculiar characteristics of mind. He sets them in contrast with the given data of sense experience, which he regards as brute fact, unlimited and unaffected by the conceptual structure. But these givens would be unintelligible without the a priori criteria of classification provided by mind, criteria which are involved not only in talk about things but even in the experience of objects. Thus, the necessary connections of concepts are embedded in perception, and analytic truths, far from being trivial and only intralinguistic, formulate the a priori structure of the world as experienced and known.

Our basic conceptual structure, and thus our a priori truths, are not fixed and eternal. They consist of deep-seated attitudes grounded in decisions that are somewhat like fiats in certain respects and like deliberate choice in others. There is nothing in our conceptual structure that is not subject to change in the face of continuing experience. This includes such basic decisions as the decision that whatever is to count as real, in contrast with the hallucinatory, must stand in causal relations with other real things. Even the laws of logic, "the parliamentary rules of intelligent thought and action," are subject to change. The only test applicable is pragmatic, the achievement of intelligible order with simplicity, economy, and comprehensiveness in a way that will be conducive to the long-run satisfaction of human needs. Thus, Lewis holds to a pragmatic theory of a priori truth but not of empirical truth.

Philosophy, according to Lewis, is a reflective, critical study of mind and its a priori principles as found in "the thick experience of everyday life," and thus in "the structure of the real world which we know." Although it studies what is implicit in experience, it is analytic and critical in method rather than descriptive. Its function is not only to formulate the conceptual structure built into experience and thought but to sharpen and to correct it. Thus philosophical claims may be analytic in character, like "There is an intelligible order in the objective world." Lewis takes this statement to be analytic on the ground that an intelligible order is an essential mark of the objective world. Whatever lacks a certain minimum order is only subjective, private experience, like dreams and hallucinations. Philosophical claims also may be critical and revisionary, recommending some change in our categorial attitudes, such as "Only the physical is real."

Lewis's theory of the a priori places the conceptual framework between two sets of givens, the presentations of sense, to which concepts apply to yield empirical knowledge, and the values in terms of which the a priori structure is pragmatically tested. It seems that both sensory experiences and values would have to be free of a priori assumptions in order to serve the function ascribed to them. This is a difficult doctrine to maintain.

VALUE CLAIMS AND NORMATIVE JUDGMENTS

The ultimate test of the a priori conceptual framework, according to Lewis, is "the long-run satisfaction of our needs in general." It would seem that value judgments would have to be independent of the conceptual framework that is being pragmatically tested if the test is to be clear-cut and not beg the question. But obviously this would be impossible in the case of basic issues. Although Lewis does not face the problem in these terms, he may be said to blunt the criticism by locating values among sense presentations and by invoking unavoidable imperatives that would be operative in any conceptual framework.

Value, in its most primitive sense, has to do with sense presentations. It is not so much a specific phenomenal quality as a mode or aspect of the given, namely, the given as gratifying or grievous. The only thing that is intrinsically good is liked or wanted subjective experience. In addition to the immediately found intrinsic value of an experience, it may be said to have contributory value by virtue of the contribution it makes to the total value quality of the conscious life of which it is a part. Such a life, he contends, is not simply a sum of its parts. So the contributory value of an experience is quite different from its intrinsic value. Objects of experience are said to be extrinsically good or bad according to their capacity to produce experiences which are satisfying or unpleasant.

Thus, for Lewis, value knowledge is a form of empirical knowledge. There are both terminating and nonterminating value judgments. The former are subjective statements of intrinsic and contributory value; the latter are objective statements about extrinsic values. Judgments of right and wrong, however, are not empirical in character. They are determinable only by reference to rules or principles that refer to values in their prescriptions. He regards the basic rational imperative to be so to think and so to act that later you will not be sorry. The only way this can be achieved is for decisions to be guided by objective knowledge rather than merely by the affective quality of immediate experience. In the area of morals, this requires that we respect others as the realities we know them to be, "as creatures whose gratifications and griefs have the same poignant factuality as our own; and as creatures who, like ourselves, find it imperative to govern themselves in light of the cognitive apprehensions vouchsafed to them by decisions which they themselves reach, and by reference to values discoverable to them."

Any attempt to prove the validity of such principles can only appeal to an antecedent recognition of them. They must be recognized by all who make decisions, all who think and act. Genuine skepticism with regard to judgments of right and wrong, good and bad, would be impossible, for on such a basis even doubt itself would be meaningless.

The question remains: Is the conceptual framework in which normative and value knowledge is formulated pragmatically testable, and, if so, just what could such a pragmatic test amount to? If it is not so testable, then it would seem that in the end Lewis is not a pragmatist after all.

See also A Priori and A Posteriori; Descartes, René; Kant, Immanuel; Knowledge, A Priori; Meaning; Modal Logic; Phenomenalism; Pragmatism; Propositions; Rationalism; Realism; Value and Valuation.

Bibliography

WORKS BY LEWIS

A Survey of Symbolic Logic. Berkeley: University of California Press, 1918.

Mind and the World-Order. New York: Scribners, 1929.

Symbolic Logic. New York: Appleton-Century, 1932. Written with C. H. Langford.

An Analysis of Knowledge and Valuation. La Salle, IL: Open Court, 1946.

The Ground and Nature of the Right. New York: Columbia University Press, 1955.

Our Social Inheritance. Bloomington: Indiana University Press, 1957.

WORKS ON LEWIS

Baylis, C. A. "C. I. Lewis, *Mind and the World-Order*." *Journal of Philosophy* 27 (1930): 320–327.

Boas, George. "Mr. Lewis's Theory of Meaning." *Journal of Philosophy* 28 (1931): 314–325.

Chisholm, Roderick M. "The Problem of Empiricism." *Journal of Philosophy* 45 (1948): 512–517.

Chisholm, Roderick M., Herbert Feigl et al. *Philosophy.* Englewood Cliffs, NJ: Prentice-Hall, 1964.

Ducasse, C. J. "C. I. Lewis' *Analysis of Knowledge and Valuation*." *Philosophical Review* 57 (1948): 260–280.

Firth, R., R. B. Brandt et al. "Commemorative Symposium on C. I. Lewis." *Journal of Philosophy* 61 (1964): 545–570.

Frankena, William. "C. I. Lewis on the Ground and Nature of the Right." *Journal of Philosophy* 61 (1964): 489–496.

Frankena, William. "Lewis's Imperatives of Right." *Philosophical Studies* 14 (1963): 25–28.

Henle, Paul. "Lewis's *An Analysis of Knowledge and Valuation*." *Journal of Philosophy* 45 (1948): 524–532.

Kusoy, B. K. *Kant and Current Philosophical Issues.* New York, 1961.

Pratt, J. B. "Logical Positivism and Professor Lewis." *Journal of Philosophy* 31 (1934): 701–710.

Schilpp, P. A. *The Philosophy of C. I. Lewis.* Vol. XIII, Library of Living Philosophers. La Salle, IL: Open Court, 1966.

Stace, W. T. "C. I. Lewis: *An Analysis of Knowledge and Valuation*." *Mind,* n.s., 57 (1948): 71–85.

White, M. G. "Value and Obligation in Dewey and Lewis." *Philosophical Review* 58 (1949): 321–329.

E. M. Adams (1967)

LEWIS, C. S. (CLIVE STAPLES)
(1898–1963)

C. S. Lewis was a British teacher, writer, and critic. He was born and raised in Belfast but spent most of his academic career at Oxford. After having volunteered for the army and subsequently getting wounded, in 1917, he returned to Oxford and took first class honors in "Greats" (philosophy and classics). Shortly thereafter he taught philosophy at Oxford as a substitute for Edgar Carrit, his former tutor in philosophy while Carrit was on leave as a visiting professor at the University of Michigan. Finding no opportunity for teaching in classics or philosophy, and having also gotten first class honors in English, Lewis was elected to a fellowship in English at Magdalene College, where he taught for thirty years. Toward the end of his academic career he was appointed to a newly created Chair of Medieval and Renaissance English at Cambridge. His strictly academic work was concentrated on the ideas rather than the literary forms of medieval and renaissance English writers.

Early in his career at Oxford Lewis became a convert, first to theism and then to Christianity. During World War II he was asked to give lectures about Christianity on the BBC: Printed in book form, these were the basis of his most famous popular work, *Mere Christianity* (2001 [1942]). Other popular works were *The Problem of Pain* (2001 [1940]), *Miracles* (2001 [1947]), and *The Screwtape Letters* (2001 [1942]). In 1945, Lewis argued with G. E. N. Anscombe about a claim in Chapter 5 of *Miracles* that naturalism is self-refuting, for it says that all our thoughts are ultimately traceable to the blind working of chance and that no thought is valid if it can be fully explained as the result of irrational causes. Anscombe distinguished between "irrational" causes and "nonrational" causes and argued that being the result of "nonrational" causes does not make our reasoning invalid. Lewis, in reply, says the "valid" in the logician's sense is not the correct word for what he meant and distinguished between "reasons" and "causes" (Hooper 1979). Some have thought that he lost that argument. He revised the chapter of *Miracles* which Anscombe had criticized, and Anscombe, at least, felt that the revision answered much of her original objections (Purtill 2004). Late in his life (in 1957), Lewis married Helen Joy Davidman, who was dying of cancer. She surprisingly (and perhaps miraculously) recovered and they spent three happy years together.

After her death, Lewis wrote (anonymously) *A Grief Observed* (2001 [1961]), which some scholars have held demonstrates that he had lost his faith, or at least his belief in the rational justification of Christianity. However, a more careful reading shows that his own description of Christianity to a friend is true: "It ends in faith, but begins with the blackest of doubts en route" (unpublished letter quoted in Purtill 2004, p. 25). It is useful to compare this book with two of his later works: *Till We Have Faces*, a fictional account of a woman who began writing a book as a complaint against the gods (the account is set in classical times) and "ends in faith"; and *Letters to Malcolm* (2002 [1964]), which touches on some of the same themes.

Lewis was, in this author's judgment as well as the judgment of other critics, a great master of English prose and a powerful writer of fiction with underlying religious themes: the seven books of the *Chronicles of Narnia*, the "space" trilogy, and *Till We Have Faces*.

Philosophically speaking, Lewis's work, both nonfiction and fiction, has a number of characteristics:

(1) He argues for his points on the basis of reason and experience. As he says in an essay, "There is, of course, no question ... of belief without evidence ... or in the teeth of evidence ... if anyone expects that, I certainly do not" (Lewis 2001 [1955], p. 17);

(2) He thinks of faith as a rational acceptance and of "temptations against faith" as emotional reactions when we find it would be much more convenient *not* to believe;

(3) He accepts miracles and uses them as evidence for Christianity, first refuting the arguments of Hume and others against the *possibility* of miracles or the possibility of knowing them, and then arguing historically that miracles have occurred;

(4) Miracles, as Lewis defines them, depend on the existence of God. Lewis argues for God's existence using variations of the moral argument and the argument from design, especially a version of what Victor Reppert has called "the argument from reason" which argues that to really trust our reason we need the existence of God. For the moral argument, Lewis agrees with other philosophers that "if God does not exist anything is permitted" and by contraposition that "if not everything is permitted [as he argues from our moral experience] then God must exist."

(5) Lewis contrasts Christianity with other forms of belief—such as naturalism, Hinduism, and so on—and argues that Christianity explains the facts of experience better than other forms of belief.

(6) Lewis grants that the problems of moral and natural evil are the most powerful against a belief in a loving, omnipotent God, and addresses both in *The Problem of Pain* and elsewhere.

Professional philosophers may find many of Lewis's arguments oversimplifications; Lewis would probably grant this for his more popular works, which were intended for intelligent nonprofessionals. However, this leads to a situation where philosophical argument can begin. What are the alleged oversimplifications and how can they be repaired? Lewis's experience with Anscombe showed he was capable of doing this, as does his work in less popular works addressed to academic or clerical audiences.

The talent that made him a good writer of fiction carries over to his nonfictional works; he is a poet, as well as a logician, and employs a gift for metaphor and analogy in his statements of arguments. Lewis has been called "perhaps the twentieth century's most popular proponent of Faith based on reason" (Nicholi 2002, p. 3). Many opponents of Christianity have taken Lewis's arguments seriously, especially those scholars who, such as Antony Flew, wish to be fair to Christianity and try to refute its best arguments. Many supporters of Christianity, both nonprofessional and academic alike, would give Lewis major credit for beginning the process that led them to Christianity.

See also Anscombe, Gertrude Elizabeth Margaret; Experience; Evil, The Problem of; Hume, David; Immortality; Miracles; Reason.

Bibliography

WORKS BY LEWIS

The Problem of Pain (1940). San Francisco: HarperCollins, 2001.

The Screwtape Letters (1942). San Francisco: HarperCollins, 2001.

Mere Christianity (1943). San Francisco: HarperCollins, 2003.

The Great Divorce (1945). San Francisco: HarperCollins, 2001.

Miracles (1947). San Francisco: HarperCollins, 2001.

"An Obstinacy in Belief." In *The World's Last Night* (1955). New York: Harcourt Harvest Books, 2002.

Till We Have Faces (1956). San Diego, CA: Harcourt Harvest Books, 2002.

A Grief Observed (1961). San Francisco: HarperCollins, 2001.

Letters to Malcolm (1964). New York: Harvest Books, 2002.

WORKS ON LEWIS

Green, Roger Lancelon, and Walter Hooper. *C. S. Lewis: A Biography*. San Diego: Harcourt Brace, 1995.

Hooper, Walter. "Oxford Bonnie Fighter." In *C. S. Lewis at the Breakfast Table*, edited by James T. Como. New York: Macmillan, 1979.

Kreeft, Peter. *C. S. Lewis for the Third Millennium: Six Essays on the Abolition of Man*. San Francisco: Ignatius Press, 1994.

Nicholi, Armand M. *The Question of God: C. S. Lewis and Sigmund Freud Debate God, Love, Sex, and the Meaning of Life*. New York: Free Press, 2002.

Purtill, Richard. *C. S. Lewis's Case for the Christian Faith*. New York: Harper Collins, 1981. New. ed., San Francisco: Ignatius Press, 2004.

Purtill, Richard. "Did C. S. Lewis Lose his Faith?" In *A Christian for All Christians: Essays in Honour of C. S. Lewis*. London: Hodder and Staughton, 1990.

Reppert, Victor. *C. S. Lewis's Dangerous Idea: A Philosophical Defense of Lewis's Argument from Reason*. Downers Grove, IL: Intervarsity Press, 1998.

Richard Purtill (2005)

LEWIS, DAVID
(1941–2001)

David Lewis was born in Oberlin, Ohio. He studied as an undergraduate at Swarthmore College before gaining a PhD in philosophy from Harvard University in 1967 where he studied with Willard van Orman Quine. His first job was at the University of California at Los Angeles, where he worked from 1966–1970, before moving to Princeton University where he worked for the rest of his career. Lewis published four monographs and more than one hundred papers, most of which have been gathered into five volumes of his collected papers. Lewis made contributions to virtually every area of contemporary Anglo-American philosophy but is probably best known for his contributions to metaphysics, in particular, his work on modality (necessity and possibility) and possible worlds and also his theories of laws of nature, causation, and chance. His work in the philosophy of mind has also been influential, as has his work on conventions and language.

MODALITY

Some of Lewis's best known work is in the metaphysics of modality: that is, his account of the nature of necessity and possibility. Lewis thought it was important to make sense of what we are doing when we talk about different possibilities that seem open, or when we say that certain facts (such that 2+2=4) are necessary, or that it is impossible for them to be otherwise. Lewis held, along with others whose claims about possibility and necessity were

to be understood as implicitly generalizing over possible worlds, complete ways things could be: To say something was possible was to say that it occurred in at least one possible world, and for something to be necessary was for it to obtain in all possible worlds. Where Lewis was nearly unique was his account of what these other possible worlds were.

According to Lewis, possible worlds were large spatiotemporal regions filled with objects and events of the same kind as those in our world, except, of course, that every possible sort of thing is found in one world or other. So Lewis's worlds contain people and trees and galaxies and tables; but also dragons, extra-spatiotemporal dimensions, ghosts, and so on. This construal of possible worlds became known as *modal realism* Despite the counterintuitive nature of this theory, Lewis showed that it brought with it many advantages, and he argued that attempts to construe possibilities as some sort of abstract object (*ersatzism* about possible worlds, in Lewis's vocabulary), failed to provide an analysis of modality, and many varieties suffered crippling internal problems.

Lewis also suggested a novel way of dealing with *de re* necessities and possibilities (possibilities or necessities for an object rather than as concerning the status of a proposition). Lewis argued that these were best analyzed using counterpart theory: where what is possible for me is what happens for one of my counterparts in another world. Since Lewis held that, strictly speaking, each possible individual was part of only one possible world, he could avoid some of the puzzles about trans-world criteria for identity. In addition, counterpart theory allowed more flexibility than literal identity would. Lewis argued, for instance, that the counterpart relation need not be transitive (so something that could happen to one of my counterparts need not be something that is possible for me) though a failure of transitivity is harder to understand if it is literal identity across possible worlds that is required for *de re* possibility (i.e., if something has to be literally happening to me in some other possible world in order for it to be possible for me). Lewis also allowed that there were multiple counterpart relations, which might give rise to multiple kinds of *de re* possibility for an object. So, for example, what the counterparts of an object are when that object is considered as a statue might be different from what the counterparts of that object are when the object is considered to be a lump of bronze. Lewis could thus allow that what we appropriately say is possible for the statue is different from what we appropriately say is possible for the piece of bronze even though the two objects might nevertheless be identical.

COUNTERFACTUALS, LAWS, CAUSATION, AND CHANCE

Issues about contrary-to-fact-conditionals, laws of nature, causation, and chance are often thought to be connected, and Lewis's contributions to these topics formed a unified neo-Humean system. Lewis's book *Counterfactuals* (1973a) offered an analysis of conditionals of the form *if* p, *it would have been the case that* q in terms of possible worlds: a conditional such as *if dolphins had had legs, they would have walked on land* is true if and only if the *nearest* possible world where dolphins have legs is one where dolphins walk on land. *Nearness*, in turn, is analyzed as overall similarity in salient respects: it is thus context-dependent, and Lewis had more to say about what sort of similarity is significant for particular sorts of these so-called counterfactual conditionals, for example the ones employed in causal reasoning.

This analysis of counterfactual claims has several advantages. It is formally tractable, yielding a logic of counterfactual judgments with some initially surprising features that do seem to correspond to features of our ordinary counterfactual judgments. For example, Lewis's system delivers the result that *strengthening the antecedent* is invalid: that is, the inference (if p then q), therefore (if p and r then q) is invalid. But consider this argument: If I leave now, I will catch the train; therefore, if I leave now and am assassinated on the way I will catch the train. The premise might well be true and the conclusion false if I run no real risk of being assassinated.

In addition, since the analysis of these conditionals does not itself appeal to, for example, dispositions or causation, it leaves the way free for counterfactual analyses of other puzzling parts of metaphysics. And, indeed, Lewis championed a counterfactual analysis of causation: At a first pass, an event C causes an event E if and only if both C and E occur and had C not occurred, E would not have occurred either. A lot more than this first pass is required for an adequate counterfactual account of causation: Sometimes E would have happened in any case, even without C, for example, if E is overdetermined. Lewis experimented with a number of counterfactual theories of causation: Their development can be seen in Lewis 1973b (and see especially the postscripts in Lewis 1986b), Lewis 1979a, and most recently Lewis 2000 and Lewis 2004.

The connection between counterfactuals and causation, on the one hand, and laws of nature, on the other hand, is slightly circuitous in Lewis, but it is another key connection in his overall system. Lewis defended a regularity theory of laws of nature: Following Ramsey, Lewis held that the laws of nature were given by the set of generalizations that provided the best tradeoff of simplicity and strength in capturing the goings-on of the world. Since the laws supervene on the patterns of particular matters of fact, at this point, at least, Lewis's metaphysical posits are minimal.

Even though the laws are only descriptions of certain privileged regularities, they make a difference to which counterfactuals are true, in Lewis's system, because similarity with respect to whether our laws hold is one of the most important components in the kind of similarity relevant for the nearness relation between possible worlds central to Lewis's analysis of counterfactuals. So when some event A would follow as a matter of law from another event B, the nearest world where A occurs will be one where B also does. Thus mere patterns of particular occurrences give rise to laws of nature, counterfactual dependencies, and so to causation—at least, if Lewis is right. Lewis extended his regularity framework to handle objective chances as well: Another member of the *nomic family* was explained, ultimately, in terms of regularities in particular events.

MIND

Lewis made contributions to several areas of the philosophy of mind. First in importance is his defense of an identity theory of the mind. Lewis characterized mental states according to the role attributed to them in our ordinary *folk* understanding of the mind: A belief, for example, is a state that tends to go together with desires with certain contents to produce certain sorts of actions. Folk psychology, when articulated, describes causal *roles* for each different sort of mental state (beliefs, desires, pains, emotions), and these roles are interdefined so that the typical causal profile of a belief is specified partly in terms of other beliefs it tends to cause, partly in terms of perceptions that tend to cause it, how it interacts with desires, and so on.

Armed with this role statement of the typical causes and effects of mental states, Lewis then argued that mental states are identical to those physical states in us that play these causal roles: So Tom's belief that it is raining is identical to the brain state of his that is typically caused by the sight and sound of rain, and typically goes together with other brain states to yield umbrella-grabbing behavior, and so on. This may well mean that which type of physical state is identical to which type of mental state may vary from subject to subject: Lewis says that which physical state is identical to a given mental state depends on what causal roles that state typically plays in the kind of thing that has it. So in humans pain will be a certain sort of brain state while in advanced robots it may be some electronic state, and in extraterrestrials it might be a matter of how gases are distributed within internal bladders.

This typical-for-the-species criterion allows both for *multiple realizability*: pain-in-aliens or pain-in-invertebrates may not be the same physical state as pain-in-humans; and we loosen the behaviorist insistence that pain must be the state, whatever it is, that produces pain behavior since, for example, an atypical human may have the state that typically causes pain reactions but makes no outward show of it, or even engages in some nonstandard behavior (imagine a *madman* who whistles, but shows no discomfort, whenever he is in the state that produces pain behavior in normal humans). The view is still a type–type identity theory, according to Lewis, because, for example, the type pain-in-humans can be identified with a particular physical property (e.g. C-fiber-firing-in-humans) even though there is no unified physical type corresponding to *pain* or *belief* simpliciter.

LANGUAGE AND CONVENTION

In Lewis's first book, *Convention* (1969), he developed a theory of conventions as patterns of mutual expectation and conditional intentions. Roughly, according to Lewis, there is a convention in a population to act in a certain way in certain circumstances if everyone does tend to behave in that way, everyone has the conditional intention to continue behaving that way, conditional on everyone else so acting, and this is common knowledge. Finally, there must also be some other alternative action that people are deciding against: We all breathe oxygen, intend to continue and know that we intend to continue, but this does not make our practice of oxygen-breathing conventional since we all have no choice. He claimed these patterns could arise fairly spontaneously (certainly without the existence of an explicit agreement) and that they tended to arise to solve coordination problems: common cases of collective action where everyone does better by coordinating their activities than if everyone does their own thing. (A decision about which side of the road to drive on is an example: The most important thing is not whether people drive on the left or right hand side but, rather, that either everyone does the one or everyone does the other.)

Lewis argued that we could understand what it was for a population to use a language as a matter of convention, in his sense. In "Language and Languages" (1975), Lewis explained how we could integrate the formal,

abstract theories of languages as functions from expressions to truth-conditions, on the one hand, with theories of language that concentrate on practices of language usage. Lewis also made significant contributions to the formal theory of language and philosophical semantics—his "General Semantics" (1970) is a prime example. Lewis was also responsible for a lot of work exploring the role of context in language: His "Scorekeeping in a Language Game" (1979b) is a classic in this area.

See also Hume, David: Metaphysics; Philosophy of Language; Philosophy of Mind; Quine, Willard Van Orman; Ramsey, Frank Plumpton.

Bibliography

MONOGRAPHS BY DAVID LEWIS
Convention: A Philosophical Study. Cambridge MA: Harvard University Press, 1969.
Counterfactuals. Oxford: Basil Blackwell, 1973a.
On the Plurality of Worlds. Oxford: Basil Blackwell, 1986a.
Parts of Classes. Oxford: Basil Blackwell, 1990.

VOLUMES OF COLLECTED PAPERS
Philosophical Papers. Vol I. Oxford: Oxford University Press, 1983.
Philosophical Papers. Vol. II. Oxford: Oxford University Press 1986b.
Papers in Philosophical Logic. Cambridge. U.K.: Cambridge University Press, 1998.
Papers in Metaphysics and Epistemology. Cambridge, U.K.: Cambridge University Press, 1999.
Papers in Ethics and Social Philosophy. Cambridge, U.K.: Cambridge University Press, 2000.

OTHER WORKS CITED
"General Semantics." *Synthese* 22 (1970): 18–67.
"Causation." *Journal of Philosophy* 70 (1973b): 556–467.
"Languages and Language." *Minnesota Studies in the Philosophy of Science* 7 (1975): 3–35.
"Counterfactual Dependence and Time's Arrow." *Nôus* 13 (1979a): 455–476.
"Scorekeeping in a Language Game." *Journal of Philosophical Logic* 8 (1979b): 339–359.
"Mad Pain and Martian Pain." In *Readings in the Philosophy of Psychology*, Vol. 1, 216–232. Cambridge MA: Harvard University Press, 1980.
"Humean Supervenience Debugged." *Mind* 103 (1994): 473–90.
"Causation as Influence." *Journal of Philosophy* 97 (2000): 182–97.
"Causation as Influence" (extended version). In *Causation and Counterfactuals*, edited by J. Collins, N. Hall, and L. Paul, 75–106. Cambridge, MA: MIT Press, 2004.

Daniel Nolan (2005)

LI AO
(774?–836)

Li Ao is perhaps the thinker in Tang China (618–907) who contributed most to a new version of Confucian philosophy that addressed issues of human nature and spiritual cultivation. By Li's time, questions in this area had been left to Buddhism and Daoism for centuries, whereas the intellectual elite in general considered Confucianism solely the authority in family and political lives. Li's importance as a thinker comes entirely from a single treatise: the *Fuxing shu* (Writings on returning to one's true nature). It is arguably the first post-Han (206 BCE–220 CE) text that gave an original treatment on the topics of human nature and spirituality from a Confucian stance.

The theme of the *Fuxing shu* is how to become a sage, the Confucian ideal of personality. Li holds that a sage is a person who has realized his "nature" (*xing*), the character of which can be described as "sincerity" (*cheng*). The nature of human beings is bestowed on them by heaven, and all people share the same nature. The reason why hardly anyone becomes a sage is that people's "emotions" (*qing*) obscure their true nature.

As to the method of becoming a sage, Li contends that if one quiets down and thus clarifies one's emotions, one's nature will be revealed and will direct one's life. One can then naturally act in a proper manner—that is, in accord with Confucian behavioral norms. The central point here is that the true nature of humans only exists in the state of tranquility. Yet tranquility of one's nature is not equivalent to suspension of emotions, because the latter will inevitably shift to a state of movement. People should learn to respond to the world directly with their true nature. The nature that is at the same time tranquil and able to have a full control of one's life exists beyond the level of emotions.

At least two issues regarding the *Fuxing shu* deserve attention here. The first is the subject of this treatise. The search for sagehood through self-cultivation was a significant notion in classical Confucianism, but went almost absent after the Han. It was owing to the Buddhist concern with Buddhahood that the perfection of human existence through spiritual cultivation became a major issue in medieval Chinese thought. Li's revival of a dormant Confucian subject is in itself an indication that the *Fuxing shu* represents a Confucian response to the centuries-old dominance of Buddhism and Daoism in the realm of metaphysical and spiritual philosophy. Li's project anticipates the endeavor of neo-Confucianism in Song times (960–1279).

Then there is the much studied and debated issue: the sources of the originality of the *Fuxing shu*. It is clear that medieval Buddhism and Daoism not only gave birth to the theme of Li's treatise, but also affected its ideas in a substantial way. The sharp contrast between "nature" and "emotions" is a case in point. This distinction is not a salient feature of classical and Han Confucianism. Even for those Confucian thinkers believing that moral values were rooted in the essence of human beings, goodness did not just exist in one's nature. It was more important to realize people's moral potential in their actual lives filled with all kinds of emotions. Simply put, in early Confucianism there was no such notion that a return to one's nature, defined as the original state of human existence, represented the perfection of human life. This idea, which is at the core of Li's theory, owed its origins principally to classical and religious Daoism. The most crucial formative force behind this idea seems to be the fundamental Daoist belief that the ideal state of life lies in its reunion with its roots—indeed with the "primordial breath" (*yuanqi*) of the universe.

Although Li borrows heavily from religious ideas current in his time, it is unmistaken that his aim is providing a theoretical framework for a Confucian way of self-cultivation. Li emphasizes that once revealed, one's nature will lead to correct knowledge and actions, that is, those in line with Confucian values. One may say that Li uses a great deal of Buddhist and Daoist material to build a Confucian house. He was one of the rare individuals in the history of ideas to really make a breakthrough.

See also Confucianism; Han Yu.

Bibliography

Barrett, Timothy Hugh. "Buddhism, Daoism and Confucianism in the Thought of Li Ao." PhD diss. Yale University, 1978.

Barrett, Timothy Hugh. *Li Ao: Buddhist, Taoist, or Neo-Confucian.* New York: Oxford University Press, 1992.

Chen, Jo-shui. "'Fuxing shu' sixiang yuanyuan zaitan: Han Tang xinxing guannian shi zhi yizhang." *Zhongyang yanjiuyuan lishi yuyan yanjiusuo jikan* 69 (3) (1998): 423–482.

Jo-shui Chen (2005)

LIAR PARADOX, THE

Attributions of truth and falsehood under certain conditions generate the "liar paradox." The most famous illustration of this comes from the Epistle to Titus, in which

St. Paul quotes approvingly a remark attributed to Epimenides: "One of themselves, even a prophet of their own, said, The Cretans are always liars, evil beasts, slow bellies. This witness is true" (King James version). Let us suppose that Epimenides, the Cretan prophet, did say that the Cretans are always liars, and let us consider the status of his utterance—call it E—under the following two conditions. (1) A Cretan utterance counts as a lie if and only if it is untrue. (2) All Cretan utterances, except perhaps E, are untrue. Now, if E is true, then, since E is a Cretan utterance, not all Cretan utterances are untrue. Hence, Cretans are not always liars (by (1)), and so E must be untrue. On the other hand, if E is untrue, then indeed all Cretan utterances are untrue (by (2)). Hence, Cretans are always liars (by (1)), and so E is true after all. Both the hypotheses, that E is true and that E is not true, yield, therefore, a contradiction. Yet the steps in the argument are all apparently valid, and the initial setup is not impossible. This is the liar paradox.

The paradox was discovered by Eubulides of Miletus (fourth century BCE) and has exercised logicians down the ages to the present time. (See Bocheński 1961, Spade 1988.) For principally two reasons, interest in the paradox was especially great in the twentieth century. First, arguments similar to that found in the liar wreaked havoc in several prominent logical systems (e.g., those of Gottlob Frege and Alonzo Church). This prompted a search for systems that were immune from paradox. Second, the rise of semantical studies created a need for a better understanding of the notions of truth, reference, and the like. The notions are fundamental to semantical investigations, but the paradoxes reveal a profound gap in our understanding of them. (The notion of reference, like other semantical notions, exhibits, under certain conditions, paradoxical behavior.)

The liar and related paradoxes raise a number of difficult conceptual problems. One is the normative problem of designing paradox-free notions of truth, reference, and the like. Another is the descriptive problem of understanding the workings of our ordinary, paradox-laden notions. The work on the paradoxes in the first half of the twentieth century is, perhaps, best viewed as addressing the normative problem. The work in the second half is best viewed as addressing the descriptive problem. Some of this work is outlined below.

Let us sharpen the descriptive problem a little. For simplicity, let us restrict our attention to a fragment, L, of our language that contains no problematic terms other than "true." All other terms in L have, let us suppose, a classical interpretation. How should "true" be interpreted? A natural demand is that the interpretation must validate the T-biconditionals, that is, all sentences of the form,

(T) "B" is true if and only if (iff) B,

where B is a sentence of L. The argument of the liar paradox shows, however, that every possible classical interpretation of "true" is bound to make some T-biconditionals false. (This is a version of Alfred Tarski's indefinability theorem.) How, then, should we interpret "true"? Should we abandon the natural demand? Or the classical framework? Or the naive reading of the T-biconditionals? Essentially, the first course is followed in the contextual approach, the second in the fixed-point approach, and the third in the revision approach.

THE CONTEXTUAL APPROACH

This approach takes "true" to be a context-sensitive term. Just as the interpretation of "fish this long" varies with contextually supplied information about length, similarly, on the contextual approach, with "true": Its interpretation also depends upon contextual information. There is no consensus, however, on the specific information needed for interpretation. In the levels theory due to Tyler Burge and Charles Parsons, the context supplies the level at which "true" is interpreted in a Tarskian hierarchy of truth predicates. In the Austinian theory of truth developed by Jon Barwise and John Etchemendy, the relevant contextual parameter is the "portion" of the world that a proposition is about. In the singularity theory of Keith Simmons, the relevant information includes certain of the speaker's intentions.

Contextual theories assign to each occurrence of "true" a classical interpretation, though not the same one to all occurrences. This has several characteristic consequences: (1) Occurrences of "true" do not express global truth for the entire language (by Tarski's indefinability theorem). They express instead restricted or "quasi" notions of truth; the former possibility is realized in the levels theory, the latter in the singularity theory. (2) Truth attributions, even paradoxical ones, have a classical truth-value. Paradox is explained as arising from a subtle, unnoticed, shift in some contextual parameter. (3) Classical forms of reasoning are preserved. But caution is in order here: Whether an argument exemplifies a classically valid form turns out to be nontrivial. For example, the argument "a is true, $a = b$; therefore, b is true" exemplifies a classically valid form only if "true" is interpreted uniformly, but this is nontrivial on the contextual approach.

THE FIXED-POINT APPROACH

This approach interprets "true" nonclassically. It rests on an important observation of Saul Kripke, Robert Martin, and Peter Woodruff. Consider again the language L, and assign to "true" an arbitrary partial interpretation $\langle U, V \rangle$, where U is the extension and V the antiextension (i.e., the objects of which the predicate is false). We can use one of the partial-valued schemes (say, Strong Kleene) to determine the sentences of L that are true (U'), false (V'), and neither-true-nor-false. This semantic reflection defines a function, κ, on partial interpretations; $\kappa(\langle U, V \rangle) = \langle U', V' \rangle$. The important observation is that κ has a fixed point: There exist $\langle U, V \rangle$ such that $\kappa(\langle U, V \rangle) = \langle U, V \rangle$.

Certain partial-valued schemes have a least fixed point, which is a particularly attractive interpretation for "true." It is also the product of an appealing iterative construction: We begin by supposing that we are entirely ignorant of the extension and the antiextension of "true"; we set them both to be $\emptyset$ (the null set). Despite the ignorance, we can assert some sentences and deny others. The rule "Assert 'B is true' for all assertible B; assert 'B is not true' for all deniable B" entitles us to a new, richer interpretation, $\kappa(\langle \emptyset, \emptyset \rangle)$, for "true." But now we can assert (deny) more sentences. The rule entitles us to a yet richer interpretation $\kappa(\kappa(\langle \emptyset, \emptyset \rangle))$. The process, if repeated sufficiently many times, saturates at the least fixed point.

Under fixed-point interpretations, the extension of "true" consists precisely of the truths and the antiextension of falsehoods. The T-biconditionals are, therefore, validated. They are not, however, expressible in L itself: fixed points exist only when certain three-valued functions, including the relevant "iff," are inexpressible in L.

THE REVISION APPROACH

This approach holds truth to be a circular concept. It is motivated by the observation that truth behaves in a strikingly parallel way to concepts with circular definitions. Suppose we define G thus:

$$x \text{ is } G =_{Df} x \text{ is a philosopher distinct from Plato } or$$
$$x \text{ is Plato but not } G.$$

The definition is circular, but it does impart some meaning to G. G has, like truth, unproblematic application on a large range of objects. It applies to all philosophers distinct from Plato and fails to apply to nonphilosophers. On one object, Plato, G behaves paradoxically. If we declare Plato is G, then the definition rules that he is not G; if we declare he is not G, the definition rules that he is

G. This parallels exactly the behavior of truth in the liar paradox.

The revision account of truth rests on general theories of definitions, theories that make semantic sense of circular (and mutually interdependent) definitions. Central to these theories are the following ideas. (1) A circular definition does not, in general, determine a classical extension for the definiendum (the term defined). (2) It determines instead a rule of revision. Given a hypothesis about the extension of the definiendum G, the definition yields a revised extension for G, one consisting of objects that satisfy the definiens (the right side of the definition). (3) Repeated applications of the revision rule to arbitrary hypotheses reveal both the unproblematic and the pathological behavior of the definiendum. On the unproblematic the revision rule yields a definite and stable verdict, irrespective of the initial hypothesis. On the pathological this ideal state does not obtain.

The ingredient needed to construct a theory of truth once we have a general theory of definitions is minimal: It is just the T-biconditionals, with "iff" read as "$=_{Df}$." This reading was suggested by Tarski, but, as it results in a circular definition, it can be implemented only within a general theory of definitions. Under the reading, the T-biconditionals yield a rule of revision. Repeated applications of this rule generate patterns that explain the ordinary and the pathological behavior of truth. The revision approach thus sees the liar paradox as arising from a circularity in truth. The approach has been developed by, among others, Anil Gupta, Hans Herzberger, and Nuel Belnap.

The three approaches, it should be stressed, do not exhaust the rich array of responses to the paradoxes in the twentieth century.

See also Church, Alonzo; Correspondence Theory of Truth; Frege, Gottlob; Kripke, Saul; Logical Paradoxes; Plato; Russell, Bertrand Arthur William; Tarski, Alfred; Types, Theory of.

Bibliography

Antonelli, A. "Non-Well-Founded Sets via Revision Rules." *Journal of Philosophical Logic* 23 (1994): 633–679.

Barwise, J., and J. Etchemendy. *The Liar: An Essay on Truth and Circularity.* New York: Oxford University Press, 1987.

Bocheński, I. M. *A History of Formal Logic.* Notre Dame, IN, 1961.

Chapuis, A. "Alternative Revision Theories of Truth." *Journal of Philosophical Logic* 24 (1996).

Epstein, R. L. "A Theory of Truth Based on a Medieval Solution to the Liar Paradox." *History and Philosophy of Logic* 13 (1992): 149–177.

Gaifman, H. "Pointers to Truth." *Journal of Philosophy* 89 (1992): 223–261.

Gupta, A., and N. Belnap. *The Revision Theory of Truth.* Cambridge, MA: MIT Press, 1993.

Koons, R. C. *Paradoxes of Belief and Strategic Rationality.* Cambridge, U.K.: Cambridge University Press, 1992.

Martin, R. L., ed. *The Paradox of the Liar,* 2nd ed. Reseda, CA: 1978. Contains a useful bibliography of material up to about 1975; for later material consult the bibliography in Gupta and Belnap, 1993.

Martin, R. L., ed. *Recent Essays on Truth and the Liar Paradox.* New York: Oxford University Press, 1984. Contains the classic papers of Parsons, Kripke, Herzberger, and others; a good place to begin the study of the three approaches.

McGee, V. *Truth, Vagueness, and Paradox.* Indianapolis: Hackett, 1991.

Priest, G. *In Contradiction.* Dordrecht: Nijhoff, 1987.

Russell, B. "Mathematical Logic as Based on the Theory of Types." In *Logic and Knowledge.* London: Allen and Unwin, 1956.

Sainsbury, R. M. *Paradoxes.* Cambridge, U.K.: Cambridge University Press, 1988.

Simmons, K. *Universality and the Liar.* New York: Cambridge University Press, 1993.

Spade, P. V. *Lies, Language, and Logic in the Late Middle Ages.* London: Variorum, 1988.

Tarski, A. "The Semantic Conception of Truth." *Philosophy and Phenomenological Research* 4 (1944): 341–376.

Visser, A. "Semantics and the Liar Paradox." In *Handbook of Philosophical Logic,* edited by D. Gabbay and F. Guenthner, Vol. 4. Dordrecht: Reidel, 1989.

Yablo, S. "Hop, Skip, and Jump: The Agonistic Conception of Truth." In *Philosophical Perspectives,* edited by J. Tomberlin, Vol. 7. Atascadero, CA: Ridgeview, 1993.

Yaqūb, A. M. *The Liar Speaks the Truth.* New York: Oxford University Press, 1993.

Anil Gupta (1996)

LIBERALISM

By definition, a liberal is one who believes in liberty, but because different people at different times have meant different things by liberty, "liberalism" is correspondingly ambiguous. The word was first heard in a political sense in England in the early nineteenth century, when "liberals" were thus named by their Tory opponents. Indeed, they were first called *liberales,* and the Spanish form was used "with the intention of suggesting that the principles of those politicians were un-English" (see *Shorter Oxford English Dictionary*). This was ironical, since the word *liberal* had been adopted by the Spaniards for policies they regarded as essentially English—that is, the Lockean prin- ciples of constitutional monarchy, parliamentary govern- ment, and the rights of man. In any event, the English- men who were called liberals (though as late as 1816 Robert Southey was still calling them *liberales*) rejoiced in the name, and what was intended to be a pejorative quickly proved to have a distinctly pleasing flavor, per- haps partly because its other significance, the Shake- spearean sense of liberal as "gross" or "licentious," had given way to the modern sense of liberal as "bountiful," "generous," or "open-hearted."

ENGLISH LIBERALISM

Traditional English liberalism has rested on a fairly sim- ple concept of liberty—namely, that of freedom from the constraints of the state. In Thomas Hobbes's memorable phrase, "The liberties of subjects depend on the silence of the law." In general, however, English liberals have always been careful not to press this notion to anarchist extremes. They have regarded the state as a necessary institution, ensuring order and law at home, defense against foreign powers, and security of possessions—the three principles John Locke summarized as "life, liberty and property." English liberals have also maintained that the law can be used to extend the liberties of subjects insofar as the law is made to curb and limit the activities of the executive government. Thus, for example, the Eng- lish laws of habeas corpus, of bail, and of police entry and arrest all constrain or restrain the executive and, in so doing, increase the freedom of the people. Some instru- ments of constitutional law have a similar effect.

The traditional form of English political liberalism naturally went hand in hand with the classical economic doctrine of laissez-faire. Toward the end of the nineteenth century, however, certain radical movements and certain English liberal theorists, such as Matthew Arnold and T. H. Green, developed, partly under foreign, left-wing influences, a different—as they claimed, a broader—con- cept of freedom, which was, to a large extent, to prove more popular in the twentieth century than traditional English liberalism with its economic gospel of laissez- faire. The central aim of this new school was utilitarian— namely, freeing men from misery and ignorance. Its exponents believed that the state must be the instrument by which this end was to be achieved. Hence, English lib- eral opinion entered the twentieth century in a highly paradoxical condition, urging, on the one hand, a free- dom that was understood as freedom from the con- straints of the state and, on the other, an enlargement of the state's power and control in order to liberate the poor from the oppressive burdens of poverty. In the political sphere this contradiction in the liberal ideology ended in the disintegration of the British Liberal Party. With the defeat of Prime Minister Herbert Henry Asquith, a disciple of the philosopher T. H. Green and an adept at reconciling contradictions, the British Liberal Party broke into two, the right-wing, or laissez-faire, element joining forces with conservatism and the radical, *étatiste* element merging with socialism. Only a "rump" remained.

FRENCH LIBERALISM

The ambiguity of the word *liberalism* is more marked in French than in any other European language. Some writers hold that as a result of events in France since the time of Louis XIV, the French people have been divided into two political camps: One that supports the Roman Catholic Church, traditional social patterns, and the Syllabus of Pius IX (1864) and one that opposes the church and favors parliament, progress, and the rights of man. Historians who see France in these terms call one side *conservateur,* the other *libéral.* Opposed to this view are those historians who see not two, but at least three, continuing traditions in French political thought: on the right, royalism and conservativism; on the left, socialism, anarchism, syndicalism, and communism; in the center, liberalism. In the first of these two analyses, *liberalisme* is understood to embrace all the creeds of the left; according to the second analysis, *liberalisme* is a political doctrine at variance with the creeds of the left.

Again, one can distinguish two distinct—indeed, opposing—schools among French theorists who claim to be liberal. One is the Lockean liberalism of Voltaire, Baron de Montesquieu, and Benjamin Constant (in effect, also that of François Guizot and the July monarchy of Louis Philippe)—the liberalism of the minimal state, individualism, and laissez-faire. But there is a second liberalism, represented by the masters of the French Revolution and by the youthful Napoleon Bonaparte, which is democratic, Rousseauesque, and *étatiste.* Whereas Lockean liberalism understands freedom as being left alone by the state, the other liberalism sees freedom as ruling oneself through the medium of a state that one has made one's own.

Both these schools of *liberalisme* contributed something to the ideology of the French Revolution, and the often unperceived contradiction between them may also be said to have contributed to the intellectual confusion of those times. The fall of Napoleon was the signal for a return to the more purely Lockean style of liberalism. Benjamin Constant not only insisted that Jean-Jacques Rousseau's concept of liberty was an illusory one but also

maintained that "*Du Contrat Social* [1762] so often invoked in favour of liberty, is the most formidable ally of all despotisms." Constant and his friends desired only to reproduce in France the Lockean Glorious Revolution of 1688. In 1830 they believed they had succeeded; Louis Philippe was enthroned on the basis of an understanding very like that on which William and Mary had been crowned in England. Politicians such as Guizot, who called themselves Libéraux, were put in charge of the kingdom. The result was not inspiring. A new bourgeoisie basked in the liberty the Lockean state introduced; the great were diminished, but the poor were not elevated. A rebellion came from the left in 1848, and the right replied with Napoleon III. Henceforth, there were few self-styled Libéraux of any importance in French politics and no liberal party. When new parties were formed later in the century, the name chosen by the center was Republicain rather than Libéral. This is not to say that liberalism died in France in 1848; rather, the word *libéralisme* thereafter ceased to call to the minds of French-speaking people any clear or distinct idea.

In 1912 Émile Faguet published a celebrated work, *Le libéralisme,* in which he took a rigidly Lockean position. "The state," he wrote, "is an evil; a lesser evil than anarchy, but nevertheless to be limited to the tasks of securing public order and safety through the justiciary, police and army." Several critics at the time attacked Faguet's definition as being outmoded; nevertheless, the definition of *libéralisme* in the 1935 edition of the *Dictionnaire de l'Académie Française* is, like Faguet's, thoroughly Lockean; it defines *libéralisme* in terms of the citizen's right to freedom of thought and to protection from government interference in private and business affairs.

One of several French theorists who attacked Faguet's exposition of liberalism (and, by implication, the academy's definition) was Jean de Grandvilliers. "How the word 'liberalism' is perverted by those who treat it as synonymous with individualism!" he wrote in *Essai sur le libéralisme allemand* (1925). "We can only reply by giving the word its true meaning." According to Grandvilliers, the true meaning of liberalism is to be found in a policy of extending the liberty of the people; he maintained that the intervention of the state is not only a useful, but also a necessary, means to achieve that end. Grandvilliers is thus a champion of the *étatiste* school of liberalism, which derived its concept of liberty from Rousseau and which argued that as long as the state belongs to the people, the enlargement of the power of the state is equally an enlargement of the power, and therefore the freedom, of its citizens.

GERMAN LIBERALISM

The word *liberal* was first heard in Germany in 1812, going there, as it went to England, from Spain. But the last years of Napoleon's power marked the decline of one tradition of German liberalism and the beginning of a new one. For in Germany, as elsewhere, we may discern not a single doctrine of liberalism but at least two main, conflicting schools, which again may be classified as the Lockean and the *étatiste*. The older German tradition was not merely derivatively Lockean; it also had contributed much to the formulation of Locke's own thought. In the sixteenth century it was a German philosopher, Johannes Althusius, who proclaimed that sovereignty derived from the people, and it was the German *Naturrechts* school of jurists that provided the bridge between the Stoic concept of *jus naturale* and the Lockean doctrine of the rights of man. But Locke, in turn, influenced the eighteenth-century German liberals, among whom Wilhelm von Humboldt was perhaps the most conspicuous. The very title of his book *Ideen zu einem Versuch, die Grenzen der Wirksamkeit des Staates zu bestimmen* (Ideas toward an investigation to determine the proper limits of the activity of the state; 1792), reveals his preoccupation with limited sovereignty and the minimal state. In this work Humboldt argued that the function of the state is not to do good but to ward off evil, notably the evil that springs from man's disregard for his neighbors' rights. The state, he said, "must not proceed a step further than is necessary for the mutual security of citizens and protection against foreign enemies; for no other object should it impose restrictions on freedom." Eighteenth-century Germany also had several liberal economists, including Christian Kraus, who considered that Adam Smith's *Wealth of Nations* (1776) was the most important book after the Bible.

In the nineteenth century a new school of liberalism, which was first and foremost nationalistic, arose in Germany. The freedom it stood for was the freedom of Germany, and the condition of the realization of this national freedom was the unification of Germany. Thus, whereas the old Lockean liberals were against the state, the new nationalist liberals wanted to create a greater state. The French declaration of 1789 proclaimed the rights of man; the German liberals inspired in 1848 a declaration of the rights of the German people. The new German liberals thought in terms of collective, rather than individual, rights. Thus, the *étatiste* German liberals saw nothing incongruous in sending a mission in 1849 from the Frankfurt parliament to Berlin to offer the crown of all Germany to a Prussian monarch, Friedrich Wilhelm, who detested democracy and who, in any event, grandly announced that he did not take crowns from commoners.

The difficulty of understanding in what sense this new German liberalism rested on a principle of freedom is that of understanding what it was that its votaries were demanding freedom from. Indeed, for many German liberals it was not a question of freedom from anything. German metaphysics of the same period was working out a concept of freedom that had nothing to do with resisting constraint. Guido de Ruggiero, a sympathetic Italian historian of German liberalism wrote:

> The eternal glory of Kant is to have demonstrated that obedience to the moral law is freedom.... It was the great merit of [G. W. F.] Hegel to have extracted from the Kantian identification of freedom with mind, the idea of an organic development of freedom, coinciding with the organisation of society in its progressively higher and more spiritual forms.... The State, the organ of coercion *par excellence,* has become the highest expression of liberty. (*History of European Liberalism*)

The idea that true freedom is to be found in obedience to the morally perfected state gave a theoretical justification (of a highly abstract kind) to the nineteenth-century German liberals' pursuit of liberty in submission to a strong and unified nation-state. But these high-thinking theorists never recovered from Friedrich Wilhelm's snub in 1849. Germany got its unity, but it was the imperialists, not the new liberals, who achieved it, and it was Otto von Bismarck, rather than Immanuel Kant, who gave the unified nation its political ethos. After the defeat of the Nazi regime in 1945, however, there was some revival of the Lockean type of liberalism in Germany.

AMERICAN LIBERALISM

In the United States the word *liberal* has never enjoyed the prestige it has in the United Kingdom, for in America there has never been, as there has in England, a national liberal party. The short-lived Liberal Republican Party of the 1870s was without a coherent program. Horace Greeley, its presidential candidate, was at once a socialist, spiritualist, vegetarian, and total abstainer; his personality led many Americans of his time to associate the word *liberal* with a visionary crank, and some still do. F. O. Matthiessen wrote in 1948: "In our nineteenth-century political life we had no such formulated division as that between the Conservatives and Liberals in England.... The key word seized upon by our native radical movement of the eighties and nineties, that of the Populists, was not 'liberal' but 'progressive'" (*From the Heart of Europe*, New York, 1948, p. 90). Again, whereas in Vernon Louis Parrington's *Main Currents in American Thought* the word *liberal* occurs on almost every page, Parrington's pupil Henry Steele Commager never once uses the words *liberal* and *liberalism* in his continuation volume, *The American Mind* (New Haven, CT, 1950).

Just as in France the word *liberal* had been used by some writers for almost any kind of left-wing opinion, so in America the word *liberal* was widely adopted after the Great Depression as a soubriquet for "socialist." In *The Liberal Imagination*, Lionel Trilling defined liberalism as meaning, among other things, "a belief in planning and international co-operation, especially where Russia is in question." This definition may not have been wholly authorized by common usage, but there can be no doubt that the word *liberal* has come to be associated in the American public's mind with *étatiste* and left-wing ideologies rather than with the Lockean notions of laissez-faire and mistrust of organized power.

Indeed, it was one of Parrington's arguments in *Main Currents in American Thought* that American liberalism, as he called it, had always been concerned with democracy in a way that Locke and his English followers had not. Yet even before the emergence of twentieth-century left-wing liberalism, two rival creeds, both of which could reasonably be called liberal, contended for political supremacy. The first, as Parrington pointed out, was close to the "English philosophy of *laissez-faire*, based on the assured universality of the acquisitive instinct and postulating a social order answering the needs of the abstract 'economic man' in which the state should function in the interests of trade." The second liberalism was Rousseauesque rather than Lockean. It was "based on the conception of human perfectibility" and looked toward an egalitarian democracy "in which the political state should function as the servant to the common well-being."

The dominant political sentiment of the American tradition derives something from both these kinds of liberalism, for it has combined a Lockean attachment to liberty from the state with a Rousseauesque belief in democracy and equality. Nevertheless, perhaps it is still not quite respectable to be an avowed liberal in America. This may be partly because there has been no traditional support for a liberal party. It is also partly because not only socialists, but also communists and communist sympathizers, have not ceased to assume the title "liberal" rather than a more explicit expression of their political commitment.

A remarkable variety of political structures has been thought by different philosophers to embody liberty, and a correspondingly mixed company has shared the name "liberal." In singling out certain main streams or schools of liberal thought, one has to be mindful of the divergences that exist even among those which can be usefully grouped together. One might broadly divide philosophers of freedom into those who think that to be free is to be able to do what one wants to do and those who think that to be free is to do what one ought to do. By a similar method, one might divide liberals into those who see freedom as something that belongs to the individual, to be defended against the encroachments of the state, and those who see freedom as something which belongs to society and which the state, as the central instrument of social betterment, can be made to enlarge and improve. It remains to be said that some of the greatest names in the history of liberal thought, including John Stuart Mill himself, are strangely poised between these two positions.

See also Althusius, Johannes; Arnold, Matthew; Censorship; Green, Thomas Hill; Hobbes, Thomas; Humboldt, Wilhelm von; Kant, Immanuel; Libertarianism; Liberty; Locke, John; Mill, John Stuart; Montesquieu, Baron de; Rights; Rousseau, Jean-Jacques; Smith, Adam; Sovereignty; Voltaire, François-Marie Arouet de.

Bibliography

Adler, Mortimer J. *The Idea of Freedom.* New York: Doubleday, 1958.

"Alain." *Le citoyen contre les pouvoirs.* Paris: Éditions du Sagittaire, 1926.

Berlin, Isaiah. *Two Concepts of Liberty.* Oxford: Clarendon Press, 1958.

Cranston, Maurice. *Freedom.* London: Longmans, Green, 1953.

Duclos, Pierre. *L'évolution des rapports politiques.* Paris: Presses Universitaires de France, 1950.

Faguet, Émile. *Le libéralisme.* Paris, 1912.

Grandvilliers, Jean de. *Essai sur le libéralisme allemand.* Paris, 1925.

Halévy, Élie. *La formation du radicalisme philosophique.* Paris, 1935.

Hallowell, John H. *The Decline of Liberalism.* London: K. Paul, Trench, Trubner, 1946.

Hartz, Louis. *Liberal Tradition in America.* New York: Harcourt Brace, 1955.

Hayek, Friedrich A. von. *The Constitution of Liberty.* Chicago: University of Chicago Press, 1960.

Hobhouse, L. T. *Liberalism.* New York: Holt, 1911.

Konvitz, M. R., and C. L. Rossiter, eds. *Aspects of Liberty.* Ithaca, NY: Cornell University Press, 1958.

Laski, Harold J. *The Rise of European Liberalism.* London: Allen and Unwin, 1936.

Martin, B. Kingsley. *French Liberal Thought in the Eighteenth Century.* London: Benn, 1929.

Neill, T. P. *Rise and Decline of Liberalism.* Milwaukee: Bruce, 1953.

Parrington, Vernon Louis. *Main Currents in American Thought.* 3 vols. New York: Harcourt Brace, 1927–1930.

Ponteil, F. *L'éveil des nationalités.* Paris, 1960.

Popper, Karl R. *The Open Society and Its Enemies.* 2 vols. London: Routledge, 1945.

Ruggiero, Guido de. *Storia del liberalismo.* Bari, Italy, 1925. Translated by R. G. Collingwood as *History of European Liberalism.* London: Oxford University Press, 1927.

Sartori, Giovanni. *Democratic Theory.* Detroit, MI: Wayne State University Press, 1962.

Schapiro, J. Salwyn. *Liberalism.* Princeton, NJ, 1953.

Thomas, R. H. *Liberalism, Nationalism and the German Intellectuals.* Chester Springs, PA, 1953.

Trilling, Lionel. *The Liberal Imagination.* Garden City, NY: Doubleday, 1953.

Waldeck-Rousseau, P. M. R. *L'état et la liberté.* Paris, 1906.

Watson, G., ed. *The Unservile State.* London: Allen and Unwin, 1957.

Maurice Cranston (1967)

LIBERALISM [ADDENDUM]

The theory of liberalism and political philosophy in general were dramatically revitalized by the publication of John Rawls's *A Theory of Justice* (1971). In that work Rawls adopts the social contract model of political theory but with several key innovations. Rawls states that his theory seeks to capture the essence of the social contract theories of Locke, Rousseau, and Kant and develop the core idea of the contract to deal with traditional criticisms of the contract model of political legitimacy. The social contract model of justifying political authority has as its core idea that the basic principles of justice are the object of an original agreement that free and rational persons concerned to further their own interests would accept in an initial position of equality.

THE ORIGINAL POSITION

For Rawls, the first question for political theory is to specify what initial conditions are right for deciding the question of justice. His answer is what he calls the "original position," a hypothetical state of nature or situation without a government designed to be the conceptual context within which the basic principles of justice will be considered and the main outlines of the distribution of rights and duties will be defined and agreed upon. Rawls sees the original position as a heuristic device or a thought experiment used to rethink and clarify our intuitions

about what justice is and what the basic structure of a just society would consist in. Rawls's concept of the original position has the following important components: the "veil of ignorance"; definition of the "people" in the original position; and, general knowledge that includes knowledge of the circumstances of justice and knowledge of the main competing theories of justice.

The overall design of the original position is based on what Rawls calls "considered judgments." These are judgments where moral capacities are likely to be manifested without distortion or prejudice. These judgments, for example, would include the beliefs that slavery, religious intolerance, and racism are wrong and ideas about fairness and human equality. Rawls terms his understanding of justification in ethics "reflective equilibrium." This model of justification rejects traditional foundationalist ideas of justification that hold that there are self-evident ethical principles from which one can derive specific moral rules and principles of justice and accepts a more coherentist model of justification. This coherence paradigm of justification holds that a theory is justified if one's considered judgments and moral and political principles cohere in a consistent belief system. By "equilibrium" Rawls means that one's judgments and principles are compatible and by "reflective" he means that one is fully and rationally aware of what our judgments and principles are and their derivation.

The veil of ignorance is a central feature of the original position. This imaginary veil is necessary, Rawls argues, because it excludes information that is not morally relevant or is a product of factors that are unjust and could be a source of prejudice. This means that information about one's social class, wealth, sex, race, abilities, personality, intelligence, particular conception of the good, health and the specific circumstances of one's society are excluded.

Though members of the original position are not allowed specific information about themselves, they are allowed certain general information. Members of the original position consider themselves free, equal, rational, and self-interested. As free, Rawls means no one is under the authority of another and as equal he means each has the same rights to make choices and decisions. As rational, Rawls means that people understand the ideas of justifying beliefs with evidence and that one should choose the most appropriate means to achieve one's goals. As self-interested, Rawls does not mean that people in the original position are selfish but rather that they are interested in their own welfare.

Members of the original position know that they need what Rawls calls "primary goods"; namely, certain basic rights, liberties, opportunities, income, wealth, and self-respect. These Rawls considers necessary means for whatever goals one may have and as such provide the motivation element in the deliberation in the original position.

Participants in the original position are also allowed knowledge of the circumstances of justice and the main competing theories of justice. The circumstances of justice include the notion that individuals coexist with roughly equal physical and mental powers, but are morally and intellectually limited with similar needs but different life goals in a world of moderate scarcity of resources.

The main competing theories of justice the members of the original position focus on are that of Rawls's theory, which he will call "justice as fairness," and utilitarianism. Rawls claims that people of the original position would reject utility as the principle of justice because, according to Rawls, the theory may allow injustice to a few to maximize utility overall.

Given his characterization of the hypothetical choice situation, Rawls believes members of the original position would agree to two principles of justice. Rawls's first principle states: "Each person is to have an equal right to the most extensive basic liberty compatible with a similar liberty for others" (1971, p. 60). The second principle holds: "Social and economic inequalities are to be arranged so that they are both, a) reasonably expected to be to everyone's advantage, and b) attached to positions and offices open to all" (1971, p. 60). According to Rawls, members of the original position would also decide that the first principle has priority over the second and cannot be sacrificed to realize the second principle more fully.

The first part of the second principle Rawls calls the "difference principle," and it requires that all inequality in economic matters benefit all members of society, especially the least advantaged. The second part of the second principle requires what Rawls calls "fair equality of opportunity." Fair equality of opportunity requires not only that there are no legal obstacles for any position in society, but it would also provide for equal starting social conditions for all. Rawls believes that all people should have an equal chance to achieve any position in society regardless of what their family background, their social class, sex, religion, and ethnic background happen to be. Government would have to make sure that people have such equal opportunity by providing an equally good education and other services intended to prevent great social inequality in income, opportunity, and wealth.

Rawls admits that to implement his two principles may mean a large role for government, but he does not demand that either socialism or capitalism would necessarily be agreed upon in the original position. He considers this an empirical decision that social conditions and economic efficiencies would dictate.

Rawls's theory has been praised and critiqued. Many applauded its robust defense of welfare liberalism, concern for the poor, and the central importance of fair equality of opportunity. Others were pleased by the interdisciplinary nature of Rawls's work and a style accessible to the ordinary educated person.

CRITICISMS OF RAWLS'S THEORY

Critics of Rawls's theory come from the political right and left. Those on the right feel he overemphasizes equality and puts too much power in the hands of government. Libertarians such as Robert Nozick (1974) claimed he has reduced liberty too greatly at the expense of equality and allowed for the violation of the right to property by allowing increased taxation of the rich to help the poor.

Critics of Rawls from the left believe he has allowed too much inequality. Socialists believe that Rawls should have realized that capitalism allows too much power in the hands of the capitalists who would control government to promote their interests. Marxists also claimed Rawls's theory of human nature is biased in favor of human nature as it exists in an alienated form under capitalism based on competitive individualism and overlooking the great power of social class in limiting freedom. Other critics such as James Sterba (2004) have questioned certain specific elements of the theory. Sterba claims the difference principle would in fact not be chosen in the original position. Sterba argues that members of the original position would choose a guaranteed minimum rather than the difference principle, but Sterba then extends that minimum to distant peoples and future generations which, he believes, will have the effect of greater equality.

Still other critics such as Michael Sandel (1982) believe that liberal philosophers such as Rawls place too much emphasis on individual rights and not enough on the role of the community and individual responsibility.

RAWLS'S LATER WORK

Rawls's later work, *Political Liberalism* (1993), still defends his principles of justice but also attempts to address some of the criticisms of his earlier work. The goals of *A Theory of Justice* (1971) were, according to Rawls, to develop justice as fairness as a superior moral and political theory to utilitarianism and use the social contract model to do so. The problem with these goals, Rawls explains in *Political Liberalism*, is that he was endorsing a comprehensive doctrine similar to Kantianism that is problematic in a world of incompatible doctrines none of which can be rationally determined to be correct. A "comprehensive doctrine" is defined by Rawls as a doctrine that encompasses all central values and beliefs about life. In this sense the main world religions and philosophical systems such as utilitarianism are comprehensive doctrines. By contrast, a "political conception" is a set of ideas that applies only to the political realm and does not assume any comprehensive doctrine but rather uses ideas found in the political culture of a society.

As Rawls puts it, the problem for his theory and political philosophy in general is: "How is it possible that there may exist over time a stable and just society of free and equal citizens profoundly divided by reasonable though incompatible religious, philosophical and moral doctrines?" (1993, p. xviii). Rawls hopes to solve this problem of reasonable pluralism of comprehensive doctrines by establishing the following: (1) to distinguish more clearly the difference between a comprehensive doctrine from a political one; (2) to emphasize the importance of stability in a well-ordered society in a world of reasonable pluralism of comprehensive doctrines; (3) to clarify that justice as fairness is not a comprehensive but a political doctrine; and (4) to show that political liberalism assumes and is compatible with a pluralism of reasonable comprehensive doctrines.

The idea of a well-ordered society is central to Rawls's answer to the problem of pluralism. For Rawls, well-ordered society is a stable society that, when realized, generates its own support from the citizenry being accepted as a fair system of cooperation based on publicly recognized rules agreed by all as just. A well-ordered society must also be one where the conception agreed to is limited to the political because of three facts. First, there is what Rawls calls the diversity of reasonable comprehensive religious, philosophical, and moral doctrines found in modern societies. The second fact is that to maintain one comprehensive doctrine as the correct one would entail the use of coercive physical state power. Third, a secure democratic government must be freely supported by at least a majority of its citizens.

Rawls believes a well-ordered society is possible because there is a limited agreement about political jus-

tice in the political culture of democratic societies. This agreement he calls an "overlapping consensus." This consensus is not a mere "modus vivendi" according to Rawls; that is, it is not merely the result of negotiation of self-interested parties, but rather it is agreed to on moral grounds found in the differing comprehensive doctrines. As such, Rawls calls his political theory of liberalism "freestanding" in that it is not based on any comprehensive doctrine.

On the one hand, many philosophers praised *Political Liberalism* as a major work dealing with the postmodern world of pluralism and ideological diversity. Critics, on the other hand, claimed that Rawls has merely assumed an overlapping consensus among comprehensive theories when in fact there is no such consensus. Others prefer his earlier work because they feel there is a need for some foundations to justify the theory that seems to be lacking in the new presentation.

Discussion of Rawls's work continues, but there is a growing consensus that his contributions to the field of political theory of liberalism will stand as a major addition to the canon of political philosophy for a long time to come.

See also Civil Disobedience; Cosmopolitanism; Multiculturalism; Postcolonialism; Republicanism.

Bibliography

Barry, B. *The Liberal Theory of Justice: A Critical Examination of the Principal Doctrines in a Theory of Justice.* Oxford: Clarendon, 1973.

Dworkin, R. *Taking Rights Seriously.* Cambridge, MA: Harvard University Press, 1977.

Freeman, S. *The Cambridge Companion to Rawls.* Cambridge, U.K: Cambridge University Press, 2003.

Freeman, S., ed. *Rawls: Collected Papers.* Cambridge, MA., 1999.

Gould, C. *Rethinking Democracy.* Cambridge, 1988.

Grcic, J. *Ethics and Political Theory.* Lanham, MD: University Press of America, 2000.

Martin, R. *Rawls and Rights.* Lawrence, KS: University Press of Kansas, 1985.

Nozick, R. *Anarchy, State and Utopia.* New York, 1974.

Rawls, John. *Justice as Fairness: A Restatement,* edited by E. Kelly. Cambridge, MA: Belknap Press of Harvard University Press, 2001.

Rawls, John. *The Law of Peoples: With, "The Idea of Public Reason Revisited."* Cambridge, MA: Harvard University Press, 1999.

Rawls, John. *Lectures on the History of Moral Philosophy,* edited by B. Herman. Cambridge, MA: Harvard University Press, 2000.

Rawls, John. *Political Liberalism.* New York: Columbia University Press, 1993. Rev. paperback ed., 1996.

Rawls, John. *A Theory of Justice.* Cambridge, MA: Belknap Press of Harvard University Press, 1971. Rev. ed., 1999.

Sandel, M. *Liberalism and the Limits of Justice.* Cambridge, U.K.: Cambridge University Press, 1982.

Sterba, J. *Triumph of Practice over Theory in Ethics.* New York: Oxford University Press, 2004.

Joseph Grcic (2005)

LIBERATION IN INDIAN PHILOSOPHY

The concept of liberation presupposes someone's state of bondage and anticipates the possibility of his or her release into a state of freedom. From the philosophical perspective bondage marks the human predicament of leading a precarious existence in an unstable world. In Indian philosophy the state of bondage is termed *saṁsāra* (global flow) and understood as a beginningless process of life of beings who are born, die, and are constantly reborn. This process is governed by the eternal law called in mainstream Hinduism *sanātana dharma*. This expression is *multivalent*, having several layers of meaning; Indian thinkers regard it as a matrix encompassing reality in its totality. In Buddhism *dharma* occurs without the attribute "everlasting," but is understood as being beyond time.

The multivalency of *sanātana dharma* gives it at least three meanings. First, as the eternal law it represents an impersonal force inherent in everything so that reality is orderly rather than chaotic; processes of reality follow the law of cause and effect. Second, the aspect of timelessness of *dharma* implies the view that even the phenomenal reality has no conceivable beginning and end, but keeps renewing itself in cycles. In other words, the global world process—including the present universe—has no fixed origin, such as a creative act of God, and will never come to an end to be replaced by the eternal "new earth and new heaven" after a day of judgment. Rather, it undergoes periodic renewals: At the beginning of each period the world process starts with the emergence (*sṛṣṭi*) of the universe from its hidden dimension into the state of manifestation; in the course of its duration (*sthiti*) it evolves to a peak, followed by decline and end in universal dissolution into the unmanifest state (*pralaya*) called cosmic night. After a period of latency, the whole process starts again.

The lives of individual beings proceed within this global framework from birth to adulthood, old age, death and rebirth in a never-ending round of *saṁsāric* exis-

tences. During the cosmic night they subsist in a kind of limbo or oblivion. Third, the concept of *dharma* also refers to the timeless and absolute reality beyond the manifested one; it represents the final goal of religious and philosophical quest equated with the ultimate truth. This truth is eternal, outside time, and independent of the changeable phases of the phenomenal reality manifested within time. The manifestation of the eternal truth or law within the universe dominated by time does not make the world everlasting in the sense of a lineal duration, but provides for its cyclic nature, its recurring rise and fall.

The concept of *dharma* understood as the absolute truth and ultimate reality has still another connotation—that of consciousness, awareness, or intelligence. Truth makes sense only if it is known. Indian philosophy, unlike Western science, has never conceived of reality without consciousness. Thus, a verse in one of the earliest Indian philosophical texts (1500–1000 BCE), the creation hymn of the *Ṛg Veda* (10, 129, 4), describes the primordial one-ness (*tad ekam*) as experiencing desire (*kāma*), the earliest seed of its mind (*manaso retaḥ*), which led to manifestation. The dimension of consciousness as an inherent quality of reality in its ultimate state evokes two fundamental insights. First, the idea of the ultimate personality (*puruṣottama*), albeit an infinite one, conceived as the personality of God, the free agent behind the world process, although not an omnipotent one. Second, it suggests that the individual human consciousness, being an instance of the universal dimension of consciousness, has—despite its present limitations—the potential of grasping reality on the ultimate level: Man has the capability to develop an understanding and vision of the absolute truth. Extricating himself thus from the conditionality of his phenomenal existence and attaining final liberation (*mokṣa, mukti*), he enters the timeless dimension of the absolute without having to participate in the world process and undergo repeated incarnations.

While in bondage, he is governed by *sanātana dharma* in all its aspects. Its aspect of causality operates in human life on a higher level as the law of karma, which is much more complicated than the law of cause and effect in the material universe, yet it can be expressed in the simple saying "as you have sown, so you will reap." Every volitional act in thought, speech, or deed generates a force that produces sooner or later—in one's present life or some future existence—results that shape one's external circumstances and appearance, forming one's character and determining one's fortune. The aspect of timelessness of *dharma* makes the lives of individual beings in the sequence of reincarnations appear to be without a conceivable beginning and end. However, the aspect of *dharma* as the timeless and absolute reality beyond the manifested world lends individual beings an affinity with the ultimate truth and the potentiality of realizing it by direct conscious experience, which brings about the termination of their bondage and the attainment of liberation outside time.

This necessitates entering a spiritual path, a training to deepen one's perception of reality up to the point of the final vision. Volitional input is essential for this purpose—as it is also within the karmic process to sow only wholesome deeds to earn future good results. The spiritual path was eventually systematized and became known as yoga.

The previous outline is valid in principle for all schools of Indian philosophy, including the earlier phases of Indian thought before the formation of philosophical systems. Despite the difference in terminology and sophistication of language, the ideas occur even in the oldest strata of Vedic scriptures in mythological guise, although nineteenth-century pioneers of Vedic scholarship failed to recognize them.

THE VEDAS AND UPANIṢADS

The *Ṛg Veda* uses the verb *muc* (hence *mokṣa* and *mukti*) in the creation myth when the god Indra periodically liberates the cosmic waters (= creative forces) from the clutches of the demon Vṛtra (10, 104, 9; 1, 32, 11; 4, 22, 7), thereby enabling the manifestation of the universe. As to humans, they are subjected to successive lives (*anūcīnā jīvitā*, 4, 54, 2), so liberation for them means being granted immortality (*amṛta, amṛtatva*). It is therefore ardently prayed for: "Lead us to immortality!" (5, 55, 4) "May I be released from death, not reft of immortality!" (7, 59, 12) "Place me in that deathless, undecaying world … make me immortal" (9, 113, 7–11). Certain "long-haired ascetics" (*keśins*) even claimed to have won immortality during their lifetime: "Due to our sagehood we have mounted upon the winds, only our bodies do you mortals see" (10, 136, 3). The pleas for immortality show that everlasting life was not automatically granted even if one reached heaven as a result of good deeds (10, 14, 8) and religious fervor (*tapas*, 10, 54, 2). Repeated death (*punarmṛtyu*) lurked even there as is later asserted by Śatapatha Brāhmaṇa (10, 4, 3, 10), so the search for immortality continues.

The ideas of rebirth under cosmic law and liberation from it are subsequently clearly spelled out in the oldest Upaniṣads (700–600 BCE): "One becomes pure by pure actions, bad by bad ones" (Bṛhadāraṇyaka Upaniṣad 3, 2,

13), and when one dies, knowledge (*vidyā*), deeds (*karmāṇi*), and previous experience (*pūrva prajñā*) follow one (4, 4, 2). One may live in higher worlds while the merits of one's actions last, but eventually returns to this world (4, 4, 4–6). But one has affinity with the Ultimate; one's inner self (*ātman*) is, at bottom, identical with the core of reality (*brahman*, 4, 4, 5). When one realizes it and can proclaim "I am *brahman*," one becomes the self of everything, including gods (1, 4, 10), and is freed from reincarnation. Thus, liberation is the result of the direct knowledge of one's inmost self and thereby of the inner essence of everything else brought about by meditational effort (*dhyāna*) and by renouncing external desires. Later Upaniṣads started developing methods of acquiring the liberating knowledge, thus foreshadowing the classical system of Yoga.

Two schools of thought and practice outside the Vedic tradition, Jainism and Buddhism, also systematized the path. Both emerged from the circles of wanderers (*śramaṇas*) striving for liberation from the round of rebirths by asceticism. In contrast to the Brahmanic tradition, they regarded the state of liberation as beyond description and used the negative term *nirvāṇa* (blowing-out) for it.

JAINISM

The term used in the teachings of Jina Mahāvīra (599–467 BCE) for individual beings is *jīva* (animate substance, soul, spirit-monad) or *ātman*. In its pure form a *jīva* is perfect, omniscient, eternal, and formless and enjoys unlimited energy and infinite bliss. When he succumbs to the influx (*āsrava*) of passions (*kaṣāya*) from the phenomenal world of modalities (*saṃsāra*), the *jīva* takes shape, assuming a body born from his actions (*karmaṇa-śarīra*), and he loses his perfection and becomes a mundane pilgrim (*saṃsāri*) through innumerable forms of life whose quality is determined by the ethical quality of his actions. Good actions secure his temporary well-being in *saṃsāra*, but do not lead to liberation. Of bad actions injury to life is the most detrimental one. Liberation (*mokṣa, mukti, nirvṛti*) is achieved by purging off (*nirjarā*) of karmic burdens accumulated by past actions and stopping (*saṃvara*) further influxes by renunciation so that the soul rises above involvement in any actions. In the last stages of ascetic practice (*tapas*), the abstention from action may involve stopping even intake of food and drink; liberation is reached on the point of death by starvation. If the *saṃsāri* achieves liberation before death, he becomes a perfect one (*siddha*) or a *tīrthaṅkara* (ford-maker, the teacher of others). Discarnate *siddhas* in *nir-*

vāṇa enjoy four infinite accomplishments: knowledge, vision, strength, and bliss. The Jain elaborate path to liberation shows overlaps with the Buddhist one and with Patañjali's Yoga.

BUDDHISM

Early Buddhist sources largely abstain from conceptual descriptions of the nature of beings, liberation, and ultimate reality. The Buddha (563–483 BCE) of the Pāli Canon maintained noble silence about such issues and focused pragmatically on analysis of the existential situation of man as it is accessible to everybody's experience and on practical procedures for gaining liberation and direct knowledge of true reality; called awakening or enlightenment (*bodhi*), this achievement does not include omniscience as in Jainism. Man's experience of himself is described in terms of five constituent groups of clinging (*upādānakkhandhas*):

(1) Bodily awareness or the experience of having a form (*rūpa*)

(2) Feelings (*vedanā*) that are pleasant, unpleasant, or neutral

(3) Perception (*saññā*) experienced through six channels—the five senses and the mind, the latter having the function of coordinating the fivefold sensory data into conceptually grasped objects

(4) Inner volitional dynamism described as the group of mental coefficients (*saṅkhāras*), such as instincts, urges, desires, wishes, decisions, and aspirations

(5) Consciousness (*viññāṇa*) or the direct awareness of being conscious of visual and other sensory objects and of mental images and concepts

None of these constituents represents the inner core, substance, or soul (*atta/ātman*) of the personality—they are *anatta*—and no such core is either postulated or denied. The structural unity of the personality is expressed by the term *nāmarūpa* (name and form), occasionally also *puggala* (Sanskrit: *pudgala*) or *purisa* (Sanskrit: *puruṣa*); its constituents constantly change, yet its individuality is preserved by its continuity as a process: The Buddha frequently referred to his and others' past lives.

Bondage to the round of births and deaths governed by the laws of karma results from ignorance (*avidyā*, *moha*) of the true nature of reality (*dhamma*). Beings are then subject to craving (*taṇhā*, *lobha*) directed to fleeting and basically substanceless pleasurable experiences and develop hate (*dosa*) if somebody obstructs their aims. The

beginning of the individuals' *saṁsāric* sojourn cannot be found, but liberation is possible when beings realize its unsatisfactoriness, recognize desire as its cause, understand that renouncing desire will free them from rebirth, and embark on the path toward that final goal.

This is the gist of the Buddha's "four noble truths," the fourth one being the eightfold path of systematic training, the first comprehensive formulation of a liberating technique. On reaching liberation a Buddha's disciple becomes an *arahat* (worthy one) and is equal to the Buddha in the acquired state of freedom, while the Buddha surpasses him in wisdom, thus enabling him to be the "teacher of gods and men." Individuals who attain liberation on their own without the guidance of a buddha become solitary enlightened ones (*paccekabuddhas*), who do not assume a teaching mission. Early Buddhism does not admit descriptions of or speculation about the state of a liberated one (*tathāgata*) after death. Here, too, the Buddha maintains "noble silence," expressly denying only the validity of the four alternatives put to him by questioners, namely that he "is," "is not," "both is and is not," and "neither is nor is not." "The final truth (*dhamma*) is deep, unfathomable, understood only by the wise" (Majjhima Nikāya 72)—an Enlightened One.

Despite this injunction, speculation did not cease and some Hīnayāna schools of thought, including Theravāda, interpreted the Buddha's description of personality factors (*khandhas*) as unsubstantial (*anatta*) to mean denial of an inner core or any other feature that would lend individuals identity in successive lives and continuity into *nirvāṇa*. This was challenged by the Pudgalavāda school, which maintained that personality (*pudgala*) as such is as eaqually undefinable as *tathāgata* and that it is independent of the individual's status, whether bound or liberated, which means that it persists throughout successive lives and into *nirvāṇa*. This doctrine was adopted by many sects and remained influential for centuries.

Mahāyāna schools of thought do not appear to have had problems with personal continuity. Innumerable *tathāgatas* are active from within their spheres of influence (*buddhakṣetras*), helping beings to liberation, assisted by *bodhisattvas*, individuals developing ten perfections (*pāramitās*) on the path to buddhahood that proceeds through ten stages (*bhūmis*). Some *bodhisattvas* vow not to enter final *nirvāṇa* until all beings are liberated "down to the last blade of grass," an innovation that envisages universal liberation. This is viewed as possible on the basis of the philosophy of emptiness (*śūnyavāda*), which developed as a result of meditational experience: The mind, emptied of all contents derived from sensory perception and conceptual activity, can make the final breakthrough into *nirvāṇa*, which is equally empty because it is inaccessible to sensory perception and undefinable. Thus, emptiness (*śūnyatā*) came to be regarded as underlying both *saṃsāra* and *nirvāṇa*, making them, at bottom, identical. Liberation occurs by shifting one's perspective.

Such tendencies to hypostatize *śūnyatā* were checked by Nāgārjuna (flourished c. 150–250), the protagonist of the Mādhyamaka school, who used the dialectical method to refute conflicting theses; truth lay in the middle, but beyond dialectics. It is accessible only to direct vision—as the Buddha taught. Tendencies to hypostatization appeared also in the Vijñānavāda school, which regards pure consciousness as the basis for not only *saṃsāra* but also *nirvāṇa*, since its achievement cannot but be a conscious experience. *Saṃsāric* phenomena are mental constructs projected from the universal storehouse consciousness (*ālaya-vijñāna*), yet the emptiness and purity of the root consciousness (*mūla-vijñāna*) and of a liberated one's consciousness remain unaffected.

HINDU SYSTEMS OF PHILOSOPHY

During the golden age of Indian civilization under the Gupta dynasty (320–510), philosophical discussions flourished between various schools of thought. Six of them came to be recognized as valid Hindu angles of viewing (*dṛṣṭi*, hence *darśana*) of reality and were systematized. All accept the basic teaching about *saṃsāric* bondage and the desirability of liberation, but differ in ontological conceptions and methodical approaches.

(1) Pūrva-Mīmāṃsā (original elucidation) regards the Vedas as eternal and pursues the path of ritual action (*karma-mārga*), which parallels cosmic processes and terrestrial events governed by the inherent law of *ṛta* (the Vedic equivalent of *dharma*), which is independent of any divine agency. Right rituals achieve anything, including rebirth in the highest existential spheres and liberation, although in advanced stages of the path ritual is interiorized and becomes a process of meditation.

(2) Vaiśeṣika (discrimination) is a kind of natural philosophy focusing on classifying reality into categories (*padārthas*). Reality is subjected to the invisible law (*adṛṣṭa dharma*) operating also in the ethical sphere independently of God (*īśvara*), an eternally free, omniscient spirit (not a creator) who can assist beings on the path of knowledge (*jñāna-mārga*) based on a meditational analysis of *saṃsāric* categories that leads to liberation from them.

(3) Nyāya (guidance) analyses logical and epistemological processes that supply beings with their picture of the world. In testing its validity, Nyāya thinkers discovered syllogism that, however, required verification by experience. Logical analysis is the start of the path of knowledge (*jñāna-mārga*). It sharpens the mind, preparing it for meditational viewing, which culminates in direct knowledge of the final truth equaling liberation.

(4) Sāṅkhya (enumeration) is a dualistic metaphysical system with no God. It recognizes an infinite number of originally pure and free eternal spirits (*puruṣas*) and the creative force of nature (*prakṛti*), which conjures up the world process for *puruṣas*. As they show interest in this spectacle, *prakṛti* creates for them bodies with senses and mental functions. The *puruṣas*, fascinated by the antics of *prakṛti*, identify with their *prakṛtic* personalities and forget their true status. When a *puruṣa* recognizes this bondage, he can liberate himself by mentally discriminating between *prakṛtic* evolutes and his original pure consciousness; this is a variety of *jñāna-mārga*. His worldly personality dissolves and he regains total freedom in isolation (*kaivalya*) from *prakṛti*.

(5) Yoga (union) as one of the six *darśanas* is chiefly a systematic eightfold path to liberation called classical Yoga, expounded by Patañjali (second century BCE). However, chapter 4 of his *Yoga Sūtras* shows that it had been a philosophical system in its own right before its ontology was overshadowed by Sāṅkhya. Still, it retained the notion of God (*īśvara*), an eternally free *puruṣa* who may assist other *puruṣas* (entangled in *saṃsāra*) struggling for liberation but is neither the Creator nor the focus of a religious cult. The discipline of the Yoga path aims at experiencing liberation as autonomy (*kaivalya*) from limiting forms of existence, accompanied by the final vision of or cognitive unification with the totality of truth (*dharmamegha-samādhi*).

(6) Uttara Mīmāṃsā (higher elucidation) or Vedānta (end of Veda, meaning Upaniṣads, its base) split into three subschools. In the Advaita (nondualistic) Vedānta of Śaṅkara (700?–750?) *brahman*, the Upaniṣadic source and core of the manifested universe, is regarded as the sole reality; the individual bondage in *saṃsāra* is an illusion (*māyā*). Liberation is achieved when this illusion is dispersed by treading

the path of knowledge (*jñāna-yoga*) that culminates in *samādhi* experienced as the unity of being, consciousness, and bliss (*sat-cit-ānanda*). The liberated one realizes that he is and has always been *brahman* and that nothing else really exists. The Viśiṣṭa Advaita (qualified nondualistic) Vedānta of Rāmānuja (c. 1077–1137) interprets the Upaniṣadic *brahman* as the eternal God who created the world out of his own subtle body by transforming it into a gross one. Beings are attributes of God, but possess their own self-conscious existence. They retain it even when liberated in mystic union with God accomplished with his grace (*prasāda*) after surrendering to him on the path of devotion (*bhakti-mārga*). Upaniṣadic passages with traces of a dualistic worldview (foreshadowing Sāṅkhya) enabled even the Dvaita (dualistic) Vedānta of Madhva (c. 1199–c. 1278) to claim Vedic authority for its interpretation. It accepts the eternal existence of *prakṛti* and the plurality of *jīvas*, who retain their individuality even in the state of liberation granted as God's grace to those who live pure lives and embrace *bhakti-mārga*. Others may transmigrate in *saṁsāra* forever. Some evildoers may even reach a point past redemption and face eternal damnation in infinite remoteness from God.

A modern approach to liberation appears in the writings of Aurobindo (1872–1950). He envisioned a new phase in the world's evolution: if enough individuals prepare themselves through yoga for receiving the cosmic consciousness, then they could bring about the spiritualization of the earth or even the whole universe. This idea of universal liberation has its origin in the vow of Mahāyāna *bodhisattvas* to liberate all beings "down to the last blade of grass."

See also Brahman; Causation in Indian Philosophy; God/Isvara in Indian Philosophy; Karma; Knowledge in Indian Philosophy; Meditation in Indian Philosophy; Mind and Mental States in Buddhist Philosophy; Negation in Indian Philosophy; Self in Indian Philosophy.

Bibliography

Blackstone, Kathryn R. *Women in the Footsteps of the Buddha: Struggle for Liberation in the Therigatha*. London: Curzon Press, 1998.

Buswell, Robert E., and Robert M. Gimello. *Paths to Liberation: The Mārga and Its Transformations in Buddhist Thought*. Delhi, India: Banarsidass, 1994.

Chakraborti, Haripada. *Asceticism in Ancient India*. Calcutta, India: Punthi Pustak, 1973.

Châu, Thích Thiên. *Les sectes personnalistes (Pudgalavādin) du bouddhisme ancien*. Paris: Université de la Sorbonne Nouvelle, 1977.

Dange, Sadashiv A. "Metempsychosis and the Ṛgveda." *Journal of the University of Bombay* 43 (79) (1974): 1–12.

Eckel, Malcolm David. *To See the Buddha: A Philosopher's Quest for the Meaning of Emptiness*. Princeton, NJ: Princeton University Press, 1992.

Fort, Andrew O. "Going on Knowledge? The Development of the Idea of Living Liberation in the Upanishads." *Indian Philosophy* 22 (4) (1944).

Fort, Andrew O. *Jīvanmukti in Transformation: Embodied Liberation in Advaita and Neo-Vedanta*. Albany: SUNY Press, 1998.

Gethin, Rupert. *The Buddhist Path of Awakening: A Study of the Bodhi-Pakkiyā Dhammā*. Leiden, Netherlands: Brill, 1992.

Gonda, Jan. *The Vision of the Vedic Poets*. The Hague, Netherlands: Mouton, 1963.

Harvey, Peter. "The Nature of the Tathāgata." In *Buddhist Studies, Ancient and Modern*, edited by P. Denwood and A. Piatigorsky. London: Curzon Press, 1983.

Jacobsen, Knut A. *Prakṛti in Sāṃkhya-Yoga: Material Principle, Religious Experience, Ethical Implications*. Delhi, India: Banarsidass, 2002.

Jaini, Padmanabha Shrivarma. *The Jaina Path of Purification*. Delhi, India: Banarsidass, 1979.

Johansson, R. *The Psychology of Nirvana*. London: Allen and Unwin, 1969.

Klostermaier, Klaus K. *Mythologies and Philosophies of the Salvation in the Theistic Traditions of India*. Waterloo, Canada: Wilfrid Laurier University Press, 1984.

Lad, Ashok Kumar. *A Comparative Study of the Concept of Liberation in Indian Philosophy*. Burhanpur, India: Girdharlal Keshavdas, 1967.

Larson, Gerald James, and Ram Shankar Bhattacharya. "Sāṅkhya: A Dualist Tradition in Indian Philosophy." In *Encyclopedia of Indian Philosophies*. Vol. 4. Princeton, NJ: Princeton University Press, 1987.

Miller, Jeanine. *The Vedas*. London: Rider, 1974.

Miller, Jeanine. *The Vision of Cosmic Order in the Vedas*. London: Routledge and Kegan Paul, 1985.

Oberhammer, Gerhard. *La Délivrance, dès Cette Vie (jīvanmukti)*. Paris: Édition-Diffusion de Boccard, 1994.

Oldmeadow, Harry. "Delivering the Last Blade of Grass: Aspects of the *Bodhisattva* Ideal in the Mahāyāna." *Asian Philosophy* 7 (3) (1997): 181–194.

Orofino, Giacomella, trans. *Sacred Tibetan Teachings on Death and Liberation*. Bridport, U.K.: Prism Press, 1999.

Verpoorten, Jean-Marie. *Mīmāṁsā Literature*. Wiesbaden, Germany: O. Harrassowitz, 1987.

Welbon, G. R. *The Buddhist Nirvāṇa and Its Western Interpreters*. Chicago: University of Chicago Press, 1968.

Werner, Karel. "*Bodhi* and *Arahattaphala*: From Early Buddhism to Early Mahāyāna." *Journal of the International Association of Buddhist Studies* 4 (1981): 70–84.

Werner, Karel. "Indian Conceptions of Human Personality." *Asian Philosophy* 6 (2) (1996): 93–107.

Werner, Karel. "Indian Concepts of Human Personality in Relation to the Doctrine of the Soul." *Journal of the Royal Asiatic Society* 1988 (1): 73–97.

Werner, Karel. "The Longhaired Sage of Ṛg Veda 10, 136: A Shaman, a Mystic, or a Yogi?" In *The Yogi and the Mystic: Studies in Indian and Comparative Mysticism*, edited by Karel Werner, 33–53. London: Curzon Press, 1989, repr. in 1994.

Werner, Karel. "A Note on *Karma* and Rebirth in the Vedas." *Hinduism* 83 (1978): 1–4.

Werner, Karel. "Symbolism in the Vedas and Its Conceptualisation." In *Symbols in Art and Religion: The Indian and the Comparative Perspectives*, edited by Karel Werner, 27–45. London: Curzon Press, 1990.

Werner, Karel. "The Vedic Concept of Human Personality and its Destiny." *Journal of Indian Philosophy* 5 (1978): 275–289.

Werner, Karel. *Yoga and Indian Philosophy*. Delhi, India: Banarsidass, 1977, reprint in 1980 and 1998.

Whicher, Ian. *The Integrity of the Yoga Darśana*. New York: SUNY Press, 1998.

Whicher, Ian, ed. *Yoga: Tradition and Transformation*. Richmond, Australia: Curzon, 2001.

Karel Werner (2005)

LIBERATION THEOLOGY

Liberation theology is the name of a movement that arose in the churches, both Catholic and Protestant, of Latin America during the last third of the twentieth century. It also describes a theological trend that is found, often under different names and with somewhat different emphases across the world, as black theology in the United States and South Africa, as Dalit theology in India, as Minjung theology in Korea, and elsewhere in other forms.

THEOLOGY

The earliest and still definitive statement of the movement is *A Theology of Liberation: History Politics, and Salvation* (1988) by Gustavo Gutiérrez. The basic principles it sets forth are:

(1) Theology is critical reflection on Christian praxis. Faith, charity, and commitment to God and to others in the struggle for humanity and justice are primary. Theology relates this praxis to the sources of revelation and the history of the church.

(2) Biblical revelation commits the church to God's "preferential option for the poor." The poor are, by their condition, involved in a struggle to realize their humanity and to become "subjects of their own history," against the political, economic, and social powers that marginalize and oppress them. This struggle is revolutionary, not reformist. The church belongs with the poor in the midst of it, doing theology in a revolutionary situation.

(3) The struggle of the poor for social justice is a work of human self-creation that finds its source, meaning, and hope in God's work. Salvation history is at the heart of human history, in creation, covenant, Christ's incarnation, and the coming kingdom of God. Political liberation is a partial salvific event, a historical realization of the kingdom, that looks forward to its ultimate fulfillment by divine grace operating in the human struggle, informing its character and directing it toward ever larger goals of human community.

This is still its basic structure. In its development and spread, however, three major issues have arisen.

CRITIQUE: DEFINING THE POOR

First, how are the poor defined? The Latin American theologians clearly have a dependent economic class in mind, created by exploiting landlords, industrialists, and bankers, along with their political and military agents. This definition, in terms of the dehumanizing dynamics of the capitalist system and class struggle against it, clearly borrows from Karl Marx. José Miguez Bonino (1976) acknowledges this explicitly as do many others. The Vatican, though affirming a preferential option for the poor, has been severely critical of this tendency to identify the poor of scripture with the proletariat that Marx defined. Liberation theologians claim, however, that this analysis is the secular expression in modern industrial society of a theme in Christian history that finds its source in the Hebrew prophets and the incarnation of Christ: the saving work of God liberating the people from the economic and political power of organized human sin. *The Kairos Document, Challenge to the Church: A Theological Comment on the Political Crisis in South Africa*—(1986), without appealing to Marx, makes the same argument concerning the apartheid system, calling it prophetic theology, as opposed to (a) state theology, which justifies the status quo, and (b) church theology, which is cautiously critical but without social analysis or a strategy for revolutionary change. Minjung theology in Korea focuses on a politically oppressed people (minjung), given hope by biblical history and promise, to strive for their liberation in a messianic kingdom where Jesus the suffering servant is lord. For Dalit theology in India, like American black theology, it is a subjugated minority, the outcastes (the dalits), to which the promise of God comes, in their conflict with an oppressive majority. Black theology draws especially on the Exodus of the

Israelites from Egypt to legitimate black people's fight for freedom.

All these movements agree that liberation is the basic theme of the Christian message. All see political, economic, cultural, and even religious powers as the instruments of oppression against which they struggle in God's name. They differ in their perception of how the poor are defined and which powers are their primary antagonists. The power analysis that Marxism provides is determinative for some and secondary for others. All of them, however, incorporate it into a more subtle and insightful guide that scripture provides to Christian understanding of the poor and to action that will realize God's promise.

CRITIQUE: THE QUESTION OF TRUTH

Second, how is the truth claim of liberation theology validated? This question arises on two levels. First, the hermeneutic of suspicion, which probes the roots of all truth claims in social experience and defines theology as a reflection on social praxis, owes much to Marx. It contradicts the teaching of St. Thomas Aquinas about the universality of reason and natural law as perfected, not destroyed by revelation. It reflects, however, the reformation understanding of reason distorted by human sin and is rooted, liberation theologians would claim, in the way God is known in the biblical history of calling, covenant, and promise.

The question remains, then, how divine revelation corrects and redeems the self-understanding also of the poor. How is truth, beyond the interests of one social group, known? Juan Luis Segundo (1976) describes the process as an expanding hermeneutical circle. Experience of reality from the perspective of the poor leads to ideological suspicion toward received structures of authority, morals, and dogma. This leads to a new awareness of God, which in turn creates a new hermeneutic for interpreting the biblical story. One does not escape ideology through this circle. But biblical revelation at one pole and the human condition of the poor at the other direct and correct it toward political and spiritual liberation. Paulo Freire develops the same line of thought as a teaching method in *Pedagogy of the Oppressed* (1970), with its emphasis on learning to be human in Christian-base communities through defining and struggling against oppressive powers while being transformed by God's saving love in the struggle.

CRITIQUE: SIN AND HOPE

Third, is liberation theology a universal message that offers hope to all, or a theology of and for the oppressed only? Vatican critiques, primarily in Pope John Paul II's speech to the Latin American bishops at the 1979 Puebla Conference in Mexico and in two "Instructions" from the Congregation for the Doctrine of the Faith 1984 and 1986, were especially strong on this point. (cf. A.T. Hennelly, *Liberation Theology: A Documentary History*, 1990). Authoritative for theology is not contemporary social analysis but the truth of the saving gospel of Christ revealed in scripture and interpreted by church tradition. The human situation must be understood in the light of the experience of the church through the ages as it responds in faith to God and the world. In this context one understands that the basic bondage is not just political oppression, but slavery to sin in all forms, that preferential option for the poor is concern for all who are caught in this bonda, and that Jesus's transforming, peacemaking, pardoning and reconciling love is the true liberation. Therefore, the church cannot sanction the violence of class war. It cannot identify God with historical achievement. It cannot understand freedom only as political.

REPLIES TO CRITICS

To these and to other criticisms, also from Protestant sources, liberation theologians reply variously. In replying to critics in his introduction to the revised edition (1988) of *A Theology of Liberation* Gutiérrez clearly addresses the community of the whole church with a call to join the poor in their struggle for liberation, confident of the reign of God, which is for all. Liberation, he says, is salvation on three levels: freedom from economic and political oppression, personal transformation, and ultimately redemption from sin. It is a movement with both historical and eschatological dimensions. However, his view of the church is less hierarchical and institutional than the Vatican critique. His emphasis on praxis as response to faith is also more social and historical.

Others, in their contexts, deal with the question in various ways. The *Kairos Document* calls the church to struggle against tyranny with appropriate force, with the hope that the coming reign of the risen Christ offers, but also with love for the oppressor and justice for all. Both Dalit theology in India and Black theology in the United States are more exclusively focused on the minority group whose faith they seek to express. Dalits, they claim, have their own participation in the liberating presence of the suffering Christ. They can only bear witness to God's promise for all people if they are not integrated into the ethos of the majority, of Hindu India, or even of the Christian church dominated by other castes. Similarly, for James H. Cone (1969, 1975), Christ's affirmation of black people is central to God's liberating purpose, and salvation for white people means identifying with this experience. Minjung theologians speak in and for the church, but they understand the experience of the people of God and the suffering messiah in the Bible as offering God's promise and hope to the suffering people of Korea today. It is the minjung who are the messianic people.

These theologies differ in their identification of oppressed peoples seeking liberation, though they communicate with and learn from one another. Their views on the relation between these peoples and the church are not the same, though all have grown out of the church and speak to it. They are not always of one mind about the use of violence in the struggle against oppressive powers, though they all would condemn hatred and seek nonviolent methods where possible. They do not all agree about the relation between the struggle of the poor for political, economic, and social liberation and the ultimate freedom promised in the coming of the kingdom of God. But for all of them Christian faith is fundamental. This means for them God's special concern for the poor in their fight for justice and freedom, God's identification with them in the servanthood and suffering of Christ, and God's promise of a world in which both oppressed and oppressors will be freed from power and domination. The movement has been called utopian, a term that Gutiérrez accepts as a provisional expression of Christian hope. Whether it is also realistic, history must judge.

See also Marxist Philosophy; Marx, Karl; Natural Law; Philosophy of Religion; Reason; Reformation; Revelation; Thomas Aquinas, St.

Bibliography

Cone, James H. *Black Theology and Black Power.* New York: Seabury Press, 1969.

Cone, James H. *God of the Oppressed.* New York: Seabury Press, 1975.

Freire, Paulo. *Pedagogy of the Oppressed.* Translated by Myra Bergman Ramos. New York: Herder and Herder, 1970.

Gutiérrez, Gustavo. *The Power of the Poor in History.* Translated by Robert R. Barr. Maryknoll, NY: Orbis Books, 1983.

Gutiérrez, Gustavo. *A Theology of Liberation: History, Politics, and Salvation.* Translated and edited by Sister Caridad Inda and John Eagleson. Maryknoll, NY: Orbis Books, 1973. Rev. ed., 1988.

Hennelly, Alfred T., ed. *Liberation Theology: A Documentary History.* Maryknoll, NY: Orbis Books, 1990.

The Kairos Document, Challenge to the Church: A Theological Comment on the Political Crisis in South Africa—. Grand Rapids, MI: Eerdmans, 1986.

Kim Yong Bock, ed. *Minjung Theology: People as the Subjects of History.* Singapore: Commission on Theological Concerns, Christian Conference of Asia, 1981.

Miguez Bonino, José. *Christians and Marxists: The Mutual Challenge to Revolution.* Grand Rapids, MI: Eerdmans, 1976.

Miguez Bonino, José. *Doing Theology in a Revolutionary Situation.* Philadelphia, PA: Fortress Press, 1975.

Nirmal, Arvind P., ed. *A Reader in Dalit Theology.* Madras, India: Gurukul Lutheran Theological College and Research Institute for the Department of Dalit Theology, 1994.

Rowland, Christopher, ed. *The Cambridge Companion to Liberation Theology.* New York: Cambridge University Press, 1999.

Segundo, Juan Luis. *The Liberation of Theology.* Translated by John Drury. Maryknoll, NY: Orbis Books, 1976.

Charles C. West (1996, 2005)

LIBER DE CAUSIS

The *Liber de Causis* (or *Liber Aristotelis de Expositione Bonitatis Purae;* Book of Causes) is a Latin translation of an Arabic work that is derived from the "Elements of Theology" of Proclus (fifth century CE). The author of the Arabic work is unknown; some scholars consider it the twelfth-century composition of David the Jew (Abraham ibn Daud or Avendeath) at Toledo, while others believe it an eighth- or ninth-century product of a school of Neoplatonism in the Near East, possibly stemming from a still earlier Syriac source.

At least one Latin translation appeared before 1187, probably the product of the Toledan translator, Gerard of Cremona. The work then came to be ascribed variously to David, al-Fārābī, or Aristotle. By 1255 the Parisian Faculty of Arts, considering it a work of Aristotle, included it in the curriculum.

Among the many doctrines contained in the 211 chapters, or Propositions, of Proclus's "Elements of Theology," the following should be noted. Proclus uses the term *theology* to mean Neoplatonic metaphysics. The latter describes the necessary procession of the world, or being, from its ultimate origins. The most important of these originative principles are: first, the gods; second, the pure spirits, or Intelligences; third, souls. The supreme god, or the One, is not describable as "being," yet it is the universal cause of every being. Before producing Intelligences, the One effects a pair of opposite principles, Limit and Infinity, and then a series of subordinate gods, or "henads," which have the causal function of Plato's Forms. The immediate effect of each principle, whether the latter be a god, a spirit, or a soul, is an attribute that is both similar to, and yet more specific than, its source. The particularity of the effect is due to its recipient. Consequently, it is difficult for the reader to see how the One can produce all things without the cooperation of its subordinates.

The thirty-two propositions of the *Liber de Causis* summarize this material with the following changes: (1) the multitude of deities (Limit, Infinity, and henads) is eliminated and divinity is reserved to the One alone; (2) the first cause is described as "being" and its causality as "creation." These changes suggest that the Neoplatonic author was either Jewish, Islamic, or Christian. Nevertheless, because the causes of Proclus act solely from the necessity of their natures and are mutually interdependent, it is questionable whether the *Liber de Causis* actually presents a monotheistic theory of free creation.

After reading William of Moerbecke's Latin translation of the "Elements of Theology" (*Elementatio Theologica*, 1268), St. Thomas Aquinas noticed for the first time that the *Liber de Causis* was not a work of Aristotle, but a modification of Proclus. Unfortunately, this discovery had to be made again during the Renaissance.

The doctrines in the *Liber de Causis* influenced many thinkers, among them: William of Auvergne, Roger Bacon, Albert the Great, John Duns Scotus, and Meister Eckhart.

See also Albert the Great; al-Fārābī; Aristotle; Bacon, Roger; Duns Scotus, John; Eckhart, Meister; Neoplatonism; Proclus; Renaissance; Thomas Aquinas, St.; William of Auvergne.

Bibliography

EDITIONS

Bardenhewer, Otto. *Die pseudo-aristotelische Schrift über das reine Gute, bekannt unter dem Namen Liber de Causis.* Freiburg im Breisgau, 1882.

Steele, Robert. *Opera Hactenus Inedita Rogeri Baconi.* Fasc. 102, "Questiones supra *Librum de Causis.*" Oxford and London: Clarendon Press, 1935.

ON THE *LIBER DE CAUSIS*

Anawati, Georges C. "Prolégomènes à une nouvelle édition du *De Causis* arabe (Kitāb al-hayr al-maḥḍ)." *Mélanges Louis Massignon* 1 (1956): 73–110.

Doresse, J. "Les sources du *Liber de Causis.*" *Revue de l'histoire des religions* 13 (1946): 234–238.

Gilson, Étienne. *History of Christian Philosophy in the Middle Ages,* 236–237. New York: Random House, 1955.

Michael W. Strasser (1967)

LIBERTARIANISM

Libertarians like to think of themselves as defenders of liberty. For example, Friedrich A. von Hayek sees his work as restating an ideal of liberty for "We are concerned with that condition of men in which coercion of some by others is reduced as much as possible in society" (1960, p. 11). Similarly, John Hospers believes that libertarianism is "a philosophy of personal liberty—the liberty of each person to live according to his own choices, provided that he does not attempt to coerce others and thus prevent them from living according to their choices" (1971, p.5). And Robert Nozick (1974) claims that, if a conception of justice goes beyond libertarian "side-constraints," it cannot avoid the prospect of continually interfering with people's lives.

Libertarians have interpreted their ideal of liberty in two basically different ways. Some, following Herbert Spencer (1820–1903), have taken a right to liberty as basic and have derived all other rights from this right to liberty. Others, following John Locke, have taken a set of rights, including typically a right to life and a right to property, as basic and have defined liberty as the absence of constraints in the exercise of these rights. Both groups of libertarians regard liberty as the ultimate political ideal, but they do so for different reasons. For Spencerian libertarians liberty is the ultimate political ideal because all other rights are derived from a right to liberty. For Lockean libertarians liberty is the ultimate political ideal because liberty is just the absence of constraints in the exercise of people's fundamental rights.

SPENCERIAN AND LOCKEAN LIBERTARIANS

Consider the view of Spencerian libertarians, who take a right to liberty to be basic and define all other rights in terms of this right to liberty. According to this view liberty is usually interpreted as being unconstrained by other persons from doing what one wants or is able to do. Interpreting liberty this way, libertarians like to limit constraints to positive acts (i.e., acts of commission) that prevent people from doing what they otherwise want or are able to do. In contrast, welfare liberals and socialists interpret constraints to include, in addition, negative acts (acts of omission) that prevent people from doing what they otherwise want or are able to do. In fact, this is one way to understand the debate between defenders of *negative liberty* and defenders of *positive liberty*. This is because defenders of negative liberty interpret constraints to include only positive acts of others that prevent people from doing what they otherwise want or are able to do, while defenders of positive liberty interpret constraints to include both positive and negative acts of others that prevent people from doing what they otherwise want or are able to do.

Suppose then we interpret constraints in the manner favored by libertarians to include only positive acts by others that prevent people from doing what they otherwise want or are able to do. Libertarians go on to characterize their political ideal as requiring that each person should have the greatest amount of liberty commensurate with the same liberty for all. From this ideal they claim that a number of more specific requirements, in particular a right to life, a right to freedom of speech, press, and assembly, and a right to property, can be derived.

Here, it is important to observe that the libertarian's right to life is not a right to receive from others the goods and resources necessary for preserving one's life. It is not a right to welfare: It is simply a right not to be killed unjustly. Correspondingly, the libertarian's right to property is not a right to receive from others the goods and resources necessary to meet one's basic needs, but a right to acquire goods and resources either by initial acquisitions or by voluntary agreements.

Of course, libertarians would allow that it would be nice of the rich to share their surplus goods and resources with the poor. Nevertheless, they deny that government has a duty to provide for such needs. Libertarians claim that some good things, such as providing welfare to the needy, are requirements of charity rather than justice. Accordingly, failure to make such provisions is neither blameworthy nor punishable. As a consequence, libertarians contend that such acts of charity should not be coercively required. For this reason they are opposed to any coercively supported welfare program.

For a similar reason libertarians are opposed to coercively supported opportunity programs. This is because the basic opportunities one has under a libertarian conception of justice are primarily a function of the property one controls, and since unequal property distributions are taken to be justified under a libertarian conception of justice, unequal basic opportunities are also regarded as justified.

The same opposition to coercively supported welfare and equal opportunity programs characterizes Lockean libertarians, who take a set of rights, typically including a right to life and a right to property, as basic and then interpret liberty as being unconstrained by other persons from doing what one has a right to do. According to this view a right to life is simply a right not to be killed unjustly; it is not a right to receive welfare. Correspondingly, a right to property is a right to acquire property either by initial acquisitions or by voluntary transactions; it is not a right to receive from others whatever goods and resources one needs to maintain oneself. Understanding a right to life and a right to property in this way, libertarians reject both coercively supported welfare programs and equal opportunity programs as violations of liberty.

A PARTIAL DEFENSE

In support of their view libertarians advance examples of the following sort. The first two are adapted from Milton Friedman (1962), and the last one is from Robert Nozick (1974).

In the first example you are to suppose that you and three friends are walking along the street and you happen to notice and retrieve a $100 bill lying on the pavement. Suppose a rich fellow had passed by earlier throwing away $100 bills, and you have been lucky enough to find one of them. Now, according to Friedman, it would be nice of you to share your good fortune with your friends. Nevertheless, they have no right to demand that you do so, and hence, they would not be justified in forcing you to share the $100 bill with them. Similarly, Friedman would have us believe that it would be nice of us to provide welfare to the less fortunate members of our society. Nevertheless, the less fortunate members have no right to welfare, and hence they would not be justified in forcing us to provide such.

The second example, which Friedman regards as analogous to the first, involves supposing that there are four Robinson Crusoes, each marooned on four uninhabited islands in the same neighborhood. One of these Crusoes happens to land on a large and fruitful island, which enables him to live easily and well. The others happen to land on tiny and rather barren islands from which they can barely scratch a living. Suppose one day they discover the existence of each other. Now, according to Friedman, it would be nice of the fortunate Crusoe to share the resources of his island with the other three Crusoes, but the other three Crusoes have no right to demand that he share those resources, and it would be wrong for them to force him to do so. Correspondingly, Friedman thinks it would be nice of us to provide the less fortunate in our society with welfare, but the less fortunate have no right to demand that we do so, and it would be wrong for them to force us to do so.

In the third example Nozick asks us to imagine that we are in a society that has just distributed income according to some ideal pattern, possibly a pattern of equality. We are further to imagine that in such a society someone with the talents of Wilt Chamberlain or Michael Jordan offers to play basketball for us provided that he receives one dollar from every home game ticket that is sold. Suppose we agree to these terms, and two million people attend the home games to see this new Wilt Chamberlain or Michael Jordan play, thereby securing for him an income of $2 million. Since such an income would surely upset the initial pattern of income distribution whatever that happened to be, Nozick contends that this illustrates how an ideal of liberty upsets the patterns required by other conceptions of justice and calls for the rejection of these conceptions of justice.

THE MINIMAL OR NIGHT-WATCHMAN STATE

Libertarians think that only a minimal or night-watchman state can be justified in terms of their ideal of liberty. The libertarian argument for the minimal or night-watchman state begins with the acceptable premise that voluntary agreements represent an ultimate ideal for social interaction. This ideal, libertarians contend, finds its fullest expression in a market economy where buyers and sellers, employers and employees, voluntarily agree to exchange the goods they possess. Thus, it is assumed that the requirements for voluntary agreements between persons with unequal resources are easily satisfied in a market economy. As long as alternative contractual arrangements make it possible for buyers and sellers, employers and employees, to take their business elsewhere, libertarians believe that agreements reached in market transactions are completely voluntary. On these grounds libertarians claim that the only significant role left for the state is to prevent and rectify departures from a market economy resulting from fraud, theft, or the use of force. Any more extensive role for the state, they contend, would restrict people's liberty; that is to say, it would restrict liberty understood negatively as the absence of interference by other persons. Accordingly, libertarians conclude that only a night-watchman state can be justified in terms of an ideal of negative liberty.

The libertarian argument for the night-watchman state also seeks to show that other social ideas cannot justify a more extensive state. Libertarians either maintain that other social ideals purporting to justify a more extensive state are themselves without justification, or they claim that these social ideals have lower priority when compared with the ideal of negative liberty. But there are not always agreements as to which critical approach is

appropriate. Thus with respect to an ideal of equality, Nozick (1974) and Hayek (1960) adopt different approaches: Nozick maintains that an ideal of equality has not been effectively justified, while Hayek maintains that the ideal has some validity but that negative liberty is the superior ideal. Allowing for such disagreements, both critical approaches could also be used by libertarians against various conceptions of positive liberty.

Nozick even goes so far as to claims that taxation of earnings from labor is on a par with forced labor. Still, libertarians are not similarly sensitive to the loss of liberty that occurs in the marketplace. For example, when an employer decides to lay someone off, Hospers (1971) claims that the employer is simply deciding against continuing a voluntary exchange and is not restricting the person's liberty. Likewise, Hayek (1960) claims that as long as workers who are laid off can find alternative employment their liberty is not being restricted. But how can requiring a person to pay $500 into a social security program under threat of greater financial loss infringe on the person's liberty when requiring a person to take a job paying $500 less under threat of greater financial loss does not infringe on the person's liberty? Surely it would seem that if one requirement restricts a person's liberty, the other will also.

To distinguish these cases, some libertarians claim that only intentional interference by others restricts a person's liberty. Requiring a person to pay $500 into a social security program under threat of greater financial loss, they contend, is intentional interference by others and hence restricts the person's liberty, while requiring a person to take a job paying $500 less under a similar threat is but the unintended result of individuals trying to better themselves in a market economy and hence does not restrict the person's liberty. But whether interference with a person's life is intentional or not is relevant only when determining the extent to which others are responsible for that interference. Although people are clearly more responsible for actions done intentionally they can still be responsible for actions done unintentionally, especially if they were morally negligent and should have foreseen the consequences of their actions. Since moral responsibility can extend to both intentional and unintentional interference with a person's life, there seems to be no reason for not considering both types of interference to be restrictions of a person's liberty. What is crucial to liberty as a social ideal is whether people are morally responsible for interfering with a person's life irrespective of whether that interference is intentional or not.

A BASIC DIFFICULTY

A basic difficulty with the libertarian's conception of justice is the claim that rights to life and property, as the libertarian understands these rights, derive from an ideal of liberty. Why should we think that an ideal of liberty requires a right to life and a right to property that excludes a right to welfare? Surely it would seem that a right to property (as the libertarian understands it) might well justify a rich person's depriving a poor person of the liberty to acquire the goods and resources necessary for meeting his or her basic nutritional needs. How then could we appeal to an ideal of liberty to justify such a deprivation of liberty? Surely we couldn't claim that such a deprivation is justified for the sake of preserving a rich person's freedom to use the goods and resources he or she possesses to meet luxury needs. By any neutral assessment it would seem that the liberty of the deserving poor not to be interfered with when taking from the surplus possessions of the rich what they require to meet their basic needs would have priority over the liberty of the rich not to be interfered with when using their surplus possessions to meet their luxury needs. But if this is the case, then a right to welfare, and possibly a right to equal opportunity as well, would be grounded in the libertarian's own ideal of liberty.

See also Justice; Liberty; Locke, John; Nozick, Robert; Philosophy of Economics; Responsibility, Moral and Legal; Rights; Social and Political Philosophy; Socialism.

Bibliography

Boas, David. *Libertarianism: A Primer.* New York: Free Press, 1997.

Friedman, Milton, with Rose D. Friedman. *Capitalism and Freedom.* Chicago: University of Chicago Press, 1962.

Hayek, Friedrich A. von. *The Constitution of Liberty.* Chicago: University of Chicago Press, 1960.

Hospers, John. *Libertarianism.* Los Angeles: Nash, 1971.

Machan, Tibor. *The Passion for Liberty.* Lanham, MD: Rowman & Littlefield, 2003.

Nozick, Robert. *Anarchy, State, and Utopia.* New York: Basic Books, 1974.

Sterba, James P. *Justice for Here and Now.* New York: Cambridge University Press, 1998.

James Sterba (2005)

LIBERTY

One of the central concerns of social and political philosophy has been the issue of what limits, if any, there are to the right of the state to restrict the "liberty" of its citizens. Unless one is convinced of the truth of anarchism, there are some actions with which the state may legitimately interfere, and unless one accords no value to personal liberty, there are some actions the state must leave to the discretion of the individual. One of the tasks of political philosophy is to develop and elaborate a theory to determine where these boundaries lie.

In his classical defense of liberalism—*On Liberty*—John Stuart Mill gave one influential answer to this question. The only reason that could justify the use of coercion against a person is to prevent harm to other people. Such a reason might not be decisive—it might be that the use of coercion would be ineffective or too costly or would violate the rights of privacy—but it brings the action in question within the scope of legitimate state power.

Other reasons, according to Mill, do not justify legal coercion. One cannot restrict someone's actions because they are harmful to that person; paternalism is not legitimate. One cannot restrict someone's actions because they are wrong or immoral (but not harmful to others); legal moralism is not legitimate. One cannot restrict someone's actions because his or her character would be improved by doing so; moral paternalism is not legitimate.

Obviously, a theory that puts such heavy weight on the notion of harm gives rise to disputes about the nature and limits of that notion. If conduct is offensive to others, does that count as harming them? If not, do we need a separate principle to justify prohibiting offensive conduct such as public nudity or racist graffiti? If we are competing for a job and you get it, am I harmed by this? Does only physical damage count as harm or emotional damage as well? Am I harmed by simply knowing that behind the walls of your house you are engaged in activities that I would find repulsive or wicked? If someone defaces the flag, is anyone harmed by this? If I consent to some action that is otherwise damaging to me, am I still harmed? Can I be harmed after my death—for example, by attacks on my reputation?

One of the most fully developed views that seeks to provide answers to these and similar questions is that of Joel Feinberg. He argues that any notion of harm that is going to play a role in answering normative questions will itself be normative in character. He accordingly defines the notion of harm in terms of a wrongful setback to a person's interests. To some extent, naturally, this shifts philosophical attention to the concept of interests.

PATERNALISM

The normative issue raised by paternalism is when, if ever, the state or an individual is entitled to interfere with a person for that person's good. Examples of laws that have been justified in paternalistic terms include requiring motorcyclists to wear helmets, forcing patients to receive blood transfusions against their wishes, or requiring individuals to save for their retirement (Social Security).

The reasons that support paternalism are those that support any benevolent action—promoting the welfare of a person. The reasons against are those that militate against any interference with the autonomy of individuals—respect for their desire to lead their own lives. Normative debates about the legitimacy of paternalism involve disputes about many issues including the nature of welfare (can we produce good for a person against that individual's preferences and evaluations?), the correctness of various normative theories (consequentialism vs. autonomy or rights-based theories), and the relevance of hypothetical consent (in Mill's famous example of the man walking across a bridge that, unknown to him, is about to collapse, we may stop him, since he would not want to cross the bridge if he knew its condition).

LEGAL MORALISM

The issue of whether the state may enforce morality—the subject that was brought to philosophical prominence by the debate between Lord Devlin and H. L. A. Hart—is present in discussions of the legalization of homosexuality, pornography, surrogate motherhood, and active euthanasia. The focus of such discussion is not the harm of such activities but their immorality and whether if they are immoral that is sufficient reason for the state to proscribe them. Since it is clearly the case that one of the grounds for proscribing murder is its immorality, the question arises as to what it might mean to deny that the state should take morality into account in limiting liberty. The best answer is that we may distinguish within the immoral different realms—for example, matters having to do with rights as opposed to matters having to do with ideals of conduct. Those who are opposed to the enforcement of morality are really opposed to enforcing certain areas of morality. Much of the discussion goes on under the heading of the "neutrality" of the liberal state.

See also Anarchism; Consequentialism; Euthanasia; Feinberg, Joel; Hart, Herbert Lionel Adolphus; Liberalism; Mill, John Stuart; Paternalism; Rights; Social and Political Philosophy.

Bibliography

Acton, Lord. *Essays in the History of Liberty.* Edited by J. R. Frears. Indianapolis: Liberty Classics, 1985.

Berlin, Isaiah. *Four Essays on Liberty.* Oxford: Oxford University Press, 1969.

Devlin, P. *The Enforcement of Morals.* London: Oxford University Press, 1965.

Dworkin, G. "Paternalism." *Monist* 56 (1972): 64–84.

Feinberg, J. *The Moral Limits of the Criminal Law.* 4 vols. New York: Oxford University Press, 1984–1988.

Hart, H. L. A. *Law, Liberty, and Morality.* Stanford, CA: Stanford University Press, 1963.

Mill, J. S. *On Liberty.* London, 1959.

Miller, David, ed. *Liberty.* Oxford: Oxford University Press, 1991.

Gerald Dworkin (1996)
Bibliography updated by Philip Reed (2005)

LICHTENBERG, GEORG CHRISTOPH
(1742–1799)

Georg Christoph Lichtenberg, the German satirist, scientist, and philosopher, studied mathematics and science at the University of Göttingen and was a professor there from 1767 to the end of his life. On two occasions Lichtenberg visited England. His impressions from these visits are recorded in his diaries and letters.

Lichtenberg's original contributions to mathematics and to pure and experimental science are not of great importance. The Lichtenberg figure in the theory of electricity was named after him. He was very successful as a teacher; among his pupils were Alexander von Humboldt and Christian Gauss. It has been said that his fame as a lecturer and demonstrator surpassed that of any other German scientist of his time.

His literary reputation with his contemporaries rested mainly on his satirical criticism of the writers of the *Sturm und Drang* movement and of the Swiss clergyman Johann Lavater's quasi-scientific psychology of character. Lichtenberg's own favorites and models in art were Englishmen: William Shakespeare; David Garrick, the actor; and William Hogarth, the painter. His analyses and descriptions of Garrick on the stage and his detailed "explanations" of Hogarth's etchings have become famous. Most of Lichtenberg's literary output during his lifetime appeared in two periodicals, of which he was the editor, the *Göttinger Taschen-Calender* and the *Göttingisches Magazin der Wissenschaften und Litteratur.*

By far the most valuable part of Lichtenberg's literary work, however, consisted of his "aphorisms," or scattered thoughts on psychological, philosophical, scientific, and many other topics. They were written down in notebooks but were never systematically arranged by the author. Nor were they used as raw material to any great extent for the more systematic work that Lichtenberg was constantly planning but never carried out. *Vermischte Schriften,* a comprehensive selection of his remarks, was published soon after his death.

Philosophically, Lichtenberg was not attached to any school or movement. The thinkers who made the deepest impressions on him were Benedict de Spinoza and Immanuel Kant. It is noteworthy that Lichtenberg was an early reviver of the great Jewish philosopher and one of the first to understand and acknowledge the revolutionary significance of Kant's transcendental philosophy. Furthermore, the versatility of his philosophical intellect is shown by his acute understanding of the work of Jakob Boehme.

Lichtenberg has had but a modest influence on the development of thought, but it is evident from the observations of Kant and Alexander von Humboldt, among others, that his contemporaries greatly prized his philosophical intellect. Subsequent generations were first made aware of his status as an independent thinker through the observation of Ernst Mach (in his *The Analysis of Sensations*) that Lichtenberg had anticipated the empiriocritical solution of the ego problem with his critique of the Cartesian *cogito ergo sum.* (In another work, "Die Leitgedanken meiner naturwissenschaftlichen Erkenntnislehre" [The primary ideas of my scientific epistemology], 1919, p. 5, Mach even hinted that he had been influenced by Lichtenberg.) Moreover, the affinity of Lichtenberg's ideas with modern linguistic philosophy has been indicated by various writers, for example, Friedrich Waismann in the preface to Moritz Schlick's *Gesammelte Aufsätze* and Richard von Mises in *Positivism.*

PHILOSOPHY OF MATHEMATICS

Lichtenberg, in contradistinction to Kant, distinguished sharply between pure and applied mathematics and separated mathematics as a logicodeductive formalism from mathematics as a theory of reality.

The truths of pure mathematics are not only certain in a strict sense but are derived (in principle) independently of experience and empirical observation. A blind man, for instance, could discover the laws of light by means of the calculus, for as soon as the fundamental facts of refraction and reflection are discovered experi-

mentally, "the whole of dioptrics and catoptrics becomes a purely geometrical problem," which can be treated without further knowledge of natural processes. For this reason the ideal form of a scientific theory is that of a logicodeductive system. Lichtenberg stated: "The aim of the physicists is to prepare the way for mathematics."

In his conception of pure mathematics, Lichtenberg approached the notion of the analytical, or tautological, character of mathematical truths. He did not take a positive stand on Kant's view of the synthetic a priori character of mathematics, but it is evident from his remarks that he viewed it with suspicion.

Mathematics shapes its own world. The business of the physicist is to decide which "of the innumerable suppositions possible" is the single true one. The results of mathematical deduction cannot be asserted in advance to agree with the results of physical inquiry. "Their agreement is a purely *empirical* coincidence, nothing else." (It is apparent from his manuscript that Lichtenberg ascribed great importance to this remark.) Thus Lichtenberg renounced all a priori claims concerning the application of mathematics to reality.

Instead of being astounded at the actual success of mathematics in the exploration of natural phenomena, Lichtenberg emphasized the approximate character of mathematical laws of nature and warned of the temptation to read more mathematics into things than is actually there. "All mathematical laws that we find in nature, despite their beauty, are doubtful to me." The forms in which nature covers herself are too manifold and changeable to be comprehended exhaustively by our own conceptual apparatus. These thoughts, which had come early to Lichtenberg, were closely connected with his highly developed talent for observation and his acute feeling for the concrete.

It is characteristic that the work with which Lichtenberg qualified for his professorship was devoted to the study of an alleged discrepancy between theory and experience. This work, "Considerations about Some Methods for Removing a Certain Difficulty in the Calculation of Probability in Gambling" (not mentioned in J. M. Keynes's bibliography in his *Treatise on Probability*), concerned a famous problem of the theory of probability, the so-called Petersburg paradox, which engaged many leading mathematicians of the eighteenth century, among others, Jean Le Rond d'Alembert and Daniel Bernoulli. It is erroneous, however, to see in this problem, as Lichtenberg and others have done, a contradiction between the mathematical calculus and the actual course of events.

Recognition is due Lichtenberg for his scientific genius in being one of the first to see the possibility of denying, without contradiction, the Euclidean axioms. That between two points only one straight line can be drawn is indeed an accepted axiom, but it is by no means necessary. One can also conceive of the possibility that several distinct lines might pass through the same two points. The manner in which Lichtenberg attempted to show this possibility was, indeed, less significant: He imagined one could take arcs with the radii ∞, ∞^2, ∞^3, and so on, so that they proceed through two fixed points, describing distinct straight lines.

Interestingly enough, Lichtenberg also expressed some thoughts about the deflection of light through gravitation. As an adherent of Isaac Newton's corpuscular theory, he assumed that light has mass, from which it follows that a beam of light must deviate from a straight path because of its weight. "Light alone appears to be an exception (viz., to the curved path of most bodies); however, since it is probably heavy, it will be deflected as a result."

EPISTEMOLOGY OF THE EXACT SCIENCES

Lichtenberg realized the great significance of the discovery of structural identities among qualitatively different domains of theoretical research into nature. His idea of *paradigmata* (patterns), according to which processes were to be "declined," seems to have approached James Clerk Maxwell's view of the significance of analogy and to have anticipated the concept of isomorphism. Lichtenberg called discovery through *paradigmata* the most fruitful of all the heuristic devices of science. As an example of an application he suggested that one might use Newton's *Optics* as a model in the theory of the calcination of metals.

Lichtenberg had a clear view of the logic of constructing hypotheses: "If we want to understand nature," he said, "we must begin with sensible appearances." Hypotheses that transcend the evidence of the senses may only be constructed insofar as they can be tested within the domain of appearances. Concepts whose presence or absence in the individual case can never be demonstrated but only assumed are not permissible in science. The concept of ether in physics belongs to this category. The ether, which "no one has seen or felt, ... condensed, rarefied, etc.," is like the notion of the world soul: Since it has no experiential consequences, it must be eliminated once and for all from a rational physics.

In spite of his opposition in principle to hypothesis making in physics, Lichtenberg did not agree with the view that all assumptions should be discarded if, although they have testable consequences, they do not literally correspond to sensible reality. Assumptions of this kind may nonetheless be useful as pictures of complicated courses of events, and thus facilitate the application of mathematics to nature. (The notion of "picture," reminiscent of Heinrich Hertz's *Principles of Mechanics,* turns up often in Lichtenberg.) "If someone could make a clock that presented the movements of the heavenly bodies as exactly as actually obtains, would he not deserve much credit, even though the world does not operate by means of cog-wheels? Through this machine he could discover many things that he would not have believed to be present in it." In addition to such mechanical models, the two theories of light and atomic theory also belong to this category.

The truth content of scientific assumptions of the type mentioned above is proportional to their explanatory power and to their relative simplicity. Lichtenberg quite aptly noted that with theories as complex as that of light "it can no longer be merely a question of what is true, but of what manner of explanation is the simplest." And he added, "The door to truth is through simplicity." Moreover, his speculation that one could attempt to combine the corpuscular and wave theories sounds very modern.

The falsification of such hypotheses can not be established beyond question by empirical circumstances. A single negative instance does not in general make it necessary to renounce a comprehensive scientific theory that has otherwise been well confirmed. "One should take special note of contradictory experiences," wrote Lichtenberg, "until there are enough of them to make constructing a new system worthwhile."

SOUL AND MATTER, REALISM AND IDEALISM

Early in his career Lichtenberg rejected the idea of the soul as a substance. Before enough was understood to explain the phenomena of the world scientifically, spirits were accepted as explanations of phenomena. As our knowledge of the physical world increased, however, the boundaries of the spiritual realm shrank until finally "that which haunts our body and produces effects in it" was the only thing left that required a ghost for an explanation. The case of the "soul" is like that of phlogiston: In the end both substances dissipate into nothingness. What remains is a "bare word" comparable to the word *state* (*Zustand*), to which, however, one may at least attribute heuristic value as a picture and as a type of idea innate in the human being.

According to Lichtenberg, the thesis of materialism is "the asymptote of psychology." In psychology, he linked himself closely with the materialistic-mechanistic association theories of the Englishmen David Hartley and Joseph Priestley. A one-to-one correspondence obtains between the mental occurrence and the state of the brain, so that the former can, in principle, be inferred from the latter.

Lichtenberg, however, did not accept metaphysical materialism. Parallel with his critique of the concept of the soul went a critique of the concept of matter. Soul and inert matter are mere abstractions, he wrote in a letter in 1786; we know of matter and of soul only on the basis of the *forces* (*Kräfte*) through which they manifest themselves and "with which they are identical." We postulate for these forces in one case "an inert receptacle and call it matter." Through such a hypostatization, which is just a "chimera" of the brain, arises "the infamous dualism in the world": the division of being into body and soul, spirit and matter. But in reality everything is one.

This acknowledgment of monism still bore a metaphysical character. It is probable that the influence of Spinoza had its effect on the position taken by Lichtenberg in 1786, since the letter of that year referred directly to Spinoza. But we may observe that, much earlier, Lichtenberg had expressed the same opinion almost word for word. However, it is not impossible that the influence of Spinoza was already at work then. Even in his earliest books of aphorisms there were remarks of a Spinozistic character, although the name of the great thinker was not mentioned.

Later, Lichtenberg's monism took a more epistemological turn in that he clearly indicated how the basis of his monistic system should be interpreted. "We are aware only of the existence of our sensations, ideas, and thought," he said and expressed the same thought with the words, "Everything is feeling (*Gefühle*)." We experience a part of our impressions as dependent upon us, another as independent of the perceiving subject: in this way we arrive at the difference between the inner and outer worlds.

To argue from sensations to an "ego" as their bearer, as René Descartes does, is not logically warranted. Lichtenberg remarked very perceptively: "One should say, 'There is thinking,' just as one says, 'There is lightning.'" To say *cogito* is to say too much; for as soon as one translates it as "I think," it seems necessary to postulate an ego.

Lichtenberg's earlier critique of the idea of the soul culminates here in a critique of the self, somewhat reminiscent of the position of David Hume.

It took considerable effort on Lichtenberg's part to attain clarity on the question of how we proceed from our sensations to things outside us. He perceived the significance of the problem from his study of Kant, and in his treatment of it we can generally discern Kant's influence.

At first it was very difficult for Lichtenberg to rid himself of the idea that something in the actual world might correspond to our representations, although we can have "no conception at all of the true nature of the outside world." But later he recognized that the question "whether things outside ourselves really exist and exist as we see them" is in fact "completely meaningless." It is just as foolish as asking whether the color blue is really blue. We are compelled by our nature—this compulsion he termed, with Kant, *die Form der Sinnlichkeit* (form of sensibility)—to express ourselves in such way that we speak of certain objects of our perception as being outside ourselves and of others as being within us. "What is outside? What are objects *praeter nos*? What is the force of the preposition *praeter*? It is a purely human invention; a name to indicate a difference from other things which we call 'not-*praeter nos*.'" "There is probably no one in the world who does not perceive this *difference*, and probably no such person will ever exist; and for philosophy that is enough. Philosophy need not go beyond this."

Is not this standpoint "idealism"? Lichtenberg clearly perceived that, just as his critique of the idea of the "soul" did not result in metaphysical materialism, so his attitude toward the question of the reality of the outer world should not be confused with metaphysical idealism. Rather his doctrine stood beyond idealism and materialism in their traditional senses. "It is truly of little consequence to me whether one wants to label this idealism. Names have no significance. It is at least an idealism which, through idealism, acknowledges that there are things outside us." What more can one ask? For human beings, "at least for the philosophical ones," there is no other reality than the one so constituted. It is true that one is satisfied in ordinary life with some other, "lower station," but whenever one begins to philosophize, one cannot but accept this enlightened point of view. "There is no other alternative," he concluded.

LICHTENBERG'S CONCEPTION OF PHILOSOPHY

"Our entire philosophy," wrote Lichtenberg, "is a correction of linguistic usage." What he meant by that is especially evident in his treatment of the question of realism. As indicated above, Lichtenberg's conception should not be understood as an attempt to deny the existence of things outside ourselves. That would have been a senseless undertaking. His intention was only to discover the meaning of the distinction between outer and inner objects by clearly presenting the facts that underlie this distinction. It turns out that the root of the traditional difficulty about the question of realism is that in ordinary life we attach a contradictory meaning to the expression "outside ourselves." When we have become conscious of this contradiction and have undertaken the proper correction of our linguistic usage, the difficulty vanishes of itself.

Philosophy, then, is a critique of language. Its goal, however, is not definitions of concepts. Lichtenberg was not of the opinion that one could, for philosophical use, replace the common language with an ideal language, perhaps in the sense of Gottfried Wilhelm Leibniz's *characteristica universalis*. Attempts to reform the nomenclature of the sciences did not find much favor with him. "To clarify words does not help," he said. Why? Because the interpretation of the clarified concepts takes place, in the final analysis, in the vernacular. But the vernacular, by its nature, is imbued with our false philosophy. The rectification of colloquial usage, which leads to true philosophy, is thus undertaken in the language of false philosophy: "We are therefore constantly teaching true philosophy with the language of the false one." The common philosophy, then, always maintains a certain superiority over the enlightened one, for the former is in possession of the "declensions and conjugations" of our language, and these are not changed by the clarification of meanings of words. "The invention of language preceded philosophy, and it is just this that makes philosophy difficult, particularly when one wishes to make it understandable to those who do not think much for themselves. Philosophy, whenever it speaks, is forced to speak the language of nonphilosophy.… Pure philosophy still imperceptibly enjoys the pleasure of love with the impure (and cannot avoid doing so)."

The philosopher, then, speaks with the words of the common language about things that are beyond it. He is thus compelled to express himself, to a certain degree, in metaphors (*Gleichnissen*). He is supposed to direct our attention with his sentences to the false logic of our language, so that we learn to see the world correctly. He does not teach us a new language but helps us to express ourselves clearly with our own. "The peasant," said Lichtenberg, "uses all the sentences of the most abstract philosophy, only they are entangled, hidden, confined, latent, as the physicist and chemist say; the philosopher gives us the pure sentences."

It should be evident from the above that Lichtenberg anticipated the conception of philosophy that has been represented in the twentieth century by Ludwig Wittgenstein. Wittgenstein knew Lichtenberg's work well and esteemed it highly. It is hardly possible, however, to speak of Lichtenberg as an influence on the philosophy of Wittgenstein. Nevertheless, a rare congeniality between the two men can be noted—not only in view of their conceptions of philosophy but also in view of their entire intellectual talents and temperaments.

See also Alembert, Jean Le Rond d'; Boehme, Jakob; Descartes, René; Hartley, David; Idealism; Kant, Immanuel; Keynes, John Maynard; Lavater, Johann Kaspar; Leibniz, Gottfried Wilhelm; Mach, Ernst; Materialism; Mathematics, Foundations of; Maxwell, James Clerk; Newton, Isaac; Priestley, Joseph; Schlick, Moritz; Spinoza, Benedict (Baruch) de; Wittgenstein, Ludwig Josef Johann.

Bibliography

Lichtenberg's works in German include *Vermischte Schriften*, edited by L. C. Lichtenberg and F. Kries, 5 vols. (Göttingen: Dieterich, 1800–1803); *Physikalische und mathematische Schriften*, edited by L. C. Lichtenberg and F. Kries, 4 vols. (Göttingen, 1803–1806); *Neue Original-Ausgabe*, 14 vols. (Göttingen, 1844–1853); *Aus Lichtenbergs Nachlass*, edited by Albert Leitzmann (Weimar, 1899); *Aphorismen, nach den Handschriften*, edited by Albert Leitzmann, 5 vols. (Berlin, 1902–1908); *Lichtenbergs Briefe*, edited by Albert Leitzmann and Carl Schüddelkopf, 3 vols. (Leipzig, 1901–1904).

Lichtenberg's remarks on questions of mathematics and physics have been printed only in part. It is most unfortunate that all of his notes from the years 1779–1788 and the greater part of those from 1793–1796, which existed at the time of the first edition of the *Vermischte Schriften*, had been lost when Albert Leitzmann, in the beginning of the twentieth century, edited the *Aphorismen, nach den Handschriften*. This loss greatly complicates the task of reconstructing the course of development of Lichtenberg's thought. The selection of aphorisms in the *Vermischte Schriften* shows that some of his most important philosophical remarks were among those subsequently lost.

For literature on Lichtenberg, see J. Dostal-Winkler, *Lichtenberg und Kant* (Munich, 1924); P. Hahn, *Georg Christoph Lichtenberg und die exakten Wissenschaften* (Göttingen: Vandenhoeck and Ruprecht, 1927); F. H. Mautner, "Amintors Morgenandacht," in *Deutsche Vierteljahrsschrift für Litteraturwissenschaft und Geistesgeschichte* 30 (1956); F. H. Mautner and F. Miller, "Remarks on G. C. Lichtenberg, Humanist-Scientist," in *Isis* 43 (1952); A. Neumann, "Lichtenberg als Philosoph und seine Beziehungen zu Kant," in *Kantstudien* 4 (1900); A.

Schneider, *Georg Christoph Lichtenberg, précurseur du romantisme,* Vol. I, *L'homme et l'oeuvre,* Vol. II, *Le penseur* (Nancy, 1954); J. P. Stern, *Lichtenberg: A Doctrine of Scattered Occasions* (Bloomington: Indiana University Press, 1959); and G. H. von Wright, "Georg Christoph Lichtenberg als Philosoph," *Theoria* 8 (1942): 201–217, of which the present entry is an adaptation.

Georg Henrik von Wright (1967)
Translated by David H. DeGrood and Barry J. Karp

LIEBERT, ARTHUR
(1878–1946)

Arthur Liebert, the German neo-Kantian philosopher, was born Arthur Levi in Berlin. The son of a merchant, he spent six years in business after completing his secondary education in 1895. He then entered the University of Berlin, where he received his doctorate in 1908. After teaching at the Berlin Handelshochschule, Liebert lectured at the University of Berlin, becoming extraordinary professor in 1925. From 1918 to 1933 he was coeditor with Paul Menzer of *Kantstudien,* which became under their guidance an instrument of growing international cooperation in philosophy. Forced to leave Germany in 1933, when the National Socialists came to power, he was appointed professor of philosophy at the University of Belgrade and there founded the journal *Philosophia: Philosophorum Nostri Temporis Vox Universa,* which appeared at irregular intervals from 1936 to 1939. When the German armies invaded the Balkans, he found refuge in England, where he published *Das Wesen der Freiheit* (1944) and, together with other refugees, organized the Freier deutscher Kulturbund in Grossbrittanien. At the end of World War II he returned to his restored professorship at Berlin, but he died shortly thereafter.

Liebert was influenced by the realistic interpretation given Immanuel Kant at Berlin by Friedrich Paulsen, Alois Riehl, and especially by Wilhelm Dilthey, who stressed the historical aspects of the *Geisteswissenschaften* (cultural sciences). Within this realistic neo-Kantian orientation, Liebert turned to the ethical problems of value and freedom and to the search for a dialectic movement of ethical and metaphysical categories in history. Many of his writings, particularly in his later years, were devoted to the promotion of worldwide philosophical cooperation as "the free guardian of freedom" and particularly to the development of a philosophical organization, "an Areopagus of mankind," within which the new humanism was to be promoted. This is the theme of "On the Duty of Philosophy in Our Age" (*Von der Pflicht der*

Philosophie in unserer Zeit), published during his exile in 1938.

Liebert's philosophical efforts to work out his critical metaphysics as a dialectic were to have taken the form of a large work titled *Geist und Welt der Dialektik,* of which only the first volume, *Grundlegung der Dialektik,* appeared (Berlin, 1929). To be distinguished from science, philosophy must accept as its field not simply being (*Sein*) but value (*Geltung*), for being not merely *is,* but *is valid* (*gilt*), or validates, itself. In opposition to the Baden neo-Kantians, Liebert rejected obligation (*Sollen*) as the ground of value, finding a new basis for metaphysics in the Kantian concern for the validation of judgments. "The right of metaphysics and the right to a metaphysics," he wrote, "flow from the idea and right of philosophy itself." The task of metaphysics thus becomes that of a historical "critical phenomenology" that "tests its own possibility and justification and derives its presuppositions and conclusions through reason."

Such a metaphysics does not merely use dialectic as the basis of metaphysical criticism but is itself dialectic. Its categories must include both philosophical ideas and the social and cultural contexts out of which they arise. "The idea of dialectic is at once the a priori condition and the definitive force (*massgebende Kraft*) for the construction of metaphysics, and also the distinctive instrument for penetrating into the nature of metaphysics, and for studying and understanding it." This dialectic must include within the scope of its critical and dynamic movement four motives: the intellectual, moral, aesthetic, and religious. Metaphysics is no longer "ontological-dogmatic" but "actualistic-critical"; the movement of its categorical structures of value combines temporal and supratemporal viewpoints. Its task is apparently never completed, because historical change outgrows the adequacy of every a priori structure. In particular, the modern world with its conflicts prevents a return to the classical humanizing harmonies of thought; the historical-normative dialectic that modern life calls forth must take the form of tragedy.

Liebert's lectures and seminars were devoted to the development and illustration of this conception of metaphysics. The *Grundlegung der Dialektik* provided only an introduction, in which Liebert traced the beginnings of the metaphysical dialectic in the thought of his contemporaries—practitioners of the *Geisteswissenschaften;* metaphysicians and theologians; and neo-Kantians and neo-Hegelians.

The Kantian identification of freedom with reason remained for Liebert the fixed a priori point of view of his "actualistic-critical" metaphysics. He persistently attacked the currently popular forms of *Lebensphilosophie* as relativistic, irrational, and sacrificing philosophical freedom. Philosophers were called upon to fulfill their vocation by turning to metaphysics and ethics as guides for individual and organizational action against the forces of irrationalism and cultural decay.

Liebert's thought has received little attention since his death. His most important writings are those in which he sought to formulate the principles of his own historical metaphysics of value.

See also Dilthey, Wilhelm; Geisteswissenschaften; Kant, Immanuel; Metaphysics; Neo-Kantianism; Paulsen, Friedrich; Riehl, Alois; Value and Valuation.

Bibliography

ADDITIONAL WORKS BY LIEBERT

Das Problem der Geltung. Berlin, 1906.

Der Geltungswert der Metaphysik. Berlin: Reuther and Reichard, 1915.

Wie ist kritische Philosophie überhaupt möglich? Leipzig, 1919.

Die geistige Krisis der Gegenwart. Berlin: Heise, 1923.

Von der Pflicht der Philosophie in unserer Zeit. Zürich, 1946.

L. E. Loemker (1967)

LIEBMANN, OTTO
(1840–1912)

Otto Liebmann, the German neo-Kantian philosopher, was born at Löwenberg (Lwowek Slaski), Silesia, and became successively *Privatdozent* at Tübingen (1865), extraordinary professor at Strassburg (1872), and professor at Jena (1882). He served as a volunteer during the siege of Paris in 1870 and 1871 and published a memoir of his experiences.

In a *Festschrift* dedicated to Liebmann on his seventieth birthday, various thinkers discussed the aspects of his work that were of particular interest to them. Each interpreted him differently; for example, Bruno Bauch stressed transcendental-methodological aspects, Erich Adickes empirical openness, Wilhelm Windelband critical-metaphysical insight. Such variegated criticism was not without foundation, for Liebmann's thought had many facets and did not evolve so much as oscillate between impulsive outbursts and great restraint, passing from problem to problem.

In his notable early book, *Kant und die Epigonen* (1865), Liebmann swept aside the academic philosophy of his day and preached a return to Immanuel Kant. He simplified Kantian thought and streamlined the post-Kantian systems. The essence of the Kantian revolution, he claimed, was the discovery of the transcendental, which, however, must be freed from the *caput mortuum* of the thing-in-itself. The systematic effort of the great successors of Kant failed because Johann Gottlieb Fichte's Ego, Friedrich Schiller's Absolute, G. W. F. Hegel's Spirit, Johann Friedrich Herbart's "reals," and Arthur Schopenhauer's Will all represent the thing-in-itself, whereas J. F. Fries mistook the transcendental for the psychological. For Liebmann the only reality, immanent in consciousness and sufficient, is experience, which is both empirical reality and transcendental ideality. But could such simplified views be unequivocally developed?

In a subsequent essay, *Über den individuellen Beweis für die Freiheit des Willens* (1866), Liebmann dealt with the freedom of the will, in opposition to Schopenhauer. Are we, it can be asked, on the level of the transcendental or of the individual ego in dealing with this problem? Reexamining the question in 1901 (*Gedanken und Tatsachen*, Vol. II, p. 88), he referred it to the individual.

In *Über den objektiven Anblick* (1869) Liebmann distinguished three factors in perception: the sensitive, the intellectual, and the transcendent. The transcendent factor in perception "is the relationship between an unknown X and a likewise unknown Y, which appears to us as our body, and from which in turn there spring into our consciousness those sensitive qualities which our intellect transforms, according to a priori laws, into perceptible nature, a phenomenon of the external material world" (p. 153). In this work the thing-in-itself is not eliminated; on the contrary, two things-in-themselves—X and Y—are admitted.

Liebmann's major works, *Analysis der Wirklichkeit* (1876) and *Gedanken und Tatsachen* (2 vols., 1882–1907), are collections of problems, not only in the critique of knowledge but also in *Naturphilosophie*, psychology, aesthetics, and ethics. In all of these, self-consciousness recognizes its limits; but the resulting agnosticism is superseded by a program of "critical metaphysics."

In this connection Liebmann denounced as a *doktrinäre Fiktion* the neo-Baconian ideal (or idol) of pure experience, itself a notion that Liebmann took from Richard Avenarius and from the evolutionary genetic psychology of Herbert Spencer and others. Every experience and every science, Liebmann claimed, is possible only by means of certain nonempirical premises, such as the principles of real identity, of the continuity of existence, of constant causality or legality, and of the temporal continuity of becoming, or, in general, by means of fundamental a priori forms or principles, which constitute the organization of human cognitive powers but from whose transcendental validity by no means necessarily follows its transcendent reality.

Liebmann distinguished three types of theories, which seek explanatory principles in the immediate empirical data, in hypotheses by which the phenomena are deduced, or in absolute metaphysical realities. He rejected the first and third, and admitted the hypotheses, if and as long as the facts confirm them. This is true not only of scientific but also of philosophical theories, especially of critical metaphysics as a "strict discussion of human views, human hypotheses on the essence of things." Liebmann concentrated on the theories of science and their metaphysical pronouncements or assumptions. He claimed, for example, that the biological point of view is more than a mere postulation of an as-if; it is a positive affirmation of entelechies. Darwinism abounds with metascientific problems and teleological claims; but not even the transcendental philosopher can escape the problems posed by nature, with its own immanent logic (*Weltlogik*), its dynamic causality that achieves an increase in perfection, even though he knows that every hypothesis and system is a product of the specifically human thinking apparatus. A study of space and time that Liebmann undertook to come to grips with non-Euclidean viewpoints led him to problems that appeared to Windelband as idle fancies.

In dealing with the problem of the multiplicity of subjects, Liebmann developed but did not elaborate upon a distinction between three conceptions of the ego: the metaphysical substrate, an objective never attained by dogmatic metaphysics; the individual ego, a tacit assumption of psychology; and the transcendental ego, a "typical" subject of the intelligence of the human species and a fundamental condition of the empirical world. The problem of psychophysical parallelism led him to postulate a coincidence of natural and logical laws on the metaphysical plane of *natura naturans*, but he did not draw the necessary methodological distinctions to adequately treat this problem.

See also Avenarius, Richard; Darwinism; Determinism and Freedom; Fichte, Johann Gottlieb; German Philosophy; Hegel, Georg Wilhelm Friedrich; Herbart, Johann Friedrich; Kant, Immanuel; Natural Law; Neo-Kantianism; Schiller, Friedrich; Schopenhauer, Arthur; Windelband, Wilhelm.

Bibliography

WORKS BY LIEBMANN

Kant und die Epigonen. Stuttgart: Schober, 1865; 2nd ed., Berlin: Reuther & Reichard, 1912.

Über den individuellen Beweis für die Freiheit des Willens. Stuttgart: Schober, 1866.

Über den objektiven Anblick. Stuttgart, 1869.

Zur Analysis der Wirklichkeit. Strassburg, 1876; 4th enlarged ed., Strassburg: Trübner, 1911.

Über philosophischen Tradition. Strassburg, 1883.

Die Klimax der Theorien. Strassburg, 1884.

Gedanken und Tatsachen, 2 vols. Strassburg, 1882–1901; 2nd ed., Strassburg: Trübner, 1899–1904.

Immanuel Kant. Strassburg, 1904.

WORKS ON LIEBMANN

Meyer, Adolf. *Über Liebmanns Erkenntnislehre und ihr Verhältniss zu Kant*. Jena, Germany, 1916. Dissertation.

Zum 70. Geburtstag Otto Liebmanns. A Festschrift in *Kantstudien* 15 (1910). Contains works by Adickes, Bauch, Hans Driesch, Windelband, and others.

Mariano Campo (1967)
Translated by Robert M. Connolly

LIFE, MEANING AND VALUE OF

To the questions "Is human life ever worthwhile?" and "Does (or can) human life have any meaning?" many religious thinkers have offered affirmative answers with the proviso that these answers would not be justified unless two of the basic propositions of most Western religions were true—that human life is part of a divinely ordained cosmic scheme and that after death at least some human beings will be rewarded with eternal bliss. Thus, commenting on Bertrand Russell's statement that not only must each individual human life come to an end but that life in general will eventually die out, C. H. D. Clark contrasts this "doctrine of despair" with the beauty of the Christian scheme. "If we are asked to believe that all our striving is without final consequence," then "life is meaningless and it scarcely matters how we live if all will end in the dust of death." According to Christianity, on the other hand, "each action has vital significance." Clark assures us that "God's grand design is life eternal for those who walk in the steps of Christ. Here is the one grand incentive to good living…. As life is seen to have purpose and meaning, men find release from despair and the fear of death" (*Christianity and Bertrand Russell*, p. 30). In a similar vein, the Jewish existentialist Emil Fackenheim claims that "whatever meaning life acquires" is derived from the encounter between God and man. The meaning thus conferred upon human life "cannot be understood in terms of some finite human purpose, supposedly more ultimate than the meeting itself. For what could be more ultimate than the Presence of God?" It is true that God is not always "near," but "times of Divine farness" are by no means devoid of meaning. "Times of Divine nearness do not light up themselves alone. Their meaning extends over all of life." There is a "dialectic between Divine nearness and Divine farness," and it points to "an eschatological future in which it is overcome" ("Judaism and the Meaning of Life").

Among unbelievers not a few maintain that life can be worthwhile and have meaning in some humanly important sense even if the religious world view is rejected. Others, however, agree with the religious theorists that our two questions must be given negative answers if there is no God and if death means personal annihilation. Having rejected the claims of religion, they therefore conclude that life is not worthwhile and that it is devoid of meaning. These writers, to whom we shall refer here as "pessimists," do not present their judgments as being merely expressions of certain moods or feelings but as conclusions that are in some sense objectively warranted. They offer reasons for their conclusions and imply that anybody reaching a contradictory conclusion is mistaken or irrational. Most pessimists do not make any clear separation between the statements that life is not worthwhile and that life is without meaning. They usually speak of the "futility" or the "vanity" of life, and presumably they mean by this both that life is not worth living and that it has no meaning. For the time being we, too, shall treat these statements as if they were equivalent. However, later we shall see that in certain contexts it becomes important to distinguish between them.

Our main concern in this entry will be to appraise pessimism as just defined. We shall not discuss either the question whether life is part of a divinely ordained plan or the question whether we survive our bodily death. Our question will be whether the pessimistic conclusions are justified if belief in God and immortality are rejected.

SCHOPENHAUER'S ARGUMENTS

Let us begin with a study of the arguments offered by the pessimists, remembering that many of these are indirectly endorsed by religious apologists. The most systematic and probably the most influential, though in fact not the gloomiest, of the pessimists was Arthur Schopenhauer. The world, he wrote, is something that ought not to exist: The truth is that "we have not to rejoice but rather to mourn at the existence of the world; that its non-existence would be preferable to its existence; that it is something which ought not to be." It is absurd to speak of life as a gift, as so many philosophers and thoughtless people have done. "It is evident that everyone would have declined such a gift if he could have seen it and tested it beforehand." To those who assure us that life is only a lesson, we are entitled to reply: "For this very reason I wish I had been left in the peace of the all-sufficient nothing, where I would have no need of lessons or of anything else" (*The World as Will and Idea*, Vol. III, p. 390).

Schopenhauer offers numerous arguments for his conclusion. Some of these are purely metaphysical and are based on his particular system. Others, however, are of a more empirical character and are logically independent of his brand of metaphysical voluntarism. Happiness, according to Schopenhauer, is unobtainable for the vast majority of humankind. "Everything in life shows that earthly happiness is destined to be frustrated or recognized as illusion." People either fail to achieve the ends they are striving for or else they do achieve them only to find them grossly disappointing. But as soon as a man discovers that a particular goal was not really worth pursuing, his eye is set on a new one and the same illusory quest begins all over again. Happiness, accordingly, always lies in the future or in the past, and "the present may be compared to a small dark cloud which the wind drives over the sunny plain: before and behind it all is bright, only it itself always casts a shadow. The present is therefore always insufficient; but the future is uncertain, and the past is irrevocable" (ibid., p. 383). Men in general, except for those sufficiently rational to become totally resigned, are constantly deluded—"now by hope, now by what was hoped for." They are taken in by "the enchantment of distance," which shows them "paradises." These paradises, however, vanish like "optical illusions when we have allowed ourselves to be mocked by them." The "fearful envy" excited in most men by the thought that somebody else is genuinely happy shows how unhappy they really are, whatever they pretend to others or to themselves. It is only "because they feel themselves unhappy" that "men cannot endure the sight of one whom they imagine happy."

On occasions Schopenhauer is ready to concede that some few human beings really do achieve "comparative" happiness, but this is not of any great consequence. For aside from being "rare exceptions," these happy people are really like "decoy birds"—they represent a possibility that must exist in order to lure the rest of humankind into a false sense of hope. Moreover, happiness, insofar as it exists at all, is a purely "negative" reality. We do not become aware of the greatest blessings of life—health, youth, and freedom—until we have lost them. What is called pleasure or satisfaction is merely the absence of craving or pain. But craving and pain are positive. As for the few happy days of our life—if there are any—we notice them only "after they have given place to unhappy ones."

Schopenhauer not infrequently lapsed from his doctrine of the "negative" nature of happiness and pleasure into the more common view that their status is just as "positive" as that of unhappiness and pain. But he had additional arguments that do not in any way depend on the theory that happiness and pleasure are negative. Perhaps the most important of these is the argument from the "perishableness" of all good things and the ultimate extinction of all our hopes and achievements in death. All our pleasures and joys "disappear in our hands, and we afterwards ask astonished where they have gone." Moreover, a joy that no longer exists does not "count"—it counts as little as if it had never been experienced at all:

> That which *has been* exists no more; it exists as little as that which has *never* been. But of everything that exists you may say, in the next moment, that it has been. Hence something of great importance in our past is inferior to something of little importance in our present, in that the latter is a *reality,* and related to the former as something to nothing. ("The Vanity of Existence," in *The Will to Live,* p. 229)

Some people have inferred from this that the enjoyment of the present should be "the supreme object of life." This is fallacious; for "that which in the next moment exists no more, and vanishes utterly, like a dream, can never be worth a serious effort."

The final "judgment of nature" is destruction by death. This is "the last proof" that life is a "false path," that all man's wishing is "a perversity," and that "nothing at all is worth our striving, our efforts and struggles." The conclusion is inescapable: "All good things are vanity, the world in all its ends bankrupt, and life a business which does not cover its expenses" (*The World as Will and Idea,* Vol. III, p. 383).

THE POINTLESSNESS OF IT ALL

Some of Schopenhauer's arguments can probably be dismissed as the fantasies of a lonely and embittered man who was filled with contempt for humankind and who was singularly incapable of either love or friendship. His own misery, it may be plausibly said, made Schopenhauer

overestimate the unhappiness of human beings. It is frequently, but not universally, true that what is hoped for is found disappointing when it is attained, and while "fearful envy" of other people's successes is common enough, real sympathy and generosity are not quite so rare as Schopenhauer made them out to be. Furthermore, his doctrine that pleasure is negative while pain is positive, insofar as one can attach any clear meaning to it, seems glaringly false. To this it should be added, however, that some of Schopenhauer's arguments are far from idiosyncratic and that substantially the same conclusions have been endorsed by men who were neither lonely nor embittered and who did not, as far as one can judge, lack the gift of love or friendship.

DARROW. Clarence Darrow, one of the most compassionate men who ever lived, also concluded that life was an "awful joke." Like Schopenhauer, Darrow offered as one of his reasons the apparent aimlessness of all that happens. "This weary old world goes on, begetting, with birth and with living and with death," he remarked in his moving plea for the boy-murderers Richard Loeb and Nathan Leopold, "and all of it is blind from the beginning to the end" (*Clarence Darrow—Attorney for the Damned,* edited by A. Weinberg, New York, 1957). Elsewhere he wrote: "Life is like a ship on the sea, tossed by every wave and by every wind; a ship headed for no port and no harbor, with no rudder, no compass, no pilot; simply floating for a time, then lost in the waves" ("Is Life Worth Living?," p. 43). In addition to the aimlessness of life and the universe, there is the fact of death. "I love my friends," wrote Darrow, "but they all must come to a tragic end." Death is more terrible the more one is attached to things in the world. Life, he concludes, is "not worth while," and he adds (somewhat inconsistently, in view of what he had said earlier) that "it is an unpleasant interruption of nothing, and the best thing you can say of it is that it does not last long" ("Is the Human Race Getting Anywhere?," p. 53).

TOLSTOY. Lev Tolstoy, unlike Darrow, eventually came to believe in Christianity, or at least in his own idiosyncratic version of Christianity, but for a number of years the only position for which he could see any rational justification was an extreme form of pessimism. During that period (and there is reason to believe that in spite of his later protestations to the contrary, his feelings on this subject never basically changed) Tolstoy was utterly overwhelmed by the thought of his death and the death of those he cared for and, generally, by the transitory nature of all human achievements. "Today or tomorrow," he wrote in "A Confession," "sickness and death will come to those I love or to me; nothing will remain but stench and worms. Sooner or later my affairs, whatever they may be, will be forgotten, and I shall not exist. Then why go on making any effort?" Tolstoy likened the fate of man to that of the traveler in the Eastern tale who, pursued by an enraged beast, seeks refuge in a dry well. At the bottom of the well he sees a dragon that has opened its jaws to swallow him. To escape the enraged beast above and the dragon below, he holds onto a twig that is growing in a crack in the well. As he looks around he notices that two mice are gnawing at the stem of the twig. He realizes that very soon the twig will snap and he will fall to his doom, but at the same time he sees some drops of honey on the leaves of the branch and reaches out with his tongue to lick them. "So I too clung to the twig of life, knowing that the dragon of death was inevitably awaiting me, ready to tear me to pieces.... I tried to lick the honey which formerly consoled me, but the honey no longer gave me pleasure.... I only saw the unescapable dragon and the mice, and I could not tear my gaze from them. And this is not a fable but the real unanswerable truth."

These considerations, according to Tolstoy, inevitably lead to the conclusion that life is a "stupid fraud," that no "reasonable meaning" can be given to a single action or to a whole life. To the questions "What is it for?" "What then?," "Why should I live?" the answer is "Nothing can come of it," "Nothing is worth doing," "Life is not worthwhile."

What ways out are available to a human being who finds himself in this "terrible position"? Judging by the conduct of the people he observed, Tolstoy relates that he could see only four possible "solutions." The first is the way of ignorance. People who adopt this solution (chiefly women and very young and very dull people) have simply not or not yet faced the questions that were tormenting him. Once a person has fully realized what death means, this solution is not available to him. The second way is that of "Epicureanism," which consists in admitting the "hopelessness of life" but seizing as many of life's pleasures as possible while they are within reach. It consists in "disregarding the dragon and the mice and licking the honey in the best way, especially if much of it is around." This, Tolstoy adds, is the solution adopted by the majority of the people belonging to his "circle," by which he presumably means the well-to-do intellectuals of his day. Tolstoy rejects this solution because the vast majority of human beings are not well-to-do and hence have little or no honey at their disposal and also because it is a matter of accident whether one is among those who have

honey or those who have not. Moreover, Tolstoy observes, it requires a special "moral dullness," which he himself lacked, to enjoy the honey while knowing the truth about death and the deprivations of the great majority of men. The third solution is suicide. Tolstoy calls this the way of "strength and energy." It is chosen by a few "exceptionally strong and consistent people." After they realize that "it is better to be dead than to be alive, and that it is best of all not to exist," they promptly end the whole "stupid joke." The means for ending it are readily at hand for everybody, but most people are too cowardly or too irrational to avail themselves of them. Finally, there is the way of "weakness." This consists in seeing the dreadful truth and clinging to life nevertheless. People of this kind lack the strength to act rationally and Tolstoy adds that he belonged to this last category.

STRENGTHS OF THE PESSIMIST POSITION. Is it possible for somebody who shares the pessimists' rejection of religion to reach different conclusions without being plainly irrational? Whatever reply may be possible, any intelligent and realistic person would surely have to concede that there is much truth in the pessimists' claims. That few people achieve real and lasting happiness, that the joys of life (where there are any) pass away much too soon, that totally unpredictable events frequently upset the best intentions and wreck the noblest plans—this and much more along the same lines is surely undeniable. Although one should not dogmatize that there will be no significant improvements in the future, the fate of past revolutions, undertaken to rid man of some of his apparently avoidable suffering, does not inspire great hope. The thought of death, too, even in those who are not so overwhelmed by it as Tolstoy, can be quite unendurable. Moreover, to many who have reflected on the implications of physical theory it seems plain that because of the constant increase of entropy in the universe all life anywhere will eventually die out. Forebodings of this kind moved Bertrand Russell to write his famous essay "A Free Man's Worship," in which he concluded that "all the labors of the ages, all the devotion, all the inspiration, all the noonday brightness of human genius, are destined to extinction in the vast death of the solar system, and the whole temple of man's achievement must inevitably be buried beneath the debris of a universe in ruins." Similarly, Wilhelm Ostwald observed that "in the longest run the sum of all human endeavor has no recognizable significance." Although it is disputed whether physical theory really has such gloomy implications, it would perhaps be wisest to assume that the position endorsed by Russell and Ostwald is well-founded.

COMPARATIVE VALUE JUDGMENTS
ABOUT LIFE AND DEATH

Granting the strong points in the pessimists' claims, it is still possible to detect certain confusions and dubious inferences in their arguments. To begin with, there is a very obvious inconsistency in the way writers like Darrow and Tolstoy arrive at the conclusion that death is better than life. They begin by telling us that death is something terrible because it terminates the possibility of any of the experiences we value. From this they infer that nothing is really worth doing and that death is better than life. Ignoring for the moment the claim that in view of our inevitable death nothing is "worth doing," there very plainly seems to be an inconsistency in first judging death to be such a horrible evil and in asserting later on that death is better than life. Why was death originally judged to be an evil? Surely because it is the termination of life. And if something, y, is bad because it is the termination of something, x, this can be so only if x is good or has positive value. If x were not good, the termination of x would not be bad. One cannot consistently have it both ways.

To this it may be answered that life did have positive value prior to one's realization of death but that once a person has become aware of the inevitability of his destruction life becomes unbearable and that this is the real issue. This point of view is well expressed in the following exchange between Cassius and Brutus in William Shakespeare's *Julius Caesar* (III.i.102–105):

CASSIUS.   Why he that cuts off twenty years of life—
Cuts off so many years of fearing death.

BRUTUS.   Grant that, and then is death a benefit:
So are we Caesar's friends that have abridged
His time of fearing death.

There is a very simple reply to this argument. Granting that some people after once realizing their doom cannot banish the thought of it from their minds, so much so that it interferes with all their other activities, this is neither inevitable nor at all common. It is, on the contrary, in the opinion of all except some existentialists, morbid and pathological. The realization that one will die does not in the case of most people prevent them from engaging in activities which they regard as valuable or from enjoying the things they used to enjoy. To be told that one is not living "authentically" if one does not brood about death day and night is simply to be insulted gratuitously. A person who knows that his talents are not as great as he would wish or that he is not as handsome as he would have liked to be is not usually judged to live "inauthenti-

cally," but on the contrary to be sensible if he does not constantly brood about his limitations and shortcomings and uses whatever talents he does possess to maximum advantage.

There is another and more basic objection to the claim that death is better than life. This objection applies equally to the claim that while death is better than life it would be better still not to have been born in the first place and to the judgment that life is better than death. It should be remembered that we are here concerned with such pronouncements when they are intended not merely as the expression of certain moods but as statements that are in some sense true or objectively warranted. It may be argued that a value comparison—any judgment to the effect that A is better or worse than B or as good as B—makes sense only if *both* A and B are, in the relevant respect, in principle open to inspection. If somebody says, for example, that Elizabeth Taylor is a better actress than Betty Grable, this seems quite intelligible. Or, again, if it is said that life for the Jews is better in the United States than it was in Germany under the Nazis, this also seems readily intelligible. In such cases the terms of the comparison are observable or at any rate describable. These conditions are fulfilled in some cases when value comparisons are made between life and death, but they are not fulfilled in the kind of case with which Tolstoy and the pessimists are concerned. If the conception of an afterlife is intelligible, then it would make sense for a believer or for somebody who has not made up his mind to say such things as "Death cannot be worse than this life" or "I wonder if it will be any better for me after I am dead." Achilles, in the *Iliad*, was not making a senseless comparison when he exclaimed that he would rather act

… as a serf of another,
A man of little possessions, with scanty means of subsistence,
Than rule as a ghostly monarch the ghosts of all the departed.

Again, the survivors can meaningfully say about a deceased individual "It is better (for the world) that he is dead" or the opposite. For the person himself, however, if there is no afterlife, death is not a possible object of observation or experience, and statements by him that his own life is better than, as good as, or worse than his own death, unless they are intended to be no more than expressions of certain wishes or moods, must be dismissed as senseless. At first sight the contention that in the circumstances under discussion value comparisons between life and death are senseless may seem implausible because of the widespread tendency to think of death as a shadowy kind of life—as sleep, rest, or some kind of homecoming. Such "descriptions" may be admirable as poetry or consolation, but taken literally they are simply false.

IRRELEVANCE OF THE DISTANT FUTURE

These considerations do not, however, carry us very far. They do not show either that life is worth living or that it "has meaning." Before tackling these problems directly, something should perhaps be said about the curious and totally arbitrary preference of the future to the present, to which writers such as Tolstoy and Darrow are committed without realizing it. Darrow implies that life would not be "futile" if it were not an endless cycle of the same kind of activities and if instead it were like a journey toward a destination. Tolstoy clearly implies that life would be worthwhile, that some of our actions at least would have a "reasonable meaning," if the present life were followed by eternal bliss. Presumably, what would make life no longer futile as far as Darrow is concerned is some feature of the destination, not merely the fact that it is a destination; and what would make life worthwhile in Tolstoy's opinion is not merely the eternity of the next life but the "bliss" that it would confer—eternal misery and torture would hardly do. About the bliss in the next life, if there is such a next life, Tolstoy shows no inclination to ask "What for?" or "So what?" But if bliss in the next life is not in need of any further justification, why should any bliss that there might be in the present life need justification?

THE LOGIC OF VALUE JUDGMENTS. Many of the pessimists appear to be confused about the logic of value judgments. It makes sense for a person to ask about something "Is it really worthwhile?" or "Is it really worth the trouble?" if he does not regard it as intrinsically valuable or if he is weighing it against another good with which it may be in conflict. It does not make sense to ask such a question about something he regards as valuable in its own right and where there is no conflict with the attainment of any other good. (This observation, it should be noted, is quite independent of what view one takes of the logical status of intrinsic value judgments.) A person driving to the beach on a crowded Sunday, may, upon finally getting there, reflect on whether the trip was really worthwhile. Or, after undertaking a series of medical treatments, somebody may ask whether it was worth the time and the money involved. Such questions make sense because the discomforts of a car ride and the time and money spent on medical treatments are not usually judged to be valuable for their own sake. Again, a woman who has given up a career as a physician in order to raise a family may ask herself whether it was worthwhile, and in this case the question would make sense not because she regards the raising of a family as no more than a means, but because she is weighing it against another good. However, if somebody is very happy, for any number of reasons—because he is in love, because he won the Nobel Prize, because his child recovered from a serious illness—and if this happiness does not prevent him from doing or experiencing anything else he regards as valuable, it would not occur to him to ask "Is it worthwhile?" Indeed, this question would be incomprehensible to him, just as Tolstoy himself would presumably not have known what to make of the question had it been raised about the bliss in the hereafter.

It is worth recalling here that we live not in the distant future but in the present and also, in a sense, in the relatively near future. To bring the subject down to earth, let us consider some everyday occurrences: A man with a toothache goes to a dentist, and the dentist helps him so that the toothache disappears. A man is falsely accused of a crime and is faced with the possibility of a severe sentence as well as with the loss of his reputation; with the help of a devoted attorney his innocence is established, and he is acquitted. It is true that a hundred years later all of the participants in these events will be dead and none of them will then be able to enjoy the fruits of any of the efforts involved. But this most emphatically does not imply that the dentist's efforts were not worthwhile or that the attorney's work was not worth doing. To bring in considerations of what will or will not happen in the remote future is, in such and many other though certainly not in all human situations, totally irrelevant. Not only is the finality of death irrelevant here; equally irrelevant are the facts, if they are facts, that life is an endless cycle of the same kind of activities and that the history of the universe is not a drama with a happy ending.

This is, incidentally, also the answer to religious apologists like C. H. D. Clark who maintain that all striving is pointless if it is "without final consequence" and that "it scarcely matters how we live if all will end in the dust of death." Striving is not pointless if it achieves what it is intended to achieve even if it is without final consequence, and it matters a great deal how we live if we have certain standards and goals, although we cannot avoid "the dust of death."

THE VANISHED PAST. In asserting the worthlessness of life Schopenhauer remarked that "what has been exists as little as what has never been" and that "something of great importance now past is inferior to something of little importance now present." Several comments are in order here. To begin with, if Schopenhauer is right, it must work both ways: If only the present counts, then past sorrows no less than past pleasures do not "count." Furthermore, the question whether "something of great importance now past is inferior to something of little importance now present" is not, as Schopenhauer supposed, a straightforward question of fact but rather one of valuation, and different answers, none of which can be said to be mistaken, will be given by different people according to their circumstances and interests. Viktor Frankl, the founder of "logotherapy," has compared the pessimist to a man who observes, with fear and sadness, how his wall calendar grows thinner and thinner as he removes a sheet from it every day. The kind of person whom Frankl admires, on the other hand, "files each successive leaf neatly away with its predecessors" and reflects "with pride and joy" on all the richness represented by the leaves removed from the calendar. Such a person will not in old age envy the young. "'No, thank you,' he will think. 'Instead of possibilities, I have realities in my past'" (*Man's Search for Meaning*, pp. 192–193).

This passage is quoted not because it contains any great wisdom but because it illustrates that we are concerned here not with judgments of fact but with value judgments and that Schopenhauer's is not the only one that is possible. Nevertheless, his remarks are, perhaps, a healthy antidote to the cheap consolation and the attempts to cover up deep and inevitable misery that are the stock in trade of a great deal of popular psychology. Although Schopenhauer's judgments about the inferior value of the past cannot be treated as objectively true propositions, they express only too well what a great many human beings are bound to feel on certain occasions. To a man dying of cancer it is small consolation to reflect that there was a time when he was happy and flourishing; and while there are undoubtedly some old people who do not envy the young, it may be suspected that more often the kind of talk advocated by the prophets of positive thinking is a mask for envy and a defense against exceedingly painful feelings of regret and helplessness in the face of aging and death and the now-unalterable past.

THE MEANINGS OF THE "MEANING OF LIFE"

Let us now turn to the question whether, given the rejection of belief in God and immortality, life can nevertheless have any "meaning" or "significance." Kurt Baier has called attention to two very different senses in which people use these expressions and to the confusions that result when they are not kept apart. Sometimes when a person asks whether life has any meaning, what he wants to know is whether there is a superhuman intelligence that fashioned human beings along with other objects in the world to serve some end—whether their role is perhaps analogous to the part of an instrument (or its player) in a symphony. People who ask whether history has a meaning often use the word in the same sense. When Macbeth exclaimed that life "is a tale/Told by an idiot, full of sound and fury,/Signifying nothing," he was answering this cosmic question in the negative. His point evidently was not that human life is part of a scheme designed by a superhuman idiot but that it is not part of any design. Similarly, when Fred Hoyle, in his book *The Nature of the Universe* (rev. ed., New York, 1960), turns to what he calls "the deeper issues" and remarks that we find ourselves in a "dreadful situation" in which there is "scarcely a clue as to whether our existence has any real significance," he is using the word *significance* in this cosmic sense.

On the other hand, when we ask whether a particular person's life has or had any meaning, we are usually concerned not with cosmic issues but with the question whether certain purposes are to be found in his life. Thus, most of us would say without hesitation that a person's life had meaning if we knew that he devoted himself to a cause (such as the spread of Christianity or communism or the reform of mental institutions), or we would at least be ready to say that it "acquired meaning" once he became sufficiently attached to his cause. Whether we approve of what they did or not, most of us would be ready to admit—to take some random examples—that Dorothea Dix, Louis Pasteur, V. I. Lenin, Margaret Sanger, Anthony Comstock, and Winston Churchill led meaningful lives. We seem to mean two things in characterizing such lives as meaningful: We assert, first, that the life in question had some dominant, overall goal or goals that gave direction to a great many of the individual's actions and, second, that these actions and possibly others not immediately related to the overriding goal were performed with a special zest that was not present before the person became attached to his goal or that would not have been present if there had been no such goal in his life.

It is not necessary, however, that a person should be devoted to a cause, in the sense just indicated, before we call his life meaningful. It is sufficient that he should have some attachments that are not too shallow. This last expression is of course rather vague, but so is the use of the word *meaning* when applied to human lives. Since the depth or shallowness of an attachment is a matter of degree, it makes perfectly good sense to speak of degrees of meaning in this context. Thus, C. G. Jung writes that in the lives of his patients there never was "sufficient meaning" (*Memories, Dreams, Reflections,* New York and Toronto, 1963, p. 140). There is nothing odd in such a locution, and there is equally nothing odd in saying about a man who has made a partial recovery from a deep depression that there is now again "some" meaning in his life.

Although frequently when people say about somebody that his life has or had meaning, they evidently regard this as a good thing, this is not invariably the case. One might express this point in the following way: Saying that attachment to a certain goal has made a man's life meaningful is not tantamount to saying that the acts to which the goal has given direction are of positive value. A man might himself observe—and there would be nothing logically odd about it—"As long as I was a convinced Nazi (or communist or Christian or whatever) my life had meaning, my acts had a zest with which I have not been able to invest them since, and yet most of my actions were extremely harmful." Even while fully devoted to his cause or goal the person need not, and frequently does not, regard it as intrinsically valuable. If challenged he will usually justify the attachment to his goal by reference to more fundamental value judgments. Thus, somebody devoted to communism or to medical research or to the dissemination of birth-control information will in all likelihood justify his devotion in terms of the production of happiness and the reduction of suffering, and somebody devoted to Christianity will probably justify his devotion by reference to the will of God.

Let us refer to the first of the two senses we have been discussing as the "cosmic" sense and to the second as the "terrestrial" sense. (These are by no means the only senses in which philosophers and others have used the word *meaning* when they have spoken of the meaning or meaninglessness of life, but for our purposes it is sufficient to take account of these two senses.) Now if the theory of cosmic design is rejected it immediately follows that human life has no meaning in the first or cosmic sense. It does not follow in the least, however, that a particular human life is meaningless in the second, or terrestrial, sense. This conclusion has been very clearly summarized by Baier: "Your life or mine may or may not have meaning (in one sense)," he writes, "even if life as such has none (in the other).... The Christian view guarantees a meaning (in one sense) to every life, the scientific view [what

we have simply been calling the unbeliever's position] does not in any sense" (*The Meaning of Life,* p. 28). In the terrestrial sense it will be an open question whether an individual's life has meaning or not, to be decided by the particular circumstances of his existence. It may indeed be the case that once a person comes to believe that life has no meaning in the cosmic sense his attachment to terrestrial goals will be undermined to such an extent that his life will cease to be meaningful in the other sense as well. However, it seems very plain that this is by no means what invariably happens, and even if it did invariably happen the meaninglessness of a given person's life in the terrestrial sense would not logically follow from the fact, if it is a fact, that life is meaningless in the cosmic sense.

This is perhaps the place to add a few words of protest against the rhetorical exaggerations of certain theological writers. Fackenheim's statement, quoted earlier, that "whatever meaning life acquires, it derives from the encounter between God and man" is typical of many theological pronouncements. Statements of this kind are objectionable on several grounds. Let us assume that there is a God and that meetings between God and certain human beings do take place; let us also grant that activities commanded by God in these meetings "acquire meaning" by being or becoming means to the end of pleasing or obeying God. Granting all this, it does not follow that obedience of God is the only possible unifying goal. It would be preposterous to maintain that the lives of all unbelievers have been lacking in such goals and almost as preposterous to maintain that the lives of believers never contain unifying goals other than obedience of God. There have been devout men who were also attached to the advance of science, to the practice of medicine, or to social reform and who regarded these ends as worth pursuing independently of any divine commandments. Furthermore, there is really no good reason to grant that the life of a particular person becomes meaningful in the terrestrial sense just because human life in general has meaning in the cosmic sense. If a superhuman being has a plan in which I am included, this fact will make (or help to make) my life meaningful in the terrestrial sense only if I know the plan and approve of it and of my place in it, so that working toward the realization of the plan gives direction to my actions.

IS HUMAN LIFE EVER WORTHWHILE?

Let us now turn to the question of whether life is ever worth living. This also appears to be denied by the pessimists when they speak of the vanity or the futility of human life. We shall see that in a sense it cannot be established that the pessimists are "mistaken," but it is also quite easy to show that in at least two senses that seem to be of importance to many people, human lives frequently are worth living. To this end, let us consider under what circumstances a person is likely to raise the question "Is my life (still) worthwhile?" and what is liable to provoke somebody into making a statement like "My life has ceased to be worth living." We saw in an earlier section that when we say of certain acts, such as the efforts of a dentist or a lawyer, that they were worthwhile we are claiming that they achieved certain goals. Something similar seems to be involved when we say that a person's life is (still) worthwhile or worth living. We seem to be making two assertions: First, that the person has some goals (other than merely to be dead or to have his pains eased) which do not seem to him to be trivial and, second, that there is some genuine possibility that he will attain these goals. These observations are confirmed by various systematic studies of people who contemplated suicide, of others who unsuccessfully attempted suicide, and of situations in which people did commit suicide. When the subjects of these studies declared that their lives were no longer worth living they generally meant either that there was nothing left in their lives about which they seriously cared or that there was no real likelihood of attaining any of the goals that mattered to them. It should be noted that in this sense an individual may well be mistaken in his assertion that his life is or is not worthwhile any longer: He may, for example, mistake a temporary indisposition for a more permanent loss of interest, or, more likely, he may falsely estimate his chances of achieving the ends he wishes to attain.

DIFFERENT SENSES OF "WORTHWHILE." According to the account given so far, one is saying much the same thing in declaring a life to be worthwhile and in asserting that it has meaning in the "terrestrial" sense of the word. There is, however, an interesting difference. When we say that a person's life has meaning (in the terrestrial sense) we are not committed to the claim that the goal or goals to which he is devoted have any positive value. (This is a slight oversimplification, assuming greater uniformity in the use of "meaning of life" than actually exists, but it will not seriously affect any of the controversial issues discussed here.) The question "As long as his life was dedicated to the spread of communism it had meaning *to him*, but was it really meaningful?" seems to be senseless. We are inclined to say, "If his life had meaning to him, then it had meaning—that's all there is to it." We are not inclined (or we are much less inclined) to say something of this kind when we speak of the worth of a person's life. We

might say—for example, of someone like Adolf Eichmann—"While he was carrying out the extermination program, his life *seemed* worthwhile to him, but since his goal was so horrible, his life *was not* worthwhile." One might perhaps distinguish between a "subjective" and an "objective" sense of "worthwhile." In the subjective sense, saying that a person's life is worthwhile simply means that he is attached to some goals that he does not consider trivial and that these goals are attainable for him. In declaring that somebody's life is worthwhile in the objective sense, one is saying that he is attached to certain goals which are both attainable and of positive value.

It may be held that unless one accepts some kind of rationalist or intuitionist view of fundamental value judgments one would have to conclude that in the objective sense of "worthwhile" no human life (and indeed no human action) could ever be shown to be worthwhile. There is no need to enter here into a discussion of any controversial questions about the logical status of fundamental value judgments. But it may be pointed out that somebody who favors a subjectivist or emotivist account can quite consistently allow for the distinction between ends that only seem to have positive value and those that really do. To mention just one way in which this could be done: One may distinguish between ends that would be approved by rational and sympathetic human beings and those that do not carry such an endorsement. One may then argue that when we condemn such a life as Eichmann's as not being worthwhile we mean not that the ends to which he devoted himself possess some nonnatural characteristic of badness but that no rational or sympathetic person would approve of them.

THE PESSIMISTS' SPECIAL STANDARDS. The unexciting conclusion of this discussion is that some human lives are at certain times not worthwhile in either of the two senses we have distinguished, that some are worthwhile in the subjective but not in the objective sense, some in the objective but not in the subjective sense, and some are worthwhile in both senses. The unexcitingness of this conclusion is not a reason for rejecting it, but some readers may question whether it meets the challenge of the pessimists. The pessimist, it may be countered, surely does not deny the plain fact that human beings are on occasions attached to goals which do not seem to them trivial, and it is also not essential to his position to deny (and most pessimists do not in fact deny) that these goals are sometimes attainable. The pessimist may even allow that in a superficial ("immediate") sense the goals which people try to achieve are of positive value, but he would add that because our lives are not followed by eternal bliss they are not "really" or "ultimately" worthwhile. If this is so, then the situation may be characterized by saying that the ordinary man and the pessimist do not mean the same by "worthwhile," or that they do mean the same in that both use it as a positive value expression but that their standards are different: The standards of the pessimist are very much more demanding than those of most ordinary people.

Anybody who agrees that death is final will have to concede that the pessimist is not mistaken in his contention that judged by his standards, life is never worthwhile. However, the pessimist is mistaken if he concludes, as frequently happens, that life is not worthwhile by ordinary standards because it is not worthwhile by his standards. Furthermore, setting aside the objection mentioned earlier (that there is something arbitrary about maintaining that eternal bliss makes life worthwhile but not allowing this role to bliss in the present life), one may justifiably ask why one should abandon ordinary standards in favor of those of the pessimist. Ordinarily, when somebody changes standards (for example, when a school raises or lowers its standards of admission) such a change can be supported by reasons.

But how can the pessimist justify his special standards? It should be pointed out here that our ordinary standards do something for us which the pessimist's standards do not: They guide our choices, and as long as we live we can hardly help making choices. It is true that in one type of situation the pessimist's standards also afford guidance—namely, in deciding whether to go on living. It is notorious, however, that whether or not they are, by their own standards, rational in this, most pessimists do not commit suicide. They are then faced with much the same choices as other people. In these situations their own demanding standards are of no use, and in fact they avail themselves of the ordinary standards. Schopenhauer, for example, believed that if he had hidden his antireligious views he would have had no difficulty in obtaining an academic appointment and other worldly honors. He may have been mistaken in this belief, but in any event his actions indicate that he regarded intellectual honesty as worthwhile in a sense in which worldly honors were not. Again, when Darrow had the choice between continuing as counsel for the Chicago and North Western Railway and taking on the defense of Eugene V. Debs and his harassed and persecuted American Railway Union, he did not hesitate to choose the latter, apparently regarding it as worthwhile to go to the assistance of the suppressed and not worthwhile to aid the suppressor. In other words, although no human action is worthwhile, some human actions and presumably some human lives are less unworthwhile than others.

IS THE UNIVERSE BETTER WITH HUMAN LIFE THAN WITHOUT IT?

We have not—at least not explicitly—discussed the claims of Schopenhauer, Eduard von Hartmann, and other pessimists that the nonexistence of the world would be better than its existence, by which they mean that a world without human life would be better than one with it.

ARGUMENTS OF A PHENOMENOLOGIST. Some writers do not think that life can be shown to have meaning in any philosophically significant sense unless an affirmative answer to this question can be justified. Thus, in his booklet *Der Sinn unseres Daseins* the German phenomenologist Hans Reiner distinguishes between the everyday question about what he calls the "need-conditioned" meaning of life, which arises only for a person who is already in existence and has certain needs and desires, and the question about the meaning of human life in general. The latter question arises in concrete form when a responsible person is faced with the *Zeugungsproblem*—the question whether he should bring a child into the world. Reiner allows that a person's life has meaning in the former or "merely subjective" sense as long as his ordinary goals (chiefly his desire for happiness) are attained. This, however, does not mean that his life has an "objective" or "existential" (*seinshaft*) meaning—a significance or meaning that "attaches to life as such" and which, unlike the need-conditioned meaning, cannot be destroyed by any accident of fate. The philosopher, according to Reiner, is primarily concerned with the question of whether life has meaning in this objective or existential sense. "Our search for the meaning of our life," Reiner writes, "is identical with the search for a logically compelling reason (*einen einsichtigen Grund*) why it is better for us to exist than not to exist" (*Der Sinn unseres Daseins*, p. 27). Again, the real question is "whether it is better that mankind should exist than that there should be a world without any human life" (p. 31). It may be questioned whether this is what anybody normally means when he asks whether life has any meaning, but Reiner certainly addresses himself to one of the questions raised by Schopenhauer and other pessimists that ought to be discussed here.

Reiner believes that he can provide a "logically compelling reason" why a world with human life is better than one without it. He begins by pointing out that men differ from animals by being, among other things, "moral individuals." To be a moral individual is to be part of the human community and to be actively concerned in the life of other human beings. It is indeed undeniable that people frequently fail to bring about the ends of morally inspired acts or wishes, but phenomenological analysis discloses that "the real moral value and meaning" of an act does not depend on the attainment of the "external goal." As Immanuel Kant correctly pointed out, the decisive factor is "the good will," the moral intent or attitude. It is here that we find the existential meaning of life: "Since that which is morally good contains its meaning and value within itself, it follows that it is intrinsically worth while. The existence of what is morally good is therefore better than its non-existence." (*Der Sinn unseres Daseins*, pp. 54–55). But the existence of what is morally good is essentially connected with the existence of free moral individuals, and hence it follows that the existence of human beings as moral agents is better than their nonexistence.

Unlike happiness, which constitutes the meaning of life in the everyday or need-conditioned sense, the morally good does not depend on the accidents of life. It is not within a person's power to be happy, but it is "essentially" (*grundsätzlich*) in everybody's power to do what is good. Furthermore, while all happiness is subjective and transitory, leaving behind it no more than a "melancholy echo," the good has eternal value. Nobody would dream of honoring and respecting a person for his happiness or prosperity. On the other hand, we honor every good deed and the expression of every moral attitude, even if it took place in a distant land and among a foreign people. If we discover a good act or a good attitude in an enemy we nevertheless respect it and cannot help deriving a certain satisfaction from its existence. The same is true of good deeds carried out in ages long past. In all this the essentially timeless nature of morality becomes evident. Good deeds cease to exist as historical events only; their value, on the other hand, has eternal reality and is collected as an indestructible "fund." This may be a metaphysical statement, but it is not a piece of "metaphysical speculation." It simply makes explicit what the experience of the morally good discloses to phenomenological analysis (*Der Sinn unseres Daseins*, pp. 55–57).

REPLIES TO REINER. There is a great deal in this presentation with which one could take issue. If one is not misled by the image of the ever-growing, indestructible "fund," one may wonder, for example, what could be meant by claiming that the value of a good deed is "eternal," other than that most human beings tend to approve

of such an action regardless of when or where it took place. However, we are here concerned primarily with the question whether Reiner has met the challenge of the pessimists, and it seems clear that he has not. A pessimist like Schopenhauer or Darrow might provisionally grant the correctness of Reiner's phenomenological analysis of morality but still offer the following rejoinder: The inevitable misery of all or nearly all human beings is so great that even if in the course of their lives they have a chance to preserve their inner moral natures or their good will, the continued torture to which their lives condemn them would not be justified. Given the pessimist's estimate of human life, this is surely not an unreasonable rejoinder. Even without relying on the pessimist's description of human life, somebody while accepting Reiner's phenomenological analysis might reach the opposite conclusion. He might, for example, share the quietist strain of Schopenhauer's teachings and object to the whole hustle and bustle of life, concluding that the "peace of the all-sufficient nothing"—or, more literally, a universe without human life—was better in spite of the fact that moral deeds could not then be performed. Since he admits the "facts" of morality on which Reiner bases his case but considers the peace of the all-sufficient nothing more valuable than morality, it is not easy to see how an appeal to the latter would show him to be mistaken. What phenomenological analysis has not disclosed, to Reiner or, as far as is known, to anybody else, is that doing good is the only or necessarily the greatest value.

WHY THE PESSIMIST CANNOT BE ANSWERED. The conclusion suggests itself that the pessimist cannot here be refuted, not because what he says is true or even because we do not know who is right and who is wrong but because the question whether a universe with human life is better than one without it does not have any clear meaning unless it is interpreted as a request for a statement of personal preference. The situation seems to be somewhat similar to what we found in the case of the question "Is my life better than my death?" when asked in certain circumstances. In some contexts indeed when we talk about human life in general, the word *better* has a reasonably clear meaning. Thus, if it is maintained that life for the human race will be better than it is now after cancer and mental illness have been conquered, or that human life will be better (or worse) after religion has disappeared, we understand fairly well what is meant, what facts would decide the issue either way. However, we do not really know what would count as evidence for or against the statement "The existence of human life as such is better than its nonexistence." Sometimes it is claimed that the question has a fairly clear meaning, namely, whether happiness outweighs unhappiness. Thus, von Hartmann supports his answer that the nonexistence of human life is better than its existence, that in fact an inanimate world would be better than one with life, with the argument that as we descend the scale of civilization and "sensitivity," we reach ever lower levels of misery. "The individuals of the lower and poorer classes and of ruder nations," he writes, "are happier than those of the elevated and wealthier classes and of civilized nations, not indeed because they are poorer and have to endure more want and privations, but because they are coarser and duller" (*Philosophy of the Unconscious,* Vol. III, p. 76). The "brutes," similarly, are "happier (i.e., less miserable)" than man, because "the excess of pain which an animal has to bear is less than that which a man has to bear." The same principle holds within the world of animals and plants:

> How much more painful is the life of the more finely-feeling horse compared with that of the obtuse pig, or with that of the proverbially happy fish in the water, its nervous system being of a grade so far inferior! As the life of a fish is more enviable than that of a horse, so is the life of an oyster than that of a fish, and the life of a plant than that of an oyster. (Ibid.)

The conclusion is inevitable: The best or least undesirable form of existence is reached when, finally, we "descend beneath the threshold of consciousness"; for only there do we "see individual pain entirely disappear" (*Philosophy of the Unconscious,* Vol. III, pp. 76–77). Schopenhauer, also, addressing himself directly to the "*Zeugungsproblem,*" reaches a negative answer on the ground that unhappiness usually or necessarily outweighs happiness. "Could the human race continue to exist," he asks (in *Parerga und Paralipomena,* Vol. II, pp. 321–322), if "the generative act were … an affair of pure rational reflection? Would not rather everyone have so much compassion for the coming generation as to prefer to spare it the burden of existence, or at least be unwilling to take on himself the responsibility of imposing such a burden in cold blood?" In these passages Schopenhauer and von Hartmann assume that in the question "Is a world with human life better than one without human life?" the word *better* must be construed in a hedonistic or utilitarian sense— and the same is true of several other philosophers who do not adopt their pessimistic answer. However, while one may stipulate such a sense for "better" in this context, it is clear that this is not what is meant prior to the stipulation. Benedict de Spinoza, for example, taught that the most miserable form of existence is preferable to nonexistence. Perhaps few who have directly observed the worst agonies and tortures that may be the lot of human beings or of animals would subscribe to this judgment, but Spinoza can hardly be accused of a self-contradictory error. Again, Friedrich Nietzsche's philosophy is usually and quite accurately described as an affirmation of life, but Nietzsche was very careful not to play down the horrors of much of life. While he did not endorse Schopenhauer's value judgments, he thought that, by and large, Schopenhauer had not been far wrong in his description of the miseries of the human scene. In effect Nietzsche maintained that even though unhappiness is more prevalent than happiness, the existence of life is nevertheless better than its nonexistence, and this surely is not a self-contradiction.

It is important to point out what does not follow from the admission that in a nonarbitrary sense of "better," the existence of the human race cannot be shown to be better than its nonexistence: It does not follow that I or anybody else cannot or should not prefer the continued existence of the human race to its nonexistence or my own life to my death, and it does not follow that I or anybody else cannot or should not enjoy himself or that I or anybody else is "irrational" in any of these preferences. It is also impossible to prove that in some nonarbitrary sense of "better," coffee with cream is better than black coffee, but it does not follow that I cannot or should not prefer or enjoy it or that I am irrational in doing so. There is perhaps something a trifle absurd and obsessive in the need for a "proof" that the existence of life is better than its nonexistence. It resembles the demand to have it "established by argument" that love is better than hate.

Perhaps it would be helpful to summarize the main conclusions reached in this essay:

(1) In certain familiar senses of "meaning," which are not usually regarded as trivial, an action or a human life can have meaning quite independently of whether there is a God or whether we shall live forever.

(2) Writers such as Tolstoy, who, because of the horror that death inspires, conclude that death is better than life, are plainly inconsistent. Moreover, the whole question of whether my life is better than my death, unless it is a question about my preference, seems to be devoid of sense.

(3) Those who argue that no human action can be worthwhile because we all must eventually die

ignore what may be called the "short-term context" of much of our lives.

(4) Some human lives are worthwhile in one or both of the two senses in which "worthwhile" is commonly used, when people raise the question of whether a given person's life is worthwhile. The pessimists who judge human life by more demanding standards are not mistaken when they deny that by their standards no human life is ever worthwhile. However, they are guilty of a fallacious inference if they conclude that for this reason no human life can be worthwhile by the usual standards. Nor is it clear why anybody should embrace their standards in the place of those commonly adopted.

(5) It appears that the pessimists cannot be answered if in order to answer them one has to be able to prove that in some nonarbitrary sense of the word *better*, the existence of life is better than its nonexistence. But this admission does not have any of the gloomy consequences that it is sometimes believed to entail.

See also Baier, Kurt; Death; Happiness; Hartmann, Eduard von; Jung, Carl Gustav; Kant, Immanuel; Lenin, Vladimir Il'ich; Meaning; Nietzsche, Friedrich; Ostwald, Wilhelm; Pessimism and Optimism; Russell, Bertrand Arthur William; Schopenhauer, Arthur; Suicide; Tolstoy, Lev (Leo) Nikolaevich.

Bibliography

The position that human life cannot be meaningful without religious belief is defended in James Martineau, *Modern Materialism and Its Relation to Religion and Theology* (New York, 1877), and more recently in C. H. D. Clark, *Christianity and Bertrand Russell* (London: Lutterworth Press, 1958), and in E. L. Fackenheim, "Judaism and the Meaning of Life," in *Commentary* 39 (1965): 49–55. Substantially similar views are expounded in Paul Althaus, "The Meaning and Purpose of History in the Christian View," in *Universitas* 7 (1965): 197–204, and in various publications by Viktor Frankl. Frankl's *Man's Search for Meaning* (Boston: Beacon Press, 1963) contains a full list of his own writings as well as those of his followers, most of whom may be described as practicing "pastoral psychology." A proreligious position is also advocated by William James in "Is Life Worth Living?," in *The Will to Believe and Other Essays in Popular Philosophy* (New York: Longmans, Green, 1897), and *The Varieties of Religious Experience* (New York: Longmans, Green, 1902), Chs. 6 and 7. A milder version of the same position is presented in Chad Walsh, *Life Is Worth Living* (Cincinnati, no date).

Schopenhauer's views about the "vanity" of life are stated in Vol. I, Bk. IV, of *Die Welt als Wille und Vorstellung* (Leipzig, 1818), translated by R. B. Haldane and J. Kemp as *The World as Will and Idea*, 3 vols. (London: Trubner, 1883), and in several of his pieces included in *Parerga und Paralipomena*, 6th ed., edited by J. Frauenstädt, 2 vols. (Berlin, 1851). Three of his essays that bear most closely on the subject of the present entry—"On the Vanity and Suffering of Life," "On the Sufferings of the World," and "The Vanity of Existence"—are available in an English translation by T. Bailey Saunders in *The Will to Live—Selected Writings of Arthur Schopenhauer*, edited by Richard Taylor (Garden City, NY: Doubleday, 1962).

Eduard von Hartmann's position is stated in Vol. III of *Die Philosophie des Unbewussten*, 3 vols. (Berlin, 1869), translated by W. C. Coupland as *Philosophy of the Unconscious* (London, 1884), in *Zur Geschichte und Begründung des Pessimismus* (Berlin, 1892), and in *Philosophische Fragen der Gegenwart* (Leipzig: Haacke, 1885), Ch. 5. Clarence Darrow's pessimism is expounded in *The Story of My Life* (New York: Scribners, 1932) and in two pamphlets, "Is Life Worth Living?" and "Is the Human Race Getting Anywhere?" (Girard, KS, no date). Tolstoy's views are stated in "A Confession," in *A Confession, the Gospel in Brief and What I Believe*, translated by Aylmer Maude (London: Oxford University Press, H. Milford, 1940). Gloomy implications are derived from the second law of thermodynamics by Bertrand Russell in "A Free Man's Worship" (1903), which is available in several books, perhaps most conveniently in Russell's *Mysticism and Logic* (London: Allen and Unwin, 1918), and by Wilhelm Ostwald, *Die Philosophie der Werte* (Leipzig: Kröner, 1913). F. P. Ramsey, in "How I Feel," in *The Foundations of Mathematics and Other Logical Essays* (London: K. Paul, Trench, Trubner, 1931), agrees with Russell and Ostwald about the physical consequences of the second law but does not share their gloomy response. Stephen Toulmin, "Contemporary Scientific Mythology," in Toulmin et al., *Metaphysical Beliefs* (London: SCM Press, 1957), questions whether the second law has the physical consequences attributed to it by Russell, Ostwald, and many others. L. J. Russell, "The Meaning of Life," *Philosophy* 28 (1953): 30–40, contains some interesting criticisms of the view that eternal existence could render any human actions meaningful.

The fullest discussions of the questions of the meaning and value of life by contemporary analytic philosophers are Kurt Baier, *The Meaning of Life* (Canberra, 1957), parts of which are reprinted in *Twentieth Century Philosophy—The Analytic Tradition*, edited by Morris Weitz (New York: Free Press, 1966); Ronald W. Hepburn, *Christianity and Paradox* (London: Watts, 1958), Ch. 8; and Antony Flew, "Tolstoi and the Meaning of Life," in *Ethics* 73 (1963): 110–118. Baier, Hepburn, and Flew support the position that life can be meaningful even if there is no God and no afterlife. This position is also defended in Eugen Dühring, *Der Werth des Lebens* (Leipzig, 1881), Chs. 6–7, and more recently in Bertrand Russell, *The Conquest of Happiness* (New York: Liveright, 1930), Ch. 2; Ernest Nagel, "The Mission of Philosophy," in *An Outline of Man's Knowledge of the Modern World*, edited by Lyman Bryson (New York: McGraw-Hill, 1960); Sidney Hook, "Pragmatism and the Tragic Sense of Life," in *Proceedings and Addresses of the American Philosophical Association* 33 (1960): 5–26; Karl R. Popper, *The Open Society and Its Enemies*, 2 vols. (5th rev. ed.,

London: Routledge and K. Paul, 1966), Vol. II, Ch. 25; and Kai Nielsen, "Examination of an Alleged Theological Basis of Morality," in *Iliff Review* 21 (1964): 39–49. Jean-Paul Sartre and Albert Camus are frequently (and rather inaccurately) described as "nihilists," but in effect they also take the position that although the universe is "absurd," human life can be meaningful. Sartre's views are found in *Being and Nothingness*, translated by Hazel E. Barnes (New York: Philosophical Library, 1956), Pt. 4. Camus's views are stated in *The Myth of Sisyphus and Other Essays*, translated by Justin O'Brien (New York: Knopf, 1955). Views very similar to those of Sartre and Camus are advocated by Flew and R. W. Hepburn in their BBC discussion "Problems of Perspective," which is printed in *Plain View* 10 (1955): 151–166. C. D. McGee, *The Recovery of Meaning—An Essay on the Good Life* (New York: Random House, 1966), Ch. 1, contains a lively and detailed discussion of some of the issues treated in the present entry. The author reaches similar conclusions but devotes far more attention to the "malaise" that inspires questions about the meaning of life. In a similar vein, Ilham Dilman, "Life and Meaning," in *Philosophy* 40 (1965): 320–333, concentrates on the psychological situations that prompt people to ask whether their own lives or the lives of others have meaning. Moritz Schlick, *Vom Sinn des Lebens* (Berlin, 1927), is concerned primarily with psychological questions, arguing that modern life tends to be spoiled by overemphasis on the achievement of distant goals. Sigmund Freud in several places alludes to the question of the meaning of life and usually dismisses it as senseless and pathological. "The moment a man questions the meaning and value of life," he wrote in a letter to Marie Bonaparte, "he is sick.... By asking this question one is merely admitting to a store of unsatisfied libido to which something else must have happened, a kind of fermentation leading to sadness and depression" (*Letters of Sigmund Freud*, translated by James Stern and Tania Stern, edited by E. L. Freud, New York: Dover, 1960, p. 436).

The Polish Marxist Adam Schaff deals with some of the issues discussed in the present entry in his *A Philosophy of Man* (London: Lawrence and Wishart, 1963). Schaff's views are criticized from a Christian point of view in Christopher Hollis, "What Is the Purpose of Life?," in *Listener* 70 (1961): 133–136. There is a discussion of the "meaning of life" from the point of view of fascism in Mario Palmieri, *The Philosophy of Fascism* (Chicago: Dante Alighieri Society, 1936). The "phenomenological" position of Hans Reiner, which was discussed in the final section of this entry, is stated in his *Der Sinn unseres Daseins* (Tübingen, 1960). Other more recent German works include *Sinn und Sein*, edited by Richard Wisser (Tübingen: Niemeyer, 1960); Reinhart Lauth, *Die Frage nach dem Sinn des Daseins* (Munich, 1953); and Johannes Hessen, *Der Sinn des Lebens* (Cologne, 1933).

Psychological studies of people who attempted or who committed suicide are contained in Margarethe von Andics, *Suicide and the Meaning of Life* (London: Hodge, 1947); Louis I. Dublin and Bessie Bunzel, *To Be or Not to Be* (New York: H. Smith and R. Haas, 1933); and E. Stengel, *Suicide and Attempted Suicide* (London: MacGibbon and Kee, 1965).

Will Durant, *On the Meaning of Life* (New York: R. Long & R.R. Smith, 1932), consists of answers by various eminent men, including Mohandas Gandhi, H. L. Mencken, Russell, and George Bernard Shaw, to the question of what they take to be the meaning of life.

Paul Edwards (1967)

LIFE, MEANING AND VALUE OF [ADDENDUM]

Paul Edwards primarily addresses the "pessimist view" that if there is no God and death is final, life has no meaning. The focus here will be on subsequent philosophical work and on issues he leaves unaddressed. Some account of nonmonotheistic religion (Buddhism, Daoism, Confucianism, and Advaita Vedanta Hinduism) should be given, especially since religious perspectives are now taken more seriously by many in the analytic philosophical tradition.

Thomas Nagel (1986) argues both that (1) human life viewed objectively is insignificant though viewed subjectively is significant and that (2) it is our capacity to recognize both (1) and our constitutional self-absorption, which makes us irreducibly absurd and our lives ironic. Against (1) David Wiggins (2002) argues that for our strivings to matter, even subjectively, there must be something we can "invest with overwhelming *importance*," and that this entails both that values are objective, though "lit up by the focus one brings to the world", and that happiness is not supremely important. Robert Nozick (1989) shares this view and imagines a hermetically sealed "experience machine" that can undetectably provide apparently real and happy experiences involving others. Would a life be better lived inside the machine in a state of perpetual happiness or outside, with the tribulation and joys of genuine connection to others? Nozick argues for the latter, distinguishing between intrinsic value and meaning. The measure of a thing's intrinsic value is the degree of its diversity and the degree of the organic unity of that diversity. Meaning comes from a thing's connection to other things with intrinsic value—the greater their value and the stronger the connection, the greater the meaning. Thus, value is proportional to both internal integration and the strength of external connections to things of great value.

Turning to religious accounts, Philip Quinn (2000) distinguishes axiological and teleological questions. He argues that an integrated life might have intrinsic or "axiological value" though it lacked any overt connection to a

ENCYCLOPEDIA OF PHILOSOPHY
2nd edition

transcendent reality that would give it "teleological value." Keith Ward argues, "What distinguishes a religious view of nontrivial purpose is that all positive human purposes are subordinate to the one objective purpose of attaining the supreme goal of union with, or fulfilling relation to, the supreme value… " (Ward 2000, p. 20). Still, a life may be intrinsically valuable, worthwhile (to oneself) and reasonably happy, without being specially valuable or meaningful, and it may be meaningful and, thus, valuable without being somehow ultimately valuable.

Now if there is a transcendent entity such as God, Brahman, Nirvana, or the Dao, then one's connectedness to it, assuming a connection of great diversity to other centers of value such as people, would bring an ultimate or teleological meaning to life, obviating the absurdity that Nagel posits. Asian philosophical traditions view normal human nature as inadequate though improvable through self-reflection and right moral action; the Indic traditions, however, offer a bleaker view of human nature than the Chinese. For both, a life of value and meaning is only possible if one aligns the self with the underlying relational structure of reality: the Dao (Chinese traditions) or the Dharma (Hinduism and Buddhism). Daoism holds that meaning is achieved by returning to the natural self in accordance with the Dao, whereas Confucianism, which developed religious notions of a transcendent reality after Mahayana Buddhism entered China, emphasizes refinement, also holding that, as Tu Wei-Ming puts it, "we can realize the ultimate meaning of life in ordinary human existence" (Tu 1985, p. 60).

For Indic traditions, an illusory view of the self leads to an attachment to this life, preventing the attainment of meaning through a transcendent being (Brahman) or a state (Nirvana), "the fullness of being" and the "fullness of emptiness," respectively. Within Hinduism, Sankara's Advaita Vedanta holds Atman (the true self) identical to Brahman. The majority Hindu position of *bhakti yoga*, espoused by Ramajuna and closer to monotheism, focuses on the key teaching that Eliot Deutsch identifies in the *Bhagavad Gita*: that nonattachment is only possible via a new attachment to that of greatest value. "One overcomes the narrow clinging to results … only when that passion is replaced by one directed to the Divine" (Deutsch 1968, p. 163). Still, even if there is a transcendent reality, the best is not an enemy of the good, so axiological and teleological meaning can be compatible and even inextricably linked. "A man who knows his own nature will know Heaven" says Mencius, and Masao Abe articulates the meaning of life in Mahayana Zen this way:

"For the sake of wisdom, do not abide in *samsara* (this life); for the sake of compassion, do not abide in *nirvana*" (Abe 2000, p. 161).

See also Brahman; Buddhism; Buddhism—Schools: Chan and Zen; Chinese Philosophy: Daoism; Indian Philosophy; Mencius; Nagel, Thomas; Nirvāṇa; Nozick, Robert; Wiggins, David.

Bibliography

Abe, Masao. "The Meaning of Life in Buddhism." In *The Meaning of Life in the World Religions*. Edited by Joseph Runzo and Nancy M. Martin. Oxford: Oneworld Publications, 2000.

Deutsch, Eliot. *The Bhagavad Gita.* Lanham: University Press of America, 1968.

Klemke, E. D., ed. *The Meaning of Life.* 2nd ed. New York: Oxford University Press, 2000.

Nagel, Thomas. *The View from Nowhere.* New York: Oxford University Press, 1986.

Nozick, Robert. *The Examined Life.* New York: Simon and Schuster, 1989.

Quinn, P. L. "How Christianity Secures Life's Meanings;" In *The Meaning of Life in the World Religions*. Edited by Runzo and Martin. Oxford: Oneworld, 2000.

Tu, Wei-Ming. *Confucian Thought: Selfhood as Creative Transformation.* Albany: State University of New York Press, 1985.

Ward, Keith. "Religion and the Question of Meaning." In *The Meaning of Life in the World Religions*. Edited by Runzo and Martin. Oxford: Oneworld, 2000.

Wiggins, David. "Truth, Invention, and the Meaning of Life." *Proceedings of the British Academy* LXII (1976). Reprinted in *Needs, Values, Truth.* 3rd ed. Oxford: Clarendon Press, 2002.

Joseph Runzo (2005)

LIFE, ORIGIN OF

Two explanations dominated prescientific thinking about the origin of life: special creation and spontaneous generation. According to the former view, supernatural intervention was essential for the creation of life; according to the latter, living organisms could form spontaneously—for example, from the mud of the Nile. Not surprisingly, special creation was usually favored as an explanation of the origin of humans and the higher animals, whereas spontaneous generation seemed adequate to explain the origin of insects, frogs, and even mice.

The theory of spontaneous generation came under attack in the seventeenth century when the Italian scientist Francesco Redi showed that maggots do not arise spontaneously in rotting meat but develop from eggs laid by flies. The spontaneous generation controversy persisted for another two hundred years or so until the classic experiments of Louis Pasteur convinced almost everyone that even microorganisms appear only as the descendents of similar microorganisms. This posed the problem of the origin of life in its modern form: How were the first organisms generated from abiotic matter?

The generally accepted answer to this question was provided by the theory of evolution through natural selection as proposed by Charles Darwin and Alfred Russell Wallace. Darwin in the final paragraph of the first edition of "On the Origin of Species" suggests that the whole complex world of life has evolved from one or a few simple kinds of organism that were formed on the Earth long ago. "There is a grandeur in this view of life with its several powers, having been originally breathed into a few forms or into one, and that, whilst this planet has gone cycling on according to the fixed law of gravity, from so simple a beginning endless forms most beautiful and most wonderful have been, and are being, evolved" (1859, chapter 14).

Darwin never published his thoughts on the origin of those earliest organisms, probably to avoid upsetting his wife, but in a much-quoted letter he speculates that life may have emerged "in some warm little pond with all sorts of ammonia and phosphoric salts, light, heat, electricity, etc., present" (1959 [1898], pp. 202–203). Thus Darwin thought that, long ago, a complex mixture of organic molecules was formed spontaneously on the Earth "in some little pond," and that they supported the appearance of the first simple living organisms. After that, the evolution of the whole biosphere was the consequence of natural selection acting on those earliest organisms and their descendants. Modern research on the origin of life is largely concerned with filling in the details of Darwin's scenario.

THE NATURE OF THE PROBLEM

The Earth is about 4.6 billion years old. The dating of the earliest fossil microorganisms remains somewhat controversial, but it seems almost certain that organisms not unlike modern bacteria or algae were already present on the Earth about 3.5 billion years ago. During the first half-billion years of Earth's history repeated impacts of comets, asteroids, and other interplanetary objects would have sterilized the Earth's surface, so up to half a billion years was available for the evolution of complex life from abiotic origins. There is no reason to doubt that this was long enough.

DNA sequencing and the comparison of the genomes of different organisms have revolutionized human understanding of the evolutionary relationships between the varied forms of life. While many details remain to be worked out, people already have a reasonable picture of the nature of the last common ancestor of all life, and a fairly detailed outline of the sequence in which the different fossil and extant forms of life evolved from it. The many gaps in the picture are likely to be filled in during the early twenty-first century. The outstanding problem, therefore, is that of the origin of the first living, replicating microorganisms. Most scientists believe that they originated on the Earth, although the possibility that they were brought here from elsewhere in the solar system cannot be dismissed out of hand.

EARLY EXPERIMENTAL STUDIES

The modern era of experimental origin-of-life studies began in 1953 with the classical experiments of Harold Urey and Stanley Miller. Alexandre Ivanovich Oparin in 1924 had suggested that the organic material needed to get life started was formed in the atmosphere of the Earth when the atmosphere was still reducing. Miller, then a graduate student working with Urey, tested this hypothesis by passing an electric discharge through a "reducing atmosphere" of methane, water, and ammonia. To the surprise of his contemporaries, Miller was able to detect among the products substantial amounts of several of the amino acids that are present in proteins. This was the first successful experiment designed to demonstrate that important components of contemporary living organisms are readily formed from simple starting materials under prebiotic conditions.

In the years following Miller's experiment, most of the organic molecules that are central to molecular biology were obtained by related methods. The discovery by Juan Oro that adenine, a component both of nucleic acids and of ATP, the energy currency of the cell, could be formed from a simple solution of ammonium cyanide was particularly impressive. However, this whole approach came under attack when it was realized that the atmosphere of the Earth could never have been as strongly reducing as Miller and Urey assumed. Whether it was ever sufficiently reducing to support similar chemistry, even if less efficiently, is uncertain.

A second possible source of the organic material needed to permit the origin of life was identified in the carbonaceous chondrites, a common class of meteorite. Careful chemical analysis showed that these stones contained abundant organic material, including amino acids and the nucleic acid bases. Many scientists believe that meteorites, comets, and interplanetary dust provided much of the organic material for the origin of life.

In the late twentieth century another possible source of prebiotic organic material was identified, namely the deep-sea vents. In the vents, superheated water containing large amounts of metal sulfides comes into contact with cold seawater causing the sulfides to precipitate. Laboratory experiments suggest that metal sulfides can act as catalysts for the formation of a mixture of a variety of organic molecules from volcanic gases. Clearly, there are several possible sources of the prebiotic organic material needed for the origin of life, but it is not clear which of them was most important.

THE RNA WORLD

The most important recent advance in our understanding of the origin of life is the realization that there once was an RNA world. The modern biological world depends on a complex, interacting system of proteins and nucleic acids in which proteins are needed to replicate nucleic acids, but the formation of proteins depends on the prior presence of nucleic acids. It is now known that the DNA/RNA/protein world was preceded by a much simpler world in which RNA, without the help of proteins, fulfilled both a genetic and a functional role.

It is now clear from laboratory experiments that RNA molecules are capable of evolution by natural selection and are capable of catalyzing a variety of difficult chemical reactions. In particular it has been possible to evolve an RNA catalyst that carries out the most important step involved in RNA replication. It seems probable, therefore, that RNA catalysts (ribozymes) once supported a fairly complex form of life, without the help of proteins. Thus the problem of the origin of life is simplified: How were the first replicating molecules of RNA synthesized on the primitive Earth?

Attempts to demonstrate the synthesis of RNA under prebiotic conditions have met with some success, but formidable difficulties remain. The monomeric components of RNA, ribonucleotides, are complicated organic molecules made up from a sugar, a heterocyclic purine or pyrimidine base, and an inorganic phosphate group. The prebiotic syntheses of the two organic components that have been reported are relatively inefficient and nonspecific, and the combination of the three elementary components to form ribonucleotides is complicated by several troublesome side reactions. A great deal of novel chemistry needs to be discovered before a plausible pre-

biotic synthesis of the nucleotides can be claimed. A number of scientists are working on the problem.

The formation of long polymers from ribonucleotides is another difficult step in the synthesis of RNA. However, substantial successes have been achieved in model systems. The most extensive studies make use of an abundant clay mineral, montmorillonite, to catalyze the polymerization of an analog of the activated nucleotides that are used in the enzymatic synthesis of RNA. This work emphasizes the important role that minerals are likely to have played in the origin of life. It seems probable that many of the most difficult reactions needed to get life started occurred on mineral surfaces rather than in solution.

The replication of DNA or RNA is dependent on specific base-pairing between adenylic acid and uridylic or thymidylic acid and between guanylic acid and cytidylic acid. Base pairing is an intrinsic property of the nucleotide bases, so that a preformed strand of RNA (DNA) will align the complementary mononucleotides in the correct sequence even in the absence of a protein enzyme. If the nucleotides are presented in an activated form suitable for incorporation into polymers, a preformed RNA (DNA) strand, therefore, will bring about the nonenzymatic synthesis of a new complementary strand. This process is known as template-directed synthesis.

Template-directed synthesis is a central theme in many scenarios for the origin of the RNA world. It has been shown, for example, that a great variety of RNA sequences can be "copied," that is a great variety of sequences will catalyze the synthesis of their complements, converting single-stranded RNA to double-stranded RNA. Thus mineral catalysis of the formation of long single-stranded RNA molecules followed by template-directed copying could, in principle, have assembled a complex mixture (library) of double-stranded RNA on the primitive Earth, but only if a supply of ribonucleotides was available.

It is possible to propose a scenario for the origin of the RNA world by optimistic extrapolation of the available experimental evidence. First nucleotides were formed abiotically; they condensed together on mineral surfaces to give single-stranded RNA that was then copied by template-directed synthesis to give a "library" of double-stranded RNA molecules. Among these was one that included an RNA polymerase that was able to get efficient RNA replication started.

The serious obstacles to the prebiotic synthesis of RNA have led many researchers to propose a different kind of solution to the problem of the origin of the RNA world. They believe that one or more much simpler biochemical worlds preceded the RNA world and "invented" RNA. The search for such simple worlds is just beginning, but there are already a number of RNA-like polymers that, although they are somewhat simpler than RNA, look as though they could have functioned as genetic systems. The search for even simple systems is an active field.

SUMMARY

It is generally accepted that once a replicating genetic polymer appeared on the early Earth, evolution through natural selection could account for the appearance of ever more complex organisms, and finally of the familiar biosphere. It is known that one such evolving world, the RNA world, preceded the world of DNA, RNA, and proteins. Scientists do not know how the RNA world came into existence. There are several theories, but none is as yet supported by strong experimental evidence. Ongoing research should provide an answer sometime in the early twenty-first century.

See also Darwinism.

Bibliography

Botta, O., and J. L. Bada. "Extraterrestrial Organic Compounds in Meteorites." *Surveys in Geophysics* 23 (2002): 411–467.

Darwin, C. R. "Letter to J. D. Hooker, [1 February] 1871. In *The Life and Letters of Charles Darwin*. Vol. II, ed. by F. Darwin [1898]. New York: Basic Books, 1959, pp. 202–203.

Darwin, Charles. *On the Origin of Species.*. London: John Murray, 1859.

Farley, J. *The Spontaneous Generation Controversy from Descartes to Oparin*. Baltimore: Johns Hopkins University Press, 1977.

Gilbert, W. "The RNA World." *Nature* 319 (1986): 618.

Johnston, W. K., P. J. Unrau, M. S. Lawrence, M. E. Glasner, and D. P. Bartel. "RNA-Catalyzed RNA Polymerization: Accurate and General RNA-Templated Primer Extension." *Science* 292 (2001): 1319–1325.

Joyce, G. F. "Nonenzymatic Template-Directed Synthesis of Informational Macromolecules." *Cold Spring Harb Symp Quant Biol* 52 (1987): 41–51.

Kasting, J. F., and L. L. Brown. "The Early Atmosphere as a Source of Biogenic Compounds." In *The Molecular Origins of Life*, edited by A. Brack, 35–56. New York: Cambridge University Press, 1998.

Miller, S. L. "A Production of Amino Acids Under Possible Primitive Earth Conditions." *Science* 117 (1953): 528–529.

Oparin, A. I. *The Origin of Life*. Translated by S. Morgulis. New York: Macmillan, 1938

Orgel, L. E. "The Origin of Life on the Earth." *Scientific American* 271 (1938): 52–61.

Oro, J., and A. Kimball. "Synthesis of Adenine from Ammonium Cyanide." *Biochem Biophys Res Commun* 2 (1960): 407–412.

Steitz, T. A., and P. B. Moore. "RNA, the First Macromolecular Catalyst: The Ribosome is a Ribozyme." *Trends Biochem Sci* 28 (2003): 411–418.

Leslie E. Orgel (2005)

LIFE, SANCTITY OF

See *Popper-Lynkeus, Josef*; *Suicide*

LIPPS, THEODOR
(1851–1914)

Theodor Lipps, a psychologist and philosopher, was born in Wallhalben, Rhineland-Palatinate. He studied theology and natural science at Erlangen, Tübingen, Utrecht, and Bonn. He obtained academic positions in Bonn (1884), Breslau (1890), and finally in Munich (1894), where he remained until his death. There he was a full professor and the teacher of Johannes Daubert and Alexander Pfänder, the founding members of the Munich circle of phenomenology. Lipps published voluminously on a large variety of topics, though his orientation in philosophy was consistently a psychological one.

In *Basic Facts of Mental Life* (1883) Lipps states his conception of philosophy as follows: "Inner experience is the basis for psychology, logic, aesthetics, ethics, and the adjunct disciplines, including metaphysics in the sense in which it is permissible to speak of it. We regard all these disciplines now as philosophical, and at least in the main they fill what is usually viewed as the range of tasks that we especially honor with the name of philosophical ones. Their objects are presentations, sensations, and volitional acts, and no intelligent person denies that such objects are different from the subject matters of other sciences and therefore require their own manner of scientific treatment" (p. 3). Thus he conceived of philosophy as equivalent to or based on psychology, with an emphasis on "inner perception."

This psychologal style of philosophy is also evident in Lipps's views on logic. These in particular became subject to attack in Husserl's critique of psychologism. By no means, however, was the close tie between philosophy and psychology unusual for the late nineteenth and early twentieth centuries. The empirically minded psychological turn that occurred in the German-speaking world at that time was an attempt to establish philosophy as a science amid the skepticism that was rife in the aftermath of the collapse of the speculative systems of German Idealism. Although Lipps's philosophical endeavors arose in this context, his approach to psychology differs significantly from the approaches of most of his contemporaries. He was, for example, willing to allow not only for inner perception but also for introspection or self-observation (*Selbstbeobachtung*), a notion that was unacceptable to many other philosopher-psychologists of the time, most notably Franz Brentano and his orthodox followers, for whom inner perception can never become self-observation.

The subject matter of psychology, according to Lipps, consists of conscious experiences (*Bewusstseinserlebnisse*), which always belong to an ego (*Ich*). It is, moreover, to be an empirical science. The ego to which conscious experiences belong—which is not to be confused with the soul (*Seele*)—is empirically given just as these experiences themselves are. "And the ego," Lipps significantly adds, "can intentionally direct its gaze upon itself. It can itself be an 'object'. It can grasp and cognize itself" (1909, p. 6). Although this acceptance of the notion of self-observation put him at odds with Brentano and other contemporaries, Lipps had much in common with Brentano, Dilthey, and others insofar as he distinguished between two aspects of psychology as an empirical science: one descriptive and analytical, the other explanatory. The latter can involve physiological considerations and laboratory experiments in order to provide causal explanations of how conscious experiences arise, whereas the former makes no use of physiology or experimentation. It was this descriptive or "pure" psychology that primarily interested Lipps.

Lipps's most outstanding and enduring contribution is his concept of empathy (*Einfühlung*). This idea is of special importance because it was adopted and critically revised in such phenomenological theories of intersubjectivity as those developed by Husserl and Edith Stein. By means of empathy we come to know not only other minds but also other important objects of experience, such as those belonging to organic nature and works of art. One empathizes when one puts oneself in the place of—and even to some extent imitates—someone or something else. Lipps asserted with particular emphasis, contrary to some of his critics, that our knowledge of other minds is first and foremost grounded in empathy and thus in feelings rather than in purely intellectual operations. The pervasive role that he gave to empathy in his wide-ranging philosophical investigations naturally led to panpsychism in metaphysics.

The philosophy that Lipps developed out of his psychological studies was by no means subjectivistic or relativistic. This was certainly not the case with his logic. Moreover, in both aesthetics and ethics he thought it was possible to formulate universally valid prescriptions on the basis of psychology. As the science of the beautiful—of that which evokes or is suited to evoke the feeling of beauty (*Schönheitsgefühl*)—aesthetics aims to establish the psychological conditions under which such a feeling arises. Ethics, according to Lipps, is concerned with universally valid morality (*Sittlichkeit*) as opposed to the morals (*Moral*) of this or that historical period, nation, class, or individual. A Kantian influence is evident in his ethical reflections, in which the moral person (*sittliche Persönlichkeit*) is given the status of the highest good. In spite of this influence from Kant, however, Lipps presented a philosophical viewpoint that should be considered on its own merits and not merely in the shadow of his predecessors.

See also Brentano, Franz; Husserl, Edmund; Pfänder, Alexander; Phenomenology.

Bibliography

Bokhove, Niels, and Karl Schuhmann. "Bibliographie der Schriften von Theodor Lipps." *Zeitschrift für philosophische Forschung* 45 (1991): 112–130.

Kesserling, Michael. "Theodor Lipps (1851–1914): Ein Beitrag zur Geschichte der Psychologie." *Psychologische Beiträge* 7 (1962): 73–100.

Lipps, Theodor. *Ästhetik. Psychologie des Schönen und der Kunst.* 2 vols. Hamburg/Leipzig: Leopold Voss, 1903/06.

Lipps, Theodor. *Grundtatsachen des Seelenlebens.* Bonn: Max Cohen & Sohn (Fr. Cohen), 1883.

Lipps, Theodor. *Leitfaden der Psychologie.* 3rd ed. Leipzig: Wilhelm Engelmann, 1909.

Lipps, Theodor. "Zur Einfühlung." In *Psychologische Untersuchungen.* Vol. 2. Edited by Theodor Lipps. Leipzig: Wilhelm Engelmann, 1913.

Robin D. Rollinger (2005)

LIPSIUS, JUSTUS
(1547–1606)

Justus Lipsius, the Flemish humanist, classical philologist, and literary critic, foremost interpreter of Stoicism in the later Renaissance, and the founder of modern neo-Stoicism, exercised a strong influence on later moral thought. Born near Louvain, he spent most of his life in exile. At the age of twenty-four, he renounced the Catholicism of his native land, accepting the chair of history and eloquence at the Protestant University of Jena (1572). After two years, he returned—ostensibly as a repentant Catholic and loyal Brabantian. Again forced to flee—this time to the Calvinist Dutch—and abjuring Catholicism a second time, he accepted the chair of history at Leiden (1579). Harassed constantly by political and religious pressures, he went to the University of Louvain, becoming one of its most prominent scholars.

The vicissitudes of his life began during the time of civil war in the Low Countries. His *Tacitus* appeared at Louvain the year after his return from Jena (1575), as did his *Antiquae Lectiones*. These commentaries on Plautus signaled his adoption of a literary style modeled after Plautus, Tacitus, and Seneca. Lipsius was profoundly influenced by the thought and prose style of Seneca and devoted the remainder of his life to the study of Stoicism. This work of Lipsius, in turn, influenced Michel Eyquem de Montaigne, Guillaume du Vair, and Pierre Charron, and in England, Francis Bacon and Joseph Hall.

The victories of Don John of Austria (Gembloux, 1578) caused Lipsius to flee to the home of his friend Christophe Plantin, and then from Antwerp to Leiden, where he became a Calvinist. Here appeared *De Constantia* (1584), an introduction to Stoicism and his most famous work. Another well-known work, *Politicorum Libri Sex* (1589), led to a bitter dispute over its advocacy of severe methods to curb unrest. His position again became intolerable; finally, he made his peace with the Jesuits (and his old friend Martin Delrio) at Mainz (1591) and returned to Catholic Europe. He accepted the chair of history and Latin literature at Louvain (1592) and was also appointed professor of Latin at the Collegium Trilingue. He published several pieces on miracles as testimonials of faith, which added little to his fame. A projected *Fax Historica*, on Greco-Roman history and the histories of the Jews, Egyptians, and others, was never completed, although several parts were published. His last works were *Manuductio ad Stoicam Philosophiam* (1604), a miscellany of Stoic moral doctrines and survey of the *Paradoxa;* and *Physiologia Stoicorum*, a careful study of the Stoic logic and physics (1604). These make clear that Lipsius was responsible for a restored Stoic philosophy and particularly for the reemphasis on natural philosophy. Although he counted himself more an eclectic than an orthodox follower of any school, Lipsius attempted to show in these works that there was no real difficulty in reconciling the Stoic *fatum* with the Christian emphasis on free will (whereas in *De Constantia*, this possibility had been rejected).

See also Bacon, Francis; Charron, Pierre; Humanism; Montaigne, Michel Eyquem de; Moral Epistemology; Renaissance; Seneca, Lucius Annaeus; Stoicism.

Bibliography

WORKS BY LIPSIUS

Opera Omnia. 4 vols. Wesel, 1675.

Tvvo Bookes of Constancie, edited by R. Kirk. Translated by Sir John Stradling. New Brunswick, NJ: Rutgers University Press, 1939.

WORKS ON LIPSIUS

Corbett, Theodore G. "The Cult of Lipsius: A Leading Source of Early Modern Spanish Statecraft." *Journal of the History of Ideas* 36 (1975): 139–152.

Croll, Morris W. "Juste Lipse et le mouvement anti-cicéronien à la fin du XVIIe siècle." *Revue du seizième siècle* 2 (1914): 200–242.

Long, A. A. "Stoicism in the Philosophical Tradition: Spinoza, Lipsius, Butler." In *Hellenistic and Early Modern Philosophy*, edited by Jon Miller. Cambridge, U.K.: Cambridge University Press, 2003.

Saunders, J. L. *Justus Lipsius: The Philosophy of Renaissance Stoicism*. New York: Liberal Arts Press, 1955.

Zanta, L. *La renaissance du stoicisme au XVIe siècle*. Paris: Champion, 1914.

Jason L. Saunders (1967)
Bibliography updated by Tamra Frei (2005)

LITERATURE, PHILOSOPHY OF

The concepts of fiction and of literature are distinct. On the one hand, there are nonfictional literary works—essays, memoirs, biographies, histories, writings about nature, and even philosophy. Perhaps we should also include some letter collections, diaries, and journals. On the other, there are nonliterary fictions both within and apart from the world of art. Cinema is full of fictional stories. Paintings represent fictional scenes. Advertising, whatever the medium it employs, often presents us with fictions. However, the concepts of fiction and literature are intertwined.

The paradigmatic literary works have steadily drifted toward being exclusively works of fiction: novels, stories, poems, and plays. When David Hume wanted to make his mark as a man of letters, he chose history and philosophy as his media. By comparison, Jean Paul Sartre made his literary mark with novels and plays while establishing his reputation as a philosopher with the contemporary equivalent of treatises and inquiries. Does this shift in literature's center of gravity reflect something important about it? Is there something about the value of literature that makes fictional works most apt to contain such value or is there perhaps an overlap between the value of fiction and literary value? We will discuss both concepts here, beginning with philosophical issues concerning fiction.

WHAT IS FICTION?

There are at least two senses of the word *fiction* that are easy to run together, but need to be distinguished for our present purpose. In one sense, a fiction can simply be a type of falsehood as when one says, "Your PhD is a fiction." By contrast, if one says that *Middlemarch* is a fiction, they are not saying that there is no such novel. They are saying that it is a certain type of book, story, or representation. It is true that there is such a book, story, or representation.

Unlike ambiguous words such as *bank*, there is probably some connection between the two senses of fiction, which explains the ease with which they are run together. Works of fiction typically contain an element of unreality. In reality, there is no such town as Middlemarch and no such people as the characters Dorothea or Casaubon who in the fiction inhabit the town. On another level, it is important to realize that the logical or semantic relationship between the two senses of fiction is loose. Fictions in the first sense can be lies and always involve falsehood. Works of fictions—a class of representations—are never lies, although they might just conceivably contain an intentional falsehood. They can refer to real things such as historical personages (Julius Caesar, Napoleon Bonaparte) and actual places (Rome, Moscow), and can contain truths about them.

The sense of fiction that primarily interests us is the second one, which refers to a class of works: works of fiction. Our job is to figure out what characterizes it and makes it distinct from other representations. Some have attempted to define fiction as a type of linguistic discourse. (Gale 1971, Urmson 1976). We know in advance that this is inadequate because of the ample existence of nonlinguistic fiction (see K. Walton [1990], for a survey and critique of this view). A second popular approach is to think of fiction as a form of pretense (though with no intent to deceive). This is on the right track, but the trick is to identify the right kind of pretense.

One might think that the standard function of a mode of representation such as language is to inform us about the actual world, to assert or show us things about it. Fiction could then be thought of as something derived from this standard use. Instead of actually asserting

something, a fictional story or its author pretends to assert it (Searle 1975). The problem with this version of the pretense view is that it is not always the right description of what artists are doing in their works. Consider a clear case of pretense: Someone is pretending to sing by lip-synching. They are doing one thing in order to pretend to do another. Is Eliot pretending to describe a real town by representing one that does not exist? That does not seem right. To adequately describe what Eliot is doing, it is enough to say that she is writing about an imaginary town. The problem is to say what *about* means in the previous sentence.

The make-believe view offers an answer (Walton 1990). In order to understand this view one has to recognize that make-believe is being used in a restricted, somewhat technical sense. Make-believe in the relevant sense involves two special features. First it involves props. Props are publicly accessible objects that guide imaginings. If, for example, children are playing school with dolls, the dolls are props. Second, make-believe, unlike some other imaginings, operates according to underlying rules about these props, which authorize or mandate certain imaginings. For example, the game of school might operate according to the rule that the number of students in the classroom is equal to the number of dolls arranged in a certain way.

According to the make-believe view, a work of fiction—whether it be a painting, novel, or poem—is a work that is intended or has the function of being a prop in a game of make-believe. What makes *Middlemarch* fictional is that it is a work—a novel in this case—intended to be or having the function of being a prop of the kind described above. It prescribes that we imagine certain things: that there is a town inhabited by such and such people. This is the sense in which it is *about* a town and its inhabitants.

The make-believe view has become one of the most widely held views about the nature of fiction (Currie 1990, Lamarque and Olsen 1994, Levinson 1996, Walton 1990), but it seems to count works as fictional items that are usually not so considered. Suppose that one writes an autobiography, but in such a way that the reader can vividly imagine the events of the writer's life. Then it appears that this work fulfills two functions. One is to inform the reader about the writer's life. A second is to enable the reader to engage in the kind of guided imagining that is constitutive of make-believe in the technical sense. Something similar happens in certain works of history and journalism, as well as nonfiction novels such as Truman Capote's *In Cold Blood*. All these works are props that authorize certain imaginings. There are some who claim that because of this, these works are fictional even if the primary purpose lies elsewhere. (Walton 1990). But this is counterintuitive: Historical novels are fictional; history is not, even if it uses techniques that produce guided imaginings. How are we to express the difference?

It might be suggested that fiction always presents some things to the imagination that are placed there simply for the purpose of being imagined. Whether or not they express truths or refer to items in the actual world is irrelevant to their proper functioning in the work. This need not be true in the nonfiction works just mentioned. This does not mean that fictions cannot contain some elements that are meant to express truth, or pick out actual people, places, or other things. It just means that not everything in the fictional work so functions. Even in a historical novel, where every character picks out a real person from the past, we are to imagine certain doings or conversations without worrying whether they occurred. So on the present proposal, something is a fiction if it is a work that is intended for, or has the function of, being a prop in a game of make-believe, and at least some of the things it mandates to be imagined are placed in the work just for the sake of being imagined.

FICTIONAL CHARACTERS

Works of fiction prescribe us to imagine people and their doings. Because of this, we say that such works, or their authors, create characters, about which we talk when describing and interpreting fictions. How should we understand such talk? How literally should we take it?

Consider the sentence, "Dorothea walked about the house with delightful emotion." A sentence such as this one normally refers to someone and says something about her, but if it appears in a work of fiction not about any actual personage, as this one does in *Middlemarch*, does it still refer to someone or, at least, to something? There are three answers to this question that currently have serious advocates: 1) the sentence still refers to someone, but a someone who does not exist; 2) the sentence does not refer to anyone, but it does refer to something (viz., a fictional character); 3) the sentence does not refer to anyone or anything.

Some proponents (Walton 1990, Lewis 1978) of the make-believe view hold the last view. Such a sentence refers to no one, but we make-believe that it does. In contrast, if we encounter in a work of fiction the sentence, "There was once a woman who was very happy," we may just make believe that there is some happy woman, at least until we are told more about her. An alternative way

of putting the third position is to say that, although the original sentence refers to nothing, it is fictionally true or true in the story that it does. (Adams, Stecker, Fuller 1997)

Proponents of the second view believe that such things as fictional characters actually exist. (Howell 1979, Lamarque and Olsen 1994, Thomasson 1999, van Inwagen 1977, Wolterstorff 1980). They posit such things more to explain the things we say about fiction than to explain fiction itself. They might even agree that the original sentence, as it occurs in the story, does not refer to anyone or anything. But in creating a work of fiction, we also create other things including characters. We can then go on to talk about them, compare them to other characters, quantify over characters, and so on. Consider the claim that Hamlet is one of the most enigmatic characters in literature. Here we appear to be saying something about Hamlet, not merely making believe something. Characters are not people, although fictional works speak of them as if they are.

The plausibility of this view hangs on whether we actually gain something by assuming fictional characters exist, that is denied to those who claim that we merely make-believe that people are being referred to in fictions, or who claim that it is merely true in the fiction, but not in reality, that such reference occurs. The latter would say that the enigmatic thing is what make believe the play *Hamlet* prescribes or what is true in the play. One thing that is gained by positing the existence of characters is a convenient way to express ourselves when we talk about fictions. The paraphrases of statements about characters in terms of what is true in a story or what make-believe is prescribed by a story will always be more cumbersome. In practice, we will always prefer character-talk. But that does not settle the question whether character-talk really refers to characters rather than works.

On the second view, characters are not what they appear to be. They are not princes, lovers, or detectives. They are not male or female. They are not people. Presumably they are abstract entities of some sort, the properties of which are all, in one way or another, parasitic on the properties of the works in which they appear. Dorothea has the property of being a character in *Middlemarch*. She, or rather it, also has the property of being ascribed the property of walking about with delightful emotion on a certain occasion. But Dorothea does not actually have the property of walking about with delightful emotion. Proponents of the first view find this counterintuitive. They claim that Dorothea is a person capable of ambulating, feeling emotion, and having a gender.

Middlemarch refers to her. In general, fictional works really do refer to people and other things, only often they are fictional people and other fictional things (i.e., people and things that do not exist) (Dilworth 2004, Parsons 1980, Zalta 1983, Zemach 1997). Dorothea and Hamlet do not exist, according to them. In this they agree with some of those who hold the make-believe view. But the people in this camp do not think that that is a reason to deny that we refer to fictional things. In fact, their chief claim is that we can refer to what does not exist including fictional people and places.

The straightforward way in which the first view treats characters is refreshing after the cumbersome paraphrases of the third view and the metaphysical abstractions of the second. Unsurprisingly, the straightforwardness comes with a cost: a highly unorthodox conception of reference. What is fair to call the majority view (which obviously does not mean it is the true one) is that one can only refer to what exists. When we refer to something, we pick it out, and what does not exist cannot be picked out because there is nothing to be picked out. If there were something, it would exist. The things we refer to are distinguished from others in virtue of their properties or characteristics, but nothing can have properties unless it exists in the first place. Existence is not just another property, but is the condition for having properties. What does (did, or will) not exist is nothing and so cannot have properties. If the first view is to get off the ground, it would have to show that the orthodox conception of reference is mistaken. Currently, there is no consensus about which of these views is the most plausible, but rather a lively, ongoing debate.

THE PARADOX OF FICTION

Whatever is the correct view regarding fictional characters, once we become imaginatively involved in stories, we develop feelings and attitudes that appear to be directed toward creatures of fiction. We commonly say that we fear Dracula, despise Casaubon, or admire Sherlock Holmes. Yet there is something paradoxical about this. Feeling fear normally involves believing both that there is something to be feared, and that it poses a danger. We do not believe that Dracula actually exists, or that he poses a danger. Yet we feel fear nevertheless.

None of the views about fictional characters discussed in the preceding section offers a solution to this paradox. Two of the three deny that characters exist. They lead us into, rather than resolve, the problem. Those who claim fictional characters exist, deny that they are people, monsters, or anything else that could stir us to feel as we do. Characters, on this view, are abstract entities, and fearing them would be akin to fearing the number five.

The paradox of fiction has provoked an enormous literature, and many proposed resolutions. Three will be discussed here. The first denies that the object of fear is really fictional. (Charlton 1984, Paskins 1977). When we say we despise Casaubon or admire Holmes, we mean that we despise or admire people like them. We despise self-absorbed people who care nothing even for those close to them. We admire people with intellects (but not necessarily opium addictions) such as Holmes. Factualism, as this view is sometimes called, has some truth to it, but it cannot solve the whole problem. We don't fear creatures such as Dracula because we have no more of a belief in vampires in general than we do in Dracula in particular. Equally important, many of the feelings we develop in the course of taking in a fictional work, are guided by the specific things we imagine as we do this, and for this reason do not generalize beyond the fiction. As Anna Karenina approaches the railroad station, we hope she will turn away rather than enter and throw herself under the train. This is not the hope that despairing lovers will turn away from train stations, or, more generally, will refrain from suicide.

A second view is a further development of the make-believe approach to fiction. (Walton 1990, Levinson 1996). The basic idea here is that fear of Dracula, for example, occurs within the game of the make-believe we play when watching a Dracula movie. Hence, it is not literally fear, any more than our thought that Dracula lives in Transylvania is literally a belief. Our make-believe may, nevertheless, be phenomenologically indistinguishable from fear. That is, it can involve the same physiological changes in the body, we can experience similar feelings, and we may have an attenuated desire to duck, hide, or flee. What we lack is the beliefs that we have with real fear, and the full range of desires and behavioral tendencies.

The last view, known as the thought theory, rebels at the idea that what we feel are not real emotions—for example, real fear. The chief claim here is that emotions such as fear and pity do not require a belief in the existence of the object of these emotions. The emotions can be caused by vivid imaginings as well (Carroll 1990, Dadlez 1997, Feagin 1996, Gron 1996, Lamarque 1996, Yanal 1999).

It is not clear that we need to take these last two views as offering genuinely distinct theories (Currie 1997). Proponents of the thought theory must admit that when imaginings cause fear, it is different in some important respects than belief-induced fear. In addition to the difference in propositional attitude (believing that versus imagining that) there are cognitive and behavioral differences as well. Proponents of the make-believe view are willing to admit we feel a real emotion, but deny it is literally fear or pity. So it is not clear that the argument between the make-believe view and the thought theory amounts to more than a dispute over the name we should give to the feelings that arise in our imaginative encounters with fiction. They appear to agree about the nature and cause of those feelings.

WHAT IS LITERATURE?

The nature of literature is just as much a matter of controversy as the nature of fiction. However, it is now widely accepted that certain definitions will not work. In the first half of the twentieth century there was the hope that literature could be defined as a special way of using language. Literature uses defamiliarized language, drawing attention to its own literary devices. (Beardsley 1958, Jakobson 1960, Wellek and Warren 1973). But on the one hand, literary works can adopt the form of any kind of writing, from the scientific report to the advertising jingle. And on the other, all sorts of nonliterary uses of language can be rife with literary devices such as figures of speech, rhetorical techniques, implicit meanings, and so on.

Three proposals will be considered for defining literature. The first defines literature in terms of a role it plays in society or a community within society. Something is a work of literature, on this view, if it is a piece of writing that fulfills this role. Different theorists in this camp define the relevant role differently. For some, the relevant community is the community of critics, and the relevant role is that of being deemed worthy, or simply being the object, of critical attention (Fish 1980). For others, the relevant community is society at large, and the relevant role is sustaining the structure of power in the society (Eagleton 1983). It is not clear, however, that this approach can succeed in defining literature, whatever insights underlie it. Consider the first version. Who are the critics in question and what does critical attention consist in? They are the literary critics of course rather than the interpreters of philosophical texts (unless they are literary interpreters of those texts from the right academic departments). There are two dangers here and it is virtually impossible to avoid both. One danger is circular definition. The critics are those whose job it is to attend to a certain body of works—works of literature. Alternatively, the critics are those who use certain techniques—but those techniques can and sometimes are used on all

sorts of things so that we get the extension of literature quite wrong.

A second approach asserts literature is a practice. Writers, readers, critics all enter into this practice by attempting to create, enjoy, or facilitate the appreciation of literary aesthetic value (Lamarque and Olsen 1994). To avoid circularity, literary aesthetic value is cashed out as the value to be found in the experience of a subject or story that has a humanly interesting content in virtue of embodying one or more perennial themes and that is given a complex form suitable to developing such a theme.

What seems right about this approach is the claim that the creation of literature is imbedded in a social practice with distinctive aims, institutions, and traditions. What is controversial about the approach is its conception of the practice in terms of aiming at a single kind of value in a way that has remained unchanged, at least since ancient Greece. When one thinks of all the various items that are relatively uncontroversial examples of literature, from ancient classics to eighteenth century essays to contemporary poetry, one must wonder whether the formula proposed by this definition really encompasses all of literature.

An alternative is to think of literature as a practice defined by an evolving set of values or functions and central art forms. Currently, these forms are the novel, short story, drama, and poetry, and in addition to their aesthetic value, we also characteristically value them in other ways such as for fulfilling certain cognitive functions, and for providing opportunities for open-ended interpretation. Anything that belongs to such an art form and is seriously intended to provide one or another of these values is a work of literature, but so are other pieces of writing that fulfill these valuable functions to a significant degree whether or not they are in one of the central literary forms. Finally, it should be recognized that our current concept of literature has itself evolved from earlier predecessor concepts, such as those of fine writing (belle lettres) and the ancient Greek or Latin classic. Items that fall under these predecessor concepts also belong to literature by a principle of inclusion implicit in our current concept. (Stecker 1996).

CRITICISM AND INTERPRETATION

Criticism is the blanket term for writing about or commenting on individual literary (or art) works. Being a blanket term, it covers different kinds of projects. One of the oldest kinds exists to orient an audience to new literary (artistic) productions as they appear. In doing this,

this kind of criticism fulfills a variety of distinct functions. It will typically identify the sort of work under discussion (e.g., an experimental novel in the manner of so and so), and acquaint a potential reader with important features of the work such as its style, plot, themes, and characters. Often implicit in these descriptions is an appreciative response (positive or negative) by the critic leading to an explicit evaluation of the work. The contemporary review is an example of this sort of criticism.

A different activity—that of analyzing and interpreting literary works—became a central critical activity in the twentieth century. This had a variety of causes. One was the rise of English and, more generally, literary studies, as an academic discipline. This generated a series of debates about the nature, content, value, and proper reception of such works, which associated a work with a great variety of ways of taking or reading it—in essence, a great variety of interpretations. Another factor was the growing prominence of difficult avant-garde works that are simply hard to understand. For such works at least, it is natural to turn to analysis and interpretation in order to understand and appreciate them. However, once we see how such analysis generates unexpected meanings or significance in these works, one suspects it might do so in any work, making any literary work a candidate for interpretation.

There are a variety of parameters along which approaches to interpreting literary works diverge. One that arose early on and has remained prominent concerns the significance of authorial intention in interpretation. Is the meaning of a work identical to such intentions, do they resolve ambiguities and other uncertainties in the work, or are they absolutely irrelevant to correctly interpreting it? Those who originally disagreed on this matter (Beardsley 1958 and 1970, Hirsch 1967) nevertheless did agree that the purpose of interpreting a work is to understand it better and that there is one best understanding that can in principle be attained. Notice there are two claims here: one about aim, one about number. These provide two further parameters about which literary theorists disagree.

Regarding the proper aim of interpretation, there are a variety of views. We have already mentioned one: understanding (Carroll 1992, Iseminger 1992, Juhl 1980, Margolis 1980, Stecker 2003). In some works, it is just difficult to grasp what is going on, and this can happen at all sorts of levels. A work can be hard to understand because of its historical or cultural distance from its audience. Alternatively, features of its style may make it difficult. There are poems where it is hard to understand what the individual lines mean. There are novels and stories where it is hard simply to follow the plot. There are others where, while it is clear that a certain series of events have transpired, there are different ways in which one could understand their significance in the story. More commonly, one knows what happens in a story or what the lines of a poem say, but one does not grasp their point or the point of various bits. There are many other ways in which one may feel one's understanding of a work is inadequate, but in all such cases one turns to interpretations of a work for greater clarity.

An alternative to understanding as the aim of interpretation, is appreciation. (Davies 1982, Goldman 1990, Lamarque 2002). The point of interpretation on this view is to create ways of taking works that enhance their aesthetic value, or that guide the reader to an appreciative experience. Just whether, and precisely how, these two aims really differ is debatable: How can one lead a reader to an appreciative experience, without offering a way of understanding a work by organizing certain features of it around a theme, by describing a character as representing a type of person, identifying the point of a series of images, and so on? The difference may be in the way one evaluates interpretations. If one's aim is understanding, perhaps one hopes to get things right, to give a correct or true interpretation, whereas if one aims to enhance the value of the work or an experience of it, the test of an interpretation is in the aesthetic enjoyment it offers to readers.

Those who think the aim of interpretation is enhanced appreciation, also tend to be pluralists about the number of acceptable interpretations a work can bear. Interpretations that are considered acceptable within this camp range from those strictly constrained by conventions in place when the work was created (Davies 1996) to a virtual free play with a text (Barthes 1989). Among those who claim that the aim of interpretation is understanding, some, such as M. Beardsley and E.D. Hirsch, are monists arguing there is a single ultimately correct understanding of a work, whereas others are pluralists. A number of writers argue that meaning is relative to the constantly changing historical moment in which the work is received (Gadamer 1975, Margolis 1980), to the responses of readers in the face of textual indeterminacy (Iser 1980), or to the assumptions of critical communities (Fish 1980; Carrier 1991).

All such relativist views imply pluralism regarding correct understanding, although pluralism does not imply relativism. An alternative to relativism about a work's meaning is a pluralism about the acceptable aims of interpretation (Stecker 1997 and 2003). Not all interpretation aims at recovering the meaning of a work. Some legitimately aims at enhancing appreciation, making a work significant to a contemporary audience, or to filling in indeterminacies in optional ways. These projects can clearly be pursued in a plurality of ways. By contrast if one's aim is to recover the intention with which the work was made, that may be a more monistic project. Perhaps, among these interpretive aims, there is one that attempts to identify a historically correct understanding of a work. There are currently a variety of proposals about what this might be (Carroll 2000, Levinson 1996, Stecker 2003).

THE VALUE OF FICTION AND LITERATURE

At the beginning of this entry, we noted that, though fiction and literature are not the same thing, the paradigmatic literary forms today are all types of fiction: poetry, the novel, the short story, and the drama. The question we raised then and turn to now is what it is about the value of literature that makes fictional work the most typical to possess that value. Is it that the value of fiction and literature tend to overlap?

The philosophical debate about the value of literature might be aptly described as between those who answer this last question affirmatively and those who answer it negatively. Fiction, clearly, can serve all sorts of purposes, and we might value it for its function in almost any of these. The chief vehicle by which it achieves these valuable purposes is imaginative engagement (i.e., the make-believe that is intimately involved in the reception of fiction). Whether or not imaginative engagement is valuable in itself, it can quickly lead to things we clearly value (e.g., the pleasure of following a story and imaginatively participating in its world).

In addition to such pleasures, imaginative engagement can also be valuable in other ways. It is plausible that it can enhance valuable abilities: to make fine discriminations, to put ourselves in the shoes of others (to empathize), and to refine the ability to identify emotional and other psychological states. A fiction also might at least contribute to acquiring propositional knowledge. What is true in a fictional world is commonly at least possibly true in the actual world. Thus we can acquire knowledge of possibilities or conceptions of how things may be. A fiction may strongly suggest that something is not only possible, but that it actually is that way, and this may help us to learn about the way things not only might be, but are.

Clearly, all of these valuable traits of fiction can be possessed by literary works, fictional or not, but we can go further and say that literary fictions are the most likely to possess, in the highest degree, the cognitive values just mentioned. While not everyone would accept this, the more controversial issue concerns whether such traits add to the literary or artistic value of these works. A view that denies this claims instead that literary value resides wholly in the aesthetic experience a work offers, where this experience is fairly narrowly conceived. For example, one view that has been vigorously defended is that the aesthetic value of a work lies in its ability to create a complex form that explores a theme of perennial human interest (Lamarque and Olsen 1994). The appreciative experience, which determines the extent to which a work possesses aesthetic value, consists in following the development of the theme in the complex formal structure of the work. What is no part of the literary value is any insight the work might offer regarding the truth about the issues it explores.

This view has the virtue of serving as a corrective to the rejection of the relevance of the aesthetic, even suspicion about its place among the central human values, that has infected large swaths of literary theory (Eagleton 1983, Scholes 1978). However, even as an account of the aesthetic value of literature, it is far too narrow. For one thing, the perennial themes—fate, free will, nature versus nurture—just are not the organizing features of all literature. Some works are more concerned with characters, some with telling a riveting story, some with exhibiting an emotion, some with precise description, and so on. Perhaps we can say that every literary work offers a conception of some aspect of human experience, and when it is good literature, it does so in such a way that one can experience what it would be like if that conception were true (Stecker 1997). However, having said this, it becomes fairly obvious that it is perverse to deny that a further way that literature can be valuable is in the cognitive value of the conceptions offered. They can be valuable for getting it right, but also for suggesting new ways of thinking or experiencing, fruitful conjectures, as it were, even if they turn out to be ultimately wrong. After all we value philosophical works for just this reason, and there are many literary works that have overtly philosophical aims.

Just as fiction can be valuable in many ways, pluralism about literary value also seems to be the most sensible view. When literary works are evaluated not only for the aesthetic experience they offer, but the cognitive, ethical, art-historical value that they possess—to mention only some additional parameters that are relevant—we are still evaluating them as literary works. Those who argue that interpretations of literary works should maximize the opportunities to appreciate them should welcome this point of view because it opens up so many new avenues from which such appreciation can develop.

See also Art, Interpretation of; Derrida, Jacques; Gadamer, Hans-Georg; Hermeneutics; Structuralism and Post-Structuralism.

Bibliography

Adams, Fred, Robert Stecker, and Gary Fuller. *The Semantics of Fictional Names.* Pacific Phiosophical Quarterly. 78 (1997): 128–48.

Barthes, Roland. *The Pleasure of the Text.* New York: Farrar, Strauss, Giroux, 1989.

Beardsley, M. *Aesthetics: Problems in The Philosophy of Criticism.* Harcourt: Brace and World, 1958.

Beardsley, M. *The Possibility of Criticism.* Detroit, MI: Wayne State University Press, 1970.

Carrier, David. *Principles of Art History.* University Park, PA: Penn State Press, 1991.

Carroll, N. "Art, Intention, and Conversation. " In *Intention and Interpretation,* edited by G. Iseminger. Philadelphia: Temple University Press, 1992.

Carroll, N. "Interpretation and Intention." *Metaphilosophy.* 31 (2000): 75–95.

Carroll, N. *The Philosophy of Horror, or Paradoxes of The Heart.* New York: Routledge, Chapman, and Hall, 1990.

Charlton, W. "Feeling for the Fictitious." *British Journal of Aesthetics* 24 (1984): 206–16.

Currie, G. *The Nature of Fiction.* Cambridge, MA: Cambridge University Press, 1990.

Currie, G. "The Paradox of Caring." In *Emotion and The Arts,* edited by M. Hjort and S. Laver. Oxford: Oxford University Press, 1997.

Dadlez, E. *What's Hecuba to Him? Fictional Events and Actual Emotions.* University Park: Pennsylvania State University Press, 1997.

Davies, S. "Interpreting Contextualities." *Philosophy and Literature* 20 (1996): 20–38.

Davies, S. "The Relevance of Painters' and Writers' Intentions." *Journal of Aesthetics and Art Criticism* 41 (1982): 65–76.

Dilworth, J. *The Double Content of Art.* Amherst, NY: Prometheus Books, 2004.

Eagleton, T. *Literary Theory.* Oxford: Blackwell, 1983.

Emt, J. "On the Nature of Fictional Entities." In *Understanding the Arts,* edited by J. Emt and G, Hermeran. Lund University Press, 1992.

Feagin, S. *Reading with Feeling.* Ithaca, NY: Cornell University Press, 1996.

Fish, Stanley. *Is There a Text in This Class?* Cambridge, MA: Harvard University Press, 1980.

Gadamer, H. *Truth and Method.* New York: Crossroads, 1975.

Gale, R. "The Fictive Use of Language." *Philosophy* 46 (1971): 324–339.

Goldman, Alan. "Interpreting Art and Literature." *Journal of Aesthetics and Art Criticism.* 48 (1990): 205–214.

Gron, E. 1996. "Defending Thought Theory from a Make-Believe Threat." *British Journal of Aesthics* 36 (1996): 311–312.

Hirsch, E. D. *Validity in Interpretation.* New Haven, CT: Yale University Press, 1967.

Howell, R. "Fictional Objects: How They Are and How They Aren't." *Poetics* 8 (1979): 129–177.

Iseminger, Gary. 1992. "An Intentional Demonstration?" In *Intention and Interpretation,* edited by G. Iseminger. Philadelphia: Temple University Press, 1992.

Iser, W. *The Act of Reading: A Theory of Aesthetic Response.* Baltimore, MD: Johns Hopkins University Press, 1980.

Jakobson, R. "Closing Statement: Linguistics and Poetics." In *Style in Language,* edited by T. Soebok. Cambridge, MA: MIT Press, 1960.

Juhl, P. D. *Interpretation: An Essay in The Philosophy of Literary Criticism.* Princeton, NJ: Princeton University Press, 1980.

Lamarque, P. "Appreciation and Literary Interpretation." In *Is There a Single Right Interpretation?,* edited by Michael Krausz. University Park, PA: Penn State Press, 2002.

Lamarque, P. *Fictional Points of View.* Ithaca, NY: Cornell University Press, 1996.

Lamarque, P., and S. Olsen. *Truth, Fiction, and Literature.* Oxford: Oxford University Press, 1994.

Levinson, J. *The Pleasures of Aesthetics.* Ithaca, NY: Cornell University Press, 1996.

Lewis, D. "Truth in Fiction." *American Philosophical Quarterly* 15 (1978): 37–46.

Margolis, J. *Art and Philosophy.* Brighton: Harvester Press, 1980.

Nussbaum, M. *Love's Knowledge.* Oxford: Oxford University Press, 1990.

Parsons, T. *Nonexistent Objects.* New Haven, CT: Yale University Press, 1980.

Paskins, B. "On Being Moved by Anna Karenina and Anna Karenina." *Philosophy* 52 (1977): 344–377.

Scholes, R. "Toward a Semiotics of Literature." In *What Is Literature?,* edited by P. Hernandi. Bloomington: Indiana University Press, 1978.

Searle, John. "The Logical Status of Fictional Discourse." *New Literary History* 6 (1975): 319–332.

Stecker, R. *Artworks: Definition, Meaning, Value.* University Park, PA: Penn State Press, 1997.

Stecker, R. *Interpretation and Construction: Art, Speech, and The Law.* Oxford: Blackwell, 2003.

Stecker, R. "What Is Literature?" *Revue Internationale de Philosophie* 50 (1996): 661–694.

Thomasson, Amie. *Fiction and Metaphysics.* Cambridge, MA: Cambridge University Press, 1999.

Urmson, J. O. "Fiction." *American Philosophical Quarterly* 13 (1976): 153–157.

van Inwagen, Peter. "Creatures of Fiction." *American Philosophical Quarterly* 14 (1977): 299–308.

Walton, K. *Mimesis as Make-Believe.* Cambridge, MA: Harvard University Press, 1990.

Wellek, R., and A. Warren. *The Theory of Literature.* 3rd ed. London: Penguin, 1973.

Wolterstorff, Nicholas. *Works and Worlds of Art.* Oxford: Oxford University Press, 1980.

Yanal, R. *Paradoxes of Emotion and Fiction*. University Park: Pennsylvania State University Press, 1999.

Zalta, E. *Abstract Objects*. Dordrecht: Reidel, 1983.

Zemach, Eddy. *Real Beauty*. University Park: Pennsylvania State University Press, 1997.

Robert Stecker (2005)

LITTRÉ, ÉMILE
(1801–1881)

Émile Littré, the French linguist and positivist philosopher, was born in Paris. From an early age Littré was interested in medicine and languages; and he received training in both. He is now best known for his *Dictionnaire de la langue française* (4 vols., Paris, 1863–1872) and his edition (with Charles Robin) of Pierre Hubert Nysten's *Dictionnaire de médecine, de chirurgie, de pharmacie, de l'art vétérinaire et des sciences qui s'y rapportent* (Paris, 1885). He was also prominent in radical political journalism (in *Le national* of Armand Carrel) and in freethinking circles. He became a member of the Académie des Inscriptions in 1838 and of the Académie Française in 1871, the latter over the violent objections of Bishop Dupanloup of Orléans. Littré was elected a deputy in 1871 and a senator for life in 1875.

These various activities and contacts enabled Littré to be unusually successful in his principal philosophical activity, the propagation of Auguste Comte's Positivism. He began to read Comte's *Cours de philosophie positive* in 1840, wrote a series of articles on it in *Le national* in 1844 and 1845 (published separately under the title *De la philosophie positive* in 1845 and later reprinted in his *Fragments de philosophie positive et de sociologie contemporaine* in Paris in 1876), and for a time became Comte's "principal disciple" and heir apparent as Director of Positivism and High Priest of the Religion of Humanity. Littré broke with Comte in 1852, however, over a combination of personal and political disagreements. Thereafter he took an increasingly independent line on Comte's doctrine as well, forming a loose group of disciples—distinct from the orthodox Comtian school—that found its principal expression in the journal *La philosophie positive*, started by Littré (with G. N. Vyrubov, the Russian positivist) in 1867. Littré himself contributed numerous important articles to the journal, but his position is stated most clearly in his *Auguste Comte et la philosophie positive* (Paris, 1863).

Littré's fundamental proposition was that during the 1840s, partly for personal reasons, Comte had abandoned the positive method for the sake of a "subjective" method that vitiated all his subsequent work. Littré proposed to cleanse Positivism of the "aberrations" of Comte's "second career" by propagating the doctrine in the pure, scientific form of the *Cours*. He insisted that "there is only one stable point and that is science." Positivism as a scientific philosophy is in one aspect a system, "which comprehends everything that is known about the world, man, and societies," and in another aspect a method, "including within itself all the avenues by which these things have become known." It has, however, a practical purpose as well: to provide a "demonstrable rallying point" and a "definite direction" for humankind. Littré differed from Comte in doubting whether Positivism was yet sufficiently advanced to serve as a basis for social and political action. He also, among other things, denied ethics its place at the apex of the hierarchy of the sciences, which Comte in his later years had given it; for Littré, ethics was not an autonomous science at all. On the other hand, Littré was inclined, against Comte, to admit psychology as an independent discipline. Littré remained committed to the evolution of the positivist Religion of Humanity into a "spiritual power" but rejected Comte's prescriptions for its actual institutionalization.

Littré and his group often found it difficult to elaborate a consistent doctrine, largely because Comte's system had in fact been conceived as a unity very early in his career, and it was therefore wrong and illogical to divide his life and work in half.

See also Comte, Auguste; Positivism; Psychology.

Bibliography

Littré's important works also include *Conservation, révolution et positivisme* (Paris, 1852; 2nd ed., 1879) and *La science au point de vue philosophique* (Paris, 1873).

For information on Littré, see É. Caro, *M. Littré et le positivisme* (Paris, 1883), which is hostile.

W. M. Simon (1967)

LLOYD, GENEVIEVE
(1941–)

Born in Cootamundra in New South Wales, Australia, Genevieve Lloyd studied philosophy at the University of Sydney and then at Oxford. Her DPhil, awarded in 1973, was on Time and Tense. From 1967 until 1987 she lectured at the Australian National University, and it was during this period that she developed her most influential ideas and wrote *The Man of Reason: "Male" and "Female" in Western Philosophy*, which was published in 1984. In 1987 she was appointed to the Chair of Philosophy at the University of New South Wales and was the first female professor of philosophy appointed in Australia.

Lloyd's contribution to feminist thought owes a good deal to Simone de Beauvoir. This is despite the fact that in *The Man of Reason* she is critical of Beauvoir's adoption of the pursuit of transcendence as the ideal of human excellence. Lloyd argues in this book that the historical notion of transcendence involves overcoming the body, which is represented as feminine, and so is a suspect value for women. At the same time her analysis of the symbolic meaning of philosophical concepts echoes Beauvoir. She follows Beauvoir in representing symbols as fundamentally dualistic, citing the Pythagorean table of opposites alluded to by Beauvoir in *The Second Sex*. Both agree that for the Pythagoreans, the male is associated with order and the right, light, and rational realm while the female corresponds to chaos and the left, dark, and irrational side of being. In an article published in *Australian Feminist Studies* in 1989, Lloyd explains that when Beauvoir speaks of woman as *other* she "is talking about the way culture has constructed the feminine—about its symbolic content" (p. 17). Likewise, Lloyd has been concerned with the ramifications of male power in the construction and control of symbolic structures. Unlike Beauvoir, however, she finds problematic the adoption by women of values traditionally symbolized as masculine. Yet she also shies away from a full endorsement of those strands of feminism of difference, which celebrate the body, emotion, and unreason as sources of essentially female values.

Though emphasizing the metaphorical association of reason with the male and reason's opposites and inferiors with the female, Lloyd is careful to avoid claiming that reason is *literally* male. In her concluding remarks to *The Man of Reason*, she says: "The claim that Reason is male need not at all involve sexual relativism about truth, or any suggestion that principles of logical thought valid for men do not hold also for female reasoners" (Lloyd 1984, p. 109). Nevertheless, she wants to avoid treating the maleness of reason as a *mere metaphor* that can easily be stripped away from the ideal of rationality. Alluding to Michèle Le Doeuff's (1948–) claim that the metaphors and images used by philosophers constitute a philosophical imaginary of marginalized tropes integral to the commitments of a text, she undermines the distinction between the literal and metaphorical. Elsewhere she evokes Jacques Derrida's deconstruction of the philosophical distinction between literal truth and metaphorical embellishment. However, Lloyd has not developed a detailed analysis of the relationship between metaphor, literal truth, rational argument, and literary effect, and this lends a certain obscurity to her position.

Despite having inspired Lloyd's line of argument, Le Doeuff has been critical of Lloyd's analysis of Francis Bacon's metaphors, arguing that the association between reason and masculinity discussed by Lloyd and found in the twentieth-century translation of Bacon is not to be found in Bacon's Latin original. She suggests in *The Sex of Knowing* that in general, historical claims that women are irrational are (false) literal claims intended to undermine women's intellectual authority.

Lloyd argues that Cartesian dualism is particularly problematic for feminism, and in her edited collection *Feminism and History of Philosophy*, sums up this suspicion. "What made the Cartesian philosophy suspect for feminists was its association with the doctrine of dualism—the rigid separation of minds and bodies as utterly distinct kinds of being. The dichotomy came to be seen as reinforcing the denigration of women, in association with the body, in opposition to the ideal of reason associated with "male 'transcendence'" (Lloyd 2000, p. 9). In her later work, Lloyd urges the fruitfulness for feminism of Benedict de Spinoza's treatment of the mind as an idea of the body, which she interprets as an ontological doctrine that undermines the polarities of the Cartesian tradition. During the 1990s she turned to working on Spinoza and published a number of books on his thought.

It is nevertheless questionable whether Cartesian dualism is literally a suspect metaphysical doctrine for feminists or whether Spinoza's form of monism would serve women better. Feminist historians such as Margaret Atherton (1943–) and Hilda Smith (1941–) have argued that historically, dualism has favored feminism. Even prior to René Descartes, women such as Christine de Pizan (1365–1431) were able to point to the immateriality of the soul as evidence that women's souls were the same as men's and so women were men's spiritual equals. Moreover, Descartes's method, with its reliance on reason and clear and distinct ideas, was accessible to women who had not had a university education. Descartes was not himself a misogynist; he took seriously the arguments of his correspondent the Princess Elizabeth of Bohemia (1630–1714), and his philosophy ushered in a period during which significant numbers of women engaged with the new philosophy.

The impact the perennial but by no means universal association between the mind and a masculine master ought to have on one's views concerning the literal materiality of the soul remains obscure. Lloyd's seminal critique of the rhetoric of the male philosophical tradition has been widely influential. The consequences that one should draw from that critique, and its significance for feminism and metaphysics, remain contested.

See also Bacon, Francis; Beauvoir, Simone de; Cartesianism; Derrida, Jacques; Descartes, René; Pythagoras and Pythagoreanism; Spinoza, Benedict (Baruch) de.

Bibliography

Atherton, Margaret. "Cartesian Reason and Gendered Reason." In *A Mind of One's Own: Feminist Essays on Reason and Objectivity*, edited by Louise M. Antony and Charlotte Witt, 19–34. Boulder, CO: Westview Press, 1993.

Beauvoir, Simone de. *The Second Sex*. Translated by H. M. Parshley. Harmondsworth: Penguin, 1983.

Broad, Jacqueline. *Women Philosophers of the Seventeenth Century*. Cambridge, U.K.: Cambridge University Press, 2002.

Le Doeuff, Michèle. *The Sex of Knowing*. London: Routledge, 2003.

Lloyd, Genevieve, ed. *Feminism and History of Philosophy, Oxford Readings in Feminism*. Oxford: Oxford University Press, 2002.

Lloyd, Genevieve. " Feminism in History of Ideas: Appropriating the Past." In *The Cambridge Companion to Feminism in Philosophy*, edited by Miranda Fricker and Jennifer Hornsby, 165–172. Cambridge, U.K.: Cambridge University Press, 2000.

Lloyd, Genevieve. "Maleness, Metaphor, and the Crisis of Reason." In *A Mind of One's Own*, edited by Louise M. Antony and Charlotte Witt, 69–83. Boulder, CO: Westview Press, 1993.

Lloyd, Genevieve. *The Man of Reason: "Male" and "Female" in Western Philosophy*. London: Methuen, 1984.

Lloyd, Genevieve. *Part of Nature: Self-knowledge in Spinoza's Ethics*. Ithaca, NY: Cornell University Press, 1994.

Lloyd, Genevieve. "Rationality." In *A Companion to Feminist Philosophy*, edited by Alison M. Jaggar and Iris Marion Young, 165–172. Oxford: Blackwell, 1998.

Lloyd, Genevieve. *Spinoza and the Ethics, Routledge Philosophy Guidebook*. London: Routledge, 1996.

Lloyd, Genevieve. "Texts, Metaphors, and the Pretensions of Philosophy." *Monist* 69 (1986): 87–102.

Lloyd, Genevieve. "Woman as Other: Sex, Gender, and Subjectivity." *Australian Feminist Studies* 10 (1989): 13–22.

Pizan, Christine de. *The Book of the City of Ladies*. Translated by Earl Jeffrey Richards. London: Picador, 1983.

Smith, Hilda L. *Reason's Disciples: Seventeenth Century English Feminists*. Urbana: University of Illinois Press, 1982.

Karen Green (2005)

LOCKE, JOHN
(1632–1704)

John Locke, English empiricist and moral and political philosopher, was born in Wrington, Somerset. Locke's father, an attorney and for a time a clerk to the justices of the peace in Somerset, fought on the parliamentary side in the first rebellion against Charles I. Locke was reared in a liberal Puritan family and early learned the virtues of temperance, simplicity, and aversion to display. Though his father was severe and remote from him in early youth, as Locke matured they became close friends.

In 1646 Locke entered Westminster School, where he studied the classics, Hebrew, and Arabic. Little time was given at Westminster to science and other studies, and its harsh discipline, rote learning, and excessive emphasis on grammar and languages were later condemned by Locke.

In 1652 Locke was elected to a studentship at Christ's Church, Oxford. He received his BA in 1656 and remained in residence for the master's degree. He was not happy with the study of Scholastic philosophy and managed to inform himself of many new areas of thought. As a master, Locke lectured in Latin and Greek and in 1664 was appointed censor of moral philosophy.

His father's death in 1661 left Locke with a small inheritance and some independence. During these years he became acquainted with many men who were to have a profound influence upon his life. From Robert Boyle, Locke learned about the new sciences and the corpuscular theory, as well as the experimental and empirical methods. Confronted with the choice of taking holy orders, continuing as a don, or entering another faculty, Locke chose medicine. Though well trained, he never practiced medicine, nor was he permitted to take the medical degree, which would have permitted him to teach the profession, until 1674, although in 1667 he began to collaborate with the great physician Thomas Sydenham.

In 1665 Locke was sent on a diplomatic mission accompanying Sir Walter Vane to the elector of Brandenburg at Cleves. He subsequently rejected a secretaryship under the earl of Sandwich, ambassador to Spain, and returned to Oxford. It was at this time that his interests began to turn seriously to philosophy. Descartes was the first philosopher whom Locke enjoyed reading and the first to show him the possibility of viable alternatives to the Schoolmen.

Locke had met Lord Ashley, earl of Shaftesbury, in 1662 at Oxford. They found much pleasure in each other's company, and the astute Shaftesbury quickly recognized Locke's talents. In 1667 he invited Locke to live with him in London as his personal physician. Later Locke served him well in many other capacities. Under Shaftesbury Locke found himself in the center of the political and practical affairs of the day. He assisted Shaftesbury in the framing of a constitution for the colony of Carolina. For a time he was secretary for the presentation of benefices and then secretary to the Council of Trade and Plantations. Locke was always at home in the world of practical affairs, and many of his philosophical attitudes reflect this interest. At the same time he became a fellow in the Royal Society, where he continued to be in touch with learning.

Locke, never robust in health, in 1675 went on a prolonged visit to France, where he made many friends and came into contact with the foremost minds of his day. His studies and criticisms of Descartes were deepened under the influence of various Gassendists.

In 1679 Locke returned to an England torn by intense political conflicts. Shaftesbury, who had become the leader of the parliamentary opposition to the Stuarts, alternated between political power and impotence. The close association with Shaftesbury brought Locke under suspicion; he was kept under surveillance. Shaftesbury was tried for treason in 1681, but acquitted. He subsequently fled England for Holland, where he died in 1683. Locke, at Oxford, uncertain of his position and fearing persecution, also fled England, arriving in Holland in September 1683. The king had demanded that Locke be deprived of his studentship at Oxford, and news of this demand caused Locke to prolong his stay. After the death of Charles II and the ascension of James II to the throne, the duke of Monmouth attempted a rebellion, which failed. Locke was denounced as a traitor, and the crown demanded of the Dutch that he be returned to England. No great effort was made to comply with the demand, and Locke remained in Holland.

During his stay in Holland, Locke again acquired a wide circle of distinguished friends and wrote extensively. He contributed an article as well as reviews to the *Bibliothèque universelle* of Jean Leclerc; these were his first published works. He wrote in Latin the *Epistola de Tolerantia*, which was published anonymously in 1689 and translated as the *First Letter concerning Toleration*. He also worked assiduously on *An Essay concerning Human Understanding*, which he had been writing off and on since 1671. In 1688 the *Bibliothèque universelle* published an abstract of the *Essay*.

These activities did not prevent him from being deeply engaged in politics. The plot to set William of Orange on the throne of England was well advanced in 1687, and Locke was, at the very least, advising William in some capacity. The revolution was accomplished in the fall of 1688, and in February 1689 Locke returned to England, escorting the princess of Orange, who later became Queen Mary.

In 1689 and 1690 Locke's two most important works, *An Essay concerning Human Understanding* and *Two Treatises of Government*, were published. From 1689 to 1691 Locke shuttled between London and Oates, the home of Sir Francis and Lady Masham, the daughter of Ralph Cudworth. He had declined an ambassadorial post only to accept a position as commissioner on the Board of Trade and Plantations. Apparently his practical wisdom was invaluable, for when he wished in 1697 to resign because of ill health, he was not permitted to do so. He remained until 1700, serving when he could, although his health was extremely poor.

In 1691 Locke made Oates his permanent residence at the invitation of Lady Masham. It was, for the aging Locke, a place of refuge and joy; there he received visits from Newton, Samuel Clarke, and others. These were productive years for Locke. *Some Thoughts concerning Education* appeared in 1693. The second edition of *Essay* was published in 1694. In the following year *The Reasonableness of Christianity* was published anonymously. He answered criticism of it in *A Vindication of the Reasonableness of Christianity* (London, 1695) and in a second *Vindication* in 1697. From 1697 to 1699 Locke engaged in an epistolary controversy with Edward Stillingfleet, bishop of Worcester.

However, Locke's health steadily failed him. After 1700, when the fourth edition of *Essay* appeared, he remained almost constantly at Oates. He was engaged in editing *Two Treatises of Government*, for no edition which pleased him had yet appeared. In his last years he wrote extensive commentaries on the epistles of St. Paul, which were published posthumously. On October 28, 1704, while Lady Masham was reading the Psalms to him, Locke died. Lady Masham wrote of him, "His death was like his life, truly pious, yet natural, easy and unaffected."

CHARACTER. The Lovelace Collection of Locke's personal papers in the Bodleian Library, Oxford, shows that Locke's character and personality were more complex than had been suspected. The great affection and respect which so many men and women had for him are testimony to his charm and wisdom. That he was modest, prudent, pious, witty, and eminently practical was long known. But he was also extremely secretive and apparently given to excessive suspicion and fears. When his lifelong friend, James Tyrrell, voiced his suspicion that Locke had written *Two Treatises*, Locke was evasive and would not admit the fact. When he suspected that Tyrrell was spreading the report that Locke was the author, Locke angrily demanded an explanation. At the same time, Locke showed great affection for many friends and a real fondness for children. In maturity he could not abide religious intolerance or suffer tyranny. He was passionately devoted to truth and strove constantly to state the truth as he saw it, but always with a caution that distrusted all dialectic, even his own, when it appeared to go beyond common sense.

INFLUENCES ON LOCKE. Locke's philosophy is grounded in medieval thought, though he, like Descartes, turned away from it as far as possible. The Cambridge Platonists, notably Ralph Cudworth and Benjamin Whichcote, influenced him greatly with respect to religious tolerance, empirical inquiry, and the theory of knowledge. Locke was indebted to Richard Hooker in his political thought. Hobbes probably influenced him somewhat, though Locke was concerned not to be classed as a Hobbist. The two most important philosophical influences upon him were Descartes and Pierre Gassendi. From Descartes he learned much that is incorporated in *Essay*, and in Gassendi and the Gassendists he found support to challenge the doctrine of innate ideas and the radical rationalistic realism of Descartes. Gassendi helped to convince Locke both that knowledge begins in sensation and that intellect, or reason, is essential to the attainment of truth and knowledge.

AN ESSAY CONCERNING HUMAN UNDERSTANDING

Locke's position in the history of Western thought rests upon *An Essay concerning Human Understanding* and *Two Treatises of Government*. He spent long years working out the thought of each, and he carefully and lovingly revised and corrected them for subsequent editions. Locke wrote two drafts of his *Essay* in 1671, and in 1685 he wrote a third. The first edition, though dated 1690, appeared in late 1689. During the years between 1671 and 1689, Locke revised and reorganized many of his original concepts. In response to criticisms of the first edition of *Essay*, he introduced a number of changes in subsequent editions. This long period of gestation and Locke's subsequent modifications of his initial public statement disclose primarily the refinement and clarification of his philosophy by way of certain important additions, but never by a radical or fundamental departure from his basic position.

From the first appearance of *An Essay concerning Human Understanding* Locke was criticized for being inconsistent in his theory of knowledge, vague in the presentation and development of many of his ideas, and wanting in thoroughness in developing other ideas. But these criticisms have in no way diminished either the importance or the influence of *Essay* on subsequent thinkers. By no means the first of the British empiricists, Locke nonetheless gave empiricism its firmest roots in British soil, where it still proudly flourishes. It must be remembered that Locke was also a rationalist, though one of quite different orientation from such Continental thinkers as Descartes, Spinoza, and Malebranche. In Locke many strands of traditional thought are rewoven into a new fabric. Subsequent thinkers, notably Berkeley, Hume, and Kant, perhaps fashioned more coherent and consistent systems, but it is doubtful whether they were more adequate to what Locke might have called the plain facts.

Locke's tendency toward inconsistency can be seen in his definition of knowledge as "the perception of the connection and agreement, or disagreement and repugnancy, of any of our ideas" (*Essay*, IV.i.2). This is plainly incompatible with his later contention that we have intuitive knowledge of our own existence, demonstrative knowledge of God's existence, and sensitive knowledge of the existence of particular things. Nonetheless, Locke would not abandon his position for the sake of consistency alone. He was persuaded that common sense and the facts justified his conviction and that whatever faults there were in his position lay in the difficulty of stating a coherent theory of knowledge, not in the reality of things. If this made him an easy prey to a skillful dialectician, like Berkeley, it also left him closer to the common conviction of most of us when we think about anything other than epistemology. It is this viewpoint, almost unique in philosophy, that accounts for the abiding interest in Locke's thought and the great extent of his influence despite the shortcomings of his work.

PURPOSE OF AN ESSAY. In "Epistle to the Reader" Locke related that some friends meeting in his chamber became perplexed about certain difficulties that arose in their discourse about a subject (left unnamed). He proposed that before they could inquire further, "it was necessary to examine our own abilities and see what objects our understandings were, or were not, fitted to deal with." This discussion in 1670 or 1671 first started Locke on the inquiries that were to continue intermittently for twenty years. What Locke first set down for the next meeting is not known, unless it was Draft A (1671) of *An Essay con-*

cerning Human Understanding. That the initial suggestion became the abiding purpose of *Essay* is clear from Locke's assertion that his purpose was "to inquire into the original, certainty, and extent of human knowledge, together with the grounds and degrees of belief, opinion, and assent" (I.i.2). At the same time he disavowed any intention to examine "the physical consideration of the mind, … wherein its essence consists, or by what motions of our spirits or alterations of our bodies we come to have any sensation by our organs or any ideas in our understandings, and whether those ideas do in their formation any or all of them depend on matter or no" (I.i.2).

Locke did not, in fact, offer any detailed or explicit accounts of these matters. He would have considered that a subject for natural philosophy. Nonetheless, he did, as indeed he had to, deal with the physical considerations of the mind, as well as all the other matters mentioned.

From the outset Locke was persuaded that our understanding and knowledge fall far short of all that exists; yet he was equally certain that men have a capacity for knowledge sufficient for their purposes and matters enough to inquire into. These convictions, pragmatic and utilitarian, set Locke apart from most of the other major philosophers of the seventeenth century, who, impressed by the new developments in mathematics and the new physical sciences, boldly plunged ahead with a rationalistic realism in the belief that their new methods would enable them in large measure to grasp reality. Locke saw that the very advances made in the new sciences put reality farther from the reach of the human mind. This did not make Locke a nominalist or an idealist in any modern sense; rather, he persistently affirmed the real objective existence of things or substances. What he denied was that the human understanding could know with certainty the real essences of substances. If "ideas" stand between reality and the understanding, it is to link them, even if only under the form of appearances. It is not to obliterate any connection between them or to justify a negation of substance—God, mind, or matter.

IDEAS. The key term in Locke's *Essay* is "idea," which he defined as "… whatsoever is the object of the understanding when a man thinks, … whatever is meant by phantasm, notion, species, or whatever it is which the mind can be employed about in thinking" (I.i.8). Any object of awareness or of consciousness must be an idea. But then how can we have any knowledge of anything other than ideas and their relationships? It is true that Locke spoke of ideas as the "materials of knowledge." Yet knowledge itself, when possessed and made the object of

the mind, must be an idea. For example, to perceive that *A* is equal to *B* is to perceive the agreement between *A* and *B*. This agreement as perceived must be an idea, or it cannot be an object of the mind when it thinks. Despite this difficulty Locke clung tenaciously to his term "idea" in his disputes with Stillingfleet. He actually intended something other than he stated, namely, that knowledge is an operation, an activity of the mind, not initially one of its objects. It would have served his purpose better had he spoken of "knowing" rather than of "knowledge," even though this would not have entirely removed the difficulty, since to set the mind at a distance where we may look at it, in order to know what knowledge is, is still to have an idea.

Locke, however, went beyond ideas to assume the real existence of things, substances, actions, processes, and operations. Ideas, except when they are the free constructs of the mind itself, signify and represent, however imperfectly, real existences and events. So deep was Locke's conviction on this point that no argument could shake him, although he constantly tried to remove the difficulties implicit in his definitions of "ideas" and "knowledge." This conviction is evident in the first two books of *Essay*, in which Locke inquired into the origin of our ideas.

NO INNATE IDEAS. It was Locke's central thesis, developed extensively in Book II of *Essay*, that we get all our ideas from experience. The whole of the first book is given to an overlong criticism, at times not germane to the subject, of the doctrine that we have innate ideas and innate knowledge.

Locke contended that there are no innate principles stamped upon the mind of man and brought into the world by the soul. In the first place, the argument that people have generally agreed that there are innate ideas, even if true, would not demonstrate the innateness of ideas. Moreover, there are no principles to which all give assent, since principles such as "Whatever is, is" and "It is impossible for the same thing to be and not to be" are not known to children, idiots, and a great part of mankind, who never heard or thought of them. Locke here assumed that innateness was equivalent to conscious perceiving and argued that to be in the mind is to be perceived or to be readily recalled to perception. Locke allowed that there is a capacity in us to know several truths but contended that this lent no support to the argument that they are innate.

To argue that all men know and assent to certain truths when they come to the use of reason proves nothing, since they will also come to know many truths that are not innate. It would appear, then, that all truth is either innate or adventitious. Again, why should the use of reason be necessary to discover truths already innately in the mind? Locke allowed that the knowledge of some truths is in the mind very early, but observation shows such truths are about particular ideas furnished by the senses; for example, a child knows the difference between the ideas of sweet and bitter before it can speak and before it knows abstract ideas. Even assent at first hearing is no proof of innateness, for many truths not innate will be assented to as soon as understood.

On the contrary, the senses first furnish us with particular ideas, which the mind by degrees becomes familiar with, remembers, and names. The mind subsequently abstracts from these particular ideas and gives names to general ideas. Thus, general ideas, general words, and the use of reason grow together, and assent to the truth of propositions depends on having clear and distinct ideas of the meaning of terms. Locke held it to be evident that particular propositions are known before the more universal and with as much certainty.

We have natural faculties or capacities to think and to reason. This is not, however, the same thing as having innate ideas, for if anyone means by innate ideas nothing but this natural capacity, he uses terms, according to Locke, in a manner plainly contrary to common usage.

In a similar fashion, Locke argued that we have no innate moral or practical principles, for there is no universal agreement about such principles; great varieties of human vice have been at one time or place considered virtues. We all have a desire for happiness and an aversion to misery, but these inclinations give us no knowledge or truth. Locke was persuaded that there are eternal principles of morality, which men may come to know through the use of reason about experience. This, however, is far from proving them innate.

In the third chapter of Book I Locke argued that no principles can be innate unless the ideas contained in them are innate, that is, unless men can be conscious of them. Impossibility and identity are hardly innate, yet without them we cannot understand the supposedly innate principle of identity, that it is impossible for the same thing both to be and not be. Similarly, the proposition that God is to be worshipped cannot be innate, for the notion of God is so diverse that men have great difficulty agreeing on it, while some men have no conception of God whatsoever.

Locke's target. Who was Locke criticizing in his long and repetitious attack on the doctrine of innate ideas? Was the position he denounced held by anyone in the form in which he presented the theory? Why did he examine the question at such length?

Since *Essay* was first published tradition has held that Locke's target was Descartes and the Cartesians. Certainly Leibniz thought so, as did others after him. In the late nineteenth century, critics pointed to Locke's own rationalism and noted that his recognition of men's natural faculties and innate powers to think and reason is not far from the position of Descartes, who wrote, "Innate ideas proceed from the capacity of thought itself," and "I never wrote or concluded that the mind required innate ideas which were in some sort different from its faculty of thinking." Various other possible objects of Locke's attacks were suggested, the Cambridge Platonists, certain groups in the universities, and various clergymen. Recently R. I. Aaron has argued persuasively that the older tradition, that Descartes, the Cartesians, and certain English thinkers were the targets of Locke's attack, is the correct one and that Locke was not simply striking at a straw man of his own making.

Reasons for attacking innate ideas. Locke suggested that the doctrine of innate ideas lends itself to a certain authoritarianism and encourages laziness of thought, so that the foundations of knowledge are not likely to be examined. The expression "innate ideas" is an unfortunate one and admittedly extremely vague. It carries with it the suggestion that certain ideas and knowledge are, in Locke's sense, imprinted on the mind and are in no way dependent on experience. Certainly there are passages in Descartes which strongly suggest that certain ideas are innately in the mind, and more than a few thinkers took this to be Descartes's meaning. Furthermore, Locke wished to prepare the ground for his own thesis that all ideas and all knowledge are acquired. If he overemphasized the crude sense of the theory of innate ideas, he also showed that even the refined doctrine is unnecessary in accounting for knowledge.

There is another point that Locke discussed later in *Essay*. Descartes asserted that the essence of the mind is to think. To Locke this meant that the mind could not both be and not think. He argued that the mind does not think always and that its real essence cannot be thinking. If the mind thinks always, either some ideas must be innate or the mind comes into being only after it has been furnished with ideas by experience. Neither alternative was acceptable to Locke.

ENCYCLOPEDIA OF PHILOSOPHY
2nd edition

SOURCE OF IDEAS. Locke, in his positive thesis in Book II, valiantly and sometimes awkwardly endeavored to show that every idea we have is ultimately derived from experience, either from sensation or reflection. Locke began by asserting that a man is conscious of two things, the fact "that he thinks" and "the ideas" in the mind about which he thinks. Locke's initial concern was with the question of how a man comes by his ideas; and he made an assumption in terms of several similes. "Let us then suppose the mind to be, as we say, white paper, void of all characters, without any ideas. How comes it to be furnished? … Whence has it all the materials of reason and knowledge?" (II.i.2). Locke replied to his own questions that we get all our ideas from experience, the two fountainheads of which are sensation and reflection. Our senses are affected by external objects (bodies) and afford us ideas, such as yellow, white, heat, cold, soft, hard, bitter, and sweet. Perceiving the operations of our own minds when we reflect, we are furnished with ideas of perception, thinking, doubting, believing, reasoning, knowing, and willing.

The ideas that are furnished by experience are the materials of reason and knowledge. These materials are either the immediate objects of sense, such as color, or the unexamined but direct awareness of such acts as doubting or knowing. Locke's meaning becomes explicitly clear in his account of solidity. He held that we get the idea of solidity by touch. "That which … hinders the approach of two bodies, when they are moving one towards another, I call solidity" (II.iv.1). He sharply distinguished this sense from the purely mathematical use of the term. Impenetrability is an acceptable alternative name for solidity. It is clearly distinct from space and hardness. After an extensive discussion Locke stated, "If anyone asks me what this solidity is, I send him to his senses to inform him. Let him put a flint or a football between his hands and then endeavour to join them, and he will know" (II.iv.6). All philosophical and scientific discourse about solidity, however complex and sophisticated it may be, must ultimately refer back to that from which it began, namely the experience or sensation we have when we put something such as a flint or a football between our hands. Similarly, we cannot by discourse give a blind man the idea of color or make known what pain is to one who never felt it. All knowledge about the physics of light and color or sound refers back to what we perceive when we see and hear. It is in this sense, then, that we get all our ideas from sensation and reflection. Locke nowhere, however, suggested that we can or should stop there. Once the mind is furnished with ideas, it may perform various operations with them.

IDEAS AND THE REAL WORLD. Throughout the first book of *Essay* Locke assumed the real existence of an external physical world and the substantial unity of a man in body and mind. He undoubtedly accepted the thesis that the external physical world is corpuscular and acts by bodies in motion that possess only those qualities which Locke called primary. Locke spoke of secondary qualities as powers in bodies to produce in our minds ideas that are signs of these powers but that in no way resemble the powers that produce them. Often he suggested that if we had the means of observing the minute motions of the particles making up gross bodies, we might have a clearer notion of what we mean when we call secondary qualities powers. Locke's position here is physical realism. It is not simply a manner of speaking. The ideas we have do represent real things outside of us and do constitute the links by which we know something of the external physical world.

Identity. Among the bodies that exist are those of plants, animals, and men. Existence itself constitutes the principle of individuation. Identity is not applied in the same way to a mass of matter and a living body. The identity of an oak lies in the organization of its parts, which partake of one common life. So it is with animals. Again, "the identity of the same man consists: viz. in nothing but a participation of the same continued life, by constantly fleeting particles of matter, in succession vitally united to the same organized body" (II.xxvii.6).

Origin of sensation. With these controlling hypotheses in *Essay* in view, we may return to Locke's invitation to consider the mind as a blank sheet of paper without any ideas. Is a mind without ideas anything but a bare capacity to receive ideas? If we ask what a man is without ideas, we can say he is an organized body existing in a world of other bodies and interacting with them. Experience is a matter of contact of the organized human body with other bodies before it is a matter of sensation or perception. Not every body impinging on our body gives rise to sensation; if it does not, we take no notice of it. However, if some external bodies strike our senses and produce the appropriate motions therein, then our senses convey into the mind several distinct perceptions. How this takes place Locke avoided considering, but that it takes place he was certain; a man, he asserted, first begins to think "when he first has any sensation" (II.i.23).

SIMPLE AND COMPLEX IDEAS. Locke proceeded to distinguish between simple and complex ideas. A simple idea is "nothing but one uniform appearance or conception in the mind, and is not distinguishable into different ideas" (II.ii.1). A color seen, a sound heard, warmth felt, an odor smelled, are all simple ideas of sense. Once it is furnished with a number of simple ideas, the mind has the power to repeat, compare, and unite them into an almost infinite variety of combinations; but it is utterly incapable of inventing or framing a new simple idea. Thus, with respect to simple ideas the mind is mostly passive; they are simply given in experience. The ideas are given not in isolation from each other but in combinations, as when we simultaneously feel the warmth and softness of wax or the coldness and hardness of ice; nevertheless, simple ideas are distinct from each other in that the mind may mark off each from the other, however united the qualities may be in the things that cause the simple ideas in the mind. Moreover, only those qualities in things that produce ideas in us can ever be imagined at all. Thus, our knowledge of existence is limited by the ideas furnished by experience. Had we one sense less or more than we now do, our experience and knowledge would be respectively decreased or increased.

We have certain ideas, such as color or odor, from one sense only; others, like figure and number, from more than one sense. Reflection alone provides us with experience of thinking and willing. Other ideas, such as pleasure, pain, power, existence, and unity, we have from both sensation and reflection.

PRIMARY AND SECONDARY QUALITIES. Locke made a second basic distinction—between primary and secondary qualities. In doing so he clearly went beyond ideas. He wrote, "Whatsoever the mind perceives in itself, or is the immediate object of perception, thought, or understanding, that I call idea; and the power to produce any idea in our mind, I call quality of the subject wherein that power is" (II.viii.8). Primary qualities, he argued, are utterly inseparable from body. They are known to be primary because sense constantly finds them there if body can be perceived at all, and the mind by critical reflection finds them inseparable from every particle of matter. Solidity, extension, figure, and mobility are all primary qualities. Our ideas of these qualities resemble the qualities themselves, and these qualities really exist in body, whether or not they are perceived. Berkeley was to show that to speak of resemblance supposes that a comparison, an observation, can be made. Locke was aware of the difficulty, as is shown in his *Examination of Malebranche*. Apparently he believed it was the only explanation plausible in spite of its difficulties.

Secondary qualities, in Locke's terms, were nothing but powers to produce various sensations. Bodies do so by the action of their bulk, figure, and texture, and by the motion of their insensible parts on our senses. Somehow they produce in us such ideas as color, odor, sound, warmth, and smell. These ideas in no way resemble the qualities of bodies themselves. They are but signs of events in real bodies. Locke also frequently called these ideas secondary qualities. He would have been clearer had he called them sensory ideas of secondary qualities, preserving the distinction between qualities as attributes of a subject and ideas as objects in the mind. A third class of qualities (sometimes called tertiary) is the power of a body to produce a change in another body, for example, the power of the sun to melt wax.

Nowhere is Locke's physical realism more evident than in his distinction between primary and secondary qualities. Whatever epistemological difficulties the distinction might entail, Locke was persuaded that the new physics required it. Indeed, the distinction was made by Boyle, Descartes, Galileo, and others before him and was thoroughly familiar in his day. Admittedly there is a problem in the assertion that a certain motion in body produces in us the idea of a particular color. Nevertheless, Locke was persuaded that it was so. In such difficult cases Locke fell back upon the omnipotence and wisdom of God and the fact that our knowledge is suited to our purpose.

IDEAS OF REFLECTION. Locke observed that perception is the first faculty of the mind and without it we know nothing else. Hence, the idea of perception is the first and simplest idea we have from reflection. What perception is, is best discovered by observing what we do when we see, hear, or think. Locke added that judgment may alter the interpretation we make of the ideas we receive from sensation. Thus, if a man born blind gains his sight, he must learn to distinguish between a sphere and a cube visually, though he can do so readily by touch. By habit the ideas of sensation are gradually integrated into the unified experience of complex ideas, and by judgment we come to expect things that look a certain way to also feel or smell a certain way. It is worth noting that Locke was persuaded that animals have perception and are not, as Descartes held, mere automatons.

Memory and contemplation. The second faculty of the mind that Locke held indispensable to knowledge is the retention manifested in both contemplation and memory. Contemplation consists in holding an idea before the mind for some time. Memory, however, gave Locke some difficulties. He asserted that "our ideas being nothing but actual perceptions in the mind—this laying up of our ideas in the repository of the memory signifies no more but this: that the mind has a power in many cases to revive perceptions which it has once had, with this additional perception annexed to them, that it has had them before" (II.x.2). The inadequacy of this statement is at once evident. It proposes no more than a kind of subjective conviction that may often be in error. Locke's analysis of memory was more psychological than philosophical. He passed over the consideration of how memory is possible at all and the criteria by which a true memory may be distinguished from a false memory. He did say, however, that attention, repetition, pleasure, and pain aid memory and are the conditions under which memory is strengthened or weakened. Again he asserted that animals have memory.

Other ideas of reflection. Other faculties of the mind are discerning and distinguishing one idea from another, comparing and compounding, naming, and abstracting. Locke considered each point also in respect to animals, holding, for example, that animals compare and compound ideas only to a slight extent and do not abstract ideas at all. At the conclusion of this chapter (II.xi.15) Locke asserted that he thought he had given a "true history of the first beginnings of human knowledge."

COMPLEX IDEAS. Locke next considered complex ideas. Just as the mind observes that several combinations of simple ideas are found together, so too, it can by its own action voluntarily join several simple ideas together into one complex idea. There are three categories of complex ideas—modes, substances, and relations. Modes are dependencies or affections of substances. Simple modes are variations or different combinations of one simple idea, whereas in mixed modes several distinct ideas are joined to make a complex idea. Ideas of substances represent distinct particular things subsisting in themselves. Complex ideas of relation consist in comparing one idea with another.

This classification is not entirely satisfactory because ideas of modes invariably entail relations in the broadest sense. Locke seems to have been closer to Aristotle than to modern usage in his employment of the term "relation." Under modes Locke included space, duration and time, number, infinity, motion, sense qualities, thinking, pleasure and pain, power, and certain mixed modes. Under substance he placed the idea of substance in general, the ideas of particular substances, and collective ideas of substances. In the category of relation, he considered a number of ideas, including cause and effect, relations of place

and time, identity and diversity, and others that he classified as proportional, natural, instituted, and moral.

The greater number of these concepts have in other philosophies been credited with some a priori and extraempirical character. They are not direct objects of sensory experience; and they appear to have a certainty not found in the mere coexistence of sensory ideas. They are more abstract and universal than the simple ideas of sensation and reflection. Locke's broad use of the term "ideas" tends to confuse and obscure the distinction between sensory percept and concept. Nevertheless, Locke undertook to show how the mind actively constructs these complex ideas, abstract and conceptual though they may be, out of the materials of knowledge, the simple ideas of sensation and reflection. In this undertaking Locke's rationalism was most evident, for he held that while the mind constructs complex ideas, it cannot do so arbitrarily. In this sense, Locke could claim for them an objective reality.

The mode of space. Examination here will be limited to only those complex ideas that are most important and difficult. Among modes, only space, duration, number, thinking, and power will be considered. Locke contended that the modifications of a simple idea are as much distinct ideas as any two ideas can be. Space in its first manifestation is a simple idea, since in seeing and touching we immediately perceive a distance between bodies and the parts of bodies. Though the idea of space constantly accompanies other sensory ideas, it is distinguishable from them. All our modes of the idea of space derive from the initial sensory experience. Thus space considered as length is called distance, considered three-dimensionally is capacity, considered in any manner is termed extension. Each different distance, especially when measured by stated lengths, is a distinct idea, including the idea of immensity, which consists in adding distance to distance without ever reaching a terminus. So too, figure allows an endless variety of modifications of the simple idea of space. Place is distance considered relative to some particular bodies or frame of reference.

Locke disagreed with Descartes's assertion that extension is the essence of matter, although he agreed that we cannot conceive of a body that is not extended. But a body has solidity, and solidity is distinct from the notion of space; for the parts of space are inseparable in thought and in actuality and are immovable, whereas a solid body may move and its parts are separable. Descartes's argument that the physical universe is a plenum was dismissed by Locke as unsound, for there is no contradiction in the conception of a vacuum. If body is not infinite, we can conceive of reaching out beyond the physical limits of the universe to a place unoccupied by matter. The idea of pure space is necessarily infinite, for we can conceive of no limit or terminus to it. Locke professed not to know whether space was a substance or an accident and offered to answer the question when the ideas of substance and accident were clarified. He was more confident of the idea of pure space than he was of the traditional philosophical categories. Locke placed a great load on the simple idea of space, and by the activity of his reason he went beyond the bounds of possible experience.

Duration and time. The idea of duration is broader than that of time. If we consider the train of ideas that passes through our minds, we observe that one idea constantly succeeds another, and so we come by the idea of succession. By reflection we acquire the idea of duration, which we may then apply to motion and sensory ideas. Where there is no perception of the succession of ideas in our minds, there is no sense of time. Locke insisted that motion does not furnish us with the idea of duration, and he directly opposed Aristotle's definition that "time is the measure of motion with respect to before and after."

Once we have the idea of duration, we need a measure of common duration. Time is the consideration of duration marked by certain measures such as minutes, hours, and days. The most convenient measures of time must be capable of division into equal portions of constantly repeated periods. We cannot be certain of the constancy of motions or of the time spans they measure. Locke was concerned with liberating time from motion. Consequently, he argued that we must consider duration itself as "going on in one constant, equal, uniform course; but none of the measures of it which we make use of can be known to do so" (II.xiv.21). Once time is liberated from motion, Locke held, we can conceive of infinite duration even beyond creation. Thus we can expand by endless addition the idea of duration to come to the notion of eternity.

Were it not for the implicit realism of Locke's arguments, it would be possible to agree with those scholars who have seen in his arguments about duration and expansion a vague groping for a position somewhat similar to Kant's a priori aesthetic. For both men, space becomes the framework of body, and duration or time the structure of the mind, or the inner sense.

Number. The idea of unity is everywhere suggested to the mind, and no idea is more simple. By repeating it we come to the complex modes of number. Once we have learned to perform this operation, we cannot stop short of the idea of infinity. Locke regarded both finite and infi-

nite as modes of quantity. Because we are able to apply the idea of number to space and time, we are capable of conceiving of them as infinite. The idea of infinity is essentially negative, since we come to it by enlarging our ideas of number as much as we please and discover that there is no reason ever to stop. We may know that number, space, and duration are infinite, but we cannot positively know infinity itself. Locke insisted that however remote from the simple ideas of sensation and reflection these ideas may be, they have their origin in those simple ideas.

The modes of thinking. Locke gave only casual and formal attention to the modes of thinking, such as sensation, remembrance, recollection, contemplation, attention, dreaming, reasoning, judging, willing, and knowing. Equally superficial was his consideration of modes of pleasure and pain, which consisted of little more than definitions of various emotions.

Power. The chapter on power is the longest in *Essay*, and Locke felt obliged to rewrite portions of it time and again, for each new edition. It is evident that power is not perceived as such. Locke observed that the mind, taking note of the changes and sequences of our ideas and "concluding from what it has so constantly observed to have been, that the like changes will for the future be made in the same things, by like agents, and by the like ways … comes by that idea which we call power" (II.xxi.1). From this it hardly seems that the idea of power is a simple idea, unless Locke meant no more than that the idea of power is only the observation of the regular order and connection of our ideas. But Locke wrote that "since whatever change is observed, the mind must collect a power somewhere able to make that change, as well as a possibility in the thing itself to receive it" (II.xxi.4). Here the idea of power is a necessary idea of reason, grounded in certain other experiences. Locke never made clear this distinction. He admitted that the idea of power included some kind of relation but insisted that it was a simple idea.

Power is both passive and active. Whether or not matter has any active power, Locke pointed out, we have our idea of active power from the operations of the mind itself. We find by direct observation that we have the power to begin, continue, or stop certain actions of our minds and motions of our bodies. This power we call will, and the actual exercise of this power, volition, or willing. Action is voluntary or involuntary insofar as it is or is not consequent upon the order or command of the mind.

Locke proceeded to explore the ideas of will, desire, and freedom in terms of the idea of power. "The idea of liberty is the idea of a power in any agent to do or forbear any particular action, according to the determination or thought of the mind, whereby either of them is preferred to the other" (II.xxi.8). Where this power is absent, a man is under necessity. Locke consequently dismissed as unintelligible the question of whether or not the will is free. The only intelligible question is whether or not a man is free. Freedom is one power of an agent and will is another; one power cannot be the power of another. "As far as this power reaches, of acting or not acting, by the determination of his own thought preferring either, so far is a man free" (II.xxi.21). Freedom then, for Locke, was the absence of constraint. If we distinguish will from desire, we cannot make the mistake of thinking the will is free.

What then determines the will with respect to action is some uneasiness in a man that may be called the uneasiness of desire. Good and evil work on the mind but do not determine the will to particular actions. The only thing that can overcome the uneasiness of one desire is the greater uneasiness of another. The removal of uneasiness is the first and necessary step to happiness. Since it is present desire that moves the will to action, good and evil contemplated and known in the mind can move us to action only when that knowledge is accompanied by a greater uneasiness than any other. Since we have many desires and can have knowledge of desired good in the future as well as feared evil, we can suspend the pursuit of any desire until we have judged it. Thus, government of our passions is possible whenever there is a greater uneasiness in not doing so. This power is the ground on which we hold men responsible for their actions. Good and bad are nothing but pleasure or pain, present or future. Error in choice is usually due to the greater strength of present pleasure or pain in comparison with future pleasure and pain. A true knowledge of what contributes to our happiness can influence a choice only when to deviate from that choice would give greater uneasiness than would any other action. Thus it is possible to change the pleasantness and unpleasantness of various actions by consideration, practice, application, and custom.

Locke's conception of power, like his ideas of cause and effect, was inadequate and vague. It was both a simple idea and a complex one; it was the notion of regular sequence and that of efficacious cause; and it was at once given and a priori. The rational and empirical elements in Locke were at war here. Locke was at his best in showing how the word "power" is commonly used. His analysis of the will and freedom was likewise involved in difficulties.

The will is not free and thus man's actions are determined; but at the same time we can suspend the execution of any desire by our judgment. Locke was aware of these difficulties, but he saw no satisfactory alternative.

Mixed modes. Mixed modes are made by the mind and are exemplified by drunkenness, a lie, obligation, sacrilege, or murder. To a great degree we get these ideas by the explanation of the words that stand for them.

SUBSTANCE. Of all the ideas considered by Locke none gave him more difficulty than that of substance, and nowhere was his empiricism more in conflict with his rationalism. The diverse trends of Locke's thought concerning substance and the problems he raised prepared the ground for Berkeley, Hume, Kant, and many others who struggled with the same questions. At every opportunity throughout *Essay* he returned to consider particular substances and the general idea of substance. Locke held that we are conversant only with particular substances through experience; yet his rationalism and realism would not permit him to abandon the general idea of substance.

The mind is furnished with many simple ideas by the senses, and it observes by reflection that certain of them are constantly together. It then presumes that these belong to one thing and for convenience gives them one name. In this way the mind arrives at the complex idea of particular substances, such as gold, which we observe to be yellow and malleable, to dissolve in aqua regia, to melt, and not to be used up in fire. A substance so defined gives us only a nominal definition.

Locke added that "not imagining how these simple ideas can subsist by themselves, we accustom ourselves to suppose some substratum wherein they do subsist, and from which they do result; which therefore we call substance" (II.xxiii.1). This idea of a substratum is extremely vague, and Locke called it a "something we know not what." Our ideas do not reach, and we cannot have, a knowledge of the real essence of substances. Nonetheless, Locke continued to believe that real essences do exist, although our knowledge comes short of them.

Our knowledge of corporeal substances consists of ideas of the primary and secondary qualities perceived by the senses and of the powers we observe in them to affect or be affected by other things. We have as clear an idea of spirit as of body, but we are not capable of knowing the real essence of either. Locke observed that we know as little of how the parts of a body cohere as of how our spirits perceive ideas or move our bodies, since we know nothing of either except our simple ideas of them. Locke even suggested that God could if he wished, as far as we know, add to matter the power to think, just as easily as he could add to matter a separate substance with the power to think.

Even our idea of God is based on simple ideas that are enlarged with the idea of infinity. God's infinite essence is unknown to us. We can only know that he exists.

RELATIONS. The mind can consider any idea as it stands in relation to any other; and thus we come by ideas of relation, such as father, whiter, older. Frequently, the lack of a correlative term leads us to mistake a relative term for an absolute one. Locke distinguished the relation from the things related and appears to have made all relations external. Indeed, he held that many ideas of relation are clearer than ideas of substances; for example, the idea of brothers is clearer than the perfect idea of man.

Though there are many ideas and words signifying relations, they all terminate in simple ideas. There is a difficulty here. If the idea of relation is not a simple idea or a combination of simple ideas, then it is distinct from them. Like the general idea of substance, it is a concept derived from reason. No doubt the mind is capable of comparing the relation of one idea with another, but our perception of this operation must have for its object either a simple idea or the operation itself. On this point Locke was obscure and evasive and avoided the difficulties by the vague assertion that all relations terminate in simple ideas.

Causation. The relation to which Locke first turned was cause and effect. His discussion was inadequate and marked by the duality found in his consideration of other ideas. We observe the order and connection of our ideas and the coming into existence of things and qualities. In pointing this out Locke was on strictly empirical grounds. When, however, he defined cause as "that which produces any simple or complex idea," and "that which is produced, effect" (II.xxvi.1), he went beyond experience and rested his argument on reason. Locke undoubtedly saw the difficulties of his position. He was concerned, on the one hand, to show how we have the ideas of cause and effect from experience. On the other hand, he was not satisfied with a mere sequence theory. The difficulty arose, as it did with power and substance, because he was persuaded that there is a reality beyond the ideas manifest to us. It is a reality, however, about which he could say little in terms of his representationalism.

Identity and diversity. Under relation Locke also examined identity and diversity, by which he meant the

relation of a thing to itself, particularly with respect to different times and places. As was stated above, the identity of a plant, an animal, or a man consists in a participation in the same continued life. To this Locke added an examination of personal identity. He argued that personal identity is consciousness of being the same thinking self at different times and places. Locke also discussed other relations, such as proportional, natural, instituted, and moral, which are not essential to the main argument of *Essay* and which will, therefore, not be discussed here.

The remaining chapters of Book II of *Essay* are devoted to "Clear and Obscure, Distinct and Confused Ideas," "Real and Fantastical Ideas," "Adequate and Inadequate Ideas," "True and False Ideas," and "The Association of Ideas." All of them have merit in clarifying other parts of *Essay* but add little that is new and not discussed elsewhere. Consequently, they will be passed over.

LANGUAGE. At the end of Book II of *Essay* Locke related that he had originally intended to pass on to a consideration of knowledge. He found, however, such a close connection between words and ideas, particularly between abstract ideas and general words, that he had first to examine the "nature, use, and signification" of language, since all knowledge consists of propositions. Book III, therefore, was incorporated into *Essay*.

The merits of Book III are the subject of some controversy. Most scholars have dismissed it as unimportant and confused. Some, such as Aaron, see many merits in it despite its manifest inadequacies.

The primary functions of language are to communicate with our fellow men, to make signs for ourselves of internal conceptions, and to stand as marks for ideas. Language is most useful when general names stand for general ideas and operations of the mind. Since all except proper names are general, a consideration of what kinds of things words stand for is in order. "Words, in their primary' or immediate signification, stand for nothing but the ideas in the mind of him that uses them" (III.ii.2). We suppose they stand for the same ideas in the minds of others. Words stand for things only indirectly. General words stand for general ideas, which become general by separation from other ideas and from particular circumstances. This process Locke called abstraction.

Definition. Definition by genus and differentia is merely a convenience by which we avoid enumerating various simple ideas for which the genus stands. (In this, Locke prepared the way for descriptive definition, which makes no pretense of defining the real essence of things.) It follows that general or universal ideas are made by the understanding for its own use. Thus the essences of so-called species are nothing but abstract ideas. Locke asserted that every distinct abstract idea is a distinct essence. This must not be taken in a Platonic sense, for it is the mind itself that makes these abstract ideas. If essences are distinguished into nominal and real, then with respect to simple ideas and modes there is no difference between nominal and real essence. In substances, they are decidedly different, in that the real essence of substance is unknowable to us.

Names. Locke asserted that the names of simple ideas are not definable. One wonders, Is blue a general idea? If so, what is this blue as against that blue? What is separated out? What retained? Locke never examined these questions, with the result that his conception of abstraction is vague and vacillating. Locke gave several distinct meanings to such terms as "general ideas" and "universal ideas," shifting from one meaning to another and never clarifying them.

Complex ideas consisting of several simple ideas are definable and intelligible provided one has experience of the simple ideas that compose them. Without experience how can a blind man understand the definition of a rainbow?

Simple ideas are "perfectly taken from the existence of things and are not arbitrary at all" (III.iv.17). Ideas of substances refer to a pattern with some latitude, whereas ideas of mixed modes are absolutely arbitrary and refer to no real existence. They are not, however, made at random or without reason. It is the name that ties these ideas together, and each such idea is its own prototype.

Since names for substances stand for complex ideas perceived regularly to go together and supposed to belong to one thing, we necessarily come short of the real essences, if there are any. One may use the word "gold" to signify the coexistence of several ideas. One man may use the term to signify the complex idea of A and B and C. Another man of more experience may add D, or add D and leave out A. Thus, these essences are of our own making without being entirely arbitrary. In any case, the boundaries of the species of substances are drawn by men.

Connective words In a brief chapter, "Of Particles," Locke pointed out that we need words signifying the connections that the mind makes between ideas or propositions. These show what connection, restriction, distinction, opposition, or emphasis is given to the parts of discourse. These words signify, not ideas, but an action of the mind. Again a difficulty arises. If "is" and "is not"

stand for the mind's act of affirming or denying, then either the mind directly apprehends its own actions in some way or we do have ideas of affirmation or denial. If we do have ideas of the mind's acts, then these words ought to signify the ideas of these acts; if we do not have ideas that these words signify, then either we do not apprehend them or something besides ideas is the object of the mind when it thinks. The remainder of Book III concerns Locke's thoughts on the imperfection of words, the abuse of words, and his suggested remedies for these imperfections and abuses.

KNOWLEDGE. The first three books of *Essay* are largely a preparation for the fourth. Many scholars see a fundamental cleavage between Book II and Book IV. Yet Locke saw no conflict between the two books, and whatever split existed in Locke's thought runs throughout *Essay*, as J. W. Yolton and others have pointed out. An effort can be made to reconcile Locke's empiricism and his rationalism, his grounding of all ideas and knowledge in experience and his going beyond experience to the existence of things.

Many of Locke's difficulties stem from his definition of "idea." It is so broad that anything perceived or known must be an idea. But Locke showed, in Books I and II, that we get all our ideas from experience, not in order to claim that nothing exists except ideas, but to show that there is an alternative to the theory of innate ideas. For Locke, experience is initially a contact of bodies and subsequently a reflection of the mind. He never doubted the existence of an external physical world, the inner workings of which are unknown to us.

Sources of knowledge. There are two sources of knowledge—sensation and reflection. The ideas we have from reflection are in some important ways quite different from those we have from sensation. In Book II Locke asserted that the mind "turns its view inward upon itself and observes its own actions about those ideas it has (and) takes from thence other ideas" (II.vi.1). The important point here is that in reflection the mind observes its own action. It is true that Locke spoke of modes of the simple ideas of reflection, such as remembering, discerning, reasoning, and judging. Nonetheless, if the mind does observe its own action, then something more than ideas are the object of the mind in reflection, or else ideas of reflection are somehow importantly different from the ideas of sensation. This point will show up in a consideration of Locke's theory of knowledge.

Propositions. Locke defined knowledge as "the perception of the connection and agreement, or disagreement and repugnancy, of any of our ideas" (IV.i.2). This agreement or disagreement is in respect to four types: identity and diversity, relation, coexistence or necessary connection, and real existence. Perceiving agreement or disagreement is quite different from just barely perceiving the ideas that are said to agree or disagree. Strictly speaking, this perception must be a distinct idea of either agreement or disagreement. Yet this was not Locke's meaning. Where there is knowledge, there is judgment, since there can be no knowledge without a proposition, mental or verbal. Locke defined truth as "the joining or separating of signs, as the things signified by them do agree or disagree one with another" (IV.v.2). There are two sorts of propositions: mental, "wherein the ideas in our understandings are, without the use of words, put together or separated by the mind perceiving or judging of their agreement or disagreement" (IV.v.5); and verbal, which stand for mental propositions.

Judgments. In this view, ideas are the materials of knowledge, the terms of mental propositions. They are, insofar as they are given in sensation and reflection, the subject matter of reflection. If perception of agreement or disagreement in identity and diversity is the first act of the mind, then that act is a judgment. If we infallibly know, as soon as we have it in our minds, that the idea of white is identical with itself and different from that of red, and that the idea of round is identical with itself and different from that of square, we must distinguish between the bare having of these ideas and the knowledge of their identity and diversity. The knowledge of their identity and diversity is a judgment. It is reflective, and in it the mind perceives its own action or operation. There can be no distinction between the judgment and the idea of it. This is perhaps Locke's meaning, which is unfortunately obscured by his broad use of the term "idea." This perception of its own action is quite distinct from the abstract idea of the power of judgment. We may be uncertain as to how the mind makes judgments, what determines it to judge, or in what kind of a substance this power inheres, but we may be sure that in the actual making of a true judgment the mind perceives its own act. This position may be beset with difficulties, but it makes some sense out of Locke's definition of knowledge.

Degrees of knowledge. Locke recognized two degrees of knowledge, in the strict sense of the term—intuition and demonstration. Of the two, intuition is more fundamental and certain. "The mind perceives the agreement or disagreement of two ideas immediately by themselves, without the intervention of any other" (IV.ii.1). Such knowledge is irresistible and leaves no room for hesita-

tion, doubt, or examination. Upon it depends all the certainty and evidence of all our knowledge. Here, clearly, what the mind perceives is not any third idea, but its own act. In demonstration the mind perceives agreement or disagreement, not immediately, but through other mediating ideas. Each step in demonstration rests upon an intuition. This kind of knowledge is most evident in, but is not limited to, mathematics.

A third degree of knowledge is "employed about the particular existence of finite beings without us, which going beyond bare probability and yet not reaching perfectly to either of the foregoing degrees of certainty, passes under the name of knowledge" (IV.ii.14). Locke called this sensitive knowledge. Fully aware of the dialectical difficulty entailed in this position, he grounded his reply to critics on common sense. The differences between dreaming and waking, imagining and sensing, are strong enough to justify this conviction. Hunger and thirst should bring a skeptic to his senses. For Locke, it was enough that common sense supported him, for he always took sensory ideas to be signs or representations of something beyond themselves.

Limits of knowledge. Locke asserted that knowledge extends no farther than our ideas and, specifically, no further than the perception of the agreement or disagreement of our ideas. We cannot have knowledge of all the relations of our ideas or rational knowledge of the necessary relations between many of our ideas. Sensitive knowledge goes only as far as the existence of things, not to their real essence, or reality. Two examples were given. In the first, Locke argued that though we have the ideas of circle, square, and equality, we may never find a circle equal to a square and know them to be equal. In the second, he observed that we have ideas of matter and thinking but may never know whether mere material being thinks. This has been discussed earlier.

In his controversy with Stillingfleet, Locke never abandoned this latter thesis. And throughout this section (IV.iii) Locke showed that many relations of coexistence give us no certainty that they will or must continue to be so. He seemed persuaded that the continued discovery of new knowledge suggests that there are vast horizons of reality that we may advance upon but can never reach. With respect to the relations between abstract ideas we may hope to advance very far, as in mathematics. To this he added the belief that a demonstrable science of morality is possible. On the other hand, he held that we can have no certain knowledge of bodies or of unembodied spirits.

Knowledge of existents. Locke argued that though our knowledge terminates in our ideas, our knowledge is real. "Simple ideas are not fictions of our fancies, but the natural and regular productions of things without us, really operating upon us; and so carry with them all the conformity which is intended; or which our state requires" (IV.iv.4). On the other hand, he argued: "All our complex ideas, except those of substances, being archetypes of the mind's own making, not intended to be copies of anything, nor referred to the existence of anything, as to their originals, cannot want any conformity necessary to real knowledge" (IV.iv.5).

Universal propositions, the truth of which may be known with certainty, are not concerned directly with existence. Nonetheless, Locke argued that we have intuitive knowledge of our own existence. Here the argument is much the same as Descartes's, and it is valid only if we accept the view that the mind in reflection perceives its own acts. This knowledge of our own existence has the highest degree of certainty, according to Locke.

We have a demonstrable knowledge of God's existence, Locke held. He used a form of the Cosmological Argument: Starting with the certainty of his own existence, he argued to the necessary existence of a being adequate to produce all the effects manifest in experience. The argument assumed the reality of cause, the necessity of order, and the intelligibility of existence.

Of the existence of other things, as has been shown, we have sensitive knowledge. Locke felt the inconsistency of his position on this matter, yet accepted what he believed common sense required. We know of the coexistence of certain qualities and powers, and reason and sense require that they proceed from something outside themselves. Throughout these arguments about existence Locke went beyond his own first definition of knowledge.

PROBABILITY. The remaining portions of *Essay* are concerned with probability, degrees of assent, reason and faith, enthusiasm, error, and the division of the sciences. Though Locke's treatment of probability is inadequate, he recognized its importance. The grounds of probability lie in the apparent conformity of propositions with our experience and the testimony of others. Practical experience shows us that our knowledge is slight, and action requires that we proceed in our affairs with something less than certainty.

Faith was, for Locke, the acceptance of revelation. It must be sharply distinguished from reason, which is "the discovery of the certainty or probability of such propositions or truths, which the mind arrives at by deduction made from such ideas which it has got by the use of its natural faculties, viz. by sensation or reflection" (IV.xviii.2). Though reason is not able to discover the truth of revelation, nevertheless, something claimed to be revelation cannot be accepted against the clear evidence of the understanding. Thus, enthusiasm sets reason aside and substitutes for it bare fancies born of conceit and blind impulse.

Error. Error cannot lie in intuition. Locke found four sources of error: the want of proofs, inability to use them, unwillingness to use them, and wrong measures of probability. Locke concluded *Essay* with a brief division of science, or human knowledge, into three classes—natural philosophy, or φυσική practical action and ethics, or πρακτική, and σημειωτκή, or the doctrine of signs.

INFLUENCE OF ESSAY. Many minds of the seventeenth century contributed to the overthrow of the School philosophies and the development of the new sciences and philosophies. Descartes and Locke between them, however, set the tone and direction for what was to follow. Certainly Locke was the most prominent figure in the early eighteenth century, the indispensable precursor of Berkeley and Hume as well as a fountainhead for the French Encyclopedists. If it is said that the two strains of Cartesian rationalism and Lockian empiricism met in Kant, it can be added that Hume built on Locke's foundation and Kant formalized much that was first a vague groping in Locke. Though Locke was not a wholly satisfactory thinker, his influence on thought in England and America has never completely abated, and even now there appears to be a revived interest in *Essay*.

POLITICAL THOUGHT

Locke's earliest known political writings were *Essays on the Law of Nature*, written in Latin between 1660 and 1664 but not known until the Lovelace Collection was examined in 1946. They were first published in 1954 with a translation by W. von Leyden. Though much in these essays appears in *An Essay concerning Human Understanding* and *Two Treatises of Government*, there remain many points at which the early essays are in conflict with parts of both later works. This fact and the bother of translating them may have deterred Locke from publishing them, despite the urging of Tyrrell. Since von Leyden can find no evidence of direct influence of these essays on anyone other than Tyrrell and Gabriel Towerson, the student of Locke is referred to von Leyden's publication for additional information.

TWO TREATISES. *Two Treatises of Government* appeared anonymously in 1690, written, it is said, to justify the revolution of 1688, or, according to the preface, "to establish the Throne of Our Great Restorer, our present King William; to make good his Title, in the Consent of the People." Locke acknowledged his authorship only in a codicil in his will listing his anonymous works and giving to the Bodleian Library a corrected copy of *Two Treatises.* He never felt that any of the editions printed during his lifetime had satisfactorily rendered his work. Only in 1960 did Peter Laslett publish a critical edition based on the Coste master copy of *Two Treatises.*

THE FIRST TREATISE. It has long been suspected that the first treatise was written in 1683 and that the second treatise was written in 1689. Laslett has presented much evidence to show that the second treatise was the earlier work, written between 1679 and 1681. If his thesis is correct, it was a revolutionary document, whose purpose was not primarily to philosophize but to furnish a theoretical foundation for the political aims and maneuvers of Shaftesbury and his followers in their struggle with Charles II. Only further scholarly probing will resolve this question.

In his preface, Locke stated that the greater part of the original work had been lost. He was satisfied that what remained was sufficient, since he had neither the time nor the inclination to rewrite the missing sections. The evidence is clear that it was portions of the first treatise that were lost.

The first treatise is a sarcastic and harsh criticism of Sir Robert Filmer's *Patriarcha*, which argued for the divine right of kings. Locke's treatise is more of historical than philosophical importance. It argued that Adam was not, as Filmer claimed, divinely appointed monarch of the world and all his descendants. Neither was the power of absolute monarchy inherited from Adam. Adam had no absolute rights over Eve or over his children. Parents have authority over children who are dependent upon them and who must learn obedience as well as many other things for life. The function of the parent is to protect the child and to help him mature. When the child comes to maturity, parental authority ends. In any case, the relation of parent and child is not the same as that of sovereign and subject. Were Filmer right, one would have to conclude that every man is born a slave, a notion that was utterly repugnant to Locke. Even if Filmer were correct, it would be impossible to show that existing rulers, especially the English kings, possess legitimate claims to their sovereignty by tracing it back to lawful descent from Adam.

THE SECOND TREATISE. Locke began the second treatise with the proposition that all men are originally in a state of nature, "a state of perfect freedom to order their actions, and dispose of their possessions, and persons as they think fit, within the bounds of the Law of Nature, without asking leave, or depending upon the Will of any other man" (II.ii.4). Although Locke sometimes wrote as if the state of nature were some period in history, it must be taken largely as a philosophical fiction, an assumption made to show the nature and foundation of political power, a fiction at least as old as Plato's treatment of the Prometheus myth in the *Protagoras.* It is a state of equality but not of unbounded license. Being rational and being a creature bound by God, man must be governed by the law of nature.

Natural law. Though the concept of the law of nature is as old as antiquity, it flourished in the seventeenth century in the minds of a considerable number of ethical and political thinkers. In general it supposed that man by the use of reason could know in the main the fundamental principles of morality, which he otherwise knew through Christian revelation. Locke was extremely vague about the law of nature, but in his *Essays on the Law of Nature* he held that that law rests ultimately on God's will. Reason discovers it. It is not innate. When, however, Locke spoke of it as "writ in the hearts of all mankind," he suggested some kind of innateness. There are obvious difficulties here, for sense and reason may fail men, even though the law of nature is binding on all. Moreover, the various exponents of the law of nature differ on what it consists of, except that it presupposes the brotherhood of man and human benevolence.

State of nature. In a state of nature, according to Locke, all men are bound to preserve peace, preserve mankind, and refrain from hurt to one another. The execution of the law of nature is the responsibility of each individual. If any man violates this law, he thereby puts himself in a state of war with the others, who may then punish the offender. The power that one man may hold over another is neither absolute nor arbitrary and must be restrained by proportion. The state of nature was for Locke a society of men, as distinct from a state of government, or a political society.

Social contract. There are certain inconveniences in a state of nature, such as men's partiality and the inclination on the part of some men to violate the rights of others. The remedy for this is civil government, wherein men

ENCYCLOPEDIA OF PHILOSOPHY
2nd edition

by common consent form a social contract and create a single body politic. This contract is not between ruler and ruled, but between equally free men. The aim of the contract is to preserve the lives, freedom, and property of all, as they belong to each under natural law. Whoever, therefore, attempts to gain absolute power over another puts himself at war with the other. This holds in the political state as well as the state of nature. When a ruler becomes a tyrant, he puts himself in a state of war with the people, who then, if no redress be found, may make an appeal to heaven, that is, may revolt. This power is but an extension of the right of each to punish an aggressor in the state of nature. Unlike Hobbes, Locke was persuaded that men are capable of judging whether they are cruelly subjected and unjustly treated. Since one reason for men entering into the social contract is to avoid a state of war, the contract is broken when the sovereign puts himself into a state of war with the people by becoming a tyrant.

Slavery. Curiously, Locke justified slavery on the grounds that those who became slaves were originally in a state of wrongful war with those who conquered them and, being captive, forfeited their freedom. Apart from being bad history, this argument ignores the rights of the children of slaves. Locke's inconsistency here may mercifully be passed over.

Property. Property was an idea that Locke used in both a broad and a narrow sense. Men have a right to self-preservation and therefore to such things as they need for their subsistence. Each man possesses himself absolutely, and therefore that with which he mixes his labor becomes his property. "God has given the earth to mankind in common." No man has original, exclusive rights to the fruits and beasts of the earth. Nevertheless, man must have some means with which to appropriate them. This consists of the labor of his body and the work of his hand. By labor, man removes things from a state of nature and makes them his property. Without labor, the earth and things in general have but little value. However, only so much as a man improves and can use belongs to him, nor may a man deprive another of the means of self-preservation by overextending his reach for property.

Though the right to property is grounded in nature, it is not secured therein. It is one of the primary ends of the state to preserve the rights of property, as well as to make laws governing the use, distribution, and transference of property. In communities or countries under government, there are fixed boundaries to the common territory, and there is land and property held in common which no one may appropriate to himself and to which those not members of the community have no right at all.

Money, being something that does not spoil, came into use by mutual consent, serving as a useful means of exchange. At the same time it made possible the accumulation of wealth greater than warranted by need or use.

Political society. Having established several rights and duties belonging to men by nature and having shown certain inconveniences and disadvantages of the state of nature, Locke turned to political society. The first society consists of the family, whose aims are not initially or primarily those of political society, but which may be included under political society.

In political society "any number of men are so united into one Society, as to quit everyone his Executive power of the law of nature, and to resign it to the public" (II.vii.89). The legislative and executive powers are "a right of making laws with penalties of Death, and consequently all less Penalties, for the regulating and preserving of property, and of employing the force of the community, in the execution of such laws, and in the defense of the commonwealth from foreign injury, and all this only for the public good" (II.i.3). By the social contract men give up, not all their rights, but only the legislative and executive right they originally had under the law of nature. This transference of power is always subordinate to the proper and true ends of the commonwealth, which are "the mutual preservation of their lives, liberties and estates."

Each man must voluntarily consent to the compact either explicitly or implicitly. An individual who at age of discretion remains a member of the community tacitly consents to the compact.

Since the compact is made between the members of the community, sovereignty ultimately remains with the people. The sovereign, in the form of a legislative body, and executive, or both, is the agent and executor of the sovereignty of the people. The community can act only by the rule of the majority, and everyone is bound by it, because an agreement of unanimity is virtually impossible. It is the people who establish the legislative, executive, and judiciary powers. Thus, an absolute monarch is incompatible with civil society.

Locke's theories so far are compatible with either monarchy, oligarchy, or democracy so long as it is recognized that ultimate sovereignty lies with the people. He believed that a constitutional monarchy with executive power, including the judiciary, in the hands of the monarch, and legislative powers in a parliamentary assembly elected by the people was the most satisfactory form of government. The supreme power he held to be the legislative, for it makes the laws that the executive must carry out and enforce. Whenever the executive violates the trust that he holds, no obligation is owed him and he may be deposed. The legislature may also violate its trust, though Locke believed it less likely to do so. Whenever this occurs, the people have a right to dissolve it and establish a new government. For this reason a regularly elected legislative body is desirable.

Rebellion. Locke explicitly recognized, as the events during his lifetime had shown, that men may become tyrants to those whom they were bound to serve. It may be a king, an assembly, or a usurper that claims absolute power. In such cases the people have a right to rebellion if no other redress is possible. Locke was not unmindful of the fact that the executive needs latitude and prerogative so that he may govern, and that the legislative body must deliberate and make laws that they believe to be in the public good. The right to rebellion is warranted only in the most extreme conditions, where all other means fail. Locke did not believe that men would lightly avail themselves of this power, for men will suffer and endure much before they resort to rebellion.

In transferring to the government the right to make and execute law and make war and peace, men do not give up the natural light of reason, by which they judge good and evil, right and wrong, justice and injustice. In specific laws or executive decisions judgment must be allowed to the legislature and the executive. If, however, a long train of acts shows a tyrannical course, then men, judging that the sovereign has put himself into a state of war with them, may justly dethrone the tyrant. On the other hand, the legislative and executive power can never revert to the people unless there is a breach of trust.

The dissolution of government is not the dissolution of society. The aim of revolution is the establishment of a new government, not a return to a state of nature. The dissolution of a government may occur under many circumstances, but foremost among them are when the arbitrary will of a single person or prince is set in place of the law; when the prince hinders the legislature from due and lawful assembly; when there is arbitrary change in elections; when the people are delivered into subjection by a foreign power; and when the executive neglects and abandons his charge. In all such cases sovereignty reverts to the society, and the people have a right to act as the supreme power and continue the legislature in themselves, or erect a new form, or under the old form place sovereignty in new hands, whichever they think best. On the other hand, "the power that every individual gave the society, ... can never revert to the individuals again, as long as the society lasts" (II.xix.243). As theory, Locke's second treatise is full of inadequacies, but its magnificent sweep of ideas prepared the ground for popular and democratic government.

EDUCATION AND RELIGION

Locke's thought on education and religion was not presented in strictly philosophical terms. It was, however, deeply rooted in the fundamental concepts of *Essay* and *Two Treatises*. His works in these areas display clearly the liberal bent of his mind as well as his love of freedom, tolerance, and truth. His attitude was pragmatic and based on considerable psychological insight into the motives, needs, passions, and follies of men. *Some Thoughts concerning Education*, several letters on toleration, and *The Reasonableness of Christianity* profoundly affected educational and religious thought in the eighteenth century and after. Two of these works, *Some Thoughts concerning Education* and the first *Letter on Toleration*, continue to be fresh and relevant.

EDUCATION. When Locke was in Holland, he wrote a number of letters to Edward Clark advising him on the education of his son, a young man of no particular distinction. Locke had in mind the education of a gentleman who would one day be a squire. In 1693 Locke modified these letters somewhat and published the contents as *Some Thoughts concerning Education* in response to "so many, who profess themselves at a loss how to breed their children." His thought was marked by a ready understanding of, and warm sympathy with, children. Three main thoughts dominate the work. First, the individual aptitudes, capacities, and idiosyncrasies of the child should govern learning, not arbitrary curricular or rote learning taught by the rod. Second, Locke placed the health of the body and the development of a sound character ahead of intellectual learning. In the third place, he saw that play, high spirits, and the "gamesome humor" natural to children should govern the business of learning wherever possible. Compulsory learning is irksome; where there is play in learning, there will be joy in it. Throughout he placed emphasis on good example, practice, and use rather than on precepts, rules, and punishment. The work was an implicit criticism of his own education at Westminster and Oxford, which he found unpleasant and largely useless.

Writing almost as a physician, Locke advised "plenty of open air, exercise, and sleep; plain diet, no wine or strong drink, and very little or no physic; not too warm and strait clothing; especially the head and feet kept cold, and the feet often used to cold water and exposed to wet." The aim in all was to keep the body in strength and vigor, able to endure hardships.

Locke urged that early training must establish the authority of the parents so that good habits may be established. The prime purpose is the development of virtue, the principle of which is the power of denying ourselves the satisfaction of our desires. The child should be taught to submit to reason when young. Parents teach by their own example. They should avoid severe punishments and beatings as well as artificial rewards. Rules should be few when a child is young, but those few should be obeyed. Mild, firm, and rational approval or disapproval are most effective in curbing bad behavior. Children should be frequently in the company of their parents, who should in turn study the disposition of the child and endeavor to use the child's natural desire for freedom and play to make learning as much like recreation as possible. High spirits should not be curbed, but turned to creative use. Curiosity too should be encouraged, and questions should be heard and fairly answered. Cruelty must always be discouraged and courageousness approved.

As the child grows, familiarity should be increased so that the parent has a friend in the mature child. Virtue, breeding, and a free liberal spirit as well as wisdom and truthfulness were the goals set by Locke in all his advice. Affection and friendship were for him both means and ends of good education.

Learning, though important, Locke put last. First, he would have the child learn to speak and read his own language well by example and practice, not by grammar. In the study of all languages, he would put off the study of grammar until they can be spoken well. He would begin the learning of a second modern language early. Reluctantly he would allow a gentleman's son to learn Latin, but he did not recommend much time on Greek, Hebrew, Arabic, rhetoric, or logic, which constituted the curricula of the universities of his day. Rather, time should be given to the study of geography, arithmetic, astronomy, geometry, history, ethics, and civil law. Dancing he encouraged, and music as well, in moderation. He was less sympathetic to poetry. Remarkably, he urged that everyone learn at least one manual trade and make some study of accounting. Finally, travel was valuable if not done before one could profit by it.

If much of this is familiar and even trite, it must be remembered that Locke was among the first to formulate these ideas. His influence on educational thought and practice was enormous and is still very much with us in its fundamental outlook and method.

RELIGION. Locke saw some merits in all the competing claims of various religious groups. He also saw the destructive force that was released when these claims sought exclusive public dominion at the expense of individual conscience. He looked in several directions at once. This tendency has earned for him the reputation of being timorous and compromising. Nonetheless, it is on this trait of mind that much of his great influence and reputation rests. For Locke, fidelity to the evidence at hand always outweighed cleverness, consistency, and dialectic. It is the chief testimony to his claim that truth was always his aim, even when he might have won an easy victory by dogmatic consistency.

Locke's writings on religion are voluminous. When he died he was working on extensive commentaries on the *Epistles of St. Paul*, as well as a draft of a fourth *Letter on Toleration*. Earlier he had written and published three letters on toleration, *The Reasonableness of Christianity* (1695), and two *Vindications* (1695 and 1697) of the latter work. Moreover, Locke's three letters to Stillingfleet, the bishop of Worcester, are concerned with religious questions as well as epistemological ones.

Religious tolerance. Locke's first *Letter concerning Toleration* stated his position clearly, and he never deviated from it substantially. It was originally written in Latin as a letter to his Dutch friend Philip van Limborch. In 1689 it was published on the Continent in Latin, and in the same year a translation of it by William Popple appeared in English.

Locke was not the first to write in advocacy of religious toleration. His was, however, a powerful, direct, and passionate plea. It was linked with *Essay* by its recognition of the limits of human knowledge and human fallibility, and with *Two Treatises* by his deep commitment to individual rights and freedom.

Locke took toleration to be the chief characteristic mark of the true church, for religious belief is primarily a relation between each man and God. True religion regulates men's lives according to virtue and piety, and without charity and love religion is false to itself. Those who persecute others in the name of Christ abjure his teachings, seeking only outward conformity, not peace and holiness. Who can believe that in torture and execution the fanatic truly seeks the salvation of the soul of his victim? Moreover, the mind cannot be forced or belief compelled. All efforts to force or compel belief breed only hypocrisy and contempt of God. Persuasion is the only lever that can truly move the mind.

A church is "a voluntary society of men, joining themselves together of their own accord in order to the public worshipping of God in such manner as they judge acceptable to Him, and effectual to the salvation of their souls." It is sharply distinct from a state, or commonwealth. The state is concerned with the public good, protecting life, liberty, and property. It has no authority in matters of the spirit. "Whatever is lawful in the commonwealth cannot be prohibited by the magistrate in the church."

It is to be doubted that any man or group of men possess the truth about the one true way to salvation. In the Scriptures we have all that may reasonably be claimed by Christians to be the word of God. The rest are the speculations and beliefs of men concerning articles of faith and forms of worship. Sincere and honest men differ in these matters, and only tolerance of these differences can bring about public peace and Christian charity. Jews, pagans, and Muslims are all equally confident in their religious faith. Mutual tolerance is essential where such diversity exists. This is most evident when we observe that it is the most powerful party that persecutes others in the name of religion. Yet in different countries and at different times power has lain in the hands of different religious groups. It is physical power, not true faith, which decides who is persecuted and who persecutes.

Throughout Locke's argument the liberty of person and the liberty of conscience are decisive. He limited this liberty only by denying to religion the right to harm directly another person or group or to practice clearly immoral rites. By a curious and probably prudential exception, he denied tolerance to atheists, because promises, covenants, and oaths would not bind them, and to any church so constituted "that all those who enter into it do thereby *ipso facto* deliver themselves up to the protection and service of another prince."

Despite these limitations, Locke's letter moved subsequent generations to a greater spirit of tolerance in religious matters. It is still part of the liberal democratic ideal and transcends the time of its composition.

Faith and reason. The *Reasonableness of Christianity* and *Vindications* are works more bound to Locke's own time. Locke was probably neither a Socinian nor a deist, even though certain deists and Unitarians found comfort and inspiration in his work. He was a sincere Christian, who tried to diminish the flourishing schisms and sects by proposing a return to the Scriptures and an abandonment of the interminable theological disputes of his day. He accepted the divine inspiration of the Bible. Nevertheless, he held that even revelation must be tested by reason. In

the New Testament, Christianity is rational and simple. The core of Christian faith lies in the belief in the fatherhood of God, the divinity of Christ the Messiah, and the morality of charity, love, and divine mercy. Justification by faith means faith in Christ, whose essential revelation is that God is merciful and forgives the sinner who truly repents and strives to live a life of Christian morality. The Mosaic law, God's mercy, and Christian morality are all consonant with human reason. Revelation discloses to man what unaided reason could not discover—the mysteries, the Virgin Birth, the Resurrection, the divinity of Christ. But when disclosed, these do not violate the canons of reason. Here as elsewhere, Locke's emphasis on reason was circumscribed, reason must be followed where possible, but it does not carry us far enough by itself.

Locke's influence was wide and deep. In political, religious, educational, and philosophical thought he inspired the leading minds of England, France, America, and to some extent, Germany. He disposed of the exaggerated rationalism of Descartes and Spinoza; he laid the groundwork for a new empiricism and advanced the claims for experimentalism. Voltaire, Montesquieu, and the French Encyclopedists found in Locke the philosophical, political, educational, and moral basis that enabled them to prepare and advance the ideas that eventuated in the French Revolution. In America, his influence on Jonathan Edwards, Hamilton, and Jefferson was decisive. Locke's zeal for truth as he saw it was stronger than his passion for dialectical and logical niceness, and this may account for the fact that his works prepared the ground for action as well as thought.

See also Animal Mind; Authority; Berkeley, George; Boyle, Robert; Cambridge Platonists; Clarke, Samuel; Cudworth, Ralph; Descartes, René; Edwards, Jonathan; Empiricism; Encyclopédie; Ethics, History of; Filmer, Robert; Gassendi, Pierre; Hobbes, Thomas; Hooker, Richard; Hume, David; Jefferson, Thomas; Kant, Immanuel; Leibniz, Gottfried Wilhelm; Malebranche, Nicolas; Montesquieu, Baron de; Natural Law; Newton, Isaac; Personal Identity; Philosophy of Education, History of; Social Contract; Spinoza, Benedict (Baruch) de; Stillingfleet, Edward; Voltaire, François-Marie Arouet de; Whichcote, Benjamin.

Bibliography

WORKS BY LOCKE

Essays on the Law of Nature. Translated from the Latin and edited by W. von Leyden. Oxford, 1954. Also gives an account of the Lovelace Collection.

An Early Draft of Locke's Essay (Draft A). Edited by R. I. Aaron and J. Gibb. Oxford, 1936. Valuable as a study of the development of *Essay*.

An Essay concerning the Understanding, Knowledge, Opinion and Assent (Draft B). Edited by B. Rand. Cambridge, MA: 1931. Valuable, but superseded by manuscript in Bodleian Library.

Epistola de Tolerantia. Gouda, 1689. Translated by William Popple as *A Letter concerning Toleration*. London, 1689. Several defenses appeared in the 1690s and fragments of a fourth in 1706.

An Essay concerning Human Understanding. London, 1690; 2nd ed. with large additions, London, 1694; 3rd ed., London, 1695; 4th ed., with large additions, London, 1700; 5th ed., with many large additions, London, 1706. Best modern edition, from which all quotes in this article are taken, is a reprint of the fifth edition, J. W. Yolton, ed., 2 vols. New York and London, 1961.

Two Treatises of Government. London, 1690. The critical and collated edition of Locke's corrected copy by Peter Laslett (Cambridge, 1960) surpasses all previous editions.

Some Considerations of the Consequences of the Lowering of Interest and the Raising of the Value of Money. London, 1692. Two additional papers on money appeared in 1695.

Some Thoughts concerning Education. London, 1693.

The Reasonableness of Christianity. London, 1695. Defenses of this work were published in 1695 and 1697.

A Letter to the Right Rev. Edward Ld. Bishop of Worcester, concerning Some Passages relating to Mr. Locke's Essay of Humane Understanding. London, 1697. Two further letters appeared, in 1697 and 1699.

A Paraphrase and Notes on the Epistles of St. Paul to the Galatians [etc.]. London, 1705.

Posthumous Works of Mr. John Locke, 6 vols. London, 1706.

The Remains of John Locke. Edited by E. Curl. London, 1714.

Works of John Locke. 3 vols. London, 1714; 10th ed., 10 vols., London, 1801.

The Correspondence of John Locke and Edward Clarke. Edited by B. Rand. Oxford, 1927.

For the remainder of Locke's published and unpublished papers, consult the works listed below by Aaron, Christopherson, von Leyden, Long, Ollion, and Yolton. See von Leyden and Long particularly for the Lovelace Collection.

WORKS ON LOCKE

Biographies

Bourne, H. R. Fox. *Life of John Locke*. 2 vols. London: H. S. King, 1876. Excellent, but inadequate since Lovelace Collection became available.

Cranston, Maurice. *John Locke, a Biography*. London and New York: Longmans, Green, 1957. A thorough study of the life of Locke, using all materials available at present.

King, Lord Peter. *The Life and Letters of John Locke*. London: H. Coburn, 1829. Not good, but contains original material.

Critical Commentaries

Aaron, R. I. "Locke's Theory of Universals." *PAS*, Vol. 33 (1932/1933). Useful and enlightening.

Aaron, R. I. *John Locke*. Oxford: Oxford University Press, 1937; rev. ed., Oxford, 1955. Best general commentary.

Adamson, J. W. *The Educational Writings of John Locke*. Cambridge, U.K.: 1922.

Bastide, C. *John Locke, ses théories politiques et leur influence en Angleterre*. Paris: Leroux, 1906. Still valuable work on Locke's political philosophy.

Christopherson, H. O. *A Bibliographical Introduction to the Study of John Locke*. Oslo, 1930. Incomplete.

Clapp, J. G. *Locke's Conception of the Mind*. PhD diss., Columbia University. New York, 1937.

Cranston, Maurice. "Men and Ideas; John Locke." *Encounter* 7 (1956): 46–54.

Czajkowski, C. J. *The Theory of Private Property in Locke's Political Philosophy*. Notre Dame, IN, 1941. Useful on the labor theory of value.

DeMarchi, E. "Locke's Atlantis." *Political Studies* 3 (1955): 164–165.

Gibson, James. *Locke's Theory of Knowledge*. Cambridge, U.K.: Cambridge University Press, 1917. Emphasizes Locke's rationalism.

Gibson, James. *John Locke*. British Academy, Henriette Hertz Lecture, 1933.

Gierke, Otto von. *Naturrecht und deutsches Recht*. Translated and edited by Ernest Barker as *Natural Law and the Theory of Society*. 2 vols. Cambridge, U.K.: 1934. A major study.

Gough, J. W. *John Locke's Political Philosophy. Eight Studies*. Oxford, 1950. Important.

Jackson, Reginald. "Locke's Distinction Between Primary and Secondary Qualities." *Mind* 38 (1929): 56–76.

Jackson, Reginald. "Locke's Version of the Doctrine of Representative Perception." *Mind* 39 (1930): 1–25.

James, D. G. *The Life of Reason: Hobbes, Locke, Bolingbroke*. London and New York: Longman, Green, 1949.

Krakowski, E. *Les sources médiévales de la philosophie de Locke*. Paris: Jouve, 1915. One of the few studies of influences on Locke.

Lamprecht, S. P. *The Moral and Political Philosophy of John Locke*. New York: Columbia University Press, 1918.

Laslett, Peter. "The English Revolution and Locke's Two Treatises of Government." *Cambridge Historical Journal* 12 (1956). Interesting and controversial.

Leibniz, G. W. *Nouveaux essais sur l'entendement humain*. Leipzig and Amsterdam, 1765. Translated by A. G. Langley as *New Essays concerning Human Understanding*. New York and London: Macmillan, 1896. An important critique of Locke by a contemporary.

Leyden, W. von. "John Locke and Natural Law." *Philosophy* 31 (1956). A useful examination.

Long, P. *A Summary Catalogue of the Lovelace Collection of Papers of John Locke in the Bodleian Library*. Oxford, 1959.

O'Connor, D. J. *John Locke*. Harmondsworth, U.K.: Penguin, 1952.

Ollion, H. *Notes sur la correspondance de John Locke*. Paris: A. Picard, 1908.

Polin, R. *La politique de John Locke*. Paris, 1960. Interesting contrast to Laslett.

Pollock, Sir Frederick. "Locke's Theory of the State." In his *Essays in the Law*. London: H. M. Stationery Office, 1922. Ch. 3.

Ryle, Gilbert. *Locke on the Human Understanding*. Oxford: Oxford University Press, 1933.

Smith, N. K. *John Locke*. Manchester, U.K.: Manchester University Press, 1933.

Ware, C. S. "The Influence of Descartes on John Locke." *Revue internationale de philosophie* (1950): 210–230.

Webb, T. E. *The Intellectualism of Locke. An Essay*. Dublin: W. McGee, 1857. Presents Locke as a precursor to Kant.

Yolton, J. W. "Locke's Unpublished Marginal Replies to John Sergeant." *Journal of the History of Ideas* 12 (1951): 528–559.

Yolton, J. W. "Locke and the Seventeenth-Century Logic of Ideas." *Journal of the History of Ideas* 16 (1955): 431–452.

Yolton, J. W. *Locke and the Way of Ideas*. Oxford: Clarendon Press, 1956. A careful study.

Yolton, J. W. "Locke on the Law of Nature." *Philosophical Review* 67 (1958): 477–498.

RECENT EDITIONS OF LOCKE'S WORKS

Goldie, Mark, ed. *John Locke: Selected Correspondence*. Oxford: Oxford University Press, 2002.

Nuovo, Victor, ed. *John Locke: Writings on Religion*. Oxford: Clarendon Press, 2002.

RECENT WORKS ON LOCKE

Bennett, Jonathan. "Ideas and Qualities in Locke's *Essay*." *History of Philosophy Quarterly* 13 (1996): 73–88.

Bolton, Martha Brandt. "Locke, Leibniz, and the Logic of Mechanism." *Journal of the History of Philosophy* 36 (1998): 189–213.

Coventry, Angela. "Locke, Hume, and the Idea of Causal Power." *Locke Studies* 3 (2003): 93–111.

Downing, Lisa. "The Status of Mechanism in Locke's *Essay*." *Philosophical Review* 107 (1998): 381–414.

Garrett, Don. "Locke on Personal Identity, Consciousness, and 'Fatal Errors'." *Philosophical Topics* 31 (2003): 95–125.

Jacovides, Michael. "Locke's Resemblance Theses." *Philosophical Review* 108 (1999): 461–496.

Jacovides, Michael. "The Epistemology under Locke's Corpuscularianism." *Archiv für Geschichte der Philosophie* 84 (2002): 161–189.

Langton, Rae. "Locke's Relations and God's Good Pleasure." *Proceedings of the Aristotelian Society* 100 (2000): 75–91.

Lowe, E. "J. Locke: Compatibilist Event-Causalist or Libertarian Substance-Causalist?" *Philosophy and Phenomenological-Research* 68 (2004): 688–701.

Martin, Raymond. "Locke's Psychology of Personal Identity." *Journal of the History of Philosophy* 38 (2000): 41–61.

McCann, Edwin. "Locke's Theory of Substance Under Attack!" *Philosophical Studies* 106 (2001): 87–105.

Newman, Lex. "Locke on the Idea of Substratum." *Pacific Philosophical Quarterly* 81 (2000): 291–324.

Ott, Walter. *Locke's Philosophy of Language*. Cambridge, U.K.: Cambridge University Press, 2003.

Owen, David. "Locke and Hume on Belief, Judgment and Assent." *Topoi* 22 (2003): 15–28.

Rogers, G. A. J., ed. *Locke's Philosophy: Content and Context*. Oxford: Clarendon Press, 1996.

Rozemond, Marleen, and Gideon Yaffe. "Peach Trees, Gravity and God: Mechanism in Locke." *British Journal for the History of Philosophy* 12 (2004): 387–412.

Stuart, Matthew. "Locke on Natural Kinds." *History of Philosophy Quarterly* 16 (1999): 277–296.

Stuart, Matthew. "Locke's Colors." *Philosophical Review* 112 (2003): 57–96.

Thiel, Udo, ed. *Locke: Epistemology and Metaphysics*. Brookfield: Ashgate: 2002.

Tuckness, Alex. *Locke and the Legislative Point of View: Toleration, Contested Principles, and the Law*. Princeton, NJ: Princeton University Press, 2002.

Wilson, Robert A. "Locke's Primary Qualities." *Journal of the History of Philosophy* 40 (2002): 201–228.

Wolterstorff, Nicholas. *John Locke and the Ethics of Belief*. New York: Cambridge University Press, 1996.

Yaffe, Gideon. *Freedom Worth the Name: Locke on Free Agency*. Princeton: Princeton University Press, 2000.

Yolton, Jean S. *John Locke: A Descriptive Bibliography*. Bristol: Thoemmes, 1998.

Yolton, John. "Locke's Man." *Journal of the History of Ideas* 62 (2001): 665–683.

James Gordon Clapp (1967)
Bibliography updated by Don Garrett (2005)

LOCKE, JOHN [ADDENDUM]

John Locke has been, for the last three decades, the subject of a rapid expansion of interest, stimulated by Oxford University Press's Clarendon edition of his works. The eight-volume edition of Locke's correspondence has opened new areas of information and exploration. So far in that series, we have definitive editions of *Essay* (including editions of the drafts and other relevant writings), the work on education, his paraphrases of St. Paul's epistles, and the papers on money, and well as *The Reasonableness of Christianity*, and the journals (again, opening a vast and important insight into Locke's reading, book buying, travels, opinions), and other works will follow. These editions, and the research that went into their production, have provided new resources for work on almost all aspects of Locke's life and writings, as well as material relating to his intellectual environment.

Antedating the Clarendon series was another medium for interest in Locke: *The Locke Newsletter*, founded and edited by Roland Hall. Beginning in 1970, published once per year (more or less), the newsletter has published articles on all aspects of Locke's thought. Included in each number is a list of recent (as of 1996) books and articles on Locke in many languages. This is a valuable source for keeping up to date on the publications about Locke. Another source of information on publications about Locke is the *Reference Guide* by Yolton and Yolton. Two other bibliographic resources are Attig's listings of Locke editions and the much fuller descriptive

ENCYCLOPEDIA OF PHILOSOPHY
2nd edition

bibliography of all editions of Locke's publications by Jean S. Yolton. The latter, a work long overdue, describes many different copies of Locke editions, which were located and examined in many different libraries and countries.

Among the topics in Locke's *Essay*, three have received special attention: the representative theory of perception, personal identity, and matter theory. The first of these in recent discussions has involved a debate over the nature of ideas: Are they special entities (e.g., images) standing between perceivers and objects, or are they simply the means for our access to the physical world? On the second topic it is becoming increasingly recognized that memory is not the crux of Locke's concept of person; it is consciousness, a wider and richer process (one with clear moral overtones) that focuses our awareness of self. A person for Locke is a moral being composed of the thoughts, feelings, and actions performed throughout a life. Consciousness is not a property of some immaterial substance, at least not so far as we can discover. The third topic has been given detailed attention via Locke's use of the corpuscular theory (see Alexander 1985). Some recognition has been given to Locke's movement toward the Newtonian concept of matter as force and power. Locke anticipated this development in his talk of the qualities of body being primarily powers. The substantiality of matter begins to fade under Locke's analysis of primary and secondary qualities. The chapter on power in *Essay*, the power of persons and the power of matter, is the longest and most complex chapter in that work (see J. W. Yolton 1993).

Locke's social and political thought has received even more attention throughout the decades, especially during the 1980s and 1990s. Laslett's early dating of *Two Treatises* and his locating that work in its historical context have been developed by writers such as Dunn, Harris, and Marshall. The central role of property and the relation of that concept to the person is generally recognized (see Tully 1980). His *Two Treatises* elaborates a concept of property that starts with each person's having property in his person. Acquisition of other possessions is a function of that original self-property. The tension between the interests and rights of the individual and those of society (or the community of mankind) is much discussed (see especially Gobetti 1992). The focus on consciousness as defining the person in his *Essay* indicated the central place of the individual in Locke's civil society. At the same time majority decisions were allowed to restrain individual actions. The power of the people is sanctioned by a social contract that obliges the ruler or legislative body to act for the good of the citizens, in conformity with the laws of nature. The interconnections between Locke's moral views and his social and political thought have been discussed by Marshall (1984). The issue of religious toleration has focused some of the recent treatments of Locke's political and religious writings, but all of the toleration writings by Locke await their inclusion in the Clarendon editions.

Locke's religious interests in the Bible and in what is required of a Christian have been clarified by recent studies (e.g., Wainwright's edition of the *Paraphrases*, 1987), but this area will be further illuminated when the Clarendon edition of *Reasonableness* appears. Locke's relation to the Latitudinarians and the role of original sin in his thinking have been explored by Spellman (1988). Coleman's (1983) systematic study of Locke's moral theory set the stage for some of the recent attention to this aspect of Locke's thought.

Another newly developing area of Locke studies concerns the reception of his doctrines in Europe, especially in France. The difficulties the French had with the term "consciousness" when translating this English term have been interestingly analyzed by Davies (1990). Reactions to Locke's books in French-language journals and the impact of his doctrines (especially thinking matter) on Enlightenment thinkers have been presented by several writers (Hutchison 1991; Schøsler 1985, 1994; J. W. Yolton 1991). The full story of the reception of Locke's doctrines in Europe (especially in Germany, Portugal, and Holland) in the eighteenth century has yet to be written. Fruitful research programs are waiting for scholars. A number of collections of articles can be consulted to fill out this brief sketch of newer developments in Locke studies (Chappell 1994, Harpham 1992, Thompson 1991).

See also Consciousness; Perception; Personal Identity; Power; Primary and Secondary Qualities; Property; Social Contract; Toleration.

Bibliography

RECENT EDITIONS OF LOCKE'S WORKS

De Beer, E. S., ed. *The Correspondence of John Locke*. 8 vols. Oxford: Oxford University Press, 1976–189.

Kelly, P., ed. *Several Papers Relating to Money, Interest, and Trade*. Oxford: Oxford University Press, 1991.

Laslett, P., ed. *Two Treatises of Government*. 3rd ed. Cambridge U.K.: Cambridge University Press, 1989.

Nidditch, P. H., ed. *An Essay concerning Human Understanding*. Oxford: Oxford University Press, 1975.

Nidditch, P. H., and G. A. J. Rogers, eds. *Drafts for the Essay concerning Human Understanding and Other Philosophical*

Writings. Vol. 1. Oxford: Oxford University Press, 1990. Includes drafts A and B: other volumes planned.

Wainwright, A. P., ed. *Paraphrases and Notes on the Epistles of St. Paul.* 2 vols. Oxford: Oxford University Press, 1987.

Yolton. J. W., and J. S. Yolton, eds. *Some Thoughts concerning Education.* Oxford: Oxford University Press, 1989.

WORKS ON LOCKE

Alexander, P. *Ideas, Qualities, and Corpuscles: Locke and Boyle on the External World.* Cambridge, U.K., and New York: Cambridge University Press, 1985.

Ashcraft, R. *Revolutionary Politics and Locke's "Two Treatises of Government."* Princeton, NJ: Princeton University Press, 1986.

Attig, J. C., ed. *The Works of John Locke: A Comprehensive Bibliography from the Seventeenth Century to the Present.* Westport, CT: Greenwood, 1985.

Ayers, M. *Locke.* 2 vols. London, 1991.

Chappell, V., ed. *The Cambridge Companion to Locke.* Cambridge, U.K., and New York: Cambridge University Press, 1994.

Colman, J. *John Locke's Moral Philosophy.* Edinburgh: Edinburgh University Press, 1983.

Davies, C. *"Conscience" as Consciousness: The Self of Self-Awareness in French Philosophical Writing from Descartes to Diderot.* Studies on Voltaire and the Eighteenth Century, 272. Oxford, 1990.

Dunn, J. *The Political Thought of John Locke: An Historical Account of the Argument of the "Two Treatises of Government."* Cambridge, U.K.: Cambridge University Press, 1969.

Franklin, J. H. *John Locke and the Theory of Sovereignty: Mixed Monarchy and the Right of Resistance in the Political Thought of the English Revolution.* Cambridge, U.K., and New York: Cambridge University Press, 1978.

Gobetti, D. *Public and Private: Individuals, Households, and Body Politic in Locke and Hutcheson.* London, 1992.

Goyard-Fabre, S. *John Locke et la raison raisonnable.* Paris: Bordas, 1986.

Harpham, E. J., ed. *John Locke's "Two Treatises of Government": New Interpretations.* Lawrence: University of Kansas Press, 1992.

Harris, I. *The Mind of John Locke: A Study of Political Theory in Its Intellectual Setting.* Cambridge, U.K., and New York: Cambridge University Press, 1994.

Hutchison, R. *Locke in France, 1688–1734.* Studies on Voltaire and the Eighteenth Century, 290. Oxford: Voltaire Foundation of the Taylor Institution, 1991.

Mackie, J. L. *Problems from Locke.* Oxford: Clarendon Press, 1976.

Marshall, J. *John Locke: Resistance, Religion, and Responsibility.* Cambridge Studies in Early Modern British History. Cambridge, U.K., and New York: Cambridge University Press, 1994.

Passmore, J. "Locke and the Ethics of Belief." *Proceedings of the British Academy,* 64 (1978): 185–208.

Rogers, G. A. J. "Locke, Anthropology, and Models of the Mind." *History of the Human Sciences* 6 (1993): 73–87.

Rogers, G. A. J., ed. *Locke's Philosophy: Content and Context.* Oxford: Clarendon Press, 1994.

Schochet, G. J. "Toleration, Revolution, and Judgment in the Development of Locke's Political Thought." *Political Science* 40 (1988): 84–96.

Schøsler, J. *La bibliothèque raisonnée (1728–1753): Les Réactions d'un périodique français à la philosophie de Locke au XVIIIe siècle.* Odense: L'universite D'ordense, 1985.

Schøsler, J. "Le Christianisme raisonnable et le débat sur le 'Socianisme' de John Locke dans la presse française de la première moitié du XVIIIe siècle." *Lias* 21 (2) (1994): 295–319.

Schouls, P. A. *Reasoned Freedom: John Locke and Enlightenment.* Ithaca, NY: Cornell University Press, 1992.

Spellman, W. M. *John Locke and the Problem of Depravity.* Oxford: Clarendon Press, 1988.

Thiel, U. *Locke's Theorie der personalen Identität.* Bonn, 1983.

Thompson, M. P., ed. *John Locke und Immanuel Kant.* Berlin: Duncker and Humblot, 1991.

Tomida, Y. "Idea and Thing: The Deep Structure of Locke's Theory of Knowledge." *Analecta Husserliana* 66 (1995): 3–143.

Tuck, R. *Natural Rights Theories: Their Origin and Development.* Cambridge, U.K., and New York: Cambridge University Press, 1979.

Tully, J. *A Discourse on Property: John Locke and His Adversaries.* Cambridge, U.K., and New York: Cambridge University Press, 1980.

Vaughn, K. I. *John Locke, Economist and Social Scientist.* Chicago: University of Chicago Press, 1980.

Vienne, J.-M. *Expérience et raison: Les fondements de la morale selon Locke.* Paris: Vrin, 1991.

Walmsley, P. "Locke's Cassowary and the Ethos of the Essay." *Studies in Eighteenth-Century Culture* 22 (1992): 253–267.

Walmsley, P. "Dispute and Conversation: Probability and the Rhetoric of Natural Philosophy in Locke's *"Essay."* *Journal of the History of Ideas* 54 (1993): 381–394.

Winkler, K. P. "Locke on Personal Identity." *Journal of the History of Philosophy* 29 (1991): 201–226.

Wood, N. *The Politics of Locke's Philosophy: A Social Study of "An Essay concerning Human Understanding."* Berkeley: University of California Press,1983.

Yolton, J. S. *John Locke: A Descriptive Bibliography.* Bristol, U.K.: Toemmes Press, 1996.

Yolton, J. S., and J. W. Yolton. *John Locke: A Reference Guide.* Boston: G. K. Hall, 1985.

Yolton, J. W. *Locke and the Compass of Human Understanding: A Selective Commentary on the Essay.* Cambridge, U.K.: Cambridge University Press, 1970.

Yolton, J. W. *Locke and French Materialism.* Oxford: Clarendon Press, 1991.

Yolton, J. W. *A Locke Dictionary.* Oxford and Cambridge, MA: Blackwell, 1993.

John W. Yolton (1996)

LOGIC, COMBINATORY

See *Combinatory Logic*

LOGIC, HISTORY OF

The mainstream of the history of logic begins in ancient Greece and comes down through the Arabian and European logic of the Middle Ages and through a number of post-Renaissance thinkers to the more or less mathematical developments in logic in the nineteenth and twentieth centuries. In the period after the fall of Rome many of the ancient achievements were forgotten and had to be relearned; the same thing happened at the end of the Middle Ages. Otherwise this Western tradition has been fairly continuous. Indian and Chinese logic developed separately. Today logic, like other sciences, is studied internationally, and the same problems are treated in the Americas, western and eastern Europe, and Asia and Australasia. The story of the development of logic will be told here under the following headings:

ANCIENT LOGIC
LOGIC AND INFERENCE IN INDIAN
   PHILOSOPHY
CHINESE LOGIC
LOGIC IN THE ISLAMIC WORLD
MEDIEVAL (EUROPEAN) LOGIC
THE INTERREGNUM (BETWEEN MEDIEVAL
   AND MODERN LOGIC)
PRECURSORS OF MODERN LOGIC
MODERN LOGIC: THE BOOLEAN PERIOD
MODERN LOGIC: FROM FREGE TO GOËDEL
MODERN LOGIC: SINCE GOËDEL

Bibliography

HISTORY OF LOGIC

(In general, texts by and studies on individual logicians are listed only if they do not appear in the bibliographies to the separate entries on these people. Most works cited in the body of this entry are not repeated below.)

General Works

Bocheński, I. M. *Formale Logik*. Freiburg: Alber, 1956. Translated and edited by Ivo Thomas as *History of Formal Logic*. Notre Dame, IN, 1961. Contains extensive bibliographies.

Enriques, Federigo. *L'évolution de la logique*. Paris, 1926.

Kneale, William C., and Martha Kneale. *The Development of Logic*. Oxford: Clarendon Press, 1962.

Kotarbiński, Tadeusz. *Wyklady z Dziejów Logiki* (Lectures on the history of logic). Lodz: Zaklad Narodowy im Ossolinskich we Wroclawiu, 1957. Translated into French as *Leçons sur l'histoire de la logique*. Paris: Presses Universitaires de France, 1964.

Prantl, Carl. *Geschichte der Logik im Abendlande*. 4 vols. Leipzig: Hirzel, 1855–1870; reprinted (3 vols.), Graz, 1955. Covers the history up to 1600, with numerous quotations from the sources.

Scholz, Heinrich. *Abriss der Geschichte der Logik*. Berlin, 1931. Translated by K. F. Leidecker as *Concise History of Logic*. New York: Philosophical Library, 1961.

Works on Post-Medieval and Later Developments

Jørgensen, Jørgen. *A Treatise of Formal Logic*, Vol. I: *Historical Development*. Copenhagen: Levin and Munksgaard, 1931.

Jourdain, P. E. B. "The Development of the Theories of Mathematical Logic and the Principles of Mathematics." *Quarterly Journal of Pure and Applied Mathematics* 41 (1910): 324–352; 43 (1912): 219–314; 44 (1913): 113–128.

Lewis, C. I. *A Survey of Symbolic Logic*. Berkeley: University of California Press, 1918; reprinted, New York, 1960.

Nidditch, P. H. *The Development of Mathematical Logic*. New York: Free Press of Glencoe, 1962.

Prior, A. N. *Formal Logic*, 2nd ed. Oxford: Clarendon Press, 1962.

Shearman, A. T. *Development of Symbolic Logic*. London: Williams and Norgate, 1906.

(A. N. P.)

ANCIENT LOGIC

THE BEGINNINGS

Logic as a discipline starts with the transition from the customary use of certain logical methods and argument patterns to the reflection on and inquiry into these and their elements, including the syntax and semantics of sentences. In antiquity, logic as a systematic discipline begins with Aristotle. However, discussions of some elements of logic and a focus on methods of inference can be traced back to the late fifth century BCE.

SYNTAX AND SEMANTICS. Some of the Sophists classified types of sentences (*logoi*) according to their force. So Protagoras (485–415), who included wish, question, answer, and command (Diels-Kranz 80.A1, Diogenes Laertius 9.53–4), and Alcidamas (pupil of Gorgias, fl. fourth century BCE), who distinguished assertion (*phasis*), denial (*apophasis*), question, and appellation (Diogenes Laertius 9.54). Antisthenes (mid-5th–mid-4th cent.) defined a sentence as "that which indicates what a thing was or is" (Diogenes Laertius 6.3, Diels-Kranz 45) and stated that someone who says what is speaks truly (Diels-Kranz 49). Perhaps the earliest surviving passage on logic is found in the *Dissoi Logoi* or Double arguments (Diels-Kranz 90.4, c.400 BCE). It is evidence for a debate over truth and falsehood. Opposed were the views that: (1) truth is a—temporal—property of sentences, and that a sentence is true (when it is said), if and only if things are as the sentence says they are when it is said, and false if they are not; and (2) truth is an atemporal property of what is said, and that what is said is true if and only if the things are the case, and false if they are not the case. These are rudimentary formulations of two alternative correspondence theories of truth. The same passage also displays awareness of the fact that self-referential use of the truth-predicate can be problematic—an insight also documented by the discovery of the Liar paradox by Eubulides of Miletus (mid fourth century BCE) shortly thereafter.

Some Platonic dialogues contain passages whose topic is indubitably logic. In the *Sophist*, Plato analyzes simple statements as containing a verb (*rhēma*, which indicates action) and a name (*onoma*, which indicates the agent) (Soph.261E–262A). Anticipating the modern distinction of logical types, he argues that neither a series of names nor a series of verbs can combine into a statement (Soph.262A–D). Plato also divorces syntax (*what is a statement?*) from semantics (*when is it true?*). Something (e.g., *Theaetetus is sitting*) is a statement if it both succeeds in specifying a subject and says something about this subject. Plato thus determines subject and predicate as relational elements in a statement and excludes statements containing empty subject expressions. Something is a true statement if with reference to its subject (Theaetetus) it says of what is (e.g., sitting) that it is. Something is a false statement if with reference to its subject it says of something other than what is (e.g., flying) that it is. Here Plato produces a sketch of a reductionist theory of truth (Soph.262E–263D; cf. also Crat. xxx). He also distinguishes negations from affirmations and takes the negation particle to have narrow scope: It negates the predicate, not the whole sentence (Soph.257B–C). There are many passages in Plato where he struggles with explaining certain logical relations. For example, his theory that things participate in Forms corresponds to a rudimentary theory of predication; in the *Sophist* and elsewhere, he grapples with the class relations of exclusion, union, and coextension; also with the difference between the *is* of predication (being) and the *is* of identity (sameness); and in *Republic* 4 he anticipates the law of noncontradiction. But his explications of these logical questions are cast in metaphysical terms and so can, at most, be regarded as protological.

ARGUMENT PATTERNS AND VALID INFERENCE. Pre-Aristotelian evidence for reflection on argument forms and valid inference are harder to come by. Both Zeno of Elea (c.490 BCE) and Socrates (470–399) were famous for the ways in which they refuted an opponent's view. Their methods display similarities with *reductio ad absurdum*, but neither of them seems to have theorized about their logical procedures. Zeno produced arguments (*logoi*) that manifest variations of the pattern *this* (that is, the opponent's view) *only if that. But that is impossible. So this is*

impossible. Socratic refutation was an exchange of questions and answers in which the opponents would be led, on the basis of their answers, to a conclusion incompatible with their original claim. Plato institutionalized such disputations into structured, rule-governed, verbal contests that became known as dialectical argument. The development of a basic logical vocabulary for such contests indicates some reflection upon the patterns of argumentation.

The fifth and fourth centuries BCE also see great interest in fallacies and logical paradoxes. Besides the Liar, Eubulides is said to have been the originator of several other logical paradoxes, including the Sorites. Plato's *Euthydemus* contains a large collection of contemporary fallacies. In attempts to solve such logical puzzles, a logical terminology develops here, too, and the focus on the difference between valid and invalid arguments sets the scene for the searching for a criterion of valid inference. Finally, it is possible that the shaping of deduction and proof in Greek mathematics that begins in the later fifth century BCE served as an inspiration for Aristotle's syllogistic.

ARISTOTLE

Aristotle is the first great logician in the history of logic. His logic was taught by and large without rival from the fourth to the nineteenth centuries CE. Aristotle's logical works were collected and put in a systematic order by later Peripatetics who titled them the *Organon* or *tool* because they considered logic not as a part but rather an instrument of philosophy. The *Organon* contains, in traditional order, the *Categories*, *De Interpretatione*, *Prior Analytics*, *Posterior Analytics*, *Topics*, and *Sophistical Refutations*. In addition, *Metaphysics* Γ is a logical treatise that discusses the principle of noncontradiction, and some further logical insights are found scattered throughout Aristotle's other works. Some parts of the *Categories* and *Posterior Analytics* would today be regarded as metaphysics, epistemology, or philosophy of science rather than logic. The traditional arrangement of works in the *Organon* is neither chronological nor Aristotle's own. The original chronology cannot be fully recovered since Aristotle often inserted supplements into earlier writings at a later time. However, by using logical advances as criterion, we can conjecture that most of the *Topics*, *Sophistical Refutations*, *Categories*, and *Metaphysics* Γ predate the *De Interpretatione*, which in turn precedes the *Prior Analytics* and parts of the *Posterior Analytics*.

DIALECTICS. The *Topics* provide a manual for participants in the contests of dialectical argument as instituted in the Academy by Plato. Books 2–7 provide general procedures or rules (*topoi*) about how to find an argument to establish or refute a given thesis. The descriptions of these procedures—some of which are so general that they resemble logical laws—clearly presuppose a notion of logical form, and Aristotle's *Topics* may thus count as the earliest surviving logical treatise. The *Sophistical Refutations* are the first systematic classification of fallacies, sorted by what logical flaw each type manifests (e.g., equivocation, begging the question, affirming the consequent, *secundum quid*) and how to expose them.

SUB-SENTENTIAL CLASSIFICATIONS

Aristotle distinguishes things that have sentential unity through a combination of expressions (a horse runs) from those that do not (horse, runs); the latter are dealt with in the *Categories* (the title really means Predications). They have no truth value and signify one of the following: substance (*ousia*), quantity (*poson*), quality (*poion*), relation (*pros ti*), location (*pou*), time (*pote*), position (*keisthai*), possession (*echein*), doing (*poiein*), and undergoing (*paschein*). It is unclear whether Aristotle considers this classification to be one of linguistic expressions that can be predicated of something else, or of kinds of predication, or of highest genera. In *Topics* 1 Aristotle distinguishes four relationships a predicate may have to the subject: It may give its definition, genus, unique property, or accidental property. These are known as predicables.

SYNTAX AND SEMANTICS OF SENTENCES.

When writing the *De Interpretatione*, Aristotle had worked out the following theory of simple sentences: A (declarative) sentence (*apophantikos logos*) or declaration (*apophansis*) is delimited from other pieces of discourse such as prayer, command, and question by its having a truth value. The truth bearers that feature in Aristotle's logic are thus linguistic items. They are spoken sentences that directly signify thoughts (shared by all humans) and, through these, indirectly, things. Written sentences in turn signify spoken ones. Sentences are constructed from two signifying expressions that stand in subject-predicate relation to each other: a name and a verb (Callias walks) or two names connected by the copula *is*, which cosignifies the connection (Pleasure is good) (*Int.* 3). Names are either singular terms or common nouns. Both can be empty (Cat. 10, *Int.* 1). Singular terms can only take subject position. Verbs cosignify time. A name-verb sentence can be rephrased with the copula (Callias is [a] walking [thing]) (*Int.* 12). As to their quality, a sentence is either an affir-

mation or a negation, depending on whether it affirms or negates its predicate of its subject. The negation particle in a negation has wide scope (Cat. 10). Aristotle defines truth separately for affirmations and negations: An affirmation is true if it says of that which is that it is; a negation is true if it says of that which is not that it is not (Met.Γ. 7((1011b25ff). These formulations can be interpreted as expressing either a correspondence or a reductionist conception of truth. Either way, truth is a property that belongs to a sentence *at a time*. As to their quantity, sentences are singular, universal, particular, or indefinite. Thus Aristotle obtains eight types of sentences, which are later dubbed *categorical sentences*; the following are examples, paired by quality:

Singular:	Callias is just.	Callias is not just.
Universal	Every human is just.	No human is just.
Particular:	Some human is just.	Some human is not just.
Indefinite:	(A) human is just.	(A) human is not just.

Universal and particular sentences contain a quantifier, and both universal and particular affirmatives are taken to have existential import. The logical status of the indefinites is ambiguous and controversial (*Int.* 6–7).

Aristotle distinguishes between two types of sentential opposition: contraries and contradictories. A contradictory pair of sentences (*antiphasis*) consists of an affirmation and its negation (that is, the negation that negates of the subject what the affirmation affirms of it). Aristotle assumes that—normally—one of these must be true, the other false. Contrary sentences are such that they cannot both be true. The contradictory of a universal affirmative is the corresponding particular negative; that of the universal negative the corresponding particular affirmative. A universal affirmative and its corresponding universal negative are contraries. Aristotle thus has captured the basic logical relations between monadic quantifiers (*Int.* 7).

Since Aristotle regards tense as part of the truth bearer (as opposed to merely a grammatical feature), he detects a problem regarding future tense sentences about contingent matters and discusses it in the famous chapter nine of his *De Interpretatione*: Does the principle that, of an affirmation and its negation one must be false, the other true, apply to these? What, for example, is the truth value now of the sentence *There will be a sea battle tomorrow*? Aristotle may have suggested that the sentence has no truth value now and that bivalence thus does not hold—despite the fact that it is necessary for there either to be or not to be a sea battle tomorrow, so that the principle of excluded middle is preserved.

NONMODAL SYLLOGISTIC. Aristotle's nonmodal syllogistic, the core of which he develops in the first seven chapters of Book One of his *Prior Analytics*, is the pinnacle of his logic. Aristotle defines a syllogism as "an argument (*logos*) in which, certain things having been laid down, something different from what has been laid down follows of necessity because these things are so." This definition appears to require that (1) a syllogism consists of at least two premises and a conclusion, (2) the conclusion follows of necessity from the premises, and (3) the conclusion differs from the premises. Aristotle's syllogistic covers only a small part of all arguments that satisfy these conditions.

Aristotle restricts and regiments the types of categorical sentence that may feature in a syllogism. The admissible truth bearers are now defined as each containing two different terms (*horoiv*) conjoined by the copula, of which one (the predicate term) is said of the other (the subject term) either affirmatively or negatively. Aristotle never comes clear on the question whether terms are things (nonempty classes) or linguistic expressions for these things. Only universal and particular sentences are discussed. Singular sentences seem excluded, and indefinite sentences are mostly ignored.

Another innovation in the syllogistic is Aristotle's use of letters in place of terms. The letters may originally have served simply as abbreviations for terms, as we can see for example in his *Posterior Analytics*, but in the syllogistic they seem mostly to have the function either of schematic term letters or of term variables with universal quantifiers assumed but not stated. Where he uses letters, Aristotle tends to express the four types of categorical sentences in the following way (with common later abbreviations in brackets):

"A holds of every B"	(A*a*B)
"A holds of no B"	(A*e*B)
"A holds of some B"	(A*i*B)
"A does not hold of some B"	(A*o*B)

Instead of *holds* he also uses *is predicated*.

All basic syllogisms consist of three categorical sentences in which the two premises share exactly one term, called the middle term, and the conclusion contains the other two terms, sometimes called the extremes. Based on the position of the middle term, Aristotle classified all possible premise combinations into three figures (*schemata*): The first figure has the middle term (B) as subject in the first premise and predicated in the second; the second figure has it predicated in both premises; the third has it as subject in both premises:

A holds of B	B holds of A	A holds of B
B holds of C	B holds of C	C holds of B

A is also called the major term and C the minor term. Each figure can further be classified according to whether or not both premises are universal. Aristotle went systematically through the fifty-eight possible premise combinations and showed that fourteen have a conclusion following of necessity from them. His procedure was this: He assumed that the syllogisms of the first figure are complete and not in need of proof since they are evident. By contrast, the syllogisms of the second and third figures are incomplete and in need of proof. He proves them by reducing them to syllogisms of the first figure and thereby *completing* them. For this he makes use of three methods: (1) Conversion (*antistrophē*)—a categorical sentence is converted by interchanging its terms. Aristotle recognizes and establishes three conversion rules: "from A*e*B infer B*e*A"; "from A*i*B infer B*i*A"; and "from A*a*B infer B*i*A." All second- and third-figure syllogisms but two can be proved by premise conversion. (2) *Reductio ad impossibile* (*apagogē*)—the remaining two are proved by reduction to the impossible, where the contradictory of an assumed conclusion together with one of the premises is used to deduce by a first-figure syllogism a conclusion that is incompatible with the other premise. Using the semantic relations between opposites established earlier, the assumed conclusion is thus established. (3) Exposition (*ekthesis*)—this method, which Aristotle uses additionally to (1) and (2), is controvertible both as to what exactly it was and as to whether it is proof.

For each of the thirty-four premise combinations that allow no conclusion, Aristotle proves by counterexample that they allow no conclusion. As overall result, he acknowledges four first-figure syllogisms (later called Barbara, Celarent, Darii, Ferio), four second-figure syllogisms (Camestres, Cesare, Festino, Baroco), and six third-figure syllogisms (Darapti, Felapton, Disamis, Datisi, Bocardo, Ferison); these were later called the modes or moods of the figures. (The names are mnemonics: e.g., each vowel indicates in order whether the first and second premises and the conclusion were sentences of type *a*, *e*, *i*, or *o*.) Aristotle implicitly recognized that by using the conversion rules on the conclusions we obtain eight further syllogisms (AnPr. 53a3–14), and that of the premise combinations rejected as nonsyllogistic, some (five, in fact) will yield a conclusion in which the minor term is predicated of the major (AnPr. 29a19–27, Fapesmo, Frisesomorum, Firesmo, Fapemo, Frisemo). Moreover, in the *Topics*, Aristotle accepted the rules "from A*a*B infer A*i*B" and "from A*e*B infer A*o*B." By using these on the conclusions, five further syllogisms could be proved though Aristotle did not mention this.

Going beyond his basic syllogistic, Aristotle reduced the third and fourth first-figure syllogisms to second-figure syllogisms, thus de facto reducing all syllogisms to Barbara and Celarent; later, in the *Prior Analytics*, he invokes a type of cut-rule by which a multipremise syllogism can be reduced to two or more basic syllogisms. From a modern perspective, Aristotle's system can be represented as an argumental natural deduction system *en miniature*. It has been shown to be sound and complete if one interprets the relations expressed by the categorical sentences set theoretically as a system of nonempty classes as follows: A*a*B is true iff the class A contains the class B. A*e*B is true iff the classes A and B are disjoint. A*i*B is true iff the classes A and B are not disjoint. A*o*B is true iff the class A does not contain the class B. The vexing textual question of what exactly Aristotle meant by *syllogisms* has received several rival interpretations, including one that they are a certain type of conditional propositional form. Most plausibly, perhaps, Aristotle's complete and *incomplete* syllogisms taken together are understood as formally valid premise-conclusion arguments; and his complete and *completed* syllogisms taken together as (sound) deductions.

MODAL LOGIC. Aristotle is also the originator of modal logic. In addition to quality and quantity, he takes categorical sentences to have a mode; this consists of the fact that the predicate is said to hold of the subject either actually or necessarily or possibly or contingently or impossibly. The latter four are expressed by modal operators that modify the predicate, for example: "It is possible for A to hold of some B"; "A necessarily holds of every B."

In *De Interpretatione* (12–13), Aristotle:

(1) Concludes that modal operators modify the whole predicate (or the copula, as he puts it), not just the predicate term of a sentence;

(2) States the logical relations that hold between modal operators, such as that "it is not possible for A not to hold of B" implies "it is necessary for A to hold of B";

(3) Investigates what the contradictories of modalized sentences are and decides that they are obtained by placing the negator in front of the modal operator.

(4) Equates the expressions *possible* and *contingent*, but wavers between a one-sided interpretation (where necessity implies possibility) and a two-sided interpretation (where possibility implies nonnecessity).

Aristotle develops his modal syllogistic in chapters eight to twenty-two of the first book of his *Prior Analytics*. He settles on two-sided possibility (contingency) and tests for syllogismhood all possible combinations of premise pairs of sentences with necessity (N), contingency (C), or no (U) modal operator: NN, CC, NU/UN, CU/UC, and NC/CN. Syllogisms with the last three types of premise combinations are called mixed modal syllogisms. Apart from the NN category, which mirrors unmodalized syllogisms, all categories contain dubious cases. For instance, Aristotle accepts:

A necessarily holds of all B.

B holds of all C.

Therefore A necessarily holds of all C.

This and other problematic cases were already disputed in antiquity, and since the mid-1930s, they have sparked a host of complex, formalized reconstructions of Aristotle's modal syllogistic. As Aristotle's theory is conceivably internally inconsistent, the formal models that have been suggested may all be unsuccessful.

THE EARLY PERIPATETICS: THEOPHRASTUS AND EUDEMUS

Aristotle's pupil and successor Theophrastus of Eresus (c. 371–c. 287 BCE) wrote more logical treatises than his teacher, with a large overlap in topics. Eudemus of Rhodes (later fourth century BCE) wrote books titled *Categories*, *Analytics*, and *On Speech*. Of all these works only a number of fragments and later testimonies survive, mostly in Aristotle commentators. Theophrastus and Eudemus simplified some aspects of Aristotle's logic and developed others where Aristotle left us only hints.

IMPROVEMENTS AND MODIFICATIONS OF ARISTOTLE'S LOGIC. The two Peripatetics seem to have redefined Aristotle's first figure so that it includes every syllogism in which the middle term is subject of one premise and predicate of the other. In this way, five types of nonmodal syllogisms only intimated by Aristotle later in his *Prior Analytics* (Baralipton, Celantes, Datibis, Fapesmo, and Frisesomorum) are included, but Aristotle's criterion that first-figure syllogisms are evident is given up (fr. 91). Theophrastus and Eudemus also improved Aristotle's modal theory. Theophrastus replaced Aristotle's two-sided contingency by one-sided possibility so that possibility no longer entails nonnecessity. Both recognized that the problematic universal negative ("A possibly holds of no B") is simply convertible (fr. 102A). Moreover, they introduced the principle that in mixed modal syllogisms the conclusion always has the same modal character as the weaker of the premises (frs.106 and 107), where possibility is weaker than actuality, and actuality than necessity. In this way Aristotle's modal syllogistic is notably simplified, and many unsatisfactory theses, like the one mentioned above, disappear.

PROSLEPTIC SYLLOGISMS. Theophrastus introduced the so-called prosleptic premises and syllogisms (fr. 110). A prosleptic premise is of the form:

For all X, if $\Phi(X)$, then $\Psi(X)$

where $\Phi(X)$ and $\Psi(X)$ stand for categorical sentences in which the variable X occurs in place of one of the terms. For example:

1) A <holds> of all of that of all of which B <holds>.

2) A <holds> of none of that which <holds> of all B.

Theophrastus considered such premises to contain three terms, two of which are definite (A, B) and one indefinite (*that*, or the bound variable X). We can represent (1) and (2) as:

$$\forall X \ \ BaX \to AaX$$

$$\forall X \ \ XaB \to AeX$$

Prosleptic syllogisms then come about as follows: They are comprised of a prosleptic premise and the categorical premise obtained by instantiating a term (C) in the antecedent *open categorical sentence* as premises, and the categorical sentences one obtains by putting in the same term (C) in the consequent *open categorical sentence* as conclusion. For example:

A <holds> of all of that of all of which B <holds>.

B holds of all C.

Therefore, A holds of all C.

Theophrastus distinguished three figures of these syllogisms, depending on the position of the indefinite term (also called *middle term*) in the prosleptic premise; for example (1) produces a third-figure syllogism, (2) a first-figure syllogism. The number of prosleptic syllogisms was presumably equal to that of types of prosleptic sentences: With Theophrastus's concept of the first figure, these would be sixty-four (that is, 32+16+16).

Theophrastus held that certain prosleptic premises were equivalent to certain categorical sentences, for example, (1) to "A is predicated of all B." However, for many, including (2), no such equivalent can be found, and prosleptic syllogisms thus increased the inferential power of Peripatetic logic.

FORERUNNERS OF *MODUS PONENS* AND *TOLLENS*. Theophrastus and Eudemus considered complex premises that they called *hypothetical premise* and that had one of the following two forms (or similar):

If something is F, it is G.

Either something is F or it is G. (with exclusive *or*)

They developed arguments with them that they called "mixed from a hypothetical premise and a probative premise" (fr. 112A) These arguments were inspired by Aristotle's syllogisms from a hypothesis (*An.Pr.* 1.44); they were forerunners of *modus ponens* and *modus tollens* and had the following forms: (frs.111 and 112):

If something is F, it is G.	If something is F, it is G.
a is F.	*a* is not G.
Therefore, *a* is G.	Therefore, *a* is not F.
Either something is F or it is G.	Either something is F or it is G.
a is F.	*a* is not F.
Therefore, *a* is not G.	Therefore, *a* is G.

Theophrastus also recognized that the connective particle *or* can be inclusive (fr. 82A); and he considered relative quantified sentences such as those containing *more*, *fewer*, and *the same* (fr. 89), and seems to have discussed syllogisms built from such sentences, again following up upon what Aristotle said about syllogisms from a hypothesis (fr. 111E).

WHOLLY HYPOTHETICAL SYLLOGISMS. Theophrastus is further credited with the invention of a system of the later so-called *wholly hypothetical syllogisms* (fr. 113). These syllogisms were originally abbreviated term-logical arguments of the kind:

If [something is] A, [it is] B.

If [something is] B, [it is] C.

Therefore, if [something is] A, [it is] C.

and at least some of them were regarded as reducible to Aristotle's categorical syllogisms, presumably by way of the equivalences to "Every A is B," and so on. In parallel to Aristotle's syllogistic, Theophrastus distinguished three figures, each of which had sixteen modes. The first eight modes of the first figure are obtained by going through all permutations with "not X" instead of "X" (with X for A, B, C); the second eight modes are obtained by using a rule of contraposition on the conclusion:

(CR) From "if X, Y" infer "if the contradictory of Y then the contradictory of X"

The sixteen modes of the second figure were obtained by using (CR) on the schema of the first premise of the first figure arguments, for example:

If [something is] not B, [it is] not A.

If [something is] B, [it is] C.

Therefore, if [something is] A, [it is] C.

The sixteen modes of the third figure were obtained by using (CR) on the schema of the second premise of the first figure arguments, for example:

If [something is] A, [it is] B.

If [something is] not C, [it is] not B.

Therefore, if [something is] A, [it is] C.

Theophrastus claimed that all second- and third-figure syllogisms could be reduced to first-figure syllogisms. If Alexander of Aphrodisias reports faithfully, any use of (CR) that transforms a syllogism into a first-figure syllogism was such a reduction. The large number of modes and reductions can be explained by the fact that Theophrastus did not have the logical means for substituting negative for positive components in an argument. In later antiquity, after some intermediate stages, and possibly under Stoic influence, the wholly hypothetical syllogisms were interpreted as propositional-logical arguments of the kind:

If p, then q.

If q, then r.

Therefore, if p, then r.

DIODORUS CRONUS AND PHILO THE LOGICIAN

In the later fourth to mid third centuries BCE, a loosely connected group of philosophers, sometimes referred to as dialecticians and possibly influenced by Eubulides, conceived of logic as a logic of propositions. Their best-known exponents were Diodorus Cronus and his pupil Philo (sometimes called Philo of Megara) although no writings of theirs are preserved. They each made ground-breaking contributions to the development of proposi-

tional logic, in particular to the theories of conditionals and modalities.

A conditional (*sunēmmenon*) was considered as a nonsimple proposition comprised of two propositions and the connecting particle *if*. Philo, who may be credited with introducing truth-functionality into logic, provided the following criterion for their truth: A conditional is false *when* and only *when* its antecedent is true and its consequent is false, and it is true in the three remaining truth-value combinations. The Philonian conditional resembles material implication except that—since propositions were conceived of as functions of time that can have different truth values at different times—it may change its truth value over time. For Diodorus, a conditional proposition is true if it neither was nor is possible that its antecedent is true and its consequent false. The temporal elements in this account suggest that the possibility of a truth-value change in Philo's conditionals was meant to be improved on. With his own modal notions (see below) applied, a conditional is Diodorean true now if and only if it is Philonian true at all times. Diodorus's conditional is thus reminiscent of strict implication. Philo's and Diodorus's conceptions of conditionals led to variants of the *paradoxes* of material and strict implication—a fact the ancients were aware of (S.E.M. 109–117).

Philo and Diodorus each considered the four modalities possibility, impossibility, necessity, and nonnecessity. These were conceived of as modal properties or modal values of propositions, not as modal operators. Philo defined them as follows:

Possible is that which is capable of being true by the proposition's own nature ... necessary is that which is true, and which, as far as it is in itself, is not capable of being false. Non-necessary is that which as far as it is in itself, is capable of being false, and impossible is that which by its own nature is not capable of being true (Boethius, *In librum Aristotelis De interpretatione: secunda editio*, p. 234).

Diodorus's definitions were these: "Possible is that which either is or will be <true>; impossible that which is false and will not be true; necessary that which is true and will not be false; non-necessary that which either is false already or will be false" (Boethius, *In librum Aristotelis De interpretatione: secunda editio*, p. 234). Both sets of definitions satisfy the following standard requirements of modal logic:

(1) Necessity entails truth and truth entails possibility;

(2) Possibility and impossibility are contradictories, and so are necessity and nonnecessity;

(3) Necessity and possibility are interdefinable;

(4) Every proposition is either necessary or impossible or both possible and nonnecessary.

Philo's definitions appear to introduce mere conceptual modalities whereas with Diodorus's definitions, some propositions may change their modal value. Diodorus's definition of possibility rules out future contingents and implies the counterintuitive thesis that only the actual is possible. Diodorus tried to prove this claim with his famous Master Argument, which sets out to show the incompatibility of (1) "every past truth is necessary," (2) "the impossible does not follow from the possible," and (3) "something is possible which neither is nor will be true" (Epictetus *Discourses* II.19). The argument has not survived, but various reconstructions have been suggested. Some affinity with the arguments for logical determinism in Aristotle's *De Interpretatione* 9 is likely.

THE STOICS

The founder of the Stoa, Zeno of Citium (335–263 BCE), studied with Diodorus. His successor, Cleanthes, (331–232) tried to solve the Master Argument by denying that every past truth is necessary and wrote books—now lost—on paradoxes, dialectics, argument modes, and predicates. Both philosophers considered logic as a virtue and held it in high esteem, but they seem not to have been creative logicians. By contrast, Cleanthes's successor, Chrysippus of Soli (c.280–207), is without doubt the second great logician in the history of logic. It was said of him that if the gods used any logic, it would be that of Chrysippus, and his reputation as a brilliant logician is amply testified. Chrysippus wrote more than 300 books on logic, on virtually any topic contemporary logic concerns itself with, including speech act theory, sentence analysis, singular and plural expressions, types of predicates, demonstratives, existential propositions, sentential connectives, negations, disjunctions, conditionals, logical consequence, valid argument forms, theory of deduction, propositional logic, modal logic, tense logic, logic of suppositions, logic of imperatives, ambiguity, and logical paradoxes—in particular, the Liar and the Sorites (Diogenes Laertius 7.189–199). Of all these, only two badly damaged papyri have survived, luckily supplemented by a considerable number of fragments and testimonies in later texts, in particular in Diogenes Laertius, book 7, sections 55–83; and Sextus Empiricus, *Outlines of Pyrrhonism*, book 2, and *Against the Mathematicians*, book 8

(both of which appear in *Works*). Chrysippus's successors, including Diogenes of Babylon (c.240–152) and Antipater of Tarsus, appear to have systematized and simplified some of his ideas, but their original contributions to logic seem small. Many testimonies of Stoic logic do not name any particular Stoic. Hence the following paragraphs simply talk about the Stoics in general; but we can be confident that a large part of what has survived goes back to Chrysippus.

LOGICAL ACHIEVEMENTS BESIDES PROPOSITIONAL LOGIC. The subject matter of Stoic logic are the so-called sayables (*lekta*): They are the underlying meanings in everything we say and think, but—like Gottlob Frege's senses—subsist also independently of us. They are distinguished from linguistic expressions: What we *utter* are those expressions, but what we *say* are the sayables (Diogenes Laertius 7.57). There are complete and deficient sayables. Complete sayables, if said, do not make the hearer feel prompted to ask a question(Diogenes Laertius 7.63). They include assertibles (the Stoic equivalent for propositions), interrogatives, imperativals, inquiries, hypotheses, and more. The accounts of the different complete sayables all had the general form *a so-and-so sayable is one in saying which we perform an act of such-and-such*. For instance: An imperatival sayable is one in saying which we issue a command; an interrogative sayable is one in saying which we ask a question; a declaratory sayable (that is, an assertible) is one in saying which we make an assertion. Thus, according to the Stoics, each time we say a complete sayable, we perform three different acts: we utter a linguistic expression, we say the sayable, and we perform a speech-act.

Assertibles (*axiōmata*) differ from all other complete sayables by having a truth value: At any one time they are either true or false. Truth is temporal and assertibles may change their truth value. The Stoic principle of bivalence is hence temporalized, too. Truth is introduced by example: the assertible "it is day" is true *when* it is day, and at all other times false (Diogenes Laertius 7.65). This suggests a reductionist view of truth, as does the fact that the Stoics identify true assertibles with facts but define false assertibles simply as the contradictories of true ones (S.E.M. 8.85).

Assertibles are simple or nonsimple. A simple *predicative* assertible, such as *Dion is walking*, is generated from the predicate *is walking*, which is a deficient assertible since it elicits the question *who*, and a nominative case (Dion's individual quality or the correlated sayable), which falls under the predicate (Diogenes Laertius 7.63

and 70). There is thus no interchangeability of predicate and subject terms as in Aristotle; rather, predicates—but not the things that fall under them—are defined as deficient and thus resemble propositional functions. It seems that whereas some Stoics took the Fregean approach that singular terms had correlated sayables, others anticipated the notion of direct reference. Concerning demonstratives, the Stoics took a simple *definite* assertible such as *this one is walking* to be true when the person pointed at by the speaker is walking (S.E.M. 100). When the thing pointed at ceases to be, so does the assertible though the sentence used to express it remains (Alex.Aphr.An.Pr. 177–8). A simple *indefinite* assertible such as *someone is walking* is said to be true when a corresponding definite assertible is true (S.E.M. 98). Aristotelian universal affirmatives ("Every A is B") were to be rephrased as "If something is A, it is B" (S.E.M. 9.8–11). The past tense assertible *Dion walked* is true when there is at least one past time at which *Dion is walking* was true. The negation of *Dion is walking* is *(It is) not (the case that) Dion is walking*, and not *Dion is not walking*. The latter is analyzed in a Russellian manner as *Both Dion exists and not: Dion is walking'* (Alex.Aphr.An.Pr. 402).

SYNTAX AND SEMANTICS OF COMPLEX PROPOSITIONS.
Thus the Stoics concerned themselves with several issues we would place under the heading of predicate logic; but their main achievement was the development of a propositional logic, that is, of a system of deduction in which the smallest substantial unanalyzed expressions are propositions, or rather, assertibles.

The Stoics defined negations as assertibles that consist of a negative particle and an assertible controlled by this particle (S.E.M. 103). Similarly, nonsimple assertibles were defined as assertibles that either consist of more than one assertible or of one assertible taken more than once (Diogenes Laertius 7.68–9) and that are controlled by a connective particle. Both definitions are recursive and allow for assertibles of indeterminate complexity. Three types of nonsimple assertions feature in Stoic syllogistic. Conjunctions are nonsimple assertibles put together by the conjunctive connective *both ... and ... and ...* . They have two or more conjuncts, all on a par. Disjunctions are nonsimple assertibles put together by the disjunctive connective *either ... or ... or ...* . They have two or more disjuncts, all on a par. Conditionals are nonsimple assertibles formed with the connective *if ..., ...*; they consist of antecedent and consequent (Diogenes Laertius 7.71–2). What type of assertible an assertible is is determined by the connective particle that controls it, that is, that is, that has the largest scope. *Both not p and q*

is a conjunction; *Not both p and q* a negation. Stoic language regimentation asks that sentences expressing assertibles always start with the logical particle or expression characteristic for the assertible. Thus the Stoics introduced an implicit bracketing device similar to that used in Jan Łukasiewicz's (1878–1956) Polish notation.

Stoic negations and conjunctions are truth-functional. Stoic (or at least Chrysippean) conditionals are true when the contradictory of the consequent is incompatible with its antecedent (Diogenes Laertius 7.73). Two assertibles are contradictories of each other if one is the negation of the other (Diogenes Laertius 7.73) or when one exceeds the other by a pre-fixed negation particle (SEM 8.89). The truth-functional Philonian conditional was expressed as a negation of a conjunction: that is, that is, not as *if p, q* but as *not both p and not q*. Stoic disjunction is exclusive and non-truth-functional. It is true when necessarily precisely one of its disjuncts is true. Later Stoics introduced a non-truth-functional inclusive disjunction (Gellius.N.A. 16.8.13–14).

Like Philo and Diodorus, Chrysippus distinguished four modalities and considered them as modal values of propositions rather than modal operators; they satisfy the same standard requirements of modal logic. Chrysippus's definitions are: An assertible is possible when it is both capable of being true and not hindered by external things from being true. An assertible is impossible when it is either not capable of being true <or is capable of being true, but hindered by external things from being true>. An assertible is necessary when, being true, it either is not capable of being false or is capable of being false but hindered by external things from being false. An assertible is nonnecessary when it is both capable of being false and not hindered by external things <from being false> (Diogenes Laertius 7.75). Chrysippus's modal notions differ from Diodorus's in that they allow for future contingents and from Philo's in that they go beyond mere conceptual possibility.

ARGUMENTS.
Arguments are—normally—compounds of assertibles. They are defined as a system of at least two premisses and a conclusion (Diogenes Laertius 7.45). Syntactically, every premise but the first is introduced by *now* or *but*, and the conclusion by *therefore*. An argument is valid if the (Chrysippean) conditional formed with the conjunction of its premises as antecedent and its conclusion as consequent is correct (S.E.P.H. 2.137, DL 7.77). An argument is *sound* (literally: *true*) when in addition to being valid, it has true premises. The Stoics defined so-called argument modes as a sort of schema of an argu-

ment (Diogenes Laertius 7.76). A mode of an argument differs from the argument itself by having ordinal numbers taking the place of propositions. A mode of the argument:

> If it is day, it is light.
> But it is not the case that it is light.
> Therefore it is not the case that it is day.

is

> If the 1st, the 2nd.
> But not: the 2nd.
> Therefore not: the 1st.

The modes functioned first as abbreviations of arguments that brought out their logically relevant form and second, it seems, as representatives of the form of a class of arguments.

STOIC SYLLOGISTIC. Stoic syllogistic is an argumental deductive system consisting of five types of indemonstrables or axiomatic arguments and four inference rules, called *themata*. An argument is a syllogism precisely if it either is an indemonstrable or can be reduced to one by means of the *themata* (Diogenes Laertius 7.78). Syllogisms are thus certain types of formally valid arguments. The Stoics explicitly acknowledged that there are valid arguments that are not syllogisms but assumed that they could be somehow transformed into syllogisms.

All basic indemonstrables consist of a nonsimple assertible as leading premiss and a simple assertible as coassumption and have another simple assertible as conclusion. They were defined by five standardized metalinguistic descriptions of the forms of the arguments (S.E. M. 8.224–5; D.L.7.80–81):

(1) A first indemonstrable is an argument composed of a conditional and its antecedent as premises, having the consequent of the conditional as conclusion.

(2) A second indemonstrable is an argument composed of a conditional and the contradictory of its consequent as premises, having the contradictory of its antecedent as conclusion.

(3) A third indemonstrable is an argument composed of a negated conjunction and one of its conjuncts as premises, having the contradictory of the other conjunct as conclusion.

(4) A fourth indemonstrable is an argument composed of a disjunctive assertible and one of its disjuncts as premises, having the contradictory of the remaining disjunct as conclusion.

(5) A fifth indemonstrable, finally, is an argument composed of a disjunctive assertible and the contradictory of one of its disjuncts as premises, having the remaining disjunct as conclusion.

Whether an argument is an indemonstrable can be tested by comparing it with these metalinguistic descriptions. For instance:

> If it is day, it is not the case that it is night.
> But it is night.
> Therefore it is not the case that it is day.

comes out as a second indemonstrable, and

> If five is a number, then either five is odd or five is even.
> But five is a number.
> Therefore either five is odd or five is even.

as a first indemonstrable. For testing, a suitable mode of an argument can also be used as a stand-in. A mode is syllogistic, if a corresponding argument with the same form is a syllogism (because of that form). However, there are no five modes that can be used as inference schemata that represent the five types of indemonstrables. For example, the following are two of the many modes of fourth indemonstrables:

> Either the 1st or the 2nd.   Either the 1st or not the 2nd.
> But the 2nd.   But the 1st.
> Therefore not the 1st.   Therefore the 2nd.

Although both are covered by the metalinguistic description, neither can be singled out as *the* mode of the fourth indemonstrables: If we disregard complex arguments, there are thirty-two modes corresponding to the five metalinguistic descriptions; the latter thus prove noticeably more economical.

Of the four *themata* only the first and third are extant. They, too, were metalinguistically formulated. The first *thema*, in its basic form, was:

> When from two <assertibles> a third follows, then from either of them together with the contradictory of the conclusion the contradictory of the other follows (Apul.*Int.* 209.9–14).

This is an inference rule of the kind today called antilogism. The third *thema*, in one formulation, was:

> When from two <assertibles> a third follows, and from the one that follows <that is, the third> together with another, external assumption, another follows, then this other follows

from the first two and the externally coassumed one (Simp.Cael. 237.2–4).

This is an inference rule of the kind today called cut rule. It is used to reduce chain syllogisms. (The second and fourth *themata* are also cut rules, and reconstructions of them can be provided since we know what arguments they. together with the third *thema*, were thought to be able to reduce.) A reduction shows the formal validity of an argument by applying to it the *themata* in one or more steps in such a way that all resultant arguments are indemonstrables. This can be done either with the arguments or their modes (S.E. M. 8.230–8). For instance, the argument mode:

> If the 1st and the 2nd, the 3rd.
> But not the 3rd.
> Moreover, the 1st.
> Therefore not: the 2nd.

can be reduced by the third *thema* to (the modes of) a second and a third indemonstrable as follows:

> When from two assertibles ("If the 1st and the 2nd, the 3rd." and "But not the 3rd.") a third follows ("Not: both the 1st and the 2nd."—by a second indemonstrable) and from the third and an external one ("The 1st.") another follows ("Not: the 2nd."—by a third indemonstrable), then this other ("Not: the 2nd.") also follows from the two assertibles and the external one.

The second *thema* reduced, among others, arguments with the following modes (Alex.Aphr.An.Pr. 164.27–31):

Either the 1st or not the 1st.   If the 1st, if the 1st, the 2nd.
But the 1st.   But the 1st.
Therefore the 1st.   Therefore the 2nd.

The Peripatetics chided the Stoics for allowing such useless arguments, but the Stoics rightly insisted that if they can be reduced, they are valid. The four *themata* can be used repeatedly and in any combination in a reduction. Thus propositional arguments of indeterminate length and complexity can be reduced. Stoic syllogistic has been formalized, and it has been shown that the Stoic deductive system shows strong similarities with relevance logical systems such as those by Storrs McCall. Like Aristotle, the Stoics aimed at proving nonevident, formally valid *arguments* by reducing them by means of accepted inference rules to evidently valid *arguments*. Thus, although their logic is a propositional logic, they did not intend to provide a system that allows for the deduction

of all propositional-logical truths but, rather, a system of valid propositional-logical arguments with at least two premises and a conclusion. Nonetheless, it is evidenced that the Stoics independently recognized many simple logical truths, including excluded middle, double negation, and contraposition.

LOGICAL PARADOXES. The Stoics recognized the importance of both the Liar and the Sorites paradoxes (Cic.*Acad.* 2.95–8, Plut.*Comm.Not.* 1059D–E, Chrys.*Log. Zet.*col.IX, S.E.*M.*1.68&7.244-246&7.416.). Chrysippus may have tried to solve the Liar as follows: There is an uneliminable ambiguity in the Liar sentence ("I am speaking falsely," uttered in isolation)between the assertibles (1) 'I falsely say I speak FALSELY' and (2) 'I *am* speaking falsely' (that is, I am doing what I'm saying), of which at any time the Liar sentence is said precisely one is true, but it is arbitrary which one: (2) entails (3) 'I *am* speaking truly' and is incompatible with (2) and (4) I truly say I speak falsely' (2) entails (4) and is incompatible with (1) and (3). Thus bivalence is preserved. Chrysippus's stand on the Sorites seems to have been that vague borderline sentences uttered in the context of a Sorites series have no assertibles corresponding them, and that it is obscure to us where the borderline cases start, so that it is rational for us to stop answering while still on safe ground. The latter remark suggests Chrysippus was aware of the problem of higher-order vagueness. Again, bivalence of assertibles is preserved.

LATER ANTIQUITY

Very little is known about the development of logic from c. 100 BCE to c. 250 CE. It is unclear when Peripatetics and the Stoics began taking notice of the logical achievements of each other. Sometime during that period, the terminological distinction between *categorical syllogisms*, used for Aristotelian syllogisms, and *hypothetical syllogisms*, used not only for those by Theophrastus and Eudemus but also for the Stoic propositional-logical syllogisms, gained a foothold. In the first century BCE, the Peripatetics Ariston of Alexandria and Boethus of Sidon wrote about syllogistic. Ariston is said to have introduced the so-called *subaltern* syllogisms (Barbari, Celaront, Cesaro, Camestrop and Camenop) into Aristotelian syllogistic (Apul.*Int.* 213.5–10), that is, the syllogisms one gains by applying the subalternation rules (that were acknowledged by Aristotle in his *Topics*):

> From "A holds of every B" infer "A holds of some B"

From "A holds of no B" infer "A does not hold of some B"

to the conclusions of the relevant syllogisms. Boethus suggested substantial modifications to Aristotle's theories: He claimed that all categorical syllogisms are complete and that hypothetical syllogistic is prior to categorical (Gal.Inst.Log. 7.2), although we are not told prior in which way. The Stoic Posidonius (c.135–c.51 BCE) defended the possibility of logical or mathematical deduction against the Epicureans and discussed some syllogisms he called *conclusive by the force of an axiom*, which apparently included arguments of the type "As the 1st is to the 2nd, so the 3rd is to the 4th; the ratio of the 1st to the 2nd is double; therefore the ratio of the 3rd to the 4th is double," which was considered conclusive by the force of the axiom "things which are in general of the same ratio, are also of the same particular ratio" (Gal. *Inst. Log.*18.8). At least two Stoics in this period wrote a work on Aristotle's *Categories*. From his writings we know that Cicero was knowledgeable about both Peripatetic and Stoic logic; and Epictetus's discourses prove that he was acquainted with some of the more taxing parts of Chrysippus's logic. In all likelihood there existed at least a few creative logicians in this period, but we do not know who they were and what they created.

The next logician of rank, if of lower rank, of whom we have sufficient evidence is Galen (129–199 or 216 CE), whose greater fame was as a physician. He studied logic with both Peripatetic and Stoic teachers and recommended to avail oneself of parts of either doctrine, as long as it could be used for scientific demonstration. He composed commentaries on logical works by Aristotle, Theophrastus, Eudemus, and Chrysippus, as well as treatises on various logical problems and a major work titled *On Demonstration*. All these are lost except for some information in later texts, but his *Introduction to Logic* has come down to us almost in full. In *On Demonstration*, Galen developed, among other things, a theory of compound categorical syllogisms with four terms, which fall into four figures, but we do not know the details. He also introduced the so-called relational syllogisms, examples of which are "A is equal to B, B is equal to C; therefore A is equal to C" and "Dio owns half as much as Theo; Theo owns half as much as Philo. Therefore Dio owns a quarter of what Philo owns." (Gal. *Inst. Log.* 17–18). All relational syllogisms Galen mentions have in common that they are not reducible in either Aristotle's or Stoic syllogistic, but it is difficult to find further formal characteristics that unite them all. In general, in his *Introduction to Logic*, he merges Aristotelian Syllogistic with a strongly Peripatetic reinterpretation of Stoic propositional logic.

The second ancient introduction to logic that has survived is Apuleius's (second century CE) *De Interpretatione*. This Latin text, too, displays knowledge of Stoic and Peripatetic logic; it contains the first full presentation of the square of opposition, which illustrates the logical relations between categorical sentences by diagram. Alcinous, in his *Handbook of Platonism* 5, is witness to the emergence of a specifically Platonist logic, constructed on the Platonic notions and procedures of division, definition, analysis, and hypothesis, but there is little that would make a logicians heart beat faster. Sometime between the third and sixth century CE, Stoic logic faded into oblivion to be resurrected only in the twentieth century in the wake of the (re)discovery of propositional logic.

The surviving, often voluminous, Greek commentaries on Aristotle's logical works by Alexander of Aphrodisias (fl. c.200 CE), Porphyry (234–c.305), Ammonius Hermeiou (fifth century), John Philoponus (c. 500), and Simplicius (sixth century), and the Latin ones by Anicius Manlius Severinus Boethius (c.480–524) have their main importance as sources for lost Peripatetic and Stoic works. Still, two of the commentators deserve special mention: Porphyry, for writing the *Isagoge* or *Introduction* (that is, to Aristotle's *Categories*), in which he discusses the five notions of genus, species, differentia, property, and accident as basic notions one needs to know to understand the *Categories*. For centuries, the *Isagogē* was the first logic text a student would tackle, and Porphyry's five predicables (which differ from Aristotle's four) formed the basis for the medieval doctrine of the *quinque voces*.

The second is Boethius. In addition to commentaries, he wrote a number of logical treatises, mostly simple explications of Aristotelian logic, but also two very interesting ones: (1) His *On Topical Differentiae* bears witness of the elaborated system of topical arguments that logicians of later antiquity had developed from Aristotle's *Topics* under the influence of the needs of Roman lawyers. (2) His *On Hypothetical Syllogisms* systematically presents wholly hypothetical and mixed hypothetical syllogisms as they are known from the early Peripatetics; it may be derived from Porphyry. Boethius's insistence that the negation of "If it is A, it is B" is "If it is A, it is not B" suggests a suppositional understanding of the conditional, a view for which there is also some evidence in Ammonius, but that is not attested for earlier logicians. Historically, Boethius is most important because he translated all of Aristotle's *Organon* into Latin, and thus these texts (except the *Posterior Analytics*) became available to philosophers of the medieval period.

See also Alcinous; Alexander of Aphrodisias; Antisthenes; Aristotle; Boethius, Anicius Manlius Severinus; Chrysippus; Cicero, Marcus Tullius; Cleanthes; Diodorus Cronus; Diogenes Laertius; Epictetus; Epicureanism and the Epicurean School; Frege, Gottlob; Galen; Gorgias of Leontini; Peripatetics; Philo of Megara; Philoponus, John; Plato; Porphyry; Posidonius; Protagoras of Abdera; Sextus Empiricus; Simplicius; Socrates; Stoicism; Theophrastus; Zeno of Citium; Zeno of Elea.

Bibliography

TEXTS AND TRANSLATIONS

Ackrill, J. L., trans. *Aristotle's Categories and De Interpretatione.* Oxford: Oxford University Press, 1961.

Alcinous. *Enseignement des doctrines de Platon.* Edited and translated into French by John Whittaker. Paris: Les Belles Lettres, 1990.

Alcinous. *The Handbook of Platonism.* Translated by John Dillon. Oxford: Oxford University Press, 1993.

Apuleius. *Peri Hermeneias.* Edited by Claudio Moreschini. Stuttgart/Leipzig: Teubner, 1991.

Barnes, Jonathan, ed. *The Complete Works of Aristotle,* 2 vols. Princeton: Princeton University Press, 1984.

Barnes, Jonathan, trans. *Porphyry's Introduction.* Oxford: Oxford University Press, 2003.

Boethius. *De hypotheticis syllogismis.* Edited and translated into Italian by L. Obertello. Brescia, Italy: Paideia, 1969.

Boethius. *In librum Aristotelis De interpretatione: secunda editio.* Edited by C. Meiser. Leipzig: Teubner, 1880.

Burnet, J., ed. *Platonis Opera,* vols. I–V. Oxford: Oxford University Press, 1901–1991.

Cooper, John M., and D. S. Hutchinson, eds. *Plato Complete Works.* Indianapolis, IN: Hackett, 1997.

Diels, Hans, and Walther Kranz, eds. (DK) *Die Fragmente der Vorsokratiker.* Berlin: Weidmann, 1951.

Diogenes Laertius. *Lives of the Philosophers,* 2 vols. Edited by M. Marcovich. Stuttgart & Leipzig: Teubner, 1999.

Döring, Klaus, ed. *Die Megariker. Kommentierte Sammlung der Testimonien.* Amsterdam: Grüner. 1972.

Dorion, Louis-Andre, trans. *Aristote: Les refutations sophistique.* Paris: J. Vrin, 1995.

Galen. *Institutio Logica.* Edited by C. Kalbfleisch. Leipzig: Teubner, 1896.

Giannantoni, G. *Socratis et Socraticorum Reliquiae,* 4 vols. *Elenchos* 18, Naples, Italy: Bibliopolis, 1990.

Huby, P. M., and Dimitri Gutas, eds. and trans. *Theophrastus: Logic.* In *Theophrastus of Eresus: Sourses for his Life, Writings, Thought and Influence,* edited by William W. Fortenbaugh, 114–275. Leiden, U.K.: Brill, 1992.

Hülser, Karlheinz, ed. *Die Fragmente zur Dialektik der Stoiker,* 4 vols. Stuttgart-Bad Cannstadt: Frommann-Holzboog, 1987–1988.

Kieffer, John Spangler, trans. *Galen's Institutio Logica.* Baltimore, MD: Johns Hopkins University Press, 1964.

Robinson, Thomas M. ed. *Contrasting Arguments: An Edition of the* Dissoi Logoi. London: Arno Press, 1979.

Ross, W. D., et al., eds. *Aristotelis Opera.* Oxford: Oxford University Press, 1890–1991.

Sextus Empiricus. *Works.* Edited by H. Mutschmann and J. Mau. Leipzig: Teubner, 1914–1961.

Smith, Robin, trans. *Aristotle, Topics I, VIII, and Selections.* Oxford: Oxford University Press, 1997.

Smith, Robin, trans. *Aristotle's Prior Analytics.* Indianapolis, IN: Hackett, 1989.

Stump, Eleanor, trans. *Boethius's 'De topicis differentiis'.* Ithaca, NY: Cornell University Press, 1978.

Weidemann, Hermann, trans. *Aristoteles, De Interpretatione.* Berlin: Akademie Verlag, 1994.

Works of Alexander of Aphrodisias, Porphyry, Ammonius, Simplicius, and Philoponus are found in: *Commentaria in Aristotelem Graeca.* Edited by H. Diels. Berlin: Reimer 1882–1909.

SECONDARY LITERATURE: GENERAL

"Ancient Logic, Overview." *Stanford Encyclopedia of Philosophy.* Available from http://www.plato.stanford.edu/.

Barnes, Jonathan. *Truth, etc..* Oxford: Oxford University Press, 2005.

Kneale, Martha, and William Kneale. *The Development of Logic.* Oxford: Oxford University Press, 1962.

SECONDARY LITERATURE: THE BEGINNINGS

Frede, Michael. "Plato's *Sophist* on False Statements." In *The Cambridge Companion to Plato.* Edited by Kraut Richard. Cambridge, U.K.: Cambridge University Press, 1992.

Kapp, Ernst. *Greek Foundations of Traditional Logic.* New York: Columbia University Press, 1942.

Mueller, Ian. "Greek Mathematics and Greek Logic." In *Ancient Logic and its Modern Interpretation. Proceedings of the Buffalo Symposium on Modernist Interpretations of Ancient Logic, 21 and 22 April, 1972.* Edited by John Corcoran. Dordrecht, Holland: Reidel, 1974.

Robinson, Richard. *Plato's Earlier Dialectic,* 2nd ed. Ithaca, NY: Cornell University Press, 1953.

Salmon, W. C. *Zeno's Paradoxes.* Indianapolis, IN: Hackett, 2001.

SECONDARY LITERATURE: ARISTOTLE

Corcoran, John. "Aristotle's Natural Deduction System." In *Ancient Logic and its Modern Interpretation. Proceedings of the Buffalo Symposium on Modernist Interpretations of Ancient Logic, 21 and 22 April, 1972.* Edited by John Corcoran. Dordrecht, Holland: Reidel. 1974.

Frede, Dorothea. "The Sea-Battle Reconsidered." *Oxford Studies in Ancient Philosophy* 3 (1985): 31–87.

Frede, Michael. "Categories in Aristotle." In *Essays in Ancient Philosophy,* 29–48. Minneapolis: University of Minnesota Press, 1987.

Lear, Jonathan. *Aristotle and Logical Theory.* Cambridge, U.K.: Cambridge University Press, 1980.

Patterson, Richard. *Aristotle's Modal Logic: Essence and Entailment in the Organon.* Cambridge, U.K., Cambridge University Press, 1995.

Patzig, Günther. *Aristotle's Theory of the Syllogism.* Translated by Jonathan Barnes. Dordrecht, Holland: Reidel, 1969.

Primavesi, Oliver. *Die aristotelische Topik.* Munich, Germany: Beck, 1996.

Smiley, Timothy. "What Is a Syllogism?" *Journal of Philosophical Logic* 1 (1974): 136–154.

Smith, Robin. "Logic." In *The Cambridge Companion to Aristotle.* Edited by Jonathan Barnes. Cambridge, U.K.: Cambridge University Press, 1994.

Striker, Gisela. "Aristoteles über Syllogismen 'Aufgrund einer Hypothese.'" *Hermes* 107 (1979): 33.

Striker, Gisela. "Modal vs. Assertoric Syllogistic." *Ancient Philosophy* Spec. issue (1994): 39–51.

Whitaker, C. W. A. *Aristotle's De Interpretatione: Contradiction and Dialectic.* Oxford: Oxford University Press, 1996.

SECONDARY LITERATURE: THEOPHRASTUS AND EUDEMUS

Barnes, Jonathan. "Theophrastus and Hypothetical Syllogistic." In *Aristoteles: Werk und Wirkung* I. Edited by J. Wiesner. Berlin, 1985.

Bobzien, Susanne. "Pre-Stoic Hypothetical Syllogistic in Galen." *Bulletin of the Institute of Classical Studies* Suppl (2002):57–72.

Bobzien, Susanne. "Wholly Hypothetical Syllogisms." *Phronesis* 45 (2000): 87–137.

Bochenski, I. M. *La Logique de Théophraste.* Fribourg, Switzerland: Publications de l'Universite de Fribourg en Suisse, 1947.

Lejewski, Czesław. "On Prosleptic Syllogisms." *Notre Dame Journal of Formal Logic* 2 (1961): 158–176.

SECONDARY LITERATURE: DIODORUS CRONUS AND PHILO THE LOGICIAN

Bobzien, Susanne. "Chrysippus' Modal Logic and its Relation to Philo and Diodorus." In *Dialektiker und Stoiker.* Edited by K. Döring and Th. Ebert. Stuttgart: Franz Steiner, 1993.

"Dialectical School." *Stanford Encyclopedia of Philosophy.* Available from http://www.plato.stanford.edu/.

Prior, A. N. *Past, Present, and Future,* chaps. II.1–2, III.1. Oxford: Clarendon Press, 1967.

Sedley, David. "Diodorus Cronus and Hellenistic Philosophy." *Proceedings of the Cambridge Philological Society* 203 (1977): 74–120.

SECONDARY LITERATURE: THE STOICS

Atherton, Catherine. *The Stoics on Ambiguity.* Cambridge Classical Studies. Cambridge, U.K.: Cambridge University Press, 1993.

Bobzien, Susanne. "Chrysippus and the Epistemic Theory of Vagueness." *Proceedings of the Aristotelian Society* 102 (2002): 217–238.

Bobzien, Susanne. "Stoic Logic." In *The Cambridge History of Hellenistic Philosophy.* Edited by J. Barnes, J. Mansfeld, and M. Schofield. Cambridge, U.K.: Cambridge University Press, 1999.

Bobzien, Susanne. "Stoic Syllogistic." *Oxford Studies in Ancient Philosophy* 14 (1996): 133–192.

Brunschwig, Jacques. "Remarks on the Classification of Simple Propositions in Hellenistic Logics." In *Papers in Hellenistic Philosophy.* Cambridge, U.K.: Cambridge University Press, 1994.

Cavini, Walter. "Chrysippus on Speaking Truly and the Liar." In *Dialektiker und Stoiker.* Edited by K. Döring and Th. Ebert. Stuttgart: Franz Steiner, 1993.

Crivelli, Paolo "Indefinite Propositions and Anaphora in Stoic Logic." *Phronesis* 39 (1994): 187–206.

Frede, Michael. *Die stoische Logik.* Goettingen: Vandenhoeck & Ruprecht, 1974.

Frede, Michael. "Stoic vs. Peripatetic Syllogistic." *Archiv für Geschichte der Philosophie* 56 (1975): 132–154.

Gaskin, Richard. "The Stoics on Cases, Predicates, and the Unity of the Proposition." In *Aristotle and After.* Edited by R. Sorabji. London: Institute of Classical Studies, 1997.

Lloyd, A. C. "Definite Propositions and the Concept of Reference." In *Les Stoïciens et leur logique,* edited by Jacques Brunschwig. Paris: 1978.

Long, A. A. "Language and Thought in Stoicism." In *Problems in Stoicism.* Edited by A. A. Long. London: Athlone Press, 1971.

Schenkeveld, D. M. "Stoic and Peripatetic Kinds of Speech Act and the Distinction of Grammatical Moods." *Mnemosyne* 37 (1984): 291–351.

SECONDARY LITERATURE: LATER ANTIQUITY

Barnes, Jonathan. "A Third Sort of Syllogism: Galen and the Logic of Relations." In *Modern Thinkers and Ancient Thinkers.* Edited by R. W. Sharples. Boulder, CO: Westview Press, 1993.

Barnes, Jonathan. *Logic and the Imperial Stoa.* Leiden: Brill, 1997.

Bobzien, Susanne. "Hypothetical Syllogistic in Galen— Propositional Logic Off the Rails?" *Rhizai Journal for Ancient Philosophy and Science* 2 (2004): 57–102.

Bobzien, Susanne. "The Development of *Modus Ponens* in Antiquity: From Aristotle to the 2nd Century AD." *Phronesis* 47 (2002): 359–394.

Ebbesen, Sten. "Boethius as an Aristotelian Commentator." In *Aristotle Transformed—The Ancient Commentators and their Influence.* Edited by R. Sorabji. London: Duckworth, 1990.

Ebbesen, Sten. "Porphyry's Legacy to Logic." In *Aristotle Transformed—The Ancient Commentators and Their Influence.* Edited by R. Sorabji. London: Duckworth, 1990.

Sullivan, W. M. *Apuleian Logic. The Nature, Sources and Influences of Apuleius' Peri Hermeneias.* Amsterdam: North Holland, 1967.

Susanne Bobzien (2005)

LOGIC AND INFERENCE IN INDIAN PHILOSOPHY

By the fifth century BCE great social change was taking place in India and a period of intense intellectual activity came into being. Rational inquiry into a wide range of topics was under way, including agriculture, architecture, astronomy, grammar, law, logic, mathematics, medicine, phonology, and statecraft. Aside from the world's earliest extant grammar, Pāṇini's (c. 400 BCE) *Aṣṭādhyāyī,* however, no works devoted to these topics actually date from this period. Nonetheless, scholars agree that incipient versions of first extant texts on these topics were being formulated.

One text dating from this period and important to tracing the development of logic in classical India is a Buddhist work, Moggaliputta Tissa's *Kathā-vatthu* (Points of controversy; third century BCE), which exhibits awareness of the fact that the form of argument is crucial to its being good. The text gives the refutation of some 200 propositions over which the Sthavīravāda, one of the Buddhist schools, disagreed with various Buddhist schools. The treatment of each point comprises a debate between a proponent and opponent. Throughout book 1, chapter 1, one finds refutations of precisely the following form:

Proponent:	Is A B?
Opponent:	Yes.
Proponent:	Is C D?
Opponent:	No.
Proponent:	Acknowledge defeat, since if A is B, then C is D.

The author clearly presumes it to be self-evident, first, that it is wrong to hold inconsistent propositions and, second, that the propositions assented to—corresponding to the propositional schemata of α, $\neg B$, $\alpha \rightarrow B$—are indeed inconsistent.

The first 500 years of the Common Era saw the redaction of treatises devoted to the systematic exposition of the technical subjects mentioned earlier, as well as of philosophical treatises in which proponents of diverse religious traditions put forth systematic versions of their worldview. These latter works bear witness, in a number of different ways, to the intense interest of the period in argumentation. To begin with, the authors of many of these texts submit arguments and, in doing so, explicitly appeal to such well-known logical principles as those of noncontradiction, of excluded middle and of double negation, though they adduce them, not as principles of logic, but as self-evident ontic facts. Thus, the Buddhist philosopher Nāgārjuna (c. 150–250) often invokes an ontic principle of noncontradiction, saying such things as "when something is a single thing, it cannot be both existent and non-existent" (*Mūlamadhyamakakārikā* chapter 7, verse 30), which is clearly reminiscent of Aristotle's own ontic formulation of the principle of noncontradiction, namely, "that a thing cannot at the same time be and not be" (*Metaphysics* book 3, chapter 2996b29–30).

Next, many of the arguments formulated correspond to such well-recognized rules of inference as *modus ponens* (i.e., from α and $\alpha \rightarrow B$, one infers B), *modus tollens* (i.e., from $\neg B$ and $\alpha \rightarrow B$, one infers $\neg\alpha$), disjunctive syllogism (i.e., from $\neg\alpha$ and $\alpha \vee B$, one infers B), constructive dilemma (i.e., from $\alpha \vee B$, $\alpha \rightarrow \gamma$ and $B \rightarrow \gamma$, one infers γ), categorical syllogism (i.e., from $\alpha \rightarrow B$ and $B \rightarrow \gamma$, one infers $\alpha \rightarrow \gamma$), and *reductio ad absurdum* (i.e., if something false follows from an assumption, then the assumption is false). This last form of argument, termed *prasaṅga* in Sanskrit, is extremely common. Indeed, so common are such arguments in Nāgārjuna's works that his follower, Buddhapālita (470–540), took all of Nāgārjuna's arguments to be *prasaṅga* arguments. As a result, Buddhapālita and his followers were and are referred to as *prāsaṅgikas* (absurdists).

Finally, many of the texts are either devoted to, or have passages devoted to, the enumeration, definition, and classification of public discussion, or debate (*vāda*). The same texts or passages also identify the parts of argument, the flaws found in poor arguments, including such fallacies as circularity (*anyonya-āśraya*, reciprocal dependence) and infinite regress (*an-avasthā*, ungroundedness), as well as quibbles (*chala*) and sophistical refutations (*jāti*) (see Solomon 1976, vol. 1, chapter 5). They also set down ways in which a discussant's behavior warrant his or her being judged the loser of the debate (*nigraha-sthāna*) (see Solomon 1976, vol. 1, chapter 6).

One of the earliest examples of an argument in a form that clearly adumbrates the canonical form the classical Indian inference eventually takes is found in a passage in the *Caraka-saṃhitā* (CS book 2, chapter 8, section 31), a medical text, which defines an argument to have five parts: the proposition (*pratijñā*), the ground or reason (*hetu*), the corroboration (*dṛṣṭānta*), the application (*upanaya*), and the conclusion (*nigamana*). The following is an example:

Proposition:	The soul is noneternal
Ground:	because it is detectable by the senses.
Corroboration:	It is like a pot.
Application:	As a pot is detectable by the senses, and is noneternal, so is the soul detectable by the senses.
Conclusion:	Therefore, the soul is noneternal.

This form of the argument clearly reflects the debate situation. First, one propounds a proposition, that is, one sets forth a proposition to be proved. One then states the ground, or reason, for the proposition one is propounding. Next, one corroborates with an example the connection implicit between the property mentioned in the proposition and the property adduced as its ground. The immediately ensuing step, the application, spells out the analogy between the example and the subject of the proposition. Notice that this part of the argument retains the vestiges of the analogical reasoning that is no doubt its predecessor. Finally, one asserts the proposition.

As was obvious to the thinkers of this period, not all arguments of this form are good arguments. However, no clear criteria are set forth whereby good arguments or inferences can be distinguished from bad ones. At best, some authors simply list good arguments, as does the Buddhist idealist Asanga (flourish fourth–fifth century CE) in a section at the end of a chapter of his *Yogācārabhūmi-śāstra* (Treatise on the stages of yogic practice). Other works provide lists of both good and bad arguments, the latter often referred to as nongrounds (*a-hetu*) or pseudogrounds (*hetu-ābhāsa*) (see Solomon 1976, vol. 1, chapter 7). It is difficult to be sure what the basis for the classification is in these early texts. In the *Nyāya-sūtra* (Aphorisms on logic), a work attributed to Gautama Akṣapāda (flourished second century CE), the author gives neither a definition nor an example. Even in cases where definitions and examples are given, as in the *Caraka-saṃhitā* mentioned earlier, the modern reader is rarely sure of what is intended.

Other passages from these earliest texts treat inference. In these passages inference is taken to be knowledge of one fact arising from knowledge of another. Often, as in the passages of the *Caraka-saṃhitā* (CS book 1, chapter 11, sections 21–22) and the *Nyāya-sūtra* (NS book 1, chapter 1, aphorism 5), no mention is made of any knowledge of what links the two facts. Moreover, the classification of inference in these two texts seems to be based on characteristics completely extrinsic to the logical features of the inferences adduced, for example, according to whether the property permitting the inference precedes, is simultaneous with, or succeeds the property to be inferred.

In contrast, passages from other texts of this period provide definitions of inference that require, besides knowledge of the two states of affairs, knowledge of the relation linking the two. However, instead of providing a formal relation, they provide a miscellany of material relations. The *Ṣaṣṭi-tantra* (Sixty doctrines), which is attributed by some to Pañcaśikha (flourished second century BCE) and by others to Varṣaṇya (fl. after the second century CE), enumerates seven such relations, while the *Vaiśeṣika-sūtra* (Aphorisms pertaining to individuation;

VS book 9, aphora 20), a text attributed to Kaṇāda (flourished first century CE), enumerates five: the relation of cause to effect, of effect to cause, of contact, of exclusion, and of inherence. In each of these texts the miscellany of material relations serves to classify inferences. Thus, although in these two works the parts of an inference have been made explicit, the formal connection among these parts remained implicit.

The works of the Buddhist philosopher Vasubandhu (flourished fourth century CE) seem to be the earliest extant works that provide a formal characterization of the inference. He holds that inference has only three parts: a subject (*pakṣa*) and two properties, the property to be established (*sādhya*) in the subject and another that is the ground (*hetu*). Exploiting an idea ascribed by his coreligionist Asanga in his *Shùn Zhèng Lùn* to an unknown school (thought by at least one scholar to be the Sāṃkhya school), Vasubandhu maintained that a ground in an inference is a proper one if, and only if, it satisfies three conditions—the so-called *tri-rūpa-hetu* (the grounding property *hetu* in its three forms). The first form is that the grounding property (*hetu*; H) should occur in the subject of an inference (*pakṣa*; p). The second is that the grounding property (H) should occur in those things similar to the subject insofar as they have the property to be established (*sādhya*; S). And third, the grounding property (H) should not occur in any of those things dissimilar from the subject insofar as they lack the property to be established (S). These conditions can be viewed as a partial specification of the validity of inferences of this form:

Thesis:	p has S.
Ground:	p has H.
Indispensability:	Whatever has H has S.

The first condition corresponds to the premise labeled *ground* in the schema above, while the second two correspond to the premise labeled *indispensability*. In his *Vāda-vidhi* (Rules of debate) Vasubandhu makes clear that the relation, knowledge of which is necessary for inference, is not just any in a miscellany of material relations, but a formal relation, which he designates, in some places, as *a-vinā-bhāva*—literally, not being without (compare to the Latin expression sine qua non)—and in others, as *nāntarīyakatva*—literally, being unmediated.

The following are two examples of inferences satisfying the previous schema:

Thesis:	p has fire.
Ground:	p has smoke.
Pervasion:	Whatever has smoke has fire.
Thesis:	p is a tree (i.e., has tree-ness).
Ground:	p is an oak (i.e., has oak-ness).
Pervasion:	Whatever is an oak (i.e., has oak-ness) is a tree (i.e., has tree-ness).

The previous schema is the one that Buddhist thinkers insisted on for all sound inference or argument. Brahmanical thinkers came to insist on a the form found in the *Caraka-saṃhitā*, but with the form of the application modified to express a universal claim, thereby giving it the same logical core as the form accepted by the Buddhists.

It is important to note that, no matter how different the metaphysical assumptions of the various philosophical schools, they all used a naive realist's ontology to specify the states of affairs used to study inference. According to this view, the world consists of individual substances or things (*dravya*), universals (*sāmānya*), and relations between them. The fundamental relation is the one of occurrence (*vṛtti*). The relata of this relation are known as substratum (*dharmin*) and superstratum (*dharma*), respectively. The relation has two forms: contact (*saṃyoga*) and inherence (*samavāya*). So, for example, one individual substance, a pot, may occur on another, say the ground, by the relation of contact. In this case the pot is the superstratum and the ground is the substratum. Or, a universal, say brownness, may occur in an individual substance, say a pot, by the relation of inherence. Here, brownness, the superstratum, inheres in the pot, the substratum. The converse of the relation of occurrence is the relation of possession.

Another important relation is the relation that one superstratum bears to another. This relation, known as pervasion (*vyāpti*), can be defined in terms of the occurrence relation. One superstratum pervades another just in case where ever the second occurs the first occurs. The converse of the pervasion relation is the concomitance relation.

As a result of these relations, the world embodies a structure: If one superstratum, designated as H, is concomitant with another superstratum, designated as S, and if a particular substratum, say p, possesses the former superstratum, then it possesses the second. This structure is captured by both the inferential schema for Buddhist thinkers and the inferential schema for Brahmanical thinkers.

Dignāga (flourished fifth century CE), another Buddhist philosopher, consolidated and systematized the insights into the formal basis of inference found in Vasubandhu's works. First, distinguishing between inference for oneself and inference for another, he made explicit what had previously been only implicit, namely, that inference, the cognitive process whereby one increases one's knowledge, and argument, the device of persuasion, are but two sides of a single coin. Second, he undertook to make the three forms of the grounding property (*tri-rūpa-hetu*) more precise, pressing into service the Sanskrit particle *eva* (only). And third, and perhaps most strikingly, he created the *hetu-cakra* (wheel of reasons), a three-by-three matrix, set up to classify pseudogrounds in light of the last two forms of the three forms of a proper ground. On the one hand, there are the three cases of the grounding property (H) occurring in some, none, or all of substrata where the property to be established (S) occurs. On the other hand, there are the three cases of the grounding property (H) occurring in some, none, or all of substrata where the property to be established (S) does not occur. Letting S be the substrata in which S occurs and $\bar{S}$ be the substrata in which S does not occur, one arrives at the following table:

H occurs in:	all S all $\bar{S}$	all S no $\bar{S}$	all S some $\bar{S}$
H occurs in:	no S all $\bar{S}$	no S no $\bar{S}$	no S some $\bar{S}$
H occurs in:	some S all $\bar{S}$	some S no $\bar{S}$	some S some $\bar{S}$

Dignāga's works set the framework within which subsequent Buddhist thinkers addressed philosophical issues pertaining to inference and debate. Thus, Śankarasvāmin (flourished sixth century CE) wrote a brief manual of inference for Buddhists, called the *Nyāya-praveśa* (Beginning logic), based directly on Dignāga's work. Not long thereafter, Dharmakirti (flourished seventh century CE), the great Buddhist metaphysician, also elaborated his views on inference and debate within the framework found in Dignāga.

Dharmakirti made at least two contributions to the treatment of inference. Recall that one of the developments found in Vasubandhu's work was the identification of the formal contribution of what corresponds with the premise labeled indispensability in the inferential schema above making explicit that the corresponding relation is a formal one. One of Vasubandhu's terms for it, namely, *a-vinābhāva* (not being without), made it clear that inference involves some form of necessity. The question raised by Dharmakirti is: What is the basis for the necessity? Recognizing that the necessity does not arise from a simple enumeration of cases, Dharmakirti postulated two relations to vouchsafe the necessity of inference: causation (*tadutpatti*) and identity (*tādātmya*). A second contribution was his attempt to bring knowledge of absences, or roughly negative facts, within the purview of inference.

Another important Buddhist thinker who treated inference was Dharmottara (flourished eighth century CE), who wrote a useful commentary on Dharmakirti's widely read *Nyāya-bindu*.

Dignāga not only had a profound influence on his Buddhist followers but he also influenced his non-Buddhist contemporaries and their followers. It would be wrong, however, to conclude that every adoption of ideas similar to those used by Dignāga in his works should be attributed to him. After all, one cannot be certain that Dignāga's contemporaries did not arrive at similar ideas independently or that they might not have got their ideas from sources common to them and Dignāga. In any event, Praśastapāda (flourished sixth century CE), an adherent of the Vaiśeṣika school and a near contemporary of Dignāga, also defined inference in a way that not only made clear its formal nature but also used the quantificational adjective *sarva* (all) to make the formal connection precise.

At the same time, some authors of this period seem to have retained a view of inference akin to the one found in the *Ṣaṣṭi-tantra* and the *Vaiśeṣika-sūtra*, in which the formal role of what corresponds with the inferential schema's pervasion (*vyāpti*) had yet to have been identified. This is true both of Vātsyāyana (flourished fifth century CE), the author of the earliest extant commentary on the *Nyāya-sūtra* and of Śabara (flourished sixth century CE), the author of the earliest extant commentary on Jaimini's *Mīmāṃsā-sūtra*. However, it was not long before the advocates of both *Nyāya* and *Mīmāṃsā* adapted to the formal view of inference. On the one hand, one finds that the *Mīmāṃsā* thinker Kumārila Bhaṭṭa (flourished 730 CE), adopted, without special comment, the formal perspective. On the other hand, one also finds that, though the *Nyāya* thinker Uddyotakara (flourished late sixth century CE) argued vigorously against many of Dignāga's views, he nonetheless advocated a view that presupposed the formalization found in Dignāga's works. Thus, Uddyotakara classified grounds (*hetu*) as: concomitant (*anvaya*), where nothing distinct from particular substratum p (in the inferential schema) fails to have the property S; exclusive (*vyatireka*), where nothing distinct from

p (in the inferential schema) has the property S; and both concomitant and exclusive, where some things distinct from p have the property S and some fail to have the property S. This classification becomes the standard classification for the adherents of *Nyāya* during the scholastic period.

See also Knowledge in Indian Philosophy; Mind and Mental States in Buddhist Philosophy; Negation in Indian Philosophy; Truth and Falsity in Indian Philosophy; Universal Properties in Indian Philosophical Traditions.

Bibliography

Annambhaṭṭa. *Tarkasaṁgraha-dīpikā on Tarkasaṁgraha by Annaṁbhaṭṭa*. Translated by Gopinath Bhattacharya. Calcutta, India: Progressive, 1976. Originally published under the title *Tarka-saṁgraha*.

Bochenski, I. M. *Formale Logik*. Freiburg, Germany: Karl Alber, 1956. Translated and edited by Ivo Thomas as *A History of Formal Logic*. 2nd ed. New York: Chelsea House, 1970.

Ganeri, Jonardon, ed. *Indian Logic: A Reader*. Richmond, U.K.: Curzon, 2001.

Gillon, Brendan S. "Dharmakiirti and His Theory of Inference." In *Buddhist Logic and Epistemology: Studies in the Buddhist Analysis of Inference and Language*, edited by Bimal K. Matilal and Robert D. Evans, 77–87. Dordrecht, Netherlands: D. Reidel, 1986.

Gillon, Brendan S., and Martha Lile Love. "Indian Logic Revisited: *Nyaayaprave'sa* Reviewed." *Journal of Indian Philosophy* 8 (1980): 349–384.

Potter, Karl H. "Introduction to the Philosophy of Nyaya-Vaisesika." *Encyclopedia of Indian Philosophies*, Vol. 2. Edited by Karl H. Potter, et al. Princeton, NJ: Princeton University Press, 1977.

Randle, H. N. *Indian Logic in the Early Schools: A Study of the Nyāyadarśana in Its Relation to the Early Logic of Other Schools*. London: H. Milford, 1930.

Solomon, Esther A. *Indian Dialectics: Methods of Philosophical Discussion*. 2 vols. Ahmedabad, India: B. J. Institute of Learning and Research, 1976–1978.

Stcherbatsky, Fedor Ippolitovich. *Buddhist Logic*. 2 vols. New York: Dover, 1962.

Vidyabhusana, Satis Chandra. *A History of Indian Logic: Ancient, Medieval, and Modern*. Calcutta, India: Calcutta University, 1921.

Brendan S. Gillon (2005)

CHINESE LOGIC

Systematic argument in Chinese philosophy began with the Moist school, founded in the fifth century BCE by the first anti-Confucian thinker, Mozi (c. 470–c. 391 BCE). He laid down three tests for the validity of a doctrine: ancient authority, common observation, and practical effect. At first the controversies of the various schools over moral and political principles led to increasing rigor in argument; then to an interest in dialectic for its own sake, as evidenced in Hui Shih's paradoxes of infinity and in Kung-sun Lung's sophism "A (white) horse is not a horse"; and still later to the antirationalism of the Daoist Zhuangzi (born c. 369 BCE), who rejected all dialectic on the grounds that names have only an arbitrary connection with objects and that any point of view is right for those who accept the choice of names it assumes.

LOGIC OF MOISM

In the third century BCE the Moists responded to Zhuangzi's skepticism by systematizing dialectic in the "Moist Canons" and the slightly later *Ta-ch'ü* and *Hsiao-ch'ü*.

"MOIST CANONS." The "Canons" confined dialectic to questions of the form "Is it this or is it not?" or, since they assumed that the proposition is merely a complex name for a complex object, "Is it or is it not the case that … ?" (The form is distinguished in Chinese by a verbless sentence with a final particle, not by a verb "to be.") In true dialectic the alternatives are paired ("Is it an ox or not?") so that one and only one fits the object. Dialectic excludes such questions as "Is it an ox or a horse?" (it may be neither) and "Is it a puppy or a dog?" (it may be both). Its solutions are absolutely right or wrong; being or not being "this," unlike being long or short, is not a matter of degree, since nothing is more "this" than this is. The Moists further argued that it is self-contradictory to deny or to affirm all propositions: the statement "All statements are mistaken" implies that it is itself mistaken, and one cannot "reject rejection" without refusing to reject one's own rejection.

Names are of three types, distinguished by their relations to "objects," which are assumed to be particular. "Unrestricted" names (such as "thing") apply to every object. Names "of kinds" (such as "horse") apply to every object resembling the one in question. "Private" names (for example, the proper name "Tsang") apply to one object. Whether a name fits an object is decided by appeal to a "standard." There may be more than one standard for an object; for "circle" the standard may be a circle, one's mental picture of a circle, or a compass. Some standards fit without qualification: A circle has no straight lines. Some fit only partially: In deciding whether someone is a "black man" it is not enough to point out his black eyes and hair. The "Canons" began with seventy-five definitions, evidently offered as "standards," of moral, psycho-

logical, geometrical, and occasionally logical terms. An example of a definition of a logical term is "'All' is 'none not so'" (supplemented in the *Hsiao-ch'ü* by "'Some' is 'not all'"). The first of the series is "The 'cause' is what is required for something to happen." ("*Minor cause*: With this it will not necessarily be so; without this it necessarily will not be so. *Major cause*: With this it will necessarily be so.") The "Canons" also distinguish the senses of twelve ambiguous terms. Thus, "same" is (1) identical ("two names for one object"), (2) belonging to one body, (3) together, and (4) of a kind ("the same in some respects").

"TA-CH'Ü" AND "HSIAO-CH'Ü." The Moist *Ta-ch'ü* further refined the classification of names. Names indicating "number and measure" cease to apply when their objects are reduced in size; when a white stone is broken up it ceases to be "big," although it is still "white." Names indicating "residence and migration" do not apply when the population moves, as in the case of names of particular states ("Ch'i") or of kinds of administrative divisions ("country"). The claim that one knows *X* only if one knows that an object is *X* applies only to names indicating "shape and appearance" ("mountain," but not "Ch'i" or "county").

The *Ta-ch'ü*, and still more the *Hsiao-ch'ü*, also showed a shift of interest from the name to the sentence and to the deduction of one sentence from another. The Chinese never analyzed deductive forms, but the Moists noticed that the formal parallelism of sentences does not necessarily entitle us to infer from one in the same way as from another, and they developed a procedure for testing parallelism by the addition or substitution of words. For example, "Asking about a man's illness is asking about the man," but "Disliking the man's illness is not disliking the man"; "The ghost of a man is not a man," but "The ghost of my brother is my brother." In order to reconcile the execution of robbers with love for all men some Moists maintained that although a robber is a man, "killing robbers is not killing men." Enemies of Moism rejected this as sophistry, on the assumption that one can argue from "A robber is a man" to "Killing robbers is killing men," just as one can argue from "A white horse is a horse" to "Riding white horses is riding horses." The *Hsiao-ch'ü* replied that there are second and third sentence types of the same form, which do not allow such an inference—for example, "Her brother is a handsome man," but "Loving her brother is not loving a handsome man"; "Cockfights are not cocks," but "Having a taste for cockfights is having a taste for cocks." A four-stage procedure was used to establish that "A robber is a man" belongs to the second type:

(1) Illustrating the topic ("robber") with things ("brother," "boat") of which formally similar statements may be made.

(2) Matching parallel sentences about the illustrations and the topic—for instance, "Her brother is a handsome man, but loving her brother is not loving a handsome man"; "A boat is wood, but entering a boat is not entering wood"; "A robber is a man, but abounding in robbers is not abounding in men, nor is being without robbers being without men."

(3) Adducing supporting arguments for the last and most relevant parallels by expanding them and showing that the parallelism still holds: "Disliking the abundance of robbers is not disliking the abundance of men; wishing to be without robbers is not wishing to be without men."

(4) Inferring, defined as "using its [the topic's] similarity to what he [the person being argued with] accepts in order to propose what he does not accept": "Although a robber is a man, loving robbers is not loving men, not loving robbers is not not loving men, and killing robbers is not killing men."

XUNZI

Outside the Moist school only the Confucian Xunzi (c. 313–c. 238 BCE) left a consecutive treatise on logical questions. According to his "Correct Use of Names" the purpose of names is to point out objects, thereby distinguishing the noble from the base and the similar from the different. Names are fixed by convention and are mutable, but to use them idiosyncratically when their usage is fixed is a crime akin to falsifying weights and measures. Objects are different if they differ in place although not in form; they remain the same if they change in form without dividing. Objects of the same kind are perceived by the senses as similar and are given the same name. Names may be of any degree of generality; we may assimilate objects under the name "thing" or distinguish them as "bird" and "beast." (Like the Moists, Xunzi took for granted a nominalist position.) The sentence is a series of names conveying one idea, and a name is understood when we grasp both the object to which it points and its interconnections in the sentence.

Xunzi distinguished three sorts of fallacies, which he illustrated with unexplained examples (two are explained by his refutations of them in his "Treatise of Corrections"). Fallacies that abuse names are exposed by an appeal to established usage, and fallacies that abuse objects are exposed by an appeal to the evidence of the senses. The first fallacy, "confusing names by misuse of names," Xunzi illustrated by "To be insulted is not disgraceful." This is a violation of the established use of "disgrace" in two senses, for social and for moral degradation. The second fallacy, "confusing names by misuse of objects," was exemplified by "Our genuine desires are few." Xunzi criticized this as a factual error about humankind. The third fallacy is "confusing objects by misuse of names." Kung-sun Lung (born 380 BCE) had defended the sophism "A (white) horse is not a horse" on grounds which assume that the question is one of identity, not one of class membership. Xunzi would presumably have replied simply that a white horse is commonly called a "horse."

LATER LOGICAL THOUGHT

The classical period of Chinese philosophy ended about 200 BCE. The next important movement, the neo-Daoism of the third and fourth centuries CE, revived the study of the sophists and the Moist "Canons." Indian treatises on logic were available in translation from the seventh century on; Buddhists wrote commentaries on them during the Tang dynasty (618–907), and in Japan they have continued to do so. But there is little evidence of progress by either Daoists or Buddhists. Neo-Confucianism, the main philosophical movement after the Song dynasty (960–1279), entirely neglected logical inquiry.

CHINESE NEGLECT OF LOGIC

It is well known that almost all Chinese philosophical "systems" are practical, moral, or mystical philosophies of life, indifferent to abstract speculation. It is therefore not surprising that Chinese thinkers have cared little for the forms of reasoning, except under the pressure of the acute controversies of the third century BCE. What is surprising is the almost exclusive interest of Chinese philosophers in the problem of names and the fact that even those who advanced from the name to the sentence studied the parallelism of sentences rather than their analysis.

A reason for this interest can be found in the Chinese language, which organizes uninflected words solely according to word order and the placing of particles. Without the inflections that expose the structure of Sanskrit, Greek, or Arabic sentences and encourage the simultaneous growth of grammar and logic the Chinese sentence, until recently, almost defied analysis; the Chinese have been lexicographers but not grammarians. On the other hand, strict parallelism of clauses—in which noun is matched with noun, adjective with adjective, adverb with adverb, verb with verb—is part of the ordinary resources of the Chinese language and easily calls attention to the logical dangers of formal parallelism.

See also Chinese Philosophy; Gongsun Long; Hui Shi; Mozi; Proper Names and Descriptions; Xunzi; Zhuangzi.

Bibliography

CHINESE LOGIC

Chao, Y. R. "Notes on Chinese Grammar and Logic." *Philosophy East and West* 20 (2) (1970): 137–154.

Cheng Chung-ying. "On Implication (*tse*) and Inference (*ku*) in Chinese Grammar and Chinese Logic." *Journal of Chinese Philosophy* 2 (1975): 225–244.

Chmielewski, Janusz. "Notes on Early Chinese Logic." *Rocznik Orientalistyczny* 26 (1) (1962): 7–21; 26 (2) (1963): 91–105; 27 (1) (1963): 103–121; 28 (2) (1965): 87–111; 29 (2) (1965): 117–138; 30 (1) (1966): 31–52; 31 (1) (1968): 117–136; 32 (2) (1969): 83–103.

Graham, Angus C. *Disputers of the Tao*. La Salle, IL: Open Court, 1989.

Graham, Angus C. *Later Mohist Logic, Ethics and Science*. Hong Kong: Chinese University Press, 1978; reprinted, 2003.

Hansen, Chad. *Language and Logic in Ancient China*. Ann Arbor: University of Michigan Press, 1983.

Harbsmeier, Christoph. *Science and Civilisation in China*, Vol. 7: *The Social Background*, Part 1: *Language and Logic in Traditional China*. Cambridge, U.K.: Cambridge University Press, 1998.

Hu Shi. *The Development of the Logical Method in Ancient China*. Shanghai: Oriental, 1922.

Lau, D. C. "On Mencius' Use of the Method of Analogy in Argument." *Asia Major* 10 (1963). Reprinted in D. C. Lau, tr. *Mencius*. London: Penguin, 1970, pp. 235–263.

Lau, D. C. "Some Logical Problems in Ancient China." *PAS*, n.s. 53 (1952–1953): 189–204.

Lenk, Hans, and Gregor Paul, eds. *Epistemological Issues in Classical Chinese Philosophy*. Albany: State University of New York Press, 1993.

Leslie, Donald. *Argument by Contradiction in Pre-Buddhist Chinese Reasoning*. Canberra: Australian National University, 1964.

Reding, Jean-Paul. *Les fondements philosophiques de la rhétorique chez les sophistes grecs et chez les sophistes chinois*. Bern: Peter Lang, 1985.

A. C. Graham (1967)
Bibliography updated by Huichieh Loy (2005)

LOGIC IN THE ISLAMIC WORLD

Arabic logic, like the rest of medieval Arabic science and philosophy, is entirely Western and has nothing to do with Oriental philosophy. It developed wholly in the wake of the classical Greek tradition as preserved in and transmitted through late Greek Aristotelianism. The present account briefly traces the evolution of Arabic logic from its inception in the late eighth century to its stultification in the sixteenth century, mentioning only the most important trends, figures, and achievements. Information on individual writers can be found in Carl Brockelmann's monumental *Geschichte der arabischen Litteratur*, cited hereafter as *GAL* (2 vols.—I, II—Weimar, 1890; Berlin, 1902; 2nd ed., Leiden, 1943–1949; 3 supp. vols.—SI, SII, SIII—Leiden, 1937–1942).

TRANSMISSION OF GREEK LOGIC TO THE ARABS

After their conquest of Syria-Iraq the Arabs came into contact with Greek learning as it continued to be nursed by various Christian sects—primarily the Nestorians and the Monophysites, or Jacobites—that had transplanted there (via such centers as Antioch, Edessa, and Nisibis) the Hellenistic scholarship of Alexandria. Thus, the first writers on logic in Arabic were Syrian Christian scholars, and their tradition of logical studies—closely linked to medicine—was transferred to an Arabic-language setting and laid the foundation for the development of Arabic logic.

The Syriac expositors of Aristotelian logic arrived at the following standard arrangement of logical works: *Isagoge* (by Porphyry), *Categories, De Interpretatione, Prior Analytics, Posterior Analytics, Topics, De Sophisticis Elenchis, Rhetoric*, and *Poetics*. These nine works were thought of as dealing with nine distinct branches of logic, each based on its own canonical text. This construction of Aristotelian logic was taken over by the Arabs, resulting in the following organization of the subject matter of logic:

Branch	Arabic Name	Basic Text
(1) Introduction	*al-īsāghūjī*	*Isagoge*
(2) Categories	*al-maqūlāt*	*Categories*
(3) Hermeneutics	*al-'ibārah*	*De Interpretatione*
(4) Analytics	*al-qiyās*	*Prior Analytics*
(5) Apodictics	*al-burhān*	*Posterior Analytics*
(6) Topics	*al-jadal*	*Topics*
(7) Sophistics	*al-mughālitah* (or *al-safsatah*)	*De Sophisticis Elenchis*
(8) Rhetoric	*al-khitābah*	*Rhetoric*
(9) Poetics	*al-shi'r*	*Poetics*

The totality of this organon was referred to as the nine books of logic, or as the eight books with the *Poetics* (or sometimes *Isagoge*) excluded. The first four of these logical treatises were apparently the only ones translated into Syriac prior to 800 and into Arabic prior to 850. They were called the four books of logic, and they constituted the object of logical studies in the basic curriculum of the Syrian academies.

Arabic translations of Aristotle's logical treatises and of several Greek studies and commentaries on them prepared the ground for the first indigenous Arabic writer on logic, the philosopher Abū-Yūsuf Yaʿqūb ibn Isḥāq al-Kindī (c. 805–873; *GAL*, I, pp. 209–210). His logical writings, however, probably amounted to little more than summaries of the writings of others about the Aristotelian texts.

SCHOOL OF BAGHDAD

In the late ninth and the tenth centuries Arabic logic was virtually the monopoly of a single school of logicians centered at Baghdad. The founders of this school belonged to a closely knit group of Syrian Christians, including the teachers of Abū Bishr Mattā ibn Yūnus and the teachers of these teachers. Its principal continuators were the pupils of Abū Bishr's pupil Yaḥyā ibn ʿAdī and the pupils of these pupils. Virtually all of these men—with the notable exception of al-Fārābī, a Muslim—were Nestorian Christians.

Abū Bishr Mattā ibn Yūnus (c. 870–c. 940; *GAL*, I, p. 207) was the first specialist in logical studies to write in Arabic. He produced the first Arabic translations of *Posterior Analytics* and *Poetics* and translated several Greek commentaries on Aristotelian works (such as Themistius on *Posterior Analytics*). In addition he wrote logical commentaries and treatises of his own, which unfortunately have not survived.

Abū Naṣr al-Fārābī (c. 873–950; *GAL*, I, pp. 210–213) was perhaps the most important logician of Islam. His commentaries, only a fraction of which survive, covered the entire Aristotelian *Organon* in great detail. All later Arabic logicians—even those who, like Avicenna, have opposed al-Fārābī's influence—have seen Aristotle through his eyes. Among the points of special interest in the commentaries of al-Fārābī are (1) a strong emphasis on *ecthesis* (the setting out of terms) as a principle of syllogistic reduction, (2) an increased resort to noncategorical (for instance, hypothetical and disjunctive) types of syllogism, (3) an elaborate treatment of inductive uses of syllogistic reasoning, especially the application of the categorical syllogism in argument by analogy, and (4) a detailed treatment of the problem of future contingency, providing for a reading of Chapter 9 of *De Interpretatione* that does not deny prior truth status to future contingents (anticipating the position of Peter Abelard).

Yaḥyā ibn ʿAdī (893–974; *GAL*, I, p. 207), who studied logic and philosophy with both Abū Bishr and al-Fārābī, not only translated Greek works from Syriac into Arabic but also taught virtually half of the Arabic logicians of the tenth century. He wrote various independent works (including a commentary on *Prior Analytics* that devoted special attention to modal syllogisms), almost none of which have survived.

The three principal achievements of this school of Baghdad are (1) completion of the series of Arabic translations of Greek logical works, (2) the masterly commentaries of al-Fārābī (and possibly others) on the logical treatises of Aristotle, and (3) the elaborate study of certain extra-Aristotelian topics by Abū Bishr Mattā and al-Fārābī (for instance, theory of "conditional," or hypothetical and disjunctive, syllogisms along lines already found in Boethius, and the syllogistic reduction of inductive modes of argument).

AVICENNA AND HIS INFLUENCE

Despite the demise of the school of Baghdad around 1050, the ultimate survival of logical studies in Islam was assured by the fact that logic had, through the mediation of medicine, become an integral constituent of the Arabic medicophilosophical tradition as taken over from the Syrian Christians. From a quantitative standpoint the eleventh century was a low ebb in the history of Arabic logic. Yet this period produced perhaps the most creative logician of Islam, the great Persian scholar Abū ibn Sīnā, known as Avicenna (980–1037; *GAL*, I, pp. 452–458).

Avicenna made a daring innovation. Although greatly indebted to the school of Baghdad, he had nothing but contempt for it because it regarded logic as the study of the Aristotelian texts. Avicenna disapproved of this orientation toward the text rather than the subject. For him, and for the tradition he dominated, a logic book was no longer a commentary on Aristotle but an independent, self-sufficient treatise or handbook that covered the ground after its own fashion. Avicenna's masterpiece is a series of treatises in his monumental *Kitāb al-shifāʾ* dealing with the nine parts of the Arabic logical organon.

An example of Avicenna's originality is the following: In Aristotle and in the Stoics one finds a temporal construction of the modality of necessity that construes "All *X*'s are *necessarily Y*'s" as "At any time *t* all *X*'s-at-*t* are *Y*'s-at-*t*." This construction works well for, say, "All men are necessarily animals" but clearly not for "All men necessarily die." Avicenna distinguished between such cases as:

(1) At every time during its existence every X is a Y ("All men are necessarily animals").

(2) At most times during its existence every X is a Y ("All men are necessarily breathing beings").

(3) At some time during its existence every X is a Y ("All men are necessarily dying beings").

He then constructed a detailed theory of syllogistic inference from temporally modalized propositions of this sort.

Avicenna styled his own work in logic (and philosophy) as Eastern, in deliberate contrast with the Western approach of the school of Baghdad. This Eastern logic espoused by Avicenna differs from that of, say, al-Fārābī not so much in matters of substance as in emphasis and in willingness to depart from Aristotelian precedent. Thus, Avicenna imported into his logic a certain amount of material derived probably from Galen (including an at least grudging recognition of the fourth figure of the categorical syllogism) and certainly from the Stoics (for example, quantification of the predicate of categorical propositions, elaboration of quality and quantity for "conditional" propositions, and a treatment of singular propositions in the manner of the Stoics).

Avicenna's call to study logic from independent treatises rather than via the Aristotelian texts met with complete success in Eastern Islam. Only in Muslim Spain did the tradition of Aristotelian studies of the school of Baghdad manage—for a time—to survive.

LOGICIANS OF ANDALUSIA

During the late eleventh and the twelfth centuries Andalusia (Muslim Spain) was the principal center of logical studies in Islam. Muḥammad ibn ʿAbdūn (c. 930–c. 995; Heinrich Suter, *Die Mathematiker und Astronomen der Araber und ihre Werke*, Leipzig, 1900–1902, no. 161; not in *GAL*), a Spanish Muslim who studied medicine and philosophy in Baghdad, was instrumental in transplanting to Córdoba the teachings of the school of Baghdad in Aristotelian logic. In the medico-logical tradition of Andalusia these teachings stayed alive for more than two and a half centuries, surviving well past their extinction in Eastern Islam.

Abū'l-Ṣalt (1068–1134; *GAL*, I, pp. 486–487) wrote an influential logic compendium that follows al-Fārābī closely; like most other Spanish Arab logicians, he seems to have had special interest in modal syllogisms. The detailed study of the writings of Aristotle was revitalized by Ibn Bājja (or Avempace; c. 1090–1138; *GAL*, I, p. 460),

who wrote an important series (extant but unpublished) of discussions of Aristotle's works based on the commentaries of al-Fārābī.

Ibn Rushd (or Averroes; c. 1126–c. 1198; *GAL*, I, pp. 461–462) was unquestionably the most important of the Arabic logicians of Spain. His elaborate commentaries on the treatises of Aristotle's logical *Organon* rival (and conceivably surpass) those of al-Fārābī in their detailed understanding of Aristotle's logic. Averroes stands, as he considered himself to stand, heir to the masters of the school of Baghdad and successor to the heritage of al-Fārābī.

Among the points of special interest in the Aristotelian commentaries of Averroes are (1) certain historical data—for instance, regarding Galen's origination of the fourth syllogistic figure—taken from the last writings of al-Fārābī, (2) anti-Avicennist polemics that afford us a view of the points of dispute between Avicenna and his opponents, (3) the detailed account of the Aristotelian theory of modal syllogisms, and (4) in general, his effort to systematize as unified doctrine the teachings of the Aristotelian *Organon*.

After Averroes the logical tradition of Muslim Spain entered a period of decline. Arabic logic became extinct in Spain because there—in contrast to Eastern Islam, where logic achieved a modus vivendi with religious orthodoxy—popular and theological hostility toward logic and philosophy as an integral part of "alien learning" continued unabated.

QUARREL OF THE EASTERN AND WESTERN SCHOOLS

Avicenna's criticisms of the school of Baghdad and his shift away from Aristotelian orthodoxy were not received with universal acceptance. A Western school arose to oppose Avicenna's innovations. Its principal exponents were the prolific Persian scholar Fakhr al-Dīn al-Rāzī (1148–1209; *GAL*, I, pp. 506–508) and his followers al-Khūnajī (1194–1249; *GAL*, I, p. 463) and al-Urmawī (1198–1283; *GAL*, I, p. 467). These logicians not only offered detailed criticisms of Avicenna's departures from Aristotle but also wrote handbooks of logic that became standard textbooks both during the lifetime of their school and later.

Opposed to these Westerners, the school of the Easterners, which supported Avicenna, continued to be active throughout the thirteenth century. Its leading exponent was the eminent and versatile Persian scholar Kamāl al-Dīn ibn Yūnus (1156–1242; *GAL*, SI, p. 859). His position was supported by his pupils al-Abharī (1200–1264; *GAL*, I, pp. 464–465) and Naṣīr al-Dīn al-Ṭūsī (1201–1274; *GAL*, I, pp. 508–512), as well as by the pupils of the last-named scholar, especially the logician al-Qazwīnī al-Kāt-ibī (c. 1220–c. 1280; *GAL*, I, pp. 466–467). These logicians produced polemical treatises to attack the theses of the Westerners, as well as textbooks and handbooks to facilitate the teaching of logic according to their conceptions.

Amid this disputation and textbook writing the logical treatises of Aristotle were completely lost sight of. In effect, Avicenna carried the field before him; in Eastern Islam, Aristotle's logical writings were utterly abandoned. Ibn Khaldūn (1332–1406) could lament, "The books and methods of the ancients are avoided, as if they had never been, although they are full of the results and useful aspects of logic." The handbooks of the two thirteenth-century schools provided a basis for all future study in Islam, completely replacing the works of Aristotle. But very little produced at this stage has any significance for logic as a science rather than as a field of instruction.

FINAL PERIOD

The period 1300–1500 may be characterized as the final period of Arabic logic, when its ossification became complete. It was a time not of creative logicians but of teachers of logic writing expository commentaries and supercommentaries on the thirteenth-century handbooks, now basic to all Arabic instruction in logic.

Underlying this development was the effort of al-Tustarī (c. 1270–c. 1330; *GAL*, SI, p. 816) and his disciple al-Taḥtānī (c. 1290–1365; *GAL*, II, pp. 209–210) to effect an arbitration between the Eastern and Western schools. As a result, later Arabic logicians were free to draw on both sectors of the tradition and to use the handbooks of both schools for the teaching of logic. The flood of glosses and supercommentaries on commentaries on the thirteenth-century logic handbooks marks the final, disintegrative phase of the evolution of logic in Islam.

CONTRIBUTIONS OF ARABIC LOGIC

Some of the original contributions made by the Arabic logicians to logic as a science are (1) al-Fārābī's syllogistic theory of inductive argumentation, (2) al-Fārābī's doctrine of future contingency, (3) Avicenna's theory of "conditional" propositions, (4) Avicenna's temporal construction of modal propositions, and (5) Averroes's careful reconstruction of Aristotle's theory of modal syllogistic. Many of the prominent "innovations" of medieval Latin logic are in effect borrowings or elabora-tions of borrowings of Arabic ideas (for example, the distinction between the various modes of *suppositio* and the distinction between modality *de dicto* and *de re*).

However, in speaking of the "original contributions" of Arabic logic two qualifications are necessary. In the first place, our knowledge of late Greek logic is so incomplete that any "original" item of Arabic work could turn out to be a mere elaboration of a Greek innovation. Second, an emphasis on originality in discussing Arabic logic is somewhat misplaced in that all the Arabic logicians—even Avicenna, the most original of them all—viewed their logical work as the reconstruction of a Greek teaching rather than as an enterprise of innovation.

See also al-Fārābī; al-Kindī, Abū-Yūsuf Yaʿqūb ibn Isḥāq; Aristotelianism; Aristotle; Averroes; Avicenna; Boethius, Anicius Manlius Severinus; Ibn Bājja; Naṣīr al-Dīn al-Ṭūsī; Porphyry.

Bibliography

ARABIC LOGIC

A complete bibliography of Arabic logic can be found in Nicholas Rescher, *The Development of Arabic Logic* (Pittsburgh: University of Pittsburgh Press, 1964). On the transmission of Greek logic to the Arabs, see Max Meyerhof, "Von Alexandrien nach Baghdad," in *Sitzungsberichte der Preussischen Akademie der Wissenschaften*, Philosophisch-historische Klasse 23 (1930): 389–429. The conflict between logic and Islamic religion is detailed in Ignaz Goldziher, "Stellung der alten islamischen Orthodoxie zu den antiken Wissenschaften," in *Abhandlungen der Königlichen Preussischen Akademie der Wissenschaften*, Philosophisch-historische Klasse, Jahrgang 1915 (Berlin, 1916). For the Arabs' familiarity with Aristotle's logical works, see R. Walzer, "Arisṭū" (Aristotle), in *Encyclopedia of Islam* (London, 1960), Vol. I; and Ibrahim Madkour, *L'organon d'Aristote dans le monde arabe* (Paris: Vrin, 1934).

Some representative Arabic logical texts accessible in European languages are D. M. Dunlop, translations of several logical *opuscula* of al-Fārābī in *Islamic Quarterly*, 2 (1955)–5 (1959); Nicholas Rescher, *Al-Fārābī's Short Commentary on Aristotle's "Prior Analytics"* (Pittsburgh, 1963); A. M. Goichon, *Avicenne: Livre de directives et remarques* (Paris, 1951); Mohammad Achena and Henri Massé, *Avicenne: Le livre de science*, Vol. I (Paris, 1955); *Aristotelis Opera cum Averrois Commentariis* (Venice, 1550 and later; 1562–1574 ed. reprinted photographically, Frankfurt: Minerva, 1962).

Substantive study of the contributions of Arabic logicians has only begun. In addition to Prantl, *Geschichte der Logik im Abendlande*, Vol. II, above, consult T. J. de Boer, "Manṭik," in *Encyclopedia of Islam*, 1st ed.; and Nicholas Rescher, *Studies in the History of Arabic Logic* (Pittsburgh: University of Pittsburgh Press, 1963).

Nicholas Rescher (1967)

LOGIC IN THE ISLAMIC WORLD [ADDENDUM]

For more on everything in the entry, see especially Hans Daiber's *Bibliography of Islamic Philosophy* (1999). Few scholars would now accept that Arabic logic is "entirely Western"; it grew out of Greek texts, but developed differently from both Hellenistic and Latin logic.

TRANSMISSION OF GREEK LOGIC TO THE ARABS

Research on the translation of the books of the *Organon* and their attendant commentaries is presented in summary essays in Goulet (1989–2003, pp. 502ff).

THE SCHOOL OF BAGHDAD

The leading representative of the textual Aristotelianism of Baghdad was al-Fārābī, and much of his extant work is now either edited or translated (see Lameer 1994).

AVICENNA AND HIS INFLUENCE

The many new editions, translations, and studies of Avicenna are listed by Jules L. Janssens (1999). An attempt to deal philosophically with his modal syllogistic is made by Paul Thom (2003, chapter 4 and idem). See also his essay "Logic and Metaphysics in Avicenna's Modal Syllogistic" (forthcoming).

LOGICIANS OF ANDALUSIA

Averroes, though without much influence in the Islamic world, is the most acute of the Andalusian logicians. See Thom (2003, chapter 5) for a philosophical treatment of his later modal syllogistic.

QUARREL OF THE EASTERN AND WESTERN SCHOOLS

There certainly were major differences among the post-Avicennan logicians, but Nicholas Rescher's use of "Eastern" and "Western" schools to gather them into opposing camps is misleading (see Street 2004, pp. 567ff).

FINAL PERIOD

One cannot assume the tradition ossified because its most common genre became the commentary. The task ahead is to read and appraise the profusion of texts written from the 900s until after the colonial invasions of the nineteenth century. For a study of the attitudes to logic in this period, see Khaled El-Rouayheb's "Sunni Muslim Scholars on the Status of Logic, 1500–1800" (2004).

See also al-Fārābī; Averroes; Avicenna; Islamic Philosophy; Rescher, Nicholas.

Bibliography

Daiber, Hans. *A Bibliography of Islamic Philosophy*. Leiden, Netherlands: Brill, 1999.

El-Rouayheb, Khaled. "Sunni Muslim Scholars on the Status of Logic, 1500–1800." *Islamic Law and Society* 11 (4) (2004): 213–232.

Goulet, Richard, ed. *Dictionnaire des philosophes antiques*, Vol. 1. Paris: Éditions du Centre national de la recherche scientifique, 1989–2003.

Janssens, Jules L. *An Annotated Bibliography on Ibn Sīnā: First Supplement (1990–1994)*. Louvain-la-Neuve: Fédération Internationale des Instituts d'études médiévales, 1999.

Lameer, Joep. *Al-Fārābī and Aristotelian Syllogistics: Greek Theory and Islamic Practice*. Leiden, Netherlands: Brill, 1994.

Street, Tony. "Arabic Logic." In *Handbook of the History of Logic, Vol. 1: Greek, Indian, and Arabic Logic*, edited by Dov M. Gabbay and John Woods, 523–596. Amsterdam: Elsevier, 2004.

Thom, Paul. "Logic and Metaphysics in Avicenna's Modal Syllogistic." In *The Unity of Science in the Arabic Tradition: Metaphysics, Logic and Epistemology and Their Interactions*, edited by Shahid Rahman, Tony Street, and Hassan Tahiri. Dordrecht, Netherlands: Kluwer-Springer, forthcoming.

Thom, Paul. *Medieval Modal Systems: Problems and Concepts*. Aldershot, U.K.: Ashgate, 2003.

Tony Street (2005)

MEDIEVAL (EUROPEAN) LOGIC

Although some elementary work was done in the ninth and tenth centuries it was not until the end of the eleventh century that medieval logic really began to develop a character of its own. It started as glosses and commentaries on some of a small number of texts that had survived from antiquity. These included Boethius's translations of Porphyry's *Isagoge*, Aristotle's *Categories* and *De interpretatione*, and two works written by Boethius himself, a treatise, *De Topicis Differentiis*, on topical inference based on the work of Themistius and Cicero, and another, *De divisione*, devoted to the various forms of division employed in logic. In the thirteenth century these works were collectively known as the *logica vetus*.

In addition logicians at the beginning of the twelfth century possessed Boethius's very extensive commentaries on the *Isagoge, Categories*, and *De interpretatione*, his two-part epitome of Aristotle's *Prior Analytics*, 1–7, *Introductio ad syllogismos categoricos* and *De syllogismo categorico*, his treatise on hypothetical syllogisms, *De hypotheticis syllogismis*, and his commentary on Cicero's *Topica, In Topica Ciceronis.*

Also important in the early development of logic were Marius Victorinus's *De diffinitionibus*, Saint Augustine's *De dialectica*, and, at least in the ninth and tenth centuries, *De decem categoriae*, a fourth-century Latin translation of a Greek paraphrase of Aristotle's *Categories* attributed to Augustine. In addition, Priscian's *Institutiones grammaticae*, with the eleventh- and twelfth-century glosses on it known as the *Glossulae*, were an important influence in the twelfth century on the development of philosophical semantics and in particular of theories of the substantive verb *to be.*

Boethius's translations of Aristotle's *Sophistical Refutations, Topics*, and *Prior Analytics* were recovered before the middle of the twelfth century. Along with the translation of the *Posterior Analytics* made then by James of Venice they provided logicians with what was distinguished from the *logica vetus* as the *logica nova*. Apart from the *Sophistical Refutations*, however, it was not until the beginning of the thirteenth century that the works of the *logia nova* had a significant impact on the development of logic. Although some parts of Avicenna's logical works were translated into Latin, unlike other areas of philosophy, Arabic writing had little impact on the development of logic.

From the middle of the twelfth century logicians developed their discipline in various ways and produced works characteristic of what would much later be referred to as the *logica modernorum*. These dealt, for example, with the properties of terms, and in particular the theory of supposition, syncategorematic words, modality, *obligationes, insolublia*, consequences, and sophisms of various kinds, each of which is discussed in this entry.

THE BOETHIAN BACKGROUND

Based as it was upon the texts of the *logica vetus* medieval logic included a great deal that has to do with ontology and philosophical semantics rather than with logic more narrowly construed as the theory of valid argumentation. Boethius gave medieval logicians much of their terminology but his commentaries on Aristotle and even more so his own works are essentially elementary, often confused, and sometimes inconsistent. It was these, however, which provided twelfth-century logicians with the material from which they constructed their new formal and philosophical logics. In particular, the remarkable developments they made in theory of inference had their beginnings in reflection on Boethius's *De Topicis Differentiis* and *De hypotheticis syllogismis.*

TOPICAL INFERENCE. Medieval logic at least in the first half of the twelfth century was characterized by an intense interest in conditional propositions and in the nature of topical inference as formulated by Boethius in *De Topicis Differentiis.* Logicians at this time were not generally concerned to regiment arguments into the modes and figures of the categorical syllogism but everywhere they classified inferences in accordance with lists of topics, based upon those given by Boethius.

In his treatise Boethius proposes to show how arguments may be discovered to settle any given question. What has to be found, he claims, is what Cicero, in his *Topica*, calls an "*argumentum*"—defined as a "reason which brings conviction where something is in doubt." An argument (*argumentatio*) is the expression in speech or writing of the proof of a conclusion constructed with the required *argumentum*. A *locus*, or topic, is the "site," or "source," of *argumenta* (*Diff. Top.* I, 1174D).

Argumenta are invoked by Boethius to warrant the enthymematic inference of a categorical conclusion from categorical premises or the direct proof of a conditional proposition. In each case what is needed is a principle that is not itself provable, called by Boethius a *maximal proposition*, and a relevant fact about the items mentioned in the conclusion. For example, by appealing to the maximal proposition "a genus is predicated of whatever its species is predicated" and the truth that animal is the genus of human being we may either infer from the premiss that Socrates is a human being the conclusion that he is an animal or, directly, the corresponding conditional.

The various relationships which Boethius holds may exist between the predicate and subject of a true categorical proposition or between the antecedent and consequent of a true conditional provide him with his *loci* (*Diff. Top.* II, 1186C). With each *locus* there are associated all the maximal propositions warranting inferences which may be made on the basis of that relationship. The enthymeme above, for example, would be characterized as holding "from species," that is, in virtue of the relationship in which a species stands to its genus.

Boethius gives the lists and classifications of the *loci* provided by both Themistius and Cicero. They are divided into those which are intrinsic, that is, having to do only with the things themselves about which a question is asked, and those which are extrinsic, having no such connection with them. (*Diff. Top.* II, 1186D) Examples of intrinsic *loci* are that from species, given above, and that from what is defined, for which one maximal proposition is: "of that of which what is defined is not predicated, the definition is not predicated." Examples of extrinsic *loci* are that from authority, which justifies inferences from the authority of the majority of people, or the relevant experts, and *loci* from various kinds of opposition.

Argumenta drawn from the locus from authority are not necessary according to Boethius but they are probable in the sense of being generally convincing. Where Aristotle had taken probability and necessity to be properties of the premises and conclusion of a dialectical syllogism, however, Boethius takes them to characterize the nature of the inference from the premiss, or premisses, to the conclusion of an argument and the corresponding connection between the antecedent and consequent of a conditional (*Diff. Top.* I, 1180C).

THE THEORY OF CONDITIONAL PROPOSITIONS. In *De Topicis Differentiis*, Boethius classifies conditional propositions according to the quality of the antecedent and consequent. He accepts what we would now call a principle of contraposition and so maintains that a topical relationship warrants a conditional of the form "if something's an *A*, then it's a *B*" if and only if it warrants one of the form "if something's not a *B*, then it's not an *A*," where *A* and *B* are general terms such as "human being" and "animal." Conditionals of the form "if something's an *A*, then it's not a *B*" are true, he maintains, only for items which are "opposites," that is, opposed exclusively but not exhaustively. For example, "if something's a human being, then it's not a donkey." Those of the form "if something's not an *A*, then it's a *B*" hold only for items which are "immediates," that is, opposed exclusively and exhaustively. For example, "if something's not well, then it's ill" (*Diff. Top.* I, 1179C).

With *De hypotheticis syllogismis* Boethius provided twelfth-century logicians with an account of the logic of certain conditional and disjunctive propositions but neither he nor any other ancient source provided them with what we would recognize as a propositional logic. Boethius had no clear understanding of the nature of either propositionality or propositional operation (Martin 1991).

In his general treatment of compound propositions in his long commentary on *De interpretatione*, Boethius thus denies that the copulative conjunction "and" does anything other than punctuate a list (*2 In Peri. Herm.*, 5, 109). In the same work he also explicitly rejects the Stoic practice of preposing a negative particle to a categorical proposition as ambiguous between the negation of the subject and predicate terms (*2 In Peri. Herm.*, 10, 261–2).

Without a notion of propositionality, Boethius has no notion a propositional form or of the substitution of propositional contents into propositional contexts to obtain new contents of arbitrary complexity. In *De hypotheticis syllogismis* he thus lists all the various kinds of hypothetical syllogism which he accepts for each different quality of the component categorical propositions. There, just as everywhere else where Boethius employs it, the negative particle preposed to a conditional never takes the whole of the following conditional proposition for its scope but always acts only on the consequent.

Boethius designates a conditional as affirmative if its consequent is affirmative and negative if it is negative no matter what the quality of the antecedent (*Hyp. Syll.* 1.9.6). The only compound propositions he considers are simple conditionals and disjunctions, that is those whose components are both categorical, and compound conditionals of which one or more component is a simple conditional. The most complex form of conditional he considers has simple conditionals for both its antecedent and consequent. These compound conditionals, again, have nothing to do with propositional logic as it is now understood. Conditionalized instances of contraposition, for example, are not true instances of the form since Boethius requires for the truth of "if (if something's an *A*, then it's a *B*), then (if something's a *C*, then it's a *D*)" that both "if something's an *A*, then it's a *C*" and "if something's a *B*, then it's a *D*" are true (*Hyp. Syll.* 3.9.1).

In *De hypotheticis syllogismis* Boethius gives the basic truth-condition for a conditional proposition, or consequence (*consequentia*), which will be accepted throughout the middle ages. To "destroy" such a proposition, that is, to show that it is false, he says, one must show that it is possible for the consequent to be false when the antecedent is true. A conditional is thus true only if the truth of the antecedent is inseparable from that of the consequent. A simple disjunction, "something's an *A* or it's a *B*," is equivalent, according to Boethius, to a simple conditional with a negative antecedent and affirmative consequent and so holds only for terms connected to one another as immediates (*Hyp. Syll.* 1.3.3).

In addition to stating the inseparability condition for their truth Boethius makes a distinction between conditionals which has profound consequences for the development of medieval logic and metaphysics. He claims that a relation of consequence may be indicated with either "*si*" ("if") or equivalently with "*cum*." The latter, however, usually means *when*, or *whenever* in Latin and that is how it is translated here.

The truth of an antecedent, Boethius notes, will be inseparable from that of a consequent if both are necessarily true even if there is no explanatory connection between them as, for example, "whenever (*cum*) fire is hot, then the heavens are spherical." Boethius does not notice, however, nor does any other ancient source available in the twelfth century, that the inseparability requirement is apparently also satisfied by any conditional whose antecedent is impossible, or whose consequent is necessary.

Boethius designates as "accidental consequences" conditionals formed with "whenever" which meet the inseparability requirement merely on account of the truth-value of their components. He contrasts them with "natural consequences," formed with "if," in which the truth of the antecedent is inseparable from that of the consequent in virtue of an explanatory connection between them. For example "if something's a human being, then its an animal" (*Hyp. Syll.* 1.3.6).

Finally, although Boethius correctly observes that Aristotle wrote nothing about hypothetical syllogisms, he takes from *Prior Analytics*, II. 4, as basic for the logic of conditional propositions what has been called Aristotle's Principle: No two conditionals of the form "if something's *A*, then its *B*" and "if something's not *A*, then its *B*" can both be true (*Hyp. Syll.* 1.4.1).

ABELARD AND THE DISCOVERY OF PROPOSITIONALITY

Peter Abelard, the first significant, and arguably the greatest, of all medieval logicians taught in Paris at various times between 1101 and 1140. Although most logical writing which we have from the twelfth century has been transmitted anonymously and with no certainty about its date of production, very fortunately both Abelard's own survey of logic, the *Dialectica*, written probably around 1116, his *Logica*, consisting of commentaries on Porphyry, Aristotle, and Boethius, written around 1120, and his *Glossulae* on Porphyry, written in the 1120s, have survived more or less intact. The following account of logic in the first half of the twelfth century is thus mainly an account of Abelard's work. He was, however, certainly not the only logician active at the time and much of his writing consists of arguments against sophisticated but unnamed opponents.

Most important, Abelard understood the distinction between the propositional content of a sentence and the force with which it is uttered (Martin 2004). The propositional content "that Socrates is running," for example, may be asserted with an assertive utterance of "Socrates is

running" or it may contribute to the meaning without itself being asserted in an assertive utterance of the conditional "if Socrates is running, then he is moving." Since Boethius treats "proposition" (*propositio*) and "assertion" (*enuntiatio*) as synonyms, however, it was rather difficult for Abelard to formulate clearly the distinction for an assertion between force and content.

Abelard uses the term "proposition" (*propositio*) to refer to a token propositional sentence. In his early writings he borrows from Priscian the expression "the being of the thing" (*essentia rei*) to speak about propositional content and identifies it with a state-of-affairs. In later writings he refers rather to the *dictum* of a proposition, that is, to "what is said" with it. For Abelard it is *dicta* which are in the first place the bearers of truth and falsity and so, for example, a conditional is true if and only if the truth of the *dictum* of the consequent follows from the truth of the *dictum* of the antecedent.

The distinction between force and content, which Peter Geach has called the *Frege Point* in deference to its supposed discoverer, is crucial for the development of genuinely propositional logics. Abelard saw this and consequently rejected Boethius's views on copulative conjunction. To the contrary, he insists that a copulative conjunction of propositions is itself a single proposition and may thus be subject to a further propositional operation. "It's not the case that (*p* and *q*)" where "*p*" and "*q*" are propositions is just as much a single proposition, he insists, as "it's not the case that (if *p*, then *q*)."

ABELARD'S TWO NEGATIONS. Negation is the simplest propositional operation. If it is defined truth-functionally, it takes any propositional content and produces another, its contradictory, false if the first is true and true if it is false.

The invention of this operation in Latin logic cannot quite be claimed with certainty for Abelard. It is possible that it was used by his predecessors since it appears in very limited way in a discussion of the appropriate way to negate a simple conditional proposition in the *Dialectica* of Garlandus Compotista, apparently written in the second decade of the twelfth century roughly contemporary with Abelard's *Dialectica*.

Abelard, however, is the first Latin writer known to us who discusses propositional negation in general and applies it both to simple and compound propositions (Martin 2004). He distinguishes, indeed, two kinds of negation. First, and principally, propositional negation, which he calls "destructive" negation, and which has the whole of the following propositional content for its scope. Second, and derivatively, a negation, which he refers to as "separative" which in the case of affirmative categoricals is obtained by negating the predicate (*Dial.* II.2, 173 sq.). Abelard follows Boethius in classifying conditionals as affirmative according the quality of their consequents. The separative negation of a given affirmative conditional is obtained by negating its consequent either destructively or separatively.

A necessary condition for the truth of both an affirmative categorical and its separative negation is that the subject term is not empty. There is no such requirement for the truth of its destructive negation.

With this distinction between negations Abelard constructs an account of the relationships between quantified propositions which results in effect in a rectangle of opposition rather than the famous square of Aristotle as Boethius understood it. Aristotle gives "not every *A* is *B*" as the contradictory opposite of "every *A* is *B*" in *De interpretatione* but in the *Prior Analytics* "some *A* is not *B*" and according to Boethius the meaning is the same.

Abelard, however, argues that "some *A* is not *B*" is not the contradictory of "every *A* is *B*" but rather "it is not the case that every *A* is *B*." He thus avoids the problem typically raised against Aristotle's logic of quantified terms, that since it requires for the truth of a universal affirmation that the subject term is not empty, given there are no chimeras, an affirmation such as "every chimera is conversing" is false. It follows that its contradictory is true. Since "some chimera is not conversing" is true, however, only if the subject term is not empty, there must be some chimeras for it to be true of! For Abelard this is not a problem since on his account both propositions are false (*Log.* "Ingred." *sup. Perierm.* 7, 408–11).

THE MANIPULATION OF MODALITY. Once the notion of propositional content was available the difference between two different interpretations of modal propositions could be formulated precisely. In his *Dialectica* Abelard notes that a mode may appear in a categorical proposition either as an adverb or an adjective as, for example, in "Socrates is possibly a bishop" and "that Socrates is a bishop is possible" (Knuutila 1993). Abelard holds that though they differ syntactically these two propositions are semantically equivalent and it is the first which properly expresses the intended meaning since possibility is properly attributed to things (*de rebus*) (*Dial.* II.2, 191sq.). The adverb serves to indicate that the inherence of the predicate in the subject is modified in some way. Later medieval logicians will refer to this as the *de re* reading of the modal claim.

In the case of true *de re* claims about possibility there is of course no actual inherence to modify and Abelard holds that such propositions are true just in case the nature of the subject is compatible with the predicate. Human nature is compatible with being a bishop so "Socrates is possibly a bishop" is true even though he never has been nor never will be one (*Dial.* II.2, 193).

Abelard records that one of his masters proposed an alternative account of propositions with adjectival modes. They are to be understood, he held, as claims about the possibility, necessity, etc. of the sense (*de sensu*), that is the propositional content, of the simple propositions from which they "descend." Against this interpretation Abelard, in effect, argues that if we substitute for a given propositional content an equivalent one, the truth-value of the proposition will remain the same. Since universal negatives convert simple, "no blind man is a seeing man" is equivalent to "no seeing man is a blind man." While his opponents accept, however, that "no blind man is possibly a seeing man" is true, since they agree that the blind do not regain their sight, they claim that "no seeing man is possibly a blind man" is false. The *de sensu* reading, however, requires them to have the same truth value (*Dial* II.2, 196).

Although he maintains in the *Dialectica* the *de sensu* reading is in general not the proper way to interpret modal propositions, Abelard does allow that it is correct for the adjectival modes "true" and "false" since these, he argues, they are properly predicated of propositional contents (*Dial.* II.2, 204–6).

Abelard discusses the same questions at length in his *Logica* in commenting on Aristotle's account of the relations between modalities in *De interpretatione*, 12. He notes, in the first twelfth-century reference to the *Sophistical Refutations*, that the distinction he is interested corresponds to that made by Aristotle between reading a proposition such as "a standing man is possibly sitting" in a composite (*per compositionem*), or a divided way (*per divisionem*). Here, however, Abelard does not insist on the reading *de rebus* but rather works out in detail the relations between modal claims of both kinds (Abelard 1958, 13).

ABELARD ON ENTAILMENT. In his logical works Abelard sought to unify into a single theory of inference the disconnected remarks on topics and the consequence relation which he found in Boethius (Martin 2004). To do this he provides a new general definition of a *locus* as the force of, or as we would say, the warrant for an entailment (*vis inferentiae*) (*Dial.* III.1, 253). He then devotes hundreds of pages of his logical works to investigating the role of *loci* thus conceived in proving conditionals and validating the corresponding enthymemes.

According to Abelard, a proposition *p* entails a proposition *q*, just in case the corresponding conditional, or consequence, *if p, then q* expresses a relationship of following, or "consecution" (*consecutio*). For this to be so, he holds, the sense of the antecedent, that is, its propositional content, must contain that of the consequent. Abelard characterizes this kind of connection as necessary but insists that it must be distinguished from the satisfaction of the inseparability condition which it guarantees, and which alone provides only the necessity of what he calls association (*comitatio*) (*Dial.* III.2, 459).

Entailments are divided by Abelard into the perfect and the imperfect. Perfect entailments satisfy the containment requirement in virtue of the form, or structure, of the propositions involved. Imperfect entailments are those in which the sense of the antecedent contains that of the consequent but does not do so in virtue of their form (*Dial.* III.1, 253).

Abelard makes the notion of perfection, and so form, more precise, and anticipates modern definitions of logical truth, by giving as a necessary condition for perfect entailment that consecution is preserved through all uniform substitutions of terms or propositional contents. He does not, however, regard the condition as sufficient and, in particular, although he classifies the conditionalizations of all valid categorical and hypothetical syllogisms as perfect, he holds that instances of the principle of reflexivity, *if p, then, p*, are imperfect, presumably because they fail to have a canonical syllogistic form. Like all other imperfect entailments, according to Abelard, they must thus be warranted as instances of an appropriate maximal proposition (*Dial.* III.1, 255).

By far the greatest part of Abelard's *Dialectica* is concerned with establishing just which conditional propositions express imperfect entailments. Boethius in *De Topicis Differentiis* says that he will explore which *loci* are suited to which syllogisms and according to Abelard this led some logicians to hold that even the canonical syllogistic figures needed topical warrants. He and his mid-twelfth century followers known, probably because of their views on universals, as the *Nominales*, rejected this. They held rather that putative principles cited to support categorical and hypothetical syllogism are simply their metalinguistic formulation as rules. They contain no term indicating a topical relationship, that is no *locus differentia*, upon which the inference in question rests (*Dial.* III.1, 256–263).

Imperfect entailments, according to Abelard, are conditionals and the corresponding enthymemes, which satisfy the two conditions necessary and sufficient for following for a restricted range of terms. The topical difference specifies the relevant substitution class and the maximal proposition warrants the inference for substitutions from that class. For example, the conditional "if Socrates is a human being, then Socrates is an animal" is true and so are all substitutions for "human being" and "animal" which stand in the relationship of species to genus. For example, "if Socrates is a pearl, then Socrates is a stone," warranted by the maximal proposition "of whatever a species is predicated, so is its genus" (*Dial.* III.1, 315).

NECESSITY. Abelard's main task in his discussion of topical inference is to establish just which topical relations and which maximal propositions warrant true conditionals. He argues in the *Dialectica* that since what is being proved are conditional propositions, even though their surface form may be categorical, maximal propositions must in fact be general conditionals "containing" each of the proved conditionals as their instances. His treatment of this question involves a sophisticated discussion of how relative pronouns function in quantified propositions and the rules for logically manipulating them.

Since Boethius had allowed that some *argumenta* are probable but not necessary certain of Abelard's contemporaries had, he tells us, accepted as true any conditionalization of an enthymeme supported by a probable maximal proposition. In particular they took to be true conditionals warranted by maximal propositions which guarantee the inseparability of association but not the following or consecution which Abelard requires for entailment (*Dial.* III.1, 271 sq.).

Against them Abelard invokes the principle from the *Prior Analytics* mentioned above. His opponents accept conditionals warranted by appeal to the *locus* from immediates and the maximal proposition "of that from which one of a pair of immediates is removed the other is predicated." They must thus accept the following argument: [I1] if something does not exist, then it is not well (by the *locus* from part to whole, since "not-well" is predicated of all non-existent things as well as all existing things which are not well); [I2] if something is not well, then it is sick (from immediates); [I3] if something is sick, then it exists (from part to whole); so, by transitivity, [I4] if something does not exist, then it is sick, and thus [I5] if something does not exist, then it exists. [I5], however, contradicts Aristotle's principle and, Abelard maintains, is obviously impossible (*Dial*. III.1, 276).

Abelard investigates in detail various proposals to modify [I2] to block the embarrassing inference while retaining its warrant from immediates. In particular he considers various ways of adding what he calls a "temporal" qualification, indicated with "when" ("*cum*"), to form propositions such as "if (when something's an animal, it's not well), then it's sick."

Boethius, as noted, claims that "if" and "when" are equivalent as indicators of a conditional connection and in *De hypotheticis syllogismis* he invariably gives the conditional components of compound conditionals with "when." For example, "if (when something's an *A*, it's a *B*), then it's a *C*." This practice allows Abelard to treat the embedded propositions as temporal rather than conditional in interpreting Boethius claims about the hypothetical syllogism (*Dial*. IV.1, 472 sq.).

The problem for Abelard is that having insisted that one destroys a conditional by showing that it is possible for the antecedent to hold without the consequent, Boethius apparently assumes that an affirmative simple conditional and the corresponding negative conditional are contradictory opposites. He thus claims to be valid, for example, syllogisms of the form "if (when something's an *A*, its a *B*), then it's a *C*, but it's not a *C*; therefore when something's an *A*, it's not a *B*."

Abelard in the end rejects Boethius's account of the hypothetical syllogism. In this case, for example, he maintains, contrary to Boethius, that the valid argument is rather an instance of *modus tollens* (*if p, then q, not:q; therefore not:p*) which concludes with the propositional negation of the antecedent: "if (when something's an *A*, it's *B*), then it's a *C*, but it's not a *C*; therefore it is not the case that (when something's an *A*, it's *B*)." Abelard thus, in effect, replaces Boethius's account of the hypothetical syllogism with a genuinely propositional theory which takes *modus ponens* (*if p, then q, p; therefore q*) and transitivity (*if p, then q, if q, then r; therefore if p, then r*) as basic principles and *modus tollens* as a derived principle and holds that all uniform substitution instances, no matter how complex, are valid (*Dial*. IV.1, 498 sq.).

Abelard was unable to save Boethius's account of the hypothetical syllogism and so he replaced it with the correct one. Apparently no one else could to do any better and *De hypotheticis syllogismis* disappeared from the logic curriculum some time in the twelfth century. It is not until Walter Burley (1274–1344) published *De puritate artis logicae* in about 1325 that hypothetical syllogisms

were discussed in any detail again, and there the conditional premises are always simple conditionals.

RELEVANCE. Abelard accepts that the *locus* from immediates and many others guarantee the inseparability of association, but he also requires a relevant connection between antecedent and consequent for the conditional to be true (Martin 2004). He does not, however, insist on relevance for the validity of an argument. So long as it is impossible for the premises to be true and the conclusion at the same time false, true premises will guarantee a true conclusion and that is all that an argument is asked to produce. Abelard thus denies as a general principle what we would now call the Deduction Theorem, that an argument *p; therefore q* is valid if and only if the corresponding conditional *if p, then q* is true (*Dial*. III.2, 455).

Abelard's distinction between association and following or consecution as two kinds of necessary connection is based on the account given in the *Isagoge* of the relationship between substances and their accidents. According to this a substance does not require a particular accident in order to exist and so accidents are separable from their subjects. The problem is that while a given substance may undergo a change with respect to certain of its accidental features there are others, according to Porphyry, which must always be present. Blackness, for example, in the case of crows, and the property of being able to laugh in the case of humans. Neither of these are included in the account of what it is to be a crow or to be human but there is no natural possibility of their subjects existing without them. Such "inseparable" accidents can, however, it is claimed, be removed in the sense that we can conceive of a crow without conceiving its blackness. They are thus contrasted with definitional features which are included as part of its essence, in the definitional account of what it is to be a particular kind of thing (*Log.* "Ingred." sup. Porph. 6, 93).

Abelard's two necessities are a generalization of this distinction between actual and conceptual inseparability. He points out in his own discussion of inseparable accidents that although the antecedent and consequent of "if Socrates is a stone, then Socrates is a pearl," are inseparable, a pearl being classified as a kind of stone, nevertheless the conditional is false. The antecedent and consequent are inseparable, and Abelard is the first medieval logician we know of to make this point, merely because the antecedent is impossible. He goes to point out that if the inseparability of association were sufficient as well as necessary for following, then any conditional with an impossible antecedent would be true. For example, "if Socrates is a stone, then Socrates is a donkey" (*Dial.* III.1, 285).

Abelard does not, however, formulate the famous principles that anything follows from an impossibility and that a necessity follows from anything. He could not be expected to do so, however, since given his definition of following they are false.

Abelard believes that his own account of the semantics of the conditional generates what we would today call a connexive logic, a logic, that is, for which no proposition can entail or be entailed by its contradictory opposite. These principles entail, Abelard recognizes, both the propositional version of Aristotle Principle and what we may call Abelard's Principle: No two conditionals of the form *if p, then q* and *if p, then not:q*, can both be true.

Abelard accepts simplification (*if (p and q), then p* and *if (p and q), then q*), contraposition (*if (if p, then q), then (if not:q, then not:p)*), and transitivity (*if p, then q, if q, then r; therefore if p, then r* is valid). Suppose, then, that Abelard's Principle is false for some p and q, that is both (1) *if p, then q* and (2) *if p, then not: q* are true. But then if (3) *if (p and not:q), then p* is true and likewise (4) *if q, then not:(p and not:q)*, we may infer by transitivity that *if (p and not:q), then not:(p and not:q)*, an instance of *if p, then not:p*, which Abelard insists is a paradigm of impossibility. Abelard's Principle is thus necessarily true and he gives a similar argument to prove Aristotle's Principle (*Dial.* III.1, 290).

From these principles there follows the most characteristic feature of the logical theory advocated by Abelard and the *Nominales*: No conditional can be true of which the antecedent and the consequent differ in quality. For example if *if p, then not: q* were true, for some p and q, then *if (p and q), then not:(p and q)* would true by transitivity and contraposition.

Most famously Abelard argued against the *locus* from opposites in this way. If the *locus* warranted a true conditional then the conditional "if Socrates a human being, then Socrates is not a donkey" would we be true and we could infer the impossibility "if Socrates is a human being and a donkey, then it is not the case that Socrates is a human being and a donkey." He sees too, and explicitly acknowledges, that it follows from the principles of his logic that the conditional principle of double negation (*p if and only if not:not:p*) is false in both directions (*Dial.* II.2, 179).

Unfortunately Abelard's various intuitions about the propositional connectives are inconsistent (Martin 1987). In particular the principles which he holds to govern

negation are incompatible with simplification. This point seems to have been first noticed the 1130s by Alberic of Paris who confronted Abelard with the following argument: The conditional [A0] "if Socrates is a human being, then he is an animal" is a paradigm of entailment according to Abelard. He must also accept each of the following: By simplification [A1] if Socrates is human and Socrates is not an animal, then Socrates is not an animal; by contraposition, [A2] if Socrates is not an animal, then Socrates is not a human being; again by contraposition, [A3] if Socrates is not a human being, then it is not the case that Socrates is human being and Socrates is not an animal; so by transitivity, [A4] if Socrates is human being and Socrates is not an animal, then it is not the case that Socrates is a human being and not an animal—contradicting a fundamental principle of Abelard's logic. Alberic's proof of inconsistency precipitated a crisis in the history of logic.

THE PARISIAN SCHOOLS AND THE CRISIS OVER THE CONDITIONAL

In middle decades of the twelfth century a number famous logicians were active at Paris and with each of was associated a school (Martin 1987). In some cases very substantial treatises have survived from these schools, illustrating that this was a period of intense activity in logic. Unfortunately most of these and certainly the most important are still unpublished. The schools may be distinguished by their response to Alberic's proof of the inconsistency of Abelard's system.

Abelard's own followers, the *Nominales*, continued to maintain the correctness of his account of the conditional and the connexive principles. Their strategy seems to have been to take negation to be a cancellation of content so that nothing follows from *p and not:p* rather than both *p* and *not:p*.

The followers of Alberic, the *Montani*, so-called because their school was located on Mont Ste. Geneviève, held that the argument failed because the conjunction of contraries in [A1] undermined the relationship on which [A0] was based. In a different context Abelard himself anticipates this objection to impossible antecedents and argues at length against it that since the antecedent is not asserted, and the argument is formally valid, the conclusion follows.

The school of Gilbert of Poitiers, the *Porretani*, held that the problem lay in the unrestricted principle of simplification. They required, as do twentieth century connexive logics, that both conjuncts play a role in such an inference. The most surprising response was that of the followers of Robert of Melun, the *Melidunenses*, who took as their basic principle for the logic of the conditional the rule "nothing follows from the false."

The solution that eventually won the day, however, was that proposed by the followers of Adam of the Little Bridge, the *Parvipontani*, so called again because of the location of their school in Paris. They accepted that the argument was sound because they apparently held that inseparability alone is both necessary and sufficient for the truth of a conditional. Aristotle's Principle thus fails when the consequent is necessary and Abelard's when the antecedent is impossible.

John of Salisbury tells us in his *Metalogicon* (1159) that one of his students, William of Soissons, had gone on to join the *Parvipontani* and discovered the twelfth-century version of one of the twentieth century's most famous arguments, the proof that *ex impossibli quodlibet*, the so-called paradox of strict implication, according to which anything follows from an impossibility (*Metalogicon* II.10).

In his *De naturis rerum* written at the end of the twelfth century Alexander Neckham gives the argument as follows: [S1] if Socrates is a human being and Socrates is not a human being, then Socrates is a human being; [S2] if Socrates is a human being, then Socrates is a human being or Socrates is a stone; [S3] if Socrates is a human being and Socrates is not a human being, then Socrates is not a human being; therefore [S4] if Socrates is a human being and Socrates is not a human being, then Socrates is a stone (*De Naturis Rerum* cixxiii, 288–89).

The outcome of the crisis provoked by Alberic was a complete change in the understanding of the logical connectives. John of Salisbury tells us that he could not conceive why any one would think that anything follows from an impossibility but according to Alexander Neckham nothing was more obvious.

Abelard had insisted that a genuine connection was required for the truth of conditionals and disjunctions. Alexander's argument, on the other hand, assumes only inseparability for the conditional and much less for the disjunction. [S2] is the so-called Principle of Addition characteristic of the disjunction defined as true if one of the disjuncts is true. The disjuncts are no longer required to be related as immediates.

The conditional and disjunction were standardly defined in this way for the rest of the middle ages. Until the end of the thirteenth century, however, a contrast continued to be drawn between an accidental consequence which held wherever the inseparability condition

was met and a natural consequence in which the sense of the antecedent contained the consequent. This stronger connection was needed because it was necessary to reason about impossibilities.

THE RECEPTION OF THE *LOGICA VETUS* AND THE DEVELOPMENT OF THE *LOGICA MODERNORUM*

Some time towards the end of the twelfth century the various different schools disappeared as the independent masters formed themselves into the corporation that became the University of Paris. Teaching and research in logic was the preserve there of the Faculty of Arts and its results appear in the introductory textbooks of the *logica modernorum*. To the traditional topics these add extensive discussions of fallacies and the properties of terms.

FALLACIES. Although Abelard had some limited access to the *Sophistical Refutations* it was not until around 1140 that the analysis of fallacies became a major concern for logicians. From the beginning, however, a short list was available in Boethius's discussion of Aristotle's remark in *De interpretatione* 6, that the putative negation of a given proposition may fail to have the required opposite truth value because the subject or predicate terms have different meanings in the two propositions (De Rijk 1962–1967).

Although Boethius's list of the ways in which this might occur ceased to be of much interest once the *Sophistical Refutations* were easily available, one of his fallacies was particularly important for the later development of logic. With no further explanation Boethius gives as an example of what he calls *univocation* the propositions "homo ambulat" ("human being walks") and "homo non ambulat" ("human being does not walk"). He claims that they are true together when the first is true of an individual, or particular man, and the second is true of "special man."

Abelard notes that univocation arises because the context in which a term is used may affect its meaning. For example, since medieval Latin has no articles or quotation marks it cannot distinguish between the occurrences of "homo" in "homo est albus," "homo est vox," and "homo est species," in the way in which we distinguish in their translations between "a human is white," "'human' is a word," and "human is a species" (De Rijk 1962–1967, I, pp. 51–56).

Logicians in the second half of the twelfth century commented at length on and refined Aristotle's account of fallacy in the *Sophistical Refutations*. By the end of the century the results of their work are clear in theology where the theory of fallacy is frequently invoked to explain and resolve errors in argumentation. In addition to the standard fallacies logicians also developed as a special form of argument the idea of counter instances (*instantiae*) which they found in the *Sophistical Refutations*, *Topics*, and *Prior Analytics*. With these the principles advocated by one or another of the schools were shown to lead to a conclusion which was unacceptable to it.

Once the works of the *logica nova* were available logicians seem to have turned their attention from the theory of consequences and topical inference to issues in philosophical semantics. Here a distinction was made between categorematic words, or terms, that is words which on their own can be the subject or predicate of a categorical proposition, and all other words which can occur in any kind proposition. The latter were called syncategorematic words.

THE PROPERTIES OF TERMS. Termist logic, so called because of its interest in the semantical properties of terms, seems to have developed in rather different ways in Paris and Oxford. The most famous Parisian termist was certainly Peter of Spain (c. 1205–1277), whose *Tractatus*, or *Summulae logicales*, written around 1235, was much commented on and remained the standard introductory text in logic in continental Europe and Scotland for the rest of the middle ages. It seems, however, not to have been greatly used in England, where the University of Oxford had its own textbooks. The *Introductiones in logicam* (c. 1245) by William of Sherwood (c. 1210–c. 1270) perhaps also belongs in the Oxford tradition. Another text belonging to the Parisian tradition is the *Summa Lamberti* (c. 1255) of Lambert of Auxerre (fl. 1250s) on which the following remarks are based.

IMPOSITION AND SIGNIFICATION. Medieval logicians developed their philosophical semantics in the first place from Boethius's commentaries on the first chapter of *De interpretatione*: Spoken words are introduced to bring to mind mental items, understandings (*intellectus*), which are obtained from the things which exist in the extra-mental world and are likenesses of them. For substantial common terms such as "human being" the corresponding understandings are the mental correlates of the forms which in the world make individuals to be the kinds of things that they are. For accidental terms such as "whiteness" they are the forms which cause individuals to have the accidental features that they do.

Words were held to acquire their meaning through acts of baptism, known as *imposition* (*impositio*), or *institution* (*institutio*) (Kretzmann et al. 1982, ch. 9). In the case of individual humans literally so. For general terms the impositor introduces a name in the presence of a paradigmatic sample with the intention that all and only individuals of the kind in question bear the same name. Adam's naming of the beasts of the field and the fowls of the air (Genesis 2:19) provided a suitable example. Although medieval accounts of imposition do not seem to have been very developed there are obvious similarities to modern causal theories of reference.

The immediate and proper signification of a common term is the understanding constituted when it uttered in the mind of a listener who speaks the language. Just what a given philosopher thought about the things understood and their relationship to individuals in the world depended on where he stood on the question of universals. Lambert, for example, was a realist. The term "human being," he claims, signifies immediately the understanding of the form which makes humans to be human and mediately the form itself. It does not signify individual human beings (*Logica*, 206).

SUPPOSITION. "Supposition" is used in the thirteenth century to refer to what earlier writers had called "appellation," it is a property which an already significant term has in virtue of its use. Corresponding to the three different contextual meanings recognized in the fallacy of univocation there are three forms of supposition. With no change in the signification established by its original imposition, the term "*homo*" thus supposits, or stands for three different kinds of things in the propositions "*homo est albus*," "*homo est vox*," and "*homo est species*."

In the first, according to Lambert, "*homo*" has personal supposition because it stands for the individuals "contained under" the form which it indirectly signifies. In the other two, he says, its supposition is simple (*Logica*, 209). In the second it stands for the thing which the term signifies indirectly—a form according to Lambert, and a "universal thing" according to Peter of Spain. In the third proposition the terms stands for itself.

William of Sherwood gives a slightly different classification. According to him in the third proposition "*homo*" has material supposition and in the other two formal supposition. In the first this formal supposition is personal and in the second it is simple (*Introductiones*, 75).

Personal supposition is the semantical property which most interested logicians since their task was to say in general what determines the truth or falsity of a given proposition and to do so they needed to decide what the terms in the proposition stand for.

THE DIVISIONS OF SUPPOSITION. Treatises on the properties of terms make many distinctions and precisions within personal supposition. Supposition properly speaking is a property of a substantive noun which it has when it stands for something. An adjective in use, on the other hand, couples something and so is said to have the property of copulation.

Supposition in general, according to Lambert, is either natural and accidental. The imposition of a term connects it mediately with a form and, at a second remove, prior to any contextual determination to all the individuals which have done, do, or will share in that form. These are what it naturally supposits for (*Logica*, 208).

Accidental supposition is supposition determined by context and may, as noted, according to Lambert, be simple, or personal. Personal supposition is further divided into discrete supposition, the supposition had by proper names, and common supposition, the supposition of common terms.

The common supposition of a term such as "human being" is further determined by its interaction with the syncategorematic words of quantity and quality, and may be either determinate or confused. Logicians offered various accounts of these forms of supposition but by the fourteenth century typically explained them in terms of their inferential relations (Kretzmann et al. 1982, ch. 9)

Supposition is determinate when the term is the subject of an indefinite or particular affirmative, such as "a human being is running" and "some human being is running." Here we may descend from the particular or indefinite proposition to the propositional disjunction of singulars whose subjects are the *supposita* of the common term and ascend from any one of those singulars to the general proposition. So from "some human being is running" we may infer "Socrates is running or Plato is running or …" and from the truth of any one of the disjuncts we may infer that some human being is running.

In confused supposition, a common term stands for all its *supposita* together. It may do this in one of two ways, either as with the subject of a universal affirmative where the supposition is distributive, and one may descend to, and ascend from, the propositional conjunction of each of the corresponding singulars. For example from "every human being is running" to "Socrates is running and Plato is running and …" and conversely.

The other form of confused supposition, merely confused supposition, is exemplified by a common term occurring as the predicate of a universal affirmative proposition. Here the term again stands for all supposita but taken together in such way that one can descend only to the predicate disjunction but ascend from any singular. For example from "every human being is an animal" to "every human being is (this animal or that animal or …)" and from "every human being is this animal" to every man is an animal.

Negation distributes any simple term to which it is applied, so both the subject and predicate of no man is running, that is, every man is not running, have confused and determinate supposition (Lambert, *Logica*, 210).

Historians have puzzled about the relationship between supposition theory and modern quantification theory but this seems to miss the point. Supposition theory does not aim to state truth-conditions for propositions but to determine which of the supposita of a term occurring in a proposition someone uttering it should be understood as referring to and in what way.

AMPLIATION AND RESTRICTION. The propositions given above to illustrate the divisions of supposition all have simple subjects and predicates with the verb in the present tense and not modified in any way. A term is said to appellate those of its *supposita* which actually exist and in the case of all these propositions appellation and supposition coincide. The qualification of a substantive with an adjective restricts its supposition to suitably qualified things. In "a white human being is running," for example, "human being" has determinate supposition only for those of its *appellate* which are white (Lambert, *Logica*, 226).

Tense affects the supposition of terms by ampliating them to stand for *supposita* other than their *appellata*, though these may also be included in the supposition. For example in "an old man was a young man" the predicate term has merely confused supposition for those of its *supposita* which existed in the past but do not now exist. The subject term has determinate supposition for its *appellate* and its past *supposita*.

There is no suggestion in the twelfth century termists named that a term might supposit for possibilia which never exist. Lambert and Peter of Spain hold, for example, that in the modal proposition "some man might be the Antichrist" "man" supposits for past and future men (Lambert, *Logica*, 228). Ampliation to pure possibilia is allowed, however, in the *Summa logicae* (c. 1324) of William of Ockham (c. 1285–1349) and *Summulae de dialectica* (1330s) of John Buridan (c. 1300– c. 1360). The change in theory of ampliation reflects a radically new conception of possibility introduced in the work of John Duns Scotus (c. 1265–1308) at the beginning of the fourteenth century. Against the assumption that all possibilities must be realized in time Scotus famously argued for the logical possibility that things could now be otherwise than they in fact are and so that there are possibilities that are never realized.

SYNCATEGOREMATIC WORDS. Both Peter of Spain and William of Sherwood as well as other termist logicians produced treatises entirely devoted to syncategorematic words (Kretzmann et al. 1982, ch. 11). These treatises do not deal with all words that are not categorematic but only with a relatively small and fairly standard set. In addition to the definition by exclusion, syncategorematic words are further characterized as semantically incomplete in that they acquire a signification only by being combined in some way with categorematic terms. For this reason they are said to be *consignificant*.

It is in the treatises on *syncategoremata* that termist logicians deal with the difficult words whose presence may affect the validity of a principle of inference and allow the construction of sophisms. As, for example, in the proof by Sherwood that no man lectures at Paris unless he is an donkey: "A man lectures at Paris unless he is an donkey" is a false conditional since the antecedent "a man is not a donkey" is necessarily true and consequent may be false. Therefore the contradictory of the conditional is true (*Syncategoremata* 82–3). In the fourteenth century such puzzles and their resolutions were collected together in separate works devoted to grammatical, logical, including modal and epistemic, and physical sophisms. Their resolution often required that the inner structure of a syncategorematic term be exposed by what was called *exposition*. "Socrates is beginning to be white," for example, might be expound as 'Socrates is not now white and after now Socrates will be white' leading on to a discussion of tense, change, and the structure of time.

Included among the *syncategoremata* in these treatises we find the propositional connectives and confirmation the twelfth century insight into their nature had not been lost. William of Sherwood, for example, discusses both negation and the copulative conjunction. He clearly distinguishes, extinctive, or propositional negation and argues that if the conjunction "Socrates is running and Plato is arguing" is negated with a preposed particle the result is true just in case one of the coupled propositions is false (*Syncategoremata* 86).

MODISM

In the last quarter of the thirteenth century the termist semantics of supposition was replaced by what is known as modism, or speculative, that is, theoretical, grammar (Marmo 1994, Kelly 2002). The proponents of this theory, the *modisti*, for example Martin of Dacia (d. 1304), Boethius of Dacia (fl. 1275), and Thomas of Erfurt (fl. 1300) were concerned to say something more general about the meaning of both categorematic and syncategorematic terms than their termist predecessors. They held that all meaningful words are characterized by certain modes of signifying and that these correspond to the traditional parts of speech. Corresponding to each modes of signifying, is a mode of understanding, and a mode of being.

According to the modists a proper name like "Socrates" as well as signifying Socrates, carries information about the essential character of what it signifies. It signifies it as a substance, for example, in the *modus substantiae*, though not as an existent, since we use nouns to speak about presently non-existent and fictional items. A verb, on the other hand, signifies what it signifies in the mode of change and becoming. Grammatical features which were regarded as less fundamental, for example, number and tense, were held to correspond to accidental modes of signifying, understanding, and being (Kretzman et al. 1982, ch. 13).

On the basis of their distinction between modes the *modisti* developed an account of grammatical congruity—the modes have to fit together in the right way. They sought to go beneath the surface structure of their language to locate the underlying relationship between the components of propositions. Their idea was that the order required by Latin grammar did not properly represent the real relationships between the things signified. Though twelfth century logicians had already explored some of these ideas especially with regard to pronouns, the *modisti* deserve credit for being the first to attempt to develop a systematic theory of syntax.

Although the modists distinguished between the full signification of a word including its mode of signifying and the things in the world to which it applies, they made no use of the idea of supposition. They seem not to have developed an account of the contextual dependence of reference to compete with that of termists and in the end it was the semantics of termism which won the day (Kretzman et al. 1982, ch. 13).

OBLIGATIONS

The earliest treatises on what were known as obligations (*obligations*) date from the second half of the twelfth century (Martin 1993). In obligational disputation one participant, the respondent, is required to agree to a hypothesis and to reply consistently with it in the face of questions put to him by the opponent. The aim of the opponent is make the respondent contradict himself.

The most important form of obligation was the one known as *positio*, in which the opponent posits to be true something which is in fact false. In the twelfth and thirteenth centuries it had two forms depending on whether the *positum* was false but possibly true, possible *positio*, or an impossibility, impossible *position*. The original motivation for the latter seems to have been Boethius's proposal in *De hypotheticis syllogismis* that an impossibility be posited in order to see what follows (*Hyp. Syll.* I.2.6).

The earliest surviving treatise on impossible *positio*, the *Tractatus Emmeranus*, recognizes that no coherent argumentation is available under such an hypothesis if one accepts that anything follows from an impossibility. It stipulates instead that reasoning in impossible *positio* should rely only on consequences in which the consequent is contained in the antecedent and so not employ those with an affirmative antecedent and negative consequent—the theory uniquely characteristic of Abelard and the *Nominales* (De Rijk 1974). Later treatments of *impossible position* require only that they be conducted using consequences satisfying the containment condition.

In accounts of possible *positio* written before 1330s the respondent's answers are required to be consistent with everything that has gone before. He must thus concede a *propositum* which follows from the conjunction of the *positum* with all *proposita* already conceded and the contradictories of those which have been denied and deny a *propositum* whose contradictory follows from this conjunction. A *propositum* is irrelevant if neither it nor its contradictory follows from the conjunction and the respondent is required, if it is true, to concede it and, if it is false, to deny it (Kretzmann et al. 1982, ch. 16A).

A well conducted *positio* thus yields a set of propositions cotenable with the original *positum* and so an account of how the world might be. In treatises on possible *positio* written before the beginning of the fourteenth century we find a rule to the effect that if *n* is the present time, the *propositum* "*n* is the present time" must be denied, since it is not possible for things now to be other than now they are. Duns Scotus rejects this principle in

setting out his new account of possibility and it is no longer found in fourteenth century accounts of *positio*.

Possible *positio* provides a way of testing the respondent's reasoning skills but also of constructing alternative possible world-histories. This application is common in fourteenth century treatments of reconciliation of divine foreknowledge with the possibility that things might be otherwise than they will be.

In the mid-1330s a group of logicians at Oxford proposed modifications to the principles of *position*. Richard Kilvington (c. 1305–1361) in his *Sophismata* required that the respondent answer an irrelevant positum not in accordance with his beliefs about its actual truth-value but rather in accordance with the beliefs he would have if the *positum* were true. Kilvington noticed that these may well differ if the *positum* refers to the respondent's epistemic states (Kretzmann et al. 1982, ch. 16B).

Roger Swineshead (d. 1356) went much further in his *Obligationes* (1340s?) and proposed what became known as the "new response" (Kretzmann et al. 1982, ch. 16B). For reasons which remain obscure he required the respondent simply to concede a *propositum* if it follows from the *positum* alone and to deny it if is incompatible. Everything else is irrelevant. This change, however, undermines the constructive character of *position* since, for example, if some false proposition p is posited and q is an irrelevant truth, the respondent must concede both p and q when they are proposed but go on to deny their conjunction p *and* q. Swineshead's account of *position* seems to have enjoyed some limited success but it is not mentioned after the end of the fourteenth century.

INSOLUBLES

The most famous example of what medievals called insolubles, sentences difficult but not impossible to solve, is the Liar: "This sentence is false" (Spade 1988). The difficulty is to assign it a truth-value since it seems that if it is true, then it is false, and if it is false, then it is true. The problem is first noticed the middle ages in the *Ars disserendi* of Adam of the Little Bridge published in 1132 and its medieval origins may well lie in reflection on possible *positio*.

Both the *Tractatus Emmeranus* and another treatise from the second half of the twelfth century, the *Obligationes Parisiensis* (De Rijk 1975), note that if a respondent accepts as a *positum* "the *positum* is false" or an equivalent, then the opponent will be able to force him to contradict himself (Martin 1993). Both works go on to discuss propositions such as "a falsehood is conceded" which may be certainly be posited but cannot then be conceded as the rules of *position* require since if it is, it becomes a Liar. The appropriate response, they claim, is to reply "You are not saying anything" (*nugaris*).

The earliest known treatise entirely devoted to the Liar, the *Insolubilia Monacensis*, from roughly the same date, adopts the same solution, voiding (*cassatio*): A self-referential utterance of "this sentence is false" fails to assert anything (De Rijk 1966). This solution continued to be invoked in the thirteenth century but is no longer employed in the heyday of insoluble literature, the first half of the fourteenth century.

Many different solutions were proposed to the problem and Thomas Bradwardine (c. 1295–1349) lists eight others besides *cassatio* in his *Insolubilia* (Spade 1988). These include, for example:

1) *Secundum quid et simpliciter* (qualified and unqualified): Distinguish between the qualified and unqualified possession of a property as Aristotle does in the *Sophistical Refutations* discussing the puzzle of a man who takes an oath to break his oath. The Liar is false without qualification, but relatively true.

2) *Transcasus* (change of situation): The claim made in uttering the Liar refers to an instant before the utterance. The Liar is simply false since the speaker said nothing then.

3) *Restrictio* (restriction): The supposition of the term "false" in the Liar is restricted to standing only for sentences other than the Liar or sentences equivalent to it. Since uttering the Liar utters only that sentence, it is simply false.

Bradwardine rejected all the theories in his list and offered a new one which set the agenda for later discussions. He maintained, first, that a proposition is true if it signifies things *only* as they are but is false if it signifies things as other than they are—it may well also signify them as they are. Second, he held, and seems to have been the first to do so that a proposition signifies just what follows from it. Bradwardine concluded that if a proposition signifies itself to be false, then it signifies itself to be true. The Liar thus signifies itself to be both true and false and so is false (Roure 1970).

CONSEQUENCES

Treatises devoted to consequences seem to be product of the fourteenth century and, although one was written by the great Parisian logician John Buridan, they are almost exclusively a British production. The second or third decade of the fourteenth century marks a turning point in the history of consequences as important as the resolution of the twelfth-century crisis (Martin 2005).

Duns Scotus was not a logician but he put logic to the service of metaphysics when he located a formal distinction between any two items which are actually inseparable but conceptually separable. If being B follows accidentally but not naturally from being A, then being A is formally but not existentially distinct from being A.

Ockham's rejection of the formal distinction seems to explain his introduction of an entirely new theory of consequences. In his *Summa logicae* rather than distinguishing between natural and accidental consequences by appealing to *loci* which guarantee containment in contrast to those which do not, he takes basic logical distinction to be between what he calls material and formal consequences (*Sum. Log.* III.3.1).

All consequences must satisfy the inseparability requirement. Material consequences satisfy it merely in virtue of truth-values of the antecedent and consequent and so include all the paradoxical consequences. Formal consequences hold in virtue of there being a connection between antecedent and consequent guaranteed by a middle, another name for a *locus*. The middle, however, is required only to guarantee non-trivial inseparability.

There is thus no logical distinction between consequences for Ockham corresponding to that between natural and accidental consequences. It is replaced by an appeal to the epistemological notion of evidence but this does not partition the class of true consequences in the way the natural—accidental distinction does. Nor, more importantly, can it be used to argue for the formal distinction.

In an alternative classification of consequences Ockham invokes a distinction already made the thirteenth century to consequences which satisfy the Inseparability condition in virtue of the necessity of the present. He holds that if the conjunction *p and not:q* is now false but at some time will be true, the truth of the antecedent is now inseparable from that of the consequent and so *if p, then q* is a consequence *ut nunc* (as-of-now). If *p and not:q* is false at all times, past, present, and future, according to Ockham, *if p, then q* is a simple consequence (*Sum. Log.* III.3.1).

Ockham's new theory of consequences seems to have very rapidly supplanted the old one and natural consequences are not mentioned in logic texts after the first quarter of the fourteenth century. Nor for that matter is impossible *positio*.

While Ockham's examples of the middles which provide the guarantee of formal consequence are all what we would classify as formal in that they hold for all uniform substitution instances of terms, his practice indicates that some middles hold only for limited classes of terms. This possibility is absent in later writers such as Buridan who explicitly defines formal consequence in terms of the uniform substitution of any terms satisfying the inseparability conditions.

By the middle of the fourteenth century the logic of consequences is thus fully formal in the modern sense and treatises on the subject contain many of the rules recognized in classical modal propositional logic.

THE LOGIC OF MODALITY

While the *Prior Analytics* offered logicians nothing on categorical syllogisms not already available in Boethius what Aristotle had to say about modal forms was extremely problematic (Lagerlund 2000). The difficulty is that he accepts modal conversion principles such as accidental conversion: *if every A is necessarily a B, then some B is necessarily an A* but also claims that while *every B is necessarily C and every A is B; therefore every A is necessarily C* is valid *every B is a C and every A is necessarily B; therefore every A is necessarily C* is not. The conversion seems only to hold only if the modality is understood in the composite sense while the claim about the syllogisms requires the divided sense.

The first known medieval solution is found in the commentary on the *Prior Analytics* written Robert Kilwardby (1215–1279) in the 1240s (Thom 2003). Aristotle had designated as *per se* predications in which the subject contains the predicate and Kilwardby claims that modality may be uniformly construed in the divided sense if the conversion principles are restricted to those in which the antecedents are per se predications. Thus "every man is necessarily an animal" converts accidentally with "some animal is necessarily human' but "every literate (man) is necessarily a man" does not convert in this way with "every man is necessarily literate." Kilwardby thus makes just the distinction between modal claims that was made between natural and accidental consequences.

Ockham in his *Summa logicae* explores the relationship between divided and composite readings on the basis of his claim that these do not differ in the case singular propositions (Normore 1999). He derives syllogisms for composite modals by applying to categorical syllogism the principles of modal inference, for example "if the premises are all necessary, then so is the conclusion." Ockham goes on to examine syllogisms formed with divided modals and with mixtures of both divided and composite (*Sum. Log.* III.1.20–46). He holds that divided claims are equivocal. Thus in "every A is possibly B," according to Ockham, the predicate is always ampliated by the mode but the supposition of subject may be understood to be only for what are now actually A or as ampliated for what can be A.

The most important development in syllogistics in the middle ages is in the work of Buridan. Buridan goes beyond Ockham in taking the theory of the syllogism to be simply an instance of the general theory of formal consequence (King 1985). He shows how the validity of the moods of the categorical syllogism can be proved from basic principles governing the semantics of general terms. The theory of modal syllogism with composite modality is, as with Ockham, quite straightforward. Buridan's treatment of divided modals is complex and of great interest since it reveals his attitude to the iteration of modalities and seems to commit him to the same principles as that of the modern system of strict implication known as S5.

Treatises on each of the subjects mentioned above continued to be produced through the fourteenth and fifteenth centuries by vast numbers of logicians. None of them, however, were of the stature of Abelard, Ockham, or Buridan, and originality in logic gave way at the end of the period to mere pedantry.

See also Abelard, Peter; Aristotle; Augustine, St.; Avicenna; Boethius, Anicius Manlius Severinus; Boetius of Dacia; Bradwardine, Thomas; Buridan, John; Burley, Walter; Cicero, Marcus Tullius; Conditionals; Duns Scotus, John; Gilbert of Poitiers; John of Salisbury; Kilwardby, Robert; Kilvington, Richard; Liar Paradox, The; Modality and Language; Peter of Spain; Porphyry; Proper Names and Descriptions; Propositions; Swineshead, Richard; Themistius; William of Ockham; William of Sherwood.

Bibliography

PRIMARY WORKS

Abaelard. Peter. *Dialectica*, edited by Lambertus De Rijk. Assen: Van Gorcum, 1970.

Abaelard. Peter. *Peter Abelard's Philosophische Schriften*, edited by B. Geyer. *Beiträge zur Geschichte der Philosophie des Mittelalters* 21, 1–4. Münster: Aschendorff: 1919–1927.

Abaelard. Peter. *Scritti di Logica*, edited by Mario Dal Pra. Florence: La Nuova Italia, 1969.

Abaelard. Peter. *Twelfth Century Logic II: Abaelardiana Inedita*, edited by Lorenzo Minio-Paluello. Rome: Edizioni Di Storia E Litteratura, 1958.

Boethius, Anicius Manlius. *Commentarium in Librum Aristotelis Perihermenias.* 2nd ed., edited by Karl Meiser. Leipzig: Tuebner, 1880.

Boethius, Anicius Manlius. *De Hypotheticis Syllogismis*, edited by Luca Orbetello. Brescia: Paideia, 1969.

Boethius, Anicius Manlius. *De Topicis Differentiis.* Translated with notes and essays on the text by Eleonore Stump. Ithaca, NY: Cornell University Press, 1978.

Buridan, Jean. *Sophisms on Meaning and Truth.* Translated by Theodore Scott. New York: Appleton-Century-Crofts, 1966.

Buridan, Jean. *Summulae De dialectica.* An annotated translation with an introduction by Gyula Klima. New Haven, CT: Yale University Press, 2001.

Burley, Walter. *On the Purity of the Art of Logic.* Translated by Paul Vincent Spade. New Haven, CT: Yale University Press, 2001.

Compotista, Garlandus. *Dialectica*, edited by Lambertus De Rijk. Assem: Van Gorcum, 1959.

De Rijk, Lambertus. *Logica Modernorum: A Contribution to the History of Early Terminist Logic.* 2 vols. Assen: Van Gorcum, 1962–1967.

De Rijk, Lambertus. "Some Notes on the Mediaeval Tract *De Insolubilibus*, with an Edition of a Tract Dating from the End of the Twelfth Century." *Vivarium* 4 (1966): 83–115.

De Rijk, Lambertus. "Some Thirteenth Century Tracts on the Game of Obligation I." *Vivarium* 12 (1974): 94–123.

De Rijk, Lambertus. "Some Thirteenth Century Tracts on the Game of Obligation II." *Vivarium* 13 (1975): 22–54.

Hughes, George. *John Buridan on Self-Reference: Chapter Eight of Buridan's Sophismata Translated, with an Introduction and a Philosophical Commentary.* Cambridge, MA: Cambridge University Press, 1982.

John of Salisbury. *Metalogicon*, edited by D. McGary, J. Hall, and K. Keats-Rohan. Turnhout: Brepols, 1991.

King, Peter. *John Buridan's Logic: The Treatise on Supposition, the Treatise on Consequences.* Dordrecht: Reidel, 1985.

Kilvington. Richard. *The Sophismata of Richard Kilvington.* Introduction, translation, and commentary by Norman Kretzmann and Barbara Ensign Kretzmann. Cambridge, MA: Cambridge University Press, 1990.

Lambert of Auxerre. *Logica (Summa Lamberti) a cura di Franco Alessio.* Firenze: La Nuova Italia, 1971.

Neckham, Alexander. *De Naturis Rerum*, edited by Thomas Wright. London: Longman, 1863.

Peter of Spain. *Syncategoreumata.* Translated by Joke Spruyt. Edited by Lambertus De Rijk. Leiden: Brill, 1992.

Peter of Spain. *Tractatus, called afterwards Summule logicales*, edited by Lambertus De Rijk. Assen: Van Gorcum, 1972.

Roure, Marie Louise. "La problématique des propositions insolubles au XIIIe siècle et au début du XIVe, suivie de l'édition des traités de W. Shyreswood, W. Burleigh et Th. Bradwardine." *Archives d'histoire doctrinale et littéraire du moyen age* 37 (1970): 205–326.

William of Ockham. *Summa Logicae*, edited by Philotheus Boehner, Gedeon Gál, and Stephan Brown. In *Opera Philosophica.* Vol. 1., edited by Guillelmi de Ockham. St. Bonaventure: The Franciscan Institute, 1974.

William of Sherwood. "De Introductiones in Logicam des Wilhelm von Shyreswood." *Sitzungsberichte der Bayerischen Akademie der Wissenschften, Phil.-hist. Abteilung* Heft 10, Munich, 1937.

William of Sherwood. "The Syncategoremat of William of Sherwood," edited by J. Reginald O'Donnell. *Medieval Studies* 3 (1941): 47–93.

William of Sherwood. *William of Sherwood's Introduction to Logic.* Translated by Norman Kretzmann. Minneapolis: University of Minnesota Press, 1966.

William of Sherwood. *William of Sherwood's Treatise on Syncategorematic Words.* Translated by Norman Kretzmann. Minneapolis: University of Minnesota Press, 1968.

SECONDARY WORKS

Bochenski, Innocentius. *A History of Formal Logic.* Edited and translated by Ivo Thomas. Notre Dame, IN: University of Notre Dame Press, 1961.

Boh, Ivan. *Epistemic Logic in the Later Middle Ages.* London: Routledge, 1993.

Kelly, Loius G. *The Mirror of Grammar: Theology, Philosophy, and the Modistae.* Amsterdam: Benjamins, 2002.

Kneale, William, and Martha Kneale. *The Development of Logic.* Oxford: Clarendon Press, 1984.

Knuutila, Simo. *Modalities in Medieval Philosophy.* London: Routledge, 1993.

Kretzmann, Norman, Anthony Kenny, and Jan Pinborg. *The Cambridge History of Later Medieval Philosophy.* Cambridge, U.K.: Cambridge University Press, 1982.

Kretzmann, Norman, Anthony Kenny, and Jan Pinborg. *Meaning and Inference in Medieval Philosophy: Studies in Memory of Jan Pinborg.* Boston: Kluwer Academic Publishers, 1988.

Kretzmann, Norman, and Eleonore Stump, eds. *Logic and the Philosophy of Language.* Cambridge, U.K.: Cambridge University Press, 1988.

Lagerlund, Henrik. *Modal Syllogistics in the Middle Ages.* Leiden: Brill, 2000.

Martin, Christopher J. "Embarrassing Arguments and Surprising Conclusions in the Development of Theories of the Conditional in the Twelfth Century." In *Gilbert de Poitiers et ses contemporains*, edited by Jean Jolivet and Alain de Libera. Naples: Bibliopolis, 1987.

Martin, Christopher J. "Logic." In *The Cambridge Companion to Abelard*, edited by Jeff Brower and Kevin Guilfoy. Cambridge, U.K.: Cambridge University Press, 2004.

Martin, Christopher J. "Formal Consequence in Scotus and Ockham: Towards an Account of Scotus' Logic." In *Duns Scot à Paris 1302–2002.* Brepols: Turnhout, 2005.

Martin, Christopher J. "The Logic of Negation in Boethius." *Phronesis* 36 (1991): 277–304.

Martin, Christopher J. "Obligations and Liars." In *Sophisms in Medieval Logic and Grammar*, edited by Stephen Read. Dordrecht: Kluwer, 1993.

Marmo, Costantino. *Semiotica e linguaggio nella scolastica: Parigi, Bologna, Erfurt, 1270–1330.* La semiotica dei modisti. Roma Istituto storico italiano per il Medio evo, 1994.

Moody, Ernest. *The Logic of William of Ockham.* London: Sheed & Ward, 1935.

Moody, Ernest. *Truth and Consequence in Medieval Logic.* Amsterdam: North-Holland Publishing Co., 1953.

Normore, Calvin. "Some Aspects of Ockham's Logic." In *The Cambridge Companion to Ockham*, edited by Paul Spade. Cambridge, U.K.: Cambridge University Press, 1999.

Pinborg, Jan. *Logik und Semantik im Mittelalter: ein Überblick.* Stuttgart-Bad Cannstatt: Frommann-Holzboog, 1972.

Pinborg, Jan. *Medieval Semantics: Selected Studies on Medieval Logic and Grammar.* London: Variorum Reprints, 1984.

Spade, Paul. *Lies, Language, and Logic in the Later Middle Ages.* London: Variorum Reprints, 1988.

Thom, Paul. *Medieval Modal Systems: Problems and Concepts.* Aldershot: Ashgate, 2003.

Yrönsuuri, Mikko, ed. *Medieval Formal Logic: Obligations, Insolubles, and Consequences.* Dordrecht: Kluwer Academic Publishers, 2001.

Christopher J. Martin (2005)

INTERREGNUM (BETWEEN MEDIEVAL AND MODERN)

The interregnum between medieval scholastic logic and modern mathematical logic may be taken as having begun about the middle of the fifteenth century. There is no clear mark of division; the change was a shift away from the characteristic interests of the twelfth to the fifteenth century, with nothing of comparable importance arising to take their place. At the same time, certain less desirable trends in scholastic logic were perpetuated. The result is that formal logic was reduced almost entirely to a very imperfectly presented syllogistic. Medieval influences continued to operate in the early years of the sixteenth century, and medieval authors were still sometimes read in the seventeenth, but by the time that William of Ockham's *Summa Logicae* was printed at Oxford in 1675, no one had written creatively in the idiom of scholastic logic for many years.

The interregnum was characteristically sterile, a cause for despondency when one thinks of the large place logic continued to occupy in the educational curriculum and of the innumerable writers who put manuals of logic on the market. The tendency to publish at all costs was encouraged by the post-Reformation and post-Tridentine growth of universities, colleges, and seminaries.

VALLA

The first author to consider is the humanist Lorenzo Valla (1407–1457), best remembered for his writing on the forged donation of Constantine. In his *Dialecticarum Libri Tres* (1441), Valla gave no definitions of syllogistic figures and moods, evidently assuming that the reader would know about these. His aim was to confine the syllogistic to the first two figures, without the five moods of

Theophrastus and Eudemus. To do this he would have had to reject subalternation, conversion, and reductio ad absurdum. About subalternation he was inconsistent; conversion he rejected as lacking brevity, ease, pleasantness, and utility; reductio ad absurdum he largely neglected. The five offending moods were called "Agrippine births," and of them all the most monstrous was "Frisemomorum, forsooth!"

Here we see the common humanist objection to the barbarity of scholastic terminology, but of course Valla was not objecting merely to comparatively recent Scholastics. His fullest invective was saved for the six moods of the third figure, which he thought insane and never found in use, unlike the first-figure and second-figure moods, which he accepted as dictated by nature to everyone, "even peasants, even women, even children." The standard means of reduction are but "remedies for sick syllogisms." The standing of the third figure would remain a point of dispute for a hundred years, until Ramus undercut Valla's argument by declaring that the figure was in obvious fact very commonly used (*Institutionum Dialecticarum Libri Tres*, Paris, 1554). Thus, Philipp Melanchthon (*Compendiaria Dialectices Ratio*, Basel, 1521) could not make up his mind on the subject.

MELANCHTHON

In Melanchthon (1497–1560), a most influential writer, the rhetorical approach to logic already appeared at a high state of development, although he retained some Aristotelian doctrine. The rhetorical tradition, derived from Cicero and Quintilian, had a place, albeit a very subordinate one, in scholastic logic. We can see it beginning to predominate in the *Dialectica ad Petrum de Medicis* (edited by D. M. Inguanez and D. G. Muller, Monte Cassino, 1943; composed about 1457), by Joannes Argyropulos, who held that the detail of the theory of *suppositio*, which was the distinctive and most original scholastic contribution to logic, offered almost nothing to oratorical practice.

Thus, scholastic logic, which in its origins had borrowed considerably from grammar, began to yield to the third member of the trivium, rhetoric. Accordingly Melanchthon declared the fruit of dialectic to be the ability to speak with propriety and exactness on any theme, and he expounded the Ciceronian syllogism, with its five parts—*propositio, approbatio, assumptio, assumptionis approbatio,* and *complexio*—before the Aristotelian. (A century later a similar five-part syllogism, with proposition, reason, example, application, and conclusion, came into favor in the New Nyāya school of Indian logic.) In general, Melanchthon said, the natural reasoning common to the learned, children, and ordinary people is to be preferred to the "rancid commentaries of dialecticians." From this time on it was often felt desirable to include comparative lists of terminology, ancient and modern, as was done by a commentator on Rodolphus Agricola in 1538, by John Seton in 1572, and by John Sanderson in 1589.

RAMUS

The syllogistic as a deductive system underwent considerable attrition in the rhetorical treatment of logic, but this cannot be ascribed exclusively to the new interests. John Dolz's *Sillogismi* (Paris, 1511), a work of purely scholastic inspiration, methodically examines arguments in the different moods and figures as though they had nothing to do with one another. Dolz gave thirty-two sets of objections to Barbara before going on to Celarent "to avoid prolixity." Although logic applied to itself was by no means unknown in Scholasticism, the idea of a closed logical system was little developed, and hence the piecemeal treatment so characteristic of the scholastic *sophismata* was easily extended to encroach on the systematic character of syllogistic. The fact that Aristotle began by presenting syllogisms in lists probably also contributed to this encroachment.

The process of fragmentation was given new impetus by Pierre de la Ramée (Peter Ramus, 1515–1572). This great master of Latin rhetorical style and innovator of educational theory developed a massive attack on the Aristotelian tradition in logic and an alternative corpus of logical material that quickly gave rise to a widespread Ramist scholasticism.

ATTACK ON ARISTOTELIAN TRADITION. Ramus's *Animadversiones Aristotelicae* (Paris, 1556) tells in twenty books how Ramus turned from the clarity of Plato to the comparative chaos of Aristotle. Pretending to be analytical, Aristotle was almost completely deficient in that (Ramist) analysis that consists in systematic definition and division, and his doctrines are not supported by examples (are not, in fact, established by rhetorical syllogisms!). These are the standards Ramus applied as he worked through the *Prior Analytics* in his Book VII, firing off a broadside at every detail of Aristotelian or scholastic doctrine that occurred to him on the way. The typically rhetorical teaching that experience, observation, and usage are the proper guides in logic is prominent. Variables seldom make their appearance in this milieu, but Ramus's express attack on abecedarian examples—which,

being examples of nothing, can be adapted to nothing—is remarkable.

RAMIST LOGIC. The *Dialecticae Libri Duo* (Paris, 1556) is divided between invention, or discovery, and judgment, a distinction derived immediately from Agrippa and mediately from Cicero and Boethius. This distinction had been recalled among Scholastics—for example, at the opening of Kilwardby's popular thirteenth-century commentary on the *Prior Analytics*, often printed under the name of Giles of Rome. Like Descartes, whose methodological ideas supplanted his own, Ramus could not escape his antecedents. The first book covers topics, or loci; the second expounds the Ramist syllogistic, divided into the contracted syllogism (an enthymematic version of the Aristotelian third figure) and the explicated syllogism (comprising the second and first figures, in that order). There are no signs of quantification, all unquantified propositions that are not singular being deemed universal. A mood is general if it contains no singular term, special if it contains one, and proper if it contains two. Examples are taken from classical rhetoric and poetry; the propriety of such sources was vigorously attacked by a little-known anti-Ramist, Thomas Oliver of Bury, in his *De Sophismatum Praestigiis Cavendis* (Cambridge, U.K., 1604), on the ground that logic has very little place in poetry or forensic oratory.

This whole early version of an ordinary-language approach to logic was admirably countered by Gisbertus Isendoorn (*Cursus Systematicus*, Oxford, 1658). Writing directly against the famous Cambridge Ramist George Downame, Isendoorn said (p. 613): *Observa ... orationem et popularem discurrendi usum non esse mensuram et normam Logicae, sed rectam rationem et accuratam artem viamque concludendi* (Mark that popular speech and usage are not the standard and norm of logic, but right reason and an exact method of reaching conclusions).

MANUALS OF LOGIC

With all the effort of the mid-sixteenth century to simplify logic, it is not surprising that vernacular manuals began to appear, although sparsely, at that time. In England there were Thomas Wilson's *The Rule of Reason* (London, 1551), Ralphe Lever's *The Arte of Reason rightly termed Witcraft* (London, 1573), Abraham Fraunce's *The Lawiers Logike* (London, 1588), and Thomas Blundevile's *The Arte of Logicke* (London, 1599); in France there was Philippes Canaye's treatise *L'organe* (Paris, 1589). Little further seems to have been published in English until John Newton's *The English Academy* (London, 1677).

ENCYCLOPEDIA OF PHILOSOPHY
2nd edition

Wilson's pioneer effort is interesting chiefly for its novel terminology; for example, the major, minor, and middle terms are called the "terme at large," the "severall terme," and the "double repeate." Blundevile introduced an arithmetical syllogism and used a catechetical method. This method had been used by Matthias Flacius Illyricus in *Paralipomena Dialectices* (Basel, 1558; composed 1550), which gives a very detailed treatment of the venerable *pons asinorum*. Canaye's book was also devoted largely to the *pons asinorum*, being distinguished by the dissection of the traditional rectangular figure into two circular ones. The same subject had been dealt with in Christopher Corner's *Ratio Inveniendi Medium Terminum* (Basel, 1549), which set a new standard of scholarship by appending a Greek text of relevant chapters of Aristotle. Thus, Aristotelian subjects were being pursued, in somewhat new ways, at the same time that the widespread Ramist innovations were taking hold.

Something of the same development can be seen in commentaries on the *Prior Analytics*, from the sixteenth-century editions of Kilwardby, through the work of Lefèvre d'Étaples (Faber Stapulensis), with his emphasis on tabular presentation; that of Agostino Nifo (Niphus Suessanus), who professed to follow the Greek commentators but wrote a long treatise on conversion in the scholastic manner; Burana's urbane commentary, with lengthy appendixes by his teacher Bagolinus and an interesting prefatory glimpse of the logical curriculum in a north Italian university; Monlorius's commentary, relatively brief but careful; to that of Pacius, with its businesslike presentation, schemes, and figures, a work praised by Sir David Ross in his own commentary. Within this developing tradition of Aristotelian scholarship we may also put the *Apparatus Syllogistici Synopsis* of Joannes Albanus (Bologna, 1620), which elaborately examined the crescent-shaped and triangular diagrams that descended from Greek sources to the Aristotelians of the Renaissance.

In a field in which syllogistic occupied so large a place one must note widespread incompetence in the matter of classification by figure. This is, of course, a point settled by definition, as Lorenzo Maiolo (*Epiphyllides in Dialecticis*, Venice, 1497) and John Wallis (*Institutio Logicae*, Oxford, 1687) saw. These two were exceptional, however. Franciscus Titelmans (*De Consideratione Dialectica Libri Sex*, Paris, 1544) found the distinction between major and minor premises a hard thing for youths; Richard Crakanthorp (*Logicae Libri Quinque*, London, 1622) omitted the fourth figure without rejecting it and found it hard to determine the number of

moods. The basic trouble was that the later medievals, following a lead given by Boethius, defined the major premise as the first stated, the major term as the extreme therein, and so on, whereas Philoponus had defined the major term as the predicate of the conclusion, the major premise as the premise containing the major term, and so on. Each of the schemes can be worked out consistently, but they give different classifications and are mutually incompatible. This was seldom understood; it was a common fault to speak of indirect conclusions in connection with Philoponian definitions or to define with Philoponus and then take, for example, Balnama as fourth figure, instead of first figure with transposed premises.

In the Oxford logicians one does not find twenty-four moods in four figures correctly worked out on a Philoponian basis until Henry Aldrich (*Artis Logicae Compendium*, Oxford, 1691; this first edition was anonymous). The principles of the matter remained so little understood that even Augustus De Morgan (*Formal Logic*, 1847) could say, "Consider the fourth and first figures as coincident and the arbitrary notion of arrangement by major and minor vanishes," and W. S. Jevons (*Elementary Lessons in Formal Logic*, 1876) described fourth-figure syllogisms as ill arranged and imperfect and unnatural in form. "Unnatural" as a description of fourth-figure syllogisms was first used by Averroes, and his opinion was reinforced by Giacomo Zabarella (1533–1589); both meant to make a point of genuine formal logic, but they used some phrases that permitted a psychological interpretation. Sir William Hamilton's treatment of the matter (*Lectures on Logic*, 1860, Vol. IV), with lists of authors for and against the fourth figure and indirect moods of the second and third, is useless without knowledge of these authors' definitions and therefore of what they were favoring or opposing. A writer of a very different style was John Hospinianus (1515–1575), who proceeded on a combinatory basis and found that by admitting singular and indefinite propositions to the syllogistic and by identifying certain moods, he could obtain thirty-six valid moods out of a possible 512.

Extremely influential on manuals of the eighteenth and nineteenth centuries was *Logique, ou l'art de penser* (1662; *The Port-Royal Logic*), by Antoine Arnauld and Pierre Nicole. Even Aldrich, who disliked its novel terminology and Cartesian standpoint, may well have been prompted by it to his strict deductive treatment, for he shows no acquaintance with any other likely influence. The authors' epistemological interests certainly contributed much to the psychologism that was soon to infect logic, but such headings as conception, judgment, and reasoning were not new in promoting this tendency. Canaye had already spoken of syllogism as the third operation of the mind, which *leaves* the premises and *arrives* at the conclusion. Such terminology is symptomatic of a change that occurred in the mid-seventeenth century. The Port-Royal section on method—a most popular subject in this period—more explicitly opened the way to the discursive excesses that would soon masquerade as logic, culminating, perhaps, in Henry Kett's *Logic Made Easy, or A Short View of the Aristotelic System of Reasoning, and Its Application to Literature, Science, and the General Improvement of the Mind* (Oxford, 1809).

A book praised by Leibniz and rather above the average, although not completely out of the common rut, is the *Logica Hamburgensis* (Hamburg, 1638), by Joachim Jung, or Jungius. One notable feature of this book is the marking of the lines of a syllogistic demonstration by letters, which are then used as references for showing by what principles which line follows from which others. Such a rather exact method of proof was very exceptional in logic before modern times, but contemporaneously with Jung, Pierre Hérigone introduced a similar method in mathematics (*Cursus Mathematicus*, Paris, 1634–1637). Jung was thoroughly acquainted with the possible use of contraposition as a means of syllogistic proof but was no more successful in his discussion of the fourth figure than so many others had been. Under the medieval heading of consequences he noted the argument *a recto ad obliquum*, which can be found in Aristotle's *Topics* II, 8, 114a18.

Some considerations, usually brief, of such standard medieval subjects as consequences and supposition theory continued to appear—for instance, those of Chrysostom Javellus (*Compendium Logicae*, Lyons, 1580), Robert Sanderson (*Logicae Artis Compendium*, Oxford, 1618), and Henry Aldrich—but these were exceptions. Arnold Geulincx hoped to repopularize such treatises by his *Logica Fundamentis Suis a Quibus Hactenus Collapsa Fuerat Restituta* (Leiden, 1662). He was able to relate alternation, conjunction, and negation by means of their truth conditions according to the laws that are often called after De Morgan or William of Ockham but that go back, at least in part, to the *Syncategoremata* of Peter of Spain. These laws were also known to the mathematician Gerolamo Saccheri, whose *Logica Demonstrativa* (Turin, 1697) is outstandingly original in its high degree of organization, its reflections on the assumptions necessary to logic, and its use of indirect proof, in the pattern of the so-called *mirabilis consequentia*, to the effect that what follows from its own negation is true. Unfortunately the few signs of revival and advance discernible at the close of the seventeenth century did not produce any general or permanent result, and even the work of Leibniz met with little response.

See also Agrippa; Aristotelianism; Aristotle; Arnauld, Antoine; Averroes; Boethius, Anicius Manlius Severinus; Cicero, Marcus Tullius; De Morgan, Augustus; Descartes, René; Geulincx, Arnold; Giles of Rome; Hamilton, William; Jevons, William Stanley; Jungius, Joachim; Kilwardby, Robert; Leibniz, Gottfried Wilhelm; Melanchthon, Philipp; Nicole, Pierre; Ramus, Peter; Theophrastus; Valla, Lorenzo; William of Ockham.

Bibliography

INTERREGNUM

Dürr, Karl. "Die Syllogistik des Johannes Hospinianus (1515–1575)." *Synthese* 9 (1952): 472–484.

Hamilton, William. "Logic: The Recent English Treatises on That Science" (1833). In *Discussions on Philosophy and Literature, Education and University Reform*, 116–174. London and Edinburgh: Longman, Brown, Green and Longmans, 1852.

Howell, W. S. *Logic and Rhetoric in England, 1500–1700*. Princeton, NJ: Princeton University Press, 1956.

Ong, W. J. *Ramus, Method, and the Decay of Dialogue*. Cambridge, MA: Harvard University Press, 1958.

Risse, Wilhelm. *Die Logik der Neuzeit*, Vol. I (1500–1640). Stuttgart and Bad Cannstatt: Frommann, 1964.

Thomas, Ivo. "The Later History of the Pons Asinorum." In *Contributions to Logic and Methodology in Honor of J. M. Bocheński*. Amsterdam: North-Holland, 1965.

Thomas, Ivo. "The Liar: A New Historical Detail." *Notre Dame Journal of Formal Logic* 6 (1965): 201–208.

Thomas, Ivo. "Medieval Aftermath: Oxford Logic and Logicians of the Seventeenth Century." In *Oxford Studies Presented to Daniel Callus*. Oxford: Clarendon Press, 1964.

Thomas, Ivo. "The Setting of Classical Logic." *Notre Dame Scholastic* 101 (1960): 16–17.

Ivo Thomas (1967)

PRECURSORS OF MODERN LOGIC

Modern logic, or the logic that is loosely called "mathematical," began in a serious and systematic way with Augustus De Morgan's *Formal Logic* and George Boole's *Mathematical Analysis of Logic*, both published in 1847.

But a number of earlier writers were already "modern" in spirit, and of these, four stand out especially sharply—Leibniz, Euler, Lambert, and Bolzano.

See also Bolzano, Bernard; Boole, George; De Morgan, Augustus; Lambert, Johann Heinrich; Leibniz, Gottfried Wilhelm.

(A. N. P.)

LEIBNIZ

Gottfried Wilhelm Leibniz (1646–1716) was distinguished in many fields, but in none more than in logic. There, however, his worth was not fully appreciated until the twentieth century. He early began to investigate Aristotelian syllogistic and never completely escaped from the syllogistic point of view. In 1666 he wrote a *Dissertatio de Arte Combinatoria*, a juvenile work that was not free of mistakes, as he later realized, but that showed a new, high sense of organization and a genuine feeling for formal logic, very rare at the time. In one part of this book Leibniz worked out for himself the calculations of Hospinianus (1560) relative to the possible and the valid moods of syllogism. He differed from Hospinianus in making singular propositions equivalent to universal ones, as did Wallis and Euler. He arrived at twenty-four strictly Aristotelian syllogisms, six in each of four figures, which he arranged in a neat tableau suggestive of certain deductive relationships. Leibniz's standard method of proof in this context was reductio ad absurdum, as suggested to him by his teacher Jakob Thomasius (1622–1684), author of *Erotemata Logica* (Leipzig, 1670), but he also recognized the need for conversion. He wrongly credited Ramus with a method actually known in the thirteenth century, the device of proving laws of conversion and subalternation by means of syllogism and the laws of identity "All *a* is *a*" and "Some *a* is *a*."

Leibniz often returned to syllogistic and was periodically vexed by semantic considerations, namely whether to think of the matter in extension or in intension— whether in "All *a* is *b*" it is the *a*'s which are said to be contained in the *b*'s or the property *a* which contains the property *b*. Leibniz had something of a fixation on the intensional approach, although he often suspected that extension was more effective and logically satisfactory. One thing that pushed him in the direction of extensionality was a fondness for experimenting with spatial interpretations. Thus, we find several attempts at diagrammatic representation, some using ruled and dotted lines and some using circles. He found it impossible to carry through such interpretations when thinking in intension.

THEORY OF COMBINATIONS. The theory of combinations is highly relevant to logic. Chrysippus is reported to have shown some interest in combinations, Kilwardby and others in the thirteenth century repeatedly made combinatory summaries of assertoric and modal syllogistic, and semantic interpretations of logical formulas in finite domains employ the theory. Besides the syllogistic computations described, Leibniz considered how many predicates can be truly asserted of a given subject or how many subjects set under a given predicate. Such problems need some preliminary arrangements, and Leibniz supposed that a composite concept is analyzable into a number of ultimate simples, just as an integer is uniquely decomposable into its prime factors. Correlating the simple concepts with prime numbers, we can say that a predicate is truly attributable to its subject if the product associated with the predicate divides that associated with the subject. The essentials of this idea have been used in modern times to obtain a decision procedure for syllogistic, and unique decomposition into primes plays an essential part in Gödel numbering.

UNIVERSAL LANGUAGE. The idea of decomposing concepts into "prime factors" suggested to Leibniz the possibility of following up the initial steps toward a universal language taken by John Wilkins (1668), Jean Joachim Becher (1661), George Dalgarno (1661), Athanasius Kircher (1663), and others. He wanted such a language not merely to be practically or commercially useful, as were many of the pioneer efforts, but to be logically constructed so as to have general scientific import. Leibniz later distinguished a universal language from a logical calculus and desired to base his language on a thorough analysis of the communicative function of the various parts of speech, tenses, suffixes, and so on (an anticipation of modern theories of syntactical categories), and at one point (*Analysis Linguarum*, 1678) he envisaged a basic Latin rather in the style of C. K. Ogden and I. A. Richards's basic English.

In saying that nouns express ideas and verbs express propositions Leibniz radically altered the Aristotelian basis of the distinction and gave, in germ, the concept of a propositional function. Such reflections led him to a reductionist program, with adverbs reduced to (derived from) adjectives and adjectives to nouns, and with the copula taken as the only fundamental verb. He recognized that particles, connectives, and prepositions are of especial importance to linguistic structure. In taking us out of the syllogistic area this theory recalls the medieval doctrine of syncategorematic terms and Thomas Aquinas's analysis of many prepositions, while it adumbrates the logic of truth-functional connectives and of relations. Leibniz knew that not all arguments are syllogistic, in this matter acknowledging a debt to Jung, but the dominance of a syllogistic point of view in Leibniz's thought is shown by his curious distinction between syllogistic and "grammatical" consequences.

This part of Leibniz's thought constitutes a distinct chapter in the history of the relations between grammar and logic. Grammar had been influential in the constitution of scholastic logic, but in the interregnum it had yielded to the third member of the medieval trivium, rhetoric, as a dominant power. In the projects for a universal and rational language we see grammar reasserting itself. But Leibniz was not content to confine logic to the "trivial" arts.

LOGICAL CALCULUS. The idea that logic might be quadrivial, and notably mathematical, was not new with Leibniz. Leibniz considered Aristotle to have been, in his logic, the first to write mathematically outside mathematics (letter to Gabriel Wagner, 1596). Roger Bacon (thirteenth century)—who also wished to reduce the trivial art of grammar to the quadrivial one of music—stated in his *Opus Maius* that "all the predicaments depend on the knowledge of quantity, with which mathematics deals, and therefore the whole of logic depends on mathematics." It is in the light of this that one should read the statement in his *Communia Mathematica* that "the mere logician cannot accomplish anything worthwhile in logical matters" (*nihil dignum potest purus logicus in logicalibus pertractare*). William of Ockham had been of the opposite opinion, and in *De Sacramento Altaris* he described mathematicians as among those less skilled in logic. Ramón Lull had written a combinatorial work, *Ars Magna* (which captured Leibniz's imagination, though he soon came to understand its deficiencies), and Thomas Hobbes had elaborated suggestively, if ineffectively, on the theme "by ratiocination I mean computation" ("Computatio Sive Logica," in *De Corpore*).

There is little doubt, however, that Leibniz's ideas, which far outstripped in detail and understanding any earlier hints, were his own spontaneous creation. "While I was yet a boy with a knowledge only of common logic, and without instruction in mathematics, the thought came to me, I know not by what instinct, that an analysis of ideas could be devised, whence in some combinatory way truths could arise and be estimated as though by numbers" (*Elementa Rationis*). He was thereafter constantly occupied with such notions and attempted to contrive an alphabet of thought, or *characteristica universalis*, which would represent ideas in a logical way, not things in a pictorial way, and would be mechanical in operation,

unambiguous, and nonquantitative; this alphabet of thought would be a means of discovery, a support to intuition, and an aid in ending disputes.

Leibniz regarded his great invention of the infinitesimal calculus (1675) as emerging from such researches, and the calculus led him to reflect still more intently on the properties desirable in such a characteristic. Exactly what he meant by "mechanical" and "calculation" is still in question, and he no doubt underestimated the task he set himself, but the imaginative fervor with which he always wrote of it reveals, as we can now appreciate, a true prophetic instinct. He often used an image from mythology to summarize his intentions, saying that his method was to be a *filum Ariadnes*, a thread of Ariadne. Many authors had long envisaged logic as a Cretan maze in need of such a clue—and that this should be so in an age when logic was scarcely existent does them little credit—but from the pen of Leibniz the allusion was more than a literary elegance and condensed a program of "palpable demonstrations, like the calculations of arithmeticians or the diagrams of geometers." (For Leibnizian references to the *filum*, see Louis Couturat, *La Logique de Leibniz*, pp. 90–92, 124; for other authors, see Ivo Thomas, "Medieval Aftermath.")

ENCYCLOPEDIA. One may ask what the theory of combinations was meant to combine, what the logical calculus was meant to calculate with, or where the analyses presupposed by the unified language of science were to be found. Leibniz was not content to leave such analysis in the state of a general project. The enormous range of his knowledge and interests, which included unity in religion, international relations, cooperation among scientists and scholars, and jurisprudence, as well as the not unrelated ordering of thought, prompted his lasting interest in the construction of an encyclopedia. T. Zwinger's *Theatrum Vitae Humanae* (1565) and Johann Heinrich Alsted's *Encyclopaedia* (1608) provided Leibniz with a basis for early schematisms, and sketches and fragments from about 1668 to the end of his life show an unceasing interest in the plan, which he believed had failed of completion through his own distractions and the lack of younger assistants. Appeals to monarchs and to learned societies met with little response. The project was, of course, a gigantic one, impossible of immediate fulfillment, but it should not be supposed that Leibniz thought it could be perfected quickly. Rather, its elaboration was to proceed gradually, along with that of the universal language and a calculus of logic. In later drafts this calculus took an ever more prominent place.

STRUCTURE OF THE CALCULUS. The main stages (1679, 1686, 1690) of Leibniz's many experiments in logical algebra have often been expounded and commented on. Here only some laws which were constant features will be mentioned.

(1) *a* is *a*;

(2) If *a* is *b* and *b* is *c*, then *a* is *c*.

Propositions of the form "*a* is *b*" are intended as universal affirmatives, "All *a* is *b*," which Leibniz normally thought of as meaning that the property *a* contains the property *b*. Sometimes he wrote "*a* contains *b*" instead of "*a* is *b*." Accordingly, rule (1) is one of the syllogistic laws of identity which, as was said above, he used from the start in syllogistic demonstrations, and rule (2) is the Barbara syllogism. Today we know that by means of the calculus of quantifiers and some definitions all asserted laws of the syllogistic can be obtained from rules (1) and (2) alone. Leibniz lacked those aids, but he admitted negative terms that obey the laws

(3) *a* is interchangeable with not-not-*a*;

(4) *a* is *b* if and only if not-*b* is not-*a*.

Rule (4) is the law of contraposition familiar to the Scholastics and, for Leibniz, most recently given prominence by Jung. From rules (1) to (4), with some definitions and Leibniz's favorite method of reductio ad absurdum, the whole syllogistic can be obtained. Leibniz did not use exactly that method but adopted at one time a rather similar one based on a restatement of rule (1), *a* = *aa*, and rule (5), below. Identity has the substitutive property described below; "*a* is *b*" is made equivalent to "*a* = *ab*"; and "Some *a* is *b*" is written "S*a* = *b*." Compound terms such as *ab* were thought of as signifying the addition of properties *a* and *b*. They obey the laws

(5) *ab* is *a*;

(6) *ab* is *b*;

(7) If *a* is *b* and *a* is *c*, then *a* is *bc*.

It has been pointed out by Karl Popper that if rules (5) and (6) are made the premises of the mood Darapti, we have the conclusion "Some *a* is *b*." This does not render the system inconsistent, but it does show that the system is already more extensive and more trivial than Leibniz presumably intended. From rules (1), (2), (5), (6), and (7) it is easy to deduce, as Leibniz did,

(8) If *a* is *bc*, then *a* is *b*, and *a* is *c*, which is the converse of (7), and

(9) If *a* is *b*, then *ac* is *bc* (using rules 2, 5, 6, and 7);

(10) If *a* is *b* and *c* is *d*, then *ac* is *bd* (using rule 9 twice and then rule 2).

Rule (10), which was known to Abelard in the twelfth century, Leibniz called *praeclarum theorema*, a very notable theorem.

Identity of terms was introduced in various ways, but always so that it was equivalent to the conjunction of "*a* is *b*" and "*b* is *a*" and so that identical terms could be substituted for one another in all contexts of the calculus. The first definition in the *Non Inelegans Specimen Demonstrandi in Abstractis*, for instance, posits that *a* = *b* holds if and only if *a* and *b* can be substituted for each other without altering the truth of any statement. The "only if" part is commonly called the principle of the identity of indiscernibles; for its converse W. V. Quine has suggested "the indiscernibility of identicals." As a principle of general application it has given rise to much discussion, although it is normally accepted in logic. While it is commonly attributed to Leibniz, Aristotle presented it in essentials in the *Topics* (VII, 1, 152a31 ff.) and *De Sophisticis Elenchis* (Ch. 24, 179a37 ff.).

An algebraic calculus requires that substitution for variables be possible, and Leibniz explicitly recognized this, in what was certainly the clearest statement in logic of the principle up to his time. Some medievals—Albert the Great, for instance—had shown their understanding of the generality conferred by variables when they called them "transcendental terms." Three more laws important for the calculus were known to Leibniz, following from rules (1), (5), (6), and (7):

(11) *ab* is *ba* (using 5, 6, and 7);

(12) *a* is *aa* (using 5);

(13) *aa* is *a* (using 1 and 7).

In the course of his experiments Leibniz came to see that particular propositions have existential import, whereas universals may not, and it was a puzzle to him what the existential import might be—factual existence or logical possibility—and whether it was built into his system or had to be further provided for. This problem had been raised by medieval logicians from the time of Abelard. One of Leibniz's solutions—that subalternation is invalid if the universal states a relation of concepts and the particular states a matter of fact but holds if we stay in one of those domains—is essentially that of Paul of Venice, who required the subjects of both propositions to have the same *suppositio*.

At a late stage Leibniz used the addition sign in place of, and with the sense of, multiplication; that is, he used *a*

+ *b* instead of *ab*. But he knew that such expressions could be interpreted as logical disjunctions, and there is also an early hint that the calculus could be interpreted propositionally, the antecedent of a conditional being said to contain the consequent. This hint may serve as a summary indication of Leibniz's position in the history of logic. Aristotle had used "antecedent" and "consequent" for "subject" and "predicate"; among medievals (such as Abelard and Kilwardby) it is often hard to tell whether the words were used of propositions or of terms; Leibniz offered a glimpse of the two domains as distinct but analogous. If his work had not gone long unpublished (we still have no complete edition), we might not have had to wait so long for the full light of Boolean day.

Bibliography

Baylis, C. A. Review of various articles on the identity of indiscernibles. *Journal of Symbolic Logic* 21 (1960): 86.

Couturat, Louis. *La Logique de Leibniz d'après des documents inédits*. Paris: Alcan, 1901; reprinted, Hildesheim, 1961.

Dürr, Karl. *Leibniz' Forschungen im Gebiet der Syllogistik. Leibniz zu seinem 300. Geburtstag*. Berlin, 1949.

Kauppi, Raili. *Über die Leibnizsche Logik mit besonderer Berücksichtigung des Problems der Intension und der Extension*. Helsinki, 1960.

Rescher, Nicholas. "Leibniz's Interpretation of His Logical Calculi." *Journal of Symbolic Logic* 19 (1954): 1–13. Reviewed by M. A. E. Dummett in *Journal of Symbolic Logic* 21 (1960): 197–199.

Ivo Thomas (1967)

EULER

The noted mathematician Leonhard Euler (1707–1783) is remembered in logic chiefly for his geometrical illustrations of syllogistic, "Euler's diagrams" or "Euler's circles." Similar devices were used by J. C. Sturm (1661), Leibniz (see Bocheński, *History of Formal Logic*, plate facing p. 260), Joachim Lange (1712), and Gottfried Ploucquet (1759), and in a very general way the idea of spatial illustration goes back at least to Juan Luis Vives, who used triangles to illustrate the Barbara syllogism ("De Censura Veri," in *Opera*, Basel, 1555). But because of Euler's fame as a mathematician and the popularity of his charming *Lettres à une princesse d'Allemagne* (the relevant letters are CII ff., dated 1761) such diagrams are traditionally named for him.

Euler used proper inclusion for the universal affirmative proposition, exclusion for the universal negative, and intersection for both the particulars. If his interpretation is followed systematically, it correctly decides the validity or invalidity of all three-term syllogisms with all terms distinct but fails for the laws of identity and con-

tradition and for degenerate syllogisms depending on them. Apparently nobody developed full syllogistic along these lines until J. D. Gergonne (1816), whose five relations give a complete system and can indeed be defined by three of them (see Ivo Thomas, "Eulerian Syllogistic," and references supplied there), but not by Euler's three. The extensional approach evidenced by Euler's interpretation of the universal affirmative was a healthy influence.

Euler also lent his authority to the doctrine that singular propositions are equivalent to universal ones (*Lettres*, CVII), a thesis propounded by John Wallis (from 1638; see Appendix to his *Institutio Logica*, Oxford, 1687). Bertrand Russell severely criticized this doctrine as confusing class membership with inclusion, but of course we can get an inclusive proposition equivalent to a membership proposition by taking the unit class of the singular subject.

See also Leibniz, Gottfried Wilhelm; Ploucquet, Gottfried; Propositions; Russell, Bertrand Arthur William; Vives, Juan Luis.

Bibliography

Faris, J. A. "The Gergonne Relations." *Journal of Symbolic Logic* 20 (1955): 207–231.

Gardner, Martin. *Logic Machines and Diagrams*. New York: McGraw-Hill, 1958.

Hamilton, William. *Lectures on Logic*. London, 1860.

Hocking, W. E. "Two Extensions of the Use of Graphs in Elementary Logic." *University of California Publications in Philosophy* 2 (2) (1909): 31–44.

More, Trenchard. "On the Construction of Venn Diagrams." *Journal of Symbolic Logic* 24 (1959): 303–304.

Thomas, Ivo. "Eulerian Syllogistic." *Journal of Symbolic Logic* 22 (1957): 15–16.

Thomas, Ivo. "Independence of Faris-Rejection-Axioms." *Notre Dame Journal of Formal Logic* 1 (1959): 48–51.

Venn, John. *Symbolic Logic*. 2nd ed. London: Macmillan, 1894.

Ivo Thomas (1967)

LAMBERT AND PLOUCQUET

Johann Heinrich Lambert (1728–1777), German physicist, mathematician, and astronomer, devoted a number of essays to the enterprise of making a calculus of logic, which he evidently thought of in connection with the tree of Porphyry. His standpoint is, as is usual with the early investigators, intensional. Let *a* and *b* be any concepts, $a + b$ their combination into a compound concept, and *ab* their common part. The letters γ and δ can be multiplied with conceptual variables, so that $a\gamma$ and $a\delta$ are read as "the genus of *a*" and "the difference of *a*." The intended meaning suggests that γ and δ are descriptive operators;

yet Lambert sometimes treated them as though they were placeholders for generic or differential concepts. At any rate Lambert, following an elementary intuition, posited $a = a\gamma + a\delta = a(\gamma + \delta)$. Wanting to descend the tree to subordinate species as well as to ascend to superordinate genera and differences, he used the notation $a\gamma^{-1}$ or a/γ, which should mean "the genus under a." Waiving the fact that a concept containing a may be an ultimate species, we reflect that although $a\gamma$ is unique, $a\gamma^{-1}$ may not be so. This accounts for the trouble that Lambert found in applying multiplication and division, for $(a/\gamma)\gamma$, "the genus of a species of a," is identical with a whereas $(a\gamma)/\gamma$, "a species of the genus of a," need not be a itself. Lambert used subtraction to obtain the removal of a concept. He did not account for the appearance of coefficients and, in general, did not question the logical appropriateness of the algebraic operations to which his basic intuitions gave rise. Boole met with similar difficulties but reflected on them.

In syllogistic Lambert started not from the Aristotelian relations but from the five that are now attributed to Gergonne. This is feasible, but Lambert failed to achieve a satisfactory notion for the mutual exclusion of two terms. His most promising innovation lay in his attention to the relative product, but he did not develop this in any practical way.

Lambert, like Leibniz, experimented with sets of ruled and dotted lines to illustrate the relationships of syllogistic terms, in part trying to correct the defect in Euler's circles of not allowing for $a = b$. Some stages of his investigations were criticized by his correspondents G. J. von Holland (whose extensional standpoint was remarkable for the time) and Gottfried Ploucquet (1716–1790), both of whom were making their own efforts to evolve a logical calculus. Ploucquet, who was a teacher of Hegel, claimed independence of Euler in his use of closed figures—he used squares (1759)—and seems to have been the first to base his syllogistic on thoroughgoing quantification of the predicate. One of his notations, "$A \rangle B$" for "No A is B," strangely, enjoyed some popularity.

See also Boole, George; Hegel, Georg Wilhelm Friedrich; Lambert, Johann Heinrich; Leibniz, Gottfried Wilhelm; Ploucquet, Gottfried; Porphyry.

Bibliography

Bök, F. A., ed. *Sammlung der Schriften welche den logischen Calcul des Herrn Professor Ploucquet betreffen.* Tübingen, 1773.

Dürr, Karl. "Die Logistik Johann Heinrich Lamberts." In *Festschrift ... Dr. A. Speiser.* Zürich, 1945.

Venn, John. *Symbolic Logic.* London, 1881; 2nd ed., London: Macmillan, 1894.

Ivo Thomas (1967)

BOLZANO

The most important logician of the first half of the nineteenth century was Bernard Bolzano (1781–1848). His views are closest to those of Leibniz, who preceded him by more than a century (Bolzano was sometimes called the Bohemian Leibniz). Although he quoted often and extensively from philosophers and logicians of his own generation and the preceding one, among them Kant, Salomon Maimon, Hegel, J. F. Fries, J. G. E. Maass, and K. L. Reinhold, he did this almost always in order to criticize them, and rightly so from our modern point of view, because orders of magnitude separate Bolzano as a logician from his contemporaries.

One may doubt whether he deserves to be called a forerunner of mathematical logic and modern semantics. His approach is in many respects rather crude and old-fashioned in comparison with those of George Boole and Gottlob Frege, one and two generations later, respectively. But many points first made by Bolzano look strikingly modern. Unfortunately most of these were either not noticed or not understood during his lifetime or were forgotten by later generations.

For Bolzano logic was mainly the theory of science. To investigate science he used a partly formalized language consisting of ordinary German extended by various types of constants and variables, as well as by certain technical terms which for the most part he was at great pains to define as carefully as possible.

The fundamental entities with which logic has to deal, according to Bolzano, are terms and the propositions they constitute. These abstract entities are carefully distinguished from the corresponding linguistic and mental entities. Because a single proposition can be expressed in an indefinite number of ways, Bolzano's first aim was to normalize such linguistic expressions, to reduce all of them to canonical forms prior to their purely formal treatment.

Bolzano's solution was highly idiosyncratic. Deviating radically from tradition, he claimed that all sentences (complex and compound sentences as well as simple ones) are reducible to the single form "A has b," where "A" is the subject term, "b" the predicate term, and "has" the copula. Although this reduction works reasonably well with such sentences as "John is hungry," which can easily be rendered as "John has hunger," it sounds less convincing in the case of reducing "This is gold" to "This has goldness" (although Bolzano presented reasons why such words as "goldness" had not been created in natural languages) and still less so when "John is not hungry" is reduced to "John has lack-of-hunger." The reduction of the compound sentence "Either P or Q" to "The-term-One-of-P-and-Q-is-true has the-property-of-being-a-singular-term" or "The-term-One-of-P-or-Q-is-true has nonemptiness" (depending on whether the original expression "Either … or …" is interpreted from its context as denoting exclusive or inclusive disjunction) looks rather strange in its verbal formulation, although it looks much less strange in some appropriate symbolism. And reducing "Some A is B" to "The-term-An-A-which-is-B has nonemptiness" may appear fantastic at first sight, although it looks much more familiar when symbolized as $A \cap B \neq 0$. Nevertheless, Bolzano did not attempt to present a full set of rules for such conversions and relied instead on the reader's willingness to believe in the existence of such reductions after being shown how to perform them on certain representative samples, including some rather recalcitrant cases.

This reduction played a small role in the further development of Bolzano's work in logic. His major innovation was his introduction of the technique of variation into what amounts essentially to the logical semantics of language, even though the semantic approach, in its modern sense, was foreign to him. Starting with a proposition, true or false, he investigated its behavior with regard to truth and falsehood under substitution for any of its terms of all other fitting (that is, propositionhood-preserving) terms. (In modern terminology, he investigated all models of sentential forms.) When the number of such variants was finite he defined the degree of validity of a proposition with respect to one or more of its constituent terms as the ratio of the number of its true variants to the number of all variants. When this ratio is 1, the proposition is universally valid; when 0, universally contravalid; when greater than 0, consistent.

After extending these notions to propositional classes Bolzano was able to define an amazing number of interesting, and sometimes highly original, metalogical notions, including compatibility, dependency, exclusion, contradictoriness, contrariety, exclusiveness, and disjointness. By far the most important notion introduced in this way is that of derivability with respect to a given class of terms, defined as holding between two propositions P and Q if and only if Q is consistent and every model of Q is a model of P with respect to this class of terms; with respect to propositional classes it is defined similarly. This

definition differs only in the unfortunate consistency clause from Tarski's definition, given in 1937, of what he called the consequence relation.

Kant had defined an "analytic" affirmative judgment as one in which the predicate concept was already contained in the subject concept. Rejecting this definition as clearly inadequate for explicating logical truth, Bolzano defined a proposition to be analytically true when universally valid with respect to at least one of its constituent terms, analytically false when universally contravalid, etc., and as analytic when either analytically true or analytically false. Bolzano was aware that this definition of analytical truth was too broad as an explication of logical truth, and he therefore went on to define a proposition as being logically analytic when (again in modern terminology) all its descriptive (extralogical) constituent terms occur in it vacuously, an anticipation of a well-known definition by W. V. Quine (1940).

Bolzano's views of probability are also strikingly modern. To define the probability of the proposition M on the assumptions $A, B, C, D, \cdots$ (with respect to certain terms $i, j, \cdots$) he used the relative degree of validity of M with respect to $A, B, C, D, \cdots$, which he defined as the ratio of the number of true variants of the set $M, A, B, C, D, \cdots$ to the number of true variants of the set $A, B, C, D, \cdots$. This conception, tenable, of course, only when the numbers involved are finite, is an important refinement of Laplace's well-known conception of probability, standard in Bolzano's time, in that it elegantly sidesteps the problem of circularity involved in the notion of equipossibility.

See also Bolzano, Bernard; Boole, George; Frege, Gottlob; Fries, Jakob Friedrich; Hegel, Georg Wilhelm Friedrich; Kant, Immanuel; Laplace, Pierre Simon de; Leibniz, Gottfried Wilhelm; Maimon, Salomon; Quine, Willard Van Orman; Reinhold, Karl Leonhard; Semantics; Tarski, Alfred.

Bibliography

Bar-Hillel, Yehoshua. "Bolzano's Propositional Logic." *Archiv für mathematische Logik und Grundlagenforschung* 1 (1952): 65–98.

Berg, J. *Bolzano's Logic.* Stockholm: Almqvist and Wiksell, 1962.

Bolzano, Bernard. *Grundlegung der Logik.* Hamburg, 1964. A useful selection by Friedrich Kambartel from the first two volumes of the *Wissenschaftslehre*.

Bolzano, Bernard. *Wissenschaftslehre*, 4 vols. Sulzbach, 1837; Leipzig: Meiner, 1929–1931 (edited by W. Schulz).

Scholz, Heinrich. "Die Wissenschaftslehre Bolzanos." *Abhandlungen des Friesschen Schule*, n.s., 6 (1937): 399–472.

Yehoshua Bar-Hillel (1967)

MODERN LOGIC

THE BOOLEAN PERIOD

The eighteenth-century and early nineteenth-century logicians considered in the preceding section were all Continental Europeans, and those who were also philosophers, namely Leibniz and Bolzano, were representatives of Continental rationalism. The British empiricism of the same period produced no logicians. On the contrary, it was antilogical. The empiricists attacked formal logic—by which they meant the attenuated syllogistic to which much of the science had shrunk during the interregnum—as trivial and sometimes as circular. This antilogicism largely echoed John Locke, whose scornful treatment of logic in his *Essay concerning Human Understanding* had provoked one of Leibniz's minor defenses of it, in the *Nouveaux Essais*. In the early nineteenth century the common logic was rescued from oblivion by Richard Whately but was not enlarged by him. Its enlargement, however, came soon after and, despite the British antilogical tradition, was at first largely a British affair, spreading later to the United States (C. S. Peirce) and then to Germany (Ernst Schröder).

See also Bolzano, Bernard; Empiricism; Leibniz, Gottfried Wilhelm; Locke, John; Peirce, Charles Sanders; Rationalism; Whately, Richard.

Bibliography

Appraisals of Hamilton's logic are to be found in John Venn, *Symbolic Logic*; C. I. Lewis, *A Survey of Symbolic Logic*; Jørgen Jørgensen, *A Treatise of Formal Logic*, Vol. I; and A. N. Prior, *Formal Logic*. Hamilton's principles, if not his practice, have found a recent defender in P. T. Geach, *Reference and Generality* (Ithaca, NY: Cornell University Press, 1962); his quantification has been analyzed in some detail by Władysław Bednarowski, "Hamilton's Quantification of the Predicate," in *PAS* 56 (1956): 217–240.

Except for *Formal Logic*, all the works by De Morgan cited in the section on him are reprinted in *On the Syllogism, and Other Logical Writings*, edited by Peter Heath (London: Routledge and K. Paul, 1966). The best modern accounts of De Morgan are to be found in Lewis, op. cit.; Jørgensen, op. cit.; and Prior, op. cit.

On Boole, see Lewis, op. cit.; Jørgensen, op. cit.; and William C. Kneale and Martha Kneale, *The Development of Logic*. The best earlier expositions are by P. E. B. Jourdain, in "The Development of the Theories of Mathematical Logic and the Principles of Mathematics"; Venn, op. cit.; and Alexander MacFarlane, in *Principles of the Algebra of Logic* (Edinburgh: Douglas, 1879). A. T. Shearman, *Development of Symbolic Logic*, is also useful.

Jørgensen, Lewis, and Jourdain all give some account of Jevons. For earlier criticism, see Shearman, above, and F. H. Bradley, *Principles of Logic* (London: K. Paul, Trench, 1883).

On Jevons's machine, see Wolfe Mays and D. P. Henry, "Jevons and Logic," in *Mind* 62 (1953): 484–505; and Martin Gardner, *Logic Machines and Diagrams*.

There are appraisals of Venn in the works by Jørgensen, Jourdain, and Shearman. On Venn diagrams, see Lewis, op. cit.; Prior, op. cit.; Gardner, op. cit.; J. N. Keynes, *Studies and Exercises in Formal Logic*, 4th ed. (London: Macmillan, 1906); and almost any elementary logic text.

In addition to his book, MacColl published a series of seven papers, "The Calculus of Equivalent Statements," in *Proceedings of the London Mathematical Society* (1877–1898); a series of eight papers, "Symbolic Reasoning," in *Mind* (1880–1906); and "The Existential Import of Propositions," in *Mind* 30 (1905): 401–402, 578–580. On MacColl, see Jourdain, op. cit.; Prior, op. cit.; and Bertrand Russell's review of MacColl's *Symbolic Logic and Its Applications*, in *Mind* 30 (1906): 255–260.

Most of Peirce's logical writings are to be found in Vols. II, III, and IV of his *Collected Papers*, edited by Charles Hartshorne, Paul Weiss, and Arthur W. Burks, 8 vols. (Cambridge, MA: Harvard University Press, 1931–1958), but there is a discussion of logical paradoxes in Vol. V, Book 2, Paper 3, and one of the history of logic in Vol. VII, Book 2, Ch. 3, Sec. 10. His most developed and comprehensive logical paper is "On the Algebra of Logic: A Contribution to the Philosophy of Notation," Vol. III, Paper 13. "The Critic of Arguments," Paper 14 in the same volume, is comparatively easy reading and has a purple patch on rhemes and demonstratives. Peirce's existential graphs, which he thought were his most important contribution to logic, are the subject of Vol. IV, Book 2. *The Collected Papers* do not include some of Peirce's contributions to the *Century Dictionary*, such as the very suggestive article "Syllogism."

(A. N. P.)

HAMILTON. The nineteenth-century revival of logic in Britain, inaugurated by Whately and continued by, among others, George Bentham, chrétien, and Solly, owed much of its later impetus to the cosmopolitan learning and reforming zeal of Sir William Hamilton (1788–1856). A severely critical article by Hamilton on Whately and his followers, in the *Edinburgh Review* (1833; reprinted in his *Discussions*, London and Edinburgh, 1852), established his authority in the field, which was chiefly exercised thereafter in oral teaching from his Edinburgh chair. His scattered and largely polemical writings, including even the posthumous *Lectures on Logic* (Edinburgh and London, 1861), give a very imperfect account of his system, which acquired such order as it possessed from the works of his pupils and disciples: William Thomson and H. L. Mansel at Oxford; T. S. Baynes, John Veitch, and William Spalding in Scotland; and Francis Bowen in America. Hamilton's main service was to insist, following Kant, on the formal nature of logic and to break with the prevailing European tradition by exhibiting its forms primarily as relations of extension between classes. He also attempted to maintain a parallel logic of intension (or comprehension) for concepts, as the inverse of extension, but this approach, like others of its kind, was a predictable, if pardonable, failure.

Hamilton's most celebrated innovation, though it was far from being his invention, was the "thoroughgoing quantification of the predicate." By attaching the quantifiers "all" ("any") and "some" to the predicate, he obtained eight propositional forms, in place of the AEIO of tradition:

(1) All *A* is all *B*.

(2) All *A* is some *B*.

(3) Some *A* is all *B*.

(4) Some *A* is some *B*.

(5) Any *A* is not any *B*.

(6) Any *A* is not some *B*.

(7) Some *A* is not any *B*.

(8) Some *A* is not some *B*.

If "some" is read as "some only," these are all simply convertible and can thus be represented as the affirmations or denials of equations. The syllogisms made up of such propositions arrange themselves, tidily enough, into 108 valid moods, 12 positive and 24 negative, in each of 3 figures (Hamilton rejected the fourth). With this arrangement, a consolidated rule of inference, and a quasi-geometrical symbolism to depict it all, Hamilton claimed to have effected a major simplification—indeed, completion—of the Aristotelian scheme.

These hopes were not borne out in the sequel. His own vacillations in the use of "some" and neglect of the differences between "all" and "any" threw even professed Hamiltonians into confusion, and the status of his propositional forms (not to mention the validity of some of his syllogisms) was much disputed. The first, for example, has no contradictory in the set and appears (on the ordinary view of "some") to be a compound of (2) and (3). The two particular affirmatives, (3) and (4), found acceptance with some writers, such as Thomson and Spalding; but of the new negatives, (6) made few friends, and (8) none at all; since it is compatible with any of the others, it says so little as to be well-nigh vacuous. A more serious objection is that since forms (1) to (5) represent all the possible ways in which two classes can be related in extension (that is, the Gergonne relations), the last three must necessarily be ambiguous or redundant.

See also Hamilton, William; Kant, Immanuel; Mansel, Henry Longueville; Whately, Richard.

P. L. Heath (1967)

DE MORGAN. The above criticisms of Hamilton's system are primarily due to Augustus De Morgan (1806–1871), whom Hamilton, in 1846, had misguidedly accused of plagiarizing his quantification. In the famous and protracted controversy that ensued, De Morgan was led into a thorough dissection of the whole system, and subsequent critics, from Mill, Peirce, and Venn onward, have taken most of their ammunition from him.

Though greatly superior as to insight and technical ability, the logic of De Morgan has affinities with that of his rival in that it, too, lays stress on the autonomy of logic and on the extensional point of view. It equally shares Hamilton's interest in reforming and enlarging the traditional syllogistic, an enterprise now outdated, which has caused it to fall into unmerited neglect. Apart from his early *Formal Logic* (London, 1847; 2nd ed., Chicago, 1926), the bulk of De Morgan's logical writings are to be found in five memoirs (plus a sixth, still unpublished) contributed to the *Cambridge Philosophical Transactions* between 1846 and 1862. The *Syllabus of a Proposed System of Logic* (London, 1860) gives a cursory account of his scheme, as does his article "Logic" in the *English Cyclopaedia* (*Arts and Science Division*, V, London, 1860, pp. 340–354).

The basis of common logic, for De Morgan, consists in relations of partial or total inclusion, or exclusion, among classes. Where information about a majority of class members is available or where, as in the "numerically definite" syllogism, precise numbers are given, it is possible, as he shows, to draw valid conclusions of a non-Aristotelian type. But these conditions are seldom realized. A more radical departure is the admission into ordinary propositions of negative terms and class names (symbolized by lower-case letters), such that a term *X* and its "contrary" *x* between them exhaust the "universe of discourse" (a useful device that has since been generally adopted). Assuming these classes to have at least notional members, it follows that two classes and their contraries can be related in eight possible ways:

(1) All *X*'s are *Y*'s.

(2) All *x*'s are *y*'s.

(3) All *X*'s are *y*'s.

(4) All *x*'s are *Y*'s.

(5) Some *X*'s are *Y*'s.

(6) Some *x*'s are *y*'s.

(7) Some *X*'s are *y*'s.

(8) Some *x*'s are *Y*'s.

These can be rewritten without negative symbols as:

(1) All *X*'s are *Y*'s.

(2) All *Y*'s are *X*'s.

(3) No *X*'s are *Y*'s.

(4) Everything is either *X* or *Y*.

(5) Some *X*'s are *Y*'s.

(6) Some things are neither *X*'s nor *Y*'s.

(7) Some *X*'s are not *Y*'s.

(8) Some *Y*'s are not *X*'s.

Of these the contradictory pairs are (1) and (7), (2) and (8), (3) and (5), and (4) and (6). Since the distribution of terms is given or implied throughout, these forms are simply convertible by reading them in reverse. "Contraversion" (or obversion) is obtained by altering the distribution of a term, replacing it by its contrary, and denying the result. "All *X*'s are *Y*'s" becomes successively "No *X*'s are *y*'s," "All *y*'s are *x*'s," and "Everything is either *x* or *Y*." The procedure is the same for the other seven forms, making 32 possibilities in all.

De Morgan's rule of syllogism is either that both premises should be universal or, when only one is, that the middle term should have different quantities in each. Inference takes place by erasing the middle term and its quantities. Since, including the syllogisms of weakened conclusion, there are 4 basic patterns, and since 3 terms and their contraries can be paired off, in premises and conclusion, in 8 different ways, there are 32 valid syllogisms, of which half have two universal premises and 8 a universal conclusion.

To remedy the "terminal ambiguity" whereby the undistributed term in the universal "All *X*'s are *Y*'s" may refer indifferently to some or all of the *Y*'s, De Morgan investigated the complex propositions produced by combining pairs of elementary forms. It is in this connection that he gives the well-known rules for negation of conjunctions which have since received his name—though he did not, in fact, invent them.

In endeavoring to patch up Hamilton's quantified system De Morgan made further distinctions between "cumular" (collective) and "exemplar" (distributive) forms of predication; struggled, unavailingly, to bring the intensional interpretation of terms (as attributes) into

line with the extensional and to subsume both under a pure logic of terms (the "onymatic" system); and explored in passing such nontraditional forms of inference as the syllogisms of "undecided assertion" and "transposed quantity." More important is his recognition that the copula performs its function in inference, not as a sign of identity, but only through its role as a transitive and convertible relation.

De Morgan's generalization of the copula leads on, in his fourth Cambridge memoir, to a pioneer investigation of relations in general, which is the foundation of all subsequent work in the field. He there distinguishes a relation (say, "lover of") from its denial, its contrary, and its converse ("loved by"); proceeds to compound relations, or relative products ("*L* of *M* of"), and to quantified versions of these ("*L* of every *M*," "of none but *M*'s," etc.); and discusses a variety of equivalences that hold between these different sorts of relations and the rules for their discovery and manipulation. The purpose of this, typically enough, was to exhibit the syllogism in its most general form, as a series of combinations of relations. Despite the ingenuity and resource with which he treated it, this devotion to the syllogism was something of a weakness in De Morgan's work. It tethered him too closely to tradition, so that it was not until others exploited them that his own most fruitful discoveries were seen for what they were.

See also De Morgan, Augustus; Hamilton, William; Mill, John Stuart; Peirce, Charles Sanders; Venn, John.

P. L. Heath (1967)

BOOLE. George Boole (1815–1864) was the founder of modern mathematical logic. Nevertheless, few of his ideas are currently accepted in mainstream logic in the forms originally proposed by him. His learned and fertile mind conceived of several important hypotheses, the testing and modification of which changed the face of logic irrevocably. One of his most important hypotheses was that every proposition can be expressed using an algebraic equation suitably reinterpreted: that logic and algebra share a common uninterpreted formal language and thus also that they have similar problem types and similar methods.

The universal affirmative, or A proposition, "Every square is a rectangle" was expressed by $x = xy$, where x is the class of squares, y the class of rectangles, and xy the "Boolean or logical product" of x with y, the class of common members of x and y. The universal negative, or E proposition, "No rectangle is a circle" was expressed by $yz = 0$, where z is the class of circles and 0 is the empty class—an idea Boole introduced into logic. The conclusion "No square is a circle," $xz = 0$, which Aristotle and previous logicians deduced in one "intuitive" step, was derived by Boole using a chain of algebraic manipulations—illustrating another of his hypotheses, namely that on some level reasoning was mechanical or algorithmic.

He used 1 for the universe, or "universe of discourse," a ubiquitous expression in modern logic that Boole coined. He used the minus sign for "logical subtraction": $1 - x$ is the class of objects in the universe that are not in the class x. Using the above symbols, expression of the particular affirmative, or I proposition, "Some rectangle is a square" and the particular negative, or O proposition, "Some rectangle is not a square" as *inequalities* would have been easy: $yx \neq 0$ and $y(1 - x) \neq 0$. This is a point that Boole never mentioned and probably did not notice—Boole's hypothesis was that algebraic *equations* were sufficient. Instead, he conceived of a logical operator, now called Boole's vee, or the vee, which was to produce from a class x a resultant class vx supposed by him to be "indefinite in every respect except that it contains some individuals of the class [x in this case] to whose expression it is prefixed." Using the vee, Boole "expressed" the above $vy = vx$ and $vy = v(1 - x)$. The vee itself as well as the two "translations" have been criticized by later logicians—mainstream logic has not adopted Boole's vee, although its similarity to other more recent nonstandard operators has been noted—for example, the Hilbert epsilon.

Using the algebraic formal language, Boole was able to express several "laws of thought" analogous to laws of algebra; indeed some were expressed by the same equations used for laws of algebra—for example, the commutative law $xy = yx$. He employed his laws of thought in two unprecedented ways. First, regarding the equations as conditions on "unknowns," he created a wholly new theory of logical equation-solving using the laws of thought the way laws of algebra are used in numerical equation-solving. Second, regarding the most basic of his laws of thought as laws of logic, he created an axiomatization of logic. Boole realized that no "class logic" as such could treat the arguments now dealt with in truth-functional proposition logic. To meet this deficiency he proposed an ingenious reinterpretation of his system that, in his view, transformed it into something akin to propositional logic. In the process, he discovered key ideas now incorporated into modern truth-function logic, establishing himself as the first modern figure in any history of propositional logic. These are but three of Boole's many revolutionary innovations.

See also Aristotle; Boole, George; Propositions.

John Corcoran (2005)

JEVONS. It was the aim of William Stanley Jevons (1835–1882), himself a pupil of De Morgan, to render Boole's calculus more simple and "logical" by removing those of its features that he found "mysterious" and by reducing its operations to mechanical routine. He also professed, officially, to reject the extensional standpoint in favor of a "pure logic" of terms, or "qualities," though the result in practice was still effectively a class or propositional logic, conceived rather in the manner of De Morgan's "onymatic" system. These views are set forth in two pamphlets, *Pure Logic* (London and New York, 1864) and *The Substitution of Similars* (London, 1869; both reprinted in *Pure Logic and Other Minor Works*, London, 1890), and at greater length in *The Principles of Science* (2nd ed., London, 1887) and *Studies and Exercises in Deductive Logic* (London, 1884).

Jevons takes over the Boolean notations for conjunction and identity (AB, $A = B$) and admits negative classes, which he symbolizes, like De Morgan, by a small a, but makes no use of 1, the universal class, and dismisses as uninterpretable both the operations of subtraction and division and the various ill-favored symbols—$(1 - x)$, x/y, $0/0$, $1/0$, etc.—that result from their use. In the case of disjunction (written + or, more generally, $\cdot|\cdot$) Jevons follows the minority view of De Morgan and a few others in proposing to read it inclusively, so that $A + B$ is permitted to have common members, and $A + A = A$ (law of unity). The importance of this reform, almost universally accepted since, is that it abolishes the need for numerical coefficients, establishes the symmetry between conjunction and disjunction exhibited, for example, in De Morgan's laws, $\overline{AB} = a + b$ and $\overline{A + B} = ab$, and makes possible such other useful rules of simplification as the "law of absorption," $A + AB = A$.

Jevons conceives of classes as groups of individuals, and of propositions about such classes, or about qualities, as equations asserting a complete or partial identity between them. Thus, "All A is B" identifies all A's with those that are B—that is, $A = AB$—and the corresponding E-proposition is $A = Ab$. He symbolizes particular propositions, on occasion, by an arbitrary prefix, but pays little attention to them—or, indeed, to the problems of quantification in general. Inference consists merely of what he calls the "substitution of similars"—that is, the replacement of any term by another, stated in a premise to be identical to it. Thus, $A = AB$ and $B = BC$ yield, by substitution, $A = ABC = AC$, the conclusion.

Of more interest is the Jevonian method of indirect inference, based on what he calls the "logical alphabet." This alphabet, which amounts to no more than a Boolean expansion of 1, is constructed by listing all the possible combinations of the terms *A, B, C*, etc., together with their negatives, thus:

ABC	*aBC*
ABc	*aBc*
AbC	*abC*
Abc	*abc*

Any given premise, say *A = BC*, on being combined with each line in turn will be found inconsistent with some— that is, will yield an expression equal to 0. These lines being struck out, the remainder give the conclusion, though it still remains to consider the "inverse problem" (which Jevons saw but did not solve) of expressing the results in a single concise formula. Particular propositions are somewhat troublesome to handle on this scheme, which actually works better for propositions than for classes. But with many terms the process soon becomes tedious in either case, and it was to remedy this that Jevons invented his "logical abacus" and "logical piano," contrivances which operate mechanically on the same principle, namely the employment of the premises to eliminate inconsistent combinations from a matrix already set up on the machine. The development of the modern computer has revived interest in Jevons's pioneer device and in his very able description of its workings. For the rest, Jevons's "equational logic," though famous in its day, is now remembered chiefly for the technical improvements on Boole's procedure that it helped to bring into use.

See also Logic Machines.

P. L. Heath (1967)

VENN. The logic of John Venn (1834–1923), sketched briefly in the *Princeton Review* (1880) and more fully elaborated in his *Symbolic Logic* (London, 1881), shows a greater understanding of George Boole's intentions and a better acquaintance with the historical background than had yet been displayed by anyone else. Though he did not suppose the new methods to have any great practical advantage over the old, he saw no reason, either, to suspect them of being anything more than a generalization of traditional practices, couched, for convenience, in a mathematical form. He therefore resisted the Jevonian simplifications and was at pains to bring out the logical significance of such operations as subtraction and division, though the latter is admitted to merit inclusion

more on grounds of consistency than for any use made of it in the reasoning of everyday life.

Venn's own account of the matter proceeds from what he calls the "compartmental," or "existential," view of logic, whose purpose is to set out the possible ways in which the four classes designated by *x, y,* and their negatives, in combination, may have one or more of their components empty. Omitting the case where all four compartments are unoccupied, this yields fifteen forms of proposition, compared with the four that arise on the traditional, or predication, view, whereby an attribute is asserted or denied of a class, and the five that emerge from diagrammatic consideration of the ways in which two nonempty classes may include, exclude, or overlap one another. Each view has its merits, in Venn's opinion, the choice between them being ultimately a conventional one.

This leads Venn to the discussion of another vexed issue, the "existential import" of propositions. Traditional logic must in consistency assume that its classes have members and nonmembers alike, and its universal propositions are thereby rendered hypothetical. To Venn it was clearer what the universal denies than what it asserts, and he therefore proposed to write A, "All *x* is *y*," as $x\bar{y} = 0$ and E, "No *x* is *y*," as $xy = 0$. These propositions are definite, yet they do not require members in *x* or *y* to make them true, since they deny only the existence of members in the common class. Particular propositions do, however, imply the presence of members in each class, since they contradict the universals; they are therefore to be written I, $xy \neq 0$, and O, $x\bar{y} \neq 0$, respectively. This was an improvement on Boole's use of indefinite symbols and has since been generally adopted, though one consequence of it (also noted by Hugh MacColl) is that subalternation ceases to be valid and that the "syllogisms of weakened conclusion" which depend on it have therefore to be rejected.

Venn was not much enamored of the syllogism, but he deserves the gratitude of all beginners in the subject for what is probably his best-known contribution to logic, the diagrams that bear his name. These are, in effect, graphical representations of the algebraic processes introduced by Boole and mechanically illustrated in Jevons's alphabet: The partitioning of a universe in terms of the possible combinations of *x, y,* and so on, and the elimination of those subdivisions inconsistent with the premises given. For two terms a pair of intersecting circles (*x* and *y*) on a ground give the four compartments $xy + x\bar{y} + \bar{x}y + \bar{x}\bar{y} = 1$ (Figure 1). Three interlaced circles (Figure 2) depict the eight combinations of Jevons's table,

FIGURE 1

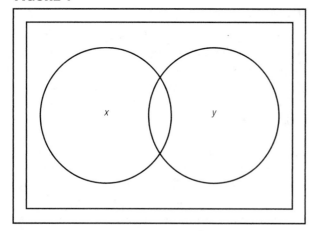

FIGURE 2

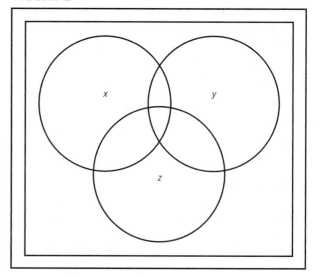

given earlier. The effect of a universal premise is to declare one or more compartments to be empty, shown by shading the area in question. A particular premise indicates that one or more compartments have occupants, shown by a cross (which may lie ambiguously on the boundary between two areas). The conclusion can then be read off, in various ways, by inspection. By the use of ellipses the same principle can be employed for up to five terms, but it then becomes unwieldy, especially in the "inverse problem" of formulating the outcome, so that one or another of the square diagrams devised by later authors is at that stage generally preferable. With suitable modifications the method can also be extended to the calculus of propositions. Though Venn did not carry this extension far, he was led by it to an early realization of the truth-functional character of the relation of material implication.

The merit of Venn's work lies not in its original departures, which are few, but rather in the light it throws on the obscurities of Boole's procedure and in its very careful and fair discussion of opposing views.

See also Boole, George; Jevons, William Stanley; Venn, John.

P. L. Heath (1967)

CARROLL. The contributions of Lewis Carroll (Charles L. Dodgson, 1832–1898) to logic consist of several pieces published between 1887 and 1899. *The Game of Logic* (London, 1887) is a book written for young people to teach them to reason logically by solving syllogisms using diagrams and colored counters. His diagrammatic method is a visual logic system that we know now to be sound and complete.

In *Symbolic Logic, Part I* (London, 1896) Carroll developed two formal methods to solve syllogisms and

sorites. The first is the Method of Underscoring that is dependent on his idiosyncratic algebraic notation that he called the Method of Subscripts. The second is his Method of Diagrams, which he extended to handle more than three terms (classes), but without providing examples. However, his diagrammatic system is an improvement over that of his contemporary, John Venn, because first, unlike Venn's system, Carroll's can handle existential statements. Second, as A. Macula showed in 1995, diagrams for ten terms (sets) or more can be drawn more easily than Venn diagrams for a large number of sets. Finally, the diagrams are self-similar and can be generated by a linear iterative process. Carroll used his method to reduce the nineteen or more valid forms of inference codified by medieval Aristotelian logicians first to fifteen forms and then to just three formulas.

Carroll published two pieces in the journal *Mind*. The first, "A Logical Paradox" (N. S. vol. 3, 1894, 436–438) is an example of hypothetical propositions. W. W. Bartley III remarks in the second edition of his book, *Lewis Carroll's Symbolic Logic* (1986, p. 505) that for about eighty years eminent logicians and philosophers failed to see this problem as little more than a routine exercise in Boolean algebra. Of the eleven questions Dodgson sent to *The Educational Times* (ten on mathematical topics) the substance of one, Question 14122, (February 1, 1899, vol. lii, p. 93) on his logical paradox, had appeared as a "Note" to his 1894 *Mind* article. H. MacColl and H. W. Curjel provided (different) solutions. The second piece in *Mind*, "What the Tortoise Said to Achilles" (N. S. vol. 4, 1895, 278–280) is a humorous example of an important problem about logical inference that Carroll was perhaps the first to recognize: the rule allowing a conclusion to be drawn from a set of premises cannot itself be treated as an additional premise without generating an infinite regress.

We see in Bartley's 1986 publication of Carroll's lost book, *Symbolic Logic, Part II*, that Carroll introduced two additional methods of formal logic. The first, the method of barred premises, a direct approach to the solution of problems involving multiliteral statements is an extension of his Method of Underscoring. The second and most important, the Method of Trees, a mechanical test of validity using a *reductio ad absurdum* argument, is the earliest modern use of a truth tree to reason in the logic of classes. It uses one inference rule (binary resolution) and a restriction strategy (set of support) to improve the efficiency of the construction. His tree method is a sound and complete formal logic system for sorites.

See also Carroll, Lewis; Logic Diagrams; Venn, John.

Bibliography

Abeles, Francine F. "Lewis Carroll's Formal Logic." *History and Philosophy of Logic* 26 (2005): 33–46.

Bartley, William W., III, ed. *Lewis Carroll's Symbolic Logic.* 2nd ed. New York: Clarkson N. Potter, 1986.

Beth, Evert W. *The Foundations of Mathematics.* Amsterdam: North Holland, 1965.

Macula, Anthony J. "Lewis Carroll and the Enumeration of Minimal Covers." *Mathematics Magazine* 69 (1995): 269–274.

Wos, Larry, et al. *Automated Reasoning.* Englewood Cliffs, NJ: Prentice-Hall, 1984.

Francine F. Abeles (2005)

PEIRCE. The logical work of Charles Sanders Peirce (1839–1914) was an unusual blend of the traditional and the modern. His early paper "Memoranda concerning the Aristotelian Syllogism," read and distributed in 1866, adapted to the second and third syllogistic figures Kant's description of first-figure reasoning as the subsumption of a case under a rule, and in later papers he exhibited analogy and induction as probabilistic weakenings of the second and third figures thus conceived. In 1867, independently of Jevons, Peirce improved Boole's logical algebra by identifying logical addition with the inclusive rather than the exclusive sense of "either-or." In 1870, inspired by De Morgan's pioneer work on the logic of relations, he extended Boole's method of algebraic analogy to this discipline, noticed that there are three-termed as well as two-termed relations, and introduced the sign "—<" for class inclusion, considered an analogue of the arithmetical "≤."

In 1880, Peirce began to use the symbol "—<" indifferently for class inclusion, implication, and the "therefore" of inference. It became one of his persistent themes that the distinction between terms, propositions, and inferences is of little logical importance. For him all propositions are, in the end, implications (this thesis is bound up with his pragmatic theory of meaning) and as such are simply inferences deprived of an element of assertiveness; terms, at least general terms, are propositions deprived of a subject. General terms are "rhemes," or, as we would now say, "open sentences," sentences with gaps where names might go. Such sentences with gaps are in a broad sense relative terms, the number of gaps indicating what Peirce called the "adinity" of the relation. Thus, "— loves —" represents a "dyadic" relation,"— gives — to —" a "triadic" one, and so on. Extending this conception downward, Peirce described an ordinary predicative term, such as "— is a man," as representing a "monadic" relation and a complete sentence, with no gaps at all, as representing a "medadic" one.

As Frege did with his "concepts," Peirce compared his "rhemes" to unsaturated chemical radicals having various valencies. Unlike Frege, however, he did not subsume rhemes under functions, like "The square of —," as the special case in which the value of the function for a given argument is a truth-value. Frege's procedure underlined the resemblance between a completed proposition and a name; for Peirce a completed proposition was rather a special case of a predicate. Nevertheless, Peirce pioneered (in 1885) the use of truth-value calculations in establishing logical laws and also foreshadowed many-valued logic by suggesting that there might be an infinity of degrees of falsehood, with truth as the zero.

A gap in a rheme may be filled, in the simplest case, by what Peirce called an "index." He divided signs into indices, which operate through some physical connection with what they signify; icons, which operate through some resemblance to what they signify; and symbols, which acquire their meaning by convention. An ordinary proper name is an "icon of an index"; it is (when uttered) a noise that resembles the noise that was made when we were introduced to the person named. A simple index would be, for example, a demonstrative pronoun accompanied by a pointing gesture. Peirce regarded the phrase "demonstrative pronouns" as an inaccurate description—it would be more appropriate to call a noun a "prodemonstrative." A common noun, for Peirce, is only an inseparable element in a rheme (for example, "man" in "is a man").

Instead of directly filling a gap in a rheme with an index, we may say either "I can find you an object such that it—" ("is a man," "loves Susan," etc.) or "Take anything you like and it —" ("is mortal if human," etc.). These are the particular and universal quantifiers, which Peirce introduced into his logic—independently of Frege, but with some debt to his own student O. H. Mitchell—in 1883. He represented them with the mathematical symbols "Σ" and "$\prod$" for continued sums and products. If we write "$a = 0$" for "a is false" and "$a \to 0$" for "a is true," $\Sigma_i a_i$ or "For some individual i, a_i," will have for its value the sum of the values of the possible a_i's and therefore will be $\to 0$ (that is, true) if and only if at least one of the a_i's is $\to$ 0, whereas $\prod_i a_i$ or "For any individual i, a_i," will have for its value the product of the values of the possible a_i's and therefore will be $\to 0$ if and only if all of the a_i's are $\to 0$. Peirce was aware of the possibility of putting any quantified expression into what is now called prenex normal form, with all the quantifiers at the beginning. He also, in what he called second-intentional logic, quantified over variables other than those standing for indices.

Every implication, Peirce came to believe, has an implicit or explicit initial quantifier—that is, is of the form $\prod_i(a_i \prec b_i)$, "For any i, if a_i, then b_i." The i's may be either ordinary individuals *of* which our a and b may be true, or instants *at* which they may be true, or possible states of affairs *in* which they may be true; for example, "If it rains it pours" may mean "For any instant i, if it rains at i, it pours at i" or "For any possible state of affairs i, if it rains in i, it pours in i." But in the latter case we may consider wider or narrower ranges of possibility, and if we limit ourselves to the actual state of affairs, the quantifier may be dropped.

Peirce made several attempts to define negation in terms of implication, and in 1885 he produced a set of axioms for the propositional calculus with implication accepted as an undefined operator and negation defined as the implication of a proposition from which anything at all would follow. This was the second set of axioms sufficient for the propositional calculus to be produced in the history of the subject (the first being Frege's of 1879) and the first set to use the curious law $((a \prec b) \prec a) \prec a$, now called Peirce's law. But Peirce experimented with other types of systems also, and in 1880 he anticipated H. M. Sheffer in showing that all truth-functions can be defined in terms of "Neither — nor —" and "Not both — and —." The "not" within a proposition (as opposed to "It is not the case that —," governing the whole), which forms the "negative propositions" of traditional logic, he regarded as expressing the relation of otherness, and he

worked out what properties of this relation are reflected in traditional logical laws. For example, the law of contraposition, "'Every A is a B' entails that whatever is not a B is not an A," follows from the mere fact that otherness is a relation, for whatever relative term R may be, if every A is a B, then whatever is an R (for instance, an other) of every B is an R of every A.

Peirce thought it desirable that logical formulas should reflect the structure of the facts or thoughts which they express and so be, in his sense, "icons"—that is, signs operating by resemblance to what they signify—and he sought constantly to develop symbolisms that were genuinely "iconic." In his later years he came to regard this as best achieved by a system of diagrams which he called "existential graphs." Typically, he attempted to represent his graph for "If A then B" as basic, but in fact his diagrams are most easily understood as starting from the representation of "and" by juxtaposition and of "not" by enclosure in a bracket or circle or square. $(A(B))$, which is his graph for "If A then B," reads off naturally as "Not both A and not B." Rules of inference are represented as permissions to alter the graphs by insertions and erasures; for example:

(R1) We may insert or remove double enclosures at will, provided that there is no symbol caught between the two enclosures; for instance, we may pass from A to $((A))$, i.e., to "Not not A," and back, but not from $(A(B))$ to AB.

(R2) Any symbol may be removed from an evenly enclosed graph (including a completely unenclosed one) or added to an oddly enclosed one; for instance, we may pass from AB, i.e., "A and B," to A, or from $(A(BC))$ to $(A(B))$, i.e., from "If A then both B and C" to "If A then B," or from (A) to (AB), i.e., from "Not A" to "Not both A and B."

(R3) We may repeat a symbol across an enclosure immediately interior to the symbol's own, and if a symbol is already thus repeated, we may remove it from the inner enclosure; for instance, we may pass from $(A(B))$ to $(A(AB))$, i.e., from "If A then B" to "If A then both A and B," or from $A(AB)$ to $A(B)$, i.e., from "A and not both A and B" to "A and not B."

If a graph is such that these permissions will enable us to transform it into any graph at all, that graph is "absurd" and its negation a logical truth. For example, $A(A)$, "Both A and not A," leads by R2 to $A((B)A)$, where B is any graph you please, and this leads by R3 to $A((B))$, this by R2 to $((B))$, and this by R1 to B. Hence, $(A(A))$, "If A then A," is a logical truth. For clarity Peirce suggested drawing rectangular enclosures, with evenly enclosed symbols written on the left and oddly enclosed ones on the right. For example, Figure 3 is a representation of $(A(B(C))$, "If A then (B but not C)." This arrangement makes it clear that Peirce was, in effect, setting up what are nowadays called "semantic tableaux," in the manner of E. W. Beth.

Peirce also thought of logical truth as represented by the blank sheet on which his graphs were drawn and absurdity by an enclosure with nothing but the blank graph sheet inside it. Since by R2 we may inscribe anything whatever in such an otherwise blank enclosure, this enclosure would in fact represent an absurdity in the previous sense of a graph that can be transformed into any graph whatsoever. "If A then absurdity," Peirce's favorite definition of "Not A," would then be strictly "$(A((\quad)))$" ("If A then B" is "$(A(B))$," and here we put "$(\quad)$" for B), but this assumes that in representing the absurd as "$(\quad)$" we already understand simple enclosure as negation, and in attempting to modify his symbolism in ways which would avoid this assumption Peirce was led into occasional unnecessary trouble.

Although Peirce was one of the inventors of bound variables, in his graphs for quantified formulas he explicitly dispensed with them in favor of what he called "lines of identity," a device recently put to the same purpose, though informally, by W. V. Quine and Peter Geach. A monadic rheme may be written as "— A" or "A —," the single valency line being close enough to be thought of as part of the symbol, and on its own this symbol is read as "Something is A." If "— B" is added to this, the whole, "A — — B," of course, means "Something is A and something is B." But if the valency lines are joined by a "line of identity," to give us "A —— B," this means "Something is A and *that same thing* is B," or "Something is at once A and B." In the common systems this identification of the subjects of which A and B are predicated is effected by attaching these predicates to the same bound variable, thus: "For some x, x is A and x is B." Again, "If anything is A then *that same thing* is B" is distinguished in the common systems from the more indefinite "If anything is A then something is B" by writing the former with a common bound variable, thus: "For any x, if x is A then x is B." In Peirce's graphs this is done by tightening "(— A (— B))" to "$(A(B))$" or "$(A —(B))$." To give some examples with dyadic rhemes, "Every A is an R of some B" comes out as "$(A —(R — B))$"; "Some B is R'd by every A" as "$(A —(R)— B$"; and "Every A is an R of itself" as "$(A —(R))$" or "$(A ——(R)$."

This "Beta part" of Peirce's graphs, of course, contains special rules for the transformation of lines of iden-

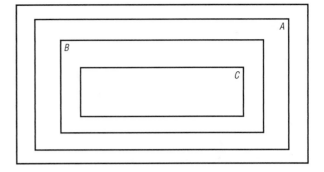

FIGURE 3

tity. For example, the additions and erasures of terms permitted by R2 may be extended to terms attached to others by lines of identity; thus, we may pass from "A —— B," "Something is at once A and B," to the plain "— B," "Something is B." Peirce said that the blank sheet—which is left here when "A —" with its line of identity is removed and which represents accepted truth when considered as a medad—represents an accepted existent when considered as a monad.

Since lines of identity may themselves be treated as dyadic rhemes and subjected to enclosure, the graphs cover identity theory and, therefore, the arithmetic of specific integers, as well as the theory of first-order quantification. For example, "There are at least two A's" will be "A —(—)— A"—that is, "Something is an A, and something that *is not* that thing is also an A." But the graphs do not readily lend themselves to the representation of higher-order quantifications, such as "Some qualities belong to everything and others to some things only," although Peirce made some rather clumsy efforts in this direction. More successful, but only adumbrated in outline, was his extension of his method to modal logic by using separate sheets for different possible worlds. This procedure is very like that now adopted by S. A. Kripke) and also echoes medieval theories of "ampliation."

There is probably no logical writer who has been more rich in original suggestions than Peirce, and his papers are a mine that has still to be fully worked. He was, at the same time, more aware than any of his contemporaries of the contributions made by their ancient and medieval predecessors. He held and persuasively supported a theory that Aristotle had anticipated (in a chapter of the *Prior Analytics* (now missing) later derivations of simple conversion from the laws of identity and syllogism, and he saw the significance of the Megarian controversy over the nature of implication and of the distinctions drawn by the Schoolmen in their theory of *consequentiae*.

Peirce's immediate circle in America included two logicians of some distinction: O. H. Mitchell, from whom Peirce derived the germ of his device of quantification, and Christine Ladd Franklin (1847–1930), who used eight "copulae" to construct De Morgan's eight categorical forms and exhibited syllogisms in different figures as derivable from "inconsistent triads," or "antilogisms." An antilogism states that a certain three propositions—for example, "Every Y is a Z," "Every X is a Y," and "Not every X is a Z"—cannot all be true: hence (syllogism 1), the first and second jointly imply the denial of the third; also (syllogism 2), the first and third jointly imply the denial of the second; also (syllogism 3), the third and second jointly imply the denial of the first.

See also Boole, George; De Morgan, Augustus; Existence; Frege, Gottlob; Jevons, William Stanley; Kant, Immanuel; Modal Logic; Peirce, Charles Sanders; Quine, Willard Van Orman.

A. N. Prior (1967)

THE HERITAGE OF KANT AND MILL. The development of logic, at least of formal logic, in the nineteenth century was largely independent of the general development of philosophy during the same period. Of the logicians considered in the preceding section only C. S. Peirce and perhaps William Hamilton were of importance in branches of philosophy other than logic, and the persons who were of most importance in other branches of philosophy contributed nothing whatsoever to technical developments of the sort here described. These persons did not ignore logic altogether, however, nor did competent logicians entirely ignore them. It will be helpful, therefore, to break the chronological order at this point and to glance back at these philosophical developments and influences.

In the nineteenth century, as in the eighteenth, there were divergent Continental and British philosophical influences, but the Continental stream, stemming from Immanuel Kant (1724–1804), was now not so much rationalistic as idealistic, and in logic it was increasingly antiformal, antimathematical, and antitechnical. Kant himself could not be described as antiformal; he had a quite exalted view of the place of formal logic in philosophy. Unfortunately, however, he thought of formal logic not as a field for new developments but as the first science to have reached perfection—it had reached perfection, he said, with the work of Aristotle. Even Kant's "Aristotelianism" was of the sadly truncated variety that had been characteristic of the interregnum. Slightly systematizing what he took to be Aristotelian logic, he divided "judgments" according to their "quantity" into universal, par-

ticular, and singular; according to their quality into affirmative (X is Y), negative (X is-not Y) and infinite (X is not-Y); according to what he called "relation" into categorical, hypothetical (that is, conditional), and disjunctive; and according to modality into apodictic (asserting necessity or impossibility), assertoric, and problematic (asserting possibility). The division according to quality is particularly absurd; where would one put, for example, the forms "X is-not not-Y" and "Not-X is Y"? More influential was his subdivision of affirmative categoricals into "analytic," in which the predicate concept is implicitly contained in the subject concept, and "synthetic," in which it is not. "Body is extended," for example, is analytic because what is meant by a body is precisely an extended substance.

The empiricism that had characterized British philosophy in the eighteenth century was still in evidence in the nineteenth in the work of John Stuart Mill (1806–1873), but Mill was not, as the eighteenth-century British empiricists had been, antilogical or antimathematical. He did not personally advance the young science of mathematical logic, but he was not hostile to it, and in the later nineteenth century it was possible for J. N. Keynes and W. E. Johnson to develop a logical style that was indebted almost equally to Mill and to the mathematicians.

Mill's own formal logic, like Kant's, was rather thin, and for details he referred his readers to Richard Whately; the greater part of his *System of Logic* (London, 1843) is devoted to what would now be called scientific method. Its first two books, however, contain well-developed theories about the meaning of various types of words and sentences and about the nature of syllogistic reasoning. It may be added here that the propositions corresponding to what Kant called analytic judgments were described by Mill as "merely verbal."

In the later nineteenth century there was considerable crossing of geographical and philosophical boundaries. Christoph Sigwart (1830–1904), in Germany, was indebted to Mill as well as to Kant; Franz Brentano (1838–1917), in Austria, owed much to Mill and nothing at all to Kant. The antimathematical logical tradition of Kant and G. W. F. Hegel was carried further in England by F. H. Bradley and Bernard Bosanquet, just when logic as an exact science was being given in Germany a new impetus by Gottlob Frege.

See also Aristotle; Bosanquet, Bernard; Bradley, Francis Herbert; Brentano, Franz; Empiricism; Frege, Gottlob; Hamilton, William; Hegel, Georg Wilhelm Friedrich;

Johnson, William Ernest; Kant, Immanuel; Logic, Traditional; Mill, John Stuart; Peirce, Charles Sanders; Sigwart, Christoph; Whately, Richard.

Bibliography

TEXTS

Hegel, G. W. F. *Wissenschaft der Logik*, Vol. I: *Die objektive Logik*, 2 vols. Nuremberg, 1812–1813. Vol. II: *Die subjektive Logik*. Nuremberg, 1816. Translated by W. H. Johnson and L. G. Struthers as *The Science of Logic*, 2 vols. London, 1929.

Kant, Immanuel. *Kritik der reinen Vernunft*. Riga: Hartknoch, 1781; 2nd ed., 1787. Translated by Norman Kemp Smith as *Critique of Pure Reason*. London: Macmillan, 1929.

Lotze, R. H. *Logik*. Leipzig, 1880. Translated by Helen Dendy as *Logic*. Oxford, 1884.

Mill, J. S. *An Examination of Sir William Hamilton's Philosophy*, 2nd ed. London: Longman, Green, Longman, Roberts and Green, 1865.

Mill, J. S. *A System of Logic*. London, 1843; 8th ed., 1872.

Sigwart, Christoph. *Logik*, 2 vols. Tübingen, 1873–1878. Translated by Helen Dendy as *Logic*, 2 vols. London, 1890.

A. N. Prior (1967)

KEYNES. John Neville Keynes (1852–1949) was for a large part of his long life registrar of the University of Cambridge. His first contribution to logic was an article in *Mind* in 1879, in which he defended formal logic as a substantial discipline distinguishable alike from the philosophical logic being pursued by the heirs of Kant and Hegel, from the "empirical" (largely inductive) logic developed by the heirs of J. S. Mill, and from the mathematical logic lately started on its career by Boole and De Morgan.

In 1884, Keynes's view of the subject was exhibited in greater detail in the first edition of his *Studies and Exercises in Formal Logic*. This work dealt, in the traditional manner, successively with terms, judgments, and syllogisms, but it had a fourth part in which essentially Boolean material was presented as a logic of categorical propositions with conjunctive, disjunctive, and negative terms and conjunctive and disjunctive compounds of these propositions. Each chapter in the book consisted of a number of well-constructed exercises, sometimes with introductory remarks and often with lengthy comments. Part I, on terms, was much influenced by the treatment of names in Book I of Mill's *System of Logic*. Part II was distinguished by a very judicious discussion, in Chapter 8, of the problems raised by Brentano and Venn about the existential import of categorical propositions.

In successive revisions and enlargements in 1887, 1894, and 1906 the chapters took on the more normal shape of extended discussions with exercises at the end.

Part IV (on compound and complex propositions) was transformed into a long appendix, and much new material was incorporated. W. E. Johnson, in the preface to his own logic, was able to refer to the final product as "Dr. Keynes's classical work, in which the last word has been said on most of the fundamental problems of the subject." To this result Johnson himself generously contributed; he and Keynes had frequent and regular discussions of logical problems, and many of the footnotes in Keynes's third and fourth editions express his indebtedness to Johnson. For example, Keynes owed to Johnson the distinction between "conditional" and "true hypothetical" propositions that Russell later dealt with more precisely as one between formal and material implication.

Keynes's literary style was of singular clarity and distinction, and he dealt urbanely but decisively with the many sophistries and confusions that were current, especially among logical writers of a broadly idealist stamp, such as Bosanquet and Bradley. At the same time, he paid attention, particularly in his final edition, to the broadly "intensional" considerations to which these writers were perhaps more sensitive than many whose standards of logical rigor were higher. He handled modal distinctions, for example, with the same neatness and skill which he brought to other topics, and he anticipated C. I. Lewis in drawing attention to what are now called the paradoxes of strict implication.

The development of Keynes's thought from edition to edition, as he brought it to bear on one topic after another, is fascinating to examine. For instance in dealing with what Mill called the connotation and denotation of general names he distinguished even in the first edition between (1) the connotation proper—that is, the set of attributes that we select by convention as those that an object must have if we are to give the name to it—and (2) the totality of attributes possessed in common by all the attributes to which the name applies. In the second edition he suggested that for (2) we might use the Port-Royalists's term "comprehension." Thus, the connotation being selected by convention, objective facts determine the name's denotation, that is, which objects have the attributes entitling them to the name, and further objective facts determine the comprehension, that is, which attributes beyond the connotation these objects have in common. But in the third edition Keynes noted that we might alternatively fix the application of a name by an "exemplification," a selection not of attributes but of objects, with respect to which we decide that we will give a certain name to anything which possesses all the attributes that these objects have in common (making an exception, as Johnson reminded Keynes that we would have to do, of such attributes as that of having been selected for this purpose). When we proceed this way convention fixes the exemplification, and the facts determine the comprehension and then the denotation.

See also Boole, George; Bosanquet, Bernard; Bradley, Francis Herbert; Brentano, Franz; De Morgan, Augustus; Existence; Hegel, Georg Wilhelm Friedrich; Kant, Immanuel; Lewis, Clarence Irving; Mill, John Stuart; Modal Logic; Russell, Bertrand Arthur William; Venn, John.

A. N. Prior (1967)

JOHNSON. Keynes's collaborator William Ernest Johnson (1858–1931) did not publish Part I of his own *Logic* until 1921 (Part II, 1922; Part III, 1924), although he had published a series of three articles titled "The Logical Calculus" in *Mind* in 1892 (17: 3–30, 235–250, 340–357) and two titled "The Analysis of Thinking" in *Mind* in 1918 (27: 1–21, 133–151). In the first series the variables in Boolean equations were explicitly given the propositional interpretation, the logical product ("x and y") being represented by juxtaposition and negation by a superimposed bar. The logical product and negation being taken as primitive, "If x then y" is defined as "Not (x and not y)"—that is, $\overline{x\bar{y}}$—the logical sum "x or y" as "Not (not x and not y)," and universal and particular quantification as continued logical multiplication and addition. "The Analysis of Thinking" is more philosophical and seems to reflect the influence of G. F. Stout's *Analytic Psychology*.

Johnson's *Logic* exhibits an attractive combination of the formal elegance of his 1892 articles with the philosophical penetration of those of 1918. In some ways—for example, in his extensive discussion of "problematic induction" (that is, scientific generalization)—he played Mill to Keynes's Whately. His book is now best known for its development of the distinction between "determinables" and "determinates," in Part I, Chapter 11. A "determinable" is one of the broad bases of distinction that may be found in objects, such as color, shape, size. Under each of these fall more or less determinate characteristics, such as red, blue, and so on, under color (and scarlet, crimson, etc. as more determinate forms of red). Johnson used this distinction as the basis of many further developments. In Part II, Chapter 10, for example, Johnson discussed what he called "demonstrative induction," in which a universal conclusion is deduced from a singular premise by the help of an "all-or-nothing" proposition. From "Either every S is P or every S is not P" and

"This S is P" we can infer "Every S is P." A natural extension is the form of reasoning in which the major premise asserts that every S exhibits the same determinate form of the determinable P (for instance, every specimen of a given element has the same atomic number) and the minor that this S exhibits the determinate form p of this determinable; hence, every S is p. (Cf. Mill on "uniform uniformities" in his *System of Logic*, Book III, Ch. 4, Sec. 2.)

Johnson presented many critical asides concerning Russell's *Principles of Mathematics*, the most valuable being in Part II, Chapter 3, "Symbolism and Functions."

See also Mill, John Stuart; Russell, Bertrand Arthur William; Stout, George Frederick; Whately, Richard.

Bibliography

WORKS ON JOHNSON

Acute and careful, as well as captious, criticism of Johnson is contained in H. W. B. Joseph's "What Does Mr. W. E. Johnson Mean by a Proposition?," in *Mind* 36 (1927): 448–466, and 37 (1928): 21–39. Johnson's views are also discussed in A. N. Prior's "Determinables, Determinates and Determinants," in *Mind* 58 (1949): 1–20, 178–194. There is a fine informative obituary of Johnson by C. D. Broad in *Ethics and the History of Philosophy* (London: Routledge, 1952).

A. N. Prior (1967)

FROM FREGE TO GÖDEL

Twentieth-century logic, and even late nineteenth-century logic, cannot be properly understood without some acquaintance not only with earlier nineteenth-century logic but also with nineteenth-century mathematics. The final section of our survey therefore begins with a sketch of the influence of nineteenth-century mathematics on the major logical developments of both the Boolean and the more recent periods. This will be followed by discussions of particular logicians.

Bibliography

(Secondary material on the logicians discussed in the final section of the article is to be found mainly in the first two parts of the bibliography.)

Carnap, Rudolf. *Foundations of Logic and Mathematics.* Chicago: University of Chicago Press, 1939. This is Vol. I, no. 3, of *International Encyclopedia of Unified Science.*

Carnap, Rudolf. *Introduction to Semantics.* Cambridge, MA: Harvard University Press, 1942.

Carnap, Rudolf. *Meaning and Necessity.* 2nd, enl. ed. Chicago: University of Chicago Press, 1956.

Church, Alonzo. *Introduction to Mathematical Logic.* Vol. I. Princeton, NJ: Princeton University Press, 1956.

Church, Alonzo. "A Note on the Entscheidungsproblem." *Journal of Symbolic Logic* 1 (1936): 40–41. See also the correction, ibid., 101–102.

Church, Alonzo. "An Unsolvable Problem of Elementary Number Theory." *American Journal of Mathematics* 58 (1936): 345–363.

Frege, Gottlob. *Translations from the Philosophical Writings of Gottlob Frege*, edited by Peter Geach and Max Black. New York: Philosophical Library, 1952.

Gentzen, Gerhard. "Beweisbarkeit und Unbeweisbarkeit von Anfangsfällen der transfiniten Induktion in der reinen Zahlen-theorie." *Mathematische Annalen* 119 (1943): 140–161.

Gentzen, Gerhard. "Neue Fassung des Widerspruchsfreiheitsbeweises für die reine Zahlentheorie." *Forschungen zur Logik und zur Grundlegung der exakten Wissenschaften*, n.s., 4 (1938): 19–44.

Gentzen, Gerhard. "Untersuchungen über das logische Schliessen." *Mathematische Zeitschrift* 39 (1934): 176–210, 405–431. Translated into French, with commentary, by R. Feys and J. Ladrière as *Recherches sur la déduction logique.* Paris, 1955.

Gentzen, Gerhard. "Die Widerspruchsfreiheit der reinen Zahlentheorie." *Mathematische Annalen* 112 (1936): 493–565.

Gödel, Kurt. Articles on intuitionist logic and number theory. *Ergebnisse eines mathematischen Kolloquiums* 4 (1933): 34–38, 40.

Gödel, Kurt. *The Consistency of the Axiom of Choice and of the Generalized Continuum-Hypothesis with the Axioms of Set Theory.* Princeton, NJ: Princeton University Press, 1940; rev. ed., 1951.

Gödel, Kurt. "What Is Cantor's Continuum Problem?" *American Mathematical Monthly* 54 (1947): 515–525.

Herbrand, Jacques. "Sur le Problème fondamental de la logique mathématique." *Comptes rendus des séances de la Société des Sciences et des Lettres de Varsovie*, Classe III, 24 (1931): 12–56.

Hilbert, David. *Gesammelte Abhandlungen.* 3 vols. Berlin: Springer, 1932–1935.

Hilbert, David, and Paul Bernays. *Grundlagen der Mathematik.* 2 vols. Berlin: Springer, 1934–1939.

Post, Emil. "Formal Reductions of the General Combinatorial Decision Problem." *American Journal of Mathematics* 65 (1943): 197–215.

Post, Emil. "Recursively Enumerable Sets of Positive Integers and Their Decision Problems." *Bulletin of the American Mathematical Society* 50 (1944): 284–316.

Post, Emil. "Recursive Unsolvability of a Problem of Thue." *Journal of Symbolic Logic* 12 (1947): 1–11.

Quine, W. V. *Set Theory and Its Logic.* Cambridge, MA: Harvard University Press, 1963.

Ramsey, F. P. *The Foundations of Mathematics and Other Logical Essays*, edited by R. B. Braithwaite. New York: Harcourt Brace, 1931.

Skolem, Thoralf. "Einige Bemerkungen zur axiomatischen Begründung der Mengenlehre." In *Wissenschaftlicher Vorträge, gehalten auf dem Fünften Kongress der Skandinavischen Mathematiker in Helsingfors 1922,*217–232. Helsinki, 1923.

Skolem, Thoralf. "Logisch-kombinatorische Untersuchungen über die Erfüllbarkeit oder Beweisbarkeit mathematischer Sätze nebst einem Theoreme über dichte Mengen." In *Skrifter Utgit av Videnskapsselskapet i Kristiania, I. Matematisk-naturvidenskapelig Klasse 1919*, no. 4, 1–36. Oslo, 1920.

Skolem, Thoralf. "Über die Nicht-Charakterisierbarkeit der Zahlenreihe mittels endlich oder abzählbar unendlich vieler Aussagen mit ausschliesslich Zahlenvariablen." *Fundamenta Mathematicae* 23 (1934): 150–161.

Skolem, Thoralf. "Über die Unmöglichkeit einer vollständigen Charakterisierung der Zahlenreihe mittels eines endlichen Axiomsystems." *Norsk Matematisk Forenings Skrifter*, series 2 (10) (1933): 73–82.

Skolem, Thoralf. "Über einige Grundlagenfragen der Mathematik." In *Skrifter Utgit av det Norske Videnskaps-akademi i Oslo, I. Matematisk-naturvidenskapelig Klasse*, no. 4, 1–49. Oslo, 1929.

Wittgenstein, Ludwig. *Philosophische Bemerkungen*, edited by Rush Rhees. Oxford: Blackwell, 1964.

(A. N. P.)

NINETEENTH-CENTURY MATHEMATICS. Mathematics in the nineteenth century was characterized by reorganization in every field, effected both by generalization, which led to the viewing of areas once considered discrete as special instances of the same general case, and by the examination of foundations, either in terms of basic concepts or by an axiomatic approach. Apart, therefore, from any specific contributions that mathematicians made to modern logic, the atmosphere was highly favorable to an explicitly logical investigation both of mathematics in general and of its various branches, including, by the end of the century, mathematical logic itself. At the same time, the growth of abstract algebra encouraged the persistence of Leibniz's ideal of mathematizing deductive logic; his ideas, although most were unpublished, maintained a steady, if at first tenuous, foothold. Thus, the early mathematical logicians, having caught the idea of a new kind of algebra, tended to work on it as a specialized branch of mathematics. By the end of the nineteenth century it had become an instrument sufficiently perfected to be able to discard its traditional algebraic appearance, even to forget momentarily its self-concern, and to apply itself to the articulation of the increasingly well-organized mathematical material. Only in the twentieth century did it catch up to its own axiomatic origins and fruitfully rejoin its algebraic ones.

Peacock. As early as 1821, A. L. Cauchy (1789–1857), in his influential *Cours d'analyse* (Paris, 1821, introduction, p. ii), attacked the current use of algebraic reasonings in geometry because "they tend to make one attribute an indefinite range to the algebraic formulas, while in reality most of these formulas hold uniquely under certain conditions, and for certain values of the quantities concerned." This thought was adopted, in a more positive version, by George Peacock (1791–1858) in *A Treatise on Algebra* (2 vols., London, 1842–1845), elaborating a work of 1830. Instead of merely rejecting such illegitimate, or at any rate unjustified, extensions of the ranges of algebraic formulas, he distinguished between two kinds of algebra, arithmetical and symbolic.

> Arithmetical algebra is the science which results from the use of symbols and signs to denote numbers and the operations to which they may be subjected; those numbers or their representatives, and the operations upon them, being used in the same sense and with the same limitations as in common arithmetic. [In symbolical algebra] the symbols which are used are perfectly general in their representation, and perfectly unlimited in their values; and the operations upon them, in whatever manner they are denoted, or by whatever name they are called, are universal in their application. (Vol. I, Ch. 1)

The relationship of the two is more fully explained in the introduction:

> The generalizations of arithmetical algebra are generalizations of reasoning not of form. ... Symbolical algebra adopts the rules of arithmetical algebra, but removes altogether their restrictions. ... It is this adoption of the rules of the operations of arithmetical algebra as the rules for performing the operations which *bear the same names* in symbolical algebra, which secures the absolute identity of the results in the two sciences so far as they exist in common. ... This principle, in my former Treatise on Algebra, I denominated the "principle of the permanence of equivalent forms."

Peacock expressed his conviction that the convention by which such permanence had been commonly assumed had both delayed the emergence of his symbolical algebra as a science in its own right and resulted in consequent confusion and false reasoning such as Cauchy had complained of. By contrast to arithmetical algebra, "the results of symbolical algebra, which are not common to arithmetical algebra, are generalizations of form, and not necessary consequences of the definitions" which introduce special conditions according as the variables denote lines, forces, periods of time, and so on.

Boole. It is not hard to see the influence of Peacock's thoughts on George Boole. In the introduction to *The Mathematical Analysis of Logic* (1847), Boole wrote:

> Those who are acquainted with the present state of the theory of symbolical algebra, are aware, that the validity of the process of analysis does not depend upon the interpretation of the symbols which are employed, but solely upon the laws of their combination. Every system of interpretation which does not affect the truth of the relation supposed, is equally admissible. ... That to the existing forms of analysis a quantitative interpretation is assigned, is the result of the circumstances by which those forms were determined, and is not to be construed into a universal condition of analysis. It is upon the foundation of this general principle, that I purpose to establish the calculus of logic, and that I claim for it a place among the acknowledged forms of mathematical analysis, regardless that in its object and in its instruments it must at present stand alone.

In this passage we see mathematical logic struggling to be born, aware of its parentage, but still uncertain, as it continued to be for some time, of its status. Boole himself interpreted his calculus in relation to both classes and propositions. Thus, "The symbol $1 - x$ selects those cases in which the proposition X is false" (*The Mathematical Analysis of Logic*, "Of Hypotheticals"), and "Let us for simplicity of conception give to the symbol x the particular interpretation of *men*, then $1 - x$ will represent the class of 'not-men'" (*An Investigation of the Laws of Thought*, London, 1854, Ch. 3 in Prop. iv).

Peacock's work drew increased attention to the formal properties of operations, and Boole regarded his subject from this point of view.

> The laws we have established ... are sufficient for the base of a calculus. From the first of them it appears that the elective symbols are *distributive,* from the second that they are *commutative;* properties which they possess in common with symbols of *quantity,* and in virtue of which, all the processes of common algebra are applicable to the present system." (*The Mathematical Analysis of Logic*, "First Principles")

These terms actually antedate Peacock; they may have been introduced by F. J. Servois (see *Annales des mathématiques,* 5 [1814]: 93). "Associativity" has been ascribed to Sir William Rowan Hamilton (see Hermann Hankel's *Theorie der complexen Zahlensysteme*, Leipzig, 1867).

Gergonne. The new trend in algebra was already evidenced by the "Essai de dialectique rationelle" (in *Annales des mathématiques* 7 [1816–1817]: 189–228) of J. D. Gergonne (1771–1859). In this he wrote:

> In the same way that an algebraic calculation can be carried out without one having the least idea about the meaning of the symbols on which one is operating, it is possible to follow a course of reasoning without any knowledge of the meaning of the terms in which it is expressed, or without adverting to it if one knows it.

Such a formalistic approach would have been more in order when fields of application were better charted, and Karl Weierstrass was still fighting for this point of view many years later. Gergonne later did important work on duality in geometry, which shows again his ability to distinguish structure from interpretation. He offered a new analysis of the fundamental ideas of syllogistic and used an inverted C for inclusion, now standardized as the hook, $\subset$.

De Morgan. Augustus De Morgan, a contemporary of Peacock and Boole, took a special interest in the organization of mathematics for didactic purposes. After *Elements of Arithmetic* (1830) he wrote *On the Study and Difficulties of Mathematics* (1831), *First Notions of Logic* (1839), which was designed to help beginning students of geometry, and *Formal Logic* (1847). In *Trigonometry and Double Algebra* he investigated symbolic calculuses. A remarkable text ("On the Syllogism, III") shows De Morgan striking out element after element in the material proposition "Every man is animal" till he is left with X——Y, showing the "pure form of the judgment"; thus, he made a start on the extension of the mathematical notion of function, to which Boole, Peirce, and most notably Frege also contributed. De Morgan's right parenthesis, as used in "X)" to mean "every X," yielding "X)Y"—that is, every X is Y—is reminiscent of Gergonne's inverted C, although Gergonne's symbol means "is contained in" and operates on two terms rather than one.

Grassmann. One of the creators of a new form of algebra was H. G. Grassmann (1809–1877). Grassmann's *Ausdehnungslehre* (Leipzig, 1844; rev. ed., 1862), fundamental to vector analysis, anticipated W. R. Hamilton's work through its greater generality and influenced Alfred North Whitehead's *A Treatise on Universal Algebra with Applications* (Cambridge, U.K., 1898). Giuseppe Peano's *Calcolo geometrico* (Turin, 1888) was written "according to the *Ausdehnungslehre* of H. Grassmann, preceded by the operations of deductive logic."

Non-Euclidean geometry. In geometry the great breakthrough was the effective creation of non-Euclidean systems. The chief figures were János Bolyai (1802–1860), Nikolai Ivanovich Lobachevski (1793–1856), and Bernhard Riemann (1826–1866). Bolyai's work on non-Euclidean geometry was titled *Appendix Scientiam Spatii Absolute Veram Exhibens; A Veritate aut Falsitate Axiomatis XI Euclidei (A Priori Haud Unquam Decidenda) Independentem.* Written in 1823, it was published in 1833 at Maros-Vásárhely in the second volume of the *Tentamen* of his father, F. Bolyai. Lobachevski wrote *Geometrische Untersuchungen zur Theorie der Parallellinien* (Berlin, 1840), an elaboration of ideas first presented in a lecture delivered at Kazan in 1826. Riemann's inaugural lecture *Ueber die Hypothesen, welche der Geometrie zu Grunde liegen* (1854) was published at Göttingen in 1867. Each seems to have done his work independently of the others, but behind all of them appears the great, although in this matter somewhat enigmatic, figure of Karl Friedrich Gauss (1777–1855), friend of Bolyai's father and of Lobachevski's teacher Bartels and teacher of Riemann. Gauss's correspondence shows him long to have had ideas on the subject, and to him we owe the word *non-Euclidean* (in a letter to Taurinus, 1824).

Bolyai, as the title of his work indicates, simply dropped Euclid's axiom of parallels; Lobachevski adopted its denial. Both required the infinity of the straight line. Riemann, approaching the matter from an analytic point of view, wished to determine the general conditions of spaces in which the measure of distance would remain everywhere constant and figures could move freely without deformation. He was thus led to consider spaces of constant curvature and more than three dimensions, with Euclidean space a special case. Riemann's work was immediately taken up by Hermann von Helmholtz (1821–1894), in *Über die thatsächlichen Grundlagen der Geometrie* (1868–1869) and *Über die Thatsachen, die der Geometrie zu Grunde liegen* (1868), and was further refined by Sophus Lie (1842–1899). Lie was one of the principal developers of the theory of groups, which Felix Klein (1849–1925) applied to geometry in his *Erlanger Programm, Vergleichende Betrachtungen über neuere geometrische Forschungen* (Erlangen, 1872; translated by M. W. Haskell as "A Comparative Review of Recent Researches in Geometry," in *Bulletin of the New York Mathematical Society* 2 [1892–1893]: 215–249).

Independence. Though Bertrand Russell (in 1897), Whitehead (in 1898), and David Hilbert (in 1899) all wrote on geometry, and Hilbert's later foundational work (*Grundlagenforschung*) provided the basis for all subsequent investigations, these pioneers of mature mathematical logic failed to secure independence for their propositional axioms. This is remarkable after all the attention that had been devoted to the independence of Euclid's axiom of parallels. Frege, too, failed in this matter. Alessandro Padoa, in 1901, gave directives for establishing the independence of concepts within an axiom system—an idea that influenced Peano—but no general method for securing the independence of propositional axioms was attained until Jan Łukasiewicz (1925) and Paul Bernays (1926), independently, found the method of interpretation by matrices.

Many-valued logics and proof theory. Non-Euclidean geometries are often mentioned in discussions of the status of many-valued logics, but they appear to have had no direct influence. (Łukasiewicz was brought to the idea by Aristotle's *Peri Hermeneias*.) It is likely that the theory of groups (closed systems of operations)—which was already finding widespread application by the end of the nineteenth century—and the rise of different algebras did much to create the climate of thought in which proof theory, and in general the metalogical investigation of the properties of entire deductive systems, could be developed. Such investigation seems to be one of the most notable characteristics differentiating mathematical logic from the logic of any other period. Proof theory stems mainly from Hilbert.

Schröder. The early, algebraic period of mathematical logic ended with Ernst Schröder (1841–1902). After a paper on algorithms for solving equations (1870) and a textbook on arithmetic and algebra, Schröder devoted himself more and more to the algebra of logic, his two chief works being *Der Operationskreis des Logikkalküls* (Leipzig, 1877) and *Vorlesungen über die Algebra der Logik* (3 vols., Leipzig, 1890–1905). Much of his work was a tidying up of the past. He discarded Boole's subtraction and division, which were subject to too many restrictions to be satisfactory inverse operations; used (as had W. S. Jevons) the sign of addition in the sense of inclusive rather than exclusive alternation; and introduced at the beginning a sign for inclusion. In this last matter he independently duplicated Frege's abandonment of the algebraic form in *Begriffsschrift* (Halle, 1879), which later became standard with *Principia Mathematica* (3 vols. Cambridge, U.K., 1910–1913). But Schröder remained interested in the solution of equations; his results for the Boolean system were taken over by Whitehead in *A Treatise on Universal Algebra*. Like Peirce, Schröder noticed a

duality between logical multiplication and addition and similarly between the null and the universal classes. Duality in geometry had been brought to the fore by J. V. Poncelet (1822), enunciated with greater generality by Gergonne (1827), and skillfully exploited by Jakob Steiner (1830).

Schröder explicitly rejected those syllogisms that are invalid when the terms are null, Boole having merely passed them over. Besides using the method of $1 - 0$ evaluation, which goes back to Boole, he developed a process of reduction to normal form. Schröder introduced two novelties. Unlike those of his contemporaries mentioned above, he was interested in independence, wishing particularly to have the distributive law independent of his other axioms, and he was thus brought to perhaps the first idea of a nondistributive lattice. He also had a clear view of the need for a theory of logical types:

> By that process of arbitrary selection of classes of individuals of the manifold originally envisaged, there arises a new, much more extensive manifold, namely that of the domains or classes of the previous one. ... [It] is necessary from the start that among the elements given as individuals there should be no classes comprising as elements individuals of the same manifold. (*Vorlesungen*, Vol. I, p. 247)

This foreshadows Russell's vicious-circle principle.

Schröder worked on Peirce's algebra of dyadic relatives as an extension of Boole's algebra, but the result was unsatisfactory, and, indeed, by the time Peirce reviewed it Schröder had already abandoned the algebraic form (though not the name) in favor of what is essentially first-order functional calculus. The Schröder-Bernstein theorem, to the effect that if each of two classes is similar to a part of the other, then they are similar to each other, was proved by Schröder in 1896 and independently by Felix Bernstein in 1898.

Peano. Schröder deplored the lack of use for the logical tool he had developed and experimented with the application of his theory of relation to Dedekind's chains. Giuseppe Peano, primarily interested in the rigor of mathematical proof, applied Schröder's instrument to comprehensive mathematical material in successive volumes of his *Formulaire de mathématiques* (5 vols., Turin, 1892–1908). He prefaced the work with a section on mathematical logic (a phrase that he originated), distinguished class membership from inclusion, which Schröder had not done, and expressed all theorems as implications rather than as equations. He still did not isolate propositional logic as a deductive preliminary, but he stated a generalized form of *modus ponens,* to the effect that a true proposition could be suppressed when it occurred as an antecedent or as part of a conjunction of antecedents in a theorem.

Peano had already obtained his five axioms of arithmetic, which contain the principle of mathematical induction, by 1889, when he published *Arithmetices Principia Nova Methodo Exposita.* The year before, J. W. R. Dedekind had reached substantially the same result in *Was sind und was sollen die Zahlen?* (Brunswick, Germany, 1888) with the induction principle provable, however, owing to his having started further back in logic, with sets and projections, rather than with sets, number, and successor. Frege, as Dedekind did not know at that time, had gone still further in the same direction. The fact that Peano, even in 1908, did not refer to either Frege or Dedekind but explicitly left the possibility of defining "number" an open question may indicate that he continued to be interested in logic more as a means of attaining brevity and rigor, and an occasional new insight, than as material from which the basic arithmetical notions might be constructed.

Cantor. Peano did draw on the theory of sets of Georg Cantor (1845–1918), including Cantor's proofs that the algebraic numbers can be put in one-to-one correspondence with the positive integers and that the real numbers cannot be so made to correspond (the "diagonal" proof). Cantor's work had grown out of a reorganization of analysis parallel to that of algebra and geometry. He was influenced, of course, by the work of Cauchy, Riemann, and Hankel on functions of complex variables, but his principal predecessor was Karl Weierstrass (1815–1897), who was greatly interested in foundational matters, especially in regard to irrational numbers and points of condensation of infinite sets. Cantor became convinced that without extending the concept of number to actually infinite sets it would hardly be possible to make the least step forward without constraint. The arithmetic that he thus created was welcomed by Frege; its influence is widely apparent and was acknowledged in Russell's *Principles of Mathematics* (Cambridge, U.K., 1903), which plotted the future progress of *Principia Mathematica.*

See also Aristotle; Boole, George; Cantor, Georg; De Morgan, Augustus; Frege, Gottlob; Geometry; Helmholtz, Hermann Ludwig von; Hilbert, David; Jevons, William Stanley; Łukasiewicz, Jan; Many-Valued Logics; Peano, Giuseppe; Peirce, Charles Sanders; Proof Theory; Russell, Bertrand Arthur William; Whitehead, Alfred North.

Bibliography

R. C. Archibald, "Outline of the History of Mathematics," in *American Mathematical Monthly* 56 (1949), cites standard histories of nineteenth-century mathematics. See also the general histories of logic listed above, as well as Roberto Bonola, *Non-Euclidean Geometry* (New York: Dover, 1955); Alonzo Church, "Schroder's Anticipation of the Simple Theory of Types," in *Erkenntnis* 9 (1939): 149–152; Georg Cantor, *Contributions to the Founding of the Theory of Transfinite Numbers,* translated, with an introduction, by P. E. B. Jourdain (Chicago: Open Court, 1915); Ettore Carruccio, *Mathematics and Logic in History and in Contemporary Thought,* translated by Isabel Quigly (Chicago: Aldine, 1965); H. B. Curry, *Foundations of Mathematical Logic* (New York: McGraw-Hill, 1963); and Giuseppe Peano, *Formulario Mathematico* (Turin, 1908; facsimile reprint, Rome: Edizioni Cremonese, 1960).

Ivo Thomas (1967)

FREGE. Modern logic began with the publication in 1879 of the *Begriffsschrift* of Gottlob Frege (1848–1925). In the *Begriffsschrift* we find for the first time a comprehensive treatment of the ideas of generality and existence, because sentence forms which were hitherto accommodated only by complicated ad hoc theories are here provided with an adequate symbolization by the device of quantification, rules for which are adjoined to the first complete formalization of the classical propositional calculus. The result closely approximates a modern formal axiomatic theory. It meets Frege's aim of a codification of the logical principles used in mathematical reasoning, although the rules of inference (substitution and *modus ponens*) and the definition of other logical constants in terms of the primitives (negation, implication, the universal quantifier, and identity) are not explicitly formalized but are mentioned as obviously justified by reference to the intended interpretation. A proof of completeness was not to be had in Frege's day, but he demonstrated the power of his system by deriving a large number of logical principles from his basic postulates and took an important step toward the formulation of arithmetical principles by showing, with the aid of second-order quantification, how the notion of serial order may be formalized.

After the *Begriffsschrift,* Frege's next major work was *Die Grundlagen der Arithmetik* (Breslau, 1884), an analysis of the concept of cardinal number presented largely in nontechnical terms. It opens the way for Frege's theories with a devastating criticism of the views of various writers on the nature of numbers and the laws of arithmetic. Difficulties encountered in the analyses of number find explanation and resolution in the celebrated claim that a statement of number contains an assertion about a concept. To say, for instance, that there are three letters in the word *but* is not, on Frege's view, to attribute a property to the actual letters; it is to assign the number 3 to the concept "letter in the word 'but.'" If we now say that two concepts *F* and *G* are numerically equivalent (*gleichzahlig*) if and only if there is a one-to-one correspondence between those things which fall under *F* and those which fall under *G*, we can define the number that belongs to a concept *F* as the extension of the concept "numerically equivalent to the concept *F*."

In terms of this definition any two numerically equivalent concepts, such as "letter in the word 'but'" and "letter in the word 'big,'" can be seen to determine the same extension, and therefore the same number, and it remains only to specify concepts to which the individual numbers belong. In sketching this and subsequent developments Frege found that the notions used appear to allow of resolution into purely logical terms. He concluded that it is probable that arithmetic has an a priori, analytic status, a view that places him in opposition to Immanuel Kant, who held that propositions of arithmetic were synthetic a priori, and to J. S. Mill, who regarded them as inductive generalizations.

In papers published after the *Grundlagen*, Frege turned his attention to problems of a more general philosophical nature, and the development of his thought in this period led to a revised account of his logic, which is incorporated in his most ambitious work, *Die Grundgesetze der Arithmetik* (2 vols., Jena, Germany, 1893–1903), in which he extended and formalized the theory of number adumbrated in the *Grundlagen*. In the *Begriffsschrift* he had rejected the traditional subject-predicate distinction but had retained one predicate, "is a fact" (symbolized "⊢"), which indicated that the judgment which it prefaced was being asserted. In his essay "Über Sinn und Bedeutung" this view was abandoned on the ground that the addition of such a sign, conceived as a predicate, merely results in a reformulation of the same thought, a reformulation which in turn may or may not be asserted.

The logic of the *Grundgesetze* is based on Frege's theory of sense and reference, the interpretation of the symbolism of the *Begriffsschrift* being modified accordingly. The formal system of the *Begriffsschrift* is further changed by replacing certain of the axioms with transformation rules, but a more important innovation is the extension of the earlier symbols to cover classes. Corresponding to any well-defined function $\Phi(\xi)$ is the range, or course of values (*Wertverlauf*), of that function, written $\acute{\epsilon}\Phi(\epsilon)$,

which Frege introduced via an axiom stipulating that $\acute{\epsilon}\Phi(\epsilon)$ is identical with $\epsilon\psi(\epsilon)$ if and only if the two associated functions $\Phi(\xi)$ and $\psi(\xi)$ agree in the values which they take on for all possible arguments ξ. In particular, this axiom licenses the passage from a concept to its extension, the course-of-values notation providing a means of representing classes and foreshadowing Bertrand Russell's class-abstraction operator, $\hat{z}(\phi z)$. Another device that found a close analogue in Russell's logic is Frege's symbol $\backslash\xi$. If a course of values ξ has a unique member, then $\backslash\xi$ is this member; otherwise $\backslash\xi$ is the course of values ξ itself. In the first case $\backslash\xi$ provides a translation of expressions of the form "the *F*" and so corresponds to Russell's description operator, $(\imath x)(\phi x)$; the second case ensures that when ξ has no unique member, $\backslash\xi$ is nevertheless well defined.

The preliminary development of logic and the theory of classes is followed by the main subject of the *Grundgesetze*, the theory of cardinal number, developed with respect to both finite and infinite cardinals. The theory of real numbers is begun in the second volume but the treatment is incomplete, and Frege was probably loath to advance further in this direction after learning, while the second volume was in the press, that the very beginnings of his theory harbored a contradiction. This contradiction, discovered by Russell, resulted from the axiom allowing the transition from concept to class, an axiom in which Frege had not had the fullest confidence. Russell's communication is discussed in an appendix to the second volume, where an emended version of the axiom is put forward. This emendation was not, in fact, satisfactory, and although Frege apparently did not know that a contradiction could still be derived, he eventually abandoned his belief that the program of the *Grundgesetze* could be carried out successfully and claimed that geometry, not logic, must provide a basis for number theory.

See also Frege, Gottlob; Kant, Immanuel; Mill, John Stuart; Russell, Bertrand Arthur William.

Bede Rundle (1967)

PEANO. Giuseppe Peano (1858–1932), professor of infinitesimal analysis at Turin and a prolific writer on a wide range of mathematical topics, contributed to the early development of both logicism and the formalism to which it is partly opposed. His first book, published under the name of a former teacher, Angelo Genocchi, was devoted to the calculus and featured a careful, systematic treatment of the subject that contrasted favorably with customary texts in rejecting loosely phrased definitions and theorems and in substituting rigorous proof for appeals to intuition. Peano was particularly insistent that the acceptability of a mathematical proposition should depend not on its intuitive plausibility but on its derivability from stated premises and definitions, and he devised a remarkable illustration of the way in which what appears evident to intuition may nonetheless be contradicted by formally incontrovertible considerations. This is his well-known space-filling curve, introduced in 1890 in the paper "Sur une Courbe, qui remplit toute une aire plaine" (*Mathematische Annalen* 36 [1890]: 157–160). About ten years earlier Camille Jordan had defined a curve as a continuous and single-valued image of the unit segment. This definition accords well enough with our intuitive conception of a curve, but Peano showed that a curve in conformity with this definition could in fact pass through every point in a square based on the unit segment and so would appear as a uniformly shaded surface if plotted on a graph.

Convinced that the development of mathematics must proceed independently of intuitive considerations, Peano embarked upon a program of refounding the various branches of mathematics. Not only geometry and analysis, where we are particularly inclined to make an appeal to what can be grasped pictorially, but even elementary number theory was to be purified of common-sense preconceptions. The entities of a mathematical theory (numbers, points, and so forth) would have to enter into the theory not as idealizations of objects given to intuition but as postulated or defined entities, having only those properties which are explicitly listed or which can be grounded on the initial definitions. To ensure the exclusion of misleading intuitive associations, Peano devised a new symbolic language in which to formalize definitions and other postulates. Principles of reasoning employed within mathematics, as well as conceptions forming the substance of mathematical theories, are transcribed into the new notation. It is at this point that mathematical logic enters into Peano's work, and although he did not carry the development of his system very far, the basic ideas and notation were taken over by Whitehead and Russell as a starting point for the system of logic presented in great detail in *Principia Mathematica*.

Also important for subsequent developments was Peano's presentation of arithmetic. It is based on a set of postulates known as the Peano axioms, although, as has been noted, Richard Dedekind had published them earlier. The axioms were intended to free the concept of number from dependence on intuition. The essentials of Peano's treatment are embodied in these five axioms:

(1) 0 is a number.

(2) The successor of any number is a number.

(3) No two numbers have the same successor.

(4) 0 is not the successor of any number.

(5) Any class which contains 0 and which contains the successor of n whenever it contains n includes the class of numbers.

The Peano axioms are commonly taken as a basis for the arithmetic of the natural numbers, supplemented by recursive definitions of such arithmetical operations as addition, multiplication, and exponentiation. Peano himself made considerable use of recursive definition, an analogue, for definitions, of the axiom of mathematical induction given by (5), which allows us to calculate the value of a function $f(n)$ step by step, given an explicit definition of $f(0)$ along with a definition of $f(n')$ in terms of $f(n)$—here "n" means "the successor of n." Thus, for addition Peano provided the two recursion equations $a + 0 = a$ and $a + n' = (a + n)'$. Rewriting the second of these as $a + (n + 1) = (a + n) + 1$, we can see that we have here a particular case of the associative law for addition, $x + (y + z) = (x + y) + z$, which can in fact be derived from the recursion equations by means of axiom (5). Multiplication is defined in similar fashion by means of the equations $a \cdot 0 = 0$ and $a \cdot b' = a \cdot b + a$, and once more familiar arithmetical laws can be extracted by means of induction.

With the assistance of a number of colleagues, including Cesare Burali-Forti, Peano succeeded in reformulating much of existing mathematical theory in accordance with his criteria of rigor and precision, the results of these investigations appearing in the journal *Rivista di Matematica* (later also *Revue de mathématiques* and *Revista de mathematica*) from 1891 to 1906 and in Peano's *Formulaire de mathématiques* (5 vols., Turin 1892–1908). The detailed coverage of algebra, arithmetic, set theory, geometry, and other branches of mathematics argues convincingly for Peano's approach, but it is questionable whether it vindicates a formalist philosophy of mathematics, since further metamathematical investigation, notably by Thoralf Skolem, has shown that if Peano's axioms are embedded in an axiomatization of set theory, they do not serve to characterize the natural numbers to the exclusion of other progressions. At the same time, it should be noted that Peano was not himself concerned with advancing either a formalist or a logicist philosophy; his approach was determined by a desire for technical improvements in the presentation of mathematics.

See also Mathematics, Foundations of; Peano, Giuseppe; Russell, Bertrand Arthur William; Whitehead, Alfred North.

Bede Rundle (1967)

WHITEHEAD AND RUSSELL. In *The Principles of Mathematics*, published in 1903, Bertrand Russell (1872–1970) set out to establish the logicist view that "all pure mathematics deals exclusively with concepts definable in terms of a very small number of fundamental logical concepts, and that all its propositions are deducible from a very small number of logical principles" (2nd ed., p. xv) and also to explain "the fundamental concepts which mathematics accepts as indefinable" (ibid.). In the *Principles* this program is pursued with minimal recourse to symbolism, the systematic formal presentation being reserved for a proposed second volume. What in fact appeared as the sequel was the classic *Principia Mathematica* (3 vols., Cambridge, U.K., 1910–1913), written in collaboration with Alfred North Whitehead. The subject matter of *Principia Mathematica* considerably overlaps that covered by Frege in his *Grundgesetze der Arithmetik*, a work to which the authors acknowledge their chief debt on questions of logical analysis; in some respects, such as the demarcation between logical and metalogical theses, *Principia Mathematica* falls short of the standards of rigor observed in Frege's masterpiece. The symbolism adopted in *Principia Mathematica* derives largely from Peano, and the development of arithmetic and the theory of series is based on the work of Cantor.

We shall concentrate on the most important feature distinguishing *Principia Mathematica* from Frege's work, the attempt to avoid the contradictions which Russell found implicit in the fifth axiom of the *Grundgesetze*. This axiom licensed the transition from a concept to its extension and from an extension to the concept, a transition that appears to do no more than give formal expression to a platitude. For instance, the proposition "Stravinsky is a member of the class of composers" appears to be no more than a circumlocution for "Stravinsky is a composer." In general, it would seem reasonable to lay down as a law that x is a member of the class of ϕ's if and only if x is ϕ—in Russellian notation, $x \, \epsilon \hat{z}(\phi z). \equiv .\phi x$. But despite its platitudinous appearance, this principle turns out to harbor a contradiction, since corresponding to the concept "is not a member of itself" we have the class of all such things—that is, the class of all classes which are not members of themselves—and if we

now ask whether this class is or is not a member of itself, we find that either way a contradiction arises: If it is a member of itself, then it satisfies the defining condition of such members, so it is not a member of itself, and if it is not a member of itself, it belongs to the class of such classes and so is a member of itself.

This contradiction was noted by Russell in 1901, and in subsequent years finding ways to avoid it formed one of his major concerns. His final analysis, incorporated into *Principia Mathematica*, attributed the contradiction, along with a number of analogous paradoxes, to a mode of reasoning involving a vicious circle, a circle that arises when we postulate a collection of objects containing members definable only by means of the collection as a whole. Russell regarded such collections as illegitimate totalities, to be avoided by observing his "vicious-circle" principle, "Whatever involves *all* of a collection must not be one of the collection." Appealing to this principle, Russell claimed that the values of a function cannot contain terms definable only by means of the function, and in place of an indiscriminate application of functions to arbitrary arguments he defined an ascending hierarchy of types, beginning with individuals and progressing through functions of individuals, functions of functions of individuals, and so forth, the only arguments which a function can significantly take being those of the immediately preceding type. In particular, a class cannot significantly be taken as an argument to its defining function, and the derivation of Russell's paradox is accordingly obstructed by ruling out both "$x \, \epsilon \, x$" and its negation as ill-formed.

Apart from enabling us to block the derivation of paradoxes, Russell claimed, the theory of types based on the vicious-circle principle has a certain consonance with common sense. However, the principle itself (in the various nonequivalent forms given by Russell) can be challenged on the ground that it rules out circular procedures which are in no way vicious.

If the vicious-circle principle is rejected, it is natural to regard Russell's paradox as no more than a straightforward contradiction, the absurdities resulting from the abstraction schema $(\exists x)(y)(y \, \epsilon \, x \equiv \phi(y))$ being no different in kind and requiring no different an explanation from those yielded by $(\exists x)(y)(Fyx \equiv \phi(y))$, where the membership relation is replaced by an arbitrary dyadic predicate. On this view the problem of finding consistent instances of the abstraction schema reduces to the analogous problem for the uninterpreted version, but although such an approach has its merits, it loses sight of an important feature of the system which the vicious-circle principle shapes via the theory of types. That is, the form of theory which the principle determines conforms to a natural conception of classes according to which they are, or at least could be, generated by a step-by-step procedure, the superstructure of classes of classes of classes, and so on, resting ultimately on the initial elements of lowest type. On the other hand, although it is natural to conceive of a domain of classes as initially secured by such a procedure, it would seem equally natural to relax this constructivist approach to the extent of allowing the specification of particular classes in the domain to proceed by characterizations in terms of the given totality, provided only that the consequent reflexivity does not embody a contradiction.

See also Cantor, Georg; Frege, Gottlob; Logical Paradoxes; Russell, Bertrand Arthur William; Whitehead, Alfred North.

Bede Rundle (1967)

POST. Besides provoking reactions in the form of rival philosophies of mathematics, the work of Whitehead and Russell stimulated new technical developments. For example, although Whitehead and Russell made free use, in *Principia Mathematica*, of the notions of truth-value and truth-function, they failed to incorporate these notions into a systematic technique for evaluating formulas of the propositional calculus. Such a technique, the method of truth tables, was presented by Emil Post (1897–1954) in his dissertation of 1920, published as "Introduction to a General Theory of Elementary Propositions" in the *American Journal of Mathematics* (43: 163–185) in 1921, the year in which Wittgenstein independently presented the same method in his *Tractatus Logico-Philosophicus*. The method dates back, in fact, to Peirce, but Post considered truth tables in their application not only to classical logic but also to systems in which any number of values are allowed, the primitive connectives of *Principia Mathematica*, "~" and "∨," having in these systems the generalized analogues "$\sim_m$" and "$\vee_m$," where $\sim_m P$ takes the values $t_2, t_3, \cdots, t_m, t_1$ as P takes the values $t_1, t_2, \cdots, t_m$, and $P \vee_m Q$ takes that of the two values assigned to P and Q which bears the lesser subscript. Classical two-valued logic is accordingly a particular case of the many-valued logics so constructed. Post provided definitions of consistency and completeness, and for the first time a formulation of the propositional calculus was proved to have these properties, the method of truth tables providing a basis for the proofs.

In his 1920 dissertation Post showed how both truth tables for classical logic and associated postulate sets may be generalized. These postulate sets were treated as uninterpreted formal systems, an approach which Post maintained and extended in the direction of even greater generality in later works, where the derivation of theorems from axioms is represented as the production of strings—that is, finite sequences of symbols—from certain other strings of specified form. Most mathematical theories can be transcribed into the canonical forms admitted by Post, and he was able to show that the rules of any theory so expressed can be reduced to productions of a particularly simple type, a reduction that greatly simplifies investigations into the syntax of formal systems.

This approach leads directly to a formulation of recursive enumerability (a set is recursively enumerable if its members can be generated as the values of an effectively calculable function) and thence to one of recursiveness (a set is recursive if both it and its complement are recursively enumerable); Post provided illuminating proofs of results concerning decidability and related topics and introduced and developed a number of important concepts in this field. In 1947 he showed the recursive unsolvability of the word problem for semigroups. That is, he proved that it is impossible to determine whether or not two arbitrarily given strings are equivalent (where A and B are equivalent if B can be obtained from A by starting with A and applying a finite sequence of specified operations prescribing the production of one string from another). This result, published independently and in the same year by A. A. Markov, is an interesting example of the resolution, by techniques of mathematical logic, of an outstanding problem in the field of mathematics proper.

See also Russell, Bertrand Arthur William; Whitehead, Alfred North; Wittgenstein, Ludwig Josef Johann.

Bede Rundle (1967)

RAMSEY. Frank Plumpton Ramsey (1903–1930), a brilliant Cambridge philosopher and logician, attempted to give a satisfactory account of the foundations of mathematics in accordance with the method of Frege, Russell, and Whitehead, defending their view that mathematics is logic while proposing revisions in the system of *Principia Mathematica* suggested by the work of Wittgenstein.

According to Russell, pure mathematics consists of "the class of all propositions of the form 'p implies q' where p and q are propositions containing one or more variables, the same in the two propositions, and neither p nor q contains any constants except logical constants" (*The Principles of Mathematics*, p. 3). Ramsey agreed with this definition insofar as it characterizes the generality that is a feature of pure mathematics, but he claimed that it takes no account of an equally important mark of mathematics, its tautological character. The term *tautological* in the relevant sense derives from Wittgenstein, who applied it to formulas of the propositional calculus which come out true no matter what combinations of the values *true* and *false* are assigned to the component propositions. Ramsey extended the term to apply to valid formulas of the predicate calculus. Thus, the formula "$(x) . \phi x : \supset : \phi a$" is tautological, since "ϕa" expresses one of the possibilities which go to make up the possibly infinite conjunction abbreviated by "$(x) . \phi x$."

Admittedly we cannot write down the fully expanded versions of quantified formulas, but this inability does not affect the tautological character of truths formulated in the compressed notation. Similarly, Ramsey maintained, the inability of human beings to list the members of an infinite class is no bar to our conceiving of classes whose members could be indicated only in this way and not via the specification of a defining predicate. Indeed, the possibility of such indefinable classes is an essential part of the extensional attitude of modern mathematics, and Ramsey regarded the neglect of this possibility in *Principia Mathematica* as one of the work's three major defects. Thus, as interpreted in the system of *Principia Mathematica* the multiplicative axiom (axiom of choice) is logically doubtful, but on an extensional view of classes it is, according to Ramsey, an evident tautology.

The second major defect that Ramsey found in *Principia Mathematica* concerns Russell's attempt to overcome the paradoxes, in particular his postulation of the axiom of reducibility. Ramsey accepted the simple theory of types as an unquestionably correct measure for avoiding the logical contradictions, such as Russell's paradox and the Burali-Forti paradox, but he claimed that the contradictions that the hierarchy of orders had been introduced to avoid are of no concern either to logic or to mathematics. These contradictions—for instance, the Richard paradox and Weyl's contradiction concerning the word *heterological*—cannot be stated in logical terms alone but contain some further reference to thought, language, or symbolism. Rejecting Russell's conception of orders, Ramsey put forward a less restrictive theory based on his extensional view of propositional functions. Just as "$(x) . \phi x$" represents an infinite conjunction of atomic propositions "$\phi a . \phi b . \cdots$" so "$(\phi)\phi a$" expands to "$\phi_1 a . \phi_2 a . \cdots$" and similarly with disjunctions replacing conjunctions for existential quantifiers. Accordingly, if we start with truth-functions of atomic formulas, then no matter how often or in what respect we generalize upon

them, we shall never pass to propositions significantly different from these elementary truth-functions; the only difference will lie in the notation introduced with the quantifiers. There is consequently no need for the axiom of reducibility—which, Ramsey claimed, could anyhow be false—and although the resultant theory countenances definitions of propositions in terms of totalities to which they belong, such definitions are in Ramsey's eyes no more vicious than an identification of a man as the tallest in a group of which he is a member.

The third great defect in *Principia Mathematica* which Ramsey proposed to rectify concerns Russell's definition of identity, according to which it is impossible for two objects to have all their properties in common. Ramsey held that this consequence shows that identity has been wrongly defined, and he advanced a definition of "$x = y$" designed to render the phrase tautological when x and y have the same value and contradictory otherwise.

See also Frege, Gottlob; Identity; Logical Paradoxes; Ramsey, Frank Plumpton; Russell, Bertrand Arthur William; Types, Theory of; Whitehead, Alfred North; Wittgenstein, Ludwig Josef Johann.

Bede Rundle (1967)

BROUWER AND INTUITIONISM. The intuitionist conception of mathematics was developed by the Dutch mathematician Luitzen Egbertus Jan Brouwer (1881–1966). According to Brouwer mathematics is not a system of formulas and rules but a fundamental form of human activity, an activity that has its basis in our ability to abstract a conception of "twoness" from successive phases of human experience and to see how this operation may be indefinitely repeated to generate the infinitely proceeding sequence of the natural numbers. In the system of mathematics based on this primordial intuition, language serves merely as an aid to memory and communication and cannot of itself create a new mathematical system; our words and formulas have significance only insofar as they are backed by an essentially languageless activity of the mind. In particular, the wording of a theorem is meaningful only if it indicates the mental construction of some mathematical entity or shows the impossibility of the entity in question. Brouwer's conception of proof as essentially mental is useful as a corrective to a narrow formalist account that would construe proof as proof in a given formal system, although his psychologism is philosophically questionable—Wittgenstein's work has rendered more than doubtful the thesis that language is only an incidental accompaniment to thought, required solely for purposes of memory and communication. What is important in intuitionism is not so much its psychologistic features as its emphasis on constructibility and the form of mathematics which its criterion of meaningfulness determines.

Implicit in classical mathematics is the notion that to know the meaning of a statement it is sufficient to know the conditions under which the statement is true or false, even though these conditions may be such that we could never be in a position to determine whether or not they held. The possibility of a gap between what can be meaningfully stated and what can be recognized either as true or as false is not admitted by the intuitionists. On their theory we can know the meaning of a statement only when we can recognize a proof of it; indeed, to understand a statement simply is to know what constitutes a proof or verification of that statement.

This emphasis on verification leads to an explanation of the logical constants and of a number of mathematical concepts that results in the rejection or reinterpretation of large parts of classical mathematics. Thus, whereas in classical mathematics the truth-table definition is adequate to giving the meaning of the constant "$\lor$" ("or"), for the intuitionist we can explain the meaning of a statement of the form "$A \lor B$" only by indicating under what conditions we should be warranted in asserting such a statement. These conditions are that we should be warranted in asserting A or that we should be warranted in asserting B, and it is clear that neither condition may hold, even when A is the negation of B.

Assume, for instance, that A is an existentially quantified statement, $\exists x P(x)$, with the quantifier ranging over the natural numbers. To suppose that this holds is to suppose that we can actually construct a number with the required property. On the other hand, what is it to suppose that $\exists x P(x)$ is false? It cannot mean that a case-by-case examination of the numbers will provide a refutation of the statement, since a case-by-case investigation of an infinite totality is not a real possibility—it is a picture to which the classical mathematician is wedded by a mistaken analogy with finite totalities. But if $\sim \exists x P(x)$ is to have a meaning which we can grasp, it can mean only that there is a contradiction in the idea of a number's having the property P. Given this explanation of the sense of the proposition and its negation, we are obliged to abandon Aristotelian logic as no longer trustworthy in this context, for asserting the disjunction $\exists x P(x) \lor \sim \exists x P(x)$ is tantamount to asserting that we either are in a position to construct a suitable number or can show the impossibility of such a construction. We are not entitled to assert a priori that at least one of these possibilities must obtain,

but to do so would simply be to commit ourselves to the unfounded belief that all mathematical problems are solvable.

This insistence on the identification of existence with constructibility can be traced back to Leopold Kronecker (1823–1891), and a precise formulation of principles of intuitionist logic was carried out in 1930 by a pupil of Brouwer's, Arend Heyting (1898–1980). Several branches of mathematics have been redeveloped from the intuitionist standpoint, but the reconstructions are often complicated, and in some cases, particularly where set-theoretic notions are involved, there has been a question of outright rejection, rather than reconstruction, of classical mathematics. Thus, impredicative definitions, hierarchies of transfinite numbers, and nonconstructive postulates such as the axiom of choice (and hence the well-ordering theorem), while important classically, are rejected in toto by the intuitionists, a rejection which has led many mathematicians to discount the claims of intuitionism without giving sufficient attention to the arguments, admittedly often obscurely expressed, on which they are based.

See also Brouwer, Luitzen Egbertus Jan; Intuitionism and Intuitionistic Logic.

Bede Rundle (1967)

HILBERT AND FORMALISM. The leading exponent of the formalist philosophy of mathematics was David Hilbert (1862–1943), who pioneered in a development of logic known as proof theory or metamathematics. From the time of his first papers on the foundations of mathematics, Hilbert stressed the importance of the axiomatic method and its superiority over the genetic approach, by which concepts are extended piecemeal as the need arises. Once a theory is axiomatized, however, it invites a number of general questions concerning the logical relations holding between its propositions, and Hilbert was soon to consider as central among such questions the problem of establishing consistency, or freedom from contradiction. Hilbert did not himself think that there was any support for the allegations of inconsistency in analysis, as made by Hermann Weyl. Nevertheless, he wished to consolidate once and for all the foundations of mathematics and to give them such clarity that the axiom of choice would be as perspicuous as the simplest arithmetical truth. To this end he needed to devise consistency proofs. He had, in 1899, shown the consistency of Euclidean geometry relative to the theory of real numbers, but proofs of this form do no more than shift the problem of consistency to the system to which the original theory has been reduced. Some new, more direct method seemed to be called for.

Despite his confidence in the consistency of classical mathematics, Hilbert contended that operating in an abstract way with mathematical concepts had proved insecure, and his remedy was to interpret number theory as relating to the observable domain of such signs as 1, 11, 111. Elementary number theory is thereby assured of a concrete interpretation—"3 > 2," for example, can be understood as asserting that the concatenation of three strokes extends beyond the concatenation of two strokes. However, the possibility of such an interpretation does not extend to all branches of classical mathematics, for such entities as transfinite cardinals do not allow of representation as sequences of strokes.

Hilbert's solution to this difficulty was to treat such numbers as "ideal" elements. Thus, appealing to Kant, he argued that one precondition for the application of logical laws is a domain of extralogical concrete objects, given in actual perception and capable of being exhaustively surveyed. Nowhere in nature is an actual infinity to be found; therefore, whereas for finite numbers a perceptually given basis could be given, transfinite numbers had a place in mathematics only as ideal elements, much like the ideal factors introduced to preserve the simple laws of divisibility for algebraic whole numbers. Such a reduction was, Hilbert claimed, a natural extension of the work of Weierstrass, who had shown that reference to infinity in the context of calculus involved merely a *façon de parler*, replaceable by a theory of limits requiring a potential infinite rather than an actual one. Similarly, the infinities introduced by Cantor, though apparently irreducible, had to be shown to be indispensable, and arguments proceeding via the infinite had to be replaced by finite methods that achieve the same goal. Again, since the transfinite enters with the use of unbounded quantifiers, statements containing these had to be regarded as ideal statements.

With this approach Hilbert hoped to partially vindicate classical mathematics against the attacks of the intuitionists. Complete vindication, however, required a proof of consistency, and the method that Hilbert proposed for obtaining such a proof is closely related to his method for providing elementary number theory with a sound basis. That is, just as he had considered numbers as sequences of strokes, so he now regarded formulas and proofs as sequences of uninterpreted signs. In this way he provided a concrete subject matter for a proof of consistency, a proof that was to invoke only logical principles whose security and perspicuity are equal to the security and perspicuity of the perceptually given domain on which they are to operate.

Thus, the consistency of some given formalization of a branch of mathematics could be unquestionably established if it could be shown by finite combinatorial methods that no manipulation of the symbols which represents a passage from axioms to theorems could result in the derivation of the expression "0 = 1" or of some other concatenation of symbols which, when interpreted, is seen to be an absurdity. The theory itself might contain symbols for transfinite cardinals and other ideal elements, but this would be no obstacle to a consistency proof, since in such a proof we are required only to treat these symbols as perceptually given objects and to show that they will never figure in a formula whose negation is also provable. On the other hand, Hilbert believed that although nonfinitary concepts are allowable within mathematics proper, they are not to be countenanced in the theory of proof that is to ensure consistency.

The formalist school, which included Wilhelm Ackermann, Paul Bernays, and John von Neumann, succeeded in establishing a number of metamathematical results of considerable significance, but without completing Hilbert's original program, for although successively stronger systems of arithmetic were proved consistent, no proof was forthcoming for the full system required by classical number theory. And, indeed, results obtained by Kurt Gödel in 1931 indicate that no finitary consistency proof is possible, since any proof of consistency must make an appeal to principles which are more general than those provided by the system and accordingly are as much open to question as those principles whose consistency we wish to establish. Attempts were subsequently made to prove consistency by means which were as close to being finitary as possible, notably by Gerhard Gentzen in 1936, but even if "finitary" were thought to apply to the methods used—in this case an application of transfinite induction—it would not follow that classical mathematics had been vindicated against the intuitionists, since to their way of thinking the mere consistency of mathematics would not suffice to confer a clear meaning on the crucial concepts of classical mathematics.

See also Gödel's Incompleteness Theorems; Hilbert, David; Kant, Immanuel; Mathematics, Foundations of; Neumann, John von; Proof Theory; Weyl, (Claus Hugo) Hermann.

Bede Rundle (1967)

LÖWENHEIM. A number of significant results concerning the first-order functional or predicate calculus (with identity) date from a paper published in 1915 by Leopold Löwenheim (1878–1957), a mathematician of Schröder's school. In this paper, "Über Möglichkeiten im Relativkalkül" (*Mathematische Annalen* 76 [1915]: 447–470), Löwenheim showed how the problem of deciding the validity of formulas in this calculus reduces to the problem of determining the validity of formulas in which only two-place predicate letters occur. Since (from the point of view of decidability) such formulas are accordingly no less general than arbitrary formulas of the calculus, we know from a later result, by Alonzo Church, that the decision problem for this class is unsolvable. However, Löwenheim was able to provide a decision procedure for a more restricted class of formulas, those in which only one-place predicate letters occur. He also showed that no formula of this restricted class could be valid in every finite domain, yet not be valid in an infinite domain, and his most famous result, known as Löwenheim's theorem, states that any formula of the full calculus which is valid in a denumerable domain is valid in every nonempty domain.

Although it is not difficult to show that if a formula is valid in a given domain, it is valid in any smaller domain, we cannot in general claim that validity in a given domain establishes validity in a larger domain. But as Löwenheim recognized, a formula may be valid in every domain comprising only finitely many of the natural numbers, yet not be valid in the domain of all natural numbers. The significance of Löwenheim's result is thus that validity in a denumerable domain guarantees validity not simply in any smaller domain but in domains which, like that of the real numbers, are of even greater cardinality than the set of natural numbers.

Bede Rundle (1967)

SKOLEM. The Norwegian mathematician Thoralf Skolem (1887–1963) made extensive contributions to the development of logic, maintaining a steady output of important papers from 1920 until his death. Skolem's first major result was an extension of the above-mentioned theorem of Löwenheim that if a formula of the first-order functional calculus (with identity) is valid in a denumerably infinite domain, it is valid in every nonempty domain and that, equivalently, if such a formula is satisfiable at all, then it is satisfiable in a domain comprising at most a denumerable infinity of elements. In 1920, Skolem generalized this theorem to the case of classes (possibly infinite) of formulas, establishing that if a class of formulas is simultaneously satisfiable, then it is satisfiable in a denumerably infinite domain. Skolem's proof makes use of the axiom of choice and the Skolem normal form of a

formula—a type of prenex normal form in which no universal quantifier precedes an existential quantifier—but both these devices were subsequently dropped, and a more constructive version of the proof was given in 1928, a version which led to the developments of Herbrand and to Gödel's completeness proof.

Skolem was led by his work on Löwenheim's theorem to consider set-theoretic concepts as in a certain sense relative. This view derives from the fact that suitable axiomatizations of set theory can be written in the notation of first-order logic, the only symbol foreign to this logic—the epsilon of membership—being replaced by a dyadic predicate letter. The result is a set of formulas which, if consistent, has by Löwenheim's theorem an interpretation within a denumerably infinite domain. At the same time, within the system of set theory we can establish, by Cantor's theorem, the existence of nondenumerably infinite sets. This apparent conflict between the magnitude of the sets in the axiomatic theory and the more limited domain in which it is modeled is known as the Löwenheim–Skolem paradox. Skolem's way out of this paradox was to suggest that the distinction between denumerable and nondenumerable be taken as relative to an axiom system, a set which is nondenumerable in a given axiomatization perhaps being denumerable in another.

The possibility of an enumeration not available within the original axiom system has led to the description of Löwenheim's theorem as the first of the modern incompleteness theorems, but Skolem's resolution of his paradox does not represent the only possibility. In the first place, it is not clear how the required enumeration could be devised even outside the system in question. To take an analogous case, Cantor's theorem shows that the members of a set containing three elements cannot be paired off with the members of the power set of this set. Since the power set in this case contains eight elements, Cantor's result is in no way surprising, but there is no inclination to say that further mappings might be devised which would yield a one-to-one correspondence between the three-member set and the eight-member set. In the second place, Löwenheim's theorem does not require us to suppose that the axiomatized theory guarantees an enumeration of the sets, since the reinterpretation of the original symbolism with respect to a denumerable domain results in a revision of the propositions implying or asserting the existence of a nondenumerable infinity of sets. By hypothesis, such propositions go over into propositions which hold in the denumerable model, but although their truth is preserved, their original meaning is altered: they could not without contradiction assert the nondenumerability of the new model.

The set-theoretic relativism that Skolem inferred from the Löwenheim–Skolem theorem led him to doubt whether mathematical concepts could be completely characterized axiomatically, and in 1934 he published a result confirming these doubts by demonstrating that no categorical system of postulates for the natural numbers can be expressed in the notation of quantification theory. Any attempt to give a unique characterization of the natural numbers by means of propositions expressed in this notation is bound to fail, even if a denumerable infinity of such propositions is allowed, since there will always be other systems of entities conforming to the structure so defined. Although this result was uncongenial to those who had hoped to delineate the numbers from a formalist standpoint, the nonstandard models which are yielded by such proofs have become increasingly important, and their application to such topics as independence proofs and mathematical analysis promises to be fruitful.

Skolem also made important contributions to the theory of recursive functions. His work in this field dates from a pioneering paper of 1923, in which he sought to develop arithmetic in a logic-free calculus. Essentially this meant the elimination of quantifiers, an elimination that Skolem proposed to effect by the extensive use of recursive definitions. For instance, instead of defining "$a < b$" as "$(\exists x)(a + x = b)$," we can avoid the use of the existential quantifier by means of the joint stipulation of (i) $-(a < 1)$ and (ii) $a < (b + 1) \leftrightarrow (a < b) \vee (a = b)$. In this and subsequent papers Skolem advanced such reductions as part of a finitistic program for securing the basis of arithmetic.

Also important are Skolem's contributions to set theory. The Zermelo–Fraenkel system is commonly presented with his modifications, and in his last years he took up the study of set-theoretic contradictions from the standpoint of systems of many-valued logic.

See also Cantor, Georg; Many-Valued Logics; Set Theory.

Bede Rundle (1967)

HERBRAND. Despite a tragically short life—he was killed in a mountaineering accident in 1931 at the age of twenty-three—Jacques Herbrand made substantial contributions to the development of mathematical logic, especially to investigations in the metatheory of logic that were the particular concern of Hilbert and his school. The bulk of Herbrand's contributions is to be found in his University of Paris dissertation of 1930, *Recherches sur la*

théorie de la démonstration (published in *Travaux de la Société des Sciences et des Lettres de Varsovie*, Classe III (33) [1930]: 33–160). This work has much in common with the later "Untersuchungen über das logische Schliessen" of Gerhard Gentzen, but the presentation of proofs and explanations is much less perspicuous than Gentzen's, and even now some aspects of Herbrand's work await further clarification and elaboration.

Herbrand's starting point is the system of classical propositional logic presented in Whitehead and Russell's *Principia Mathematica*, but the extension of this to functional calculi of first and higher orders is effected by the addition of further rules in place of axioms. The resultant calculi, in which mathematical theories may be embedded, are investigated from a Hilbertian proof-theoretic viewpoint, with emphasis on such syntactic notions as derivability and to the exclusion of semantic questions that cannot be given a finistic interpretation. New proofs are given of a number of results already known, such as those concerning solvable cases of the decision problem, and for the first time the idea and proof of the deduction theorem is presented for a particular system of logic. That is, Herbrand showed that a necessary and sufficient condition for the derivability of a proposition P in his theory with hypotheses H is that $H \supset P$ should be derivable in the logic without hypotheses.

Herbrand's most powerful result concerns the necessity and sufficiency of certain conditions for the provability of a quantificational schema. He showed, in fact, that such a schema is provable if and only if a quantifier-free tautology of a prescribed form is constructible from it. The proofs of the various theses that go to make up this result are somewhat complicated, but the form of tautology which is associated with a provable formula can be indicated in the following way: First, a given quantificational schema is so transformed that each quantifier has its minimum scope or, alternatively, each has its maximum scope. Taking just the first case, then, all the quantifiers are placed initially and have a scope that extends to the far right of the formula.

Suppose we are given a schema in this form—for example, $\exists x \, \exists y \, \forall z \, [Fx \rightarrow (Fy \, \& \, Fz)]$—which we shall call "A." The necessary and sufficient condition of A's holding is that it be false that for any x and y there is a value of z for which the matrix of A is false. Accordingly, if x and y both take the value a_1, say, there must be some value a_2 of z that results in the falsity of the matrix if A is to be false; further, if x takes the value a_1 and y takes the value a_2, then for some value a_3 of z the matrix must be false; again, if x takes the value a_2 and y takes the value a_1, the matrix must be false for some value a_4 of z, and so on. But if we find that at least one of the substitution instances of the matrix so generated must be true, we have shown the failure of a necessary condition for the falsity of A. In fact, this is the outcome of the present example, since the disjunction of the cases so far considered, $[Fa_1 \rightarrow (Fa_1 \& Fa_2)] \vee [Fa_1 \rightarrow (Fa_2 \& Fa_3)] \vee [Fa_2 \rightarrow (Fa_1 \& Fa_4)]$, is a tautology—thus, if Fa_2 is true, the first disjunct is true, and if Fa_2 is false, the last disjunct is true.

Herbrand showed how such disjunctions can be constructed from a formula in prenex normal form with the quantifiers occurring in any number and order. He showed, too, that the original formula can be retrieved from such a disjunction by the application of a few simple rules, without use of *modus ponens*. And, indeed, it is clear from the example given that the only rules required for the derivation of the original formula from the tautology are rules allowing for the insertion of quantifiers before the disjuncts and a rule allowing us to erase repetitions of identical disjuncts. The final result allows us to assert that the constructibility of a tautologous disjunction is both a necessary and a sufficient condition for the provability of the associated quantified schema.

In addition to shedding considerable light on the structure of quantification theory, Herbrand's theorem is the source of a number of important metatheoretic results. Löwenheim's theorem is an immediate consequence—accepted by Herbrand only when reinterpreted finitistically—and certain cases of the decision problem allow of simple resolution. Important for Herbrand's aims was the application of his theorem to the question of the consistency of arithmetic, and he was able to show that if we have a model for a set of hypotheses, an interpretation with respect to some domain under which all these hypotheses are true, then no contradiction can arise in the theory deduced from the axioms. Suppose hypotheses $H_1, H_2, \cdots, H_n$ give rise to a contradiction while having a true interpretation within the model. Since $H_1 \& H_2 \& \cdots \& H_n$ comes out true in the model, the model brings the negation of this conjunction out false, and if a formula is false in some domain, it is not associated with a quantifier-free tautology. If, on the other hand, $H_1, H_2, \cdots, H_n$ yield a contradiction, then $\sim(H_1 \& H_2 \& \cdots \& H_n)$ is provable and thus is associated with a tautologous disjunction. This form of consistency proof was discussed further by Herbrand in his later article "Sur la Non-contradiction de l'arithmétique" (*Journal für die reine und angewandte Mathematik* 166 [1931]: 1–8), and the same idea appears in Gentzen's "Untersuchungen über das logische Schliessen."

See also Quantifiers in Formal Logic; Russell, Bertrand Arthur William; Whitehead, Alfred North.

Bede Rundle (1967)

GÖDEL. Kurt Gödel (1906–1978), a major figure in the history of logic, is best known for his celebrated incompleteness theorem presented in "Über formal unentscheidbare Sätze der Principia Mathematica und verwandter Systeme I" (*Monatshefte für Mathematik und Physik* 38 [1931]: 173–198) and his associated proof of the impossibility of establishing the consistency of customary formulations of arithmetic by methods formalizable within the systems themselves. In addition to these results (discussed in the entry Gödel's Theorem), Gödel made important contributions to several other branches of logic, and prior to his 1931 paper he had already presented the first completeness proof for the first-order functional calculus (in "Die Vollstandigkeit der Axiome des logischen Funktionkalküls," *Monatshefte für Mathematik und Physik* 37[1930]: 349–360). Making use of a normal form devised by Thoralf Skolem, Gödel elaborated a proof along lines that were followed by Jacques Herbrand to a similar end in a publication of the same year (*Recherches sur la théorie de la démonstration*, in *Travaux de la Société des Sciences et des Lettres de Varsovie*, Classe III [33] [1930]: 33–160), but he went further than Herbrand in his method for showing how any unprovable formula may be falsified.

Intuitionistic as well as classical logic has been one of Gödel's major concerns, and his results in this field are of importance to an understanding of the formalizations of this logic initiated by Arend Heyting in 1930. The intuitionist propositional calculus is naturally thought of as a subsystem of classical logic, obtained by omitting from the latter those theses that are intuitionistically unacceptable. Gödel indicated that this picture could in a sense be reversed, since it is possible to define all two-valued truth-functions by means of the connectives for negation and conjunction, and he was able to show that any formula involving only these connectives is provable within intuitionistic logic if it is provable classically. Gödel showed, further, that even classical number theory, if suitably interpreted, can be thought of as included within intuitionistic number theory. He also proved that the intuitionist propositional calculus has no finite characteristic matrix. That is, although the two-valued truth tables for classical logic serve to verify all and only those theses provable in this logic, it is impossible, according to Gödel's result, to devise truth tables having any finite number of values that will perform the same service for the intuitionist system.

Two propositions that have been at the center of much investigation and controversy are the axiom of choice and Cantor's generalized continuum hypothesis. It was Gödel who proved that both are consistent with the axioms of set theory provided only that these axioms are themselves consistent. The axiom of choice is a highly nonconstructive axiom licensing the selection of an unspecified element from each of a (possibly infinite) family of sets and the formation of a set comprising just the elements so selected. The generalized continuum hypothesis, which in fact implies the axiom of choice, states that $2^{\aleph_\alpha} = \aleph_{\alpha+1}$; that is, starting with $\aleph_0$, which is the number of the natural numbers, the series of increasingly higher cardinals is successively generated by raising 2 to the power of the preceding aleph. The system Σ of set theory that Gödel used derives from John von Neumann and Paul Bernays. Gödel showed that if it were possible to derive a contradiction from the axiom of choice and the continuum hypothesis in Σ, then the axioms of Σ alone would suffice for the derivation of a contradiction. This result is obtained by constructing a model Δ within Σ itself, where Δ is such that the propositions asserting that the axioms of Σ hold for Δ are demonstrable in Σ and the similar relativizations to Δ of the axiom of choice and the generalized continuum hypothesis are likewise demonstrable in Σ. Paul J. Cohen showed, in 1963, that the negations of these propositions are also consistent with the axioms of set theory. In other words, the axiom of choice and the generalized continuum hypothesis are now known to be independent of the other axioms of set theory.

See also Cantor, Georg; Gödel, Kurt; Neumann, John von; Set Theory.

Bede Rundle (1967)

SINCE GÖDEL

The pace of development in logic picked up rapidly after Gödel's incompleteness theorems, and five branches emerged: set theory, model theory, proof theory, computability theory, and nonclassical logics.

Gödel's theorems were formulated for type theory, but this was soon displaced as the framework for mathematics by Zermelo-Frankel set theory with choice (ZFC). Gödel's theorems still apply, and imply the existence of set-theoretic statements that can be neither proved nor disproved. Gödel himself showed that Cantor's continuum hypothesis cannot be disproved, and conjectured that it cannot be proved, as was established in the 1960s

by Paul Cohen. Since then the search for new axioms to settle questions left open by ZFC has flourished.

Gödel's results on the unprovability of the consistency of a formal theory within the theory itself were followed by Tarski's work on the undefinability of truth for a formal language within the language itself. Tarski's work also for the first time gave a rigorous definition, in a *meta*-language, of truth for a sentence of formal language, relative to an interpretation, which is needed for a fully rigorous statement even of Gödel's earlier *completeness* theorem. With his truth definition Tarski laid the foundations for a general theory of models, a model of a formal theory being an interpretation that makes it true.

Gödel showed the unachievability of the original aim of proof theory: to establish the consistency of infinitistic mathematics by finitist means; but this leaves open the possibility of establishing *relative* consistency through the interpretation of ostensibly stronger in ostensibly weaker theories. Gödel himself contributed to this program, and in the mid-1930s the powerful new methods were introduced by Gerhardt Gentzen (1909–1945).

Gödel used in his work the auxiliary notion of a primitive recursive function, which include many but not all functions that are effectively computable in an intuitive sense. Two equivalent proposed characterizations of the full class of effectively computable functions followed. Recursive function theory was developed in collaboration with his student S. C. Kleene (1909–1994) by Alonzo Church, who proved there is no effectively computable function that will tell whether a given formula is logically valid. Turing machines were developed by Alan Turing, who proved the possibility in principle of a universal programmable computer, a possibility that began to be realized during the Second World War.

Gödel contributed not only to the areas just enumerated, which together constitute *mathematical logic*, but also to the study of modal and other nonclassical logics, often called *philosophical logic*. Mathematical logic was characterized by explosive growth after 1945. Philosophical logic grew more slowly until the development of a usable model theory for nonclassical logics with the work of Saul Kripke and others circa 1960, after which development speeded up and important connections with theoretical computer science emerged.

Much of the growth in all five branches has occurred in areas far removed from philosophy, but if the volume of philosophically oriented work has decreased in relative terms, still it has increased in absolute terms owing to the overall growth of logic.

See also Cantor, Georg; Church, Alonzo; Gödel, Kurt; Kripke, Saul; Logic, Non-Classical; Tarski, Alfred; Turing, Alan M.

John P. Burgess (2005)

GENTZEN. The first systematic formulations of the propositional and predicate calculi were presented axiomatically, on the analogy of certain branches of mathematics. In 1934, Gerhard Gentzen (1909–1945), a logician of Hilbert's school, published a formalization of logical principles more in accordance with the way in which these principles are customarily applied. (A similar approach was developed independently by S. Jaśkowski; see below, section on Polish logicians.) In illustrating his technique Gentzen considered how we might establish as valid the schema $(X \vee (Y \& Z)) \supset (X \vee Y) \& (X \vee Z)$. Assuming that the antecedent holds, either X is true, or $Y \& Z$ is true. In the former case we can pass to each of $X \vee Y$ and $X \vee Z$ and hence to their joint assertion. Assuming now $Y \& Z$, we may infer Y, whence $X \vee Y$, and likewise Z, whence $X \vee Z$. In this case the conjunction is once more derivable. Since it is derivable from each disjunct of the original assumption, we may assert the implication unconditionally.

In this simple form of argument the justification of the schema has been broken down into a series of uncomplicated steps, each involving either the introduction or the elimination of a logical connective. Extracting the rules that were applied and supplementing them with similar rules governing the use of the other connectives, we arrive at a system of "natural" deduction—either *NJ* (intuitionist logic) or *NK* (classical logic). Gentzen considered the former more natural than the latter, but whichever we opt for, it appears that the resultant codification of logical principles is more natural, on at least two counts, than a codification presented in axiomatic fashion.

In the first place, we avoid the devious moves that may be necessary to establish a logical principle from an axiomatic basis and follow more closely a pattern of reasoning that we should intuitively adopt. In the second place, the conception of logic as a system of axioms and theorems adjoined to some given subject matter appears inappropriate, since, in their application to, say, a branch of mathematics, principles of logic function not as true statements forming part of the theory in question but as rules of inference allowing us to establish relations of consequence between propositions of the theory.

In addition to the systems *NJ* and *NK*, Gentzen devised related formalizations of logic, the *L*-systems, in which derivable formulas are shown to possess a particularly direct form of proof. These systems contain the "cut" rule, a generalized form of *modus ponens* that, like *modus ponens*, has the disadvantage that we cannot work back from a schema to premises from which it could have been derived. However, although the cut rule is crucial in showing the equivalence of the *L*-systems with the earlier *N*-systems, Gentzen showed that the cut rule can be eliminated from any proof in the *L*-systems. This powerful metatheorem simplifies the reconstruction of proofs of valid formulas, yielding a decision procedure for the propositional fragments of *LJ* and *LK* and greatly facilitating the search for proofs in the full calculi. Gentzen further applied his *Hauptsatz* to proofs of consistency; in particular, he showed one formalization of arithmetic to be noncontradictory. The formalization in question does not contain a schema of unrestricted induction, but in later works Gentzen remedied this defect, overcoming the obstacle to such proofs presented by Gödel's results by making use of a principle of transfinite induction which cannot be reduced to ordinary induction within the system. It is a matter of controversy whether such a proof represents the attainment of one of Hilbert's goals, a finitary consistency proof for classical number theory.

See also Gödel, Kurt; Hilbert, David; Induction.

Bede Rundle (1967)

CHURCH. From the beginning of the twentieth century questions concerning the decidability of logical and mathematical theories have held a special interest for logicians, mathematicians, and philosophers. A number of important concepts and far-reaching results in this field have come from Alonzo Church (1903–1995), author of a definitive text on logic and noted writer on the history of logic.

The notion of decidability is not one which a beginner in mathematics could explicitly formulate, but both this and related notions, such as that of effective calculability, have a place in the description of the most elementary mathematical concepts. Often our understanding of a particular numerical predicate is inextricably tied to our ability to determine whether or not an arbitrary number satisfies that predicate, and in many cases terms expressing the result of a calculation or computation can be fully grasped only by one who has the ability to carry out the sorts of computation in question. Thus, with the division of numbers into odd and even there is intimately associated a technique for determining which of these predicates applies to an arbitrary whole number; similarly, a person's grasp of the concepts of sum and product is measured by his ability to calculate sums and products. But although the grasp of concepts and the mastering of techniques may go hand in hand in many cases, the symbolism of arithmetic allows us to formulate propositions whose truth-value may resist determination by any obvious methods of computing or reasoning in general, a situation that frequently arises with the introduction of unrestricted quantification.

Consider, for instance, the proposition P, "There is at least one odd perfect number." A perfect number is a number that is equal to the sum of its divisors, itself excluded. Thus, 6 is perfect, being equal to the sum of 1, 2, and 3; so is 28, being equal to the sum of 1, 2, 4, 7, and 14. Like "x is odd," the predicate "x is perfect" is a decidable predicate, in the sense that given any number n, we can, after a finite number of steps, respond with an unambiguous *yes* or *no* to the question "Is n perfect?" But although both of the predicates entering into P are decidable, the infinitude of the positive integers is an obstacle to an immediate determination of the truth-value of P which would make use of the decidability of these predicates together with a case-by-case examination of the integers. Indeed, proposition P, along with Fermat's last theorem, Goldbach's conjecture, and many other propositions of elementary number theory, has as yet been neither proved nor disproved. Accordingly we may well wonder whether it is possible to devise a technique that, when applied to an arbitrary proposition of this class, would enable us to determine the truth or provability of the proposition. Now, for all we know, any one of these outstanding problems may eventually be resolved, but Church showed that no general technique could be devised which would allow us to ascertain in an effective manner the truth or provability of an arbitrary arithmetical proposition.

By a direct application of the method of diagonalization (a procedure whereby a hypothesized function is shown to differ from each member of a class of functions of which it must be a member if it is to exist), Church demonstrated not simply that such a technique has proved elusive but that the supposition of its existence involves an absurdity. In this respect arithmetic contrasts with the propositional calculus, but although the propositional calculus does have a decision procedure—the method of truth-tables—Church showed that the first-order functional calculus fares no better than arithmetic, it being impossible to find a method that allows us to recognize as provable or refutable an arbitrary formula of this calculus. It may prove—indeed, in many cases it has already been shown—that fragments of these systems are

decidable, but Hilbert's aim of a general technique which would banish ignorance from mathematics appears to be unattainable.

In demonstrating his theorem Church was obliged to provide a formal counterpart of the intuitive notion of effective calculability, and he proposed that this notion be identified with that of recursiveness. The notion of a recursive function (of positive integers) was introduced by Gödel, acting on a suggestion of Herbrand, and was analyzed in detail by S. C. Kleene. A function is said to be (general) recursive (a generalization of the notion of primitive recursive) if, roughly speaking, its value for given arguments can be calculated from a set of equations by means of two rules, one allowing the replacement of variables by numerals, the other allowing the substitution of equals for equals. As Church remarks, the intuitive status of effective calculability rules out any complete justification of his proposal (since known as Church's thesis), but he adduces reasons for regarding the identification as plausible, and the plausibility of his thesis has subsequently been reinforced by the discovery that despite their apparent dissimilarity, various alternative attempts to characterize the intuitive concept have all proved equivalent to that of general recursiveness.

Thus, at the time Church put forward his thesis the Church-Kleene notion of λ-definability was already known to provide an equivalent, and Turing's "computability," Post's "1-definability" and "binormality," and Markov's "computability" provide alternatives defined with respect to machines and combinatorial operations. It should be mentioned, however, that Church's thesis has not met with universal support; a summary and criticism of a number of objections can be found in Elliot Mendelson's "On Some Recent Criticism of Church's Thesis" (in *Notre Dame Journal of Formal Logic* 4 [1963]: 201–205).

See also Church, Alonzo; Gödel, Kurt; Number; Turing, Alan M.

Bede Rundle (1967)

TURING AND COMPUTABILITY THEORY. In the late 1930s Alan M. Turing was one of the founders of computability theory. His main contributions to this field were published in three papers that appeared in the span of a few years, and especially in his ground-breaking 1936–1937 paper, published when he was twenty-four years old.

As indicated by its title, "On Computable Numbers, with an Application to the Entscheidungsproblem," Turing's paper deals ostensibly with real numbers that are computable in the sense that their decimal expansion "can be written down by a machine." As he pointed out, however, the ideas carry over easily to computable functions on the integers or to computable predicates.

The paper was based on work that Turing had carried out as a Cambridge graduate student, under the direction of Maxwell Newman (1897–1984). When Turing first saw a 1936 paper by Alonzo Church, he realized at once that the two of them were tackling the same problem—making computability precise—albeit from different points of view. Turing wrote to Church and then traveled to Princeton University to meet with him. The final form of the paper was submitted from Princeton.

In a space of thirty-six pages, the paper manages to accomplish the following six goals:

(1) A formalization of what it means to be "calculable by finite means," in terms of an idealized computing device—now known of course as a Turing machine.

(2) The construction of a "universal computing machine," which when supplied with the "standard description" of a machine M on its tape, will simulate the operation of M.

(3) The proof of the unsolvability of the halting problem and proofs of the unsolvability of other problems, such as the problem of deciding, given a machine M, whether or not M will ever print the symbol 0.

(4) Three kinds of arguments for Turing's thesis, that is, the claim that his formulation in terms of machines is successful in capturing the idea of "processes which can be carried out in computing" (249). It should be noted that Kurt Gödel and others have found Turing's arguments here completely convincing.

(5) A proof of Church's theorem that David Hilbert's Entscheidungsproblem can have no solution, that is, the problem of deciding whether or not a given formula is derivable in the predicate calculus is unsolvable.

(6) An outline, in an appendix, of the equivalence of computability by Turing machines to computability as formulated by Church in terms of the λ-calculus. (This proof was given in further detail in Turing's 1937 paper, "Computability and λ-Definability.")

Turing's paper remains a readable introduction to his ideas. How might a diligent clerk carry out a calculation by following instructions? The clerk might organize the work in a notebook. At any given moment his or her attention is focused on a particular page. Following the instructions, he or she might alter that page, and then might turn to another page. And the notebook is large enough that he or she never comes to the last page.

The alphabet of symbols available to the clerk must finite; if there were infinitely many symbols, then there would be two that were arbitrarily similar and so might be confused. One can then, without loss of generality, regard what can be written on one page of notebook as a single symbol. And one can envision the notebook pages as being placed side by side, forming a paper tape, consisting of squares, each square being either blank or printed with a symbol. At each stage of the work, the clerk—or the mechanical machine—can alter the square under examination, can turn attention to the next square or the previous one, and can look to the instructions to see what part of them to follow next. Turing describes the latter as a change of state of mind.

Turing writes, "We may now construct a machine to do the work" (251). Such a machine is of course now called a Turing machine, a phrase first used by Church in his review of Turing's paper in *The Journal of Symbolic Logic*. The machine has a potentially infinite tape, marked into squares. Initially, the tape is blank. (Alternatively, if one wants to compute some function, the input word or number can be written on the tape.) The machine is capable of being in any one of finitely many states (the phrase *of mind* being inappropriate for a machine).

At each step of the calculation, depending on its state at the time, the machine can change the symbol in the square under examination at that time, can turn its attention to the square to the left or to the right, and can then change its state to another state.

The program for this Turing machine can be given by a table. Where the possible states of the machine are $q_1, \ldots, q_r$, each line of the table is a quintuple (q_i, S_j, S_k, D, q_m) that is to be interpreted as directing that whenever the machine is in state q_i and the square under examination contains the symbol S_j, then that symbol should be altered to S_k and the machine should shift its attention to the square on the left (if $D = L$) or on the right (if $D = R$), and should change its state to q_m. For the program to be unambiguous, it should have no two different quintuples with the same first two components. One of the states, say q_1, is designated as the initial state—the state in which the machine begins its calculation. If one starts the machine running in this state, it might (or might not), after some number of steps, reach a state and a symbol for which its table lacks a quintuple having that state and symbol for its first two components. At that point the machine halts.

In particular, where 0 and 1 are among the symbols in the alphabet, the machine might run on and on, sometimes printing a 0 or 1 on the tape (besides printing whatever other markers are needed for the computation). In this way, the machine might generate an infinite binary string. One can interpret this binary string as giving the binary expansion of a real number in the unit interval. Say that a real number is computable if it differs by an integer from a number in the unit interval whose binary expansion can be generated by some Turing machine.

Alternatively, if one wants the machine to compute a function, one can, after starting the machine with the input word or number on the tape, wait for it to halt and then look at the tape (starting with the square then under examination) to see what the output word or number is.

Turing shows how to construct a "universal computing machine" that, when supplied with the "standard description" of a machine M on its tape, will simulate the operation of M. This allows him to apply a diagonal argument to show that there can be no computable way to determine whether or not a given machine will continue to print 0's and 1's forever. In effect, he shows the unsolvability of the halting problem.

Turing argues that his formulation of the computability concept includes all sequences that would informally be considered to be computable. That is, he argues for what is now called Turing's thesis, the Church-Turing thesis, or Church's thesis, depending on the context. He gives three kinds of arguments: First, he shows how his machines can capture the informal idea of a step-by-step process, as indicated briefly earlier. Second, he shows that certain changes to his definition of a machine would have no effect at all on what sequences would be computable. And third, he gives examples of large classes of numbers that are computable: the real algebraic numbers, e, π, the real zeros of the Bessel functions, and so forth. Of course, as he emphasizes, only countably many real numbers can be computable.

Turing's 1939 paper, "Systems of Logic Based on Ordinals," is based on his PhD dissertation, written under Church's supervision during Turing's two-year stay at Princeton.

Gödel's incompleteness theorems had shown that any sufficiently strong formal system was incomplete, and in particular could not prove its own consistency. One can then add to this formal system the sentence expressing its consistency, thereby obtaining a stronger system.

And this process can be iterated. The iteration can be transfinite, making use of ordinal notations for the constructive ordinals. This topic, which was later taken up by Solomon Feferman (1928–) in the 1950s, does not directly pertain to computability theory.

In the process, however, Turing introduced the important concept of computability relative to an oracle. He gave the basic definitions and indicated how his work on computability could be adapted to incorporate the idea of calculations that, at any stage, could utilize a hypothetical fixed body of information. This idea later led to work on the classification (of problems or of sets or of functions) according to degree of unsolvability. Moreover, the degrees of unsolvability are partially ordered, under what is now called Turing reducibility.

After 1939 Turing's work on computability stopped while Turing, now back in England, threw himself into wartime cryptographic work. There was an urgent need to break the German battlefield Enigma code. The success of Turing and the British cryptographic team was of enormous military importance throughout World War II. But nothing was known publicly about this work until it was declassified several years after Turing's suicide in 1954.

After the war Turing turned to computation topics, both practical and theoretical, outside the field of computability theory. On the practical side, he was involved in hardware and software design for early digital computers. On the theoretical side, he published important work on artificial intelligence.

See also Church, Alonzo; Computability Theory; Computationalism; Gödel, Kurt; Hilbert, David; Machine Intelligence; Turing, Alan M.

Bibliography

Church, Alonzo. "An Unsolvable Problem of Elementary Number Theory." *American Journal of Mathematics* 58 (1936): 345–363.

Turing, A. M. "Computability and λ-Definability." *The Journal of Symbolic Logic* 2 (1937): 153–163.

Turing, A. M. "On Computable Numbers, with an Application to the Entscheidungsproblem." *Proceedings of the London Mathematical Society* 42 (1936–1937): 230–265. A correction, 43 (1937): 544–546.

Turing, A. M. "Systems of Logic Based on Ordinals." *Proceedings of the London Mathematical Society* 45 (3) (1939): 161–228.

Herbert B. Enderton (2005)

DECIDABLE AND UNDECIDABLE THEORIES. Suppose T is a theory (i.e., a set of sentences) in a formal language

L of logic. A decision procedure for *T* is a mechanical procedure for calculating whether any given sentence of *L* is a logical consequence of *T*. We say that *T* is decidable if it has a decision procedure and undecidable if not. The decision problem for *T* is to determine whether or not *T* is decidable. (One can avoid the slightly vague notion of a mechanical procedure by noting that a theory *T* is decidable if and only if the set of its logical consequences is computable.

Quantifier elimination and related model-theoretic techniques have yielded proofs that many important first-order theories are decidable. Examples are the theory of addition of integers (Presburger 1930), the theories of real-closed fields and algebraically closed fields (Tarski 1951), the theory of abelian groups (Szmielew 1955), and—if a number-theoretic conjecture of Schanuel is true—the theory of the field of real numbers with exponentiation (Macintyre and Wilkie 1996). The first theory shown to be undecidable was first-order Peano arithmetic; Kurt Gödel proved its undecidability in 1931. Many other undecidable theories are known, but the proofs of undecidability are all based directly or indirectly on Gödel's ideas. In 1970 Yuri V. Matiyasevich (1993) improved Gödel's result by showing that the set of diophantine sentences true in the natural numbers is not computable (a diophantine sentence is one of the form "There are natural numbers *m*, *n*, and so on such that *E* is true," where *E* is an arithmetical equation using *m*, *n*, and so on). Part 3 of "Decidable and Undecidable Theories" of J. Donald Monk (1976) gives many examples.

We say that a formal language *L* of logic is decidable if the empty theory in *L* is decidable—in other words, if there is a mechanical test to determine which sentences of *L* are valid. Gödel's ideas led to a proof that if *L* is a nontrivial first-order language, for example, with at least one binary relation symbol besides equality, then *L* is undecidable (Church 1936). Later research extended this result to various important sublanguages of first-order languages. But there are also decidable languages, for example, languages of propositional logic and a number of languages with monadic predicate symbols (e.g., the language of syllogisms). See Egon Börger, Erich Grädel, and Yuri Gurevich (1997) for full information on decidable and undecidable languages. After their book appeared, a new family of decidable languages was discovered, the guarded languages, whose decidability implies the decidability of various modal logics (see Grädel, Hirsch, and Otto 2002).

The decision problem for logical languages is also known as the Entscheidungsproblem. See Paulo Mancosu (1999, §8) on the place of this problem in early twentieth-century thinking about the foundations of mathematics, particularly within the school of David Hilbert.

See also Computability Theory; First-Order Logic; Gödel's Theorem; Model Theory.

Bibliography

Börger, Egon, Erich Grädel, and Yuri Gurevich. *The Classical Decision Problem*. Berlin: Springer, 1997.

Church, Alonzo. "A Note on the Entscheidungsproblem." *Journal of Symbolic Logic* 1 (1936): 40–41. Correction *ibid*: 101–102.

Gödel, Kurt. "Über formal unentscheidbare Sätze der Principia Mathematica und verwandter Systeme I." *Monatshefte für Mathematik und Physik* 38 (1931): 173–198. Edited and translated in *Kurt Gödel. Collected Works Volume I: Publications 1929–1936*, ed. Solomon Feferman, et al, pp. 144–195. New York: Oxford University Press, 1986.

Grädel, Erich, Colin Hirsch, and Martin Otto. "Back and Forth between Guarded and Modal Logics." *ACM Transactions on Computational Logics* 3 (2002): 418–463.

Macintyre, Angus, and Alex Wilkie. "On the Decidability of the Real Exponential Field." *Kreiseliana*, edited by P. Odifreddi, pp. 441–467. Wellesley, MA: A.K. Peters, 1996.

Mancosu, Paolo. "Between Russell and Hilbert: Behmann on the Foundations of Mathematics." *Bulletin of Symbolic Logic* 5 (1999): 303–330.

Matiyasevich, Yuri V. *Hilbert's Tenth Problem*. Cambridge, MA: MIT Press, 1993.

Monk, J. Donald. *Mathematical Logic*. New York: Springer, 1976.

Presburger, Mojżesz. "Über die Vollständigkeit eines gewissen Systems der Arithmetik ganzer Zahlen, in welchem die Addition als einzige Operation hervortritt." *Comptes Rendus du Premier Congrès des Mathématiciens des Pays Slaves, Warszawa 1929*. Warsaw (1930): 92–101; supplementarty note *ibid*: 395.

Szmielew, Wanda. "Elementary Properties of Abelian Groups." *Fundamenta Mathematicae* 41 (1955): 203–271.

Tarski, Alfred. *A Decision Method for Elementary Algebra and Geometry*. Berkeley: University of California Press, 1951.

Tarski, Alfred, Andrzej Mostowski, and Raphael M. Robinson. *Undecidable Theories*. Amsterdam: North-Holland, 1953.

Wilfrid Hodges (2005)

MODEL THEORY

Tarski. The Polish-American logician Alfred Tarski (1901–1983) was born Alfred Teitelbaum in Warsaw; he changed his surname to Tarski in 1924. That same year he obtained his doctorate at the University of Warsaw for a thesis in logic under the supervision of Stanisław Leśniewski; he had also studied under Tadeusz Kotarbiński, Kazimierz Kuratowski, Jan Łukasiewicz, Stefan Mazurkiewicz and Wacław Sierpiński. At the University of Warsaw he was Docent and then Adjunct Professor from

1924 to 1939; simultaneously he taught in a high school from 1925 to 1939. From 1942 to his retirement in 1969 he held posts at the University of California at Berkeley.

Through his own work and that of his students, Tarski stands along with Aristotle and Frege as one of the creators of the discipline of logic. Andrzej Mostowski, Julia Robinson, Robert Vaught, Chen-Chung Chang, Solomon Feferman, Richard Montague, Jerome Keisler, and Haim Gaifman, among others, wrote their theses under his supervision.

In print Tarski was reluctant to place himself in any philosophical tradition. He described himself as "perhaps a philosopher of a sort." In 1930 he said that he agreed in principle with Leśniewski's "intuitionistic formalism," but in 1954 he reported that this was no longer his attitude. His philosophical reticence was certainly deliberate and reflected a view that careful formalization can resolve or at least avoid problems thrown up by philosophical speculation.

Tarski had many research interests within logic. He maintained most of them throughout his career and integrated them to an extraordinary degree. The setting of most of his work in Warsaw from 1926 to 1938 was the notion of a deductive theory. Such a theory develops a certain subject matter, starting from primitive terms together with axioms and proceeding by definition and logical deduction, all within a formally defined language. Tarski saw these theories as a paradigm for research in mathematical subjects. Like David Hilbert with his metamathematics, Tarski proposed to take the theories themselves as subject matter. But unlike Hilbert, Tarski did so by developing metatheories (that is, deductive theories about deductive theories) without any restriction to finitary means. For example the notion of "true sentence of the deductive theory T" must be defined in a metatheory T'. Tarski chose as primitive notions of T' those of T together with notions from set theory and syntax, and he showed how to write a definition in the metatheory which exactly characterizes the class of true sentences of T. He proposed similar metatheoretic definitions of "satisfies," "definable," and (with less confidence) "logical consequence." His later characterization of "logical notion" was published posthumously. His influential English exposition of his definition of truth in 1944 is still the best nontechnical introduction.

At the same time Tarski developed methodologies for creating deductive theories of particular topics, and for settling the decision problem for particular deductive theories. His method of elimination of quantifiers, based on work of Thoralf Skolem and others, guided him to an axiomatisation of the first-order theory of the field of real numbers. As a byproduct he found an algorithm for deciding the truth of first-order statements about the field of real numbers (or, as he later realized, any real-closed field). Responding to the work of Alonzo Church and Alan Turing on undecidability, Tarski developed methods for proving the undecidability of a deductive theory T by interpreting a known undecidable theory within T.

In the 1940s Tarski turned his attention to the application of metatheorems of logic in mathematics. In parallel with Anatolii Mal'tsev and Abraham Robinson, he showed that the compactness theorem of first-order logic could be used to prove purely mathematical facts. During the early 1950s he recast his notion of deductive theory to fit the new program. A deductive theory was no longer about a particular subject matter. Rather it was in a formal language with primitive symbols that could be interpreted as one pleases. An interpretation that makes all the axioms of the theory true is called a *model* of the theory. We can study those classes of structures which consist of all the models of a particular theory; in 1954 Tarski proposed the name *theory of models* for this line of research. Tarski adapted his definition of truth to define the relation "Sentence ϕ is true in structure A." He published this new model-theoretic truth definition in a joint paper with Vaught, which also included fundamental theorems about elementary embeddings between structures.

Particular theories that Tarski had studied in connection with quantifier elimination or undecidability became central to model-theoretic research. Some of them, such as the theories of real-closed fields and algebraically closed fields, remained central fifty years on. Tarski also stated several problems that strongly influenced the direction of model-theoretic research. For example he asked for a quantifier elimination for the field of reals with an exponentiation function, and for algebraic necessary and sufficient conditions for two structures to be elementarily equivalent.

Tarski's further contributions during his American period were perhaps more scattered but no less important. He was closely involved in the theory of large cardinals. He also worked with students and colleagues on relation algebras and cylindrical algebras. During the 1960s he studied finite axiomatisations of equational classes, picking up a theme from his work with Łukasiewicz during the 1920s on propositional logics. He never lost his interest in formal theories of geometry. Students of his recall that he looked back with particular pride to the work that he did during the 1940s with Bjarni

Jónsson on decompositions of finite algebras. With the help of colleagues in Europe and the United States, he was instrumental in the setting up of the series of International Congresses in Logic, Methodology and Philosophy of Science, which first met at Stanford in 1960.

See also Aristotle; Frege, Gottlob; Hilbert, David; Kotarbiński, Tadeusz; Leśniewski, Stanisław; Łukasiewicz, Jan; Model Theory; Montague, Richard; Set Theory.

Bibliography

Feferman, Anita Burdman, and Solomon Feferman. *Alfred Tarski: Life and Logic*. New York: Cambridge University Press, 2004.

Givant, Steven R. "A Portrait of Alfred Tarski." *The Mathematical Intelligencer* 13 (1991): 16–32.

Suppes, Patrick. "Philosophical Implications of Tarski's Work." *Journal of Symbolic Logic* 53 (1988): 80–91.

Tarski, Alfred. *O logice matematycznej i metodzie dedukcyjnej*, Biblioteczka Mat. 3–5. Lwów and Warsaw: Ksiąznica-Atlas, 1936. Translated and revised as *Introduction to Logic and to the Methodology of the Deductive Sciences*. New York: Oxford University Press, 1994.

Tarski, Alfred. "The Semantic Conception of Truth." *Philosophy and Phenomenological Research* 4 (1944): 13–47.

Tarski, Alfred. *Logic, Semantics, Metamathematics*. Translated by J. H. Woodger. 2nd ed., edited by John Corcoran. Indianapolis: Hackett, 1983.

Tarski, Alfred. *Pisma Logiczno-Filozoficzne*. Vol. 1, *Prawda*; Vol. 2, *Metalogika*, edited by Jan Zygmunt. Warsaw: Wydawnictwo Naukowe, 1995, 2001.

Tarski, Alfred. "What Are Logical Notions?" *History and Philosophy of Logic* 7 (1986): 143–154.

Tarski, Alfred. *Collected Papers*. 4 vols., edited by S. R. Givant and R. N. McKenzie. Basel: Birkhäuser, 1986.

Tarski, Alfred, and Robert L. Vaught. "Arithmetical Extensions of Relational Systems." *Compositio Mathematica* 13 (1957): 81–102.

Woleński, Jan. *Logic and Philosophy in the Lvov-Warsaw School*. Dordrecht: Kluwer, 1989.

Wilfrid Hodges (2005)

Robinson. Abraham Robinson (1918–1974) was a logician and mathematician. Born in Waldenburg (Silesia), he moved to Palestine in 1933, where he studied mathematics at the Hebrew University in Jerusalem and also joined the Haganah. In 1940 he fled to Britain as a wartime refugee and enlisted with the Free French Air Force. He took his PhD in London in 1949 while teaching aerodynamics at the Cranfield College of Aeronautics. He held posts successively in Toronto, Jerusalem, Los Angeles, and finally Yale, where he died of cancer. His eventful life is described by Joseph W. Dauben (1995).

Robinson's PhD thesis on applications of logic in mathematics led to an invitation to speak at the International Congress of Mathematicians in 1950. The talks of Robinson and Alfred Tarski at this congress became founding documents of the new discipline that Tarski named model theory. Throughout his career Robinson was one of the most fertile contributors of programs, techniques, and results to model theory.

Robinson's thesis contains his independent discovery of the compactness theorem for first-order languages of any cardinality. In the proof he introduced constant symbols to stand for the elements of the model to be constructed. He noticed that if these constant symbols corresponded to the elements of a given structure A, and the theory contained sentences expressing all the relations of the structure A, then any model of the theory would contain an isomorphic copy of A. This observation became the method of diagrams, which Robinson used systematically as a way of creating models of a theory with prescribed embeddings between them. Diagrams immediately became one of the fundamental techniques of model theory (for many applications, see Robinson 1963).

Robinson switched from one branch of mathematics to another with extraordinary ease. There were certain topics that he kept returning to from different angles. Two in particular were elementary embeddings and algebraically closed fields. Combining the two, he noted that every embedding between algebraically closed fields is elementary. He coined the term *model-complete* for theories whose models have this property and devised tests to show when a theory is model-complete.

Observing the role of algebraically closed fields in field theory, he looked for analogous structures within other classes. Model completions, model companions, infinite forcing companions, and finite forcing companions were notions that he proposed at various times as generalizations of algebraic closure. He identified the classes of real-closed fields and differentially closed fields as the model completions of the ordered fields and the differential fields, respectively, and axiomatized the class of differentially closed fields (though the usual axioms are an improved version due to Lenore Blum). In 1965 the notion of model completion played a central role in the proofs by James Ax and Simon Kochen, and independently by Yuri Ershov, of a number-theoretic conjecture of Emil Artin.

Around 1960 he noticed that any proper elementary extension of the field of real numbers contains infinitesimals. He quickly developed this insight into a powerful and intuitively natural approach to mathematical analysis that he named nonstandard analysis. Nonstandard analysis is one of the few innovations in logic that were entirely the work of a single individual.

Not long before his death, Robinson collaborated with the number theorist Peter Roquette to apply model-theoretic methods in number theory. This work gave a first hint of the deep interactions between model theory and diophantine geometry that came to light in the 1990s, sadly too late for Robinson to contribute. In fact, Robinson died before he could take on board the stability theory pioneered by Michael Morley and Saharon Shelah, though his students, Greg Cherlin and Carol Wood, did contribute to this field, bringing with them Robinson's lifelong eagerness to apply model theory to algebra, algebraic geometry, and mathematics in general.

Though unable himself to believe in any kind of existence for infinite totalities, he strongly defended the right of mathematicians to proceed as if such totalities exist. His discussion (Robinson 1965) of mathematical and epistemological considerations that favor one or another of the traditional views in philosophy of mathematics is thoughtful but seems not to reveal a thoroughly worked out position. His anti-Platonistic attitude may have helped him to create nonstandard analysis by allowing him to be relaxed about what the "real" real numbers are.

In Robinson's *Selected Papers* (1979), the bibliography lists ten books, more than a hundred papers, and a film. One in seven of his papers are in wing theory and aeronautics.

See also Infinitesimals; Model Theory; Tarski, Alfred.

Bibliography

Dauben, Joseph W. *Abraham Robinson: The Creation of Nonstandard Analysis—A Personal and Mathematical Odyssey*. Princeton, NJ: Princeton University Press, 1995.

Robinson, Abraham. "Formalism 64." In *Proceedings of the International Congress for Logic, Methodology, and Philosophy of Science, Jerusalem 1964*, edited by Y. Bar-Hillel, 228–246. Amsterdam, Netherlands: North-Holland, 1965.

Robinson, Abraham. *Introduction to Model Theory and to the Metamathematics of Algebra*. Amsterdam, Netherlands: North-Holland, 1963.

Robinson, Abraham. *Selected Papers*. 3 vols, edited by H. J. Keisler et al. Amsterdam, Netherlands: North-Holland, 1979.

Wilfrid Hodges (2005)

SET THEORY SINCE GÖDEL See *Set Theory*

THE PROLIFERATION OF NONCLASSICAL LOGICS.

The twentieth century, and especially its second half, was marked by a fairly spectacular proliferation of what are sometimes called nonclassical logics. To understand this, one needs to see the matter in its historical context. There have been three great periods in the history of European logic: ancient Greece, medieval Europe, and, starting toward the end of the nineteenth century, the current period. Each period has been marked by the production of novel theories of the nature and extent of logical validity. Thus, in the ancient period, Aristotle, the Megarian, and the Stoic logicians offered different accounts of validity, the conditional, and modality. The medieval period tried to reconcile some of the differences in their heritage, and in the process produced numerous different accounts of the nature of the connectives, consequence, and supposition. Not surprisingly, in both periods there was active and lively debate concerning the theories that were produced.

The periods between the great periods were characterized not just by a lack of interest in logic, but by a forgetting of much of the significant prior developments. In particular, all that remained of logic in about the middle of the nineteenth century—so-called traditional logic—was a somewhat bowdlerized form of the theory of the syllogism and some of its medieval accompaniments. It was at this time that mathematical logic came into existence. It was mathematical in two senses. The first is that the logicians who produced it were interested in the analysis of the reasoning of the mathematics of their time (and its foundations). The second is that they applied mathematical techniques to the subject in a novel way, such as those of abstract algebraic, set theory, and combinatorics.

Out of this, principally at the hands of Gottlob Frege and Bertrand Russell, developed a novel theory of logic. This was streamlined, organized, and simplified by a number of logicians in the first part of the twentieth century—notably, David Hilbert, Alfred Tarski, and Gerhard Gentzen. The result was an account of inference that was so much more powerful than traditional logic that is soon superseded it as the standard canon. This is so-called classical logic.

It had hardly appeared, however, before some logicians realized that a number of assumptions that were packed into it were contentious—especially once one goes beyond the kind of mathematical reasoning out of which classical logic arose. One of these was the principle of bivalence: that every (declarative) sentence is either true or false. In the 1920s the first many-valued logics were produced by Jan Łukasiewicz, Emil Post, Tarski, and others. In many-valued logics, sentences can be assumed to be neither true nor false, both true and false, have an infinity of degrees of truth, and so on.

Another assumption that is packed into classical logic is truth-functionality: that the truth value of a compound sentence is a function of the truth values of its parts. This is obviously not true of modal notions, and in the 1920s Clarence Irving Lewis presented in axiomatic form the first modern systems of modal logic. Modal logic was given an enormous boost with the discovery of world-semantics by, in particular, Saul Kripke in the 1960s. This allowed for the production of logics for other non-truth-functional notions (so called intentional logics), such as tense-operators (by Arthur Prior), epistemic and doxastic notions (by Jaako Hintikka), and deontic notions (by Henrik von Wright).

Another early critique of classical logic was provided by mathematical intuitionists, such as Luitzen Brouwer and Arend Heyting, who, driven by the view that existence should not be asserted unless people can construct the object in question, produced a system of formal logic in which a number of propositional and quantifier inferences that are valid in classical logic fail.

In the second half of the century, various critics of classical logic attacked the account of the (material) conditional it employs (as had Lewis). This produced the relevant logics of Alan Anderson and Nuel Belnap, and the conditional logics of Robert Stalnaker and David Lewis. These logics both have world-semantics. The world semantics for relevant logics were produced by, in particular, Richard Routley (later Sylvan) and Robert Meyer. The central feature of such semantics (it can be seen in retrospect) is the deployment of the notion of an impossible world.

The principle of inference of classical logic that everything entails a contradiction came under attack in its own right by logicians in the same period, including Stanisław, Jaśkowski, Newton da Costa, and Graham Priest. This produced a number of paraconsistent logics, which may be many-valued, modal, relevant, or of other kinds.

The development of nonclassical logics received further momentum from the advent of computer science and information technology after the 1960s. This produced new constructivist systems (such as linear logic), intentional logics (such as dynamic logic), and paraconsistent logics (such as various resolution systems). Research in Artificial Intelligence has also produced new epistemic logics, as well as the whole new area of formal non-monotonic (i.e., non-deductive) inference.

Thus, at the start of the twenty-first century there is a wide range of logics embodying different metaphysical presuppositions and potential applications. What to make of this is another matter. Perhaps most obvious is that the revolution in logic that occurred around the turn of the twentieth century was not so much the production of a novel logical theory—important though this was. It was instead the deployment of mathematical techniques to logic in a novel way. This allowed the development of classical logic, but the techniques were so powerful and versatile that they could be used to produce many other logics as well.

Which of all these logics is right, and, indeed, the meaning of that question, are matters to be determined only by detailed philosophical argument. Such arguments have been much part of the philosophical landscape since about the middle of the twentieth century. Indeed, the twenty-first century is seeing disputes in philosophical logic of a depth and acuity not seen since medieval logic. Whatever their outcome, the presence of the multitude of logical systems serves to remind that logic is not a set of received truths, but a discipline in which competing theories concerning validity vie with each other. The case for each theory—including a received theory—has to be investigated on its merits.

See also Aristotle; Brouwer, Luitzen Egbertus Jan; Conditionals; Frege, Gottlob; Hintikka, Jaako; Hilbert, David; Intuitionism and Intuitionistic Logic; Kripke, Saul; Lewis, Clarence Irving; Lewis, David; Logic, Non-Classical; Łukasiewicz, Jan; Many-Valued Logics; Megarians; Modal Logic; Non-Monotonic Logic; Paraconsistent Logics; Prior, Arthur Norman; Relevance (Relevant) Logics; Russell, Bertrand Arthur William; Stoicism; Tarski, Alfred; Wright, Georg Henrik von.

Bibliography

Gabbay, Dov M., and John Woods, eds. *Handbook of the History of Logic*. Vol. 6: *Logic and Modalities in the Twentieth Century*. Amsterdam, the Netherlands: Elsevier, 2005.

Gabbay, Dov M., and John Woods, eds. *Handbook of the History of Logic*. Vol. 7: *The Many-Valued and Non-Monotonic Turn in Logic*. Amsterdam, the Netherlands: Elsevier, 2005.

Haack, Susan. *Deviant Logic, Fuzzy Logic: Beyond the Formalism*. Chicago, IL: University of Chicago Press, 1996.

Priest, Graham. *Introduction to Non-Classical Logic*. Cambridge, U.K.: Cambridge University Press, 2001.

Read, Stephen. *Thinking about Logic: An Introduction to the Philosophy of Logic*. Oxford, U.K.: Oxford University Press, 1994.

Graham Priest (2005)

KRIPKE AND KRIPKE MODELS. See *Kripke, Saul*

FRIEDMAN AND REVERSE MATHEMATICS. During the second half of the twentieth century, many mathematicians lost interest in the foundations of mathematics. One of the reasons for this decline was an increasingly popular view that general set theory and Gödel-style incompleteness and independence results do not have much effect on mathematics as it is actually practiced. That is, as long as mathematicians study relatively concrete mathematical objects, they can avoid all foundational issues by appealing to a vague hybrid of philosophical positions including Platonism, formalism, and sometimes even social constructivism. Harvey Friedman (born 1948) has continually fought this trend, and in 1984 he received the National Science Foundation's Alan T. Waterman Award for his work on revitalizing the foundations of mathematics.

One of Friedman's methods of illustrating the importance of foundational issues is to isolate pieces of mathematics that either display the incompleteness phenomenon or require substantial set theoretic assumptions and which most mathematicians would agree fall within the scope of the central areas of mathematics. For example, he has created numerous algebraic and geometric systems that make no explicit reference to logic but which, under a suitable coding, contain a logical system to which Gödel's incompleteness theorems apply. Furthermore, these systems look similar to many systems used by mathematicians in their everyday work. Friedman uses these examples to argue that incompleteness cannot be dismissed as a phenomenon that occurs only in overly general foundational frameworks contrived by logicians and philosophers.

Friedman has also done a large amount of work concerning the necessary use of seemingly esoteric parts of Zermelo-Frankel set theory and its extensions. He has found theorems concerning concrete objects in mathematics that require the use of uncountably many iterations of the power set axiom and others that require the use of large cardinal axioms. These investigations have culminated in what Friedman calls Boolean relation theory.

In his 1974 address to the International Congress of Mathematicians, Friedman started the field of reverse mathematics by suggesting a three-step method for measuring the complexity of the set theoretic axioms required to prove any given theorem T. First, formalize the theorem T in some version of set theory. (Typically a formal system called second order arithmetic is used.) Second, find a collection of set theoretic axioms S which suffices to prove T. Third, prove the axioms in S from the theorem T (while working in a suitably weak base theory). If the third step is successful, then the equivalence between S and T shows that S is the weakest collection of axioms which suffices to prove T. If the third step fails, then the second step must be repeated until a proof of T is found using only axioms that can be proved from T. Because the third step involves proving axioms from theorems as opposed to the usual action of proving theorems from axioms, this type of analysis is now called reverse mathematics. It is frequently possible to draw a number of foundational conclusions concerning a theorem T once the equivalent collection S of set theoretic axioms has been isolated.

See also Gödel's Incompleteness Theorems; Mathematics, Foundations of; Platonism and the Platonic Tradition; Reverse Mathematics.

Bibliography

Friedman, H. "Some Systems of Second Order Arithmetic and Their Use." *Proceedings of the 1974 International Congress of Mathematicians*, vol. 1, 235–242. Montreal: Canadian Math Congress, 1975.

Harrington, L. A., M. D. Morley, A. Scedrov, and S. G. Simpson, eds. *Harvey Friedman's Research on the Foundations of Mathematics*. Studies in Logic and the Foundations of Mathematics, vol. 117. Amsterdam: North Holland Press, 1985.

Peter Cholak (2005)
Reed Solomon (2005)

LOGIC, MATHEMATICAL

See *Logic, History of*

LOGIC, MODAL

See *Modal Logic*

LOGIC, NON-CLASSICAL

The purpose of this entry is to survey those modern logics that are often called "non-classical," classical logic being the theory of validity concerning truth functions and first-order quantifiers likely to be found in introductory textbooks of formal logic at the end of the twentieth century.

For the sake of uniformity I will give a model-theoretic account of the logics. All of the logics also have proof-theoretic characterizations, and in some cases (such as linear logic) these characterizations are somewhat more natural. I will not discuss combinatory logic, which is not so much a non-classical logic as it is a way of expressing inferences that may be deployed for both classical and non-classical logics. I will use A, B, … for arbitrary sentences; $\wedge$, $\vee$, $\neg$, and $\rightarrow$, for the standard conjunction, disjunction, negation, and conditional operators for whichever logic is at issue. "Iff" means "if and only if." For references see the last section of this article.

EXTENSIONS VERSUS RIVALS

An important distinction is that between those non-classical logics that take classical logic to be alright as far as it goes, but to need extension by the addition of new connectives, and those which take classical logic to be incorrect, even for the connectives it employs. Call the former *extensions* of classical logic, and the latter *rivals*. Thus modal logics, as now usually conceived, are extensions of classical logic. They agree with classical logic on the extensional connectives (and quantifiers if these are present) but augment them with modal operators. By contrast, intuitionist and relevant logics are more plausibly thought of as rivals. Thus $A\vee\neg A$ is valid in classical logic but not intuitionist logic, and $A\rightarrow(B\rightarrow A)$ is valid in classical logic but not relevant logic.

The distinction must be handled with care however. Modern modal logics can be formulated, not with the modal operators, but with the strict conditional, $\dashv$ (from which modal operators can be defined), as primitive; and $A\dashv(B\dashv A)$ is not valid. From this perspective modal logic is a rival to classical logic (which is the way it was originally intended). Similarly it is (arguably) possible to add a negation operator, $, to relevant logics which behaves as does classical negation. Classical logic is, then, just a part of this logic, identifying the classical $\neg A$ and $A\rightarrow B$ with the relevant A and $A \vee B$, respectively. From this perspective, in a relevant logic, $\rightarrow$ and $\neg$ are operators additional to the classical ones, and relevant logic is an extension of classical logic.

What these examples show is that whether or not something is an extension or a rival of classical logic is not a purely formal matter but a matter of how the logic is taken to be applied to informal reasoning. If, in a modal logic, one reads $A\dashv B$ as "if A then B" then the logic is a rival of classical logic. If one reads $A\rightarrow B$ as "if A then B" and $A\dashv B$ as "necessarily, if A then B," it is an extension. If, in a relevant logic, one reads $A\rightarrow B$ as "if A then B," and $\neg A$ as "it is not the case that A," the logic is a rival to classical logic; if one reads $A \vee B$ as "if A then B" and A as "it is not the case A," it is an extension. (The examples also raise substantial philosophical issues. Thus both a relevant logician and an intuitionist are liable to deny that $ is a connective with any determinate meaning.)

MANY-VALUED LOGICS

A central feature of classical logic is its bivalence. Every sentence is exclusively either true (1) or false (0). In *many-valued logics*, normally thought of as rivals to classical logic, there are more than two semantic values. Truth-functionality is, however, maintained; thus the value of a compound formula is determined by the values of its components. Some of the semantic values are *designated*, and a valid inference is one in which, whenever the premises are *designated*, so is the conclusion.

A simple example of a many-valued logic is that in which there are three truth values, 1, i, 0; and the truth functions for the standard connectives may be depicted as follows:

	$\neg$
*1	0
i	i
0	1

$\rightarrow$	1	i	0
1	1	i	0
i	1	1	i
0	1	1	1

$\vee$	1	i	0
1	1	1	1
i	1	i	i
0	1	i	1

$\wedge$	1	i	0
1	1	i	0
i	i	i	0
0	0	0	0

The only designated value is 1 (which is what the asterisk indicates). This is the Łukaziewicz 3-valued logic, $Ł_3$. If the middle value of the table for $\rightarrow$ is changed from

1 to i we get the Kleene 3-valued logic K_3. The standard interpretation for i in this logic is *neither true nor false*. If in addition i is added as a designated value, we get the paraconsistent logic *LP*. The standard interpretation for i in this is *both true and false*.

$Ł_3$ can be generalized to a logic, $Ł_n$, with n values, for any finite n, and even to one with infinitely many values. Thus the continuum-valued Łukasiewicz logic, $Ł_\aleph$, has as semantic values all real numbers between 0 and 1 (inclusive). Normally only 1 is designated. If we write the value of A as $v(A)$, $v(A \vee B)$ and $v(A \wedge B)$ are the maximum and minimum of $v(A)$ and $v(B)$, respectively; $v(\neg A)=1-v(A)$; $v(A \rightarrow B)=1$ if $v(A) \le v(B)$ and $v(A \rightarrow B)=1-(v(A)-v(B))$ otherwise. Standardly the semantic values are thought of as degrees of truth (so that 1 is *completely true*). Interpreted in this way $Ł_\aleph$ is one of a family of many-valued logics called *fuzzy logics*.

MODAL LOGICS

Another family of non-classical logics maintains bivalence, but rejects truth-functionality. *Modal logics* augment the connectives of classical logic with the operators □ (it is necessarily the case) and ◇ (it is possibly the case). The truth-values of □A and ◇A depend on more than just the truth value of A.

Standard semantics for modal logics invoke a set of (possible) worlds, augmented with a binary relation, R. wRw' means, intuitively, that from the state of affairs as it is at w, the state of affairs as it is at w' is possible. (In first-order modal logics each world comes also with a domain of quantification.) The extensional connectives are given their usual truth conditions with respect to a world, but if we write the value of A at world w as $v_w(A)$:

$v_w(□A)=1$, iff for all w' such that wRw', $v_{w'}(A)=1$

$v_w(◇A)=1$, iff for some w' such that wRw', $v_{w'}(A)=1$

Validity is defined in terms of truth preservation at all worlds. (This is for *normal* modal logics. *Non-normal* modal logics have also a class of non-normal worlds, at which the truth conditions of the modal operators are different.)

Different modal logics are obtained by putting constraints on R. If R is arbitrary we have the system K. If it is reflexive (validating □$A \rightarrow A$), we have T; if transitivity is also required (validating □$A \rightarrow$ □□A), we have $S4$; if symmetry is added (validating $A \rightarrow$ □◇A), we have $S5$. (Alternatively, in this case, R may be universal: For all w and w', wRw'.) If we have just the condition that every world is related to some world or other (validating □$A \rightarrow$ ◇A), we have D.

The notion of possibility is highly ambiguous (logical, physical, epistemic, etc.). Arguably, different constraints on R are appropriate for different notions.

INTENSIONAL LOGICS

World semantics have turned out to be one of the most versatile techniques in contemporary logic. Generally speaking, logics that have world-semantics are called *intensional logics* (and are normally thought of as extensions of classical logic). There are many of these in addition to standard modal logics.

□ may be interpreted as "it is known that", in which context it is usually written as K and the logic is called *epistemic logic*. (The most plausible epistemic logic is T.) It may be interpreted as "it is believed that," in which case it is usually written as B, and the logic is called *doxastic logic*. (Though even the logic K seems rather too strong here, except as an idealization to logically omniscient beings.) □ may be interpreted as "it is obligatory to bring it about that," in which case it is written as O, and the logic is called *deontic logic*. The standard deontic logic is D.

One can also interpret □ as "it is provable that." The best-known system in this regard is usually known as *GL* and called *provability logic*. This logic imposes just two constraints on the accessibility relation. One is transitivity; the other is that there are no infinite R-chains, that is, no sequences of the form w_0Rw_1, w_1Rw_2, w_2Rw_3, ... This constraint verifies the principle □(□$A \rightarrow A) \rightarrow$ □A, but not □$A \rightarrow A$. The interest of this system lies in its close connection with the way that a provability predicate, *Prov*, works in standard systems of formal arithmetic. By Gödel's second incompleteness theorem, in such logics one cannot prove $Prov(\langle A \rangle) \rightarrow A$ (where $\langle A \rangle$ is the numeral for the gödel number of A); but Löb's theorem assures us that if we can prove $Prov(\langle A \rangle) \rightarrow A$ we can prove A, and so $Prov(\langle A \rangle)$. It is this idea that is captured in the characteristic principle of *GL*.

Another possibility is to interpret □ and ◇ as, respectively, 'it will always be the case that,' and 'it will be the case at some time that.' In this context the operators are normally written as G and F, and the logic is called *tense logic*. In the world-semantics for tense logics, worlds are thought of as times, and the accessibility relation, R, is interpreted as a temporal ordering. In these logics there are also past-tense operators: H and P ("it has always been the case that" and "it was the case at some time that," respectively). These are given the reverse truth conditions. Thus for example:

$v_w(HA)=1$, iff for all w' such that $w'Rw$, $v_{w'}(A)=1$

The past and future tense operators interact in characteristic ways (e.g., $A \rightarrow HFA$ is logically valid). The basic tense logic, K_t, is that obtained when R is arbitrary. As with modal logics, stronger systems are obtained by adding constraints on R, which can now represent the ideas that time is dense, has no last moment, and so on.

Of course it is not necessary to have just one family of intensional operators in a formal language: One can have, for example, modal and tense operators together. Each family will have its own accessibility relation, and these may interact in appropriate ways. Systems of logic with more than one family of modal operators are called *multi-modal*. One of the most important multi-modal logics is *dynamic logic*. In this there are operators of the form $[\alpha]$ and $\langle\alpha\rangle$, each with its own accessibility relation, R_α. In the semantics of dynamic logic, the worlds are thought of as states of affairs or of a computational device. The αs are thought of as (non-deterministic) actions or programs, and $wR_\alpha w'$ is interpreted to mean that starting in state w and performing the action α (or running the program α) can take one to the state w'. Thus $[\alpha]A$ ($\langle\alpha\rangle A$) holds at state w, just if performing α at w will always (may sometimes) lead to a state in which A holds. The actions themselves are closed under certain operations. In particular, if α and β are actions, so are $\alpha;\beta$ (perform α and then perform β); $\alpha\cup\beta$ (perform α or perform β, non-deterministically); α^* (perform α some finite number of times, non-deterministically). There is also an operator, ? ("test whether"), which takes sentences into programs. The corresponding accessibility relations are: $xR_{\alpha;\beta}y$ iff for some z, $xR_\alpha z$ and $zR_\beta y$; $xR_{\alpha\cup\beta}y$ iff $xR_\alpha y$ or $xR_\beta y$; $xR_{\alpha*}y$ iff for some $x=x_1, x_2, ..., x_n=y$, $x_0R_\alpha x_1$, $x_1R_\alpha x_2$, ..., $x_{n-1}R_\alpha x_n$; $xR_{A?}y$ iff ($x=y$ and $v_x(A)=1$). Because of the * operator, dynamic logic can express the notion of finitude in a certain sense. This gives it some of the expressive strength of second-order logic.

CONDITIONAL LOGICS

Another family of logics of the intentional variety was triggered by some apparent counter-examples to the following inferences:

$A \rightarrow B \vdash (A \wedge C) \rightarrow B$

$A \rightarrow B, B \rightarrow C \vdash A \rightarrow C$

$A \rightarrow B \vdash \neg B \rightarrow \neg A$

which are valid for the material conditional. (For example: "If you strike this match it will light; hence if you strike this match and it is under water it will light.") Log-

ics of the conditional that invalidate such principles are called *conditional logics*. Such logics add an intentional conditional operator, $>$, to the language. In the semantics there is an accessibility relation, R_A, for every sentence, A (or one, R_X, for every proposition, that is, set of worlds, X). Intuitively $wR_A w'$ iff w' is a world which A holds but is, *ceteris paribus*, the same as w. The truth conditions for $>$ are:

$v_w(A>B)=1$ iff for all w' such that $wR_A w'$, $v_{w'}(B)=1$

The intuitive meaning of R motivates the following constraints:

$wR_A w'$ then $v_{w'}(A)=1$

if $v_w(A)=1$, then $wR_A w$

Stronger logics in the family are obtained by adding further constraints to the accessibility relations. A standard way of specifying these is in terms of "similarity spheres"—neighbourhoods of a world containing those worlds that have a certain degree of similarity to it.

The natural way of taking a conditional logic is as a rival to classical logic (giving a different account of the conditional). Some philosophers, however, distinguish between indicative conditionals and subjunctive/counterfactual conditionals. They take the indicative conditional to be the material conditional of classical logic, and $>$ to be the subjunctive conditional. Looked at this way conditional logics can be thought of as extensions of classical logic.

INTUITIONIST LOGIC

There are a number of other important non-classical logics that, though not presented originally as intentional logics, can be given world semantics. One of these is *intuitionist logic*. This logic arose out of a critique of Platonism in the philosophy of mathematics. The idea is that one cannot define truth in mathematics in terms of correspondence with some objective realm, as in a traditional approach. Rather one has to define it in terms of what can be proved, where a proof is something that one can effectively recognize as such. Thus, semantically, one has to replace standard truth-conditions with proof-conditions, of the following kind:

$A \vee B$ is provable when A is provable or B is provable.

$\neg A$ is provable when it is provable that there is no proof of A

$\exists xA(x)$ is provable when we can effectively find an object, n, such that $A(n)$ is provable

Note that in the case of negation we cannot say that $\neg A$ is provable when A is not provable: We have no effective way of recognizing what is not provable; similarly, in the case of the existential quantifier, we cannot say that $\exists x A(x)$ is provable when there is some n such that $A(n)$ is provable: we may have no effective way of knowing whether this obtains.

Proceeding in this way produces a logic that invalidates a number of the principles of inference that are valid in classical logic. Notable examples are: $A \lor \neg A$, $\neg\neg A \to A$, $\neg \forall x A(x) \to \exists x \neg A(x)$. For the first of these, there is no reason to suppose that for any A we can find a proof of A or a proof that there is no proof of A. For the last, the fact that we can show that there is no proof of $\forall x A(x)$ does not mean that we can effectively find an n such that $A(n)$ can be proved.

In the world-semantics for intuitionist logic, interpretations have essentially the structure of an $S4$ interpretation. The worlds are interpreted as states of information (things proved), and the accessibility relation represents the acquisition of new proofs. We also require that if $v_w(A)=1$ and wRw', $v_{w'}(A)=1$ (no information is lost), and if x is in the domain of quantification of w and wRw' then x is in the domain of quantification of w' (no objects are undiscovered). Corresponding to the provability conditions we have:

$v_w(A \lor B)=1$ iff $v_w(A)=1$ or $v_w(A)=1$

$v_w(\neg A)=1$ iff for all w' such that wRw', $v_{w'}(A)=0$

$v_w(\exists x A(x))=1$ iff for all n in the domain of w, $v_w(A(n))=1$

Unsurprisingly, given the above semantics, there is a translation of the language of intuitionism into quantified $S4$ that preserves validity.

Another sort of semantics for intuitionism takes semantic values to be the open sets of some topology. If the value of A is x, the value of $\neg A$ is the interior of the complement of x.

RELEVANT LOGIC

Another logic standardly thought of as a rival to classical logic is *relevant* (or *relevance*) *logic*. This is motivated by the apparent incorrectness of classical validities such as: $A \to (B \to B)$, $(A \land \neg A) \to B$. A (propositional) relevant logic in one in which if $A \to B$ is a logical truth A and B share a propositional parameter. There are a number of different kinds of relevant logic, but the most common has a world-semantics. The semantics differs in two major ways from the world semantics we have so far met.

First it adds to the possible worlds a class of logically impossible worlds. (Though validity is still defined in terms of truth-preservation over possible worlds.) In possible worlds the truth conditions of $\to$ are as for $\exists$ in $S5$:

$v_w(A \to B)=1$ iff for all w' (possible and impossible) such that $v_{w'}(A)=1$, $v_{w'}(B)=1$

In impossible worlds the truth conditions are given differently, in such a way that logical laws such as $B \to B$ may fail at the world. This may be done in various ways, but the most versatile technique employs a three-place relation, S, on worlds. If w is impossible, we then have:

$v_w(A \to B)=1$ iff for all x, y such that $Swxy$, if $v_x(A)=1$, $v_y(B)=1$

This clause can be taken to state the truth conditions of $\to$ at all worlds, provided that we add the constraint that, for possible w, $Swxy$ iff $x=y$. With no other constraints on S, this gives the basic (positive) relevant logic, B. Additional constraints on S give stronger logics in the family. Typical constraints are:

$\exists x(Sabx \text{ and } Sxcd) \Rightarrow \exists y(Sacy \text{ and } Sbyd)$

$Sabc \Rightarrow Sbac$

$Sabc \Rightarrow \exists x(Sabx \text{ and } Sxbc)$

Adding all three gives the (positive) relevant logic, R. Adding the first two gives RW, R minus Contraction ($A \to (A \to B) \vdash A \to B$). The intuitive meaning of S is, at the time of this writing, philosophically moot.

The second novelty of the semantics is in its treatment of negation. It is necessary to arrange for worlds where $A \land \neg A$ may hold. This may be done in a couple of ways. The first is to employ the Routley * operator. Each world, w, comes with a "mate," w^* (subject to the constraint that $w^{**}=w$, to give Double Negation). We then have:

$v_w(\neg A)=1$ iff $v_{w^*}(A)=0$

(If $w=w^*$, this just delivers the classical truth conditions.) Alternatively, we may move to a four-valued logic in which the values at a world are *true only*, *false only*, *both*, *neither* ($\{1\}, \{0\}, \{1,0\}, \emptyset$). We then have:

$1 \in v_w(\neg A)$ iff $0 \in v_w(A)$

$0 \in v_w(\neg A)$ iff $1 \in v_w(A)$

The semantics of relevant logic can be extended to produce a (relevant) *ceteris paribus* conditional, $>$, of the kind found in conditional logics, by adding the appropriate binary accessibility relations.

DISTRIBUTION-FREE LOGICS

There are some logics in the family of relevant logics for which the principle of Distribution, $A \wedge (B \vee C) \vdash (A \wedge B) \vee (A \wedge C)$, fails. To achieve this the truth conditions for disjunction have to be changed. In an interpretation, let $[A]$ be the set of worlds at which A holds. Then the usual truth conditions for disjunction can be written:

$$v_w(A \vee B) = 1 \text{ iff } w \in [A] \cup [B]$$

To invalidate Distribution, the semantics are augmented by a closure operator, $\mathfrak{C}$, on sets of worlds, x, satisfying the following conditions:

$$X \subseteq \mathfrak{C}(X)$$

$$\mathfrak{C}\,\mathfrak{C}(X) = \mathfrak{C}X$$

$$\text{if } X \subseteq Y \text{ then } \mathfrak{C}(X) \subseteq \mathfrak{C}(Y)$$

The truth conditions of disjunction can now be given as:

$$v_w(A \vee B) = 1 \text{ iff } w \in \mathfrak{C}([A] \cup [B])$$

Changing the truth conditions for disjunction in RW in this way (and using the Routley * for negation) gives linear logic (LL). LL is usually formulated with some extra intentional connectives, especially an intentional conjunction and disjunction. These connectives can be present in standard relevant logics too. Intuitionist, relevant, and linear logics all belong to the family of *substructural logics*. Proof-theoretically, these logics can be obtained from a sequent-calculus for classical logic by weakening the structural rules (especially Weakening and Contraction).

Another logic in which distribution fails is *quantum logic*. The thought here is that it may be true (verifiable) of a particle that it has a position and one of a range of momenta, but each disjunct attributing to it that position and a particular momentum is false (unverifiable). The states of a quantum system are canonically thought of as members of a Hilbert space. In the world-semantics for quantum logic, the space of worlds is taken to be such a space, and sentences are assigned closed subsets of this. $[A \wedge B] = [A] \cap [B]$, $[A \vee B] = \mathfrak{C}([A] \cup [B])$, where $\mathfrak{C}(X)$ is the smallest closed space containing X; and $[\neg A] = [A]^{\perp}$. $X^{\perp}$ is the space comprising all those states that are orthogonal to members of X. (It satisfies the conditions: $X = X^{\perp\perp}$, if $X \subseteq Y$ then $Y^{\perp} \subseteq X^{\perp}$, and $X \cap X^{\perp} = \emptyset$.) In quantum logic $A \rightarrow B$ can be defined in various ways. Perhaps the most plausible is as $\neg A \vee (A \wedge B)$. (The subspaces of a Hilbert space also have the structure of a partial Boolean algebra. Such an algebra is determined by a family of Boolean algebras collapsed under a certain equivalence relation,

which is a congruence relation on the Boolean operators. Partial Boolean algebras can be used to provide a slightly different quantum logic.)

PARACONSISTENT LOGICS

Before we turn to quantifiers there is one further kind of logic to be mentioned: *paraconsistent logic*. Paraconsistent logic is motivated by the thought we would often seem to have to reason sensibly from information, or about a situation, which is inconsistent. In such a case, the principle $A, \neg A \vdash B$ (*ex falso quodlibet sequitur*, Explosion), which is valid in classical logic, clearly makes a mess of things. A paraconsistent logic is precisely one where this principle fails.

There are many different families of paraconsistent logics—as many as there are ways of breaking Explosion. Indeed many of the techniques we have already met in this article can be used to construct a paraconsistent logic. The 3-valued logic *LP* is paraconsistent, as is the Łukasiewicz continuum-valued logic, provided we take the designated values to contain 0.5. The ways that negation is handled in relevant logic also produce paraconsistent logics, as long as validity is defined over a class of worlds in which A and $\neg A$ may both hold. Another approach (*discussive logic*) is to employ standard modal logic and to take A to hold in an interpretation iff A holds at some world of the interpretation. In this approach the principle of Adjunction ($A, B \vdash A \wedge B$) will generally fail, since A and B may each hold at a world, whilst $A \wedge B$ may not. Another approach ("positive plus") is to take any standard positive (negation free) logic, and add a non-truth-functional negation—so that the values of A and $\neg A$ are assigned independently. In these logics, the principle of Contraposition ($A \leftrightarrow B \vdash \neg B \leftrightarrow \neg A$) will generally fail. Yet another is to dualise intuitionist logic. In particular one can take semantic values to be the closed sets in some topology. If the value of A is X, the value of $\neg A$ is the closure of the complement of X.

SECOND-ORDER QUANTIFICATION

We now turn to the issue of quantification. In classical logic there are quantifiers $\forall$ and $\exists$. These range over a domain of objects, and $\forall x A(x)$ [$\exists x A(x)$] holds if every [some] object in the domain of quantification satisfies $A(x)$. All the propositional logics we have looked at may be extended to first-order logics with such quantifiers. Other non-classical logics may be obtained by adding to these (or replacing these with) different kinds of quantifiers.

Perhaps the most notable of these is second-order logic. In this there are bindable variables (X, Y, …) that can stand in the place where a monadic first-order predicate can stand and which range over sets of objects in the first-order domain—canonically all of them. (There can also be variables that range over the n-ary relations on that domain, for each n, as well as variables that range over n-place functions. The second-order extension of classical logic is much stronger than the first-order version. It can provide for a categorical axiomatization of arithmetic and consequently is not itself axiomatizable.

Monadic second-order quantifiers can also be given a rather different interpretation, as plural quantifiers. The idea here is to interpret $\exists X\, Xa$ not as "There is a set such that a is a member of it," but as "There are some things such that a is one of them." The proponents of plural quantification argue that such quantification is not committed to the existence of sets.

OTHER SORTS OF QUANTIFIERS

There are many other non-classical quantifiers. For example one can have a binary quantifier of the form $Mx(A(x),B(x))$, "most As are Bs." This is true in a finite domain if more than half the things satisfying $A(x)$ satisfy $B(x)$. It is not reducible to a monadic quantifier plus a propositional connective.

Another sort of quantifier is a cardinality quantifier. The quantifier "there exist exactly n things such that" can be defined in first-order logic with quantification and identity in a standard way. The quantifier "there is a countable number of things such that" (or its negation, "there is an uncountable number of things such that") cannot be so defined—let alone the quantifier "there are κ things such that," for an arbitrary cardinal, κ. Such quantifiers can be added, with the obvious semantics. These quantifiers extend the expressive power of the language towards that of second-order logic—and beyond.

Another kind of quantifier is the branching quantifier. When, in first-order logic, we write:

$$\forall x_1 \exists y_1 \forall x_2 \exists y_2 A(x_1, x_2, y_1, y_2)$$

y_2 is in the scope of x_1, and so its value depends on that of x_1. To express non-dependence one would normally need second-order quantification, thus:

$$\exists f_1 \forall x_1 \exists f_2 \forall x_2 A(x_1, x_2, f_1(x_1), f_2(x_2))$$

But we may express it equally by having the quantifiers non-linearly ordered, thus:

$$\begin{matrix} \forall x_1 \exists y_1 \\ \forall x_2 \exists y_2 \end{matrix} \; A(x_1, x_2, y_1, y_2)$$

As this would suggest, branching quantifiers have something of the power of second-order logic.

A quite different kind of quantifier is the substitutional quantifier. For this there is a certain class of names of the language, C. $\Pi x A(x)$ [$\Sigma x A(x)$] holds iff for every [some] $c \in C$, $A(c)$ holds. This is not the same as standard (objectual) quantification, since some objects in the domain may have no name in C; but first-order substitutional quantifiers validate the same quantificational inferences as first-order objectual quantifiers. Note that the notion of substitutional quantification makes perfectly good sense for any syntactically well-defined class, including predicates (so we can have second-order substitutional quantification) or binary connectives (so that $\Sigma x(AxB)$ can make perfectly good sense).

Finally in this category comes free quantifiers. It is standard to interpret the domain of objects of quantification (at a world) as comprising the objects that exist (at that world). It is quite possible, however, to think of the domain as containing a bunch of objects, some of which exist, and some of which do not. Obviously this does not change the formal properties of the quantifiers. But if one thinks of the domain in this way one must obviously not read $\exists x$ as 'there exists an x such that'; one has to read it simply as 'for some x'. Given this set-up, however, it makes sense to have existentially loaded quantifiers, $\forall^E$ and $\exists^E$, such that $\forall^E A(x)$ [$\exists^E A(x)$] holds (at a world) iff all [some] of the existent objects (at the world) satisfy $A(x)$. If there is a monadic existence predicate, E, these quantifiers can be defined in the obvious way, as (respectively): $\forall x(Ex \rightarrow A(x))$ and $\exists x(Ex \wedge A(x))$. Clearly, existentially loaded quantifiers will not satisfy some of the standard principles of quantification, such as $\forall^E x A(x) \rightarrow A(c)$, $A(c) \rightarrow \exists x^E A(x)$ (since the object denoted by 'c' may not exist). Some logics do not have the existentially unloaded quantifiers, just the loaded ones. These are usually called *free logics*.

NON-MONOTONIC LOGICS

It remains to say a word about one other kind of logic that is often categorized as non-classical. In all the logics we have been considering so far:

if $\Sigma \vdash A$ then $\Sigma \cup \Delta \vdash A$

(where Σ and Δ are sets of formulas): Adding extra premises makes no difference. This is called *monotonicity*. Logics in which this principle fails are called *non-monotonic logics*. Non-monotonic inferences can be thought of as inferences that are made with certain default assumptions. Thus I am told that something is a bird, and I infer that it can fly. Since most birds fly this is a reasonable conclusion. If, however, I also learn that the bird weighs 20 kg. (and so is an emu or an ostrich), the conclusion is no longer a reasonable one.

There are many kinds of non-monotonic logics, depending on what kind of default assumption is implemented, but there is a common structure that covers many of them. Interpretations, I, of the language come with a strict partial ordering, $>$ (often called a *preference ordering*). Intuitively, $I_1 > I_2$ means that the situation represented by I_1 is more normal (in whatever sense of normality is at issue) than that represented by I_2. (In particular cases it may be reasonable to suppose that $>$ has additional properties.) I is a *most normal model of* Σ iff every $B \in \Sigma$ holds in I, and there is no $J > I$ for which this is true. A follows from Σ iff A holds in every most normal model of Σ. As is clear a most normal model of Σ is not guaranteed to be a most normal model of $\Sigma \cup \Delta$. Hence monotonicity will fail. As might be expected there is a close connection between non-monotonic logics and conditional logics, in which the inference $A \rightarrow B \vdash (A \wedge C) \rightarrow B$ fails. Though non-monotonic logic has come to prominence in modern computational logic, it is just a novel and rigorous way of looking at the very traditional notion of non-deductive (inductive, ampliative) inference.

HISTORY, PERSONS, REFERENCES

We conclude this review of non-classical logics by putting the investigations discussed above in their historical context. References that may be consulted for further details are also given at the end of each paragraph. For a general introduction to propositional non-classical logics, see Priest (2001). Haack (1996) is a discussion of some of the philosophical issues raised by non-classical logics.

The first modern many-valued logics, the Ł$_n$ family, were produced by Jan Łukasiewicz in the early 1920s. (Emil Post also produced some many-valued logics about the same time.) Łukasiewicz's major philosophical concern was Aristotle's argument for fatalism. In this context he suggested a many-valued analysis of modality. Logics of the both/neither kind were developed somewhat later. Canonical statements of K_3 and LP were given (respectively) by Stephen Kleene in the 1950s and Graham Priest in the 1970s. Ł$_\aleph$ was first published by Łukasiewicz and Alfred Tarski in 1930. The intensive investigation of fuzzy logics and their applications started in the 1970s. A notable player in this area was Lotfi Zadeh. (Rescher 1969, Urquhart 2001– , Hájek 1998, Yager and Zadeh 1992.)

Modern modal logics were created in an axiomatic form by Clarence Irving Lewis in the 1920s. Lewis's concern was the paradoxes of the material conditional, and he suggested the strict conditional as an improvement. Possible-world semantics for modal logics were produced by a number of people in the 1960s, but principally Saul Kripke. The semantics made possible the systematic investigation of the rich family of modal logics. (Bull and Segerberg 2001– , Garson 2001– , Hughes and Cresswell 1996.)

The idea that the techniques of modal logics could be applied to notions other than necessity and possibility occurred to a number of people around the middle of the twentieth century. Tense logics were created by Arthur Prior, epistemic and doxastic logic were produced by Jaakko Hintikka, and deontic logics by Henrik von Wright. Investigations of provability logic were started in the 1970s by George Boolos and others. Dynamic logic was created by Vaughn Pratt and other logicians particularly interested in computation, including David Harrel, in the 1970s. (van Bentham 1988, Burgess 2001– , Thomason 2001– , Meyer 2001– , Åqvist 2001– , Boolos 1993, Harrel, Kozen, and Tiuryn 2001– .)

Conditional logics (with "sphere semantics") were proposed by David Lewis and Robert Stalnaker in the 1970s. They were formulated as multi-modal logics by Brian Chellas and Krister Segerberg a few years later (Harper, Stalnaker, and Pearce 1981, Nute and Cross 2001–).

The intuitionist critique of classical mathematics was started by Luitzen Egbertus Jan Brouwer in the early years of the twentieth century. This generated a novel kind of mathematics: intuitionist mathematics. Intuitionist logic, as such, was formulated by Arend Heyting and Andrei Kolmogorov in the 1920s. The intuitionist critique of mathematical realism was extended to realism in general by Michael Dummett in the 1970s (Dummett 1977, van Dalen 2001–).

Systems of relevant logic, in axiomatic form, came to prominence in the 1960s because of the work of Alan Anderson, Nuel Belnap and their students. World-semantics were produced by a number of people in the 1970s, but principally Richard Routley (later Sylvan) and Robert Meyer. The semantics made possible the investigation of the rich family of relevant logics. The four-valued semantics for negation is due to J. Michael Dunn (Dunn and Restall 2001– , Mares 2004).

Linear logic was produced by Jean-Yves Girard in the 1980s. Although many members of the class of sub-structural logics had been studied before, the fact that they could be viewed in a uniform proof-theoretic way, was not appreciated until the late 1980s. The formulation of quantum logic in terms of Hilbert spaces is due, essentially, to George Birkhoff and John von Neumann in the

1930s. The use of an abstract closure operator to give the semantics for non-distributive logics is due to Greg Restall. (Troelstra 1992, Restall 2000, Paoli 2002, Chihara and Giuntini 2001, Hughes 1989).

The first paraconsistent logic (discussive logic) was published by Stanisław Jaśkowski in 1948. Other non-adjunctive logics were later developed in the 1970s by Peter Schotch and Raymond Jennings. Newton da Costa produced a number of different paraconsistent logics and applications, starting with positive-plus logics in the 1960s. The paraconsistent aspects of relevant logic were developed by Priest and Routley in the 1970s. (Priest, Routley and Norman 1989, Priest 2001, Carnielli et al. 2001, Mortensen 1995).

Second-order quantification goes back to the origins of classical logic in the work of Gottlob Frege and Bertrand Russell. Its unaxiomatizability put it somewhat out of fashion for a number of years, but it made a strong come-back in the last years of the twentieth century. The notion of plural quantification was made popular by George Boolos in the 1980s. (Shapiro 1991, 2001–; Boolos 1984).

Quantifier phrases other than "some A" and "all A" are pervasive in natural language; and since Frege provided an analysis of the quantifier many different kinds have been investigated by linguists and logicians. Branching quantifiers were proposed by Jaakko Hintikka in the 1970s. Substitutional quantification came to prominence in the 1960s, put there particularly in connection with quantification into the scope of modal operators by Ruth Barcan Marcus. It was treated with suspicion for a long time, but was eventually given a clean bill of health by Kripke. Free logics were first proposed in the 1960s, by Karel Lambert and others (van der Does and van Eijck 1996, Barwise 1979, Kripke 1976, Bencivenga 2001–).

Non-monotonic logics started to appear in the logic/computer-science literature in the 1970s. There are many kinds. The fact that many of them could be seen as logics with normality orderings started to become clear in the 1980s (Shoham, 1988; Crocco, Fariñas del Cerro, and Herzig 1995; Brewka, Dix, and Konolige, 1997).

See also Aristotle; Brouwer, Luitzen Egbertus Jan; Combinatory Logic; Dummett, Michael Anthony Eardley; First-Order Logic; Frege, Gottlob; Fuzzy Logic; Gödel's Incompleteness Theorems; Hintikka, Jaako; Intensional Logic; Intuitionism and Intuitionistic Logic; Kripke, Saul; Lewis, Clarence Irving; Lewis, David; Łukasiewicz, Jan; Many-Valued Logics; Modal Logic; Neumann, John von; Non-Monotonic Logic; Platon-

ism and the Platonic Tradition; Prior, Arthur Norman; Provability Logic; Quantifiers in Natural Language; Quantum Logic and Probability; Russell, Bertrand Arthur William; Second-Order Logic; Semantics; Tarski, Alfred; Wright, Georg Henrik von.

Bibliography

Åqvist, Leonard. "Deontic Logic." In Gabbay and Guenthner (2001–), vol. 8.

Bencivenga, Ermanno. "Free Logic." In Gabbay and Guenthner (2001–), vol. 5.

van Bentham, Johan. *A Manual of Intensional Logic*. Stanford, CA: CSLI, 1988.

van Bentham, Johan. "On Branching Quantifiers in English." *Journal of Philosophical Logic* 8 (1979): 47–80.

Boolos, George. *The Logic of Provability*. Cambridge, U.K.: Cambridge University Press, 1993.

Boolos, George. "To Be Is to Be the Value of a Variable (Or Some Values of Some Variables)." *Journal of Philosophy* 81 (1984): 430–449. Reprinted in Boolos's *Logic, Logic, and Logic*. Cambridge, MA: Harvard University Press, 1998.

Brewka, Gerhard, Jürgen Dix, and Kurt Konolige. *Non-Monotonic Logic: An Overview*. Stanford, CA: CLSI, 1997.

Bull, Robert A., and Krister Segerberg. "Basic Modal Logic." In Gabbay and Guenthner (2001–), vol. 3.*

Burgess, John A. "Basic Tense Logic." In Gabbay and Guenthner (2001–), vol. 7.*

Chihara, Maria-Luisa D., and Roberto Giuntini. "Quantum Logics." In Gabbay and Guenthner (2001–), vol. 6.*

Crocco, Gabriella, Luis Fariñas del Cerro, and Andreas Herzig. *Conditionals: From Philosophy to Computer Science*. Oxford: Oxford University Press, 1995.

van Dalen, Dirk. "Intuitionistic Logic." In Gabbay and Guenthner (2001–), vol. 5.*

van der Does, Jaap, and Jan van Eijck. "Basic Quantifier Theory." In *Quantifiers, Logic, and Language*, edited by Jaap van der Does and Jan van Eijck. Stanford, CA: CLSI, 1996.

Dummett, Michael. *Elements of Intuitionism*. Oxford: Oxford University Press, 1977.

Gabbay, Dov, and Franz Guenthner, eds. *Handbook of Philosophical Logic*. 2nd ed. Dordrecht: Kluwer Academic, 2001–. Articles marked * are (possibly) revised versions of chapters in the much shorter first edition, Dordrecht: Reidel, 1983–89.

Garson, James. "Quantification in Modal Logic." In Gabbay and Guenthner (2001–), vol. 3.*

Haack, Susan. *Deviant Logic, Fuzzy Logic: Beyond the Formalism*. Chicago: University of Chicago Press, 1996.

Hájek, Petr. *Metamathematics of Fuzzy Logic*. Dordrecht: Kluwer Academic, 1998.

Harper, William, Robert Stalnaker, and Glenn Pearce, eds. *Ifs: Conditionals, Belief, Decision, Chance, and Time*. Dordrecht: Kluwer Academic, 1981.

Harrel, David, Dexter Kozen, and Jerzy Tiuryn. "Dynamic Logic." In Gabbay and Guenthner (2001–), vol. 4.*

Hughes, George, and Max Cresswell. *A New Introduction to Modal Logic*. London: Routledge, 1996.

Hughes, R. I. G. *The Structure and Interpretation of Quantum Mechanics*. Cambridge, MA: Harvard University Press, 1989.

Kripke, Saul. "Is There a Problem about Substitutional Quantification?" In *Truth and Meaning*, edited by Gareth Evans and John McDowell. Oxford: Oxford University Press, 1976

Mares, Edwin. *Relevant Logic*. Cambridge, U.K.: Cambridge University Press, 2004.

Meyer, John Jules. "Modal Epistemic and Doxastic Logic." In Gabbay and Guenthner (2001–), vol. 10.

Mortensen, Chris. *Inconsistent Mathematics*. Dordrecht: Kluwer Academic, 1995.

Paoli, Francesco. *Substructural Logics: A Primer*. Dordrecht: Kluwer Academic, 2002.

Priest, Graham. *Introduction to Non-Classical Logic*. Cambridge, U.K.: Cambridge University Press, 2001.

Priest, Graham, Richard Routley, and Jean Norman. *Paraconsistent Logic: Essays on the Inconsistent*. Munich: Philosophia Verlag, 1989.

Rescher, Nicholas. *Many-Valued Logic*. New York: McGraw Hill, 1969.

Restall, Greg. *An Introduction to Substructural Logics*. London: Routledge, 2000.

Shapiro, Stewart. *Foundations without Foundationalism: A Case for Second-Order Logic*. Oxford: Oxford University Press, 1991.

Shoham, Yoav. *Reasoning about Change*. Cambridge, MA: MIT Press, 1988.

Thomason, Richmond H. "Combinations of Tense and Modality." In Gabbay and Guenthner (2001–), vol. 7.*

Troelstra, Anne. *Lectures on Linear Logic*. Stanford, CA: CSLI, 1992.

Urquhart, Alasdair. "Basic Many-Valued Logic." In Gabbay and Guenthner (2001–), vol. 2.*

Yager, Ronald R., and Lotfi A. Zadeh. *An Introduction to Fuzzy Logic Applications in Intelligent Systems*. Dordrecht: Kluwer Academic, 1992.

Graham Priest (2005)

LOGIC, SYMBOLIC

See *Logic, History of*

LOGIC, TRADITIONAL

In logic, as in other fields, whenever there have been spectacular changes and advances, the logic that was current in the preceding period has been described as "old" or "traditional," and that embodying the new material has been called "new" or "modern." The Stoics described themselves as "moderns" and the Aristotelians as devotees of the "old" logic, in the later Middle Ages the more adventurous writers were called *moderni,* and since the latter part of the nineteenth century the immensely expanded logic that has developed along more or less mathematical lines ("mathematical logic," "symbolic logic," "logistics") has been contrasted with the "traditional" logic inherited from the sixteenth and seventeenth centuries. In every case the logic termed "old" or "traditional" has been essentially Aristotelian, but with a certain concentration on the central portion of the Aristotelian *corpus,* the theory of categorical syllogism—the logic of Aristotle himself having been rather less circumscribed than that of the "tradition," especially of the sixteenth to the nineteenth century.

THE LOGIC OF TERMS

To begin with the categorical syllogism, an inference, argument, or syllogism (traditionally, all arguments are assumed to be syllogistic) is a sequence of propositions (premises followed by a conclusion), such as "All animals are mortal; all men are animals; therefore, all men are mortal." Propositions, in turn, are built up from terms—for example, "animals," "mortals," "men." The traditional order of treatment, therefore, begins with the study of terms (or, in writers with a psychological or epistemological bias, ideas) and goes on to the study of propositions (or judgments), concluding with that of syllogisms (or inferences).

The terms from which the propositions principally studied in the traditional logic are built up are common nouns (*termini communes*), such as "man" and "horse," although some attention is also paid to singular terms, such as "Socrates," "this man," and "the man next door." Much of the traditional theory is devoted to the arrangement of common nouns in an order of comprehensiveness, and here a distinction is made between two aspects of their functioning—their "extension" (as the logicians of Port-Royal called it) or "denotation" (John Stuart Mill) and their "intension" (Sir William Hamilton), "comprehension" (Port-Royalists), or "connotation" (Mill). The extension or denotation of a common noun is the set of individuals to which it applies, its intension or connotation the set of attributes that an individual must possess for the common noun to be applicable to it. Thus, the connotation of the term *man* consists of the attributes of being an animal, being rational, and perhaps possessing a certain bodily form; its denotation consists of all objects that possess these attributes.

Broadly, the connotation of a term is its meaning, the denotation its application. The analysis of the meaning of a term is described as definition, and the breaking up of the set of objects to which it applies into subsets is described as division. The subsets of the set of individuals to which a given term applies are called the species of the genus denoted by the given term. The attribute that marks off a particular species from others of the same genus is called its differentia. The species is said by scholastic logicians to "fall under" its genus, and the standard way of defining a species is by giving its genus and its differentia.

The ordering of terms into species and genera is often thought of as having an upper and a lower limit. The upper limit, or *summum genus,* will be a broad category such as "thing" (*substantia*)—horses are animals, animals are organisms, organisms are bodies, bodies are things. More abstract terms will come to an end in more abstract categories, such as "quality" or "relation" (scarlet is a species or kind of red, red is a color, color is a quality). The *infima species,* or lower limit, is a more difficult concept. Man, for example, is commonly given as an *infima species,* but are not men divisible into, for instance, dark-haired and fair-haired men? This is answered, from the point of view of intension, by dividing the attributes of an individual into those that constitute its essence or nature and those that are merely accidental, and genuine species are said to be marked off by "essential" attributes only; further subdivisions differentiated by "accidental" attributes, such as the color of a man's hair, are not counted as genuine species. This distinction is not recognized by some writers. Gottfried Wilhelm Leibniz counted all attributes of an individual as essential, so that someone would not be *that* individual if he were in the least respect different from what he is. At the other extreme, Mill said that "individuals have no essences," although he had a use for the term *essence* in connection with general terms: It is of the essence of being a man, for example, to be an animal, if being an animal is one of the attributes commonly employed in fixing the application of the word *man.*

An allied doctrine of Mill's is that the proper names of individuals, by contrast with common nouns, have no connotation, only denotation. We may not be able to think of a named individual without thinking of him as having certain attributes, but the purpose of a proper name is not to convey the fact that he has those attributes but only to identify him as *that* individual. This view has been criticized by various writers, on the ground, among others, that we cannot identify an object at all without knowing at least its *infima species.* Mill has also been criticized for using the same term, "denotation," both for the application of a common noun and for what is named by a proper name.

Common terms can be simple or complex. Some kinds of complexity are of logical interest—for example, the conjunctive combination exemplified by "blind man" (i.e., what is both blind and human) and the disjunctive combination exemplified by "man-or-beast." This kind of complexity is of interest because, for one thing, it links up with the previous topic, a blind man being a species (in the broad though not the narrow sense) of man and a man being a species (again in the broad sense) of man-or-beast (i.e., of animal). Again, the term "son-of-Philip" is compounded of the relative expression "son of" and the proper name "Philip," and this, too, links with the preceding topic, a son of Philip being a species (in the broad sense) of son. But the logical behavior of complex terms of these types is a topic of modern rather than traditional logic. Even traditional logic, however, has something to say about negative terms, such as "non-man" (i.e., what is not human), as will be shown in what follows.

The distribution of terms is a subject that will be more intelligible after propositions and syllogisms have been considered.

THE LOGIC OF PROPOSITIONS

OPPOSITION. The division of traditional logic called the logic of propositions is not to be confused with what is now called the propositional calculus. The propositional calculus studies the logical behavior of propositions formed from simpler propositions by means of various connectives (for example, "Either all men are liars or no men are"), as opposed to propositions formed not from other propositions but from terms (for example, "No men are liars"). The traditional logic of propositions or judgments, on the other hand, is chiefly concerned with the classification and simpler interrelations of precisely the second class of propositions, although it normally also touches on "compound" or "hypothetical" propositions, without going beyond their simplest types and the simplest inferences involving them.

Propositions not compounded of other propositions are called categorical. This word has the force of "unconditional," the implied contrast being with forms like "*If all that the Bible says is true, all men are mortal*" or "*Either not all that the Bible says is true, or all men are mortal.*" Categoricals have a *subject term* and a *predicate term* ("men" is the subject term and "mortal" the predicate term of "All men are mortal") and are subdivided in two main ways—according to quantity, into universals ("All men are mortal," "No men are mortal") and particulars ("Some men are mortal," "Some men are not mortal"), and according to quality, into affirmatives ("All men are mortal," "Some men are mortal") and negatives ("No men are mortal," "Some men are not mortal"). These are often displayed in a square, with universals at the top, particulars at the bottom, affirmatives on the left, negatives on the right:

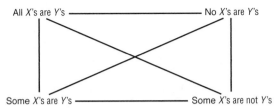

All *X*'s are *Y*'s ———————— No *X*'s are *Y*'s

Some *X*'s are *Y*'s ———————— Some *X*'s are not *Y*'s

Universal affirmatives are called A-propositions, particular affirmatives I-propositions, universal negatives E-propositions, and particular negatives O-propositions (the vowels being taken from the words *affirmo* and *nego*). Two other "quantities" are commonly mentioned, namely *singular* and *indefinite*. Singular propositions, such as "Socrates is mortal," are a genuinely distinct type, which we shall touch upon at appropriate points; indefinites, such as "Men are mortal," seem merely to be universals or particulars in which the quantity is left unstated. The expressions other than terms which enter into these forms are called "syncategorematic"; they are divided into the signs of quantity "all" and "some" and the copulas "is" or "are" and "is not" or "are not." ("No" is both a sign of quantity and a sign of negation.)

These types of propositions—A, E, I, and O—are the traditional "four forms," and as a preliminary to logical manipulation it is customary to restate given sentences in some standard way that will make their quantity and quality immediately evident. The forms given above, with "all," etc., and with plural common nouns for terms, are the most widely used, but it is in some ways less misleading to use "every," etc., and the terms in the singular—"Every *X* is a *Y*," "No *X* is a *Y*," "Some *X* is a *Y*," "Some *X* is not a *Y*." What is important is to understand that "some" means simply "at least one"; "Some men are mortals" or "Some man is a mortal" must be understood as neither affirming nor denying that more than one man is a mortal and as neither affirming nor denying that all men are (i.e., "some" does *not* mean "only some").

A square of the type shown earlier is called a *square of opposition*, and propositions with the same terms in the same order may be "opposed" in four ways. Universals of opposite quality ("Every *X* is a *Y*," "No *X* is a *Y*") are said to be *contraries*; these cannot be jointly true. Particulars of opposite quality ("Some *X* is a *Y*," "Some *X* is not a *Y*") are said to be *subcontraries*; these cannot be jointly false. Propositions opposed only in quantity are said to be *subalterns*, the *subalternant* universal implying (without being implied by) the *subalternate* particular ("Every *X* is a *Y*" implies "Some *X* is a *Y*," and "No *X* is a *Y*" implies "Some *X* is not a *Y*"). Propositions opposed in both quantity and quality ("Every *X* is a *Y*" and "Some *X* is not a *Y*," and "No *X* is a *Y*" and "Some *X* is a *Y*") are *contradictories*;

they cannot be jointly true or jointly false—the truth of a given proposition implies the falsehood of its contradictory; its falsehood implies the contradictory's truth.

EQUIPOLLENCE. Closely connected with the theory of opposition is that of the equipollence of propositions with the same terms in the same order but with negative particles variously placed within them. Since contradictories are true and false under reversed conditions, any proposition may be equated with the simple denial of its contradictory. Thus, "Some *X* is not a *Y*" has the same logical force as "Not every *X* is a *Y*," and, conversely, "Every *X* is a *Y*" has the force of "Not (some *X* is not a *Y*)," or, to give it a more normal English expression, "Not any *X* is not a *Y*." Similarly, "Some *X* is a *Y*" has the force of "Not (no *X* is a *Y*)" and "No *X* is a *Y*" that of "Not (some *X* is a *Y*)"—that is, "Not any *X* is a *Y*." Also, since "no" conveys universality and negativeness at once, "No *X* is a *Y*" has the force of "Every *X* is not-a-*Y*," and, conversely, "Every *X* is a *Y*" has the force of "No *X* is not-a-*Y*." Writers with an interest in simplification have seen in these equivalences a means of dispensing with all but one of the signs "every," "some," and "no." Thus the four forms may all be expressed in terms of "every," as follows: "Every *X* is a *Y*" (A), "Every *X* is not-a-*Y*" (E), "Not every *X* is not-a-*Y*" (I), "Not every *X* is a *Y*" (O).

Of singular propositions all that need be said at this point is that they divide into affirmatives ("Socrates is mortal," "This is a man," "This man is mortal") and negatives ("Socrates is not mortal," etc.) and that when their subject is formed by prefixing "this" to a common noun (as in "This man is mortal"), the singular form is implied by the corresponding universal ("Every man is mortal") and implies the corresponding particular ("Some man is mortal"). Some of the traditional logicians attempted to assimilate singular propositions to particulars, some to assimilate them to universals, but these attempts are not very impressive, and it is one of the few merits of the Renaissance logician Peter Ramus that he and his followers treated them consistently as a type of their own.

CONVERSION OF PROPOSITIONS. With regard to pairs of propositions of the same form and with the same terms, but in reverse order—for example, "No *X* is a *Y*" and "No *Y* is an *X*"—these are sometimes equivalent and sometimes not. Where they are, as in the case just given, they are said to be *converses* of one another, and the forms are said to be convertible. E and I are convertible; A and O are not. That every man is an animal, for example, does not imply that every animal is a man, and that some animal is not a horse does not imply that some horse is not an animal. Conversion, the inference from a given proposition to its converse ("Some men are liars; therefore, some liars are men"), is a type of immediate inference—that is, inference involving only one premise (as opposed, for instance, to syllogisms, which have two). Other immediate inferences are those from a given proposition to an "equipollent" form in the sense of the preceding section (for example, "Every man is mortal; therefore, not any man is not") and from a subalternant universal to its subalternate particular ("Every man is mortal; therefore, some man is mortal").

The conversion just described is "simple" conversion; with universals (even A, though it is not "simply" convertible) there is also a conversion *per accidens,* or *subaltern* conversion—that is, a legitimate inference to the corresponding particular form with its terms transposed. Thus, although "Every man is an animal" does not imply that every animal is a man, it does imply that some animal is.

Other forms of immediate inference arise when negative terms are introduced. The simultaneous interchange and negation of subject and predicate is called *conversion by contraposition,* or simply contraposition. It is a valid process with A's and O's, not with E's and I's. ("Every man is an animal" implies "Every non-animal is a non-man"—whatever is not an animal is not a man—and "Not every animal is a man" implies "Not every non-man is a non-animal," but "No horse is a man" does not imply "No non-man is a non-horse"; "Some X is a Y" is true and "Some non-Y is a non-X" false if the X's and the Y's overlap and between them exhaust the universe.) All of the four forms may be "obverted" (Alexander Bain's term)—that is, have their quality changed and the predicate negated ("Every X is a Y" implies "No X is a non-Y," "No X is a Y" implies "Every X is a non-Y," and similarly with the particulars). A variety of names are given to the results of repeated successive obversion and conversion.

THE LOGIC OF SYLLOGISM

A categorical syllogism is the inference of one categorical proposition, the conclusion, from two others, the premises, each premise having one term in common with the conclusion and one term in common with the other premise—for example:

Every animal is mortal;
Every man is an animal;
Therefore, every man is mortal.

The predicate of the conclusion (here "mortal") is called the major term, and the premise that contains it (here written first) the major premise. The subject of the conclusion ("man") is the minor term, and the premise that contains it (here written second) the minor premise. The term common to the two premises ("animal") is the middle term.

FIGURES AND MOODS. Syllogisms are divided into four figures, according to the placing of the middle term in the two premises. In the first figure the middle term is subject in the major premise and predicate in the minor; in the second figure predicate in both; in the third figure subject in both; in the fourth predicate in the major and subject in the minor. The following schemata, with P for the major term, S for the minor, and M for the middle, sum up these distinctions:

Figure 1	Figure 2	Figure 3	Figure 4
$M-P$	$P-M$	$M-P$	$P-M$
$S-M$	$S-M$	$M-S$	$M-S$
$S-P$	$S-P$	$S-P$	$S-P$

Within each figure, syllogisms are further divided into *moods,* according to the quantity and quality of the propositions they contain.

Not all of the theoretically possible combinations of propositions related as above constitute valid syllogisms, sequences in which the third proposition really follows from the other two. For example, "Every man is an animal; some horse is an animal; therefore, no man is a horse" (mood AIE in Figure 2) is completely inconsequent (even though all three propositions happen in this case to be true). During the Middle Ages those syllogistic moods that are valid acquired certain short names, with the mood indicated by the vowels, and all of them were put together in a piece of mnemonic doggerel, of which one of the later versions is the following:

Barbara, Celarent, Darii, Ferioque prioris;
Cesare, Camestres, Festino, Baroco secundae;
Tertia *Darapti, Disamis, Datisi, Felapton,*
Bocardo, Ferison habet. Quarta insuper addit
Bramantip, Camenes, Dimaris, Fesapo, Fresison.

Here Bocardo, for example, means the mood OAO in Figure 3, of which an illustration (C. S. Peirce's example) would be

Some patriarch (viz., Enoch) is not mortal;
Every patriarch is a man;
Therefore, some man is not mortal.

There is also a group of moods (Barbari and Celaront in Figure 1, Cesaro and Camestrop in Figure 2, Camenop in Figure 4) in which a merely particular conclusion is drawn although the premises would warrant our going further and making the conclusion universal (the "subaltern" moods). The Ramists added special moods involving singulars (if we write S and N for affirmative and negative singulars, we have ASS and ESN in Figure 1, ANN and ESN in Figure 2 and SSI and NSO in Figure 3). It may be noted that every syllogism must have at least one universal premise, except for SSI and NSO in Figure 3—the so-called expository syllogisms, for example, "Enoch is not mortal; Enoch is a patriarch; therefore, not every patriarch is mortal." Moreover, every syllogism must have at least one affirmative premise, and if either premise is negative or particular, the conclusion must be negative or particular, as the case may be ("the conclusion follows the weaker premise," as Theophrastus put it, negatives and particulars being considered weaker than affirmatives and universals).

REDUCTION. The mnemonic verses serve to indicate how the valid moods of the later figures may be "reduced" to those of Figure 1—that is, how we may derive their conclusions from their premises without using any syllogistic reasoning of other than the first-figure type. (This amounts, in modern terms, to proving their validity from that of the first-figure moods taken as axiomatic.) In the second-figure mood Cesare, for example, the letter s after the first e indicates that if we *simply convert* the major premise we will have a pair of premises from which we can deduce the required conclusion in Figure 1, and the initial letter C indicates that the first-figure mood employed will be Celarent. An example of a syllogism in Cesare (EAE in Figure 2) would be

No horse is a man;
Every psychopath is a man;
Therefore, no psychopath is a horse.

This conclusion may equally be obtained from these premises by proceeding as follows:

No horse is a man—s——▸No man is a horse;
Every psychopath is a man → Every psychopath is a man;
Therefore, no psychopath is a horse.

Here the right-hand syllogism, in which the first premise is obtained from the given major by simple conversion and the second is just the given minor unaltered, is in the mood Celarent in the first figure. Festino "reduces" similarly to Ferio, and Datisi and Ferison (in the third figure) reduce to Darii and Ferio, though in the third-figure cases it is the minor premise that must be simply converted. Darapti and Felapton reduce to Darii and Ferio by conversion of the minor premise, not simply, but *per accidens* (this is indicated by the s of the other moods being changed to p).

Camestres (Figure 2) and Disamis (Figure 3) are a little more complicated. Here we have not only an s, for the simple conversion of a premise, but also an m, indicating that the premises must be transposed, and a further s at the end because the transposed premises yield, in Figure 1, not the required conclusion but rather its converse, from which the required conclusion must be obtained by a further conversion at the end of the process. An example in Disamis would be the following:

Some men are liars;
All men are automata;
Therefore, some automata are liars.

If we convert the major premise and transpose the two, we obtain the new pair

All men are automata;
Some liars are men,

and from these we may obtain in the first-figure mood Darii not immediately the conclusion "Some automata are liars" but rather "Some liars are automata," from which, however, "Some automata are liars" does follow by simple conversion.

Baroco and Bocardo are different again. In both of them neither premise is capable of simple conversion, and if we convert the A premises *per accidens* we obtain pairs IO and OI, and there are no valid first-figure moods with such premises—in fact, no valid moods at all with two particular premises. We therefore show that the conclusion follows from the premises by the device called reductio ad absurdum. That is, we assume for the sake of argument that the conclusion does not follow from the premises—that is, that the premises can be true and the conclusion false—and from this assumption, using first-figure reasoning alone, we deduce impossible consequences. The assumption, therefore, cannot stand, so the conclusion does after all follow from its premises.

Take, for example, the following syllogism in Baroco (AOO in Figure 2):

Every man is mortal;
Some patriarch (viz., Enoch) is not mortal;
Therefore, some patriarch is not a man.

Suppose the premises are true and the conclusion is not. Then we have

(1) Every man is mortal;
(2) Some patriarch is not mortal;
(3) Every patriarch is a man.

(This is the contradictory of the conclusion.) But from (1) and (3), in the first-figure mood Barbara, we may infer

(4) Every patriarch is mortal.

However, the combination of (2) and (4) is impossible. Hence, we can have both (1) and (2) only if we drop (3)—that is, if we accept the conclusion of the given second-figure syllogism.

It is possible to "reduce" all the second-figure and third-figure moods to Figure 1 by this last method, and although this procedure is a little complicated, it brings out better than the other reductions the essential character of second-figure and third-figure reasoning. Figure 1 is governed by what is called the *dictum de omni et nullo,* the principle that what applies to all or none of the objects in a given class will apply or not apply (as the case may be) to any given member or subclass of this class. As Immanuel Kant preferred to put it, first-figure reasoning expresses the subsumption of cases under a rule—the major premise states some affirmative or negative rule ("Every man is mortal," "No man will live forever"), the minor asserts that something is a case, or some things are cases, to which this rule applies ("Enoch and Elijah are men"), and the conclusion states the result of applying the rule to the given case or cases ("Enoch and Elijah are mortal," "Enoch and Elijah will not live forever"). Hence, in Figure 1 the major premise is always universal (that being how rules are expressed) and the minor affirmative ("Something *is* a case").

Second-figure reasoning also begins with the statement of a rule ("Every man is mortal") but in the minor premise denies that we have with a given example the result which the rule prescribes ("Enoch and Elijah are *not* mortal," "Enoch and Elijah *will* live forever") and concludes that we do not have a case to which the rule applies ("Enoch and Elijah cannot be men"). It combines, in effect, the first-figure major with the contradictory of the first-figure conclusion to obtain the contradictory of the first-figure minor (compare the "reduction" of Baroco). A second-figure syllogism, in consequence, must have a universal major, premises opposed in quality, and a negative conclusion. Its practical uses are in refuting hypotheses, as in medicine or detection ("Whoever has measles has spots, and this child has no spots, so he does not have measles"; "Whoever killed X was a person of great strength, and Y is not such a person, so Y did not kill X").

In the third figure we begin by asserting that something or other does not exhibit the result which a proposed rule would give ("Enoch and Elijah are *not* mortal," "Enoch and Elijah *will* live forever"), go on to say that we nevertheless do have here a case or cases to which the rule would apply if true ("Enoch and Elijah *are* men"), and

conclude that the rule is not true ("Not all men are mortal," "Some men do live forever"). A third-figure syllogism, consequently, has an affirmative minor (the thing is a case) and a particular conclusion (the contradictory of a universal being a particular); its use is to confute rashly assumed rules, such as proposed scientific laws.

This rather neat system of interrelations (first clearly brought out by C. S. Peirce) concerns only the first three figures; it was not until the later Middle Ages, in fact, that a distinct fourth figure was recognized. The common division of figures assumes that we are considering completed syllogisms, with the conclusion (and its subject and predicate) already before us; however, the question Aristotle originally put to himself was not "Which completed syllogisms are valid?" but "Which pairs of premises will yield a syllogistic conclusion?" Starting at this end, we cannot distinguish major and minor premises as those containing, respectively, the predicate and subject of the conclusion. Aristotle distinguished them, in the first figure, by their comparative comprehensiveness and mentioned what we now call the fourth-figure moods as odd cases in which first-figure premises will yield a conclusion wherein the "minor" term is predicated of the "major." Earlier versions of the mnemonic lines accordingly list the fourth-figure moods with the first-figure ones and (since the premises are thought of as being in the first-figure order) give them slightly different names (Baralipton, Celantes, Dabitis, Fapesmo, Frisesomorum).

DISTRIBUTION OF TERMS. Terms may occur in A-, E-, I-, and O-propositions as distributed or as undistributed. The rule is that universals distribute their subjects and particulars distribute their predicates, but what this means is seldom very satisfactorily explained. It is often said, for example, that a distributed term refers to all, and an undistributed term to only a part, of its extension. But in what way does "Some men are mortal," for example, refer to only a part of the class of men? Any man whatever will do to verify it; if any man whatever turns out to be mortal, "Some men are mortal" is true. What the traditional writers were trying to express seems to be something of the following sort: A term t is distributed in a proposition $f(t)$ if and only if it is replaceable in $f(t)$, without loss of truth, by any term "falling under it" in the way that a species falls under a genus. Thus, "man" is distributed in

> Every man is an animal;
> No man is a horse;
> No horse is a man;
> Some animal is not a man,

since these respectively imply, say,

Every blind man is an animal;
No blind man is a horse;
No horse is a blind man;
Some animal is not a blind man.

On the other hand, it is undistributed in

Some man is keen-sighted;
Some man is not disabled;
Every Frenchman is a man;
Some keen-sighted animal is a man,

since these do not respectively imply

Some blind man is keen-sighted;
Some blind man is not disabled;
Every Frenchman is a blind man;
Some keen-sighted animal is a blind man.

In this sense A- and E- propositions do distribute their subjects and E- and O-propositions their predicates. John Anderson pointed out that the four positive results above may be established syllogistically, given that all the members of a species (using the term widely) are members of its genus—in the given case, that all blind men are men. From "Every man is an animal" and "Every blind man is a man," "Every blind man is an animal" follows in Barbara; with the second example the syllogism is in Celarent, with the third in Camestres, with the fourth in Baroco. Note, however, that the mere prefixing of "every" to a term is not in itself sufficient to secure its "distribution" in the above sense; for example, "man" is not distributed in "Not every man is disabled," since this does not imply "Not every blind man is disabled."

For a syllogism to be valid the middle term must be distributed at least once, and any term distributed in the conclusion must be distributed in its premise (although there is no harm in a term's being distributed in its premise but not in the conclusion). Many syllogisms can quickly be shown to be fallacious by the application of these rules. "Every man is an animal; every horse is an animal; therefore, every horse is a man," for example, fails to distribute the middle term "animal," and it is clear that any second-figure syllogism with two affirmative premises would have the same fault (since in the second figure the middle term is predicate twice, and affirmatives do not distribute their predicates). Other special rules for the different figures, such as that in Figures 1 and 3 the minor premise must be affirmative, can be similarly proved from the rules of distribution together with the rules of quality (that a valid syllogism does not have two negative premises, and that a conclusion is negative if and only if one premise is). Logicians have endeavored to prove some

of these rules from others and to reduce the number of unproved rules to a minimum.

EULER'S DIAGRAMS. One device for checking the validity of syllogistic inferences is the use of certain diagrams attributed to the seventeenth-century mathematician Leonhard Euler, although their accurate employment seems to date rather from J. D. Gergonne, in the early nineteenth century.

From the traditional laws of opposition and conversion it can be shown that the extensions of any pair of terms X, Y will be related in one or another of five ways: (α) every X is a Y and every Y is an X, that is, their extensions coincide; or (β) every X is a Y, but not every Y is an X, that is, the X's form a proper part of the Y's; or (γ) every Y is an X, but not every X is a Y, that is, the Y's form a proper part of the X's; or (δ) some but not all X's are Y's and some but not all Y's are X's, that is, the X's and Y's overlap; or (ϵ) no X's are Y's and so no Y's are X's, that is, the X's and Y's are mutually exclusive. These five cases are represented by the following diagrams:

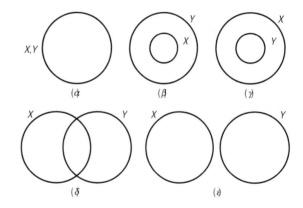

"Every X is a Y" (A) is true if and only if we have either (α) or (β); "Some X is not a Y" (O) if and only if we have either (γ) or (δ) or (ϵ); "No X is a Y" (E) if and only if we have (ϵ); and "Some X is a Y" (I) if and only if we have either (α) or (β) or (γ) or (δ). From these facts it follows that A and O are in no case true together and in no case false together, and similarly for E and I; that I is true in every case in which A is and also in two cases in which A is not, and similarly for O and E; that A and E are in no case true together but in two cases are both false; and that O and I are in no case both false but in two cases are both true. After working out analogous truth conditions for the forms with reversed terms, we will see that they are the same for the two I's and the two E's (showing that these are simply convertible) but not for the two A's and the two O's (showing that these are not). Given which of the five relations holds between X and Y and which between Y and Z, we can work out by compounding diagrams what will be the possible relations between X and Z. For example, if we know that every X is a Y and every Y a Z, then we must have either $(\alpha)XY$ and $(\alpha)YZ$ or $(\alpha)XY$ and $(\beta)YZ$ or $(\beta)XY$ and $(\alpha)YZ$ or $(\beta)XY$ and $(\beta)YZ$; that is, we must have

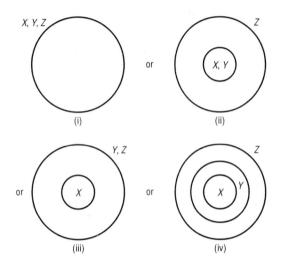

Inspection will show that for X and Z we have in every case either

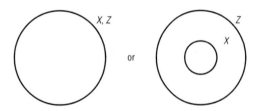

so in every case every X is a Z. Hence, Barbara is valid.

When employing this procedure it is essential to consider all the possible cases involved. Barbara is not validated, for example, by considering case (iv) alone, as popular expositions of this method sometimes suggest.

POLYSYLLOGISMS, ENTHYMEMES, AND INDUCTION. In an extended argument the conclusion of one inference may be used as a premise of another, and the conclusion of that as premise of a third, and so on. In presenting such an argument we may simply omit the intermediate steps and list all the premises together. For example, the sequence of categorical syllogisms "Every X is a Y, and every Y is a Z, so every X is a Z; and every Z is a T, so every X is a T" may be condensed to "Every X is a Y, every Y is a Z, and every Z is a T; therefore, every X is a T." Such a condensed chain of syllogisms is called a polysyllogism or sorites. The theory of chains of two syllo-

gisms was thoroughly studied by Galen, as reported in an ancient passage unearthed by Jan Łukasiewicz. Galen showed that the only combinations of the Aristotelian three figures that could be thus used were 1 and 1, 1 and 2, 1 and 3, and 2 and 3. His discovery of these four types of compound syllogism was misunderstood by later writers as an anticipation of the view that single syllogisms may be of four figures.

Even when it is not a conclusion from other premises already stated, one of the premises of an inference may often be informally omitted (for example, "Enoch and Elijah are men; therefore, Enoch and Elijah are mortals"). Such a truncated inference is often called an enthymeme. This is not Aristotle's own use of the term, though he did mention that a premise is often omitted in the statement of an enthymeme in his sense. An Aristotelian enthymeme is a merely probable argument—that is, one in which the conclusion does not strictly follow from the premises but is merely made more likely by them. When the claim made for an argument is thus reduced, the normal rules may be relaxed in certain directions; in particular, the second and third figures may be used to yield more than merely negative results. Thus, Figure 2 may be used not only to prove that something is not a case falling under a given rule but also to suggest that it is one—to use a modern example:

Any collection of particles whose movement is accelerated will occupy more space than it did;

A heated gas will occupy more space than it did;

Therefore, a heated gas may be a collection of particles whose movement is accelerated.

Figure 3 may be similarly used not only to prove that some rule does not hold universally but also to suggest that it does hold universally—for instance:

X, Y, Z are all of them white;
X, Y, Z are all of them swans;
Therefore, perhaps all swans are white.

If the second premise here is strengthened to "X, Y, Z are all the swans there are," the conclusion will follow without any "perhaps" (of course, the new premise is in this case a false one, and the conclusion is also false). The form of inference

X, Y, Z, etc., are all of them P's;
X, Y, Z, etc., are all the S's there are;
Therefore, all S's are P's

was called by Aristotle "induction"; more accurately, he used this term for a similar passage from all the subspecies to their genus ("The *X*'s, the *Y*'s, and the *Z*'s are all of them *P*'s and are all the *S*'s; therefore, ..."). He observed that the "conversion" of the second premise to "All the *S*'s are the *X*'s, the *Y*'s, and the *Z*'s" will turn such an induction into a syllogism in Barbara.

The term *induction* being extended in the more recent tradition to cover the merely probable inference given just previously, we distinguish Aristotelian induction by calling it "formal" or "perfect" induction or (as W. E. Johnson called it) "summary" induction. The Figure 2 type of merely probable inference is one of the things meant by the term "argument from"—or "by"—"analogy" (or just "analogy"); C. S. Peirce called it "hypothesis."

SKEPTICAL CRITICISMS OF SYLLOGISTIC REASONING. In the latter part of the nineteenth century, under the influence of J. S. Mill, textbooks of the traditional type came to have two main divisions, "formal" or "deductive" logic (dealt with more or less as above) and "inductive" logic or "scientific method." With the details of inductive logic we are not concerned here, but we may glance at the view of some writers that merely probable induction and analogy are the only genuine types of reasoning, "formal" or syllogistic reasoning being useless or spurious because it is inevitably circular, assuming in the premises what it sets out to prove as the conclusion.

The second-century skeptic Sextus Empiricus suggested that in the syllogism "Every man is an animal; Socrates is a man; therefore, Socrates is an animal," the only way to establish the major premise is by induction; however, if the induction is incomplete the examination of a new instance—for example, of Socrates—might prove it false, and if it is complete the conclusion ("Socrates is an animal") must already have been used in establishing it. This argument was repeated by such writers as George Campbell, in the eighteenth century, who supplemented it with another, to cover the case in which the major is established not by induction but simply by definition or linguistic convention: "Of course every man is an animal, for being an animal is part of what we mean by being a man." In this case it is the minor premise, "Socrates is a man," that cannot be established without first establishing the conclusion (that he is an animal). The same point was urged by another Scottish philosopher, Thomas Brown. It is allied to an argument used by Sextus to show not that syllogism is circular but that the major premise is superfluous. If, he said, every man is an animal because it follows from an object's being a man that it is an animal, then the allegedly enthymematic

"Socrates is a man; therefore, Socrates is an animal" must be valid as it stands.

Richard Whately, answering Campbell's arguments in the early nineteenth century, complained that Campbell had confined himself to examples in which the syllogistic argument was indeed superfluous and countered them with some in which it was not—for example, the case of some laborers, ignorant of the fact that all horned animals are ruminant, digging up a skeleton which they, but not a distant naturalist, could see to be horned, the laborers and the naturalist thus separately providing premises which were both required to obtain the conclusion that the skeleton was of a ruminant animal. Whately admitted that the sense in which we may make a "discovery" by drawing a syllogistic conclusion is different from that in which we make a discovery by observation, but it can be a genuine discovery none the less; there are "logical" as well as "physical" discoveries.

After Whately, J. S. Mill took up the argument, but it is not entirely clear what side he was on. Sometimes he treated a universal major as already asserting, among other things, the conclusion:

> Whoever pronounces the words, All men are mortal, has affirmed that Socrates is mortal, though he may never have heard of Socrates; for since Socrates, whether known to be so or not, really is a man, he is included in the words, All men, and in every assertion of which they are the subject. (*System of Logic*, Book II, Ch. 3, p. 8, note)

"Included in the *meaning* of the words," he must have meant (for it is obvious that neither Socrates the man nor "Socrates," his name, forms any part of the words "All men"), but this contradicts Mill's own insistence that the meaning of general terms like "men" lies wholly in their "connotation" and that "All men are mortal" means that wherever the attributes of humanity are present, mortality is present, too. He rightly chided Brown, who thought that the meaning of "Socrates is mortal" (like that of "Socrates is an animal") is already contained in the minor premise "Socrates is a man," for failing to distinguish the actual connotation of "man" (i.e., the attributes by which its application is determined) from other attributes (such as mortality) which we may empirically discover these to be attended with, but his own view in the passage cited is similarly negligent.

Mill's main point, however, is different and more defensible. When careful and extensive observation warrants the conclusion that, say, all men are mortal, and we then observe that the duke of Wellington is a man and conclude that he is therefore mortal, we have in effect an induction followed by a syllogism. Mill pointed out that if this procedure is justified at all, the introduction of the syllogistic major is superfluous. For if the original body of evidence really does warrant the inference that all men are mortal, it is certainly sufficient to warrant the inference that the duke of Wellington is mortal, given that he is a man. In other words, if we really are justified in the move from particular observations to the general proposition, and from there to new particulars, we would be equally justified in moving directly "from particulars to particulars."

What the syllogistic major does, Mill argued, is simply to sum up in a single formula the entire class of inferences to new particulars which the evidence warrants. That is, "All men are mortal" means, in effect, that if we ever find anyone to be a man we are justified in inferring, from the observations we have previously amassed, that he is mortal. "The conclusion is not an inference drawn *from* the formula"—that is, from "All men are mortal" thus understood—"but an inference drawn *according to* the formula" (ibid., p. 4). Mill here anticipated Gilbert Ryle's treatment of "lawlike statements" as "inference licenses" and echoed Sextus's point that it is inconsistent to require that such licenses be added to the premises of the inferences they permit, since what they license is precisely the drawing of the conclusion from those premises.

Mill in fact here shifted the discussion from Sextus's first skeptical "topic" to his second—from the charge of circularity to the question of what distinguishes a rule of inference from a premise. On this point more was said later in the nineteenth century by C. S. Peirce. Peirce, like Mill, distinguished sharply between the premise or premises from which, and the "leading principle" according to which, a conclusion is drawn. He also noted, as did Mill, that what is traditionally counted as a premise may function in practice as a "leading principle." But it need not, and, indeed, what is traditionally counted as a "leading principle" (say the *dictum de omni et nullo*) may sometimes be, conversely, treated in practice as a premise. Certainly, since *all men are mortal* (leading principle 1), we are justified in inferring the mortality of Socrates (or the duke of Wellington, or Elijah) from his humanity. But equally, since *all members of any class are also members of any class that contains the former as a subclass* (leading principle 2), we are justified in inferring the mortality of Socrates from his being a man *and* from men's being a subclass of mortals. For the very same reason (that all members of any class are also members of any class that

contains the former as a subclass) we are justified in inferring the mortality of Socrates from his being a member of a subclass of the class of mortals *and* from the membership of any member of a class in all classes of which it is a subclass. In this last example we have one and the same proposition functioning as a premise and as a leading principle in the same inference (not merely, like "All men are mortal" in the preceding two examples, as a leading principle in one and a premise in another); to be capable of this, Peirce thought, is the mark of a "logical" leading principle.

It is not certain that Peirce's method of distinguishing "logical" from other sorts of "leading principles" will bear inspection. However, he seems to have established his basic point, that what it would be fatal to require in all cases—the treatment of a leading principle as a premise—we may safely permit in some. There may be useful and valid reasoning about subjects of all degrees of abstraction, including logic itself.

HYPOTHETICAL AND DISJUNCTIVE SYLLOGISMS.
Traditional textbooks, aside from developing the theory of categorical propositions and syllogisms, have a brief appendix mentioning "hypothetical" (or "conditional") and "disjunctive" propositions and certain "syllogisms" to which they give rise.

"Hypothetical" syllogisms are divided into "pure," in which premises and conclusion are all of the form "If p then q" (notably the syllogism "If p then q, and if q then r; therefore, if p then r," analogous to Barbara), and "mixed," in which only one premise is hypothetical and the other premise and the conclusion are categorical. The mixed hypothetical syllogism has two valid "moods":

(1) *Modus ponendo ponens*: If p then q, and p; therefore, q.

(2) *Modus ponendo tollens*: If p then q, but not q; therefore, not p.

In both these moods the hypothetical premise is called the major, the categorical the minor. *Ponere,* in the mood names, means to affirm, *tollere* to deny. In (1), by affirming the antecedent of the hypothetical we are led to affirm its consequent; in (2), by denying its consequent we are led to deny its antecedent. The fallacies of "affirming the consequent" and "denying the antecedent" (i.e., of doing these things *to start with,* in the minor premise) consist in reversing these procedures—that is, in arguing "If p then q, and q; therefore, p" and "If p then q, but not p; therefore, not q."

"Disjunctive" syllogisms—that is, ones involving "Either-or" propositions—have the following two "mixed" moods:

(3) *Modus tollendo ponens*: Either *p* or *q*, but not *p*; therefore, *q* (or, but not *q*; therefore, *p*).

(4) *Modus ponendo tollens*: Either *p* or *q*, and *p*; therefore, not *q* (or, and *q*; therefore, not *p*).

Mood (4) is valid only if "Either *p* or *q*" is interpreted "exclusively"—that is, as meaning "Either *p* or *q* but not both"—whereas (3) is valid even if it is interpreted as "Either *p* or *q* or both." There is also a *modus tollendo ponens* with the simple "Not both *p* and *q*" as major and the rest as in (4).

DILEMMAS. Hypothetical and disjunctive premises may combine to yield a categorical conclusion in the *dilemma*, or "horned" syllogism (*syllogismus cornutus*), with its two forms:

(5) *Constructive*: If *p* then *r*, and if *q* then *r*, but either *p* or *q*; therefore, *r*.

(6) *Destructive*: If *p* then *q*, and if *p* then *r*, but either not *q* or not *r*; therefore, not *p*.

These basic forms have a number of variations; for instance, *q* in (5) may be simply "not *p*," making the disjunctive premise the logical truism "Either *p* or not *p*"; or *p* may imply *r* and *q* imply *s*, giving as conclusion "Either *r* or *s*" rather than the categorical *r*; or the disjunctive premise may be conditionalized to "If *s* then either *p* or *q*," making the conclusion "If *s* then *r*."

A typical dilemma is that put by Protagoras to Euathlus, whom he had trained as a lawyer on the understanding that he would be paid a fee as soon as his pupil won a case. When the pupil simply engaged in no litigation at all, Protagoras sued him for the fee. His argument was "If Euathlus wins this case, he must pay my fee by our agreement, and if he loses it he must pay it by the judge's decision (for that is what losing this case would mean), but he must either win or lose the case; therefore, in either case he must pay."

"Escaping between the horns" of a dilemma is denying the disjunctive premise; for example, Euathlus might have argued that he would neither win nor lose the case if the judge refused to make any decision. "Taking a dilemma by the horns" is admitting the disjunction but denying one of the implications, as Euathlus might have done by arguing that if he won he would still not be bound by the agreement to pay Protagoras, because this was not the sort of case intended in the agreement.

"Rebutting" a dilemma is constructing another dilemma drawing upon the same body of facts but leading to an opposite conclusion. This is what Euathlus did, arguing that if he won the case he would be dispensed from paying by the judge's decision, and if he lost it the agreement would dispense him, so either way he was dispensed from paying. Rebuttal, however, is possible only if one of the other moves (though it may not be clear which) is also possible, for a single set of premises can lead by equally valid arguments to contradictory conclusions only if they contain some fault in themselves.

Dilemmatic reasoning obtains a categorical conclusion from hypothetical and disjunctive premises; the Port-Royalists pointed out that we may also obtain hypothetical conclusions from categorical premises. For in any categorical syllogism we may pass directly from one of the premises to the conclusion stated not categorically but conditionally on the truth of the other premise; for instance, from "Every man is mortal" we may infer that if Socrates is a man he is mortal, and from "Socrates is a man" that if every man is mortal Socrates is, and similarly with all other syllogisms. This "rule of conditionalization" is much used in certain modern logical systems.

TRADITIONAL AND MODERN LOGIC

Not only the "rule of conditionalization" but the whole subject of hypothetical and disjunctive reasoning fits more comfortably into modern than into traditional logic, being an inheritance from the Stoics, the first "modern" logicians, rather than from Aristotle. Traditionalists have often been worried at its finding any place at all in their general *corpus* and have sometimes attempted to justify it by "reducing" hypothetical and disjunctive propositions and syllogisms to "categorical" ones.

Disjunctives, to begin with, may be eliminated as a distinct form by equating "Either *p* or *q*" with the conditional "If not *p* then *q*," and the conditional form does sometimes look as if it might be a mere verbal variant of the categorical universal. This last is especially true where the conditional is introduced not by the plain "if" but by "if ever" or "if any"; "If ever a gas is heated it expands" and "If any gas is heated it expands" seem simply variants of "Every heated gas expands." But here the antecedent and consequent of the conditional are not, as J. N. Keynes put it, complete propositions with an "independent import"—"it expands" is not on its own a comprehensible sentence; the "it" refers back to the heated gas of the antecedent. Keynes suggested that the term *conditional* be used for precisely this type of "If-then" statement and the term *true hypothetical* confined to cases in which the antecedent and consequent do have "independent import," such as "If Socrates is damned, then there is no justice in heaven." And the representation of "true hypotheticals" as categorical universals is not easy.

In modern logic, from the Stoics through some of the medieval *moderni* to the "logisticians" of our own century, "the stone which the builders rejected has been made the head of the corner." "Pure hypotheticals," together with other forms in which entire propositions are linked by various "connectives," have been made the subject of the most elementary part of logic, the propositional calculus. Aristotelian universals and particulars are built out of these forms (by means of prefixes called "quantifiers") rather than vice versa. (Details are given in the entries Logic, Modern and Russell, Bertrand, section on logic and mathematics.) The essential procedure is to read "Every A is a B" as "For every individual x, if x is an A then x is a B" and "Some A is a B" as "For some individual x, x is an A and x is a B." Here, instead of a Keynesian "conditional" being explained as a categorical universal in disguise, the explanation is reversed, and the components which, as Keynes said, are "not propositions of independent import" are represented as "propositional functions" in which the place taken in a genuine proposition by an individual name is taken by a variable ("bound" by the initial quantifier "for all x"). But the "if" which links these components is the very same "if" which in the "pure hypotheticals" of the propositional calculus links genuine propositions. This "if" is not explained in terms of anything else (except perhaps other connectives) but is taken as fundamental.

In this way the traditional themes are not banished from modern logic but are incorporated into a much larger subject. When the Aristotelian forms are thus interpreted, however, their laws seem to require modification at some points. In particular, the A-form "For any x, if x is an A then x is a B" does not seem to imply the I-form "For some x, x is an A and x is a B," for the former does not imply that any x in fact is an A (it says only that if any x is an A it is a B), whereas the latter does imply this (if some x both is an A and is a B, then that x is at least an A). This eliminates inference by subalternation and whatever else in the traditional theory depends on it, such as subaltern conversion and syllogisms, like Darapti, which require this for reduction to Figure 1.

Modern logic, however, is not at all monolithic in character, and the sketch just given is a little stylized, depicting modern logic not as a living discipline but rather as a new "tradition" that has displaced the old and against which there are already dissentient voices that give

the older tradition a measure of justification (rather like that accorded to pre-Copernican astronomy by the more radical forms of relativity theory). We cannot go back to the prison that would confine all logic to the Aristotelian syllogism, but it is possible to defend (a) something like the view that the form "Every X is a Y" is more fundamental than either "For all x, f(x)" or "If p then q" and (b) the traditional ignoring (in inference by subalternation, etc.) of terms that have no application.

As to (a), we now know how to define both "for all x" and "if" in terms of a single undefined logical operator which amounts to "for all x, if"; for we can take as our fundamental logical complex the form "Anything such that α is such that β" and read "If p then q" as the special case of this in which α and β are "propositions with independent import," and "For all x, β" as the special case in which α is logically true anyway (for instance, in which it has the form "Anything such that β is such that β") and so can he ignored as a "condition" of β's truth. C. S. Peirce—at almost every point the most imaginative and flexible of the "moderns," although he died in 1914—always regarded some such reduction as possible in principle and saw the difference between the "terms" out of which categorical propositions are constructed and the "propositions" out of which we construct hypotheticals as a point of little logical importance.

Peirce, moreover, gave a highly modern justification for the traditional view that within syllogistic logic only the first figure is strictly necessary. Traditional methods of "reducing" other figures to the first do indeed involve another form of inference, namely conversion, and although this can be represented as a kind of enthymematic syllogism, it comes out as syllogism that is already in the second and third figures. For we do it by letting the term B be the same as A in the two syllogisms

No C is a B (i.e., an A);
Every A is a B (i.e., an A);
Therefore, no A is a C

(Cesare, Figure 2) and

Every B (i.e., A) is an A;
Some B (i.e., A) is a C;
Therefore, some C is an A

(Datisi, Figure 3). The replacement of B by A turns the universal affirmative premise into the logical truism "Every A is an A," which can be dropped, and the conclusion into the converse of the remaining premise.

We can, however, derive second-figure syllogisms from first-figure ones by a variant of the reductio ad absurdum method, employing nothing but Barbara in its terminal and propositional forms, the forms

(a) Every A is a B, and every B is a C; therefore, every A is a C; and

(b) If p then q, and if q then r; therefore, if p then r,

together with freedom to rearrange our premises and to "conditionalize" and "deconditionalize" conclusions, that is, to make such passages as that from (a) to, and to (a) from,

(c) Every A is a B; therefore, if every B is. a C then every A is a C

and from (b) to, and to (b) from,

(d) If p then q; therefore, if (if q then r) then if p then r.

As a special case of (d) we have

(e) If every B is a C then every A is a C; therefore, if (if every A is a C I am much mistaken) then if every B is a C I am much mistaken.

Forms (c) and (e) will take us from the premise to the conclusion of

(f) Every A is a B; therefore, if (if every A is a C I am much mistaken) then if every B is a C I am much mistaken.

But "If X then I am very much mistaken" just amounts to "Not X," and (f) therefore amounts to

(g) Every A is a B; therefore, if not every A is a C, not every B is a C,

that is, a conditionalized form of Bocardo, Figure 3.

The equation of "Not X" with "If X then I am much mistaken" is Peirce's variant, at this point, of one account of denial. It makes it possible to present the other traditional forms as complexes of "if" and "every" (and "if" and "every," as was shown, are basically the same form of linkage), as follows:

Not every X is a Y (O) = If every X is a Y I am much mistaken.

No X is a Y (E) = Every X is not-a-Y = Every X is such that if it is a Y I am much mistaken.

Some X is a Y (I) = Not (no X is a Y) = If every X is such that if it is a Y I am much mistaken, then I am much mistaken.

Syllogisms, in all figures, involving these forms are derivable from Barbara by methods similar to that used to

obtain Bocardo above, although the derivations will often be more complicated than the one given. For some of them we require Barbara in yet another form besides (a) and (b) above, namely the mixed terminal and propositional

Every X is a Y; therefore, anything such that if it is a Y, then p, is such that if it is an X, then p,

and a kind of terminal principle of *modus ponens*,

Whatever is an X is a thing such that if its being an X implies that p, then p.

Modern logic will not admit that Barbara gives us all the logic there is, but its techniques do bring out anew the extreme fecundity of this ancient form.

Turning now to the failure of certain traditional forms of inference when terms without application are employed, there have been two more recent lines of attack on the view that traditional logic is simply "wrong" in accepting such forms as "Every X is a Y; therefore, some X is a Y." One, used by Łukasiewicz, is formalistic in character; it is a mistake, Łukasiewicz says, to interpret the traditional propositional forms in terms of modern quantification theory in the ways above indicated, or in any other ways. If we just take them as they stand, without interpretation, we can find a rigorous symbolism for them and show that the traditional laws form a self-consistent system; worries about their interpretation are extralogical. T. J. Smiley, on the other hand, thinks the interpretation of the traditional forms in quantification theory worth attempting but points out that quantification theory, as now developed, offers us wider choices of interpretation than was once thought. For quantification theory now handles cases of the form "For all x, f(x)" in which the range of the variable x is restricted to objects of some particular sort, each sort of object having its own type of variable. We need not, therefore, interpret "Every man is mortal," say, in the standard modern way as "For any individual object x, if that object is human it is mortal" but may read it, rather, as "For any *human* individual m, that human individual is mortal" (with no "ifs" about it). This interpretation, when embedded in a suitable theory of "many-sorted" quantification, will yield all the traditional results.

See also Negation.

Bibliography

Peter of Spain's *Summulae Logicales* (modern reprint, edited by I. M. Bocheński, Turin, 1947), Tractatus I–V and VII, is the best-known medieval compendium of the traditional material. In the post-Renaissance epoch the most influential work has been the so-called Port-Royal logic, Antoine Arnauld and Pierre Nicole's *Logique, ou l'art de penser* (translated by T. S. Baynes as *The Port-Royal Logic,* Edinburgh: Sutherland and Knox, 1851). Richard Whately's crisp, homely, and pugnacious *Elements of Logic,* which appeared in successive editions in the first half of the nineteenth century, is another classic. But the most comprehensive treatment of logic along traditional lines is J. N. Keynes's *Studies and Exercises in Formal Logic* (London and New York, 1884; 4th ed., London: Macmillan, 1906).

J. S. Mill's views on the denotation and connotation of terms are developed in his *System of Logic* (London, 1843), Book I, Chs. 2, 5, and 6; his views on the uses of the syllogism are in Book II, Ch. 3. The views of C. S. Peirce are in his *Collected Papers,* edited by Charles Hartshorne, Paul Weiss, and Arthur W. Burks (8 vols., Cambridge, MA: Harvard University Press, 1931–1958), 2.455–516 and 3.154–197, and in his article "Syllogism" in the *Century Dictionary* (6 vols., New York: Century, 1889–1891).

For modern systematizations and interpretations, see Jan Łukasiewicz, *Aristotle's Syllogistic* (2nd ed., Oxford: Clarendon Press, 1957); J. C. Shepherdson, "On the Interpretation of Aristotle's Syllogistic," in *Journal of Symbolic Logic* 21 (1956): 137–147; and T. J. Smiley, "Syllogism and Quantification," in *Journal of Symbolic Logic* 27 (1962): 58–72.

A. N. Prior (1967)

LOGIC, TRANSCENDENTAL

See *Kant, Immanuel*

LOGICAL ATOMISM

See *Analysis, Philosophical; Russell, Bertrand Arthur William; Wittgenstein, Ludwig Josef Johann*

LOGICAL EMPIRICISM

See *Logical Positivism*

LOGICAL FORM

One can use sentences to present arguments, some of which are valid. Sentences are complex linguistic expressions that exhibit grammatical structure. And the grammatical properties of sentences need not be obvious. As discussed in this entry, certain arguments seem to be valid because the relevant premises and conclusions exhibit nonobvious logical structure. But this raises questions about what logical structure is and how it is related to grammatical structure.

PATTERNS OF REASONING

An ancient thought is that premises and conclusions have parts and that valid arguments exhibit valid forms, like the following: **Q** if **P**, and **P**; so **Q**. One can say that the variables (in bold) range over propositions, leaving it open for now what propositions are: sentences of some (perhaps unspoken) language, abstract states of affairs, or whatever. One can also assume that declarative sentences can be used, in contexts, to indicate or express propositions. But each sentence of English is presumably distinct from the potential premise/conclusion indicated with that sentence in a given context. Different speakers can use *I swam today* at different times to indicate various propositions, each of which could be expressed in other languages. Nonetheless, propositions seem to be sentence-like in some respects, especially with regard to being composite.

The conclusion of (1)

(1) Chris swam if Pat swam, and Pat swam; so Chris swam.

is evidently part of the first premise, which has the second premise as another part. But simple propositions, without propositional parts, also seem to have structure. Aristotelian schemata like the following are valid: Every *P* is *D*, and every *S* is a *P*; so every *S* is *D*. The italicized variables are intended to range over predicates—logical analogs of nouns, adjectives, and other classificatory terms (like *politician, deceitful,* and *senator*). Simple propositions appear to have subject-predicate structure; where a subject can consist of a predicate and a quantifier (indicated with a word like *every, some,* or *no*).

Medieval logicians explored the hypothesis that all propositions are composed of simple propositions and a few special elements, indicated with words like *or* and *only*. While they expected some differences between grammatical and propositional structure, the idea was that sentences reflect the important aspects of logical form. The medieval logicians also made great strides in reducing Aristotelian schemata to more basic inferential principles: one concerning replacement of a predicate with a less restrictive predicate, as in *Rex is a brown dog, so Rex is a dog;* and one concerning converse examples, like *Rex is not a dog, so Rex is not a brown dog.*

Nonetheless, traditional logic/grammar was inadequate. If Juliet kissed Romeo, then Juliet kissed someone. And predicates containing quantifiers were problematic.

If *respects some doctor* and *respects some senator* indicate nonrelational proposition-parts, like *is tall* and *is ugly*, then the argument indicated with (2)

> (2) Some patient respects some doctor, and every doctor is a senator; so some patient respects some senator.

has the following form, which is not valid: Some *P* is *T*, and every *D* is an *S*; so some *P* is *U*. One can introduce a variable *R* ranging over relations and offer schemata like the following: Some *P* **R** some *D*, and every *D* is an *S*; so some *P* **R** some *S*. But this is not a basic inference pattern; and such schemata do not capture the validity of inferences like the following: Every patient who met every doctor is tall, and some patient who met every doctor respects every senator; so some patient who respects every senator is tall. Relative clauses posed difficulties as well. If sentence (3) is true, so is sentence (4):

> (3) Every patient respects some doctor.

> (4) Every old patient respects some doctor.

But in (5) and (6) the direction of valid inference is reversed:

> (5) No lawyer who saw every patient respects some doctor.

> (6) No lawyer who saw every old patient respects some doctor.

FUNCTIONS AND ARGUMENTS

Gottlob Frege showed how to deal with these examples and more. But on his view, propositions have function-argument structure. Let *S* stand for the successor function. Frege interpreted the arithmetic expression *S*(3) as having a semantic value: the value of the relevant function given the relevant argument; that is, the number four. The division function can be represented as a mapping from ordered pairs of numbers to quotients: $Q(x, y) = x/y$. Functions can also be specified conditionally; consider the function that maps every even integer onto itself, and every odd integer onto its successor. On Frege's view, *Mary sang* indicates a proposition with the following structure: Sang(Mary). And he took the relevant function to be a conditional mapping from individuals in a given domain to truth values: $Sang(x) = \mathbf{t}$ if x sang, and $\mathbf{f}$ otherwise; where for each individual x, $Sang(x) = \mathbf{t}$ if and only if (iff) x sang, and $Sang(x) = \mathbf{f}$ iff x did not sing. The proposition that John admired Mary, like the proposition that Mary was admired by John, was said to have the following structure: Admired(John, Mary); where $Admired(x, y) = \mathbf{t}$ if x admired y, and $\mathbf{f}$ otherwise.

Frege's treatment of quantification departed more radically from tradition. Let F be the function indicated by *sang*, so that someone sang iff some individual x is such that $F(x) = \mathbf{t}$. Using modern notation, someone sang iff $\exists x[Sang(x)]$; where the quantifier binds the variable. Every individual in the domain sang iff F maps each individual onto $\mathbf{t}$; in modern notation, $\exists x[Sang(x)]$. With regard to the proposition that some politician is deceitful, subject-predicate grammar suggests the division *Some politician / is deceitful*. But for Frege the logically important division is between the existential quantifier and the rest, with the quantifier binding two occurrences of its variable: $\exists x[P(x) \& D(x)]$; some individual is both a politician and deceitful. Likewise with regard to the proposition that every politician is deceitful: $\forall x[P(x) \to D(x)]$; everyone is such that if he or she is a politician then he or she is deceitful. In which case, *every politician* does not indicate a constituent of the proposition. Grammar also masks a logical difference between the existential and universal propositions: predicates are related conjunctively in the former, but conditionally in the latter.

The real power of Frege's logic is most evident in his discussion of how the proposition that every number has a successor is logically related to more basic arithmetic truths. But just consider the following analyses of (3a–6a):

> (3a) $\forall x\{P(x) \to \exists y[D(y) \& R(x,y)]\}$

> (4a) $\forall x\{[O(x) \& P(x)] \to \exists y[D(y) \& R(x,y)]\}$

> (5a) $\neg\exists x\{Lx \& \forall y[P(y) \to S(x,y)] \& \exists z[D(z) \& R(x,z)]\}$

> (6a) $\neg\exists x\{Lx \& \forall y\{[O(y) \& P(y)] \to S(x,y)\} \& \exists z[D(z) \& R(x,z)]\}$

Given Frege's rules of inference, (3a) implies (4a), while (5a) follows from (6a). Frege concluded that natural language is not suited to the task of representing propositions perspicuously. On his view, premises/conclusions have function-argument structure, which is often masked in natural language. But one can try to invent languages whose sentences depict true propositional structure.

Frege originally took propositional constituents to be the relevant functions and (ordered n-tuples of) entities that such functions map to truth-values. But he later refined this view, taking the sense of an expression to be a mode of presentation of the corresponding semantic value. Frege identified propositions—or what he called thoughts (*Gedanken*)—with senses of sentences in an ideal language, which allowed him to distinguish the proposition that Hesperus is bright from the proposition that Phosphorus is bright. Thus, Frege could deny that the inference *Hesperus is Hesperus, so Hesperus is Phosphorus* is an instance of the valid form *P, so P.*

DESCRIPTIONS AND MISMATCH

One might think that the logical form of any proposition indicated with *The boy from Canada sang* is *Sang(b)*, where *b* stands for the individual in question. But this makes elements of the description logically irrelevant. And if the boy from Canada sang, then a boy sang. Moreover, *the* implies uniqueness (at least within a context). So Bertrand Russell (1919) held that a proposition expressed with *The boy sang* has the following structure: $\exists x\{Boy(x)$ $\& \forall y[Boy(y) \rightarrow y = x] \& Sang(x)\}$; where the middle conjunct is one way, among many, of expressing uniqueness. According to Russell, even if a speaker refers to a certain boy when saying *The boy sang*, that boy is not a constituent of the indicated proposition—which has the form of an existential quantification, as opposed to a function saturated by the boy. In this respect, *the boy* is like *some boy*. Though on Russell's view, not even *the* indicates a propositional constituent. This extended Frege's idea that natural language is misleading, while letting Russell account for the meaningfulness of descriptions that describe nothing.

Let **Frank** be the proposition indicated (now) with *The (present) king of France is bald*. If **Frank** consists of some function saturated by an entity indicated with *The king of France*, there must *be* such an entity. But instead of appealing to nonexistent kings, or ways of presenting them, Russell held that **Frank** is of the form $\exists x\{K(x) \&$ $\forall y[K(y) \rightarrow y = x] \& B(x)\}$. In which case, the true negation of **Frank** is not of the form $\exists x\{K(x) \& \forall y[K(y) \rightarrow y =$ $x] \& \neg B(x)\}$. This invited the thought, developed by Ludwig Wittgenstein (1922, 1953) and others, that many philosophical puzzles might dissolve if one properly understood the logical forms of one's claims. Russell also held that one bears a special relation to constituents of propositions one can entertain and that one typically does not bear this relation to the individuals one refers to with names. This led Russell to say that names are disguised descriptions. On this view, *Hesperus* is associated with a complex predicate—say, for illustration, of the form $E(x) \& S(x)$. Then *Hesperus is bright* indicates a proposition of the form $\exists x\{[E(x) \& S(x)] \& \forall y\{[E(y) \& S(y)] \rightarrow y = x]\} \& B(x)\}$. It follows that Hesperus exists iff $\exists x[E(x) \& S(x)]$; and this was challenged by Saul Kripke (1980). But Russell could say that "Phosphorus is bright" indicates a proposition of the form $\exists x\{[M(x) \& S(x)] \&$ $\forall y\{[M(y) \& S(y)] \rightarrow y = x]\} \& B(x)$; where $E(x)$ and $M(x)$ indicate different functions, specified in terms of evenings and mornings, leaving room to discover that $E(x) \& S(x)$ and $M(x) \& S(x)$ both indicate functions that map Venus alone to the truth-value **t**.

Positing unexpected logical forms thus had payoffs. But if mismatches between sentential and propositional structure are severe, one wonders how one manages to indicate propositions. This worry was exacerbated by increasing suspicion that talk of propositions is (at best) a way of talking about how one should regiment one's verbal behavior for purposes of scientific inquiry and that one should regiment natural language in first-order predicate calculus. From this perspective, associated with Willard Van Orman Quine (1950), mismatches between logical and grammatical form are to be expected. Another strand of thought, inspired by Wittgenstein's later work, also suggested that a single sentence could be used (on different occasions) to express different kinds of propositions. Peter Strawson (1950) argued, contra Russell, that a speaker could use an instance of *The F is G* to express a singular proposition about the F in the context at hand. Keith Donnellan (1966) contended that a speaker could even use an instance of *The F is G* to express a singular proposition about an individual that is not an F. Various considerations suggested that relations between spoken sentences and propositions are at best very complex and mediated by speakers' intentions.

With hindsight, though, one can see that the divergence between logical and grammatical form was exaggerated. Consider again the proposed regimentation of the proposition indicated with *Some boy sang*: $\exists x[Boy(x)$ $\& Sang(x)]$. With restricted quantifiers, one can offer another logical paraphrase that parallels the grammatical division between *some boy* and *sang*. Let $\exists x:Boy(x)$ be an existential quantifier that binds a variable ranging over boys in the domain. Then $\exists x:Boy(x)[Sang(x)]$ means that for some individual x such that x is a boy, x sang. Likewise, $\forall x:[Tall(x) \& Boy(x)]\{Sang(x)\}$ is logically equivalent to $\forall x\{[Tall(x) \& Boy(x)] \rightarrow Sang(x)\}$. And $\exists x:[Boy(x) \& \forall y:Boy(y)[x = y]]\{Sang(x)\}$ means that for some boy x such that x is identical with every boy, x sang. Richard Montague (1974) offered a similar rewrite of Russell's hypothesis about the logical form of *The boy sang*. On this view, *The boy* corresponds to a propositional constituent, even though the boy referred to (if such there be) does not.

Still, the subject-predicate structure of *Mary trusts every doctor* diverges from the function-argument structure of $\forall y:Doctor(y)[Trusts(Mary, y)]$. Grammatically, *trusts* and *every doctor* form a phrase; though logically, *trusts* combines with *Mary* and a variable to form a complex predicate that in turn combines with a restricted quantifier. Given Montague's (1974) techniques, one can provide algorithms that systematically associate quantificational sentences of natural language (described in subject-predicate terms) with Fregean propositional structures. But it seemed that mismatches between grammatical and logical form remained, at least in cases of complex predicates with quantificational constituents.

TRANSFORMATIONAL GRAMMAR AND LF

One must not, however, assume a naive conception of grammar when thinking about its relation to logic. For example, the grammatical form of a sentence need not be determined by the order of its words. Using brackets to indicate phrasal structure, one can distinguish sentence (7) from the homophonous sentence (8).

(7) {Mary [saw [the [boy [with binoculars]]]]}

(8) {Mary [[saw [the boy]] [with binoculars]]}

The direct object of (7) is *the boy with binoculars*, while in (8), *saw the boy* is modified by an adverbial phrase. And a leading idea of modern linguistics is that many grammatical structures are transformations of others.

Expressions often appear to be displaced from positions canonically associated with certain grammatical relations. In (9), *who* seems to be associated with the direct-object position of *saw*.

(9) Mary wondered who John saw

And (9) can be glossed as *Mary wondered which person is such that John saw him*. This invites the hypothesis that the structure of (9) is as shown in (9-SS), reflecting a transformation of the simpler expression shown in (9-DS):

(9-SS) {Mary [wondered [who$_i$ {John [saw (_)$_i$]}]]]}

(9-DS) {Mary [wondered {John [saw who]}]}

where coindexing indicates a grammatical relation between the coindexed positions. The idea was that each sentence has a surface structure and a deep structure and that the former will differ from the latter when expressions like *who* are displaced as in (9). As an illustration of the kind of data relevant to such hypotheses about grammar, note that (10–12) are perfectly fine sentences, while (13) is not:

(10) The boy who sang was happy

(11) Was the boy who sang happy

(12) The boy who was happy sang

(13) Was the boy who happy sang

The ill-formedness of (13) is striking, since one can ask whether or not the boy who was happy sang. This suggests that (11-SS) is the result of a permissible transformation, but (13-SS) is not:

(11-SS) Was$_i$ {[the [boy [who sang]]] [(_)$_i$ happy]}

(13-DS) Was$_i$ {[the [boy [who [(_)$_i$ happy]]]] sang}

As transformational grammars were elaborated, many linguists posited another level of grammatical structure—LF, intimating logical form—obtained by displacing quantificational expressions. In particular, it was proposed that structures like (14-SS) were transformed, as in (14-LF):

(14-SS) {Pat [trusts [every doctor]]}

(14-LF) {[every doctor]$_i$ {Pat [trusts (_)$_i$]}}

Clearly, (15-LF) does not reflect the pronounced word order in English. But there is independent evidence for covert (inaudible) quantifier-raising in natural language. The suggestion was that each sentence has a PF (intimating phonological form) that determines pronunciation, and an LF that determines interpretation. On this view, the scope of a quantifier must be determined at LF, as in (14-LF). And one can say this, while also saying that the pronunciation of *Pat trusts every doctor* reflects the untransformed surface structure (14-SS). Many apparent examples of grammar-logic mismatches were thus rediagnosed as mismatches between different aspects of grammatical structure. This preserves the idea that surface appearances are often misleading with regard to propositional structure. But it also suggests that grammatical form and logical form converge, once one moves beyond traditional subject-predicate conceptions of structure with regard to both logic and grammar. And further simplification may be possible.

Given a conception of grammar according to which each sentence has a PF and an LF, perhaps involving different transformations, it is not obvious that one needs to posit other levels of grammatical analysis. Each expression of a natural language may just be a PF-LF pair that can be generated in accordance with certain constraints on how expressions can be combined and transformed. One can hypothesize that a sentence like (9) is formed in stages, including stages like those depicted in (9-DS) and (9-SS), without saying that any one stage is special in ways that deep structure and surface structure were said to be. On this view, (10–12) correspond to natural ways of associating a PF with an LF, but the string of words in (13) does not. From this perspective, urged by Noam Chomsky and others, talk of PFs and LFs need not be understood in terms of interlevel transformations (Chomsky 1995, Hornstein 1995). Rather, PFs and LFs can be viewed simply as generable linguistic structures that reflect pronunciation and meaning. In which case questions about grammatical form and linguistic meaning are largely questions about LFs.

Nonetheless, there is still an important conceptual distinction between the linguist's notion of LF and the logician's notion of logical form. The LF of a sentence may, in various ways, underdetermine the structure of the proposition a speaker expresses with that sentence (in a given context). The LF may, however, provide a scaffolding that can be elaborated in particular contexts, with little or no mismatch between basic sentential and propositional structure. These issues remain unsettled. But discoveries of rich grammatical structure reinvigorated the idea that natural languages are semantically compositional.

Prima facie, *Every tall sailor respects some doctor* and *Some short boy likes every politician* exhibit common modes of linguistic combination. So a natural hypothesis is that the meaning of each sentence is somehow fixed by these modes of combination, given the word meanings. Inspired by Alfred Tarski's development of Frege in 1956, Donald Davidson (1967) conjectured that there are recursively specifiable theories of truth for natural languages. And while there are many apparent objections, the conjecture has been fruitful. This raises the possibility that talk of logical forms should be construed in terms of the structure(s) that speakers impose on words to understand natural language systematically. From this tendentious perspective, the phenomenon of valid inference would be largely a reflection of semantic compositionality.

At this point, many issues become germane. Given any sentence of natural language, one can ask interesting questions about its grammatical structure and what it can be used to say. (Modal claims and propositional attitude reports have been studied intensively.) It is not obvious how one should characterize meanings or logical relations. (Are theories of meaning theories of truth? Which valid inferences, if any, cannot be captured in first-order terms?) The role of context is large and ill understood. But it seems clear that the traditional questions—what kinds of structures do propositions and sentences exhibit, and how do thinkers who also speak relate these struc-

tures—must be addressed in terms of increasingly sophisticated conceptions of logic and grammar.

See also Events in Semantic Theory; Modality and Quantification; Semantics; Syntax.

Bibliography

Beaney, Michael, ed. *The Frege Reader*. Oxford, U.K.: Blackwell, 1997.

Boolos, George. *Logic, Logic, and Logic*. Cambridge, MA: Harvard University Press, 1998.

Chomsky, Noam. *Aspects of the Theory of Syntax*. Cambridge, MA: MIT Press, 1965.

Chomsky, Noam. *Knowledge of Language: Its Nature, Origin, and Use*. New York: Praeger, 1986.

Chomsky, Noam. *The Minimalist Program*. Cambridge, MA: MIT Press, 1995.

Davidson, Donald. "Truth and Meaning." *Synthese* 17 (1967): 304–323.

Donnellan, Keith. "Reference and Definite Descriptions." *Philosophical Review* 75 (1966): 281–304.

Fodor, Jerry. "Propositional Attitudes." *The Monist* 61 (1975): 501–523.

Grice, H. Paul. "Logic and Conversation." In *Syntax and Semantics*. Vol. 3, edited by P. Cole and J. Morgan. New York: Academic Press, 1975.

Hornstein, Norbert. *Logical Form: From GB to Minimalism*. Oxford, U.K.: Blackwell, 1995.

Kneale, William, and Martha Kneale. *The Development of Logic* (1962). New York: Oxford University Press, 1984.

Kripke, Saul. *Naming and Necessity*. Cambridge, MA: Harvard University Press, 1980.

May, Robert. *Logical Form: Its Structure and Derivation*. Cambridge, MA: MIT Press, 1985.

Montague, Richard. *Formal Philosophy*. New Haven, CT: Yale University Press, 1974.

Preyer, Gerhard, and Georg Peters, eds. *Logical Form and Language*. New York: Oxford University Press, 2002.

Quine, W. V. *Methods of Logic*. New York: Henry Holt, 1950.

Russell, Bertrand. *Introduction to Mathematical Philosophy*. London: George Allen and Unwin, 1919.

Sainsbury, Mark. *Logical Forms*. Oxford, U.K.: Blackwell, 1991.

Strawson, Peter. "On Referring." *Mind* 59 (1950): 320–344.

Tarski, Alfred. *Logic, Semantics, Metamathematics*. 2nd ed. Translated by J. H. Woodger; edited by John Corcoran. Indianapolis, IN: Hackett, 1983.

Wittgenstein, Ludwig. *Philosophical Investigations*. Translated by G.E.M. Anscombe. New York: Macmillan, 1953.

Wittgenstein, Ludwig. *Tractatus Logico-Philosophicus*. Translated by D. Pears and B. McGuinness. London: Routledge and Kegan Paul, 1922.

Zalta, Edward. "Frege (Logic, Theorem, and Foundations for Arithmetic)." *The Stanford Encyclopedia of Philosophy*. Stanford, CA: Metaphysics Research Lab, Stanford University, 2003. Available at http://plato.stanford.edu/archives/fal12003/entries/frege-logic.

Paul M. Pietroski (2005)

LOGICAL KNOWLEDGE

"Logical knowledge" can be understood in two ways: as knowledge of the laws of logic and as knowledge derived by means of deductive reasoning. Most of the following is concerned with the first of these interpretations; the second will be treated briefly at the end. Furthermore, only deductive logic will be treated: As yet, there is no set of laws of inductive logic enjoying the kind of consensus acceptance accorded to deductive logic.

To begin with, we must specify what is a law of logic—not an entirely straightforward task. There are three, not all mutually exclusive, conceptions of logic laws. First, one could take them to be valid schemata (of statements), such as the familiar law of excluded middle, "p or not p". A second conception is that they are valid rules of inference, such as the familiar *modus ponens*— that is, from "$p{\rightarrow}q$" and p infer q. The third conception of logic law, due to Gottlob Frege and Bertrand Russell, takes them to be maximally general, true (not valid) second-order quantified statements (see Goldfarb, 1979). The following discussion is confined, by and large, to the second conception; but the philosophical problems canvassed arise with respect to the other conceptions as well.

In order to appreciate the problems involved in the analysis of knowledge of logical laws, note first that, however these laws are conceived, knowledge of them appears to be propositional. That is, to know a law of logic is to know that a rule of inference (or a schema) is valid (or a statement true). But, given the classical analysis of knowledge as justified true belief, it follows that knowledge of the validity of a rule of inference requires justification. There are two uncontroversially entrenched forms of justification: inductive and deductive justification. By the nature of inductive reasoning an inductive justification of validity shows, at best, that a rule of inference usually leads from true premises to a true conclusion (or that it is sufficiently highly likely to do so). This is too weak; a valid rule of inference, as noted above, necessarily leads from true premises to true conclusions. So it appears that the justification of validity must be deductive.

On the basis of this conclusion it can be shown that the justification of the validity of any rule of inference either is circular or involves an infinite regress. The argument has two parts. To begin with, there certainly are deductive justifications of rules of inference that raise no serious philosophical questions. Take the justification of the rule "existential specification" in Benson Mates's widely used *Elementary Logic*: "To justify this rule,... we observe that ... we may ... obtain the inference it permits [using certain basic rules] ... Assuming ... that the basic rules ... are [valid], ... the above description of how any [existential specification] inference can be made using only [those] rules ... shows that [existential specification] is [valid], too" (Mates, 1972, p. 123). The rule is justified by explicitly assuming the validity of other rules, so the justification here is only relative. If all logical laws are justified in this way, then, plausibly, the justification of any given rule will be either circular, by explicitly assuming its own validity, or will involve an infinite regress.

One might conclude from this that there must be some set of rules that are not justified on the basis of the assumed validity of other rules. Let us call these rules fundamental. Unfortunately, there is a simple argument that the justification of fundamental rules will involve a similar circularity or infinite regress.

What counts as a deductive justification of a proposition depends on what forms of inference are taken to be valid. For, if any rule of inference used in an argument is invalid, then the argument could not constitute a deductive justification of anything. Let us formulate this point as: A deductive argument presupposes the validity of the rules of inference it employs. Given this formulation, we can state an intuitive principle: If an argument for the validity of a rule of inference presupposes the validity of that very rule, then the argument is circular. To distinguish this notion of circularity from the one used above, let us call this pragmatic circularity, and the former, direct circularity.

Suppose a fundamental rule of ρ is justified by an argument π. Now either π employs nonfundamental rules, or it does not. Suppose π employs a nonfundamental rule σ. By the first part of the argument, σ is justified by assuming the validity of fundamental rules. Again, either the justification of σ assumes the validity of ρ or it does not. Now assume further that if an argument employs a rule whose justification assumes the validity of another, then it presupposes the validity of the second. Thus, in the first case, the justification of ρ is pragmatically circular. In the second case, the justification of ρ presupposes the validity of a set of other fundamental rules.

Now suppose that π does not employ nonfundamental rules. Then, either it employs ρ or it does not. In the first case the justification is pragmatically circular. In the second, again, the justification of ρ presupposes the validity of a set of other fundamental rules. Hence, the justification of any fundamental rule either is pragmatically circular or involves an infinite regress. (See Goodman 1983, pp. 63–64; see also Bickenbach 1978, Dummett 1973, and Haack 1976.)

One might object to the notion of circularity of argument used in the second part of the argument. Unlike the more familiar variant of circularity, the conclusion in this case is not actually assumed as a premise but is presupposed by the inferential transitions. Thus, it is unclear that this sort of circular argument suffers from the principal difficulty afflicting the more familiar sort of circular argument, namely, that every conclusion is justifiable by its means.

This, however, is not a very strong objection. One might reply, to begin with, that pragmatically circular arguments are just as objectionable as directly circular ones in that both assume that the conclusion is not in question, by assuming its truth in the one case and by acting as if it were true in the other. Moreover, while it is unclear that every rule of inference is justifiable by a pragmatically circular argument, it is clear that such an argument can justify both rules that we take to be valid and rules that we take to be fallacies of reasoning. For example, the following is an argument demonstrating the validity of the fallacy of affirming the consequent (see Haack, 1976):

1. Suppose "$p \rightarrow q$" is true.

2. Suppose q is true.

3. By the truth table for "$\rightarrow$," if p is true and "$p \rightarrow q$" is true, then q is true.

4. By (2) and (3), p is true and "$p \rightarrow q$" is true.

5. Hence, p is true.

Second, one might accept that deductive justification is not appropriate for fundamental logical laws but conclude that there is another kind of justification, neither deductive nor inductive, for these laws. There have been two proposals about a third kind of justification.

One proposal, due to Herbert Feigl (1963), claims that fundamental logical laws require pragmatic, instrumental justification. An immediate difficulty is, What counts as a pragmatic justification of a logical law? Surely, if there is anything that a rule of inference is supposed to do for us, it is to enable us to derive true conclusions from true premises. So, it looks as if to justify a logical law pragmatically is to show that it is suited for this purpose. And that seems to require showing that it is valid. Feigl is aware of this problem and argues that, in the context of a pragmatic justification, circularity is not a problem, since all that such a justification is required to do is provide a recommendation in favor of doing things in some particular way, not a proof that this way necessarily works. It is not clear, however, that this constitutes a compelling response to the philosophical problem of justifying

deduction, since, far from needing a letter of reference before employing deductive reasoning, its use is inescapable.

Another proposal for a third kind of justification is due to J. E. Bickenbach (1978), who argues that rules of inference are justified because they "fit with" specific instances of arguments that we accept as valid; for this reason he calls this kind of justification "instantial." The problem with this approach is that, in the case of rules of inference having some claim to being fundamental, such as *modus ponens*, it is plausible that we take the validity of the rule to be conceptually prior to the validity of any instance of it. For example, in the case of *modus ponens*, where there appear to be counterinstances to the rule, such as the sorites paradox, we take the problem to lie not in *modus ponens* but in vague concepts. Hence, whatever force "instantial" justification has, it seems incapable of conferring on fundamental rules of inference the kind of conceptual status we take them to have.

One might simply accept the conclusion of the argument, that fundamental logical laws cannot be justified, as indicating the philosophical status of these laws: They are simply constitutive rules of our practice of deductive justification. That is, there is no such thing as deductive justification that fails to conform to these rules, just as there is no such thing as the game of chess in which the queen is allowed to move in the same way as the knight. This third response leads to at least two philosophical questions: (1) How do we identify the fundamental laws of logic? (2) Is there such a thing as criticism or justification, as opposed to mere acceptance of a deductive practice?

A natural way to answer the first question is to take the fundamental rules to be determined by the meanings of the logical constants. This answer has been developed in some detail by Dag Prawitz (1977) and Michael Dummett (1991). Following Gerhard Gentzen (1969), they take the natural deduction introduction and elimination rules for a logical constant to be determined by the meaning of that constant. (More detail on the answer is provided in the final paragraph of this article.) Part of an answer to the second question has been provided by A. N. Prior (1967) and Nuel Belnap (1961), who showed that there exist sets of rules of inference that we can recognize as internally incoherent.

This third response has the consequence that our relation to the fundamental laws of logic is not one of knowledge classically construed and, hence, is different from our relation to other laws, such as the laws of physics, or of a country.

We turn now to the notion of knowledge derived from deductive reasoning. The question this notion raises, first studied by J. S. Mill (1950, bk. 2, chap. 3), is to explain how deductive reasoning could be simultaneously necessary and informative. It is undeniable that we can understand the premises and the conclusion of an argument without knowing that the former implies that latter; this is what makes it possible for us to gain information by means of deductive reasoning. This fact does not by itself conflict with the necessity of deductive implication, since there is no conflict between the existence of something and our lack of knowledge thereof. But, a problem can arise if the explanation of the necessity of deductive implication entails constraints on the notion of understanding. The following are two ways in which the problem of deduction arises.

First, consider Robert Stalnaker's (1987) analysis of the notions of proposition and of understanding. The proposition expressed by a statement is a set of the possible worlds, the set of those worlds in which the proposition is true. To understand a statement is to know the proposition it expresses; hence, to understand a statement is to know which possible worlds are those in which the proposition it expresses is true. These claims have two consequences: First, that all necessary statements, and hence all deductive valid statements, express the same proposition, namely, the set of all possible worlds; second, to understand any necessary statement is to know that the proposition it expresses is the set of all possible worlds. From these consequences it would seem to follow that in virtue of understanding any valid statement, one would know that it is necessarily true. It seems plausible that if one understands the premises and the conclusion of a valid argument, then one must also understand the conditional whose antecedent is the conjunction of the premises and whose consequent is the conclusion. But if the argument is valid, so is this conditional. Hence, if an argument is valid, then anyone who understood its premises and conclusion would know that this conditional expressed a necessary truth. It is now plausible to conclude that one can know whether an argument is valid merely on the basis of understanding its premises and conclusion by knowing whether the corresponding conditional expressed a necessary truth.

Next, consider Dummett's (1973, 1991) analysis of deductive implication. According to this analysis, deductive implication is based on the meanings of the logical constants. Thus, for example, the fact that p and q imply "p and q" is explained by the fact that the meaning of "and" is such that the truth condition of "p and q" is sat-

isfied just in case those of p and of q are. Similarly, the meaning of the existential quantifier is such that if the truth condition of "a is F" is satisfied, then so must the truth condition of "There is an F". Thus, corresponding to each logical constant, there is an account of the truth conditions of logically complex statements in which that constant occurs as the principal connective, in terms of the truth conditions of its substatements. This account explains the validity of rules of inference to those statements from their substatements and hence determines the set of fundamental rules, rules whose validity must be acknowledged by anyone who understands the meanings of the logical constants. But there are, as we have seen, cases in which we can understand the premises and the conclusion of an argument without knowing that the former implies the latter. So, how is deductive implication to be explained in those cases? This question is easy to answer if all the inferential transitions in these arguments are instances of fundamental rules determined by the senses of the constants. But the fact is otherwise; we acknowledge a number of rules of inference that are not reducible to fundamental rules. The problem is thus not an epistemological one; it arises because our conception of deductive implication includes rules whose necessity is not explainable on the basis of our understanding of the logical constants.

See also A Priori and A Posteriori; Dummett, Michael Anthony Eardley; Frege, Gottlob; Induction; Mill, John Stuart; Prior, Arthur Norman; Russell, Bertrand Arthur William.

Bibliography

Belnap, N. "Tonk, Plonk, and Plink." In *Philosophical Logic*, edited by P. F. Strawson. Oxford: Oxford University Press, 1967.

Bickenbach, J. E. "Justifying Deduction." *Dialogue* 17 (1979): 500–516.

Dummett, M. A. E. "The Justification of Deduction." In *Truth and Other Enigmas.* Cambridge, MA: Harvard University Press, 1978.

Dummett, M. A. E. *The Logical Basis of Metaphysics.* Cambridge, MA: Harvard University Press, 1991.

Feigl, H. "De Principiis Non Disputandum...?" In *Philosophical Analysis,* edited by M. Black. Englewood Cliffs, NJ: Prentice-Hall, 1963.

Gentzen, G. "Investigations into Logical Deduction." In *Collected Papers,* edited by M. E. Szabo. Amsterdam: North-Holland, 1969.

Goldfarb, W. D. "Logic in the Twenties." *Journal of Symbolic Logic* 79 (1979): 1237–1252.

Goodman, N. *Fact, Fiction, and Forecast.* Cambridge, MA: Harvard University Press, 1983.

Haack, S. "The Justification of Deduction." *Mind* 85 (1976): 112–119.

Mates, B. *Elementary Logic.* 2nd ed. New York: Oxford University Press, 1972.

Mill, J. S. *A System of Logic.* In *Philosophy of Scientific Method,* edited by E. Nagel. New York: Hafner, 1950.

Prawitz, D. "Meaning and Proof: On the Conflict between Classical and Intuitionistic Logic." *Theoria* 48 (1977): 2–4.

Prior, A. N. "The Runabout Inference Ticket." In *Philosophical Logic,* edited by P. F. Strawson. Oxford: Oxford University Press, 1967.

Stalnaker, R. *Inquiry.* Cambridge, MA, 1987.

Strawson, P. F., ed. *Philosophical Logic.* Oxford: Oxford University Press, 1967.

Sanford Shieh (1996)

LOGICAL PARADOXES

A paradox is an argument that derives or appears to derive an absurd conclusion by rigorous deduction from obviously true premises. Perhaps the most famous is Zeno's paradox of the runner, who, before she can reach her destination, first has to reach the point halfway there, and who, before reaching the halfway point, has to reach the quarter point, before which she must reach the point one-eighth of the way to the destination, and so on. The conclusion is that no runner ever reaches her goal, or even gets started.

To contemporary ears the argument does not sound so irresistible, since we can attribute its appeal either to an ambiguity in the use of "never" ("at no point in time" *versus* "at no point in the sequence") or to a dubious hidden premise that it is impossible to perform infinitely many tasks in a finite time, perhaps because there is a positive minimum to the length of time each task requires. To the ancients, however, the paradox was deeply disturbing. The most influential response was that of Aristotle, who concluded that it was not possible to partition the runner's path into infinitely many parts. Any segment of the runner's course can be divided in two, so that there is no finite bound on how many pieces the path contains, but the process of partitioning the path never concludes in a path with infinitely many parts. The number of segments that make up the path is said to be *potentially infinite.* The moral Aristotle drew from Zeno is that there is, in nature or in mathematics, no *actual infinite.* "Potentially infinite" is not like "potentially hot." When we say that a poker is potentially hot, we mean that, at some time and circumstance, it could be actually hot, whereas when we say that a line is potentially infinite, we mean that it can

always be made longer but not that there is any time at which it is actually infinite.

Aristotle's doctrine commanded wide adherence among philosophers and mathematicians, but toward the end of the nineteenth century it came widely to be seen as too restrictive. New mathematics embraced not only infinitely long lines, but also an analysis of a line as made up of infinitely many points, as well as infinite sets, infinite numbers, and infinite-dimensional geometry.

The new mathematics brought a spate of new paradoxes, which, in their formal structure, resemble the semantic paradoxes, the first of which appeared in the sixth century BCE when Epimenides, himself a Cretan, declared that Cretans always lie. Provided Epimenides' neighbors are sufficiently mendacious, we are driven to the conclusion that, if his statement is true, it is false, and if false, true. Deep problems, or perhaps a single deep problem in different manifestations, afflict the foundations of both mathematics and linguistics.

COUNTING BEYOND THE FINITE

Broadly speaking there were two reasons for repudiating of Aristotle's prohibition of the actual infinite. First as mathematics became vastly more general, finitistic techniques came to be seen as confining. The ancient Greeks had a marvelously sophisticated theory of polygons and conic sections, but a fully general theory of shapes requires such techniques as approximating an unruly curve by an infinite sequence of curves that are better behaved.

The second reason was the so-called arithmetization of geometry, brought about by the investigation of alternatives to Euclid's axiom that, given a line and a point not on the line, there is on their plane exactly one line through the point that never intersects the given line, no matter how far the two lines are extended. Once alternatives to Euclidean geometry emerged, one could no longer be fully confident that Euclid's axioms correctly described the world around us (and, indeed, these suspicions are confirmed by the general theory of relativity). The theory of real numbers remained at the center of modern mathematics, but since one could no longer identify the positive real numbers as the ratios of lengths of physical line segments, one was no longer sure what the theory referred to.

A strategy for answering this question can be found in William Hamilton's treatment of the complex numbers. Extending the real number system by introducing a fictitious solution to the equation "$x^2 + 1 = 0$" proves enormously useful mathematically, but one cannot help fretting that addressing algebraic problems with make-believe solutions is more an exercise in wishful thinking than legitimate science. Hamilton proposed to soothe this consternation by taking "complex number" to refer not to new and ontologically dubious entities but to familiar mathematical objects thought of in a new way. Namely, we treat a complex number as an ordered pair of ordinary real numbers, with appropriate operations.

Hamilton's construction presupposed the real numbers, but we can apply the same technique to secure the real numbers on a firmer basis. The starting point is easy enough. We can identify the positive rational numbers as ordered pairs of relatively prime positive integers, but the rationals have gaps—$\sqrt{2}$, for instance—and the modern theory of continuity and limits requires a number system without gaps. More precisely we want assurance that the *least upper bound principle*, according to which every nonempty set of real numbers that is bounded above has a least upper bound, is satisfied. Richard Dedekind solved this problem by identifying the real number with pairs $\langle A,B \rangle$ that partition the rationals into nonempty, nonoverlapping sets with every member of A less than every member of B.

Dedekind's construction succeeded in securing the real numbers on a foundation that did not presuppose the truth of Euclidean geometry, but it required the unapologetic acceptance of infinite sets. It permitted real analysis to be seen as built upon a foundation in the theory of sets, and indeed set theory is widely perceived as providing a uniform foundation for all of mathematics.

The elevation of set theory to its central role received its greatest impetus from the work of Georg Cantor (1895, 1897) who extended elementary-school arithmetic so that infinite as well as finite sets could be counted. Doing so required him to confront Galileo's paradox. Two sets have the same number of elements if there is a one-one correspondence by which each member of one set is paired off with one and only one member of the other. It follows that there are just as many perfect squares as there are nonnegative integers, since we can pair off n with n^2. But it seems obvious that there are more nonnegative integers than there are squares. A lot more, in fact, since as N grows the proportion of perfect squares among the first N integers becomes vanishingly small. The moral Galileo drew from this is that the notions of more and fewer cannot be applied to the infinite.

Overcoming Galileo's paradox was largely a matter of raw intellectual courage. Cantor had to resolve to follow the computations where they led, no matter how strongly

the results he obtained contravened the intuitions obtained from grade-school experience with finite numbers. Stipulating that the cardinal number of S is equal to the cardinal number of T (in symbols, $\#(S) = \#(T)$) if and only if S and T can be put in one-one correspondence and that $\#(S) \leq \#(T)$ if and only if S has the same cardinal number as a subset of T, we find that the familiar laws of order carry over directly, with one glaring exception. As Galileo's paradox illustrates, you can have $\#(S) \leq \#(T)$ even though T is a proper subset of S. Defining, for S and T disjoint, $\#(S) + \#(T) = \#(S \cup T)$, we find that the familiar laws of addition are largely upheld, but that particular computations yield wildly unexpected results. If we let $\aleph_0$ be the number of natural numbers, we find that $\aleph_0 + \aleph_0 = \aleph_0$ Similarly if we define $\#(S) \cdot \#(T)$ to be the cardinal number of the set of ordered pairs $\langle s,t \rangle$ with $s \in S$ and $t \in T$, we find $\aleph_0 \cdot \aleph_0 = \aleph_0$. In fact for any infinite numbers κ and λ, we have $\kappa + \lambda = \kappa \cdot \lambda = \max(\kappa,\lambda)$.

It is starting to look as if infinite arithmetic is remarkably easy: Whatever the question, the answer is "$\aleph_0$." This happy impression is dispelled when we turn to infinite exponentiation. Defining $\#(S)^{\#(T)}$ to be the number of functions from T to S, we find that $2^{\#(T)}$, which is the cardinal number of the *power set* of T (the set $\wp(T)$ of subsets of T), is strictly greater than $\#(T)$. That is, $2^{\#(T)} \geq (T)$ and $2^{\#(T)} \neq \#(T)$. That $\#(\wp(T)) \geq \#(T)$ is easy; use the function that takes an element x of T to $\{x\}$. To see that $\#(T) \neq \#(\wp(T))$, let F be a function from $\wp(T)$ to T. We want to see that F is not one-one, that is, that there exist distinct subsets U and V of T with $F(U) = F(V)$, which we do by assuming F were one-one and deriving a contradiction. Define a binary relation E on T by stipulating that xEy if and only if x is an element of some set W with $y = F(W)$. Then for any element x of T and any subset V of T, we have $xEF(V)$ if and only if Vx. (Why? If $xEF(V)$, then there is a W with $F(V) = F(W)$ and Wx; because F is one-one, we must have $V = W$, hence Vx. Conversely if Vx, then we can find our set W with $F(V) = F(W)$ and Wx by setting W equal to V.) In particular if we let R be the set of all elements of T that do not bear the relation E to themselves, we have, for any x, $xEF(R)$ if and only if Rx, which happens if and only if not xEx. Taking x equal to $F(R)$ reveals a contradiction.

In particular, the number of real numbers is $2^{\aleph_0}$ so that there are more real numbers than there are natural numbers. To see that the real numbers are equinumerous with the numbers in the interval from 0 to 1, use the function that takes x to $\frac{1}{2}(\frac{x}{|x|+1}+1)$. The proof that the real numbers between 0 and 1 are equinumerous with the sets of natural numbers uses the function that takes a real number to the set of places in its binary decimal expansion where 1s appear, although one has to tinker a bit to make allowance for numbers like ⅜, which has two different binary decimal expansions, 0.10100000000 … and 0.10011111111 … .

There are two fundamental ways we apply the counting numbers: To measure the size of a set, and to mark positions in a queue. For the first purpose we employ the English nouns, "one," "two," "three," and so on, whereas for the second we use the adjectives "first," "second," "third." … To generalize the first concept into the infinite Cantor developed his theory of infinite cardinal numbers, and for the second he introduced a theory of infinite so-called *ordinal numbers*. First some definitions. A binary relation L on a set S is an *ordering* if it meets the following three conditions, for any x, y, and z in S: If xLy and yLz, then xLz; not xLx; and either xLy, yLx, or $x = y$. The usual way of ordering the real numbers is an ordering, but it doesn't distinguish a first, second, and third real number. In order for the members of an ordered set to be counted by ordinal numbers, a further condition is required: A binary relation L on a set S is *well-founded* just in case every nonempty subset R of S has an L-least element, an element x of R such that there in no element y of R with yLx; equivalently there is no infinite sequence s_0, s_1, s_2, s_3, … with $s_{n+1}Ls_n$. A well-founded ordering is a *well-ordering*. Cantor's second great innovation was to extend the notion of ordinal number to infinite well-orderings.

If L well-orders a set S and M well-orders T, an *order isomorphism* from L to M is a one-one correspondence that preserves the order relation, so that, for any x and y in S, we have: xLy if and only if $f(x)Mf(y)$. Two well-orderings have the same ordinal number if and only if they are order isomorphic. If α is the ordinal number of an ordering L on S and β is the ordinal number of an ordering M on T, we say that $\alpha \leq \beta$ if and only if L is order-isomorphic to an initial segment of M. This provides a well-ordering of the ordinals, which supplies for each ordinal α a well-ordering of the ordinals less than α; its ordinal number is α. If L is a well-ordering of a set S there is a unique ordinal number associated with each element x of S that marks its position, namely the ordinal number of the well-ordering we get by restricting L to $\{y \in S: yLx$ and $y \neq x\}$.

Ernst Zermelo discovered a deep connection between cardinal and ordinal numbers: The cardinal numbers are well-ordered, so that the infinite cardinals can be placed in a sequence, $\aleph_0$, $\aleph_1$, $\aleph_2$, $\aleph_3$, …, and every cardinal number has the form $\aleph_\alpha$, for some ordinal α.

MR. RUSSELL'S BARBER

The program of securing the theory of sets on a unified axiomatic basis was trenchantly pursued by Gottlob Frege. A prerequisite for such a program is a system of logic that is both highly powerful and fully explicit, and before Frege there was no such logic. Frege's program has a philosophical motive. He wanted to show that the laws of arithmetic are analytic, so that, by providing suitable definitions, the laws of arithmetic can be reduced to pure logic. The key idea is that to say Traveler is a horse and to say that Traveler is an element of $\{x: x$ is a horse$\}$ are two ways of saying the same thing, just like "Lee rode Traveler" and "Traveler was ridden by Lee."

The specific form taken by Frege's reduction of arithmetic to logic depends on his doctrine of concepts and objects. Proper names (such as "Traveler"), definite descriptions (such as "the horse Lee rode into battle"), and sentences (such as "Traveler is a horse") are *saturated* expressions, and they denote *objects*. Under Frege's rather eccentric usage, sentences are a species of name; they denote either the True or the False, which are objects. Open sentences, like "x is a horse" and "Lee rode x into battle," are *unsaturated*, and they denote *concepts*. When we complete an open sentence by replacing the variable by a name, we get a sentence that denotes either the True or the False. Open sentences are a special case of *function sign*, an unsaturated expression whose completion yields a name. A concept is a special kind of function, one that cannot take any values other than the True and the False. There are, in addition, functions that demand more than one argument, represented by such multiply unsaturated phrases as "x rode y," and so-called *second-level* functions that take ordinary functions as arguments.

The fundamental principle of Frege's set theory, his Basic Law V (Basic Laws I through IV are unexceptionable principles of logic), associates a set, the object $\{x: Fx\}$, with each concept F in such a way that, for any concepts F and G, $\{x: Fx\}$ is equal to $\{x:Gx\}$ if and only if, for every object x, we have Fx if and only if Gx. The left-to-right direction of this axiom is the axiom of extensionality, which has proven harmless. Extensionality is what distinguishes sets from properties. The property of being a human being is different from the property of being a featherless biped, even though $\{x: x$ is a featherless biped$\}$ = $\{x: x$ is a human being$\}$. The right-to-left direction has proven deeply problematic. It asserts that the second-level function taking the concept F to $\{x: Fx\}$ is one-one. On the basis of this axiom we can define "$\in$": $z \in y$ if and only if, for some F, $y = \{x: Fx\}$ and Fz, and we can derive the so-called *comprehension principle* that, for any F and

$z, z \in \{x: Fx\}$ if and only if Fz, just as in the proof of Cantor's theorem, and just as before, we can derive a contradiction by asking whether $\{x: x \notin x\}$ is an element of itself.

Bertrand Russell discovered the paradox and communicated it to Frege just as the second volume of Frege's monumental *Grundegesetze der Arithmetic* was going to press. Frege regarded it as devastating. "With the loss of my Basic Law V," he wrote in reply to Russell (1902, pp. 127–128), "not only the foundations of my arithmetic, but also the sole possible foundations of arithmetic, seem to vanish." Later scholarship, led by George Boolos, has seen the devastation as not quite so complete as Frege took it. Roughly speaking there are two principal components to the *Grundgesetze*: First the employment of Basic Law V (together with suitable definitions) to derive what Frege calls Hume's Principle, that, for any concepts F and G, the numbers associated with F and G are equal if and only if there is a one-one correspondence between the objects that fall under F and those that fall under G; and second the derivation from Hume's Principle of the fundamental laws of arithmetic. The latter component is a substantial mathematical accomplishment that is unharmed by Russell's paradox.

A couple of other set-theoretic paradoxes emerged at about the same time, one, due to Cantor, involving cardinal numbers, and the other, due to Cesare Burali-Forti, about ordinal numbers.

For Cantor's paradox, let V be the set of all sets. Since every set of sets is a set, $\wp(V)$ is a subset of V, and so $\#(\wp(V)) \leq \#(V)$. Yet Cantor's theorem tells us that $\#(\wp(V)) > \#(V)$. Cantor concluded from the contradiction that there is no set of all sets, invoking a distinction reminiscent of Aristotle's distinction of potentially and actually infinite. The sets measured by the $\aleph_\alpha$s are transfinite, whereas the set of all sets, if there were such a thing, would be absolutely infinite. There is no such thing as V because the sets do not form a completed whole. There is no absolute infinity in mathematics; absolute infinity is the province of God alone.

For Burali-Forti's paradox, consider that the ordinals are well-ordered, and so they have an ordinal number. Call it α. α also the ordinal of the collection of ordinals less than α and so there is an order-isomorphism f from the collection of all the ordinals to the collection of ordinals less than α. $f(\alpha) < \alpha$, and so, since the ordering on the ordinals is well-founded, there has to be a least ordinal β with $f(\beta) \neq \beta$. We have $f(\beta) =$ the least ordinal greater than all the members of $\{f(\gamma): \gamma < \beta\}$ = the least ordinal greater than all the members of $\{\gamma: \gamma < \beta\}$; = β.

Mirimanoff's paradox emerged a little later. Let us say that a set is *hereditarily well-founded* if it belongs to a collection C with the following properties: Every element of an element of C is an element of C; and the elements of C are well-founded (that is, the restriction to an element of C of the elementhood relation is well-founded). It is easy to verify that the collection of all hereditarily well-founded sets is hereditarily well-founded. But this gives us the absurd prospect of a well-founded set that is an element of itself.

Russell illustrated the logical structure of his paradox with an amusing example. Imagine a village whose barber (an adult male villager) shaves all and only the adult male villagers who do not shave themselves. A contradiction arises when we inquire whether the barber shaves himself, by reasoning exactly analogous to the thinking that gets Russell's paradox. Unlike the set-theoretic paradox, however, the puzzle about the barber has an easy solution. There can be no such barber, however plausible the story that said there was one sounded on first hearing. One would like to obtain a similar resolution to Russell's paradox, denying that there is such a set as $\{x: x \notin x\}$ (and, presumably, also that there are such sets as V, the set of all ordinals, and the set of all hereditarily well-founded sets) by restricting the range of open sentences that can be substituted for "F" in the comprehension principle. The trick is to do this in a principled, credible way that avoids contradictions while maintaining the set existence principles required to do mathematics. Before asking how this might be done, let us examine the semantic analogues of the set-theoretic paradoxes.

SEMANTIC PARADOXES

Semantics, as Alfred Tarski characterized it, is the branch of linguistics that studies the connections between expressions of a language and the things or states of affairs those expressions refer to. Its principal theoretical concepts are *truth*, *reference*, and *satisfaction*. A name, like "Traveler" or "Robert E. Lee's horse," refers to (or *names* or *denotes*) an object, in this case a stallion. An open sentence, like "x is a horse," represents a concept. The sentence got by substituting a name for the variable in an open sentence is true just in case the object referred to by the name falls under the concept represented by the open sentence. Because Traveler falls under the concept *horse*, the sentence "Traveler is a horse" is true. The reason for using the variable "*x*" to mark the place in the open sentence where a name needs to be supplied is to accommodate open sentences like "x rode y into battle," which represent concepts with more than one argument. The account of satisfaction needs to be complicated a bit to allow for such open sentences, but that need not concern us here.

Another, more substantial, complication is that one should not really speak of a sentence being true, but rather of a sentence being true in a language in a context, or perhaps of a sentence expressing, in a language in a context, a proposition that is true. "I am now riding Traveler" is true when Lee says it while riding his horse, but it is false in most other contexts. This complication too can be set aside here.

Here our concern is with the semantic paradoxes. Epimenides is credited with the earliest formulation, although it is doubtful that he recognized that his statement was paradoxical. Someone acutely aware of the paradox was Eubulides of Miletas (a contemporary of Aristotle), who asked, "A man says that he is lying; is what he says true or false?" Eubulides formulated other notorious paradoxes, among them the *Bald Man* (The observation that plucking a single hair from a man who is not bald will not make him bald leads, by multiple application, to the conclusion that not even a man with no hair at all is bald) and the *Hooded Man* (You know who your father is, and you do not know who the hooded man is, even though, unknown to you, the hooded man is your father; this violates the law of identity, which allows the exchange of names that denote the same thing).

To avoid fretting about indexicals and also to avoid consternation that only purposefully false statements count as "lies," let us consider what we may call the Liar Sentence, the sentence "The Liar Sentence is not true." We would naively expect the notion of truth to be governed by the (T)-schema, "'_____' is true if and only if _____;" "Traveler is a horse," for example, is true if and only if Traveler is a horse. However filling the blank with "The Liar Sentence is not true," and noting that "The Liar Sentence is not true" = the Liar Sentence, results in contradiction.

The Liar paradox does not have a direct set-theoretic analogue, but there are paradoxes involving satisfaction and reference that have such analogues. The analogue to Russell's paradox is due to Kurt Grelling. We would intuitively expect satisfaction to be governed by a principle exactly parallel to the comprehension principle in set theory, telling us, for example, that, for any y, y satisfies "x is a horse" if and only if y is a horse. The phrase "x is a horse" is not a horse, and so "x is a horse" does not satisfy itself, whereas "x is an open sentence" does satisfy itself.

For any y, y satisfies "x is an open sentence that does not satisfy itself" if and only if y is an open sentence that does not satisfy itself. Taking y to be the open sentence "x is an open sentence that does not satisfy itself" yields a contradiction.

Cantor's paradox is obtained by generalizing Cantor's argument that there are more real numbers between 0 and 1 than there are positive integers, which proceeds by assuming for *reductio ad absurdum* that there were a list that enumerated all the real numbers between 0 and 1, then asking where on the list there appears the number r given by stipulating that the nth digit in the binary decimal expansion of r is equal to one if and only if zero is the nth digit in the binary decimal expansion of the nth number on the list. *Richard's paradox* invites us to consider, in particular, the list gotten by enumerating the English expressions that denote real numbers between 0 and 1 in alphabetical order. Cantor's argument gives us a real number between 0 and 1 that is not named by any expression of English. But is Cantor's number not named by the expression "the number r, between 0 and 1, such that the nth binary digit of r is equal to one if and only if zero is the nth binary digit of the number named by the alphabetically nth English phrase that names a real number between 0 and 1"?

The number of English expressions that name ordinal numbers is $\aleph_0$ since the expressions are finite strings of words from a finite vocabulary. There are more than $\aleph_0$ ordinals, so there are ordinals not named by an expression of English, and hence a least ordinal number not named by an expression of English. But "the least ordinal number not named by an expression of English" names it. This is *König's paradox*. *Berry's paradox* is the finitary version, got by noting that "the least natural number that cannot be named by an English expression of fewer than thirty syllables" is an English expression that names a natural number in twenty-eight syllables.

PRINCIPIA MATHEMATICA

Alfred North Whitehead and Bertrand Russell undertook to solve simultaneously both the set-theoretic paradoxes and the semantic paradoxes. The aim of their highly ambitious *Principia Mathematica* was to secure all of mathematics on a basis in pure logic. In their system the role hitherto played by sets was taken over by *propositional functions*, which are a kind of amalgam of Frege's concepts and Frege's propositions. *Propositions* are, for Frege, the objects of belief and judgment, the sort of thing referred to by "that" clauses in English. According to Russell if you prefix the word "that" to an open sentence, you get an expression that names a propositional function, a function taking objects to propositions. If you supply an object as argument, the output is the proposition you would express if you substituted a name of that object into the open sentence. With Traveler as argument, the propositional function designated by "that Lee rode x into battle" yields the proposition that Lee rode Traveler into battle.

This account was considered and rejected by Frege on the basis that it would yield the result that the proposition that Traveler is white is identical to the proposition that the horse Lee rode into battle is white, in spite of the fact that someone who did not realize that Traveler is the horse Lee rode into battle might believe one but not the other. For Frege, the argument of the propositional function is not the horse Traveler but the sense (*Sinn*) of the name "Traveler." Russell thought he could thwart Frege's objection by a logical analysis according to which "the horse Lee rode into battle" is, despite appearances, not a denoting phrase. The relative merits of Frege's and Russell's conceptions of propositional functions have been much debated.

Whitehead and Russell proposed to avert the paradoxes by adopting the *vicious circle principle* (which they attribute to Henri Poincaré), according to which you cannot have a proposition that refers to itself since before you could formulate such a proposition you would have to already possess the proposition you were trying to formulate. You cannot have a propositional function that has itself or any of its values as argument, nor can you have a propositional function in whose formulation you are required to talk about the propositional function or any of its arguments. To formulate an analogue to Russell's paradox in terms of propositional functions, you would have to suppose that the phrase "that x is a propositional function not true of itself" denoted a propositional function, and such a propositional function would violate the vicious circle principle. Whitehead and Russell adopted a (maddeningly elaborate) formalism in which such phrases were grammatically ill-formed.

The vicious circle principle evades the paradoxes (as far an anyone knows), but it also rules out ordinary mathematics. If r is the least upper bound of a given collection of real numbers then it is the least element of a totality that includes r itself.

In *Principia Mathematica*, the propositional functions are arrayed in layers, where the level of a given function is determined by the levels of its possible arguments and also by the levels of the propositional functions utilized in defining the given function. A propositional func-

tion is said to be *predicative* if it is at the lowest level it could possibly be at, given what its arguments are. Either it is defined without referring to anything beyond its potential arguments (say, by giving a list), or the things referred to are sufficiently low-level that they do not affect the level of the function. Whitehead and Russell obtained the least upper bound principle by adopting the *axiom of reducibility*, according to which for every propositional function there is a predicative propositional function true of the same things. Given a collection C of real numbers, take a predicative function Fx that is coextensive with "x is an upper bound of C," we get the least upper bound of C as the least number that satisfies Fx.

The justification of the axiom of reducibility is purely pragmatic—it is needed for mathematics—and its adoption seriously undermines Whitehead and Russell's claim to have reduced mathematics to logic.

Once we have the axiom of reducibility on board, there in no longer any useful purpose in having the position in the hierarchy of a propositional function depend on the positions of the things we refer to in defining the function as well as on the positions of the potential arguments. We can obtain both the same mathematical results and the same degree of insulation from paradox simply by taking the type of a propositional function to be immediately above the types of its arguments, no matter how the propositional function is defined. Frank Ramsey first recognized this, effecting an enormous simplification in the system. W. V. Quine took the observation a step further, noticing that there was no longer any benefit in supposing coextensive propositional functions to be distinct, so that we could take the things the "Ramsey-fied" theory was about to be sets and relations, rather than propositional functions of one or more variables.

The system can be further streamlined by replacing talk about binary relations between individuals with talk about sets of ordered pairs of individuals, replacing talk about ternary relations with talk about sets of ordered triples, and so on. There is no need to take ordered triples as primitive, since we can define $\langle a,b,c \rangle$ as the ordered pair $\langle a,\langle b,c \rangle \rangle$. In fact—this is an ingenious observation of Norbert Weiner—there is no need to take ordered pairs as primitive, since we can define $\langle a,b \rangle$ as $\{\{\{a\},\emptyset\},\{\{b\}\}\}$. This stipulation enables us to derive the principle that, for any a, b, c, and d, $\langle a,b \rangle = \langle c,d \rangle$ if and only if $a=c$ and $b=d$, which is the only thing one ever needs to know about ordered pairs. The resulting system is arrayed in a simple hierarchy. There are individuals, sets of individuals, set of sets of individuals, and so on. It is this hierarchical structure, rather than the vicious circle principle, that precludes paradox.

ZERMELO-FRAENKEL SET THEORY

The most prominent of *Principia Mathematica*'s rivals originates, not in a philosophical analysis of methods of reasoning that lead to the paradoxes, but in a mathematical examination of ways of reasoning that never cause problems. Zermelo's 1904 proof that every set can be well-ordered, with its corollary that the cardinal numbers are well-ordered, met considerable resistance. It was felt that it skirted too close the edge of the newly discovered paradoxes. Poincaré, for example, complained about vicious circularity. Zermelo replied that the methods of forming sets that figure in the paradoxes are far removed from the methods that are gainfully employed by working mathematicians, and that the principles that figure in the deduction of the well-ordering theorem fall into the latter category. To make this reply more precise Zermelo wrote down axioms of set theory sufficient to derive the well-ordering theorem, in the hope that all could see that the proof required only well-established principles of workaday mathematics that had never been implicated in paradox.

Zermelo's axioms did not come equipped with a diagnosis of the paradoxes, but a couple of widely accepted further principles do have diagnostic import. Although Zermelo's axioms are immensely powerful, they omit some common and apparently harmless mathematical practices, like forming infinite sequences of the form $\langle s_0, s_1, s_2, s_3 \ldots \rangle$. Abraham Fraenkel proposed to rectify this situation by adopting the *replacement axiom schema*, which says that for any open sentence that defines a function, if the inputs to the function form a set, so do the outputs. In Frege's logic, in which there was one style of variables ranging over sets and other objects and another style ranging over functions, the replacement axiom would be expressed by saying the restriction of a function to a set domain invariably has a set as its range. Fraenkel is only able to produce a schema that applies to definable functions because his logical resources are restricted to the first-order predicate calculus, which only has variables ranging over individuals. The new principle is formulated as a formula that contains a schematic letter, so understood that the formulas of the language of set theory obtained by substituting a formula for the schematic letter are regarded as axiomatic. This retreat to first-order logic results from relinquishing the program of trying to produce a logic so powerful that set theory can be reduced to it. The existence of sets cannot be established by logic alone, and the first-order formulation makes set theory's existence assumptions fully explicit.

The replacement axioms assure us that an open sentence has a set as its extension unless the things that satisfy it are more numerous than the members of any set. The doctrine of *limitation of size* has it that things form a set unless there are too many of them, and that the paradoxes arise from attempts to form sets that are too large to hang together. The Burali-Forti paradox, for example, tells us that the ordinals are too numerous to form a set.

Mirimanoff's paradox distinguishes the hereditarily well-founded sets—what Mirimanoff calls the *ordinary sets*—from the others. It turns out that extraordinary sets (if there are any) are never needed for mathematics, and if we restrict our attention to ordinary sets, adopting an axiom that the elementhood relation is well-founded, an attractive picture of the universe of set appears. Sets are built up in stages. At the bottom level the so-called *urelements* are whatever non-sets you may want to count or measure. (For pure, as opposed to applied, mathematics, no urelements are needed.) At the second level are sets of urelements. At the third level are sets whose elements are urelements and sets of urelements. And so on. At each stage the available building blocks are the urelements and the sets built at earlier stages, and every set is constructed at some, possibly transfinite, stage. Because new sets and new ordinals are added at every stage, there is no stage at which one constructs a set that contains all the ordinals or a set that contains all the sets that do not contain themselves (which would be a set that contained all sets). The purported sets that threaten paradox never appear.

The two strategies for blocking the paradoxes—limitation of size and construction in stages—are by no means in conflict. Indeed one could argue (although it is certainly not obvious) that the stage construction ensures that no stage ever produces a set large enough to violate the limitation of size. On the other hand Peter Aczel (1988) has devised an alternative to standard set theory, provably consistent if ordinary set theory is, that upholds limitation of size but allows non-well-founded sets in great profusion.

The Whitehead-Russell system and the Zermelo-Fraenkel system are by no means the only extant responses to the set-theoretic paradoxes—Quine, for example, devised a method for restricting the comprehension principle so as to allow a universal set, without apparent contradiction—but they are the most prominent. Their rivalry is not so implacable as first appears. Indeed Kurt Gödel (1944/1983) has noted that we can think of the Zermelo-Fraenkel system as obtained from

Principia Mathematica, as simplified by Ramsey, Quine, and Weiner, by generalizing in two directions. First we allow the types to be cumulative, so that the possible elements at a type level are not just the sets of the immediately preceding type but sets of all the preceding types. Second we allow the type levels to extend into the transfinite.

One question the axiomatizations leave unanswered is how comprehensive the theory of sets is intended to be. Not all collections are sets. A stamp collection for example can survive the acquisition of a new stamp, whereas when you add a stamp to a set of stamps, you get a different set. But perhaps set theory accounts for all extensional collections. If not then the set theorist has two tasks: To say what extensional collections there are, and to say which of the extensional collections are sets. John von Neumann gave such an account. His theory has two kinds of *classes*, namely, sets and *proper classes*. Classes are made up of sets and urelements, and a class is a set if and only if it is not equinumerous with the class of all ordinals. The proper classes form the top element of the cumulative hierarchy.

Zermelo has a different perspective, reminiscent of Aristotle's doctrine that a line or the integers never form a completed whole. The universe of set theory does not form a completed whole, according to Zermelo. Candidates for the "universe" of set theory are only provisional, and one can always advance to a higher perspective from which a candidate universe is seen as a set within a larger universe.

SEMANTIC PARADOXES

In looking at possible solutions to the set-theoretic paradoxes, the semantic paradoxes have been set aside. One cannot happily say about the Liar Sentence the same thing one wants to say about the alleged set of all ordinals, namely, that there is no such sentence. One might want to say that what goes wrong with the Liar Sentence is that it does not express a proposition, but any satisfaction this gives us is short-lived. A propositionalist theory of truth has to account for two things, the truth conditions for propositions and the connection between a sentence and the proposition it expresses, and the latter relation remains troublesome. Consideration of the Propositional Liar Sentence ("The Propositional Liar Sentence does not express a true proposition") seems to force us the self-defeating conclusion that the Propositional Liar Sentence does not express a proposition, and hence that it does not express a true proposition.

The standard response to the semantic paradoxes was given by Alfred Tarski, who insists that, in developing a semantic theory, the language one employs (the *metalanguage*) must be richer in expressive power than the language one is talking about (the *object language*), so that one can never formulate the theory of truth, reference, and satisfaction for a language within the language itself.

A number of ingenious extensions of Tarski's basic idea have been developed. Notable among them is Saul Kripke's (1975) demonstration that, thinking of such troubled sentences as the Liar as neither true nor false, one can add the predicate "true" to a language and partition the sentences of the resulting language in such a way that a sentence S is counted as true, false, or undecided according as the statement that S is true is accounted true, false, or undecided. The enriched language cannot, however, express the equivalence of S with the statement that S is true, nor can it express the proof that the Kripke construction yields the equivalence. These things can only be said within a richer metalanguage. Indeed, in the best known version (there are a number of variants), the addition of the truth predicate results in a drastic restriction in the range of truth-preserving inferences, so that the object language has an enervated logic in which nothing resembling ordinary mathematical or philosophical reasoning can be carried on (as Solomon Feferman's investigations have made abundantly clear). Hartry Field (2003) has proposed enriching the Kripke construction by adding a new, nonclassical conditional, which behaves enough like the everyday "if..., then" to accommodate a substantial range of familiar inferences. With Field's novel interpretation of "if and only if," the (T)-sentences are all counted as true.

Field's construction is too complicated to describe here, but its key idea comes from revision theory, which employs full classical logic but regards the "if and only if" that appears in the (T)-sentences as a special connective that represents definitional equivalence. Developed by Anil Gupta and Nuel Belnap (1993) on a foundation laid down independently by Gupta and Hans Herzberger, revision theory treats the (T)-sentences as defining "true," and it ascribes to the "if and only if" of definition a special logic that allows for circular definitions. If "F" is defined by "$F(x)$ if and only if _____," where the defined predicate "F" appears in the blank, and if C is proposed as a possible candidate for the extension of "F," then the map that takes C to {x: x satisfies _____ when C is taken as the extension of "F"} gives us, by iteration, better and better candidates for the extension of

"F." Throughout the revision process, the Liar sentences keeps flip-flopping between true and false, but sentences that have an intuitively correct truth value eventually settle down to their intuitively expected values, even in the presence of extensive self-reference and cross-reference. Tarski's restriction is still observed, inasmuch as the entire construction is developed within a richer metalanguage.

Tarski's doctrine works happily for formal languages, but it leaves us unable to understand how the notion of truth and reference apply to natural languages, since "true in English" is a phrase of English and not some unnatural metalanguage.

Some progress has been made by adapting the *Principia Mathematica* idea of subscripted "true"s. There is a predicate "$true_0$" that applies to sentences that contain no semantic notions; a predicate "$true_1$" that applies to sentences with no semantic notions other than "$true_0$;" "$true_2$" that applies to sentences with no semantic notion other than "$true_0$" and "$true_1$" and so on. Tyler Burge (1979) and Charles Parsons (1974) have proposed applying this notion to English by supposing that the English word "true" is ambiguous, and that disambiguating subscripts are tacitly ascribed by contexts in such a way that a truth attribution is supplied a subscript one greater than the maximum of those that appear in the sentences one is talking about. Eubulides's derivation of a contradiction is seen as committing a fallacy of equivocation, inasmuch as the tacit subscript changes during the course of his argument.

The *Principia*-inspired approach still has limitations. For one thing there does not appear to be any uniform, non-arbitrary way of coping with situations in which A talks about all the things B says at the same time B talks about all things A says. For another the description of the subscripting machinery lies outside the object language, so that we are provided with no good way of dealing with "This sentence is not $true_\alpha$, for any α."

A different approach tries to consolidate the Liar paradox and the Bald Man by developing the idea that, if Harry is a borderline case of "bald," "Harry is bald" should be neither true nor false. "'Harry is bald' is either true or false" follows logically (defining falsity as truth of the negation) from the conditionals we get by substituting "Harry is bald" and "Harry is not bald" into the right-to-left direction of the (T)-schema. Allowing that "Harry is bald" is neither true nor false requires restricting the right-to-left direction of (T) so that it does not apply to such things as border applications of vague terms, which are semantically defective. This restriction yields an attractive response to the Bald Man, but the answer to the Liar is problematic. The left-to-right direction of (T) ("If 'The Liar Sentence is not true' is true then the Liar Sentence is not true") suffices to yield the conclusion that the Liar Sentence is untrue, and hence, because the right-to-left (T)-schema fails for it, that the statement that Liar Sentence is untrue is semantically defective. This result is unwelcome, because it tells us that a conclusion can be derived by rigorous, careful deduction from secure premises and still be semantically defective.

The argument of the previous paragraph is adapted from Richard Montague's (1960) argument that a Liar-type paradox can be obtained for necessity in place of truth. Also, as Montague and David Kaplan (1960) showed, for knowledge. It seems safe to say that the semantic paradoxes are currently less well-managed than the set-theoretic paradoxes.

See also Aristotle; Cantor, Georg; Frege, Gottlob; Galileo Galilei; Gödel, Kurt; Hamilton, William; Kaplan, David; Kripke, Saul; Liar Paradox, The; Montague, Richard; Neumann, John Von; Poincaré, Jules Henri; Quine, Willard van Orman; Ramsey, Frank Plumpton; Relativity Theory; Russell, Bertrand Arthur William; Set Theory; Tarski, Alfred; Whitehead, Alfred North; Zeno of Elea.

Bibliography

Aczel, Peter. *Non-Well-Founded Sets.* Stanford, CA: CSLI, 1988.

Aristotle. *Physics.* 2 vols. Translated by Philip H. Wicksteed and Francis M. Cornford. Cambridge, MA: Harvard University Press, 1929 and 1934.

Boolos, George S. *Logic, Logic, and Logic.* Cambridge, MA, and London: Harvard University Press, 1998.

Burali-Forti, Cesare. "Una Questione sui Numeri Transfiniti." *Rendiconti del Circolo Matematico di Palermo* 11 (1897): 154–164. English translation by Jean van Heijenoort in van Heijenoort, 104–111.

Burge, Tyler. "Semantical Paradox." *Journal of Philosophy* 76 (1979): 169–198. Reprinted in Martin, 83–117.

Cantor, Geog. "Beiträge zur Begründung der transfiniten Mengenlehre." *Mathematische Annalen* 46 (1895): 481–512 and 49 (1897): 312–356. English translation by Philip E. B. Jourdain. New York: Dover, 1955.

Dedekind, Richard. *Stetigkeit und irrationale Zahlen.* Braunschweig: F. Veiwig, 1872. English translation by Wooster W. Beeman in Dedekind *Essays on the Theory of Numbers,* 1–27. New York: Dover, 1963.

Feferman, Solomon. "Toward Useful Type-Free Theories, I." *Journal of Symbolic Logic* 49 (1984): 75–111. Reprinted in Martin, 237–287.

Field, Hartry. "A Revenge-Immune Solution to the Liar Paradox." *Journal of Philosophical Logic* 32 (2003): 139–177.

Fraenkel, Abraham. "Über die Zermelosche Begründung der Mengenlehre." *Jahresbericht der Deutchen Mathematiker-Vereinigung* 3011 (1921): 97–98.

Fraenkel, Abraham. "Zu den Grundlagen der Cantor-Zermeloschen Mengenlehre." *Mathematische Annalen* 86 (1922): 230–237.

Frege, Gottlob. *Begriffsschrift*. Halle: Nebert, 1879. Translated by Stefan Bauer-Mengelberg in van Heijenoort, 1–82.

Frege, Gottlob. "Funktion und Begriff." 1881. English translation by Peter Geach and Max Black in *Translations*, 21–41.

Frege, Gottlob. "Über Sinn und Bedeutung." *Zeitschrift für Philosophie und philosophische Kritik* 50 (1892): 25–50. English Translation by Peter Geach and Max Black in *Translations*, 56–78.

Frege, Gottlob. *Grundgesetze der Arithmetik*, 2 vols. Jena: Pohle, 1893 and 1903. Partial translation by Montgomery Furth. Berkeley and Los Angeles: University of California Press, 1964.

Frege, Gottlob. "Letter to Russell." 1902. English translation by Beverly Woodward in van Heijenoort, 126–128.

Frege, Gottlob. *Translations from the Philosophical Writings*. 2nd. ed. Oxford: Basil Blackwell.

Galileo Galilei. *Discorsi e dimostrazioni matematiche*. Translated by Henry Crew and Alfonso de Salvio. New York: Dover, 1956.

Gödel, Kurt. "Russell's Mathematical Logic." In *The Philosophy of Bertrand Russell*, edited by Paul A. Schilpp, 125–153. Evanston and Chicago: Northwestern University Press, 1944. Reprinted in Paul Benacerraf and Hilary Putnam, eds., *Philosophy of Mathematics* 2nd ed., 447–469. Cambridge, U.K.: Cambridge University Press, 1983.

Grelling, Kurt, and Leonard Nelson. "Bemerkungen zu den Paradoxien von Russell und Burali-Forti." *Abhandlungen der Fries'schen Schule neue Folge* 2 (1908): 301–334.

Gupta, Anil. "Truth and Paradox." *Journal of Philosophical Logic* 11 (1982): 1-60. Reprinted in Martin, 175–235.

Gupta, Anil, and Nuel Belnap. *The Revision Theory of Truth*. Cambridge, MA: MIT Press, 1993.

Hallett, Michael. *Cantorian Set Theory and Limitation of Size*. Oxford: Clarendon, 1984.

Herzberger, Hans G. "Notes on Naïve Semantics." *Journal of Philosophical Logic* 11 (1992): 61-102. Reprinted in Martin, 133–174.

König, Julius. "Über die Grundlagen der Mengenlehre und das Kontinuumproblem." *Mathematische Annalen* 61 (1905): 156–160. Translated by Stefan Bauer-Mengelberg in van Heijenoort, 145-149.

Keefe, Rosanna, and Peter Smith, eds. *Vagueness: A Reader*. Cambridge, MA, and London: MIT Press, 1996.

Kripke, Saul A. "Outline of a Theory of Truth." *Journal of Philosophy* 72 (1975): 690–716. Reprinted in Martin, 53–81.

McGee, Vann. *Truth, Vagueness, and Paradox*. Indianapolis: Hackett, 1991.

Martin, Robert L., ed. *Recent Essays on Truth and the Liar Paradox*. Oxford and New York: Oxford University Press.

Mirimanoff, Dimitry. "Les antinomies de Russell et de Burali-Forti et le problème fondamental de la théorie des ensembles." *L'enseignement Mathématique* 19 (1917): 37–52.

Montague, Richard. *Formal Philosophy*. New Haven, CT: Yale, 1974.

Montague, Richard. "Syntactic Treatments of Modality, with Corollaries on Reflection Principles and Finite Axiomatizability." *Acta Philosophical Fennica* 16 (1963): 153–167. Reprinted in Montague, *Formal Philosophy*, 286–302.

Montague, Richard, and David Kaplan. "A Paradox Regained." *Notre Dame Journal of Formal Logic* 1 (1960): 79–90. Reprinted in Montague, *Formal Philosophy*, 270–285.

Parsons, Charles. "The Liar Paradox." *Journal of Philosophical Logic* 3 (1974): 381–412. Reprinted in Martin, 9–45.

Quine, Willard van Orman. "New Foundations for Mathematical logic." *American Mathematical Monthly* 44 (1937): 70–80. Reprinted in Quine, *From a Logical Point of View*. Cambridge, MA: 1953, 80–101.

Quine, Willard van Orman. *The Logic of Sequences: Harvard Dissertations in Philosophy*. New York: Garland, 1990.

Ramsey, Frank Plumpton. "The Foundations of Mathematics." *Proceedings of the London Mathematical Society* 25 (1925): 338–384. Reprinted in Ramsey, *The Foundations of Mathematics and Other Logical Essays*. London: Routledge and Kegan Paul, 1931: 1–61, and in Ramsey, *Philosophical Papers*. Cambridge, U.K.: Cambridge University Press, 1990, pp. 164–224.

Richard, Jules. "Les principes de mathématiques et le problème de ensembles." *Revue Générale des Sciences Pures et Appliquées* 16 (1905): 541. English translation by Jean van Heijenoort in van Heijenoort, 142–144.

Russell, Bertrand. "Letter to Frege." 1902. In van Heijenoort, 124–125.

Russell, Bertrand. "On Denoting." *Mind* n. s. 14 (1905): 479–493. Reprinted in Russell, *Logic and Knowledge*. London: Allen and Unwyn, 1956: 41–56.

Tarski, Alfred. "Grundlegung der wissenschaftlichen Semantik." *Actes du Congrès International de Philosophie Scientifique* 3 (1930): 1–8. English translation by J. H. Woodger in Tarski, *Logic, Semantics, Metamathematics*, 401–408.

Tarski, Alfred. *Logic, Semantics, Metamathematics*. 2nd ed. Indianapolis: Hackett, 1983.

Tarski, Alfred. "Der Wahrheitsbegriff in den formalisierten Sprachen." *Studia Philosophica* 1 (1935): 261–405. English translation by J. H. Woodger in Tarski, *Logic, Semantics, Metamathematics*, 152–278.

Van Heijenoort, Jean, ed. *From Frege to Gödel*. Cambridge, MA, and London: Harvard University Press, 1967.

Von Neumann, John. "Eine Axiomatisierung der Mengenlehre." *Journal für die reine und angewandte Mathematik* 154 (1925): 219–240. English translation by Stefan Bauer-Mengelberg and Dagfinn Føllesdal in van Heijenoort, 393–413.

Whitehead, Alfred North, and Bertrand Russell. *Principia Mathematica*. 2nd ed. 3 vols. Cambridge, U.K.: Cambridge University Press, 1925 and 1927.

Wiener, Norbert. "A Simplification of the Logic of Relations." *Proceedings of the Cambridge Philosophical Society* 17 (1914): 387–390. Reprinted in van Heijenoort, 224–227.

Zermelo, Ernst. "Beweis, daß jede Menge wohlgeordnet werden kann." *Mathematische Annalen* 59 (1904): 514–516. English translation by Stefan Bauer-Mengelberg in van Heijenoort, 139–141.

Zermelo, Ernst. "Neuer Beweis für die Möglichkeit einer Wohlordnung." *Mathematische Annalen* 65 (1908): 107–28.

English translation by Stefan Bauer-Mengelberg in van Heijenoort, 183–198.

Zermelo, Ernst. "Über Grenzzahlen und Mengenbereiche." *Fundamenta Mathematicae* 16 (1930): 29–37.

Zermelo, Ernst. "Untersuchungen über die Grundlagen der Mengenlehre I." *Mathematische Annalen* 65 (1908): 261–281. English translation by Stefan Bauer-Mengelberg in van Heijenoort, 199–215.

Vann McGee (2005)

LOGICAL POSITIVISM

"Logical positivism" is the name given in 1931 by A. E. Blumberg and Herbert Feigl to a set of philosophical ideas put forward by the Vienna circle. Synonymous expressions include "consistent empiricism," "logical empiricism," "scientific empiricism," and "logical neopositivism." The name logical positivism is often, but misleadingly, used more broadly to include the "analytical" or "ordinary language" philosophies developed at Cambridge and Oxford.

HISTORICAL BACKGROUND

The logical positivists thought of themselves as continuing a nineteenth-century Viennese empirical tradition, closely linked with British empiricism and culminating in the antimetaphysical, scientifically oriented teachings of Ernst Mach. In 1907 the mathematician Hans Hahn, the economist Otto Neurath, and the physicist Philipp Frank, all of whom were later to be prominent members of the Vienna circle, came together as an informal group to discuss the philosophy of science. They hoped to give an account of science that would do justice—as, they thought, Mach did not—to the central importance of mathematics, logic, and theoretical physics, without abandoning Mach's general doctrine that science is, fundamentally, the description of experience. As a solution to their problems, they looked to the "new positivism" of Jules Henri Poincaré; in attempting to reconcile Mach and Poincaré they anticipated the main themes of logical positivism.

In 1922, at the instigation of members of the "Vienna group," Moritz Schlick was invited to Vienna as professor, like Mach before him (1895–1901), in the philosophy of the inductive sciences. Schlick had been trained as a scientist under Max Planck and had won a name for himself as an interpreter of Albert Einstein's theory of relativity. But he was deeply interested in the classical problems of philosophy, as Mach had not been.

Around Schlick, whose personal and intellectual gifts particularly fitted him to be the leader of a cooperative discussion group, the "Vienna circle" quickly established itself. Its membership included Neurath, Friedrich Waismann, Edgar Zilsel, Béla von Juhos, Felix Kaufmann, Feigl, Victor Kraft, Philipp Frank—although he was by now teaching in Prague—Karl Menger, Kurt Gödel, and Hahn. In 1926 Rudolf Carnap was invited to Vienna as instructor in philosophy, and he quickly became a central figure in the circle's discussions; he wrote more freely than the other members of the circle and came to be regarded as the leading exponent of their ideas. Carnap had been trained as a physicist and mathematician at Jena, where he had come under Gottlob Frege's influence. Like other members of the circle, however, he derived his principal philosophical ideas from Mach and Bertrand Russell.

Ludwig Wittgenstein and Karl Popper were not members of the circle but had regular discussions with its members. In particular, Wittgenstein was in close contact with Schlick and Waismann. Wittgenstein's *Tractatus Logico-Philosophicus* had a profound influence on the deliberations of the circle, where it was interpreted as a development of British empiricism.

The circle ascribed to Wittgenstein the "verifiability principle"—that the meaning of a proposition is identical with the method of verifying it—that is, that a proposition means the set of experiences that are together equivalent to the proposition's being true. Wittgenstein, they also thought, had shown how an empiricist could give a satisfactory account of mathematics and logic. He had recognized that the propositions of logic and mathematics are tautologies. (The logical positivists paid no attention to Wittgenstein's distinction between tautologies and identities.) They are "independent of experience" only because they are empty of content, not because, as classical rationalists had argued, they are truths of a higher order than truths based on experience.

In the German-speaking countries, the Vienna circle was a small minority group. For the most part, German-speaking philosophers were still committed to some variety of "German idealism." Neurath, with his strong sociopolitical interests, was particularly insistent that the circle should act in the manner of a political party, setting out to destroy traditional metaphysics, which he saw as an instrument of social and political reaction.

In 1928 the significantly named Verein Ernst Mach (Ernst Mach Society) was set up by members of the circle with the avowed object of "propagating and furthering a scientific outlook" and "creating the intellectual instruments of modern empiricism." To welcome Schlick back to Vienna in 1929 from a visiting professorship at Stanford, California, Carnap, Hahn, and Neurath prepared a manifesto under the general title *Wissenschaftliche Weltauffassung, Der Wiener Kreis* (The Scientific World View: The Vienna Circle). This manifesto traced the teachings of the Vienna circle back to such positivists as David Hume and Mach, such scientific methodologists as Hermann Ludwig von Helmholtz, Poincaré, Pierre Maurice Marie Duhem, and Einstein, to logicians from Gottfried Wilhelm Leibniz to Russell, utilitarian moralists from Epicurus to John Stuart Mill, and to such sociologists as Ludwig Feuerbach, Karl Marx, Herbert Spencer, and Menger. Significantly absent were any representatives of the "German tradition"—even, although somewhat unfairly, Immanuel Kant.

In order to make its conclusions familiar to a wider world, the circle organized a series of congresses. The first of these was held in Prague in 1929 as a section of a mathematical and physical, not a philosophical, congress. It was jointly sponsored by the Ernst Mach Society and the Society for Empirical Philosophy, a Berlin group led by Hans Reichenbach and with such members as Walter Dubislav, Kurt Grelling and Carl Hempel, which stood close in its general approach to the Vienna circle.

Meanwhile, the international affiliations of the circle were increasing in importance. American philosophers like C. W. Morris emphasized the link between logical positivism and American pragmatism; Ernest Nagel and W. V. Quine visited Vienna and Prague. In Great Britain, logical positivism attracted the interest of such Cambridge-trained philosophers as L. Susan Stebbing and John Wisdom and the Oxford philosophers Gilbert Ryle and A. J. Ayer, the latter participating for a time in the deliberations of the circle. In France such philosophers of science as Louis Rougier were attracted by logical positivism, as were a group of neo-Thomists led by General Vouillemin, who welcomed the positivist critique of idealism. In Scandinavia, where the way had been prepared by the antimetaphysical philosophy of Axel Hägerström, a number of philosophers sympathized with the aims of the logical positivists; Eino Kaila, Arne Naess, Åke Petzäll, and Jørgen Jørgensen were prominent representatives of the international movement centering on logical positivism. The Polish logicians, especially Alfred Tarski, exerted a considerable influence on members of the circle, particularly on Carnap. German philosophers, except for Heinrich Scholz of Münster and the Berlin group, remained aloof. Undoubtedly, the organizational energies of the circle did much to bring into being in the 1930s an international community of empiricists; this was largely a consequence of the circle's isolation within the German countries themselves.

Meanwhile the circle was publishing. In 1930 it took over the journal *Annalen der Philosophie* and renamed it *Erkenntnis*. In the period from 1930 to 1940 it served as a "house organ" for members of the Vienna circle and their associates. In addition, the circle prepared a series of monographs under the general title *Veröffentlichungen des Vereines Ernst Mach* (from 1928 to 1934) and *Einheitswissenschaft* (edited by Neurath from 1934 until 1938).

During the 1930s, however, the Vienna circle disintegrated as a group. In 1931 Carnap left Vienna for Prague; in that year Feigl went to Iowa and later to Minnesota; Hahn died in 1934; in 1936 Carnap went to Chicago and Schlick was shot by a mentally deranged student. The meetings of the circle were discontinued. The Ernst Mach Society was formally dissolved in 1938; the publications of the circle could no longer be sold in German-speaking countries. Waismann and Neurath left for England; Zilsel and Kaufmann followed Feigl, Carnap, Menger, and Gödel to the United States. *Erkenntnis* moved in 1938 to The Hague, where it took the name *Journal of Unified Science*; it was discontinued in 1940. Logical positivism, too, disintegrated as a movement, absorbed into international logical empiricism.

CRITIQUE OF TRADITIONAL PHILOSOPHY

Mach denied that he was a philosopher. He was trying, he said, to unify science and, in the process, to rid it of all metaphysical elements; he was not constructing a philosophy. The general attitude of the Vienna circle was very similar. Schlick was the exception. With logical positivism, he argued, philosophy had taken a new turn, but logical positivism was nonetheless a philosophy. Carnap, in contrast, wrote that "we give no answer to philosophical questions and instead *reject all philosophical questions*, whether of Metaphysics, Ethics or Epistemology" (*The Unity of Science*, p. 21). Philosophy, on his view, had to be destroyed, not renovated.

Undoubtedly, this intransigent attitude to philosophy can in part be explained by the peculiar character of German idealism and its hostility to science. The logical positivists thought of themselves as extending the range of science over the whole area of systematic truth and as needing for that purpose to destroy the claim of idealist philosophers to have a special kind of suprascientific access to truth.

METAPHYSICS. Of the traditional branches of philosophy, the positivists rejected transcendental metaphysics on the ground that its assertions were meaningless, since there was no possible way of verifying them in experience. Nothing that we could possibly experience, they argued, would serve to verify such assertions as "The Absolute is beyond time." Therefore, the positivists held, it tells us nothing. The rejection of transcendental metaphysics was not a novelty; Hume had described transcendental metaphysics as "sophistry and illusion" and had alleged that it makes use of insignificant expressions; Kant and the neo-Kantians had rejected its claim to be a form of theoretical knowledge; Mach had sought to remove all metaphysical elements from science. But whereas earlier critics of metaphysics had generally been content to describe it as empty or useless or unscientific, the logical positivists took over from Wittgenstein's *Tractatus* the rejection of metaphysics as meaningless. The propositions of metaphysics, they argued, are neither true nor false; they are wholly devoid of significance. It is as nonsensical to deny as to assert that the Absolute is beyond time.

EPISTEMOLOGY. Neo-Kantians had sometimes suggested that philosophy could be reduced to epistemology or "theory of knowledge," which discussed such topics as "the reality of the external world." But assertions about the external world, the positivists argued, are quite as meaningless as assertions about the Absolute or about things-in-themselves. For there is no possible way of verifying the assertion that there is, or the assertion that there is not, an external world independent of our experience. Realism and idealism, considered as epistemological theses, are equally meaningless. So far as epistemology has any content, it reduces to psychology, to assertions about the workings of the human mind, and these have nothing to do with philosophy.

ETHICS. The logical positivists disagreed about ethics. Of course they all rejected any variety of transcendental ethics, any attempt to set up a "realm of values" over and above the world of experience. Assertions about values, thus conceived, fall within the general province of transcendental metaphysics and had therefore to be rejected as nonsensical. But whereas Schlick sought to free ethics from its metaphysical elements by converting it into a naturalistic theory along quasi-utilitarian lines, Carnap and Ayer argued that what are ordinarily taken to be ethical assertions are not assertions at all. To say that "stealing is wrong," for example, is neither, they suggested, to make an empirical statement about stealing nor to relate

stealing to some transcendental realm. "Stealing is wrong" either expresses our feelings about stealing, our feelings of disapproval, or, alternatively (positivists' opinions differ about this), it is an attempt to dissuade others from stealing. In either case, "stealing is wrong" conveys no information.

PHILOSOPHICAL MEANINGLESSNESS. In general, the positivists explained, when they said of philosophical assertions that they were meaningless, they meant only that they lacked "cognitive meaning." Ethical and metaphysical assertions have emotional associations; this distinguishes them from mere jumbles of words. Such statements as "God exists" or "Stealing is wrong" are, on the face of it, very different from a collocation of nonsense syllables. But the fact remains, the positivists argued, that such "assertions" do not convey, as they purport to do, information about the existence or character of a particular kind of entity. Only science can give us that sort of information.

Not all philosophers, however, have devoted their attention to describing pseudo entities such as "the Absolute" or "values" or "the external world." Many of them have been mainly concerned with empirical-looking concepts such as "fact," "thing," "property," and "relation." Russell's lectures on logical atomism and Wittgenstein's *Tractatus* are cases in point.

Wittgenstein suggested, however, that the sections in the *Tractatus* in which he talked about facts, or attempted to show how propositions can picture facts, must all in the end be rejected as senseless—as attempts to say what can only be shown. For it is impossible in principle to pass beyond our language in order to discuss what our language talks about. Philosophy is the activity of clarifying; it is not a theory.

Schlick carried to its extreme Wittgenstein's *Tractatus* doctrine that philosophy is an activity. Philosophy, he suggested, consists in the deed of showing in what the meaning of a statement consists; that is, philosophy is a silent act of pointing. The ultimate meaning of a proposition cannot consist in other propositions. To clarify, therefore, we are forced in the end to pass beyond propositions to the experience in which their meaning consists.

This view won few adherents. It was generally agreed that philosophers could not avoid making the sort of ontological assertions Wittgenstein made in the *Tractatus* and that it is altogether too paradoxical to suggest that all propositions about, for example, the relation between facts and language are nonsensical, even if "important" nonsense. Neurath, in particular, insisted that nonsense cannot be "important," cannot act as a ladder by which we arrive at understanding, as Wittgenstein had said.

STATEMENTS ABOUT LANGUAGE. Carnap suggested that Wittgenstein was mistaken in supposing that his ontological assertions were without any sense. They were, however, meaningful assertions about language, not about a world beyond language. No doubt, Carnap admits, ontological statements have the appearance of being about the world or, at least, about the relation between language and the world. But this is so only because they have been wrongly formulated in what Carnap calls "the material mode."

Carnap distinguishes three classes of sentences: object sentences, pseudo object sentences, and syntactical sentences. Any ordinary sentence of mathematics or science is an object sentence. Thus, for example, "Five is a prime number" and "Lions are fierce" are both object sentences. Syntactical sentences are sentences about words and the rules governing the use of words. For example, "Five is not a thing-word but a number-word" and "Lion is a thing-word" are syntactical sentences. Pseudo object sentences are peculiar to philosophy; they look like object sentences but if rightly understood turn out to be syntactical sentences. To understand them rightly we have to convert them from the "material mode" into the "formal mode," that is, from sentences that look as if they are about objects into sentences that are obviously about words. Examples are "Five is not a thing but a number" and "Lions are things." Once these sentences are converted out of the "material mode" into the corresponding "formal" (or syntactical) mode, they can be discussed; in the material mode they are quite undiscussable.

But how are syntactical disputes to be settled? Suppose one philosopher asserts and another denies that "numerical expressions are class-expressions of the second level"—Carnap's "translation" of "numbers are classes of classes"—how is it to be determined which is correct? All such statements, Carnap argues, are relative to a language; they are either statements about the characteristics of some existing language or proposals for the formation of a new language. Fully expressed, that is, they have the form "In language *L*, such-and-such an expression is of such-and-such a type." It can be immediately determined whether such a syntactical statement is true by examining the language in question.

PROBLEMS OF POSITIVISM

VERIFIABILITY. The course taken by the subsequent history of logical positivism was determined by its attempts to solve a set of problems set for it, for the most part, by its reliance on the verifiability principle. The status of that principle was by no means clear, for "The meaning of a proposition is the method of its verification" is not a scientific proposition. Should it therefore be rejected as meaningless? Faced with this difficulty, the logical positivists argued that it ought to be read not as a statement but as a proposal, a recommendation that propositions should not be accepted as meaningful unless they are verifiable. But this was an uneasy conclusion. For the positivists had set out to destroy metaphysics; now it appeared that the metaphysician could escape their criticisms simply by refusing to accept their recommendations.

Recognition of this difficulty led Carnap to suggest that the verifiability principle is an "explication," a contribution to the "rational reconstruction" of such concepts as metaphysics, science, and meaning, to be justified on the quasi-pragmatic grounds that if we ascribe meaning only to the verifiable we shall be able to distinguish forms of activity that are otherwise likely to be confused with one another. It is not, however, by any means clear in what way the verifiability principle can be invoked against a metaphysician who takes as his point of departure that his propositions clearly have a meaning. The most that can be said is that the onus is then on the metaphysician to distinguish his propositions from others that he would certainly have to admit to be meaningless.

A second set of problems hinged on the nature of the entities to which the verifiability principle applies. Since "proposition" had ordinarily been defined as "that which can be either true or false," it seemed odd to suggest that a proposition might be meaningless. Yet it was no less odd to suggest that a sentence—a set of words—could be verified, even if there was no doubt that it could be meaningless. Ayer suggested as an alternative the word *statement,* and he wrote as if the problem were a purely terminological one. But it is a serious question whether "true," "false," and "meaningless" are alternative descriptions of the same kind of occurrence or whether to describe a sentence as "meaningless" is not tantamount to denying that any statement has been made, any proposition put forward. This would have the consequence that we can consider whether a statement is verifiable only after we have settled the question of the meaning of the sentence used to make the statement.

The logical positivists themselves were much more concerned about the fact that the verifiability principle threatened to destroy not only metaphysics but also science. Whereas Mach had been happy to purge the sciences, the logical positivists ordinarily took for granted the substantial truth of contemporary science. Thus, it was a matter of vital concern to them when it became apparent that the verifiability principle would rule out as meaningless all scientific laws.

For such laws are, by the nature of the case, not conclusively verifiable; there is no set of experiences such that having these experiences is equivalent to the truth of a scientific law. Following Frank Plumpton Ramsey, Schlick suggested that laws should be regarded not as statements but as rules permitting us to pass from one singular statement to another singular statement. In Ryle's phrase, they are "inference-licenses." Neurath and Carnap objected to this on the ground that scientific laws are used in science as statements, not as rules. For example, attempts are made to falsify them, and it is absurd to speak of "falsifying a rule." Furthermore, Carnap pointed out, ordinary singular statements are in exactly the same position as laws of nature; there is no set of experiences such that if I have these experiences there must be, for example, a table in the room.

For these and comparable reasons "verifiability" was gradually replaced by "confirmability" or by the rather stronger notion of "testability." Whereas at first the meaning of a proposition had been identified with the experiences that we would have to have in order to know that the proposition is true, now this was reduced to the much weaker thesis that a proposition has a meaning *only if it is possible to confirm it,* that is, to derive true propositions from it. Carnap, in accordance with his "principle of tolerance," was prepared to admit that a language might be constructed in which only verifiable propositions would count as meaningful. He was content to point out that such a language would be less useful for science than a language that admits general laws. But most positivists, interested as they were in the actual structure of science, simply replaced the verifiability principle by a confirmability principle.

If, however, the original principle proved to be too strong, the new principle threatened to be too weak. For, on the face of it, the new principle admitted as meaningful such metaphysical propositions as "Either it is raining or the Absolute is not perfect." Whether the confirmability principle can so be restated as to act as a method of distinguishing between metaphysical statements as meaningless and scientific statements as meaningful remains a question of controversy.

UNIFICATION OF SCIENCE. A further set of problems hinges on the question of what sort of things act as "ver-

ifiers" or "confirmers." One of Mach's main concerns, which the logical positivists shared, had been to unify science, especially by rejecting the view that psychology is about an "inner world" that is different from the "outer world" that physical science investigates. The doctrine that both physics and psychology describe "experiences" made such a unification possible. In his earlier writings Carnap tried to show in detail how "the world" could be constructed out of experience, linked together by relations of similarity. But then a new difficulty arose; one about how it is possible to show that one person's experiences are identical with another's. On the face of it, an experience-based science is fundamentally subjective; science is verified only at the cost of losing its objectivity.

To overcome this difficulty, Schlick drew a distinction between "content" and "structure." We can never be sure, he argued, that the content of our experience is identical with the content of any other person's experience, for example, that what he sees when he says that he sees something red is identical with what we see when we say we see something red. For scientific purposes, however, this does not matter in the slightest. Science is interested only in the structure of our experience, so that provided, for example, we all agree about the position of red on a color chart, it is of no importance whether our experience of red differs.

Yet Schlick still thought that such "experiences" are what gives content, meaning, to science, converting it from a conceptual frame into real knowledge. Thus, it appears that the ultimate content of science lies beyond all public observation. There is no way of verifying that another person is even experiencing a content, let alone a content that is like or unlike the content of my experience.

PHYSICALIST THEORIES. Profoundly dissatisfied with the conclusion that the ultimate content of scientific truths is private, Neurath was led to reject the view—which logical positivists had so far taken for granted—that it is "experiences" which verify propositions. Only a proposition, he argued, can verify a proposition. Carnap accepted this conclusion and developed the conception of a "protocol statement," the ultimate resting point of verifications, a statement of such a nature that to understand its meaning and to see that it is true are the same thing. Carnap still suggested, however, that a protocol statement records a private experience, even though every such statement—indeed every statement—can be translated into the public language of physics. Statements of the form "Here now an experience of red" can, he argued, be translated into statements about the physical state of the body of the person who has the experience of red. (Subsequently this "physicalist" thesis was expressed in the weaker form, that every statement is linked by means of correspondence rules with the statements of physics.)

Neurath was still dissatisfied. Protocol statements, he argued, must form part of science as distinct from merely being translatable into its language. Otherwise, science still rests on essentially private experience. In fact, protocol statements must take some such form as "Otto Neurath reports that at 3:15 p.m. there was a table in the room perceived by Otto." The effect of this suggestion, as Schlick remarked with horror, is to leave open the possibility that the basic protocol statements may not be true. They, rather than some natural law with which they are incompatible, can be rejected as false. Schlick persisted in arguing that the ultimate confirmations of scientific propositions must be experiences of the form "here, now, blue"—which he described as "the only synthetic statements which are not hypotheses." Carnap came to agree with Neurath, however, that all synthetic statements are hypotheses.

At first, indeed, Carnap replied to Neurath by invoking his principle of tolerance. One has a free choice, he argued, between a language that incorporates protocol statements and a language into which they can be translated. Subsequently he has moved more and more in Neurath's direction. Statements of the form "the body Carnap is in a state of green-seeing," he now suggests, are sufficient to act as confirmations, and it is not necessary at any point to use the "phenomenal language" that Mach had thought to be the basic language of science. But Carnap still writes as if the issue between physicalist and nonphysicalist hinges on the choice of a language. Logical positivism, we might say, split into three groups, one asserting physicalism, the second rejecting it, and the third expressing a preference for the physicalist language.

In his *Logical Syntax of Language* Carnap had argued that all statements about the "meaning" or "significance" of statements are of the "pseudo object" type and should be translated into a syntactical form. Thus, for example, "This letter is about the son of Mr. Miller" has to be read as asserting that in this letter a sentence occurs which has the expression "the son of Mr. Miller" as its subject. This was a highly implausible doctrine, since, clearly, a letter can be about the son of Mr. Miller without using the phrase "the son of Mr. Miller." Under Tarski's influence Carnap decided that his original thesis had been unduly restrictive; philosophy had to refer to the semantical as well as the syntactical characteristics of language in order

to give a satisfactory explication of, for example, the conception of "truth." Now Carnap found himself in opposition to Neurath. To try to pass beyond language to what language signifies, Neurath argued, is at once to reintroduce the transcendental entities of metaphysics. The subsequent development of semantics at Carnap's hands would have done nothing to relieve Neurath's qualms. Languages can be constructed, Carnap argues, in a variety of ways, and the question whether, for example, one accepts a language that includes names for abstract entities is a matter of practical convenience, not admitting of argument at any other level. The influence of Mach on Carnap's thinking has now been almost entirely dissipated; he writes, rather, in the spirit of a Poincaré or a Duhem.

THE INFLUENCE OF POSITIVISM

Logical positivism, considered as the doctrine of a sect, has disintegrated. In various ways it has been absorbed into the international movement of contemporary empiricism, within which the disputes that divided it are still being fought out. Originally, it set up a series of sharp contrasts: between metaphysics and science, logical and factual truths, the verifiable and the nonverifiable, the corrigible and the incorrigible, what can be shown and what can be said, facts and theories. In recent philosophy, all these contrasts have come under attack, not from metaphysicians but from philosophers who would in a general sense be happy enough to describe themselves as "logical empiricists." Even among those philosophers who would still wish to make the contrasts on which the logical positivists insisted, few would believe that they can be made with the sharpness or the ease that the logical positivists at first suggested.

Logical positivism, then, is dead, or as dead as a philosophical movement ever becomes. But it has left a legacy behind. In the German-speaking countries, indeed, it wholly failed; German philosophy, as exhibited in the works of Martin Heidegger and his disciples, represents everything to which the positivists were most bitterly opposed. In the United States, Great Britain, Australia, the Scandinavian countries, and in other countries where empiricism is widespread, it is often hard to distinguish the direct influence of the positivists from the influence of such allied philosophers as Russell, the Polish logicians, and the British "analysts." But insofar as it is widely agreed that transcendental metaphysics, if not meaningless, is at least otiose, that philosophers ought to set an example of precision and clarity, that philosophy should make use of technical devices, deriving from logic, in order to solve problems relating to the philosophy of science, that philosophy is not about "the world" but about the language through which men speak about the world, we can detect in contemporary philosophy, at least, the persistence of the spirit that inspired the Vienna circle.

See also Absolute, The; Analysis, Philosophical; Ayer, Alfred Jules; Basic Statements; Carnap, Rudolf; Duhem, Pierre Maurice Marie; Einstein, Albert; Emotive Theory of Ethics; Empiricism; Epicurus; Epistemology, History of; Frege, Gottlob; Gödel, Kurt; Heidegger, Martin; Helmholtz, Hermann Ludwig von; Hempel, Carl Gustav; Hume, David; Kant, Immanuel; Language; Leibniz, Gottfried Wilhelm; Mach, Ernst; Metaphysics; Mill, John Stuart; Neo-Kantianism; Neurath, Otto; Planck, Max; Poincaré, Jules Henri; Popper, Karl Raimund; Positivism; Ramsey, Frank Plumpton; Reichenbach, Hans; Russell, Bertrand Arthur William; Ryle, Gilbert; Schlick, Moritz; Tarski, Alfred; Utilitarianism; Verifiability Principle; Wittgenstein, Ludwig Josef Johann.

Bibliography

The essays by leading logical positivists included along with an introduction by Ayer and an extensive bibliography in Alfred J. Ayer, ed., *Logical Positivism* (Glencoe, IL: Free Press, 1959), are the best introduction to the movement as a whole. Other representative writings by members of the Vienna circle and its associates include the following: Alfred J. Ayer, *Language, Truth and Logic* (London: Gollancz, 1936; 2nd ed., 1946). Rudolf Carnap, *Der Logische Aufbau der Welt* (Berlin: Weltkreis, 1928), translated by R. George as *The Logical Structure of the World* (London: Routledge and Kegan Paul, 1967); "Die physikalische Sprache als Universalsprache der Wissenschaft," in *Erkenntnis* 2 (5–6) (1932): 423–465, translated by Max Black as *The Unity of Science* (London: Kegan Paul, 1934); *Logische Syntax der Sprache* (Vienna: Springer, 1934), translated by Amethe Smeaton as *The Logical Syntax of Language* (London and New York: Kegan Paul, 1937); *Philosophy and Logical Syntax* (London: Kegan Paul, 1935); "Testability and Meaning," in *Philosophy and Science* 3 (4) (1936): 419–471, and 4 (1) (1937): 1–40; *Meaning and Necessity* (Chicago: University of Chicago Press, 1947); "Empiricism, Semantics and Ontology," in *Revue internationale de philosophie* 4 (11) (1950), reprinted in *Semantics and the Philosophy of Language,* edited by Leonard Linsky (Urbana: University of Illinois Press, 1952), pp. 208–228; and "Intellectual Autobiography" and "Reply to My Critics," in *The Philosophy of Rudolf Carnap,* edited by P. A. Schilpp (La Salle, IL: Open Court, 1963).

See Herbert Feigl and May Brodbeck, eds., *Readings in the Philosophy of Science* (New York: Appleton-Century-Crofts, 1953), and Herbert Feigl and Wilfrid Sellars, eds., *Readings in Philosophical Analysis* (New York: Appleton-Century-Crofts, 1949), for articles by Carnap, Feigl, Reichenbach, Hempel, Frank, and Zilsel. See also Philipp Frank, *Modern Science and Its Philosophy* (Cambridge, MA: Harvard University Press, 1949); Victor Kraft, *Der Wiener Kreis, Der Ursprung des Neopositivismus* (Vienna: Springer-Verlag, 1950), translated by Arthur Pap as *The Vienna Circle* (New York: Philosophical Library, 1953); Jørgen Jørgensen, *The Development of Logical Empiricism* (Chicago: University of Chicago Press, 1951); Charles W. Morris, *Logical Positivism, Pragmatism and Scientific Empiricism* (Paris: Hermann, 1937); Otto Neurath, *Einheitswissenschaft und Psychologie* (Vienna: Gerold, 1933) and *Le développement du Cercle de Vienne et l'avenir de l'empiricisme logique* (Paris: Hermann, 1935); Hans Reichenbach, *The Rise of Scientific Philosophy* (Berkeley: University of California Press, 1951); Karl Raimund Popper, *Logik der Forschung* (Vienna: Springer, 1935), translated with new appendices by the author, with the assistance of Julius Freed and Lan Freed, as *Logic of Scientific Discovery* (London: Hutchinson, 1959); Moritz Schlick, *Allgemeine Erkenntnislehre* (Berlin: Springer, 1918), *Fragen der Ethik* (Vienna: Springer, 1930), translated by D. Rynin as *Problems of Ethics* (New York: Prentice Hall, 1939), and *Gesammelte Aufsätze* (Vienna: Gerold, 1938), partially republished as *Gesetz Kausalität und Wahrscheinlichkeit* (Vienna: Gerold, 1948); and Ludwig Wittgenstein, *Tractatus Logico-Philosophicus,* German version as *Logisch-Philosophische Abhandlung* in *Annalen der Naturphilosophie* 14 (1921): 185–262, English translation by C. K. Ogden (London: Routledge, 1922; rev. ed., New York: Humanities Press, 1961); *Philosophical Investigations* (Oxford: Blackwell, 1953).

See also Richard von Mises, *Kleines Lehrbuch der Positivismus* (The Hague: W. P. van Stockum, 1939), translated as *Positivism: A Study in Human Understanding* (Cambridge, MA: Harvard University Press, 1951); G. Bergmann, *The Metaphysics of Logical Positivism* (London: Longmans Green, 1954); Frederick C. Copleston, *Contemporary Philosophy* (London: Burns and Oates, 1956); Ernest Nagel, *Logic without Metaphysics* (Glencoe, IL: Free Press, 1956); John Arthur Passmore, "Logical Positivism," in *Australasian Journal of Psychology and Philosophy* 21 (1943): 65–92, 33 (1944): 129–153, and 26 (1948): 1–19, and *A Hundred Years of Philosophy* (London: Duckworth, 1957); James O. Urmson, *Philosophical Analysis* (Oxford: Clarendon Press, 1956); and Julius R. Weinberg, *An Examination of Logical Positivism* (London: Kegan Paul, 1936).

John Passmore (1967)

LOGICAL TERMS

The two central problems concerning "logical terms" are demarcation and interpretation. The search for a demarcation of logical terms goes back to the founders of modern logic, and within the classical tradition a partial solution, restricted to logical connectives, was established early on. The characteristic feature of logical connectives, according to this solution, is truth-functionality, and the totality of truth functions (Boolean functions from n-tuples of truth values to a truth value) determines the totality of logical connectives. In his seminal 1936 paper, "On the Concept of Logical Consequence," Alfred Tarski demonstrated the need for a more comprehensive criterion by showing that his semantic definition of logical consequence—the sentence σ is a logical consequence of the set of sentences Σ iff (if and only if) every model of Σ is a model of σ—is dependent on such a demarcation. (Thus suppose the existential quantifier is not a logical term, then its interpretation will vary from model to model, and the intuitively logically valid consequence, "Rembrandt is a painter; therefore there is at least one painter," will fail to satisfy Tarski's definition. Suppose "Rembrandt" and "is a painter" are both logical terms, then the intuitively logically invalid consequence, "Frege is a logician; therefore Rembrandt is a painter," will satisfy Tarski's definition.) Tarski, however, left the general demarcation of logical terms an open question, and it was not until the late 1950s that the first steps toward developing a systematic criterion for logical predicates and quantifiers were taken.

In his 1957 paper, "On a Generalization of Quantifiers," A. Mostowski proposed a semantic criterion for first-order logical quantifiers that generalizes Frege's analysis of the standard quantifiers as second-level cardinality predicates. Technically, Mostowski interpreted a quantifier, Q, as a function from universes (sets of objects), A, to A-quantifiers, Q_A, where Q_A is a function assigning a truth-value to each subset B of A. Thus, given a set A, the existential and universal quantifiers are defined by: for any $B \subseteq A, \exists_A(B) = T$ iff $B \neq \phi$ and $\forall_A(B) = T$ iff $A - B = \phi$. Intuitively, a quantifier is logical if it does "not allow us to distinguish between different elements" of the underlying universe. Formally, Q is logical iff it is invariant under isomorphic structures of the type <A,B>, where $B \subseteq A$; that is, Q is a logical quantifier iff for every structure <A,B> and <A',B'>:if<A,B>≅<A',B'>, then $Q_A(B) = Q_{A'}(B')$. Quantifiers satisfying Mostowski's criterion are commonly called *cardinality quantifiers,* and some examples of these are "!δx" ("There are exactly δ individuals in the universe such that …"), where δ is any cardinal, "Most x" ("There are more x's such that … than x's such that not …"), "There are finitely many x," "There are uncountably many x," and so forth.

In 1966, P. Lindström extended Mostowski's criterion to terms in general: A term (of type n) is logical iff it is invariant under isomorphic structures (of type n). Thus, the well-ordering predicate, W, is logical since for any A,A', $R \subseteq A^2$ and $R' \subseteq A'^2$: if <A,R>≅<A',R'>, then

$W_A(R) = W_{A'}(R')$. Intuitively, we can say that a term is logical iff it does not distinguish between isomorphic arguments. The terms satisfying Lindström's criterion include identity, n-place cardinality quantifiers (e.g., the 2-place "Most," as in "Most A's are B's"), relational or polyadic quantifiers like the well-ordering predicate above and "is an equivalence relation," and so forth. Among the terms not satisfying Lindström's criterion are individual constants, the first-level predicate "is red," the first-level membership relation, the second-level predicate "is a property of Napoleon," and so forth. Tarski (1966) proposed essentially the same division.

The Mostowski-Lindström-Tarski (MLT) approach to logical terms has had a considerable impact on the development of contemporary model theory. Among the central results are Lindström's characterizations of elementary logic, various completeness and incompleteness theorems for generalized (model-theoretic, abstract) logics, and so forth. (See Barwise and Feferman 1985). But whereas the mathematical yield of MLT has been prodigious, philosophers, by and large, have continued to hold on to the traditional view according to which the collection of (primitive) logical terms is restricted to truth-functional connectives, the existential and/or universal quantifier and, possibly, identity. One of the main strongholds of the traditional approach has been Willard Van Orman Quine, who (in his 1970 book) justified his approach on the grounds that (1) standard first-order logic (without identity) allows a remarkable concurrence of diverse definitions of logical consequence, and (2) standard first-order logic (with or without identity) is complete. Quine did not consider the logicality of nonstandard quantifiers such as "there are uncountably many," which allow a "complete" axiomatization. L. H. Tharp (1975), who did take into account the existence of complete first-order logics with nonstandard generalized quantifiers, nevertheless arrived at the same conclusion as Quine's.

During the 1960s and 1970s many philosophers were concerned with the interpretation rather than the identity of logical terms. Thus, Ruth Barcan Marcus (1962, 1972) and others developed a substitutional interpretation of the standard quantifiers; Michael Anthony Eardley Dummett (1973) advocated an intuitionistic interpretation of the standard logical terms based on considerations pertaining to the theory of meaning; many philosophers (e.g., van Fraassen) pursued "free" and "many-valued" interpretations of the logical connectives; Jaako Hintikka (1973, 1976) constructed a game theoretic semantics for logical terms. In a later development, G.

Boolos (1984) proposed a primitive (non-set-theoretic) interpretation of "nonfirstorderizable" operators, which has the potential of overcoming ontological objections to higher-order logical operators (e.g., by Quine).

In the mid-1970s philosophers began to search for an explicit, general philosophical criterion for logical terms. The attempts vary considerably, but in all cases the criterion is motivated by an underlying notion of logical consequence. Inspired by Gerhard Gentzen's proof-theoretic work, Ian Hacking (1979) suggests that a logical constant is introduced by (operational) rules of inference that preserve the basic features of the traditional deducibility relation: the subformula property (compositionality), reflexivity, dilution (stability under additional premises and conclusions), transitivity (cut), cut elimination, and so forth. Hacking's criterion renders all and only the logical terms of the ramified theory of types genuinely logical. A. Koslow's (1992) also utilizes a Gentzen-like characterization of the deducibility relation. Abstracting from the syntactic nature of Gentzen's rules, he arrives at a "structural" characterization of the standard logical and modal constants. Both Koslow and Hacking incorporate lessons from an earlier exchange between A. N. Prior (1960, 1964) and N. Belnap (1962) concerning the possibility of importing an inconsistency into a hitherto consistent system by using arbitrary rules of inference to introduce new logical operators.

C. Peacocke (1976) approaches the task of delineating the logical terms from a semantic perspective. The basic property of logical consequence is, according to Peacocke, a priori. α is a logical operator iff α is a non-complex n-place operator such that given knowledge of which objects (sequences of objects) satisfy an n-tuple or arguments of α, $<\beta_1,\ldots,\beta_n>$, one can know a priori which objects satisfy $\alpha(\beta_1,\ldots,\beta_n)$. Based on this criterion Peacocke counts the truth-functional connectives, the standard quantifiers, and certain temporal operators ("In the past …") as logical, while identity (taken as a primitive term), the first-order membership relation, and "necessarily" are nonlogical. Peacocke's criterion is designed for classical logic, but it is possible to produce analogous criteria for nonclassical logics (e.g., intuitionistic logic). T. McCarthy (1981) regards the basic property of logical constants as topic neutrality. He considers Peacocke's condition as necessary but not sufficient, and his own criterion conjoins Peacocke's condition with Lindström's invariance condition (MLT). The standard first-order logical vocabulary as well as various nonstandard generalized quantifiers satisfy McCarthy's criterion, but cardinality quantifiers do not (intuitively, cardinality quantifiers are not topic-neutral).

Sher (1991) considers necessity and formality as the two characteristic features of logical consequence. Treating formality as a semantic notion, Sher suggests that any formal operator incorporated into a Tarskian system according to certain rules yields consequences possessing the desired characteristics. Viewing Lindström's invariance criterion as capturing the intended notion of formal operator, Sher endorses the full-fledged MLT as delineating the scope of logical terms in classical logic.

The theory of logical terms satisfying Lindström's criterion has led, with various adjustments, to important developments in linguistic theory: a systematic account of determiners as generalized quantifiers (Barwise and Cooper, Higginbotham and May); numerous applications of "polyadic" quantifiers (van Benthem, Keenan); and an extension of Henkin's 1961 theory of standard branching quantifiers, applied to English by Hintikka (1973), to branching generalized quantifiers (Barwise and others).

See also Dummett, Michael Anthony Eardley; Frege, Gottlob; Hintikka, Jaako; Logic, History of; Marcus, Ruth Barcan; Model Theory; Prior, Arthur Norman; Quine, Willard Van Orman; Tarski, Alfred.

Bibliography

Barwise, J. "On Branching Quantifiers in English." *Journal of Philosophical Logic* 8 (1979): 47–80.

Barwise, J., and R. Cooper. "Generalized Quantifiers and Natural Language." *Linguistics and Philosophy* 4 (1981): 159–219.

Barwise, J., and S. Feferman, eds. *Model-Theoretic Logics.* New York: Springer-Verlag, 1985.

Belnap, N. "Tonk, Plonk, and Plink." *Analysis* 22 (1962): 130–134.

Boolos, G. "To Be Is to Be a Value of a Variable (or to Be Some Values of Some Variables)." *Journal of Philosophy* 81 (1984): 430–449.

Dummett, M. "The Philosophical Basis of Intuitionistic Logic." In *Truth and Other Enigmas.* Cambridge, MA: Harvard University Press, 1978.

Hacking, I. "What Is Logic?" *Journal of Philosophy* 76 (1979): 285–319.

Henkin, L. "Some Remarks on Infinitely Long Formulas." In *Infinitistic Methods.* Warsaw, 1961.

Higginbotham, J., and R. May. "Questions, Quantifiers and Crossing." *Linguistic Review* 1 (1981): 41–79.

Hintikka, J. "Quantifiers in Logic and Quantifiers in Natural Languages." In *Philosophy of Logic,* edited by S. Körner, 208–232. Oxford, 1976.

Hintikka, J. "Quantifiers vs. Quantification Theory." *Dialectica* 27 (1973): 329–358.

Keenan, E. L. "Unreducible n-ary Quantifiers in Natural Language." In *Generalized Quantifiers,* edited by P. Gärdenfors. Dordrecht: Reidel, 1987.

Koslow, A. *A Structuralist Theory of Logic.* Cambridge, U.K.: Cambridge University Press, 1992.

Lindström, P. "First Order Predicate Logic with Generalized Quantifiers." *Theoria* 32 (1966): 186–195.

Marcus, R. Barcan. "Interpreting Quantification." *Inquiry* 5 (1962): 252–259.

Marcus, R. Barcan. "Quantification and Ontology." *Noûs* 6 (1972): 240–250.

McCarthy, T. "The Idea of a Logical Constant." *Journal of Philosophy* 78 (1981): 499–523.

Mostowski, A. "On a Generalization of Quantifiers." *Fundamenta Mathematicae* 42 (1957): 12–36.

Peacocke, C. "What Is a Logical Constant?" *Journal of Philosophy* 73 (1976): 221–240.

Prior, A. N. "Conjunction and Contonktion Revisited." *Analysis* 24 (1964): 191–195.

Prior, A. N. "The Runabout Inference-Ticket." *Analysis* 21 (1960): 38–39.

Quine, W. V. O. *Philosophy of Logic.* Englewood Cliffs, NJ: Prentice-Hall, 1970.

Sher, G. *The Bounds of Logic: A Generalized Viewpoint.* Cambridge, MA: MIT Press, 1991.

Tarski, A. *Logic, Semantics, Metamathematics,* 2nd ed. Indianapolis: Hackett, 1983.

Tarski, A. "On the Concept of Logical Consequence" (1936). In *Logic, Semantics, Metamathematics,* 2nd ed., 409–420. Indianapolis: Hackett, 1983.

Tarski, A. "What Are Logical Notions?" (1966). *History and Philosophy of Logic* 7 (1986): 143–154.

Tharp, L. H. "Which Logic Is the Right Logic?" *Synthese* 31 (1975): 1–21.

van Benthem, J. "Polyadic Quantifiers." *Linguistics and Philosophy* 12 (1989): 437–464.

van Fraassen, B. C. "Singular Terms, Truth-Value Gaps, and Free Logic." *Journal of Philosophy* 63 (1966): 481–495.

Gila Sher (1996)

LOGICAL TERMS, GLOSSARY OF

This glossary is confined, with few exceptions, to terms used in formal logic, set theory, and related areas. No attempt has been made to cover what is often called "inductive logic," although several terms in this field have been included for the convenience of the reader.

It should be noted that many topics dealt with very briefly here are treated in full in various other entries in this encyclopedia. Cross references to these will be enclosed in quotation marks; cross references to other glossary entries will be indicated by boldface italics (e.g., "see *relation*").

abduction. (1) A syllogism whose major premise is known to be true but whose minor premise is merely probable. (2) C. S. Peirce's name for the type of reasoning that yields from a given set of facts an explanatory hypothesis for them.

abstraction. (1) In traditional logic, the process of deriving a universal from particulars. (2) In set theory, the process of defining a set as the set of all objects that have a particular property.

abstraction, axiom of (axiom of comprehension). An axiom in set theory stating that for any predicate P, there exists a set of all and only those objects that satisfy P. It was the unrestricted use of this axiom that led to the paradoxes of set theory.

abstract term. In traditional logic, a term that is a name of the common nature of many individuals, considered apart from them or from what distinguishes them from one another. A common example of an abstract term is "humanity."

accident. See *predicables.*

actual infinite. The infinite regarded as a completed whole.

a fortiori. A nonsyllogistic mediate inference of the form "B is greater than C; A is greater than B; hence, A is greater than C." It is clear that the validity of this argument follows from the transitivity of the relation "greater than," and therefore some authors extend the term to cover all relational syllogisms whose validity depends on the transitivity of the relation involved. See *relation.*

aggregate. A collection of objects satisfying a given condition.

alephs. The symbols, introduced by Georg Cantor, that designate the cardinality of infinite sets (see entry "Set Theory"). Aleph-null ($\aleph_0$) designates the cardinality of the smallest infinite set, aleph-one ($\aleph_1$) the cardinality of the next largest infinite set, etc. See *continuum hypothesis*; entry "Set Theory."

algebra of logic. A system in which algebraic formulas are used to express logical relations. In such a system many familiar algebraic laws that hold for numbers are not retained. The work of George Boole contains the first important example of an algebra of logic.

algorithm. A mechanical procedure for carrying out, in a finite number of steps, a computation that leads from certain types of data to certain types of results. See *decision problem; effectiveness.*

alternation. See *disjunction, exclusive.*

alternative denial. See *Sheffer stroke function.*

ambiguity. Capability of being understood in two or more ways. The term is strictly applied only in cases where the possibility of different interpretation is due not to the expression itself but to some feature of the particular use of the expression; when this possibility is due to the expression itself the expression is called *equivocal.* Many authors, however, do not make this distinction.

amphiboly. An equivocation that arises not out of an equivocation in a word or phrase but because the grammatical structure of the sentence or clause leaves the place of the phrase in the whole not entirely determinate. An example is "The shooting of the hunters was finished quickly."

ampliation. In medieval logic, the extension of a common term from a narrow supposition to a wider one.

analogy. A comparison between two or more objects that indicates one or more respects in which they are similar. An *argument from analogy* is an inference from some points of resemblance between two or more objects to other such points. The method of *refutation by logical analogy* is a method for showing that an argument is fallacious by giving an example of another argument of the same form whose invalidity is immediately apparent.

analysis, mathematical. The theory of real and complex numbers and their functions.

analytic. Used of a proposition whose denial is self-contradictory. Such a proposition is true either by virtue of its logical form alone (in which case it is called a *logical truth,* or *logically necessary*) or by virtue of both its logical form and the meaning of its constituent terms. An instance of a logical truth is "It is raining or it is not raining"; an example of an analytic truth that is not a logical truth is "All bachelors are unmarried." Analytic propositions cannot be false and are therefore said to be *necessary truths.* Whether there are necessary truths that are not also analytic truths is a matter of much dispute. See entry "Analytic and Synthetic Statements."

ancestral relation. For a given relation *R,* the relation *R** that exists between two objects *x* and *y* if and only if *y* has every *R*-hereditary property that *x* has. A property is said to be *R-hereditary* when, if it is correctly predicated of *b* and if *aRb,* then it is also correctly predicated of *a.* For example, let *R* be the property "is the successor of." Then "is a natural number" (where this property also applies to 0) is *R*-hereditary, since if *b* is a natural number and *a* is the successor of *b,* then *a* is also a natural number. Given this fact, we can define the property "is a natural number" as the property of all objects that bear the ancestral relation to 0 for the relation "is the succes-

sor of"—that is, as the property of all objects that have every "is the successor of"-hereditary property that 0 has. One of these properties is "is a natural number," and therefore only the natural numbers can meet this definition.

It should be noted that the above definition is an example of an *impredicative definition,* since "is a natural number" is defined in terms of the class of "is the successor of"-hereditary properties, a class of which it is a member.

antecedent. The part of a hypothetical proposition that precedes the implication sign.

antilogism. A triad of propositions such that the joint truth of any two of the propositions implies the falsity of the third. Christine Ladd-Franklin's principle of the syllogism states that a valid syllogism is one whose premises taken with the contradictory of the conclusion constitute an antilogism. Thus, the syllogism whose premises are "All men are mortal" and "Socrates is a man" and whose conclusion is "Socrates is mortal" is a valid syllogism, for the joint assertion of any two of the three propositions that constitute the premises and the contradictory of the conclusion implies the falsity of the third proposition.

antinomy. See *paradox.*

apodictic (apodeictic) proposition. See *modality.*

appellation. In medieval logic a term is said to have appellation if it is applicable to some existing thing. Thus, "the present queen of England" has appellation, but "the present queen of the United States" does not.

A-proposition. In traditional logic, a universal affirmative categorical proposition. An example is "All men are mortal."

Archimedean property. The property of a system of numbers whereby for any two numbers *a* and *b,* if *a* is less than *b,* then there is a number *c* such that *a* multiplied by *c* is greater than *b.*

argument of a function. A member of the domain of a given function.

arithmetical predicate. A predicate that can be explicitly expressed in terms of the truth-functional connectives of propositional calculus, the universal and existential quantifiers, constant and variable natural numbers, and the addition and multiplication functions.

arithmetization of mathematics (arithmetization of analysis). The definition, which was developed by Karl Weierstrass, Richard Dedekind, and Georg Cantor, of the nonnatural numbers as certain objects construed out of the natural numbers and set-theoretic objects and the corresponding reduction of the properties of the former to the properties of the latter.

arithmetization of syntax. The process of correlating the objects of a formal system with some or all of the natural numbers and then studying the relations and properties of the correlated numbers so as to gain information about the syntax of the formal system. This was done systematically by Kurt Gödel in the researches that led to his incompleteness theorems. See entry "Gödel's Theorem."

ars combinatoria. A technique of deriving complex concepts by the combination of relatively few simple ones, which are taken as primitive. This technique was proposed by Gottfried Wilhelm Leibniz as a valuable aid for the study of all subjects. He proposed the development of a universal language (*characteristica universalis*) containing a few primitive symbols in terms of which all other symbols would be defined. A universal mathematics (*mathesis universalis*)—that is, a universal system of reasoning—would then be added, and all subjects could be studied in this language. Leibniz program is often viewed as an early forerunner of the formalization of various disciplines.

assertion sign. The sign ⊢, introduced by Gottlob Frege to indicate in the object language that a proposition is being judged as true and is not merely being named. Some authors now use this sign in the metalanguage to express that the formula to which it is prefixed is a theorem in the object language.

assertoric proposition. See *modality.*

associativity. The property of a relation R that consists in the identity of "$aR(bRc)$" and "$(aRb)Rc$," where a, b, and c are any elements of the field of R. Addition has this property, since "$a + (b + c)$" is the same as "$(a + b) + c$."

attribute. Although it is now often used synonymously with "property," this term was traditionally confined to the essential characteristics of a being.

Aussonderungsaxiom. An axiom in set theory, first introduced by Ernst Zermelo, which states that for any set a and any predicate P, there exists a set containing all and only those members of a that satisfy the predicate P.

axiom. A basic proposition in a formal system that is asserted without proof and from which, together with the other such propositions, all other theorems are derived according to the rules of inference of the system. See *postulate.*

axiomatic method. The method of studying a subject by beginning with a list of undefined terms and a list of axioms and then deriving the truths of the subject from these postulates by the methods of formal logic.

axiom schema. A representation of an infinite number of axioms by means of an expression containing syntactical variables and having well-formed formulas as values. Every value of the expression is to be taken as an axiom.

axiom schema of separation. See *Aussonderungsaxiom.*

Barbara. See *mnemonic terms.*

Baroco. See *mnemonic terms.*

biconditional. A binary propositional connective (↔, ≡), usually read "if and only if" (often abbreviated "iff"), whose truth table is such that "A if and only if B" is true when A and B are either both true or both false and is false when one is true and the other false. "A if and only if B" is equivalent to "if A then B, and if B then A."

binary connective. See *connective.*

Bocardo. See *mnemonic terms.*

Boolean algebra. The first algebra of logic. It was invented by George Boole and given its definitive form by Ernst Schröder.

Boolean functions. Functions that occur in Boolean algebra. The more important ones are the class-union function, the class-intersection function, and the class-complement function.

bound occurrence of a variable. An occurrence of a variable a in a well-formed part of a formula A either of the form "for all a, B" or of the form "there is an a such that B."

bound of a set. For a given relation R, a *lower* bound (or first element) of a set a is any member of a that bears the relation R to all members of a; an upper bound of a is any member of a to which all members of a bear the relation R. A *greatest lower bound* of a set a (or *infimum* of a) is a lower bound of a to which all lower bounds of a bear the relation R; a *least upper bound* of a (or *supremum* of a) is an upper bound of a that bears the relation R to all upper bounds of a.

bound variable. A bound variable of a formula A is a variable that has a bound occurrence in A.

Bramantip. See *mnemonic terms.*

Burali-Forti's paradox. See *paradox.*

calculus. Any logistic system. The two most important types of logical calculi are *propositional* (or sentential) calculi and *functional* (or predicate) calculi. A propositional calculus is a system containing propositional variables and connectives (some also contain propositional constants) but not individual or functional variables or constants. In the *extended* propositional calculus, quantifiers whose operator variables are propositional variables are added. Among the *partial* propositional calculi, in which not all the theorems of the standard propositional calculus are obtainable, the most important are David Hilbert's *positive* propositional calculus (this contains all those parts of the standard propositional calculus that are independent of negation) and the *intuitionistic* propositional calculus (in this system axioms about negation acceptable from the intuitionistic point of view are added to the positive propositional calculus). A functional calculus is a system containing, in addition to the symbols of propositional calculus, individual and functional variables and/or constants, as well as quantifiers that take some of these variables and constants as their operator variables. In a *first-order* functional calculus (or *first-order logic*) the quantifiers have as their operator variables only individual variables, and the functions have as their arguments only individual variables and/or constants. In a *second-order* functional calculus (or second-order logic) the operator variables of the quantifiers can be functional variables. After that, each odd order adds functional variables and/or constants some of whose arguments are of the type introduced two orders below, and each even order allows the use of the variables introduced one order below as operator variables for the quantifiers. When there are no individual or functional constants present the functional calculus is called *pure*; when either is present it is called applied.

Camenes. See *mnemonic terms.*

Camestres. See *mnemonic terms.*

Cantor's paradox. See *paradox.*

Cantor's theorem. The theorem stating that for any given set a, the power set of a has a greater cardinality than a has.

cardinality (power). For a given set, the cardinal number associated with it.

cardinal number. An object a that is associated with all and only the members of a set of equipollent sets. Various authors disagree on what this object is. The *Frege-Russell definition* of cardinal number is simply the identification of a with the set of equipollent sets.

Cartesian product. For a given set a, the set whose members are all and only the sets that contain one member from each member of a.

categorematic. In traditional logic, used of a word that can be a term in a categorical proposition. In contemporary logic, used of any symbol that has independent meaning. An example of a categorematic word is "men." Cf. *syncategorematic.*

categorical proposition. See *proposition.*

category. A general or fundamental class of objects or concepts about whose members assertions can significantly be made which differ from those that can significantly be made about nonmembers of this class. The two most famous lists of categories are those of Aristotle and Immanuel Kant. Aristotle's list comprises substance, quantity, quality, relation, activity, passivity, place, time, situation, and state. Kant's comprises unity, plurality, and universality (categories of quantity); reality, negation, and limitation (categories of quality); substantiality, causality, and reciprocity (categories of relation); and possibility, actuality, and necessity (categories of modality).

Celarent. See *mnemonic terms.*

Cesare. See *mnemonic terms.*

choice, axiom of (multiplicative axiom). An axiom in set theory stating that if a is a disjoint set which does not have the null set as one of its members, then the Cartesian product of a is different from the null set. It can be proved that this axiom is equivalent to the well-ordering theorem.

choice function. A function R whose domain includes (or, according to some authors, is identified with the set of) all the nonempty subsets of a given set a and whose value is a member of any such subset.

Church's theorem. The theorem, stated and proved by Alonzo Church, that there is no decision procedure for determining whether or not an arbitrary well-formed formula of the first-order functional calculus is a theorem of that system.

Church's thesis. The thesis that every effectively calculable function (effectively decidable predicate) is general recursive.

circular reasoning. See *fallacy.*

class. (1) An aggregate. (2) In Gödel–von Neumann–Bernays set theory, where a distinction is made between sets and classes, a class is an object that can contain members but cannot be a member of any object. See *set.*

classification. Two of the issues of concern to traditional logicians were the nature of the process of grouping individuals into classes of individuals (*species*), these classes into further classes, and so on (the process of classification), and the nature of the reverse process (the process of *division*)—breaking a class down into its subclasses, these into their subclasses, and so on, until the simplest classes are broken down into the individuals that are their members.

In the process of classification one begins with a group of individuals and arranges them into classes, called *infimae species,* none of which can be broken down into species but only into individuals. One then groups the *infimae species* into other classes, of which the *infimae species* are subclasses. (For any species the class of which it is a subclass is called the *proximum genus.*) The grouping continues until one reaches the class of which all the original individuals are members. This is the *summum genus,* and when one reaches it the process of classification is finished. (All the classes between the *infimae species* and the *summum genus* are called the *subaltern genera.*)

In the process of division one begins with the *summum genus* and breaks it down into its subclasses, continuing until one reaches the *infimae species.* Finally, these are broken down into the individuals that are their members.

Several rules were set up for classification and division: (1) at each step only one principle may be used for breaking down the classes or grouping them together; (2) no group may be omitted at any step; (3) no intermediate step may be omitted. When applied to division this last rule is known as the rule of *division non faciat saltum.*

A *dichotomy* is a form of division (or of classification) in which at each stage the genus is divided into species according to whether or not the objects possess a certain set of differentiae. The two species formed (*proxima genera*) are therefore mutually exclusive and jointly exhaustive.

closed sentence (closed schema). A sentence (or schema) that has no free variables.

closed with respect to (closed under) a relation. A set is closed under a relation R if and only if for all a, if aRb and if a is a member of the set, then b is a member of the set.

closure of a formula. A formula formed by placing before an original formula A quantifiers binding all variables that occur freely in A. A *universal* closure is the formula formed when only universal quantifiers are used, and an *existential* closure is the formula formed when only existential quantifiers are used.

collective term. In traditional logic, a term that denotes a collection of objects regarded as a unity. An example is "the Rockies."

combinatory logic. A branch of mathematical logic where variables are entirely eliminated, their place being taken by certain types of functions that are unique to this branch of logic.

commutativity. The property of a relation R that consists in the equivalence of aRb and bRa, where a and b are any elements of the field of R.

comparability, law of (law of trichotomy). The principle in set theory that the cardinality of two sets is always comparable; that is, for any two sets a and b, a is greater than b or equal to b or less than b.

complement of a set (negate of a set). The set of all and only those objects that are not members of a given set a.

completeness. The word *completeness* is used in varying senses. In the strongest sense (E. L. Post) a logistic system is said to be complete if and only if for any well-formed formula A, either A is a theorem of the system or the system would become inconsistent upon the addition of A as an axiom (without any other changes); in this sense propositional calculus, but not pure first-order functional calculus, is complete. In a second, weaker sense (Kurt Gödel) a logistic system is said to be complete if and only if all valid well-formed formulas are theorems of the system; in this sense both propositional calculus and pure first-order functional calculus are also complete. In a third, and still weaker, sense of completeness (Leon Henkin) a logistic system is said to be complete if and only if all secondarily valid well-formed formulas are theorems of the system; in this sense the pure second-order functional calculus and functional calculi of higher order are complete.

complete set. A set all of whose members are subsets of it.

composition, fallacy of. See *fallacy.*

comprehension, axiom of. See *abstraction, axiom of.*

computable function. See *Turing-computable.*

conclusion. That which is inferred from the premises of a given argument.

concrete term. In traditional logic, a term that is the name of an individual or individuals. An example of such a term is "Socrates."

condition. A *necessary condition* is a circumstance in whose absence a given event could not occur or a given thing could not exist. A *sufficient condition* is a circumstance such that whenever it exists a given event occurs or a given thing exists. A *necessary and sufficient condition* for the occurrence of a given event or the existence of a given thing is therefore a circumstance in whose absence the event could not occur or the thing could not exist and which is also such that whenever it exists the event occurs or the thing exists.

This terminology is sometimes extended to the formal relations that exist between propositions. Thus, the truth of a proposition *A* is said to be a necessary condition for the truth of another proposition *B* if *B* implies *A,* and the truth of *A* is said to be a sufficient condition for the truth of *B* if *A* implies *B.*

conditional. See *implication.*

conditional proof. A proof that begins by making certain assumptions, $A_1, A_2, \cdots, A_n$, deducing *B* from them, and then asserting on the basis of this the truth of the hypothetical proposition "if A_1, then if A_2, then if …, then if A_n, then *B.*" The *rule of conditionalization* is the rule that allows one to make this last step on the basis of the preceding ones.

conjunction. A binary propositional connective (&, .), usually read "and," whose truth table is such that "*A* and *B*" is false when *A* or *B* or both are false and is true when both are true.

connective. A symbol that is used with one or more constants or forms to produce a new constant or form. When the constants or forms are propositional ones the connective is known as a *propositional connective* (or *sentential connective*). The most common propositional connectives are negation, conjunction, disjunction, implication, and biconditional. They are classified as *singulary, binary,* etc., according to the number of propositional constants or forms with which they combine.

connotation. See *meaning, Frege's theory of.*

consequence. Any proposition that can be deduced from a given set of propositions. Thus, given the set of propositions {*A,* if *A* then *B*}, the proposition *B* is a consequence of the set, since it can be deduced from the members of the set by one application of *modus ponens.*

consequent. The part of a hypothetical proposition that follows the implication sign or the "then."

consequentia. The name given by medieval logicians to a true hypothetical proposition. *Formal* consequentiae (those which hold for all substitutions of the categore-matic terms) were distinguished from *material* consequentiae (those holding only for particular categorematic terms).

consistency. A set of propositions has consistency (or is consistent) when no contradiction can be derived from the joint assertion of the propositions in the set. A logistic system has consistency when no contradiction can be derived in it. Two syntactical definitions of the consistency of a logistic system are Alfred Tarski's, that a system is consistent if not every well-formed formula is a theorem, and E. L. Post's, that a system is consistent if no well-formed formula consisting of only a propositional variable is a theorem. There is, in addition, a semantical definition of consistency, according to which a set of propositions (or a logistic system) is consistent if there is a model for that set of propositions (or for the set of all the theorems of the system). It must not be assumed that any of these definitions are equivalent; in any case where it is claimed that they are, a proof is required.

constant. A symbol that, under the principal interpretation, is a name for something definite, be it an individual, a property, a relation, etc.

constructive existence proof. A proof of the existence of a mathematical object having a property *P* that gives an example of such an object or at least a method by which one could find such an example.

contingent. Logically possible. See *logical possibility.*

continuity. An ordered dense class all of whose non-empty subsets which have an upper bound have a least upper bound has continuity (or is continuous). See entry "Continuity."

continuum hypothesis. The hypothesis, proposed by Georg Cantor, that the cardinality of the power set of a set whose cardinality is aleph-null ($\aleph_0$) is aleph-one ($\aleph_1$)—that is, that there is no set whose cardinality is greater than aleph-null but less than the cardinality of the power set of a set whose cardinality is aleph-null. The *generalized continuum hypothesis* is the hypothesis that for the cardinality of any infinite set, the next highest cardinality is the cardinality of its power set.

contradiction. The joint assertion of a proposition and its denial.

contradiction, law of. See *laws of thought.*

contradictory. Two propositions are contradictory if and only if their joint assertion would be a contradiction. "All men are mortal" and "Some men are not mortal," for example, are contradictory propositions. Two terms are contradictory when they jointly exhaust a universe of discourse and are mutually exclusive. In the domain of natural numbers other than 0, for example, "odd" and "even" are contradictory terms. See *contrary*.

contraposition. In traditional logic, a type of immediate inference in which from a given proposition another proposition is inferred that has as its subject the contradictory of the original predicate. (It should be noted that a change of quality is involved in some cases.) *Partial* contraposition results in a new proposition that is the same as the subject of the original proposition; *full* contraposition results in a predicate of the new proposition that is the contradictory of the subject of the original proposition. The process of contraposition (whether partial or full) yields an equivalent proposition only when the original proposition is an A- or O-proposition; when it is an E-proposition traditional logicians allowed for contraposition *per accidens* (or by limitation)—that is, contraposition plus a change in the quantity of the proposition from universal to particular—claiming that the proposition formed is equivalent to the original proposition. The process of contraposition yields no equivalent proposition when the original proposition is an I-proposition. See entry "Logic, Traditional."

contrary. Applied to two propositions that cannot both be true but can both be false. "All men are mortal" and "No men are mortal," for example, are contrary propositions. Also applied to two terms that are mutually exclusive, but need not be jointly exhaustive, in a universe of discourse. In the domain of natural numbers, for instance, "less than 7" and "more than 19" are contrary terms. See *contradictory*.

contrary-to-fact (counterfactual) conditional. A conditional proposition whose antecedent is known to be false.

converse domain of a relation (range of a relation). For any relation R, the set of all objects a such that there exists an object b such that bRa.

converse of a relation (inverse of a relation). For any relation R, the relation R* such that aR*b if and only if bRa.

conversion. In traditional logic, a type of immediate inference in which from a given proposition another proposition is inferred that has as its subject the predicate of the original proposition and as its predicate the subject of the original proposition (the quality of the proposition being retained). The process of conversion yields an equivalent proposition only when the original proposition is an E- or I-proposition; when it is an A-proposition traditional logicians allowed for conversion *per accidens*

(or by limitation)—that is, conversion plus a change in the quantity of the proposition from universal to particular. Thus, the E-proposition "No men are immortal" yields "No immortals are men," but the A-proposition "All men are mortal" can be converted only by limitation, yielding "Some mortals are men." The process of conversion yields no equivalent proposition if the original proposition is an O-proposition. See entry "Logic, Traditional."

copula. In traditional logic, the term that connects the subject and predicate in a categorical proposition. It is always a form of the verb "to be."

corollary. A proposition that follows so obviously from a theorem that it requires little or no demonstration.

counterfactual conditional. See *contrary-to-fact conditional.*

course-of-values induction. An argument from mathematical induction such that in the induction step one proves that "if the property P holds for all numbers before a, it holds for a as well," where a is any number.

Darapti. See *mnemonic terms.*

Darii. See *mnemonic terms.*

Datisi. See *mnemonic terms.*

decision problem. The problem of finding an algorithm (a *decision procedure*) that enables one to arrive, in a finite number of steps, at an answer to any question belonging to a given class of questions. For a logistic system in particular, this is the problem of finding a decision procedure for determining, for any arbitrary well-formed formula of the system, whether or not it is a theorem of the system.

A positive solution to a decision problem consists of a proof that a decision procedure exists. A negative solution to a decision problem consists of a proof that no such procedure is possible. An example of a positive solution is the proof that the truth tables provide a decision procedure for the propositional calculus; an example of a negative proof is Church's theorem.

decision procedure. See *decision problem.*

Dedekind finite. See *finite set.*

Dedekind infinite. See *finite set.*

deducible. A set of propositions is said to be deducible from another set of propositions if and only if there is a valid deductive inference which has the latter set as its premises and the former set as its conclusion.

deduction. A form of inference such that in a valid deductive argument the joint assertion of the premises and the denial of the conclusion is a contradiction.

deduction theorem. For a given logistic system, the metatheorem that states that if there is a proof in the system of A_{n+1} from the assumptions $A_1, A_2, \cdots, A_n$, then there is also a proof in the system of the proposition "if A_n, then A_{n+1}" from the assumptions $A_1, \cdots, A_{n-1}$.

definiendum. That which is defined in a definition.

definiens. That which, in a definition, defines the definiendum.

definite descriptions, theory of. A definite description is a description which, by virtue of the meanings of the words in it, can apply to only one object. A standard example of a definite description is "the author of *Waverley*." The theory of definite descriptions, introduced by Bertrand Russell, aims at eliminating definite descriptions. Unlike most other eliminative theories, Russell's does not attempt to offer a way of explicitly defining definite descriptions. Instead, it shows how in any given context the description together with the context can be eliminated in such a way that the resulting linguistic expression is equivalent to the original one. It is for this reason that Russell's theory is said to offer a way of contextually defining definite descriptions.

If we symbolize the definite description as "$(x)P$" ("the unique x such that P," where P is any well-formed expression), Russell's theory can be stated as follows (unless otherwise indicated, it will be supposed that the scope of the occurrence of a definite description is the smallest well-formed part of the formula that contains that occurrence of the definite description): Let us symbolize the scope of the definite description as M and the whole formula as A. M is replaced by the expression "$(\exists y)(z)[(Pz \equiv z = y). M']$," where y and z are the first two variables not occurring in A and M' is the result of substituting y for every occurrence of "$(\imath x)P$" in M. The resulting formula, A', is equivalent to A but lacks the definite description that we set out to eliminate.

The motivation for this theory is to be found in certain difficulties that arose for Russell's theory of meaning, the theory that the meaning of a term is its reference. It has been suggested, primarily by W. V. Quine, that since similar difficulties can arise for names in general, this theory should be extended to all names. Russell, however, thought that there was a class of names, *logically proper names*, for which these difficulties could not arise; he therefore favored retaining names of this class. See entry "Proper Names and Descriptions."

definition. The description or explanation of the meaning of a word or phrase. Various types of definitions have been distinguished by logicians. To begin with, there is the distinction between a *lexical* definition (a report of a meaning the word already has) and a *stipulative* definition (a proposal to assign a meaning to a word). One must also distinguish, with traditional logicians, the following techniques for defining: (1) *dictionary* definition, giving a word or phrase that is synonymous with the definiendum; (2) *ostensive* definition, giving examples of objects to which the word or phrase is properly applied; and (3) definition *per genus et differentiam*, giving the genus of the objects to which a word or phrase is properly applied and the differentiae that distinguish these objects from the other members of the genus. See *predicables.*

Some new types of definition that have been discussed by contemporary logicians include (4) definition *by abstraction*, defining a class term by specifying the properties that an object must have in order to be a member of the class, and (5) *recursive (inductive)* definition, defining a number-theoretic function or predicate term by giving the value or values of the function or predicate when 0 is the argument and then giving the value or values when the successor of any number a is the argument in terms of a and the value when a is the argument (cf. *recursive function*). Finally, one must distinguish (6) *contextual* definitions, which give meaning to the definiendum only in particular contexts, not in isolation.

definition, Aristotelian theory of. See *predicables.*

demonstration (derivation). A deductive proof offered for a given set of propositions.

De Morgan's laws. The theorems of propositional calculus that assert the material equivalence of "not (A or B)" with "not-A and not-B" and "not (A and B)" with "not-A or not-B." De Morgan, in his book *Formal Logic*, did not actually state these laws; he gave, instead, the corresponding laws for the logic of classes. It should be noted that some of the medieval logicians stated these theorems for the logic of propositions.

denotation. See *meaning, Frege's theory of.*

dense. Used of an ordered set such that between any two elements of the set there is another element of the set.

denumerable set. A set whose cardinality is aleph-null ($\aleph_0$). Some authors extend "denumerable" so as to make it synonymous with "enumerable."

derivable. See *deducible.*

derivation. See *demonstration.*

derived rule of inference. A metalinguistic theorem asserting that under certain conditions there is a proof in the object language for a certain type of well-formed formula. The point of such theorems is that they enable us to state that certain well-formed formulas are theorems of the object language without having to find a proof in the object language for these formulas.

descending induction. An argument that shows that a certain property holds for no number by demonstrating that if it held for any number, it must hold for a lesser number.

diagonal proof. The proof, given by Georg Cantor, that there are infinite sets that cannot be enumerated.

dichotomy. See *classification.*

dictum de omni et nullo. The principle of syllogistic reasoning that asserts that whatever is distributively predicated (whether affirmatively or negatively) of any class must be predicated of anything belonging to that class.

difference of sets. For any two sets *a* and *b,* the set of all and only those objects that are members of *a* but not of *b.*

differentia. See *predicables.*

dilemma. An argument whose major premise is the conjunctive assertion of two hypothetical propositions and whose minor premise is a disjunctive proposition. If the minor premise alternatively affirms the antecedents of the major premise, the dilemma is said to be *constructive*; if the minor premise alternatively denies the consequents of the major premise, the dilemma is said to be *destructive.* Constructive dilemmas are divided into *simple constructive* dilemmas (the antecedents of the major premise are different and the consequents are the same) and *complex constructive* dilemmas (both the antecedents and the consequents of the major premise are different). Destructive dilemmas are divided into *simple destructive* dilemmas (the consequents of the major premise are different and the antecedents are the same) and *complex destructive* dilemmas (both the consequents and the antecedents of the major premise are different).

Dimaris. See *mnemonic terms.*

Disamis. See *mnemonic terms.*

discreteness. The property possessed by all ordered sets that lack the property of continuity.

disjoint sets. Sets that have no members in common.

disjunction, exclusive (alternation). A binary propositional connective, one possible interpretation of "or," whose truth table is such that "*A* or *B*" is true if and only if one of the two propositions is true and the other false.

disjunction, inclusive. A binary propositional connective ($\vee$), one possible interpretation of "or," whose truth table is such that "*A* or *B*" is true in all cases except where both *A* and *B* are false.

distributed term. In a categorical proposition the occurrence of a term is distributed if and only if the term as used in that occurrence covers all the members of the class that it denotes. In a universal categorical proposition the subject is distributed; in a negative categorical proposition the predicate is distributed.

distributivity. The relation that exists between two relations R and R^* when "$aR(bR^*c)$" is identical with "$(aRb)R^*(aRc)$."

division. See *classification.*

division non faciat saltum. See *classification.*

domain of a relation. For any relation R, the set of all objects a such that there exists an object b such that aRb.

domain of individuals. For a given interpretation of a given logistic system, the set of objects that is the range of the individual variables.

duality. The relation that exists between two formulas that are the same except for the interchanging of the universal with the existential quantifier, the symbol for the null class with that for the universal class, sum of sets with product of sets, and conjunction with disjunction (where conjunction, disjunction, and negation are taken as primitive, all other propositional connectives being defined in terms of them). The two formulas are said to be the duals of each other. "A and B" and "A or B," for example, are duals.

dyadic relation. A two-place relation.

effectiveness. A notion is said to be effective if there exists an algorithm for determining, in a finite number of steps, whether or not the notion applies to any given object. For example, in a logistic system the notion of a proof is effective, since there is a mechanical procedure for determining, in a finite number of steps, whether or not in that system a given sequence of well-formed formulas constitutes a proof of another given well-formed formula.

element. A member of a given set.

elementary number theory. The theory of numbers insofar as it does not involve analysis.

empty set. See *null set.*

entailment. The relation that exists between two propositions one of which is deducible from the other.

enthymeme. A syllogism in which one of the premises or the conclusion is not explicitly stated. An example of an enthymeme is the inference of "Socrates is mortal" from "All men are mortal," the missing premise being "Socrates is a man."

enumerable set. A set that either is finite or has a cardinality of aleph-null ($\aleph_0$). Cf. *denumerable set.*

epagoge. In traditional logic, the process of establishing a general proposition by induction.

epicheirema. A syllogism in which one or more of the premises is stated as the conclusion of an enthymematic prosyllogism. See *polysyllogism.*

episyllogism. See *polysyllogism.*

E-proposition. In traditional logic, a universal negative categorical proposition. An example is "No men are mortal."

epsilon. In set theory, the name of the symbol (ϵ) for set-membership.

equality. A relation that exists between two or more sets, equated by some authors with *identity* and by others with *equivalence relation.*

equipollent. Used of sets between which there exists a one-to-one correspondence.

equivalence relation. A relation that is reflexive, symmetric, and transitive (see *relation*). Identity is a standard example of an equivalence relation.

equivalent. Used of two propositions that are so related that one is true if and only if the other is true. Some authors also use this term, as applied to sets, synonymously with "equipollent."

equivocation. See *fallacy.*

eristic. The art of fallacious but persuasive reasoning.

essence. See *predicables.*

Euler's diagrams. The representations, generally attributed to Leonhard Euler, of relations among classes by relations among circles. See entry "Logic Diagrams."

excluded middle, law of. See *laws of thought.*

existential generalization, rule of. The rule of inference that permits one to infer from a statement of the form "Property P holds for an object a" a statement of the form "There exists an object such that property P holds for it."

existential import. The commitment to the existence of certain objects that is entailed by a given proposition.

existential instantiation, rule of. The rule of inference that permits one to infer from a statement of the

form "There exists an object such that property P holds for it" a statement of the form "Property P holds for an object a." Because this inference is not generally valid, restrictions have to be placed on its use.

existential quantifier. The symbol (E) or ($\exists$), read "there exists." It is used in combination with a variable and placed before a well-formed formula, as in "($\exists a$) _____" ("There exists an object a such that _____").

extension. Although often used synonymously with "denotation," this term is sometimes used to refer to the set of species that are contained within the genus denoted by a given term. In the first sense the extension of "men" is the set of all men; in the second sense it is the set of sets into which humankind can be divided.

extensional. Used of an approach to a problem which in some respect confines attention to truth-values of sentences rather than to their meanings. Thus, a logic in which, for purposes of deductive relations, truth-values may be substituted for sentences is an extensional logic. Cf. *intensional.*

extensionality, axiom of. An axiom in set theory stating that for any two sets a and b, if for all c, c is a member of a if and only if c is a member of b, then a is identical with b.

fallacy. An argument that seems to be valid but really is not. There are many possible types of fallacy; traditional logicians have discussed the following ones: (1) *accentus,* a fallacy of ambiguity, where the ambiguity arises from the emphasis (accent) placed on a word or phrase; (2) *affirmation of the consequent,* an argument from the truth of a hypothetical statement and the truth of the consequent to the truth of the antecedent; (3) *ambiguity,* an argument in the course of which at least one term is used in different senses; (4) *amphiboly,* a fallacy of ambiguity where the ambiguity involved is of an amphibolous nature; (5) *argumentum ad baculum,* an argument that resorts to the threat of force to cause the acceptance of the conclusion; (6) *argumentum ad hominem,* an argument that attempts to disprove the truth of what is asserted by attacking the asserter or attempts to prove the truth of what is asserted by appealing to the opponent's special circumstances; (7) *argumentum ad ignorantiam,* an argument that a proposition is true because it has not been shown to be false, or vice versa; (8) *argumentum ad misericordiam,* an argument that appeals to pity for the sake of getting a conclusion accepted; (9) *argumentum ad populum,* an argument that appeals to the beliefs of the multitude; (10) *argumentum ad verecundiam,* an argument in which an authority is appealed to on matters outside his field of authority; (11) *begging the question (circular reasoning)*, an argument that assumes as part of the premises the conclusion that is supposed to be proved; (12) *composition*, an argument in which one assumes that a whole has a property solely because its various parts have that property; (13) *denial of the antecedent*, an argument in which one infers the falsity of the consequent from the truth of a hypothetical proposition and the falsity of its antecedent; (14) *division*, an argument in which one assumes that various parts have a property solely because the whole has that property; (15) *equivocation*, an argument in which an equivocal expression is used in one sense in one premise and in a different sense in another premise or in the conclusion; (16) *ignoratio elenchi*, an argument that is supposed to prove one proposition but succeeds only in proving a different one; (17) *illicit process*, a syllogistic argument in which a term is distributed in the conclusion but not in the premises; (18) *many questions*, a demand for a simple answer to a complex question; (19) *non causa pro causa*, an argument to reject a proposition because of the falsity of some other proposition that seems to be a consequence of the first but really is not; (20) *non sequitur*, an argument in which the conclusion is not a necessary consequence of the premises; (21) *petitio principii*, see (11) *begging the question*; (22) *post hoc, ergo propter hoc*, argument from a premise of the form "*A* preceded *B*" to a conclusion of the form "*A* caused *B*"; (23) *quaternio terminorum*, an argument of the syllogistic form in which there occur four or more terms; (24) *secundum quid*, an argument in which a proposition is used as a premise without attention given to some obvious condition that would affect the proposition's application; (25) *undistributed middle*, a syllogistic argument in which the middle term is not distributed in at least one of the premises. See entry "Fallacies."

Felapton. See *mnemonic terms.*

Ferio. See *mnemonic terms.*

Ferison. See *mnemonic terms.*

Fesapo. See *mnemonic terms.*

Festino. See *mnemonic terms.*

field of a relation. The union of the domain and the converse domain of a given relation.

figure. A way of classifying categorical propositions. According to most traditional logicians, since figure depends on the position of the middle term in the premises, there are four possible figures. In the first figure the middle term is the subject of the major premise and the predicate of the minor premise. In the second figure the middle term is the predicate of both premises and in the third figure the subject of both premises. In the fourth figure the middle term is the predicate of the major premise and the subject of the minor premise. Aristotle allowed only three figures and treated as being indirectly in the first figure those syllogisms that later logicians placed in the fourth. See entry "Logic, Traditional."

finitary method. The type of method to which David Hilbert and some of his followers restricted themselves in their metamathematical research. The clearest statement of the restrictions was made by Jacques Herbrand, who insisted that the following conditions be met: (1) One must deal only with a finite and determined number of objects and functions. (2) These are to be so defined that there is a univocal calculation of their values. (3) One should never affirm the existence of an object without indicating how to construct it. (4) One must never deal with the set of all the objects of an infinite totality. (5) That a theorem holds for all of a set of objects means that for every particular object it is possible to repeat the general argument in question, which should then be treated as only a prototype of the resulting particular arguments.

finite set (inductive set). A set that either is empty or is such that there exists a one-to-one correspondence between its members and the members of the set of all natural numbers less than a specified natural number. A set which is not finite is said to be *infinite.*

Richard Dedekind introduced a different characterization of finite and infinite sets. A *Dedekind finite* set is one that has no proper subset such that there exists a one-to-one correspondence between the elements of the set and the elements of that proper subset. A *Dedekind infinite* set (or *reflexive* set) is one that is not Dedekind finite. It can be shown that Dedekind's characterization is equivalent to the previous one; the proof, however, involves the axiom of choice.

first element of a set. See *bound of a set.*

first-order logic. First-order functional calculus. See *calculus.*

formalism. The doctrine, advanced as a program by David Hilbert and his followers, that the only foundations necessary for mathematics are its formalization and a proof by finitary methods that the system thus produced is consistent. See entry "Mathematics, Foundations of."

formalization. The construction of a logistic system whose intended interpretation is such that under it the truths of a given body of knowledge are the interpreted theorems of the system.

formalized language. A logistic system with an interpretation.

formally imply. A proposition *A* is said to formally imply a proposition *B* in a given logistic system if there is, in that system, a valid proof of *B* from *A* taken as a hypothesis.

formal system. See *logistic system.*

formation rules. For a given logistic system, the rules that determine which combinations of symbols are well-formed formulas and which are not.

formula. For a given logistic system, any sequence of primitive symbols.

foundation, axiom of (Axiom der fundierung, axiom of regularity). An axiom in set theory stating that every nonempty set *a* contains a member *b* which has no member in common with *a*.

free occurrence of a variable. For a given variable *a* that occurs in a given well-formed formula *A,* an occurrence of *a* in no well-formed part of *A* which is of the form "For all *a, B*" or of the form "There exists an *a, B*."

free variable. A free variable of a formula *A* is a variable in *A* that has no bound occurrence in *A.*

Fresison. See *mnemonic terms.*

function. A many-one correspondence.

functional calculus. See *calculus.*

future contingents, problem of. The problem, first discussed by Aristotle, of whether any contingent statement about the future has a truth-value prior to the time it refers to.

Galenian figure. The fourth syllogistic figure, supposedly introduced by Galen.

generalization, rule of. The rule of inference that allows one to infer from every proposition another proposition that is the same as the original one except that it is preceded by a universal quantifier binding any variable.

general term. A term that is predicable, in the same sense, of more than one individual.

Gentzen's consistency proof. The proof, first given by Gerhard Gentzen in 1936, of the consistency of classical pure number theory with the unrestricted-induction postulate. The proof employs transfinite induction up to the ordinal ϵ_0.

Gentzen system. A system of logic characterized by the introduction into the object language of a new connective (symbolized by →) that has properties analogous to the ordinary metalinguistic idea of "provable in the system." The rules of inference of such a system apply to *Sequenzen*—that is, to formulas of the form "$A_1, A_2, \cdots, A_n \to B_1, B_2, \cdots, B_m$," where *m* and *n* are equal to or greater than 0, and $A_1, A_2, \cdots, A_n, B_1, B_2, \cdots, B_m$ are formulas of ordinary logical systems.

genus. See *predicables.*

Gödel-numbering. The assignment of a natural number to each entity of a formal system. See *arithmetization of syntax.*

Gödel's completeness theorem. The theorem, first introduced by Kurt Gödel in 1930, that every valid well-formed formula of pure first-order functional calculus is a theorem of that system.

Gödel's incompleteness theorems. Two theorems that were first proved by Kurt Gödel in 1931. One states that any ω-consistent system adequate for elementary number theory is such that there is a valid well-formed formula of the system not provable in the system. J. B. Rosser, in 1936, extended this result to any consistent system. The second theorem states that any consistent system adequate for elementary number theory is such that there can be no proof of the consistency of the system within the system. See entry "Gödel's Theorem."

Gödel–von Neumann–Bernays set theory. The form of axiomatic set theory that avoids the paradoxes of set theory by distinguishing between sets (collections that can also be elements of other collections) and classes (collections that cannot be elements of other collections) and ensuring that all the objects leading to paradoxes (for example, the universal class) are classes and not sets.

Henkin's completeness theorem. The theorem, proved by Leon Henkin in 1947, that every secondarily valid well-formed formula of pure second-order functional calculus is a theorem of that system.

hereditary property. See *ancestral relation.*

Hilbert program. See *formalism.*

ideal mathematics. For David Hilbert, the nonfinitary part of mathematics, which, although necessary, was suspect and therefore required a consistency proof. See *real mathematics.*

idempotency. A binary operation is idempotent if and only if that operation, when performed on any element with itself, results in just that element.

identically false. Used of a well-formed formula of propositional calculus whose truth-value is falsehood for all possible values of its constituent well-formed formulas.

identically true. Used of a well-formed formula of propositional calculus whose truth-value is truth for all possible values of its constituent well-formed formulas.

identity. A relation that holds only between an object and itself.

identity, law of. See *laws of thought.*

identity of indiscernibles. Gottfried Wilhelm Leibniz's principle that two objects are identical if for every class, one object belongs to the class if and only if the other does. This is not to be confused with what W. V. Quine has called the *indiscernibility of identicals,* the principle that if two objects are identical, they belong to the same classes.

iff. A common abbreviation for "if and only if." See *biconditional.*

ignoratio elenchi. See *fallacy.*

image. The members of the converse domain of a relation that are values of the relation when its argument is a member of a set that is part of its domain.

immediate inference. An inference of a conclusion from a single premise. Traditional logicians discussed two types: (1) *opposition of propositions,* the inference, from the truth or falsity of one proposition, of the truth or falsity of another proposition having the same subject and predicate (such inferences involve contradictory, contrary, subalternate, and subcontrary propositions), and (2) *eductions,* the inference, from one proposition, of another differing from it in subject or predicate or in both (these involve obversion, conversion, contraposition, and inversion).

imperfect figures. The second and third syllogistic figures, the valid arguments of which, according to Aristotle, are such that their validity can be known only by their reduction to valid syllogisms in the perfect first figure.

implication (conditional). A binary propositional connective (→, ⊃), usually read "if-then," of which there are two major interpretations: (1) *Material implication.* Under this interpretation, "If A then B" is true in all cases except when A is true and B false. (2) *Strict implication.* Under this interpretation, "If A then B" is true only when B is deducible from A. *Philonian* implication is the Stoic version of material implication, and *Diodorean* implication is the Stoic interpretation of "if-then" according to which "If A then B" is true if whenever (in the past, present, or future) A is true, B is also true.

implicit definition. A set of axioms implicitly define the undefined terms in them by, in effect, confining the references of these terms to the intended ones. The axioms do this by stating conditions satisfiable by only one set of objects.

The idea that a set of axioms can implicitly define the undefined terms in them is usually credited to J. D. Gergonne (1819). It was once thought that the basic terms of arithmetic could be implicitly defined by the axioms (namely, Peano's postulates) containing them; however, it is now known that this cannot be done, since Peano's postulates admit of more than one interpretation.

impredicative definition. Definition of an object in terms of a totality of which it is a member. For an example of impredicative definition, see *ancestral relation.*

inclusion. A relation that holds between two sets when all the members of one are members of the other. The relation of set-inclusion must be distinguished from that of set-membership.

inconsistent. Used of a set of propositions from which, or a logistic system in which, a contradiction can be derived.

indemonstrables. The Stoics' name for the axioms of their propositional logic.

independence. An axiom A of a given logistic system is independent (or has independence) if and only if in the system obtained by omitting A from the axioms of the given system, A is not a theorem. A rule of inference R of a given logistic system is independent if and only if in the system obtained by omitting R from the rules of inference of the given system, R is not a derived rule of inference.

indirect proof (reductio ad absurdum). An argument that proves a proposition A by showing that the denial of A, together with accepted propositions $B_1, B_2, \cdots, B_n$, leads to a contradiction. Strictly speaking, this fails to prove the truth of A, since one of the previously accepted premises may be false; the force of the argument therefore rests on using premises that are far better established than the denial of A, so that the denial of A will be rejected and A accepted.

individual (particular). (1) Anything considered as a unit. (2) In the theory of types, any member of the lowest type.

induction. Among acceptable inferences, logicians distinguish those in which the joint assertion of the premises and the denial of the conclusion is a contradiction from those in which that joint assertion is not a contradiction. The former are deductive inferences; inductive inferences are to be found among the latter.

Much has been written about the precise nature of inductive inferences, but few definite results have been obtained. It is likely that there is a wide variety of types of inductive inferences. Two quite different types are the inference from observational data to theoretical conclusions and the inference from the composition of a sample to the composition of a whole population.

induction, mathematical. An inference of the form "0 has the property P; if any natural number a has the property P, then its successor has the property P; therefore, every natural number has the property P." The first step is called the *basis,* or the *zero step,* of the induction, and the second is called the *induction step.*

inductive set. See *finite set.*

inference. Derivation of a proposition (the conclusion) from a set of other propositions (the premises). When the inference is acceptable the premises afford good reasons to assert, or render certain, the conclusion.

infima species. See *classification.*

infinite set. See *finite set.*

infinity, axiom of. An axiom in set theory that guarantees the existence of an infinite number of individuals. This axiom takes various forms, all having in common the property of being valid in at least one infinite domain of individuals while not being valid in any finite domain of individuals.

initial ordinal. An ordinal that is not equipollent with any smaller ordinal.

insolubilia. The medieval name for antinomies. The antinomies that are usually referred to by this name are variants of the Liar paradox.

intension. A term sometimes used by traditional authors as synonymous with "connotation." In contemporary logical works "intension" has come to be synonymous with "sense." See *meaning, Frege's theory of.*

intensional. (1) Used of an approach which in some respect considers the meaning as well as the truth-value of a formula. A characteristic of such systems is that some propositions in them are referentially opaque. Systems of modal logic are usually intensional systems.

(2) Used of a proposition that contains a referentially opaque part. Cf. *extensional.*

intention, first (primary). In medieval logic, signs that signify things and not other signs are said to have first intention. See entry "Logic, Traditional."

intention, second (secondary). In medieval logic, signs that signify other signs and not things are said to have second intention. See entry "Logic, Traditional."

interpretation. An interpretation of a set A of well-formed formulas consists of a nonempty set (the *domain of the interpretation*) and a function which assigns to each individual constant appearing in any of the members of A some fixed element in the domain, to each n-place predicate letter appearing in any of the members of A some n-place relation in the domain, and to each n-place function letter appearing in any member of A some function whose arguments are n-tuples of elements of the domain and whose values are also elements of the domain. The individual variables are thought of as ranging over the elements of the domain, and the connectives are given some meaning. Such an interpretation provides meaning for the members of A.

The *principal* interpretation is the intended interpretation. The *secondary* interpretations of a set of well-formed formulas are all the interpretations, other than the principal one, such that under them all the members of the set are true.

intersection of sets (product of sets). The set of all the objects that are elements of all the sets $a_1, a_2, \cdots, a_n$ (symbolized "$a_1 \cap a_2 \cap \cdots \cap a_n$").

intuitionism. The doctrine, advanced by L. E. J. Brouwer and his followers, whose key thesis is that a mathematical entity with a particular property exists only if a constructive existence proof can be given for it. As a result the actual infinite is ruled out of mathematics, and only denumerably infinite sets, viewed as potentially infinite, are allowed. Furthermore, the law of excluded middle is rejected in the sense that when infinite classes are being dealt with, a disproof of a universal statement is not automatically a proof of its denial—that is, an existential statement. See entry "Mathematics, Foundations of."

intuitive set theory. The form of set theory that is based on an unrestricted use of the axiom of abstraction. The paradoxes of set theory were generated within a system of intuitive set theory.

inverse of a relation. See *converse of a relation.*

inversion. In traditional logic, a type of immediate inference in which from a given proposition another proposition is inferred whose subject is the contradictory of the subject of the original proposition. See entry "Logic, Traditional."

iota operator. The definite description operator, ⍳. It is read: "The unique _____ such that _____."

I-proposition. In traditional logic, a particular affirmative categorical proposition. An example is "Some men are mortal."

joint denial. A binary propositional connective ($\downarrow$) whose truth table is such that "*A* joint-denial *B*" is true if and only if both *A* and *B* are false. Joint denial and the Sheffer stroke function are the only binary propositional connectives that are adequate for the construction of all truth-functional connectives.

judgment. (1) The affirming or denying of a proposition. (2) The proposition affirmed or denied.

Lambert's diagrams. The representation, introduced by J. H. Lambert, of relations among classes by relations among straight lines.

law of logic. Any general truth of logic.

laws of thought. Three laws of logic that were traditionally treated as basic and fundamental to all thought. They were (1) *the law of contradiction,* that nothing can be both *P* and not-*P*, (2) *the law of excluded middle,* that anything must be either *P* or not-*P*; and (3) *the law of identity,* that if anything is *P*, then it is *P*.

lekton. The Stoic name for the sense of a formula.

lemma. A theorem proved in the course of, and for the sake of, the proof of a different theorem.

level (order). In the ramified theory of types, a class of objects that is composed of all and only those objects such that the definition of one of them requires no reference to a totality containing other members of the class. A hierarchy of levels is built up by beginning with the class of those objects that can be defined without reference to any totality and continuing with succeeding levels, members of each of which are defined in terms of totalities of objects of the previous level.

Liar paradox. See *paradox, Epimenides' paradox.*

limit. For a given sequence of numbers, the number *a* such that for any arbitrarily small number *b* greater than 0 there exists a number *c* such that for any number *d* larger than *c* the absolute value of the difference between the *d*th member of the sequence and *a* is less than *b*.

limit number. An ordinal number that is not 0 and is such that if *a* is a member of it, then the successor of *a* is also a member of it.

limit ordinal. See *limit number.*

logic. The study of the validity of different kinds of inference. This term is often used synonymously with *deductive* logic, the branch of logic concerned with inferences whose premises cannot be true without the conclusion's also being true. The other major branch of logic, *inductive* logic, is concerned with inferences whose premises can be true even if the conclusion is false.

logical fiction. The apparent denotation of a symbol that really has no denotation. Formulas containing such symbols are translatable into formulas containing no symbol or symbols that even appear to have this denotation.

logical form. It is commonly said that logic is concerned with the form, not the matter, of a proposition or argument. The distinction between form and matter is, however, seldom made precise; it can therefore best be seen by consideration of an example:

If it is raining, people will carry umbrellas.

It is raining.
People will carry umbrellas.

Analysis of this inference shows that it is valid because it is of the form "If *A*, then *B*; *A*; therefore, *B*." The values of the variables make no difference in the validity of the argument. Formal logic is concerned with inferences, like this one, whose validity depends on their form.

As the example shows, the form of a proposition is nothing more than the result of substituting, in the proposition, free variables for the constants, whereas the *matter of a proposition* is that for which the variables are substituted. The form of an argument is the result of substituting, in all the premises and in the conclusion of the argument, free variables for constants.

In some contemporary works any formula that contains one or more free variables is called a form.

logical implication. The relation that holds between two propositions when one is deducible from the other.

logically necessary. See *analytic.*

logical possibility (possible truth). A proposition that is not self-contradictory. Some authors restrict this term to propositions that are also not logically necessary.

logical truth. See *analytic.*

logic diagram. A diagram used to represent logical relations. See entry "Logic Diagrams."

logicism. The doctrine, advanced by Gottlob Frege and Bertrand Russell, that all the concepts of mathematics can be derived from logical concepts through explicit definitions and all the theorems of mathematics can be derived from logical axioms through purely logical deduction. See entry "Mathematics, Foundations of."

logistic method. The method of studying a subject by formalizing it.

logistic system (formal system). A system whose primitive basis is explicitly stated in the metalanguage.

Löwenheim's theorem. See *Skolem-Löwenheim theorem.*

major premise. In a categorical syllogism, the premise that contains the major term.

major term. In a categorical syllogism, the term that is the predicate of the conclusion.

many-one correspondence. A relation R such that for every element a of its domain there is only one member b of its converse domain such that aRb. "Son of" is a many-one correspondence since for every member of its domain (for every son) there is only one member of the converse domain (his father) of which it is true that the member of the domain is the son of the member of the converse domain.

many-valued logic. A system of logic in which each formula has more than two possible truth-values.

map of one set into another. A one-to-one correspondence between two sets whose domain is the first set and whose converse domain is a proper subset of the second set.

map of one set onto another. A one-to-one correspondence between two sets whose domain is the first set and whose converse domain is the second set.

material implication. See *implication.*

mathematical induction. See *induction, mathematical.*

matter of a proposition. See *logical form.*

meaning, Frege's theory of. According to this theory, propounded by Gottlob Frege in 1892, the meaning of a proper name has two aspects, the *sense* and the *reference.* The reference of a proper name is that which it is a name of. Thus, the reference of "Sir Walter Scott" is Sir Walter Scott. Frege claimed that there must be, besides the reference, another aspect of the meaning of such a name. "Sir Walter Scott" and "the author of Waverley" have the same reference, but it would be most implausible to say that they have the same meaning. The aspect of meaning that distinguishes "Sir Walter Scott" from "the author of Waverley" is called the sense of the proper name.

It should be noted that this is a theory of the meaning of proper names, not common names. It is for common names that John Stuart Mill first introduced his distinction between *denotation* (the objects to which the common name is properly applied) and *connotation* (the characteristic or set of characteristics that determines to which objects the common name properly applies). Unlike Frege, Mill thought that the meaning of a proper name is simply that which it denotes.

mediate inference. An inference in which the conclusion follows from two or more premises.

membership. The relation that exists between a set and its elements. The relation of set-membership must be distinguished from the relation of set-inclusion.

mention of a term. An occurrence of a linguistic expression in quotation marks for the purpose of talking about that linguistic expression. For example, in "'Cicero' has six letters" it is not the orator himself but the word referring to him that is being discussed.

This is to be contrasted with *use of a term,* the occurrence of a linguistic expression for the purpose of talking about something other than the expression.

metalanguage. A language used to talk about an object language; a *meta-metalanguage* is a language used to talk about a metalanguage, and so forth. Derivatively, a proposition is said to be in the metalanguage if and only if it is about an expression in the object language.

metamathematics (proof theory). The study of logistic systems. Some authors restrict this term to investigations employing finitary methods.

metatheorem. A theorem in a metalanguage.

metatheory. The metamathematical investigations relating to a given logistic system.

method of construction. Bertrand Russell's name for the method of introducing new types of numbers by defining them in terms of previously introduced numbers and the usual logical and set-theoretic notation. Opposed to the method of construction is the *method of postulation,* whereby one introduces new types of numbers as primitive terms with appropriate axioms.

middle term. In a categorical syllogism, the term that occurs in both premises but not in the conclusion.

minor premise. In a categorical syllogism, the premise that contains the minor term.

minor term. In a categorical syllogism, the term that is the subject of the conclusion.

mnemonic terms. The names that the medieval logicians introduced for the valid syllogisms. One such term is "Barbara." The key for these mnemonics is as follows: The three vowels respectively indicate the three constituent propositions of the syllogism as A, E, I, or O. For first-figure syllogisms the initial consonants are arbitrarily the first four consonants; for the other figures the initial consonants indicate to which of the first-figure syllogisms the syllogism in question may be reduced. Other consonants occurring in second-, third-, and fourth-figure mnemonics indicate the operation that must be performed on the proposition indicated by the preceding vowel in order to reduce the syllogism to a first-figure syllogism. The key for this is as follows: "*s*" indicates simple conversion, "*p*" indicates conversion *per accidens*, "*m*" indicates metathesis (interchanging of the premises), "*k*" indicates obversion, and "*c*" indicates *convertio syllogism* (that is, the syllogism is to be reduced indirectly). In mnemonic terms the only meaningless letters are "*r*," "*t*," "*l*," "*n*," and noninitial "*b*" and "*d*." More elaborate mnemonics have been devised for syllogisms in which two or more of the premises exhibit modality. See entry "Logic, Traditional."

Mnemonic Terms

Name	Figure	Major premise	Major premise	Conclusion
Barbara	first	A	A	A
Baroco	second	A	O	O
Bocardo	third	O	A	O
Bramantip	fourth	A	A	I
Camenes	fourth	A	E	E
Camestres	second	A	E	E
Celarent	first	E	A	E
Cesare	second	E	A	E
Darapti	third	A	A	I
Darii	first	A	I	I
Datisi	third	A	I	I
Dimaris	fourth	I	A	I
Disamis	third	I	A	I
Felapton	third	E	A	O
Ferio	first	E	I	O
Ferison	third	E	I	O
Fesapo	fourth	E	A	O
Festino	second	E	I	O
Fresison	fourth	E	I	O

modality. (1) The characteristic of propositions according to which they can be described as "apodictic," "assertoric," or "problematic." An *assertoric* proposition asserts that something is the case; an *apodictic* proposition asserts that something must be the case; a *problematic* proposition asserts that something may be the case. This type of modality was called by the medieval logicians *modality sine dicto* (*de re*).

(2) The characteristic of propositions according to which they can be described as "necessary," "impossible," "possible," or "not-necessary." Medieval logicians called this type *modality cum dicto* (*de dicto*).

modal logic. The study of inferential relations among propositions which are due to their modality. Most logicians treat systems of modal logic as intensional, basing them upon strict implication. An alternative approach is to treat these systems as extensional, basing them upon a many-valued logic. See entry "Modal Logic."

model. An interpretation of a given set of well-formed formulas according to which all the members of the set are true. The *standard* model corresponds to the principal interpretation, and a *nonstandard* model corresponds to a secondary interpretation. See *interpretation.*

modus ponendo tollens. An inference of the form "Either *A* or *B*; *A*; therefore, not-*B*." This type of inference is valid only if "or" is interpreted as exclusive disjunction.

modus ponens. An argument of the form "If *A* then *B*; *A*; therefore, *B*." Some authors use the term to designate the rule of inference that allows arguments of this form.

modus tollendo ponens. An argument of the form "Either *A* or *B*; not-*A*; therefore, *B*."

modus tollens. An argument of the form "If *A* then *B*; not-*B*; therefore, not-*A*." Some authors use the term to designate the rule of inference that allows arguments of this form.

mood. A way of classifying categorical syllogisms according to the quantity and quality of their constituent propositions.

multiplicative axiom. See *choice, axiom of.*

name. In traditional logic, a word or group of words that can serve as a term in a proposition. A *general* name is one that can be significantly applied to each member of a set of objects, a *singular* name is one that can be significantly applied to only one object, and a *collective* name is one that can be significantly applied to a group of similar things regarded as constituting a single whole.

natural number. A member of a certain subset of the cardinal numbers. There are various ways of defining this subset so that it contains all and only the desired objects (namely 0, 1, 2, 3, $\cdots$); the most common way is to define it as the set of all objects that belong to all sets containing 0 and closed under the successor relation.

necessary condition. See *condition.*

necessary truth. See *analytic.*

negate of a set. See *complement of a set.*

negation. A singulary propositional connective ($\neg$, $^-$, $\sim$, $-$), usually read "not," whose truth table is such that "not-*A*" is true if and only if *A* is false.

negative name. In traditional logic, a name that implies the absence of one or more properties or that denotes everything with the exception of some particular thing or set of things. An example of such a name is "non-Briton."

non sequitur. See **fallacy.**

normal system of domains. A system of domains such that the axioms of second-order functional calculus are valid in them and the rules of inference of second-order functional calculus preserve validity in them.

null set (empty set). A set with no members.

number. See **cardinal number; natural number; rational number; real number;** entry "Number."

object language. A language used to talk about things, rather than about other languages. Derivatively, a proposition is said to be in the object language if and only if it is not about any linguistic expression. "Socrates was a philosopher" is therefore in the object language, whereas "'Socrates' has eight letters" is not.

obversion. In traditional logic, a type of immediate inference in which from a given proposition another proposition is inferred whose subject is the same as the original subject, whose predicate is the contradictory of the original predicate, and whose quality is affirmative if the original proposition's quality was negative and vice versa. Obversion of a proposition yields an equivalent proposition when applied to all four types (A, E, I, and O) of propositions that traditional logicians considered. See entry "Logic, Traditional."

omega. The smallest infinite ordinal (denoted by ω), the order type associated with the set of all natural numbers as ordered in their natural order.

omega-complete. Used of a system which, if it contains the theorems that property P holds of 0, of 1, of 2, and so on, contains the theorem that P holds of all numbers.

omega-consistent. Used of a system which, if it contains the theorems that property P holds of 0, of 1, of 2, and so on, does not contain the theorem that P holds of all numbers.

one-many correspondence. A relation R such that for every member a of its converse domain, there is more than one object b that is a member of its domain such that bRa. "Father of" is an example of a one-many correspondence, since for every member of its converse domain (everyone who has a father) there is only one member of its domain (that person's father) such that the member of the domain is the father of the member of the converse domain.

one-to-one correspondence. A relation R such that for every member a of its converse domain, there is only one object b that is a member of its domain such that bRa. A one-to-one correspondence is said to be *order-preserving* if both its domain and its converse domain are simply ordered and if, for all c and d that are members of its domain and are such that c precedes d in the ordering of the domain, it is the case that their respective images e and f in the converse domain are such that e precedes f in the ordering of the converse domain.

open schema. A formula containing free individual and functional variables.

open sentence. A formula containing free individual variables.

operator. A symbol or combination of symbols that is syncategorematic under the principal interpretation of the logistic system it occurs in and that may be used with one or more variables and one or more constants or forms or both to produce a new constant or form. Universal and existential quantifiers are the most common examples of operators.

O-proposition. In traditional logic, a particular negative categorical proposition. An example is "Some men are not mortal."

order. See **Level.**

ordered, partially. A set a is partially ordered if and only if there is a relation R such that for all b, c, and d that are members of a, (1) if bRc and cRd, then bRd, and (2) it is not the case that bRb.

ordered, simply. A set a is simply ordered if and only if there is a relation R such that a is partially ordered by R and for all b and c that are members of a and are not identical, either bRc or cRb.

ordered, well. A set a is well ordered if and only if there is a relation R such that a is simply ordered by R and for every nonempty subset of a, there is a first element of that nonempty subset.

ordered pair. For given objects a and b, the ordered pair (a,b) is the pair set of which one member is the unit set whose only member is a and the other member is the pair set whose members are a and b.

order-preserving. See **one-to-one correspondence.**

order type. The set of all sets that are ordinally similar to a given set.

ordinally similar. Two or more sets are ordinally similar if and only if there exists between them a one-to-one order-preserving correspondence.

ordinal number. An order type of a well-ordered set.

pairing axiom. An axiom in set theory stating that for any two objects *a* and *b*, there is a set *c* whose members are *a* and *b* only.

pair set. A set that contains exactly two members.

paradox (antinomy). A statement whose truth leads to a contradiction and the truth of whose denial leads to a contradiction. Since F. P. Ramsey it has been customary to distinguish between *logical paradoxes* (often called *paradoxes of set theory*), which can arise in the object language because they involve only the usual logical and set-theoretic symbols, and *semantic paradoxes*, which can arise only in the metalanguage because they involve semantic concepts.

The most prominent logical paradoxes are the following: (1) *Russell's paradox.* Consider the set of all objects that are not members of themselves. Is that set a member of itself? If it is, then it is not. If it is not, then it is. (2) *Cantor's paradox.* Consider the set of all sets. Is it equal to or greater than its power set? If it is equal, then there is a contradiction, since there is a proof that the power set of any set is greater than the set itself. If it is not, then there is a contradiction, since the power set of any set is a set of sets and must therefore be a subset of the set of all sets, and there is a proof that the subset of a set cannot be greater than the set itself. (3) *Burali-Forti's paradox.* Consider the set of all ordinals. Does it have an ordinal number? If it does not, there is a contradiction, since by the "less than" relation it is well ordered, and there is a proof that all well-ordered sets have ordinal numbers. If it does, there is a contradiction, since it can be proved that the set's ordinal number must be both equal to and less than its image in the mapping of the set of all ordinals onto the set of all ordinals less than its own ordinal.

The most prominent of the semantic paradoxes are the following: (1) *Berry's paradox.* Consider the expression "the least natural number not namable in fewer than 22 syllables." Is the number it denotes namable in fewer than 22 syllables? If it is, there is a contradiction, since by definition it cannot be. If it is not, there is a contradiction, since we can produce a way of naming it in 21 syllables—the way we named it in stating this paradox. (2) *Epimenides' paradox.* Consider the sentence "This sentence is not true." Is it true? If it is, then it is not; if it is not; then it is. (3) *Grelling-Nelson paradox of heterologicality.* A predicate is heterological if the sentence ascribing the predicate to itself is false. Is the predicate "heterological" itself heterological? If it is, then it is not; if it is not, then

it is. (4) *Paradox of the Liar.* See *Epimenides' paradox* (although the name is often used to refer to the nearly identical paradox beginning with the sentence "This statement expresses a lie"). (5) *Richard's paradox.* Consider the set of all real numbers between 0 and 1 that can be characterized in a finite number of English words. This set has only denumerably many members. It can be shown, in a manner very similar to Cantor's diagonal proof, that we can specify in a finite number of English words a number that cannot belong to the set. Does it belong to the set? If it does, there is a contradiction, since it cannot. If it does not, there is a contradiction, since it can be characterized in a finite number of English words, and all such numbers belong to the set. See entry "Logical Paradoxes."

paradoxes of material implication. These so-called paradoxes consist in the fact that if "if _____ then _____" is taken in the sense of material implication, then any proposition of that form is true if the antecedent is false no matter what the consequent is or if the consequent is true no matter what the antecedent is. Thus, "If Eisenhower were premier of France, then the moon would be made of cheese" and "If 2 + 2 = 17, then Johnson is the president of the United States" are both true propositions if "if-then" is interpreted in the sense of material implication.

paralogism. Any fallacious reasoning.

particular. See *individual.*

Peano's postulates. A system of five postulates from which one can derive the rest of arithmetic. The five postulates are (1) 0 is a number; (2) the successor of any number is a number; (3) there are no two numbers with the same successor; (4) 0 is not the successor of any number; (5) every property of 0 also belonging to the successor of any number that has that property belongs to all numbers.

per accidens. Used of a predication to the subject of one of its accidents.

perfect figure. The first figure of the syllogism. According to Aristotle, this is the only figure to which the *dictum de omni et nullo* is directly applicable.

per se. Used of a predication to the subject of one of its essential attributes.

petitio principii. See *fallacy,* (11) *begging the question.*

polysyllogism. A series of syllogisms so linked that the conclusion of one is a premise of another. In such a series a syllogism is said to be a *prosyllogism* if its conclusion is a premise of the syllogism with which it is connected and an *episyllogism* if one of its premises is the conclusion of the syllogism with which it is connected. See *sorites*.

possible truth. See *logical possibility*.

post hoc, ergo propter hoc. See *fallacy*.

postulate. Although often used synonymously with "axiom," this term is sometimes confined to the basic propositions of a particular discipline, with the axioms being the basic propositions common to all disciplines (for example, the laws of logic). The distinction arises only when one is concerned not merely with a formal system but also with its interpretation.

postulation, method of. See *method of construction*.

potential infinite. The infinite regarded as a limiting concept, as something becoming rather than as something completed.

power. See *cardinality*.

power set. The set of all subsets of a given set.

power-set axiom. An axiom in set theory stating that for any given set, its power set exists.

pragmatics. See *semantics, formal*.

predicables. A classification of things and concepts as predicated of subjects, first made by Aristotle. His four predicables were definition, genus (in which he included differentia), proprium, and accident. Medieval logicians, following Porphyry, offered a list of five predicables—species, differentia, genus, proprium, and accident—which was adopted by most traditional logicians.

For Aristotle one defined a term by stating the *essence* of the object that it names (this statement is called the *definition*). The essence of a thing is that property which makes it the type of thing it is and not some other type of thing. The essence has two aspects: the *genus* is that which is predicable essentially of other kinds of things as well, and the *differentia* is that which is possessed essentially only by things of one type (members of one species) and not by things of any other type. Thus, in "Man is a rational animal" the genus is "animal," and the differentia is "rational."

Aristotle distinguished between the essence of a thing and other properties which belong only to that type of thing but are not part of its essence; such a property is called a *proprium*. The precise manner in which he hoped to make this distinction is not very clear. He also recognized that a thing might have a property that it need not have. He called such a property an *accident*.

predicate. Traditionally, the word or group of words in a categorical proposition that connote the property being attributed to the subject or denote the class which the subject is being included in or excluded from. The term is often extended, in contemporary works, to cover all words or groups of words that connote properties or relations in any type of proposition. Thus, in "All men are mortal" the predicate is "mortal."

predicate calculus. See *calculus*.

predication. The attributing of a property to a subject.

premise. A member of the set of propositions, assumed for the course of an argument, from which a conclusion is inferred.

primitive basis. The list of primitive symbols, formation rules, axioms, and rules of inference of a given logistic system.

primitive symbols. Those symbols of a given logistic system that are undefined and are not divided into parts in the course of operating within the system. One can, following John von Neumann, divide these symbols into constants, variables, connectives, operators, and bracket-like symbols.

privative name. A name that implies the absence of a property where it has been or where one might expect it to be.

problematic proposition. See *modality*.

product of sets. See *intersection of sets*.

proof. For a given well-formed formula A in a given logistic system, a proof of A is a finite sequence of well-formed formulas the last of which is A and each of which is either an axiom of the system or can be inferred from previous members of the sequence according to the rules of inference of the system.

proof from hypothesis. A proof from a given set of hypotheses $A_1, A_2, \cdots, A_n$ in a given logistic system is a sequence of well-formed formulas the last of which is the conclusion of the proof and each of which is either an axiom of the system or one of $A_1, A_2, \cdots, A_n$ or a formula that can be inferred from previous formulas in the sequence by the rules of inference of the system.

proof theory. See *metamathematics*.

proper class. An object which contains members but which cannot itself be a member of any object.

proper subset. A subset of a given set that is not identical with the given set.

proposition. There is no uniform use of the word *proposition* among logicians and philosophers. Many writers distinguish a proposition from a sentence; thus, "Socrates was a philosopher" and "Socrates war ein Philosoph" would be two different sentences that express the same proposition. Other writers use *sentence* and *proposition* interchangeably. To avoid some of the associations of the word *proposition* some contemporary philosophers abandon the term altogether in favor of *statement.* For a discussion of some of the philosophical controversies arising in this connection, see entry "Propositions." For present purposes it is assumed that the reader has a rough idea of what the term *proposition* means. This discussion will accordingly confine itself to an account of the different kinds of propositions distinguished by logicians.

Propositions may be classified in many ways. To begin with, one must distinguish *simple* (or *atomic* or *elementary*) propositions, propositions that do not have other propositions as constituent parts, from *compound* (or *molecular*) propositions, propositions that do have other propositions as constituent parts.

Among simple propositions the more important types are *categorical* (or *subject-predicate*) propositions, which affirm or deny that something has a property or is a member of a class, and *relational* propositions, which affirm or deny that a relation holds between two or more objects. A categorical proposition is *singular* when its subject is the name of an individual and *general* when its subject is the name of a property or class, affirmative when its predicate is affirmed of the subject and *negative* when its predicate is denied of the subject. A general categorical proposition is *universal* when it is talking about all the members of the subject class or all the objects that have the subject property and *particular* when it is talking about only some of the members of the subject class or some of the objects that have the subject property.

Among compound propositions the most important types are *alternative* (or *disjunctive*) propositions, which are of the form "A or B," *conditional* (or *hypothetical*) propositions, of the form "If A then B," *conjunctive* propositions, of the form "A and B," and *negative* propositions, of the form "Not-A." Many propositions that seem to be simple turn out under proper analysis to be compound. Such propositions are known as *exponible* propositions.

Kant, and many logicians following him, distinguished a class of *infinite* (or *limitative*) propositions, affirmative propositions with a negative term as predicate. This distinction has been challenged by many

authors. A more widely accepted addition to our classification is the *indefinite* proposition, a proposition that is equivocal because no indication is given of whether it is universal or particular. Finally, modality provides still another means of classifying propositions.

propositional calculus. See *calculus.*

propositional connective. See *connective.*

propositional function. A function whose range of values consists exclusively of truth-values. Thus, "*a* is the father of George Washington" is a propositional function, since for any argument for *a*, the value of the whole unit is truth or falsehood, depending on whether or not the argument is the name of George Washington's father.

proprium. See *predicables.*

prosyllogism. See *polysyllogism.*

protothetic. A form of the extended propositional calculus, first introduced by Stanisław Leśniewski, to which have been added variables whose values are truth-functions and a notation for the application of a function to its argument or arguments, and in which the quantifiers are allowed to have variables of any kind as operator variables. In the *higher* protothetic, variables whose values are propositional functions of truth-functions are added.

proximum genus. See *classification.*

quality of a proposition. The characteristic that makes a proposition affirmative or negative. Kant, and logicians following him, added a third type, infinite propositions. See *proposition.*

quantification of the predicate. The prefixing of a sign of quantity, "some" or "all," to the predicate of a proposition in the same way as to the subject, a device introduced by Sir William Hamilton. The claim was that this would make explicit what was implicit in the proposition.

quantifier. An operator of which it is true that both the constant or form it is used with and the constant or form produced are propositions or propositional forms. Thus, an existential quantifier, when joined to a proposition or propositional form A, produces a new proposition or propositional form "(∃a)M."

quantity of a proposition. The characteristic that makes a proposition universal or particular. Kant and others considered singular propositions as being a third, distinct type of quantity.

Quine's set theories. A group of set theories proposed by W. V. Quine, combining some of the features of type theory with some of the features of the Zermelo-Fraenkel and Gödel–von Neumann–Bernays set theories. As in the set theories, the axiom of abstraction is not retained in its full power, and the formation rules of intuitive set theory are not modified; as in type theory, the notion of stratification is used, since in certain key axioms only stratified formulas generate sets.

range of a relation. See *converse domain of a relation.*

range of values. The class of those things that are ambiguously named by a given variable.

rational number. A number that can be put into the form *a/b,* where *a* is any integer and *b* any natural number.

real mathematics. For David Hilbert, that part of mathematics that is finitary in character, has therefore a clear and intuitive meaning, and poses no problem about its foundation except for the fact that when ideal mathematics is adjoined to it the possibility of inconsistency arises. See *ideal mathematics.*

real number. Any number which can be represented by an unending decimal.

recursive function. There are various types of recursive functions. In order to explain them we must first introduce some terminology: a *constant function* is a function that has the same value for all of its arguments; a *successor function* has as its value for any given argument the successor of that argument; an *identity function* is a function of *n* arguments whose value is always the *i*th argument. All such functions are known as *fundamental functions.*

A function of *n* arguments is defined by *composition* when, given any set of previously introduced functions of *n* arguments, the value of the new function is equal to the value of a previously introduced function whose arguments in any particular case are the values of each of the members of the set of functions when their arguments are the arguments of the newly introduced function in that particular case. In symbols, where *P* is the new function being defined by composition, $P(a_1, a_2, \cdots, a_n) = R(S_1(a_1, a_2, \cdots, a_n), S_2(a_1, a_2, \cdots, a_n), \cdots, S_m(a_1, a_2, \cdots, a_n))$, where *R* and $S_1, S_2, \cdots, S_m$ are previously introduced functions.

A function is defined by *recursion* in the following circumstances: (1) A value is assigned to the function for the case where one of its arguments is 0 in terms of a previously introduced function whose arguments, except for 0, are in any particular case all and only the arguments of the new function in that particular case. In symbols, where *P* is the new function and *R* the previously introduced function, $P(a_1, a_2, \cdots, a_n, 0) = R(a_1, a_2, \cdots, a_n)$. (2)

A value is given to the new function when 0 is not one of its arguments and when one of its arguments is the successor of any number *b,* in terms of a previously introduced function *S,* whose arguments, except for the successor of *b,* are in any particular case all the arguments of the newly introduced function, *b* itself, and the value of the new function when its arguments are all and only the arguments already given for *S.* In symbols, $P(a_1, a_2, \cdots, a_n, b + 1) = S(a_1, a_2, \cdots, a_n, b, P(a_1, a_2, \cdots, a_n, b))$.

Any numerical function that is a fundamental function or can be obtained, by composition or recursion or both, from the fundamental functions by a finite sequence of definitions is a *primitive recursive numerical function.* A function *P* is introduced by the *least-number operator* if its value for a given set of arguments is the least number *b* such that the value of a previously introduced function *R,* whose arguments in any particular case are the arguments of *P* in that case and *b,* is equal to 0 provided that there is such a *b;* if there is no such *b,* the function is undefined for those arguments. In symbols, $P(a_1, a_2, \cdots, a_n) =$ the least *b* such that $R(a_1, a_2, \cdots, a_n, b) = 0$, provided that there is a *b* such that $R(a_1, a_2, \cdots, a_n, b) = 0$. Any numerical function that either is a fundamental function or can be obtained from the fundamental functions by a finite sequence of definitions by composition, recursion, and the least-number operator (when this operator is used in defining a general recursive function, it must be the case that for all $a_1, a_2, \cdots, a_n$ there is a *b* such that $R(a_1, a_2, \cdots, a_n, b) = 0$) is a *general recursive numerical function.*

recursively enumerable. Used of a set or class that is enumerated (allowing for repetitions) by a general recursive function. That is, there is a general recursive function whose converse domain has the same members as the set when its domain is the set of natural numbers.

recursive number theory. The development of number theory, instituted by Thoralf Skolem, in which no quantifiers are introduced as primitive symbols, in which universality is expressed by the use of free variables, and in which functions are introduced through definitions by recursion.

recursive set. A set that is enumerated (allowing for repetitions) by a general recursive function and whose complement is also enumerated (allowing for repetitions) by a general recursive function.

reducibility, axiom of. An axiom, introduced by Bertrand Russell and A. N. Whitehead in *Principia Mathematica,* which says that for any propositional function of arbitrary level there exists a formally equivalent propositional function of the first level.

reductio ad absurdum. (1) See **indirect proof.** (2) The method of proving a proposition by showing that its denial leads to a contradiction. In this sense it is often known as a *reductio ad impossibile.*

reduction of syllogisms. The process whereby syllogisms in imperfect figures are expressed in the first figure. Reduction is *direct* when the original conclusion follows from premises in the first figure derived by conversion, obversion, etc., from premises in an imperfect figure. Reduction is *indirect* when a new syllogism is formed which establishes the validity of the original conclusion by showing the illegitimacy of its contradictory. See entry "Logic, Traditional."

reference. See **meaning, Frege's theory of.**

referential opacity. An occurrence of a word or sequence of words such that one cannot in general supplant the word or sequence of words with another word or sequence of words that refers to the same thing while preserving the truth-value of the containing sentence. For example, although "9 is necessarily greater than 7" is true, the result of substituting for "9" a sequence of words that refers to the same thing, "the number of planets," is the false proposition "The number of planets is necessarily greater than 7." Therefore, in this occurrence "9" is referentially opaque.

reflexive relation. See **relation.**

reflexive set. See **finite set.**

regularity, axiom of. See **foundation, axiom of.**

relation. This term is not adequately defined in traditional logic. The failure to offer an adequate definition is symptomatic of the lack of serious consideration, on the part of traditional logicians, of the significant differences between categorical and relational propositions. Augustus De Morgan and C. S. Peirce were the first logicians in the contemporary period to study the logic of relational propositions. Since their time this subject has become an important part of logic. In contemporary works, particularly in works on set theory, a relation is defined as a set of ordered pairs.

A relation R is *reflexive* if "aRa" holds for all a that are members of the field of R, *irreflexive* if "aRa" holds for no members of the field of R, and *nonreflexive* if "aRa" holds for some but not all members of the field of R. For example, "is a member of the same family as" is a reflexive relation, "is not a member of the same family as" is an irreflexive relation, and "loves" is a nonreflexive relation.

A relation R is *symmetric* if for all a and b that are members of the field of R, aRb if and only if bRa, *asymmetric* if for all a and b that are members of the field of R, aRb if and only if not-bRa, and *nonsymmetric* when "aRb" and "bRa" hold for some but not all a and b that are members of the field of R. For example, "is a member of the same family as" is a symmetric relation, "is a child of" is an asymmetric relation, and "is a brother of" is a nonsymmetric relation.

A relation R is *transitive* when for all a, b, and c that are members of the field of R, if aRb and bRc, then aRc, *intransitive* when for all a, b, and c that are members of the field of R, if aRb and bRc, then not-aRc, and *nontransitive* when if aRb and bRc, then "aRc" holds for some but not all of the a, b, and c that are members of the field of R. For example, "is a descendant of" is a transitive relation, "is a child of" is an intransitive relation, and "is not a brother of" is a nontransitive relation.

The foregoing classifications are said to apply to a relation in a set if the corresponding properties hold for all members of the field of a relation that are members of the set. A relation is *connective* in a set if for all distinct a and b that are members of the set, either aRb or bRa.

The study of relational propositions has raised many philosophical issues—and has greatly influenced discussions of older issues—about the nature of relations. On these matters, see entry "Relations, Internal and External."

replacement, axiom of (axiom of substitution). An axiom in set theory stating that for any set a and any single-valued function R with a free variable b, there exists a set that contains just the members $R(b)$, with b being a member of a.

representative of a cardinal number. A set that has a given cardinal number as its cardinality.

Richard's paradox. See **paradox.**

rule of inference (transformation rule). For a given logistic system, any rule in its metalanguage of the form "From well-formed formulas of the form $A_1, A_2, \cdots, A_n$, it is permissible to infer a well-formed formula of the form B."

Russell's paradox. See **paradox.**

Russell's theory of definite descriptions. See **definite descriptions, theory of.**

Russell's vicious-circle principle. The principle according to which impredicative definitions are not allowed.

satisfiable. A well-formed formula that is satisfiable in some nonempty domain of individuals.

satisfiable in a domain. A well-formed formula is satisfiable in a given domain of individuals if and only if it has the value truth for at least one system of possible values of its free variables.

Schröder-Bernstein theorem. The theorem, first conjectured by Georg Cantor and proved by Felix Bernstein and Ernst Schröder, which states that if a and b are sets such that a is equipollent with a subset of b and b is equipollent with a subset of a, then a and b are equipollent.

scope of a quantifier. For a given occurrence of a quantifier as part of a well-formed part of a well-formed formula, the rest of that well-formed part.

secondarily satisfiable. Used of a well-formed formula that is satisfiable in some normal system of domains.

secondarily valid. Used of a well-formed formula that is valid in every normal system of domains.

second-order logic. Second-order functional calculus. See *calculus.*

section of a set. See *segment of a set.*

segment of a set (section of a set). The subset of a given set ordered by a given relation whose members are those members of the set that precede a given member in the given ordering.

selection set. A set that contains one member from each subset of a given set.

self-contradiction. A proposition that in effect both asserts and denies some other proposition.

semantical rule. Any rule in the metalanguage that concerns the meaning of expressions in the object language.

semantics, formal (semiotics). The study of linguistic symbols. Following C. W. Morris, it is customary to divide formal semantics into three areas: (1) *Syntax,* the study of the relations between symbols. The study of the ways in which the symbols of a given language can be combined to form well-formed formulas is one part of syntax. (2) *Semantics,* the study of the interpretation of symbols. Following W. V. Quine, it is customary to distinguish between the theory of reference, which studies the reference or denotation of symbols, and the theory of meaning, which studies the sense or connotation of symbols. (3) *Pragmatics,* the study of the relations between symbols, the users of symbols, and the environment of the users. Thus, the study of the conditions in which a speaker uses a given word is part of pragmatics. See entry "Semantics."

sense. See *meaning, Frege's theory of.*

sentential calculus. See *calculus.*

sentential connective. See *connective.*

sequence. A function whose domain is a subset, not necessarily a proper one, of the set of natural numbers. Some authors extend the term to any function whose domain is ordered.

set. (1) An aggregate. (2) In Gödel–von Neumann–Bernays set theory, where a distinction is made between sets and classes, sets are those objects that can both contain members and be members of some other object.

Sheffer stroke function (alternative denial). A binary propositional connective (|), whose truth table is such that "A stroke-function B" is false if and only if A and B are both true. The Sheffer stroke function and joint denial are the only binary propositional connectives adequate for the construction of all truth-functional connectives.

simultaneously satisfiable. A class of well-formed formulas is said to be simultaneously satisfiable if there is some nonempty domain of individuals such that for all the free variables in all the formulas that are members of the class, there exists at least one system of values in that domain for which every formula in the class has the value truth.

singular term. A term that, in the sense in which it is being used, is predicable of only one individual. For example, any definite description is a singular term.

singulary connective. See *connective.*

Skolem-Löwenheim theorem. In 1915, Leopold Löwenheim proved that if a well-formed formula is valid in an enumerably infinite domain, it is valid in every nonempty domain. A corollary is that if a well-formed formula is satisfiable in any nonempty domain, it is satisfiable in an enumerably infinite domain. In 1920, Thoralf Skolem generalized this corollary—and thus completed the theorem—by proving that if a class of well-formed formulas is simultaneously satisfiable in any nonempty domain, then it is simultaneously satisfiable in an enumerably infinite domain.

Skolem's paradox. The seemingly paradoxical fact that systems in which Cantor's theorem is provable, and which therefore have nondenumerable sets, must, by virtue of the Skolem-Löwenheim theorem, be satisfiable in an enumerably infinite domain.

sorites. A chain of syllogisms in which the conclusion of each of the prosyllogisms is omitted. If each of the conclusions forms the minor premise of the following episyllogism, the sorites is an *Aristotelian* sorites; if each of the conclusions forms the major premise of the following episyllogism, it is a *Goclenian* sorites.

sound. Used of an interpretation of a logistic system such that under the interpretation all the axioms either denote truth or always have the value truth, and all the rules of inference are truth-preserving.

species. See *classification.*

square of opposition. A diagrammatic representation of that part of the traditional doctrine of immediate inferences between categorical propositions that went under the name of the opposition of propositions. See entry "Logic, Traditional."

stratification. The substitution of numerals for variables in a formula (the same numeral for each occurrence of a single variable) in such a way that the symbol for class-membership is flanked always by variables with consecutive ascending numerals.

subalternation. The relation between a universal and a particular proposition of the same quality. Traditionally this relation has been viewed in such a way that the universal proposition implies the particular proposition. The universal proposition is called the *subalternant*; the particular proposition is called the *subalternate.*

subaltern genera. See *classification.*

subcontrary propositions. Two propositions that cannot both be false but may both be true. Any I- and O-propositions with the same subject and the same predicate form a pair of subcontrary propositions.

subject. The word or words in a categorical proposition that denote the object to which a property is being attributed or the class which is either included in or excluded from some other class.

subset. Any set *b* such that all the members of *b* are members of a given set *a.*

substitution, axiom of. See *replacement, axiom of.*

substitution, rule of. A rule of inference that allows one to infer from a given formula *A* another formula *B* that is the same as *A* except for certain specified changes of symbols. The various rules of substitution differ in the types of changes they allow.

successor. For a given number, the number that follows it in the ordinary ordering of the numbers. In Peano's axiomatic treatment of arithmetic "successor" is treated as a primitive term. In the various set-theoretic treatments of arithmetic it is defined differently. For example, "the successor of *a*" is sometimes defined as the unit set whose only member is *a.*

sufficient condition. See *condition.*

summum genus. See *classification.*

sum of sets. See *union of sets.*

sum set. For a given set *a*, the set whose members are all and only those objects which are members of members of *a.*

sum-set axiom. An axiom in set theory stating that for any set *a*, its sum set exists.

supposition. Roughly, the property of a term whereby it stands for something; the doctrine of supposition was extensively developed by the medieval logicians. *Material* supposition is possessed by those terms that stand for an expression, and *formal* supposition is possessed by those terms that stand for what they signify. Among terms having formal supposition, those that are common terms have *common* supposition, and those that are properly applicable to only one individual have *discrete* supposition. When in a given occurrence a common term stands for the universal, it has *simple* supposition; opposed to this is *personal* supposition, a property possessed by a common term in those occurrences where it stands for particular instances.

syllogism. A valid deductive argument having two premises and a conclusion. The term is often restricted to the case where both premises and the conclusion are categorical propositions that have between them three, and only three, terms. More careful authors distinguish this case by referring to it as a *categorical* syllogism. A *hypothetical* syllogism is one whose premises and conclusions are hypothetical propositions, and a *disjunctive* syllogism is one whose premises and conclusion are disjunctive propositions. All of these cases, where the three propositions are of the same type, are *pure* syllogisms. A *mixed* syllogism is one in which there occur at least two types of propositions.

A *strengthened* syllogism is one in which the same conclusion could be obtained even if we substitute for one of the premises that is a universal proposition its subalternate. Thus, the syllogism whose premises are "All men are mortal" and "All baseball players are men" and whose conclusion is "Some baseball players are mortal" is a strengthened syllogism, since it would have been sufficient to have as a premise "Some baseball players are men." A *weakened* syllogism is one whose premises imply a universal proposition but whose conclusion is the subalternate of that universal proposition. The above example is also an example of a weakened syllogism, since the premises, as they stand, imply "All baseball players are mortal."

symbol, improper. A symbol that is syncategorematic under the principal interpretation of the logistic system it occurs in. An example of such a symbol is "and."

symbol, proper. A symbol that is categorematic under the principal interpretation of the logistic system it occurs in. Any individual constant is a proper symbol.

symmetrical relation. See *relation.*

syncategorematic. In traditional logic, used of a word which cannot be a term in a categorical proposition and which must be used along with a term in order to enter into a categorical proposition. An example of this is "all." In contemporary logic the term refers to any symbol that has no independent meaning and acquires its meaning only when joined to other symbols. Cf. *categorematic.*

syntactical variable. A variable ranging over the names of symbols and formulas.

syntax. See *semantics, formal.*

synthetic. Used of a proposition that is neither analytic nor self-contradictory.

systematic ambiguity (typical ambiguity). A convention, introduced by Bertrand Russell and A. N. Whitehead, whereby one does not specify the type or order to which the variables in a formula belong, thus allowing one formula to represent an infinite number of formulas, namely all those formulas that are exactly like it except for the fact that their variables are assigned orders and types in such a manner that the formula formed is well-formed according to the formation rules of the ramified theory of types.

tautology. A compound proposition that is true no matter what truth-values are assigned to its constituent propositions. Thus, "A or not-A" is a tautology, since if "A" is true, then the whole proposition is true, and if "A" is false, then "not-A" is true, and therefore the whole proposition is still true.

term. Traditionally, the subject or predicate in a categorical proposition. Some authors extend the word *term* to cover all occurrences of categorematic words or expressions which, although not propositions by themselves, are parts of a proposition.

tertium non datur. The law of excluded middle. See *laws of thought.*

theorem. Any well-formed formula of a given logistic system for which there is a proof in the system.

theorem schema. A representation of an infinite number of theorems by means of an expression that contains syntactical variables and has well-formed formulas as values. Every value of the expression is to be taken as a theorem.

theory of types. The theory, introduced by Bertrand Russell and A. N. Whitehead in *Principia Mathematica,* which avoids the paradoxes of set theory by modifying the formation rules of intuitive set theory. In the *simple theory of types* the only modification is that every variable is assigned a number that signifies its type, and formulas of the form "a is a member of b" are well-formed if and only if a's type-number is one less than b's. In *ramified type theory* each variable is also assigned to a particular level, and certain rules are introduced about the levels of variables; these rules are such as to exclude classes defined by impredicative definitions. See entry "Types, Theory of."

tilde. The name of the symbol for negation ($\sim$).

token. A specified utterance of a given linguistic expression or a written occurrence of it. An expression-*type,* on the other hand, is an entity abstracted from all actual and potential occurrences of a linguistic expression. In "John loves John," for example, there are three word-tokens but only two word-types.

transfinite cardinals. All cardinal numbers equal to or greater than aleph-null ($\aleph_0$).

transfinite induction. A proof by course-of-values induction where the numbers involved are the ordinal numbers. This type of proof is important because it can be used to show that a property holds not only for the finite ordinals but for the transfinite ordinals as well.

transfinite ordinal. The order-type of an infinite well-ordered set.

transfinite recursion. A definition of a function by recursion in such a way that a value is assigned not only when the argument is a finite ordinal but also when it is a transfinite ordinal.

transformation rule. See *rule of inference.*

transitive relation. See *relation.*

transposition. A rule of inference that permits one to infer from the truth of "A implies B" the truth of "Not-B implies not-A," and conversely.

trichotomy, law of. See *comparability, law of.*

truth-function. A function whose arguments and values are truth-values. A compound proposition is said to be a truth-functional proposition if the connective that is adjoined to the constituent propositions to form the compound proposition has a truth-function associated with it. In such a case, since the only arguments of the function are truth-values, the truth-value of the compound proposition depends only on the truth-values of its constituent propositions.

truth table. A table that shows the truth-value of a compound proposition for every possible combination of the truth-values of its constituent propositions.

truth-value. One of two abstract entities, truth and falsehood, postulated in Fregean semantics to serve as the reference of true and false sentences. In many-valued logics other truth-values are introduced.

Turing-computable. Used of a function whose value for any given argument a Turing machine can compute. The notion of Turing computability, due to A. M. Turing, is often introduced as a way of making precise the notion of an effectively computable function.

Turing machine. A machine that is capable of being in any one of a finite number of internal *states* at any particular time. The machine is supplied with a linear tape divided into squares on which symbols (from a fixed finite alphabet) may or may not be printed. It scans one, and only one, square at any given time and can erase a symbol from the scanned square and print some other symbol on it. The machine's behavior (in terms of changing what is on the scanned square, changing its internal state, and moving the tape so as to scan a different square) is governed by a *table* of instructions that determines what the machine is to do, given any *configuration* (a combination of the state the machine is in and the symbol on the scanned square) of the machine.

type. (1) See *token.* (2) In the theory of types, a class of objects all of whose members are such that they can be members of the same object. The lowest type is composed of all individuals, the next type of all sets of individuals, and each succeeding type of sets whose members are objects of the immediately preceding type.

typical ambiguity. See *systematic ambiguity.*

union of sets (sum of sets). The set whose members are all and only those objects that are members of at least one of two or more sets.

unit set. A set with only one member.

universal generalization, rule of. The rule of inference that permits one to infer from a formula of the form "Property *P* holds for an object *a*" a formula of the form "Property *P* holds for all objects." Because this inference is not generally valid, restrictions have to be placed on its use.

universal instantiation, rule of. The rule of inference that permits one to infer from a statement of the form "Property *P* holds for all objects" a statement of the form "Property *P* holds for an object *a.*"

universal quantifier. The symbol (   ) or (∀   ), read "for all." It is used in combination with a variable and placed before a well-formed formula, as in "(*a*) _____" ("For all *a,* _____").

universal set. A set such that there is no object *a* that is not a member of the set.

universe of discourse. Those objects with which a discussion is concerned.

univocal. A linguistic expression is univocal if and only if it is neither ambiguous nor equivocal.

use of a term. See *mention of a term.*

valid formula. A well-formed formula that is valid in every nonempty domain. A well-formed formula is said to be valid for a given domain of individuals if it is true for all possible values of its free variables.

valid inference. An inference the joint assertion of whose premises and the denial of whose conclusion is a contradiction.

value. A member of the range of values of a given variable.

value of a function. That member of the converse domain of a function with which a given argument is paired under the function.

variable. A symbol that under the principal interpretation is not the name of any particular thing but is rather the ambiguous name of any one of a class of things.

Venn diagram. A modification, first introduced by John Venn, of Euler's diagrams. The key differences between Euler's diagrams and Venn's diagrams stem from the fact that Venn, and many other logicians, wanted to deny the traditional assumption that propositions of the form "All *P* are *Q*" or "No *P* are *Q*" imply the existence of any *P*'s. For details, see entry "Logic Diagrams."

vicious-circle principle. See *Russell's vicious-circle principle.*

well-formed formulas. Those formulas of a given logistic system of which it can sensibly be asked whether or not they are theorems of the system. In any particular system, rules are given that define the class of well-formed formulas and enable one to determine mechanically whether or not a given string of symbols is a well-formed formula of the system.

well-ordering theorem. The theorem stating that for any set there is a relation that well-orders it. See *choice, axiom of.*

wff. A common abbreviation for "well-formed formula."

Zermelo-Fraenkel set theory. That form of axiomatic set theory that avoids the paradoxes of set theory by dropping the axiom of abstraction and substituting for it a set of axioms about set-existence.

Boruch A. Brody (1967)

LOGIC AND THE FOUNDATIONS OF MATHEMATICS

A very detailed account of main developments of logic will be found in *Logic, History of.* Brief explanations of many of the terms commonly used by logicians will be found in *Logical Terms, Glossary of.* The Encyclopedia also features the following articles dealing with questions in logic and the foundations of mathematics: *Artificial and Natural Languages; Combinatory Logic; Computability Theory; Computing Machines; Decision Theory; Definition; Existence; Fallacies; Geometry; Gödel's Theorem; Identity; Infinity in Mathematics and Logic; Laws of Thought; Logical Paradoxes; Logic Diagrams; Logic Machines; Many-Valued Logics; Mathematics, Foundations of; Modal Logic; Negation; Number; Questions; Semantics; Set Theory; Subject and Predicate; Synonymity; Syntactical and Semantical Categories; Types, Theory of;* and *Vagueness.* See "Logic" and "Mathematics, Foundations of," in the index for entries on thinkers who have made contributions in this area.

LOGIC DIAGRAMS

"Logic diagrams" are geometrical figures that are in some respect isomorphic with the structure of statements in a formal logic and therefore can be manipulated to solve problems in that logic. They are useful teaching devices for strengthening a student's intuitive grasp of logical structure, they can be used for checking results obtained by algebraic methods, and they provide elegant demonstrations of the close relation of logic to topology and set theory.

Leonhard Euler, the Swiss mathematician, was the first to make systematic use of a logic diagram. Circles had earlier been employed, by Gottfried Wilhelm Leibniz and others, to diagram syllogisms, but it was Euler who, in 1761, first explained in detail how circles could be manipulated for such purposes. Euler's contemporary Johann Heinrich Lambert, the German mathematician, in his *Neues*

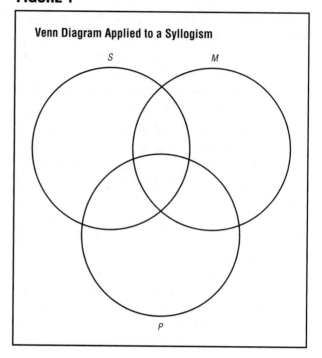

FIGURE 1

Venn Diagram Applied to a Syllogism

Organon (1764) used straight lines, in a manner similar to Euler's use of circles, for diagramming syllogisms.

VENN DIAGRAMS

The Euler and Lambert methods, as well as later variants using squares and other types of closed curves, are no longer in use because of the great improvement on their basic conception which was introduced by the English logician John Venn. The Venn diagram is best explained by showing how it is used to validate a syllogism. The syllogism's three terms, *S, M,* and *P,* are represented by simple closed curves—most conveniently drawn as circles—that mutually intersect, as in Figure 1. The set of points inside circle *S* represents all members of class *S,* and points outside are members of class not-*S*—and similarly for the other two circles. Shading a compartment indicates that it has no members. An X inside a compartment shows that it contains at least one member. An X on the border of two compartments means that at least one of the two compartments has members.

Consider the following syllogism:

Some *S* is *M.*

All *M* is *P.*

Therefore, some *S* is *P.*

The first premise states that the intersection of sets *S* and *M* is not empty. This is indicated by an X on the bor-

FIGURE 2

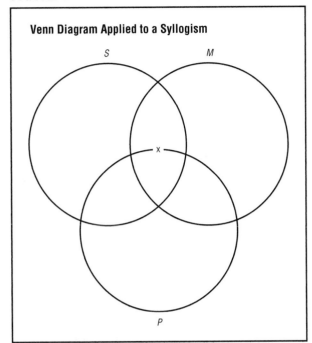

Venn Diagram Applied to a Syllogism

FIGURE 3

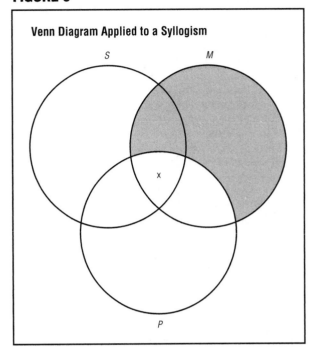

Venn Diagram Applied to a Syllogism

der dividing the two compartments within the overlap of circles *S* and *M* (Figure 2). The second premise states that the set indicated by that portion of circle *M* that lies outside of *P* is empty. When this area is shaded (Figure 3) the X must be shifted to the only remaining compartment into which it can go. Because the X is now inside both *S* and *P*, it is evident that some *S* is *P*; therefore, the syllogism is valid.

Venn did not restrict this method to syllogisms. He generalized it to take care of any problem in the calculus of classes, then the most popular interpretation of what is now called Boolean algebra. For statements with four terms he used four intersecting ellipses, as shown in Figure 4. Since it is not possible for five ellipses to intersect in the desired manner, statements with five or more terms must be diagramed on more complicated patterns. Various methods of forming nonconvex closed curves for Venn diagrams of statements with more than four terms have been devised.

RECTANGULAR CHARTS

Statements involving a large number of terms are best diagramed on a rectangle divided into smaller rectangles that are labeled in such a way that the chart can be manipulated efficiently as a Venn diagram. Many different methods of constructing such charts were worked out in the late nineteenth and early twentieth centuries, each

with merits and defects. The first to be published was that of Allan Marquand in 1881. Figure 5 shows a Marquand chart for four terms. Alexander Macfarlane preferred a narrow strip, which he called a "logical spectrum," subdivided and labeled as in Figure 6. Later, in "Adaptation of the Method of the Logical Spectrum to Boole's Problem" (in *Proceedings of the American Association for the Advancement of Science* 39 [1890]: 57f.), Macfarlane used his chart for solving a complicated problem in George Boole's *Laws of Thought* (1854).

Other types of rectangular charts were devised by William J. Newlin, William E. Hocking, and Lewis Carroll. Carroll introduced his chart in a book for children, *The Game of Logic* (London and New York, 1886). Instead of shading compartments, he proposed marking them with counters of two colors, one for classes known to have members, the other for null classes.

An elaborate diagrammatic method designed to cover all types of logic, including modal logics, was devised in 1897 by the American philosopher Charles Sanders Peirce and later discussed in several brief, obscurely written papers. Although Peirce considered these "existential graphs," as he called them, his greatest contribution to logic, they aroused little interest among later logicians and have yet to be fully explicated and evaluated.

FIGURE 4

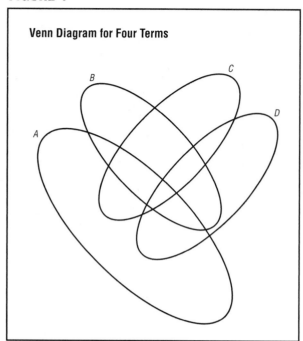

Venn Diagram for Four Terms

FIGURE 5

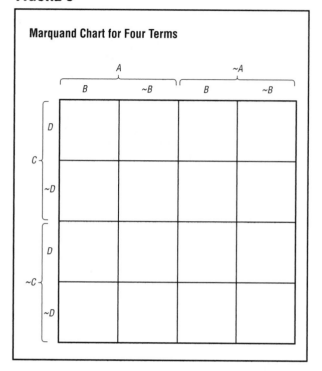

Marquand Chart for Four Terms

DIAGRAMS FOR THE PROPOSITIONAL CALCULUS

In the early twentieth century the class interpretation of Boolean algebra was supplemented by a more useful interpretation in which classes are replaced by propositions that are either true or false and related to one another by logical connectives. The Venn diagrams, as well as their chart extensions, work just as efficiently for the propositional calculus as for the class calculus, but cultural lag has prevented this fact from entering most logic textbooks. For example, the class statement "All apples are red" is equivalent to the propositional statement "If x is an apple, then x is red." The same Venn diagram is therefore used for both statements (Figure 7). Similarly, the class statement "No A is B" is equivalent to the propositional statement "Not both A and B," symbolized in modern logic by the Sheffer stroke. Both statements are diagramed as in Figure 8.

A major defect of the Venn system is that it is difficult to distinguish the shading of one statement from the shading of another, so that one loses track of individual premises. This is best remedied by diagramming each statement on a separate sheet of transparent paper and superposing all sheets on the same basic diagram. Such a method using cellophane sheets shaded with different colors and superposed on a rectangular diagram was devised by Karl Döhmann, of Berlin.

A network method for solving problems in the propositional calculus, designed to keep statements separate and to bring out visually the nature of the logical connectives, is given in Martin Gardner's *Logic Machines and Diagrams* (1958), Chapter 3. Each term is represented by two vertical lines, one for "true," the other for "false." A connective is symbolized by "shuttles" that connect truth-value lines in the manner indicated by the "true" lines of a truth table for that connective. Figure 9 shows the diagram for implication.

A "Boole table," devised by Walter E. Stuerman, also keeps individual statements separate and can be used for graphing any type of Boolean algebra. It combines features of Macfarlane's chart with Lambert's linear method. John F. Randolph has developed a simple method of handling a Marquand diagram by sketching nested cross marks and using dots to indicate nonempty compartments.

Although the Venn circles and their various chart extensions can obviously be given three-dimensional forms, no three-dimensional techniques for diagramming Boolean algebra have been found useful because of the extreme difficulty of manipulating solid diagrams. In this connection, however, mention should be made of a curious cubical chart, devised by C. Howard Hinton in 1904, that is constructed with 64 smaller cubes and used for identifying valid syllogisms.

FIGURE 6

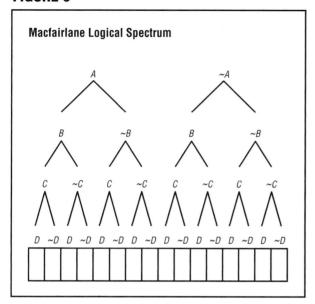

Macfairlane Logical Spectrum

FIGURE 7

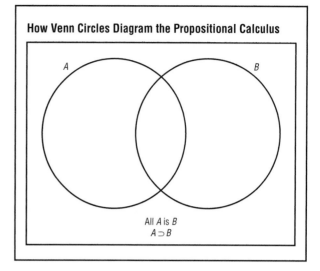

How Venn Circles Diagram the Propositional Calculus

All *A* is *B*
$A \supset B$

Boolean algebra is now known to be a special type of lattice, which in turn is a certain type of partially ordered set. A lattice diagram for a Boolean algebra of two terms is easily drawn, and although of little use in problem solving, it displays graphically many features of the propositional calculus.

In the logic of relations a large variety of useful diagrams have been widely used. The tree graph, for example, which goes back to ancient Greece, is an efficient way to indicate a familiar type of relation. Examples include the tree of Porphyry, found in medieval and Renaissance logics, the later tree diagrams of Peter Ramus, diagrams showing the evolution of organisms, family tree graphs, and graphs of stochastic processes in probability theory. The topological diagrams in Kurt Lewin's *Principles of Topological Psychology* (1936), as well as modern "sociograms," transport networks, and so on, may be called logic diagrams if "logic" is taken in a broad sense. However, such diagrams are now studied in the branch of mathematics called graph theory and are not generally considered logic diagrams. In a wide sense any geometrical figure is a logic diagram since it expresses logical relations between its parts.

AREAS FOR EXPLORATION

All diagrams for Boolean algebras work most efficiently when the statements to be diagramed are simple binary relations. Compound statements with parenthetical expressions are awkward to handle unless the statements are first translated into simpler expressions. Attempts

have been made to extend the Venn diagrams and other types of Boolean graphs to take care of parenthetical statements directly, but in all cases the diagrams become too complex to be useful. Perhaps simpler methods will be found by which traditional diagrams can be made to accommodate parenthetical expressions.

Little progress has been made in developing good diagrammatic methods for minimizing a complex logical statement—that is, for reducing it to a simpler but equivalent form. Several chart methods for minimizing have been worked out. The closest to a diagrammatic technique is the Karnaugh map, first explained by Maurice Karnaugh in 1953. The map is based on an earlier diagram called the Veitch chart, in turn based on a Marquand chart.

Work on better methods of minimizing is still in progress. The work has important practical consequences because electrical networks can be translated into Boolean algebra and the expression minimized and then translated back into network design to effect a simplification of circuitry. It is possible that a by-product of new minimizing methods may be a diagrammatic method superior to any yet found.

Another field open to exploration is the devising of efficient ways to diagram logics not of the Boolean type, notably modal logics and the various many-valued logics.

See also Boole, George; Carroll, Lewis; Geometry; Hocking, William Ernest; Lambert, Johann Heinrich; Leibniz, Gottfried Wilhelm; Logic, History of; Logic Machines; Peirce, Charles Sanders; Porphyry; Ramus, Peter; Renaissance; Venn, John.

FIGURE 8

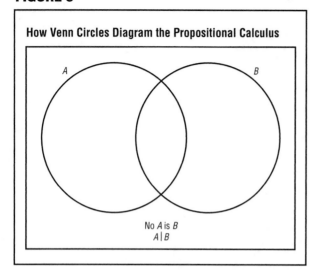

How Venn Circles Diagram the Propositional Calculus

No *A* is *B*
A | *B*

FIGURE 9

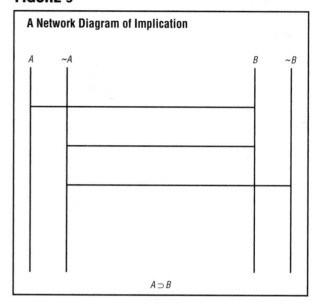

A Network Diagram of Implication

A ⊃ *B*

Bibliography

Venn's *Symbolic Logic,* rev. 2nd ed. (London: Macmillan, 1894), remains the best single source for the early history of logic diagrams. It also contains the fullest exposition of his own method, which he first presented in "On the Diagrammatic and Mechanical Representation of Propositions and Reasonings," *Philosophical Magazine* 10 (July 1880): 1–18. For more recent history and references, consult Martin Gardner, *Logic Machines and Diagrams* (New York: McGraw-Hill, 1958).

Euler's explanation of his circles can be found in his *Lettres à une princesse d'Allemagne,* Vol. II, letters 102–108 (St. Petersburg: Academie Impériale des Sciences, 1768). Lambert's method, in an improved form, is explained in J. N. Keynes, *Studies and Exercises in Formal Logic.* 4th ed. (London: Macmillan, 1906), p. 243.

For Venn diagrams of statements with more than four terms, see W. E. Hocking, "Two Extensions of the Use of Graphs in Elementary Logic," in *University of California Publications in Philosophy* 2 (2) (1909): 31–44; Edmund C. Berkeley, "Boolean Algebra and Applications to Insurance," in *Record, American Institute of Actuaries* 26 (1937): 373–414, and 27 (1938): 167–176 (reprinted, New York, 1952); Trenchard More Jr., "On the Construction of Venn Diagrams," in *Journal of Symbolic Logic* 24 (1959): 303–304; and Stephen Barr, *Experiments in Topology* (New York: Crowell, 1964), p. 206. A method of drawing five irregular but congruent convex pentagons intersecting in the required manner is explained by David W. Henderson in "Venn Diagrams for More Than Four Classes," *American Mathematical Monthly* 70 (1963): 424–426.

On rectangular Venn charts, see Allan Marquand, "A Logical Diagram for *n* Terms," in *Philosophical Magazine* 12 (1881): 266–270; Alexander Macfarlane, "The Logical Spectrum," in *Philosophical Magazine* 19 (1885): 286–289; William J. Newlin, "A New Logical Diagram," in *Journal of Philosophy, Psychology, and Scientific Methods* 3 (1906): 539–545; and the Hocking paper mentioned above. Carroll's method is further developed in his *Symbolic Logic* (London and New York, 1896; paperback ed., New York, 1958). Peirce's papers are reprinted in the *Collected Papers of Charles Sanders Peirce,* edited by Charles Hartshorne and Paul Weiss, Vol. IV (Cambridge, MA: Harvard University Press, 1933).

An explanation of how Venn circles can be used to handle problems in the propositional calculus appears in Gardner's *Logic Machines and Diagrams* (op. cit.), pp. 48–54. Döhmann explained his method in a privately printed booklet, *Eine logistische Farbenquadrat-Methode* (Berlin, 1962). Stuerman described his "Boole table" in "Plotting Boolean Functions," *American Mathematical Monthly* 67 (1960): 170–172, and in "The Boole Table Generalized," *American Mathematical Monthly* 68 (1961): 53–56. Randolph's method is given in "Cross-Examining Propositional Calculus and Set Operations," *American Mathematical Monthly* 72 (1965): 117–127. Hinton explained his cubical chart in his eccentric book *The Fourth Dimension* (London: Sonnenschein, 1904), pp. 100–106. John Evenden presented a two-term lattice diagram for Boolean algebra in "A Lattice-Diagram for the Propositional Calculus," *Mathematical Gazette* 46 (1962): 119–122.

Karnaugh first explained his map in "The Map Method for Synthesis of Combinational Logic Circuits," *Transactions of the American Institute of Electrical Engineers,* Part 1, 72 (1953): 593–599. E. W. Veitch explained his earlier diagram in "A Chart Method for Simplifying Truth Functions," *Proceedings of the Association for Computing Machinery* (May 2 and 3, 1952), 127–133.

Martin Gardner (1967)

LOGICISM

See *Mathematics, Foundations of*

LOGIC MACHINES

Because logic underlies all deductive reasoning, one might say that all computers are logic machines. In a wider sense, any mechanical device is a logic machine (for example, an eggbeater spins clockwise "if and only if" its crank turns clockwise). Generally, however, the term is restricted to machines designed primarily or exclusively for solving problems in formal logic. Although a digital computer, or even a punch-card data-processing machine, can be programmed to handle many types of logic, it is not considered a logic machine in the strict sense.

The rotating circles of Ramón Lull, thirteenth-century Spanish mystic, cannot be called logic machines even though they were used as reasoning aids. The first true logic machine was a small device called a "demonstrator," invented by Charles Stanhope, third Earl Stanhope, an eighteenth-century English statesman. By sliding two panels (one of gray wood, the other of transparent red glass) behind a rectangular opening, he could test the validity of traditional syllogisms, as well as syllogisms with such quantified terms as "Most of *a*" and "8 of 10 of *a*." Stanhope also used his device for solving elementary problems in what he called the logic of probability.

JEVONS'S MACHINE

The first logic machine capable of solving a complicated problem faster than a human could solve it without the aid of a machine was the "logical piano" invented by the nineteenth-century economist and logician William Stanley Jevons. The machine was built for him by a clockmaker at Salford in 1869 and first demonstrated by Jevons in 1870 at a meeting of the Royal Society of London. The device (now owned by the Oxford Museum of the History of Science) resembles a miniature upright piano, about three feet high, with a keyboard of 21 keys. On the face of the piano are openings through which one can see the 16 possible combinations of 4 terms and their negatives. A statement in logic is fed to the machine by pressing keys according to certain rules. Internal levers and pulleys eliminate from the machine's face all combinations of terms inconsistent with the statement. When all desired statements have thus been fed to the machine the face is inspected to determine what term combinations, if any, are consistent with the statements.

Jevons believed that this machine, designed to handle Boolean algebra, provided a convincing demonstration of the superiority of George Boole's logic over the tradi-

tional logic of Aristotle and the Schoolmen. John Venn's system of diagramming follows essentially the same procedure as Jevons's machine. In both cases the procedure gives what are today called the valid lines of a truth table for the combined statements under consideration. Neither the Venn diagrams nor Jevons's machine is capable of reducing these lines to a more compact form. This criticism of the machine was stressed by the English philosopher F. H. Bradley in his *Principles of Logic* (1883).

OTHER MECHANICAL DEVICES

Jevons's logical piano was greatly simplified by Allan Marquand, who built his first model in 1881, when he was teaching logic at Princeton University. Like Jevons's, Marquand's machine is limited to 4 terms, but the 16 possible combinations are exhibited on its face by 16 pointers, each with a valid and an invalid position, arranged in a pattern that corresponds to Marquand's chart for 4 terms (see the entry "Logic Diagrams," Figure 5). The number of keys is reduced to 10, and the device is about a third the height of Jevons's machine. Both Marquand and Jevons interpreted Boolean algebra primarily in class terms, but their machines operate just as efficiently with the propositional calculus.

A third machine of the Jevons type was invented in 1910 by Charles P. R. Macaulay, an Englishman living in Chicago. It is a compact, ingenious boxlike device with interior rods operated by tilting the box a certain way while pins on the side are pressed to put statements into the machine. Consistent combinations of four terms and their negatives appear in windows on top of the box.

A curious contrivance for evaluating the 256 combinations of syllogistic premises and conclusions was constructed in 1903 by Annibale Pastore, a philosopher at the University of Genoa. It consists of three wheels, representing a syllogism's three terms, joined to one another by an arrangement of endless belts appropriate to the syllogism being tested. If the syllogism is valid, all three wheels turn when one is cranked.

GRID CARDS

Logic grid cards are cards that can be superposed so that valid deductions from logical premises are seen through openings on the cards. A set of syllogism grid cards invented by the Englishman Henry Cunynghame, a contemporary of Jevons, was depicted by Jevons in Chapter 11 of *Studies in Deductive Logic* (London, 1884). A differently designed set is shown in Martin Gardner's "Logic Machines" (in *Scientific American* 186 [March 1952]: 68–73). A more elaborate set, indicating the nature of the fallacy when a syllogism is invalid, can be found in Gardner's *Logic Machines and Diagrams* (New York, 1958) and Richard Lampkin's *Testing for Truth* (Buffalo, NY, 1962). Triangular-shaped grid cards, for binary relations in the propositional calculus, are described in Gardner's book and in H. M. Cundy and A. P. Rollett's *Mathematical Models* (2nd ed., Oxford, 1961; see pp. 256–258). Gardner described a simple way to make punch cards that can be sorted in such a manner as to solve logic problems in "Mathematical Games" (in *Scientific American* 203 [December 1960]: 160–168).

ELECTRICAL MACHINES

Marquand sketched an electrical circuit by which his machine could be operated, but the electrical version was probably never built. Benjamin Burack, a psychologist at Roosevelt College, Chicago, was the first actually to construct an electrical logic machine, in 1936. His device tested all syllogisms, including hypothetical and disjunctive forms. Since then many different kinds of electrical syllogism machines have been constructed.

In 1910, in a review in a Russian journal, Paul Ehrenfest pointed out that because a wire either carries a current or does not, it would be possible to translate certain types of switching circuits into Boolean algebra. Work along such lines was done by the Russian physicist V. I. Šestakov in 1934–1935, but his results were not published until 1941. Similar views were set forth independently in 1936, in a Japanese journal, by Akira Nakasima and Masao Hanzawa. It was the mathematician Claude E. Shannon, however, who impressed the engineering world with the importance of this isomorphism by his independent work, first published in 1938.

Shannon's paper inspired William Burkhart and Theodore A. Kalin, then undergraduates at Harvard University, to design the world's first electrical machine for evaluating statements in the propositional calculus. The Kalin-Burkhart machine was built in 1947. Statements with as many as twelve terms are fed into it by setting switches. The machine scans a truth table for the combined statements, and a set of twelve small bulbs indicates the combination of true and false terms for each truth-table row as it is scanned. If the combination is consistent with the statements, this is indicated by another bulb. The machine is thus an electrical version of Jevons's device but handles more complex statements and presents valid truth-table rows in serial time sequence rather than simultaneously.

A three-term electrical machine was built in England in 1949 without knowledge of the Kalin-Burkhart machine. Advances in switching components made possible more sophisticated logic machines in the United States and elsewhere during the early 1950s. Of special interest is a ten-term machine built at the Burroughs Research Center in Paoli, Pennsylvania, using the parenthesis-free notation of Jan Łukasiewicz.

DIGITAL COMPUTERS

While the special machines were being developed it became apparent that statements in Boolean algebra could easily be translated into a binary notation and analyzed on any general-purpose digital computer. As digital computers became more available, as well as faster and more flexible, interest in the design of special-purpose logic machines waned. Since 1955 almost all machine-aided investigations in logic have been conducted with digital computers. In 1960, Hao Wang described how he used an IBM 704 computer to test the first 220 theorems of the propositional calculus in *Principia Mathematica*. The machine's total running time was under three minutes.

The similarity between switching circuits and the nets of nerve cells in the brain suggests that the brain may think by a process that could be duplicated by computers. Much work is being done in programming computers to search for proofs of logic theorems in a manner similar to the heuristic reasoning of a logician—that is, by an uncertain strategy compounded of trial and error, logical reasoning, analogies with remembered experience, and sheer luck. The work is closely related to all types of learning machines. Such work may prove useful in exploring logics for which there is no decision procedure—or no known decision procedure—but no special machines have yet been built for such a purpose. Work is also under way on the more difficult problem of designing a machine, or programming a digital computer, to find new, nontrivial, and interesting theorems in a given logic.

Attempts have been made to design machines capable of reducing a statement in Boolean algebra to simpler form. A primitive minimizing machine was constructed by Daniel Bobrow, a New York City high school student, in 1952. At about the same time, Shannon and Edward F. Moore built a relay circuit analyzer that makes a systematic attempt to simplify circuits, a problem closely related to the logic minimizing problem.

No special machines are known to have been constructed for handling many-valued logics, but many papers have been published explaining how such machines could be built, as well as how digital computers could be programmed to handle such logics. Kurt Gödel's undecidability proof has ruled out the possibility of an ultimate logic machine capable of following a systematic procedure for testing any theorem in any possible logic, but whether the human brain is capable of doing any kind of creative work that a machine cannot successfully imitate is still an open, much debated question.

See also Aristotle; Boole, George; Bradley, Francis Herbert; Computing Machines; Gödel, Kurt; Gödel's Incompleteness Theorems; Jevons, William Stanley; Logic, History of; Łukasiewicz, Jan; Lull, Ramón; Machine Intelligence; Venn, John.

Bibliography

For a history of logic machines, see Martin Gardner, *Logic Machines and Diagrams* (New York: McGraw-Hill, 1958), and Rudolf Tarján, "Logische Maschinen," in *Digital Information Processors,* edited by Walter Hoffmann (New York: Interscience, 1962), which includes a bibliography of 119 references. Stanhope's machine is discussed in Robert Harley, "The Stanhope Demonstrator," *Mind* 4 (1879): 192–210.

Jevons described his logical piano in "On the Mechanical Performance of Logical Inference" (1870), reprinted in his *Pure Logic and Other Minor Works* (London: Macmillan, 1890); a briefer discussion appears in his *Principles of Science* (London: Macmillan, 1874; reprinted, New York, 1958). Marquand discussed his machine in "A New Logical Machine," *Proceedings of the American Academy of Arts and Sciences* 21 (1885): 303–307. Marquand's machine was praised by C. S. Peirce in "Logical Machines," *American Journal of Psychology* 1 (November 1887): 165–170. Pastore wrote an entire book about his device, *Logica formale, dedotta della considerazione di modelli meccanici* (Turin, 1906). The book was reviewed at length by André Lalande in *Revue philosophique de la France et de l'étranger* 63 (1907): 268–275.

Wolfe Mays, "The First Circuit for an Electrical Logic-Machine," in *Science* 118 (1953): 281–282, and George W. Patterson, "The First Electric Computer, a Magnetological Analysis," in *Journal of the Franklin Institute* 270 (1960): 130–137, describe Marquand's sketches. A description of Macaulay's device is in his U.S. patent, No. 1,079,504, issued in 1913.

Burack first described his 1936 machine in "An Electrical Logic Machine," *Science* 109 (1949): 610–611. Shannon's historic paper on the isomorphism of Boolean algebra and certain types of switching circuits is "A Symbolic Analysis of Relay and Switching Circuits," in *Transactions of the American Institute of Electrical Engineers* 57 (1938): 713–723. The Kalin-Burkhart machine is described in Edmund C. Berkeley, *Giant Brains* (New York: Wiley, 1949). The English three-term machine is discussed in Wolfe Mays and D. G. Prinz, "A Relay Machine for the Demonstration of Symbolic Logic," *Nature* 165 (1950): 197. The Burroughs machine is discussed in A. W. Burks, D. W. Warren, and J. B. Wright, "An Analysis of a Logical Machine Using Parenthesis-Free

Notation," *Mathematical Tables and Other Aids to Computation* 8 (1954): 53–57, and in William Miehle, "Burroughs Truth Function Evaluator," *Journal of the Association for Computing Machinery* 4 (1957): 189–192.

Hao Wang's description of his use of the IBM 704 is in "Toward Mechanical Mathematics," *IBM Journal of Research and Development* 4 (1960): 2–22, reprinted in *The Modeling of Mind,* edited by Kenneth Sayre and Frederick J. Crosson (Notre Dame, IN: University of Notre Dame Press, 1963). On computer simulation, see Allen Newell and H. A. Simon, "Computer Simulation of Human Thinking," in *Science* 134 (1961): 2011–2017, and references cited there. On the Shannon-Moore relay circuit analyzer, see Shannon and Moore's "Machine Aid for Switching Circuit Design," in *Proceedings of the Institute of Radio Engineers* 41 (1953): 1348–1351.

Martin Gardner (1967)

LOGOS

The Greek term *logos* is multiply ambiguous. The unabridged Greek dictionary gives five and a half long columns of definitions and examples. *Logos* is a noun corresponding to the verb *legein* (say), signifying, among other things, speech, statement, sentence, account, definition, formula, calculation, ratio, explanation, reasoning, and faculty of reason. Early studies of the term tended to talk about a concept of *logos,* as if there were some single concept or theory associated with it. In fact, the term was employed in different ways by different thinkers. Yet, there is a kind of interplay in concepts associated with the term that makes a single study worthwhile.

Scholars sometimes speak of a change from *mythos* to *logos;* roughly, a transition in expression from storytelling in myths, usually expressed in poetry, to scientific, philosophical, or historical accounts, usually expressed in prose. Philosophers of the sixth century BCE were among the first Western writers to compose treatises in prose. The new medium of expression permitted a more analytic and detached view of things, and it embodied a revolution in thinking about the world. Although *logos* (plural: *logoi*) could signify a story, increasingly *logoi* were taken to be scientific accounts in contrast to *mythoi* "stories" and *epea* "verses" (see Plato *Timaeus* 26e). But for the sophists, a *mythos* can be used to express a *logos* (Plato *Protagoras* 320c)—but only insofar as *logos* is seen as a more basic kind of explanation.

THE PRESOCRATICS

Logos soon came to signify something of the content of rational discourse as well as the medium, and it is this sense, or set of senses, that this entry will focus on. Heraclitus (c. 500 BCE) was the first philosopher to raise *logos* to the level of a principle. He opens his book by saying, "Of this *Logos*'s being forever do men prove to be uncomprehending, both before they hear and once they have heard it. For although all things happen according to this *Logos* they are like the unexperienced experiencing words and deeds such as I explain when I distinguish each thing according to its nature and show how it is" (fr. 1). Heraclitus's *logos* can be shared with people, and indeed he explicates it in his own treatise; but he anticipates that most people will fail to understand the message. "Although this *Logos* is common," Heraclitus writes, "the many live as if they had a private understanding" (fr. 2). Somehow the *logos* is publicly available but ignored by the many, who lack philosophical insight. The *logos* has a particular message, or implication: "Listening not to me but to the *Logos* it is wise to agree that all things are one" (fr. 50). Heraclitus regards the *logos* as transcending his own personal communication, and teaching the unity of things.

Heraclitus's *logos* is a kind of structural principle as well as a message, a reciprocal law of exchange. It has a kind of syntax like language that orders the changes of the world. Heraclitus plays with statements that are syntactically ambiguous, as if to show that the same words can make different statements, which at another level complement each other. So the world is based on a single structure that manifests itself in contraries. Language provides a model for the world.

In the early fifth century BCE, Parmenides presented an argument against change, in the form of a revelation from a goddess. Yet the goddess tells the narrator, "Judge by *logos* the contentious refutation spoken by me" (fr. 7). Here *logos* seems to mean something like *reasoning*, which clearly becomes the key to philosophical truth. For, despite the religious imagery and associations of his poem, Parmenides's message is above all an argument addressed to the reason.

In the latter half of the fifth century BCE the sophists traveled about Greece teaching practical skills to help young men succeed in politics and, above all, the art of public speaking. They saw a knowledge of *logos*—and especially, for them, the spoken word—as the key to controlling emotions and hence the reactions of audiences to a message. As Gorgias observed, "*Logos* is a great potentate, who by means of the tiniest and most invisible body is able to achieve the most godlike results" (fr. 11, section 8). Sophists composed contradictory arguments (*antilogikoi logoi*) on a single topic to teach skill in argumentation, and sometimes studied elements of language and argumentation.

PLATO AND ARISTOTLE

By the fourth century BCE *logos* is established not only as speech and the like, but as the faculty of reason. Speech becomes the manifestation of reason, and reason the source of speech. According to Plato an understanding of rhetoric presupposes a knowledge of souls—what would later be called psychology—and the use of dialectic to implant truth in souls (*Phaedrus*). In fact, thinking (*dianoia*) is just internal speech (*Sophist* 263e, *Theaetetus* 189e). Thus speech becomes a model for thought, and ultimately a representation for the world; for a sentence (*logos*), such as "Theaetetus is sitting," is true just in case it correctly describes an action or condition of Theaetetus (*Sophist* 263a–b). In another context, Plato suggests that one can more safely study the world in *logoi* than by means of sensations, and he consequently adopts a method of hypothesis (*Phaedo* 99d–100a).

The sign that one has knowledge is one's ability to give an account (*logos*) or explanation (*Phaedo* 76b), and one who can give an adequate account is a dialectician (*Republic* 534b). At one point Plato considers as a definition of *knowledge* "true judgment accompanied by an account [*logos*]," but rejects this in part because a satisfactory explanation of *logos* cannot be given independently of knowledge (*Theaetetus* 201c ff.). While the ability to give a rational account provides evidence of knowledge, the account is no mere component of knowledge.

Aristotle accepts Plato's view of the relation between language and the world along with some of Plato's terminology (*Categories* 2–4; *On Interpretation* 1–7). He recognizes, if somewhat obscurely, the two relationships that allow language to connect to reality: reference (*semainein*) and predication (*katêgoria*)—the latter primarily a link between a substance and its attributes, but mirrored in the link between grammatical subject and predicate. The basic unit of communication is the sentence (*logos*), which when it makes an assertion (*apophantikos*) is the bearer of truth or falsity. Whereas reference connects words with things, (grammatical) predication asserts that the things are connected in a certain way; if the assertion corresponds to the way things are, it is true; otherwise it is false. Building on this basic theory of language, Aristotle developed the first system of logic, showing how certain propositions follow logically from certain other propositions (*Prior Analytics*). Moreover, he conceived of a science as a set of propositions arranged in a logical order with axioms and definitions as starting points, and theorems as conclusions (*Posterior Analytics* I)—laying out this ideal structure that would be realized by the axiomatization of geometry a generation or two after his death. Thus in a certain sense Aristotle saw the world as possessing a thoroughgoing logical structure that could be captured in language. Indeed, whereas contemporary logicians often think of logical systems as arbitrary human constructs, some of which are useful for capturing certain linguistic relationships, Aristotle thinks of his logic as having its basis in the nature of things (*Prior Analytics* I 27).

HELLENISTIC PHILOSOPHY

According to the Stoics, the world is ultimately composed of fire, which is identical with God. Fire pervades the world and functions as a world-soul. Reason (*logos*) is found in the world-soul, which orders and controls the world; it is the active principle and is identical with God (Diogenes Laertius 7.134). Soul is found in all animals, and in humans there is also a ruling principle that possesses reason. Thus *logos* in the human mind is like *logos* in the cosmos. Through the activity of fire, reason controls the creation and the history of the world. The world periodically perishes in a conflagration that turns all the elements back into fire, from which a new world arises, seeded by seminal *logos*, a structural principle that directs the cosmogony (Diogenes Laertius 136). The events of the world are ultimately under the control of reason, so that the world is governed by providence (Diogenes Laertius 138–9). The Stoics distinguish between uttered discourse (*prophorikos logos*) and internal discourse (*endiathetos logos*); the former humans have in common with parrots, but the latter is peculiar to humans (Sextus Empiricus *Against the Professors* 8.275).

Philo of Alexandria (early to mid-first century CE), combining Judaism and Platonism by using Plato's theory to explicate the Bible, recognizes *logos* as an image of the invisible God, and human beings as created in the image of the *logos* (*On Dreams* 239, *The Confusion of Tongues* 147). God also acts by his word, for "His word is his deed" (*The Sacrifices of Able and Cain* 65). The world is itself the product of a plan in the mind of God, consisting of the Platonic Forms (*On the Creation* 17–19), which are thus conceived of as present in the mind of God. From this model of the world the creator makes first an invisible world, then a visible one (29–36).

CHRISTIANITY AND NEOPLATONISM

The Gospel according to John begins by affirming the central role of the *Logos*, or Word: "In the beginning was the Word, and the Word was with God, and the Word was God. ... All things were made by him; and without him was not any thing made that was made. ... And the Word

was made flesh, and dwelt among us" (John 1.1, 3, 14). It may be that the *Logos* of John derives from Jewish rather than Greek conceptions, yet the notion was close enough to Greek philosophical conceptions to allow early Christian thinkers to see in it a point of contact between their scriptures and pagan philosophy. They saw Philo as an inspired writer who shared their vision of the Word of God as an intermediary between God and humans. Jesus of Nazareth was the Word of God, who manifested the power of God on earth and prepared the way for his disciples to become sons of God (1.12).

In the mid-second century Justin Martyr identifies Jesus as the *Logos* that wise men, including philosophers, partake of. He finds references to the *Logos* in Plato's *Timaeus*, and more general instances of divine reason in Heraclitus and the Stoics (*First Apology* 5, 40; *Second Apology* 8, 10, 13). He explains that Christians "call Him [Jesus] the Word, because He carries tidings from the Father to men: but maintain that this power is indivisible and inseparable from the Father" (*Dialogue with Trypho* 128). In the most systematic statement of the early church fathers, Origen (third century), commenting on the opening lines of Hebrews, says that Jesus as Word is the invisible image of the invisible God—apparently apprehensible only by reason—who "interpret[s] the secrets of wisdom, and the mysteries of knowledge, making them known to the rational creation" (*On Principles* 1.2.6–7).

Plotinus borrowed from the Stoics at least the general conception of *logos* in a seed to account for the influence Soul has on the visible world. The world "was ordered according to a rational principle [*kata logon*] of soul potentially having throughout itself power to impose order according to rational principles [*kata logous*], just as the principles in seeds shape and form living creatures like little worlds" (*Enneads* 4.3.10). This also helps one understand how Mind orders things by comparing its operation to that of a seed with a rational principle; in such a way reason (*logos*) flows out from Mind to the world (3.2.2). And one can understand how timeless realities have foresight over the world of change by supposing that events unfold according to an archetype, which is effortlessly realized by the imposition on matter of rational principles (4.4.12). Indeed, Plotinus proclaims in a theodicy, "The origin [of events in the world] is *logos* and all things are *logos*," even if they seem to be irrational or evil to our limited view (3.2.15).

In the early fifth century Augustine argued that a word in the heart precedes the articulate word of speech. This inner word is a likeness of the Word of God, by whom God carried out the creation of the world, and which came to be embodied in flesh in a way analogous to that in which the inner word becomes articulated in language. Thus the preverbal cognition that humans have in themselves an image of the Word of God (*On the Trinity* 15.11.20).

Although in Greek philosophy many different versions of how language, reason, and rational principles connect with the world can be found, what is remarkable is the widespread commitment to some view whereby reason is imbedded in the cosmos. Human reason does not simply impose some extraneous order on the world, but it discovers in nature a structure that mind has in common with the world.

See also Aristotle; Augustine, St.; Diogenes Laertius; Hellenistic Thought; Heraclitus of Ephesus; Neoplatonism; Parmenides of Elea; Patristic Philosophy; Philo Judaeus; Plato; Platonism and the Platonic Tradition; Plotinus; Semantics, History of; Sextus Empiricus; Sophists; Stoicism.

Bibliography

Aall, Anathon. *Geschichte der Logosidee in der griechischen Philosophie.* 2 vols. Leipzig, Germany: O. R. Reisland, 1896–1899. Reprint, Frankfurt, Germany: Minerva, 1968.

Boeder, Heribert. "Der frühgriechische Wortgebrauch von *Logos* und *Aletheia.*" *Archiv für Begriffsgeschichte* 4 (1959): 82–112.

Frede, Michael, and Gisela Striker, eds. *Rationality in Greek Thought.* Oxford: Clarendon Press, 1996.

Kittel, Gerhard, et al. "Lego." In *Theologisches Wörterbuch zum Neuen Testament,* edited by Gerhard Kittel, vol. 4, 69–140. Stuttgart, Germany: W. Kohlhammer, 1942. Abridged in *Theological Dictionary of the New Testament.* Translated by Geoffrey W. Bromiley, 505–514. Grand Rapids, MI: W. B. Eerdmans, 1985.

Mourelatos, Alexander P. D. "Heraclitus, Parmenides, and the Naive Metaphysics of Things." In *Exegesis and Argument,* edited by E. N. Lee, A. P. D. Mourelatos, and R. Rorty. Assen, Netherlands: Van Gorcum, 1973.

Robb, Kevin, ed. *Language and Thought in Early Greek Philosophy.* La Salle, IL: The Hegeler Institute, 1983.

Daniel W. Graham (2005)

LOISY, ALFRED
(1857–1940)

Alfred Loisy, the French biblical exegetist, was the best-known and most controversial representative of the Modernist movement in France at the end of the nineteenth and beginning of the twentieth centuries. His scholarly investigation led him to the kind of destructive criticism of the Gospel narratives and Christian dogmas carried on earlier by such scholars as D. F. Strauss and Ernest Renan, whose lectures at the Institut Catholique Loisy attended from 1882 to 1885. Loisy's long career, from his entry into the priesthood in 1879 to shortly before his death, was one of much controversy and progressive estrangement from personal religion.

Loisy was born at Ambrière, Marne, and died at Ceffonds, Haute Marne. He became professor of Hebrew in 1881, and of Holy Scripture in 1889, at the Institut Catholique. Loisy's views on the date of the book of Proverbs soon aroused misgivings, and he was warned that continuation of such unorthodoxy would place him in danger of official censure.

Loisy's superior, Monsignor d'Hulst, was an enlightened man and not intolerant of the work of the modern critical school, but as head of the Institut Catholique he was in a responsible and difficult position. The head of the College of St. Sulpice had forbidden his students to attend the heterodox Loisy's lectures, and when in 1892 Loisy started his own periodical, *L'enseignement biblique,* for the instruction of young priests, d'Hulst felt obliged to urge caution. In 1892, soon after Renan's death, d'Hulst himself wrote an article on Renan in *Le correspondant.* Without condoning Renan's break with Catholicism, d'Hulst upheld his complaint, in *Souvenirs d'enfance et de jeunesse,* that the instruction given at such seminaries as St. Sulpice was out of touch with modern scholarship and the modern world. A further article by d'Hulst, aimed at promoting tolerance of the more searching kind of biblical criticism, gave offense in orthodox quarters, and d'Hulst felt obliged to clear his institute of any suspicion of unorthodoxy. Therefore, when Loisy continued to declare his critical independence of dogma and revelation, and to present a historical Jesus apart from the Christ of faith, he was forced to resign his chair in 1893.

As a reply to modernist exegesis, the pope issued the encyclical *Providentissimus Deus* (November 18, 1893), denying that error is compatible with divine authorship. Loisy wrote to Leo XIII, professing submission to the encyclical's demand that the truth of the Bible should not be questioned. His insincerity can be inferred, however, for his activities remained unchanged. In fact, on receiving a reply in a mollified tone that invited him to devote himself to less contentious studies, Loisy openly expressed his impatience.

Loisy criticized the Protestant scholar Carl Gustav Adolf von Harnack's *Wesen des Christentums* (Leipzig, 1900) in his *L'évangile et l'église* (Paris, 1902), which was condemned by the archbishop of Paris as undermining faith in the authority of Scripture and the divinity of Jesus Christ. Loisy wrote an apology, *Autour d'un petit livre* (Paris, 1903), which, with four other works of his, was condemned by the Holy Office and placed on the Index in 1903. The papal secretary of state required the archbishop of Paris to demand that Loisy withdraw the five offending volumes, but Loisy refused.

He wrote in conciliatory terms to Pope Plus X, but the development of his religious ideas—or, in Catholic eyes, the disintegration of his faith—could ultimately lead only to his exclusion from the Roman communion. He regarded such mysteries as the incarnation of God as mere metaphors and symbols, and described his own religious belief as pantheistic, positivistic, or humanitarian rather than Christian. He conceived the basic problem facing the man torn between belief and doubt to be whether the world contains or embodies any spiritual principle apart from man's own consciousness.

In 1907 the papal secretary of state called upon Loisy to repudiate certain propositions, attributed to him and condemned in the decree *Lamentabili* (July 2, 1907), and to disown Modernism, condemned in Plus X's encyclical *Pascendi Dominici Gregis* (September 6, 1907). Loisy replied that where his views were not misrepresented in the decree, he felt obliged to stand by them, since he regarded them as true. The demands were repeated, and Loisy was required to submit within ten days. He still refused and was thereupon excommunicated.

Loisy's break with the church in 1908 put an end to what had become a false and increasingly impossible position. In 1909 he was appointed professor of the history of religion at the Collège de France, a chair that he held until 1927 and that allowed him to continue publishing in freedom. He published memoirs of his most controversial years in *Choses passées* (Paris, 1913).

His *Naissance du christianisme* (Paris, 1933) drew together and presented more intransigently views that he had held and expressed earlier, but his disbelief in the truth of the Gospel narratives and the Acts of the Apostles was now more pronounced. The supernatural elements were discredited, and the view of the historical Jesus was not very different from those of Strauss and Renan. A prophet appeared in Galilee and was crucified while Pontius Pilate governed Judaea. The rest—the alleged events of Jesus' life and his subsequent deification by his followers—belonged, for Loisy as for Renan, to the realm of myth and Messianic aspiration in search of its symbolic figure.

See also Harnack, Carl Gustav Adolf von; Modernism; Renan, Joseph Ernest; Strauss, David Friedrich.

Bibliography

ADDITIONAL WORKS BY LOISY
Histoire du canon de l'Ancien Testament. Paris: Letouzey and Ané, 1890.
Histoire du canon du Nouveau Testament. Paris: Maisonneuve, 1891.
Histoire critique du texte et des versions de l'Ancien Testament. Paris: Letouzey and Ané, 1892.
Le quatrième évangile. Paris: A. Picard, 1903.
Les évangiles synoptiques. Paris, 1908.
Jésus et la tradition évangélique. Paris, 1910.
À propos d'histoire des religions. Paris: Nourry, 1911.
Les mystères païens et le mystère chrétien. Paris: Nourry, 1914.
La paix des nations et la religion de l'avenir. Paris: Nourry, 1920.
La morale humaine. Paris: Nourry, 1923.

WORKS ON LOISY
Petre, M. D. *Alfred Loisy: His Religious Significance*. Cambridge, U.K.: Cambridge University Press, 1944.
Vidler, A. R. *The Modernist Movement in the Roman Church*, 67–139. Cambridge, U.K.: Cambridge University Press, 1934.

Colin Smith (1967)

LOMBARD, PETER

See *Peter Lombard*

LONGINUS (PSEUDO)

From its first publication in 1554 until the early nineteenth century, the fragmentary text *Peri hupsous* was all but unquestioningly attributed to Cassius Longinus, a Greek of the third century CE. Prevalent scholarly opinion now places the origin of the text in the first half of the first century; but, nothing beyond the text itself being known of its actual author, and nothing of comparable interest being known to have been written by the historical Longinus, the use of the latter name for the author of the text has stuck.

Problems of interpretation of the text begin with its title. Although the word *hupsēlos* is commonly translated as "sublime," Longinus, in contrast with modern writers, uses it neither as a quasi-technical term nor as the expression of an aesthetic concept coordinate with "the beautiful" but as an ordinary term of praise (even if special praise) for compositions of words. A case has even been made for taking the term, as he uses it, to signify nothing more specific than greatness or excellence in discourse (Grube 1957).

However, there are also grounds for supposing that Longinus has in mind a specific literary virtue. The sublime, he says, is the echo of a great mind; its effect is to transport us; it fills us with joy and pride as if we ourselves had produced what we hear. Some of these passages may give the modern reader a faint tingle of Kant, but Longinus, however often he compares sublime writing to thunderbolts, volcanoes, and the like, never applies the word *hupsēlos* to natural phenomena—only to verbal productions. Even where he compares writing to painting and to music, he never attributes sublimity to products of those media, but only to works of words. In short, the Longinian *hupsos*, unlike the modern "sublime," is a quality of discourses only.

At the same time, Longinus holds that the power to produce sublime discourse is more a product of nature than of art (*technē*), the latter being understood as a teachable, specialized form of know-how.For Longinus, whatever contribution is made by the calculated use of figures, diction, and word arrangement—devices whose exposition in fact takes up the major part of *Peri hupsous*—the chief source of sublimity is the inborn power to form great conceptions. (Longinus's term for this power, *megalophuia*, usually translated "genius," literally means "great-naturedness.") Sublime discourse thus turns out to be discourse in which the natural greatness of the mind of the writer or speaker is seemingly imparted to the reader or hearer.

Peri hupsous enjoyed a great vogue following the publication of Nicholas Boileau's French translation in 1674, then passed out of fashion over the next century as the application of the term *sublime* shifted from discourse to nature, and the underlying conception from rhetoric to psychology. One can argue, however, that by explaining sublimity of discourse in terms of the nature of the author and the mind of the audience, Longinus himself provided the basis for that shift.

See also Aesthetics, History of; Beauty; Ugliness.

Bibliography

WORKS BY LONGINUS (PSEUDO)

On Great Writing (1957). Translated by G. M. A. Grube. Indianapolis: Hackett, 1991. Does a better job than most English translations of avoiding the imposition of alien meanings, though at the price of excluding the word "sublime."

"Longinus" on the Sublime, edited by D. A. Russell. Oxford: Clarendon Press, 1964. Greek text with commentary.

WORKS ON LONGINUS (PSEUDO)

Grube, G. M. A. "Notes on the *Peri Hupsous.*" *American Journal of Philology* 78 (1957): 355–374. A collection of remarks on matters of translation and interpretation, particularly on the meaning of the word *hupsos*.

Macksey, Richard. "Longinus Reconsidered." *Modern Language Notes* 108 (1993): 913–934. A concentrated summary account of the text and its influence.

Olson, Elder. "The Argument of Longinus' *On the Sublime*." In *Critics and Criticism, Ancient and Modern*, edited by R. S. Crane. Chicago: University of Chicago Press, 1952. (Originally published in *Modern Philology* 39 (1942): 225–258.) A defense of Longinus's claim to be explaining the *art* (in the classical sense) of sublime writing.

Miles Rind (2005)

LOPATIN, LEO MIKHAILOVICH

See *Lopatin, Lev Mikhailovich*

LOPATIN, LEV MIKHAILOVICH
(1855–1920)

Lev Mikhailovich Lopatin, the Russian philosopher and psychologist, was one of a number of Russian thinkers—such as A. A. Kozlov—to advance a pluralistic idealism or personalism inspired by the monadology of Gottfried Wilhelm Leibniz. Lopatin was for many years professor of philosophy at Moscow University, president of the Moscow Psychological Society, and editor of the leading Russian journal, *Voprosy Filosofii i Psikhologii* (Problems of Philosophy and Psychology). He wrote extensively and is famous for the clarity and beauty of his style. His thought owed much not only to Leibniz (and to Rudolf Hermann Lotze) but also to his longtime friend, the Russian philosopher Vladimir Solov'ëv.

Lopatin held that every activity or process presupposes an agent. In his metaphysics there is a plurality of agents, which are spiritual entities (monads), supratemporal, and thus indestructible (since destruction involves cessation of existence in time). He held that God is related to this plurality as its unifying ground, but he did not develop fully the character of this relationship. Lopatin's chief contributions to the general doctrine of monads are his view of the substantiality of the individual spirit and his doctrine of "creative causality." According to the former, the individual spirit is neither a substance that is separate from its phenomena nor a pure succession of absolute states; each of these conceptions is fundamentally self-contradictory. Rather, the spirit is a substance that is immanent in its phenomena; its phenomena are the direct realization of its nature. Each individual spirit, moreover, is a "creative" or productive cause; temporal, mechanical causality, and necessity, as well as all material properties—such as extension—are derivatives of the primary causality of supratemporal spirit.

Lopatin was the first of the Russian Leibnizians to give thorough attention to the moral sphere. The doctrine of creative causality gave him a basis for asserting the freedom of the will and for developing an ethical personalism in which moral phenomena represent the highest manifestation of the creative activity of individual spirit. Thus moral phenomena have metaphysical significance, and despite the evil and the inefficacy of good that we observe in the world, reality contains a moral order and is not "indifferent to the realization of the moral ideal."

Just as in ethics Lopatin maintained that unaided experience is not an adequate guide, so in epistemology generally, he discounted pure empiricism in favor of "speculative" principles, defining speculative philosophy as "the knowledge of real things in their principles and in their ultimate signification." Man's immediate inner experience is the source of his knowledge of real things, but philosophy works on this experience and goes beyond it through rational speculation.

See also Agent Causation; Ethics, History of; Kozlov, Aleksei Aleksandrovich; Leibniz, Gottfried Wilhelm; Russian Philosophy; Solov'ëv (Solovyov), Vladimir Sergeevich.

Bibliography

WORKS BY LOPATIN

Polozhitel'nyye zadachi filosofii (The positive tasks of philosophy). 2 vols. Moscow, 1886–1891.
Filosofskie kharakteristiki i rechi (Philosophical characterizations and speeches). Moscow: Academia, 1995.
'The Philosophy of Vladimir Soloviev." *Mind* 25 (October 1916): 425–460.

WORKS ON LOPATIN

Ognev, A. *Lev Mikhailovich Lopatin*. Petrograd, 1922.
Zen'kovskii, V. V. *Istoriia russkoi filosofii*. 2 vols. Paris: YMCA Press, 1948–1950. Translated by George L. Kline as *A History of Russian Philosophy*. 2 vols. New York: Columbia University Press, 1953.

James P. Scanlan (1967)
Bibliography updated by Vladimir Marchenkov (2005)

LOSEV, ALEKSEI FËDOROVICH
(1893–1988)

Aleksei Fëdorovich Losev was a Russian philosopher and classicist and the author of numerous works on ancient and early modern aesthetics, language, symbolism, myth, and music aesthetics. A native of Novocherkassk, he graduated from Moscow University in 1917 with degrees in philosophy and classical philology and later taught at the University of Nizhnii Novgorod and Moscow Conservatory. Before they ceased to exist in 1922 he attended the meetings of the Vladimir Sergeevich Solov'ëv (Solovyov) Religious-Philosophical Society and Nikolai Aleksandrovich Berdyaev's Free Academy of Spiritual Culture, where he met the leading figures of the so-called religious-philosophical renaissance.

During the 1920s Losev forged his own version of Christian neoplatonism for which he drew on ancient Platonists, Greek church fathers, German idealism (especially Friedrich Wilhelm Joseph von Schelling and Georg Wilhelm Friedrich Hegel), Russian religious-philosophical thought, and Edmund Husserl. The later, largely forced, assimilation of Marxism was neither purely cosmetic nor did it cause any fundamental shift in his outlook. Losev accepted the valuable aspects of Marxism but eschewed its limitations. In 1929 he secretly took monastic vows. Between 1927 and 1930 he published eight volumes on ancient philosophy, philosophy of language, mathematics, music aesthetics, and philosophy of myth. The last book in this series, *Dialektika mifa* (The dialectics of myth; 1930), became the cause of Losev's arrest and sentence of ten years in labor camps. He was freed, almost totally blind, in 1933 and for the next twenty years he was not allowed to publish his own work or teach philosophy. After teaching part time at provincial universities he became a professor at Moscow University in 1942 and was even awarded a doctorate in classical philology. The appointment was soon withdrawn, however, on charges of idealism and Losev was transferred to Moscow State Pedagogical Institute, where he remained until retirement. He resumed publishing in 1953 and eventually established himself, against considerable official resistance, as one of the most respected authors on ancient philosophy and culture in the Soviet Union. By the end of his life Losev's oeuvre included more than 30 monographs and 400 scholarly publications. Posthumous editions have increased this number almost twofold. The crowning achievement of his life's labor was an eight-volume study on ancient aesthetics—an original interpretation of antiquity without precedent, in scope and size, in world classical scholarship.

Losev's output over his lifetime is marked by a remarkable continuity. The themes of antiquity, language, symbol, myth, mathematics, and music remained constant from his earliest to his last publications. His vast oeuvre, however, still requires much study and any judgment of it must remain provisional at this stage.

METHOD

Losev elaborated his phenomenological-dialectical method in the 1920s and later only supplemented it by new influences, among which Marxism and structuralism were perhaps most notable. In Marxism Losev found support for his conviction about a meaningful link between socioeconomic and intellectual processes but, in contrast to Marxism, he did not reduce the latter to the former. He considered the eidos of classical phenomenology, which he described as "the integral semantic face (smyslovoi lik) of a thing" (1927a, p. 53), too static and supplemented it by establishing dynamic dialectical relations among its constituent parts. Like Hegel, Losev understood dialectics as the rhythm of both thinking and objective reality, but his own version of dialectics was derived largely from ancient and Christian neoplatonist sources.

Losev had a penchant for developing multilayered analytic structures of the phenomena that he studied. Often, the key element in these conceptual constructions is what he calls the dialectical tetraktis: the development of meaning via the four steps of unity, multiplicity, the ideal synthesis of the two, and, finally, the fact in which this synthesis is realized.

Throughout his life Losev argued strenuously against the dogmatic one-sidedness of both materialism and idealism and strove to position himself above these abstract divisions.

LANGUAGE

Central to Losev's entire outlook was the philosophy of language articulated in *Filosofiia imeni* (Philosophy of the name; 1927b). Losev's view was informed by onomatodoxy (*imiaslavie*), a trend in Orthodox theology centered on the veneration of God's name. He understood language in terms of ontological symbolism, that is, as access to the reality of being. "The name," he argued, "is life. … The mystery of the word consists precisely in that it is the tool of our intimate and conscious encounter with the inner life of things. … The world is created and is held together by the name and the word" (1993, pp. 617, 642,

746). The name, according to Losev, embraces being in its entirety, from the meonic formlessness of pure matter, to the rational, eidetic formation of all natural and social phenomena, to the suprarational regions of thinking where it passes into "noetic ecstasy" (pp. 676–677). Losev's meticulous gradations of this phenomenological-neoplatonist terrain are held together by a dialectical hierarchy of various "moments" in the structure of words. Later in life Losev attentively studied structuralism with which the eidetic aspect of his analysis of language had much in common. He consistently objected, however, to all nondialectical treatments of language, be they positivist, neo-Kantian, or structuralist.

SYMBOL

Losev's theory of the symbol was inspired by the thought of Pavel Aleksandrovich Florenskii and Viacheslav Ivanovich Ivanov, but it also absorbed other influences as it evolved from his early work, such as *Antichnyi kosmos i sovremennaia nauka*, to later writings, such as *Problema simvola i realisticheskoe iskusstvo* (The problem of symbol and realistic art, 1976). In the latter Losev analyses in detail the structure of symbol and argues that symbols are means of practical, creative "re-making of reality" (pp. 15–17). In Losev's view a symbol is the perfect fusion of inner meaning and its external expression. It is this balance that distinguishes it from allegory, where the image outweighs the abstract idea, or from a scheme, where the idea is rich but its representation arid.

MYTH

Losev regards myth as a necessary category of consciousness and defines it as "unfolded magical name" (2003, pp. 186–187)—a formula that highlights myth's verbal (narrative) form, personalistic nature, and the presence of the miraculous in it. As a story about reality it is distinct from poetry and art in general; as a prereflexive story about a miraculous reality, myth is distinct from science and metaphysics. Myths form the foundations of people's outlooks, Losev argues, and thus determine cultural and historical processes on the most fundamental level. He views the history of culture as a constant struggle among various mythologies, and one of his tasks is to uncover the inner logic of this process. "Whatever one's view of myth, any critique of mythology is always merely a profession of another, new mythology" (1927b, p. 771). According to Losev no historical epoch is free of mythology and, despite its hostility toward myth, modernity is emphatically mythological. Modern cosmology advances, he impugns, a vision of the world as an infinite dark void, ruled by a "blind, deaf, and dead" monster, that is, matter. Losev's other targets among modern myths include titanic Prometheanism that he critiqued at length in *The Problem of Symbol and Realistic Art*. The key notion in Losev's critique of modernity was what he called in *Estetika Vozrozhdeniia* (Renaissance aesthetics; 1978) "the absolutization of the human subject."

The reconciliation of myth and philosophy is Losev's goal in his essay "Absoliutnaia mifologiia = absoliutnaia dialektika" (Absolute mythology = absolute dialectics; 1929–1930, published in 2000). Taken by themselves, both myth and dialectics are limited and an adequate outlook can be based, Losev insists, only on their synthesis. Dialectics inevitably comes up against the ultimate limit of rational cognition, and in the suprarational realm beyond this boundary it should be fused with mythology (p. 275). In his early period Losev found the optimal candidates for such a synthesis in the mythology of Eastern (Orthodox) Christianity and Russian religious-philosophical thought.

Losev applied his theoretical ideas to numerous analyses of specific myths ranging from ancient Greco-Roman to modern mythology (*Ocherki antichnogo simvolizma i mifologii* [Essays on ancient symbolism and mythology; 1930]; *Mifologiia grekov i rimlian* [The mythology of the Greeks and Romans; 1930s, published in 1996]; and *The Problem of Symbol and Realistic Art*).

ANTIQUITY

In *Istoriia antichnoi estetiki* (History of ancient aesthetics; 1963–1994) Losev's point of departure is that all ancient philosophizing, from pre-Socratics to Proclus, is based "on the intuitions of a thing, rather than of personhood" (*Istoria antichnoi filosofii v konspektivnom izlozhenii* [History of ancient philosophy: a conspectus], p. 155). He emphasizes the link between the "material-thingly" (*material'no-veshchestvennaia*) basis of thinking and ancient slave-owner economy but rather than a particular economic order the ultimate intuitive ground of ancient philosophy was "the sensible, material cosmos" (p. 15). From this impersonal absolute stems ancient fatalism that gradually evolves, via Stoics and other schools, toward providentialism. Ancient philosophy ends, Losev claims, when this original, astronomical intuition is replaced by the personalistic and historical vision of reality in Christianity. Losev argues for a dialectical view of this process, in which ancient philosophy grows out of specific mythological intuitions in the late archaic and early classical period, and in the end returns to embrace and justify this original mythology on rational grounds—

only to yield to a new mythology and a philosophy that evolves on its basis.

MUSIC

Losev's philosophy of music combines Pythagoreanism and Romanticism, both refracted through his dialectical phenomenology. Eventually, he also explored Marxist themes, such as music and ideology—especially in his philosophical prose of the early 1930s (published posthumously). The culmination of Losev's early philosophy of music was *Muzyka kak predmet logiki* (Music as the subject of logic; 1927), where music is defined as the expression of "the life of numbers." In its depth this life is a total "coincidence of opposites" and "extreme formlessness" that defies all categories of the understanding (1990, p. 209). At the same time a musical work possesses an "eidetic completeness" (p. 269). Fused with the chaos of "pure musical being," this mathematically determined fullness of form makes music "the eidos of the alogical" (p. 279). Losev further evokes Plotinus to define time as "the alogical becoming of the number" (p. 328) and links this idea with the temporal nature of music. The closing passages of the book are devoted to deriving from these insights such elements of musical form as melody, rhythm, harmony, and even timbre. Losev both used and further elaborated his philosophy of music in a number of essays, written in the course of his lifetime, on specific composers, such as Nikolai Rimsky-Korsakov (1844–1908), Aleksandr Scriabin (1872–1915), and Richard Wagner (1813–1888).

Losev is one the key philosophers—perhaps *the* key philosopher—who preserved the continuity of Russian religious-philosophical tradition in Russia against a concerted effort by the Soviet regime to destroy it. In the post-Soviet period Losev emerged as one of the central figures of twentieth-century Russian thought—a position confirmed by numerous editions of his works and his broad influence on the current philosophical discourse. The significance of his work, however, reaches far beyond the Russian context. While the strikingly broad reach of his thought makes the recognition of his contribution difficult, it also comprises highly valuable insights into the nature of thinking, history, personhood, and expression.

See also Berdyaev, Nikolai Aleksandrovich; Florenskii, Pavel Aleksandrovich; Hegel, Georg Wilhelm Friedrich; Husserl, Edmund; Idealism; Ivanov, Viacheslav Ivanovich; Marxist Philosophy; Myth; Neoplatonism; Patristic Philosophy; Philosophy of Language; Platonism and the Platonic Tradition; Pre-Socratic Philosophy; Proclus; Russian Philosophy; Schelling, Friedrich Wilhelm Joseph von; Solov'ëv (Solovyov), Vladimir Sergeevich.

Bibliography

WORKS BY LOSEV

Antichnyi kosmos i sovremennaia nauka (The ancient cosmos and modern science). Moscow: Author, 1927a.

Filosofiia imeni (Philosophy of the name). Moscow: Author, 1927b.

Istoriia antichnoi estetiki (History of ancient aesthetics), Vol. 1. Moscow: Vysschaia shkola, 1963; Vols. 2–8. Moscow: Iskusstvo, 1969–1994.

Iz rannkikh proizvedenii (Early writings). Moscow: Pravda, 1990.

Bytie, Imia, Kosmos (Being, name, cosmos). Moscow: Mysl', Rossiiskii otkrytyi universitet, 1993.

Forma, Stil', Vyrazhenie (Form, style, expression). Moscow: Mysl', 1995.

The Dialectics of Myth. Translated by Vladimir Marchenkov. London: Routledge, 2003.

Istoriia antichnoi filosofii v konspektivnom izlozhenii (A history of ancient philosophy: a conspectus), Moscow: Mysl', 1989.

Problema simvola i realisticheskoe iskusstvo (The problem of the symbol and realistic art), Moscow: Iskusstvo, 1976.

WORKS ABOUT LOSEV

"Aleksej Fedorovich Losev: Philosophy and the Human Sciences." *Studies in East European Thought* 56 (2–3) (June 2004) (Special Issue).

Haardt, Alexander. "Aleksei Losev and the Phenomenology of Music." In *Russian Thought after Communism: The Recovery of a Philosophical Heritage*, edited by James P. Scanlan, 197–205. Armonk, NY: M. E. Sharpe, 1994.

Haardt, Alexander. *Husserl in Russland: Phänomenologie der Sprache und Kunst bei Gustav Spet und Aleksej Losev.* Munich, Germany: Fink Verlag, 1993.

Jubara, Annett. *Die Philosophie des Mythos von Aleksej Losev im Kontext "Russischer Philosophie"* Wiesbaden, Germany: Harrassowitz Verlag, 2000.

Vladimir Marchenkov (2005)

LOSSKII, NIKOLAI ONUFRIEVICH
(1870–1965)

Nikolai Losskii (Lossky), a Russian religious philosopher, was born in the province of Vitebsk in western Russia. He studied history, philology, and natural sciences at St. Petersburg University (1891–1898), as well as philosophy under the neo-Kantian Aleksandr Vvedenskii (1856–1925). Losskii continued his philosophical education in Germany (1901–1903) with Wilhelm Windel-band, Wilhelm Wundt, and Georg Müller. He received his master's degree in 1903, and his doctorate in philosophy four years later. From 1900 Losskii taught at St. Petersburg University, where he was appointed to a chair of philosophy in 1916. In 1921 Losskii was dismissed from the university for his religious beliefs, and in 1922 he was exiled by the Soviet government from the homeland. From 1922 to 1945 he settled in Czechoslovakia, where he taught in universities in Prague, Brno, and Bratislava. From 1946 Losskii lived in the United States and taught at St. Vladimir's Orthodox Theological Seminary in New York (1947–1950).

Losskii was a systematic philosopher and prolific writer whose works have been translated into many foreign languages. His writings cover most of the traditional philosophical disciplines, though he gave special emphasis to epistemology, metaphysics, and ethics. His philosophy is variously labeled as intuitivism, hierarchical personalism, or ideal-realism, depending on what part of his comprehensive system the commentator focuses on. The central idea of Losskii's philosophy is, in his own words, the insight that "everything is immanent in everything" (Zenkovsky 1953, p. 668). In his religious views Losskii adhered to Christian doctrine, though some of his views, such as his teachings about reincarnation and creation, seem incompatible with the Orthodox tradition.

In his epistemology, Losskii rejected the possibility of transcendent knowledge and affirmed that in the process of cognition, subject and object must be connected. In acts of knowing, the object of knowledge is not a representation of an entity but the actual entity itself. The subject or self becomes cognizant of the world of nonself by a special act that Losskii called "epistemological coordination." Although the object of knowledge is part of the process of knowing, the content of knowledge contains more than its own object; rather, it is the result of the subject's efforts at comparing and distinguishing. Hence, the truth that one can achieve in the cognitive process is never complete, because the process of differentiating, however strong it may be, always leaves unexplored some part of reality.

In Losskii's theory of knowledge, named "intuitivism," intuition is not merely one aspect of cognition, but permeates all cognitive processes. Though all knowledge is intuitive by nature, knowledge can be differentiated by the type of intuition. Losskii distinguished three types of intuition: sensuous, intellectual, and mystical, corresponding respectively to the real, ideal, and metalogical levels of existence.

In his ontology, Losskii defended an "organic," or holistic, worldview. In his view, any object constitutes a system by virtue of a principle that lies beyond that system. As a systemic unity, the world requires a principle that stands beyond it and represents its foundation. This principle is called "the Absolute" in philosophy and "God" in religion. No positive definition grasps the Absolute as such, but philosophers can study its manifestations in the created world.

In the created realm, Losskii distinguished three levels of reality: the real, the abstract, and the concretely ideal, the last of which consists of living agents, whom he sometimes referred to as concrete ideal entities, substances, or, more precisely, substantival agents. As compared with the abstract ideal, which includes, for instance, abstract relations, ideal entities are active agents who independently determine their own manifestations in time. The human self is one such substantival agent. As an entity that transcends space and time, it is responsible for creating psychic processes in time and realizing material events in a spatiotemporal framework.

In Losskii's view, God's creation stops with substantival agents, who are free to choose their own evolution. The original sin of self-centeredness, symbolically described in the Biblical story of the fall of Adam and Eve, does not signify that humanity once attained perfection and then freely lost it. The life of the spirit has to result from efforts exercised by the creature itself; otherwise the creature's freedom is falsified. Those substantival agents who choose selfishness and prefer their own interests to God's will must continue their evolution on the lower levels of reality and are subjected to a long and difficult process of redemption.

Since the universe is an integral holistic system, an organism, all substantival agents are interconnected with each other. Their consubstantiality is crowned with and headed by the cosmic substance, which Losskii, following the Solov'evian tradition, called "Sophia." Though not identified with the Absolute, this supreme substance, like all other creatures belonging to the created realm, is perfect and unites the multiplicity of creation into one cosmic whole. The kingdom of God, led by Sophia, represents the ontological basis of absolute values and the ultimate goal for every substantival agent. The existence of the spiritual kingdom makes it possible for fallen beings to restore their original divine identities and to partake of the heavenly life. In the kingdom of God, everyone is in harmony with all, and everyone is all. In the life of the kingdom of God, headed by Sophia, every member experiences constant growth in all possible dimensions that ideally complement and enrich one another.

Though Losskii wrote comparatively little on political philosophy, in his few articles on the subject he consistently stood for democratic values. According to him, in the course of an increasingly complex social life, the state is unified more securely by the dispersion of power and by constitutional limits on the absolute power of the monarch. The ultimate choice between monarchy and republic depends on which can best balance the united will of the nation with the rights and development of its members.

See also Intuition; Personalism; Russian Philosophy; Solov'ëv (Solovyov), Vladimir Sergeevich; Sophia; Windelband, Wilhelm; Wundt, Wilhelm.

Bibliography

WORKS BY LOSSKII

Mir kak osushchestvlenie krasoty: Osnovy estetiki (The world as the manifestation of beauty: principles of aesthetics). Moscow: Progress Publishers, 1996.

Chuvstvennaia, intellektual'naia i misticheskaia intuitsiia (Sensory, intellectual, and mystical intuition). Moscow: Respublika, 1995. Includes the following works: *Tipy mirovozzrenii: Vvedenie v metafiziku* (Types of worldviews: an introduction to metaphysics; 1931); *Chuvstvennaia, intellektual'naia i misticheskaia intuitsiia* (Sensory, intellectual, and mystical intuition; 1938); *Obshchedostupnoe vvedenie v filosofiiu* (A general introduction to philosophy; 1956), pt. 1 and pt. 3, chap. 21.

Bog i mirovoe zloi (God and worldly evil). Moscow: Respublika, 1994. Includes the following works: *Dostoyevski i ego khristianskoe miroponimanie* (Dostoyevsky and his Christian worldview; 1953); *Tsennost' i bytie: Bog i Tsarstvo Bozhie kak osnova tsennostei* (Value and existence: God and the kingdom of God as the basis of values; 1931); translated by S. Vinokooroff as pt. 1 of *Value and Existence*, by N. O. Lossky and J. S. Marshall (London: Allen and Unwin, 1935); *Bog i mirovoe zlo: Osnovy teoditsei* (God and worldly evil: principles of theodicy; 1941).

Istoriia russkoi filosofii. Moscow: Progress, 1994. Translated as *History of Russian Philosophy* (New York: International Universities Press, 1951). Includes Losskii's summary of his own philosophy.

Usloviia absoliutnogo dobra (Conditions of the absolute good). Moscow: Politicheskaia literatura, 1991. Includes the following works: *Usloviia absoliutnogo dobra: Osnovy etiki* (Conditions of the absolute good: principles of ethics; 1949); *Kharakter russkogo naroda* (The character of the Russian people; 1957).

Izbrannoe (Selected works). Moscow: Pravda, 1991. Includes the following works: *Obosnovaniia intuitivizma* (1906), translated by N. Duddington as *The Intuitive Basis of Knowledge: An Epistemological Inquiry* (London: Macmillan, 1919); *Mir kak organicheskoe tseloe* (1917), translated by N.

Duddington as *The World as an Organic Whole* (London: Oxford, 1928); *Svoboda voli* (1927), translated by N. Duddington as *Freedom of Will* (London: Williams and Norgate, 1932).

WORKS ON LOSSKII

Lossky, Boris, and Nadejda Lossky. *Bibliographie des œuvres de Nicolas Lossky*. Paris: Institut d'études slaves, 1978. A complete bibliography of works by Losskii and translations of his works. Includes a detailed chronology of his life.

Zenkovsky, V. V. *A History of Russian Philosophy*. Vol. 2, 630–676. Translated by George L. Kline. London: Routledge and Kegan Paul, 1953.

Mikhail Sergeev (2005)

LOTMAN, IURII MIKAILOVICH
(1922–1993)

Iurii Mikailovich Lotman was a specialist in the theory of literature and aesthetics, the history of Russian literature, semiotics, and study of culture. He was born in Petrograd (now St. Petersburg). In 1939 he commenced his studies in the philology department of Leningrad University. In the fall of 1940 he joined the army and fought in World War II from 1941 to 1945. In 1946 he continued his studies at the university, finishing them in 1950. Because of the anti-Semitic campaign in the Soviet Union, Lotman was not able to work in Leningrad and moved to Estonia. From 1950 to 1954 he taught at the Tartu Pedagogical Institute. In 1952 he defended his dissertation in philology on the ideas of A. N. Radishchev and N. M. Karamzin. In 1954 he was named docent of Tartu University, and from 1960 to 1977 he was the head of the Department of Russian Literature there. In 1961 he received a doctorate in philology by defending the dissertation titled *Puti razvitiia russkoi literatury preddekabristskogo perioda* (Paths of the development of Russian literature in the pre-Decembrist period).

FROM THE HISTORY OF LITERATURE TO SEMIOTICS

Lotman's chief historical works are devoted to the history of Russian literature from the eighteenth century to the mid-nineteenth century. He examines this literature in conjunction with other cultural phenomena, particularly philosophical thought, history, and sociopolitical life. From the beginning of the 1960s Lotman develops a structural-semiotic approach to the study of works of art, organized the publication of the series *Trudy po znakovym sistemam, Semiotika* (*Sign Systems Studies,*

Semiotics), and directed regularly held "summer schools," conferences, and seminars on the semiotic study of various domains of culture. The combination of these activities, which included the participation not only of Tartu scholars but also of scholars from Moscow and other cities, became the internationally known Tartu-Moscow School of Semiotics (Grzybek 1989). The first issue of *Sign Systems Studies* included his *Lektsii po struktural'noi poetike* (Lectures on structural poetics) (Lotman 1964).

The works of Lotman and those of his colleagues and followers on the semiotic analysis of various cultural texts, including artistic texts in particular, are united by the idea of "secondary modeling systems," where the text is interpreted as a unity of models of objective and subjective reality, as well as in the capacity of a sign system secondary in relation to the signs of natural languages, which represent the "primary modeling system." Headed by Lotman, the "Tartu school" of semiotics continues the traditions of the Russian "formal school," especially Iurii Tynianov, and structural linguistics (Ferdinand de Saussure and Roman Jakobson), taking into account the efforts to develop semiotic structuralism in various countries. However, the Tartu school does not limit itself to the study of the formal structure of works of art; it focuses primarily on the semantics of sign structures (Lotman 1970, Shukman 1977). Together with his semiotic studies, Lotman also continues his historico-literary investigations, in which he employs a structural-semiotic methodology. The novelty of his work is that he attempts to combine structuralism with historicism, the premise being that a semiotician must also be a historian. Lotman's work in the history of literature is characteristically theory-laden.

FROM SEMIOTICS TO THE STUDY OF CULTURE

At the beginning of the 1970s Lotman arrived at the view that the semiotic object must be adequately understood not simply as a separate sign but as a text existing in culture—as a text constituting "a complex device storing multiple and diverse codes, capable of transforming received messages and of generating new ones, like an information generator possessing traits of intellectual personality" (Lotman 1981, p. 132). Taking this as his point of departure, Lotman considers culture itself in its semiotic aspect, in the multiplicity of its communicative connections (Lotman 1970–1973). By analogy with V. I. Vernadskii's concepts of "biosphere" and "noosphere," Lotman introduced the concept of "semiosphere," which is characterized by the limits of semiotic space, its structural heterogeneity and internal diversity, forming a structural hierarchy whose components are in a dialogic interrelationship (Lotman 1984). Lotman thus realized the transformation of the initial semiotics and overcomes its total schematism. But he did this not through post-structuralism and "deconstruction" (in the spirit of Jacques Derrida) but through a semiotic interpretation of cultural texts, taking into account their uniqueness, creative character, and intertextual dialogues. Not only is culture as a whole understood as a text, but any text is viewed as a product of culture.

Lotman's theoretical views take into account the development of contemporary scientific knowledge, especially information theory, cybernetics, the theory of systems and structures, the theory of the functional asymmetry of the brain, and the ideas of synergetics (Lotman 1990, 1992). At the same time these views also rely on the abundant material of world culture, primarily Russian culture, which is considered in its typological significance. Lotman's works on the history of Russian culture are of great value. Highly popular was his series of television broadcasts on Russian culture, aired posthumously in 1994 (Lotman 1994).

PHILOSOPHICAL POSITION

Lotman did not explicitly declare his philosophical views. In the presemiotic period of his activity, philosophy interested him only as an object of historical study. But semiotic and culturological studies presupposed a theoretico-philosophical self-definition. Lotman had a broad knowledge of philosophy and closely studied the ideas of Gabriel de Mably, Jean-Jacques Rousseau, and Alexander Radischev (Lotman 1958, 1960). He also identified in a masterful way the philosophical content of the work of literary artists (Lotman 1987, 1988). His own philosophical-methodological ideas underwent a specific evolution (Kim Soo Hwan 2003). In the 1960s the adherents of the "Tartu school" held positivist views, maintaining that semiotics was in fact their philosophy (Stolovich 1994). But later Lotman began to search for a philosophy that would correspond to his semiotic culturology. He turned to Leibniz's monadology, proposing that the semiosphere consists of a multiplicity of "semiotic monads" as intellectual units—that is, bearers of Reason. In his own words, "man not only thinks but also finds himself within a thinking space, just as a bearer of speech is always immersed in a certain language space." The existence of the external world is accepted, but it too is "an active participant in the semiotic exchange" (Lotman 1989, pp. 372, 375). God for Lotman is a universally significant phenomenon of culture. Although his attitude toward religion was respectful, he himself was a theological agnostic (Egorov 1999, pp. 236–237).

Lotman keenly absorbed the ideas of various thinkers, including Leibniz, Rousseau, Kant, Hegel, and Freud. In 1967 and 1971 he published in the journal *Semiotics* certain works of the Russian religious philosopher and scientist Pavel Florenskii, who had been repressed by the Soviet authorities. Lotman also reacted positively to Bakhtin's conception of dialogue (Egorov 1999, pp. 243–258). However, Lotman's own philosophical views cannot be reduced to any one system, be it Platonism (Vetik 1994), Kantianism (M. Lotman 1995), Hegelianism, or Marxism. His philosophical views can be defined as a type of "systemic pluralism," which presupposes the combination of heterogeneous ideological components in a specific system.

Living and being educated in the Soviet Union, Lotman could not fail to feel the influence of Marxism. He assimilated that aspect of Marxism that was related to Hegel's dialectic, the principle of historicism, and the social factor in the development of culture. But the ideological content of Marxism was alien to Lotman (Gasparov 1996, pp. 415–426). His structural-historical studies provoked the suspicion and displeasure of official circles (at the beginning of the 1970s, he was even interrogated by the KGB and his belongings were searched). At the same time his popularity grew immensely and he was considered a scholar of the first rank and a brilliant personality in intellectual circles both in the Soviet Union and abroad. He was elected as a corresponding member of the British Academy, as an academician of the Norwegian, Swedish, and Estonian academies of science, and as vice president of the International Semiotics Association. The institute for Russian and Soviet culture in Germany was named after him: Lotman-Institut für russische und sowjetische Kultur, Ruhr-Universität Bochum.

See also Aesthetics, History of; Bakhtin, Mikhail Mikhailovich; Cybernetics; Derrida, Jacques; Florenskii, Pavel Aleksandrovich; Freud, Sigmund; Hegel, Georg Wilhelm Friedrich; Hegelianism; Historicism; Information Theory; Kant, Immanuel; Leibniz, Gottfried Wilhelm; Marxist Philosophy; Monad and Monadology; Neo-Kantianism; Platonism and the Platonic Tradition; Radishchev, Aleksandr Nikolaevich; Rousseau, Jean-Jacques; Russian Philosophy; Structuralism and Post-structuralism.

Bibliography

WORKS BY LOTMAN

Radishchev i Mabli [Radishchev and Mably]. 1958. In *Izbrannye stat'i* [Selected articles], by Yu. M. Lotman. Vol. 2, 100–123. Tallinn, Estonia: Aleksandra, 1992.

Russo i russkaja kul'tura v XVIII–nachala XIX veka [Rousseau and Russian culture from the 18th century to the the early 19th century]. In *Traktaty* [The treatises], by Jean-Jacques Rousseau. Moscow: Nauka, 1969.

Lektsii po struktural'noii poetike [Lectures on structural poetics]. Tartu, Estonia, 1964.

Struktura khudozhestvennogo teksta [The structure of the artistic text]. Moscow: Iskusstvo, 1970. Translated by Gail Lenhoff and Ronald Vroon as *The Structure of the Artistic Text*. Michigan Slavic Contributions 7. Ann Arbor: University of Michigan, Department of Slavic Languages and Literatures, 1977.

Stat'i po tipologii kul'tury [Articles on the typology of culture]. Vols. 1–2. Tartu, Estonia, 1970–1973.

Analiz poeticheskogo teksta [Analysis of the poetic text]. 1972. Translated by D. Barton Johnson as *Analysis of the Poetic Text*. Ann Arbor, MI: Ardis, 1976.

Semiotika kino i problemy kinoestetiki [Semiotics of cinema and problems of a film-aesthetics]. Tallinn, Estonia: Eesti raamat, 1973. Translated by Mark Suino as *Semiotics of Cinema*. Michigan Slavic Contributions. Ann Arbor: University of Michigan Press, 1976.

"*Semiotika kultury i poniatie teksta*" [Semiotics of culture and the concept of the text] [1981]. In *Izbrannye stat'i* [Selected articles], by Yu. M. Lotman. Vol. 1, p. 132. Tallinn, Estonia: Aleksandra, 1992.

"*O semiosfere*" [On the semiosphere]. 1984. In *Izbrannye stat'i* [Selected articles], by Yu. M. Lotman. Vol. 1, 11–24. Tallinn, Estonia: Aleksandra, 1992.

Sotvoreni? Karamzina [The creative works of Karamzin]. Moscow: Kniga, 1987.

Iz razmyshlenii nad tvorcheskoi evoliutsiei Pushkina [From reflections on the creative evolution of Pushkin]. 1988. In *Izbrannye stat'i* [Selected articles], by Yu. M. Lotman. Vol. 2, 473–478. Tallinn, Estonia: Aleksandra, 1992.

Kul'tura kak sub'ekt i sama-sebe ob'ekt. 1989. In *Izbrannye stat'i* [Selected articles], by Yu. M. Lotman. Vol. 3. Tallinn, Estonia: Aleksandra, 1993. Translated by Lotman Juri as "Culture as a Subject and an Object in Itself." *Trames* 1 (1) (1997): 7–16.

Universe of the Mind: A Semiotic Theory of Culture. Translated by Ann Shukman. Introduction by Umberto Eco. London: Tauris, 1990. 2nd ed., 2001.

Kultura i vzryv [Culture and explosion]. Moscow: Gnosis-Progress, 1992.

Besedy o russkoi kul'ture: Byt i traditsii russkogo dvorianstva; XVIII–nachalo XIX veka [Conversations on Russian culture: The life and traditions of the Russian nobility from the 18th century to the early 19th century). St. Petersburg: Iskusstvo, 1994.

Vnutri mysliashchikh system: Chelovek-Tekst-Semiosfera-Istoriia [Inside thinking systems: man-text-semiosphere-history]. Moscow: Iazyki russkoi kul'tury. 1996.

REFERENCES AND FURTHER READING

Egorov, B. F. *Zhizn' i tvorchestvo Iu M. Lotmana* [Life and creativity of Yu. M. Lotman]. Moscow: Novoe literaturnoe obozrenie, 1999.

Gasparov, M. L. *Lotman and Marxism* [1996]. In *Vnutri myslyashchikh system: Chelovek-Tekst-Semiosfera-Istoriya*, by Yu. M. Lotman. Moscow: Iazyki russkoi kul'tury, 1996.

Grzybek, P. *Studium zum Zeichenbegriff der sowjetischen Semiotik (Moskkauer und Tartuer Schule).* Bochum, Germany, 1989.

Kim Soo Hwan. *Osnovnye aspekty tvorcheskoi evoliutsii Y. M. Lotmana* [The main aspects of Lotman's creative evolution]. Moscow: Novoe literaturnoe obozrenie, 2003.

Lotman, M. Yu. *Zametki o filosofskom fone tartuskoi semiotiki* [Notes on the philosophical background of semiotics in Tartu]. In: *Lotmanovskii sbornik*, vol. 1. 214–222. Moscow: ITS-Garant, 1995.

Shukman, Ann. *Literature and Semiotics: A Study of the Writings of Yu. M. Lotman.* Amsterdam: North-Holland, 1977.

Stolovich, L. N. "*A. F. Losev o semiotike v Tartu*" [A. F. Losev on semiotics in Tartu]. *Novoe literaturnoe obozrenie* 8 (1994): 99–104.

Vetik, R. "Platonism of Yu. Lotman." *Semiotika* 99 (1–2) (1994).

Leonid N. Stolovich (2005)
Translated by Boris Jakim

LOTZE, RUDOLF HERMANN
(1817–1881)

Rudolf Hermann Lotze, the German idealist metaphysician, was born in Bautzen He studied medicine and philosophy at the University of Leipzig, taking his doctorates in both fields. He studied mathematics and physics with E. H. Weber, W. Volckmann, and G. T. Fechner and philosophy with C. H. Weisse, who influenced him greatly. In 1841 he became instructor in medicine at Leipzig, where he subsequently taught philosophy. While at Leipzig he published two short works, the *Metaphysik* (Leipzig, 1841) and *Logik* (Leipzig, 1843), which adumbrated the essentials of his later philosophy. In 1844 Lotze succeeded Johann Friedrich Herbart as professor of philosophy at the University of Göttingen. He remained there until 1881, when he was called to the University of Berlin. Shortly after joining the faculty at Berlin, he contracted pneumonia and died.

Lotze pursued his interests in the medical sciences, psychology, philosophy, the arts, and literature throughout his life. As a result of his medical training, he developed a strong love for exact investigation and precise knowledge, but art and literature made him particularly sensitive to the central role of feeling and value in the total life of a culture. He wanted nothing to interfere with the growth of the exact sciences in all areas of human experience, yet he insisted that both intellect and scientific knowledge were essentially the means and tools of feeling, emotion, and intuition.

NEW CONCEPTION OF METAPHYSICS

Like many thinkers born in the first two decades of the nineteenth century, Lotze faced three great schisms: the schism between science and Christianity, which was known at that time as the conflict between science and religion; the schism between reason and feeling; and the schism between knowledge and value. To Lotze, these schisms had to be rationally harmonized in some manner. It seemed impossible to him for any rational man to reject any one of the trinity that composes the total culture of man: science, art, and value. Each has its place in the life of man and the universe, and none can be eliminated without distorting and destroying that life. However, Lotze felt that their proper relationship cannot be established by the older metaphysical methods. There is no possibility of rationally deducing the basic categories and values of existence by any sort of logical dialectic, either Platonic or Hegelian. Knowledge of existence depends upon knowledge of fact acquired through observation and experimentation. Consequently, the empirical sciences are the proper investigators of existence. All that metaphysics can do is to analyze, clarify, and order those concepts and theories that the sciences create into as adequate a system as the facts permit. Metaphysics cannot go beyond this in any scientific sense. Nevertheless, Lotze admitted that metaphysics has another, broader purpose. The urge to be metaphysical is not to be found in metaphysics itself but in ethics, in the desire to know and attain some ultimate good. Thus, metaphysics involves speculating beyond what is scientifically warrantable in order to include that which drives men to write metaphysics: the experience of ultimate goodness.

Because metaphysics must be founded upon science, Lotze objected to any philosophical system that claimed completeness. All philosophical systems, like his own, must remain open and undogmatic. They must not even provide provisional answers to profound questions for which not even provisional answers exist. He thought it was far better for a philosopher to raise questions and to stimulate inquiry than to offer sterile answers lacking any reasonable foundation in fact.

IDEALISTIC MONADISM, MECHANISM, AND GOD

Lotze was essentially an idealist, but his idealism was tempered by his respect for science and his emphasis upon feeling as the dominant element guaranteeing meaning to the life of man.

From the beginning, Lotze considered thought as one aspect of the soul. Thought is aware only of ideas about reality; it does not know reality, for knowledge and reality can never be identical. Neither are experience and thought to be identified. Identity with reality or object can be achieved as experience, never as thought, for thought is purely representative. Truth is attained in ways different from thought. Thought must fuse with the total feeling experience, since it is in feeling that we have direct awareness of good and evil, beauty and ugliness, worth and unworth, contradiction and harmony; these rest in the soul's original capacity to experience pain and pleasure. Consequently, Lotze thought that feeling is the ultimate arbiter of consistency and intellectual harmony, the ultimate judge of the worth of anything, and the ultimate creator of imagination and its works. Moreover, feeling is the nisus that drives man to seek whatever total unity of comprehension and action is possible for him. His love of knowledge, goodness, and beauty arises from, and finds its fulfillment in, feeling. Thus, the essential nature of feeling is love, which constantly drives man toward a greater overall comprehension, of his life and the cosmos. "If … love did not lie at the foundation of the world … this world … would be left without truth and without law."

Feeling convinced Lotze that the world is psychical and thus consists of souls as well as a personal deity. A soul is not simply a stream of impressions united by memory; it is a substantival entity, causally related to the body and interacting with it. Nevertheless, the soul is the greater influence and governs the body in ways closed to it. Both soul and body act according to law, but the laws of bodies as such are purely physical. The laws of the soul are on a higher level; they are teleological and unite the physical and the mental. They do not contradict the laws of the physical world, but they do control and reorder them.

A personal deity, God, follows from the existence of souls and ends. How else can they be explained? The world and everything in it is the personal creation of God and the means by which he attains his ends and the ends of his creatures. However, Lotze tempered this conviction by insisting that God attains his ends through the mechanisms or causal nexuses that science discovers, and he further insisted that these mechanisms are characteristic of both the living and the nonliving.

Lotze rejected the notion that telic and nontelic explanations are incompatible with each other. He opposed the older forms of vitalism popular in his day. He argued that mechanisms are simply the instruments, or tools, by which God accomplishes his ends in the world. Although it is true that God might have used other means, he preferred mechanism as a way of establishing universal law in both the physical and psychic realms.

Lotze argued further that the thesis of mechanism should not be identified with materialism. Mechanism does not imply the nonexistence of ends or of psychic beings; it implies only the existence of uniform modes by which things come into being. The world can just as easily be psychic as material, but the psychic interpretation is rationally to be preferred because it does not make a mystery or a paradox of the presence of feeling and values in the world.

In the *Mikrokosmus*, Lotze continued to elaborate this position. Mechanism is simply a method of research; it is not a fundamental explanation of life and mind. Only the most exhaustive survey of the life of man can provide such an explanation and relate his life to the cosmos and God. Furthermore, mechanism does not repudiate free will; it is simply the necessary condition for the will to express its autonomy.

For Lotze, there are three realms of observations: the realm of fact, the realm of universal law, and the realm of values, which serve as standards of meaning for the world. These realms are only logically separable; they cannot be separated in reality. Fact and law are the means, the mechanisms, by which values are attained in this world; they are also the means by which men discover that certain values are foolish, contradictory, unrealizable, or in other words, false. Since fact and universal law are not existentially separable from value, God must also be the creator of everything and the quintessence of whatever deserves to exist for its own sake. Moreover, since feeling is fundamental, a sort of pluralistic idealism in which the only realities are living spirits and God in interaction is justified. All other realities are so only secondarily, as manifestations of these spiritual activities.

Lotze ultimately accepted a variant of Leibnizian monadism as a correct interpretation of experience. There is no single unity or oneness to existence. Direct experience reveals an irreducible multiplicity of things. Reality is always in flux, always involving constant doing and suffering. Nevertheless, the flux, the doing, and the suffering occur within a fixed order, a preestablished harmony between God and the multitude of spirits.

Lotze recognized that this metaphysical theory is neither a logical deduction from experience nor completely intelligible, but he believed it to be a reasonable inference from the manner in which the valid experiential concepts of our thought, the flux of facts, and the order of values interconnect in our experience. To limit ourselves to what science understands is to exclude unjustifiably the realms of feeling and values, and to exclude the latter is to render our experience unintelligible.

PIETY

To Lotze, nature and the social life are the two fundamental sources for religious ideas. From nature we derive the concept of God; from our social life, the concepts of ethical living. Paganism has tended to emphasize the cosmological; Christianity, the ethical. Christianity has sought to fuse both into one complete theological scheme. In this it is mistaken. To Lotze, the ethical element in religion is far more significant than the cosmological (which can properly be left to science), even though the emphasis upon cosmology leads to recognition of God. The true mark of the religious man is not his cosmology but his feeling for, and search after, what ought to be, his passion for, and loyalty to, the highest possible ideals. This passion and loyalty, however, are not so much activistic as contemplative.

Piety, for Lotze, is found in the inner life, in a feeling for the holy that attains so high a state of intuitive comprehension that logic, reason, becomes futile and inessential. Piety lies beyond any sectarian interest, Christian or not, for it drives men to seek a totality of feeling in which truth is completely fused with goodness and beauty. In consequence, the holy is not merely what men think it is; it is rather the unattained, the beyond in our lives that is without contradiction, defect, or dissonance. It is manifested in the endless striving for that immortal sea that is the infinite parent of all things. In this contemplative striving, in this endless search for total harmony and for the ought-to-be lies the possibility of progressively uniting science, religion, and art. However, the overwhelming realization of this unity occurs only at particular moments when one is moved by the experience of total beauty. In such moments, one knows absolutely that the fusion has, as far as possible, been accomplished.

INFLUENCE

Lotze's influence in Germany, France, and England was considerable during his lifetime. Philosophers became more empirical-minded, less dogmatic. More consideration was given to the feeling, experiential aspects of human life. Nevertheless, Lotze left few, if any, disciples, and no Lotzean school of philosophers arose.

In America, Lotze's influence during the 1870s and 1880s was felt both in church and philosophical circles. The Reverend Joseph Cook of Boston made him widely popular, hailing him as the seer who had made the microscope the instrument of immortality and science the humble servant of the Bible. Leading American philosophers such as B. P. Bowne, G. T. Ladd, and Josiah Royce were particularly influenced, for he offered them an experiential mode of reconciling their strong Christian commitments with the methods and conclusions of science.

See also Bowne, Borden Parker; Fechner, Gustav Theodor; Herbart, Johann Friedrich; Metaphysics; Psychology; Royce, Josiah; Value and Valuation.

Bibliography

The principal writings of Lotze include *Allgemeine Pathologie und Therapie als mechanische Naturwissenschaften* (Leipzig, 1842); *Medicinische Psychologie oder Physiologie der Seele* (Leipzig: Weidmann, 1852); *Mikrokosmus*, 3 vols. (Leipzig, 1856–1864), translated by E. Hamilton and E. E. C. Jones as *Microcosmus*, 2 vols. (Edinburgh. 1885–1886); and *Die Geschichte der Aesthetik in Deutschland* (Munich, 1868). Lotze planned a comprehensive account of his philosophy in three volumes titled *System der Philosophie.* The first part was *Logik* (Leipzig: Hirzel, 1874), and the second, *Metaphysik* (Leipzig: Hirzel, 1879). These were translated into English and edited by Bernard Bosanquet as *Lotze's System of Philosophy* (Oxford: Clarendon Press, 1884). The third volume, which was to have covered religion, art, and practical philosophy, was incomplete at the time of his death. See also *Kleine Schriften*, edited by D. Peipers, 3 vols. (Leipzig, 1885–1891).

For literature on Lotze, see Karl Robert Eduard von Hartmann, *Lotzes Philosophie* (Leipzig: Friedrich, 1888); Henry Jones, *A Critical Account of the Philosophy of Lotze* (Glasgow, 1895); J. W. Schmidt-Japing, *Lotzes Religionsphilosophie in ihrer Entwicklung ...* (Göttingen, 1925); E. E. Thomas, *Lotze's Theory of Reality* (London: Longmans, Green, 1921); and Max Wentscher, *H. Lotze. Lotzes Leben und Werke,* Vol. I (Heidelberg: Winter, 1913).

Rubin Gotesky (1967)

LOVE

"Love" as a concept enters philosophy at one point through religion, particularly when the origin of the world is expressed as an act of procreation or the Creator is conceived of as loving his creation either as a whole or in part (i.e., the human race). But the concept of love is also a subject for philosophic meditation in regard to ethical problems. Love, as one of the most powerful of human impulses, was early seen to be much in need of control, especially if man as rational animal was to be able to use his rational capacities. Much of the ethical writing on love is designed to suggest some means whereby the pleasures and other values of loving may be preserved without entailing the supposed evils of intemperate sexuality. This type of speculation ran from Plato through the Neoplatonists—those of both the early Christian period and the Italian Renaissance. In the Platonic tradition love had a unique metaphysical status, for it existed in both the material and the ideal worlds. Love can take on many forms, from gross sexual passion to a devotion to learning, but, it was argued, the ultimate object of love is the beautiful. The goodness that God sees in his creation is its beauty and to feel the beauty of the world is to love it and its Creator.

CLASSICAL MYTHOLOGY

The word *eros* as it is found in Homer is not the name of a god but simply a common noun meaning "love" or "desire." In Hesiod's *Theogony* Eros becomes one of the three primordial gods, the other two being Chaos and Earth. Although Eros has no offspring and seems to play no role in the genealogy of the gods, he has the greatest power over his fellow immortals. He unnerves the limbs and overcomes the reason of both gods and men. When Aphrodite is born from the sperm of Uranus (Heaven), Eros and Himeros (desire, longing, lust) accompany her into the council of the gods. Whether Hesiod was talking in terms of personalized abstractions or was actually thinking of anthropomorphic beings is not clear, for the *Theogony* is a curious mixture of both kinds of expression. For the history of philosophy, the importance of Hesiod's brief mention of Eros lies in the attribution to him of a power that is the enemy of reason. Something similar is to be found in Sophocles' *Antigone* in the chorus that is sung just after Creon has announced that Antigone must die for having buried her brother's body. Eros is addressed as the god who has brought about Antigone's tragedy. He is described as unconquerable, destructive, roaming over the sea and among the dwellers of the wilderness. Neither the gods nor ephemeral humankind can escape him; he drives his victims to madness and turns the just to evil. An even stronger denunciation of the god may be found in Euripides' *Hippolytus,* along with the additional warning that whether one surrenders to love or refuses to capitulate to it, one is doomed. And indeed, Phaedra, whose successors are obviously Vergil's Dido and Racine's Phèdre, became the prototype of a woman ruined by Eros.

Such poetic passages reflect certain observations about human nature and human behavior. They point to a struggle within man's psyche between a rational, controllable, prudent, and wise agent and an irrational, uncontrollable, mad, and foolish agent. When the former is in control, man will behave in praiseworthy fashion, but when the latter gains the upper hand, he will act like a beast. He will abandon reason that, according to most of the ancients, alone distinguishes him from the beasts. Although man also has an animal nature, to yield to its demands is to betray his essential nature. The notion that Eros might reinforce the human element in man does not appear in the pre-Platonic writers.

EARLY PHILOSOPHIC REFLECTIONS

The Greeks admitted several forms of love, including heterosexual and homosexual passion; parental, filial, and conjugal affection; fraternal feeling; friendship; love of country; and the love of wisdom. All were associated with either Eros or *Philia* (fondness or friendship). Love was believed to be a power capable of uniting people in a common bond. And since not only people but also animals and the elements were thus united, it was appropriate to conceive of this power as lodged in a single agent that governed the whole cosmos. According to Parmenides, Love was created by the goddess Necessity, and in the writing of Empedocles, love emerges as one of the two universal forces (the other being strife) that explain the course of cosmic history. These two agents—the one of union, the other of decomposition—are not simply names for the fact that composition and decomposition occur; on the contrary, love and strife are not resident in things but are external to them and act upon them. According to Empedocles, the cosmos, so to speak, is held in tension between the forces of harmony and disunion. Were the two forces to be synchronously present, the world would clearly be in a state of disorder. Hence, Empedocles introduced the idea of cycles into his philosophy, as well as the concept of world history as an alternation of the reigns of Love and Strife. When Love is in control, the elements form compounds out of which arise more complex units and, eventually, animate beings. In the primitive period of the cycle, men worship Aphrodite, are innocent of slaughter and, presumably, of war, and are, moreover, vegetarians. "The altar did not reek of the unmixed blood of bulls, but this was the greatest abomination among men, to snatch out the life and eat the

goodly limbs" (Fragment 128). But when Strife is dominant, disorganization, the ultimate disaggregation of the elements, and war and all its attendant evils, take the place of the blessings of love. As far as we can tell from the surviving fragments, Empedocles believed that the cyclical process was everlasting.

The attribution of peace and harmony to the goddess Aphrodite (Empedocles' name for love) is clearly a renunciation of the early poets' idea of love. Empedocles' conception of her resembles the *alma* Venus of Lucretius. Yet she remains the goddess of sexual love, for sexual love has become one example of the universal power of union: It provides the philosopher with empirical evidence of a metaphysical principle.

PLATO. For a complete expression of a philosophic concept of love, one must turn to Plato's *Symposium*. Probably no other document in European literature has had as much influence on the philosophy of love. The various speeches that are reported in this dialogue represent points of view with which Plato does not always agree but which he apparently thought important enough to be presented as typical. These speeches range from an encomium of love's effect on morality to a description of its effect on knowledge. Phaedrus likened the passionate attachment between Achilles and Patroclus to the conjugal affection between Alcestis and Admetus. In both cases it is the lover, not the beloved, who has gained virtue through his or her love. In the following speech, by Pausanias, two kinds of love are distinguished, that of the heavenly Aphrodite and that of the earthly Aphrodite, or the love of the soul and the love of the body. The former is more likely to be the love of a young man (not a boy) at the time when his reason begins to develop and his beard begins to grow. In this speech honorable love is clearly the attraction that a man has for a virtuous soul and is fused in the mind of the speaker with philosophy itself, which is the love of wisdom. It is this honorable love that Eryximachus then describes as the source of harmony and the preserver of the good.

The conclusion drawn from these encomiums is that love is in essence the love of beauty and that beauty is nothing material; it is an ideal. But no man desires the ideal until he has been educated through philosophic training. In the final speech, which supposedly reports the philosophy of the seeress Diotima, we find that there is a scale of beauty, progressing from that of bodies through that of forms, thoughts, minds, institutions and laws, the sciences, to absolute or ideal beauty.

Beauty, for Plato, was the one bridge between the two realms of the material and the ideal, particulars and universals. (This appears clearly enough in the *Phaedrus*; what the *Symposium* adds is a discussion of the power that draws men to beauty in its many modes.) The two realms present not simply a duality of kind but also of value, for the ideal and the universal, which are perfect and eternal, are always to be preferred to the material and the particular. Sexual love itself, although lowest on the scale of love, is nevertheless the seed of ideal love, since what attracts a man to the beloved is beauty.

ARISTOTLE. Plato's account of love, insofar as it concerns friendship, was amplified by Aristotle in the eighth and ninth books of the *Nicomachean Ethics*. But Aristotle treated chiefly the ethical and psychological aspects of the matter. He also utilized the metaphor of the attractive power of love in explaining the motion of the planetary spheres, the Unmoved Mover being the beloved and the planetary system the lover. With important differences that will be mentioned below, the Unmoved Mover became a part of the Christian concept of God.

TRANSITION TO CHRISTIANITY

In the *Magna Moralia*, which was probably composed at least in part by Aristotle, it is written that "It would be strange if one were to say that he loved Zeus.... It is not love towards God of which we are in search … but love towards things with life, that is, where there can be a return of affection." God then is thought to be incapable of returning our love for him, assuming that we can have love for him. In fact, although there are myths in which gods and mortals have been in love with each other, the gods always first disguise themselves as mortals, as Aphrodite did when she fell in love with Anchises, or take on various other forms, which was the habit of Zeus. These myths all deal with sexual intercourse, not with friendship or paternal affection. Omitting the culture heroes, there was no god or goddess in ancient mythology who had any love for humankind. Prometheus is an exception, but he was punished for his help to mortals, and in all probability the historic Greeks thought of him as simply a personification of forethought.

There is no god in classical religion who could be called "our father in heaven." The attitude that Lucretius tried to foster in the minds of his fellow Romans was supposed to be an antidote to their fear of the gods. According to the legends, however, there was good reason to fear them. Ceres and Bacchus may have given men bread and wine, but most of the divinities did little more than take

revenge on the human race for the injuries they had received from their fellow gods. In Judaism and Christianity, however, a new relationship to the divinity was established. As early as Deuteronomy 6:5 the commandment was laid down to love God "with all thine heart, and with all thy soul, and with all thy might," a commandment repeated by Jesus (Matthew 22:37) as the first and great commandment, followed by the second, "Thou shalt love thy neighbor as thyself." It will be observed that now love is not seen as a power that destroys man's reason, but rather, as an emotional attitude that can be voluntarily produced. It is praised in the Psalms (for example, 91:14) and also in the First Epistle to the Corinthians and the First Epistle of John (I John 4:16–20). Both epistles cite the power of love to heal discord and fear, and love is represented as a bond between God and man. According to the Gospel of John (3:16), it is because of God's love for the world that redemption is brought to man.

That man could love God, even if he could not love Zeus, had been seen by Philo Judaeus in his *Questions on Genesis* (XVIII, 16) in which he says that once a man has received a clear impression of God and God's powers, his soul is filled with longing for union with God. Thus, in the First Epistle of John, God is identified with love, "and he that dwelleth in love dwelleth in God, and God in him" (I John 4:16). This idea was also found in non-Christian theologians of Hellenistic times, for example, in the *Hermetica (Asclepius* II, Sec. 21), in which all things, including God, are said to be bisexual, a unity that is approximated by men and women in sexual love. This unity is admittedly incomprehensible and what "you might correctly call either Cupid or Venus." But in both Philo and the *Hermetica,* as in Plotinus and Cleanthes' "Hymn to Zeus," the original stimulus to the love of God is knowledge, not sexual love. In *Asclepius* (XIII, 9) the love of God is reduced to worship, sacrifice, prayer, and reverence, and these follow upon a knowledge of the divine nature. In Plotinus the union with God, although aided by ascetic practices, is nevertheless the climax of cognition. Since knowledge occurs only between similar beings, to know God is to be like him; since God is unique, one must become absorbed into his being in order to know him. This may seem to be suggested in the verses from the First Epistle of John cited above, but actually in John the love of God, although it unites man and God, is an act of will similar to the love for one's fellow man. It would presumably be made manifest by one's acts and one's faith; it is not the conclusion or fulfillment of a metaphysical system.

Although the Church Fathers came closest to an identification of God with Aristotle's Unmoved Mover and later Christian philosophers gave God the attributes of that ontological principle, there were differences that have too often been obscured. The Unmoved Mover was neither a person nor a creator; he was uniquely able to produce change without being altered himself, and he could thus suffer no emotions whatsoever. The biblical God was the very antithesis of this. But in order to give an analogy of the way in which the Unmoved Mover moves the world, Aristotle took recourse to the metaphor of the beloved who attracts the lover. This, of course, became in time Dante Alighieri's "love which moves that sun and the other stars." For Aristotle, however, the Unmoved Mover could not return the love of the beings who are below him. In Christianity, as in Judaism, it was essential that God love his creatures as they love him, and, as previously mentioned, love seems to have been thought of as subject to volition. According to Plato (to limit the discussion to him), love arose involuntarily at the sight of a beautiful body. A man's erotic education consisted in a denial, after an analysis of the nature of beauty, of the acts that usually follow such a sight. Once that denial became a part of a man's character, he could rise to allegedly nobler beauties until the final goal—the contemplation of absolute beauty completely detached from anything corporeal—was reached.

The early Christians had more confidence in man's will than had their pagan contemporaries. Both love of God and religious faith were thought to be subject to volition. The concept of believing in order to understand, as St. Augustine put it, was based on the assumption that belief was not the effect but the source of understanding. To what extent the early Christian writers were aware of the psychological effect of practicing certain rites, as Pascal later was, is difficult to say. But since great emphasis was put upon ceremonious expressions of devotion and upon the refusal to carry out pagan rites, we can assume that the practices were believed to induce the appropriate emotions. The most famous of such ceremonies was the Christian agape, in which the devout met to share a supper and to rejoice in their common beliefs. The word *agape* means both love and the object of love, although the pagan satires treated it as if it meant a sexual orgy. The participants in the agape probably thought of it as a ceremony of brotherly love commemorating the Last Supper, although according to the testimony of the Epistle of Jude (12), it was abused at a fairly early date. Whatever its origin and its primitive significance, it is clear that it was supposed to be a ceremony of affection, and it reinforced the friendliness that members of the same religion might be expected to have toward one another. Two emotional factors that seem to have been absent from paganism thus came into prominence in early Christianity—fraternal love as an essential of piety and filial love to a divine father, both of which were reciprocated. These forms of love were strengthened by the persecutions to which the early Christians were subjected—persecutions that bound them together in a special community and led to self-sacrifice in the various forms of martyrdom.

AUGUSTINE. Of the Church Fathers, it is St. Augustine who gives us the most detailed analysis of love, ranging from his youthful sexual escapades to his final love of God. The famous opening of Book II of the *Confessions* described his condition as one of utter subservience to the flesh. Just as he was capable of enjoying sin (in his case, petty theft), not for the loot it brought him but for the joy of sinning, so he enjoyed love not for the sake of his beloved, but for the sake of his own self-centered pleasure. He described in vivid terms the loathing that invaded him while satisfying his passion. The death of a dear friend aroused in him a realization of the egocentricity of his passion, and in planning to organize a small group of fellow Christians who would live in charity and share their belongings (a plan that came to nothing), he first approached unselfish love. Through self-knowledge he learned to look upon the eternal light and ultimately came to the complete love of God, which he described in the tenth book of the *Confessions*. The fruit of this love was knowledge of the divine. Whereas for Plato and Philo cognition led to love, for Augustine it was love that led to cognition. This theme was developed in the twelfth century by such writers as William of Saint Thierry and St. Bernard of Clairvaux.

MIDDLE AGES

The ecstatic loss of self that accompanies sexual love was also assumed to be one of the features of the beatific vision. It is apparent in mystical literature that erotic language is especially effective in communicating mystical experience, and the similarities between religious and sexual ecstasy are manifest in, for example, the Song of Solomon. One should not conclude, however, that the medieval mystics were actually aware of the similarity between the beatific vision and sexual union, for those who are supposed to have made "mystic marriages," like the two St. Catherines, had presumably never had a corporeal marriage. Nonetheless, in mysticism the climax of the love of God was self-annihilation, much as in the Indian *mithuna,* and although the church never encouraged mystic practices, it had to admit their importance when they led to the immediate knowledge of God.

Thus, love in itself became an object of study, and the casuistry of love was elaborated in textbooks and poems as early as the twelfth century. Most of these writings seem to have taken as their source the *De Amore* of André le Chapelain which, whether intended to be serious or not, was taken seriously by most of its readers. It would appear to be a manual on seduction and to have only the most remote relevance to love. The time of its publication, however, coincided with the appearance of many commentaries on the Song of Solomon, and its influence on the rituals of the courts of love has been admitted by most medievalists. As the etiquette of the courts of love developed, love became an end in itself and was not necessarily to be gratified by sexual experience. The lover was supposed to serve his lady with no recompense other than the consciousness of his having served her.

One can only guess at how faithfully the precepts of courtly love were carried out, but as a set of ideas they form an important part of European moral philosophy. By elevating women to a position of irrefragable sovereignty over men, the ideals of courtly love became interwoven with the religious ideal of unquestioned loyalty to church and to God. The sovereign woman became identified with the Blessed Virgin to whom were applied many of the epithets of the bride in the Song of Solomon—rose of Sharon, the closed garden, the tower of ivory—phrases whose symbolical meaning had already been elaborated by St. Bernard. In the thirteenth century the question of the relative primacy of God's reason and will was disputed. For those who believed in the primacy of God's will, it followed that obedience rather than understanding was to be given the higher value. This was also true of courtly love and of chivalry as a doctrine.

DANTE. The culmination of the medieval writing on love is, for modern readers, Dante's *Vita nuova*. However else this book may be interpreted, it is the story of how love that begins with the sight of a girl's beauty ends with a vision which Dante intimated was to be that of the *Divine Comedy*. For Dante the Johannine phrase "God is love" was of essential importance in religion. In ending the *Divine Comedy* with the love that moves the sun and the other stars, he identified his own love and all love with the love that the cosmos has for its Creator. His "new life" was not to be fulfilled in a union with the woman whom he loved but in her guiding him through paradise. Few words occur more frequently in the poems of Dante than "amore." Sometimes he seems to be writing in the vein of

courtly love, sometimes in the mystical vein of St. Bernard, but in both cases love is represented as a force that attracts man to a nobler life. Dante does not overlook the sufferings of a man in love; indeed, he emphasizes them. But to suffer because of love appears to be analogous to the sufferings of the martyrs—an abnegation of the self for a value that transcends egoism.

RENAISSANCE NEOPLATONISM

In Plotinus a distinction was made between three forms of love—love as a god, as a daemon, and as a passion. The first of these was again divided into the celestial and terrestrial Aphrodite. The celestial Aphrodite inspires the love of ideas and is the soul of the intelligible world. The terrestrial Aphrodite presides over marriage and is the soul of the sensible world. Love as a demon is identified with the souls of individual human beings. As a passion it is the love of beauty in temperate men and the love of sexual pleasure in those who dwell exclusively in the material world of ugliness. All love, however, is the love of some degree of beauty. Plotinus adopted the scale of beauties that had been outlined in the *Symposium* and read into it a hierarchy of being. At the apex stood the One; the "way up" to the One led from the beauty of material objects to that of ideas. In this instance one sees again the fusion of the erotic passion with the ecstasy of the mystic vision. Paradoxically, an experience that is intimately associated with our bodily life was thought of as the one escape from it.

This complex of confused ideas permeated Renaissance Neoplatonism. Philosophers such as Marsilio Ficino and Count Giovanni Pico della Mirandola constantly emphasized the power of love to free the soul from its bodily prison. They took over the theme of the two Venuses, and they assigned separate human faculties to each. They gave different names to the kinds of love—namely, divine, human, and animal.

LEONE EBREO. The philosophy of love expounded by Ficino and Mirandola was most fully developed by Leone Ebreo (Judah Abrabanel) in his *Dialoghi d'amore* (1501–1502), a work that circulated extensively not only in Italy but (in translation) through all Europe. Leone tied together the religious, philosophic, and literary traditions into a single network of ideas.

In the *Dialogues* the two interlocutors are Philo and Sophia, obviously elements of the word *philosophia*. Philo is the lover, and Sophia is the beloved. The first dialogue distinguishes between love and desire and describes the various forms of love; the second discusses the presence of love in all natural operations, from the synthesis of the four elements to the movements of the planetary spheres; and the third deals with the love of God as the force that holds the universe together. Thus, it is asserted that love is a single principle permeating all things, from the material through the spiritual, and that this principle is the dynamic factor in cosmic change. There is no difference in essence between the attraction the elements have for one another and the forms of love that exist in human beings. The appraisal of the kinds of love is based on the objects of love, and Leone, like most of his contemporaries, thought that wisdom was inherently more valuable than pleasure.

It should be noted that the concept of a single dynamic power, whether it was called love or force or attraction, became more and more widely used as time went on. Its most extreme form was the *Sehnsucht* ("longing") of some German romantic philosophers, the *Streben* ("striving") of Johann Gottlieb Fichte, and Novalis's endless and unfulfilled search for the blue flower. One of the characteristics of love, at least in the mind of Leone, is its inability ever to be satisfied. Though Philo in the *Dialogues* pleads with Sophia to tell him that she responds to his love, she will not do so.

MODERN PERIOD

During the seventeenth and eighteenth centuries the interest in love was largely psychological and was expressed mainly in novels, poems, and maxims. While love of neighbor and God was approved, sexual love was morally more problematic. The ideal of female chastity was still upheld; in English novels, such as those of Samuel Richardson, a man was allowed to love a woman as long as he did not infringe upon her virginity. Whereas André le Chapelain graded sexual relations according to the social ranks of the maiden and her seducer, Richardson put all men and women on the same level in this respect. Thus, love was democratized. Sexual love was not to be condoned unless sanctified by the sacrament of marriage.

In such French novels as *Le grand Cyrus* by Madeleine de Scudéry, *Les liaisons dangereuses* by Choderlos de Laclos, and *La nouvelle Héloïse* by Jean-Jacques Rousseau, one finds more subtle distinctions and analyses. These authors continue the Renaissance casuistry about the different kinds of love and their respective values, but it must be remembered that their psychology of love was developed against the background of Christian moral principles. There is a constant conflict between the fervent religious and moral desire not to satisfy one's longings (described in

La nouvelle Héloïse) and an awareness of the almost unlimited force of the individual's erotic desires (treated in *Les liaisons dangereuses*).

SPINOZA. The *Ethics* of Benedict de Spinoza was published in Holland in 1677. In this posthumous work, as in earlier publications, Spinoza emphasized man's need of perfection—that is, the fulfillment of both his intellectual and his emotional powers, which indeed were not existentially separate. He maintained that the more adequate an idea, the more it is pleasing, liberating, and intrinsically human. The culmination of the ethical life—that is, the life devoted to freedom of the intellect—is found in the "intellectual love of God." This phrase may have come from Leone Ebreo, but the idea goes back to St. Augustine. Both the *Confessions* and the *Ethics* are built on premises that are discovered by the intuitive process. The God of Spinoza is far from being the God of St. Augustine, but the method of finding him in the inner life and becoming aware of his presence is curiously similar. Both philosophers present a similar paradox: One must lose oneself in order to find oneself, but in so doing, one finds that what one has really discovered is God.

OTHER WRITERS. The analysis of love now passes into the hands of psychologists. Comte Destutt de Tracy and the novelist Stendhal both wrote books on love in which they attempted to probe its motivation and its effects upon conduct, but neither attempted to do more than to discuss love as a sexual experience. Destutt de Tracy's *De l'amour* was not published until 1926, although it may have been known in manuscript form; Stendhal's *On Love*, however, was published in 1822, and although it had no popular success at the time, it was later widely read. In Germany, on the other hand, such books as Johann Wolfgang von Goethe's *Sorrows of Young Werther*, *Elective Affinities*, and, of course, *Faust* gave a quasi-religious tone to the sexual experience. The impossibility of attaining complete satisfaction led men of this tendency to idealize Don Juan as a perfectionist who seeks a goal that he can never reach, for the ideal is precisely that which ought to be and never is. K. W. F. Schlegel's *Lucinde* is a perfect example of this interpretation of love as the ever-sought and unrealizable ideal.

SCHOPENHAUER. Arthur Schopenhauer was unique in condemning all forms of love on the grounds that they tie one to the will-to-live. But he found this will even in the subanimate world of nature; thus, he was reverting to the ancient tradition of an omnipresent principle and was more interested in the metaphysical status of this principle than in the details of human psychology. Although Schopenhauer's condemnation of love follows from his general metaphysical position, he supplemented this condemnation with an essay, "Metaphysics of the Love of the Sexes," in which he tried to show that poets and novelists had recognized the evil of loving, although they had not formulated the abstract principles that would justify this point of view. Love drives men and women to suicide, madness, and extremes of sacrifice. Pointing out that he has no philosophic precedents to guide him, Schopenhauer flatly declares that all forms of love are rooted in sexuality and that, obviously, the existence of future generations depends upon its gratification. But the sexual instinct can disguise itself in various ways, especially as "objective admiration," although in reality the will-to-live is aiming at the production of a new individual. Because sexual union exists for the benefit of the species, not for the individuals involved in it, marriages should not be made for love but for convenience. Thus, he says, there is guilt in loving, for its culmination is simply the perpetuation of the will-to-live, with all its attendant miseries.

FREUD. Historically, Schopenhauer's influence on Sigmund Freud is more important than his theory of the will-to-live in itself. Freud renamed the will-to-live the libido and at one time even saw its goal as death. The concept of the death wish paralleled Schopenhauer's emphasis on art and pity as the two ways of escape from life, and it had no great success in psychological circles. The libido as a term for generalized desire, on the other hand, has become part and parcel of the terminology of psychodynamics. Like most philosophic concepts, it has been distorted by both its supporters and its adversaries, but by reintegrating humanity and its strivings into the natural world, it has revived in a new form the kernel of Diotima's speech in the *Symposium*. Freud, along with most Platonists, would deny this. However, since love in the *Symposium* is found not only in sexual attraction but also in scientific research and philosophic meditation, there is only a verbal difference between the two philosophies. Freud, to be sure, does not preach the denial of bodily love, but at the same time he never denied the need for self-restraint and self-discipline. Although he may have said that the scientist is dominated by an anal-erotic urge, he did not deprecate science in these terms; rather, he explained what he thought was its general etiology. He also opened the door to a franker discussion of human motivations, and his contribution to ethics can hardly be overestimated. He attempted to show men how to realize the ideal of self-knowledge that philosophers had advocated for centuries without indicating how one might attain it. By pointing out the universality of love in its various forms and suggesting how it becomes deformed and alienated from its natural goals, Freud laid the foundation for an ethics that would be freed from ecclesiastical dogmatism. Although his followers have modified some of his ideas, as was inevitable, they have not denied either the preeminence of the libido as a driving power in human affairs or its ability to mask itself. One cannot overlook Freud's contribution toward giving men the ability to understand both one another and themselves—a type of understanding that had been preached over the centuries but always on the assumption that human nature could be observed in conscious behavior.

As is always the case in intellectual history, ancient beliefs survive and take on new forms. This is as true of the history of the idea of love as it is of other ideas. It is obvious that although no one believes any longer in the myth of the two Aphrodites as anthropomorphic deities each of whom is accompanied by a special Eros, the distinction between the two still persists as the contrast between carnal and spiritual love. The First Epistle of John and the Gospel of John have been by no means discarded in the Occident, nor has the commandment to love God and one's neighbor been forgotten. *Caritas* as both brotherly love and charity is still preached, if not practiced, and the Neoplatonic notion that through love we shall have harmony and through harmony, peace, is as potent a force in social education as it has ever been. Philosophy sometimes takes as its goal the rationalization of common sense, or at least of widely held beliefs, and according to the available evidence, no one has ever maintained that the whole duty of man consists in hating, provoking disorder, and disobeying what are at various times called the laws of God or of nature. Philosophers writing on love have attempted in numerous ways, first, to describe the unique part it plays in human life; second, to seek its similarity to other impulses; third, to appraise the ends that it wishes to achieve; and finally, to work out a systematic account of all these distinctions and put them into a logical network of ideas.

See also Aristotle; Augustine, St.; Beauty; Bernard of Clairvaux, St.; Dante Alighieri; Destutt de Tracy, Antoine Louis Claude, Comte; Empedocles; Fichte, Johann Gottlieb; Ficino, Marsilio; Freud, Sigmund; Goethe, Johann Wolfgang von; Neoplatonism; Parmenides of Elea; Pascal, Blaise; Perfection; Pico della Mirandola, Count Giovanni; Plato; Plotinus; Rousseau, Jean-Jacques; Schlegel, Friedrich von; Schopenhauer, Arthur; Spinoza, Benedict (Baruch) de.

Bibliography

PRIMARY SOURCES

Aristotle. *Nicomachean Ethics.* Translated by W. D. Ross. Oxford, 1925. Books 7–8.

Augustine. *Confessions.* Translated by E. B. Pusey. London, 1907. Book 1, Ch. 12; Book II, Chs. 1 and 6; Book III, Ch. 1; Book IV, Ch. 6; Book VI, Ch. 14; Book VII, Ch. 10; Book VIII, Ch. 2; Book X, Ch. 7.

Bernard. *De Diligendo Deo*; Sermon, *In Cantica Canticorum.* In *Patrologia Latina,* edited by J. P. Migne. Paris, 1844–1864. Vols. 182–183, respectively.

Chapelain, André le. *De Amore.* Edited by E. Trojel. Havniae, 1892.

Cleanthes. *Hymn to Zeus.* Translated by George Boas in *Rationalism in Greek Philosophy.* Baltimore: Johns Hopkins Press, 1961. P. 251.

Dante. *Divine Comedy.* Translated by H. F. Carey, 2nd ed. London, 1819.

Dante. *Il convivio.* Translated by P. H. Wicksteed as *The Convivio of Dante Alighieri.* London: Dent, 1903.

Dante. *Vita nuova.* Translated by Dante Gabriel Rossetti as *The New Life of Dante Alighieri.* London, 1901.

Empedocles. Fragments 115, 128, 130. In *Early Greek Philosophy,* by J. Burnet, 3rd ed. London, 1920; New York, 1957.

Euripides. *Hippolytus.*

Freud, Sigmund. *A General Introduction to Psycho-Analysis.* Translated by Joan Riviere. Garden City, NY, 1943.

Freud, Sigmund. *Three Contributions to the Theory of Sex* and *Totem and Taboo.* In *The Basic Writings of Sigmund Freud.* New York: Random House, 1938.

Hermetica (Asclepius II, 21). Edited by A. D. Nock and A. J. Festugière. Paris, 1960. Vol. II.

Laclos, Choderlos de. *Les liaisons dangereuses.* Garden City, NY: Doubleday, 1961.

Leone Ebreo. *The Philosophy of Love.* Translated by F. Friedberg-Seelye and Jean H. Barnes. London: Soncino Press, 1937.

Lucretius. *De Rerum Natura,* Book I, 1–49. In *The Stoic and Epicurean Philosophers,* by W. J. Oates. New York: Modern Library, 1957.

Plato. *Symposium.* In *Plato: Dialogues,* edited by B. Jowett, 4th rev. ed. Oxford, 1953.

Pseudo-Aristotle. *Magna Moralia.* Translated by St. George Stock. Oxford, 1915. 1208 b, 31.

Schopenhauer, Arthur. *The World as Will and Idea.* Translated by R. B. Haldane and J. Kemp, 6th ed. London, 1907. See especially Vol. III, Ch. 44, "Supplements to the Fourth Book." London, 1909.

Spinoza, Benedict de. *Ethics,* Part 5. In *The Chief Works of Spinoza,* translated by R. H. M. Elwes, 2 vols. New York, 1955.

SECONDARY SOURCES

Bruyne, Edgar de. *Études d'esthétique médiévale.* Bruges: De Tempel, 1946. Vol. III, Book IV, Ch. 2.

Gilson, Étienne. *The Spirit of Mediaeval Philosophy.* Translated by A. H. C. Downes. New York, 1940. Ch. 14.

Mackail, J. W. *Select Epigrams from the Greek Anthology.* London, 1906. See especially the introduction, Sections vi–vii, pp. 32–41.

Panofsky, Erwin. *Studies in Iconology.* New York: Oxford University Press, 1939. Chapters 5–6.

George Boas (1967)

LOVE [ADDENDUM]

Since the middle of the twentieth century, analytic philosophers have taken diverse interests in love. Philosophers of mind have asked what kind of psychological state love is. A natural answer is that love is an emotion like any other. Some philosophers, however, find love to be an anomalous emotion, or even not to be an emotion at all. Most types of emotions seem to be triggered by, or partially to consist in, a belief that the emotion is warranted by some fact about its object. Fear of something, for example, typically involves the thought that the thing feared is dangerous or threatening. Love seems to be an exception, since it is unclear what fact about one's beloved might warrant one's love for this person. Some are willing to accept love as an emotion despite this anomaly, while others insist that love must be a psychological state of a different kind. The most commonly proposed alternative is that love is a desire, or set of desires, regarding one's beloved.

The view that love is an anomalous emotion stems from a perception that nothing warrants or justifies it. This raises a second issue that has occupied philosophers: whether there are reasons for love, and if so, what these reasons might be. The most natural candidates for reasons for love would seem to be properties or qualities of the beloved, such as wit, beauty, or kindness. Among many problems with this proposal, three have attracted especially close attention. First, some find the proposal fetishistic, or at least misdirected. It appears to represent love as focused on the beloved's accidental properties, rather than on that person's essence. Second, if one's reasons for loving the beloved are properties, then one's love ought to wane as the beloved loses those properties. This seems at odds with the thought, famously expressed by William Shakespeare, that "Love is not love/Which alters when it alteration finds." Finally, if one's reasons for loving the beloved are properties, then insofar as one's love is responsive to those reasons, it will soon migrate to another person with those properties in sufficient proportion. This too seems antithetical to love.

Impressed by some of these problems, Harry Frankfurt concludes that while love creates reasons, there are no reasons for love. Love is a structure of desires for which there is no antecedent justification. Love is focused on the particular person whom one loves; it is not a response to some generalizable, justifying property that the person has. Since Jane, say, is the particular person she is and she can neither lose this trait nor share it with anyone else, one's love for her does not alter as it alteration finds, nor does it transfer to her twin. David Velleman (1999), resisting Frankfurt's conclusion, suggests that love is a response to a justifying feature that is also identical with the beloved's essence: Jane's rational nature or capacity for valuation, for instance. However, this suggestion seems to leave one's beloved vulnerable to being replaced—indeed, replaced by any other person with a rational nature. A different strategy for avoiding Frankfurt's conclusion is to suggest that love is a response to the reasons provided by one's shared history with the person one loves. This would explain why one's love does not alter as the beloved's wit or beauty fades, and why one's love does not accept a substitute with whom no such history is shared. However, the appeal to shared history again threatens to make love focused on the beloved's accidental properties, rather than on that person's essence. It also seems to put the cart before the horse. Love seems to precede many relationships, rather than develop with them.

Moral philosophers have been particularly concerned that love, and similar attitudes such as friendship, are in tension with morality, at least as understood in certain theories. The tension is thought to arise because these moral theories—most notably, utilitarianism and Kantianism—require one to be impartial, that is, to give equal weight to everyone's interests. Love, in contrast, seems to impel one to be partial: to give greater weight to the interests of one's beloved. The tension has been thought to be more acute at the level of deliberation than at the level of action. While there may be utilitarian and Kantian justifications for permissions, or even requirements, to act as love directs, deliberating in terms of such justifications seems incompatible with love. This incompatibility has generally been seen as a problem for such moral theories, rather than as a problem for love. The incompatibility makes these moral theories seem self-defeating or overly demanding, or it reveals that they fail to take into account something of genuine value.

In defense of these moral theories, some philosophers have insisted that the incompatibility is only apparent. Indirect utilitarians have pointed out that while utilitarianism requires one to do what is best from an impartial standpoint, utilitarianism need not require one to deliberate in impartial terms. Indeed, there may be strong utilitarian reasons for not so deliberating. Kantians have similarly observed that the moral agent need not always be guided by specific reflection on what it is morally permissible to do. A less concessive Kantian response appears in Velleman's work. Love, he argues, is a "moral emotion," by which he seems to mean, at least in part, that love is animated by the same value that underlies morality itself.

Other philosophers, however, have insisted that the incompatibility is real. Some of these philosophers urge rejecting impartial moral theories, perhaps in favor of a virtue-based approach. Others see the incompatibility as casting doubt not on the impartiality of morality, but instead on its authority over our lives.

See also Friendship; Moral Psychology; Virtue and Vice; Virtue Ethics.

Bibliography

Frankfurt, Harry. *Necessity, Volition, and Love.* Cambridge, U.K.: Cambridge University Press, 1999.

Frankfurt, Harry. *The Reasons of Love.* Princeton, NJ: Princeton University Press, 2004.

Green, O. H. "Is Love an Emotion?" In *Love Analyzed*, edited by Roger E. Lamb. Boulder, CO: Westview Press, 1997.

Keller, Simon. "How Do I Love Thee? Let Me Count the Properties." *American Philosophical Quarterly* 37 (2) (2000): 163–173.

Kolodny, Niko. "Love as Valuing a Relationship." *Philosophical Review* 112 (2) (2003): 135–189.

Taylor, Gabriele. "Love." *Proceedings of the Aristotelian Society* 76 (1975–1976): 147–164.

Velleman, David. "Love as a Moral Emotion." *Ethics* 109 (2) (1999): 338–374.

Williams, Bernard. "Persons, Character, and Morality." In his *Moral Luck.* Cambridge, U.K.: Cambridge University Press, 1981.

Wolf, Susan. "Morality and Partiality." *Philosophical Perspectives* 6 (1992): 243–259.

Niko Kolodny (2005)

LOVEJOY, ARTHUR ONCKEN
(1873–1962)

Arthur Oncken Lovejoy, the American philosopher and historian of ideas, was born in Berlin, Germany, the son of the Reverend W. W. Lovejoy of Boston and Sara

Oncken of Hamburg. Educated at the University of California (Berkeley) and at Harvard, where he received his MA, Lovejoy began his teaching career at Stanford University (1899–1901) and then taught for seven years at Washington University in St. Louis. After short periods at Columbia University and the University of Missouri, he went to Johns Hopkins in 1910 as professor of philosophy, remaining there until his retirement in 1938. In 1927 he gave the Carus Lectures, published as *The Revolt against Dualism* in 1930, and the William James Lectures, published as *The Great Chain of Being* in 1933. Lovejoy was widely known as an epistemologist, a philosophic critic, a historian of ideas, and a man of action. He helped to organize the Association of American University Professors, in which he served for many years as chairman of the group that investigated all charges of violation of academic freedom. In this connection he wrote the article "Academic Freedom" for the *Encyclopaedia of the Social Sciences*.

Lovejoy's works fall into two main groups—those on epistemology and those on intellectual history—although he also wrote essays on ethics, religion, and social problems.

PHILOSOPHICAL WORKS

For many years Lovejoy confined his writings to articles, a great number of them critical. These were often directed against various forms of anti-intellectualism: "The Thirteen Pragmatisms" (1908), "Some Antecedents of the Philosophy of Bergson" (1913), and "The Paradox of the Thinking Behaviorist" (1922). These articles, however, were frequently examinations of certain contemporary movements in philosophy, such as the New Realism: "Reflections of a Temporalist on the New Realism" (1911) and "On Some Novelties of the New Realism" (1913). Some were even on the supposed philosophical implication of the theory of relativity: "The Travels of Peter, Paul and Zebedee" (1932) and "The Paradox of the Time-Retarding Journey" (1931).

It was not until 1930 that Lovejoy published his major work, *The Revolt against Dualism*, in which he attempted to defend epistemological dualism against the reigning modes of monism. He began by sketching what he called naive dualism, which assumes that (1) many possible objects of knowledge (*cognoscenda*) are at places external to the body of the percipient; (2) man must have real traffic with things that existed in the past and may exist in the future; (3) man can have knowledge of things as they would be if they were not directly known; (4) other minds and experiences exist; and (5) *cognoscenda* in

other places and at other times are apprehensible by other knowers. The book analyzed this naive dualism and defended a corrected form of it. On the whole, although not in detail, Lovejoy was more interested in the duality of two existents (of two five-cent stamps, for instance) than qualitative duality such as of red and green. The duality of two things is demonstrated, he wrote, by the fact that one of the supposed pair has a spatial, a temporal, or a spatiotemporal position that is inconsistent with that empirically exhibited by the other. If, then, it can be shown that our ideas of objects have positions that can be shown not to be those of the objects, then the two cannot rightly be believed to be one. Qualitative duality would be demonstrated in analogous fashion, but the inconsistency would lie between two sets of qualities.

In his autobiographical essay, "A Temporalistic Realism," in Volume II of *Contemporary American Philosophy*, edited by G. P. Adams and W. P. Montague (London and New York, 1930), Lovejoy pointed out that one of his earliest philosophical theses was that experience itself is temporal. Any philosophical position that overlooks or denies this, or conflicts with it, would, in his opinion, be condemned as contradicting a manifest truth. (This does not, of course, assert that any philosophy—such as that of Henri Bergson—that admits the empirical reality of time is thereby proved.) The various forms of monism fail to evade, and cannot evade, the consequences of this fact. For instance, the date at which a visual datum occurs is not the date of the object that one is seeing. There is a time lag between the emission of light rays from a star and their arrival at the retina of a human eye, to say nothing of the arrival of the nerve current stimulated by them at the cerebral cortex, where it apparently causes a visual image to appear. Indeed, some stars that we perceive now may have become extinct many light-years ago. Analogous statements can be made about sound, odor, and taste.

Although Lovejoy also used other criteria, this criterion of duality suffices to establish existential duality between object and sensum. To deny the duality, Lovejoy asserted, would be equivalent to asserting that two particulars can each be in two places at the same time, that one particular has or consists of many shapes and other inconsistent qualities at the same time, that it has two dates in the same temporal order, that it can be at the same time both the beginning and the end of a causal series, and, finally, that error is impossible. Lovejoy discussed each of these theses in connection with epistemological positions widely held at the time the book was written: the New Realism, objective relativism, Alfred

North Whitehead's denial of simple location, and Bertrand Russell's epistemology as given in *The Analysis of Mind* (London and New York, 1921) and *The Analysis of Matter* (London and New York, 1927).

Lovejoy's dualism differed from that of the naive dualist in that the latter is likely to believe that his objects are qualitatively, if not existentially, identical with the objects of others. Our ideas, Lovejoy held, do not necessarily have properties identical with the properties of anything in the physical world, but we are not therefore condemned to know nothing whatsoever of that world. We cannot prove beyond doubt that some of the properties of our ideas are also properties of the physical world, but such is "a natural assumption which no one can prove to be false" (*Revolt against Dualism*, p. 273). Qualities that vary with percipients must be held to be subjective, but there are certain residual properties—extension, shape, relative position, temporal succession, and motion—that may reasonably be said to characterize both our ideas and their objects. The reasonableness of the hypothesis rests on its ability to give us grounds for framing a "coherent, simple, unifying, scientifically serviceable" set of hypotheses for explaining both the rise of our sensory data and their peculiar characteristics. It will, in short, account for a world that is causally efficacious, that exists between our perceptual moments, and that has a past and future independent of any percipients.

INTELLECTUAL HISTORY

To separate Lovejoy's philosophical views from his historical studies is artificial, for his philosophy is based on a wide knowledge of history, and his historiography is based on his belief in the existence and efficacy of ideas. However, such a distinction may be made for purposes of classification.

Lovejoy was the chief promoter in the United States of the historiography of ideas. His continuing interest in this area dated back at least to his monograph *The Dialectic of Bruno and Spinoza* (Berkeley, CA, 1904). He was the originator and first editor of the *Journal of the History of Ideas*. He studied such general ideas as romanticism, evolutionism, naturalism, and primitivism, showing the ambiguities resident in them and their ingression into fields that have no ostensible logical connection with them.

In the preface to *Essays in the History of Ideas*, Lovejoy defined his conception of the historiography of ideas: (1) It studies the presence and influence of the same ideas in very diverse provinces of thought and in different periods; thus, an idea that may have originated in logic may

turn up in biology, or vice versa. (2) There are certain catchwords, such as *nature*, that have taken on new meanings over time, although the people using them are seldom aware of their ambiguities. The historian of ideas will analyze these various meanings as they occur. An example from fairly recent history (not one of Lovejoy's own) would be the eulogistic usage of the word *organic*. (3) It has also been noticed that a given author will prove susceptible to the emotional aura of certain terms and, probably because of this, will waver between a valid meaning of an idea and an incongruous meaning. It is usually assumed that the thought of a given writer must be consistent and unified; but by accepting this assumption, a historian may overlook precisely those thoughts expressed by a writer that were in fact influential. A fuller explanation of the program is given in Lovejoy's essay "The Historiography of Ideas," first published in 1938 and republished as the opening chapter in *Essays in the History of Ideas*.

THE GREAT CHAIN OF BEING. Lovejoy's most influential single contribution to the history of ideas is *The Great Chain of Being*. The idea whose fortunes he traced in this book was first expressed by Plato in the *Timaeus*. There Plato maintained that the Demiurge, being good, was not jealous and, not being jealous, wanted the world to lack nothing; therefore, if the world were to lack nothing, all possibilities must be realized. The realization of all possibilities is the great chain of being, and the principle it rests upon was called by Lovejoy the principle of plenitude.

This apparently simple idea, contained in a creation myth, was introduced into Christian theology through Neoplatonism and into cosmography by Hasdai Crescas with his supposition of many worlds, by Johannes Kepler, by Nicholas of Cusa with his theory of a boundless universe, and, above all, by Giordano Bruno with his open acceptance of the principle as it applies to stellar bodies. In Benedict de Spinoza it appeared as the doctrine that all ideas of God must be realized, and in Gottfried Wilhelm Leibniz as the principle of sufficient reason. Lovejoy showed how the principle entered into biological speculations in the eighteenth century and how it was "temporalized." In the idea of the great chain of being, which he presented with a richness of erudition, Lovejoy found one of the most fertile yet neglected ideas in Western philosophy and masterfully traced its ramifications and subsequent history.

PRIMITIVISM. A second dominant idea, the study of whose history Lovejoy initiated, is that cluster of notions known as primitivism. Primitivism has two forms—a chronological form, exemplified in the myth of the Golden Age, and a cultural form, best exemplified in cynicism and in all attempts to rediscover the so-called natural life. Each of these forms has two subspecies, "hard" primitivism and "soft" primitivism. Hard primitivism maintains that the state of nature (man's primordial condition) was rugged and unencumbered with superfluities, a state very close to that of the legendary noble savage. Soft primitivism, on the contrary, maintains that the state of nature was agreeably gentle, that earth gave man her fruits spontaneously without any labor on his part, and that there was no private property and hence no covetousness, no war, no foreign trade, none of the complications that the arts and sciences introduce.

Lovejoy urged as early as 1917 that there would be more progress in philosophical studies if there were more cooperation among philosophers ("On Some Conditions of Progress in Philosophical Inquiry"). A documentary history of primitivism provided, it seemed, an ideal opportunity for such cooperation. Lovejoy and three other scholars formed a team and agreed to publish a four-volume work, to be titled *A Documentary History of Primitivism and Related Ideas*, covering the ground from early Greek times to the recent past. Of this projected work only one volume, *Primitivism and Related Ideas in Antiquity*, written by Lovejoy with George Boas, was completed, although a number of smaller works by various scholars came out as contributions to the subject. The published volume contained, along with documents and commentaries, two supplementary essays—"Primitivism in Ancient Western Asia," by W. F. Albright, and "Primitivism in Indian Literature," by P.-E. Dumont—and an appendix by Lovejoy—"Some Meanings of 'Nature.'" Although the original four-volume plan was never carried out, what did appear may have shown historians of philosophy that primitivism was a philosophic theme neglected by the historical tradition that had nevertheless permeated Occidental thought.

See also Bruno, Giordano; Crescas, Hasdai; History and Historiography of Philosophy; Kepler, Johannes; Leibniz, Gottfried Wilhelm; Neoplatonism; Nicholas of Cusa; New Realism; Realism; Russell, Bertrand Arthur William; Whitehead, Alfred North.

Bibliography

WORKS BY LOVEJOY

"The Thirteen Pragmatisms." *Journal of Philosophy* 5 (1908): 1–12, 29–39.

"Reflections of a Temporalist on the New Realism." *Journal of Philosophy* 8 (1911): 589–599.

"Some Antecedents of the Philosophy of Bergson." *Mind*, n.s. 22 (1913): 465–483.

"On Some Novelties of the New Realism." *Journal of Philosophy* 10 (1913): 29–43.

Bergson and Romantic Evolutionism. Berkeley, CA, 1914.

"On Some Conditions of Progress in Philosophical Inquiry." *Philosophical Review* 26 (1917): 123–163.

"The Paradox of the Thinking Behaviorist." *Philosophical Review* 31 (1922): 135–147.

The Revolt against Dualism: An Inquiry concerning the Existence of Ideas. La Salle, IL: Open Court, 1930.

"The Paradox of the Time-Retarding Journey." *Philosophical Review* 40 (1931): 48–68, 152–167.

"The Travels of Peter, Paul and Zebedee." *Philosophical Review* 41 (1932): 498–517.

Primitivism and Related Ideas in Antiquity. Written with G. Boas. Baltimore, MD: Johns Hopkins Press, 1935.

The Great Chain of Being: A Study of the History of an Idea. Cambridge, MA: Harvard University Press, 1936.

Essays in the History of Ideas. Baltimore, MD: Johns Hopkins Press, 1948. Contains a list of Lovejoy's articles up to and including 1947.

Reflections on Human Nature. Baltimore, MD: Johns Hopkins Press, 1961.

The Reason, the Understanding, and Time. Baltimore, MD: Johns Hopkins Press, 1961. Deals with the Romantic theory of knowledge.

Essays in the History of Ideas. Baltimore, MD: John Hopkins Press, 1970.

WORKS ON LOVEJOY

Boas, George. "A. O. Lovejoy as Historian of Philosophy." *Journal of the History of Ideas* 9 (4) (October 1948): 404–411.

Mandelbaum, Maurice. "Arthur O. Lovejoy and the Theory of Historiography." *Journal of the History of Ideas* 9 (4) (October 1948): 412–423.

Montague, W. P. "My Friend Lovejoy." *Journal of the History of Ideas* 9 (4) (October 1948): 424–427.

Montague, W. P. "Professor Lovejoy's Carus Lectures." *Journal of Philosophy* 25 (11) (May 24, 1928): 293–296.

Murphy, Arthur E. "Mr. Lovejoy's Counter-revolution." *Journal of Philosophy* 28 (1931): 29–42, 57–71.

Nicholson, Marjorie. "A. O. Lovejoy as Teacher." *Journal of the History of Ideas* 9 (4) (October 1948): 428–438.

Spencer, Theodore. "Lovejoy's *Essays in the History of Ideas*." *Journal of the History of Ideas* 9 (4) (October 1948): 439–446.

Taylor, H. A. "Further Reflections on the History of Ideas: An Examination of A. O. Lovejoy's Program." *Journal of Philosophy* 40 (May 27, 1943): 281–299.

Wiener, Philip P. "Lovejoy's Rôle in American Philosophy." In *Studies in Intellectual History*, 161–173. Baltimore: Johns Hopkins Press, 1953. A collection of essays by a group of Lovejoy's colleagues.

George Boas (1967)
Bibliography updated by Michael J. Farmer (2005)

LOYALTY

"Loyalty," as a moral rather than a political concept, has received scant attention in philosophical literature. In fact, at the present time [1967] it seems banished from respectable ethical discussions, owing, no doubt, to its historical association with an obsolete metaphysics (idealism) and with such odious political movements as the extreme nationalism of Nazism. However, the supposed implications suggested by these disreputable associations are ill-founded. On the contrary, loyalty is an essential ingredient in any civilized and humane system of morals.

Philosophical issues regarding loyalty may be separated into the question of the object of loyalty, and the question of the moral value of loyalty.

THE OBJECT OF LOYALTY

Granted that loyalty is the wholehearted devotion to an object of some kind, what kind of thing is this object? Is it an abstract entity, such as an idea or a collective being? Or is it a person or group of persons?

The idealist contends that loyalty is "the willing and practical and thoroughgoing devotion of a person to a cause" (Josiah Royce, *The Philosophy of Loyalty,* p. 17). Its object is "a cause beyond your private self, greater than you are … impersonal and superpersonal" (ibid., pp. 19–20). As a cause it is something that transcends the individual, "an eternal reality." Apart from familiar metaphysical and logical objections to this concept of a superpersonal reality, this view has the ethical defect of postulating duties over and above our duties to individual men and groups of men. The individual is submerged and lost in this superperson not only ontologically but also morally, for it tends to dissolve our specific duties and obligations to others into a "superhuman" good.

Opposing the idealistic position is the view, characteristic of social atomism (empiricism or utilitarianism, for example), that denies any distinctive status to loyalty on the grounds that metaphysically there can be no such superpersonal entity to serve as its object. Insofar as the concept of loyalty has any validity at all, it reduces to other kinds of relations and dispositions, such as obedience or honesty. Most empiricists are inclined to agree with David Hume, however, that loyalty is a virtue that holds "less of reason, than of bigotry and superstition."

Thus, it is generally assumed that we must either accept the notion of a superperson or some other abstract entity as the object of loyalty or reject the notion of loyalty altogether as founded on an illusion. This assumption is open to question.

In answer to the idealists, it should be pointed out that in our common moral language, as well as historically, "loyalty" is taken to refer to a relationship between persons—for instance, between a lord and his vassal, between a parent and his children, or between friends. Thus, the object of loyalty is ordinarily taken to be a person or group of persons.

Loyalty is conceived as interpersonal, and it is also always specific; a man is loyal to *his* lord, *his* father, or *his* comrades. It is conceptually impossible to be loyal to people in general (to humanity) or to a general principle, such as justice or democracy.

The social atomist fails to recognize the special character and significance of the ties that bind individuals together and provide the basis for loyalties. Loyalty is not founded on just any casual relationship between persons, but on a specific kind of relationship or tie. The special ties involved arise from the twofold circumstance that the persons so bound are comembers of a specific group (community) distinguished by a specific common background and sharing specific interests, and are related in terms of some sort of role differentiation within that group. A friendship, a family, or such a highly organized group as a political, priestly, or military community illustrates the presence of these conditions. Special ties of this sort provide both the necessary and the sufficient conditions for a person to be a proper object of loyalty.

The impersonal or objective element mentioned by Royce and other idealists is explained by the fact that it is the ties, the mutually related roles, rather than any particular personal characteristics of the individuals involved that provide the grounds for loyalty. Why should I be loyal to X? Because he is *my R* (friend, father, leader, comrade). More purely personal characteristics of $X,$ such as his kindness, courage, amiability, honesty, or spirituality cannot serve as *grounds* for loyalty. That the conditions of loyalty abstract from the personal characteristics of the individuals concerned does not, of course, entail that loyalty must relate to a superpersonal entity (cause, whole) any more than the fact that an algebraic formula contains a variable within it (such as Fx) entails that there must be some kind of supernumber to satisfy the function.

THE MORAL VALUE OF LOYALTY

Is loyalty something good in itself? Is it always good? Can there be bad loyalties?

On these questions the idealist takes an extreme position, for he holds that loyalty is the highest moral good. According to Royce, a man's wholehearted devotion to a cause is *eo ipso* good and becomes evil only when it conflicts with other loyalties. The supreme good is loyalty to loyalty: "so choose and so serve your individual cause as to secure thereby the greatest increase of loyalty amongst men" (ibid., p. 121).

The view that loyalty has an inner value, "whatever be the cause to which this man is loyal," can be used to redeem the most evil acts of men. Such a belief outrages our moral feelings, for we want to say that a cause which demands injustice or cruelty as the price of devotion renders that devotion an evil in itself. It is impossible to separate logically the moral quality of devotion from the moral quality of its object, if that object is a cause. (Incidentally, a distinction must be made between devotion to a thoroughly evil purpose and devotion that is simply misdirected, in the sense that it is well-intentioned but wrong for some other reason.)

Even assuming that the problem of bad loyalties can be resolved by invoking "loyalty to loyalty," the idealist may still be accused of turning morality, which properly concerns man's relations to his fellows, into service of an abstract principle or a cause, thus treating man as a mere means rather than as an end-in-itself.

The social atomist, on the other hand, regards the moral value of loyalty, construed as devotion or obedience to persons or institutions, entirely as a function of its benign or mischievous consequences. This view, however, robs loyalty of any special moral significance. It fails to account, for example, for the admirable side of a mother's loyalty to her son even when, considering the total picture, it is not entirely justified morally.

We must ask what loyalty demands of a person. The etymology of the word *loyalty* gives a clue, for it comes from the French word *loi* and thus means something akin to *legality*. Loyalty, strictly speaking, demands what is morally due the object of loyalty. A loyal subject is one who wholeheartedly devotes himself to his duties to his lord. What is due or owed is defined by the roles of the persons concerned. The fact that loyalty gives what is due also explains why we can demand the loyalty of others.

It follows that mere blind obedience to every wish of the person who is the object of loyalty is not loyalty; it is a perversion of loyalty. There is no moral value to it at all, since it is not something that is morally due. A loyal Nazi is a contradiction in terms, although a loyal German is not.

There are, to be sure, conflicts of loyalties, but this fact does not entail that any of the loyalties involved are improper or invalid. It is simply a logical consequence of the fact that there are conflicts of duties; my duty to my parents may conflict with my duty to my wife or to my fellow countrymen. Sometimes there are clear ways of resolving these conflicts and sometimes there are not, but we cannot eliminate the problem of conflicting loyalties either by a metaphysical trick or by the mechanical application of a value calculus.

One final observation must be made concerning the distinction between loyalty and fidelity. Loyalty includes fidelity in carrying out one's duties to the person or group of persons who are the object of loyalty; but it embraces more than that, for it implies an attitude, perhaps an affection or sentiment, toward such persons. Furthermore, at the very least, loyalty requires the complete subordination of one's own private interest in favor of giving what is due, and perhaps also the exclusion of other legitimate interests. In this sense, loyalty may often be one-sided, although it need not be. If we could not count on the loyalty of others or give them our loyalty, social life would be not only bleak but also impossible.

See also Atomism; Empiricism; Hume, David; Idealism; Royce, Josiah; Utilitarianism.

Bibliography

Aristotle. "On Friendship." In *Nicomachean Ethics.* Books VIII and IX.

Bryant, Sophie. "Loyalty." In James Hasting's *Encyclopaedia of Religion and Ethics.* Vol. VIII, 183–188. New York: Scribners, 1916.

Rashdall, Hastings. *Theory of Good and Evil.* Vol. 1, 188 and 273. London: Oxford University Press, H. Milford, 1924. For the social atomist view of the moral value of loyalty.

Royce, Josiah. *The Philosophy of Loyalty.* New York, 1924.

Sidgwick, Henry. *Methods of Ethics,* 254. 7th ed. London, 1922. For the social atomist view of the moral value of loyalty.

John Ladd (1967)

LU CHIU-YÜAN

See *Lu Xiangshan*

LUCIAN OF SAMOSATA
(c. 115–c. 200)

Lucian of Samosata, the philosophical satirist and satirist of philosophy, was born at Samosata (Samsat) on the Euphrates and was educated there. He then studied rhetoric in Asia Minor, after which he was a lawyer for a while, toured Greece and Italy as a lecturer, and held a chair of literature in France. In middle age he settled in Athens, where he wrote and gave public readings of his most successful dialogues, many of which were on philosophical themes. Late in life he joined the staff of the Roman governor of Egypt. Nothing is known of his death except that it occurred after 180.

Lucian's philosophical position is not easy to define because he expresses contradictory attitudes, and his persistent irony and his obvious wish to entertain make it hard to know how seriously to take his statements. The contradictions have been used as a basis for several different theories of his intellectual development, but the chronological order of his works is too uncertain for any such interpretation to be wholly convincing.

In *The Fisher*, Lucian claimed to be a champion of philosophy, which he described elsewhere as a civilizing and morally improving study; however, he constantly criticized pseudo philosophers for their greed, bad temper, sexual immorality, and the general inconsistency between their preaching and their practice. The historical occasion for such attacks was the encouragement of philosophy by Marcus Aurelius, which had made philosophers almost as numerous as monks and friars were in the Middle Ages.

Lucian's favorite target was the Stoic, but he also savagely attacked such Cynics as Peregrinus, and in *The Sale of Lives* he made fun of every school. However, he sometimes wrote approvingly of individual philosophies. The *Nigrinus* appears to be a eulogy of Platonism, although this may be ironical or simply an excuse for satirizing Roman society. The *Cynicus* is a less ambiguous defense of Cynicism, and in several dialogues Lucian speaks through a character called Cyniscus or through that of the Cynic Menippus. Diogenes is once mentioned favorably, and in the *Alexander* there is enthusiastic praise for Epicurus, "a really great man who perceived, as no one else has done, the beauty of truth."

The *Hermotimus* rejects all philosophical systems on the grounds that they are mutually contradictory and thus cannot all be right, and life is too short to discover which of them is nearest to the truth. The wisest course is to get on with the business of living, guided by common sense. Tiresias in the *Menippus* gives the same advice.

In general, Lucian disliked philosophies that encourage superstition, such as Platonism and Stoicism, and preferred materialists like Democritus and Epicurus. Although he made fun of the Skeptics, he was temperamentally inclined to skepticism, or to an eclecticism of the kind described in the *Life of Demonax*.

His own positive ideas included a conception of society free from racial, social, and economic distinctions. He valued such human qualities as sincerity, courage, cheerfulness, and kindness; and he continually stressed the importance of facing facts, especially the fact of death.

Lucian's influence on later thought was exerted largely, but not entirely, through the medium of literary technique. He facilitated the spread of humanism in the sixteenth century by suggesting one of the basic themes (the absurdity of plutocracy) and some of the incidental jokes in Thomas More's *Utopia*, but his main contributions were the lighthearted manner, the form (a fantastic journey described in a familiar dialogue), and the trick of using proper names that etymologically imply nonexistence or nonseriousness. He also aided in the Reformation by providing literary precedents and humorous devices for the satire on ecclesiastics, theologians, monks, and superstitions in Desiderius Erasmus's *Encomium Moriae* and in the work of François Rabelais. Voltaire's *Candide* is Lucianic in both manner and theme (the refutation of philosophical theory by reality), and its final moral is identical with that of the *Menippus*. The *Conversation between Lucian, Erasmus and Rabelais in the Elysian Fields* shows that Voltaire regarded Lucian as one of his masters in the strategy of intellectual revolution.

Bacon called Lucian a contemplative atheist, and as such Lucian evidently interested David Hume, who described him as a very moral writer, quoted him with respect when discussing ethics and religion, and read him on his deathbed. Since then, professional philosophers have tended to ignore him, but perhaps his spirit is still alive in those who (as Bertrand Russell did), are prepared to flavor philosophy with wit.

See also Cynics; Diogenes of Sinope; Epicurus; Erasmus, Desiderius; Humanism; Hume, David; Leucippus and Democritus; More, Thomas; Platonism and the Platonic Tradition; Rabelais, François; Russell, Bertrand Arthur William; Skepticism; Stoicism; Voltaire, François-Marie Arouet de.

Bibliography

TEXTS

Luciani opera. 4 vols, edited by M. D. Macleod. Oxford Classical Texts, 1972–1987.

Harmon, A. M. With facing Greek text. 8 vols., 1968–1979, Loeb Classical Library. Vol. 6 translated by K. Kilburn; vols. 7–8 translated by M. D. Macleod.

Macleod, Matthew D. "Lucianic Studies since 1930." *Aufstieg und Niedergang der Römischen Welt* 2.34.2 (1994): 1362–1421.

STUDIES

Anderson, Graham. *Lucian: Theme and Variation in the Second Sophistic*. Leiden: Brill, 1976.

Baldwin, Barry. *Studies in Lucian*. Toronto: Hakkert, 1973.

Bernays, J. *Lukian und die Kyniker*. Berlin, 1879.

Billault, Alain. *Lucien de Samosate*. Lyon: Centre d'Études Romaines et Gallo-Romaines 13, 1994.

Bompaire, J. *Lucien écrivain: Imitation et création*. Paris: Bibliothèque des Écoles Françaises d'Athènes et de Rome, 1958.

Branham, R. B. *Unruly Eloquence: Lucian and the Comedy of Traditions*. Cambridge, MA: Harvard University Press, 1989.

Camerotto, A. *Le metamorfosi della parola: studi sulla parodia in Luciano di Samosata*. Pisa: Istituti editoriali e poligrafici internazionali, 1998.

Caster, M. *Lucien et la pensée religieuse de son temps*. Paris: Société d'édition "Les belles lettres," 1937.

Clay, Diskin. "Lucian of Samosata, Four Philosophical Lives (Nigrinus, Demonax, Peregrinus, Alexander Pseudomantis)." *Aufstieg und Niedergang der Römischen Welt* 2.36.5: 3406–3450.

Edwards, Mark J. "Lucian and the Rhetoric of Philosophy: The Hermotimus." *Acta Classica* 62 (1993): 195–202.

Georgiadou, A., and D. H. J. Lamour. *Lucian's Science Fiction Novel True Histories: Interpretation and Commentary*. Leiden: Brill, 1998.

Helm, R. *Lucian und Menipp*. Leipzig: Teubner, 1906; reprinted, Hildesheim, 1967.

Jones, C. P. *Culture and Society in Lucian*. Cambridge, MA: Harvard University Press, 1986.

Peretti, A. *Luciano: Un intellettuale greco contro Roma*. Florence: Nuova Italia, 1946.

Robinson, Christopher. *Lucian and His Influence in Europe*. Chapel Hill: University of North Carolina Press, 1979.

Tackaberry, W. H. *Lucian's Relation to the Post-Aristotelian Philosophers*. Toronto, 1930.

Paul Turner (1967)
Bibliography updated by David Konstan (2005)

LUCRETIUS
(?–c. 55 BCE)

Little is known of Lucretius (d. ca. 55 BCE [Donatus, *Life of Virgil*] or perhaps a few years later; cf. Hutchinson 2001) apart from his poem in six books, *On the Nature of Things* (*De rerum natura*), an exposition in Latin hexameters of the doctrines of the Greek philosopher Epicurus, who lived two centuries earlier. Saint Jerome, in his *Chronicle* (Olympiad 171.3), claims that he committed suicide as a result of taking a love potion, and that he wrote his poem "in intervals of insanity," presumably meaning between, rather than during, such episodes.

Jerome also asserts that Cicero "emended" Lucretius' text, that is, corrected it for publication, after his death (as Jerome gives it) in 51/50. It is possible that this is an inference from a letter of Cicero's to his brother (2.9, February 54 BCE), in which he praises Lucretius' poem, though Cicero himself had translated the Greek poet Aratus into Latin hexameters, and might well have taken an interest in a fellow poet's work.

Internal evidence reveals some repetitions and inconsistencies (e.g., the doublet at 4.45–53 and 4.26–44), which Lucretius would doubtless have eliminated in a final version; Lucretius also states that he will treat in greater detail the nature and habitation of the gods (5.155), but no such passage survives. Some scholars have supposed that he planned to include it in a seventh or even later book, and that accordingly the poem as we have it is radically incomplete; in particular, Lucretius did not intend to conclude with the depressing spectacle of the Athenian plague (summary of views in Boyancé 1963: 79–83). But there are good justifications for this ending, and Lucretius could have changed his mind about the theological section, or treated it briefly within the compass of the poem as we have it. In the proem to Book 6 (91–94) he indicates plainly that he is approaching the end of the poem.

The Pre-Socratic philosophers Parmenides and Empedocles had written treatises in verse, and Empedocles' poem, which Lucretius regarded highly enough to deem its author "godlike" (1.716–741), may have borne the same title (*Peri phuseôs*, or perhaps the even closer *Peri phuseôs tôn ontôn*: Sedley 1998: 21–22; the title may not have been Empedocles' own: Schmalzriedt 1970), and may have extended to several thousand lines (Diogenes Laertius 8.77). Empedocles' proem was likely a model for Lucretius' own (Gale 1994: 59–74; Sedley 1998: 1–34). Later, the medium for philosophy was decidedly prose, and Epicurus himself was suspicious of poetry (fr. 229 Usener; cf. Gale 1994: 14–18). In the Hellenistic period (third–first centuries BCE), didactic poetry was composed on a variety of topics, from astronomy and farming to poisonous snakes, but these genre pieces were not usually intended to provide serious instruction; Lucretius' poem was. He succeeds remarkably in conveying rigorous arguments concerning such matters as the constitution of the universe, which for the Epicureans was composed solely of atomic matter and empty space (Books 1–2), the materialist basis of perception and cognition (Books 3–4), and the evolution of the earth and of human civilization (Book 5), along with such special topics as the nature of magnetism (Book 6), even as he struggles with the relative poverty of the Latin philosophical vocabulary, as opposed to Greek (1.136–39, 832, 3.260; cf. Cicero *De finibus* 3.51).

Given the mainly fragmentary or hostile character of our sources concerning Epicurus' doctrines (three short essays by Epicurus in the form of letters are reproduced by Diogenes Laertius, Book 10), Lucretius provides the single extended exposition of Epicurean physics that survives by a follower of the school. Doubtless, the medium of verse imposed some limitations, and Lucretius' understanding of certain points was perhaps faulty, but the poem is immensely valuable for the history of philosophy. It is also a magnificent work of literature, shot through with a moral passion that brightens even the most painstaking arguments about atoms and void.

SOURCES AND ORIGINALITY

This said, it is obviously important to determine what sources Lucretius himself employed, and over this question there is considerable controversy. It is in principle possible that Lucretius relied on no particular text but composed an independent poetical treatise based on his immersion in Epicureanism (Clay 1983: 31). David Sedley (1998), in turn, has argued forcefully that Lucretius adhered principally to a single treatise by Epicurus—*On Nature*—and was almost completely indifferent to or unaware of more recent currents in Epicureanism, or of ongoing debates with other schools, above all the Stoics (he dubs Lucretius a "fundamentalist" in this respect; cf. Furley 1967). Other scholars have seen clear indications of later influences in Lucretius' poem, for example in his attack on skepticism (Vander Waerdt 1989, Lévy 1997), his account of socio-political evolution (Schrijvers 1996 detects the influence of Polybius' theory of constitutions), and his arguments against teleology (Schmidt 1990: 152–160). Some have found it implausible that Lucretius should have been wholly isolated from the contemporary revival of Epicureanism in Italy, and have sought to demonstrate parallels between Lucretius' poem and the treatises of Philodemus (Kleve 1997), burned and buried in the eruption of Vesuvius in 79 CE, but still partly legible. Evidence that Lucretius' poem was among the scrolls in Philodemus' library remains inconclusive.

No one denies that Lucretius composed more freely in the proems with which he prefaced each of the six books, where, for example, he speaks of Venus as the ancestress of the Romans (1.1), and often too in the conclusions, or that he sometimes resorted to other sources than Epicurus (e.g., the description of the plague, based closely on Thucydides 2.47–54; cf. the analysis of pas-

sionate love at the end of Book 4, esp. vv. 1121–1191, and the personification of Nature scolding the man who fears death at 3.931–977, both indebted to Greek styles of diatribe [Wallach 1976, Reinhardt 2002]). So too, his choice of imagery in technical passages is frequently his own, for instance his illustration of the flow of thin membranes or simulacra from the surface of objects by reference to the colors cast on the audience by the awnings stretched above a Roman amphitheater (4.75–83). Some passages are more difficult to decide. When Lucretius explains the drive to accumulate wealth as a function of the fear of death, he says that poverty is imagined the "antechamber to hell" (3.65–69). Is this a Lucretian metaphor, or a piece of Epicurean doctrine? So too, Lucretius affirms that the legendary torments in the underworld, like Tantalus' perpetual hunger and the Danaids' task of carrying water in leaky pails, are really images of the forever frustrated pursuit of wealth and power in this world (3.978–1023). This may be a poetical flourish, but conceivably it reflects a genuine Epicurean explanation of the fear of punishment in the afterlife (Konstan 1973: 13–27).

Apart from such passages, in its broad outline Lucretius' poem conforms to the subjects that we know Epicurus treated in his principal statement of his views, above all his *On Nature* (*Peri phuseôs*), of which some substantial, though lacunose, fragments have been recovered on papyrus (see Sedley 1998: 133 for a possible reconstruction). To all appearances, Lucretius set about to versify a treatise on the atomic theory, and its implications for human psychology and society. He did not incorporate into his poem substantial arguments from Epicurus' ethical writings (for example, *On Lives* or *On the End*; cf. Diogenes Laertius 10.30). What is more, he shows no interest in many of the issues with which Philodemus was concerned, such as rhetoric, literary theory, virtues and vices, governance, semiotics, or the right methods for training disciples, which became central concerns of the school after the founder's death. Nor does he engage systematically and polemically with later opponents of Epicureanism, or with dissident views within the school, as Philodemus does (cf. the debates that Cicero stages between Epicureans, Stoics, and Academics); if indeed there are traces of such controversies in his poem, it is nonetheless remarkable that the philosophers whom he refutes explicitly and at length are Empedocles, Heraclitus, Anaxagoras, and Democritus: no mention of later thinkers. His poem purports to present classical Epicureanism in a palatable but accurate form to a Roman public—sweetening the spoon of medicine, in Lucretius' image (1.936–950, 4.11–25). He describes himself as planting his feet in Epicurus' footprints (3.3–4, 5.55–56), and this seems a fair statement of his intentions.

This fidelity to Epicurus' major exposition of his doctrine need not be taken as a sign of intellectual narrowness or a quasi-religious commitment to the word of the Master (Sedley 1998: 93). It was the custom of Hellenistic didactic poets to take as their source a scientific treatise, as Aratus, for example, did in his *Phaenomena* or *Constellations*, where he followed Eudoxus' work of the same name (fr. 3a Lasserre), even as he modelled his style on that of the archaic poet Hesiod. The Roman poet Ennius, whom Lucretius praises extravagantly despite his mistaken belief in the underworld (1.117–126), did something similar when he rendered into prose the pseudo-scientific narrative of Euhemerus. Lucretius was writing as much in the sophisticated Alexandrian tradition as in that of the pre-Socratic poet-philosophers.

It is a separate question whether Lucretius sometimes altered Epicurus' order of presentation, and with this his chain of reasoning, and whether he added to or modified the arguments of the Master here and there, either independently or by mining other works of Epicurus or early Epicureans. He seems to claim some responsibility for the sequence in which he presents a series of proofs (1.52, 3.419–420; cf. Clay 1983: 38). Sedley (1998: 148–152) speculates that Lucretius planned a more extensive rearrangement of topics, but did not live to finish revising the entire poem. Lucretius may have been influenced also by the order of subjects in standard collections of doctrines, whether doxographies or rhetorical disquisitions (Runia 1997; on rhetoric, Classen 1986: 371).

LUCRETIUS AND EPICUREAN DOCTRINE

No doubt, Lucretius' vivid analogies and images are not without philosophical interest, though some will have had antecedents in Epicurus' works or elsewhere; for example, the proof of atomic motion from the visible vibration of dust motes in a sunbeam (2.114–141), comparable to Brownian motion, was evidently already proposed by Democritus (cf. Aristotle *De anima* 404a3–4). The image of a flock of sheep on a distant hillside (2.317–322), by which Lucretius illustrates how a compound may be seen as proceeding slowly although its constituent particles are moving rapidly, was likely Lucretius' own. Epicureanism tended, more than other ancient schools, to admit proof by analogy—a principal means of inferring the properties of the invisible atomic world from perceptible events—and this favored the probative value of similes (cf. 2.112–113). Isolating philo-

sophically significant innovations in Lucretius, however, is a delicate task, given the scrappy condition of his principal source or sources (even where he composed freely rather than drawing on specific texts), and a novel comparison does not necessarily constitute a new argument.

In the circumstances, there are several ways to proceed. First, one may identify arguments in Lucretius that have no known parallel in Epicurus' own writings or those of later Epicureans; these at least are possible candidates for Lucretian innovation. Second, one may demonstrate Lucretius' dependence on some other, non-Epicurean source, e.g., Polybius or Thucydides, bearing in mind that Lucretius' references to early writers may have been filtered through Epicurus. Third, one may note specifically Roman or personal nuances of the sort that alter or affect in some measure orthodox Epicurean doctrine. Finally, one may discover places where Lucretius seems to disagree with what we know to have been Epicurus' view. The last is certainly the most dramatic, and indeed there is one apparent case of such a discrepancy: Lucretius speaks of four components of the soul (3.231–245)—air, ether, fire, and an unnamed, superfine element—whereas Epicurus, in the *Letter to Herodotus* (63), mentions just three, and in somewhat different terms. It is hardly likely that Lucretius is silently introducing here a modification of Epicurean doctrine. Conceivably, he was simply mistaken; alternatively, and more probable, Epicurus' account in the *Letter* is compressed, and he elaborated the fuller view in the relevant, now lost, passage in *On Nature* (Sedley 1998: 71n47).

Given the state of Epicurean texts, Lucretius is often our best guide to Epicurean doctrine, especially since there is not sufficient reason to suppose that his treatment is original. For example, Lucretius appeals to the so-called swerve of atoms, by which they shift by a minimal amount in their downward course at no determinate time or place (2.216–293), to account for free will and also for the initial interaction of atoms, which could not have collided had they maintained their natural downward motion at uniform speed. The latter argument seems particularly weak, since there is no beginning to the Epicurean universe, but it may nevertheless have been broached by Epicurus himself (cf. Fowler 2002: 301–309). Lucretius' account of the development of human civilization departs from parallel treatments known from other writers (Cole 1967), among other ways by inserting passages on the origin of religion and of language; again, this sequence may very well go back to Epicurus himself (Konstan 1973: 44–55; Campbell 2003: 15–18, 283–293). But Lucretius inclines to multiplying arguments—for example, he offers 28 or 29 different proofs for the mortality of the soul (3.417–614)—and it is plausible that he may have added several to the common Epicurean stock, especially since only one or two are attested in Epicurus (Boyancé 1986: 141–142).

Epicurus discouraged active participation in politics because it produced the kinds of psychological tensions that his teachings were designed to eliminate. Lucretius, however, expresses a desire for peace (1.21–49) so that Memmius, the Roman aristocrat to whom he addresses his poem, will not have to engage in public service (perhaps an allusion to his praetorship in 58 BCE; Hutchinson (2001) sees a reference to the civil war that began in 49 BCE, and dates the poem to this period); in this way, Memmius will be free to dedicate himself to philosophy and achieve the tranquillity that Epicureanism held to be the goal of life. Epicureanism had a certain vogue among Roman nobles who had no intention of giving up their political status and activities—Julius Caesar himself is said to have been an adherent —and Lucretius was no doubt adapting his advice here to the outlook and social realities of his time (as did Philodemus). Whether this represents a change of principle or simply a tactical shift of rhetoric is difficult to say (cf. Fowler 1989).

Epicurus affirmed that sex should be avoided, since it has never done any good and is often harmful (Diogenes Laertius 10.118, fr. 62 Usener; *VS* 51); he also discouraged marriage (Diogenes Laertius 10.119 [textually corrupt], Epictetus *Discourses* 3.7.19–20, etc.). Lucretius' attitude toward love and sex is not inconsistent with Epicurus' own, though Epicurus' surviving writings are not so fervent on the subject, but he appears, at the end of Book IV (1278–1287), to introduce a newly positive view of matrimony and parenthood (Nussbaum 1994: 185–187; Brown 1987: 87–91, 118–122 sees no discrepancy here between Epicurus and Lucretius). Again, the fear of death, and of punishment in the afterlife, was the central cause of mental perturbation, according to Epicurus, and here too Lucretius is wholly in agreement; but his approach seems "more personal and emotional" than Epicurus' (Segal: 1990: 6; cf. 27–33, 51–54, 113; for the arguments, see Warren 2004); indeed, the Roman poet Statius spoke of the "burning passion of learned Lucretius" (*Silvae* 2.7.76). Further, Lucretius' anguished distress at the needless suffering of his fellow men (2.14–19) lends his poetry a proselytizing fervor, and this, like the shuddering pleasure (3.25–30) he experiences at the vision of a world without a hell, may seem to admit into Epicureanism a passion at odds with its goal of quietude.

Why did Lucretius end his poem with the grisly description of the plague that struck Athens in 429 BCE? Some scholars have supposed that it serves as a "final exam" in Lucretius' course on Epicureanism, testing whether readers have learned the lesson that death holds no terrors. This seems an adequate explanation (cf. Commager 1957, Bright 1971), even without an explicit moral to point the message. The plague is an accelerated image of life itself, which invariably terminates in death. Since Epicurus taught that pleasure does not increase with length of time (*Principal Doctrines* 18–20; Lucretius 3.944–945, 1080–1081), a life cut short by illness is not cause for apprehension.

Lucretius' poem immediately became famous: Virgil (*Georgics* 2.490–492) wrote, "Blessed is he who is able to know the causes of things," with obvious reference to Lucretius (*Ovid Amores* 1.15.23–24). Its rediscovery in the Renaissance inspired philosophical didactic poetry down through the eighteenth century, when the genre came to an end.

See also Empedocles; Epicurus.

Bibliography

TEXTS AND TRANSLATIONS

Bailey, Cyril. *Titi Lucreti Cari De Rerum Natura Libri Sex.* 3 vols. Oxford: Oxford University Press, 1947.

Humphries, Rolfe. *The Way Things Are: The De Rerum Natura of Titus Lucretius Carus.* Bloomington: University of Indiana Press, 1969.

Melville, Sir Ronald. *Lucretius, On the Nature of the Universe.* With introduction and notes by D. and P. Fowler. Oxford: Clarendon Press, 1997.

Smith, Martin Ferguson. *Lucretius: De Rerum Natura.* With English translation by W. H. D. Rouse, revised with new text, introduction, and notes. Cambridge, MA: Harvard University Press (Loeb Classical Library), 1975.

STUDIES

Algra, Keimpe A., Pieter W. van der Horst, and David T. Runia, eds. *Polyhistor: Studies in the History and Historiography of Ancient Philosophy.* Presented to Jaap Mansfeld on his Sixtieth Birthday. Leiden: E. J. Brill, Philosophia Antiqua 72, 1996.

Algra, K.A., M.H. Koenen and P. H. Schrijvers, eds. *Lucretius and his Intellectual Background.* Amsterdam: Royal Netherlands Academy of Arts and Sciences, 1997.

Boyancé, Pierre. "La théorie de l'âme chez Lucrèce." In *Probleme der Lukrezforschung*, edited by Carl Joachim Classen, 131–150. Hildesheim: Olms, 1986 (orig. 1958).

Boyancé, Pierre. *Lucrèce et L'Épicurisme.* Paris: Presses Universitaires de France, 1963.

Bright, David F. "The Plague and the Structure of the *De rerum natura.*" *Latomus* 30 (1971): 607–632.

Brown, Robert D., ed. *Lucretius on Love and Sex. A Commentary on De Rerum Natura IV, 1030–1287*. Leiden: E. J. Brill, 1987.

Campbell, Gordon. *Lucretius on Creation and Evolution: A Commentary on De Rerum Natura Book Five Lines 772–1104*. Oxford: Oxford University Press, 2003.

Classen, Carl Joachim. "Poetry and Rhetoric in Lucretius." In *Probleme der Lukrezforschung*, 331–373. Hildesheim: Olms, 1986.

Classen, Carl Joachim, ed. *Probleme der Lukrezforschung*. Hildesheim: Olms, 1986.

Clay, Diskin. *Lucretius and Epicurus*. Ithaca NY: Cornell University Press, 1983.

Cole, Thomas. *Democritus and the Sources of Greek Anthropology*. Cleveland: Press of Western Reserve University, 1967.

Commager, Henry Steele, Jr. "Lucretius' Interpretation of the Plague." *Harvard Studies in Classical Philology* 62 (1957): 105–121.

Fowler, Don P. "Lucretius and Politics." In *Philosophia Togata: Essays on Philosophy and Roman Society*, edited by Miriam Griffin and Jonathan Barnes, 120–150. Oxford: Clarendon Press, 1989.

Fowler, Don. *Lucretius on Atomic Motion. A Commentary on De Rerum Natura 2.1–332*. Oxford: Oxford University Press, 2002.

Furley, David J. *Two Studies in the Greek Atomists*. Princeton, NJ: Princeton University Press, 1967.

Gale, Monica. *Myth and Poetry in Lucretius*. Cambridge, U.K.: Cambridge University Press, 1994.

Hutchinson, G. O. "The Date of *De rerum natura*." *Classical Quarterly* 51 (2001): 150–162.

Kleve, Knut. "Lucretius and Philodemus." In *Lucretius and his Intellectual Background*, edited by Algra et al., 49–66. Amsterdam: Royal Netherlands Academy of Arts and Sciences, 1997.

Konstan, David. *Some Aspects of Epicurean Psychology*. Leiden: E. J. Brill, Philosophia Antiqua 25, 1973.

Lévy, Carlos. "Lucrèce avait–il lu Enésideme?" In *Lucretius and his Intellectual Background*, edited by Algra et al. 115–124. Amsterdam: Royal Netherlands Academy of Arts and Sciences, 1997.

Nussbaum, Martha C. *The Therapy of Desire: Theory and Practice in Hellenistic Ethics*. Princeton, NJ: Princeton University Press, 1994.

Reinhardt, Tobias. 2002. "The Speech of Nature in Lucretius' De Rerum Natura 3.931–71." *Classical Quarterly* 52: 291–304.

Runia, David T. "Lucretius and Doxography." In *Lucretius and his Intellectual Background*, edited by Algra et al., 93–103. Amsterdam: Royal Netherlands Academy of Arts and Sciences, 1997.

Schmalzriedt, Egidius. *Peri physeos: Zur frühgeschichte der Buchtitel*. Munich: Fink Verlag, 1970.

Schmidt, Jürgen. *Lucrez, der Kepos, und die Stoiker*. Frankfurt am Main: Peter Lang, Studien zur klassischen Philologie 53, 1990.

Schrijvers, Piet H. "Lucretius on the Origin and Development of Political Life (De Rerum Natura 5.1105–1160)." In *Polyhistor: Studies in the History and Historiography of Ancient Philosophy*, 220–230. Presented to Jaap Mansfeld on his sixtieth birthday. Leiden: E. J. Brill, Philosophia Antiqua 72, 1996.

Schrijvers, Piet H. *Lucrèce et les sciences de la vie*. Leiden: Brill, Mnemosyne Supplement 186, 1999.

Sedley, David. *Lucretius and the Transformation of Greek Wisdom*. Cambridge, U.K.: Cambridge University Press, 1998.

Segal, Charles. *Lucretius on Death and Anxiety*. Princeton, NJ: Princeton University Press, 1990.

Vander Waerdt. "Colotes and the Epicurean Refutation of Skepticism." *Greek Roman and Byzantine Studies* 30 (1989): 225–267.

Wallach, Barbara Price. *Lucretius and the Diatribe against the Fear of Death*. Leiden: Brill, Mnemosyne Supplement 40, 1976.

Warren, James. *Facing Death: Epicurus and His Critics*. Oxford: Oxford University Press, 2004.

David Konstan (2005)

LU HSIANG-SHAN

See *Lu Xiangshan*

LUKÁCS, GEORG
(1885–1971)

Georg (György) Lukács, the Hungarian Marxist philosopher and literary critic, was professor of aesthetics and the philosophy of culture at the University of Budapest from 1945 to 1956. Lukács was born in Budapest into a rich and eminent family (before he became a communist he wrote under the family name "von Lukács"). He took a doctorate in philosophy in Budapest (1906) and then studied under Georg Simmel at Berlin and under Max Weber at Heidelberg. Since Lukács was recognized as one of Europe's leading literary critics when he joined the Communist Party of Hungary in December 1918, he was offered the post of people's commissar for culture and education in the communist regime of Béla Kun (March–August 1919). After the fall of Kun, Lukács took refuge in Vienna, where he edited the review *Kommunismus* and carried on a struggle with Kun (exiled in Moscow) for control of the Hungarian underground movement. Publication in Berlin in 1923 of Lukács's collection of essays, *Geschichte und Klassenbewusstsein*, decided the issue in favor of Kun—for the book was denounced as "deviationist." Lukács was ousted from the central committee of the Communist Party and from the editorship of *Kommunismus* after publishing his "self-criticism." He took refuge in Russia when Adolf Hitler came to power and, after a further and more thorough act of self-criticism, worked in the Institute of Philosophy of the Soviet Academy of Science from 1933 to 1944. Returning to Hungary, he became a member of parliament and professor of aesthetics. In 1956 Lukács was a leader of the Petofi circle, which played a role in the anti-Russian insurrection, and then minister for culture in the short-lived Imre Nagy government. After the defeat of the revolution, Lukács was deported to Romania, but he was allowed to return to Budapest in April 1957 to live in retirement and to devote himself to a monumental work on aesthetics, of which one volume was published, in Hungarian.

AESTHETICS AND CRITICISM

Lukács's fame as one of the few philosophers produced by the Marxist movement rests on a book that he repudiated soon after its publication, *Geschichte und Klassenbewusstsein* (History and class consciousness). His later work—some thirty books and hundreds of articles—constitutes an attempt to found a Marxist aesthetic that could be used to criticize modernist, formalist, and experimental art in the name of socialist realism. This critical work entailed some confusion of literary criticism with political polemic, of which the following judgment on Kafka is typical: "no work of art based on *Angst* (anxiety) can avoid—objectively speaking—guilt by association with Hitlerism and the preparations for atomic war" (*The Meaning of Contemporary Realism*, p. 81). Lukács's influence as a critic has been intensely conservative, for he held that "realism is not one style among others; it is the basis of literature" (p. 48).

In his first aesthetic studies, *Die Seele und die Formen* (The soul and the forms) and *Die Theorie des Romans* (The theory of the novel), Lukács was still a neo-Kantian. He held that literature was the striving for expression of the irrational soul in and through an alien and hostile reality. He stressed the value of "inwardness" and the uselessness of society to the individual. These works have been claimed as among the sources of existentialism, but Lukács himself denounced them as "false and reactionary" upon his conversion to communism. Thereafter he contrasted Marxism, as a philosophy that integrated the individual in society, with all modern "philosophies of crisis and evasion," and in particular with existentialism, which isolated men outside social and economic relations.

Lukács's stress on social relationships became the basis of his aesthetics. Form, he argued, should be determined by content (therefore abstract art and formalism are degenerate), and "there is no content of which Man

himself is not the focal point" (*The Meaning of Contemporary Realism*, p. 19). Since man exists only in a social and historical context, aesthetics inevitably is concerned with politics. If the subject of a work of art is man seen statically, then that work declines into subjectivism and allegory. Literature must be dynamic, setting characters in historical perspective in order that they might be shown as having direction, development, and motivation. For literature to be dynamic, the major historical movement of the day must be taken into account. In the twentieth century that movement was socialism. The only valid contemporary literary styles are socialist realism, which is practiced inside the socialist movement, and critical realism, which is practiced by authors sympathetic to socialism. Lukács's theories naturally entailed condemnation of most twentieth-century art, literature, and music, but they were fruitfully applied to the historical novel.

SOCIAL AND HISTORICAL ANALYSIS

Geschichte und Klassen-bewusstsein, the censored masterpiece of communist thought, became the classic text of Western Marxism as contrasted with Soviet orthodoxy. It led to a revaluation of Marxism by setting it in a Hegelian context. Lukács was the first to see that Karl Marx's theory of history and even his economics could be read as an application of the Hegelian dialectic. He did this a decade before the discovery and publication of Marx's *Economic and Philosophic Manuscripts of 1844*, which amply confirmed his theory, at least with regard to the young Marx. Having meanwhile disowned his book, Lukács could not claim credit for that brilliant piece of philosophical reconstruction, but he later could show the profound similarity between the philosophies of G. W. F. Hegel and Marx (*Der junge Hegel*). His idealist reading of Marx clashed with the accepted Leninist version, and, since Lukács worsened his case in 1923 by revealing the influence of Georges Sorel and Rosa Luxemburg on his thought, his book was condemned with a ferocity unusual even in communist polemics.

Lukács had rejected Friedrich Engels's and V. I. Lenin's conception of the Marxist dialectic as a set of laws applying to nature, and he rejected too the notion that historical materialism deduces all social and moral life from the economic base. Historical materialism and the dialectic, he said, both mean the same thing, namely that in society subject and object are one. When men know (or enter into any other relation with) social entities—whether these are institutions or economic goods or another age's culture—the relation established is not the sort of relation they have with the natural objects studied by physical science. Social entities are reified personality or alienated spirit, while men themselves are the product of historical forces. The knower and the known, subject and object, are moments of one entity, society, and their relations are necessarily ambiguous, two-way, or dialectical.

Marx had said, "As personal interests become autonomous in the shape of class interests, the personal conduct of the individual becomes reified and alienated and thereby becomes a thing apart from him, an independent force." It is just such alienated forms of conduct that make up society. In the nineteenth century in particular, because of the development of industry, "material forces were saturated with spiritual life, while human existence was made animal, became a material force." Marx meant, said Lukács, that spirit had become thing and things were steeped in spirit, so that history was a fabric of meanings-become-forces. This dialectical relation of subject and object was most marked in the case of the proletariat because the proletariat had been reduced by capitalism to labor, a mere economic commodity, and yet it could still take cognizance of itself as a commodity by acquiring class consciousness. Thereupon, it saw through the supposed natural laws of economics and revolutionized capitalism. "For this class, self-knowledge means at the same time correct knowledge of the whole of society … so this class is at once subject and object of knowledge" (*Geschichte und Klassenbewusstsein*). Its self-knowledge is history knowing itself, and in that total clarity lies the promise of a return from alienation.

The difficulties raised by historical relativism—difficulties that had been seen by all who asked how Marxism alone among social opinions could escape being vitiated by its relation to a given class and age—can be resolved only by going right to the extreme of relativism. That is to say, historical materialism must be applied to itself until it is seen as relative and provisional. This means abandoning the notion of absolute truth and denying the complete opposition of true and false. History is a dialectical totality of knowers and things known, and every piece of culture, no matter how deformed by class position and historical situation, reflects that totality. Truth exists, but it exists only in the future tense; it is the presumptive totality to be attained by permanent self-criticism. "The criterion of truth is grasp of reality. But reality is not at all to be confounded with empirical being, what actually exists. Reality *is* not; it becomes—and not without the collaboration of thought" (*Geschichte und Klassenbewusstsein*). Rejecting the representative theory of knowledge made orthodox for Marxists by the examples of Engels and Lenin (the "concepts in our heads" are

"true images of reality"), Lukács held that truth is not something to be reflected but something to be made by us by collaborating with what is new and progressive in historical forces. The vague notion of a moving totality of things, of the whole of history, is essential to this "relativization of relativism." Lukács did not clearly delineate this notion, but it evidently bears a resemblance to the Hegelian Absolute.

Lukács's three main doctrines—the dialectical unity of subject and object in society; the promise of a return from alienation when society, through the proletariat, attains self-knowledge; and the notion of truth as a totality yet to be achieved—were attractive to some Western existentialists. Lukács complained that their "treacherous" use of his work was a "falsification of a book forgotten for good reason." Another line of influence was through his former associate Karl Mannheim, who developed the relativization of all ideologies into the sociology of knowledge. Within the communist world, the only doctrine of Lukács's censored book to enjoy some surreptitious authority was his "proof" of the communist intellectual's duty to accept the Communist Party as the supreme expression of proletarian class consciousness and thus as endowed with the correct view of history. This doctrine Lukács himself practiced rigorously, even to the extent of repudiating his own major contribution to modern thought.

See also Aesthetics, History of; Communism; Critical Realism; Critical Theory; Engels, Friedrich; Existentialism; Hegel, Georg Wilhelm Friedrich; Historical Materialism; Kafka, Franz; Lenin, Vladimir Il'ich; Mannheim, Karl; Marxist Philosophy; Marx, Karl; Neo-Kantianism; Simmel, Georg; Socialism; Sorel, Georges; Weber, Max.

Bibliography

WORKS BY LUKÁCS

Philosophy
Die Seele und die Formen. Berlin: Fleischel, 1911.
Die Theorie des Romans. Berlin: Cassirer, 1920.
Geschichte und Klassenbewusstsein. Berlin: Malik, 1923.
Der junge Hegel. Zürich: Europa, 1948; rev. ed., Berlin, 1954.
Existentialismus oder Marxismus? Berlin: Aufbau, 1951.
Beiträge zur Geschichte der Aesthetik. Berlin: Aufbau, 1954.
Die Zerstörung der Vernunft. Berlin: Aufbau, 1955.

Literary Criticism
Essays über Realismus. Berlin: Aufbau, 1948. Translated by E. Bone as *Studies in European Realism.* London: Hillway, 1950.
Thomas Mann. Berlin, 1949. Translated by S. Mitchell as *Essays on Thomas Mann.* London: Merlin Press, 1964.

The Historical Novel. Translated by H. Mitchell and S. Mitchell. London: Merlin Press, 1962.

The Meaning of Contemporary Realism. Translated by J. Mander and N. Mander. London: Merlin Press, 1963.

WORKS ON LUKÁCS

Arato, A., and P. Breines. *The Young Lukács and the Origin of Western Marxism*. New York: Seabury Press, 1979.

Carbonara, C. *L'estetica del particolare di G. Lukacs*. Naples, 1960.

Goldmann, Lucien. *Le dieu caché*. Paris: Gallimard, 1955. Translated by P. Thody as *The Hidden God*. New York: Humanities Press, 1964.

Goldmann, Lucien. "Introduction aux premiers écrits de Georges Lukacs." In Lukács's *La théorie du roman*. Geneva, 1963.

Heller, A., ed. *Lukács Revisited*. Oxford: Blackwell, 1983.

Jung, W. *Georg Lukács*. Stuttgart: Metzler, 1989.

Kadarkay, A. *Georg Lukács Life, Thought, and Politics*. Oxford: Blackwell, 1991.

Lukács, Georg et al. *Georg Lukács: Zum Siebzigsten Geburtstag*. Berlin: Aufbau-Verlag, 1955.

Merleau-Ponty, Maurice. *Les aventures de la dialectique*. Paris: Gallimard, 1955. Translated as *Adventures of the Dialectic*. Evanston, IL: Northwestern University Press, 1972.

Mészáros, L. *Lukács' Concept of the Dialectic*. London: Merlin, 1972.

Watnick, Morris. "Relativism and Class Consciousness: Georg Lukács." In *Revisionism*, edited by Leopold Labedz. New York: Praeger, 1962.

Zitta, Victor. *Georg Lukács's Marxism*. The Hague: Nijhoff, 1964.

Neil McInnes (1967)
Bibliography updated by Thomas Nenon (2005)

ŁUKASIEWICZ, JAN
(1878–1956)

Jan Łukasiewicz, the Polish philosopher and logician, was born in Lvov. After studying mathematics and philosophy at the University of Lvov he was graduated in 1902 with a PhD in philosophy. Łukasiewicz taught philosophy and logic first at Lvov and from 1915 at the University of Warsaw. In 1918 he interrupted academic work to accept a senior appointment in the Polish ministry of education in Ignacy Paderewski's cabinet. At the end of that year, however, he returned to the university and continued as professor of philosophy until September 1939. During that period he served twice as rector of the university (1922/1923 and 1931/1932). Toward the end of World War II Łukasiewicz left Warsaw. After some time in Münster and then in Brussels, in 1946 he accepted an invitation from the Irish government to go to Dublin as professor of mathematical logic at the Royal Irish Academy, an appointment that he held until his death.

Łukasiewicz held honorary degrees from the University of Münster and from Trinity College, Dublin. He was a member of the Polish Academy of Sciences in Kraków, the Society of Arts and Sciences in Lvov, and the Society of Arts and Sciences in Warsaw.

EARLY WRITINGS

Łukasiewicz studied under Kazimierz Twardowski, who was occupied with conceptual analysis. The rigorous, clear thinking Twardowski advocated is easily recognizable in the first major essays published by Łukasiewicz. Of these works, *O zasadzie sprzeczności u Arystotelesa* (On the principle of contradiction in Aristotle; Kraków, 1910) was one of the most influential books in the early period of the twentieth-century logical and philosophical revival in Poland. It must have stood high in the author's own estimation, for in 1955 he began translating it into English. The main point of the book is that in Aristotle's work one can distinguish three forms of the principle of contradiction: ontological, logical, and psychological. The ontological principle of contradiction is that the same property cannot both belong and not belong to the same object in the same respect. The logical principle says that two contradictory propositions cannot both be true, and the psychological principle of contradiction holds that no one can, at the same time, entertain two beliefs to which there correspond two contradictory propositions. Łukasiewicz supported his findings with quotations from the writings of Aristotle and then examined the validity of Aristotle's argumentation. One chapter brought to the notice of Polish readers Bertrand Russell's antinomy concerning the class of all classes that are not members of themselves. The appendix contains an elementary exposition of the algebra of logic, as well as an original and interesting methodological classification of the ways of reasoning, a problem with which at least two of Łukasiewicz's early papers were concerned.

Łukasiewicz's writings published before 1918 suggest that until that time he was in quest of topics to which he could devote all his intellectual resources. He found such topics in the logic of propositions and in the logic of the ancient Greeks. From 1918 onward, deviations from this double line of research are few and of little significance.

LOGIC OF PROPOSITIONS

MANY-VALUED LOGICS. The first and perhaps most important result obtained by Łukasiewicz in the logic of propositions was his discovery of three-valued logic in 1917. Our ordinary logic of propositions is two-valued, presupposing only two logical values, truth and falsity, and it tacitly adheres to the principle of bivalence, that a propositional function holds of any propositional argument if it holds of the constant true proposition (usually symbolized by 1) and if it holds of the constant false proposition (represented by 2). If we use δ as a functorial variable that, when followed by a propositional argument, forms a propositional expression, then we can express the principle of bivalence by saying "if $\delta 1$ then if $\delta 2$ then δp," where p is a propositional variable. The meaning of the logical constants forming such expressions as, for instance, Cpq ("if p then q"), Kpq ("p and q"), Apq ("p or q"), and Np ("it is not the case that p") are, in two-valued logic, conveniently and adequately determined by means of the familiar two-valued truth tables:

$$C11 = C21 = C22 = 1$$
$$C12 = 2$$
$$K11 = 1$$
$$K12 = K21 = K22 = 2$$
$$A11 = A12 = A21 = 1$$
$$A22 = 2$$
$$N1 = 2$$
$$N2 = 1$$

In three-valued logic the principle of bivalence does not hold. It is replaced by the principle of trivalence, which presupposes three logical values: the constant true proposition represented by 1, the constant false proposition by 3, and the constant "possible" proposition by 2. The principle then says "if $\delta 1$ then if $\delta 2$ then if $\delta 3$ then δp." As a consequence the meanings of implication, conjunction, alternation, and negation have to be readjusted, and the following three-valued truth tables suggest themselves for the purpose:

$$C11 = C21 = C22 = C31 = C32 = C33 = 1$$
$$C12 = C23 = 2$$
$$C13 = 3$$
$$K11 = 1$$
$$K12 = K21 = K22 = 2$$
$$K13 = K23 = K31 = K32 = K33 = 3$$
$$A11 = A12 = A13 = A21 = A31 = 1$$
$$A22 = A23 = A32 = 2$$
$$A33 = 3$$
$$N1 = 3$$
$$N2 = 2$$
$$N3 = 1$$

In this logic alternation and conjunction can be defined as follows: $Apq = CCpqq$, and $Kpq = NANpNq$. All expressions involving only C and N and verified by the new truth tables can be constructed into a deductive system based on the axioms $CpCqp$, $CCpqCCqrCpr$, $CCCpNppp$,

and $CCNpNqCqp$. This was shown by Mordchaj Wajsberg, who had studied logic under Łukasiewicz in Warsaw. Wajsberg's system, however, does not enable us to define all the functors available in three-valued logic. In particular the functor T, whose truth table says that $T1 = T2 = T3 = 2$, cannot be defined in terms of C and N. Jerzy Słupecki, who had also been a pupil of Łukasiewicz, subsequently proved that by adding $CTpNTp$ and $CNTpTp$ to Wajsberg's axioms we get a functionally complete system of three-valued logic, in which any functor can be defined.

The conception of three-valued logic was suggested to Łukasiewicz by certain passages in Aristotle. Purely formal considerations, such as those that led E. L. Post to comparable results, played a subordinate role in Łukasiewicz's thinking. By setting up a system of three-valued logic Łukasiewicz hoped to accommodate the traditional laws of modal logic. He also hoped to overcome philosophical determinism, which he believed was entailed by the acceptance of the bivalence principle and which he had always found repulsive. Interestingly enough, he modified his views in the course of time and saw no incompatibility between indeterminism and two-valued logic.

Once a system of three-valued logic had been constructed, the possibility of four-valued, five-valued, ..., n-valued, and, finally, infinitely many-valued logics was obvious. At one time Łukasiewicz believed that the three-valued and the infinitely many-valued logics were of greater philosophical interest than any other many-valued logic, for they appeared to be the least arbitrary. In the end, however, he interpreted Aristotelian modal logic within the framework of a four-valued system.

The philosophical significance of the discovery of many-valued logic can be viewed in the following way: The laws of logic had long enjoyed a privileged status in comparison with the laws propounded by natural sciences. They had been variously described as a priori or analytic, the purpose of such descriptions being to point out that the laws of logic were not related to reality in the same way as were the laws of natural sciences, which had often been corrected or discarded in the light of new observations and experiments. The laws of logic appeared unchallengeable. By discovering many-valued logics Łukasiewicz showed that even at the highest level of generality—within the field of propositional logic—alternatives were possible. By adhering to the principle of bivalence or any other n-valence principle we run the same risk of misrepresenting reality that the scientist does when he offers any of his generalizations.

THE CLASSICAL PROPOSITIONAL LOGIC.

Although Łukasiewicz contemplated the possibility that a nonclassical logic of propositions applied to reality, he made the classical propositional logic the principal subject of his research. He showed that the axiom systems of the calculus of propositions proposed by Frege, Russell, and Hilbert each contained a different redundant axiom. He proved that all the theses of the *CN*-calculus could be derived from the three mutually independent axioms *CCNppp*, *CpCNpq*, and *CCpqCCqrCpr*. He solved the problem of the shortest single axiom for the *E*-calculus and the *C*-calculus by showing that the *E*-calculus, whose only functor means "if and only if," with $E11 = E22 = 1$ and $E12 = E21 = 2$ as its truth table, could be based on any of *EEpqEErqEpr*, *EEpqEEprErq*, and *EEpqEErpEqr* and on no shorter thesis and by proving that *CCCpqrCCrpCsp* is the shortest thesis strong enough to yield the *C*-calculus. The first single axiom for *CN*-calculus, consisting of 53 letters, was discovered by Alfred Tarski in 1925. It was soon followed by a series of successive simplifications devised by Łukasiewicz and by Bolesław Sobociński. The latest in this series is a 21-letter axiom, *CCCCCpqCNrNsrtCCtpCsp*, discovered by C. A. Meredith, Łukasiewicz's Irish colleague. It is likely to prove to be the shortest possible axiom for the *CN*-calculus.

CONSISTENCY, COMPLETENESS, AND INDEPENDENCE.

The metalogical study of deductive systems of the logic of propositions includes the study of consistency and completeness, and, in the case of systems based on several axioms, the mutual independence of the axioms has also to be considered. Independently of Post, Łukasiewicz developed both a method of proving consistency and one of proving the completeness of systems of the calculus of propositions. The completeness proof was based on the idea that if the system under consideration is not complete, there must be independent propositions, that is, propositions not derivable from the axioms of the system which on being adjoined to the axioms lead to no contradiction. If there are independent propositions, then there must be a shortest one among them. Following Łukasiewicz's method, one tries to show that any proposition that is meaningful within the system either is derivable from the axioms or is longer than another proposition inferentially equivalent to it. This method dispenses with the concept of "normal expressions" and is very useful for proving weak completeness of partial systems. Mutual independence of theses is usually established by an appropriate reinterpretation of the constant terms occurring in them. Many such reinterpretations have been provided by Łukasiewicz's many-valued logics.

The wealth of metalogical concepts and theorems worked out in Łukasiewicz's logical seminar in Warsaw by Łukasiewicz himself, Tarski, Adolf Lindenbaum, Sobociński, and Wajsberg can best be seen in "Untersuchungen über den Aussagenkalkül," which summarizes the results obtained there between 1920 and 1930.

FUNCTORIAL CALCULUS.

In Dublin, Łukasiewicz became interested in a two-valued calculus of propositions involving functorial variables. Since he used only functorial variables requiring one propositional argument to form a propositional expression, his new calculus was only a part of what Stanisław Leśniewski had called protothetic. A very strong rule of substitution invented by Łukasiewicz, together with the usual substitution rules for propositional variables, allows us, for instance, to use a thesis of the form δa to infer not only Na but also such theses as $Cp\alpha$, $C\alpha p$, $C\alpha CN\alpha p$, $C\alpha\alpha$, and α. By means of the new rule Łukasiewicz was able to base the calculus on the single axiom $C\delta C22C\delta 2\delta p$. This axiom is identical with the principle of bivalence, because $C22 = 1$. Meredith succeeded in showing that Łukasiewicz's axiom could be replaced by $C\delta\delta 2\delta p$ or by $C\delta pC\delta Np\delta q$. He was also able to prove completeness of the system.

ANCIENT LOGIC

Concurrently with his investigations of the logic of propositions Łukasiewicz was engaged in a thorough reappraisal of ancient logic. For centuries the logic of the Stoics had been regarded as a sort of appendage to the Aristotelian syllogistic. Łukasiewicz was the first to recognize in it a rudimentary logic of propositions. He found evidence that the main logical functions, such as implication, conjunction, exclusive disjunction, and negation, were known to the Stoics, who, following Philo of Megara, interpreted them as truth-functions, just as we do now. He pointed out that the Stoics, unlike Aristotle, had given their logic the form of schemata of valid inferences. Some of these schemata had been accepted axiomatically and others were rigorously derived from them. He subjected to severe but justified criticism the treatments of Stoic logic by such authorities as Carl Prantl, Eduard Zeller, and Victor Brochard. His preliminary investigations of medieval logic showed beyond doubt that in this field too there was room for fruitful research.

Equally successful was Łukasiewicz's inquiry into Aristotle's syllogistic. No sooner had he mastered the elements of symbolic logic for himself than he realized that the centuries-old traditional treatment of the Aristotelian syllogistic called for revision. A new presentation of the logic of Aristotle was before long included in his regular lectures at the university and then published in *Elementy logiki matematycznej* (Elements of mathematical logic; Warsaw, 1929). Łukasiewicz completed a detailed monograph on the subject in Polish in the summer of 1939, but the manuscript and all printed copies were lost during the war. *Aristotle's Syllogistic* (1951) is a painstaking reconstruction undertaken by Łukasiewicz on his arrival in Dublin. The monograph can rightly be called revolutionary. In it Łukasiewicz argued that Aristotelian syllogisms are logical laws rather than schemata of valid inferences, as is taught in traditional textbooks. He put in historical perspective Aristotle's introduction of variables and, referring to a forgotten Greek scholium, gave a plausible explanation of the problem of the so-called Galenian figure. Among more formal results, we owe to Łukasiewicz the first modern axiomatization of syllogistic. The system he set up, based on the axioms *Aaa* ("every *a* is *a*"), *Iaa* ("*some a* is *a*"), *CKAbcAabAac*, and *CKAbcIbalac*, seems to be in perfect harmony with Aristotle's own treatment of the subject in the *Analytica Priora*. The axioms are jointly consistent and mutually independent. Moreover, Słupecki has ingeniously solved the decision problem for the system.

MODAL LOGIC

During the last few years of his life Łukasiewicz devoted much attention to modal logic. The results are presented in "A System of Modal Logic," and in the second edition of *Aristotle's Syllogistic* (1957) they serve as the basis for a critical examination of Aristotle's theory of modalities. Łukasiewicz's principal idea is that of "basic modal logic," obtained by adding to the classical calculus of propositions the axioms *CpMp* and *EMpMNNp* and by axiomatically rejecting *CMpp* and *Mp*. In these formulas *Mp* stands for "it is possible that *p*." According to Łukasiewicz any modal system must contain basic modal logic as a part. This condition is fulfilled by the four-valued modal system based on *CδpCδNpδq* and *CpMp* as the only axioms, with *CMpp* and *Mp* axiomatically rejected.

The logical symbolism used in this entry was worked out by Łukasiewicz in the early 1920s. It requires no punctuation signs, such as brackets or dots, which from the point of view of metalogical investigations is its greatest merit. At the same time Łukasiewicz worked out a simple and perspicuous method of setting out proofs in the logic of propositions and in syllogistic. Both his symbolism and his proof technique have been adopted by many logicians outside Poland.

Łukasiewicz was not only a resourceful and imaginative scholar but also a gifted and inspiring teacher. He was one of the founders, and the life and soul, of the Warsaw school of logic. Tarski, Lindenbaum, Stanisław Jaśkowski, Wajsberg, Father Jan Salamucha, Sobociński, Słupecki, and Meredith have been his most outstanding pupils or collaborators.

See also Aristotle; Frege, Gottlob; Hilbert, David; Logic, History of; Modal Logic; Philo of Megara; Propositions; Russell, Bertrand Arthur William; Tarski, Alfred; Truth; Twardowski, Kazimierz.

Bibliography

PRINCIPAL WORKS BY ŁUKASIEWICZ

"Analiza i konstrukcja projecia przyczyny" (Analysis and construction of the concept of cause). *Przegląd Filozoficzny* 9 (1906): 105–179.

O zasadzie sprzeczności u Arystotelesa. Kraków, 1910.

Die logischen Grundlagen der Wahrscheinlichkeitsrechnung. Kraków: Akademie der Wissenschaften, 1913.

"Opojeciu wielkości" (On the concept of magnitude). *Przeglad Filozoficzny* 19 (1916): 1–70.

"O logice trójwartościowej" (On three-valued logic). *Ruch Filozoficzny* 5 (1920): 170–171.

"Logika dwuwartościowa" (Two-valued logic). *Przegląd Filozoficzny* 23 (1921): 189–205.

"Démonstration de la compatibilité des axiomes de la théorie de la déduction." *Annales de la Société Polonaise de Mathématique* 3 (1925): 149.

Elementy logiki matematycznej. Warsaw, 1929; 2nd ed., Warsaw, 1958. Translated by Olgierd Wojtasiewicz as *Elements of Mathematical Logic.* New York, 1963.

"Untersuchungen über den Aussagenkalkül." *Comptes rendus des séances de la Société des Sciences et des Lettres de Varsovie,* Classe III 23 (1930): 30–50. In collaboration with Alfred Tarski. English translation by J. H. Woodger in *Logic, Semantics, Metamathematics,* by Alfred Tarski, 38–59. Oxford: Clarendon Press, 1956.

"Philosophische Bemerkungen zu mehrwertigen Systemen des Aussagenkalküls." *Comptes rendus des séances de la Société des Sciences et des Lettres de Varsovie,* Classe III 23 (1930): 51–77.

"Ein Vollständigkeitsbeweis des zweiwertigen Aussagenkalküls." *Comptes rendus des séances de la Société des Sciences et des Lettres de Varsovie,* Classe III 24 (1931): 153–183.

"Zur Geschichte der Aussagenlogik." *Erkenntnis* 5 (1935–1936): 111–131.

"Der Äquivalenzenkalkül." *Collectanea Logica* 1 (1939): 145–169.

"Die Logik und das Grundlagenproblem." In *Les entretiens de Zurich sur les fondements et la méthode des sciences mathématiques 6–9 Décembre 1938,* 82–100. Zürich, 1941.

"The Shortest Axiom of the Implicational Calculus of Propositions." *Proceedings of the Royal Irish Academy* 52, Section A (1948): 25–33.

"On Variable Functors of Propositional Arguments." *Proceedings of the Royal Irish Academy* 54, Section A (1951): 25–35.

Aristotle's Syllogistic. Oxford, 1951; 2nd ed., Oxford: Clarendon Press, 1957.

"A System of Modal Logic." *Journal of Computing Systems* 1 (1953): 111–149.

Z zagadnień logiki i filozofii (Problems of logic and philosophy). Edited by Jerzy Słupecki. Warsaw: Panstwowe Wydawn, 1961. Essays. Contains bibliography.

In addition to the above, Łukasiewicz published about twenty papers and over fifty notes and reviews.

WORKS ON ŁUKASIEWICZ

Borkowski, Ludwik, and Jerzy Słupecki. "The Logical Works of J. Łukasiewicz." *Studia Logica* 8 (1958): 7–56.

Jordan, Z. A. *The Development of Mathematical Logic and of Logical Positivism in Poland between the Two Wars.* Oxford, 1945.

Kotarbiński, Tadeusz. "Jan Łukasiewicz's Works on the History of Logic." *Studia Logica* 8 (1958): 57–62.

Kotarbiński, Tadeusz. *La logique en Pologne.* Rome: Signorelli, 1959.

Prior, A. N. "Łukasiewicz's Contributions to Logic." In *Philosophy in the Mid-century,* edited by Raymond Klibansky, 53–55. Florence, 1958.

Sobociński, Bolesław. "In Memoriam Jan Łukasiewicz." *Philosophical Studies* (Ireland) 6 (1956): 3–49. Contains bibliography.

Sobociński, Bolesław. "La génesis de la Escuela Polaca de Lógica." *Oriente Europeo* 7 (1957): 83–95.

Czesław Lejewski (1967)

LULL, RAMÓN
(c. 1232–1316)

Ramón Lull (or Llull), the Franciscan philosopher, was born in Palma de Mallorca in the Balearic Islands. Lull received the education of a rich knight of the period, but was converted from dissipation to a devout life in about 1263. At that time Majorca was largely populated by Muslims, and Islam was still the great rival of Christianity. Lull resolved to dedicate himself to the conversion of Muslims and to seek martyrdom for their sake. After selling almost all his possessions and undertaking various pilgrimages, Lull spent nine years (c. 1265–1274) in Majorca, acquiring a profound knowledge of Arabic. In 1274 he had a vision that revealed to him the Principles on which his combinatory Art should be based. In 1275 James II of Majorca had Lull's early writings examined for orthodoxy, and in 1276 James founded at Miramar in Majorca a monastery where Franciscans could study Arabic and Lull's Art to prepare for missions to Islam.

Lull appears to have divided his time in the years 1276–1287 between Miramar and Montpellier. In 1287 he began a series of journeys to the courts of kings and popes with the hope of persuading them to support his missionary, his reforming, and (later) his crusading projects. Lull placed his hopes principally in the papacy and in the kings of France and Aragon. His only apparent success was when the Council of Vienne (1311–1312) ordained the creation of chairs for Hebrew, Arabic, and "Chaldean" in five centers. Lull also undertook missions to Tunis (1293), to Bougie, in Algeria (1307), and again to Tunis (1314–1315). The traditional account of his martyrdom at Bougie cannot be sustained. He seems to have died in Majorca before March 25, 1316. He has been beatified by the Roman Catholic Church.

In the years 1288–1289, 1297–1299, 1309–1311, and probably 1306, Lull taught at the University of Paris; he also lectured publicly at Naples and Montpellier. Starting about 1272, he began to write incessantly. Some 240 of his approximately 290 works have survived. About 190 are only preserved in Latin (over 100 of these Latin works remaining unpublished until recently), although most of them were originally written in Catalan. Some of his works were originally written in Arabic; all these Arabic versions, however, are lost.

The desire to bring about the conversion of Muslims and Jews, as well as pagan Tartars, which inspired Lull's ceaseless activity, also inspired his writings. The desire for the reunification of the church (divided into hostile East and West), and for the complete reunification of humankind, through Christianity, dominated Lull's life. Lull's Art and his whole philosophy are apologetic and Franciscan, aimed at conversion by peaceful persuasion. Lull's advocacy of an armed crusade came late in his life; it was intended as subsidiary to missions. Lull's life was a continual battle with Islam, not only in Spain and North Africa, but also, from 1298, in Paris, with the "Averroists." In opposition to the "double-truth" theory imputed to such rationalist philosophers as Boethius of Dacia and Siger of Brabant, whose master was Aristotle as interpreted by Averroes, Lull sought to reestablish the unity of truth in philosophy and theology.

THE ARS COMBINATORIA

According to Lull, God, insofar as he can be known to men, consists of a series of divine attributes, or "Dignities," which are also the absolute Principles of Lull's Art. These Dignities (in the later works goodness, greatness, eternity, power, wisdom, will, virtue, truth, glory) are the instruments of God's creative activity, the causes and archetypes of all created perfection. The essence of the Art does not (as is often thought) consist in demonstration, but in the metaphysical reduction of all created things to the Dignities, which are Principles of knowing as well as of Being, and in the comparison of particular things between themselves in the light of the Dignities, by means of such relative predicates as difference, agreement, contrariety, beginning, middle, end, majority, equality, minority. The absolute and relative predicates together form the self-evident principles common to all the sciences. These principles are combined in circular figures, where letters are substituted for their names ($B =$ goodness, and so on).

Lull's treatises on different sciences (cosmology, physics, law, medicine, astronomy, geometry, logic, psychology) are applications of his general Art. Lull made continual efforts to simplify and popularize his Art, from the primitive version in the *Ars Magna* of about 1274 to the final *Ars Generalis Ultima* of 1308. The latter work and also the *Arbre de ciència (Arbor Scientiae)* of 1296 are more philosophical and less polemical in purpose than the original Art. A vast encyclopedia that found favor in the Renaissance, the *Arbre* is an attempt to classify all knowledge under a unified plan. Lull's influence was acknowledged by Gottfried Wilhelm Leibniz in the later philosopher's search for the *caracteristica universalis* and *ars combinatoria,* which he hoped would make possible the deduction of all truths from basic concepts. Despite the clear analogies between the two systems, Leibniz only took over part of Lull's ideas, omitting Lull's original purpose of the Art as a means of converting infidels.

Lull was the first Christian philosopher of the Middle Ages to use a language other than Latin for his major works. Although he did not receive a university training, he enjoyed advantages denied to the great Scholastics. Of the three Mediterranean cultures of his time he knew Latin Christianity and Islam well and was aware of Greek Christianity. The basis of Lull's philosophy was Neoplatonic realism as transmitted through the Augustinian tradition: his exact use of John Scotus Erigena, Anselm, the Victorines, Bonaventure, and Roger Bacon is still debated. Lull was also familiar with the writings and beliefs of his Jewish and Muslim contemporaries.

All Lull's contemporaries shared a vision of the world based on Neoplatonism. The common belief in a hierarchy, or ladder, of creation, the theories of the four elements and of the spheres, the organization of reality by numerical-geometrical symbolism, the idea of man as a microcosm, were all incorporated by Lull into his system. That excellent scholars have seen the inspiration of Lull's theory of the Dignities in the Muslim *hadras* or in the Jewish kabbalist *sefirot* (both terms for the divine attributes) shows that Lull's doctrine (although of Christian derivation) provided a reasonable basis for a dialogue with the Muslim and Jewish elites. Much the same is true of the doctrine of correlative principles, developed in Lull's later works, by which each attribute unfolds into a triad of interconnected principles, agent, patient, and the action itself, expressing the relations between God, a creature, and God's action. Lull probably took this doctrine from the Arabic writer al-Ghazālī, whose *Logic* he translated. It is more probable that Lull derived the idea for the figures that illustrate his Arts from contemporary Spanish kabbalists or from the circular figures of Isidore of Seville's well-known cosmological treatise *De Natura Rerum* than from Ibn al-'Arabī of Murcia, who has been suggested as his source.

Two of the most striking characteristics of Lull's philosophy and theology—his "rationalism" and his emphasis on the importance of action, shown in his constant appeals to Christian rules—owe their prominence in his system to its polemical inspiration. Lull's "necessary reasons," by which he proposed to "prove" the articles of faith, are reasons of congruence and analogy, not purely deductive principles. In opposition to Islamic scholastic theology (the *kalam*), which tried to demonstrate the Faith, Lull sought to show that the Muslim, who began with a belief in monotheism and the divine attributes, must proceed to Christianity. Despite the nondeductive character of his works, Lull's thought is deeply rational. Only seldom in his mystical writings does love eclipse the intellect or obscure its powers. For him, contemplation issues in action. *Blanquerna* and *Felix* are the first philosophical-social novels of Europe. In *Blanquerna* Lull sketched his plan for a *Pax Christiana,* a society of nations presided over by the papacy.

See also al-Ghazālī, Muhammad; Anselm, St.; Aristotle; Augustinianism; Bacon, Roger; Boetius of Dacia; Bonaventure, St.; Erigena, John Scotus; Ibn al-'Arabī; Islamic Philosophy; Jewish Philosophy; Kabbalah; Leibniz, Gottfried Wilhelm; Logic, History of; Medieval Philosophy; Neoplatonism; Realism; Siger of Brabant.

Bibliography

Lull's Latin works may be found in a new critical edition, *Raimundi Lulli Opera latina* (vols. 1–5, Palma, 1959–1967; vols. 6–, Turnhout, Belgium, 1978–; at present 28 vols. have appeared). Reprint editions have made two important earlier collections of Lull's Latin works available, one by the printer Zetzner, *Raimundus Lullus, Opera* (2 vols., Strasbourg, 1651; reprinted, Stuttgart, 1996), another by Ivo Salzinger, *Raymundi Lulli Opera omnia* (8 vols., Mainz, 1721–1742; reprinted, Frankfurt am Mainz, 1965). Dr. Viola Tenge-Wolf has undertaken the digitalization of the over 2,000 microfilms of Lullian manuscripts in the Raimundus-Lullus-Institut of the University of Freiburg im Breisgau.

Editions of Lull's Catalan works include *Obres de Ramón Lull* (21 vols., Palma and Barcelona, 1906–1950) and the supplementary *Nova edició de les obres de Ramon Llull* (Palma, 1990–, in progress). A handy edition is *Ramon Llull, Obres essencials* (2 vols., Barcelona, 1957–1960). *Selected Works of Ramon Lull* have been translated into English by Anthony Bonner (2 vols., Princeton, NJ, 1985; who has also published the Catalan texts in 2 vols., Palma, 1989; these volumes include an important chronological catalog of Lull's Works, pp. 1257–1304 in the English edition). A complete catalog of the printed editions of Lull's works has been published by Elíes Rogent and Estanislau Duràn, *Bibliografía de les impressions lul.lianes* (Barcelona, 1927).

For studies of Lull's life and work see Tomás y Joaquín Carreras y Artau, *Historia de la filosofía española*, vol. 1 (Madrid: Real Academia de Ciencias Exactas, Físicas y Naturales, 1939) pp. 231–640; vol. 2 (Madrid, 1943) contains a valuable history of Lullism. For an English biography of Lull see E. Allison Peers, *Ramon Lull: A Biography* (London, 1929), which should now be supplemented by Jocelyn N. Hillgarth, *Ramon Lull and Lullism in 14th-Century France* (Oxford, 1971). A general introduction to Lull's worldview is provided by Robert Pring-Mill, *El microcosmos lul.lià* (Palma: Editorial Moll, 1962; in German, Stuttgart, 2001). For the intellectual and religious context in which Lull's Art developed see Harvey J. Hames, *The Art of Conversion: Christianity and Kabbalah in the 13th Century* (Leiden, 2000). For Lull's influence in the sixteenth century see Frances A. Yates, *Lull & Bruno: Collected Essays* (2 vols., London, 1982).

Rudolf Brummer has published a *Bibliographia lulliana: Ramon-Llull-Schriftum, 1870–1973* (Hildesheim, 1976); which has been supplemented for the years 1974–1984 by Marcel Salleras i Carolà in *Randa* (Barcelona) 19 (1986): 153–198. Current bibliography may also be found in the review *Estudios lulianos* (now *Studia lulliana*), published in Palma since 1957.

Jocelyn Nigel Hillgarth (1967)
Bibliography updated by Charles Lohr (2005)

LUNACHARSKI, ANATOLI VASILYEVICH

See *Lunacharskii, Anatolii Vasil'evich*

LUNACHARSKII, ANATOLII VASIL'EVICH
(1875–1933)

Anatolii Vasil'evich Lunacharskii (also Lunacharsky), the Marxist philosopher and literary critic and Soviet administrator, joined the Russian Social Democratic Party in Kiev in 1892. Because of his political activities as a secondary school student, he was denied admission to Russian universities. He attended lectures at Kiev University and at the University of Zürich, where in 1894–1895 he studied under Richard Avenarius, who converted him to empiriocriticism. Lunacharskii returned to Moscow in 1897, was exiled to Vologda (1899–1902), and spent several years in western Europe between 1904 and 1917. He was the first Soviet people's commissar for education (1917–1929).

Lunacharskii's contributions to philosophy are concentrated in value theory (which he rather misleadingly called biological aesthetics), ethics, and philosophy of religion. Like the positivists, he denied the adjudicability of value disputes. "In order to show," he wrote, "that a given type of valuation is in its very root worse than another type, the scientist must oppose one criterion to another, but the choice between criteria is a matter of *taste*, not *knowledge*" ("K voprosu ob otsenke" [On the question of valuation], 1904, reprinted in *Etiudy*, Moscow, 1922, p. 55).

In ethics and social philosophy Lunacharskii was a "Nietzschean Marxist." He called himself an aesthetic amoralist and rejected the categories of duty and obligation, stressing instead free creative activity, the "artistic" shaping of ends and ideals. "Nietzsche," he declared, "and all the other critics of the morality of duty, have defended the autonomy of the individual person, the individual's right to be guided in his life solely by his own desires" ("'Problemy idealizma'…," [Problems of idealism…] in *Obrazovanie* 12 [2] [1903]: 133).

Lunacharskii called his individualism macropsychic, or "broad-souled," to distinguish it from "narrow-souled" (micropsychic) individualism. It approached collectivism in its stress on the historical community of the creators of culture.

Traditional religious attitudes and institutions, according to Lunacharskii, could and should be given a new, socialist content. The old religions—supernatural, authoritarian, "antiscientific"—must be replaced by a new religion that will be humanistic, libertarian, and "scientific." The building of socialism and the shaping of the high human culture of the future will be a building of God (*bogostroitel'stvo*). "Scientific socialism," Lunacharskii declared, "is the most religious of all religions, and the true Social Democrat is the most deeply religious of men" ("Budushchee religii" [The future of religion], p. 23). The religion of God-building will soften the sting of mortality by intensifying man's awareness of the "universal connectedness of life, of the *all-life* which triumphs even in death" ("Eshche o teatre i sotsializme [Once more on the theater and socialism], in *Vershiny*, Vol. I, 1909, p. 213). The new religion, imparting a sense of "joyous union with the triumphant future of our species," will be full of drama and passion, having its own "saints and martyrs." It will be worthy to stand beside medieval Christianity in the "universal arsenal of art and inspiration" (*R. Avenarius: Kritika chistogo opyta v populiarnom izlozhenii A. Lunacharskovo* [R. Avenarius: *Critique of Pure Experience*, Expounded for the layman by A. Lunacharskii], Moscow, 1905, p. 154).

See also Avenarius, Richard; Marxist Philosophy; Marx, Karl; Positivism; Russian Philosophy; Socialism; Value and Valuation.

Bibliography

WORKS BY LUNACHARSKII

On Education: Selected Articles and Speeches. Moscow: Progress Publishers, 1981.

On Literature, and Art. Translated by Avril Pyman and Fainna Glagoleva. Moscow: Progress Publishers, 1973.

WORKS ON LUNACHARSKII

Fitzpatrick, S. *The Commissariat of Enlightenment: Soviet Organization of Education and the Arts under Lunacharsky, October 1917–1921.* Cambridge, U.K.: Cambridge University Press, 2002.

O'Connor, T. E. *The Politics of Soviet Culture: Anatolii Lunacharskii.* Ann Arbor, MI: UMI Research Press, 1983.

Tait, A. L. *Lunacharskii: Poet of the Revolution (1875–1907).* Birmingham: Department of Russian Language and Literature, University of Birmingham, 1984.

George L. Kline (1967)
Bibliography updated by Vladimir Marchenkov (2005)

LUTHER, MARTIN
(1483–1546)

Martin Luther, the German theologian and leader of the Protestant Reformation, was born at Eisleben, Saxony. His father came of peasant stock, but established himself during Luther's boyhood as a successful copper miner in Mansfeld. From 1501 to 1505 Luther attended the University of Erfurt, and then, at his father's wish, he began the study of law; but a spiritual crisis, occasioned by a violent thunderstorm, induced him to enter the Erfurt monastery of the Augustinian Friars. Despite conscientious and even overscrupulous attention to his monastic duties, Luther was obsessed by dread of God's anger, and his superior tried to direct the young man's energies and undoubted ability into a scholar's calling. From 1512 he was biblical professor at the new University of Wittenberg, a position he held, despite interruptions, until his death.

THEOLOGICAL DEVELOPMENT

Three stages may be distinguished in Luther's theological development. Between 1512 and 1517, and probably (in the judgment of most scholars) not later than 1515, his biblical studies led to a theological reorientation, at the center of which was an interpretation of the justice of God in Romans 1:17, not as a divine attribute expressed in punishment and reward, but as the activity by which God makes men just ("justifies" them). This justice of God is identical with His grace: It is not conditional upon human merit, but is received by faith alone (faith itself being a work of God in man). The working out of this basic insight made Luther increasingly critical of late scholastic theology and of ecclesiastical abuses. The appearance of the Ninety-five Theses on indulgences (1517), although they were not intended as "un-Catholic," was interpreted by Luther's opponents as ecclesiastically disloyal and subversive. Luther had, indeed, touched on the heart of medieval piety, the sacramental system, since indulgences belonged to the sacrament of penance.

The second period of Luther's development, from 1517 to 1521, was marked by his struggle with the Roman authorities, during which he abandoned the theory of papal, and even ecclesiastical, infallibility. In his *Babylonian Captivity* (1520), he made a systematic attack on the sacramental system, reinterpreting a sacrament as, like preaching, a form of the divine Word, by which God offers man His justice and creates the response of faith. The "church" is defined, not in terms of hierarchical authority, but as the communion of those whom Christ rules with His Word, all of whom are priests. Luther's basic insight into the character of Christian justice (or righteousness) was sharpened during this same period by greater precision in the distinction (already made before 1517) between Law and Gospel. The Law of God can only demand and condemn; it cannot be used by man as a means of self-salvation through strict obedience. The security of man before God lies solely in the Gospel, with its word of free forgiveness.

During the third period, after 1521, Luther's attention was turned to rival reformers who departed from him on particular points, or who demanded a more radical transformation of the church than he was prepared to countenance. Many of the radicals sought to establish communities in which the ethic of the Sermon on the Mount should be the sole rule of social conduct. Against them, Luther again argued for the distinction between Law and Gospel. Just as it is wrong to place Law between God and the conscience, so it is wrong to regulate society by the Gospel. The conscience needs the gospel of forgiveness, but society can only be founded upon the law of retributive justice (though Law should always be the agency of love). The two "realms," or "kingdoms," of Heaven and Earth—that is, the two ways in which God rules over the world of men—are not to be confused.

In his controversy with the humanist leader Desiderius Erasmus, which also belongs within the third stage of his development, Luther again believed himself to be fighting for the gospel of forgiveness. He acknowledged that Erasmus's selection of the theme to be debated—namely, the freedom of the will—came closer to the decisive issue than did the questions of the papacy, purgatory, and indulgences. Luther was not, of course, interested in the psychology of human action as such but in preserving his original insight into the agency of divine grace. He acknowledged a measure of human freedom in matters that do not concern salvation, but refused to make salvation depend at any point on the inherent possibilities of human nature. He therefore located the power of man's decision for God in the Gospel itself, and in the secret influence of the Holy Spirit. For Luther, this did not mean that God acts coercively, thereby doing violence to man's will, but that God is sovereign over the will and can direct it to His ends. Man acts voluntarily (that is, as he wills) even in those matters that concern his salvation. But the will itself is controlled by God. It cannot change itself from an evil to a good will: It must *be* changed under the influence of the Spirit.

Luther was not, of course, a philosopher. He was primarily a theologian, obliged by circumstances to become a rebel and a reformer. Indeed, it is often supposed that he was an implacable enemy of philosophy, and to this problem the remainder of this article will be devoted. It will appear how closely Luther's views on reason and philosophy are related to the central theological concerns (Christian justice and the two realms of Heaven and Earth) that have been sketched above.

ATTITUDE TOWARD PHILOSOPHY

It is not hard to document from Luther's own writings the common accusation that he was an anti-intellectualist. His description of reason as "the Devil's Whore" is well known, and he recommended that the faithful sacrifice reason, or slay it, as the enemy of God. Many have seen in this apparent antirationalism evidence of Luther's Ockhamist heritage, but this is an oversimplification of an intricate historical problem. Luther did not invariably decry reason. In his celebrated appearance before the Diet of Worms (1521) he seemed to appeal to a double norm—Scripture and reason. (He refused to recant unless convinced by "the testimonies of Scripture or by evident reason.") And sometimes he showered extravagant praise upon reason as the greatest of God's gifts, as the "inventress and mistress of all the arts, of medicine and law, of whatever wisdom, power, virtue and glory men possess in this life."

Luther accepted the traditional view that reason set man apart from the brute beasts and gave him dominion over the world. Clearly, the problem is to explain, not an extreme one-sidedness, but a strange ambivalence. And the appeal to Luther's alleged Ockhamist heritage cannot help to explain his attitude until the Ockhamist understanding of reason is itself clarified and the extent of Luther's overall dependence upon nominalism is carefully assessed. The persistent image of nominalist theology as antirational and un-Catholic requires reconsideration in the light of recent studies, and verbal echoes of nominalism in Luther's writing may prove of no great significance. In any case, the primary historical task is to examine Luther's actual utterances on reason and philosophy and to view them in relation to the inner structure of his thought.

THE CONCEPT OF REASON. The apparent ambiguities in Luther's utterances on reason can be explained, in part, by his fundamental distinction between the two realms of human existence. At one and the same time, man lives toward God in the Heavenly Kingdom and toward his natural and social environments in the Earthly Kingdom. Luther judges human reason to be an adequate instrument for dealing with earthly affairs, that is, the maintaining of physical subsistence (*oeconomia*) and the regulation of life in society (*politia*). In this realm, reason is legitimately exercised and affords the only light man needs. But in spiritual affairs the situation is quite different. Reason has no understanding of what it is that commends a man to God. Therefore God has given His Word (in the Scriptures), and reliance upon reason could, in this realm, only be perverse and presumptuous. The way of salvation could never have been thought out by rational enquiry, for all God's works and words transcend reason. The Word of God is apprehended, not by reason, but by faith.

This does not mean that, for Luther, reason must be totally excluded from theology. He allowed for the possibility of taming reason's presumptuousness. It then becomes the handmaid of faith. Luther spoke of reason as illumined by faith, regenerated, or born anew. Sometimes the notion of regenerate reason tended to coalesce with the notion of faith itself. But generally, Luther seemed to think of regenerate reason as the human capacity for orderly thought being exercised upon material provided by the Word. Perhaps this is what he meant by the correlation of Scripture and reason in his answer before the Diet of Worms: He was willing to be persuaded either by direct biblical citations or by plain inferences from them. He certainly did not mean to set reason beside Scripture as an independent and supplementary source of theological knowledge.

The doctrine of the two realms provides, then, the framework for a threefold distinction by means of which Luther's various utterances on reason may, for the most part, be harmonized. We have to distinguish between natural reason, ruling within its own domain (the Earthly Kingdom); presumptuous reason, encroaching on the domain of faith (the Heavenly Kingdom); and regenerate reason, serving faith in subjection to the Word of God. Luther does not represent an anti-intellectualist dismissal of disciplined thought; he tries to formulate a theological critique of reason, in which the boundary lines of reason's competence are sharply drawn. Only in the second of these three contexts does reason appear as "the Devil's Whore." In the first it is the greatest of God's gifts; in the third, an excellent instrument of godliness.

It is necessary, however, to carry the analysis further and to show that Luther's invective against reason is focused upon a quite specific blunder that reason makes when it trespasses, unregenerate, upon the domain of faith. It then appears that the *sacrificium intellectus* for which he calls cannot be understood simply as an epistemological doctrine, but rests upon a more strictly theological (or soteriological) concern. For in many passages from his writings, what Luther meant to express by his colorful invective against reason, was his constant astonishment at the heart of his own gospel: the unconditioned character of God's grace. Reason must be "put to death" because it cannot comprehend the miracle of divine forgiveness, and therefore stands in the way of man's receiv-

ing the justice of God. Reason became identified in Luther's mind with the religious attitude of the natural (that is, unregenerate) man, who can conceive only of a strictly legalistic relationship to God. *Ratio* became virtually synonymous with a definite *opinio*, and it is by no means accidental that the two words can be found side by side in several passages. Nor, of course, was this usage wholly eccentric, since Lewis and Short's Latin-English dictionary gives as one of the meanings of *ratio* a "view or opinion resting upon reasonable grounds." And Luther fully acknowledged a certain reasonableness about the assumption that a just God must require "good works" as the precondition of communion with Him.

Consequently, the proclamation of an unconditioned grace—which demands nothing, save the acceptance of faith—can be greeted by reason only with incredulity. What needs to be "sacrificed," therefore, is not human rationality, without qualification, but rather the legalistic mentality of the natural man. As Luther put it, grace must "take us out of ourselves," and we must learn to "rise above reason." In short, Luther's concept of reason (at least, when his remarks about it are pejorative) is not formal, but material. *Ratio* is a concrete attitude rather than the faculty or structure of reasoning. When the natural man turns his thoughts to religion, he carries over into the Heavenly Kingdom presuppositions that, however appropriate in dealing with his social existence in the Earthly Kingdom, no longer apply. For the Kingdom of Christ is a realm, not of law, but of grace (*das Reich der Gnaden*).

THE CONCEPT OF PHILOSOPHY. Because Luther's views on reason are set in a theological context, they are not always directly relevant to the problem of faith and reason as the philosopher normally understands it. But Luther's standpoint certainly had consequences for the philosophy of religion, and more particularly for the problem of a natural theology. For Luther there could be no question of treating the truths of reason as a kind of foundation for the truths of revelation. The continuity between nature and grace, as presented in the classical scholastic scheme, is broken. There is no rational preamble to faith, because reason is not a neutral instrument for the discovery of objective truths; it is misled by its own bias and even corrupted by sin—that is, by the egocentricity of the unredeemed man. For man in sin actually prefers a God of law, upon whom he can establish a claim. Revelation does not confirm or supplement reason: It stands in contradiction to reason, until the natural man is "born anew." The religion of reason is not merely insufficient or imperfect, but perverted and erroneous. Luther does not deny that a limited knowledge of God is available to reason; but the egocentricity of man in sin is a fatal defect, productive of idolatry and superstition. Reason makes God as it wills Him to be, and turns this natural knowledge into idolatry. The god of reason is a false God.

In general, Luther's direct statements about philosophy closely parallel his judgment on reason. As early as the Lectures on Romans (1515–1516) he had come to see his mission as a protest against philosophy, and his writings are interspersed with abusive descriptions of Aristotle ("the stinking philosopher," "the clown of the High Schools," "the blind pagan," etc.). Thomas Aquinas, who symbolized the attempt to synthesize Aristotle and the Christian faith, is treated with similar disrespect. Nevertheless, Luther could on occasion speak deferentially of philosophy and even of Aristotle. He approved of much that the Greek philosopher had written on social ethics and ranked Cicero's ethics even higher. He freely acknowledged that the Christian had much to learn from philosophy in this area.

The key to Luther's ambivalence lies, as with his concept of reason, in the distinction between the two realms. The boundaries are carefully drawn. Philosophy is an excellent thing in its own place, but if philosophical categories are transferred into theology, the result can only be confusion. Luther saw philosophy as tied to the empirical world (the Earthly Kingdom), whereas theology is concerned with things unseen (the Heavenly Kingdom). He was not, strictly speaking, hostile to Aristotle, but to the theological application of Aristotelianism by the Schoolmen. Of course, some of the Greek philosopher's doctrines already had a theological bearing (for example, on the immortality of the soul and on divine Providence). These Luther dismissed. But he approved Aristotle's treatises on the sermonic arts (logic and rhetoric) and, with qualifications, those on moral philosophy.

Perhaps the most important illustration of Luther's attitude toward Aristotle is afforded by his discussions of moral "habit" (Latin, *habitus*; Greek, *hexis*). In the *Nicomachean Ethics*, Aristotle taught that "we become just by performing just acts." Luther's opponents apparently gave this doctrine a theological application: That is, it was used to support the claim that good works must precede justification. In assailing the concept of habit, Luther is not offering a philosophical critique of Aristotle, but rejecting the theological application of Aristotelian doctrines. A philosophical theory belongs within the Earthly Kingdom. The Schoolmen mix the kingdoms.

COMPARISON WITH NOMINALISM. Luther's distinction between two spheres of knowledge (philosophy and theology) and between two organs of knowing (reason and faith) certainly invites comparison with late medieval Scholasticism. There is perhaps a prima facie probability that Luther's views on reason and philosophy were under the influence of the nominalists. His main instructors at Erfurt were nominalists, and it is noteworthy that Luther could speak of William of Ockham with apparent respect, even calling him "my dear master." He adopted the nominalist view of universals, and he explicitly owned a debt to the nominalist Pierre d'Ailly in the doctrine of the Real Presence. Other possible debts have been argued with more or less plausibility, although it can hardly be denied that Luther left nothing unchanged that he borrowed from others. At least the possibility is open that at the outset the sharp distinction between faith and reason may have been suggested to him by his familiarity with the Ockhamist school.

It may be that the separation of theology and philosophy in Luther is to be explained partly by his acceptance, along with the nominalists, of a strict Aristotelian concept of science. Against Thomas, Luther agreed with the nominalists that since theology rests upon assertions of faith, it cannot be classed as a science. Philosophy (which is the sum total of rational knowledge and embraces the various sciences) deals with the visible world, which is accessible to reason. Theology deals with an invisible world, accessible only to faith. Such points of agreement between Luther and the Ockhamists cannot, however, conceal the sharp differences between them. Quite apart from the fact that Luther developed a divergent concept of faith, his standpoint represents a different basic concern. The interest of the Ockhamists in the problem of faith and reason was primarily epistemological. Hence they devoted considerable thought to relating the cognition of reason to the cognition of faith, and sought in various ways to bridge the gap that they had apparently cut between the two. Nominalist theologians tried to comprehend both faith and reason within a single epistemological scheme. They regarded theological propositions (once established) as subject to rational scrutiny, believed that merely probable arguments could lead to faith when the will cooperates, and argued that revelation was given precisely to those who made maximum use of their rational capacities. Luther, on the other hand, was not interested in narrowing the epistemological gap. On the contrary, the problem for him was graver, because he allowed for the corruption of reason by human sinfulness. Hence his restrictions on reason, even if they were built on a nominalist view of science, go beyond it in what is primarily a theological, rather than philosophical, concern.

THE THEORY OF "DOUBLE TRUTH." The nominalist distinction between the spheres of faith and of reason has commonly been interpreted as though there were a disharmony, or even a contradiction, between them. Indeed, the doctrine of a "double truth"—that is, that a proposition may be true in theology, but false in philosophy—has been attributed to the nominalist theologian Robert Holkot. Properly speaking, double truth seems never to have been a consciously adopted "doctrine" in the Middle Ages, but rather an accusation leveled against theological opponents. There does not seem to be adequate reason to attribute it to any of the nominalists. True, they admitted some apparent conflicts, for instance, that the Christian belief in the Trinity, when formulated according to the rules of Aristotelian logic, contained real contradictions. But this simply prompted the quest for a higher logic, which could embrace both the traditional Aristotelian rules and also the rules appropriate to the peculiarities of theological truth.

A doctrine of double truth could, however, be attributed to Luther with some plausibility, since he explicitly said that "the same thing is not true in different disciplines" (*Disputation on the Proposition, "The Word became flesh,"* 1539). But Luther himself did not use the expression "double truth," and a close inspection of his argument suggests that, despite appearances, he really had a rather different thesis in mind. What he was trying to defend might better be called a "theory of multiple meaning." Neither "twofold" nor "truth" quite pinpoints Luther's thesis, and perhaps even "manifold truth" (Bengt Hägglund's phrase) is still misleading. If we may paraphrase the drift of Luther's argument, he seems to be saying that *homo loquens* reflects and communicates, not by means of a single, universally valid language, but by means of several languages, which are relative to particular disciplines or areas of experience. Hence the meaning of a term or proposition is determined by the area of discourse: If transferred from one area of discourse to another, a term may acquire a different meaning, or have no meaning at all. To use Luther's own examples, it makes no sense to ask the weight of a line or the length of a pound.

Whether correct or not, this argument bears a close resemblance to ideas that played an important role in twentieth-century linguistic philosophy, and is therefore not likely to be dismissed as obscurantism or anti-intellectualism. Unfortunately, Luther's argument is not developed with adequate precision, either in this *Disputation* or elsewhere. But it is not an isolated argument. The basic thesis—that the same form of words may have different meanings in different disciplines—underlies many of his remarks about the relation of ethics and theology. For example, the proposition that fallen man can do no good is fundamental to Luther's teaching on justification. But Luther admits that this is true only in a theological, not in an ethical, context, for in each context the word *good* means something different. This is, perhaps, a statement of double truth, but only because it rests on a theory of multiple meaning. Thus interpreted, "double truth" does not imply contradiction, but excludes it, since real contradiction is possible only within a single realm of discourse. As Luther put it in the first thesis of the *Disputation*: "Although we must hold to the saying, 'One truth agrees with another,' nevertheless the same thing is not true in different disciplines."

See also Ailly, Pierre d'; Aristotelianism; Aristotle; Averroism; Cicero, Marcus Tullius; Erasmus, Desiderius; Faith; Holkot, Robert; Reason; Reformation; Thomas Aquinas, St.; William of Ockham.

Bibliography

WORKS BY LUTHER

The definitive German edition of Luther's writings in Latin and German is *D. Martin Luthers Werke. Kritische Gesamtausgabe* (Weimar, 1883–). The most comprehensive English version is *Luther's Works: American Edition*, edited by Jaroslav Pelikan and Helmut T. Lehmann (St. Louis: Concordia, 1955–1986, 55 vols.).

WORKS ON LUTHER

Recent Studies

Three twentieth-century books dealing with Luther's views on reason and philosophy are Bengt Hägglund, *Theologie und Philosophie bei Luther und in der occamistischen Tradition. Luthers Stellung zur Theorie von der doppelten Wahrheit* (Lund: Gleerup, 1955); Bernhard Lohse, *Ratio und Fides. Eine Untersuchung über die Ratio in der Theologie Luthers* (Göttingen: Vandenhoeck and Ruprecht, 1958); and B. A. Gerrish, *Grace and Reason: A Study in the Theology of Luther* (Oxford: Clarendon Press, 1962). One of the most adequate treatments of Luther's intellectual background is still Otto Scheel, *Martin Luther, Vom Katholizismus zur Reformation*, Vol. I, 1st ed. (Tübingen: n.p., 1916); Vol. II, 3rd and 4th eds. (Tübingen, 1930).

Luther and Nominalism

The literature dealing with the general question of Luther's relation to nominalism is sketched in Leif Grane, *Contra Gabrielem. Luthers Auseinandersetzung mit Gabriel Biel in der Disputatio contra scholasticam theologiam 1517* (Copenhagen: Gyldendal, 1962). Grane's own discussion is focused on the theological rather than on the philosophical points, as is the work of Reinhard Schwarz, *Fides, Spes und Caritas beim jungen Luther unter besonderer Berücksichtigung der mittelalterlichen Tradition* (Berlin: De Gruyter, 1962). The work of Heiko Augustus Oberman in *The Harvest of Medieval Theology: Gabriel Biel and Late Medieval Nominalism* (Cambridge, MA: Harvard University Press, 1963) is intended to lay the foundations for a study of nominalism in relation to the beginnings of Reformation theology.

Additional Background

For the wider aspects of Luther's thought, see the articles and bibliographies under "Luther" in *Die Religion in Geschichte und Gegenwart*, 3rd ed. (Tübingen, 1960), Vol. IV, pp. 480–523, which may be brought up to date by the annual listings of the *Luther-Jahrbuch*.

B. A. Gerrish (1967)

LUTHER, MARTIN [ADDENDUM]

The renaissance of Luther studies enjoyed by the twentieth century continues apace. The massive critical, or Weimar (WA), edition of his work has recently been finished in 127 volumes. Important interpretive works have been published and discussed, including a major three-volume theological biography by Martin Brecht (1985–1993). Despite, or perhaps because of, this wide variety of scholarship, even such a seemingly simple theme as faith and philosophy in Luther has no consensus among interpreters.

There has been a welcome re-reception of Luther by Catholic scholars, starting with Joseph Lortz in 1939. A significant ecumenical consensus was reached by evangelical and Catholic scholars on the occasion of Luther's 500th birthday, noting that Vatican II reflects many of the concerns Luther addressed in his own witness to the gospel. This larger ecumenical interpretation has led to studies that appreciate the more Catholic side of Luther as a reformer and teacher of the whole church, not excluding his doctrine of justification by faith.

The importance of understanding each of Luther's distinct writings within its own historical, institutional, and rhetorical context is a major virtue of modern Luther studies. Equally important is an understanding of Luther against his late-medieval background. This has led to a new appreciation for Luther's dependence upon nominalism, especially the school of Ockham (*via moderna*). Recent scholarship has documented Luther's use of philosophy and logic in his theological arguments, including elements of nominalist logic from Gabriel Biel and Pierre d'Ailly. Luther's strong language against reason, philoso-

phy, and Aristotle were aimed at a particular target, namely, the scholastic theology of an earlier age (*via antiqua*). Unlike the Neo-Kantian and existentialist interpretations of Luther, recent scholars have argued that Luther nowhere has a complete condemnation of metaphysics or ontology in theological understanding. Indeed, some scholars now find a kind of ontology in Luther's conception of salvation.

At the heart of contemporary controversy surrounding the interpretation of Luther is the so-called Finnish school, including the work of Tuomo Mannermaa (2005). On this view, Luther taught that Christ is really and personally present in faith for the Christian. Justification is not simply alien, external, and forensic but also relational and ontological. The relationship between human being and the divine Trinity is understood not only as an external declaration of a righteousness that is not our own but also as the growth of Christ-like love through faith. The similarities of Luther's view thus understood, and the Eastern Orthodox notion of *theosis* (divinization), has been a key point in the Finnish school. Even given this new understanding, Luther consistently rejected philosophical ontology and scholastic metaphysics. When discussing the presence of Christ, he refused to go beyond what was promised in the Word. "But how He is present—this is beyond our thought; for there is darkness." (*Lectures on Galatians* [1535], WA 40/1:229). Thus, Luther appears to have used philosophical tools and concepts but refused to build theology on philosophical systems. For Luther, theology is grounded on the Word of God, not philosophical speculation.

See also Ailly, Pierre d'; Aristotle; Biel, Gabriel; Existentialism; Kant, Immanuel; Ockhamism; Ontology; Philosophy; Reason; William of Ockham.

Bibliography

Braaten, Carl, and R. W. Jenson, eds. *Union with Christ: The New Finnish Interpretation of Luther*. Grand Rapids, MI: Eerdmans, 1998.

Brecht, Martin. *Martin Luther*. 3 vols. Minneapolis: Fortress, 1985–1993.

Dieter, Theodor. *Der junge Luther und Aristoteles*. Berlin: de Gruyter, 2001.

Janz, Denis. *Luther and Late Medieval Thomism*. Waterloo, ON: Wilfrid Laurier University, 1983.

Joint Lutheran/Roman Catholic Study Commission. *Facing Unity*. Geneva: Lutheran World Federation, 1985.

Lortz, Joseph. *The Reformation in Germany*. New York: Herder & Herder, 1968 [1939].

Luther, Martin. *D. Martin Luthers Werke: Kritische Gesamtausgabe*. 4 parts in 127 vols. Weimar: H. Böhlau, 1883–2007.

Mannermaa, Tuomo. *Christ Present in Faith*. Minneapolis: Fortress, 2005.

White, Graham. *Luther as Nominalist*. Helsinki: Luther-Agricola-Society, 1994.

Wicks, Jared, ed. *Catholic Scholars Dialogue with Luther*. Chicago: Loyola University Press, 1970.

Alan G. Padgett (2005)

LU XIANGSHAN
(1139–1193)

Lu Xiangshan, also called Lu Jiuyuan, started the idealistic trend in Chinese philosophy. He emphasized the supremacy and self-sufficiency of the mind, contrary to his contemporary Zhu Xi, who stressed the need to discover reason and to acquire knowledge of the external world. He lived in the province of Jiangsi. His father was a respected member of the gentry, and from his early youth Lu was able to devote himself to the study of Confucius and Mencius. He disagreed with the views of the scholar Cheng Yi of the Northern Sung Dynasty.

Lu Xiangshan is known for the following:

When a sage arises in the East,
The mind is the same,
And so is reason.

The same is true of sages born in the West, the North, and the South and of those born thousands of generations earlier and later. What he meant is that mind is the same the world over and at all times. From this fundamental thesis he drew the conclusions that mind has priority over all things and that reason has a universal validity.

Yang Jian, a disciple of Lu and a submagistrate, asked him, "What is the Original Mind?" Lu quoted the words of Mencius concerning the four kinds of virtues—*ren* (benevolence), *yi* (righteousness), *li* (decency), and *zhi* (knowledge)—and said, "This is the Original Mind." But Yang failed to understand what Lu meant. Some time after, a lawsuit was brought by a salesman of fans for Yang's verdict, and Yang again came to Lu with the same question. Lu answered, "In trying the case of the fan salesman, you were able to judge right that which is right and wrong that which is wrong. This is the Original Mind." Yang was then convinced that the mind is self-conscious and self-evident.

Lu was firmly convinced that there is a universal mind and a universal rationality: "What fills the universe is rationality; what the scholars should search for is to render the idea of rationality clear to all. The scope of rationality is boundless." He also quoted Cheng Hao's words, "The universe is great; yet it has its limitation," and then inferred from them that what is more perfect than the universe is rationality.

Again he said: "Rationality in the universe is so evident that it is never concealed. The greatness of the universe lies in the existence of rationality which is an order publicly followed and without partiality. Man with Heaven and Earth constitutes the triad. Why should one be egocentric and not in conformity with rationality?" Lu's main idea is that since each one has a mind and reason is inherent in mind, mind is reason. Furthermore, he says: "What is the happening of the universe is the ought-to-do-duty of man; what is the ought-to-do-duty is the happening of the universe."

See also Chinese Philosophy; Mencius; Rationality; Reason; Zhu Xi (Chu Hsi).

Bibliography

Works by Lu may be found in the typescript *The Philosophy of Lu Hsiang-shan, a Neo-Confucian Monistic Idealist*, translated by L. V. Cady in 2 volumes (New York: Union Theological Seminary, 1939), which also contains discussion.

Chan, Wing-tsit. *A Source Book in Chinese Philosophy*. Princeton, NJ: Princeton University Press, 1963.

De Bary, Theodore William. *The Message of the Mind in Neo-Confucianism*. New York: Columbia University Press, 1989.

Huang, Chin-hsing. "Chu Hsi versus Lu Hsiang-shan: A Philosophical Interpretation." *Journal of Chinese Philosophy* 14, no. 2 (1987): 179–208.

Huang, Siu-chi. *Lu Hsiang-shan: A Twelfth Century Chinese Idealist Philosopher*. New Haven, CT: American Oriental Society, 1944; Westport, CT: Hyperion Press, 1977.

Carsun Chang (1967)
Bibliography updated by Huichieh Loy (2005)

LYING

Lying may be defined as the making of a declarative statement to another person that one believes to be false, with the intention that the other person believe that statement to be true, and the intention that the person believe that one believes that statement to be true. Lying may be distinguished from other forms of intentional deception insofar as it involves the use of conventional signs arranged to make a statement. Intentional deception using natural signs, such as fake smiling, shamming a limp, or wearing a disguise, does not count as lying. Intentional deception using conventional signs that are neither spoken nor written, such as deceptively nodding one's head, sending deceptive smoke signals, or deceptive signaling by semaphore, does count as lying, at least insofar as one is making a statement.

Lying requires that a statement be made; hence that form of deception that consists in withholding a statement from another person with the intention that the other person infer a believed falsehood—sometimes called a lie of omission or a concealment lie—does not count as lying. Exaggerating, being misleading, hedging, or being evasive, with the intention that the other person infer a believed falsehood, also does not count as lying. Lying does not require that the statement that is made is false, but it does require that the statement made is believed to be false rather than merely not believed to be true, or believed to be possibly false or probably false. Lying does not require that the other person is real, only that the other person is believed to be a person and is believed to be real. This does not resolve the questions of whether one can lie to no other person in particular (for example, by publishing a believed false account of an event), or whether there can be intrapersonal lying (for example, an earlier self lying to a later self).

The most important philosophical discussions of lying are to be found in St. Augustine, St. Thomas Aquinas, and Immanuel Kant. Aquinas differed from Augustine and Kant in holding that making a declarative statement to another person that one believes to be false is sufficient for lying; no further deceptive intention is needed. All three held that lying is wrong and that one should never lie; however they distinguished between not lying or being truthful, which is required, and being candid or volunteering believed truths, which is not. Augustine and Aquinas held that some lies, such as lies told to save the lives of innocents or lies told to avoid being defiled, that do not harm the particular person(s) lied to, are less egregious than other lies, such as malicious lies and lies told in the teaching of religion. All three argued that lying is a perversion of the faculty of speech, the natural end of which is the communication of thoughts. Augustine and Kant argued that in telling a lie one harms oneself, and undermines trust in society; hence there can never be a harmless lie. Kant also argued that a person cannot consent to being told a particular lie; hence in lying to another person one is necessarily treating that person as a mere means to one's end.

See also Deontological Ethics; Duty; Kantian Ethics; Moral Rules and Principles; Self-Deception; Virtue and Vice.

Bibliography

Adler, J. E. "Lying, Deceiving, or Falsely Implicating" *Journal of Philosophy* 94 (1997): 435–452.

Aquinas, St. Thomas. "Question 110: Lying." In *Summa Theologiae*, edited by Thomas Gilby. Garden City, NY: Image Books, 1969.

Augustine, St. "On Lying and Against Lying." In *Treatises on Various Subjects*, edited by R.J. Deferrari. New York: Fathers of the Church, 1952.

Bok, S. *Lying: Moral Choice in Public and Private Life.* 2nd ed. New York: Vintage Books, 1999.

Chisholm, R. M., and T. D. Feehan. "The Intent to Deceive." *Journal of Philosophy* 74 (1977): 143–159.

Frankfurt, H. G. "The Faintest Passion." In *Necessity, Volition, and Love.* Cambridge, U.K.; New York: Cambridge University Press, 1999.

Kant, I. *Immanuel Kant, Practical Philosophy*, edited by Mary Gregor and Allen W. Wood. Cambridge, U.K.: Cambridge University Press, 1996.

Mahon, J. E. "Kant on Lies, Candour, and Reticence." *Kantian Review* 7 (2003): 101–133.

Mannison, D. S. "Lying and Lies." *Australasian Journal of Philosophy* 47 (1969): 132–144.

Siegler, F. A. "Lying." *American Philosophical Quarterly* 3 (1966): 128–136.

James Edwin Mahon (2005)

LYOTARD, JEAN-FRANÇOIS
(1924–1998)

Born in Versailles, France, on August 10, 1924, Jean-François Lyotard was educated in Paris. As a child, Lyotard wanted to be a monk, painter, historian, or novelist, but settled a career in philosophy. He began teaching philosophy at the secondary school level in Constantine, Algeria, and later at La Flèche, France. From 1954 to 1966, Lyotard was a member of a leftist revolutionary group called Socialism ou Barbarie (either socialism or barbarism), eventually joining a splinter group called Pouvoir Ouvrier (Worker's Power) in 1964. He broke with the group in 1966 after becoming critical of Marxism's tendency toward universalism. He began work as a philosophy professor, and was employed at University of Paris X, Nanterre, during the student protests of May 1968. He gained a full position at the University of Paris VIII, Vincennes, where he spent many years and became an emeritus faculty member in 1987. He was also a founding member of the Collège International de Philosophie in Paris. With *The Postmodern Condition: A Report on Knowledge* (1979) he achieved international renown, and was guest lecturer at many universities throughout the world. On April 21, 1998, Lyotard died of leukemia in Paris. Lyotard's philosophical influences are diverse, including research on topics in Marxism, psychoanalysis, aesthetics, continental and analytical philosophy. An overall theme throughout his works is the inability for a single theory to capture the whole of reality, typically stressing what has been left out or forgotten in a particular theory.

Lyotard's initial writings of the 1950s and early 1960s were political and focused on the Marxist concerns of *Socialism ou Barbarie*, with particular attention to the ending the French occupation of Algeria. Additionally, he published *La phénoménologie* (*Phenomenology*) that supports many aspects of phenomenology, but is critical of its tendency to prioritize the transcendental ego in isolation from the material concerns addressed in Marxism. After attending Jacques Lacan's lectures in the 1960s, Lyotard wrote his first major work, *Discours, figure* to complete his *doctorat d'etat*. Published in 1971, *Discours, figure* compares the approaches of structuralism and phenomenology by examining the relationship between textual words of reading, and the figural or visual image of seeing that resists signification and rational concepts. Lyotard argues that text and figure cannot be neatly separated from one another, and neither word nor image should be privileged. His next important work, *Libidinal Economy*, published in 1974, is strongly influenced by Freud, Marx, and Nietzsche, though Lyotard later recants his self-professed "evil book" (*Perigrinations*, 13). *Libidinal Economy* is a break from the rest of Lyotard's work because it retreats entirely from the intellectualism of rational concepts in favor of an examination of drives, affects, intensities, and energy flows that can be ordered in a variety of ways by society.

Lyotard attained fame with the publication of *The Postmodern Condition* in 1979, which was commissioned by the Quebec government to examine the status of knowledge in highly developed societies. The publication of this book catapulted Lyotard into the international spotlight. Often, Lyotard's use of the term "postmodernism" is misunderstood as a historical era following the modern period, though in *The Postmodern Condition* Lyotard insists that the postmodern occurs within the modern period as an "incredulity toward meta-narratives" (p. xxiv). For Lyotard, modernism relies upon meta-narratives that are overarching discourses that try to explain all phenomena according to their own terms.

Lyotard utilizes Ludwig Wittgenstein's terminology of "language games" during this period to suggest that different language games follow their own rules and cannot be adequately translated to one another. While scientific discourse is denotative, ethical discourse is prescriptive, and to translate the descriptive into the prescriptive would be analogous to translating the rules of chess into those of checkers. Universal grand narratives in modernity suppose that language games are indeed commensurable and result in a kind of "terror" that cannot accept other kinds of games. Lyotard questions the hierarchical priority of scientific and technological forms of knowledge in developed societies that exclude other types of knowledge. According to Lyotard, grand narratives cannot legitimate their authority, and the postmodern breaks through the modern when grand narratives lose their credibility. The epistemological questions raised in *The Postmodern Condition* turn toward political themes in *The Differend*.

Published in 1983, *The Differend: Phrases in Dispute* is thought to be Lyotard's most important work because of its elaboration of the central concept of the book, the "differend." Lyotard defines the *différend* as a "case of conflict, between (at least) two parties, that cannot be equitably resolved for lack of a rule of judgment applicable to both arguments" (p. xi). Lyotard uses the instance of proving the horror of the gas chambers at Auschwitz as his paradigmatic model of a *différend*. Revisionist historian Robert Faurisson denies that the Holocaust occurred because there are no victims who were eyewitnesses to the atrocity. In order for there to be an eyewitness, one would have to be a victim that survived the gas chambers, making it impossible to establish the crime according to Faurisson's criterion. This situation is used as a touchstone to examine various political scenarios in which the victim cannot establish the existence of an injustice, because his or her experience does not conform to present criterion for establishing a legitimate "injustice," and for that reason, the plaintiff becomes a victim of a further wrong. A *différend* follows the structure of a double bind, where it is impossible for the plaintiff to prove damage by the rules of current authority, and differs from litigation that can be established within the present rules. For Lyotard, the *différend* is signaled by a sublime feeling because it involves an overwhelming feeling of pleasure and a feeling of pain. The pain in the sublime comes from the inability to express the wrong of the *différend*, but the feeling of pleasure arises from the potential for the creation of new idioms of discourse that can express the wrong. Lyotard uses Kant's theory of aesthetical judgments of the sublime to describe a theory of political judgment where judgments are made without recourse to a universal rule. Because of the incommensurability of language genres, the *différend* cannot be eliminated for good, but one can bear witness to *différends* and even strain to hear their call.

Much of Lyotard's later work explores Kant's theory of the sublime in greater detail. Lyotard also published many important books of essays focusing on art, literature, history, technology, politics, and postmodernism, in addition to books on several other topics. According to Geoffrey Bennington (1988), Lyotard personally believed that his major works were *Discourse, figure*, *Libidinal Economy*, and *The Differend*.

See also Postmodernism.

Bibliography

WORKS BY LYOTARD

Discours, figure. Paris: Klincksieck, 1971.

Économie libidinale. Paris: Éditions de Minuit, 1974. Translated by Iain Hamilton Grant as *Libidinal Economy* (Bloomington: Indiana University Press, 1993).

La condition postmoderne: Rapport sur le savoir. Paris: Éditions de Minuit, 1979. Translated by Geoff Bennington and Brian Massumi as *The Postmodern Condition: A Report on Knowledge* (Minneapolis: University of Minnesota Press, 1984).

Au Juste. With Jean-Loup Thébaud. Paris: Christian Bourgois, 1979. Translated by Wlad Godzich as *Just Gaming* (Minneapolis: University of Minnesota Press, 1985).

Le différend. Paris: Éditions de Minuit, 1983. Translated by Georges Van Den Abbeele as *The Differend: Phrases in Dispute* (Minneapolis: University of Minnesota Press, 1988).

The Lyotard Reader, edited by Andrew Benjamin. Oxford, U.K.: Blackwell, 1989.

L'inhuman: Causeries sur le temps. Paris: Éditions Galilée, 1988. Translated by Geoffrey Bennington and Rachel Bowlby as *The Inhuman: Reflections on Time* (Stanford, CA: Stanford University Press, 1991).

Leçons sur l'analytique du sublime. Paris: Galilée, 1991. Translated by Elizabeth Rottenberg as *Lessons on the Analytic of the Sublime* (Stanford, CA: Stanford University Press, 1994).

WORKS ABOUT LYOTARD

Bennington, Geoffrey. *Lyotard: Writing the Event*. New York: Columbia University Press, 1988.

Readings, Bill. *Introducing Lyotard: Art and Politics*. London: Routledge, 1991.

Williams, James. *Lyotard and the Political*. London: Routledge, 2000.

Karin Fry (2005)

MACH, ERNST

(1838–1916)

Mach, Ernst, Austrian physicist and philosopher, was born at Turas near Brno, Moravia (now in the Czech Republic). As with many great figures, a profound psychological experience in youth had lasting effect. Mach describes it in *The Analysis of Sensations*:

> I have always felt it as a stroke of special good fortune that early in life, at about the age of fifteen, I lighted, in the library of my father, on a copy of Kant's *Prolegomena to Any Future Metaphysics*. The book made at the time a powerful and ineffaceable impression upon me, the like of which I never afterwards experienced in any of my philosophical reading. Some two or three years later the superfluity of the role played by "the thing in itself" abruptly dawned on me. On a bright summer day in the open air, the world with my ego suddenly appeared to me as *one* coherent mass of sensations, only more strongly coherent in the ego. Although the actual working out of this thought did not occur until a later period, yet this moment was decisive for my whole view.

Examination of Mach's life and work confirms this statement. Fired by the stimulus, he studied in Vienna and became professor of mathematics at Graz in 1864. In 1867 he took a chair of physics at Prague and in 1895 became professor of the history and theory of inductive science at Vienna. In 1901, he was appointed to the upper house of the Austrian parliament. His interests were extraordinarily wide: In physics he made contributions to acoustics, electricity, hydrodynamics, mechanics, optics, and thermodynamics, and in psychology to perception and aesthetics. William James, who met Mach in 1882, reported that he appeared to have read and thought about everything. At the start of the twentieth century, he and Henri Poincaré were the two outstanding popularizers of science in the world. Lenin's main philosophical work is an onslaught on Machian thought, which was highly regarded by Russian socialists who opposed Lenin. Albert Einstein's 1916 obituary of Mach includes this comment: "His direct joy in seeing and comprehending, Spinoza's amor dei intellectualis, was so overwhelming that in high old age he still stared at the world with the inquisitive eyes of a child in order to take simple delight in understanding the connection of things." On another occasion, Einstein (1949) praised Mach's "incorruptible skepticism."

MACH'S INFLUENCE

Mach gave his name to three things in science. A crude but revealing measure of his enduring significance is given by the number of Internet entries listed by Google, at the time of writing, for each of them: the Mach number (41,400), Mach's principle (2,820), and Mach bands (1,580). For comparison, the uncertainty principle of Heisenberg has 56,500 entries. Under Ernst Mach, one finds 92,100 entries. David Hume has 249,000, and Einstein 1,070,000.

Mach has been described as a superb experimentalist but unusual theorist. The Mach number is named after him because he was the discoverer of shock waves, which he observed directly in a brilliant early use of flash photography. He explained the sonic bang first heard in the Franco-Prussian war of 1870. For this outstanding work he was twice nominated for the Noble Prize near the end of his life. However, this was at a time when discoveries were flooding in, and he never received the prize he undoubtedly deserved. For his many other experimental researches—including the discovery of Mach bands in psychology—the reader is referred to Blackmore's biography cited at the end of this entry. This article is about his influence on philosophy of science and, more significantly, natural philosophy in the great tradition of the seventeenth century.

Mach's vivid holistic experience in youth became the unifying core of his *The Science of Mechanics: A Critical and Historical Account of Its Development*. Published in 1883 and widely read ever since, it argues fiercely for the primacy of empirical facts and the need to understand the contingent historical nature of progress in science. Mach was strongly antimetaphysical and questioned the foundations of all knowledge. Physical concepts are not immutable and should always be based on universally observed connections within phenomena. Newton had given a circular definition of mass; Mach replaced it with an operational definition based on the observed accelerations that interacting bodies impart to each other. Einstein recognized the key importance of Mach's approach in his own celebrated operational definition of simultaneity in the special theory of relativity in 1905.

Perhaps even more important than this influence was Mach's intense distrust of the invisible rigid structure of absolute space and time that Newton had introduced in his *Principia* in 1687 in order to formulate his first law motion. Now known as the law of inertia, it states that every body continues in a state of rest or uniform motion in a straight line unless acted upon by external forces. Absolute space was widely attacked as a dubious concept in Newton's time, above all by Gottfried Wilhelm Leibniz and George Berkeley. However, Mach was the first person to offer a plausible alternative to the framework that Newton had introduced on the basis of rather strong empirical evidence. Mach argued that the locally observable inertial motion of force-free bodies could in reality be "guided" by the integrated physical effect of the totality of matter in the universe rather than by absolute space. Einstein dubbed this idea *Mach's principle*. It was undoubtedly the greatest single stimulus that led to the creation of his general theory of relativity in 1915. Ironically, the actual status of Mach's principle within general relativity is still controversial, although the present writer believes that the theory is almost perfectly Machian when correctly understood.

Mach also had an influence, though far less decisive, on the discovery of quantum mechanics. By the early 1920s, many physicists had come to despair of ever finding a description of atomic phenomena within the traditional framework of space and time. Strongly influenced by Mach's contention that science should solely concern itself with connections between directly observable phenomena, and impressed by Einstein's "Machian" successes, the youthful Werner Heisenberg embarked on a radical approach. The single-sentence abstract of his 1925 paper in which he created quantum mechanics in a matrix representation reveals the depth of Mach's influence: "This paper," Heisenberg wrote, "attempts to create foundations for a quantum-theoretical mechanics that is based exclusively on connections between quantities that are in principle observable." (Heisenberg 1925, p. 879) Mach also had an influence on the formulation of the so-called Copenhagen interpretation of quantum mechanics by Heisenberg and Niels Bohr in 1926 and 1927. In a decidedly Machian manner, they argued that it was the job of science to establish correlations between phenomena and not to attempt a direct description of "reality."

MACH IN THE TWENTIETH CENTURY

Although Mach's ideas manifestly played a strongly positive role in the great discoveries of twentieth-century physics, his actual philosophy of science has had a mixed and generally negative reception. There is no doubt that he underestimated the value of pure theoretical speculation in scientific discoveries, especially in physics. There are many important discoveries that clearly could never have been made had theoreticians stuck rigidly to Mach's precept that the role of science is solely to establish directly the immediate connection of phenomena. They include general relativity, Erwin Schrödinger's wave-mechanical formulation of quantum mechanics, and the modern theory of gauge interactions. Many working scientists now accept Karl Raimund Popper's contention that in physics at least significant progress is often made through a bold conjecture that can in no way be justified by direct experience. Instead, the theoretician relies on intuition and accumulated experience to create a conceptual framework from which conclusions are drawn deductively and then tested against observation. In this approach, which is alien to Mach's philosophy, theories are always tentative and liable to empirical refutation.

The weakness of Mach's approach can probably be attributed to two main factors. First, his youthful epiphany made him an idealist rather like Berkeley. The extent to which Mach claimed ontological primacy for direct sense perceptions comes out startlingly in the opening chapter of The Analysis of Sensations. The difficulty with such an approach, which does have intellectual coherence, is that it has hitherto proved impossible to go beyond purely qualitative statements. The interconnection of directly experienced phenomena is notoriously difficult to grasp, as is the nature of the phenomena themselves. The second factor is the age in which Mach lived and worked. Theories based on invisible mechanically operating microscopic constituents of matter and substances such as phlogiston and caloric had indeed had a dismal track record more or less up to Mach's time. However, Newton had already given striking examples of rigorous, mathematically based use of hypotheses and deduction, and in Mach's time theoreticians had considerably refined in their art. The twentieth century saw their skill increase still further with spectacular effect. In contrast, it is characteristic that Mach's desire to "see connections" led him to make the famous flash photographs of shock waves for which he so nearly won the Nobel Prize. This was the greatest direct triumph of his approach to science.

The article by Peter Alexander in the previous edition of this encyclopedia, with twice the length of this entry, goes into much more detail about the various aspects of Mach's philosophy of science. The present writer therefore felt it would be useful to concentrate on Mach's great influence in natural philosophy. Within the narrower confines of philosophy of science, Mach was described by Philipp Frank in his Modern Science and Its Philosophy as one of the "spiritual ancestors ... and real master of the Vienna Circle." The Vienna Circle was influential. Mach was also an important inspiration for the operationalism of Percy W. Bridgman.

See also Berkeley, George; Bohr, Niels; Bridgman, Percy William; Einstein, Albert; Energy; Force; Heisenberg, Werner; Hume, David; James, William; Laws, Scientific; Leibniz, Gottfried Wilhelm; Lenin, Vladimir Il'ich; Logical Positivism; Mass; Motion; Newton, Isaac; Phenomenology; Poincaré, Jules Henri; Popper, Karl Raimund; Quantum Mechanics; Relativity Theory; Schrödinger, Erwin; Sensationalism; Space; Spinoza, Benedict (Baruch) de.

Bibliography

WORKS BY MACH

Mach wrote numerous books, and it is a mark of his impact that several are still in print in English translations. Lack of space precludes a detailed bibliography, which can be found at the end of the article by Peter Alexander. Mach's best known work is *Die Mechanik in ihrer Entwicklung historisch-kritisch dargestellt* (1883), translated as *The Science of Mechanics* by T. J. McCormack (LaSalle, IL: Open Court, 1960). Among his more physical writings, one can certainly recommend his *Die Geschichte und die Wurzel des Satzes von der Erhaltung der Energie* (1872), translated by P. E. B. Jourdain as *History and Root of the Principle of the Conservation of Energy* (Chicago: Open Court, 1911) and the *Populärwissenschaftliche Vorlesungen*, translated by T. J. McCormack as *Popular Scientific Lectures* (Chicago: Open Court, 1894), which includes a beautiful account of his work on shock waves. Also interesting but of uneven standards are his *Space and Geometry* (Chicago: Open Court, 1894) and *Die Prinzipien der Wärmelehre*, the last of Mach's major books to be translated (*Principles of the Theory of Heat*. Dordrecht, Netherlands: D. Reidel, 1986). His most important book laying out his philosophy is undoubtedly *Die Analyse der Empfindungen* (1906) (*The Analysis of Sensations*, available from Dover Publications, 1959) and there is also *Erkenntnis und Irrtum* (1905) (*Knowledge and Error*. Dordrecht, Netherlands: D. Reidel, 1976). There is a valuable exhaustive list of Mach's scientific papers and books (and much secondary literature in German) in Joachim Thiele's "Ernst Mach-Bibliographie" published in *Centaurus* 8 (1963): 189–237.

WORKS ON MACH

Einstein's obituary of Mach appeared in the *Physikalische Zeitschrift*, Volume 17, No. 7, pp. 101–104, 1919. His comment about Mach's incorruptible skepticism appears in his "Autobiographical Notes" in *Albert Einstein: Philosopher-Scientist*, edited by P. Schilpp, New York: Harper and Row (1949), p. 1. Heisenberg's article that created the matrix formulation of quantum mechanics is: "Über quantentheoretische Umdeuting kinematischer und mechanischer Beziehungen," *Zeitschrift für Physik*, Vol. 33, No. 12, 879 (1925). Philipp Frank made his comment about Mach and the Vienna Circle in his book *Modern Science and Its Philosophy*, Harvard: Harvard University Press, 1950. The English-language secondary literature is extensive. Blackmore's biography *Ernst Mach: His Life, Work, and Influence* (Berkeley and Los Angeles: University of California Press, 1972) is a mine of information but uneven in the discussion of his philosophy. Alexander's article is another useful guide to earlier literature, but in this modern age the scholar who really wishes to make an in-depth study of the literature is probably best advised to trawl the Internet. In 1988, the Charles University in Prague organized an excellent conference to mark the 150th anniversary of Mach's birth. The conference papers *Ernst Mach and the Development of Physics* (Prague: Karolinum, 1991) are a useful compendium but probably difficult to obtain. A special conference *Mach's Principle: From Newton's Bucket to Quantum Gravity* was held at Tübingen, Germany in 1993. The proceedings, edited by Julian Barbour and Herbert Pfister, were published in 1995 by Birkhäuser (Boston) and include the present writer's article arguing that general relativity is Machian and includes much other material by physicists, historians, and philosophers.

Julian Barbour (2005)

MACHIAVELLI, NICCOLÒ
(1469–1527)

Niccolò Machiavelli, the Italian politician and political thinker, is famous for his treatise on princeship titled *The Prince* (*Il principe*) and for a discussion of how to establish a good republican government, *The Discourses* (*Discorsi sopra la prima deca di Tito Livio*). Machiavelli also wrote poems and comedies (including the *Mandragola*), a *History of Florence,* and a book titled *Art of War.* They contain many original ideas and were widely read, but today these writings arouse interest mainly because their author was the man who, with *The Prince* and *The Discourses,* inaugurated a new stage in the development of political thought.

When Machiavelli wrote *The Prince* and *The Discourses,* he was aware that he was saying things about politics that had not been expressed before; in the introduction to *The Discourses* he stated that he was resolved "to open a new route which has not yet been followed by anyone." Nevertheless, Machiavelli would not have claimed to be a systematic political philosopher. *The Prince* was written in 1512–1513; the date of *The Discourses* is less certain, but it was certainly completed by 1517. Machiavelli was then in his forties and, in the preceding years of his life, he had been a practical politician who had never shown interest in becoming a political writer or in embarking on a literary career.

In 1498, after the expulsion of the Medici from Florence and the fall of Girolamo Savonarola, Machiavelli had entered the Florentine chancellery, where his special function was to serve as the secretary of The Ten, a group of magistrates charged with the conduct of diplomatic negotiations and the supervision of military operations in wartime. In this position Machiavelli carried out a number of diplomatic missions in Italy, France, and Germany. His ability attracted the attention of Gonfalonier Piero Soderini, the official head of the Florentine government, and Machiavelli became Soderini's confidant—his "lackey," according to Soderini's enemies. Machiavelli's close relationship with Soderini became a serious handicap when, in 1512, the republican regime was overthrown and the Medici returned to Florence. Other members of the chancellery were permitted to continue in office, but Machiavelli was dismissed and forced to withdraw to a small estate near Florence, where he lived in straitened economic circumstances.

It was at this time that Machiavelli turned to literary work in the hope that through his writings he would gain the favor of influential men who might help him to regain a position in the Florentine government. *The Prince* was dedicated to Lorenzo de' Medici, a nephew of Pope Leo X and the actual ruler of Florence. *The Discourses* was dedicated to members of the Florentine ruling group, and his *History of Florence* was written at the suggestion of Cardinal Giulio de' Medici, who in 1523 became Pope Clement VII. In the 1520s Machiavelli's efforts began to bear fruit. Clement VII entrusted him with a number of minor political commissions, and Machiavelli devoted himself to this kind of work, relegating the completion of his literary projects to the background. However, in 1527, before Machiavelli had been firmly reestablished in a political position—actually, at a moment when his future had again become uncertain because the Medici had once more been driven from Florence—he died.

Thus, Machiavelli's attitude in composing *The Prince* and *The Discourses* was not that of a disinterested scholar; his aims were practical and personal. He wanted to give advice that would prove his political usefulness, and he wanted to impress those who read his treatises. Therefore, Machiavelli was inclined to make numerous startling statements and extreme formulations. A characteristic example is his saying that the prince "must abstain from taking the property of others, for men forget more easily the death of their father than the loss of their patrimony" (*The Prince,* Ch. 17).

ARTS OF WAR

Machiavelli's statements were startling not only because of their form of presentation but also because of their content. One aspect of political affairs with which Machiavelli had been particularly concerned and in which he was especially interested was the conduct of military affairs. He thought deeply about the reasons why the French had so easily triumphed over the Italians in 1494 and had marched from the north to the south of Italy without meeting serious resistance. Machiavelli's explanation was that the governments of the various Italian states, whether they were republican regimes or principalities, had used mercenary soldiers led by hired *condottieri*. He therefore recommended that in case of war the prince should lead his troops himself and that his army should be composed of his own men; that is, the Italian governments should introduce conscription. Moreover, Machiavelli polemicized against other favorite notions of his time on military affairs; for instance, he denied that artillery was decisive in battle or that fortresses could offer a strong defense against an invading army.

MORALS AND POLITICS

Machiavelli's rejection of traditional political ideas emerged most clearly in his discussions of the relation between morals and politics. The most revolutionary statements on these issues are found in chapters 15–19 of *The Prince*, which deal with the qualities a prince ought to possess. In the Mirror of Princes literature of the ancient world and of the Middle Ages, a prince was supposed to be the embodiment of human virtues; he was expected to be just, magnanimous, merciful, and faithful to his obligations, and to do everything that might make him loved by his subjects. Machiavelli objected to such demands. According to him, a prince "must not mind incurring the scandal of those vices without which it would be difficult to save the state, and if one considers well, it will be found that some things which seem virtues would, if followed, lead to one's ruin and that some others which appear vices result in one's greater security and well-being." This sentence and chapters 15–19 have frequently been understood as meaning that instead of being mild a prince ought to be cruel; instead of being loyal, treacherous; instead of aiming to be loved, he should aim to be feared. But this is a misunderstanding. A closer reading shows that Machiavelli admonishes a prince to disregard the question whether his actions would be called virtuous or vicious. A ruler ought to do whatever is appropriate to the situation in which he finds himself and may lead most quickly and efficiently to success. Sometimes cruelty, sometimes leniency, sometimes loyalty, sometimes villainy might be the right course. The choice depends on circumstances. To illustrate his point of view Machiavelli used as an example the career of Cesare Borgia, which he outlined in chapter 7 of *The Prince*.

Machiavelli's views have frequently been interpreted as meaning that wickedness is more effective than goodness. This distortion of his views has been regarded as the essence of Machiavelli's teaching, as identical with what later centuries called Machiavellism. It should be stated that Machiavelli was not concerned with good or evil; he was concerned only with political efficiency. His rejection of the *communis opinio*—whether in the special area of military affairs or in the general field of ethics—was a reflection of a new and comprehensive vision of politics. Before Machiavelli, the prevailing view had been that the task of government was distribution and maintenance of justice. Machiavelli believed that the law of life under which every political organization existed was growth and expansion. Thus, force was an integral, and a most essential, element in politics.

Machiavelli's interest in military affairs had its basis in his conviction that possession of a powerful and disciplined military force was a requisite for the preservation of political independence. Moreover, because political life was a struggle, the conduct of life according to Christian virtues could endanger political effectiveness; Christianity, by preaching meekness and selflessness, might soften men and weaken a political society. Machiavelli directed some very strong passages against the effeminacy to which Christianity had led. Political man needed not virtues but *virtù*, "vitality." The possession of *virtù* was the quality most necessary for a political leader, but according to Machiavelli both individuals and entire social bodies could and should possess *virtù*. That is why, in *The Prince*, Machiavelli could write a "handbook for tyrants," while in *The Discourses* he could advocate a free republican regime. Every well-organized, effective political organization must be permeated by one and the same spirit and must form an organic unit. There are few if any passages in Machiavelli in which he uses the word *state* (*stato*) in the modern sense of an organic unit embracing individuals and institutions. However, there can be no doubt that his concept of an organized society producing *virtù* among its members comes very close to the modern concept of state.

METHOD OF ARGUMENT

The new vision of the character of politics required a new method of political argumentation. Rules for the conduct of politics could not be formulated on the basis of theoretical or philosophical assumptions about the nature of a good society; successful political behavior could be learned only through experience. Machiavelli stated in his dedication of *The Prince* that he wanted to tell others what he had "acquired through a long experience of modern events and a constant study of the past." Thus, experience was not limited to those events in which a person participated but embraced the entire field of history. To Machiavelli the most instructive period of the past was that of republican Rome. Machiavelli thought that, because the Romans succeeded in extending their power over the entire world, no better guide for the conduct of policy could be imagined than that of Roman history. It is indeed true that previous writers on politics, particularly the humanists, had used historical examples, but to rely exclusively on historical experience in establishing political laws was an innovation; Machiavelli's writings implied that every true political science ought to be based on history.

It has been said that, in rejecting the validity of the doctrines of theology and moral philosophy for the conduct of politics, Machiavelli established politics as an autonomous field. He could do so because he regarded political bodies not as creations of human reason but as natural phenomena. In Machiavelli's opinion all political organizations, like animals, plants, and human beings, are subject to the laws of nature. They are born, they grow to maturity, they become old, and they die. Well-organized political bodies might live longer than others, but even the best-constructed political society, even Rome, could not escape decline and death. This view of the instability and impermanence of all things gives Machiavelli's recommendations their particular tenor. Men or political bodies are entitled to use all possible means and weapons because the moments when they can flourish and triumph are brief and fleeting. Despite Machiavelli's claim that political success depended on acting according to the political laws he established in his writings, he was always conscious of the role of accident and fortune in human affairs.

INFLUENCE

It is of some importance to distinguish between the shocking novelty of Machiavelli's particular recommendations and his general concepts of politics, from which his practical counsels arose. Such a distinction helps to explain the contradictory reception his ideas found in the following centuries. Machiavelli's writings soon became known in Italy and then in other European countries, particularly France and England, although in 1559 his works were placed on the Index. Generally he was considered an adviser of cruel tyrants, an advocate of evil; Cardinal Reginald Pole said that Machiavelli wrote "with the finger of the Devil." Although nobody in the sixteenth century dared publicly to express anything but abhorrence, a school of political writers arose in Italy who explained that the criteria of a statesman's or ruler's actions were the interests of the state. These advocates of the doctrine of "reason of state"—even if they did not acknowledge their obligations to Machiavelli—followed the course Machiavelli had charted. The Enlightenment, with its belief in the harmony of morality and progress, could only condemn Machiavelli's view that political necessity permitted the neglect of ethical norms. An example is the *Anti-Machiavel* that Frederick II of Prussia composed as a young man. Some eighteenth-century thinkers, however, recognized truth in Machiavelli's approach to politics. For instance, Gabriel Bonnot de Mably and Jean-Jacques Rousseau admired Machiavelli because he had realized that the strength of a political organization depends on the existence of a collective spirit that is more than a summation of individual wills.

In the nineteenth century, students of Machiavelli, following the interpretation that the German historian Leopold von Ranke had given, did not believe that Machiavelli had wanted to separate ethics and politics. Because the last chapter of *The Prince* contains an appeal for the liberation of Italy from the barbarians, they assumed that Machiavelli had permitted the violation of moral rules only for the purpose of a higher ethical goal; that his purpose had been to point the way toward the foundation of a unified Italy. Thus, in the nineteenth century Machiavelli became respectable as the prophet of the idea of the national state. In the later part of the century Machiavelli was also referred to by those who wanted to free man from the oppressive shackles of traditional morality and believed that man's faculties could be fully developed only if he placed himself "beyond good and evil." Friedrich Nietzsche's superman was supposed to have "virtue in the style of the Renaissance, *virtù*, virtue free from morality."

See also Enlightenment; Nietzsche, Friedrich; Peace, War, and Philosophy; Political Philosophy, History of; Religion and Politics; Social and Political Philosophy; Rousseau, Jean-Jacques.

Bibliography

The literature on Machiavelli is very extensive. A more recent critical edition of his works is that edited by Sergio Bertelli and Franco Gaeta and published by Feltrinelli in its Biblioteca di classici italiani. So far four volumes containing Machiavelli's literary works and three volumes containing his *Legazioni e commissarie* have appeared (1960–1964). This edition provides a critical discussion of the Machiavelli literature. The best recent translation is Allan Gilbert, *Chief*

Works, and Others, 3 vols. (Durham, NC: Duke University Press, 1965).

Older biographies have become obsolete since the appearance of Roberto Ridolfi's *Vita di Niccolò Machiavelli* (Rome, 1954), translated by Cecil Grayson as *The Life of Niccolò Machiavelli* (Chicago: University of Chicago Press, 1963). Machiavelli's intellectual development is well analyzed by Gennaro Sasso in his *Niccolò Machiavelli: Storia del suo pensiero politico* (Naples: Nella sede dell'Istituto, 1958). For the relation of Machiavelli's thought to that of his contemporaries, see Felix Gilbert, *Machiavelli and Guicciardini* (Princeton, NJ: Princeton University Press, 1965). The main lines of the influence of Machiavelli's ideas on the political thought of later centuries are traced in Friedrich Meinecke, *Die Idee der Staatsräson in der neueren Geschichte* (Berlin: R. Oldenbourg, 1924), translated by Douglas Scott as *Machiavellism* (New Haven, CT: Yale University Press, 1957). For Machiavelli's impact on English political thought, see Felix Raab, *The English Face of Machiavelli: A Changing Interpretation 1500–1700* (London: Routledge and Paul, 1964).

Felix Gilbert (1967)

MACHIAVELLI, NICCOLÒ [ADDENDUM]

Many readers come to Machiavelli with their minds made up about who he was and what he espoused. A more balanced assessment must take into account many approaches to his work and possible influences from the classical world.

EVALUATING MACHIAVELLI

In order to evaluate Machiavelli one must first decide what he was doing and second decide how to balance the assessment of the texts. The traditional assessment of Machiavelli is "expedient egoist." Under this reading one would cite passages from *The Prince* in which rulers are advised to employ deceit and cruelty for the sake of political advantage. However, it is unclear whether these passages should be taken at face value or rather as an invective set in its European historical perspective: (a) a striving to connect to the past—particularly to the Roman Empire and its eloquent Republican spokesman, Cicero; and (b) a chafing with the Papal authority over the legacy of the Roman Empire—especially the bogus "Donation of Constantine." In this forged document the Roman Emperor Constantine supposedly granted the whole of the Roman Empire to the pope who, in turn, allowed the daily duties of running the secular to fall upon the emperor. This document sought to establish a legal claim for the pope's universal secular power. It could

be that Machiavelli, in the first case, was interested in espousing the republican message of Cicero. It could also be, in the second case that Machiavelli was consciously breaking away from established forms of exposition in order to create another mode of political discourse.

In recent scholarship (over the second half of the twentieth century) Ernst Cassirer (1946) believed that Machiavelli espoused a clear and coherent argument based upon a vision that moved the modern world forward in a realistic fashion. Isaiah Berlin (1972 [1953]\) followed in asserting that Machiavelli put forth a cogent secular vision that was consistent. Leo Strauss (1958) agreed that the vision was consistent, but said that both from the points of view in *The Prince* and of *The Discourses on Livy* that Machiavelli was a teacher of evil (namely, an expedient egoist).

Certainly, the worldviews presented in *The Prince* and *The Discourses on Livy* appear both different and the same. They are *different* in that in the former case there seem to be many aphorisms that violate ethical laws whereas in the latter it seems that Machiavelli is concerned to uphold public morality—such as eliminating public corruption for the sake of the republic. One might reasonably ask whether the same person wrote both works.

However, they are *similar* in that they are both pragmatically oriented toward solving problems. Thus, we are faced with one interpretative option of which work should be seen as representing the author's "true vision"? Because of the caveats mentioned above, (a) and (b), some of the so-called "Cambridge School" (Pocock, Skinner, and Viroli) have accentuated the emphasis upon the rule of law, common good, and general republicanism as seen from the *Discourses* as evidence that Machiavelli was really a forward-thinking republican thinker.

If [this]\ reading of Machiavelli is correct, then he is a thinker who is not an advocate of expedient egoism, but rather is a thinker who saw various dead ends in the way political philosophy was being explored. To start anew he tries to jettison the views of the reigning paradigm and start afresh. This is an interesting interpretation, but it has one possible flaw: Machiavelli does not spend time on theoretical foundations. Any theory asserted to be present there must be read into the text. And so what theory might support his pragmatic observations?

Two candidates are Aristotle and Cicero. At this period of history, Aristotle's *Politics* and *Ethics* had recently been translated into Latin. Cicero had been the established authority (because of his association with

Rome and because of the rhetorical structure of the *Discourses*) and so most commentators seem to think that he is the dominant influence. Another argument along this line is that Aristotle thought that civic virtue derived from man fulfilling his nature in the context of society (so that politics flows from ethics). Machiavelli does not employ such an explanatory framework. Can his texts be read from this perspective? Perhaps, but it may be a stretch because the practicality of Machiavelli works against Aristotle's essentialism.

The candidate left standing is Cicero. If this is the case, then Cicero's presence best describes the Muse of Machiavelli. The structure of the *Discourses* seems to suggest this as it follows the classical rhetorical form: (for example, observe the titles of the first three chapters: (1) What Have been Universally the Beginnings of Any City Whatever, and What was That of Rome; (2) Of How Many Species Are Republics, and Which Was the Roman Republic; (3) What Accidents Made the Tribunes of the Plebs Be Created in Rome, Which Made the Republic More Perfect).

However, once this is accepted, then other results may follow. The postmodernists assert that literary constructions can substitute for a traditional exposition of the pursuit of a universal Truth (as per Aristotle). Instead, the use of Ciceronian rhetoric might resonate with the etymology of "rhetoric" à la speaking in public or engaging in discourse with others. If this understanding is correct, then the philosophy of discourse and *construction from discourse* as per Foucault, Ricoeur, Derrida, or Habermas might be more apropos than the use of rhetoric as a means of transmitting already settled truths.

Such an interpretation may have many advantages. First, it might resolve the contradictions between the various texts of Machiavelli. This is because contradictions are only a problem if one is creating a systematic work of philosophy, such as was aspired to by Aristotle or Thomas. Second, it might blunt the traditional "bad boy" image of Machiavelli by bringing him into the realm of merely revealing various approaches to the questions of what policies might be necessary for running a state. By bringing out various options and interacting with them, Machiavelli might be eschewing the conventional method of discourse (even though he employs traditional forms) in favor of creating a new realpolitik.

This reinvigorated conception would find its sources in the way politics are actually practiced. So, for example, *The Prince* might be seen not as a way things *ought to be*, but a description of the way things *are*. If we are to go anywhere, here is the starting point. Let us all accept this.

And in the *Discourses* if Rome is a model of a civilization that worked well for a long time, then the focus should be upon what can be done to correct the flaws that brought it down. Under this sort of reading, the exploration of politics is not about creating treatises on political theory, but instead of initiating a dialogue among readers about the "deal points" in running a state. The completion of the text lies in the audience.

See also Aristotle; Berlin, Isaiah; Cassirer, Ernst; Cicero, Marcus Tullius; Derrida, Jacques; Foucault, Michel; Habermas, Jürgen; Political Philosophy, History of; Ricoeur, Paul; Social and Political Philosophy; Thomas Aquinas, St.

Bibliography

Bertman, Martin. "Justice with Particular Reference to Hobbes." *Kriterion* 42 (103) (2001): 58–70.

Blattberg, Charles. *From Pluralist to Patriotic Politics: Putting Practice First*. New York: Oxford University Press, 2000.

Cassirer, Ernst. *The Myth of the State*. New Haven, CT: Yale University Press, 1946.

Matthes, Melissa M. *The Rape of Lucratia and the Founding of Republics: Readings in Livy, Machiavelli, and Rousseau*. University Park: Pennsylvania State University Press, 2000.

WORKS BY MACHIAVELLI

Opere Complete, edited by S. Bertelli and F. Gaeta. Milan: Feltrinelli, 1960–1965.

The Prince. Translated by Harvey C. Mansfield, Jr. Chicago: University of Chicago Press, 1985.

Florentine Histories. Translated by Laura F. Banfield and Harvey C. Mansfield, Jr. Princeton, NJ: Princeton University Press, 1988.

Machiavelli: The Chief Works and Others, edited and translated by A. Gilbert. Durham, NC: Duke University Press, 1989.

Tutte. Le Opere. Edited by Mario Martelli. Florence: Sansoni, 1992.

Discourses on Livy. Translated by Harvey C. Mansfield, Jr. and Nathan Tarcov. Chicago: University of Chicago Press, 1996.

WORKS ON MACHIAVELLI

Ascoli, Albert Russell, and Victoria Kahn. "Introduction." In *Machiavelli and the Discourse of Literature*, edited by Albert Russell Ascoli and Victoria Kahn, 1–15. Ithaca, NY: Cornell University Press, 1993.

Berlin, Isaiah. "The Originality of Machiavelli." 1953. In *Studies on Machiavelli*, edited by Myron P. Gilmore. Florence: Sansoni, 1972.

Falco, Maria J., ed. *Feminist Interpretations of Niccolo Machiavelli*. University Park: Pennsylvania State University Press, 2004.

Femia, Joseph. "Machiavelli and Italian Fascism." *History of Political Thought* 25 (1) (2004): 1–15.

Femia, Joseph. *Machiavelli Revisited*. Cardiff: University of Wales Press, 2004.

Fiore, Silvia Ruffo. *Niccolo Machiavelli: An Annotated Bibliography of Modern Criticism and Scholarship.* New York: Greenwood Press, 1990.

Fischer, Markus. *Well-Ordered License: On the Unity of Machiavelli's Thought.* Lanham, MD: Lexington Books, 2000.

Flyvbjerg, Bent. *Making Social Science Matter: Why Social Inquiry Fails and How It Can Succeed Again.* Translated by Steven Sampson. Cambridge, U.K.: Cambridge University Press, 2001.

Gilbert, Felix. *Machiavelli and Guicciardini: Politics and History in Sixteenth-Century Florence.* New York: Norton, 1984.

Gilbert, Felix. "On Machiavelli's Idea of *virtù.*" *Renaissance News* 4 (1951): 53–56.

Griffiths, Paul E. "Basic Emotions, Complex Emotions, Machiavellian Emotions." *Philosophy* 52 (2003): 39–67.

Hulliung, Mark. *Citizen Machiavelli.* Princeton, NJ: Princeton University Press, 1983.

Kahn, Victoria. "Habermas, Machiavelli, and the Humanist Critique of Ideology." *PMLA* 105 (1990): 464–476.

Kahn, Victoria. *Machiavellian Rhetoric: From the Counter-Reformation to Milton.* Princeton, NJ: Princeton University Press, 1994.

Knoll, Manuel. "Die Konservative Verantwortungsethik des Humanisten Niccolo Machiavelli." *Politisches Denken* (2003): 94–116.

Lang, Andre. "La Dialectique de la Fortune et de la Virtu chez Machiavel." *Diotima: Review of Philosophical Research.* 31 (2003): 179–188.

McCormick, John P. "Machiavelli against Republicanism: On the Cambridge School's 'Guicciardian Moments.'" *Political Theory* 31 (5) (2003): 615–643.

Montgomery-Blair, Brook. "Post-Metaphysical and Radical Humanist Thought in the Writings of Machiavelli and Nietzsche." *History of European Ideas* 27 (3) (2001): 199–238.

Nederman, Cary J. "Machiavelli and Moral Character: Principality, Republic and the Psychology of 'Virtu.'" *History of Political Thought* 21 (3) (2000): 349–364.

Pocock, J. G. A. *The Machiavellian Moment: Florentine Political Thought and the Antlantic Republican Tradition.* Princeton, NJ: Princeton University Press, 1975.

Skinner, Quentin. *Machiavelli.* New York: Hill and Wang, 1981.

Skinner, Quentin. "The Republican Ideal of Political Liberty." In *Machiavelli and Republicanism,* edited by Gisela Bock, Quentin Skinner, and Maurizio Viroli, 293–309. Cambridge, U.K.: Cambridge University Press, 1990.

Spackman, Barbara. "Politics on the Warpath: Machiavelli's *Art of War.*" In *Machiavelli and the Discourse of Literature,* edited by Albert Russell Ascoli and Victoria Kahn, 179–194. Ithaca, NY: Cornell University Press, 1993.

Strauss, Leo. *Thoughts on Machiavelli.* Chicago: University of Chicago Press, 1958.

Tarlton, Charles. "'Azioni in modo l'una dall'altra': Action for Action's Sake in Machiavelli's The Prince." *History of European Ideas* 29 (2) (2003): 123–140.

Vatter, Miguel E. *Between Form and Event: Machiavelli's Theory of Political Freedom.* Dordrecht, Netherlands: Kluwer, 2000.

Viroli, Maurizio. *Machiavelli.* Oxford: Oxford University Press, 1998.

Michael Boylan (2005)

MACHINE INTELLIGENCE

Computers beat the best human chess players. Computers guide spacecraft over vast distances and direct robotic devices to explore faraway astronomical bodies. Computers outpace humans in many respects, but are they actually intelligent? Can they think? Even if one is skeptical about the mentality of today's computers, the interesting philosophical issue remains: Might computers possess significant intelligence someday? Indeed, might computers feel or even have consciousness? And, how would we know?

THE HISTORICAL DEBATE

These issues of machine intelligence are not new to philosophy. The debate about whether a machine might think has its philosophical roots in the seventeenth and eighteenth century with the development of modern science. If the universe is fundamentally materialistic and mechanistic, as the emerging scientific paradigm suggested, it would follow that humans are nothing more than machines. Possibly, other machines might be constructed that would be capable of thought as well. Thomas Hobbes (1588–1679), who advocated a materialistic, mechanistic view, argued that reasoning is reckoning and nothing more. Humans reason by calculation with signs involving addition, subtraction, and other mathematical operations. Hobbes took these signs to be material objects that have significance as linguistic symbols. Julien La Mettrie (1709–1751), another materialist and mechanist, speculated that it might be possible to teach a language to apes and to build a mechanical man that could talk.

Not every philosopher of that era agreed with such radical predictions. René Descartes (1596–1650) held that animals are, indeed, complex machines but as such, necessarily lack thought and feeling. People have bodies that are in themselves nothing but complex machines, but people also have minds, nonmaterial entities that are in time but not space, that interact with their bodies. On this dualistic conception, intelligence and consciousness of people exist only as part of their minds, not as part of their bodies. Constructing a nonhuman machine that by itself had intelligence or consciousness was an impossibility for Descartes. Descartes admitted that a machine could be built that might give an impression of possessing intelligence, but it would be only a simulation of real intelligence and could be unmasked as a thoughtless machine. In fact, Descartes offered two certain tests by which a machine can be distinguished from a rational human being even if the machine resembled a human in appearance. First, although a machine may utter words, a machine will never reply appropriately to everything said in its presence in the way that a human can. Second, although a machine may perform certain actions as well as or even better than a human, a machine will not have the diversity of actions that a human has.

THE CONCEPTION OF COMPUTING MACHINES

The contemporary debate about the possibility of machine intelligence ignited with the advent of modern electronic computers that are accurate, reliable, fast, programmable, and complex. Nobody did more in the twentieth century to construct a coherent concept of computing and to generate the contemporary debate about the intellectual possibilities of computers than Alan Turing (1912–1954). Turing explained computability in terms of abstract mathematical machines, now called *Turing Machines*. A Turing machine consists of a potentially infinite tape, divided into individual cells, on which a read–write head travels either left or right one cell at a time. The read–write head follows instructions that are found in a table of transition rules. The table of transition rules is the program that directs the Turing machine. Each instruction in the table specifies for a given a state of the Turing machine and a particular symbol being read on the tape, what the read–write head should do (print a symbol, erase the symbol, move right, or move left), and which state the machine should go to next.

Turing showed how such simple, elegant machines could compute ordinary arithmetic functions, and he conjectured that anything that is effectively computable could be computed by such a machine. In addition, Turing developed the concept of a universal Turing machine that can compute what any Turing machine can compute. Turing also showed the limitations of his machines by demonstrating that some functions are not computable, even by a universal Turing machine. Turing's seminal work on computable numbers and computing machines provided much of the conceptual foundation for the development of the modern computer. During World War II Turing applied some of his theoretical insights in designing special computing equipment to decipher the German Enigma codes. After World War II Turing led efforts to design some of the earliest computers, including the Automatic Computing Engine (ACE) in 1945.

The concept of computing developed by Turing provided not only a theoretical foundation for computer science but also a theoretical framework for much of artificial intelligence and cognitive science. A central paradigm of these fields is that mental processes and, in particular, cognitive processes are fundamentally computational. Processes that constitute and demonstrate human intelligence and general mentality, such as perception, understanding, learning, reasoning, decision making, and action, are to be explained in terms of computations. On the computational view, a mind is an information processing device. In its strongest form the computational theory of the mind holds that an entity has a mind *if and only if* that entity has computational processes that generate mentality.

Three important aspects of the theory of computation support the possibility of machines possessing intelligence and various aspects of minds. First, computation is understood in terms of the manipulation of symbols. Symbolic manipulation can represent information inputted, information processed, information stored, and information outputted. If human intelligence depends on the ability to represent the world and to process information, then the symbolic nature of computation offers a promising environment in which to conceive and develop intelligent machines. Much, though not all, of machine intelligence work has been conducted within this framework.

Second, if intelligence and mentality are computational in nature, then it does not matter what material conducts the computations. The computational structures and processes are multiply realizable. They might be instantiated in human brains, in computers, or even in aliens comprised of a different assortment of chemicals. All may have mentality as long as they have the appropriate computational processes. Indeed, it is possible to have mixed systems comprised of different materials. Cochlear implants and bionic eyes send information to human brains from external stimuli. Humans with these implants hear and see although part of their processing channels are inorganic.

Third, the computational model suggests an account of the connection between mind and body that other theories of the mind leave mysterious. The computational model explains intelligence and overall mental activity on the basis of decreasingly complex components. A hierarchy of computational systems is hypothesized, each of which is made up of simpler computational systems, until at bottom—as in a computer—there is nothing but elementary logical components, the operations of which can be explained and easily understood in terms of physical processes.

THE TURING TEST

For many people the phrase *machine intelligence* is an oxymoron. Machines by their nature are typically regarded as unintelligent and unthinking. How could a mere machine demonstrate actual intelligence? Turing believed that computing machines could be intelligent but was concerned that our judgments of the intelligence of such machines would be influenced by our biases and previous experiences with the limitations of machines. In his seminal article, "Computing Machinery and Intelligence" (1950), Turing considered the question "Can machines think?" but did so by replacing that question with another. The replacement question is explained in terms of a game that he calls "the imitation game." The imitation game is played by a man (A), a woman (B), and a human interrogator (C). The interrogator is in a room apart from the other two and tries to determine through conversation which of the other two is the man and which is the woman. Turing suggested that a teleprinter be used to communicate to avoid giving the interrogator clues through tones of voice. In the game the man may engage in deception in order to encourage the interrogator to misidentify him as the woman. The man may lie about his appearance and preferences. Turing believed that the woman's best strategy in the game is to tell the truth.

After he explained how the imitation game is played in terms of a man, a woman, and a human interrogator, Turing introduced his replacement question(s). Turing said, "We now ask the question, 'What will happen when a machine takes the part of A in this game?' Will the interrogator decide wrongly as often when the game is played like this as he does when the game is played between a man and a woman? These questions replace our original, 'Can machines think?'" (Turing, 1950, p. 434). Although his proposed version of the imitation game, now called the *Turing test*, may seem straightforward, many questions have been raised about how to interpret it. For example, to what extent does gender play a role in the test? Some maintain that Turing intended, or should have intended, that the computer imitate a woman just as the man did in the original imitation game. The more standard interpretation of the test is that the computer takes the part of A but that the part of B is played by a human—a man or a woman. On the standard interpretation the point of the test is to determine how well a computer can match the verbal behavior of a human, not necessarily a woman. The examples of questions for the test that Turing suggested are not gender specific but rather more general inquiries about writing sonnets, doing arithmetic, and solving chess problems.

Turing neglected to elaborate on many details of his test. How many questions can be asked? How many judges or rounds of judging are there? Who is the average interrogator asking questions? What counts precisely as passing the test? And, importantly, what conclusion should be drawn from a Turing test if it were passed? Turing moved quickly to replace the initial question "Can machines think?" with questions about playing the imitation game. He suggested that the original question "Can machines think?" is "too meaningless to deserve discussion" (Turing, 1950, p. 442). He could not have been claiming that the question is literally meaningless, or his own replacement project would not make sense. What he was suggesting is that terms like *machine* and *think* are vague terms in ordinary speech, and what people typically associate with a machine is not something that has or perhaps could have intelligence. What he was proposing with his test is a way to make the overall question of machine thinking more precise so that at least in principle, an empirical test could be conducted. Still, the issue is left open as to exactly what passing the Turing test would establish. Could it ever show that a machine is intelligent or that a machine thinks or possibly even that a machine is conscious?

A widely held misconception is that Turing proposed the test as an operational definition of thinking or considered the test to give logically necessary and sufficient conditions for machine intelligence. Critics of the test frequently point out that exhibiting intelligent behavior in this test is neither a logically necessary nor logically sufficient condition for thinking. But this common objection against the test misses the mark, for Turing never said he was giving an operational definition and never argued that the test provided a logically necessary or sufficient condition for establishing machine intelligence. Indeed, Turing argued for the opposite position. He did not take his test to be a necessary condition for intelligence, for he readily admitted that a machine might have intelligence but not imitate well. He never maintained that passing the test is logically sufficient for intelligence or thinking by a machine. On the contrary, he argued that demanding certainty in knowledge of other minds would push one into solipsism, which he rejected.

A more plausible interpretation of the Turing test is to regard it as an *inductive* test. If a machine passed a rigorous Turing test with probing questioning on many topics, perhaps by different judges over a reasonably extended period of time, then good inductive evidence for attributing intelligence or thinking to the machine might exist. Behavioral evidence is used routinely to make inductive judgments about the intelligence of other humans and animals. It would seem appropriate to use behavioral evidence to evaluate machines as well. In judging human-like intelligence linguistic behavior seems particularly salient. There would be no logical certainty in such a judgment any more than there is logical certainty in scientific testing in general, and revision of judgments in light of new evidence might be required. Regrettably, other evidence like relevant to a judgment of machine intelligence, such as evidence from non-linguistic behavior and evidence about the internal operation of the machine, cannot be directly gathered within the Turing test. Turing realized this, but thought it more important to eliminate bias so that a machine would not be excluded as intelligent simply because the person making the judgment knew it was a machine.

CRITICISMS OF THE TURING TEST

Turing himself considered and replied to a variety of criticisms of his test ranging from a theological objection to an extrasensory perception objection. At least two of the objections he discussed remain popular. One is the Lady Lovelace objection based on a remark by Ada Lovelace that Charles Babbage's Analytical Engine, a nineteenth-century mechanical computer, had no pretension to originate anything. A similar point is often made by claiming that computers only do what they are programmed to do. The objection is difficult to defend in detail because computers can surprise even their programmers, are affected by their input as well as their programming, and can learn. Of course, one might argue that, at bottom, computers are merely following rules and therefore are not creative. But to firmly establish this objection, one would need to show that, at bottom, humans are not merely following rules and that anything merely following rules cannot be creative.

Another objection that Turing considered is the mathematical objection that utilizes results in mathematical logic, such as Kurt Gödel's incompleteness theorem. This argument, later developed by J. R. Lucas (1961) and by Roger Penrose (1989), maintains that fundamental limits of logical systems are limits of computers but not of human minds. But, as Turing himself pointed out, it has not been established that these logical limits do not apply equally well to humans.

In addition to these classical criticisms, a number of contemporary objections to the Turing test have been advanced. Robert French (1990) has maintained that the test is virtually useless because there will always be subtle subcognitive behavior that will allow an interrogator to identify humans from machines. If true, the Turing test would be more difficult to pass and possibly not very useful, but this outcome would also enhance the potential inductive sufficiency of the Turing test if it were passed.

In another criticism of the Turing test, Ned Block (1981) has suggested that a computer program that worked as a conversation jukebox so that it gave a stored but appropriate response to every possible remark by an interrogator throughout a conversation would pass the test. Because the test occurs during a finite period and in that period only a finite, though very large, number of responses can be made, such a program seems logically possible. Whether such a program could exist in practice given the complexity of semantic relations in a conversation and the changing facts of the world is unclear, but even taken as a thought experiment, the success of the jukebox program would at most show that the Turing test does not provide a logically sufficient condition for the possession of intelligence, a position to which Turing agreed.

John Searle (1980) developed one of the most popular contemporary objections against machine intelligence: the Chinese Room Argument. Simply put, a computer program running on a digital machine is only manipulating symbols syntactically and necessarily lacks semantics. Thus, even if a machine passed a Turing test, it would not understand anything. A digital computer might simulate intelligence, but on Searle's view it would not have a mind. Some critics of this argument have suggested that humans acquire semantics through interaction with the environment, and possibly, machines equipped with sensory inputs and motor outputs could acquire semantics in this way as well. More telling, the Chinese Room Argument does not validly establish what it claims. Searle has maintained that a human brain has the causal powers to produce a mind; the Chinese Room Argument does not demonstrate that computer programs, once loaded and running on a physical machine, could not have similar causal powers.

The Turing test is a possible test for machine intelligence and one that has received enormous philosophical discussion, but it is not the only test. Normally, the intelligence of animals and other humans is tested and inferred by examining an entity's relevant behavior in various situations. Similarly, machine intelligence can be tested based on its ability to demonstrate such processes as understanding, reasoning, and learning regardless of how well it can imitate a human. Human intelligence is not the only kind of intelligence. Along these lines Patrick Hayes and Kenneth Ford (1995) have argued that too much emphasis on passing the Turing test has actually been detrimental to progress in artificial intelligence.

THE FUTURE OF MACHINE INTELLIGENCE

Turing believed that human language and understanding of machines and mentality would shift by the year 2000, and indeed, the notion of a machine being intelligent is not as outlandish as it once was. In his 1950 article (p. 442) Turing also made a very famous specific prediction that has not fared as well. He said: "I believe that in about fifty years' time it will be possible to programme computers, with a storage capacity of about 10^9, to make them play the imitation game so well that an average interrogator will not have more than 70 per cent chance of making the right identification after five minutes of questioning." No computer has come close to meeting this standard in a rigorously conducted Turing test. But it should be noted that behind Turing's prophecy was a plan that has not come to pass. He imagined that one day a computer would learn just as a child does. And like a human the computer gradually would obtain a larger and larger understanding of the world. Machine learning in specific contexts has been a reality for decades, but general learning by a machine remains an elusive goal, and without it, the intelligence of machines will be limited.

The long-term future of machine intelligence is a matter of considerable philosophical debate. Here are four visions of the future that have been suggested. On the *android vision* some intelligent machines of the future will look like humans or at least resemble humans in their intellectual capacities. Because humans are the most intelligent creatures known, human intelligence is taken as the obvious standard. Turing's own proposals employed much of this vision. From this viewpoint it is sensible to ask whether robots someday will be the intellectual peers of humans and might deserve rights as rational beings. But some critics argue that computers will never be much like humans without similar emotional needs and desires. On the *slave vision* intelligent machines of the future will give humans increasingly sophisticated assistance but, like their not-so-intelligent predecessors, they will be slaves, possibly held in check by Isaac Asimov's well-known three laws of robotics (1991). On the *successor vision* machine intelligence will become increasingly sophisticated and machines will evolve beyond humans. Hans Moravec (1999) has argued that humans will be surpassed by machines in terms of intel-

ligence within a relatively short time. Such machines might evolve and progress rapidly through a Lamarckian transmission of culture to the next generation. Finally, on the *cyborg vision*, advanced by Rodney Brooks (2002) and others, machine intelligence will increasingly be embedded in us. Machine intelligence will be used to augment our abilities and will blend into our nature. Machine intelligence will become part of our intelligence, and we will become, at least in part, intelligent machines.

See also Artificial Intelligence; Chinese Room Argument; Computationalism; Descartes, René; Gödel's Theorem; Hobbes, Thomas; Induction; La Mettrie, Julien Offray de; Solipsism; Turing, Alan M.

Bibliography

Asimov, Isaac. *Robot Visions*. New York: Penguin Books, 1991.

Block, Ned. "Psychologism and Behaviorism." *Philosophical Review* 90 (1981): 5–43.

Boden, Margaret. *The Creative Mind: Myths and Mechanisms*. London: Routledge, 2004.

Brooks, Rodney. *Flesh and Machines: How Robots Will Change Us*. New York: Pantheon, 2002.

Copeland, Jack, ed. *The Essential Turing*. New York: Oxford University Press, 2004.

Dennett, Daniel. *The Intentional Stance*. Cambridge, MA: MIT Press, 1987.

Descartes, René. *Discourse on Method*. Translated by Donald Cress. Indianapolis, IN: Hackett, 1980.

Dreyfus, Hubert, and Stuart Dreyfus. *Mind over Machine*. New York: Free Press, 1986.

French, Robert. "Subcognition and the Limits of the Turing Test." *Mind* 99 (1990): 53–65.

Gunderson, Keith. *Mentality and Machines*. 2nd ed. Minneapolis: University of Minnesota Press, 1985.

Haugeland, John. *Artificial Intelligence: The Very Idea*. Cambridge, MA: MIT Press, 1985.

Hayes, Partick, and Kenneth Ford. "Turing Test Considered Harmful." *Proceedings of the Fourteenth International Joint Conference on Artificial Intelligence* (1995): 972–977.

Hobbes, Thomas. *Leviathan: With Selected Variants from the Latin Edition of 1668*, edited by Edwin Curley. Indianapolis, IN: Hackett, 1994.

Hodges, Andrew. *Alan Turing: The Enigma*. New York: Simon and Schuster, 1983.

La Mettrie, Julien. *L'homme Machine: A Study in the Origins of an Idea*. Princeton, NJ: Princeton University Press, 1960.

Lucas, J. R. "Minds, Machines, and Gödel." *Philosophy* 36 (1961): 120–4.

Moor, James. "The Status and Future of the Turing Test." *Minds and Machines* 11 (2001) 77–93.

Moravec, Hans. *Robot: Mere Machine to Transcendent Mind*. New York: Oxford University Press, 1999.

Penrose, Roger. *The Emperor's New Mind*. Oxford: Oxford University Press, 1989.

Searle, John. "Minds, Brains, and Programs." *Behavioral and Brain Sciences* 3 (1980): 417–457.

Sterrett, Susan. "Turing's Two Tests for Intelligence." *Minds and Machines* 10 (2000): 541–559.

Turing, Alan. "Computing Machinery and Intelligence." *Mind* 59 (1950): 433–460.

James H. Moor (2005)

MACINTYRE, ALASDAIR
(1929–)

Alasdair Chalmers MacIntyre was born in Glasgow, Scotland. He was philosophically trained at Manchester University and subsequently taught at Manchester, Leeds University, Oxford University, and the University of Essex before emigrating to the United States in 1970. Since then he has held teaching posts at Brandeis University, Boston University, Vanderbilt University, Duke University, and the University of Notre Dame.

By his late teens MacIntyre became sympathetic to Marxism as a theoretical articulation of the failures of contemporary social, economic, and political institutions, resulting in the publication of his first book, *Marxism: An Interpretation*, at the age of twenty-three. While never giving up his view that modernity merits wide-ranging criticism and that such criticism must come from a rationally defensible theoretical standpoint, he came to believe that Marxism lacked the necessary resources. What is needed, MacIntyre held, is a moral and political philosophy built on an adequate theory of human nature and the human good—though this theory would have to recognize that human nature and the human good are deeply historically conditioned. What is also needed is an adequate account of how such a theory can be shown to be rationally superior to its rivals—though, again, this account would have to recognize that standards of rationality in inquiry are themselves deeply historically conditioned. MacIntyre's mature philosophy, expressed in the series of books *After Virtue* (1981), *Whose Justice? Which Rationality?* (1988), *Three Rival Versions of Moral Enquiry* (1990), and *Dependent Rational Animals* (1999), respond to these perceived needs and exhibit the most noteworthy features of his work: his account of tradition-constituted rationality, his Aristotelian ethics of virtue, and his Aristotelian politics of local community.

TRADITION-CONSTITUTED RATIONALITY

MacIntyre's view is that the most salient feature of contemporary moral and political discourse is interminable disagreement. Defenders of rival views become ever more sophisticated in the development and advocacy of their theories, but there is no progress toward resolution of these disagreements. It seems to be the aspiration of participants in these debates to offer a defense of their respective theories that is acceptable to any rational agent. MacIntyre calls this aim of providing a defense of morality acceptable to rational agents as such The Enlightenment Project, and holds that, for all the substantive differences between figures such as David Hume and Immanuel Kant, it is their common objective to provide a basis for morality that commands rational acceptance by all. After all, one might think that the alternative is an unacceptable relativism whereby different theories are justified in terms of different standards, with no way to bring rival theories truly into competition.

MacIntyre's contribution is to argue for the existence of rival and incompatible standards of rational assessment while denying that this affirmation brings with it a commitment to relativistic conclusions. We are confronted with different traditions of rational inquiry, each with its own theories and standards for assessment of theories, and each with a history within which various positions have been forwarded, defended, and to whatever extent affirmed or rejected. There is no neutral rationality-as-such by which we can decide between these various competing traditions. But relativistic conclusions do not follow, MacIntyre argues, because it is always possible that one tradition can show itself superior to a rival tradition by showing that one's tradition fares better than the rival even in that rival's own terms.

MacIntyre's positive views in ethics and politics are versions of Aristotelianism. In keeping with his conception of rationality in inquiry, his basis for affirming these views is that Aristotelianism is more defensible than rival traditions, even on those rival traditions' own terms.

THE ETHICS OF VIRTUE

MacIntyre argues in *After Virtue* that of the classical moral theories presented by Hume, Kant, Jeremy Bentham, and John Stuart Mill, neither they nor their contemporary defenders offer anything like compelling reasons to affirm these theories, nor do we have any reason to think that such reasons are forthcoming. Should we then, MacIntyre asks, follow Friedrich Nietzsche in thinking that the institution of morality is a fraud, to be jettisoned as the institution of taboo was jettisoned?

MacIntyre holds that there is an alternative to the moral theories defended in the Enlightenment and in the wake of the Enlightenment: Aristotelianism. On Aristotle's view ethics deals with the transformation of human beings from their immature condition into a condition that constitutes their true end, the realization of their specifically human potentialities, which realization occurs through the acquisition and exercise of various moral and intellectual virtues. Aristotelianism fell by the wayside during the Enlightenment—in part because of its close identification with Roman Catholic scholasticism and in part because of the discrediting of Aristotelian science in the Scientific Revolution—but MacIntyre argues that this rejection was unwarranted, for an ethics coming out of the Aristotelian tradition is the best hope for moral philosophy.

MacIntyre's original formulation of this virtue ethics in *After Virtue* defines the virtues in terms of those qualities of character and intellect that are necessary for one's achievement of goods specific to practices (for example, games, crafts, arts, sciences, and other complex activities), for the sustenance of one's quest for the good life, and for the maintenance of one's community and one's traditions. He does not there formulate his view as part of a teleological conception of human nature and, indeed, in that work, he treats it as a desideratum for a restated Aristotelian ethics that it not rest on such a *metaphysical biology*. But in later works, most clearly *Dependent Rational Animals*, MacIntyre argues that ultimately we have to understand the virtues in terms of just such a teleological conception—a version of Aristotelianism grounded in the work of Thomas Aquinas—and that this conception is not at odds with the well-founded claims of contemporary science.

THE POLITICS OF LOCAL COMMUNITY

MacIntyre's views in political philosophy are frequently labeled *communitarian*, but this is a mistake if by communitarian we mean the position that states should be in some way guided by the ideals of the value of community. MacIntyre's position is more radical, for he holds that every conception of politics that is built on the attempt to justify the state is doomed to failure. For the state—a hierarchically structured apparatus of political control—is not justifiable; all attempts to explain why the state is authoritative have failed. This does not mean that politics is an empty enterprise or that authority is inevitably illegitimate. It means, rather, that the goods of politics are realized not through the state but through much more local communities in which people can engage in genuine argument and have effective control over how their common life is structured. Only in local communities can the politics of the common good rather than that of individual advantage or class dominance be practiced. This emphasis on the necessarily local character of good politics also marks MacIntyre's views as Aristotelian.

See also Aristotelianism; Aristotle; Bentham, Jeremy; Communitarianism; Enlightenment; Hume, David; Kant, Immanuel; Marxist Philosophy; Mill, John Stuart; Nietzsche, Friedrich; Scientific Revolutions; Social and Political Philosophy; Thomas Aquinas, St.; Virtue Ethics.

Bibliography

WORKS BY MACINTYRE

Marxism: An Interpretation. London: SCM Press, 1953.

A Short History of Ethics (1966). 2nd ed. Notre Dame, IN: University of Notre Dame Press, 1998.

After Virtue: A Study in Moral Theory (1981). 2nd ed. Notre Dame, IN: University of Notre Dame Press, 1984.

Whose Justice? Which Rationality? Notre Dame, IN: University of Notre Dame Press, 1988.

Three Rival Versions of Moral Enquiry: Encyclopaedia, Genealogy, and Tradition. Notre Dame, IN: University of Notre Dame Press, 1990.

The MacIntyre Reader, edited by Kelvin Knight. Notre Dame, IN: University of Notre Dame Press, 1998.

Dependent Rational Animals: Why Human Beings Need the Virtues. Chicago: Open Court, 1999.

WORKS ON MACINTYRE

Horton, John, and Susan Mendus, eds. *After MacIntyre: Critical Perspectives on the Work of Alasdair MacIntyre.* Notre Dame, IN: University of Notre Dame Press, 1994.

Murphy, Mark C., ed. *Alasdair MacIntyre.* New York: Cambridge University Press, 2003.

Mark C. Murphy (2005)

MACKIE, JOHN LESLIE
(1917–1981)

John Leslie Mackie was born in Sydney, Australia, and educated under John Anderson at the University of Sydney, and at Oxford, where he graduated with a First in Literae Humaniores in 1940. After the war, he returned to an academic position in the University of Sydney, and in 1955 he took up the Chair in Philosophy at the University of Otago, in Dunedin, New Zealand. In 1959 he returned to the University of Sydney to replace Anderson in the Challis Chair. After five years he left for Great Britain, going first to fill the foundation Chair of Philosophy at the new University in York. In 1967 he became Fellow of University College, Oxford, and University Reader in 1978. He remained at Oxford until his death in 1981.

Mackie's work is characterized by an acute, unwearied, and always dispassionate analysis of alternative solutions to specific philosophical problems. Striving first for full clarity in the statement of the problem, he proceeds by careful exploration and appraisal of the arguments available in support of alternative proposed solutions. Mackie applied this analytic style of reasoning across a broad range of issues. He made contributions to, among other topics, logic—and particularly the understanding of logical paradoxes; to the nature of conditionals and the theory of causality; to the interpretation of counterfactual conditionals; to the theory of space and time; to the theological problem of evil; to the theory of ethics; to the relations between reason, morality, and law; to the philosophy of mind; to the philosophy of biology; and to the interpretation of Locke's epistemology and metaphysics, and of Hume's ethics.

For many years, Mackie published a succession of important articles, but no books. This pattern of publication was transformed in 1973 with the appearance of *Truth, Probability, and Paradox,* a collection of essays on logical themes. This was followed in rapid succession by *The Cement of the Universe* (1974), which presents his views on causation, and *Problems from Locke* (1976). In this work Mackie takes up a group of characteristically Lockean themes, including primary and secondary qualities, perception, substance, universals, identity, and innate ideas, and relates them to contemporary discussion of the same issues. In *Ethics, Inventing Right and Wrong* (1977) he presents a sustained argument for a distinctive error-projection account of human moral thinking, which was provided with some additional support in his extended discussion of Hume's moral theory, which appeared in a book of that name in 1980. Lastly, posthumously, *The Miracle of Theism* was published in 1982. Its subtitle—*For and Against the Existence of God*—sufficiently indicates its contents. Though scrupulously fair, Mackie himself was firmly convinced by the case for atheism. This burst of productivity propelled Mackie to the forefront among British philosophers of his generation, and his relatively early death, while still at the height of his powers, was keenly felt.

MACKIE'S THESES

Although contributing to many debates in the course of his career, Mackie is principally celebrated for four distinctive theses. The first, in philosophical theology, is his insistence, patiently argued over many years, that all the attempts to reconcile the existence of evil with the classical Christian conception of God as omnipotent, omnis-

cient, and benevolent are failures, and that any plausible variations on them will fail also.

The second is in philosophical logic, in which Mackie argues that despite appearances, counterfactual conditionals are not actually propositions at all, but rather condensed and elliptically expressed arguments. The conditional's antecedent is the argument's premise, and its consequent is the conclusion. The counterfactual conditional is to be accepted if the argument is good as it stands, or can be made good by the supply of plausible understood additional premises.

The third thesis pertains to metaphysics, specifically causation. Recognizing that in almost every case the whole cause of an event involves multiple factors, Mackie proposed an account of causal factors. These, he held, are INUS conditions—that is: insufficient but necessary parts of unnecessary but sufficient conditions for the occurrence of the effect.

In ethics, the area of Mackie's fourth distinctive thesis, he argues that although the semantics of ordinary indicative moral discourse apparently require that there be moral facts in virtue of which human moral claims are true or false, there are no such moral facts. Moral discourse must therefore be explicated as arising from widespread error. The denial of objective moral facts is the aspect of his thought that most clearly shows the influence of his Andersonian education. Mackie argued that people's attitudes and feelings when considering their behavior and its effects lead them to assume, falsely, the existence of objective features of right or wrong, good or bad, in human situations, which correspond to, and validate, those attitudes and feelings. As there are no such validating properties, people must take on themselves the responsibility for the judgments they make.

In the years since his death, Mackie's philosophy has continued to be influential. In particular, his controversial views in ethics and philosophical theology continue to attract critical but respectful discussion.

See also Anderson, John; Causation: Metaphysical Issues; Conditionals; Counterfactuals; Evil, The Problem of; Hume, David; Locke, John; Logical Paradoxes; Noncognitivism; Philosophy of Biology; Philosophy of Mind; Space; Theism, Arguments For and Against; Time.

Bibliography

WORKS BY MACKIE

Truth, Probability and Paradox: Studies in Philosophical Logic. Oxford: Clarendon Press, 1973.

The Cement of the Universe: A Study of Causation. Oxford: Clarendon Press, 1974.

Problems from Locke. Oxford: Clarendon Press, 1976.

Ethics: Inventing Right and Wrong. Harmondsworth, U.K.: Penguin, 1977.

Hume's Moral Theory. London: Routledge and Kegan Paul, 1980.

The Miracle of Theism: Arguments For and Against the Existence of God. Oxford: Clarendon Press, 1982.

COLLECTIONS OF MACKIE'S ARTICLES

Mackie, J., and P. Mackie, eds. *Logic and Knowledge: Selected Papers. Vol. 1.* Oxford: Clarendon Press, 1985.

Mackie, J, and P. Mackie, eds. *Persons and Values; Selected Papers. Vol. 2.* Oxford: Clarendon Press, 1985.

WORKS ABOUT MACKIE

Honderich, T., ed. *Morality and Objectivity; a Tribute to J. L. Mackie.* London: Routledge and Kegan Paul, 1985. Contains a comprehensive Mackie bibliography.

Keith Campbell (1996, 2005)

MACROCOSM AND MICROCOSM

"Macrocosm" and "microcosm" are philosophical terms referring, respectively, to the world as a whole and to some part, usually man, as a model or epitome of it. According to one version of this ancient analogy, man and the universe are constructed according to the same harmonic proportions, each sympathetically attuned to the other, each a cosmos ordered according to reason. By an imaginative leap, the universe itself was thought to be, like man, living and conscious, a divine creature whose nature is reflected in human existence. Animism and panpsychism also regard the world as alive throughout, but the microcosm idea is distinct in emphasizing the unity or kinship of all life and thought in the world. If man is the microcosm of the universe, then not only is everything animated by *some* soul or other, but there is *one* world soul by which everything is animated. Thus, the followers of Pythagoras and Empedocles held, according to Sextus Empiricus, that "there is a certain community uniting us not only with each other and with the gods but even with the brute creation. There is in fact one breath pervading the whole cosmos like soul, and uniting us with them" (W. K. C. Guthrie, *A History of Greek Philosophy,* Vol. I, p. 278).

Because the word *kosmos* can mean order as well as world or world order, "microcosm" can signify not only man in relation to the universe (or in relation to the state, as in Plato's *Republic*) but also any part of a thing, espe-

cially a living thing, that reflects or represents the whole it belongs to, whenever there is a mirroring relation between the whole and each of its parts. Nicholas of Cusa's doctrine of individuals as "contractions" of the form of the universe is a microcosm theory, as is Gottfried Wilhelm Leibniz's theory of monads as "perpetual living mirrors of the universe"; similarly, to cite an example from nonphilosophical discourse, the composer Béla Bartók's collection of piano pieces *Mikrokosmos* is a little world of modern musical style and technique.

The idea of the microcosm appears in pre-Socratic philosophy in connection with the problem of relating the One and the Many. Taking all of nature to derive ultimately from a single common substance, they supposed it to have inherent in it a principle of motion and change (which they identified with life, soul). Since some of the resulting entities possess consciousness, so too must their source. And if the universal soul is eternal and divine, then the human soul, which is a "fragment" of the One, as the Pythagoreans held, must also be eternal and divine. The return of the individual soul to its divine origin could be realized by philosophical understanding of the cosmos; since like is known by like, as the cosmos becomes known the knower is assimilated to it. Thus, man is, and discovers himself to be, the part that most perfectly reveals the nature of the whole.

Man the microcosm is a commonplace of Greek thought from Anaximenes, the Pythagoreans, Heraclitus, and Empedocles to the Stoics and Neoplatonists. It is a staple theme for variation in the Orphic, Gnostic, and Hermetic texts and in the literature of mysticism, pantheism, and the occult. That man is the microcosm was, in the Renaissance, widely taken to mean that cosmic knowledge and influence might be achieved through contemplation of the powers and tendencies men find in their own imaginations. Such knowledge would be based not on mere inference from resemblance but rather on the kinship or identity of human life and consciousness with the forces governing nature as a whole.

The notion that man is the microcosm has always played both rational and mystical roles in Western thought. Well into the period of the scientific revolution, the microcosm was an image of the order and harmony pervading the world. Saying that the universe is controlled by a single principle (in the way that rational thought is the controlling principle in man) expressed the unified and self-regulating character of the world as understandable in its own terms, fit for scientific investigation. Similarly, human thought itself was conceived to be self-regulating and self-correcting—thus entered the idea of the autonomy of reason that has played an important part in the history of rationalism and of Western philosophy generally. According to Plato's recollection doctrine, "All nature is akin, and the soul has learned everything, so that when a man has recalled a single piece of knowledge—*learned* it, in ordinary language—there is no reason why he should not find out all the rest" (*Meno* 81D, E). By recollection Plato meant the recovery of systematic knowledge of necessary truths from within oneself, but it is easy to see how it could also be thought of as an intuitive, nontheoretical process—a stream of consciousness leading to memory of past reincarnations or of the soul's celestial origin.

The thought that the universe is ordered not by chance but by one spiritual principle stimulated the wish for direct mystical union with this soul, and even for influence over things through it, as easily as it encouraged the pursuit of systematic understanding of the world. The first impulse produced such exalted sentiments as those lavished upon the universe in the Hermetic religious writings; the second pushed open the door to that underground world of magic, astrology, alchemy, and spiritualism that claimed to utilize the same unifying principles assumed in science and in the astral theology of the philosophers. Perhaps something may be said for a generous interpretation of this magical view of nature, which even in antiquity was distinguishable from its rationalistic and humanistic counterpart. For the practitioners of the occult and for their opponents, the view of the world as a "be-souled" creature was neither an isolated hypothesis nor an idle conceit; the microcosm was an almost omnipresent presupposition, the basis of the very language in which the phenomena whose explanation was sought were represented. Yet there were always philosophical skeptics, and often the same writers who affirmed the world soul or the microcosm—for example, Plotinus, Giovanni Pico della Mirandola, Johannes Kepler—also tried to restrict it in ways that precluded the possibility of undesirable magical application.

ANCIENT THOUGHT

In the *Timaeus* Plato presents a mythical account of the creation of the world according to which the world's soul and body are made by the Demiurge, who copies the Form of the ideal living creature (not itself any species of animate being but embracing the types of them all). The world soul is constructed according to a complex musical pattern, and, in order to be capable of thought, the elements of discourse—sameness, difference, and existence—are blended to form its mind. The body joined to

the world soul is said to be unlike the human body or that of any animal in the world, being perfectly spherical, devoid of organs of sense, respiration, and ingestion; however, the processes of the universe are said to be reproduced even in the details of microcosmic processes, such as the moment of blood in humans. And because of the affinity between the divine part in humans and the thoughts and revolutions of the universe, the study of the rhythms of the macrocosm are recommended as a means of "correcting those circuits in the head that were deranged at birth."

A methodological discussion forms the context of a playful passage in the *Philebus* (27A–31B) in which the microcosm image also appears. All philosophers hold mind to be the king of heaven and earth, Socrates observes: "in reality they are magnifying themselves. And perhaps they are right." Socrates and Protarchus agree that the order of the world proves that the cosmos is governed by "Mind [*nous*] and a wondrous regulating Intelligence." Socrates argues further that the elements composing our bodies are but fragments produced and sustained by the elements in the universe. Because the unity of the elements in us makes up our bodies, the collective unity of elements in the universe must make up the world's body; because our bodies have souls, the body of the universe must have one, too; for where could our bodies have gotten their souls "if the body of the universe, which has elements the same as our own though still fairer in every respect, were not in fact possessed of a soul?" Strictly, this much of the argument concludes merely in the existence of a world soul that is the cause of the mixture of the body's elements—there is as yet barely a hint of the world soul's having a structure of its own apart from the body, of its being rationally ordered and the cause not just of all mixture but of all movement in the cosmos. Ultimately, the universal soul itself is said to be produced by Cause (later identified with Mind), yet this Mind cannot come into existence without soul (30C). To the extent that we can distinguish the Demiurge from the world soul (in the *Timaeus*), we can say that the Cause of the *Philebus* is probably more like the first of these.

Aristotle's physical system seems to have been designed to avoid the view of the cosmos as "besouled" or as alive in all its parts. Thus, in *De Caelo* the motion of the stars is explained not by any life in them but mainly in terms of the circular motion natural to the *aether* of which they are composed. In Book II (Ch. 2) Aristotle rejects the view that "it is by the constraint of a soul that it [the heaven] endures forever." The Demiurge as designer of the world is wholly excluded; no consciousness is needed of the rational (but unpremeditated) pattern to which nature adheres. Although there is a reference (to the views of others) in the *Physics* (Book VIII, Ch. 2), which may be the first occurrence of the Greek expression for "microcosm," Aristotle seems not to have organized his conception of nature around the view of it as an organism in any significant way. (For a contrasting account, see W. K. C. Guthrie, "Man as Microcosm.")

What is missing in Aristotle reappears (partly under Heraclitus's influence) in the thought of the Stoics—the sense of the world as an animate and conscious continuum each part of which affects all others by its *sympathy,* its "sharing of experience" with the others. The doctrine of sympathies and antipathies among the parts of the world animal guided the physical research of the Stoics and predisposed them to accept and to attempt to rationalize the particulars of astrology and divination. And man as microcosm was the source of their efforts to locate the basis of human conduct in natural law; by playing one's assigned role in the cosmos, one's logos, his "inner self," would be linked to that of the whole (Hans Jonas, *The Gnostic Religion,* p. 248).

Plotinus, like the Stoics, treated the world as a single creature, "living differently in each of its parts." If the world soul of Plato's system is thought of as operating purposefully and consciously, and if the Nature of Aristotle's system is taken to work purposefully but unconsciously, we should say that for Plotinus the world as a whole is governed consciously yet produces individual things "as in a dream," spontaneously, without reasoning, choice, or calculation. According to Plotinus only a unity of soul among us could explain our sympathetic relations to one another, "suffering, overcome, at the sight of pain, naturally drawn to forming attachments" (*Ennead* IV, ix, 3). Plotinus denied that the unity he spoke of entailed the transference of a person's emotions to places outside his body; the souls of the sufferer and of the sympathizer do not feel as one. Rather, his model of unity is that of a science, where individual truths cannot be considered apart from the whole; "the whole is in every part: … The one detail, when it is matter of science, potentially includes all" (IV, ix, 5). In geometry, for example, "the single proposition includes all the items that go to constitute it and all the propositions which can be developed from it" (IV, ix, 5). Perhaps this very strict sense of unity, which asserts that each thing is internally connected with every other thing (or that there is one thing with which each is connected) has always been latent in the microcosm doctrine; if so, it is an aspect of the doctrine that seems to offer small encouragement to the search for the actual

relations in nature. The question "Which things are causally connected, which are not?" has little point if all can affect all alike.

The general ancient view of the world as a perfect organism may have been responsible, as Samuel Sambursky suggests, for the insistence of ancient thinkers on the attempt to understand the world as a whole, in its entirety, and for their almost total avoidance of experimentation—the isolation of phenomena, or "dissection of nature," characteristic of modern science.

MEDIEVAL AND MODERN THOUGHT

Man as microcosm of the universe is not integral to Jewish and Christian doctrine in the way that it is to the Gnostic religious system, for example; thus, Philo Judaeus and Moses Maimonides employed the idea of the world soul only dialectically. In *The Guide of the Perplexed* (Pt. I, Ch. 72) Maimonides at first argues that the world is like a human being, but he then presents so many points of difference between the two that in the end it is clear that he considers the possession of a rational order to be their only common factor. As a cosmological view, the microcosm has little or no place in Augustine or in Thomas Aquinas, who treats it as a mere figure of speech. By contrast, Joseph ibn Zaddik states one of the microcosm's main attractions when he proposes to show how self-knowledge will lead to knowledge of the whole—a "short cut" through the study of man, bypassing the sciences. Bernard of Tours and other members of the school of Chartres assimilated the world soul of Plato's *Timaeus* to the Third Person of the Trinity. Drawing upon Bernard, Hildegard of Bingen, in her visionary writings, represented detailed correspondences between heavenly motions, winds, elements, humors, and bodily and spiritual states in the individual.

Plato had typically employed the microcosm image to portray the transformation of consciousness through theoretical knowledge of whatever cosmic order science reveals; Ibn Zaddik reverses the process, seeking to discover in man what the cosmic order must be. Where Plato stressed the dissimilarity between the living cosmos and the structure and functioning of any particular animal, including man, Hildegard dwells on their supposed similarity in picturesque detail. The idea that inner experience of human nature supplies a direct route to reality is prone to magical extension in a way that Plato's view is not, but it was this conception that took hold in medieval and Renaissance microcosm literature.

Renaissance speculation on the microcosm centered on the idea that human nature partakes of bodily, intellectual, and divine existence, uniting in itself the whole of the sublunary, celestial, and supercelestial realms. Human consciousness, by which man can know all things, connects him with all things; consciousness is itself a link between thought and its objects. Through consciousness man can know and become all that he wills. A similar doctrine of connections drawn from the Kabbalah underlies the various magical theories of language which asserted that quasi-physical influences join names and things, beyond the conventions of the various natural languages. Partly controllable influences also form the structure of the elaborate identities and correspondences that Agrippa von Nettesheim and Paracelsus described between minerals, animals, heavenly bodies, psychic powers, and parts of the human body. Such influences are also involved in the interaction between thought and its objects that Giordano Bruno assumed in his search for direct awareness of the sympathies controlling nature through memory and the ideas of them in his imagination.

The occult "applications" of the microcosm idea did not survive the advance of the mechanistic worldview. By the eighteenth century, occult qualities, or anything that seemed like them—for example, action at a distance—were in such wide disrepute that even Isaac Newton, to avoid the appearance of being committed to an occult doctrine, refrained from expressing fully his theory of the mode of action of atomic "Central Forces." But in the second edition of the *Principia* (1713), he described the ether as "a certain most subtle spirit which pervades and lies hid in all gross bodies … by the force and action of which spirit the particles of bodies attract one another at near distances and cohere … and all sensation is excited, and the members of animal bodies move at the command of the will, namely by vibrations of this spirit"—a view not far from that of the Stoics, as Stephen Toulmin and June Goodfield remark (*The Architecture of Matter,* p. 195).

Even later, belief in psychic planetary action had not lost all ground; thus, Franz Anton Mesmer's explanation of "animal magnetism," or hypnosis, assumed a "responsive influence … between the heavenly bodies, the earth, and animated bodies," which the hypnotist drew upon. And the idea of a psychic force in the world beyond our immediate awareness, of which our conscious lives are parts or manifestations, endured, for example, in Johann Wolfgang von Goethe's Nature philosophy and in Arthur Schopenhauer's world will—ancestors of the concept of the unconscious. Perhaps some aspects of the microcosm idea can be found in Sigmund Freud's attempts to explain

the instincts in man as repetitions of the reactions of living matter to drastic changes in the prehistoric environment. (Thus, we might say that man's instincts are a microcosm of his evolution.) Among the known "enforced alterations in the course of life … stored for repetition," Freud, along with Sándor Ferenczi, noted the drying up of the oceans which left life to adapt on land and the cultural development necessitated by the glacial epoch. These are reexperienced at birth, in the diphasic onset of man's sexual life, and in the latency period. Freud invokes the contending forces, Love and Strife, of Empedocles's "Cosmic phantasy," pointing out their similarity to Eros and Destructiveness, the two primal instincts of his biopsychical theory. These instincts, which "present the delusive appearance of forces striving after change and progress" actually impel the organism toward the reinstatement of earlier, more stable states, ultimately to inorganic existence. The originally biological principle that ontogeny recapitulates phylogeny has received very wide psychological extension in psychoanalysis; most recently, Carl Jung has (somewhat cryptically) identified his doctrine of the collective unconscious with that of "the microcosm containing the archetypes of all ideas."

Perhaps the microcosm image is not entirely the scientific dead end it has understandably been taken for; as early attempts to construct models of the embodied soul's structure, development, and dynamics, some versions of the image may stand to scientific psychological research as alchemy stands to chemistry.

See also Agrippa von Nettesheim, Henricus Cornelius; Anaximenes; Aristotle; Augustine, St.; Bernard of Tours; Bruno, Giordano; Chartres, School of; Empedocles; Freud, Sigmund; Goethe, Johann Wolfgang von; Heraclitus of Ephesus; Hildegard of Bingen; Ibn Zaddik, Joseph ben Jacob; Jung, Carl Gustav; Kabbalah; Kepler, Johannes; Leibniz, Gottfried Wilhelm; Maimonides; Neoplatonism; Nicholas of Cusa; Panpsychism; Paracelsus; Philo Judaeus; Pico della Mirandola, Count Giovanni; Plato; Plotinus; Pythagoras and Pythagoreanism; Schopenhauer, Arthur; Sextus Empiricus; Socrates; Thomas Aquinas, St.

Bibliography

Three useful histories of the microcosm theme are G. P. Conger, *Theories of Macrocosms and Microcosms in the History of Philosophy* (New York: Russell and Russell, 1922), which includes a survey of critical discussions up to 1922; Rudolph Allers, "Microcosmus, From Anaximandros to Paracelsus," in *Traditio* 2 (1944): 319–407; and W. K. C. Guthrie's "Man as Microcosm," in *Proceedings of the European Cultural Foundation* (Athens, 1966); all contain many references. W. K. C. Guthrie's discussion of the microcosm, to which this article is indebted, in *A History of Greek Philosophy* (Cambridge, U.K.: Cambridge University Press, 1962–), Vol. I, is the most important one for the period covered; this volume, *The Earlier Presocratics and the Pythagoreans*, also contains valuable remarks on Plato and Aristotle. The microcosm in Plato is discussed by F. M. Cornford throughout his commentary on the *Timaeus* in *Plato's Cosmology* (London: K. Paul, Trench, Trubner, 1937); G. M. A. Grube discusses the microcosm as part of Plato's theory of the soul in *Plato's Thought* (London: Methuen, 1935), Ch. 4; see also F. M. Cornford, "Psychology and Social Structure in the Republic of Plato," in *Classical Quarterly* (1912): 247–265; R. Hackforth's translation of the *Philebus*, with commentary, in *Plato's Examination of Pleasure* (Cambridge, U.K., 1945); and Gregory Vlastos, "Anamnesis in the *Meno*," in *Dialogue* 4 (2) (September 1965): 143–167, which interprets the recollection theory with comments on its connection with the doctrine of reincarnation. Possible oriental influences on Plato are discussed in A. Olerud, *L'idée de microcosmos et de macrocosmos dans la Timée de Platon* (Uppsala, 1951). Two valuable relevant studies of Aristotle are W. K. C. Guthrie's introduction to the text and translation of *Aristotle on the Heavens* (London, 1939) and Friedrich Solmsen's *Aristotle's System of the Physical World* (Ithaca, NY: Cornell University Press, 1960).

On the Stoics, see Samuel Sambursky, *The Physics of the Stoics* (Princeton, NJ: Princeton University Press, 1987.)

On Plotinus, see the introductions and translations in E. R. Dodds, *Select Passages Illustrating Neoplatonism* (London, 1923), and A. H. Armstrong, *Plotinus* (London: Allen and Unwin, 1953). Remarks bearing on the microcosm in ancient thought generally are contained throughout E. R. Dodds, *The Greeks and the Irrational* (Boston: Beacon, 1957); Hans Jonas, *The Gnostic Religion* (Boston: Beacon, 1963), especially Ch. 10, "The Cosmos in Greek and Gnostic Evaluation"; A.-J. Festugière, *Personal Religion among the Greeks* (Berkeley: University of California Press, 1954); E. A. Lippman, *Musical Thought in Ancient Greece* (New York: Columbia University Press, 1964); and Samuel Sambursky, *The Physical World of the Greeks* (London: Routledge and Paul, 1956). See also E. W. Beth, *The Foundations of Mathematics: A Study in the Philosophy of Science*, rev. ed. (New York, 1964), Chs. 1 and 2, "The Pre-history of Research into Foundations" and "Aristotle's Theory of Science."

Hildegard of Bingen's life and writings are examined in Charles Singer, *From Magic to Science* (New York: Dover, 1958), Ch. 6, "The Visions of Hildegard of Bingen," a rewritten chapter from *Studies on the History and Method of Science*, Vol. I (Oxford, 1917). Ernst Cassirer, *Individuum und Kosmos in der Philosophie der Renaissance* (Leipzig: Teubner, 1927), translated by Mario Domandi as *The Individual and the Cosmos in Renaissance Philosophy* (New York: Harper, 1963), is the standard discussion of the microcosm in Renaissance thought. On the difficult subject of Renaissance occult literature, see D. P. Walker, *Spiritual and Demonic Magic from Ficino to Campanella* (London: Warburg Institute, University of London, 1958). Three chapters in Frederick Copleston's *A History of Philosophy*, Vol. III, *Late Medieval and Renaissance Philosophy*, Part 2 (Westminster, MD: Newman Bookshop, 1953), are useful

surveys; Ch. 15 discusses the microcosm in Nicholas of Cusa, Chs. 16 and 17 are on the philosophy of nature. An important interpretation of Bruno is Frances Yates, *Giordano Bruno and the Hermetic Tradition* (Chicago: University of Chicago Press, 1964). There are also interesting discussions in Alexandre Koyré, *Mystiques, spirituels, alchimistes du XVIe siècle allemand* (Paris, 1955), and in Werner Pauli, "The Influence of Archetypal Ideas on the Scientific Theories of Kepler," in *The Interpretation of Nature and the Psyche* (New York: Pantheon, 1955). Microcosm and macrocosm are discussed in the context of the idea of the chain of being in E. M. W. Tillyard, *The Elizabethan World Picture* (New York, 1941); see also W. C. Curry, *Shakespeare's Philosophical Patterns* (Baton Rouge: Louisiana State University Press, 1937). On the transition from animism to mechanism in science, see E. J. Dijksterhuis, *Mechanization of the World-Picture*, translated by C. Dikshoorn (Oxford: Clarendon Press, 1961); M. B. Hesse, *Forces and Fields* (London: T. Nelson, 1961); and Stephen Toulmin and June Goodfield, *The Architecture of Matter* (New York: Harper and Row, 1962).

A brief account of Mesmer's ideas can be found in Clark L. Hull, *Hypnosis and Suggestibility* (New York: Appleton-Century, 1933), pp. 6–11. Schopenhauer's doctrine of the microcosm and its influence on Ludwig Wittgenstein are discussed in Patrick Gardiner, *Schopenhauer* (Baltimore: Penguin, 1963). Wittgenstein's remark "I am my world. (The microcosm.)" appears in the *Tractatus*, but without the connection with the world-spirit doctrine it has in his *Notebooks* (pp. 84–85). Wittgenstein's idea of an internal connection between language, thought, and reality is discussed in Erik Stenius, *Wittgenstein's Tractatus* (Oxford, 1960), and Max Black, *A Companion to Wittgenstein's Tractatus* (Ithaca, NY: Cornell University Press, 1964).

A short discussion of the microcosm image as employed by Freud and other analysts is contained in Philip Rieff's introduction to *General Psychological Theory* (New York, 1963), which is a volume in the paperback edition of Freud's *Collected Papers*; see pp. 9–17. Freud discusses Empedocles in "Analysis Terminable and Interminable," in the volume *Therapy and Technique*, edited by Philip Rieff (New York, 1963), the paperback edition of Freud's *Collected Papers*. Jung's ideas are expressed in his *Naturklärung und Psyche* (Zürich: Rasche, 1952), translated by R. F. C. Hull as *The Interpretation of Nature and the Psyche* (New York: Harcourt Brace, 1955). Ch. 3 of his essay "Synchronicity: An Acausal Connecting Principle" contains numerous quotations from earlier microcosm literature.

Problems that arise in trying to characterize the universe as a unified whole (or as a "whole" at all) on the basis of information concerning only a part and in trying to treat scientifically the nature of a necessarily unique object are presented in D. W. Sciama, *The Unity of the Universe* (Garden City, NY: Doubleday, 1959), pp. 69–205. For further discussion and bibliography, see the Cosmology and Rationalism entries.

Donald Levy (1967)

MAILLET, BENOÎT DE
(c. 1656–1738)

Benoît de Maillet was a French diplomat, traveler, and natural scientist. Information concerning the place and date of his birth, details of his life, and the significance of his works is, at best, sketchy and contradictory. A member of the impoverished nobility, Maillet presumably received the customary classical education of the day. He seems to have led an apathetic existence until his appointment to the French consulate in Cairo at the age of thirty-six. As consul, he handled the king's business well and, for services rendered, was named ambassador to Ethiopia in 1702. He declined the honor, ostensibly for reasons of health but actually because his duties would be less concerned with Franco-Ethiopian relations than with the formidable task of converting the natives to Christianity. In 1707, at his own request, he left his post in Cairo to assume charge of the French consulate in Livorno, Italy. He was so successful as consul and later as inspector of French settlements in other parts of the Mediterranean that, upon his retirement in 1724, he received a handsome pension and spent the remaining fourteen years of his life in Marseille. There, besides attending to a large correspondence, most of which is now lost, he wrote several works, including *Description de l'Egypte* (1735) and the vastly more important *Telliamed, ou entretiens d'un philosophe indien avec un missionnaire françois* (1748), which appeared posthumously.

TELLIAMED

The years of Maillet's consulships, his travels in the Mediterranean basin, and his wide readings and careful observations formed much of the background for *Telliamed* (the author's name spelled backward). First published in Amsterdam, it was closely followed by other editions in both French and English, the most important being that of the Abbé Le Mascrier (1755). The work consists of a series of conversations in which Maillet, speaking through his Indian philosopher, Telliamed, puts forth various geological and biological speculations about Earth's cosmogony and its evolution—together with the organic beings it supported—into its present state. According to Maillet's system, Earth, product of a whirlpool of cosmic dust, was for countless ages entirely covered with swirling waters. As the waters gradually receded, the primordial mountains formed by the currents of these waters slowly emerged from the depths. The crashing of the waves against these mountains formed new mountains, and with the appearance of life in the seas, fossil strata were formed.

Primitive forms of aquatic life, produced in ever-increasing abundance through the aeons, underwent gradual modifications of structure and function in keeping with changing habits and new environments. Thus, creatures along the shallow coastal waters moved into the marshes and, after much trial and error, finally emerged with wings for flying or legs for walking. Beneath this speculation lay the work's basic theme that everything in the universe, through the processes of time, was undergoing constant change. Occasionally the author's boldly imaginative thought resulted in whimsy, which was interpreted by many of his critics as folly or childish fantasy.

Telliamed immediately became a center of controversy that extended well into the nineteenth century. Maillet's heretical views, which ran counter to the tenets of Genesis, aroused the theologians of the day, while many eighteenth-century rationalists and scientists, led by Voltaire, were violently opposed to his ideas on other grounds. Disparaging criticisms continued in the writings of such eminent men of science as Étienne Geoffroy Saint-Hilaire and Georges Cuvier, Nonetheless, Comte de Buffon, Denis Diderot, Chevalier de Lamarck, and Erasmus Darwin, among others, availed themselves of Maillet's theories as a starting point for even more daring concepts of their own.

Bibliography
Collier, Katherine. *Cosmogonies of Our Fathers.* New York, 1934.

Dufrenoy, Marie-Louise. *Benoît de Maillet, précurseur de l'évolution.* Paris, 1960.

Haber, Francis C. *The Age of the World. Moses to Darwin.* Baltimore: Johns Hopkins Press, 1959.

Kohlbrugge, J. H. F. "B. de Maillet, Lamarck und Darwin." *Biologisches Zentralblatt* 32 (1912): 508–518.

Wolf, A. *A History of Science, Technology and Philosophy in the XVIIIth Century.* 2nd ed, edited by Douglas McKie. London: Allen and Unwin, 1952.

Otis Fellows (1967)

MAIMON, SALOMON
(1753–1800)

Born in 1753 in a small village in Lithuania, Shlomo ben-Yehoshua later named himself "Maimon" after the great medieval Jewish philosopher Moses Maimonides. After being married at the age of eleven and fathering a child at fourteen, Maimon left his native country around 1778 in search of "Enlightenment." Following extraordinary adventures as a wandering beggar and scholar, Maimon arrived in Berlin in March 1780. There he became acquainted with Moses Mendelssohn and his circle. Maimon formulated many of his views (on Judaism and religion in general, and on Spinoza) in overt or covert criticism of Mendelssohn. Until 1791 Maimon contributed to projects of Jewish Enlightenment (*Haskala*), which he wished to promote in the first place through scientific knowledge. Later he became estranged from Jewish affairs.

Maimon's rather coarse way of life, which offended both Jewish ceremonial law and bourgeois decorum, forced him to leave Berlin in 1783. From June 1783 until March 1785 he studied in a German high school in Altona (Hamburg), and improved his knowledge of German and mathematics as he also learned Latin, English, and French. Back in Berlin, Maimon was supported almost entirely by benefactors. By the end of 1789, following praise from Immanuel Kant, Maimon published his first German book, *Versuch über die Tranzscendentalphiloso-phie* (*An Essay on Transcendental Philosophy*), which is a critical commentary on Kant's *Critique of Pure Reason*. A prolific writer, Maimon produced a number of publications, including both books and journal articles. Almost all of Maimon's works are commentaries of a sort on different writers, a method of philosophizing that is certainly a legacy of his Jewish education. In 1795 Maimon met Graf Adolf Kalkreuth, later himself a philosophical writer, and moved into his house near Berlin, and later to his estate in Silesia. There Maimon died on November 11, 1800.

In his autobiography (1792–1793) Maimon interprets his life as a process of progressive formation (*Bildung*) leading from traditional orthodox Judaism in Lithuania to the center of Enlightenment in Berlin. This change is conceived as "spiritual rebirth" (*Gesammelte Werke* 1:301), a classical term of contemporary Pietism. This work inspired many later autobiographies of European Jews seeking Enlightenment ideals, and it sets the stage for Maimon's own brand of philosophy.

RATIONAL DOGMATISM AND EMPIRICAL SKEPTICISM

In the *Versuch*, Maimon describes his position as "rational dogmatism and empirical skepticism," and despite the oddity of the combination, this is an apt description of his views (*Gesammelte Werke* 2, 432). Maimon follows the rationalists (particularly B. Spinoza and G. W. Leibniz) in granting the principle of sufficient reason unlimited scope: There is nothing inexplicable in the world, and reason's demands are unconstrained. But at the same time, while we can be sure that the principle of sufficient reason in general holds universally, our finitude prevents us from knowing with any certainty whether any *particular* judgment we make about the world accords with this rational condition. As such, whereas rationalism is right about the nature of knowledge, skepticism infects particular knowledge claims.

The exception to this, Maimon claims, is mathematics, in which we can achieve certain knowledge, for here our situation is compared to the "divine": In our mathematical claims we create the contents of mathematical judgments, by constructing a priori the objects of geometry and arithmetic. Here we can be assured (although in geometry this is not always the case) that our concepts apply to objects, because the objects themselves are created according to the concepts. But whereas certainty is guaranteed in the field of mathematics, our empirical judgments do not rise to this level, because they can never be shown to possess the "determinable" relation between subject and predicate demanded of "real thought."

DETERMINABILITY AND REAL THOUGHT

According to Leibniz, analytic thought is governed by the law of identity or contradiction: The complete concept of the subject contains all predicates that can be truthfully predicated of it. All true propositions are hence either overtly or "virtually" analytic. Maimon maintains that if there are synthetic judgments a priori (as Kant holds), there must also be a principle of such judgments. Since Maimon rejects the thesis that synthesis is the result of the application of the understanding to intuition, he maintains that synthetic thought must have a principle in reason itself. This is his Law of Determinability. The principle distinguishes between the subject that can be thought by itself and the predicate that can be thought only in relation to a subject: It thus permits the synthesis "square table" and excludes "tablish square," because "table" can be thought by itself and the property "square" cannot.

A further, seemingly paradoxical component of the law of determinability is that in a "real synthesis" there is exactly *one* predicate for each subject term. It thus demands for "line" either "straight" or "curved" and excludes "sweet line." Finally, it positively determines that a "real synthesis" is only a synthesis that produces a new object. The hallmark of an object determined through real thought is that new consequences follow from it that flow neither from the subject nor from the predicate terms alone, but only from their synthesis. Thus a triangle has certain "consequences" (e.g., that the sum of its internal angles equals two right angles), whereas the Pythagorean theorem is a further consequence of the synthesis of "triangle" and "right angle."

Real thought then depends on a determinable relation between subject and predicate, and this in turn can be guaranteed only in cases where an object is constructed according to a concept. While this occurs in geometry, the determinable relation cannot be shown to hold in cases in which we are passively given empirical objects through sensibility. Here it is also conspicuous that "real synthesis" is equivalent to the construction of the object itself, and that it proceeds from general to particular concepts. This and the unique relation between subject and predicate imply that if we could generate predications according to the law of determinability, we would be able to (re)construct the *entire* conceptual structure of the world. Because rationalism assumes that complete knowledge exhausts its object, the generation of this conceptual structure would be tantamount to the construction of the world. In mathematics we are hence similar to God (*Gesammelte Werke* 4:42). But this divinity is sharply limited: because proper knowledge consists in such determinable relations that in empirical cases we cannot produce but are merely given, most of what we think of as empirical human knowledge does not in fact deserve the name. Our beliefs about the merely encountered world of objects fail to meet the criteria of real knowledge. This is one source of Maimon's skepticism, which plays a key role in his critique of Kant.

QUID FACTI/QUID JURIS

The difficulty Maimon finds in Kant's views on synthetic judgments a priori centers on two crucial questions that drive the Transcendental Deduction of the Categories in the *Critique of Pure Reason*. There, Kant distinguishes between the *quid facti* (or, the question of fact) and the *quid juris* (or the question of right or warrant) of the use of the pure concepts of the understanding. The first question concerns whether we indeed have certain synthetic judgments due to the application of categories to intuitions, whereas the second asks about our right or justification in doing so. Kant is largely concerned with the second question, because he assumes, according to Maimon, that our experience reveals that we in fact have certain knowledge. But Maimon calls this assumption into question, by challenging the Kantian idea that our experience really involves supposedly objective and necessary claims such as "The sun warms the stone." Kant can assume this to be the case, but this will not convince

the skeptic—yet the central argument of the Deduction needs just this supposition, Maimon argues, to establish that the categories are legitimately employed in experience. As a result, only by begging the question "*quid facti*" against a Humean skeptic can Kant's argument succeed.

Maimon also remains suspicious of Kant's answer to the question *quid juris*. Kant aims to show that the legitimate employment of the categories rests on the way in which they can be applied to the intuitive contents of experience delivered by the faculty of sensibility; this depends on his fundamental commitment to a model of experience that distinguishes between intuitions (which are singular and immediate) and concepts (which are general and mediate). Kant's system endorses a kind of cognitive dualism, in which the separate faculties of the understanding and sensibility each contribute distinct and ineliminable elements of cognition. Yet Maimon finds this dualism problematic, for it faces all the challenges and problems that traditionally confront other dualisms such as that between mind and body. For how can wholly separate faculties nonetheless interact in the way that cognition requires? Maimon claims that for this reason Kant's cognitive dualism cannot answer the *quid juris* in a satisfactory manner.

In Maimon's critique of Kant, his allegiances to both skepticism and rationalism come to the fore. The challenge to the *quid facti* draws upon a kind of Humean skepticism about the structure of experience, and calls into question the notion of experience with which Kant's project begins. The critique of the *quid juris* rests upon Maimon's rationalist commitments, for it demands that some sufficient reason or explanation be provided for what Maimon takes to be a wholly mysterious relation between concepts and intuitions. Maimon's challenge to Kant is so interesting and powerful precisely because of his odd brand of skepticism, for it allows him to mount simultaneous attacks on the critical system from both an empiricist and a rationalist position.

MAIMON AND THE TRADITION

Kant famously described Maimon as his most acute critic, and this admiration—even if tinged with occasional acrimony—was shared by a number of other figures in German philosophy. The renown provided by Kant's comments allowed Maimon to engage in conversations and disputes with a number of the leading lights of the day. Maimon corresponded with K. L. Reinhold (and later had a bitter falling out when Maimon published their letters without Reinhold's permission), and penned a series of pseudonymous responses to the then-anonymous author of *Aenesidemus* (G. E. Schulze). In all of these works Maimon pressed his version of empirical skepticism and rational dogmatism.

Maimon's most lasting influence, however, was on J. G. Fichte, who shared Kant's respect for Maimon's intellect, and who saw more clearly than others the threat that Maimon's position posed for Kant's philosophy. Fichte's formulations of his *Wissenschaftslehre* in large part stand as attempts to meet the challenge Maimon posed to Kant, in particular to answer the charge that a dualistic model of cognition cannot explain how its disparate elements interact. Fichte's solution—which turns on rejecting Kant's model of cognition in favor of the positing activity of the Absolute-I—marked the beginning of Absolute Idealism, which reached its fruition in Schelling and Hegel. Maimon himself was certainly no Absolute Idealist—in fact, in his correspondence with Fichte he distances himself from Fichte's project—but his challenge to Kant provided an important goad in the development of Fichte's *Wissenschaftslehre*, and through him the systems of Schelling and Hegel. Thus Maimon's "dogmatic rationalism" found successors but neither his "empirical skepticism" nor his unique combination of both attracted adherents.

But Maimon's combination of skepticism and rationalism is of interest not simply as a historical step on the road from Kant to Hegel, but as a fascinating and often compelling position in its own right. Maimon's skepticism is unique in being based not upon a suspicion of the claims of rational inquiry, but, perhaps paradoxically, on an uncompromising commitment to the demands of reason. The challenge Maimon poses to all accounts of cognition is to explain how the understanding can apply to the contents of sensibility (whether *a priori* or *a posteriori*). Maimon ultimately resorts to a skeptical answer to this question, yet a nonskeptical response to the challenge he presents is something contemporary theories of cognition continue to struggle to meet.

See also Epistemology.

Bibliography

WORKS BY MAIMON

Gesammelte Werke. 7 vols., edited by Valerio Verra Hildesheim, Germany: Georg Olms, 1965–1976.

Versuch über die Transzendentalphilosophie (1790), edited by Florian Ehrensperger. Hamburg, Germany: Felix Meiner Verlag, 2004.

WORKS ABOUT MAIMON

Atlas, Samuel. *From Critical to Speculative Idealism: The Philosophy of Solomon Maimon.* The Hague: Martinus Nijhoff, 1964.

Beiser, Frederick. *The Fate of Reason: German Philosophy from Kant to Fichte.* Cambridge, MA: Harvard University Press, 1987.

Bergmann, Samuel. *The Philosophy of Salomon Maimon.* Translated by Noah Jacobs. Jerusalem: Magnes Press, 1967.

Bransen, Jan. *The Antinomy of Thought: Maimonian Skepticism and the Relation between Thoughts and Objects.* Dordrecht, Netherlands: Kluwer, 1991.

Engstler, Achim. *Untersuchungen zum Idealismus Salomon Maimons.* Stuttgart-Bad Cannstatt, Germany: Frommann-Holzboog, 1990.

Freudenthal, Gideon, ed. *Salomon Maimon: Rational Dogmatist, Empirical Skeptic.* Dordrecht, Netherlands: Kluwer, 2003.

Gueroult, Martial. *La philosophie transcendental de Salomon Maimon.* Paris: Vrin, 1929.

Kuntze, Friedrich. *Die Philosophie Salomon Maimons.* Heidelberg, Germany: Carl Winter, 1912.

Gideon Freudenthal (2005)
Peter Thielke (2005)

MAIMONIDES
(1135–1204)

Maimonides was the most celebrated Jewish philosopher of the Middle Ages. "Maimonides" is the Latinized cognomen of Moses son of Maimon. Also called RaMBaM, the acronym for Rabbi Moses ben Maimon, he was born in Córdoba, which belonged at that time to Muslim Spain. His father, Maimon son of Joseph, was a distinguished scholar versed in traditional Jewish lore. At the age of thirteen, Maimonides left his native town after it was conquered by the army of the Almohads, an intolerant Muslim sect. After various journeys he and his family settled in northern Africa, under the oppressive rule of the Almohads. In 1165 they went to Egypt, where Maimonides became a court physician and leader of the Jewish community. He died in Cairo.

Maimonides was and is regarded as an outstanding authority on Jewish religious law, the Halachah. His writings in this field include a commentary in Arabic on the Mishnah that contains a treatise on ethics known as "Eight Chapters" and a list of the thirteen fundamental dogmas of the Jewish faith as established by Maimonides; another of these works, known under the two titles *Mishnah Torah* and *Yad Hazakah,* is a voluminous codification of the Law written in Hebrew, whose first portion, the "Book of Knowledge," expounds a system of religious beliefs and is markedly influenced by philosophy.

The fact that a considerable portion of Maimonides' activity was devoted to legal doctrine is by no means irrelevant in a consideration of his philosophical attitude. In a sense this was a practical activity that can be assimilated to that of a statesman; it was accordingly consonant with Maimonides' Platonizing contention that certain superior individuals are able to combine a mode of existence given over to contemplation and intellection with a life of action.

Maimonides also wrote several medical treatises in Arabic. One of them, known as *Moses' Chapters* (*Fuṣūl Mūsā*), contains a critique of Galen, part of which deals with the Greek physician's animadversions on the Law of Moses. He also composed two popular tracts, "Treatise on Resurrection" and "Epistle to Yemen," the latter treatise rebutting the claims of a pseudo Messiah who had appeared in Yemen. Maimonides is also the author of one philosophical treatise on logic, composed in his early youth.

GUIDE OF THE PERPLEXED

Maimonides' reputation as a philosopher rests squarely upon his *Guide of the Perplexed* (*Dalālat al-Hāirīn* in Arabic), a work that its author did not regard as being of a philosophical nature. The "perplexed" to whom the *Guide* is supposed to have been addressed are men who are well grounded in the Jewish religious tradition and have some knowledge of certain philosophical sciences; the disciple to whom Maimonides addresses the "Introductory Epistle" at the beginning of the *Guide* is said to be conversant with logic and mathematics but not with physics or metaphysics. These semi-intellectuals are regarded by Maimonides as being in a state of mental confusion because they consider that the theses of the Greek sciences contradict religious faith. The word *hayra,* "perplexity," which is connected with the participle *hā'irīn* figuring in the title of the work under discussion, appears to have served as a technical term denoting the state of mind induced by a tug of war between two opposed beliefs. Both al-Farabi and, in the generation before Maimonides, the Jewish philosopher Abraham ibn Da'ud also used the term *perplexed* to describe people who hesitate between the conflicting claims of philosophy and religion. In one passage of the *Guide* Maimonides seems to indicate that his purpose in writing the work was to help such of the perplexed as were endowed with the requisite intellectual capacities to achieve a full knowledge of philosophical truths without giving up the observance of the religious commandments.

Maimonides, however, like his contemporary Averroes, was convinced that philosophy could constitute a terrible threat to the social fabric if a vulgarized version of its doctrines were to spread among ordinary people and destroy simple faith in authority. Systematic treatises, giving a step-by-step account of the Aristotelian doctrines, avoided this danger through recourse to technical terms and logical argumentation, which were incomprehensible to noninitiates. Maimonides employed another method, set forth in his introduction to the *Guide.* In the case of this work his very considerable gift for literary composition, which had enabled him to succeed in the extremely difficult task of producing a well-ordered code comprising the whole of Talmudic law, was called upon to disarrange and make a jumble of the systematic expositions of Aristotle and the Aristotelians. Maimonides makes it quite clear that in order to make understanding more difficult, he carefully tore apart conceptions that belong together. The reader is thus faced with the challenge of reconstructing the original whole out of pieces dispersed in various portions of the *Guide.* Maimonides even states that on certain points he deliberately makes two contradictory assertions. These and other precautions, which were intended to confuse readers of insufficient intellectual caliber or preparation, have turned the *Guide* into an enigma; any solution of the enigma can be impugned by an appeal to some statement of Maimonides' that may or may not have been meant to be taken at its face value.

INFLUENCES ON MAIMONIDES

There is a question whether the *Guide* was meant to be an apologetic attempt to render religion intellectually respectable by exposing the limitations of human reason, beyond which lies the domain of faith in things that may be true although they are unknown to philosophers; or, alternatively, whether it was meant to demonstrate that religion has a purely practical use. If the latter, then Maimonides meant to say that theoretical truth is essentially, although perhaps not completely, revealed by philosophy and to deny that religion has anything to offer except, in the most favorable cases, myths and parables to be interpreted with the help of scientific knowledge. A knowledge of the philosophical authors whose influence was avowed by Maimonides or may be discerned in his work may help to determine what actually was the main object of the *Guide.*

In a letter to Samuel ibn Tibbon, who translated the *Guide* into Hebrew, Maimonides wrote that he considered Plato's writings to be superseded by those of Aristotle, which are the root and foundation of all philosophy.

Nevertheless, he thought that Aristotle should be studied only with the help of the commentators Alexander of Aphrodisias, Themistus, and Averroes (a contemporary of Maimonides, who was not acquainted with the Muslim philosopher's commentaries at the time the *Guide* was written). Maimonides esteemed al-Farabi above all the other Islamic philosophers (a typical attitude of the philosophers of Spain), and also praised Ibn Bājja, the Muslim Spanish Aristotelian. His reaction to Avicenna, who was the dominant philosophical influence in the Islamic East, was ambivalent.

Maimonides does adopt certain conceptions of Avicenna's. Thus, his view that existence is an accident derives from Avicenna's fundamental doctrine that essences per se are neutral with respect to existence, which supervenes on them as an accident. However, in points that have an obvious bearing on religious beliefs, Maimonides sometimes does not hesitate to prefer Aristotelian notions, although they appear to be incompatible with the Jewish tradition prevalent in his time, to views that are more easily reconcilable with this tradition and that, through Avicenna's adhesion, were given the hallmark of philosophical respectability. To cite an outstanding example, Maimonides holds no brief for Avicenna's opinion that the individual human soul survives the death of the body and is immortal. Like Alexander of Aphrodisias and other Aristotelians, he considers that in man only the actual intellect—which lacks all individual particularity—is capable of survival. In adopting this view, Maimonides clearly shows that, at least on this point, he prefers the philosophical truth as he sees it, however opposed it may seem to be to the current religious conceptions, to the sort of halfway house between theology and philosophy which, in the severe judgment of certain Spanish Aristotelians—notably Averroes—Avicenna had sought to set up.

To cite another instance, Maimonides does not give the slightest indication of recognizing, as Avicenna did, the mystical ecstatic way to God as being on the same level as the way of the intellect (the Muslim philosopher may have claimed even more for it than simple equality). According to the *Guide,* the religious commandment enjoining the love of God entails the duty of knowing whatever may be known of him, for love is proportionate to the knowledge man has of the beloved.

THEORY OF DIVINE ATTRIBUTES

What kind of cognition of God is possible to man? The *Guide* sets forth at considerable length and with stronger emphasis than in Avicenna the doctrine of negative the-

ology. According to this doctrine, nothing positive can be known about God, who has nothing in common with any other being. No predicate or descriptive term can legitimately be applied to him unless it is given a meaning that is wholly different from the one the term has in common usage and is purely negative. All statements concerning God considered in himself should, if they are to be regarded as true, be interpreted as providing an indication of what God is *not.* This applies even to the statement that God exists. Maimonides maintains that progress in this kind of negative knowledge is of considerable value, for it does away with false ideas concerning God.

On the other hand, the positive knowledge that man is capable of is concerned with quite a different domain; it deals not with God in himself but with his governance of nature, or, in other words, with the order obtaining in the cosmos and determining the events that occur in it. According to Maimonides' interpretation of Exodus 33, only this knowledge is granted to Moses, and such are the limitations of human science. As far as this conception is concerned, the acts of God may be identified with the operations of nature (or with historical happenings brought about by natural causes). Maimonides' view of the world being by and large Aristotelian, these operations are subject to the rule that they do not destroy but, rather, safeguard the perpetuity of the immutable order of nature, including the preservation of humankind and of the various other species of living beings.

Some of the operations of God (or of nature) seem, from the human point of view, to be beneficent, for instance, the operation that instills into progenitors the impulse to care for their young; others, such as earthquakes or large floods, seem destructive. Because of the anthropomorphic tendency, men witnessing happenings of the first kind speak of God as being merciful and may impute havoc and death to God's being vengeful. These are two of the so-called divine attributes of action. Quite evidently they are not concerned with the essence of God but reflect a purely human evaluation of God's, or nature's, actions. In contrast with other medieval Aristotelian philosophers, Maimonides does not recognize the divine attributes of relation.

DIVINE INTELLECTION

As the Aristotelian system of physics requires, and as Maimonides demonstrates by means of a number of proofs taken over from earlier philosophers, this world is dependent upon God (who is the Prime Mover); but, contrary to Aristotle's conception (already modified by some of the late Greek Neoplatonists, whose views reached Maimonides through the Islamic philosophers), God is regarded as the efficient and formal as well as the final cause of the cosmos. This God is pure intellectual activity, to which (in Maimonides' view as well as in Aristotle's) man's intellection bears a certain resemblance. Indeed, Maimonides seems to go out of his way to point out this similarity. In this connection a comparison between a statement of his and one of al-Farabi's is instructive. In accordance with the doctrine of Book A of Aristotle's *Metaphysics,* the Muslim philosopher states quite unequivocally that it is because God intellects only himself that the subject, object, and act of divine intellection are identical. Maimonides, too, maintains this three-fold identity with regard to God (*Guide,* Part I, Ch. 68); but he points out that it exists equally in the case of man's intellection of any object, for instance, a piece of wood, because according to an opinion of Aristotle, the actual intellect is identical with the object cognized by it. (This opinion was apparently quite unconnected with Aristotle's conception of God.) This comparison of man's cognition to God's, which argues similarity between the two, appears to be incompatible with Maimonides' negative theology. This point had already been made in the Middle Ages and must be taken into account in any interpretation of the *Guide.*

Furthermore, the fact that Maimonides uses as an example the intellection of a piece of wood seems to suggest that, unlike Aristotle and al-Farabi but in accordance with many of the medieval Aristotelians, he tends to believe that God cognizes not only himself but all the intelligibles. Since cognition involves identity, this conception would appear to entail the identification of God with the intelligible structure of the universe, regarded both as the subject and as the object of cognition. The argument does not entail the identification of matter with God or with an attribute of the Deity. To call Maimonides' position or its logical corollaries "pantheism" would therefore be to go beyond the evidence.

ORIGIN OF THE WORLD

A main theme of the *Guide* concerns the contradiction between the idea of God upon which Judaism is founded and the philosophical view of God. The philosophical view for Maimonides is the conception of God as an intellect rather than as described by the speculations of negative theology. Maimonides is fully aware of the crucial character of the issue and of the impossibility of achieving a true reconciliation between the philosophical and the religious points of view. He remarks in the *Guide*

(Part II, Ch. 20): "For to me the combination between [the world] existing in virtue of necessity and being produced in time in virtue of a purpose in the world ... comes near to being a combination of two contraries." Maimonides points out the "very disgraceful conclusions" that follow from the first opinion:

> Namely it would follow that the Deity, whom everyone who is intelligent recognises to be perfect in every kind of perfection, could as far as all beings are concerned, produce nothing new in any of them; if He wished to lengthen a fly's wing or shorten a worm's foot, He would not be able to do so. But Aristotle would say that He would not wish it and that it is impossible to will something different from what is; that it would not add to His perfection, but would perhaps from a certain point of view be a deficiency. (*Guide,* Part II, Ch. 22)

In Maimonides' interpretation of the Aristotelian position, God's will is assimilated to the divine Intellect, which is identical with God himself, and the world may be regarded as something like an intellection necessarily produced by this Intellect. A consequence of Aristotle's theory as understood by Maimonides is that every characteristic of things existing in the world must be supposed to have a cause grounded in the natural structure of the universe (as opposed to a supernatural cause not determined by this structure). It may be added that as far as bodies are concerned, Maimonides seems to believe that in cases in which a mechanistic explanation can be found, it might provide such a cause. If this were accepted, it would mean that no part of the natural order could be, or could ever have been, different from what it actually is, for its existence is guaranteed by the immutability of divine reason. In other words, the world could not have been created in time.

From this point of view Maimonides is quite consistent in describing temporal creation as the greatest of miracles and in stating that if this is admitted, the intellectual acceptance of other direct interventions of God in the natural course of events does not present any difficulties. Since it serves Maimonides' purpose to make out the best case possible for what he designates as the religious conception of God, he attempts to show that a structure of the universe that is necessary, because it is rationally determined in every respect, does not exist—or at least he seems to do so. In fact, he does not go beyond the demonstration, made at some length, that as far as the heavenly spheres are concerned, Aristotelian physics (although it gives satisfactory explanation of the phenomena of the sublunar world) is incapable of propounding a comprehensive scientific theory that can be regarded as certain and that provides cogent proof for the assumption that the cosmic order could not be different from what it actually is. In this critique of Aristotle's celestial physics he is helped by the much-debated discrepancy that exists between Aristotle's natural science and the Ptolemaic system.

Maimonides also puts forward an argument of somewhat different character. He points out that man's knowledge of the order of nature is based on the empirical data of which he is cognizant. It is, however, conceivable that the existence of the data that are known to man had a beginning in time. No man who studies this problem should ignore this possibility, for if he does so, his case would be analogous to that of a person who disbelieves on empirical grounds—because he has met only adults—that human beings are brought into the world through birth after having been embryos.

Maimonides' critique of the inconsistencies and the insufficiency of the Aristotelian physics is pertinent within its scheme of reference. However, the doctrine of the eternity of the world does not rest exclusively upon physical theory. It is also corollary to the conception of God as Intellect, and Maimonides is aware of this. It is certainly significant, and it may be a deliberate omission, that when Maimonides is dealing with the problem of the eternity of the world in the *Guide,* he does not mention this conception although other portions of the work prove he had adopted it. Thus he does not allude to God as Intellect when he proclaims in the *Guide* (Part II, Ch. 25) that he does not accept the doctrine of the eternity of the world for two reasons: (1) because it has not been demonstrated; (2) because its adoption would be tantamount to destroying the foundations of the Law, for it would mean denying the claims of the prophets and rejecting the belief in miracles.

SOURCES OF KNOWLEDGE

That Maimonides rejected the doctrine of the eternity of the world partly because (as his second reason) it would have destroyed the foundations of religious law may appear to affirm the claim of religious belief to have a decisive voice in theoretical questions that are of paramount concern to it. That is, it may appear to affirm this claim, provided that the intellect is unable to reach a fully demonstrable conclusion with regard to the moot points. Clearly such a claim can have far-reaching implications. It could be argued that this position leads to the recognition of suprarational theoretical truths or, alternatively, to the

assertion of validity of conclusions in the sphere of theory adopted only on the basis of practical reason. Maimonides himself, however, does not at all countenance such a demotion of theoretical reason. In the *Guide* (Part I, Ch. 2) he explains the superiority of theoretical reason, which is concerned with the difference between truth and falsehood, over practical reason, which deals with the distinction between good and evil. His allegorical interpretation of Adam's fall entails the conclusion that practical reason has the comparatively lowly function of curbing the appetite to which man is prone when he is not given over to theoretical contemplation.

As for prophecy and divine revelation, they cannot be regarded as sources of supraintellectual knowledge conceived as being independent of, and superior to, the system of sciences produced by theoretical reason. This comes out clearly in Maimonides' description of the characteristics peculiar to prophets. According to him, prophets must have both an outstanding intellectual capacity and an outstanding imaginative capacity. Given these two preconditions, and suitable conduct, prophecy is a natural phenomenon; the gift of prophecy can be withheld from a person having the required qualifications only by means of a miracle. The intellectual capacity of prophets is similar at least in kind to that of the philosophers; it enables them to receive what Maimonides terms a "divine overflow," an influx coming from the Active Intellect, which, according to the interpretation of the Aristotelian doctrine adopted by Maimonides, brings about the actualization of man's potential intellect. The Active Intellect is the last of the ten incorporeal Intellects; its special sphere of action is the sublunar world.

There is no suggestion that the conclusions reached by the prophets through the use of the intellect are in any way different from those of the philosophers, though the prophets may reach them more rapidly; all prophets are philosophers. This clearly applies also to Moses, in spite of a statement in the *Guide* that none of the author's assertions about the prophets pertain to Moses. In other writings Maimonides describes Moses as having attained union with the Active Intellect; according to the conception of certain Islamic Aristotelians, union with the Active Intellect represents the highest goal and is reached by the great philosophers.

Imagination is inferior to intellect for Maimonides, who was on this point an orthodox Aristotelian. Imagination enables the prophet to see veridical dreams and visions, for the divine overflow spills over from the intellectual to the imaginative sphere. But it certainly does not give access to a supraintellectual truth. In fact the superiority of Moses over all other prophets is, according to Maimonides' interpretation, partly the result of the circumstance that in his prophecy he did not have recourse to imagination.

POLITICAL PHILOSOPHY

Religious revelation thus does not procure any knowledge of the highest truth that cannot be achieved by the human intellect; it does, however, have an educative role—as well as a political one. In Maimonides' words, "The law as a whole aims at two things: the welfare of the soul and the welfare of the body" (*Guide,* Part III, Ch. 27).

Because of the great diversity of human character, a common framework for the individuals belonging to one society can be provided only by a special category of men endowed with the capacity for government and for legislation. Those who have only a strong imagination, unaccompanied by proportionate intellectual powers, are not interested in the intellectual education of the members of the state which they found or govern. On the other hand, the foremost example of an ideal lawgiver is Moses.

The law instituted by Moses had to take into account the historical circumstances—the influence of ancient Oriental paganism—and had to avoid too great a break with universal religious usage. To cite one example, sacrifices could not be abolished, because this would have been an excessively violent shock for the people. In spite of these difficulties, however, Moses succeeded in establishing a polity to which Maimonides, in the "Epistle to Yemen," applies the term *al-madīna al-fādila* ("the virtuous city") used by the Muslim philosophers to designate the ideal state of Plato's *Republic*—a work that, perhaps mainly through the mediation of al-Farabi, had a considerable impact on Maimonides' political thought.

MORAL PHILOSOPHY

The polity is not alone in regulating men's actions in the best possible way. The Scriptures by which the polity is ruled also contain hints that may guide such human individuals as are capable of understanding its hints to philosophical truths. Some of these truths are to be discovered in the beliefs taught to all those who profess Judaism; these dogmas are for evident reasons formulated in a language adapted to the understanding of ordinary unphilosophical people. There are, however, other religious beliefs that, although they are not true, are necessary for the majority of the people, to safeguard a tolerable public order and to further morality. Such are the belief that God is angry with those who act in an unjust manner and

the belief that he responds instantaneously to the prayer of someone wronged or deceived (*Guide,* Part III, Ch. 28). The morality suited to men of the common run aims at their exercising a proper restraint over the passions of the appetite; it is an Aristotelian middle-of-the-road morality, not an ascetic one. The ascetic overtones that are occasionally encountered in the *Guide* concern the philosopher rather than the ordinary man.

There is a separate morality for the elite, which is or should be called upon to rule, to which Maimonides alludes in the *Guide* (Part I, Ch. 54; Part III, Chs. 51 and 54). This ethical doctrine is connected with Maimonides' interpretation of what ought to be man's superior goal, which is to love God, and, as far as possible, to resemble him.

From the point of view of negative theology, love of God can be achieved only through knowledge of divine activity in the world, the only knowledge of God possible. This supreme goal can be reached through a study of natural science and of metaphysics, which appears to signify that the highest perfection can be attained only by a man who leads the theoretical life—the man whose superiority was proclaimed by Aristotle. However, Maimonides is at pains to show—and this seems to be a Platonic element in his doctrine—that the theoretical life can be combined with a life of action, as proved by the examples of the patriarchs and of Moses.

What is more, a life of action can constitute an imitation of God. For the prophetic legislators and statesmen endeavor to imitate the operations of nature, or God (the two are equivalent); the expression "divine or natural actions," which occurs in the *Guide,* may have been in Benedict de Spinoza's mind when he first spoke of *Deus sive natura*). Maimonides emphasizes two characteristics that belong both to the actions of God-nature and to the actions of superior statesmen. First, however beneficent or destructive—or, in ordinary human parlance, however merciful or vengeful—the actions in question appear to be, neither God nor the prophetic statesman is actuated by passions. Second, the activity of nature (or God) tends to preserve the cosmic order, which includes the perpetuity of the species of living beings, but it has no consideration for the individual. In the same way the prophetic lawgivers and statesmen, who in founding or governing a polity should imitate this activity, must have in mind first and foremost the commonweal, the welfare of the majority, and must not be deterred from following a politically correct course of action by the fact that it hurts individuals.

The imitation of the works of God (or of nature) by the prophets means (*Guide*, Part III, Ch. 32) that the prophets imitate in leadership the indirect and complicated way through which nature obtains its desired results, as seen, for instance, in the extremely intricate mechanism of living organisms. Maimonides calls this indirect method a "gracious ruse" of God and his wisdom; he may have taken the expression over from Alexander of Aphrodisias's work "Principle of the All" (extant only in Arabic translation). It is reminiscent, not only on the verbal plane, of G. W. F. Hegel's "Cunning of Reason." According to the *Guide*, Moses used the indirect method in making the sons of Israel wander for forty years in the desert instead of leading them straight to the land of Canaan, for he wanted the people to shed slavish habits and acquire in the hard school of the desert the warlike virtues necessary for conquest. He also used it in adapting the commandments to the historical and geographical circumstances.

INFLUENCE OF THE *GUIDE*

The *Guide* was first translated into Hebrew in Maimonides' lifetime, by Samuel ibn Tibbon and a little later by al-Harizi. Its first translation into Latin was also produced in the thirteenth century. Maimonides' injunction to follow his example in writing the Arabic text of the work only in Hebrew characters (and thus to prevent its being read by non-Jews) was not always observed. The work is mentioned by some later Muslim writers but does not appear to have had more than a very slight impact on Muslim thought.

In the period after Maimonides the *Guide* was the fundamental text of medieval Jewish thought and was much debated. In the thirteenth and fourteenth centuries it was violently denounced for being antireligious and as vehemently defended against this charge; commentaries upon it were written by Shem-Tov Falaquera, Joseph ibn Kaspi, Moses of Narbonne, Isaac Abravanel, and others, and its theses are discussed at length in such capital philosophical works as Gersonides' *Milhamot Adonai* (The wars of the Lord) and Hasdai Crescas's *Or Adonai* (Light of the Lord). At first blush it is therefore rather surprising that among Jewish philosophers, relatively few of Maimonides' disciples have been content to adopt his apparently agnostic attitude toward fundamental metaphysical problems and thus to leave what he believed to be a necessary loophole for religious belief. In fact, no doubt partly because of the unsystematic mode of exposition of the *Guide*, some philosophically minded commentators (notably Moses of Narbonne) expounded Averroes's conceptions rather than Maimonides' in their commentaries on the *Guide*. Other commentators—for example, Abravanel—often criticized him from a traditionalistic religious point of view.

The *Guide* had a strong influence on later Jewish philosophers, many of whom owe their introduction to philosophy to the *Guide*. This can be seen in Spinoza (a considerable portion of the *Tractatus Theologico-politicus* is devoted to a critique of Maimonides, although the explicit references to him are few) and in Salomon Maimon, who wrote a commentary on the *Guide*.

The influence of Maimonides on the medieval Christian Schoolmen seems to have been considerable; the matter has not yet been sufficiently investigated, though several studies dealing with the subject do exist. It may be noted that by elaborating the doctrine of suprarational truths the systems of Thomas Aquinas and of other Scholastics found a way of legitimating from a theoretical point of view Maimonides' decision to opt for the belief in temporal creation, because the existence of religion hinged on this belief's being generally accepted.

See also Alexander of Aphrodisias; al-Fārābī; Averroes; Avicenna; Crescas, Hasdai; Ethics, History of; Galen; Gersonides; Hegel, Georg Wilhelm Friedrich; Ibn Bājja; Jewish Philosophy; Maimon, Salomon; Medieval Philosophy; Plato; Spinoza, Benedict (Baruch) de; Thomas Aquinas, St.

Bibliography

WORKS BY MAIMONIDES

Le guide des égarés. Edited by Salomon Munk, 3 vols. Paris: A. Franck, 1856–1866. Arabic text and French translation, with many detailed notes. The French translation has been reedited. Paris: G.-P. Maisonneuve, 1960.

The Guide of the Perplexed. Translated with an introduction and notes by Shlomo Pines. Chicago: University of Chicago Press, 1963. Introductory essay by Leo Strauss.

WORKS ON MAIMONIDES

Altmann, Alexander. "Das Verhältnis Maimunis zur jüdischen Mystik." *Monatsschrift für Geschichte und Wissenschaft des Judentums* 80 (1936): 305–330.

Baron, Salo, ed. *Essays on Maimonides: An Octocennial Volume.* New York: Columbia University Press, 1941.

Diesendruck, Z. "Maimonides' Lehre von der Prophetie." In *Jewish Studies in Memory of Israel Abrahams,* edited by G. A. Kohut, 74–134. New York: Press of the Jewish Institute of Religion, 1927.

Diesendruck, Z. "Die Teleologie bei Maimonides." *Hebrew Union College Annual* 5 (1928): 415–534.

Epstein, I., ed. *Moses Maimonides: 1135–1204.* London: Soncino Press, 1935.

Guttmann, Jakob. *Der Einfluss der Maimonideschen Philosophic auf das christliche Abendland.* Leipzig, 1908.

Rohner, A. *Das Schöpfungsproblem bei Moses Maimonides, Albertus Magnus, und Thomas von Aquin.* Münster: Aschendorff, 1913.

Roth, Leon. *The Guide for the Perplexed, Moses Maimonides.* London, 1948.

Strauss, Leo. *Persecution and the Art of Writing.* Glencoe, IL: Free Press, 1952. Includes "The Literary Character of *The Guide for the Perplexed,*" also published in Baron's *Essays on Maimonides* (see above).

Strauss, Leo. *Philosophic und Gesetz.* Berlin: Schocken, 1935.

Strauss, Leo. "Quelques Remarques sur la science politique de Maimonide et de Farabi." *Revue des études juives* 100 (1936): 1–37.

Wolfson, H. A. "Hallevi and Maimonides on Design, Chance, and Necessity." *Proceedings of the American Academy for Jewish Research* 11 (1941): 105–163.

Wolfson, H. A. "Hallevi and Maimonides on Prophecy." *Jewish Quarterly Review,* n.s., 32 (1941–1942): 345–370, and n.s., 33 (1942–1943): 49–82.

Wolfson, H. A. "Maimonides and Halevi." *Jewish Quarterly Review,* n.s., 2 (1911–1912): 297–337.

Wolfson, H. A. "Maimonides on Negative Attributes." In *Louis Ginzberg Jubilee Volume,* edited by A. Marx et al., 419–446. New York: American Academy for Jewish Research, 1945.

Wolfson, H. A. "Maimonides on the Internal Senses." *Jewish Quarterly Review,* n.s., 25 (1934–1935): 441–467.

Wolfson, H. A. "The Platonic, Aristotelian, and Stoic Theories of Creation in Hallevi and Maimonides." In *Essays in Honour of the Very Rev. Dr. J. H. Hertz,* edited by Isidore Epstein, Ephraim Levine, and Cecil Roth, 427–442. London: E. Goldston, 1942.

Shlomo Pines (1967)

MAIMONIDES [ADDENDUM]

Since Shlomo Pines's entry, scholars have come to accept 1138, not 1135, as the year of Maimonides' birth. Some scholars also believe that the youthful treatise on logic (*Millot ha-Higayon*) is not by Maimonides. The major development in Maimonidean studies, however, is an interpretive one. Pines worked closely with Leo Strauss on the 1963 English translation of Maimonides' *Guide of the Perplexed*, which remains the best complete English version of his philosophical magnum opus. Strauss, who wrote the introductory essay to the translation, had an idiosyncratic way of reading many premodern thinkers, including Maimonides. In brief, Strauss understood Maimonides to be engaged in a vast project of deception, of concealing his real beliefs, in order that those incapable of understanding and accepting them not become perplexed and dislodged from their simple pieties.

Strauss's way of reading Maimonides finds its way into this article when Pines suggests that Maimonides was a closet Aristotelian who (really) believed in the eternity of the world. Never mind that Maimonides says the opposite to this; for the Straussian, this is just the point: to conceal one's real beliefs, and to suggest the opposite from what one explicitly argues for. There are still Straussian interpreters and interpretations, but they are in retreat. Philosophical scholars tend to rest content with mulling over the actual arguments that Maimonides presents. Further, in response to the Straussian position that there exists a deep divide between philosophy and the law (religion), between Athens and Jerusalem, recent scholars such as Isadore Twersky (1967) and David Hartman (1976) argue that, on the contrary, Maimonides grounds philosophy in the law and understands the law as subserving in large part suprapolitical ends.

Scholars seem less taken with the Maimonidean reaction to Avicenna (Ibn Sīnā) than Pines appears to be. The Islamic thinkers who have more recently emerged as significant for Maimonides are al-Fārābī and Ibn Bājja (Avempace). They tend to be important for their influence on Maimonides' moral and political theorizing. Pines is still good on Maimonides' practical philosophy. Especially to be noted is his insistence on a Platonic element in his view of the summum bonum. Often Maimonides is presented as endorsing Aristotle's view that human happiness is a function of contemplative activity alone. Pines rightly resists this, noting that Moses, the political prophet, is paradigmatic for Maimonides. Indeed, the end of the *Guide* makes clear that imitation of God mirrors God's providential care for the created world.

See also al-Fārābī; Aristotelianism; Aristotle; Avicenna; Ibn Bājja; Platonism and the Platonic Tradition.

Bibliography

WORKS BY MAIMONIDES

Crisis and Leadership: Epistles of Maimonides, edited by David Hartman. Translated by Abraham Halkin. Philadelphia: Jewish Publication Society, 1985.

Ethical Writings of Maimonides, edited and translated by Raymond L. Weiss and Charles E. Butterworth. New York: New York University Press, 1975.

The Guide of the Perplexed. Abridged edition, edited by Julius Guttmann. Translated by Chaim Rabin. London: East and West Library, 1952. Reprinted with a new introduction by D. H. Frank. Indianapolis: Hackett, 1995.

A Maimonides Reader, edited by Isadore Twersky. New York: Behrman House, 1972.

WORKS ON MAIMONIDES AND HIS PHILOSOPHY

Burrell, David. *Knowing the Unknowable God: Ibn Sina, Maimonides, Aquinas.* Notre Dame, IN: University of Notre Dame Press, 1986.

Cohen, Robert, and Hillel Levine, eds. *Maimonides and the Sciences.* Dordrecht, Netherlands: Kluwer, 2000.

Fox, Marvin. *Interpreting Maimonides: Studies in Methodology, Metaphysics, and Moral Philosophy.* Chicago: University of Chicago Press, 1990.

Hartman, David. *Maimonides: Torah and Philosophic Quest.* Philadelphia: Jewish Publication Society, 1976.

Kellner, Menachem. *Maimonides on Human Perfection.* Atlanta: Scholars Press, 1990.

Kellner, Menachem. *Maimonides on Judaism and the Jewish People.* Albany: State University of New York Press, 1991.

Kellner, Menachem. *Maimonides on the Decline of the Generations and the Nature of Rabbinic Authority.* Albany: State University of New York Press, 1996.

Kraemer, Joel, ed. *Perspectives on Maimonides: Philosophical and Historical Studies.* Oxford: Littman Library, 1991.

Lachterman, David. "Maimonidean Studies 1950–86: A Bibliography." *Maimonidean Studies* 1 (1990): 197–216.

Langermann, Yitzhak Z. "The Mathematical Writings of Maimonides." *Jewish Quarterly Review* 75 (1984): 57–65.

Leaman, Oliver. *Moses Maimonides.* London: Routledge, 1990.

Leibowitz, Yeshayahu. *The Faith of Maimonides.* New York: Adama Books, 1987.

Manekin, Charles. *On Maimonides.* Belmont, CA: Wadsworth, 2004.

Pines, Shlomo, and Yirmiyahu Yovel, eds. *Maimonides and Philosophy.* Dordrecht, Netherlands: Nijhoff, 1986.

Seeskin, Kenneth. *Maimonides: A Guide for Today's Perplexed.* West Orange, NJ: Behrman House, 1991.

Seeskin, Kenneth. *Searching for a Distant God: The Legacy of Maimonides.* New York: Oxford University Press, 2000.

Stern, Josef. *Problems and Parables of Law: Maimonides and Nahmanides on Reasons for the Commandments.* Albany: State University of New York Press, 1998.

Strauss, Leo. *Philosophy and Law: Contributions to the Understanding of Maimonides and His Predecessors.* Albany: State University of New York Press, 1994. Originally published as *Philosophie und Gesetz.* Berlin: Schocken, 1935.

Twersky, Isadore. *Introduction to the Code of Maimonides (Mishneh Torah).* New Haven, CT: Yale University Press, 1980.

Twersky, Isadore. "Some Non-Halakic Aspects of the *Mishneh Torah.*" In *Jewish Medieval and Renaissance Studies,* edited by A. Altmann, 95–118. Cambridge, MA: Harvard University Press, 1967.

Twersky, Isadore, ed. *Studies in Maimonides.* Cambridge, MA: Harvard University Press, 1991.

Weiss, Raymond. *Maimonides' Ethics: The Encounter of Philosophic and Religious Morality.* Chicago: University of Chicago Press, 1991.

Daniel H. Frank (2005)

MAINE DE BIRAN
(1766–1824)

Maine de Biran, the French statesman and philosopher, was born Marie François Pierre Gonthier de Biran, receiving the name "Maine" from the name of his family's property (le Maine). He attended the *collège* at Périgueux, dominated by the secular, moderate constitutional Royalists called *Doctrinaires,* and excelled there in mathematics. In 1784 he joined the king's guard and in 1789 was wounded defending Louis XVI in a mob uprising. To escape the Reign of Terror, he retired to his estate in 1793 and began intensive psychological and philosophical investigations. In 1797 he was elected to the Council of Five Hundred, and this election of a moderate royalist was a symptom of the beginning of the end of the Reign of Terror. This post and other public duties did not keep him from reaping the fruits of his earlier meditations. He became acquainted with the *Idéologues* Pierre-Jean Georges Cabanis and Comte Destutt de Tracy by winning first prize in an essay contest sponsored by the Institute of France with the essay *L'influence de l'habitude sur la faculté de penser* (*The Influence of Habit on the Faculty of Thinking*). He won membership in the institute in 1805 by gaining another first prize, for *Mémoire sur la décomposition de la penser* (The Analysis of Thought). While continuing to write outstanding philosophic and psychological essays, he intensified his political activities, became a member of the Chamber of Deputies, and was made commander in the Legion of Honor. Under the first restoration he returned to the National Assembly and was put in charge of liaison between the assembly and the king on financial matters. Despite these public activities, he was at the time of his death acknowledged by most of his distinguished contemporaries as their master (*maître à tous*) in philosophy.

His famous *Journal intime* reveals a melancholy, emotionally changeable person, of poor health, who was highly sensitive to climatic and personal surroundings. He spent much of his personal and philosophic life trying to understand and mitigate this sensitivity.

PHILOSOPHICAL DEVELOPMENT

Maine de Biran's philosophic development can be summarized briefly as a movement toward a more and more detailed conviction that man's inward experience is (1) different from his outwardly experienced "impressions," and (2) an important source and basis of knowledge. His most mature essays speak of an "inward sense" (*sens intime*) that reveals our experience of willed bodily movement (*effort voulu*); in the course of his philosophic development he gave to this experience a more and more important role, progressively more subtly analyzed. The names of John Locke, Étienne Bonnot de Condillac, and Charles Bonnet, all of whom emphasized outward impressions as the ultimate source of knowledge, occurred as frequently in his early notes as did the name of Jean-Jacques Rousseau, whose "Profession of Faith of a Savoyard Vicar" in *Émile* had aroused Maine de Biran's interest in the "inner light" (*lumiére intérieure*).

But the outwardly oriented epistemologies of Condillac and Locke and their disciples, the *Idéologues*, soon grew less adequate for Maine de Biran, as did Bonnet's explanations of perception in terms of physiological mechanisms (explanations based upon outward "impressions"). After 1802 and his first great prize essay, *The Influence of Habit on the Faculty of Thinking*, which was similar in many ways to the writings of the *Idéologues*, Maine de Biran moved into his longest and most original period of philosophizing, during which he became quite critical of his former masters and developed and defended the key doctrine of his philosophy, that the *effort voulu* is a unique source of basic knowledge. In this stage he wrote *Mémoire sur la décomposition de la penser* (which won him membership in the Institute of France) and his most mature completed philosophic work, *Essai sur les fondements de la psychologie* (Essay on the Foundations of Psychology; 1812).

From 1814 to the end of his life he developed—but never with great precision—a doctrine derived from Immanuel Kant (by way of Maine de Biran's friend André Marie Ampère), a doctrine that identified "belief" (*croyance*) as one of the inner sources of knowledge. At first Maine de Biran spoke of belief as revealing the transphenomenal substance of things, and from 1815 on he applied this notion of a "faculty of belief" to problems of theology. According to Maine de Biran, *croyance*, like the *effort voulu*, originates inwardly, but—unlike voluntary bodily movement—is always passive; its function is to receive God's grace. Still, he continued to speak of the importance of the *effort voulu*; the doctrine of the significance of the faculty of belief in relation to religious matters was not a repudiation of the significance of the activistic, individualistic capacity of the *effort voulu* in matters of natural knowledge. In fact, during this last period, from 1814 to 1824, he wrote some of his finest essays developing his doctrine that the *sens intime* is a unique and important source of knowledge. Two of his outstanding works on this subject were *Examen des leçons de philosophie de M. Laromiquière* (An Examination of

Laromiquière's Lessons in Philosophy; 1817) and his unfinished masterpiece, *Nouveaux Essais d'anthropologie* (New Essays in Anthropology; 1824), both of which cast much light on the doctrine of *effort voulu*. In fact this doctrine was far more thoroughly developed than the doctrine of *croyance*. Nevertheless, the emphasis given to belief in the last stage of his thought confirms the generalization that the whole tendency of his philosophic development was toward a more profound conviction that inward experience—whether of willed effort or of belief itself—is the richest basis of knowledge.

LEARNING AND EXPERIENCE

Condillac, the forerunner of the *Idéologues*, had insisted on clarifying terms and validating claims to knowledge by reference to simple, directly experienced outward "sensations" stripped of the increments of learning. The leader of the *Idéologues* in Maine de Biran's day, Destutt de Tracy, had continued Condillac's line of thought but had noticed that (1) some experiences get duller and vaguer by repetition, while others become more distinct; and that (2) there is a capacity to move our bodies voluntarily (Destutt de Tracy called it "*motilité*") that has a vital function in our learning to perceive objects. In addition, Destutt de Tracy's colleagues Cabanis and Bonnet had seen the importance of physiological conditions for an analysis of the human mind.

In his first prize-winning essay Maine de Biran developed all of these suggestions. He not only distinguished between outer impressions and felt effort, but he distinguished what he called "sensations" (such as tastes and smells), wherein the impression is vivacious and our voluntary bodily movement is minimal, from what he called "perceptions" (such as talking aloud and hearing ourselves), wherein the outward impresssion is less important than the inward experience of moving our organs.

But these distinctions might have no importance for an analysis of knowledge, he thought, if they do not help us to understand learning more fully. And so in his first essay he set about trying to discover whether habituation or repetition has a different effect on passive sensations than on active perceptions; if different effects were found to exist it could be assumed that the distinction between sensations and perceptions is important. He found that passively experienced sensations got vaguer with habituation, and perceptions that are involved with our willed bodily movement became more and more precise. Our sense of smell loses its refinement in a hothouse, but we walk, talk, play games better by practicing. Therefore, he concluded, in perceptions alone do we find the possibility of learning, of moving from the passive sensational confusion of the infant to the subtle distinctions of the adult mind. If Condillac's passively received outward impressions were all that was available to consciousness, the repetition of these impressions would have resulted in a vague blur. The development of mind is linked with willed bodily movement, with perceptions.

One of our most important perceptions is our experience of speaking and hearing our own words; this is the most active perception, and the least dependent upon adventitious external impressions. Sounds uttered by us are among the first signs we know; they are outwardly experienced signs of our own inward actions, and it is the inward action that constitutes the meaning of the sign. There are other signs too: We learn to associate two or more external impressions as natural, or physical, signs of each other. But for Maine de Biran the sign-relationship most directly involved in human reasoning is the relationship between spoken words or conventional signs and our inwardly experienced effort to move our organs of speech. In the course of acquiring by habituation a more subtle and distinct way of talking we acquire a more subtle and distinct mentality. Maine de Biran never lost sight of natural sign-relationships between impressions or between images of impressions as part of our learning process, but he insisted that oral, conventional sign-relationships were basic to human mentality. To describe human thinking only in terms of associated images of outward impressions is to ignore speech, the faculty that makes human thought peculiarly human.

In 1812, in his "Essay on the Foundations of Psychology," Maine de Biran set out to find a primary experience, a *fait primitif* antecedent to all learning or habituation (Condillac had sought such a fact and had claimed to find it in outward sensations). Maine de Biran held that such a basic experience must satisfy three criteria: First, it must be within the limits of awareness (although he sometimes talked of unconscious perceptions); second, it must, of course, not be learned or deduced, but must be directly experienced; finally, it must be persistent, for knowledge must have a firmer basis than the passing moment. He rejected outward impressions and inward emotions and affections because they were fleeting, and he rejected the physiological findings he had once been attracted to because they were the results of inferences or deductions, not immediately experienced. In the end he adopted as his primary experience the *effort voulu* he had found to be so crucial to the learning process: We are aware of it, although sometimes not vivaciously; it is not itself learned, although we learn how to move various mem-

bers skillfully; and this experience persists in various degrees of tension (ranging from sensations up to perceptions) throughout our waking life. The most lucidly developed part of Maine de Biran's philosophy is his explanation and defense of this triple claim involved in calling the *effort voulu* a primary experience.

SELFHOOD, CAUSALITY, AND LIBERTY

Philosophers such as Locke, Condillac, and the *Idéologues* had great difficulty accounting for our idea of a persistent, inwardly experienced self, because they assumed that experience was made up of nothing but fleeting, outward impressions. But the origin of this idea loses its mystery if we give our attention to our persistent, inward experience of our own willing against our varying bodily resistance to that willing. Throughout our lives we feel this relationship at the center of our experience in varying degrees of tension. The center is the self (*le moi*), the periphery, or the surrounding impressions, is the nonself. In fact, the unity of our own more or less resisting body as felt in the *sens intime* is the origin of our whole notion of unity or identity, whether it occurs in mathematics or elsewhere.

The felt relationship between the body and our more or less active willing to move that body is for Maine de Biran our basic experience of causation. In defending this claim he argued that the term *cause* cannot be explained by hazy references to "innate" ideas, or by question-begging, tautological assertions about effects presupposing causes; in this he agreed with David Hume. He also agreed with Hume that our disparate impressions do not reveal any instance of necessary connection. But he flatly disagreed with Hume's double assumption that outward impressions are basically similar to and are the origin of any inward experience we may have. Maine de Biran insisted that in our *sens intime* we find a unique, primary experience of necessary connection.

Hume's main objections to this claim occur in his *Enquiries concerning the Human Understanding and concerning the Principles of Morals*; he points out that in cases such as palsy or amputation we cannot be sure our own bodily movement will follow our willing. Moreover, the means by which the will and our body are united is, in Hume's word, "mysterious." How then can we be said to experience an instance of necessary connection when neither connection nor necessity is experienced here? Maine de Biran responded to these objections by using his basic distinction between impressions and the *effort voulu*, or between images, or copies of outward impressions, and our idea of inward felt effort. To the first objection he replied that bodily movement is simultaneous with the willing that is its cause, and that if there is any failure or disappointment, it is the failure or disappointment of a plan involving memory and anticipatory images concerning a succession of experiences. Willed effort itself, involving the simultaneity of cause and effect, never fails; only plans involving successive outward impressions may fail. According to Maine de Biran, Hume mistakes our *pensées* for our *effort voulu*, confuses disparate outward impressions and their images with intimately related, inwardly simultaneous willing and movement.

Hume's second objection is that no connection or "means" connecting the will to the body is present in willed effort. By "means" Hume chiefly meant physiological means that can be demonstrated through outward impressions and derived hypotheses concerning the connection between the willed effort and bodily movement. Maine de Biran answered, however, that in the face of the plainly felt experience of inward causation, one need not ask for "connecting" entities deviously derived from a different sort of experience; Hume, in doing so, simply reasserted his old prejudice in favor of outward impressions and their images. No assertion concerning our physiological structures can diminish or put in question our inwardly experienced relationship between willing and our body. To say that it does is like claiming that remarks about a Caruso's anatomy diminish or put in question the greatness of his artistry. The greatness lies in the singing itself, just as our certainty in experiencing the *effort voulu* lies in this experience itself, not in any hypothetical structures based on quite different experiences. Finally, Maine de Biran pointed out that we apply the term *cause* or *necessary connection* to outward impressions by projecting our inward experience of simultaneity into the outward world of successive impressions; our original experience of causation or necessary connection is inward; all other uses of the term *causation* are derivative from it.

The certainty of the experienced relationship between will and bodily movement is the basis of man's liberty. Deterministic arguments that have been invoked to contest man's liberty depend on causal laws that are less certain than, and indeed irrelevant to, the experience of moving our bodies ourselves. Maine de Biran was willing to assert that in varying degrees strong motives or desires incline us to will certain movements. He was even willing to agree that our passions are sometimes overwhelming, for example, under the influence of hunger or fear, but he went on to say that there are times when the crucial causal factor in any action is our will, which is capable of rejecting any given desire or inclining motive.

At those times we are free, and no dubious hypotheses concerning determining causes can hold up against the plain fact that we can and do withstand particular external or internal pressures. Our freedom does exist, although it is occasional and is tempered by the degree of inclination or pressure.

See also Ampère, André Marie; Bonnet, Charles; Cabanis, Pierre-Jean Georges; Causation; Condillac, Étienne Bonnot de; Destutt de Tracy, Antoine Louis Claude, Comte; Hume, David; Kant, Immanuel; Locke, John; Perception; Rousseau, Jean-Jacques.

Bibliography

WORKS BY MAINE DE BIRAN

The first published edition of Maine de Biran's works was *Oeuvres philosophiques de Maine de Biran*, edited by Victor Cousin, 4 vols. (Paris: Ladrange, 1841). This edition is incomplete and should be avoided, except by those who wish to account for the gross misunderstandings of Maine de Biran's thought that were current in the nineteenth century. The definitive edition of Maine de Biran's notes, essays, and letters is the one edited by Pierre Tisserand and Henri Gouhier: *Oeuvres de Maine de Biran*, 14 vols. (Paris: Alcan, 1920–1942). Gouhier has also edited the definitive edition of Maine de Biran's philosophically revealing *Journal intime* (Neuchâtel, 1954–1957). Only one of Maine de Biran's works has been translated into English—his first prize-winning essay, translated by Margaret Boehm as *The Influence of Habit on the Faculty of Thinking* (Baltimore: Williams and Wilkins, 1929).

WORKS ON MAINE DE BIRAN

No definitive biography has been written; the most detailed life now in print is that by Amable de La Vallett-Monbrun, *Maine de Biran: Essai de biographie historique et psychologique* (Paris, 1914). Sainte-Beuve's brief biography of him in *Causeries du Lundi*, Vol. VIII (Paris, undated), is famous for its eloquence.

On the development of Maine de Biran's philosophy three excellent books have been written. Henri Gouhier's *Les conversions de Maine de Biran* (Paris: Vrin, 1947) is the best account we have of the influences upon him. *Maine de Biran et son oeuvre philosophique*, by Victor Delbos (Paris: Vrin, 1931), is a lucid, impartial summary of the key works. *L'expérience de l'effort et de la grâce chez Maine de Biran*, by George Le Roy (Paris, 1934), uses a Bergsonian approach but even so is faithful and perceptive; it is the best consecutive account of his development. A perceptive, memorable account of his thought occurs in *French Philosophies of the Romantic Period*, by George Boas (Baltimore: Johns Hopkins Press, 1925).

A few useful works on specific topics include Henri Gouhier, "Maine de Biran et Bergson," in *Les études bergsoniennes*, Vol. I (Paris, 1948); Philip Paul Hallie, *Maine de Biran, Reformer of Empiricism* (Cambridge, MA: Harvard University Press, 1959); Jacques Paliard, *Le raisonnement selon Maine de Biran* (Paris, 1925); Euthyme Robef, *Leibniz et Maine de Biran* (Paris, 1927); Ian W. Alexander, Ian W. "Maine De Biran and Phenomenology," *Journal of the British Society for Phenomenology* 1 [1970]: 24–37); Francis C. Moore, Francis C., *The Psychology of Maine De Biran* (Oxford: Clarendon Press, 1970); Serge J. Morin, "Maine De Biran: A New Dualism," *Philosophical Forum* (5[1974]: 441–459); Jean Pucelle, "The Meaning of Experience in Maine De Brian's Philosophy," *International Philosophical Quarterly* (13[1973]: 25–32); Christopher C. Rodie, "Delacroix, Maine De Biran, and the Aesthetics of Romanticism." *Dialogue* (17[1974]: 13–24).

Philip P. Hallie (1967)
Bibliography updated by Tamra Frei (2005)

MAISTRE, COMTE JOSEPH DE
(1754–1821)

Comte Joseph de Maistre, the Savoyard philosopher and diplomat, was born in Chambéry. After the conquest of Savoy by the French revolutionary forces, he retired to Lausanne, where he lived for three years, devoting himself mainly to writing his *Considérations sur la France* (1796), an attack on the political philosophy of republicanism. He was then summoned to Turin by the king of Sardinia and later moved to Cagliari, the capital of the very diminished kingdom of Sardinia. In 1802 he was appointed Sardinian minister plenipoteniary to St. Petersburg and remained there for fourteen years, composing his famous *Soirées de Saint-Pétersbourg*, which was not published until the year of his death.

ULTRAMONTANISM

De Maistre is best known for his ultramontanism and traditionalism, which are most forcibly stated in *Du pape*, written in 1817, although anticipated in certain details in his *Considérations sur la France*. His presuppositions were those of any medieval Roman Catholic—the church is a divine institution; its foundation was given to St. Peter; St. Peter was the first pope; his successors have inherited the powers conferred on him by Jesus Christ himself. The book opens with a demonstration of papal infallibility. Identifying the sovereignty of the pope with that of any secular ruler, de Maistre argued that sovereignty implies infallibility, since no ruler is sovereign whose decisions can be set aside or be subject to appeal. He thus made no distinction between executive competence and validity. As parliaments exist simply to inform the sovereign of matters of which he might not be aware or to make requests and express occasional desires, so the church

councils have no power to do more than this. They are convoked and presided over by the pope, who is not bound by their decisions, for they have no real power of decision. The notion that matters of faith and doctrine can be decided by a council is as absurd as the notion that a parliament can actually rule. De Maistre maintained that when the pontiff speaks ex cathedra and without restraint to the church, he has never erred nor can he ever err in questions of faith. He might be constrained to make a false pronouncement, or he might be speaking merely as a man and not as a pope, but in his function as a sovereign monarch, it is impossible that he should ever be in error.

The reason we require any kind of government is that we are born corrupt, yet with a sense of morality. Our souls are thus in a state of conflict. Sovereigns exist in order to prevent the disasters that arise from this conflict and to keep order within the state. No man is capable of governing himself, for no man can spontaneously quell the evil that is in him; therefore, the power to do so must reside in the hands of one ruler who will be above criticism and have absolute power. This ruler, whether he is a king or a pope, does not rule by the consent of his people but because of their needs. Kings, although infallible in regard to their own provinces, are nevertheless subject to the laws of God, and the pope is the only possible judge of whether they have been faithful to them. The pope is the deputy of God, and when a secular ruler has erred, he can be deposed and his subjects can be freed from their oaths of allegiance to him by papal decree. This power, de Maistre maintained, has been used only rarely where hereditary sovereigns were involved; it was used more freely against elected sovereigns, such as the Holy Roman emperors, for they were chosen by man, not by God. The pope, it should be noted, does not interfere in purely secular problems of administration; his intervention is invoked only in morals and religion.

Nevertheless, the pope is not a universal sovereign, for his power is checked by the canons, the laws, the customs of nations, duty, fear, prudence, and opinion, "which governs the world." Is it not better, de Maistre asked, to settle disputes by the decision of a wise and prudent ruler, inspired by God himself, than by rebellions, civil wars, and all the evils that follow from them? Such an arbitrator will inevitably submit to the commands of duty and prudence, will be sensitive to custom and opinion, and will intuitively know which road to take when conflict arises.

TRADITIONALISM

A reader of *Du pape* will be impressed by de Maistre's use of tradition to justify his conclusions. The supremacy of the pope, he argued, has always been acknowledged, even by his critics. That is, they all admitted that he has done what de Maistre said he has the power to do, and, de Maistre added, no one except those who had suffered at his hands objected to his power. That something has always been done is to de Maistre proof that it has been done correctly. He even denied the right to liberty on the ground that slavery was the fate of most men until the rise of Christianity.

To de Maistre the human race is a single being, the soul of which is expressed in its language. Language develops, but so does tradition. The tradition of Catholicism is simply the fulfillment of the covenant God gave to Abraham; passed to Moses and then to Aaron, the high priest; and so on down to the promise made to Peter. But in every tradition, in spite of its development, there is a unity of idea, and the maintenance of that unity is entrusted to the pontiff.

ROYALISM

Concurrent with de Maistre's traditionalism was his royalism. He was so convinced of the need for absolute monarchs that he even maintained that since kings had a longer life expectancy than other men, royal families differ in nature from nonroyal families, as a tree differs from a shrub. A king is not a private individual and must not be judged as such. He is the nation in the same way that the pope is the church. Consequently, his power is also absolute, for when he speaks, it is the nation speaking through him. Kings alone preserve national unity. The word *unity* was a eulogistic term for de Maistre. To be unified is better than to be manifold; to remain the same is better than to change. And although de Maistre had to admit those changes that have obviously occurred and are not evil, he insisted on the unity that underlay them.

De Maistre usually carried his ideas to their logical conclusions. His famous apostrophe to the hangman in the *Soirées* is based on de Maistre's presupposition of the twofold nature of man. If the hangman is removed from society, order will give way to chaos, thrones will totter, and society will disappear. "God who is the author of sovereignty is also the author of punishment." He is the author of punishment so that corrupt man may still be redeemed. But if man is to be punished, there must be an absolute and unquestioned power to execute the punishment, and that power is the king's.

De Maistre was the first philosopher of the counterrevolution in France. With the vicomte de Bonald, he gave a set of arguments to legitimists and Catholics. But although de Maistre was admired by many for his consistency in both principle and inference, his variety of political philosophy was never popular, even during the restoration. The anti-intellectualism of François René de Chateaubriand and Mme. de Staël, as fully opposed to the extremes of revolution as was de Maistre's traditionalism, gained more adherents. Moreover, ultramontanism was disclaimed by the Vatican. This disclaimer, perhaps, was the main reason for the failure of de Maistre's thought to become popular in France.

See also Bonald, Louis Gabriel Ambroise, Vicomte de; Chateaubriand, François René de; Republicanism; Staël-Holstein, Anne Louise Germaine Necker, Baronne de; Traditionalism.

Bibliography

WORKS BY DE MAISTRE

Considérations sur la France. Neuchâtel, Switzerland, 1796.

Du pape. 2 vols. Lyons, 1819.

Soirées de Saint-Pétersbourg. 2 vols. Paris, 1821.

Oeuvres complètes. 14 vols. Lyons, 1884–1887.

The Works of Joseph de Maistre. Translated by Jack Lively. New York: Macmillan, 1965. Selections.

WORKS ON DE MAISTRE

Boas, G. *French Philosophies of the Romantic Period*. Baltimore: Johns Hopkins Press, 1925. See Ch. 3.

Ferraz, M. *Histoire de la philosophie en France au XIXe siècle*. Vol. II, *Traditionalisme et ultramontanisme*. Paris: Didier 1880.

Garrard, Graeme. "Joseph De Maistre's Civilization and its Discontents." *Journal of the History of Ideas* 57(3) (1996): 429–446.

Garrard, Graeme. "Rousseau, Maistre, and the Counter-Enlightenment." *History of Political Thought* 15(1) (1994): 97–120.

Gianturco, E. *Joseph de Maistre and Giambattista Vico*. Washington, DC, 1937.

Kochin, Michael S. "How Joseph De Maistre Read Plato's Laws." *Polis* 19(1–2) (2002): 29–43.

Kow, Simon. "Maistre and Hobbes on Providential History and the English Civil War." *Clio* 30(3) (2001): 267–288.

Laski, H. J. *Authority in the Modern State*. New Haven, CT: Yale University Press, 1919.

Lecigne, C. *Joseph de Maistre*. Paris, 1914.

Spektorowski, Alberto. "Maistre, Donoso Cortes and the Legacy of Catholic Authoritarianism." *Journal of the History of Ideas* 63(2) (2002): 283–302.

George Boas (1967)
Bibliography updated by Tamra Frei (2005)

MAJOR, JOHN
(1469–1550)

John Major, or Mair, was a Scottish theologian, active at the University of Paris for some years before and after he secured a license in theology in 1506. Major helped to revive, if only briefly, the spirit of fourteenth-century nominalism. He was entirely sympathetic with the approach of William of Ockham and Jean Buridan, even though he adopted some doctrines of John Duns Scotus and other realists.

Major came to Paris in 1493 after studying at Cambridge. He taught at the University of Paris for most of his lengthy career, with the exception of seven years at the Scottish universities of Glasgow and St. Andrews. When he arrived at Paris, scholasticism, pietism, and humanism were rivals within the university itself. Late medieval pietism was reflected in the ascetic discipline instituted at the Collège de Montaigu, the school that so repelled Desiderius Erasmus by its austerity and its logic-chopping. Major, with his frugal Scottish background, found the atmosphere of Montaigu less forbidding, and he responded with initial enthusiasm to its manner of disputing. He seems to have been little influenced by the sort of humanism being advocated at the time by Jacques Lefèvre d'Étaples, who stressed the value of knowing Aristotle and the Church Fathers in the original Greek. Major belonged to the scholastic tradition completely. His theological and philosophical works proceed entirely from a formal analysis of separate arguments. He made no use of Greek, although he clearly was conversant with Latin literature.

Major's earliest published work consisted of short treatises on terminist logic, published separately from 1500 to 1503, and then together at Lyons in 1505 as a commentary on Peter of Spain. Later he published commentaries on Aristotle's *Ethics* and *Physics*. In theology, he wrote commentaries on the *Sentences* of Peter Lombard and on the Gospels. All of these writings reflect his teaching duties, even in their style. Toward the close of his long life, Major complained mildly at having been forced to accommodate himself to the "manner of our ancestors" and admitted that students had not always found the disputatious style agreeable. In addition to the works already mentioned, Major wrote *A History of Greater Britain*, a landmark in the writing of Scottish history and a most unusual work for a nominalist theologian. Many passages in this work—such as those in defense of the "oaten bread" of Scotland or of ale as opposed to wine—suggest a personality by no means dry and pedantic. Neverthe-less, Major's philosophical style has put off scholars, and his work still awaits total and mature evaluation. Almost all present-day accounts of Major continue to be colored by humanist criticisms of theology made in the spirit of Erasmus, with little sympathy for medieval logic.

See also Aristotle; Buridan, John; Duns Scotus, John; Erasmus, Desiderius; Logic, History of: Medieval (European) Logic; Medieval Philosophy; Patristic Philosophy; Peter Lombard; Peter of Spain; Pietism; William of Ockham.

Bibliography

A reliable, although sketchy, account of Major's philosophical opinions is given by Ricardo Garcia Villoslada in *La universidad de Paris durante los estudios de Francisco de Vitoria* (Rome: Universitatis Gregorianae, 1938), pp. 127–164. Carl Prantl, in *Geschichte der Logik im Abendlande* (Leipzig, 1927), Vol. IV, pp. 247–250, gives a few excerpts from Major's logical writings. Major's views on church matters (he was a conciliarist and champion of Gallicanism) are sometimes dealt with briefly in histories of political theory. The details of his life are presented in Aeneas J. G. Mackay's biography, prefixed to an English translation of *A History of Greater Britain* (Edinburgh: Edinburgh University Press, Scottish History Society, 1892), which also contains a bibliography of Major's writings. This bibliography needs to be supplemented, however, by the additions given by Hubert Élie, *Le traité "De l'infini" de Jean Mair* (Paris: Vrin, 1938); James F. Keenan, "The Casuistry of John Major: Nominalist Professor of Paris (1506–1531)," *Annual of the Society of Christian Ethics* (1993, pp. 205–221).

Neal W. Gilbert (1967)
Bibliography updated by Tamra Frei (2005)

MALCOLM, NORMAN
(1911–1990)

Norman Malcolm, one of America's best-known philosophers, was born in Selden, Kansas, in 1911. After studying philosophy with O. K. Bouwsma at the University of Nebraska, he enrolled as a graduate student at Harvard in 1933. The decisive period for Malcolm's career, however, was probably the time he spent at Cambridge University in 1938–1939, when he met G. E. Moore and Ludwig Wittgenstein. Although Moore exerted a strong influence on him, it is perhaps not unfair to say that most of Malcolm's published work was an attempt to understand Wittgenstein, to explain his thought to others, and to apply Wittgenstein's characteristic manner of approaching philosophical questions to areas the latter did not directly treat.

Malcolm's published work deals especially with the nature of necessary truth; empirical certainty; the connections between common sense, ordinary language, and philosophy; knowledge and perception; and such topics in the philosophy of mind as memory, dreaming, and the problem of other minds. He also wrote on topics in the philosophy of religion. What follows will be confined to the first three topics.

NECESSARY TRUTH

"Are Necessary Propositions Really Verbal?" and its companion piece, "The Nature of Entailment" (in *Knowledge and Certainty*), together form an interesting statement of the linguistic theory of the a priori. In the former, Malcolm points out that some philosophers (for example, C. D. Broad, Moore, and A. C. Ewing) hold that necessary propositions state very general truths about reality—for instance, that nothing is both red and green all over. Others (for example, A. J. Ayer and the early Wittgenstein) apparently believe that if necessary propositions state anything at all, they state truths about language; they are "merely verbal." Malcolm tries to show that, although it is false, literally speaking, that necessary propositions are merely verbal, there is nonetheless considerable merit in saying that they are. He argues this point by claiming that we learn necessary truths by observing how people use certain expressions. Finding out that a pair of propositions are equivalent, for example, is the same thing as finding out that some pairs of expressions are used interchangeably. What makes a given statement necessary is some empirical fact about linguistic usage. (Although Malcolm considers the objection that on this account any necessary statement turns out to be identical with or equivalent to some contingent statement about linguistic expressions, he does not, it seems, have a clear answer to it.) Accordingly, he says, it is false that necessary statements are merely verbal or are rules of grammar or are not really propositions; it is nonetheless worthwhile to say these things in that they prevent one from supposing, for example, that there are two kinds of facts or truths, necessary and contingent, a supposition that is, literally speaking, true but nonetheless misleading. Why? Perhaps Malcolm believed that in saying this one minimizes the vast and important difference between necessary and contingent truths, the difference being that the necessary truths depend upon or reflect facts of linguistic usage in a way that the contingent truths do not.

EMPIRICAL CERTAINTY

In "The Verification Argument" and "Certainty and Empirical Statements" (in *Knowledge and Certainty*), Malcolm objects to the view that no empirical statements are ever really certain. "The Verification Argument" is a careful, clear, and very impressive examination of the arguments philosophers (in particular, C. I. Lewis, who was a teacher of Malcolm's at Harvard) have offered for this skeptical view. Where S is any empirical statement, Malcolm points out that these arguments always invoke as a premise the claim that the consequences of S may not occur and deduce from this that it is not certain that the consequences of S will occur. What Malcolm shows is that there is no interpretation of the former statement according to which it both is true and entails the latter.

ORDINARY LANGUAGE

In several essays, Malcolm dealt with certain questions about the relationships between ordinary language, common sense, and philosophy. Essentially, what he says is that if a philosopher is investigating a concept of ordinary language (for example, *seeing*) and comes to conclusions at variance with ordinary language, then we may be sure that he has made a mistake. What is it to come to a conclusion that goes against ordinary language? One way of doing this is to hold that a sentence with an ordinary use expresses a logical impossibility: some philosophers, for example, appear to insist that it is logically impossible to see physical objects. We may recognize their error by noting that such sentences as "I see the table in the corner" have a perfectly good ordinary use and therefore cannot be self-contradictory. But it is impossible to convey the full power of Malcolm's arguments without a very detailed consideration of particular cases.

See also Ayer, Alfred Jules; Broad, Charlie Dunbar; Common Sense; Dreams; Lewis, Clarence Irving; Memory; Moore, George Edward; Ontological Argument for the Existence of God; Other Minds; Wittgenstein, Ludwig Josef Johann.

Bibliography

WORKS BY MALCOLM

"Defending Common Sense." *Philosophical Review* (1949).

"Philosophy and Ordinary Language." *Philosophical Review* (1951).

"Dreaming and Skepticism." *Philosophical Review* (1956).

Ludwig Wittgenstein: A Memoir. London: Oxford University Press, 1958.

Dreaming. London: Routledge, 1959.

Knowledge and Certainty. Englewood Cliffs, NJ: Prentice Hall, 1963.

"Behaviorism as a Philosophy of Psychology." In *Behaviorism and Phenomenology,* edited by T. W. Wann. Chicago: William Marsh Rice University by the University of Chicago Press, 1964.

"Is It a Religious Belief That God Exists?" In *Faith and the Philosophers,* edited by John Hick. New York: St. Martin's, 1964.

"Scientific Materialism and the Identity Theory." *Dialogue* (1964).

Alvin Plantinga (1967)

MALEBRANCHE, NICOLAS
(1638–1715)

EARLY LIFE AND *RECHERCHE*

One of the major figures in post–René Descartes Cartesianism, Nicolas Malebranche was one of many children born to his mother, Catherine de Lauzon, the sister of a viceroy of Canada, and his father, also Nicolas Malebranche, a secretary to Louis XIII. As in the case of Descartes and Blaise Pascal, Malebranche was born in frail health. His particular afflictions were a severe malformation of the spine and weak lungs, and because of these conditions he needed to be tutored at home until the age of sixteen. Subsequently, he was a student at the Collège de la Marche, and after graduating he went to study theology at the Sorbonne. His education left him with a dislike of a scholasticism that focused on the work of Aristotle. Thus, in 1660 he decided to leave the universities and enter the Oratory, a religious congregation founded in Paris in 1611 by the Augustinian theologian Pierre Bérulle. At the Oratory Malebranche studied ecclesiastical history, linguistics, and the Bible, and with his fellow students he also immersed himself in the work of St. Augustine. Though judged to be merely a mediocre student, he was ordained a priest on September 14, 1664.

The same year he was ordained, Malebranche happened in a Paris bookstall upon a posthumous edition of Descartes's *Traité de l'homme* (*Treatise on Man*), which provides a sketch of a mechanistic account of the physiology of the human body. Malebranche's early biographer, Father Yves M. André, reports that he was so "ecstatic" on reading this account that he experienced "such violent palpitations of the heart that he was obliged to leave his book at frequent intervals, and to interrupt his reading of it in order to breathe more easily" (André 1970, pp. 11–12). Though André does not indicate why Malebranche was so moved, one can speculate that he had discovered in this text a way to investigate the natural world without relying on Aristotelian scholasticism. In any case, after his encounter with *L'homme* Malebranche devoted himself to a decade-long study of the Cartesian method and its results in mathematics and natural philosophy.

The principal fruit of this study was a two-volume work bearing the title *De la recherche de la vérité. Où l'on traitte de la nature de l'esprit de l'homme, et de l'usage qu'il en doit faire pour eviter l'erreur dans les sciences* (*The Search after Truth,* first published 1674–1675), in which is treated the nature of the human mind and the use that must be made of it to avoid error in the sciences. It is primarily this text that provides the basis for Malebranche's reputation in the early modern period. As its full title indicates, the *Recherche* focuses on the principal sources of human error and on the method for avoiding those errors and for finding the truth. The first five books enumerate the various errors deriving from the senses, — imagination, pure understanding, inclinations, and passions, respectively—and a sixth book is devoted to the Cartesian method of avoiding such errors through attention to clear and distinct ideas. The centerpiece of the third book, on pure understanding, is a defense of the claim that the ideas through which one perceives bodies exist in God. Tucked away in the final book, on method, is a critique of "the most dangerous error of the ancients," namely, the Aristotelian position that there are secondary causes in nature distinct from God.

The first volume of the *Recherche,* containing the first three books, was published in 1674 and drew an immediate response in 1675 from Simon Foucher, the canon of Sainte Chapelle of Dijon. Foucher was an "academic skeptic" who attacked the assumption that ideas in one can represent objects distinct from oneself (see Foucher 1969). The Cartesian Benedictine Robert Desgabets replied to Foucher by insisting that the Cartesian rule that clear and distinct ideas are true presupposes that one's thoughts correspond to real external objects. In brief prefaces added to various editions of the second volume of the *Recherche,* Malebranche chastised both thinkers for failing to read the work they were discussing, noting in particular that he had explicitly argued in the *Recherche* that the ideas one perceives exist in God rather than in oneself.

Malebranche solicited written responses to the *Recherche* modeled on the sets of objections published with Descartes's *Meditations.* Perhaps put off by Malebranche's harsh treatment of Foucher and Desgabets, his critics offered instead only informal objections channeled through mutual friends. In 1678 Malebranche appended to the *Recherche* a set of sixteen *Eclaircissements*, or clarifications, that respond to these objections. Among the more important objections addressed are those that concern Malebranche's assertion that one has a freedom to "consent" to certain motives for action (Eclaircissement I), his claim that reason does not yield a demonstrative argument for the existence of the material world (Eclaircissement VI), his doctrine of the vision of ideas in God (Eclaircissement X), his conclusion that one knows one's own soul through a confused consciousness rather than through a clear idea of its nature (Eclaircissement XI), and his occasionalist thesis that God is the only true cause (Eclaircissement XV). In the 1678 edition there is a final Eclaircissement that defends the importance "not only for knowledge of nature but also for knowledge of religion and morals" of the view, only hinted at in the text of the *Recherche* itself, that God acts for the most part through "general volitions" (*volontez générales*), and that He acts though "particular volitions" (*volontez particulières*) only in the exceptional case of miracles.

NATURE ET GRÂCE AND THE DEBATE WITH ARNAULD

Malebranche developed his theory of divin action in his 1680 *Traité de la nature et de la grâce* (*Treatise on Nature and Grace*). He published this work over the objections of the Jansenist theologian and Cartesian philosopher Antoine Arnauld, who was disturbed by what he saw as Malebranche's denial of the claim in the Scriptures and Catholic tradition that God attends to particular details in matters of grace. Arnauld responded to the publication of *Nature et de la grâce* by publishing a response to Malebranche, and the ensuing battle between these two individuals became one of the major intellectual events of the day. Arnauld's opening salvo was the 1683 *Des vraies et des fausses idées* (*On True and False Ideas*), which attacks not *Nature et de la grâce* but the *Recherche* (see Arnauld 1990). His strategy here is to undermine Malebranche's influence in theological matters by revealing the inadequacy of his philosophical views. In particular, Arnauld attacks Malebranche's assumption that ideas are "representative beings" distinct from one's perceptions, offering instead the position, which he plausibly ascribes to Descartes, that ideas are simply aspects of the perceptual modifications of one's soul. This argument reflects a sympathy for Descartes's views that dates back to Arnauld's set of comments on the *Meditations*.

The same year that Arnauld presented his initial critique, Malebranche published the *Méditations chretiennes*

et métaphysiques (*Christian and Metaphysical Meditations*), where "the Word" (i.e., the Second Person of the Trinity) offers a summary of Malebranche's system that highlights the central role that God plays in both metaphysics and morality. This work was in some ways a follow up to his 1677 *Conversations chrétiennes* (*Christian Conversations*). In this earlier text Malebranche presents a defense of the Christian religion that emphasizes the Augustinian theme of one's dependence on God for knowledge and happiness. In 1684 Malebranche further develop his views in moral philosophy in the *Traité de morale* (*Treatise on Ethics*), in which he argues that moral virtue requires a love of the "immutable order" that God reveals to those who seek to know it.

Also in 1684 Malebranche responded to Arnauld's *Idées*, and after a further exchange on the topic of the nature of ideas the debate turned to the religious issues of divine providence, grace, and miracles. The battle became increasingly bitter, and as a result of a campaign on the part of Arnauld and his supporters, Malebranche's *Nature et de la grâce* was put on the Catholic *Index librorum prohibitorum* (*Index of Prohibited Books*) in 1690 (the *Recherche* was added in 1709). The Malebranche-Arnauld polemic continued even after Arnauld's death in 1694, with the posthumous publication of two letters from Arnauld in 1699 and of Malebranche's responses to those letters in 1704.

ENTRETIENS AND DEBATES WITH LEIBNIZ AND RÉGIS

In 1688 Malebranche published his *Entretiens sur la métaphysique et la religion* (*Dialogues on Metaphysics and on Religion*), a concise summary of his main metaphysical doctrines of the vision in God and occasionalism that also addresses the problem of evil. In 1696 he appended to this text the *Entretiens sur la mort* (*Dialogues on Death*), which he composed after a life-threatening illness.

In 1692 Malebranche published a short study, the *Lois de la communication des mouvements* (*Laws of the Communication of Motions*), in which he endorses Descartes's law of the conservation of the quantity of motion but offers rules governing collision that, unlike Descartes's own rules, involve no appeal to a force in bodies to remain at rest. In correspondence with Malebranche, Gottfried Wilhelm Leibniz emphasized difficulties with Descartes's conservation law and that correspondence led Malebranche to insert into a 1700 edition of the *Lois* the claim that experience reveals the falsity of this law.

In 1693 Malebranche responded to the criticisms of the *Recherche* in the 1690 *Système de philosophie* (*System of Philosophy*) by the French Cartesian Pierre-Sylvain Régis. Régis defended an account of ideas similar to the one that Arnauld had defended against Malebranche during the 1680s, and Arnauld used the Régis-Malebranche exchange as an occasion to return to the issue of ideas during the last year of his life (on this exchange, see Schmaltz 2002, chapter 5). Despite their dispute, Malebranche and Régis were both appointed as honorary members of the French Académie des sciences when it was reorganized in 1699. Malebranche presented an inaugural lecture to the Académie that defends against Descartes an account of color in terms of the frequency of vibrations of light. In later published versions of the lecture Malebranche revised his discussion to take into account the theory of the nature of color in the work of the great English natural philosopher Sir Isaac Newton.

FINAL WORKS

In 1699 Malebranche published *Traité de l'amour de Dieu* (*Treatise on the Love of God*), along with *Trois lettres à Lamy* (*Three Letters to Lamy*), in which he rejects the claim of the Benedictine François Lamy (not to be confused with his Cartesian contemporary, the Oratorian Bernard Lamy) that passages from the *Traité de morale* and other texts support the quietist position, that moral action derives from a disinterested "pure love of God." This rejection of Lamy's quietism provided the basis for Malebranche's reconciliation with the French cleric and establishment figure Jacques-Bénigne Bossuet. Bossuet had earlier enlisted the aid of François de Salignac de la Mothe Fénelon in writing against Malebranche's occasionalism and his appeals to God's "general will," but later became a bitter enemy of Fénelon's quietism.

With the support of the apostolic vicar in China, Malebranche published in 1708 *Entretien d'un philosophe chrétien et d'un philosophe chinois, sur l'existence et la nature de Dieu* (*Dialogue between a Christian Philosopher and a Chinese Philosopher on the Existence and Nature of God*). In this text, Chinese philosophy is closely allied with the monism found in the early modern Dutch thinker, Benedict (Baruch) de Spinoza.

A sixth and last edition of the *Recherche* appeared in 1712, and in 1715 Malebranche published his final work, *Réflexions sur la prémotion physique* (*Reflections on Physical Premotion*), in which he responded to the claim of the abbé Laurent-François Boursier that occasionalism leads naturally to the Thomistic position that God determines one's actions by means of a "physical premotion." In his

response, Malebranche defended the claim, present from the first edition of the *Recherche*, that one's free actions involve a "consent" that God does not determine.

NATURE OF IDEAS AND THE VISION IN GOD

In a section of the third book of the *Recherche* devoted to "the nature of ideas," Malebranche argues for his famous doctrine of the vision in God. More precisely, the thesis in this section is that one sees external objects by means of ideas in God. The argument for this thesis begins with the claim at the beginning of this section that "everyone agrees that we do not perceive objects external to us by themselves" since it can hardly be the case that "the soul should leave the body to stroll about the heavens to see the objects present there" (Malebranche 1997b, III-2.i.§1). Arnauld later took exception to this starting point, countering that "ideas, taken in the sense of representative beings, distinct from perceptions, are not needed by our soul in order to see bodies" (Arnauld 1990, p. 18). His main objection is that Malebranche stacks the deck in favor of his doctrine that one sees ideas of bodies in God by assuming from the start that these ideas are distinct from one's own perceptions.

In developing his own position, Arnauld appeals to Descartes's distinction in the Third Meditation between the formal reality of an idea as a perceptual modification of mind and its objective reality as a representation of an object. Arnauld insists that a representative idea is simply the objective reality of a perception, and thus not something distinct from that perception. However, it is important to note that Malebranche's definition of an idea does not rule out such a position from the start. As he himself insists to Arnauld, the claim that one must perceive external objects through ideas leaves open the question of whether an idea is "*a modality of the soul*, according to the opinion of M. Arnauld; an *express species*, according to certain philosophers, or an *entity created with the soul*, according to others; or finally *intelligible extension rendered sensible by color or light*, according to my opinion" (Malebranche 1958–1984, p. 6:95).

Malebranche's description of his own opinion goes beyond what can be found in the original edition of the *Recherche*. However, his description of the other alternatives is drawn directly from this text. In particular, Malebranche argues that there are only four alternatives to the conclusion that one sees bodies through ideas in God: (1) bodies transmit resembling species to the soul; (2) one's soul has the power to produce ideas when triggered by nonresembling bodily impression; (3) ideas are created with the soul or produced in it successively by God; and (4) one's soul sees both the essence and the existence of bodies by considering its own perfections. Malebranche tells Arnauld that because this list constitutes "an exact division … of all the ways in which we can see objects" and because each of the alternative accounts yields "manifest contradictions," his argument from elimination serves to demonstrate the doctrine of the vision in God (Malebranche 1958–1984, p. 6:198f).

It is difficult to determine from the *Recherche* the precise source of the enumeration. However, Desmond Connell (1967) establishes that Malebranche's argument was drawn from the account of angelic knowledge in the work of the sixteenth-century Spanish scholastic Francisco Suárez. Particularly crucial for Malebranche's enumeration is Suárez's claim that angels must know material objects through species that God adds to their mind given that God alone can know them through His own substance. In light of this claim, one can take Malebranche's first three hypotheses to cover the various ways in which one can perceive bodies through immaterial species "superadded" to one's soul, and his fourth hypothesis to cover the possibility that one perceives bodies in the perfections of one's soul. In arguing against the last hypothesis Malebranche notes that because a finite being can see in itself neither the infinite nor an infinite number of beings (as Suárez argues in the case of angels), and because one in fact perceives both the infinite and infinity in external objects, it must be that one sees these objects by means of perfections contained in the only being that can possess an infinity of ideas, namely, God Himself.

Malebranche takes the conclusion here to confirm the view in "an infinity of passages" in Augustine that "we see God" in knowing eternal truths. This appeal to the Augustinian theory of divine illumination provides the basis for an argument for the vision in God that bypasses the unusual enumeration in the *Recherche*. This more direct argument is introduced in Eclaircissement X, where Malebranche urges that the ideas one perceives must exist in an "immutable and necessary Reason" because they are themselves immutable and necessary (Malebranche 1958–1984, p. 3:129f). Malebranche emphasizes that the Augustinian view that eternal truths derive from uncreated features of the divine intellect conflicts directly with the voluntarist conclusion in Descartes that these truths derive rather from God's free and indifferent will. Particularly in his exchanges with Arnauld, Malebranche attempts to present his doctrine of the vision in God as a natural consequence of Descartes's

account of ideas. However, Malebranche's own Augustinian argument serves to show that Descartes could not have accepted this doctrine. Moreover, such an argument reveals the most fundamental reason for Malebranche's rejection of Arnauld's Cartesian identification of ideas with one's own perceptions. Because Malebranche identified these ideas with necessary and immutable essences, and because he held that these ideas derive their necessity and immutability from the divine intellect, he concludes that Arnauld's position can lead only to a radical subjectivism that renders impossible any sort of *a priori* knowledge of the material world.

INTELLIGIBLE EXTENSION AND EFFICACIOUS IDEAS

Eclaircissement X also introduces the notion of "intelligible extension" mentioned in Malebranche's claim to Arnauld quoted earlier concerning his own opinion. According to this text, God has a single ideal extension that serves to represent particular bodies to Him. Arnauld objects that this position involves a retraction of the claim in the *Recherche* that one perceives bodies by means of distinct ideas in God. In response, Malebranche insists that his view all along is that God represents particular bodies by means of His own simple "absolute being." For Arnauld, however, the view that God contains extension in this way is objectionable because it is connected to the heretical view in the work of Spinoza that God is extended substance. The charge of Spinozism reappears in Malebranche's 1713–1714 correspondence with one of his former students, J. J. Dortous de Mairan, who later became the secretary of the Paris Académie des sciences (for this correspondence, see Malebranche 1995). As in the case of Arnauld, so in this correspondence Malebranche vigorously denies this charge. In both cases he responds by emphasizing that the infinite and indivisible ideal extension that exists in God differs from the finite and divisible extension in the material world.

A final feature of Malebranche's doctrine of the vision in God is connected to the notion in his writings of the "efficacious idea" (*idée efficace*). This notion became entrenched in Malebranche's system around 1695, after his encounter with his Cartesian critic Régis (see Robinet 1965). In his *Système de philosophie* Régis challenges the claim in the preface to the *Recherche* that one's mind is united to God in a manner that "raises the mind above all things" and is the source of "its life, its light, and its entire felicity." While he grants the commonplace claim that God must create and conserve one's soul, Régis denies that one is enlightened by means of a union with ideas of bodies in God. Rather, he insists that God conserves in one ideas that derive directly from the bodies they represent. In his 1693 *Réponse à Régis* (*Response to Régis*) Malebranche emphasizes his Augustinian position that one can be instructed as to the nature of bodies only through a union with God. However, he puts a new spin on this position when he notes that the union with God involves an "affecting" or "touching" of one's mind by God's idea of extension.

Already in the 1688 *Entretiens sur la métaphysique* Malebranche suggests that the union with God can be explicated in terms of a causal relation between God's ideas and one's mind. After 1695 he develops this suggestion by introducing the notion of "pure" or nonsensory intellectual perceptions that are produced by God's efficacious idea of extension. Still, he also stresses in this later period that such an idea is the causal source of one's sensations. One advantage of this extension of the doctrine of efficacious ideas to sensations is that it yields a fairly clear explanation of Malebranche's claim to Arnauld that an idea is "intelligible extension rendered sensible by color or light." Before 1695 Malebranche explained how intelligible extension is so rendered by appealing somewhat obscurely to the view that the soul "attaches" colors to a nonsensory idea. However, the theory of efficacious ideas allows him to say that this idea is rendered sensible by causing in one the appropriate sensations of light and color. The claim that one sees ideas in God is thus transformed into the claim that one's soul has intellectual and sensory perceptions that yield an understanding of the truth concerning bodies in virtue of their causal relation to God's idea of extension. One scholar concludes that while Malebranche starts with the vision *in* God, he ends with a vision *by* God (Alquié 1974, 209).

CARTESIAN DUALISM AND SENSATION

Malebranche tells Arnauld that it was Augustine's authority "which has given me the desire to put forth *the new philosophy of ideas*" (Malebranche 1958–1984, p. 6:80). By contrast, he emphasizes in the preface of the *Recherche* that Augustine failed to see that sensible qualities "are not clearly contained in the idea we have of matter," adding that "the difference between mind and body has been known with sufficient clarity for only a few years." The allusion here is to Descartes's discovery of an idea of matter that reveals that its nature consists in extension alone. This idea dictates that sensible qualities such as colors, tastes, and odors that are not reducible to modes of extension cannot exist external to mind. But since these

qualities exist in the mind, and in particular in the mind's perception of the qualities, the mind itself must be distinguished from body. In this way the Cartesian idea of matter reveals "the difference between mind and body."

In the initial book of the *Recherche*, on the errors of the senses, Malebranche proposes that the erroneous belief of the Aristotelians as well as of Augustine that sensible qualities exist in bodies has its source in a misuse of "natural judgments" that help in the conservation of the human body. Here, he is following Descartes's account in the Sixth Meditation of the "teachings of nature," and in particular the claim there that the purpose of sensations is not to teach one about the nature of bodies but simply to inform one of what is beneficial or harmful to the human composite. Just as Descartes urged that erroneous beliefs about the nature of body can be avoided by attending to the clear and distinct perceptions of the intellect, so Malebranche counsels that one avoid error by attending to what the clear idea of matter reveals to one about the nature of body. As noted earlier, Malebranche has Augustinian reasons for saying that the idea that so instructs one exists in God. By his own admission, however, the conclusion that the idea that instructs one is an idea of extension derives from Descartes's discoveries.

Malebranche emphasizes that the clear idea of extension must be distinguished from one's confused sensations. One point he wants to make is that the idea exists in God while the sensations are only modifications of one's mind. However, his emphasis that this idea is "pure" or nonsensory indicates that one's experience of the material world has an intellectual component. His late doctrine of the efficacious idea involved the position that one has pure intellectual perceptions produced by God's intellectual idea of extension. But his mature position that this idea is also the cause of one's sensations allows for the claim that one's most basic sensory contact with the material world has an intellectual component.

Malebranche's doctrine of the vision in God also conflicts with Descartes's doctrine of the creation of the eternal truths. However, there are further departures from orthodox Cartesianism that are linked to two qualifications of this doctrine. The first qualification is that God's idea of extension can reveal only the nature of bodies and not their existence. This qualification is not explicit in the initial edition of the *Recherche*, which says only that the existence of properties of bodies external to one is "very difficult to prove" (Malebranche, 1997b, I.x.§1). Foucher objected that Malebranche has no good reason to affirm the external existence of these properties. In Eclaircissement VI, Malebranche urges that the idea of extension does reveal the possible existence of the material world and that Descartes has shown that one has a probable argument for its actual existence deriving from one's natural propensity to believe that there are bodies. However, he concedes in this text—without crediting Foucher—that neither he nor Descartes can provide an argument from reason that demonstrates "with evidence" or "with geometric rigor" that this belief is true. His claim is that any conclusive argument must appeal to faith in the veracity of the report in the Scriptures that God has created the heavens and the earth.

According to the second qualification of the vision in God—which is found in the original edition of the *Recherche*—one perceives the nature of one's soul not through a clear idea in God, but only through a confused "consciousness or inner sensation" (*conscience ou sentiment intérieur*). Malebranche accepts the Cartesian commonplace that consciousness reveals immediately the existence of the soul. He allows that one knows the nature of one's soul to consist in thought; moreover, he embraces the Cartesian conclusion that the soul as a thinking substance is distinct from the body as an extended substance. Still, he insists that one knows that the soul is distinct from the body not by means of any direct insight into the nature of thought, but by seeing that thought is not contained in the idea of matter. More generally, Malebranche claims that one's lack of access to a clear idea of the soul is evident because one does not have knowledge of thought that matches one's knowledge of the mathematical features of bodies. This last point turns on its head Descartes's own conclusion in the Second Meditation that the nature of the human mind is "better known" than the nature of body; for Malebranche, it is the nature of body that is better known than the nature of mind.

In Eclaircissement XI Malebranche attempts to counter "the authority of Descartes" by arguing that the Cartesians themselves must admit that they have only a confused awareness of the nature of the sensory modifications of the soul. He notes that whereas the intellectual idea allows the various modes of extension to be related in a precise manner, there is no clear scale on which one can order one's sensations of different shades of the same color, not to mention one's sensations of sensible qualities of different kinds. Malebranche takes the confusion in the sensations to reveal a confusion in one's perception of the nature of the soul. He adds that Cartesians can discern that sensible qualities are modifications of an immaterial soul only by seeing that they are "not clearly contained in the idea we have of matter" (Malebranche 1958–1984, pp. 3:168, 170f).

OCCASIONALISM AND GENERAL VOLITIONS

Malebranche is known for his occasionalism, that is, his doctrine that God is the only causal agent and that creatures are merely "occasional causes" that prompt divine action. On the old textbook account, occasionalism was an ad hoc response to the purported problem in Descartes of how substances as distinct in nature as mind and body can causally interact. According to this account, Malebranche was driven by this problem with Cartesian dualism to propose that it is God who brings it about that one's sensations and volitions are correlated with motions in one's body.

However, occasionalism was already an old doctrine at the time that St. Thomas Aquinas wrote against it in the thirteenth century. Thomas indicated that the primary concern of the occasionalists was to strengthen the assertion of God's omnipotence. Though he allowed that God must "concur" with creatures in producing effects, he also claimed that there is reason to conclude that creatures are true secondary causes. For instance, he urged that it is more in accord with divine greatness to say that God communicates His power to creatures. Moreover, he claimed that it is simply evident to the senses that creatures have the power to bring about effects. Thomas also argued that if there were no natures in creatures that explain effects, then there could be no true scientific explanation of effects through their natural causes.

Malebranche was concerned to respond to all these arguments against occasionalism, particularly as they were developed in the work of scholastics such as Suárez. Against the first point that God's greatness requires the communication of His power, Malebranche counters that it is in fact idolatrous to attribute divine power to creatures. His argument that God alone can produce effects relies on the assumption that "a true cause … is one such that the mind perceives a necessary connection [*liaison nécessaire*] between it and its effects" (Malebranche 1997b, VI-2.iii). Malebranche claims that there is such a connection neither among bodily states, nor between bodily and mental states, nor among mental states. In all these cases one can deny the connections without contradiction. There can be a necessary causal connection in only one case, namely, the connection between the volitions of an omnipotent agent and its upshots. Thus, only such an agent, namely, God, can be a true cause.

In the *Entretiens sur la métaphysique* Malebranche offers a different argument based on Descartes's suggestion in the Third Meditation that God conserves the world by continuously creating it. The argument begins with the claim that God must create bodies in some particular place and in determinate relations of distance to other bodies. If God conserves a body by creating it in the same place from moment to moment, that body remains at rest, and if He conserves it by creating it in different places from moment to moment, it is in motion. One cannot even create motion in one's own body. Rather, it is God who must produce it on the occasion of volitional states. Moreover, it is not motions in one's brain that cause one's sensory states, but God who produces them on the occasion of the presence of such motions.

Unlike the argument from necessary connection, this argument from continuous creation is for the most part restricted to the case of body. There is a good reason for this restriction since the argument depends on the premise—dictated by a Cartesian understanding of the nature of body in terms of extension alone—that particular bodies cannot exist without bearing determinate relations of distance among themselves. As noted, Malebranche denies that one has a clear knowledge of the nature of the soul. No consideration of the soul could therefore reveal that it can exist only with a determinate set of modes. Indeed, Malebranche allows for the view that God creates souls with an indeterminate inclination toward "the good in general." Even so, he insists that God must be the cause of "everything real" in one's soul on the grounds that such real effects can be produced only by the power of creation. In this way the argument from continuous creation converges on the conclusion, which Malebranche claims to find in Augustine, that all creatures depend entirely on God.

The second scholastic argument against occasionalism appealed to the purported fact that it is evident to the senses that creatures have causal power. For Malebranche, however, this argument is no more persuasive than the argument that bodies must have qualities such as colors and tastes since one's senses tell one that they do. As indicated earlier, Malebranche offers Cartesian grounds for thinking that the purpose of one's sensations is not to reveal the true nature of the material world, but to indicate what is helpful or harmful to one's body. Malebranche holds that one's attribution of causal powers to bodies manifests in particular an attachment to the body that is an effect of original sin. Because of this attachment, one takes objects in the material world to be a cause of one's happiness rather than God.

In Eclaircissement XV Malebranche responds to the scholastic point that occasionalism renders scientific explanation impossible by appealing to the fact that God is not an arbitrary agent, but acts in accord with His wisdom. This wisdom dictates that He act "almost always" by means of a "general and efficacious will." Such a will produces effects that are perfectly lawlike. For instance, God acts by a general will in producing changes in bodies in accord with the law of the communication of motion. Malebranche does allow that God can produce miracles by "particular volitions" that are not lawlike. However, he emphasizes that there are relatively few such volitions in God. Thus, one can offer scientific explanations that appeal to the laws of motion that reflect the nature of God's general will.

Malebranche was not the first Cartesian to endorse occasionalism. There were followers of Descartes, such as Louis de la Forge and Claude Clerselier, who stressed that God must be the cause of the communication of motion in bodily collisions given the passivity of Cartesian matter. These Cartesians attempted to preserve some room for the action of finite minds on the body, but the Cartesian Géraud de Cordemoy went further in claiming that only God can cause changes in the material world. However, none of these thinkers went as far as Malebranche in asserting that God must produce all real changes in nature. Moreover, Malebranche is distinctive in providing an explanation of God's action that distinguishes His general will from His particular volitions.

THEODICY AND FREEDOM

The presence of various evils in the world is problematic for any theist who claims that this world was created by a God who has infinite power, knowledge, and goodness. However, the problem is particularly acute for an occasionalist, such as Malebranche, who holds that God is the only true cause of effects in nature. Malebranche offers a theodicy that addresses the problem of evil by stressing that in the "order of nature" God acts for the most part through His general will. In *Nature et de la grâce* he starts by admitting that God could have acted by particular volitions to prevent natural evils such as malformed offspring (a fitting example given his own malformed spine), and thus could have produced a more perfect world than He actually did create. However, he urges that God could have done so only by departing from simple laws, thereby sacrificing the simplicity and uniformity of action that is a supreme mark of His wisdom. God produces the natural evils that follow from simple laws not because He wills those particular effects, but because He wills a world that best reflects His wisdom by possessing the most effects governed by the fewest laws.

In his *Réflexions* on Malebranche's *Nature et de la grâce* Arnauld objects to what he takes to be the suggestion in his target text that God has concern only for general features of the world and does not will the details of His effects. For Arnauld, divine providence requires that God intend all the particularities of the world He creates. There is some controversy over whether Arnauld's critique is based on a proper interpretation of Malebranche. Certain commentators follow Arnauld in thinking that Malebranche's claim in *Nature et de la grâce* that God acts by relatively few general volitions involves a rejection of the position that He has volitions for each particular effect. Others insist that this claim says only that God has volitions in accord with general laws and that the doctrine of God's continual creation in the *Entretiens* in fact requires distinct volitions for distinct effects. Some evidence for the former view is provided by the fact that Malebranche emphasizes that the laws themselves are "efficacious" and that God employs relatively few volitions in producing effects in the order of nature.

Malebranche insists that God's general will is operative not only in the order of nature but also in the "order of grace." However, he notes that the production of effects in the latter order also involves human action that is free in the strong sense of not being determined by anything external to the agent. His appeal to this sort of freedom is in fact central to his solution to the problem of moral evil, that is, the compatibility of sin with God's goodness. According to Malebranche God is not responsible for sinful action since such action derives not from Him but from sinful agents. Arnauld objects that this solution is "more pelagian than anything in Pelagius" and that one must side with Augustine, who declares Pelagianism a heresy. Malebranche responds that he does not follow Pelagius in denying the importance of grace and that Augustine himself emphasizes one's freedom in action.

Malebranche also insists that it is obvious by "inner sensation" that one is genuinely free. However, there is some question whether this introspective report is compatible with Malebranche's occasionalist claim that God is the only real cause. As indicated earlier, Malebranche does hold that God alone is the cause of one's indeterminate inclination to love the good in general. However, he insists that one is free to "consent" to the stopping of that inclination at a particular object other than God. Such consent results in an "absolute and intrinsic" love of that object that is sinful given that this love is worthy only of God. The consent is free because one is always able to suspend consent and to search for objects more worthy of one's love. Malebranche claims that one's freedom to consent or suspend consent does not conflict with occasionalism since these acts produce no "real" or "physical"

change in one's mind. Sometimes he suggests that consent is nothing real because it is involves merely resting with a particular good. One problem with this suggestion is that it makes it difficult to understand how taking the opposite course of suspending consent could also involve the production of nothing real. However, Malebranche sometimes indicates that both consent and suspense produce nothing real merely in the sense that they create neither new thoughts nor an increase in inclination. He also indicates that though God determines one's "natural love" for particular objects, he leaves undetermined our "free love" for such objects.

Although Malebranche himself is less than explicit on the point, he seems at times to have left at least some room for the position that one's consent involves the determination of one's free love, whereas one's suspense involves leaving that love in its indeterminate state. In neither case is there the production of a physical change because there is no creation of new thoughts or of an increase in inclination. Whether this reflects Malebranche's own considered view is, however, a matter of scholarly dispute.

MORAL THEORY AND SELF-LOVE

The theocentrism that is evident in Malebranche's doctrines of the vision in God and occasionalism would lead one to expect that God plays a central role in his moral theory. This expectation is borne out by his remarks in the *Traité de morale*. Indeed, Malebranche's two doctrines are prominent in this work. The vision in God is reflected in the insistence that moral duties are dictated by "relations of perfection" revealed in God's wisdom. As in the case of necessary truths concerning body, so in the case of moral truths Malebranche unequivocally rejects Cartesian voluntarism. The doctrine of occasionalism is reflected in Malebranche's insistence that God is one's greatest good because He alone can cause one's happiness. This point indicates that Malebranche takes moral action to require a consideration not only of abstract relations of perfection but also of the happiness of the self.

Malebranche starts from the Augustinian position that morality concerns the proper ordering of one's love. Given the importance of human freedom for his theodicy, it is not surprising that Malebranche insists that the love required for moral action involve the free exercise of the will. In his view, the "good will" is one that freely strives to be guided in action by objective relations of perfection that hold among the various objects of love. God is the most perfect being and hence the most worthy of one's love, whereas human beings are more perfect than mere material beings and thus more worthy of one's love. When the intensity of one's love matches the order among perfections, one has a right love that provides the basis for virtue, that is, a habitual inclination to love objects according to their perfections.

Malebranche holds that because of original sin, one is inclined not to right love directed by one's perception of relations of perfection in God's wisdom, but to a disordered love directed by bodily pleasures deriving from the soul-body union. This is the counterpart to the disordered inclination of one's will to make judgments about the nature of the material world that are based on sensations deriving from the union. For Malebranche, a corrective to both of these disorders of the will is to attend to clear ideas that exist in God.

Malebranche sometimes suggested that disordered love of bodily pleasure derives from self-love. Encouraged by this suggestion, one of his followers, François Lamy, claimed that his position leads to the quietist view in Fénelon that moral conduct requires a "pure love of God" that involves no concern for the self or its pleasure. This position, which Lamy himself endorsed, was later condemned by the Catholic Church, due in large part to a campaign against Fénelon directed by his critic, Bossuet. But Malebranche insisted that such a position directly conflicts with his own view that pleasure itself is a good that is required as a motive for action. When critics such as Arnauld and Régis charged that this view results in hedonism, Malebranche responded that it is only ordered pleasures that bring the greatest good. This response is reflected in Malebranche's claim to Lamy that a disordered love of self is to be contrasted not with pure love of God, but with an ordered love that seeks happiness in the contemplation of the greatest good, God. In emphasizing the need for this sort of love of God, Malebranche was returning to his view in the preface to the *Recherche* that it is through a union with God that the mind "receives its life, its light, and its entire felicity."

HISTORICAL INFLUENCE

Malebranche's influence on seventeenth- and eighteenth-century philosophy was significant. This is clear in the case of Leibniz, who wrote to Malebranche in 1679 that "I enthusiastically approve of the two propositions that you put forward: namely, that we see all things in God and that bodies strictly speaking do not act on us." Moreover, Leibniz's discussion in his 1684 *Discours de la métaphysique* (*Discourse on Metaphysics*) bears an evident relation to Malebranche's *Nature et de la grâce*. Here, Leibniz

follows Malebranche in insisting that God acts in accord with wisdom and that He selects from among an infinity of possible worlds that world that best reflects His perfection by balancing simple laws and variety of effects. Leibniz stresses, in line with Malebranche's views, that the simplicity constraint governs both laws of nature and laws of grace.

The *Discours* also includes a section in which Leibniz comments on the Arnauld-Malebranche debate on the nature of ideas and offers some complimentary remarks concerning the Malebranchean doctrine of the vision in God. In his 1710 *Théodicée*, Leibniz highlights his agreement with the claim in *Nature et de la grâce* that natural evil exists because God's wisdom dictates that He restrict himself to a "general will." However, he also charges in this text that Malebranche's occasionalism leads to a kind of Spinozism insofar as it denies the activity and thus the substantiality of creatures. Leibniz offers his "preestablished harmony," on which creatures have the power to cause alterations in their own states. This theory, which is anticipated in the *Discours*, distinguishes Leibniz's view from Malebranche's. However, Leibniz himself sometimes presents the preestablished harmony as an internal correction to the Malebranchean system that is in accord with Malebranche's own emphasis on the perfection of divine action in creation.

Malebranche's influence extended across the Channel, where he gained admirers such as John Norris, Thomas Taylor, and Arthur Collier. His views drew a more critical reception from John Locke, who wrote *Examination of Père Malebranche's Opinion of Seeing All Things in God*, which was published posthumously in 1706. Though Malebranche himself did not respond to this work, it later received a full reply from the Savoyard cardinal, Giacinto Sigismondo Gerdil, who would have been elected pope in 1800 were it not for the veto exercised by the Austrians on political grounds. In his *Défense du sentiment du P. Malebranche*, published in 1748, Gerdil urged that Malebranche's hypothesis that God causes one's perceptions is more intelligible than Locke's own hypothesis that passive matter is the cause of these states. Because of Gerdil's influence, Malebranche's views gained a following in Italy.

During the eighteenth century Malebranche also won the grudging respect of George Berkeley and David Hume. Berkeley indeed appeared to his critics to be a "Malbranchiste de bonne foi," a view that Berkeley himself counters when he writes in the third (1734) edition of his *Three Dialogues between Hylas and Philonous* that "there are no principles more fundamentally opposed than [Malebranche's] and mine." Berkeley does differ from Malebranche in rejecting the existence of an external material world, in insisting that ideas exist in one's mind rather than in God's and in claiming that the senses reveal immediately the true nature of sensible objects. However, Berkeley follows Malebranche in rejecting the Aristotelian conception of nature and in attributing causal efficacy in natural interactions to God (though Berkeley does attempt, with questionable success, to leave room for the power of finite spirits to move their own bodies). Also, Berkeley holds with Malebranche that one's perceptions are related to certain "archetypes" in the divine mind that serve as the pattern for God's creation (Luce [1934] is the classic study of the relation between Berkeley and Malebranche).

In 1737 Hume wrote to his friend Michael Ramsey that he should prepare himself for "the metaphysical Parts" of the reasoning in the forthcoming *Treatise of Human Nature* (1739–1740) by reading "once over la Recherche de la Vérité of Pere Malebranche," along with selected works from Descartes, Berkeley, and Pierre Bayle. Malebranche is important primarily for the account of causation and causal belief in the *Treatise*. Hume relies there explicitly on Malebranche's argument for the negative conclusion that neither external nor internal experience affords one any idea of power. With Malebranche, Hume emphasizes the importance of necessary connection to the understanding of causation. Hume does reject Malebranche's own claim that God is the only real cause, noting in a famous passage from the *Enquiry concerning Human Understanding* (1748) that with such a claim "we are got into fairy land, long ere we have reached the last steps of our theory." Hume's preference is for a psychological account of causal belief that sticks closely to "common life and experience" and that emphasizes the central role of the imagination. Nonetheless, Hume's own discussion belies his remark in the *Enquiry* that "the glory of Malebranche is confined to his own nation, and to his own age."

See also Arnauld, Antoine; Aristotle; Augustine, St.; Bayle, Pierre; Berkeley, George; Bossuet, Jacques Bénigne; Cartesianism; Chinese Philosophy; Collier, Arthur; Descartes, René; Desgabets, Robert; Determinism and Freedom; Ethics, History of; Evil, The Problem of; Fénelon, François de Salignac de la Mothe; Foucher, Simon; General Will, The; Hume, David; Leibniz, Gottfried Wilhelm; Locke, John; Newton, Isaac; Norris, John; Pascal, Blaise; Pelagius and Pelagianism; Régis, Pierre-Sylvain; Spinoza, Benedict (Baruch) de; Spinozism; Suárez, Francisco; Thomism; Volition; Voluntarism.

Bibliography

WORKS BY MALEBRANCHE

Oeuvres complètes de Malebranche. 20 vols, edited by André Robinet. Paris: J. Vrin, 1958–1984.

Dialogue between a Christian Philosopher and a Chinese Philosopher on the Existence and Nature of God. Translated by Dominick A. Iorio. Washington, DC: University Press of America, 1980.

Treatise on Ethics. Trans. C. Walton. Dordrecht: Kluwer, 1993.

Malebranche's First and Last Critics: Simon Foucher and Dortous de Mairan. Translated by Richard A. Watson and Marjorie Grene. Carbondale: Southern Illinois University Press, 1995.

Dialogues on Metaphysics and on Religion. Translated by David Scott; edited by Nicholas Jolley. New York: Cambridge University Press, 1997a.

The Search after Truth. Translated and edited by Thomas M. Lennon and Paul J. Olscamp. New York: Cambridge University Press, 1997b.

WORKS ON MALEBRANCHE

Alquié, Ferdinand. *Le cartésianisme de Malebranche.* Paris: J. Vrin, 1974.

André, Yves M. *La vie du R. P. Malebranche.* Geneva: Slatkine Reprints, 1970.

Arnauld, Antoine. *On True and False Ideas.* Translated by Elmar J. Kremer. Lewiston, NY: Edwin Mellen Press, 1990.

Bardout, Jean-Christophe. *Malebranche et la métaphysique.* Paris: Presses Universitaires de France, 1999.

Brown, Stuart, ed. *Nicolas Malebranche: His Philosophical Critics and Successors.* Assen, Netherlands: Van Gorcum, 1991.

Chappell, Vere, ed. *Nicholas Malebranche.* New York: Garland, 1992.

Connell, Desmond. *The Vision in God: Malebranche's Scholastic Sources.* Louvain, Belgium: Nauwelaerts, 1967.

Easton, Patricia, Thomas M. Lennon, and Gregor Sebba, eds. *Bibliographia Malebranchiana: A Critical Guide to the Malebranche Literature into 1989.* Carbondale: Southern Illinois University Press, 1992.

Foucher, Simon *Critique de la recherche de la verité,* edited by Richard A. Watson. New York: Johnson Reprint, 1969.

Gueroult, Martial. *Malebranche.* 3 vols. Paris: Aubier, 1955–1959.

Jolley, Nicholas. *The Light of the Soul: Theories of Ideas in Leibniz, Malebranche, and Descartes.* Oxford, U.K.: Clarendon Press, 1990.

Luce, A. A. *Berkeley and Malebranche: A Study in the Origins of Berkeley's Thought.* London: H. Milford, 1934.

McCracken, Charles J. *Malebranche and British Philosophy.* Oxford, U.K.: Clarendon Press, 1983.

Moreau, Denis. *Deux cartésiens: La polemique entre Antoine Arnauld et Nicolas Malebranche.* Paris: J. Vrin, 1999.

Nadler, Steven, ed. *The Cambridge Companion to Malebranche.* Cambridge, U.K.: Cambridge University Press, 2000.

Nadler, Steven. *Malebranche and Ideas.* New York: Oxford University Press, 1992.

Pyle, Andrew. *Malebranche.* London: Routledge, 2003.

Radner, Daisie. *Malebranche: A Study of a Cartesian System.* Assen, Netherlands: Van Gorcum, 1978.

Robinet, André. *Système et existence dans l'oeuvre de Malebranche.* Paris: J. Vrin, 1965.

Rodis-Lewis, Geneviève. *Nicolas Malebranche.* Paris: Presses Universitaires de France, 1963.

Schmaltz, Tad M. *Malebranche's Theory of the Soul: A Cartesian Interpretation.* New York: Oxford University Press, 1996.

Schmaltz, Tad M. *Radical Cartesianism: The French Reception of Descartes.* New York: Cambridge University Press, 2002.

Sebba, Gregor, ed. *Nicolas Malebranche, 1638–1715: A Preliminary Bibliography.* Athens: University of Georgia Press, 1959.

Walton, Craig. *De la Recherche du Bien: A Study of Malebranche's Science of Ethics.* The Hague: Nijhoff, 1972.

Tad M. Schmaltz (2005)

MALRAUX, GEORGES-ANDRÉ

(1901–1976)

Georges-André Malraux, the French author, critic, revolutionist, and statesman, was born in Paris to a well-to-do family. He studied at the Lycée Condorcet and the Institut des Langues Orientales and early in life developed an enduring interest in archaeology, art, and Oriental languages and thought. His life and writing were characterized by a restless, questioning, quasi-apocalyptic intensity that is fully understandable only in terms of the crisis with which Western thought was confronted in the first half of the twentieth century: At grips with a fast-accumulating mass of new knowledge, Western civilization was seeking to adjust to the violent changes that had disrupted its former social, intellectual, and spiritual framework of values.

In 1923 Malraux went on an archaeological expedition into the Cambodian jungle, and soon afterward he returned to the Orient to participate in the revolutionary struggle that was transforming the Asiatic world. He seems at the time to have been in sympathy with the Marxist ideology. *La tentation de l'occident* (Paris, 1926), his first serious work, is a fictional dialogue between a Chinese and a European intellectual and shows how decisive was his first encounter with the Orient. It intensified Malraux's self-styled obsession with the notions of civilization and culture. He was always vitally concerned with the problems of the life and death of civilizations; the specificity, irreducibility, and relativity of all cultures;

their determining action in shaping the mental structures of individuals; and the bearing on his own cultural world of the observations and conclusions of historians and anthropologists such as Oswald Spengler and Leo Frobenius. This initial obsession was nourished and substantiated by Malraux's legendary familiarity with all realms of art (painting and sculpture in particular); his avid and exceptionally broad grasp of literature; and his addiction to passionate debate with leading personalities in Europe and the Orient. Although his thought was always concentrated on a present unremittingly interrogated, it developed within vast perspectives both in time and space.

In the late 1920s Malraux, as art editor for the Gallimard publishing firm in Paris, traveled widely in search of art treasures, while actively participating in the unavailing struggle of the European intellectuals against fascism, Nazism, and anti-Semitism. He later commanded a group of aviators for the Republican forces in the Spanish Civil War, was active in the French resistance after 1940, and became, first, minister of information, then minister of cultural affairs, in the cabinet of General Charles de Gaulle.

He was deliberately "committed" as a writer for intellectual reasons. Western science, he claimed, offers a set of relationships that define the cosmos but, by omitting the observer, it presents a cosmos in which man has no place. According to Malraux, psychoanalysis has revealed the blind, destructive forces at work within the self and has put into question the very notion of a fundamental human personality. To recover some concept of man, Malraux maintained that one must once again examine what man does, thereby redefining his powers. The image of the rational, detached observer—scientist or philosopher—placed outside the world he observes must therefore give way to the participant who is, as it were, a knot of relations with the world. Malraux often reiterated that man "is what he does." Participation therefore was the first and necessary stage in his search for definition.

The elucidation of an action is the theme of his novels. All revolve around the question, "What can a man best do with his life?"; all are animated by the same answer that is given in *Man's Hope*: "Transform into consciousness an experience as broad as possible." Writing is the medium through which this transformation takes place; hence the intensity of the process, the inner questioning, and the many-faceted debate that it embodies. His six widely read novels all are wrenched from stages of his own experience: *Les conquérants* (Paris, 1928); *La voie royale* (Paris, 1930); *La condition humaine* (Paris, 1933); *Le temps du mépris* (Paris, 1935); *L'espoir* (Paris, 1937);

and *Les noyers de l'Altenburg* (Lausanne, 1943), the first volume of a two-part novel whose second part was destroyed by the Nazis. These were followed by an impressive series of works on art: *Goya* (Geneva, 1947); *La psychologie de l'art* (3 vols., Geneva, 1947, 1949, 1950); *Le musée imaginaire de la sculpture mondiale* (3 vols., Paris, 1952, 1953, 1954); *Les voix du silence* (Paris, 1953); and *La métamorphose des dieux* (Paris, 1960). A number of reviews, prefaces, and speeches add to this abundant corpus of work.

Despite both the variety of his media and the obscurities inherent in his manner of writing, there is a remarkable degree of consistency and lucidity in Malraux's thought, questionable though many of his assumptions and examples may be. He posits as premise the definitive disappearance from Western civilization of the structure of values established by the Christian *Weltanschauung*. Western man is thus left face to face with a cosmos to which he cannot relate. However, he is still in possession of the inner drive that, since the Greeks, has structured his world—the need to create a coherent, intelligible image of man's fate that gives significance to each individual life. Hence the double burden of lucidity and anguish characteristic of our time, hence its "temptations." The most prevalent is the nihilism whereby Western man, living in a state of "metaphysical distraction," renounces his drive toward lucidity and submits to blind necessity and to natural and social conditioning. This, according to Malraux, is an intolerable reversion to the "demons," that is, to the blind animal instinct within us. Malraux also examined and partially rejected the Asian resorption of the individual into the cosmos (considered as divine). In preference to the Asian view, he sought to define man's power in his capacity to "leave a scar on the planet," to transform his environment. For a while he understood the process in terms of the Marxist theory of history.

Malraux's final view emerged from his meditations on art. It is a complex outlook related to the study of art styles and their migrations and metamorphoses, an approach that is characteristic of such art historians as Élie Faure and Henri Focillon. In brief, for Malraux a new planetary civilization that has destroyed all significant cultures is now in the making. The structures of values whereby each individual within a human society relates to the cosmos, to the community, and to his own actions now exist only as "relativized absolutes." This is the first agnostic civilization, the first that does not relate to some form of the divine. It also presents a new phenomenon, the "imaginary museum," in which all works of art—

whatever their origin—are available, to be perceived as significant in themselves and not for what they once signified. For Malraux this universal presence and significance testifies to a fundamental power of humankind: the power to dominate and transcend fate and to create a universe in some way accessible to all men, who are thereby freed from time, death, and blind necessity. The privileged potential image of humankind, therefore, that Malraux detects as indicative of our present orientation is that of man as creator and as forger of his own freedom. Malraux thus formulated in new terms the age-old problem of freedom and destiny, to serve as the foundation for a new ethic. His work is fundamentally relevant in an age that is deeply preoccupied with the working of the mind, considered on one hand as a form of conditioned mechanism and on the other as a principle of free activity, order, and meaning.

See also Aesthetics, History of; Agnosticism; Art, Expression in; Marxist Philosophy; Nihilism; Spengler, Oswald; Value and Valuation.

Bibliography

WORKS BY MALRAUX

The works listed below are English editions of Malraux's works in the order in which they appear in the text.

The Temptation of the West. Translated with an introduction by Robert Hollander. New York: Vintage, 1961.

The Conquerors. Translated by W. S. Whale. New York: Harcourt Brace, 1929.

The Royal Way. Translated by Stuart Gilbert. New York: Smith and Haas, 1935.

Man's Fate. Translated by Haakon Chevalier. New York: Smith and Haas, 1934.

Days of Wrath. Translated by Haakon Chevalier. New York: Random House, 1936.

Man's Hope. Translated by Stuart Gilbert and Alistair MacDonald. New York: Random House, 1938.

The Walnut Trees of Altenburg. Translated by A. W. Fielding. London: Lehmann, 1952.

Saturn: An Essay on Goya. Translated by C. W. Chilton. London: Phaidon, 1957.

The Psychology of Art. Translated by Stuart Gilbert. Vol. I: *Museum without Walls*; Vol. II: *The Creative Act.* New York: Pantheon, 1949–1951.

The Voices of Silence. Translated by Stuart Gilbert. New York: Doubleday, 1953.

The Metamorphosis of the Gods. Translated by Stuart Gilbert. New York: Doubleday, 1960.

WORKS ON MALRAUX

Blend, Charles. *André Malraux: Tragic Humanist.* Columbus: Ohio State University Press, 1963. A biography and general critical study, with a bibliography of Malraux's work and a brief critical bibliography.

Frohock, Wilbur. *André Malraux and the Tragic Imagination.* Stanford, CA: Stanford University Press, 1952. A basic work.

Lewis, R. W. B., ed. *Malraux.* Englewood Cliffs, NJ: Prentice-Hall, 1964. A collection of critical essays.

Lyotard, Jean Francois. *Soundproof Room: Malraux's Anti-Aesthetics.* Translated by Robert Harvey. Stanford: Stanford University Press, 2001.

Raymond, Gino. *Andre Malraux: Politics and the Temptation of Myth.* Aldershot: Avebury; Brookfield: Ashgate, 1995.

Righter, William. *The Rhetorical Hero: An Essay on the Aesthetics of Andre Malraux.* New York: Chilmark Press, 1964.

Vandergars, André. *La jeunesse littéraire d'André Malraux.* Paris: Pauvert, 1964. Contains a wealth of information on Malraux's Indochinese activities.

Germaine Brée (1967)
Bibliography updated by Desiree Matherly Martin (2005)

MALTHUS, THOMAS ROBERT
(1776–1834)

Thomas Robert Malthus, the English economist and moral philosopher, is most famous for his contributions to population studies. In his *Principles of Political Economy* (1820) and in his controversies with David Ricardo, Malthus seems partly to have anticipated J. M. Keynes; and Keynes himself, in his *Essays in Biography*, generously remarked that "if only Malthus, instead of Ricardo, had been the parent stem from which nineteenth century economics proceeded, what a much wiser and richer place the world would be today!"

Malthus's work on population is contained in two books, misleadingly presented as if they were merely different editions of one. The first, best referred to as the *First Essay*, is actually titled *An Essay on the Principle of Population as It Affects the Future Improvement of Society, with Remarks on the Speculations of Mr. Godwin, M. Condorcet, and Other Writers.* The second, best thought of as the *Second Essay*, was, with some reserve, offered by Malthus as a much extended second edition. But it was retitled *An Essay on the Principle of Population, or a View of Its Past and Present Effects on Human Happiness with an Inquiry into Our Prospects Respecting the Future Removal or Mitigation of the Evils Which It Occasions.* The *First Essay* is an occasional polemic against utopianism; the *Second*, a labored treatise full of detailed factual material. What they have in common is the same guiding and coordinating theoretical schema, although even this is in one respect importantly amended in the later book.

The fundamental principle is that unfreakish human populations possess a power of multiplying in a geometrical progression. The next step is to urge that this power always is and must be checked by countervailing forces; for, on the most optimistic supposition, means of subsistence could in the long run at best be increased only in an arithmetical progression. (The subsistence of checks could, of course, be inferred without recourse to this misleadingly arithmetized supposition, by referring directly to the fact that no human population ever does achieve its full multiplicative potential.) The questions then arise. What are these checks? what ought they to be?

Checks are classified in two different ways. First, they can be positive or preventive: the former by the time of the *Second Essay* being all causes of (premature) death; and the latter, correspondingly, all checks on the birth rate. The second classification is strongly normative: In the *First Essay* all checks must count as either misery or vice; but in the *Second Essay* a third option, moral restraint, is added. This is defined as "the restraint from marriage which is not followed by irregular gratifications." Malthus seems never to have entertained the possibility of restraint within marriage; and he categorically rejected any form of contraception, even within wedlock, as vice.

This scheme of ideas constituted an intellectual engine that was immensely powerful both for its primary purpose of confounding utopian optimism and for its secondary function of guiding social inquiry. We also have clear statements from both Charles Darwin and Alfred Russel Wallace that it was reading Malthus on population which independently led each to see the clue to the problem of the origin of species in natural selection through "a struggle for existence," a phrase used by Malthus himself. Against the utopians the argument was that our inordinate animal power of multiplication is bound—sooner or later, and usually sooner—to run up against the inexorably constricting walls of scarcity. All measures of intended amelioration which directly or indirectly encourage an increase of population that outstrips resources—and most do—will, in the not very distant end, merely multiply the number of bearers of misery and agents of vice. These harsh and gloomy conclusions were only modified, not upset, by the belated recognition of the option of moral restraint. For it was, and remains, hard to cherish high hopes from the preaching of such prudence; and in any society which did generally accept such preaching all but the richest would have to marry women nearing the evening of their reproductive powers.

It is, therefore, not surprising that generations of idealists hoping to reshape the present sorry scheme of things nearer to their heart's desire have released torrents of argument and abuse at "Parson Malthus" and his ideas. Yet, despite the apparent implication of his system—that God has placed humankind in a situation offering little promise of secure improvement—it would be wrong to assume that Malthus as a man or as a thinker was either insensitive or harsh. Compared with the optimistic utopians of his father's reading and acquaintance he could not but appear a jarring pessimist. But this was a matter of facing what he took to be the sober facts of the human condition, not of callous indifference to the relief of man's estate. To quote Keynes again, his work is really in "the tradition which is suggested by the names of Locke, Hume, Adam Smith, Paley, Bentham, Darwin and Mill, a tradition marked … by a prosaic sanity … and by an immense disinterestedness and public spirit." As against, say, Condorcet, who wrote of inevitable progress while under the shadow of the guillotine, Malthus was concerned first with finding what the facts are and then with discovering how, in the light of those perhaps recalcitrant facts, we are to do the best we can. It is no accident that in the first chapter of the *First Essay* he acknowledges a debt to David Hume and Adam Smith but not to the impossible and visionary Jean-Jacques Rousseau, whom his father had known and admired.

THEODICY

The same intellectual associations are seen in his theodicy. William Paley was one of the early converts to Malthus on population, and appropriately, Paley was one of Malthus's favorite theologians. So Malthus insists in the *First Essay* that "Evil exists in the world not to create despair but activity." (It was from this part of the work that Darwin and Wallace most directly derived the idea of a necessary struggle for existence.) What Malthus may have acquired from the dissenting Christians and Unitarians of his father's circle is a note of theological radicalism, a note not caught either by the hostile conventional left, represented then by William Cobbett and William Hazlitt, or by such sentimental conservative opponents as Samuel Taylor Coleridge and Robert Southey.

In the theodicy of the last chapter of the *First Essay* Malthus boldly steps away from Paley and from the whole tradition of Christian orthodoxy by insisting that "it is perfectly impossible to conceive that any … creatures of God's hand can be condemned to eternal suffering. Could we once admit such an idea, all our natural conceptions of goodness and justice would be completely overthrown, and we could no longer look on God as a merciful and righteous Being." (Malthus settles his own account with Christianity by accepting the Hobbist interpretation; that eternal death means eternal death and not eternal life in torment. The "doctrine of life and immortality which was brought to light by the gospel" is "the doctrine that the end of righteousness is everlasting life, but that the wages of sin are death." This plausible reading had been unanimously rejected by the orthodox Saints and Fathers, doubtless as being unacceptably merciful.)

CRITIQUE OF POPULATION THEORY

As a heuristic and explanatory scheme, the population theory resembles bits of classical physics, although it might also be usefully compared with that of Darwinism. The fundamental principle is like the first law of motion in that both describe not what does go on but what would go on if there were no counteracting forces; and in both cases the main theoretical function of the basic law is to generate questions about such forces and checks. Again, Malthus in classifying checks always aims at complete, exhaustive lists; and his arguments often depend on his appreciation that the values of the various checks considered as variables will be, for a given population, inversely connected: the bigger the sum of the preventive checks, the smaller the sum of the positive checks; and so on. These are similarities of which Malthus himself—thanks to his mathematical training at Cambridge—seems to have been aware. (It is doubtless to the same training that we owe his introduction of the supposition of the arithmetical progression to which, and to the consequent comparison of the two progressions, is due much of the appearance of "mathematical certainty" in his demonstrations.)

Malthus never tied up all the various minor logical loose ends in his original conceptual scheme, although he added important appendices to the third and fifth editions of his work in 1806 and 1817 and wrote the article "Population" for the 1824 supplement to the *Encyclopaedia Britannica* (revised and published separately as his last word in 1830). But the main objections to Malthus that emerged from the enormous controversy are two, one moral and one logical. The moral objection repudiates Malthus's total rejection of contraception. It is this repudiation, combined with acceptance of Malthus's warnings on the dangers of overpopulation, which makes a Neo-Malthusian. The suggestion sometimes heard that the spread of contraception has made Malthusian ideas obsolete should be seen as manifestly absurd. Contraception is one kind of preventive check; none at all would be required if the multiplicative power was not still there to be checked.

The second objection insists on a distinction, which Malthus was forever inclined to overlook, between two senses of *tendency*. A tendency to produce something may be a cause which, operating unimpeded, would produce it. But to speak of a tendency to produce something may also be to say that the result is one that may reasonably be expected to occur in fact. This point seems to have been put against Malthus for the first time by Nassau Senior in his *Two Lectures on Population* (1831) and was grudgingly accepted. It was developed in the following year by Archbishop Whateley in *Lectures on Political Economy* (ninth lecture).

If both these objections are accepted, it becomes possible to recognize the Malthusian menace but to insist that the tendency to catastrophe does not have to be a tendency in the second sense—not if people can be persuaded to employ the means which science has and will put into our hands. Yet Malthus must have the last word. For it was he who most dramatically and powerfully drew attention to an absolutely vital fact, a fact that is still persistently and often disastrously ignored. It is, in the words of Senior, that "no plan for social improvement can be complete, unless it embraces the means both of increasing production, and of preventing population making a proportionate advance."

See also Keynes, John Maynard.

Bibliography

WORKS BY MALTHUS

An Essay on the Principle of Population as It Affects the Future Improvement of Society, with Remarks on the Speculations of Mr. Godwin, M. Condorcet, and Other Writers. London: J. Johnson, 1798. Facsimile edition (London, 1926); paperback edition with introduction by K. E. Boulding (Ann Arbor: University of Michigan Press, 1959).

An Essay on the Principle of Population, or a View of Its Past and Present Effects on Human Happiness, with an Inquiry into Our Prospects Respecting the Future Removal or Mitigation of the Evils Which It Occasions. London, 1803. There is an Everyman Library edition (London and New York); the version now in print has an introduction by M. P. Fogarty.

Glass, D. V., ed. *Introduction to Malthus.* London: Watts, 1953. Includes discussion by Glass and others and an appendix of two things by Malthus.

T. R. Malthus: The Unpublished Papers in the Collection of Kanto Gakuen University.

The Malthus Library Catalogue: The Personal Collection of Thomas Robert Malthus at Jesus College, Cambridge. New York: Pergamon Press, 1983.

The Pamphlets of Thomas Robert Malthus. New York: A.M. Kelley, 1970.

An Essay on the Principle of Population: Text, Sources and Background, Criticism. New York: Norton, 1976.

Principles of Political Economy. Cambridge; New York: Cambridge University Press, 1989.

The Works of Thomas Robert Malthus. Edited by E. A. Wrigley and David Souden. London: W. Pickering, 1986, 1798.

WORKS ON MALTHUS

Bonar, J. *Malthus and His Work.* 2nd ed. New York: Macmillan, 1924.

Flew, Antony. "The Structure of Malthus' Population Theory." In *Philosophy of Science: The Delaware Seminar.* Vol. I, edited by B. Baumrin. New York: Interscience Publishers, 1963.

Keynes, J. M. "Robert Malthus: The First of the Cambridge Economists." In *Essays and Sketches in Biography.* London, 1951.

Levin, S. M. "Malthus and the Idea of Progress." *Journal of the History of Ideas* 27 (1) (1966): 92–108.

Petersen, William. *Malthus.* Cambridge, MA: Harvard University Press, 1979.

Senior, Nassau William. *Two Lectures on Population.* London, 1831.

Turner, Michael Edward. *Malthus and His Time.* New York: St. Martin's Press, 1986.

Waterman, Anthony Michael C. *Revolution, Economics, and Religion: Christian Political Economy, 1798–1833.* Cambridge, U.K.; New York: Cambridge University Press, 1991.

Whateley, Richard. *Lectures on Political Economy.* London, 1832.

Winch, Donald. *Malthus.* Oxford; New York: Oxford University Press, 1987. New York: Cambridge University Press, 1997–2004.

Antony Flew (1967)
Bibliography updated by Michael J. Farmer (2005)

MAMARDASHVILI, MERAB KONSTANTINOVICH
(1930–1990)

Merab Mamardashvili was born September 15, 1930, in Gori, Gerorgia and died November 25, 1990, in Moscow. He was a philosopher most of whose creative life passed in Moscow and Tbilisi, Georgia, in the period from the 1950s through the 1980s. He was an original thinker who received world recognition. His main spheres of inquiry were the philosophy of consciousness, the theory of transformed forms of consciousness; classical and non-classical forms of rationality; the phenomenology of life, love, and death; proof of the necessity of Cartesian, Kantian, and Husserlian themes as "elements" or dimensions of all philosophizing; problems of the existence, consciousness, and action of man under the conditions of socialism and of the Soviet regime; contemporary civilization and the "anthropological catastrophe."

Mamardashvili graduated from the philosophy department of Moscow University in 1954 and completed his graduate studies there in 1957. He was on the editorial staff of the journals *Voprosy filosofii* [Questions of philosophy] (1957–1961) and *Problemy mira isotsializma* [Problems of the world and of socialism] (1961–1966). He then worked in a number of institutes of the Academy of Sciences (the Institute of the International Workers Movement and the Institute of the History of Natural Science and of Technology); from 1968 to 1974, he was associate editor-in-chief of *Voprosy filosofii*. From 1980 to 1990, he lived in Tbilisi, where he worked in the Institute of Philosophy of the Georgian Academy of Sciences. From 1972, he was a professor of philosophy.

Having been formed in the period of the "thaw" in the 1950s and having by the 1960s become an original thinker, an opponent of socialism and of the political regime existing then in the USSR (although without being an open dissident), Mamardashvili was compelled to expound his ideas not so much in published works that were subject to censorship, as in lecture courses, which attracted hundreds of listeners. In view of his ability to expound the most complex and recondite philosophical ideas in oral form, he was called "the Georgian Socrates."

Some of Mamardashvili's lecture courses were given in France, Italy, and other countries: He was fluent in a number of foreign languages. His popularity and his recognition as a talented philosopher grew. But the opposition of the authorities, who persecuted him, also grew. That is why during his life he was able to publish only three books: *Formy i soderzhanie myshleniia. K kritike gegelevskogo ucheniia o formakh poznaniia (Forms and Content of Thought. Toward a Critique of Hegel's Doctrine of the Forms of Knowledge)*, Moscow, 1968; *Klassicheskii i neklassicheskii idealy ratsional'nosti (Classical and Non-classical Ideals of Rationality)*, Tbilisi, 1984; *Kaki ia ponimaiu filosofiiu (How I Understand Philosophy)*, Moscow, 1990; as well as articles in journals and collected works. There is a principal difficulty in assimilating and evaluating Mamardashvili's philosophical ideas: The tape recordings of his lectures that served as the basis of the works published under his name after his death were edited and modified by the editors and publishers. Because of this, these books are secondary sources whose status is ambiguous: They are integral parts of Mamardashvili's philosophical heritage, but at the same time a number of specialists view them as inauthentic.

MAMARDASHVILI'S MAIN SPHERES OF INQUIRY AND HIS PRINCIPAL IDEAS

Mamardashvili dealt in four major spheres in his lifetime. His principal ideas and concepts are outlined below and a general explanation is given for his contribution to philosophy.

I. ANALYSIS OF CONSCIOUSNESS AND OF THE TRANSFORMED FORMS OF CONSCIOUSNESS IN THE WORKS OF KARL MARX. For Mamardashvili, as well as for a number of other influential philosophers of Russia of the Soviet period, reference to Marx became a means of struggle with the dogmas of dialectical and historical materialism, as well as a means of grounding his own ideas. In Mamardashvili's exposition, the chief of these are: "The Marxian schemata give rise to the elements of a series of theories: to the elements of (1) a theoretical model of the social conditionedness of consciousness; (2) a theory of fetishism and of the symbolics of the social in consciousness; (3) a theory of ideology (the socio-philosophical critique of ideology developed by Marx was subsequently transformed into that which is now called the sociology of knowledge as an academic discipline); (4) a theory of science and of free spiritual production as particular forms of active consciousness; (5) a theory of consciousness as an instrument of man's personal development and of his responsibility in the sphere of culture and historical activity" (*How I Understand Philosophy*, Moscow, 1990, pp. 299–300). Later Mamardashvili will say that he found his way to phenomenology not through Husserl but through Marx, who revealed "the phenomenological nature of consciousness, its quasi-objective character," but—in contradiction to the phenomenology of the twentieth century—always disclosed "behind phenomena" their causal origin and "the social system of communion, which the phenomena of consciousness serve" (p. 303).

To this is appended an interpretation of the concept of "the transformed forms of consciousness," which we already encounter in Marx, but to which Mamardashvili attributes a broader and more profound theoretical significance. According to Mamardashvili, the transformed forms are characterized by the fact that "the form of manifestation acquires an 'essential' significance, is particularized, and content is replaced in the phenomenon by another relation, which merges with the property of the material bearer (substrate) of the form itself (for example, in cases of symbolism) and takes the place of the real relations" ("*Forma prevrashchennaia*" [*Transformed Form*] in *Filosofskaia entsiklopediia* [*Philosophical Ency-*

clopedia], vol. 5, Moscow, 1970, p. 387). Examples of this are capitalized cost in the system of bourgeois economics (the case of an irrational transformed form); objective appearance: the movement of the sun and planets around the earth; the operation of sign forms of culture; memory and coding units in computers; and the symbolic processing of links of consciousness (according to Freud).

II. EXISTENTIALISM AND FRENCH MARXISM. It was early on that Mamardashvili began his polemic with existentialism and with French Marxism. He personally debated Sartre and Althusser. During the 1950s and 1960s, like these French authors whom he critically analyzed, Mamardashvili based his thought on Marx's conception, but he was also developing an original conception of society and man. At the center of Mamardashvili's positive analysis was a theory of personality and alienation which rejected Sartre's conception of nature, matter, and the material in socio-historical life: "Taking as his point of departure a phenomenological analysis, Sartre can see in the manifestations of social 'matter' (i.e., the fact of the existence in society of forces and relationships which are independent of individuals and their consciousness) only an extra-human and mysterious power, which bewitches people and their relationships and weaves together with them the thread of factual history" ("Kategoriia sotsial'nogo bytiia i metod ego analiza v ekzistentsializme Sartra" [The Category of Social Being and Its Method of Analysis in Sartre's Existentialism] in Sovremennyi ekzistentializm [Contemporary Existentialism], Moscow, 1966, p. 187).

III. COMPARATIVE ANALYSIS OF RATIONALITY. Mamardashvili devoted a number of his works to a comparative analysis of the classical and non-classical types or ideals of rationality. He discerned the specific character of the classical type of rationality in the following features: (1) the concept of the "objective" in the "classical" type was identified with the external (the spatial), while the spatial was identified with the material, which had important philosophical and methodological consequences; (2) "from within the physical theory, which investigates natural phenomena and comes to a certain objective and intelligible picture of the world, we cannot (from within this theory itself) understand those means which we use to construct this picture" (The Classical and Non-classical Ideals of Rationality, p. 5). The understanding of the physical world is bought at the cost of a "lack of scientific understanding" of conscious phenomena (although, as living beings, we freely live and orient ourselves in this sphere). Other features include the princi-

ples of classical rationality: "the principle of the continuity of reproducible experience," "the self-identity of the subject" (p. 9); and reliance on the concept of "phenomenon"; de-anthropomorphization. Non-classical rationality arises under the influence of the theory of relativity and quantum mechanics; and in the social and humanitarian disciplines, it arises under the influence of the theory of Marx's ideology, Husserl's phenomenology, and Freud's psychoanalysis. The main principles and procedures of non-classical rationality are: (1) phenomenon instead of appearance, for "I return to the phenomemological level, which prohibits us from discussing something without first bringing to a stop the premises of our objectifying thought …" (p. 50); (2) the refusal to accept the existence of some "preestablished world with ready-made laws and essences" (p. 64); (3) a complete and comprehensive understanding that consciousness is "one of the inalienable elements of the very object of investigation" (p. 79).

IV. INTERPRETATIONS OF DOCTRINES OF PROMINENT PHILOSOPHERS. The central place in Mamardashvili's philosophy is occupied by a particular interpretation of the doctrines of a number of prominent thinkers and cultural figures of the past (see the posthumous Kartezianskie razmyshleniia [Cartesian Meditations]; Kantianskie variatsii [Kantian Variations], Moscow, 1997; and Lektsii o Pruste [Lectures on Proust], Moscow, 1995). The originality of this interpretation consists in a free transition from an abstractly philosophical analysis of the doctrines of Descartes or Kant to an illumination of the socio-historical content as well as the trans-historical cultural, moral, aesthetic, and personal content contained in these doctrines. As a result, the philosophical consciousness is closely interwoven with the radical problems, contradictions, and crises of civilization, with orientations of the human personality that have meaning for life. This is realized, for example, in the historico-philosophical as well as socio-philosophical figure of the three "K's": "Kartesius" (Descartes), Kant, and Kafka.

In the interpretation of Descartes the central plane is occupied by the theme of cogito, which Mamardashvili calls "the phenomenon of all phenomena," as well as by the paths leading to cogito. The consciousness of ego cogito is interpreted, on the one hand, as a limit abstraction from all that is historically concrete, even from man, a limit abstraction which implies the "permissibility" and even the inevitability of transcendentalism (in the traditions of Descartes, Kant, and Husserl). On the other hand, this "improbable abstraction" is realized, after which it "becomes in a concealed manner the foundation" of our physical knowledge and of the formulation of physical laws, although it is scarcely the case that we are always conscious of the "accomplishment" of the abstraction. Here, the abstraction of the transcendental *ego* acquires social, personal, and moral foundations and consequences. What this means is that thought is free and thus "paths of *coherent* space must be laid for thought, i.e., paths of open discussion (*glasnost*), mutual tolerance, formal legality…" (*Lektsii o Pruste*, p. 115).

The second "K" (Kant) in Mamardashvili's interpretation indicates the conditions under which man—a finite, mortal being, whose life could have become meaningless in the face of infinity—creates around himself a special world, a world which presupposes choice, evaluations, decisions; in other words, freedom. This is because everyone who is born not only enters the world of nature with its rigid causal connections, but also encounters and in part creates the world of "intelligible" objects. These latter, according to Mamardashvili, are "*images* of integralities," as if designs and projects of development.

The third "K" is a figurative reference to the "world of Kafka," i.e., to the penetration into the human world of certain "zombie-situations," attesting to the "degeneration" or "regressive variant" of the general K-principle: In opposition to *Homo sapiens*, n other words, to "man who knows good and evil," a "strange man," an indescribable man, enters the world of civilization. "Ridiculous, absurd, bizarre, dreamlike confusion and something otherworldly"—that is how Mamardashvili describes the actions of Joseph K. in Kafka's *Trial*, and this also goes for the situation of the absurd in human society. With the accumulation of the potential of the absurd in human history, including contemporary history, the result can be the most dangerous chaos of civilization, a kind of anthropological catastrophe. "Terrifying idols of passion, soil, and blood cover the world, concealing the hidden paths of order; and it is very difficult to tear oneself away from these idols, and to enter onto the radiant paths of thought, order, and harmony" (p. 210).

See also Cartesianism; Descartes, René; Existentialism; Freud, Sigmund; Husserl, Edmund; Kafka, Franz; Kant, Immanuel; Marx, Karl; Quantum Mechanics; Rationality; Relativity Theory; Russian Philosophy; Sartre, Jean-Paul.

Bibliography

Kruglikov, V., ed. *Kongenial'nost' mysli: O filosofe Merabe Mamardashvili (Congeniality of Thought: On the Philosopher Merab Mamardashvili)*. Moscow, 1999.

Kruglikor, V., and J. Schokasov, eds. *Vstrecha s Dekartom (Encounter with Descartes)*. Moscow, 1996.

Mamardashvili, Merab. *Estetika myshleniia (Aesthetics of Thought)*. Moscow, 2000.

Mamardashvili, Merab. *Méditationes cartésiennes*. Solin, 1997.

Mamardashvili, Merab. *Moi opyt netipichen (My Experience Is Atypical)*. Moscow, 2000.

Mamardashvili, Merab. *Soznanie i zivilisatija*. Moscow, 2004.

Mamardashvili, Merab. *Strela posnanija*. Moscow, 2004.

Mamardashvili, Merab. *Variationi Kantiane*. Torino, 2003.

Motroshilova, Nelly. *Raboty rasnych let. Izbrannye statji i esse*. Moscow, 2005.

Nelly Motroshilova (2005)
Translated by Boris Jakim

MANDEVILLE, BERNARD
(c. 1670–1733)

Bernard Mandeville, a physician and moralist, was probably born in Rotterdam, Holland, where he was baptized on November 20, 1670. His family was a distinguished one, his father, grandfather, and great-grandfather having been noted physicians. The family name was originally de Mandeville, but Mandeville dropped the "de" in later life. He was educated at the Erasmian School in Rotterdam and then attended the University of Leiden, where he studied philosophy and medicine. He was granted the degree of doctor of medicine in 1691. His medical specialty was the treatment of nerve and stomach disorders, or, as he called them, the "hypochondriack and hysterick passions." Dr. Johnson is said to have had a high regard for a treatise Mandeville wrote on these diseases.

A short time after taking his degree Mandeville visited London to learn English, and liking the country and the people, he chose to settle in England. Little is known about his English life beyond the bare facts that he married, that he had a son and a daughter, that he practiced medicine, and that he apparently had plenty of time for writing. His success as a writer is all the more remarkable when one remembers that English was his adopted language. His best-known work is *The Fable of the Bees*, with its slogan "private vices, public benefits." It called forth a number of replies from the outraged defenders of virtue, including George Berkeley in the *Alciphron* and Francis Hutcheson. The book was a regular source of public and private controversy in the eighteenth century. The notoriety that this work gained Mandeville doubtless explains why no very consistent account of his situation and character has come down to us from his contemporaries. But Benjamin Franklin, who once met Mandeville, reported that he was "a most facetious and entertaining companion." Mandeville died at Hackney in England.

The Fable of the Bees was twenty-four years in the making. It began as a poem of 433 lines called "The Grumbling Hive: Or, Knaves Turn'd Honest" (London, 1705). The many bitter attacks on the poem caused Mandeville to produce several expositions, elaborations, and defenses of it, all of which grew, over the years, into the book *The Fable of the Bees; Or Private Vices, Public Benefits.* In its final form, the sixth edition (1729), the *Fable* consists of two parts. Part I is the original poem followed by several essays: (1)"An Enquiry into the Origin of Moral Virtue," consisting of twenty-two remarks on various lines or words in the poem, such as luxury, pride, and so on; (2) "An Essay on Charity and Charity Schools"; (3) "A Search into the Nature of Society"; and (4) "A Vindication of the Book" against a presentment of the grand jury of Middlesex and other abuse. Part II, which is as long as the first part, consists of six dialogues in which Cleomenes instructs Horatio in the true meaning of the *Fable.*

As might be expected in a book that was put together over a long period and whose later parts are a defense of the earlier, Mandeville's targets are several, and assessing the relative importance of his ideas is not easy. His economic doctrines are certainly more thoroughly worked out than his moral theories, and he wanted politicians to take his economic views seriously. Given that a politician desires the nation he governs to be great and wealthy and given that there is a large population to be kept in employment, then a certain kind of economic life must be permitted and even fostered. The production of necessities will neither employ very many people nor by itself make a nation great. Therefore, the production of luxuries must be permitted, and their consumption on the most lavish scale possible encouraged, thus simultaneously achieving splendor and full employment. Mandeville analyzes the making of hooped and quilted petticoats in order to show not only the opportunities for labor the manufacture of this luxury provides in itself, but also the subsidiary employments (shipwright, sailor, dye-finder, and so on) that fashion calls into being.

In "An Essay on Charity and Charity Schools" Mandeville gives some hint of the structure of the society that is required to produce a great and wealthy nation. In this essay, he opposes educating the poor on the grounds that knowledge enlarges and multiplies our desires and that the fewer things a person wishes for, the more easily may his necessities be supplied. As Mandeville understood the English economic system of the eighteenth century, it required a large number of laboring poor, and he feared that education would make them dissatisfied with their lot and would consequently disrupt the system.

But Mandeville goes on to show the mixed feelings that have always troubled the analytical observer of society who is also a decent human being. He tells us that he does not wish to be thought personally cruel, but he believes that proposing to educate the poor is "to be Compassionate to excess, where Reason forbids it, and the general Interest of the Society requires steadiness of Thought and Resolution." It is, he argues, no harder on the poor to withhold education from them, even though they may have "natural parts and genius" equaling the rich, than it is to withhold money from them as long as they have the same inclinations to spend as the rich have.

Mandeville strongly favored free trade, seeing clearly that in order for one nation to buy another's goods, it must be able to sell its own. Any restriction in international trade must cause the loss of markets, with a consequent fall in the level of employment at home. In the eighteenth century Mandeville's writings became the chief source of arguments in favor of the manufacture of luxuries and against restrictions on trade, either within a given nation or between nations. Adam Smith owed much to his knowledge of *The Fable of the Bees.*

Mandeville did not choose, however, to publish these economic doctrines in a straightforward way. Instead, he offered them in his moralizing poem, "The Grumbling Hive." The bees in the poem have many vices, but their society thrives. Mandeville's notion of vice is a threefold one. First, he has in mind such character traits as envy, vanity, love of luxury, and fickleness in diet, furniture, and dress. These traits make buyers eager to spend lavishly and consume prodigiously, so that they will soon be ready to spend again. Second, Mandeville calls vice that behavior necessary to profitable trade. The seller must conceal from the prospective buyer both the original cost of his goods and the lowest price at which he is willing to sell, while the buyer must conceal the highest price at which he will buy. Mandeville believes that success will certainly require deceit on the part of both buyer and seller, not to mention sharper practices that may descend to downright fraud. Third, Mandeville counts crime as a vice that provides public benefits. Thieves are valuable on two counts. The threat of them keeps locksmiths in business, and when they do succeed, they soon squander their gains, thus contributing to the circulation of wealth. Mandeville may therefore conclude, "The worst of all the Multitude/Did something for the Common Good." In this vein he regards even wars and natural disasters as valuable to the economic system, for by destroying goods, they provide an opportunity for labor to replace them.

Against his claims for the social utility of vice Mandeville sets the following picture of virtue:

> It is certain that the fewer Desires a Man has and the less he covets, the more easy he is to himself … the more he loves Peace and Concord, the more Charity he has for his Neighbor, and the more he shines in real virtue, there is no doubt but that in proportion he is acceptable to God and Man. But let us be Just, what Benefit can these things be of, or what earthly good can they do, to promote the Wealth, the Glory and Worldly Greatness of Nations?

By a divine fiat the bees of the grumbling hive are all made honest, and their society declines into simplicity and insignificance.

Why did Mandeville present his economic doctrines in a poem praising vice, a poem that could only outrage his contemporaries? The most likely supposition is that in the first writing the motives of the moralist are uppermost. If English economic life is seen as it is and as it will be, then encouraging men to be honest and frugal is a disservice to both them and the continuation of the economic system. By praising those sorts of behavior that are ordinarily called vicious, Mandeville hoped to shock the moralist into seeing the world as it is. He gives the moralist the choice either of accepting the world as it is and changing his tune or of rejecting the world and admitting that the virtues the moralist praises require a context quite different from what is ordinarily supposed. What Mandeville takes to be economic truths thus become the basis for a program that is no less than the reform of moralizing.

As *The Fable of the Bees* grew, Mandeville came to offer bits of moral theory, largely because of his discovery of the writings of the Earl of Shaftesbury. He attacked Shaftesbury bitterly. He calls the claim that men may be virtuous without self-denial "a vast Inlet to Hypocrisy." He says that Shaftesbury's search for "a real worth and excellence" in things "is not much better than a Wild-Goose-Chase that is but little to be depended on." Mandeville's own view is that "our Liking or Disliking of things chiefly depends on Mode and Custom, and the Precept and Example of our Betters and such whom one way or other we think to be Superior to us. In Morals there is no greater certainty."

The organization of men into a society arises from the multiplicity of each man's desires and the need to overcome the great man's desires and the need to overcome the great natural obstacles that stand in the way of satisfying these desires. In society each man achieves his own ends by laboring for others. Under a government each member of society is rendered subservient to the whole, and all men, by cunning management, are made to act as one. The key to social organization is man's pride and his consequent delight in flattery. Thus, governors may flatter men into putting public interest before private interest, and men are led to be pleased with themselves for being virtuous. Indeed, this satisfaction is the reward for virtuous actions, and it is ultimately this feeling that makes virtue possible.

These doctrines place Mandeville in the moral-sense school, but his presentation of them is desultory and unsystematic. A successor, such as David Hume, would have been interested to find these views in the *Fable*. But there is something else in Mandeville's writings that is even more impressive—the large number of vignettes, anecdotes, and sketches that make the reader feel he is learning what people are really like and that must in the end make him a shrewder observer of human nature.

See also Berkeley, George; Franklin, Benjamin; Hutcheson, Francis; Johnson, Samuel; Moral Sense; Shaftesbury, Third Earl of (Anthony Ashley Cooper); Smith, Adam; Virtue and Vice.

Bibliography

The premier modern edition of *The Fable of the Bees* is that prepared by F. B. Kaye, 2 vols. (London, 1924). Kaye's researches have provided us with a balanced account of Mandeville's life, and his introductory essay on Mandeville's thought and influence should be consulted.

Mandeville's other works include *The Virgin Unmask'd: Or, Female Dialogues betwixt an Elderly Maiden Lady, and Her Niece* (London: J. Morphew, 1709); *Free Thoughts on Religion, the Church, and National Happiness* (London: T. Jauncy and J. Roberts, 1720); *A Modest Defence of Publick Stews* (1724); *An Enquiry into the Causes of the Frequent Executions at Tyburn* (London: J. Roberts, 1725); *An Enquiry into the Origin of Honour, and the Usefulness of Christianity in War* (London: J. Brotherton, 1732); and *A Letter to Dion [Berkeley], Occasion'd by His Book Call'd Alciphron* (1732).

Elmer Sprague (1967)

MANI AND MANICHAEISM

Mani, "the apostle of God," founder of one of the most widely influential religions of the ancient world, was born in southern Babylonia about 216 CE. Little is definitely known of his birthplace and parentage, since some statements should probably be discounted as malicious reports from his adversaries. He seems to have been of Persian descent and related, at least on his mother's side, to the royal house of Parthia, which was overthrown in 226 by the Sassanid Ardashir I. He is said to have received his first revelation at the age of twelve, but he did not receive his formal call to apostleship until he was twenty-four. His public activity began with a journey to India, where he founded his first community.

Upon the death of Ardashir in 241, Mani returned to Parthia, where he was welcomed by Ardashir's successor Shapur, for whom he wrote a book, the *Shapurakan*. When Shapur died thirty years later, Mani also enjoyed the favor of his successor, but when Bahram came to the throne in 272 the situation changed. Throughout Mani's career the Magian priests had been his most deadly enemies, and they now secured his impeachment and condemnation. He was executed about 276 CE, and his death apparently was followed by persecution of his adherents.

At least seven works have been ascribed to him, including the *Shapurakan*, another work titled "The Living Gospel," and the *Epistula Fundamenti*, which, on the evidence of Augustine, was used by north African Manichaeans as a handbook of doctrine. To these some Western authorities add the *Kephalaia*, which is extant in Coptic. Resources for the study of Manichaeism—once limited to the information supplied by such opponents as Augustine and Titus of Bostra and to excerpts in the works of Theodore bar Konai, in Hegemonius's *Acta Archelai*, and in such Arabic sources as the *Fihrist* of En-Nadim—had in the twentieth century been enriched by discoveries of original Manichaean documents in Turkestan and Egypt. The fragments discovered at Turfan include texts in several Iranian dialects, Turkish, and Chinese, while the Egyptian discovery includes Coptic versions of the *Kephalaia*, a psalmbook, and a collection of homilies.

THE SYSTEM OF MANI

The chief characteristic of Mani's system is a consistent dualism that rejects any possibility of tracing the origins of good and evil to one and the same source. Evil stands as a completely independent principle against Good, and redemption from the power of Evil is to be achieved by recognizing this dualism and following the appropriate rules of life. The opposition of God and Matter is seen in the realm of nature as the conflict of Light and Darkness, Truth and Error. The present world, and man in particular, presents a mixture of Good and Evil, the result of a

breach of the original limits by the powers of evil. The whole purpose of the founding of the universe was to separate the two principles and restore the original state of affairs, rendering Evil forever harmless and preventing any future repetition of the intermingling.

It is the special task of the Manichaean, the man who has been brought to the light, to collaborate in this separation. Through the God-sent mind that is in him and that sets him apart from the other creatures, he must become aware of the mixture present in all things. He must thus discover the true meaning and significance of the world and conduct himself accordingly, in such a way as to avoid any further contamination of the light and promote its release from its mixture with the darkness. The death of the body is thus redemption; and true life is the release of the soul, which is light, from its imprisonment in the body and its return to its true abode.

The Manichaean myth begins with the two primal principles of Light and Darkness, each dwelling in its own realm, coeternal but independent. Perception of the Light excites envy, greed, and hate in Darkness, and provokes it to attack the Light. In response the Father of Greatness calls forth the Primal Man, who arms himself with five powers and descends to battle with the Darkness. He is defeated, however, and the five powers of Darkness devour a part of his light and thus bring the mixture into being. In some versions this is explained as part of a deliberate plan to satisfy the powers of Darkness temporarily by the cession of a portion of the light and thus to prevent further attack. The captive portion of light, the armor of the Primal Man, is identified with the soul, which thus becomes subject to the affections of Matter.

The Primal Man appeals to the Father of Greatness, who sends the Living Spirit to deliver him. The archons, or powers of Darkness, are now overcome (although they do not lose their power of action), and heaven and earth are made from their carcasses. From the purest part of the Light in the archons the sun and moon are formed, but even so only a small part of the Light has been delivered. A fresh appeal from the powers of Light leads the Father of Greatness to send a Third Messenger, whose appearance inspires the Darkness to produce Adam and Eve in the image of his glorious form and to enclose in them the Light still at its disposal. The creation of Eve has a special purpose, in that she is more subservient to the demons and serves as their instrument for the seduction of Adam. Procreation serves the ends of Darkness, since each birth means a further dispersal of the Light, another subject for the realm of Darkness, and a prolonging of the captivity of the Light. The powers of Light accordingly send Jesus on a mission of revelation to Adam, who is still innocent but subsequently disobeys, is seduced by Eve, and so sets the chain of reproduction in motion. This protracts the drama of salvation, and with it the mission of Jesus, into the history of humankind. In one age the revelation comes to India through the Buddha, in another to Persia through Zoroaster, in a third to the West through the historical Jesus, and in the last age it comes through Mani himself, the apostle of the true God.

MANICHAEAN ETHICS

The cosmogonic myth provides the basis and substructure for the Manichaean ethics and hope of redemption. The ethics are rigorously ascetic: Since procreation only prolongs the reign of the powers of darkness, marriage must be rejected. The Manichaean must abstain from all "ensouled" things and eat only vegetables, so as to avoid, as far as possible, any injury to the Light. The full rigor of Manichaean ethics is reserved for the Elect, and the mass of adherents, the Hearers or Soldiers, are allowed to live under less rigorous rules. Correspondingly there is a difference in their destiny after death: The Elect pass at once to the Paradise of Light, but the Soldiers must return to the world and its terrors until their light is freed and they attain to the assembly of the Elect. The third class of men, the sinners who are outside the Manichaean religion, are doomed to remain in the power of Evil.

MANICHAEAN GNOSTICISM

It is clear that Manichaeism may be regarded as a form of Gnosticism. Indeed, it has been called "the most monumental single embodiment of the gnostic religious principle, for whose doctrinal and mythological representation the elements of older religions were consciously employed" (Hans Jonas, *The Gnostic Religion*, pp. 207f.). It differs, however, from such older forms of Gnosticism as Valentinianism in that here the dualism is from the beginning an integral part of the myth, and not the result of a development in the myth. In Jonas's words, "the tragedy of the deity is forced upon it from outside, with Darkness having the first initiative," whereas in the other type of Gnosticism, Darkness is the product of the divine passion, not its cause. Any attempt to identify the sources upon which Mani drew for the construction of his system is, however, fraught with difficulty, and it would be dangerous to try to establish any genetic relationship. For example, attempts have been made, on the basis of the statement that his father belonged to a Baptist sect, the *Mugtasila*, to forge a link with Mandaeism; but although Mandaean elements have been found in the Manichaean

psalmbook, the identity of the *Mugtasila* with the Mandaeans, or of either with some still older Jewish or Jewish-Christian Baptist movement, is still a matter of debate.

Another possible link is with the Zervanite heresy in Zoroastrianism, but here again caution is necessary. (On this whole subject, see Carsten Colpe, *Die Religion in Geschichte und Gegenwart*, Sec. 5.) In a general way, it may be said that Mani incorporated Christian, Buddhist, and Zoroastrian elements into his religion, but Manichaeism seems to have adapted itself to the dominant religion of a particular area. Moreover, it has been held that he had little more than a hearsay knowledge of Christianity, although he had some acquaintance with the heresies of Bardesanes and of Marcion. It appears that he intended to found not merely a sect but a new religion that could embody the best of the older faiths, fusing elements from Buddhism, Christianity, and Zoroastrianism with his own teaching.

His success is evident from the fact that Manichaeism survived so long and for a time was a serious rival to Christianity. After Mani's death it spread through Syria into the West and spread eastward deep into central Asia. Centuries later Manichaean ideas were current among the Bogomiles in the Balkans (see Dmitri Obolensky, *The Bogomils*) and among the Albigenses and Cathari in Provence (see Steven Runciman, *The Mediaeval Manichee*). There may be debate as to the historical connection of these later movements with the original Manichaeism, but some influence appears beyond dispute. Nor should it be forgotten that Augustine himself was for a time an adherent of Manichaeism. A religion that could arouse the interest of such later thinkers as Pierre Bayle, David Hume, and Voltaire must be regarded as one of profound significance for the history of thought.

See also Augustine, St.; Bayle, Pierre; Buddhism; Christianity; Evil; Evil, The Problem of; Gnosticism; Hume, David; Valentinus and Valentinianism; Voltaire, François-Marie Arouet de; Zoroastrianism.

Bibliography

TEXTS AND TRANSLATIONS

Allberry, C. R. C. *A Coptic Manichaean Psalm-Book.* Stuttgart: Kohlhammer, 1938.

Asmussen, Jes. *X^uāstvānīft.* Copenhagen: Prostant apud Munksgaard, 1965.

Boyce, Mary. *The Manichaean Hymn Cycles in Parthian.* London: Oxford University Press, 1954.

Clark, Larry. "The Manichaean Turkic Pothi-Book." *Altorientalische Forschungen* 9 (1982): 145–218.

Gardner, Iain. *The Kephalaia of the Teacher.* Leiden: Brill, 1995.

Gardner, Iain, and Samuel N. C. Lieu. *Manichaean Texts from the Roman Empire.* Cambridge, U.K.: Cambridge University Press, 2004.

Klimkeit, Hans-Joachim. *Gnosis on the Silk Road.* San Francisco: Harper, 1993.

Koenen, Ludwig, and Cornelia Römer. *Der Kölner Mani-Kodex.* Opladen: Westdeutscher, 1988.

Polotsky, Hans Joachim. *Manichäische Homilien.* Stuttgart: Kohlhammer, 1934.

Schmidt-Glintzer, Helwig. *Chinesische Manichaica.* Wiesbaden: Otto Harrassowitz. 1987.

Sundermann, Werner. *Der Sermon vom Licht-Nous.* Berlin: Akademie-Verlag, 1992.

Sundermann, Werner. *Der Sermon von der Seele.* Turnhout, Belgium: Brepols, 1997.

STUDIES

BeDuhn, Jason David. *The Manichaean Body in Discipline and Ritual.* Baltimore: Johns Hopkins Press, 2000.

Bryder, Peter. *The Chinese Transformation of Manichaeism.* Löberöd: Plus Ultra, 1985.

Gulácsi, Zsuzsanna. *Manichaean Art in Berlin Collections.* Turnhout, Belgium: Brepols, 2001.

Jonas, Hans. *The Gnostic Religion.* 2nd ed. Boston: Beacon Press, 1963.

Lieu, Samuel N. C. *Manichaeism in the Later Roman Empire and Medieval China,* 2nd ed. Tübingen: Mohr-Siebeck, 1992.

Mikkelsen, Gunner. *Bibliographia Manichaica.* Turnhout, Belgium: Brepols, 1997.

Obolensky, Dmitri. *The Bogomils.* Cambridge, U.K.: Cambridge University Press, 1948.

Pedersen, Nils Arne. *Studies in the Sermon on the Great War.* Aarhus: Aarhus University Press, 1996.

Reeves, John. *Heralds of that Good Realm.* Leiden: Brill, 1996.

Runciman, Steven. *The Mediaeval Manichee.* Cambridge: Cambridge University Press, 1947.

Widengren, Geo. *Der Manichäismus.* Darmstadt: Wissenschaftliche Buchgesellschaft, 1977.

Wurst, Gregor. *Das Bemafest der ägyptischen Manichäer.* Altenberge: Oros, 1995.

R. McL. Wilson (1967)
Bibliography updated by Jason BeDuhn (2005)

MANNHEIM, KARL
(1893–1947)

Karl Mannheim, the German sociologist, was born in Budapest and died in London. He studied at Berlin and Paris, and at Heidelberg under Max Weber, and later taught at Heidelberg, Frankfurt am Main, and, after 1933, in London.

Mannheim's thought resembles that of such philosophers as Auguste Comte and G. W. F. Hegel, who believed that in the past man had been dominated by the historical process whereas in the future he would gain ascendancy over it. Mannheim was deeply influenced by Karl Marx, but he deviated from Marxism in asserting that a better society might be achieved by nonrevolutionary means and also in de-emphasizing the interpretation of the development of society as being semiautomatic and stressing the importance of conscious political effort. He was, in addition, decisively influenced by German historicism and Anglo-Saxon pragmatism. From the former he took the belief that history is the *ens realissimum*, while from the latter he derived his criterion of truth. Both positions pointed toward a radical relativism, which, however, he strove to overcome.

In his first and most important book, *Ideologie und Utopie*, Mannheim asserted that the act of cognition must not be regarded as the effort of a purely theoretical consciousness, because the human consciousness is permeated by nontheoretical elements arising both from man's participation in social life and in the streams and tendencies of willing which work themselves out contemporaneously in that life. The influence of these active factors is all-important; even the categorial structure of the intellect does not escape it. Mannheim therefore maintained that epistemology (as practiced, for instance, by Immanuel Kant) was outdated, and must be superseded by a new discipline, the sociology of knowledge.

According to Mannheim, this new discipline revealed that all knowledge (at any rate, knowledge of things human) was situation-bound (*situationsgebunden*)—that is, tied to a given constellation of sociohistorical circumstances. Each age develops its own style of thought, and comparisons between these styles are impossible, since each posits a different basic (or, so to speak, relatively absolute) sphere. Even within each age there are conflicting tendencies toward conservation, on the one hand, and toward change on the other. Commitment to conservation tends to produce "ideologies"—to falsify thought by excessive idealization of the past and overemphasis on the factors making for stability. Intentness on change is apt to produce "utopias," which overvalue both the future and factors leading to change.

Between ideology and utopia there is at least the possibility of completely realistic (*situationsgerecht*) thought that functions without friction within the given framework of life, and is set neither on pushing forward nor on holding back the development of society. But Mannheim places little emphasis on this possibility. He sees a very strong tendency toward the polarization of society into hostile camps. Only the comparatively uncommitted intelligentsia is likely to approach nearer the truth. From its special and particularly favorable vantage point, it could, and should, elaborate a "total perspective" that would synthesize the conflicting contemporary world views and thereby neutralize, and to some extent overcome, their one-sidedness. Such a "dynamic synthesis" is the nearest possible approximation to a truly realistic attitude, within the limitations imposed upon a given epoch.

This estimate of human thought might seem to justify accusing Mannheim of skepticism, but Mannheim held himself innocent of the charge. To rebut it, he developed his doctrine of "relationism," which he opposed to skeptical relativism. Relationism, he argued, does not impugn the validity of an insight: It merely draws attention to the fact that the insight is dependent upon, and confined within, a specific sociohistorical situations. But this argument merely shifts the relativity, and does not remove it. Mannheim held that every sociohistorical situation is located at a specific point along a unilinear, ever-progressing and never-returning temporal continuum—history. Each situation is therefore unique, and the knowledge to which it gives birth, and which is true within it, is equally unique, bound to its time and place, and relative.

But Mannheim was not primarily concerned with the truth of propositions. Rather, he operated with a radically different conception of "truth." To him, truth is an attribute, not so much of discourse, as of reality. The individual who is in contact with the living forces of his age has the truth, or better, is in the truth—a conception that shows at once Mannheim's Marxism, his historicism, and his pragmatism. He was moving close to the belief that the traditional *adaequatio rei et intellectus* (correspondence of thought and reality) should be replaced by a new test, the *adaequatio intellectus et situs* (correspondence of thought and situation). He was interested in the genuineness, rather than in the truth (properly so called), of a given world view.

Mannheim was a confirmed progressivist, and he tended to prefer whatever was, at any time, emergent. After his immigration to England in 1933, he adopted a more practical and political orientation. He argued dialectically, especially in *Mensch und Gesellschaft im Zeitalter des Umbaus* (1935), that a completely unregulated society, such as he thought liberalism had created, was apt to produce its own opposite, totalitarian dictatorship. To secure the values of democracy, it was necessary to avoid the weaknesses of both liberalism and totalitarianism. As a viable synthesis, Mannheim advocated "planning for freedom," a social system that would ensure economic stability by regulating the more objective aspects of life, such as production, but at the same time grant freedom to men's subjective strivings (for example, in matters of taste), thereby releasing cultural creativity. In this context, Mannheim became interested in education as the prime means of radical democratization. Toward the end of his career, he began to feel that a modernized Christianity held out some hope for a new integration of society's value system, which had become splintered and self-contradictory.

See also Christianity; Democracy; Hegel, Georg Wilhelm Friedrich; Historicism; Ideology; Kant, Immanuel; Marxist Philosophy; Marx, Karl; Pragmatism; Sociology of Knowledge.

Bibliography

WORKS BY MANNHEIM

Ideologie und Utopie. Bonn: Cohen, 1929. Translated by Louis Wirth and Edward Shils as *Ideology and Utopia.* London: Routledge, 1936. The English edition also includes the article "Wissenssoziologie" from *Handwörterbuch der Soziologie*, edited by Alfred Vierkandt. Stuttgart: Enke, 1931.

Mensch und Gesellschaft im Zeitalter des Umbaus. Leiden: Sijthoff, 1935. Translated by Edward Shils as *Man and Society in an Age of Reconstruction.* London: Routledge, 1940.

Diagnosis of Our Time. London: Routledge, 1943.

Freedom, Power and Democratic Planning, edited by Hans Gerth and Ernest K. Bramstedt. London: Routledge, 1951.

Essays on the Sociology of Knowledge, edited by Paul Kecskemeti. London: Routledge, 1952.

Essays on Sociology and Social Psychology, edited by Paul Kecskemeti. London: Routledge, 1953.

Essays on the Sociology of Culture, edited by Ernst Mannheim and Paul Kecskemeti. London: Routledge, 1956.

Systematic Sociology, edited by J. S. Erös and W. A. C. Stewart. London: Routledge and Kegan Paul, 1957.

An Introduction to the Sociology of Education. Written with W. A. C. Stewart. London: Routledge, 1962.

Freedom, Power, and Democratic Planning. London: Routledge & K. Paul, 1968.

From Karl Mannheim, edited by Kurt H. Wolff. New York: Oxford University Press, 1971.

Die strukturanalyse der erkenntnistheorie. Vaduz/Liechtenstein: Topos Verlag, 1978.

Strukturen des Denkens, edited by David Kettler, Volker Meja, and Nico Stehr. Frankfurt am Main: Suhrkamp, 1980.

Structures of Tinking: Text and Translation, edited by David Kettler, Volker Meja, and Nico Stehr. Translated by Jeremy J. Shapiro and Shierry Weber Nicholsen. Boston, MA: Routledge & Kegan Paul, 1982.

Conservatism: A Contribution to the Sociology of Knowledge, edited by David Kettler, Volker Meja, and Nico Stehr. London: Routledge & Kegan Paul, 1986.

Collected Works of Karl Mannheim. London; New York: Routledge, 1997.

Selected Correspondence (1911–1946) of Karl Mannheim, Scientist, Philosopher, and Sociologist, edited by Éva Gábor. Lewiston, NY: Edwin Mellen, 2003.

WORKS ON MANNHEIM

Kettler, David, and Volker Meja. *Karl Mannheim and the Crisis of Liberalism: The Secret of these New Times*. New Brunswick, NJ: Transaction, 1995.

Lieber, Hans-Joachim. *Wissen und Gesellschaft*. Tübingen: Niemeyer, 1952.

Loader, Colin. *The Intellectual Development of Karl Mannheim: Culture, Politics, and Planning*. Cambridge, U.K.; New York: Cambridge University Press, 1985.

Longhurst, Brian. *Karl Mannheim and the Contemporary Sociology of Knowledge*. New York: St. Martin's Press, 1989.

Maquet, Jacques Jerome. *Sociologie de la connaissance*. Louvain: Institut de Recherches Économiques et Sociales, 1949. Translated into English by John F. Locke as *The Sociology of Knowledge*. Boston: Beacon Press, 1951.

Remmling, Gunter W. *The Sociology of Karl Mannheim: With a Bibliographical Guide to the Sociology of Knowledge, Ideological Analysis, and Social Planning*. New York: Humanities Press, 1975.

Schoeck, Helmut. "Die Zeitlichkeit bei Karl Mannheim." *Archiv für Rechts- und Sozialphilosophie* 38 (1949–1950): 371–382.

Simonds, A. P. *Karl Mannheim's Sociology of Knowledge*. Oxford: Clarendon, 1978.

Woldring, H. E. S. *Karl Mannheim: The Development of His Thought: Philosophy, Sociology and Social Ethics, with a Detailed Biography*. Assen: Van Gorcum, 1986.

Werner Stark (1967)
Bibliography updated by Michael J. Farmer (2005)

MANSEL, HENRY LONGUEVILLE

(1820–1871)

Henry Longueville Mansel, an English philosopher and divine, was educated at Merchant Taylors' School, London, and St. John's College, Oxford. He became tutor in his college, the first Wayneflete professor of moral and metaphysical philosophy at Oxford University in 1859, Regius professor of ecclesiastical history there in 1866, and dean of St. Paul's in 1868.

Mansel was at Oxford during the period when, after more than a century of slumbers, it was again beginning to take philosophy seriously. But whereas his Oxford contemporaries, such as Benjamin Jowett and T. H. Green, looked to Germany for their philosophy, Mansel looked to France and Scotland.

Indebted to various thinkers, especially to William Hamilton and Victor Cousin, Mansel was remarkably successful in assimilating their influences. When—as on the question of the perception of an external world—he occupied common ground with Hamilton, Mansel's version was marked by a superior clarity and relevance. Likewise, he more than did justice to what was genuinely original and valuable in Cousin's critique of John Locke's doctrine of judgment, making it the foundation of a subtle and thorough discussion of the relation of thinking to experience begun in the *Prolegomena Logica* and completed in the article "Metaphysics, or the Philosophy of Consciousness."

The point at issue was the relation of meaning to verification. Can we know a proposition to be true or false without first understanding the meaning of the terms involved, in the sense of being able to define each of them separately? Mansel dealt with this difficulty by making a sharp distinction between a *logical judgment,* in which the understanding of the terms precedes the judgment as to the truth or falsity of the proposition, and a *psychological judgment,* in regard to which this sharp distinction cannot be drawn, and in regard to which the understanding of the terms coincides with the judgment as to the truth of the proposition.

Mansel's main point was that the former sort of judgment must always, in the last analysis, rest upon the latter, of which the Cartesian *cogito* is the prime example. In this way the kind of clear-cut empirical knowledge with which science deals rests on the foundation of an essentially vague metaphysical knowledge embodied in the *cogito.* This doctrine, which descended through Cousin from Thomas Reid, was worked out by Mansel in the course of an excellent discussion of the problem of universals and particulars, contained in the article "Metaphysics." What nominalistic atomists had forgotten was that the individual thing is initially given in an essentially vague experience (for example, three objects seen in the far distance and just recognizably human) that withholds the details and reveals only general characteristics.

While this topic of the relation of thinking to experience was central in Mansel's work, he was equally stimulating on other questions. Somewhat in the French style, he held that the will, in the form of attention, forms an integral part of cognition. Following a suggestion of Dugald Stewart's, he tried to illuminate the difference between the presence and the absence of efforts of will by an interesting phenomenology of daydreaming and semiconsciousness. Again influenced by Reid, Mansel was aware—as few were in his time—of the complexities and difficulties of the problem of our knowledge of the existence of other minds, discussing it, appropriately enough, in connection with the moral judgment. Finally, Mansel dealt interestingly with the distinction between philosophy and science. Philosophy deals with what he called facts of consciousness, whose distinctive feature is that their *esse* is *percipi*, in the sense in which René Descartes had said that, so far as philosophy is concerned, there is no difference between seeing something and thinking one sees it.

The result of this careful phenomenological analysis (the word *phenomenology* had been introduced by Mansel's masters, Hamilton and Cousin) was that Mansel saw human experience as inherently complex and mysterious. In the background of Mansel's philosophy there was always an explicit contrast with a rival kind of reductive analysis that regarded man as being as unmysterious in his inner workings as a pocket watch. This contrast was the key to the controversies aroused by Mansel's Bampton lectures, "The Limits of Religious Thought," delivered in 1858. Mansel held that reason tells us that if evil exists, then God cannot be both perfectly good and all-powerful. However, God's omnipotence and perfect goodness must be accepted as a matter of faith. Although God is perfectly good, we cannot know the nature of his goodness. Man's finite goodness cannot explain God's infinite goodness; they are the same by analogy, not identity.

Mansel's lectures were attacked by F. D. Maurice and Goldwin Smith, and by John Stuart Mill, who devoted Chapter 7 of his *Examination of Sir William Hamilton's Philosophy* to Mansel's views. Mill wrote, "I will call no being good, who is not what I mean when I apply that epithet to my fellow creatures, and if such a being can sentence me to hell for not so calling him, to hell I will go." Mansel replied in *The Philosophy of the Conditioned*, and Mill in turn replied in numerous footnotes in later editions of the *Examination*, listing Mansel first among his critics. For Mansel man's goodness was not clear and God's goodness was inscrutable; both were equally a mystery.

Mansel's *Letters, Lectures, and Reviews,* published posthumously, contains, among other things, interesting articles on the philosophy of language and on mathematical logic.

See also Cousin, Victor; Descartes, René; Green, Thomas Hill; Hamilton, William; Locke, John; Logic, History of; Mill, John Stuart; Phenomenology; Language, Philosophy of; Reid, Thomas; Stewart, Dugald.

Bibliography

WORKS BY MANSEL

Prolegomena Logica. Oxford: W. Graham, 1851.

"Metaphysics, or the Philosophy of Consciousness." In *Encyclopaedia Britannica,* 8th ed. 1857. Published separately, Edinburgh, 1860.

The Limits of Religious Thought. Oxford and London: J. Wright for J. Murray, 1858.

The Philosophy of the Conditioned. London and New York: A. Strahan, 1866.

Letters, Lectures, and Reviews. Edited by H. W. Chandler. London: J. Murray, 1873.

WORKS ON MANSEL

Burgon, J. W. *Lives of Twelve Good Men.* London, 1888. Vol. II, pp. 149–237.

Mill, J. S. *An Examination of Sir William Hamilton's Philosophy.* London: Longmans, Green, 1865. Ch. 7.

Stephen, Leslie. "H. L. Mansel." In *Dictionary of National Biography.* London, 1893. Vol. 36, pp. 81–83.

George E. Davie (1967)

MANY-VALUED LOGICS

An orthodox assumption in logic is that (declarative) sentences have exactly one of two values, true (1) and false (0). Many-valued logics are logics where sentences may have more than two values. Aristotle (*De Interpretatione,* chapter 9) was perhaps the first logician to countenance the thought that some sentences (future contingents) may be neither true nor false; Aristotle's ideas were discussed by many logicians in the Middle Ages. However, contemporary work on many-valued logics commenced with the work of the Polish logician Jan Łukasiewicz early in the twentieth century. One hundred years later there are many well-known many-valued logics, and the properties of such logics are well established. The logics have important philosophical applications (e.g., in articulating the views that some sentences are neither true nor false, or both true and false, or that truth comes by degrees). They also have important technical applications (e.g., in establishing various independence results).

In what follows, p, q, ... will be used for propositional parameters (variables); A, B, ... for arbitrary sentences; and Σ, Δ, ... for sets of sentences. For references, see the last section of this entry.

ŁUKASIEWICZ LOGICS

To illustrate the notion of a formal many-valued logic, consider classical propositional logic with the following connectives: ∧ (conjunction), ∨ (disjunction), ¬ (negation), and → (conditional). This may be formulated as follows. The set of semantic values, *Val*, is {0, 1}. The set of designated values, *Des*, is {1}. An evaluation, *v*, assigns every propositional parameter (pp), a member of *Val*. All formulas are then assigned such values recursively by the clauses:

$$v(\neg A) = 1 - v(A)$$
$$v(A \wedge B) = Min(v(A), v(B))$$
$$v(A \vee B) = Max(v(A), v(B))$$
$$v(A \rightarrow B) = 1 \qquad \text{if } v(A) \le v(B)$$
$$\qquad\qquad = 1 - (v(A) - v(B)) \text{ otherwise}$$

(*Max*(*x*, *y*) is the maximum of *x* and *y*; *Min*(*x*, *y*) is the minimum of *x* and *y*. *v*(*A*→*B*) takes the maximum value minus any amount one has to drop to get from *A* to *B*.) The inference from Σ to *A* is valid (Σ ⊨ *A*) just if there is no evaluation that makes all the premises designated but not the conclusion (i.e., there is no *v* such that for all *B*∈Σ, *v*(*B*)∈*Des*, but *v*(*A*)∉*Des*).

If everything is exactly the same, except that *Val* = {0, ½, 1}, one has the three-valued Łukasiewicz logic Ł₃. The semantic conditions for the connectives can be depicted in the form of tables, thus:

→	1	1/2	0
1	1	1/2	0
1/2	1	1	1/2
0	1	1	1

	¬
1	0
1/2	1/2
0	1

∨	1	1/2	0
1	1	1	1
1/2	1	1/2	1/2
0	1	1/2	0

∧	1	1/2	0
1	1	1/2	0
1/2	1/2	1/2	0
0	0	0	0

More generally, if *n*>1 and everything is the same, except that *Val* = {*i*/(*n*−1) : 0≤*i*≤*n*−1}, one has the Łukasiewicz *n*-valued logic Ł*ₙ*. Finally, if everything is the same, except that *Val* = [0, 1] (the set of all real numbers between 0 and 1, inclusive), one has the Łukasiewicz continuum-valued logic Ł*ℵ*. (The relationship between these logics is that Ł*ₙ* is a [proper] sublogic of Ł*ₘ* if and only if

[iff] *m* divides *n*; and Ł*ℵ* is a [proper] sublogic of all the Ł*ₙ*. The logic in which *Val* is the set of rationals between 0 and 1 turns out to be equivalent to Ł*ℵ*.)

BOTH/NEITHER LOGICS

The values of a many-valued logic need not be numbers (and the designated values do not need to be a singleton). In another well-known family of logics, *Val* = {1, *b*, *n*, 0}. (1 can be thought of as *true and only true*; 0 as *false and only false*; *b* as *both true and false*; and *n* as *neither true nor false*.) *Des* = {1, *b*}. One can order these values as follows:

If *v* is an evaluation of the pps into *Val*, it is extended to all formulas by the following conditions:

$$v(A \vee B) = Lub \{v(A), v(B)\}$$
$$v(A \wedge B) = Glb \{v(A), v(B)\}$$

(*Lub X* is the least element of the lattice greater than or equal to every member of *X*. *Glb X* is the greatest element of the lattice less than or equal to every member of *X*.) The conditions for negation can be represented as follows:

	¬
1	0
b	*b*
n	*n*
0	1

A→*B* can be defined as ¬*A*∨*B*. Note that all these conditions agree with classical logic when the values are just 0 and 1.

These semantics give the logic often called First Degree Entailment (FDE). If one ignores the value *n*, one gets the three-valued logic LP. If one ignores the value *b*, one gets the strong Kleene three-valued logic, K₃. FDE and K₃ have no logical truths; LP (and Ł₃) does. LP and FDE are paraconsistent (i.e., the inference *A*, ¬*A*⊢*B* is not valid); K₃ is not. FDE is a sublogic of both logics, but neither is a sublogic of the other (and all three are sublogics of classical logic). The weak Kleene three-valued logic, B_3, is the same as K_3, except that any truth function with an n as an input gives n as an output.

For the first-order versions of all the logics in this section and the last, the quantifiers $\forall$ and $\exists$ can be thought of as the infinitary generalizations of $\wedge$ and $\vee$, in the usual way. Thus, if Dom, is the domain of quantification, and every $d \in Dom$, has a name, c_d, (and if not just add them):

$$v(\forall x A\ (x)) = Glb\{v(A(c_d)) : d \in Dom\}$$

$$v(\exists x A\ (x)) = Lub\{v(A\ (c_d)) : d \in Dom\}$$

where the bounds are with respect to the appropriate orderings.

GENERAL DEFINITION

In general terms, in a semantics for a formal many-valued propositional logic, there is an arbitrary set of semantic values, Val. (If the cardinality of Val is n, the logic is called n-valued; if it is finite, the logic is called finitely many-valued; if it is infinite, the logic is called infinitely many-valued.) Des, the set of designated values, is an arbitrary subset of Val. Each n-ary connective in the language, #, is assigned an n-place (total) function, $f_\#$, with inputs and outputs in Val. An evaluation of the language, v, assigns each pp a member of Val. Semantic values are assigned to all sentences recursively by the equations $v(\#(A_1, \dots, A_n)) = f_\#\ (v(A_1), \dots, v(A_n))$. An inference is valid if there is no evaluation that makes all the premises designated and the conclusion undesignated. (Slightly more general definitions are also possible here.)

For quantifiers, a domain of quantification, Dom, and denotation function, δ, are added. For every constant c, $\delta(c) \in Dom$; if P is an n-place predicate, $\delta(P)$ is a (total) n-place function with inputs and outputs in Dom. $v(Pc_1, \dots c_n) = \delta(P)(\delta(c_1), \dots, \delta(c_n))$. Each quantifier, Q, is assigned a (total) function, f_Q, with inputs that are subsets of Val and outputs in Val. Assuming that each object in the domain has a name: $v(QxA(x)) = f_Q(\{v(A(c_d)) : d \in Dom\})$.

It is not difficult to check that any many-valued logic is a Tarski consequence relation. That is, it satisfies the following properties. (Here, Σ,Δ means $\Sigma \cup \Delta$; and set braces for singletons are omitted.)

If $A \in \Sigma$, $\Sigma \vDash A$

If $\Sigma \vDash A$ and $\Sigma \subseteq \Delta$, then $\Delta \vDash A$

If $\Sigma \vDash A$ and $\Delta, A \vDash B$, then $\Sigma, \Delta \vDash B$.

If $\Sigma \vDash A$, then any uniform substitution is valid.

(A uniform substitution is obtained by replacing each occurrence of any pp with the same formula.)

In many cases, the set of values (Val), together with the operations on it (the $f_\#$s), is a special case of an algebra of a certain kind. In classical logic, these are Boolean algebras; in the case of FDE, these are De Morgan algebras; and in the case of Ł$_\aleph$, these are MV algebras. Another notion of validity can be obtained by appealing to all the algebras of a kind. At this point, many-valued logic slides into algebraic logic.

PROOF PROCEDURES

All finitely many-valued logics are decidable (and *a fortiori* axiomatizable, though not necessarily finitely axiomatizable). A uniform algorithm is a generalization of truth tables (often there are more efficient ones). Consider all the possible assignments of values to the relevant pps. In each case, compute the values of the premises and the conclusion, and see if there is any assignment in which all the premises are designated and the conclusion is not.

A simple axiom system for Ł$_3$ is as follows:

$A \rightarrow (B \rightarrow A)$

$(A \rightarrow B) \rightarrow ((B \rightarrow C) \rightarrow (A \rightarrow C))$

$(\neg A \rightarrow \neg B) \rightarrow (B \rightarrow A)$

$((A \rightarrow \neg A) \rightarrow A) \rightarrow A$

The only rule of inference is *modus ponens* $(A, A \rightarrow B \vdash B)$; $A \vee B$ is defined as $(A \rightarrow B) \rightarrow B$; and $A \wedge B$ is defined as $\neg(\neg A \vee \neg B)$. In each Ł$_n$ a family of J-functions can be defined, where $v(J_i A) = 1$ if $v(A) = i$, and $v(J_i A) = 0$ otherwise (i, here, being any value of the logic). These can be exploited to give a uniform procedure for producing an axiom system for each Ł$_n$. Similar techniques work for other finitely many-valued logics in which analogues of the J-functions can be defined. (Much technical effort has gone into investigating which functions can be defined in various many-valued systems.) An axiom system for Ł$_\aleph$ is obtained by replacing the last axiom cited earlier with:

$$((A \rightarrow B) \rightarrow B) \rightarrow ((B \rightarrow A) \rightarrow A)$$

If the designated values are changed to $[r, 1]$ (closed at the left end) or $(r, 1]$ (open at the left end), for some rational number, r, the systems are also axiomatizable. If r is an irrational number, they may not be.

Appropriate tableau and natural deduction systems for many-valued logics can often be found. For example, here is a tableau system for FDE. Lines of the tableau are of the form A: + or A: − . (Intuitively, + means "is designated" and − means "is not designated".) To test the inference $A_1, \ldots , A_n \vdash B$, start with lines of the form A_1: + , ..., A_n: + , B: − . The rules are as follows (± can be disambiguated uniformly either way):

$$\alpha \wedge \beta : + \qquad \alpha \wedge \beta : - \qquad \neg(\alpha \wedge \beta) : \pm$$
$$\downarrow \qquad \swarrow \searrow \qquad \downarrow$$
$$\alpha : + \qquad \alpha : - \quad \beta : - \qquad \neg\alpha \vee \neg\beta : \pm$$
$$\beta : +$$

$$\alpha \vee \beta : - \qquad \alpha \vee \beta : + \qquad \neg(\alpha \vee \beta) : \pm$$
$$\downarrow \qquad \swarrow \searrow \qquad \downarrow$$
$$\alpha : - \qquad \alpha : + \quad \beta : + \qquad \neg\alpha \wedge \neg\beta : \pm$$
$$\beta : -$$

$$\neg\neg\alpha : \pm$$
$$\downarrow$$
$$\alpha : \pm$$

A branch closes if it contains lines of the form A: + and A: − . Adding closure whenever there are lines of the form A: + and $\neg A$: +, gives K_3. Adding closure whenever there are lines of the form A: − and $\neg A$: −, gives LP. (Adding both gives classical logic.) The first-order versions of all the finitely many-valued logics already mentioned also have sound and complete proof procedures. However, first-order $Ł_\aleph$ is not axiomatizable. By contrast, the logics that are the same as $Ł_\aleph$, except that for some rational number, $r<1$, $Des = (r, 1]$ (open at the left end) or $[r, 1]$ (closed at the left end) are axiomatizable.

MANY-VALUED AND OTHER LOGICS

A number of important logics, notably intuitionist logic, standard modal, and relevant logics, are demonstrably not finitely many-valued. Specifically, suppose that a logic validates the inferences $\vdash A \rightarrow A$ and $A \vdash A \vee B$. Then for any $a, b \in Val$, $f_\rightarrow(a, a) \in Des$, and if $a \in Des$, $f_\vee(a, b) \in Des$. Now suppose that the logic is n-valued, and that $p_0, \ldots , p_n$ are distinct pps. Let A be the disjunction of all formulas of the form $p_i \rightarrow p_j$ (for $0 \leq i \neq j \leq n$). Consider any evaluation. For some i and j, p_i and p_j must have the same value; hence, $p_i \rightarrow p_j$, and so A, are designated. Hence, A is a logical truth. The logics just cited can be shown to have no logical truths of this form (where $\rightarrow$ is the intuitionist, strict, and relevant conditional, respectively).

However, nearly all logics have an infinitely many-valued semantics of a rather unilluminating kind. Consider the set of logical truths of any logic closed under uniform substitution. Let Val be the set of formulas of the language; $Des = \{A : \vdash A\}$; $f_\#(A_1, \ldots , A_n) = \#(A_1, \ldots , A_n)$. Then $\vdash A$ iff $\models A$.

[Proof: Suppose that A is a logical truth. Consider any interpretation, v. It is easy to check that $v(A)$ is A with every pp, p, replaced by $v(p)$. Since the logic is closed under uniform substitution $v(A)$ is a logical truth; that is, it is designated. Conversely, suppose that A is not a logical truth. Consider the interpretation, v, which maps every pp to itself. It is easy to check that $v(A) = A$, which is not designated.]

The construction can be extended to show that any Tarski consequence relation with finite sets of premises has a many-valued semantics iff it satisfies one condition. This is called uniformity, and is, loosely speaking, to the effect that pps not involved in an inference are irrelevant to it. Specifically, if $\Gamma, \Delta \models A$, then $\Gamma \models A$, provided that:

1.) Δ is nontrivial (that is, for some B, $\Delta \not\models B$)

2.) No formula in Δ contains a pp that occurs in a formula in $\Gamma \cup \{A\}$

It should be noted that not all logics are uniform. In Ingebrigt Johansson's minimal logic, $\emptyset \cup \{p, \neg p\} \models \neg q$, but $\{p, \neg p\}$ is nontrivial, and $\emptyset \not\models \neg q$.

The finiteness constraint can be dropped if the notion of uniformity is strengthened in an appropriate fashion. (Some interesting differences between single-conclusion inference and multiple-conclusion inference emerge in this case.)

PHILOSOPHICAL APPLICATIONS

Many-valued logics have been claimed to have numerous philosophical applications. Like all interesting philosophical matters, these applications are debatable.

Łukasiewicz interpreted Aristotle's argument in *De Intepretatione* (chapter 9) as showing that, though true statements about the past and present are now necessarily true, contingent statements about the future (such as "There will be a sea battle tomorrow") currently have an indeterminate truth status. He suggested deploying $Ł_3$ in an analysis of this situation, reading the truth values $\{1, ½, 0\}$ as necessarily true, indeterminate, and necessarily false, respectively. As one would expect $A \vee \neg A$ is not logically valid in $Ł_3$.

Łukasiewicz suggested adding an operator to the language, $\square$, representing necessity, whose truth conditions may be represented as follows:

	$\square$
1	1
1/2	0
0	0

Its dual, possibility, $\lozenge$, that is, $\neg\square\neg$, is as follows:

	$\lozenge$
1	1
1/2	1
0	0

This makes the inference $A \vdash \square A$ valid—which is reasonable enough on the Aristotelian picture. However, it also makes the inference $\lozenge A, \lozenge B \vdash \lozenge(A \wedge B)$ valid—which it is not, even for Aristotle. (Just let B be $\neg A$.) As has already been seen, normal modal logics are not finitely many-valued.

Future contingents are just one example of sentences that have been suggested as being neither true nor false (truth value gaps). Others include: sentences with reference failure ("The king of France is bald," "3 = 1/0"), category mistakes and other "nonsense" ("This stone is thinking of Vienna"), paradoxical sentences of self-reference ("This sentence is false"), sentences attributing a vague property in a borderline case ("This is a child"—said of someone around puberty), and sentences unverifiable by the appropriate mathematical or scientific procedure ("There are ten consecutive '7's in the decimal expansion of π", "This electron has a velocity of exactly 100 m/sec").

It is often claimed that K_3 (or, sometimes, B_3) is the appropriate logic for such cases: Gappy sentences take the value n. (In the last case, quantum logic and intuitionist logic have also been suggested to handle the matter.) In these logics $A \vee \neg A$ is not a logical truth, but neither is anything else. In particular, then, $A \wedge \neg A$ is not a logical falsity. Even if "The king of France is bald" is neither true nor false, "The king of France is bald and not bald" would seem to be logically false.

One way around this problem is to deploy the method of supervaluations. If v is any K_3 evaluation, let μ be a supervaluation of v ($v \preceq \mu$) iff:

$$\mu(p) \text{ is never } n, \text{ and if } v(p) \neq n, v(p) = \mu(p)$$

An important feature of this logic, not shared by Ł_3, is that if $v(A)$ is 1 or 0, and $v \preceq \mu$, then $\mu(A)$ has the same value.

Now define the supertruth-value, v_s of a sentence under v as follows:

$$v_s(A) = 1 \text{ if for all } \mu \text{ such that } v \preceq \mu, \mu(A) = 1$$
$$= 0 \text{ if for all } \mu \text{ such that } v \preceq \mu, \mu(A) = 0$$
$$= n \text{ otherwise}$$

Define an inference as supervaluation valid if it preserves supertruth-value 1. The inferences that are supervaluation-valid now turn out to be exactly those that are classically valid.

[Proof: If an inference is not classically valid, let v be an evaluation that makes the premises true and the conclusion false. But v is a K_3 evaluation and $v \preceq v$. Hence the inference is not supervaluation-valid. Conversely, suppose that an inference is not supervaluation valid. Then there is a K_3 valuation, v, such that every supervaluation of v gives all the premises the value 1, but not the conclusion. Hence, there is some supervaluation that gives all the premises value 1, but the conclusion value 0. This is a classical evaluation. Hence, the argument is classically invalid.]

On the other side of the street, it has been suggested that some sentences are both true and false (truth-value gluts). These include: paradoxical sentences of self-reference ("This sentence is false"), statements describing instantaneous transition states ("He is in the room"—said at the instant he is symmetrically poised between being in and out), statements of rights and obligations ("She is legally required to do such and such"—when the requirements are based on inconsistent legislation), and sentences attributing a vague property in a borderline case ("This is a child"—said of someone around puberty).

It is sometimes suggested that LP—or FDE if one wants to also take in the possibility of truth value gaps—is the appropriate logic for such cases. The glutty sentences take the value b. (Other paraconsistent logics have also been suggested for the job.) In these logics $A \wedge \neg A$ may take a designated value. In LP the negation of this is also a logical truth.

A way to regain classical logic with LP is by the use of subvaluations. Subvaluations and subvaluation validity are defined in the way dual to supervaluation (*b* replacing *n*, and *some* replacing *all*). In the case of subvaluations, one has the equivalence between classical validity and subvaluation validity only in the one-premise case. (But the duality between the two cases is exact. In a classical multiple-conclusion logic $A \lor B \vdash A,B$ is valid. It is not supervaluation-valid. The equivalence between classical and supervaluational validity holds only because in a single-conclusion inference, one is, in effect, disjoining all the conclusions. In the subvaluation case, this corresponds to conjoining all the premises, which reduces matters to the single premise case.) The technique of super/subvaluations can be generalized to FDE, where there are both gaps and gluts.

A weakness of both LP and FDE is that they do not have a detachable conditional, since $A, A \to B \nvDash B$. They can be augmented with such a conditional, though. Thus, the many-valued logic RM$_3$ augments LP with a detachable conditional, $\Rightarrow$, whose truth conditions can be represented as follows:

$\Rightarrow$	1	b	0
1	1	0	0
b	1	b	0
0	1	1	1

In the context of information processing, truth value gaps are often interpreted as incomplete information, and truth-value gluts as inconsistent information. While in the context of gaps and gluts, a word should be said about set theory. It is well known that the naive comprehension schema

$$x \in \{y : A(y)\} \leftrightarrow A(x)$$

leads to contradiction (and so triviality)—in the shape of paradoxes such as Russell's—when the underlying logic is classical. It has often been suggested that the principle might be consistent (or at least inconsistent but nontrivial) when the underlying logic is many-valued. Problems for such suggestions arise because the principle generates triviality if the logic contains contraction $((A \to (A \to B)) \to (A \to B))$ and *modus ponens*. Let $A(y)$ be $y \in y \to B$. Call the set that this defines *c*. Comprehension quickly gives: $c \in c \leftrightarrow (c \in c \to B)$. Contraction and *modus ponens* then give *B*. (This is Curry's paradox.) RM$_3$, K$_3$, B$_3$,

and Ł$_n$ (for finite *n*) all contain *modus ponens* and, if not contraction, something closely related to it that will do the same job. However, the schema based on Ł$_{\aleph}$ is consistent. If the extensionality principle ($\forall x (x \in y \leftrightarrow x \in z) \to y = z$) is added, though, then even Ł$_{\aleph}$ gives triviality. (Virtually the same comments can be made about the naive *T*-schema ("*A*" is true $\leftrightarrow A$) when self-reference is present. Though here extensionality is, of course, not an issue.)

For a final example of the philosophical application of many-valued logics: It is often claimed that the appropriate semantics for a language with vague predicates is one with degrees of truth. Such logics now usually go under the rubric of fuzzy logics. Ł$_{\aleph}$ is a paradigm one such. (It is not the only one: Ł$_{\aleph}$ is one of a family of logics in which *Val* = [0, 1]. Each is based on a so-called t-norm—essentially a function stating the truth conditions for an appropriate conjunction connective.) The only logical inference that the simplest form of the Sorites paradox uses is *modus ponens*. This is valid in Ł$_{\aleph}$; but if one changes *Des* to, say, [0.8, 1], it is not. (Let $v(p) = 0.9 \in Des$, $v(q) = 0.7 \notin Des$. Then $v(p \to q) = 0.8 \in Des$.) Note that probability theory is not a many-valued logic. The probability of a compound sentence is not determined by the probabilities of it components. (Let *a* and *b* be independent fair coins. Let A_H be "Coin *a* will come down heads"; A_T be "Coin *a* will come down tails"; and B_H be "Coin *b* will come down heads." $\text{Prob}(A_H) = \text{Prob}(A_T) = \text{Prob}(B_H) = 0.5$. But $\text{Prob}(A_H \land A_T) = 0$ and $\text{Prob}(A_H \land B_H) = 0.25$.)

TECHNICAL APPLICATIONS

Many-valued logics have various technical applications. Perhaps the most important of these, in a philosophical context, is their use in proving independence results. Thus, suppose that one has some axiom system, *T*, and wishes to know whether some formula, *A*, is deducible in it. One way to show that it is not is to construct a many-valued logic such that all the axioms of *T* always take a designated value, and all the rules of *T* preserved designated values. It follows that all theorems always take designated values. If one can find an interpretation of the logic in which *A* does not take a designated value, it follows that it cannot be proved.

For example, the following is a set of axioms for the $\to / \neg$ fragment of the relevant logic often called RW (R minus contraction). The only rule of inference is *modus ponens*:

$A \to A$

$(A \to B) \to ((B \to C) \to (A \to C))$

$A \to ((A \to B) \to B)$

$$\neg\neg A \rightarrow A$$

$$(A \rightarrow \neg B) \rightarrow (B \rightarrow \neg A)$$

Now consider the three-valued Łukasiewicz logic, Ł₃. One can check (e.g., by truth tables) that all the axioms always take the designated value and that *modus ponens* preserves that property. Now let C be the formula: $(p \rightarrow (p \rightarrow q)) \rightarrow (p \rightarrow q)$. Take an evaluation, v, in which $v(p) = \frac{1}{2}$ and $v(q) = 0$. Computation verifies that $v(C) = \frac{1}{2}$. Hence C is not provable. Since $v(\neg C) = \frac{1}{2}$ as well, $\neg C$ cannot be proved either. Hence, C is independent of RW.

A much more technically demanding example of the use of many-valued logics to prove independence is in set theory. If one takes the values of the logic to be those of any Boolean algebra, taking the top value as the only designated value, and interprets the connectives and quantifiers in appropriate ways, the logic delivered is classical logic. Choosing the Boolean algebra in an appropriately set-theoretic way, one can also show that the axioms (and so theorems) of Zermelo Fraenkel set theory, ZF, take the designated value. Choosing the algebra in more cunning fashions, one can show that various important set-theoretic principles, such as the continuum hypothesis, do not receive designated values. Hence, ZF does not entail the continuum hypothesis.

HISTORY, PERSONS, AND REFERENCES

This entry concludes by putting the investigations discussed earlier in their historical context. Relevant references that may be consulted for further details are also given at the end of each paragraph. For a gentle introduction to many-valued logics, see Graham Priest (2001, chapters 7, 8, 11); for a more detailed introduction, see Alasdair Urquhart (2001); and for further detailed technical discussions, see Richard Hähnle (2001). J. Michael Dunn and George Epstein (1977) provide a bibliography of work on many-valued logics up to 1974.

The first modern many-valued logic was Ł₃. This, and its generalization to n-valued logics, Ł$_n$, were published by Łukasiewicz around 1920. At about the same time, the U.S. mathematician Emil Post was also constructing finitely many-valued logics. (The most significant feature of Post's systems is its treatment of negation. If the values of the n-valued logic are 0, 1, … , $n-1$, then $v(\neg A) = |1 + v(A)|$ (Mod n). Philosophical applications of this many-valued logic are difficult to find.) The logic Ł$_\aleph$ was published by Łukasiewicz and Alfred Tarski in 1930. Much of the early investigation of many-valued logics and their axiomatizations were carried out by Polish logicians including Mordechaj Wajsberg and Jerzy

Słupecki. Finding a demonstrably complete axiom system for Ł$_\aleph$ turned out to be a hard problem. Reputedly, it was solved by Wajsberg, but the first proofs to be published were by Alan Rose and Berkeley Rosser and by Chen Chung Chang in the late 1950s. The unaxiomatizability of first-order Ł$_\aleph$ was proved by Bruno Scarpellini in 1962. (Łukasiewicz 1970, Rosser and Turquette 1952, Wójcicki 1988, Malinowski 1993.)

Canonical statements of the other many-valued logics mentioned in this entry were given by the following: B_3, Dmitryi Anatol'evich Bochvar, 1939; K_3, Stephen Kleene, 1952; FDE and RM₃, Alan Ross Anderson and Nuel Belnap, 1975; LP, Graham Priest, 1979. (Rescher 1969, Priest 2001.)

The proof that intuitionist logic is not many-valued was first given by Kurt Gödel in 1933. The idea was applied to modal logic by James Dugunji in 1940. The earliest versions of the idea that every logic has a many-valued semantics are usually attributed to Adolf Lindenbaum in the 1920s. Generalizations are due to Jerzy Łos and Roman Suszko in 1958. (Hughes and Cresswell 1968, Shoesmith and Smiley 1978, Wójcicki 1988.)

The applicability of many-valued logics to the view that some sentences are neither true nor false was pursued by many people in the second half of the twentieth century. These include Richard Routley, Leonard Goddard, Saul Kripke, Kit Fine, and Scott Soames. Supervaluations were invented by van Fraassen in 1969. Toward the end of the twentieth century, their application to vagueness became a very standard idea. The application of many-valued logics to the view that some sentences are both true and false, though less popular, has been pursued by various paraconsistent logicians. These include Newton da Costa, Priest, Routley, and Dominic Hyde. The generalization of supervaluation to logics with gluts as well as gaps was developed by Achille Varzi in the 1990s. (Rescher 1969, Scott 1974, Haack 1978, Dunn and Epstein 1977, Humberstone 1998, Varzi 2000, Priest 2001.)

The possibility of basing the naive comprehension schema for sets on Ł$_\aleph$ was investigated by Thoralf Skolem and Chang in the 1950s. The consistency of the schema (and the inconsistency of extensionality) was proved by Richard White in 1979. (White 1979.)

Fuzzy logics and their applicability to vagueness have been investigated fairly intensely since about the 1970s, by many people, including Kenton Machina and Patrick Grim, and, on the technical side, Lotfi Zadeh, Petr Hájek, and Daniele Mundici. (Keefe 2000, Hájek 1998, Cignoli, D'Ottaviano, and Mundici 2000.)

The use of many-valued logics in independence investigations goes back to the early years of the subject, though this has flourished with the proliferation of non-classical logics in the second half of the twentieth century. One of the earliest techniques for proving independence results in set theory is that of forcing, developed by Paul Cohen in the early 1960s. That similar things could be done with Boolean-valued models was realized by Robert Solovay, Dana Scott, and others a few years later. (Anderson and Belnap 1975, Bell 1985.)

See also Fuzzy Logic; Intuitionism and Intuitionistic Logic; Logic, History of; Logic, Non-Classical; Modal Logic; Paraconsistent Logics; Relevance (Relevant) Logics; Set Theory.

Bibliography

Anderson, Alan Ross, and Nuel D. Belnap Jr. *Entailment: The Logic of Relevance and Necessity.* Vol 1. Princeton, NJ: Princeton University Press, 1975.

Bell, John. *Boolean-Valued Models and Independence Proofs in Set Theory.* New York: Oxford University Press, 1985.

Cignoli, Roberto L. O., Itala M. L. D'Ottaviano, and Daniele Mundici. *Algebraic Foundations of Many-Valued Reasoning.* Dordrecht, Netherlands: Kluwer Academic, 2000.

Dunn, J. Michael, and George Epstein, eds. *Modern Uses of Multiple-Valued Logic.* Dordrecht, Netherlands: D. Reidel, 1977.

Haack, Susan. *Philosophy of Logics.* New York: Cambridge University Press, 1978.

Hähnle, Richard. "Advanced Many-Valued Logic." In *Handbook of Philosophical Logic,* Vol. 3. 2nd ed., edited by D. Gabbay and F. Guenthner. Dordrecht, Netherlands: Kluwer Academic, 2001.

Hájek, Petr. *Metamathematics of Fuzzy Logic.* Dordrecht, Netherlands: Kluwer Academic, 1998.

Hughes, George, and Max Cresswell. *Introduction to Modal Logic.* London: Methuen, 1968. Revised as *A New Introduction to Modal Logic.* London: Routledge, 1996.

Humberstone, Lloyd. "Many-Valued Logics, Philosophical Issues in." In *Routledge Encyclopedia of Philosophy,* Vol. 6., edited by E. Craig. London: Routledge, 1998.

Keefe, Rosanna. *Theories of Vagueness.* New York: Cambridge University Press, 2000.

Łukasiewicz, Jan. *Selected Works,* edited by L. Borkowski. Amsterdam, Netherlands; North-Holland, 1970.

Malinowski, Grzegorz. *Many-Valued Logics.* Oxford, U.K.: Clarendon Press, 1993.

Priest, Graham. *Introduction to Non-classical Logic.* New York: Cambridge University Press, 2001.

Rescher, Nicholas. *Many-Valued Logic.* New York: McGraw Hill, 1969.

Rosser, J. Barkely, and Atwell R. Turquette. *Many-Valued Logics.* Amsterdam, Netherlands: North-Holland, 1952.

Scott, Dana. "Does Many-Valued Logic Have Any Use?" In *Philosophy of Logic,* edited by S. Körner. Oxford, U.K.: Blackwell, 1974.

Shoesmith, David J., and Timothy J. Smiley. *Multiple Conclusion Logic.* New York: Cambridge University Press, 1978.

Urquhart, Alasdair. "Basic Many-Valued Logic." In *Handbook of Philosophical Logic.* Vol. 2. 2nd ed., edited by D. Gabbay and F. Guenthner. Dordrecht, Netherlands: Kluwer Academic, 2001. This is a revised version of "Many-Valued Logic" in Vol. 3 of the first ed (Dordrecht, Netherlands: D. Reidel, 1986).

Varzi, Achille. "Supervaluationism and Paraconsistency." In *Frontiers in Paraconsistent Logic,* edited by D. Batens et al. Baldock, U.K.: Research Studies, 2000.

White, Richard B. "The Consistency of the Axiom of Comprehension in the Infinite-Valued Predicate Logic of Łukasiewicz." *Journal of Philosophical Logic* 8 (1979): 509–534.

Wójcicki, Ryszard. *Theory of Logical Calculi: Basic Theory of Consequence.* Dordrecht, Netherlands: Kluwer Academic, 1988.

Graham Priest (2005)

MANY WORLDS/MANY MINDS INTERPRETATION OF QUANTUM MECHANICS

The many worlds/many minds formulations of quantum mechanics are reconstructions of Hugh Everett III's (1957a, 1957b, 1973) relative-state formulation of quantum mechanics. Each is presented as a proposal for solving the quantum measurement problem. Much of the philosophical interest in these theories derives from the metaphysical commitments they suggest. They illustrate the roles played by traditional metaphysical distinctions both in formulating and in evaluating physical theories. They also illustrate the range of metaphysical options one must consider if one wants a metaphysics that is consistent with the structure of the physical world suggested by the best physical theories.

The quantum measurement problem is a consequence of the orthodox quantum-mechanical representation of physical properties. In order to account for interference effects, the orthodox view requires that one allows for a physical system to be in a *superposition* of having mutually incompatible classical physical properties. An electron *e* might, for example, be in a superposition of being in New York City and being in Los Angeles. If the unit-length vector $(NYC)_e$ represents the electron being in New York City and if the orthogonal unit-length vector $(LA)_e$ represents the electron being in Los Angeles, then the state of the electron in a superposition of being in each city is represented by

$$(S)_e = a(NYC)_e + b(LA)_e,$$

where a and b are complex numbers, such that a-squared plus b-squared equals one. On the orthodox view, the state represented by the unit-length vector $(S)_e$ is not a state where the electron is determinately in NYC, it is not a state where the electron is determinately in LA, it is not a state where the electron is determinately in both cities, and it is not a state where the electron is determinately in neither city. Rather, on the standard interpretation of states, an electron in state $(S)_e$ simply fails to have a determinate position.

While allowing for superpositions of classical properties explains the counterintuitive empirical results of interference experiments, it leaves a puzzle: If electrons are sometimes in such superpositions of position, then why do electrons have determinate positions whenever one looks for them? In its most general form the quantum measurement problem is to explain why physical systems exhibit quantum interference effects, which typically involves talk of superpositions, and to explain why people—when they look for them—always observe physical systems to have determinate physical properties.

LINEAR DYNAMICS AND COLLAPSE DYNAMICS

The standard von Neumann-Dirac collapse formulation of quantum mechanics (1955 [1932]) explains interference effects and definite measurement results by stipulating two dynamical laws. The *linear dynamics* describes the deterministic continuous evolution of the state of a physical system when no measurement of the system is made. It is this law that describes the evolution of physical systems in superpositions of classical properties and thus explains quantum interference effects. The *collapse dynamics* describes the random discontinuous evolution of the state when a measurement is made of the physical system. It is this law that explains how one gets determinate measurement records at the end of an observation and makes the standard statistical predictions. More specifically, in the case of the electron in state $(S)_e$, if an observer M looks for the electron in NYC, the collapse dynamics predicts that the state will instantaneously and randomly evolve from

$$(Ready)_m (a(NYC)_e + b(LA)_e),$$

a state where M is ready to look for e and e is in state $(S)_e$, to either ("In NYC")$_m$ (NYC)$_e$ (with probability (a^2)), in which case e is now determinately in NYC and M determinately records this fact, or to ("Not in NYC")$_m$ (LA)$_e$ (with probability (b^2)), in which case e is now determinately in LA and M determinately records that it is not found in NYC.

In order to understand the work done by the collapse dynamics in the standard theory, consider what would happen without the collapse of the quantum-mechanical state. In the measurement above, the linear dynamics predicts that the postmeasurement state of the observer who correlate their records perfectly with the position of the electron, written in the determinate record basis, is

$$(E) = a("In\ NYC")_m (NYC)_e + b("Not\ in\ NYC")_m (LA)_e.$$

On the standard interpretation of states, M here has no determinate measurement record. Rather, without the collapse dynamics, M ends up in an entangled superposition of finding and not finding the electron. This is presumably not what happens.

So, in the standard theory, the collapse dynamics is both responsible for the theory making the standard quantum statistical predictions and for the explanation of determinate measurement results. But because the physical state that results from applying the collapse dynamics to a system is typically different from the state that results from applying only the linear dynamics, the standard formulation of quantum mechanics is at best incomplete and arguably logically inconsistent on a strict reading—unless one can stipulate strictly disjoint conditions for when each dynamical law obtains. In the context of the standard collapse theory, solving the measurement problem would require one to stipulate exactly what interactions count as measurements and hence cause collapses.

Rather than stipulating when collapses occur, Everett's proposal for solving the quantum measurement problem involved denying that there are collapses. More specifically, Everett proposed simply dropping the collapse dynamics from the standard von Neumann-Dirac theory of quantum mechanics and taking the resulting pure wave mechanics as a complete and accurate description of all physical systems. Everett then intended to deduce the standard statistical predictions of quantum mechanics—the predictions that are explained by the collapse dynamics in the standard formulation of quantum mechanics—as subjective experiences of observers who are themselves treated as ordinary physical systems within the new theory. Dropping the collapse dynamics clearly eliminates potential conflict between the two dynamical laws; but if one drops the collapse dynamics, one must then explain how we obtain determinate measurement results that exhibit the standard quantum statistics when the linear dynamics alone typically predict entangled postmeasurement superpositions such as $(E)_e$.

RECONSTRUCTING EVERETT'S THEORY

While it is clear that Everett intended for his relative-state formulation of quantum mechanics to explain why one gets determinate measurement results, it is unclear how this was supposed to work. There are several alternative reconstructions of Everett's theory in the literature, all designed to provide quantum mechanics without the collapse dynamics with determinate measurement records while somehow recovering the standard quantum statistics. The many worlds and the many minds formulations of quantum mechanics represent two general approaches to reconstructing Everett's relative-state formulation of quantum mechanics.

The splitting worlds formulation is perhaps the most popular version of the many worlds formulation. The splitting world formulation of quantum mechanics

> asserts that it makes sense to talk about a state vector for the whole universe. This state vector never collapses and hence reality as a whole is rigorously deterministic. This reality, which is described *jointly* by the dynamical variables and the state vector, is not the reality we customarily think of, but is a reality composed of many worlds. By virtue of the temporal development of the dynamical variables the state vector decomposes naturally into orthogonal vectors, reflecting a continual splitting of the universe into a multitude of mutually unobservable but equally real worlds, in each of which every good measurement has yielded a definite result and in most of which the familiar statistical quantum laws hold. (DeWitt and Graham 1973, p. v)

Proponents of this view admit that the metaphysical commitments it suggests are counterintuitive: "I still recall vividly the shock I experienced on first encountering this multiworld concept. The idea of 10^{100} slightly imperfect copies of oneself all constantly spitting into further copies, which ultimately become unrecognizable, is not easy to reconcile with common sense. Here is schizophrenia with a vengeance" (DeWitt and Graham 1973, p. 161).

But it is precisely these counterintuitive commitments that explain why observers end up recording determinate measurement results. On the splitting worlds formulation the universe splits whenever one makes a measurement in such a way that every physical possible result in fact determinately occurs in some future world. More specially, there is one world corresponding to each term in the expression of the quantum mechanical state when written in the theory's preferred basis. In choosing the preferred basis, one chooses a single preferred way from among the many different, mathematically equivalent, ways of representing quantum-mechanical states as the sum of mutually orthogonal unit-length vectors. On the splitting worlds formulation, the preferred basis is chosen so that each term in the expansion of the state describes a world where there is a determinate measurement record. The state (E) above describes two worlds: One where the observer M determinately records the measurement result "In NYC" and e is in fact in NYC and another where M determinately records "Not in NYC" and e is in fact in LA.

PROBLEMS WITH THE SPLITTING WORLDS FORMULATION. While the splitting worlds formulation of quantum mechanics does explain why there are determinate measurement records, it encounters other problems. A standard complaint is that the theory is ontologically extravagant. We presumably only ever need one physical world, our world, to explain our experiences. The reason for postulating the actual existence of a different physical world corresponding to each term in the quantum-mechanical state is that it allows one to explain our determinate experiences while taking the deterministically evolving quantum-mechanical state to be in some sense a complete and accurate description of the physical facts. But again one might wonder whether the sort of completeness one gets warrants the many-world ontology.

Another problem with the splitting worlds formulation concerns the statistical predictions of future events. The standard collapse formulation of quantum mechanics predicts that M will get the result "In NYC" with probability a-squared and the result "Not in NYC" with probability b-squared in the above experiment, and this is what is observed as relative frequencies for such experiments. Insofar as there will be two copies of M in the future, M is guaranteed to get each of the two possible measurement results. So, in this sense at least, the probability of M getting the result "In NYC" is one, which is simply not what is observed if both a and b are nonzero. A principle of indifference might lead one to assign a probability of one-half to each of the two possible measurement outcomes. But not only would such a principle be difficult to justify here, probability one-half for each possible outcome is typically not what would be observed for such experiments as relative frequencies. So while the splitting worlds formulation explains why observers get determinate measurement records, as it stands, it makes no empirical predictions for the likelihood of future events.

In order to understand what one would have to add to the theory to get the standard quantum statistical predictions for future events, one might note that the question "What is the probability that M will record the result 'In NYC'?" is, strictly speaking, nonsense—unless one has an account of the transtemporal identity of the observer M. Because there is no rule that states which worlds are which at different times, the splitting worlds theory is prevented from making statistical predictions concerning an observer's future experiences. And not being able to account for the standard quantum probabilities is a serious problem because it was the successful statistical predictions of quantum mechanics that made quantum mechanics worth taking seriously in the first place.

Another problem for the splitting worlds formulation of quantum mechanics concerns the way worlds are supposed to split. In order to explain the determinate measurement records, one must choose a preferred basis so that observers have determinate measurement records in each term of the quantum-mechanical state when written in the preferred basis. The problem is that not just any basis will make records determinate in every world (consider, for example, a basis that includes the vector (E) above). Selecting the preferred basis to use determines when worlds split, and determining when worlds split is as difficult as trying to determine when the collapse occurs in the standard formulation of quantum mechanics. This is the preferred basis problem. This problem is closely analogous to the original measurement problem in the context of the standard collapse formulation of quantum mechanics.

A popular strategy for resolving the preferred basis problem is to try to find a criterion involving the interaction between a quantum-mechanical system and its environment that would dynamically select a preferred basis for a system. As a simple example of an environmental decoherence criterion, one might take the preferred basis of a system to be the one that represents the classical property of the system to which its environment becomes most strongly correlated, whatever this may be. Insofar as a measurement record is easily read, one might argue, the environment becomes strongly with the value of the

record, so such a criterion would be expected select the determinate-record basis as preferred. One problem with having the environment of a system select the preferred basis, however, is that, in the case of the splitting worlds formulation at least, one presumably needs a preferred basis for the entire universe, which does have an environment.

THE MANY MINDS FORMULATION. David Albert and Barry Loewer's many minds formulation of quantum mechanics (1988) provides another approach for interpreting Everett's relative-state formulation of quantum mechanics. Everett said that his theory "is objectively continuous and causal, while subjectively discontinuous and probabilistic" (1973, p. 9). The many minds formulation of quantum mechanics captures this feature by distinguishing between an observer's *physical state* and its evolution, which is continuous and causal, and an observer's *mental state* and its evolution, which is discontinuous and probabilistic. This is a sort of hidden-variable theory, where the variable being added to the standard quantum-mechanical state is the mental states of observers. Stipulating determinate mental states solves the quantum measurement problem by directly providing observers with determinate, accessible measurement records.

In order to get the observer's complete mental state to supervene on her or his physical state, Albert and Loewer associate with each observer a continuous infinity of minds. The standard quantum-mechanical state always evolves in the usual deterministic linear way, but each mind evolves randomly, with probabilities determined by the particular mind's current mental state and the evolution of the quantum-mechanical state. In the experiment above, Albert and Loewer's mental dynamics predicts that the probability of each of the observer's minds becoming randomly associated with the result "In NYC" (the first term of (E)) is a-squared and that the probability of each becoming randomly associated with the result "Not in NYC" (the second term of (E)) is b-squared.

An advantage of the many minds formulation over the splitting worlds formulation is that here there is no physically preferred basis. One must choose a preferred basis in order to specify the mental dynamics completely, but this choice has nothing to do with any physical facts. Rather, it can be thought of as part of the description of the relationship between physical and mental states. Another advantage of the many minds formulation is that, unlike the splitting worlds formulation, it makes the standard probabilistic predictions for the future measurement results of each mind. Because the states of particular minds do not supervene on the physical state here, in order to talk about their states and how they evolve, one must suppose that individual minds have transtemporal identities, which in turn requires a commitment to a strong form of mind-body dualism. But it is also this strong dualism that makes the many minds theory one of the few formulations of quantum mechanics that resolves the quantum measurement problem and is manifestly compatible with special relativity.

One might wonder whether the sort of mental supervenience one gets in the many minds formulation (it is not the states of an observer's individual minds, but only the complete distribution of the states of all of these minds that can be taken to supervene on her or his physical state) is worth the trouble of postulating a continuous infinity of minds associated with each observer. Another option is to suppose that each observer has a single mind that evolves in the Albert and Loewer random way. But here one sacrifices all but the weakest sort of supervenience of mental states on physical states. Here the physical state would only tell one the probabilities of various mental states obtaining.

If one wants to avoid the mind-body dualism involved in the many minds formulation, one can use the evolution of minds to construct an alternative many worlds formulation. On one such theory, the many threads formulation of quantum mechanics, worlds do not split. Rather, one stipulates that there is one world corresponding to each possible trajectory of a single Albert-Loewer mind and that the history of that world is described by the history of the world that would be observed by the mind. Each observer then inhabits exactly one of these worlds, and the global quantum-mechanical state is used to assign prior epistemic probabilities to each physically possible world in fact being a given observer's world. These prior probabilities, concerning which possible world is an observer's actual world, might then be updated as she learns more about the history of her world. In the simplest case, she eliminates from contention all possible worlds that are incompatible with a particular observed event. Unlike the splitting worlds formulation, there is no special problem in understanding probabilities of future events on this account. A particular event is either going to happen or not in our world. The standard quantum probabilities here simply represent our posterior uncertainty concerning which world we in fact inhabit (Barrett 1999).

See also Quantum Mechanics.

Bibliography

Albert, D. Z. *Quantum Mechanics and Experience*. Cambridge, MA: Harvard University Press, 1992.

Albert, D., and B. Loewer. "Interpreting the Many Worlds Interpretation." *Synthese* 77 (1988): 195–213.

Barrett, J. *The Quantum Mechanics of Minds and Worlds*. Oxford: Oxford University Press, 1999.

DeWitt, B. S. "The Many-Universes Interpretation of Quantum Mechanics." In *Foundations of Quantum Mechanics*. New York: Academic Press, 1971. Reprinted in *The Many-Worlds Interpretation of Quantum Mechanics*, edited by B. S. DeWitt and N. Graham, 167–218. Princeton, NJ: Princeton University Press, 1973.

DeWitt, B. S., and N. Graham, eds. *The Many-Worlds Interpretation of Quantum Mechanics*. Princeton, NJ: Princeton University Press, 1973.

Dowker, F. A., and A. Kent. "On the Consistent Histories Approach to Quantum Mechanics." *Journal of Statistical Physics* 83, nos. 5–6 (1983): 1575–1646.

Everett, H. *On the Foundations of Quantum Mechanics*. Thesis. Princeton University, New Jersey. 1957a.

Everett, H. "'Relative State' Formulation of Quantum Mechanics." *Reviews of Modern Physics* 29 (1957b): 454–462.

Everett, H. "The Theory of the Universal Wave Function." In *The Many-Worlds Interpretation of Quantum Mechanics*, edited by B. S. DeWitt and N. Graham. Princeton, NJ: Princeton University Press, 1973.

von Neumann, J. *Mathematical Foundations of Quantum Mechanics*. Princeton, NJ: Princeton University Press, 1955. Translated by R. Beyer from *Mathematische Grundlagen der Quantenmechanik* (Berlin: Springer, 1932).

Jeffrey A. Barrett (2005)

MARBURG, SCHOOL OF

See *Neo-Kantianism*

MARCEL, GABRIEL
(1889–1973)

Gabriel Marcel, the French philosopher, dramatist, and critic, was born in Paris. His father, a highly cultured man, held important administrative posts in the Bibliothèque Nationale and the Musées Nationaux. Marcel's mother died when he was four. Raised in a home dominated by the cultured agnosticism of his father and the liberal, moralistic Protestantism of his aunt, and nurtured in a scholastic system concerned only with intellectual achievement, he later sought refuge in a modified type of idealism. The shaking experiences of World War I, during which he was an official of the Red Cross concerned with locating missing soldiers, brought home to him the failure of abstract philosophy to cope with the tragic character of human existence. His conversion to Catholicism in 1929 did not substantially alter the direction of his thought, although it intensified his conviction that the philosopher must take into consideration the logic interior to faith and hope.

RELATIONSHIP TO EXISTENTIALISM

Marcel's name has most often been linked with "theistic existentialism." Because of the ambiguities of this term and the association of existentialism in the popular mind with Jean-Paul Sartre's philosophy, to which his is almost diametrically opposed, Marcel has preferred the designation "Neo-Socratic" for his thought. This should not obscure Marcel's contributions to existential philosophy or his similarity to other thinkers who are ordinarily associated with it.

Before publication of the major philosophical works of Karl Jaspers and Martin Heidegger, Marcel introduced into French philosophy, in his essay "Existence and Objectivity" (1925) and in his *Metaphysical Journal*, many of the themes that later became central to existentialism. Often making use of an independently developed phenomenological method, he dealt with such themes as participation, incarnation, man as being in the world, and the priority of existence over abstraction (the *cogito*) as a starting point for philosophy.

Marcel's critique of idealism and his defense of faith resemble Søren Kierkegaard's critique of G. W. F. Hegel; Marcel, however, refuses to allow that faith is an irrational leap or that the individual stands alone in his faith. Heidegger and Marcel explore much of the same terrain in seeking to restore the "ontological weight to human experience" (*Being and Having*, p. 103). They share a common view of the nature of truth and language. Marcel, however, unlike Heidegger, includes within his ontology the assurance of fulfillment that is part of faith's apprehension of God as Absolute Presence. In many ways Martin Buber has been Marcel's closest contemporary philosophical relative. Each has independently developed a philosophy of dialogue and communion in which the distinction between the relation of an I to a thou and an I to an it or a him plays a central part.

PHILOSOPHICAL METHOD

A great injustice is necessarily done in any summary account of Marcel's thought, for the charm and the convincing power of his conclusions are inseparable from his itinerant, tentative, and exploratory philosophical method. One of the most characteristic features of his thinking is the vigor with which he combated the spirit of

abstraction and the conceptual sclerosis that he believes is an occupational hazard of systematic and academic philosophers. But despite his rejection of systematic philosophy, Marcel's work is based on an underlying principle of unity, or more accurately an underlying vision, which, seen dimly from the beginning, has been progressively more clearly apprehended. This vision, which is essentially both Platonic and Christian, expresses itself in the conviction that within the temporal and transient order *homo viator* is given a foretaste of eternal realities.

Marcel's philosophical explorations cannot be divorced from his dramatic writings or from his experimentation in music. His plays are not philosophical in the sense of being popular forums for the presentation of worked-out ideas. Rather, they present complicated situations in which persons find themselves trapped, challenged, and confused; and thus indirectly they explore the nature of the exile into which the soul enters as it becomes alienated from itself, from those it loves, and from God. Marcel believes that in music one finds a foretaste or presentiment of the perfect harmony and communion toward which all authentic human existence strives. Philosophy shares both in the tension that is the essence of drama and in the harmony which is the essence of music. Its starting point is a metaphysical "dis-ease" like that of a person in a fever who shifts around searching for a comfortable position. This search for a home in the wilderness, a harmony in disharmony, a transcendent source of assurance in a transient life takes place through a reflective process that Marcel calls secondary reflection.

THE NATURE OF THINKING

Marcel distinguishes two degrees or types of thinking, primary and secondary reflection. Primary reflection is characterized as abstract, analytical, objective, universal, and verifiable. The thinking subject in primary reflection is not the individual human person but the thinker qua mind (the *Bewusstsein überhaupt*). Primary reflection deals with the realm of the problematic. As the etymology of "problem" (*pro-ballo*) suggests, the distinguishing feature of the problematic approach to reality is the separation of the questioner from the data about which he questions. The data of primary reflection lie in the public domain and are equally available to any qualified observer. Once a problem is posed, primary reflection proceeds to abstract from the concrete data any elements that are not relevant to the solution of the particular problem under consideration. When a solution or an explanation has been found, the original curiosity and tension that motivated the thinker are alleviated.

Primary reflection, as exemplified in scientific and technical thought, has allowed us to possess and manipulate our world more completely and is therefore indispensable to human culture. However, intellectual and moral confusion results when primary reflection becomes imperialistic and claims the right to judge all knowledge and truth by criteria appropriate only to the realm of the objective and the problematic. When this happens, abstraction gives way to "the spirit of abstraction," the use of techniques gives way to technocracy, and the inexhaustible riches of a kaleidoscopic world are forced to conform to a black-and-white logic.

Secondary reflection is concrete, individual, heuristic, and open. Strictly speaking, it is concerned not with objects but with presences. Its contemplation begins not with curiosity or doubt but with wonder and astonishment. Hence, it is humble in its willingness to be conformed to categories created by that on which it is focused. It remains open to its object as a lover does to his beloved—not as a specimen of a class but as a unique being. This openness is not a methodological principle as in scientific thought but arises from the possibility of something new being created in the relationship. Secondary reflection is dialogical, not dialectical. Rather than searching for information about the other and dealing with it abstractly, secondary reflection seeks the revelation of total presence, whether the presence be that of my body, the world, the other person, or God. Thus, secondary reflection is brought to bear on data or questions from which the thinker as existing person cannot legitimately abstract himself: "Am I free?" "Is there meaning and value in life?" "Can I commit myself to this person?" In other words, secondary reflection is concerned not with problems but with mystery.

MYSTERY

According to Marcel, a mystery initially appears to be merely a problem that is difficult to solve. Reflection shows, however, that in dealing with a genuine mystery the distinction between subject and object, between what is in me and what is before me, breaks down. Faced with questions about freedom, the meaning of life, the existence of God, and so forth, no objective standpoint can be found from which a universally valid answer may be discovered. This does not mean that mystery is unknown or unknowable and lies in a realm of vague feelings over which thought has no grasp. Rather, knowledge of mystery presupposes an immediate participation, or what Marcel also calls a "blinded intuition," but this participation is understood only with the aid of a conceptual

process. Unaided intuition is not an adequate philosophical instrument. However, secondary reflection penetrates into the mystery of existence and being only when it works in conjunction with love, fidelity, faith, and the other "concrete approaches." It yields a kind of knowledge and truth that, if unverifiable, nevertheless is confirmed as it illuminates our lives. Two foci of mystery may be distinguished, although never separated, in Marcel's thinking. The mystery of existence is dealt with in "concrete" philosophy and the mystery of being in "concrete" ontology.

CONCRETE PHILOSOPHY

Marcel denies that the detached, disincarnate, Cartesian *cogito* provides a possible starting point for a concrete philosophy. It is with the existing subject, the incarnate being who is already in the world, that philosophy must begin. The experience of the inexhaustible concreteness of the existing world can be neither deduced, doubted, nor demonstrated. Existence is not a thing, a quality, or a discrete content of thought that can be isolated and pointed out; rather it is that in which the subject participates and from which thought begins its quest for meaning. The assurance of existence that we have is not of the intellectual order but is an outcome of our direct participation in the world via sensation and feeling. Because sensation and feeling are inseparable from the body, our knowledge of existence is tied up with our being incarnate.

Incarnation is the "central given of metaphysic," the absolute starting point for an existential philosophy, because it is on the analogy of my experience of my body that the world is understood. I project into the world the sense of density and presence that I experience when I become aware of my own body. The world exists for me only in the measure that I am related to it in a way similar to the way in which I am related to my own body.

As I am not even ideally separable from my body, I am likewise inseparable from my situation. Those habitual surroundings and historical conditions that shape my life enter into the very fiber of what I am. Insofar as I recognize that my situation enters into the constitution of my being, and hence that I am not able to abstract myself from it completely and view it with the objective detachment of a spectator, I may speak of the family that nurtured me or of an illness that shaped me as having a mysterious character.

A concrete philosophy must also affirm the immediacy of our being with others. The principle of the intentionality of consciousness, Marcel holds, applies in our relations both to persons and to the world. Philosophy begins not with *I am* but with *we are*.

The significance of this intersubjectivity will be determined by the type of relations that characterize one's life. The self who treats other persons as objects to be manipulated and used is condemned because of its egocentricity to live in a world lacking in ontological depth, and hence it will be prey to despair when the thrill of possession wears thin. To endeavor to allow the other person to become present as a thou is to enter into a relationship within which the assurance of fulfillment is received.

ONTOLOGY

No word used by Marcel is more difficult to define or richer in meaning than *being*. It refers neither to the sum total of all objects that exist nor to some universal substratum underlying all particulars. Being is eternal and inexhaustible. It is "that which does not allow itself to be dissolved by the dialectics of experience" (*Metaphysical Journal*, p. 181). Only by participation in being can isolation, despair, and tragedy be overcome. The quest for being is thus identical with the quest for salvation. To deny being is to say that "all is vanity," that nothing has intrinsic worth. To affirm being is to declare that corresponding to the deepest exigency of the human spirit is a fulfillment of which an earnest is given in experiences of creativity, joy, and love.

As defined by Marcel, the question of being cannot be approached objectively and problematically. Being can be affirmed only if I can discover within experience some presence that testifies to being. Two elements in human experience seem to offer such a testimony. First, at the heart of the human condition is an "ontological exigence," an impulse to transcendence that is present in all authentic human life, the exigence to penetrate to a level of experience saturated with meaning and value. The mere existence of such an exigence is no guarantee in itself that a corresponding satisfaction exists. It could be the case, as Sartre says, that man is a "useless passion." But Marcel attempted to show, by way of a phenomenological analysis, that certain experiences of love, joy, hope, and faith, as understood from *within*, present a positive testimony to the existence of an inexhaustible presence. This assuring presence, which might be called the immanence of being in human experience, is never a possession but is constantly created anew as an I enters into relations with an empirical thou or the Absolute Thou (God). Although the assurance of being never becomes conceptually clear, it provides the illumination making creative, open existence possible.

In what might be called Marcel's ontological personalism, the concrete approaches to being are identical with the approaches to other persons and to God. To enter into a loving relationship requires that a person exorcise the spirit of egocentricity and possession and become spiritually available (*disponible*) to others. A vow of creative fidelity is likewise necessary if the unconditional demands of love are to be satisfied. In approaching God, fidelity becomes faith and *disponibilité* becomes hope. In love, fidelity, hope, and faith man approaches the mystery of being and is overtaken with the assurance that he is accompanied by the eternal fulfilling Presence that he seeks to know.

See also Being; Existentialism; Hegel, Georg Wilhelm Friedrich; Heidegger, Martin; Idealism; Jaspers, Karl; Kierkegaard, Søren Aabye; Personalism; Philosophy of Religion, History of; Sartre, Jean-Paul; Thinking.

Bibliography

WORKS BY MARCEL

A thorough and updated bibliography of works by Marcel, translations of his works, and works about Marcel is maintained by the Gabriel Marcel Society at http://www.lemoyne.edu/gms.

Philosophical Works

Journal métaphysique. Paris: Gallimard, 1927. Translated by Bernard Wall as *Metaphysical Journal*. Chicago: Regnery, 1952.

Être et avoir. Paris: Aubier, 1935. Translated by Katharine Farrer as *Being and Having*. London: Dacre Press, 1949.

Du refus à l'invocation. Paris: Gallimard, 1940. Translated by Robert Rosthal as *Creative Fidelity*. New York: Noonday Press, 1964.

Homo Viator. Paris: Aubier, 1945. Translated by Emma Craufurd. New York, 1962.

The Philosophy of Existence. Translated by Manya Harari. New York: Philosophical Library, 1949. Republished as *Philosophy of Existentialism*. New York: Citadel Press, 1961. Previously uncollected essays written between 1933 and 1946. Perhaps the best short introduction to Marcel's thought.

Le mystère de l'être. 2 vols. Paris: Aubier, 1951. Translated by G. S. Fraser and René Hauge as *The Mystery of Being*. 2 vols. Chicago, 1950.

Les hommes contre l'humain. Paris: La Colombe, 1951. Translated by G. S. Fraser as *Men against Humanity*. London: Harvill Press, 1952. Republished as *Man against Mass Society*. Chicago: Regnery, 1962.

L'homme problématique. Paris: Aubier, 1955.

Présence et immortalité. Paris: Flammarion, 1959.

The Existential Background of Human Dignity. Cambridge, MA: Harvard University Press, 1963.

Plays

"The Lantern." *Cross Currents* 8 (2) (1958): 129–143.

Three Plays. Translated by Rosalind Heywood and Marjorie Gabain. New York: Hill and Wang, 1958; 2nd ed., 1965. Contains "A Man of God," "Ariadne" (*Le chemin de Crête*), and "The Funeral Pyre" (*La chapelle ardente*; in the 2nd ed., "The Votive Candle").

Translations

Creative Fidelity. Translated, with an introduction, by Robert Rosthal. New York: Farrar, Strauss, 1964.

Presence and Immortality. Translated by Michael A. Machado. Pittsburgh: Duquesne University Press, 1967.

Tragic Wisdom and Beyond. Translated by Stephen Jolin and Peter McCormick. Evanston, IL: Northwestern University Press, 1973.

WORKS ON MARCEL

Applebaum, David. *Contact and Alienation, The Anatomy of Gabriel Marcel's Metaphysical Method*. Washington, DC: Center for Advanced Research in Phenomenology & University Press of America, 1986.

Busch, Thomas. *The Participant Perspective: A Gabriel Marcel Reader*. Lanham, MD: University Press of America, 1987.

Cain, Seymour. *Gabriel Marcel*. London: Bowes and Bowes, 1963.

Gallagher, Kenneth T. *The Philosophy of Gabriel Marcel* New York: Fordham University Press, 1963.

Lapointe, Francis H., and Claire C. Lapointe. *Gabriel Marcel and His Critics: An International Bibliography (1928–1976)*. New York: Garland, 1977.

Pax, Clyde. *An Existentialist Approach to God: A Study of Gabriel Marcel* The Hague: Martinus Nijhoff, 1972.

Prini, Pietro. *Gabriel Marcel et le méthodologie de l'invérifiable*. Paris, 1953.

Ricoeur, Paul. *Gabriel Marcel et Karl Jaspers*. Paris: Éditions du Temps Present, 1947.

Schilpp, Paul A., and Lewis E. Hahn. *The Philosophy of Gabriel Marcel*. Library of Living Philosophers Vol. XVII. La Salle, IL: Open Court, 1984.

Troisfontaines, Roger. *De l'existence à l'être*. 2 vols. Paris, 1953. Essentially a concordance of what Marcel has said on any subject. Contains a complete bibliography of Marcel's work until 1953.

Samuel McMurray Keen (1967)
Bibliography updated by Thomas Nenon (2005)

MARCION
(*c. 85–c. 159*)

Marcion was one of the most significant and, in a way, perplexing figures of the second century CE—significant both for founding the Marcionite Church and for providing the stimulus for the formation of the New Testament canon, and perplexing because of the difficulty of classifying him among contemporary thinkers. He is often called a Gnostic, and there are certainly distinct affinities with Gnosticism in his cosmology and soteriology; but his lack of a mythical anthropology and of any syncretistic tendency sets him apart.

A native of Sinope in Pontus, he was born c. 85 and must have died c. 159, since there is no suggestion in our sources that he survived until the reign of the emperor Marcus Aurelius (161–180). According to the ecclesiastical writer Hippolytus, Marcion was the son of a bishop, and indeed there are indications that he grew up within the Christian faith. Excommunicated by his own father because of his unorthodox views, he traveled first to Asia Minor, then to Rome (c. 138–140), where he was at first closely associated with the church. In 144 he was again excommunicated, and he founded a church of his own that was for a time a serious menace to "orthodox" Christianity.

Marcion was a Bible critic and theologian rather than a philosopher; indeed, Adolf von Harnack describes him as "fundamentally a Biblicist and an opponent of all philosophy." The root of his teaching lies in the Pauline antithesis of Law and Gospel, but he exaggerated this contrast to the extent of distinguishing the Creator (the God of the Old Testament) from the true God, in himself unknown and alien to this world but manifested in the person of Jesus. This conception of the "alienness" of the true God Marcion shared with the Gnostics, but for him this concept developed from the study of the Scriptures rather than from philosophical speculation. Rejecting allegorical interpretation, he was unable to reconcile the Old Testament description of God with the New Testament portrayal of God as the father of Christ. Unlike the Gnostics as well as some of his followers, Marcion himself held that the Creator is not evil but merely just. Only the true God is good, a God of love. From this initial contrast the whole of Marcion's system follows naturally. This world, which is the work of the Creator, is imperfect. The Jewish law, and indeed all positive morality, is a means by which the Creator exercises control over humankind and is therefore to be rejected. Marcion's conclusions, however, led not to licentious antinomianism but to asceticism: Marriage and sexual intercourse, for example, were prohibited as devices for the continued procreation of subjects of the Creator. Salvation is deliverance from the world and its God and is effected at the price of Christ's blood, solely by God's grace and not because the redeemed were considered "akin" to the supreme good God, as the Gnostics believed.

The gospel brought by Jesus was misunderstood and falsified by the apostles: Only Paul had the truth of the matter. Marcion therefore rejected not only the Old Testament but also those parts of the New Testament that, according to him, were contaminated by Judaism. His canon consisted of ten letters of Paul, beginning with Galatians, and an expurgated Gospel of Luke. He also set out his teaching in his *Antitheses*, which was largely composed of contrasts between the two Gods. Marcion's works have not survived, and we are dependent on information provided by his opponents (especially Tertullian) His followers (especially Apelles) later modified his teachings so that they were in closer conformity with ordinary Gnosticism. Some of the "Gnostic" elements in his own theology have been attributed to the influence of the second-century Gnostic Cerdo.

Marcionism was at its height in the latter half of the second century. Thereafter it tended to decline in the West, and the remnants of Marcionite churches were often absorbed into Manichaeanism. In the East it had a longer history, surviving down to the fifth century or later.

See also Cosmology; Gnosticism; Harnack, Carl Gustav Adolf von; Mani and Manichaeism; Tertullian, Quintus Septimius Florens.

Bibliography

Blackman, Edwin C. *Marcion and His Influence.* London: S.P.C.K., 1948.

Harnack, Adolf von. *Marcion: Das Evangelium vom fremden Gott.* Leipzig: Hinrichs, 1921. A classic.

Jonas, H. *The Gnostic Religion.* New York, 1958. Pp. 137ff.

Knox, J. *Marcion and the New Testament.* Chicago: University of Chicago Press, 1942.

R. McL. Wilson (1967)

MARCUS, RUTH BARCAN

Ruth Barcan Marcus, though she has published in a number of areas, is best known for her groundbreaking papers in modal and philosophical logic. In 1946 she initiated the first systematic treatment of quantified modal logic (see Barcan, 1946), therein provoking W. V. Quine's decades-long attack upon the meaningfulness of quantification into alethic modal contexts. The ensuing dispute focused attention on the phenomenon of referential opacity and led to important developments in logic, metaphysics, and philosophy of language. In subsequent papers Marcus extended the first-order formalization to second order with identity (Barcan, 1947) and to modalized set theory (Marcus, 1963, 1974). Particularly significant theses presented in these works were the axiom

$\blacklozenge (\exists x) Fx \rightarrow (\exists x) \blacklozenge Fx$, known as the Barcan formula (Barcan, 1946), and the proof of the necessity of identity (Barcan, 1947; Marcus, 1961). It is of some historical interest that Marcus introduced the now standard "box" operator for necessity.

Marcus's response to criticisms of quantified modal logic took many forms and was a theme to which she returned repeatedly throughout her career. In her 1961 paper (and elsewhere) she sought to dispel certain puzzles about substitutivity of identity in modal contexts; she was an early advocate of a substitutional interpretation of the quantifiers for certain purposes (Marcus, 1961, 1962, 1972), as for example in modal and fictional discourse; she maintained that quantification into modal contexts involves no commitment to an objectionable essentialism (Marcus, 1961), and she later developed and defended a version of Aristotelian essentialism within a modal framework (Marcus, 1967, 1976). Finally, in the mid-1980s she offered an explicit defense of the metaphysical actualism that had informed her early papers in modal logic (Marcus, 1985–1986). Here once again Marcus employed an objectual interpretation of the quantifiers, construing our core modal discourse as counterfactual discourse about actual objects.

Allied doctrines of enduring significance either originated or evolved in other writings by Marcus. For example, she introduced a flexible notion of extensionality whereby languages and theories are extensional to the extent that they identify relatively stronger equivalence relations with relatively weaker ones (Marcus, 1960, 1961). She also proposed that ordinary proper names are contentless directly referential tags (Marcus, 1961). In so doing, Marcus rejected earlier "descriptivist" accounts, often associated with Gottlob Frege and Bertrand Russell, and laid the cornerstone of the so-called new theory of direct reference later elaborated by Saul Kripke, Keith Donnellan, David Kaplan, and others.

Writing in moral theory, Marcus exposed defects in the structure of standard deontic logic (Marcus, 1966). She also argued that moral dilemmas are real and, moreover, that their reality is compatible with the consistency of the moral principles from which they derive (Marcus, 1980). Reasoning from a straightforward analogue of semantic consistency, she called into question familiar arguments from the existence of moral dilemmas to ethical antirealism. The resulting account also yielded some second-order principles of conflict avoidance.

Finally, in a series of papers on the nature of belief (Marcus, 1981, 1983, 1990), Marcus rejected language-centered theories according to which beliefs are attitudes to linguistic or quasilinguistic entities (sentences of English or "Mentalese," for instance). Her proposal was that an agent *X* believes that *S* if and only if *X* is disposed to respond as if *S* obtains, where *S* is a possible state of affairs and what is to count as such a response is a function of environmental factors and internal states such as *X*'s needs and desires. This object-centered theory, as opposed to the language-centered views of Donald Davidson and Jerry Fodor, for example, more naturally accommodates unconscious beliefs and beliefs of infralinguals and nonlinguals. It also accommodates a more robust notion of rationality and explains, as its rivals cannot, why a fully rational agent would not believe a contradiction. In the wide sense of the term, a rational agent is one who, among other things, strives to maintain the global coherence of the behavioral—that is, verbal as well as nonverbal—indicators of his beliefs. Thus, although a rational agent might assent to a contradiction, his assent would not "go over" into a belief. Indeed, upon discovering the contradiction, he would retract his earlier (contradictory) belief claim. On Marcus's view, just as one cannot know what is false, one cannot believe what is impossible.

Marcus was professor of philosophy and chair of the department at the University of Illinois at Chicago from 1964 to 1970, professor of philosophy at Northwestern University from 1970 to 1973, and the Reuben Post Halleck Professor of Philosophy at Yale, where she succeeded her mentor Frederick B. Fitch, from 1973 to the time of her retirement in 1992. In addition to her scholarly achievements Marcus changed the face of the philosophical profession by her efforts on behalf of women. Perhaps most noteworthy in this connection was the reform of hiring practices instituted by the American Philosophical Association during her tenure as an officer and subsequently as chairman of its National Board of Officers.

See also Davidson, Donald; Fodor, Jerry A.; Frege, Gottlob; Kaplan, David; Kripke, Saul; Logic, History of; Metaethics; Metaphysics; Modal Logic; Philosophy of Language; Quine, Willard Van Orman; Rationality; Russell, Bertrand Arthur William; Set Theory.

Bibliography

WORKS BY MARCUS

Barcan, R. C. "A Functional Calculus of First Order Based on Strict Implication." *Journal of Symbolic Logic* 11 (1946): 1–16.

Barcan, R. C. "The Identity of Individuals in a Strict Functional Calculus of First Order." *Journal of Symbolic Logic* 12 (1947): 12–15.

Marcus, R. B. "Extensionality." *Mind* 69 (273) (1960): 55–62.

Marcus, R. B. "Modalities and Intensional Languages." *Synthese* 13 (1961): 303–322.

Marcus, R. B. "Interpreting Quantification." *Inquiry* 5 (1962): 252–259.

Marcus, R. B. "Classes and Attributes in Extended Modal Systems." *Proceedings of the Colloquium in Modal and Many Valued Logic, Acta philosophica fennica* 16 (1963): 123–136.

Marcus, R. B. "Iterated Deontic Modalities." *Mind* 75 (300) (1966): 580–582.

Marcus, R. B. "Essentialism in Modal Logic." *Noûs* 1 (1967): 91–96.

Marcus, R. B. "Essential Attribution." *Journal of Philosophy* 67 (1971): 187–202.

Marcus, R. B. "Quantification and Ontology." *Noûs* 6 (1972): 240–250.

Marcus, R. B. "Classes, Collections, and Individuals." *American Philosophical Quarterly* 11 (1974): 227–232.

Marcus, R. B. "Dispensing with Possibilia." Presidential address, *Proceedings of the American Philosophical Association* 49 (1976): 39–51.

Marcus, R. B. "Moral Dilemmas and Consistency." *Journal of Philosophy* 77 (3) (1980): 121–135.

Marcus, R. B. "A Proposed Solution to a Puzzle about Belief." In *The Foundations of Analytic Philosophy,* edited by P. French, T. Uehling, H. K. Wettstein. Midwest Studies in Philosophy 6. Minneapolis: University of Minnesota Press, 1981.

Marcus, R. B. "Rationality and Believing the Impossible." *Journal of Philosophy* 75 (1983): 321–337.

Marcus, R. B. "Possibilia and Possible Worlds." Edited by R. Haller. *Grazer philosophische Studien* 25–26 (1985–1986): 107–132.

Marcus, R. B. "Some Revisionary Proposals about Belief and Believing." *Philosophy and Phenomenological Research* (Supplement 1990): 133–154.

Marcus, R. B. *Modalities.* New York: Oxford University Press, 1993.

Diana Raffman (1996)
G. Schumm (1996)

MARCUS AURELIUS ANTONINUS
(121–180 CE)

Marcus Aurelius Antoninus may have wielded more political power than any other person to have an entry in this encyclopedia. Born into a prominent Roman family in 121 CE, Marcus was adopted in 138 by Emperor Hadrian's heir, Antoninus Pius (at Hadrian's behest), and he succeeded Antoninus as emperor in 161. Marcus's reign is usually judged favorably; indeed, his death in 180 is often thought to end the golden age of the Roman Empire. But it was not all wine and roses: Marcus faced troubles on the frontiers of the empire, a devastating plague, and worst of all, persistent wars that included the first Germanic invasion of Italy in centuries, a harbinger of invasions to come.

By late antiquity, Marcus Aurelius was most famous as a philosopher. This reputation has come to rest on his Greek writings *to himself*, best known in English as the *Meditations*. In Book One, Marcus offers an idealized account of the influences on his character, acknowledging gods, family, and teachers, including several philosophers, a grammarian, and the rhetorician Fronto, part of whose correspondence with Marcus survives. The remaining eleven books manifest no obvious organization and have puzzled many scholars. Their 473 chapters vary considerably in length and style, from maxims to minitreatises, with consolations, dialogues, and harangues thrown in. These chapters commonly feature first- or second-person pronouns and the imperative mood, with the aim of recommendation or rebuke. Sometimes Marcus articulates more theoretical doctrines of philosophy or even, though much less often, arguments, but even at his most explicitly theoretical, he does not stray far from commending or censuring. Scholars have conjectured that the *Meditations* are the scraps of an intended treatise, but this does not fit well with the text. Scholars have also tried to rearrange the chapters to impose a clearer organization, but no such reorganization has commanded broad acceptance. Instead, most scholars now take the *Meditations* as they are. On the consensus view, although the whole collection is informed by philosophical reflection, Marcus writes not to theorize but to bring his thoughts, feelings, and activities in line with the philosophical commitments he accepts.

The *Meditations* are therefore not like usual philosophical writing, and this is what makes them historically significant. Philosophers in ancient Greece and Rome often encourage others to engage in meditative exercises to cultivate a philosophical way of life (especially relevant is Epictetus, *Diss.* I 1.25), and Marcus's work is the best example of such exercises. It suggests that one does not cultivate a philosophical way of life by the detailed application of philosophical theory to particular dilemmas. That is why Marcus's exercises do not shed much light on the particulars of his life. When he does make practical precepts explicit, he states them in general terms that could apply to a shopkeeper in Kansas as well as a Roman emperor and in terms that target attitudes more than actions. So it seems that one cultivates philosophy by bringing about a general outlook that one will then put into action as the circumstances demand.

The philosophical outlook that Marcus cultivates is generally thought to be Stoic though he does not call himself a Stoic. His praise for Epictetus and his use of Stoic vocabulary encourage this thought, but by no means decisively, since he also cites Plato and Epicurus favorably, and by his time philosophers of many schools used Stoic vocabulary. Still, some of the most prominent themes of the *Meditations* are genuinely Stoic: strong contrasts between the value of one's mind, a part of the divine intelligence, and what is external to one's mind and indifferent to one's happiness (II 13, III 12); concerted efforts to reduce anger at others and to control impulses (II 1, VII 22); and regular insistence that one should help other members of the human community (V 33, VIII 59, IX 1.1, IX 23). Less distinctively Stoic is the persistent theme of death (II 12, III 3, IV 5, IV 6, IV 48, VI 28; XII 36), though this is a natural obsession if the *Meditations* were written (as the evidence suggests) in the last decade of Marcus' life and some of them at military camps. So on balance the impression of Stoic commitments is hard to deny.

To call Marcus a Stoic, though, one must use an undemanding litmus. First, Marcus shows very weak adherence to two-thirds of the traditional Stoic system. He ignores the epistemology, language, and formal logic of the Stoic study of reason (or logic; logikē), and he belittles the need to study nature (that is, to engage physics; physikē). He occasionally helps himself to the Stoic thought that the cosmos is providentially ordered (II 3, X 6, XI 18.1), but he is detached enough from this thought that he also tries repeatedly to claim that the same practical precept applies whether the world is providential or, as Epicurean atomism holds, not (VII 32, VIII 17, IX 39, X 6, XII 24). In general, Marcus's philosophical commitments do not much outrun his ethic.

Even Marcus's ethical reflections are so untheoretical as to suggest a departure from traditional Stoicism. For example, Stoic ethics traditionally relies on the thought that virtuous activity alone constitutes a happy life, and Stoics support this thought either by describing the natural development of concern for virtuous activity alone (and the concomitant stripping away of obstacles to a smooth flow of life) or by engaging directly in the question of what happiness is. Marcus, though, does not motivate his Stoic aims theoretically. Presumably, he does not need to. If he already has these aims, he needs only to reshape his attitudes to improve his pursuit of them. In this way, Marcus's special purpose leads him to pass over many of the issues, distinctions, and arguments of traditional Stoicism.

The Stoicism of the *Meditations* clearly owes much to Epictetus, but in its ruthless pursuit of getting the cast of mind right without dallying in logic, physics, or the distinctions among the things that are neither good nor bad, it also resembles still more Cynicizing versions of Stoicism as that of Aristo of Chios, the renegade Stoic of the third century BCE. Marcus might have been especially influenced by Aristo's work or by the Cynic revival in imperial Rome. Or perhaps the appearance of such affinity is due to his special purpose in the *Meditations* of trying to recast his general practical attitudes.

This purpose might also explain another characteristic of Marcus's Stoicism. It is often said that Marcus shows strong Platonist leanings, especially in the starkly dualistic way in which he contrasts the intellect in the soul with the body (IV 41, VIII 37, IX 24, XII 33) and the matter of the external torrent (V 10.2, VI 15, VIII 24, IX 36). Sometimes these leanings are attributed specifically to the influence of the Platonizing Stoic Posidonius (c. 135–c. 50 BCE), and sometimes they are said to anticipate Neoplatonism. But Marcus's occasionally dualistic talk and his hostility toward the body might be understood instrumentally as part of a regimen to correct his excessive attachment to his own body and not as a commitment to any dualism.

The *Meditations* were apparently not in wide circulation for several centuries after Marcus's death, and so they exhibit no obvious influence on the immediately subsequent history of philosophy. In modern times, however, the work has been widely admired, sometimes for its fresh glimpse into ancient Stoicism but more often for its intimate picture of an aging emperor's struggle with noble yet human goals, to be a better person, and to face death without fear or regret.

See also Aristo of Chios; Cynics; Epictetus; Epistemology; Ethics; Neoplatonism; Platonism and the Platonic Tradition; Posidonius; Stoicism.

Bibliography

TEXT, TRANSLATION, AND COMMENTARY
Farquharson, A. S. L. *Meditations of the Emperor Marcus Antoninus*. 2 vols. Oxford: Clarendon Press, 1944.

CORRESPONDENCE
Hout, M. P. J. van den, ed. *M. Cornelii Frontonis Epistulae*. Vol. 1. Leiden: Brill, 1954

BIOGRAPHY
Birley, Anthony. *Marcus Aurelius: A Biography*. Revised ed. New Haven: Yale University Press, 1987.

STUDIES
Asmis, Elizabeth. "The Stoicism of Marcus Aurelius." *Aufstieg und Niedergang der römischen Welt*. Part II, Vol. 36.3. Berlin: de Gruyter, 1989, pp. 2228–2252.
Brunt, P.A. "Marcus Aurelius in his *Meditations*." *Journal of Roman Studies* 64 (1974): 1–20.
Hadot, Pierre. *The Inner Citadel: The Meditations of Marcus Aurelius*. Translated by Michael Chase. Cambridge, MA: Harvard University Press, 1998.
Rutherford, R. B. *The Meditations of Marcus Aurelius: A Study*. Oxford: Clarendon Press, 1989.

Eric Brown (2005)

MARÉCHAL, JOSEPH
(1878–1944)

Joseph Maréchal, one of the most original and influential of Neo-Scholastic thinkers, was born at Charleroi, Belgium. He entered the Society of Jesus at the age of seventeen, and between 1895 and 1910, in spite of poor health, he not only successfully completed the long and exacting Jesuit course of studies in the humanities, philosophy, theology, and asceticism but also obtained his doctorate in the natural sciences from the University of Louvain (1905). After the completion of his Jesuit training, during the latter part of which he also taught biology to his younger confreres, he spent some time in Germany studying experimental psychology and psychotherapy. From the outset his main interest centered on the psychology of religious experience and its implications for metaphysics and the critical problem.

After the outbreak of war in 1914 he went to England with his Jesuit students. He did not begin teaching formally at the Jesuit scholasticate in Louvain until 1919. From then until 1935 he conducted courses in psychology, theodicy, and the history of modern philosophy. It was during these years that he published his most important works, the two-volume *Études sur la psychologie des mystiques* and the First, Second, Third, and Fifth Cahiers of the *Point de départ de la métaphysique* (the first three are somewhat abridged in his *Précis d'histoire de la philosophie moderne*). The Fourth Cahier, *Le systéme idéaliste chez Kant et les postkantiens*, was published posthumously in 1947 from manuscripts left by the author.

After 1935 and until his death Maréchal ceased teaching and writing, mostly because of poor health but partly because he felt that his work was misunderstood and ineffectual. Concerning "my epistemology," he remarked, "I have never had the means of exposing, orally or by writing, my general conception of the problem of knowledge. The Fifth Cahier states once more this problem *in terms of Kant*, which retains something artificial demanded by immediate historical antecedents. My definitive position ought to appear only at the end of the Sixth Cahier, in which there remains a new stage to overcome" (*Mélanges Maréchal*, Vol. I, p. 13; all translations are the author's). Unfortunately, the Sixth Cahier was never published.

In an article, "À propos du Sentiment de presence chez les profanes et chez les mystiques," published in 1908, the year he was ordained a priest, and later reproduced in the first volume of his *Études sur la psychologie des mystiques* (2nd ed., pp. 67–122), Maréchal for the first time indicated the distinctive trend of his philosophical thought. He pointed out that "the judgment of presence properly speaking affirms a spatial relation between a subject and an object," implying their reality, which is conditioned by "(1) a certain unity of mind, realized by (2) the coordination of representations, (3) with the concurrence of feeling" (*Études*, p. 110). Because the existential judgment cannot be founded solely on sensible experience, in view of sensible illusions, or on subjective feeling, the "psychologists" arbitrarily assume the anteriority of the subjective over objective knowledge, thus creating the pseudocritical problem of the "bridge" from thought to reality, the solution of which is thus prejudiced in favor of idealism. According to Maréchal the terms of the problem should be reversed. A more simple and more logical procedure would be "to posit as a primitive fact the *real, affirmation*, and the *objective* and to seek how this fact, in being broken up, gives birth to the secondary notions of the *unreal*, of *doubt*, and of the *subjective*. We shall thus rediscover, with a certain number of modern psychologists and under the impulse of experience, the point of view—very clear but insufficiently analyzed—of ancient Thomistic psychology" (ibid.).

Maréchal's principal work is his Fifth Cahier. The first four cahiers present a historical exposition and critical analysis of the problem of knowledge prior to Immanuel Kant, in Kant, and in post-Kantian transcendental idealism and a "historical demonstration" of the Thomistic solution. A twofold antinomy emerges, of the sensibility and understanding and of the understanding and metaphysical reason. Kant resolved the first antinomy by refuting the exaggerated claims of both the empiricists and the rationalists and by effecting a synthesis of the sensibility and understanding. However, according to Maréchal, Kant failed to resolve the second antinomy because he did not take into consideration the

role of finality and intellectual dynamism in objective knowledge, a failure revealed in his *Opus Postumum* and in Johann Gottlieb Fichte's finalism. Maréchal held that Thomas Aquinas's epistemology virtually contains the solution of the antinomy of the understanding and reason by their effective synthesis in terms of intellectual dynamism (though Thomas himself did not explicitly consider the modern critical problem). Hence, the Fifth Cahier, "Thomisme devant la philosophic critique," presents the Thomistic solution of the critical problem without pretending to present an anachronistic confrontation of Kant and Thomas.

Maréchal agreed with Kant that we have no intellectual intuition of the noumenal, but he denied Kant's conclusion that the noumenal is therefore unknowable to human reason. Even though the human mind is not intuitive, but only abstractive and constructive, in its knowledge, yet in virtue of its innate active dynamism to Absolute Being it attains the noumenal or metaphysical in its synthetic elaboration of the object of knowledge by the "active intellect."

The Fifth Cahier has two main divisions. The first part is an examination, according to the demands of modern criticism, of "the theory of knowledge in the framework of Thomistic metaphysics," which Maréchal aptly termed "a *metaphysical* critique of the object"; it is preceded by a "critical preamble," in which the author explains Thomas's "universal doubt" and refutation of skepticism. The second part is "a Thomistic critique of knowledge transposed to the transcendental plane" and therefore "a *transcendental* critique of the object," an attempt to go beyond Kant on the basis of Kant's point of departure and transcendental method, which seeks the a priori conditions of the possibility of the objective contents of human consciousness, viewed precisely as objective.

How does Maréchal's metaphysical critique of the object differ from his transcendental one? Both have as their initial point of departure the object immanent in the mind, the mental content directly revealed in consciousness, what René Descartes called the "objective reality" of the idea. However, according to the metaphysical critique, the presence of the object in the mind is intentional and therefore ontological or noumenal in its signification, whereas according to the transcendental critique there is present to the mind only a phenomenon. From either viewpoint, however, there can be no question but that this immanent object presents (1) a sensible aspect, (2) a conceptual aspect (involving the notes of universality and necessity), and (3) a transcendent aspect inexorably pointing toward Absolute Being. Unlike Kant, scholastic Thomism accepts the objective validity of the third aspect. As we shall presently see, the two critical approaches differ not as regards their philosophical methods but only as regards their formal object. The formal object of the metaphysical critique is being, viewed as being in all its fullness, universality, and necessity—namely, Absolute Being or God; the formal object of the transcendental critique is the phenomenon.

This is not to say that the transcendental method, as understood in too narrow a sense by Kant himself, does not differ from the metaphysical method of Thomism. The transcendental method seeks to determine the a priori conditions of the possibility of the "objective" contents of consciousness. But as Maréchal contended, the most important and salient of these a priori conditions (which Kant failed to recognize) is the intellectual dynamism of the subject, its activity in constructing the immanent object. This is revealed by "transcendental reflection," whereas "transcendental deduction" proves that the object immanent in consciousness cannot be truly "objective" except in terms of this a priori or objectivizing function of the dynamic intellect, whose formal object is Absolute Being. Needless to say, Kant himself never conceived the transcendental method in such a dynamic fashion. Thus, the most basic inconsistency of his methodology, according to Maréchal, is his stated purpose of disclosing by transcendental reflection the purely logical and static a priori conditions of knowledge, whereas, inadvertently or not, his procedure is often psychological and dynamic; he viewed the mind as constructive and synthetic, and therefore as active, but illogically concluded that the only a priori discoverable by transcendental reflection is purely logical, formal, and static. Hence, Maréchal refuted Kant in the first part of Cahier V by applying the transcendental method to the ontological object, thus legitimizing the Thomistic point of departure of metaphysics (namely, that the human mind directly attains the noumenal or intelligible in its necessary judgments), while in the second part he attempted to go beyond Kant's agnostic conclusions by proving the necessity of metaphysics, using this same transcendental method and basing the proof on Kant's own presupposition that the object immanent in consciousness is the phenomenal.

To constitute a noumenal "object in itself," that which is known must be something more than an abstract essence or form in the mind; it must go beyond the domain of *form* and be related to the sphere of *act*. An abstract essence can become a possible essence and there-fore represent a real essence only when the immanent form becomes an act of the dynamism of the intellect, necessarily relating the abstract form to Absolute Being, as a partial fulfillment of this dynamism.

Maréchal was not maintaining "the ontological parologism" that the proposition "Truth is" is intuitive or analytical; rather, he held that what the discursive and abstractive intellect apprehends is that the connection between truth and being must be affirmed under pain of contradiction, when our intellectual dynamism to Absolute Truth is also apprehended. (The objective validity of our abstractive knowledge is thus assured.) Only the divine intellect is intuitive, but an abstractive intellect is capable of apprehending and reducing an abstracted form, inherent in the potentially intelligible data of sense, to act by virtue of its active dynamical tendency to Pure Act, thus approximating the perfection of the exemplary divine knowledge. Since our intellectual knowledge is not a purely passive reception of abstract forms, the self-consciousness of the synthesizing knowing subject as an intellectual dynamism is the key to Maréchal's doctrine on the objectivization of human knowledge.

Maréchal's distinction between the human intellect viewed as formally cognoscitive and the same intellect viewed as a natural being or entelechy (*ut res quaedam naturae*) is very important for an understanding of his epistemology of objectivization. The strictly intentional function of the abstractive intellect, whose formal object is being as such, must be basically identified with the entitative function of the same intellect viewed as a dynamic real tendency to Absolute Being or Truth. It is only in virtue of the intellect viewed as dynamic act that the formally cognoscitive and abstractive intellect can assimilate a representative form as objective being, that is, as a partial fulfillment of the intellect's natural dynamism to the acquisition of *all being*, the intuition of Being Itself.

Granted the sensible data, it is in the formation of the concept that the synthesizing function of the knowing subject reveals itself. Thus, metaphysical concepts present themselves in our consciousness as universal and necessary and therefore as connoting a relation to Absolute Being; though they may conceptually represent a multiplicity, they necessarily signify a universal, though analogical, unity of being that is intelligible only in terms of Absolute Being. How are we to explain these elements of universality and necessity?

In a Thomistic metaphysical critique of the object, the a priori is not simply a logical function, as in Kant. Rather, it designates, in terms of Maréchal's intellectual dynamism, an a priori that is at once both metaphysical and psychological; for Maréchal the formal object of the intellect as a natural entelechy, or *res quaedam naturae*, is Absolute Being. On the conscious, elicitive, and formally cognoscitive level, being is necessarily presented as an abstract being as such, but such a representation, Maréchal contended, is possible only because the intellect naturally tends to Absolute Being as its natural entelechy or end on the preconscious and preelicitive level. The substantial unity of the knowing subject makes possible the "conversion to the phantasm," without which it could not make a judgment concerning the concrete individual.

Maréchal's transcendental critique of knowledge can be more readily understood when it is viewed in the light of his posthumously published Fourth Cahier, especially his remarks on Kant's *Opus Postumum* (pp. 225–326) and on Fichte's "Intellectual Intuition of Act or Dynamic Intuition" (pp. 348ff.) and his article "L'aspect dynamique de la méthode transcendentale chez Kant" (*Revue Néoscholastique* 42 [1939]: 341–384). In his analysis of Kant's *Opus Postumum* ("The Passage from the First Foundations of the Metaphysic of Nature to Physics")—which Kant once called his "masterpiece" but which was first published in 1920 by Erich Adickes under the title *Kants Opus Postumum, dargestellt und beurteilt*—Maréchal pointed out that Kant acknowledged that the "form" involved in human knowledge is not merely static or logical but dynamic and real in its implication. This same idea of intellectual dynamism is emphasized by Maréchal's analysis of Fichte's development of Kantianism, so much so that Maréchal has been accused of being too Fichtean and voluntaristic in his application of the Kantian transcendental method to the problem of knowledge. For Fichte, as for Maréchal, the self-reflecting self, the immediate intuition of the self as "a primary fact of consciousness … is the sole solid foundation of all philosophy" (Fourth Cahier, p. 349).

See also Descartes, René; Fichte, Johann Gottlieb; Idealism; Kant, Immanuel; Neo-Kantianism; Scotism; Thomas Aquinas, St.; Thomism.

Bibliography

WORKS BY MARÉCHAL

Le point de départ de la métaphysique. Leçons sur le développement historique et théorique du problème de la connaissance. 5 vols. Vols. I, II, III, Brugge and Paris, 1922–1923; Vol. IV, Brussels, 1947; Vol. V, Louvain and Paris, 1926.

Études sur la psychologic des mystiques. 2 vols. Vol. I, Brugge and Paris, 1924; Vol. II, Brussels, 1937. Translated in great part by Algar Thorold as *Studies in the Psychology of the Mystics*. London: Burns, Oates and Washburne, 1927.

Précis d'histoire de la philosophic moderne, Vol. I: *De la renaissance à Kant*. Louvain, 1933.

Mélanges Maréchal, Vol. I: *Oeuvres*. Brussels: Édition Universelle, 1950. Collected articles, with bibliography.

A Maréchal Reader. New York: Herder and Herder, 1970.

George Carver: Savant noir, ancien esclave. 1973.

Proust, prince des humoristes. Paris: Panthéon, 1996.

L'école de papa. Lyon: Editions Bellier, 1998.

Victor Hugo: Dictionnaire de ses idées, ses jugements, seshumeurs. Lyon: Bellier, 1999.

L'enseignement selon les anarchistes. Lyon: Bellier, 2000.

WORKS ON MARÉCHAL

Casula, M. *Maréchal e Kant.* Rome: Fratelli Bocca, 1955.

Gilson, Étienne. *Réalisme thomiste et critique de la connaissance*, 130–155. Paris: J. Vrin, 1939.

Hayen, A. "Un intérprete thomiste du kantisme: Joseph Maréchal." *Revue internationale de philosophie* (1954): 449–469.

Mélanges Maréchal. Vol. II (Paris, 1950), contains additional studies.

James I. Conway, S.J. (1967)
Bibliography updated by Michael J. Farmer (2005)

MARIANA, JUAN DE
(1535–1624)

Juan de Mariana, the neo-Scholastic political philosopher, was born at Talavera de la Reina, Spain, and died at Toledo. Entering the Society of Jesus at eighteen, he completed the Jesuit course of studies in philosophy and theology and taught theology in Rome from 1561 to 1569 and at Paris from 1569 to 1574. He then retired to Toledo to work on his "History" and other writings in practical philosophy. Mariana's *Historiae de Rebus Hispaniae* (Toledo, 1952; also published in elegant Spanish by the author, Toledo, 1601) was one of the first general histories of Spain. Also influential were his treatises *De Rege et Regis Institutione* (Toledo, 1599, translated by G. A. Moore as *The King and the Education of the King*, Washington, DC, 1948) and *De Mutatione Monetae* (On Changing the Value of Money), one of the *Tractatus Septem* (Cologne, 1609).

Accused of attacking the sovereign power of Spain in his criticism of its fiscal policies, Mariana was tried in 1609 by the Spanish Inquisition and acquitted. His philosophy is important for its handling of political, social, and economic problems. A strong advocate of the power of the people, Mariana argued that the citizens as a whole (*communitas civium*) are superior in power to the monarch. Men lived originally in an unorganized "state of nature," not needing political institutions to maintain justice; all possessions were held in common, and men naturally cooperated for their common welfare (*De Rege,* Chs. 8 and 13). With advances in arts and sciences, a division of goods developed into private possession; thus arose jealousy, pride, and strife among men. Tired of the struggle for domination, men then made a pact, delegating the ruling power to certain leaders. (Note that Mariana antedates both Thomas Hobbes and Jean-Jacques Rousseau.) The basic enactments of law can be changed only by the manifest will of the people. If the king fails to rule in accord with the law, he may be deposed by the people using prudent judgment; physical force may be employed for this purpose. Mariana was accused of trying to justify tyrannicide; his views did not endear him to the Spanish monarchists.

See also Hobbes, Thomas; Political Philosophy, History of; Rousseau, Jean-Jacques; Scotism; Thomism.

Bibliography

Laures, J. *The Political Economy of Juan de Mariana.* New York: Fordham University Press, 1928. Contains Latin text of *De Mutatione Monetae.*

Lewy, Guenter. *Constitutionalism and Statecraft during the Golden Age of Spain: A Study of the Political Philosophy of Juan de Mariana, S.J.* Geneva: Droz, 1960.

Tallmadge, G. K. "Juan de Mariana." In *Jesuit Thinkers of the Renaissance,* edited by Gerard Smith, 157–192. Milwaukee: Marquette University Press, 1939.

Ullastres Calvo, A. "La teoria de la mutación monetaria del Mariana." *Anales de economia* (15) (1944): 273–304; (20) (1945): 437–471.

Vernon J. Bourke (1967)
Bibliography updated by Philip Reed (2005)

MARÍAS, JULIÁN
(1914–)

Julián Marías is the best-known and most productive of the post–Civil War philosophers in Spain who have sought to reconcile the doctrines of their teacher, José Ortega y Gasset, with traditional theism. Born in Valladolid in 1914, Marías studied under Ortega in Madrid just before the Civil War. When Ortega returned from exile in 1948, they jointly founded the Institute of Humanities in Madrid. Marías has taught at the institute and, as visiting professor, at various American universities. The bulk of his published work concerns the history of philosophy, mainly Spanish and scholastic philosophy.

His general *Historia de la filosofía* (1941), which he wrote at the age of twenty-six, emphasizes the Aristotelian and scholastic traditions and gives a prominent position to Spanish thought. In *La escuela de Madrid* (The Madrid school; Buenos Aires, 1959), Marías presented the most comprehensive study available of such contemporary Spanish thinkers as Ortega, Miguel de Unamuno, Xavier Zubiri, and Manuel García Morente.

As a Catholic disciple of Ortega, who was explicitly irreligious and anti-Catholic, Marías gave a theistic interpretation of Ortega's "ratiovitalism" (a reconciliation of rationalism and the vitalist doctrines of the 1920s). In his major work, *Introducción a la filosofía* (1947), Marías argued that certain intellectual and spiritual "ultimates" are true biological needs of humankind. To be lived at all humanly, life requires, in addition to food and other animal necessities, "the possession of a radical and decisive certitude." That certitude serves as the foundation for numerous "partial truths." It harmonizes all our beliefs into a single clear perspective, and it also provides society with a ruling view that is needed for social stability. Men turn to philosophy for this certitude, so there is nothing more "practical," vital, or socially relevant than metaphysics, which is called upon to give men a standard to live by.

Marías accepts all the pragmatist, relativist, and historicist implications of vitalism, which usually have been regarded as destructive of religious convictions, and he argues from them back to the traditional religious outlook. Truth is what answers a vital need by removing the feeling of insecurity and perplexity. It is always relative to particular life situations and historical periods. Truth fragments into a multitude of relative truths, which contain concrete concepts as distinct from general concepts, which are obtained only by an arbitrary and schematizing process of abstraction. Yet, if the quest for completely satisfying, radical certainty is pressed tenaciously enough, it will lead beyond this complete nominalism to God, who appears as the ground or basis of being. Although the ego that carries on that quest was, for Ortega, the incarnation of "vital reason," for Marías it is the person who owns both vitality and reason. At death, that person, or soul, loses vitality and psychic activity but does not necessarily cease to exist. The mortality of the soul is a theory that remains in need of proof.

See also Ortega y Gasset, José; Rationalism; Unamuno y Jugo, Miguel de; Vitalism.

Bibliography

Works by Marías are *Obras* (Works), 10 vols. (Madrid: Revista de Occidente, 1959–1982), *Historia de la filosofía* (Madrid, 1941); and *Introdución a la filosofía* (Madrid, 1947), translated by Kenneth Reid and Edward Sarmiento as *Reason and Life* (New Haven, CT, 1956).

On Marías, see Alain Guy, "Julián Marías," in *Philosophes espagnols d'hier et d'aujourd'hui* (Toulouse, 1956), pp. 330–339.

OTHER RECOMMENDED WORKS BY MARÍAS

Meditaciones sobre la sociedad española. Madrid: Alianza Editorial, 1966.

Miguel de Unamuno. Cambridge, MA: Harvard University Press, 1966.

History of Philosophy. New York: Dover, 1967.

Nuevos ensayos de filosofía. Madrid: Ediciones de la Revista de Occidente, 1968.

Obras. Madrid: Revista de Occidente, 1969–1982.

Generations: A Historical Method. University: University of Alabama Press, 1970.

José Ortega y Gasset, Circumstance and Vocation. Norman: University of Oklahoma Press, 1970.

Metaphysical Anthropology; the Empirical Structure of Human Life. University Park: Pennsylvania State University Press, 1971.

Philosophy as Dramatic Theory. University Park: Pennsylvania State University Press, 1971.

La justicia social y otras justicias. Madrid: Seminarios y Ediciones, 1974.

A Biography of Philosophy. University: University of Alabama Press, 1984.

The Structure of Society. Tuscaloosa: University of Alabama Press, 1987.

Understanding Spain. Ann Arbor: University of Michigan Press; San Juan: Editorial de la Universidad de Puerto Rico, 1990.

La felicidad humana. Madrid: Alianza Editorial, 1995.

The Christian Perspective. Houston, TX: Halcyon Press, 2000.

Ortega y Gasset, José. *Meditations on Quixote.* Introduction and notes by Julián Marías, Urbana: University of Illinois Press, 2000, 1961.

Neil McInnes (1967)
Bibliography updated by Michael J. Farmer (2005)

MARITAIN, JACQUES

(1882–1973)

The French philosopher Jacques Maritain was a powerful force in twentieth-century philosophy and cultural life. The author of more than fifty philosophical works and of countless articles that appeared in the leading philosophical journals of the world, he was widely regarded as a preeminent interpreter of the thought of Thomas Aquinas and as a highly creative thinker in his own right.

Maritain, born in Paris, was reared in an atmosphere of liberal Protestantism. He attended the Sorbonne, where he fell briefly under the spell of teachers passionately convinced that science alone could provide all the answers to the questions that torment the human mind. It was at the Sorbonne that he met his wife-to-be, Raïssa Oumansoff, a young Russian-Jewish student who was to share his quest for truth and to become an intellectual and poet of real stature in her own right. She was also to collaborate with Maritain on a number of books. Soon disillusioned with the scientism of their Sorbonne masters, the two attended the lectures of Henri Bergson at the Collège de France. Bergson liberated in them "the sense of the absolute," and, following their marriage in 1904, they were converted (1906) to the Roman Catholic faith through the influence of Léon Bloy.

The years 1907 and 1908 were spent in Heidelberg, where Maritain studied biology under Hans Driesch. He was particularly interested at the time in Driesch's embryogenetic theory of neovitalism, a theory then little known in France. Upon returning to Paris, Maritain undertook the task of directing the compilation of a *Dictionary of Practical Life.* During the three years that he worked on this project, he also undertook a serious study of the writings of Thomas Aquinas. In 1914, he was appointed to the chair of modern philosophy at the Institut catholique de Paris.

From 1945 to 1948 Maritain was French ambassador to the Vatican. Afterward he taught at Princeton University until his retirement in 1956. He has also taught at the Pontifical Institute of Mediaeval Studies in Toronto, Columbia University, the Committee on Social Thought at the University of Chicago, and the University of Notre Dame. The Jacques Maritain Center was established at Notre Dame in 1958 for the purpose of encouraging research along the lines of his philosophy.

Maritain's thought is based on the principles of Aristotle and Thomas Aquinas but incorporates many insights found in other philosophers, both classical and modern, and also profits greatly from data supplied by such sciences of man as anthropology, sociology, and psychology.

THEORY OF KNOWLEDGE

The cardinal point in Maritain's theory of knowledge is his defense and critical elucidation of different ways of knowing reality. On the one hand, Maritain sees the richness and inexhaustibility of material reality as requiring that the mind let fall on it different noetic glances, each of which reveals to the mind a different universe of intelligibility to be explored. There is, first of all, the universe of *mobile being*—being imbued with mutability—which constitutes the sphere of the knowledge of nature and which itself calls for both an empiriological analysis, that is, a spatiotemporal analysis oriented toward the observable and measurable as such (science of nature), and an ontological analysis, that is, an analysis oriented toward intelligible being, toward the very being and intelligible structure of things (philosophy of nature). There is, second, the universe of *quantity* as such, which constitutes much of the sphere of mathematics. And there is, finally, the universe of *being as being*, which constitutes the sphere of metaphysics.

Much of Maritain's energy was devoted to giving the philosophy of nature its epistemological charter, in contrast with many Thomists in a hurry who would have it almost totally eclipsed by metaphysics, and in contrast with the many scientists who think that the only object capable of giving rise to an exact and demonstrable science is that which is sense-perceivable and can be subjected to methods of experimental and mathematical analysis. Maritain's serious study of the work of modern physicists and biologists revealed to him that scientists are led by their science itself to discover within the mysterious universe of nature problems that go beyond the experimental and mathematical analysis of sensory phenomena. It also revealed to him that the conceptual lexicon of the scientist is radically different from the conceptual lexicon of the philosopher. For these reasons, Maritain emphasized the need for, and prerogatives of, both an ontological analysis and an empiriological analysis of the sensible real. He also worked out a theory of physicomathematical knowledge that relates this knowledge to what the Scholastics called intermediary sciences (*scientiae mediae*), sciences which straddle the physical order and the mathematical order and which have more affinity with mathematics than with physics as to their rule of explanation and yet at the same time are more physical than mathematical as to the terminus in which their judgments are verified.

On the other hand, Maritain saw the human mind as having another life than that of its conscious logical tools and manifestations: "there is not only logical reason but also, and prior to it, intuitive reason." There is indeed not only the Freudian unconscious of instincts, tendencies, complexes, repressed images and desires, and traumatic memories; there is also a spiritual unconscious or preconscious, the preconscious of the spirit in its living springs. The acts and fruits of human consciousness and the clear perceptions of the mind—in other words, the universe of concepts, logical connections, rational discursus, and rational deliberation—emerge in the last analysis from the hidden workings of this preconscious life of the spirit; but there also emerge from them many genuine knowings, and many affective movements, which remain more or less *sur le rebord de l'inconscient*, as Bergson would have said—on the edge of the unconscious. Among such knowings we have the various kinds of knowledge by inclination (knowledge through connaturality)—notably, poetic knowledge, the "natural" or prephilosophical knowledge of moral values, and mystical experience. Maritain felt it to be most incumbent upon us to recognize not only the different kinds or degrees of conceptual and discursive knowledge but also these different nonconceptual and "immediate" forms of knowledge.

METAPHYSICS

Maritain held the classical view that the object of metaphysics is *being as being,* and he stressed that it is in things themselves that metaphysics finds this object. It is the being of sensible and material things, the being of the world of experience, which is the immediately accessible field of investigation for metaphysics; it is this which, before seeking its cause, metaphysics discerns and scrutinizes—not as sensible and material but as being. Before rising to what may be a realm of spiritual existents, metaphysics must grasp empirical existence, the existence of material things—not as empirical and material but as existence.

For Maritain, at the starting point of metaphysics there lies an intuition, the "metaphysical intuition of being," which may be said to consist in the intellect's seeing—through an abstractive or eidetic (idea-producing) visualization—the intelligible value *being*, being in itself and in its essential properties. The word *intuition* here has caused much difficulty for some philosophers, but it seems to be demanded by the thought that Maritain was trying to express. What must somehow be preserved is, on the one hand, that it is as true to say that this "seeing" produces itself through the medium of the vital action of our intellect—of our intellect as vitally receptive and contemplative—as to say that we produce it; and, on the other hand, that it is being more than anything else that produces this "seeing."

In his scrutiny of the being of sensible and material things, Maritain presented a highly original treatment of what Thomists and others have long considered to be the first principles of speculative reason—the principles of identity, sufficient reason, finality, and causality. He explained that the reality that is the object of the idea of being is richer than this idea, and it presses for multiplication in a manifold of notions, among them the notions of unity, of goodness, of truth: being is one, is good, is true. Each of these notions expresses to the mind nothing but being itself, to which it adds nothing but a conceptual difference. But precisely in virtue of this ideal element that differs from one to the other, these notions as such are different among themselves and are different from the notion of being; they are convertible notions but they are not identical with one another. There is thus a superabundance of being with regard to the notions in which it is objectified, and it is in terms of this superabundance that Maritain elucidated the intuitivity of the first principles.

When he turned his philosophical gaze to the problem of the "cause of being," Maritain was attentive both to specifically philosophical ways of establishing the existence of God and to nonphilosophical or prephilosophical ways of approaching God. Under the first heading he restates the five classical ways of Thomas Aquinas, divesting them of the examples borrowed from ancient physics and formulating them in a language more appropriate to modern times; then he proposes a "sixth way." In this "sixth way" we have first the complex primordial intuition, and later the rational and philosophical reflection, that the *I* who thinks, the *I* who is caught up in pure acts of intellect, cannot ever not have been, for both the intellect and the intelligible as such are above time: this *I* must always have existed, and in some personal existence, too, although not within the limits of its own personal being but rather in some transcendent and suprapersonal Being. Philosophical reflection can go on to establish how the *I* always existed in God, can establish that "the creature which is now I and which thinks, existed before itself eternally in God—not as exercising in Him the act of thinking, but as thought by Him."

But Maritain was quick to recognize prephilosophical approaches to God—the "natural," or instinctive and intuitive, approach proper to the first apperceptions of the human intellect, the approach through art and poetry, and the approach through moral experience. The inner dynamism of a man's first awakening to the intelligible value of existence causes him to see that the Being-with-nothingness that is both his own being and the being of the universal whole must be preceded by transcendent Being-without-nothingness. As concerns art and poetry, the poet or artist, in following the very line of his art, tends without knowing it to pass beyond his art; just as a plant, although lacking knowledge, directs its

stem toward the sun, the artist, however sordid his life, is oriented toward the primary source of beauty. And finally, as concerns moral experience, when a man experiences, in a primary act of freedom, the impact of the moral good, and is thus awakened to moral existence and directs his life toward the good for the sake of the good, then he directs his life, without knowing it, toward the absolute Good. In this way he knows God vitally, by virtue of the inner dynamism of his choice of the good, even if he does not know God in any conscious fashion or through any conceptual knowledge.

MORAL PHILOSOPHY

One of the most provocative sides to Maritain's thought was his theory of "moral philosophy adequately taken." His contention was that moral philosophy—however vast, necessary, and fundamental be the part that natural ethics plays in it—must, if it is to be adequate to its object (the direction or regulation of human acts), take into account the data of revelation and theology concerning the existential state of man. Human conduct is the conduct of an existent, not simply the conduct of a nature. Consequently, the moral philosopher must take into account all data that contribute to make the existential condition of man genuinely known to us. He must take into account the data of ethnology, sociology, and psychology. And he must also take into account theological data. For, in fact, as a result of the present state of human nature, man has more propensity to evil than the man of pure nature by reason of the original sin and of the concupiscence that remains even in the just; and, on the other hand, he has incomparably stronger weapons for good, by reason of divine grace. Maritain recognized that the moral philosopher who does take this situation into account will not be a *pure* philosopher but maintained that he will still be able to use the method proper to philosophy and advance with steps, so to speak, of philosophy, not of theology.

Maritain's theory of natural law was elaborated against the background of anthropological data. He held that two basic elements must be recognized in natural law: the *ontological* and the *gnoseological*; and it is perhaps in considering the second of these two that Maritain made his most fecund insights. The chief point he wished to emphasize is that the genuine concept of natural law is the concept of a law that is natural not only in the sense that it is the normality of functioning of human nature or essence but also in the sense that it is naturally known, that is, known through inclination or through connaturality, not through conceptual knowledge and by way of reasoning. The inclinations in question, even if they deal with animal instincts, are essentially human and, therefore, reason-permeated inclinations; they are inclinations refracted through the crystal of reason in its unconscious or preconscious life. And since man is a historical animal, these essential inclinations of human nature either developed or were released in the course of time; as a result, man's knowledge of natural law developed progressively and continues to develop. Thus, the fact that there is considerable relativity and variability in the particular rules, customs, and standards of different peoples is in no way an argument against natural law.

It belongs, of course, to moral philosophy to provide a scientific justification of moral values by a demonstrative determination of what is consonant with reason and of the proper finalities of the human essence and of human society.

SOCIAL AND POLITICAL PHILOSOPHY

Much of Maritain's effort was directed to working out the character of authentically Christian politics. He lays primary emphasis on man as being both an *individual* and a *person*—an individual by reason of that in him which derives from matter, and a person by reason of that in him which derives from his subsisting spirit. Man must live in society both because of his indigence as an individual and because of his abundance or root generosity as a person. As an individual, man is only a part, and as such he bears the same relation to society as the part bears to the whole. His private good as an individual is in everything inferior to the common good of the whole, so that an individual may even be required to risk his life for the sake of the good of the community. But as a person, man is a whole; and the whole that the person is surpasses the whole that society is, because the person, by reason of the subsistence of his spiritual soul, is destined for eternal union with the transcendent Whole, whereas the particular society in which the person lives, by reason of its not having a spiritual soul, is not destined for union with the transcendent Whole, but will die in time. Man is above and superior to political society, and the political community must recognize the person's orientation to an end above time and facilitate his attainment of it.

Maritain's social and political philosophy also manifested a keen sense of history. For Maritain as for Pindar, man must become what he is—man must "win his being"; man must become, in the psychological and moral order, in the social and political order, the person he is in the ontological order. Among the many truths related to this fundamental exigency of man's being is one

that Maritain sees as of absolutely essential importance—the fact that human history is made up of periods, each of which is possessed of a particular intelligible structure, and therefore of particular basic requirements.

It is Maritain's contention that the historical climate of the modern world is quite different from that of the medieval world. For him, medieval civilization was a sacral civilization, by which he means that the historical ideal of the Middle Ages was principally controlled by two dominants: On the one hand, the idea or myth of fortitude in the service of God—the lofty aim was to build up a fortress for God on earth—and on the other hand, the concrete fact that temporal civilization had a largely ministerial role as regards the spiritual—the body politic was to a large extent a function of the sacred and imperiously demanded unity of religion. In contrast, modern civilization was for Maritain a secular civilization, by which he meant that the historical ideal of modern times is largely controlled by two other dominants: On the one hand, the idea or myth of the body politic as being by nature something of the natural order and something directly concerned, therefore, only with the temporal life of men and their temporal common good; and on the other hand, the concrete fact that in pursuing this temporal common good, modern man is most intent on the attainment of freedom and the realization of human dignity in social and political life itself.

Against the background of this view of medieval and modern civilizations, Maritain reflected at length on the nature of the democratic ideal. He saw democracy as the only way of bringing about a moral rationalization of politics, and he insisted that in order to accomplish this task democracy needs the quickening ferment of Gospel inspiration. But he also insisted, no less forcefully, that the "creed of freedom" that lies at the very basis of democracy is not a religious, but rather a civic or secular, one. Furthermore, this secular creed deals with practical tenets that depend basically on simple, "natural" apperceptions of which the human heart becomes capable with the progress of moral conscience and which can be similarly adhered to by minds that may differ greatly as to the speculative and theoretical justifications. In keeping with such a conception, Maritain repeatedly asserted that men belonging to very different philosophical or religious lineages can and should cooperate in the pursuit of the common good of political life. He also maintained that the supreme principles governing the relationship between church and state should be applied less in terms of the social power than in terms of the vivifying inspiration of the church: "the superior dignity of the Church is to find its ways of realization in the full exercise of her *superior strength of all pervading inspiration."* This reflects a most basic premise in all of Maritain's thought: that immutable principles admit of, and even call for, analogical applications in different existential situations.

PHILOSOPHY OF ART

From his earliest years Maritain was the friend and confidant of numerous artists, writers, poets, and musicians, and he was considered by many as having the finest aesthetic sensibility among the major figures of modern philosophy. His long reflection on almost every facet of the artistic process culminated in his monumental *Creative Intuition in Art and Poetry,* which grew out of six lectures given in 1952 at the National Gallery of Art, Washington, where he had been invited to deliver the initial series of the A. W. Mellon Lectures in the Fine Arts.

Maritain held, like Dante Alighieri, that human art continues in its own way the labor of divine creation. But he kept reminding the modern artist that human art cannot create out of nothing; it must first nourish itself on things, which it transforms in order to make a form divined in them shine on a bit of matter. Maritain would admit that the widespread effort toward "pure art" in the latter part of the nineteenth century may have been a beneficent phase after the exasperation of sensibility provoked by impressionism, but he affirmed that in the last analysis human art is doomed to sterility and failure if it cuts itself off from the existential world of nature and the universe of man.

The deepest concern of Maritain was with the nature of poetic knowledge and poetic intuition, that is, with the nature of the knowledge immanent in and consubstantial with poetry, poetry as distinct from art and quickening all the arts. He held that poetic knowledge is a typical instance of knowledge through connaturality. Poetic knowledge, as he saw it, is nonconceptual and nonrational knowledge; it is born in the preconscious life of the intellect, and it is essentially "an obscure revelation both of the subjectivity of the poet and of some flash of reality coming together out of sleep in one single awakening." This unconceptualizable knowledge comes about, Maritain maintained, through the instrumentality of emotion, which, received in the preconscious life of the intellect, becomes intentional and intuitive, and causes the intellect obscurely to grasp some existential reality as *one* with the self (of the knower) reality has moved; and at the same time the knower grasps all that which this reality calls forth in the manner of a sign. In this way the self is known in the experience of the world and the world is known in the experience of the self, through an intuition that essentially tends toward utterance and creation. Thus, in such a knowledge it is the object created—the poem, the painting, the symphony—in its own existence as a world of its own that plays the part played in ordinary knowledge by the concepts and judgments produced within the mind.

Poetic knowledge, then, is not directed toward essences, for essences are disengaged from concrete reality in a concept, a universal idea, and are an object for speculative knowledge. Poetic intuition is directed toward concrete existence as connatural to the soul pierced by a given emotion. In a passage of great beauty Maritain wrote:

> This transient motion of a beloved hand—it exists an instant, and will disappear forever, and only in the memory of angels will it be preserved, above time. Poetic intuition catches it in passing, in a faint attempt to immortalize it in time. But poetic intuition does not stop at this given existent; it goes beyond, and infinitely beyond. Precisely because it has no conceptualized object, it tends and extends to the infinite, it tends toward all the reality, the infinite reality which is engaged in any singular existing thing. (*Creative Intuition in Art and Poetry,* p. 126)

Maritain was admired even by those who may be of very different philosophical convictions. He was admired not only for his lifelong zeal for truth and impassioned commitment to freedom but also for his exceptional qualities as a person—his humility, his charity, his fraternal attitude toward all that is. He came to be recognized as one of the great *spirituels* of his time.

See also Aesthetic Judgment; Aristotle; Being; Bergson, Henri; Dante Alighieri; Driesch, Hans Adolf Eduard; Epistemology; Epistemology, History of; Ethics, History of; Metaphysics; Poetizing and Thinking; Social and Political Philosophy; Thomas Aquinas, St.

Bibliography

WORKS BY MARITAIN

Theory of Knowledge

La philosophie bergsonienne. Paris: Rivière, 1914; 3rd ed., Paris, 1948. Translated by Mabelle L. Andison and J. Gordon Andison as *Bergsonian Philosophy and Thomism.* New York: Philosophical Library, 1955.

Réflexions sur l'intelligence et sur sa vie propre. Paris: Nouvelle Librairie Nationale, 1924.

Le docteur angélique. Paris: Desclée De Brouwer, 1930. Translated by Joseph W. Evans and Peter O'Reilly as *St. Thomas Aquinas.* New York, 1958.

Distinguer pour unir, ou Les Degrés du savoir. Paris: Desclée De Brouwer, 1932; 4th ed., Paris, 1946. Translated under the supervision of Gerald B. Phelan as *The Degrees of Knowledge.* New York, 1959.

Le songe de Descartes. Paris: Corrêa, 1932. Translated by Mabelle L. Andison as *The Dream of Descartes.* New York: Philosophical Library, 1944.

La philosophie de la nature; Essai critique sur ses frontières et son objet. Paris: Téqui, 1935. Translated by Imelda C. Byrne as *Philosophy of Nature.* New York: Philosophical Library, 1951.

The Range of Reason. New York: Scribners, 1952.

Metaphysics

Sept Leçons sur l'être et les premiers principes de la raison spéculative. Paris: Téqui, 1934. Translated as *A Preface to Metaphysics: Seven Lectures on Being.* London and New York: Sheed and Ward, 1939.

Court Traité de l'existence et de l'existant. Paris: Hartmann, 1947. Translated by Lewis Galantière and Gerald B. Phelan as *Existence and the Existent.* New York: Pantheon, 1948.

Approches de Dieu. Paris: Alsatia, 1953. Translated by Peter O'Reilly as *Approaches to God.* New York: Harper, 1954.

Moral Philosophy

Science et sagesse. Paris: Labergerie, 1935. Translated by Bernard Wall as *Science and Wisdom.* New York: Scribners, 1940.

Education at the Crossroads. New Haven, CT: Yale University Press, 1943.

Neuf leçons sur les notions premières de la philosophie morale. Paris: Téqui, 1951.

La philosophie morale, Vol. I: *Examen historique et critique des grands systèmes.* Paris: Gallimard, 1960.

Social and Political Philosophy

Humanisme intégral. Paris: Aubier, 1936. Translated by M. R. Adamson as *True Humanism.* New York: Scribners, 1938.

La personne et le bien commun. Paris: Desclée De Brouwer, 1947. Translated by John J. FitzGerald as *The Person and the Common Good.* New York: Scribners, 1947.

Man and the State. Chicago: University of Chicago Press, 1951.

The Social and Political Philosophy of Jacques Maritain. Edited by Joseph W. Evans and Leo R. Ward. New York, 1955. Selected readings.

On the Philosophy of History. New York: Scribners, 1957.

Reflections on America. New York: Scribners, 1958.

Philosophy of Art

Art et scolastique. Paris: Librairie de l'Art Catholique, 1920; 3rd ed., Paris, 1935.

"Frontières de la poésie." In his *Frontières de la poésie et autres essais.* Paris: Rouart, 1935. This and the above work were translated by Joseph W. Evans as *Art and Scholasticism and the Frontiers of Poetry.* New York, 1962.

Situation de la poésie. Paris: Desclée De Brouwer, 1938. Written in collaboration with Raïssa Maritain. Translated by Marshall Suther as *The Situation of Poetry.* New York: Philosophical Library, 1955.

Creative Intuition in Art and Poetry. New York: Pantheon, 1953.

The Responsibility of the Artist. New York, 1960.

WORKS ON MARITAIN

Bars, Henry. *Maritain en notre temps.* Paris: B. Grasset, 1959.

Bars, Henry. *La politique selon Jacques Maritain.* Paris: Les Éditions ouvrières, 1961.

Croteau, Jacques. *Les fondements thomistes du personnalisme de Maritain.* Ottawa: Éditions de l'Université d'Ottawa, 1955.

Evans, Joseph W., ed. *Jacques Maritain: The Man and His Achievement.* New York: Sheed and Ward, 1963.

Gallagher, Donald, and Idella Gallagher. *The Achievement of Jacques and Raïssa Maritain: A Bibliography, 1906–1961.* New York: Doubleday, 1962.

Maritain, Raïssa. *Les grandes Amitiés,* 2 vols. New York: Éditions de la Maison Française, 1941. Vol. I translated by Julie Kernan as *We Have Been Friends Together.* New York: Longman, 1942. Vol. II translated by Julie Kernan as *Adventures in Grace.* New York: Longman, 1945.

The Maritain Volume of the Thomist. New York, 1943. Originally published as Vol. 5 (1943) of *The Thomist,* dedicated to Maritain on the occasion of his sixtieth birthday.

Phelan, Gerald B. *Jacques Maritain.* New York: Sheed and Ward, 1937.

Tamosaitis, Anicetus. *Church and State in Maritain's Thought.* Chicago, 1959.

Joseph W. Evans (1967)

MARITAIN, JACQUES [ADDENDUM]

Jacques Maritain died in Toulouse on April 28, 1973, as a professed religious of the Petits Frères de Jesus. His wife Raissa had died in 1959 when the couple was visiting France and from that point on Maritain's center of gravity was once again Europe. In Toulouse, he taught the brothers of his community and the published works that resulted are almost exclusively theological. Thus, Maritain continued to surprise: the quintessential layman became a professed religious, the philosopher became a theologian.

His reputation with many suffered when he published *The Peasant of the Garonne* in 1966. In the immediate wake of the ecumenical council dubbed Vatican II, Maritain was severely critical of developing trends in the Catholic Church. Teilhard de Chardin and phenomenology were major targets of his criticism. Some saw in this a retrogression, remembering *Antimoderne.* It helps to distinguish Maritain's political views from his Catholic faith. He held the latter with unswerving orthodoxy from the time of his conversion. It was otherwise with his political views. His long association with *Action Francaise,* so difficult to reconcile with his earlier socialism, was followed by a resurgence of his natural liberalism in political matters. The conservatism of the *Peasant* is theological, not political.

Negative reactions to the *Peasant* are eclipsed by the upsurge of interest in Maritain during the latter part of the twentieth century. The Jacques Maritain Center at Notre Dame was founded in 1958 and seemed destined to become the repository of Maritain's papers. The bulk of his papers are to be found in Kolbsheim, the home of the *Cercle d'études Jacques et Raissa Maritain*. Under the general direction of René Mougel a magnificent sixteen volume *Oeuvres complètes* has appeared. There is another International Maritain Association centered in Rome under the aegis of Roberto Papini which has sponsored a score of publications and conferences, as well as a periodical, *Notes et Documents*. There are flourishing Maritain associations in Canada, the United States, and Latin America. Biographies have been written, collections of letters published, various monographs have appeared. A projected twenty volume set of Maritain's work in English is under way from the Jacques Maritain Center, whose web site at nd.edu can be consulted for other relevant materials.

Perhaps interest is strongest in his political, social, and aesthetic views. Given the contingency of the practical order this is surprising, perhaps, but would seem to attest to Maritain's knack of finding permanent values in the changing cultural landscape. His metaphysical views have their adherents still and there is a quickened interest on the part of physicists in Maritain's views of natural philosophy and natural science, as is evident in the institute founded by the physicist-philosopher Anthony Rizzi. Far from waning, interest in Maritain's thought seems to be increasing. For all that, it is perhaps not too much to say that it is his personality that continues to attract. Leon Bloy's line, "There is only one tragedy, not to be a saint," may seem a counter-cultural motto for a philosopher, but perhaps that is due to the all too exiguous character of recent philosophizing. In any case, as person as well as thinker, Jacques Maritain's influence is still strongly felt in the twenty-first century.

See also Aesthetics, History of; Liberalism; Phenomenology; Socialism; Teilhard de Chardin, Pierre.

Bibliography

WORKS BY MARITAIN

Jacques et Raissa Maritain Oeuvres Complétes, edited by René Mougel et. al. Strasbourg: Editions Universitaires Fribourg Suisse, 16 volumes, 1986–1999.

The Collected Works of Jacques Maritain, edited by Ralph McInerny, Bernard Doering, Fred Crosson. Notre Dame: Notre Dame University Press, 1997.

WORKS ABOUT MARITAIN

Barré, Jean-Luc. *Jacques et Raissa Maritain: Les Mendiants du Ciel*. Paris: Stock, 1995.

Doering, Bernard. *Jacques Maritain and the French Catholic Intellectuals*. Notre Dame, IN: University of Notre Dame Press, 1983.

McInerny, Ralph. *The Very Rich Hours of Jacques Maritain: A Spiritual Life*. Notre Dame: University of Notre Dame Press, 2003.

Schall, James V. *Jacques Maritain, The Philosopher in Society*. New York: Rowman and Littlefield, 1998.

Ralph McInerny (2005)

MARKOVIĆ, SVETOZAR
(1846–1875)

Svetozar Marković was a Serbian socialist, philosopher, and publicist. After prolonged uprisings between 1804 and 1815 had liberated Serbia from Turkey, a cultural revolution took place, led by the reformer of the Serbian language and orthography Vuk Karadžich (1787–1864), and socialist ideas began to spread. The first Serbian socialist writers were the economist and philosopher Živojin Žujović (1838–1870) and Svetozar Marković.

After technical studies in Belgrade, Marković continued his education in St. Petersburg, where he attended the lectures of Dmitri Pisarev and became acquainted with the ideas of the Russian revolutionary democrats. Marković went to France in 1869 and then to Zürich, where he became acquainted with the Western revolutionary workers' movement and with the works of Karl Marx. Marković became the correspondent for Serbia and the Balkans of the Marxist First International. In 1870 he returned to Serbia, where he gathered about himself a circle of young intellectuals and workers. He published *Radenik* (The Worker; 1871–1872), the first socialist newspaper in the Balkans, and later the newspapers *Javnost* (The Public) and *Glas Javnosti* (The Public Voice). After nine months' imprisonment for violating the press law, Marković, who had become seriously ill, was set free in 1875. He began publishing a new newspaper, *Oslobodjenje* (Liberation), but shortly afterward he died in Trieste.

The basic determinant of Marković's thought and activity was the Serbian social situation. The disoriented rural paupers and the small and unorganized urban proletariat had repudiated the patriarchal social order, but they disagreed on the means of improving their lot. In search of ways to solve the social problems of his countrymen, Marković developed a socialist ideology. This theory was greatly influenced by the Russian revolutionary democrats Nikolai Chernyshevskii, Nikolai Dobrolyubov, and Pisarev, and later by Marx, but its main sources were materialist philosophy and the natural sciences—French eighteenth-century materialism (particularly Baron d'Holbach, Denis Diderot, and Jean Le Rond d'Alembert); the vulgar materialism of Friedrich Büchner, Karl Vogt, and Jacob Moleschott; the positivism of Auguste Comte and John Stuart Mill; and the scientists Charles Darwin, Ernst Haeckel, Wilhelm Wundt, and Ivan Mikhailovich Sechenov, the Russian physiologist. There are also traces in Marković's thought of the utopian socialists the Comte de Saint-Simon, François Marie Charles Fourier, and Étienne Cabet, as well as of other socialists such as Pierre-Joseph Proudhon and Louis Blanc.

ATHEISM AND MATERIALISM

Lacking a deep and systematic philosophical and sociopolitical education, Marković did not intend to become a philosopher or a literary figure but strove to be the ideologist and spiritual leader of a new trend in science and life—a publicist and propagator of new ideas. Nevertheless, his theoretical outlook was relatively original and presented an integral whole.

Marković's ideology embraced first of all the general principles of scientific atheism and natural-philosophical materialism expressed in the study "Realni Pravac u Nauci Iživotu" (The Realistic Trend in Science and Life; in the journal *Letopis Matice Srpske*, 1871–1872) and other works. From Chernyshevskii and Marx he borrowed the notion of the need for building up a philosophical theory as the basis of sociopolitical knowledge and practice. He called his view "scientific materialism and realism." All phenomena, as well as the processes of nature, society, and spiritual life, were interpreted in terms of matter and its laws. Nature and society were integrally connected. Only by means of science was the people's economic and political revival possible. Marković, like Marx, contrasted his view with Bakunin's. In spite of certain elements of mechanism and agnosticism in his outlook, Marković advocated the idea of dialectical development and an evolutionistic-materialistic theory of knowledge as the basis of the social struggle of the socialist movement.

In his interpretation of man and society, Marković drew upon Darwin, Comte, the French materialists, Ludwig Feuerbach, and Chernyshevskii. Morals is founded on knowledge and science, and the development of morals is affected by the development of man's needs through the socialization of instincts. Moral feelings are not innate; man becomes individually moral and socially more morally minded as society develops. Only by constant labor can man raise himself to a height unreachable by any other organism. Marković condemned the morals of bourgeois society as being founded upon the exploitation of the lower classes. Because morality is the indispensable consequence of the social machine, only a socialist revolution can bring about a new socialist morality. Seeing the primary goal of the future socialist society as the morality of its members, Marković termed his ethical socialism "idealistic realism." He did not conceive of the idea as being determined by matter, but spoke of the idea as the primary motive force in the development of society.

AESTHETICS

Believing that a spiritual revolution must precede the political and economic revolutions, Marković held that the social revival had to be supported by literature and art. In "Pevanje i Mišljenje" (Songs and Thought; *Matica*, 1868), "Realnost u Poeziji" (Reality in Poetry; *Matica*, 1870), and many other works, Marković expounded a materialist aesthetic modeled upon that of Chernyshevskii. Literature should be realistic and rational, expressing the genuine life, needs, and interests of the people, and should have an effect upon the general social revival. Marković's views decisively affected the development of Serbian literature, turning it toward Russian and western European realism.

SOCIOPOLITICAL VIEWS

In his voluminous book *Načelo Narodne Ekonomije* (The principles of the national economy [Belgrade, 1874]), written in the vein of J. S. Mill and Chernyshevskii, Marković praised Marx for his discovery of the law of social development, but he held that these laws could not be applied to Russia, Serbia, and other economically undeveloped countries, which, in Marković's opinion, could bypass capitalism and move from patriarchal cooperatives directly to socialism. Marković's teachings on society, state, and revolution, in spite of some elements of utopianism and historical idealism, showed a high degree of accuracy. Although he gave too much weight to the roles of social consciousness, science, and philosophy, and consequently to the revolutionary intelligentsia, in the development of socialist society, his program was revolutionary and democratic. In a series of works, especially in his most original work, *Srbija na Istoku* (Serbia in the East

[Novi Sad, 1872]), Marković defended the Paris Commune and criticized the capitalistic social system of western Europe and the narrowness of the bourgeois democracies. Marković was convinced that the transition to socialism was possible only by means of a revolution of the whole people against foreign invaders and native capitalist exploiters. He developed a fragmentary theory of the smashing of the bourgeois state in the socialist revolution and the withering away of the socialist state in the process of building communism. Like Marx, he held that only in conjunction with revolutionary practice could revolutionary theory solve the social problem. He perceived the significance of the class struggle in the West, but in backward Serbia he thought that the revolutionary intelligentsia could play a more decisive role than the proletariat. He advocated federation and self-government for the southern Slav nations. He also advocated a system of cooperatives.

Although Marković was more a revolutionary democrat than a Marxist, his teachings nevertheless united general Marxian principles concerning revolution with theories concerning the specific national character of Serbia. Moreover, they stressed the need for joint action on the part of the revolutionary intelligentsia, the peasantry, and the workers. Thus, Marković was the founder and leader of the Serbian socialist movement, as well as its theoretician, philosopher, aesthetician, and literary critic.

See also Aesthetics, History of; Aesthetics, Problems of; Alembert, Jean Le Rond d'; Atheism; Chernyshevskii, Nikolai Gavrilovich; Comte, Auguste; Darwin, Charles Robert; Diderot, Denis; Feuerbach, Ludwig Andreas; Fourier, François Marie Charles; Haeckel, Ernst Heinrich; Holbach, Paul-Henri Thiry, Baron d'; Marxist Philosophy; Marx, Karl; Materialism; Mill, John Stuart; Moleschott, Jacob; Pisarev, Dmitri Ivanovich; Proudhon, Pierre-Joseph; Realism; Saint-Simon, Claude-Henri de Rouvroy, Comte de; Socialism; Wundt, Wilhelm.

Bibliography

WORKS BY MARKOVIĆ

Many of Marković's scientific and periodical papers are collected in *Sabrani Spisi*, 4 vols. (Belgrade, 1960–1965).

WORKS ON MARKOVIĆ

For literature on Marković, see Slobodan Jovanović, *Svetozar Marković* (Belgrade, 1904). Jovan Skerlić, *Svetozar Marković* (Belgrade, 1910); Veselin Masleša, *Svetozar Marković* (Belgrade, 1947); Dušan Nedeljković. "Lik Svetozara Markovića," in the journal *Glas SAN* (3) (1951): 200–207;

Dimitrije Prodanović, *Shvantanje Svetozara Markovića o državi* (Belgrade, 1961).

ADDITIONAL SOURCES

McClellan, Woodford. *Svetozar Marković and the Origins of Balkan Socialism.* Princeton, NJ: Princeton University Press, 1964.

Stoianovich, Traian. "The Pattern of Serbian Intellectual Evolution." *Comparative Studies in Society and History* 1 (3) (1959): 242–272.

Stokes, Gale. "Svetozar Marković in Russia." *Slavic Review* 31(3) (1972): 611–625.

Andrija Stojković (1967)
Bibliography updated by Philip Reed (2005)

MARSILIUS OF INGHEN
(1340–1396)

Marsilius of Inghen was a scholastic theologian, writer on logical textbooks, and prolific commentator on Aristotle. He played an important role in the foundation of the University of Heidelberg. His significance rests not only on his commentaries on Aristotle—his advocacy and popularization of the new, nominalist logic and semantics—but also on an independent-minded theology that sometimes rejected post-Scotistic positions in favor of thirteenth-century positions (such as those of Thomas Aquinas or Bonaventure).

Marsilius of Inghen was a student at Paris, matriculating there in Arts in 1362, and then in Theology in 1366. At Paris, he was influenced by the thought of John Buridan, and he undertook significant administrative work, including rectorships (1367–68, 1371) as well as representation to the Papal court (1369, 1377–78). Marsilius's whereabouts are largely unknown between 1379 and the founding of the University of Heidelberg in 1386—except, that is, for a Nijmegen banquet he attended in 1382. From 1386 to 1392, he was a Master at Heidelberg—and was also an occasional Rector—up until his death in 1396 (Hoenen 1993, pp. 7–11; Santos Noya, 2000, Vol. 87, pp. 1–26).

He read the Sentences (the standard requirements to become a Master of Theology) from 1392 to 1394. Part of the preparation for this commentary was most likely done in Paris from 1367 to 1377. (Hoenen and Braakhuis 1993, pp. 39–57; Santos Noya 2000, Vol. 87, pp. 31–32).

Marsilius was a nominalist on universals. Like Ockham and Buridan he did not believe that universals exist outside the soul, and that the direct object of each science is merely the proposition in the mind. Real objects, he believed, are the objects of sciences via the signification of the proposition. Marsilius's logic and semantics can be described reliably as Buridanist, albeit with some points of dissent and less detail. As well, he differed from Buridan on the division of supposition, the signification of chimera, his definitions of *ampliatio* and *appellatio*, and his non-adoption of *suppositio naturalis* (Bos 1983, p. 254).

Marsilius's natural philosophy is empiricist; he holds that the starting point of natural philosophy is sense data and per se known principles. From this point he then leaps from singular observations to a universal proposition if there is no expectation of a counterexample—due to the mind's inclination to truth. Thus, a causal connection can be held to be universal, though one has not experienced all its instances.

In his theology, he criticized both the Scotistic position that the Divine Ideas are formally distinct from the Divine Essence, and the Ockhamist thesis that the Ideas are identical with the objects that are known. He held the Thomistic theses that God's Ideas of created things are not distinct from his essence and that the difference between the divine attributes exists only in the human mind due to its finitude. He also held that natural reason can prove that God is the cause of all and knows created things. Marsilius brought together the critical semantico-logical tradition of the fourteenth century and the themes of thirteenth century theologians such as Aquinas and Bonaventure (Hoenen 1993, pp. 235–253).

In the fifteenth and sixteenth centuries, he was regarded as a great advocate of nominalism, and grouped with Buridan, Ockham and Gregory of Rimini. His logical treatises exist in many manuscripts, and were widely used as textbooks in the fifteenth century. His theology of grace and divine foreknowledge was well known and quoted by late-scholastic writers such as Vitoria, De Soto, Molina, and Suarez. His Aristotelian commentaries were also well known and cited up to the early-modern period. For example, both Leonardo da Vinci and Gallileo Galilei refer to his commentary on Aristotle's *De Generatione et Corruptione*.

See also Buridan, John; Thomas Aquinas, St.; William of Ockham.

Bibliography

WORKS BY MARSILIUS OF INGHEN
Quaestiones super quattuor libros Sententiarum. Super primum quaestiones 1–7 and 8–21, edited by Manuel Santos Noya, et al. (Studies in the History of Christian Thought, vols. 87–88.) Leiden, Netherlands: Brill, 1999–.

Treatises on the Properties of Terms. A first critical edition of the *Suppositiones, Ampliationes, Appellationes, Restrictiones and Alienationes*, with introduction, translation, notes, and appendices by Egbert P. Bos. (Synthese Historical Library, vol. 22.) Dordrecht, Netherlands: D. Reidel, 1983.

WORKS ABOUT MARSILIUS OF INGHEN
Braakhuis, H. A. G., and Maarten J. F. M. Hoenen, eds. *Marsilius von Inghen.* Acts of the International Marsilius of Inghen Symposium. Nijmegen, Netherlands: Ingenium, 1992.
Hoenen, Maarten J. F. M. *Marsilius of Inghen: Divine Knowledge in Late Medieval Thought.* Leiden, Netherlands: Brill, 1993.
Hoenen, Maarten J. F. M., and Paul J. J. M. Baakker, eds. *Philosophie und Theologie des ausgehenden Mittelalters: Marsilius von Inghen und das Denken seiner Zeit.* Leiden, Netherlands: Brill, 2000.

C. F. Ledsham (2005)

MARSILIUS OF PADUA
(c. 1275/1280–1342)

Marsilius of Padua (Marsilio dei Mainardini), an Italian political theorist, was born between 1275 and 1280 and died in 1342. He probably studied medicine at the University of Padua. In 1313 he was rector of the University of Paris, where he met such leading Averroists as Peter of Abano and John of Jandun. He is chiefly famous for his antipapalist treatise *Defensor Pacis* (Defender of peace; 1324), a landmark in the history of political philosophy. When his authorship of this work became known in 1326, he was forced to flee to the court of Louis of Bavaria in Nuremberg; Pope John XXII thereupon branded him a heretic. Marsilius subsequently assisted Louis in various imperial ventures in Italy.

DEFENSOR PACIS

The primary purpose of the *Defensor Pacis* was to refute the papalist claims to "plenitude of power" as these claims had been advanced by Pope Innocent IV, Egidius of Rome, and others in the thirteenth and fourteenth centuries. So crushing was the refutation produced by Marsilius that it completely reversed the papalist position. The papal position had held that secular rulers must be subject to the papacy even in "temporal" affairs, so that they must be established, judged, and, if necessary, deposed by the pope. Marsilius, in contrast, undertook to demonstrate that the papacy and the priesthood in general must be subject not only in temporal, but even in "spiritual," affairs to the whole people and to the secular ruler acting by the people's authority. The powers of the priesthood were to be reduced to the administration of the sacraments and the teaching of divine law, but even in these functions the priests were to be regulated and controlled by the people and its elected government. The upshot of Marsilius's doctrine was that the attempt to base human society on religious values under priestly control was decisively overthrown; instead, the way was opened for a purely secular society under the control of a popularly elected government. Hence, it is understandable that Marsilius has been hailed as a prophet of the modern world. His treatise exerted a marked influence during the period of the Reformation.

THEORY OF THE STATE. Equally as important as these revolutionary conclusions are the premises from which Marsilius derived them. These premises are found in his general theory of the state, which is noteworthy for its fusing of three distinct themes. The first is the Aristotelian teleological view of the state as subserving the good life. The various parts of the state, including government, are defined by the contribution they make to the rational "fulfillment" of men's natural desire for a "sufficient life." This fulfillment proceeds through the "proper proportioning" of men's actions and passions, ranging from nutritive and sensitive acts to appetitive and cognitive ones. The function of government is to regulate men's transitive acts in accordance with the law as a standard of justice. The first theme, then, stresses an affirmative and maximal utilitarianism—what is required for the attainment of the highest ends of the "sufficient life," the common benefit, and justice.

The second theme of Marsilius's political theory, in contrast, is a negative and minimal utilitarianism. It emphasizes the inevitability of conflicts among men and the consequent need for the formal instrumentalities of coercive law and government in order to regulate these conflicts. Without such regulation, Marsilius repeatedly insists, human society itself must be destroyed. In developing this theme, Marsilius presents a positivistic concept of law, which stands in contrast with his nonpositivistic conception of justice (a distinction often overlooked in discussions of his ideas). He holds that there are objective criteria of justice, which he characterizes in terms of Aristotle's analysis of rectificatory justice—moderating the excesses of men's transitive acts and "reducing them to equality or due proportion," thereby promoting the common benefit. But whereas Marsilius views law as a system of general rules concerned with the regulation of the same "excesses" and the resultant conflicts, as well as with other matters bearing on the common benefit, he emphasizes that these legal rules need not be based on "true cog-

nitions of justice." On the contrary, laws may be based on "false cognitions of the just and the beneficial," so that Marsilius, unlike most medieval political philosophers, holds that justice is not a necessary condition of law. What is necessary is that the legal rules have coercive force, such that with regard to their observance "there is given a command coercive through punishment or reward to be distributed in the present world." These rules and the government that enforces them must be unitary in the sense that, if a society is to survive, it cannot have two or more rival coercive bodies of law and government.

The third theme of Marsilius's political theory is that the people is the only legitimate source of all political authority. It is the people, the whole body of citizens or its "weightiest part," that must make the laws either by itself or through elected representatives, and it is also the people that must elect, "correct," and, if necessary, depose the government. Marsilius presents many arguments for this republican position: (1) The whole people is intellectually and emotionally superior to any of its parts, so that only from its choice will emerge the best law and government, the ones most conducive to the common benefit, as against the ones that subserve the interests of some special group; (2) self-legislation is necessary for individual freedom; (3) only if the laws and government are chosen by the people will they be obeyed; and (4) that which affects all ought to be subject to approval by all.

Although all three themes of Marsilius's general political theory were found in earlier medieval political philosophers, no other philosopher had given the second and third themes as central a position as did Marsilius. As a result of this, although Marsilius's first theme—about the ends of the "sufficient life," the common benefit, and justice—persists throughout his treatise, it is overshadowed by his emphases on coerciveness as the essence of political authority and on the republican bases of all such authority. The full consequence of these emphases emerges in the applications he makes of his general political theory to the problems of ecclesiastical politics.

APPLICATIONS OF THE THEORY. In keeping with his first theme, Marsilius views the Christian priesthood as one of the parts of the state dedicated to achieving the "sufficient life" for all believers. Unlike the other parts of the state, however, the priesthood subserves the "sufficient life" to be attained primarily "in the future world" rather than the present one. Like the other Averroists, Marsilius manifests skepticism about the rational demonstrability of such a future life; nevertheless, he officially accepts the Christian doctrine that the future life is superior to the present life. He also holds, however, that secular and religious values are in basic opposition; here he seems to be applying in the realm of the practical the Averroist doctrine of the contrariety of reason and faith in theoretic philosophy.

Taken in conjunction with the maximal, affirmative utilitarianism of his first theme, accepting that the priesthood subserves the highest end of man would have required Marsilius to accept also the papalist doctrine that the "secular" government, subserving the lesser end of this-worldly happiness, must be politically subordinate to the priesthood. At this point, however, Marsilius's second and third themes have their effect. Since the essence of political authority is the coerciveness required for the minimal end of preserving society, it follows that the higher end subserved by the priesthood does not entitle it to superior political authority. The question of the order of political superiority and inferiority is thus separated from the question of the order of moral and religious values. What determines the order of political authority is not the greater excellence of one end over another but, rather, the specifically political need for unified coercive authority in order to prevent unresolved conflicts from destroying society. Hence, the secular government, as bearer of this coercive authority, must be politically superior to the priesthood. If the priests refuse to obey the government and its laws, then they must be compelled to do so, because such disobedience threatens that unity of coercive authority without which society cannot survive. Indeed, it is because of this disobedience and because of its claim to a rival, superior "plenitude of power," that Marsilius convicts the papacy of being the gravest enemy of civil peace. In this context Marsilius presents his whole critique of the papacy as an application to fourteenth-century conditions of Aristotle's book on revolutions (*Politics* V), dealing with the ways in which threats to civil peace may be avoided.

In addition to this political argument against diverse centers of coercive power in any society, Marsilius also stresses, from within the religious tradition itself, that religious belief, in order to be meritorious, must be purely voluntary. Hence, in order to fulfill its mission, divine law and the priesthood that teaches and administers it cannot be coercive in this world.

Marsilius's third theme, republicanism, also plays an important role in the political subordination of the priesthood and papacy. The only rules and persons that are entitled to the status of being coercive laws and government officials are those ultimately chosen by the peo-

ple; hence, there can be no crediting the claims of divine law and the priesthood to a separate derivation of coercive political authority from God. It is true that Marsilius subsequently holds that secular rulers govern by divine right, but he views this only as a divine confirmation of the people's ultimate electoral authority. This republicanism operates not only in the relation of the priesthood to the secular state but also in its relation to religious affairs. Because the whole people is superior in virtue to any of its parts and because freedom requires popular consent or election, the priesthood itself must be elected by the people of each community rather than being appointed by an oligarchically chosen pope, and the pope himself must be elected by the whole of Christendom. Similarly, the whole people must elect general councils to provide authoritative interpretations of the meaning of divine law. In these ways Marsilius's general political theory leads to a republican structure for the church as against its traditional monarchic structure. In effect, this also means that the secular government, acting by the people's authority, secures hegemony over the priesthood and papacy in all spheres.

See also Aristotelianism; Aristotle; Averroism; John of Jandun; Medieval Philosophy; Political Philosophy, History of; Republicanism; Sovereignty; Utilitarianism.

Bibliography

The *Defensor Pacis* is available in two critical editions, one edited by C. W. Previté-Orton (Cambridge, U.K.: Cambridge University Press, 1928) and one edited by Richard Scholz, 2 vols. (Hanover: Hahn, 1932–1933), in the series *Fontes Juris Germanici Antiqui* of the series *Monumenta Germaniae Historica*. There is an English translation by Alan Gewirth, *Defensor Pacis* (New York: Columbia University Press, 1956).

A comprehensive bibliography of studies published to about 1950 of Marsilius's doctrines is contained in Alan Gewirth, *Marsilius of Padua and Medieval Political Philosophy* (New York: Columbia University Press, 1951), pp. 323–326.

Bibliographical information on subsequent studies will be found in Georges de Lagarde's important study, *Marsile de Padoue*, 2nd ed. (Paris, 1948), which is in the series *La naissance de l'esprit laique au déclin du moyen âge*, 3rd ed. (Paris, 1959–).

Alan Gewirth (1967)

MARSILIUS OF PADUA [ADDENDUM]

In order to understand Marsilius more fully, it is useful to examine both the classical influences upon his work and the ways he applies his own principles in the minor works such as *Defensor Minor* and *De Translatione Imperii*.

MARSILIUS AND CICERO

Most discussions of *Defensor Pacis* concentrate upon Aristotle's *Ethics* and *Politics* (which had become available in translation around 1250 and 1260, respectively). Indeed, Marsilius employs the Aristotelian distinctions of the healthy types of civil constitution: monarchy, aristocracy, and polity and their complements the diseased constitutions: tyranny, oligarchy, and extreme democracy. However, though Aristotle is certainly the primary source of many of the distinctions in Part I of *Defensor Pacis*, there are other key influences as well. Among these is Cicero's doctrine of natural duty to others from his *De officiis*. Cary Nederham has argued that this sense of natural duty is the secular analogue to theological or Christian duty. The use of parallel justifications for why a person should be committed to the community follows the general structure of the book in which Part I creates a secular justification for politics whereas Part II elaborates the foundations of ecclesiastical duty.

The secular duty to the community is a natural duty so that every person in the state must fulfill the duties of friendship and of civic society—without regard to personal welfare. This duty extends to a concern for others and a duty to rescue and assist those in need. Because the source of the duty is natural to all people, there is no national restriction on this duty. Thus, it commits each person to exhibit concern beyond his own society to others internationally.

DEFENSOR MINOR AND DE TRANSLATIONE IMPERII

These works are more conventional and do not contain the split presentation of secular argument and theological exposition that characterized *Defensor Pacis*. These minor works are more conventional dealing with parsing the jurisdictions of theology and secular government. Though these works are not as well known as the *Defensor Pacis*, they are useful to help put Marsilius's major work into perspective. For example, one of the possible motivations for Marsilius's antipapal rhetoric (though Marsilius, himself, was a priest) might be Marsilius's alliance with the Bavarian King Ludwig IV. Ludwig wanted to expand his empire and move into Italy. (It should be remembered that at this time the Pope resided in Avignon, France.) Marsilius's writing was associated with Ludwig, who appointed Marsilius as spiritual vicar of Rome and himself as the Roman Emperor. However,

this situation was short lived and soon both fled back to Germany.

The *Defensor Minor* and *De Translatione Imperii* fit into this context. They apply principles of *Defensor Pacis* to contemporary problems. For example, papal authority is questioned in regard to Ludwig's plan to marry his daughter to a close relative in order to stabilize his political prospects. Both Marsilius and William of Ockham were to weigh in on this question as an issue of authority. In *Defensor Minor* no new positions are forged, but are fine tuned so that they might be applied to cases such as the marriage of Ludwig's daughter.

Another example concerns the bogus "Donation of Constantine." In this forged document the Roman Emperor Constantine supposedly granted the whole of the Roman Empire to the Pope who, in turn, allowed the daily duties of running the secular to fall upon the emperor. This document sought to establish a legal claim for the pope's universal secular power. Marsilius argues against the Donation in both *Defensor Pacis* and *De Translatione Imperii*.

See also Aristotelianism; Aristotle; Cicero, Marcus Tullius; Duty; Political Philosophy, History of; William of Ockham.

Bibliography

Ashcraft, Richard. "Ideology and Class in Hobbes' Political Theory." *Political Theory* 6 (1978): 17–62.

Black, Antony. *Political Thought in Europe, 1250–1450.* Cambridge, U.K.: Cambridge University Press, 1992.

Black, Antony. "Society and the Individual from the Middle Ages to Rousseau: Philosophy, Jurisprudence, and Constitutional Theory." *History of Political Thought.* 1, (2) (Summer 1980): 145–166.

Luscombe, Davie E. "The State of Nature and the Origins of Society." In *The Cambridge History of Later Medieval Philosophy*, edited by N. Kretzmann, A. Kenny, and J. Pinborg. Cambridge, U.K.: Cambridge University Press, 1982.

McGrade, A. S. "Aristotle's Place in the History of Natural Rights." *Review of Metaphysics* 49 (4) (1996): 803–829.

WORKS BY MARSILIUS OF PADUA

Defensor Pacis, edited by C. W. Previté-Orton. Cambridge, U.K.: Cambridge University Press, 1928.

Defensor Pacis. Translated by Alan Gewirth. New York: Columbia University Press, 1956.

Oeuvres Minueres, edited by C. Jeudy and J. Quillet. Paris: Editions CNRS, 1979.

Writings on the Empire: Defensor minor and De translatione imperii, edited by C. J. Nederman. Cambridge, U.K.: Cambridge University Press, 1993.

WORKS ON MARSILIUS OF PADUA

Canning, Joseph. "The Role of Power in the Political Thought of Marsilius of Padua." *History of Political Thought* 20 (1) (1999): 21–34.

Coleman, Janet. "Medieval Discussions of Property: *Ratio* and *Dominium* According to John of Paris and Marsiglio of Padua." *History of Political Thought* 4 (Summer 1983): 209–228.

Condren, Conal. "Democracy and the *Defensor Pacis*: On the English Language Tradition of Marsilian Interpretation." *Il Pensiero Politico* 8 (1980): 301–316.

Condren, Conal. "Marsilius of Padua's Argument from Authority: A Study of Its Significance in the *Defensor Pacis*." *Political Theory* 5 (1977): 205–218.

D'Entrèves, A. P. *The Medieval Contribution to Political Thought: Thomas Aquinas, Marsilius of Padua, Richard Hooker*. Oxford: Oxford University Press, 1939.

Gewirth, Alan. "John of Jandun and the *Defensor Pacis*." *Speculum* 23 (1948): 267–272.

Gewirth, Alan. *Marsilius of Padua and Medieval Political Philosophy*. 2 vols. New York: Columbia University Press, 1951. Contains an extensive bibliography.

Gewirth, Alan. "Republicanism and Absolutism in the Thought of Marsilius of Padua." *Medioevo* 5 (1979): 23–48.

Grignaschi, Marc. "La Rôle de l'aristotélisme dans le 'Defensor Pacis' de Marsile de Padoue." *Revue d'Histoire ed de Philosophie Religieuse* 35 (1955): 310–340.

Kaye, Sharon. "Against a Straussian Interpretation of Marsilius of Padua's Poverty Thesis" *History of Philosophy Quarterly* 11 (3) (1994): 269–279.

Loffelberger, Michael. *Marsilius von Padua: Das Verhältnis Zwischen Kirche und Staat in "Defensor Pacis."* Berlin: Duncker and Humbolt, 1992.

Nederman, Cary J. "Character and Community in the *Defensor Pacis*: Marsiglio of Padua's Adaptation of Aristotelian Moral Psychology." *History of Political Thought* 13 (3) (1992): 377–390.

Nederman, Cary J. *Community and Consent: The Secular Political Theory of Marsiglio of Padua's 'Defensor Pacis'*. Lanham, MD: Rowman and Littlefield, 1995. Contains a good bibliography.

Nederman, Cary J. "From *Defensor Pacis* to *Defensor Minor*: The Problem of Empire I Marsiglio of Padua." *History of Political Thought* 16 (3) (1995): 312–329.

Nederman, Cary J. "Nature, Justice and Duty in the *Defensor Pacis*: Marsiglio of Padua's Ciceronian Impulse." *Political Theory* 18 (1990): 615–637.

Quillet, Jeannine. "L'aristotélisme de Marsile de Padoue." *Miscellanea Medievalia* 2 (1963): 696–706.

Quillet, Jeannine. "L'aristotélisme de Marsile de Padoue et ses rapports avec l'averroïsme." *Medioevo* 5 (1979): 81–142.

Spiers, Kerry E. "The Ecclesiastical Theory of Marsilius of Padua: Sources and Significance." *Il Pensiero Politico* 10 (1977): 3–21.

Tierney, Brian. "Marsilius on Rights." *Journal of the History of Ideas* 52 (1991): 3–17.

Wilks, Michael. "Corporation and Representation in the *Defensor Pacis*." *Studia Gratiana* 15 (1972): 251–292.

Michael Boylan (2005)

MARSTON, ROGER
(c. 1250–1303)

Roger Marston, the Augustinian Scholastic, was born in one of England's Marstons. He was educated at the Faculty of Arts and Theology at the University of Paris about 1270 and taught at Oxford and Cambridge between 1276 and 1285. He was the provincial of the English Franciscans between 1292 and 1298.

Marston's career may be characterized as a conscious effort to restore St. Augustine to his position as the great leader of Christian philosophers and theologians. In carrying out the proposals of his teacher, John Peckham (also an Augustinian), Marston exhibited a phenomenal knowledge of the writings of Augustine, as well as a fine sense of historical and textual criticism. He must have been attacked as an archconservative, because he defended himself by remarking that he did not cling to tradition out of mere habit, but that after a reasonable scrutiny of the evidence, he had formed opinions that harmonized the writings of the "saints" with the wisdom of the philosophers. Marston knew the Greek and Muslim philosophers, and interpreted them with a great deal of subtle skill, sometimes calling attention to fundamental ambiguities in their thought.

Marston needed all the resources at his command to counter the attacks directed against the Augustinian theory of divine illumination, which he deemed necessary to explain certitude. Since the attacks were made under the guise of Aristotle's authority, Marston attempted to reconcile Augustine's theory of knowledge with that of Aristotle, as seen through the latter's Islamic commentators. Thus, Roger claimed that the Eternal Light of Augustine is the same as the separate agent intellect of Avicenna and Averroes. However, the English friar would not allow man to be "dispossessed" of his own individual agent intellect, and hence he posits a double agent intellect: divine and human. This was one of the medieval solutions to the idealist-empiricist dilemma.

In the realm of the philosophy of nature, there was one doctrine of Thomas Aquinas to which Marston took serious exception—namely, the Thomistic contention that each individual being had but one form. Prior to Thomas, the far more common opinion had been that in material beings there was a plurality of forms. In man there were the forms of "vegetivity," "sensitivity," and "rationality," corresponding to the human functions of nutrition, sensation, and thought. Marston's solution to the question introduced a refinement that amounted to a synthesis of the Thomistic and traditional solutions, although it favored the latter. There is one substantial form for each being, but that single form admits of various subordinate and persisting degrees, or grades. Marston's theory of the grades of the form is the first organized version of this theory that has come down to us from the Middle Ages.

With respect to the majority of his philosophico-theological tenets, Marston followed the lead of Bonaventure. With Bonaventure (and against Thomas), he considered an eternal creature an impossibility. Prime matter can exist apart from all forms by divine intervention, because God is the "Form of all things" who conserves his handiwork just as water conforms to the intricate convolutions of a mold, as long as it is contained by the mold. On the subject of God's foreknowledge of future human acts—a perennial problem in Christian philosophy—Marston remarks that since an individual's memory of a past event does not constrain his free will with regard to the past, neither does God's foreknowledge constrain his free will with regard to the future.

For a medieval, Marston has an unusually personal style, and his remarks are often a source of valuable information for the historian.

See also Agent Intellect; Augustine, St.; Augustinianism; Averroes; Avicenna; Bonaventure, St.; Empiricism; Idealism; Medieval Philosophy; Peckham, John; Thomas Aquinas, St.; Thomism.

Bibliography

WORKS BY MARSTON

Quaestiones Disputatae, edited by Franciscani non-nominati. Quaracchi, 1932: *Bibliotheca Franciscana Scholastica VII,* lxxx + 497pp.)

Quodlibeta Quatuor, edited by G. Etzkorn and I. Brady. Grottaferrata, 1994: *Bibliotheca Franciscana Scholastica XXVI,* 2nd ed., 87 + 550 pp.). Introduction by Ignatius Brady includes a thorough treatment of Marston's life, career, and works.

WORKS ON MARSTON

Etzkorn, G. "Roger Marston, O.F.M.: An Example of Thirteenth-Century Anti-Semitic Apologetics." *Cithara* 21 (1982): 3–16.

Etzkorn, G. "Roger Marston's Grades' Theory in the Light of His Philosophy of Nature." *Miscellanea Mediaevalia* 2 (1963): 535–542.

Hissette, R. "Roger Marston a-t-il professé l'hylémorphisme universel?" *Revue de Théologie Ancienne et Médiévale* 39 (1972): 205–223.

Magnani, P. *Il problema delle Rationes Seminales in Ruggero di Marston.* Milan: Marzorati, 1992.

Pérez-Estévez, A. "La materia en Roger Marston." *Veridad y Vida* 55 (1997): 217–220.

Girard J. Etzkorn (1967, 2005)

MARTINEAU, JAMES
(1805–1900)

James Martineau, an English philosopher and religious leader, was born in Norwich. He was a brother of Harriet Martineau, the novelist and economist. James Martineau attended school in Norwich and Bristol and went on to study for the ministry under the Unitarian auspices of Manchester New College at York. He accepted a call to a congregation in Dublin in 1828 and was married later the same year. In 1832 he became minister to a dissenting congregation in Liverpool. He occupied this post for twenty-five years, but for most of that period he was also teaching philosophy and other subjects at Manchester New College, and when the college was moved to London in 1857, he moved with it. From 1869 to 1885 he served as principal of the college. Despite the criticism aroused by his views on religious and theological matters, he was regarded as the foremost spokesman of Unitarianism in England and was revered by many in other religious groups as well for his impressive contributions to the literature of hymn, private prayer, and sermon.

In accordance with the then prevailing tendency of Unitarian thought, Martineau was brought up to accept the doctrines of associationism, egoism, and necessitarianism as taught by David Hartley and Joseph Priestley. In his early teaching he used works by James Mill and Thomas Brown as texts, but the difficulties he had in defending their views, together with his own growing sense of the inadequacy of their philosophy as a basis for a Christian outlook, led him rapidly toward a new general position. By 1839 he concluded that necessitarianism was incompatible with that sense of "the personal origin and personal identity of sin" which is central to Christianity. During the next half-dozen years he worked out the implications of this point. The results were first published in 1845 and 1846 in two long reviews (reprinted in *Essays, Reviews, and Addresses*) that outlined the positions he was to develop and defend for the rest of his life. Although he learned much from a year of study in Berlin in 1848 and 1849, German philosophy did not really change his thought. He remained far more a follower of Bishop Butler and Thomas Reid than of Immanuel Kant or G. W. F. Hegel.

At the basis of all of Martineau's constructive thought is the view that we must accept as true certain deliverances of consciousness that appear to give us directly information about the external world, the self, and morality. Neither Kant nor William Hamilton nor J. S. Mill seemed to him to have given us reason to distrust the intuitions of the mind, and since these intuitions present themselves as reliable, we are entitled to have faith in them until reasons against them are produced. Martineau's intuitionism is the philosophical counterpart of the very great emphasis he placed, in interpreting religion, on personal religious experience. It is in such experience, he held, that one must look for revelation, not in messages delivered by others nor in traditions preserved by organized groups. Philosophically, both epistemology and ethics lead directly to justifications of religious belief.

From the very start of knowledge, Martineau argued, we are aware of a self and a not-self, and we are aware of these not as simply passively there but as being actively related. We thus intuit ourselves as willing and the world, in turn, as an expression of will. The former intuition is at the basis of our understanding of causality, which cannot be explained in terms of succession of phenomena, and the idea of causality finds its mature expression in the belief that God is the noumenal cause of the phenomenal order. Science, which deals only with phenomena, cannot upset our belief in God, but the increasing unity of the laws and theories that science discovers acts as a confirmation of our intuitive belief in the unity of the cause of nature.

If the "natural" attributes of God, such as omnipotence and intelligence, are revealed through our experience of the external world, the moral attributes are revealed to us primarily in our moral experience. Martineau argued very carefully that the central subject of moral judgment is motives or "springs of action," not acts or consequences. He held that whenever there is more than one motive competing to direct our action, we are intuitively aware that one of the motives is higher than the others.

"The moral faculty," he said, "is not any apprehension of invisible qualities in external actions, not any partition of them into the absolutely good and absolutely evil, not any intellectual testing of them by rules of congruity or balances of utility, but a recognition, at their very source, of a scale of *relative* values lying within ourselves," relative because a given motive may be higher in relation to one alternative, lower in relation to another. To be good is to choose to act on the relatively higher motive. Once this choice is made, consideration of consequences comes in to aid in selecting the particular act that will best express the motive in the actual circumstances. It is the first choice only that is morally relevant, though the second is, of course, important. Since the moral value of both agent and act is wholly determined by his choice of motive, Martineau went to considerable pains to defend absolute freedom of the will. The arguments rely heavily on the concept of cause developed in his epistemology. In our own willing we learn something of the nature of God's activity; the realization that there is an authoritative demand on us to act on the relatively higher motive is the chief revelation of God within our moral experience. The authoritativeness of the demand can be explained only in theistic terms, and the content of the demand reveals to us God's moral nature.

Martineau's style is extremely florid and his exposition quite diffuse. In his epistemological and metaphysical writings he seems often to have missed the point of an opposing theory or to have been content with very weak arguments for his own. But his ethics, as an account of the ethics of motive, if not highly original, is in conception and in execution one of the finest that has ever been presented.

See also Brown, Thomas; Butler, Joseph; Egoism and Altruism; Epistemology; German Philosophy; Hamilton, William; Hartley, David; Hegel, Georg Wilhelm Friedrich; Kant, Immanuel; Mill, James; Mill, John Stuart; Priestley, Joseph; Reid, Thomas.

Bibliography

Works by Martineau include *A Study of Spinoza* (London: Macmillan, 1882); *Types of Ethical Theory*, 2 vols. (Oxford: Clarendon Press, 1885); *A Study of Religion*, 2 vols. (Oxford: Clarendon Press, 1888); *The Seat of Authority in Religion* (London: Longmans, Green, 1890); and *Essays, Reviews, and Addresses*, selected and revised by Martineau himself (London: Longmans, Green, 1890–1891).

For an account of his life and philosophy, see James Drummond and C. B. Upton, *Life and Letters of James Martineau* (London: J. Nisbet, 1902); criticism of the ethics will be found in Henry Sidgwick, *Lectures on the Ethics of T. H. Green, Mr. Herbert Spencer, and J. Martineau* (London: Macmillan, 1902).

J. B. Schneewind (1967)

MARTINETTI, PIERO
(1872–1943)

Piero Martinetti, an Italian metaphysician, was professor of theoretical philosophy at the University of Milan from

1906 until 1931, when he resigned in protest against the oath imposed on university professors by the Fascist regime.

Martinetti sought to reestablish metaphysics as a valid science by a method whose validity would have to be recognized even by positivists. This project involved a refutation of positivism on its own grounds. The positivist attack on metaphysics, Martinetti claimed, is valid only against vulgar or dogmatic metaphysics. Scientific metaphysics meets all the requirements of scientific methodology. It adheres to data that all science must recognize; but it is no mere synthesis of the sciences, for it interprets scientific findings and determines their meaning rather than their mere truth. Consequently, a scientific metaphysics would achieve, on a posteriori grounds, successive unifications of empirical data until the Absolute was achieved.

The first of the successive levels in this projected unification is that of the "I" or self as a unity of sensuous consciousness. This is the constant flux of sense perception, the central point around which all perception is synthesized. At this stage no distinction is made between subject and object. The self at this level possesses a rudimentary transcendental character in the invincible conviction that its sense perceptions are identical with those of all possible subjects, but this persuasion is itself a mere datum.

This intimation of the transcendental and a priori provides a means of passage to the next level of synthesis, the logical level. But the a priori forms of synthesis are not a priori in the Kantian sense; they are "con-natural" with their empirical content. Among these forms are substance and cause, which unify respectively the coexistent and the successive. The movement from the sensible forms of unity to the logical forms is not itself a logical process; rather, it is entirely natural. Logic is the "science of the natural conformations of human thought," and logical relations are therefore empirical relations.

The third stage of synthesis, that of absolute unity, cannot be achieved in thought; it is implied in the dynamic of thought. We can have no speculative concept, but only a symbolic intuition, of it. However, it cannot be concluded, therefore, that our knowledge is limited to phenomena. The absolute unity is always present, although in an imperfect way, because it enters structurally into all levels of synthesis. This omnipresence of the Absolute Martinetti called mystical: "Our knowledge is a mystic unity with the eternal Logos."

This process of synthesis applies also to the practical order, whose transcendental principle is liberty. Morality exhibits a primary synthesis in the form of necessity freely achieved—a synthesis that is continued and extended by art and religion.

See also Absolute, The; A Priori and A Posteriori; Metaphysics; Positivism.

Bibliography

WORKS BY MARTINETTI

Introduzione alla metafisica, 2 vols. Milan, 1902–1904.

Emanuele Kant-Prolegomini. Turin, 1913. With a commentary by Martinetti.

La libertà. Milan, 1928.

Gesù Cristo ed il cristianesimo. Milan, 1934.

Ragione e fede. Turin: G. Einaudi, 1942.

WORKS ON MARTINETTI

Alessio, F. P. *L'idealismo religioso di Piero Martinetti.* Brescia: Morcelliana, 1950.

Gentile, Giovanni. "La teoria della conoscenza del Martinetti." In *Saggi critici*, 1st series. Naples, 1921.

Sciacca, M. F. *Piero Martinetti.* Brescia, 1943. Contains an excellent bibliography.

A. Robert Caponigri (1967)

MARTY, ANTON
(1847–1914)

Anton Marty was a professor of philosophy at the German University of Prague and for forty years a close associate of Franz Brentano. Marty's most important work is the *Untersuchungen zur Grundlegung der allgemeinen Sprachtheorie* (Halle, 1908), a treatise on the philosophy of language. His theory of meaning, or "semasiology," is based upon Brentano's descriptive psychology. From a contemporary point of view, the most interesting aspects of this theory are the distinction between categorematic and syncategorematic uses of words and the theory of emotive utterances.

Like Brentano, Marty appeals to the correctness of affirmation and rejection, and of love and hate (in a broad sense) to explicate the syncategorematic character of certain basic philosophical concepts. In the assertion "There is a horse," the words "a horse" *refer* to an object, but the words "there is" serve only to *express* the fact that the speaker is accepting or acknowledging the object. An object is said to have being if it may be correctly accepted; it has nonbeing if it may be correctly rejected; it is good if it may be correctly loved; it is bad if it may be correctly hated; the necessary is that which may be correctly accepted a priori; the impossible is that which may be correctly rejected a priori.

Marty rejected the view of Bernard Bolzano and Alexius Meinong, according to which there are objects that may be said to "subsist" and not to "exist." But he did contend that the objects that may be said to "exist" may be classified as being either "real" or "nonreal." Examples of nonreal objects that exist are gaps, deficiencies, holes, space, time, and what Marty called the content of a judgment. (If the judgment "There are horses" is correct, then there exists that nonreal object that is the being of horses; if it is incorrect, then there exists that nonreal object that is the nonbeing of horses.) According to Marty, nonreal objects have no causal efficacy, and their existence is always a function of the existence of certain concomitant real objects. Brentano objected to this view on the ground that sentences ostensibly referring to such nonreal objects may be translated into sentences referring only to the real objects that Marty conceded to be their concomitants ("There is an absence of food in the larder" serves only to express the rejection of food in the larder) and that hence all such "irrealia" are superfluous. But where Marty restricted "real" to a subclass of things that exist, Brentano said that judgments about unicorns are also judgments about "real objects"; these judgments are about things that, if they were to exist, would be real (in Marty's sense of "real").

The word *good*, according to Marty, serves to express one's love of an object; "bad" serves to express one's hate of an object. Marty discussed the emotive function of ethical sentences in detail and noted the ways in which such sentences are related to commands, recommendations, questions, and optatives. However, unlike contemporary emotivists, Marty held with Brentano that the emotions expressed and incited by ethical sentences are emotions that are either correct or incorrect; his theory of ethical sentences could thus be said to be emotive and also objective. He discussed in detail the relations among emotive and nonemotive sentences and the respects in which sentences of the one type may presuppose sentences of the other (for example, a man who calls "Stop thief!" asserts implicitly that there is a thief and that he is trying to get away).

See also Bolzano, Bernard; Brentano, Franz; Emotive Theory of Ethics; Meinong, Alexius; Philosophy of Language.

Bibliography

Marty's posthumously published *Raum und Zeit* (Halle: Niemyer, 1916) sets forth a comprehensive theory of space, time, and causality. His writings also include *Über den Ursprung der Sprache* (Würzburg: Stuber, 1875). *Die geschichtliche Entwicklung des Farbensinnes* (Vienna, 1879); *Die logische, lokalistische und andere Kasustheorien* (Halle, 1910); *Gesammelte Schriften*, edited by Josef Eisenmeir, Alfred Kastil, and Oskar Kraus, 2 vols. (Halle: Niemyer, 1916–1920); and *Nachgelassene Schriften*, edited by Otto Funke (Bern, 1940–1950).

See also Oskar Kraus, *Anton Marty: sein Leben und seine Werke* (Halle, 1916); and *Die Werttheorien* (Brünn: Rudolf M. Rohrer, 1937).

Roderick M. Chisholm (1967)

MARULIĆ, MARKO
(1450–1524)

Marko Marulić, the Croatian poet, historian, and philosopher, was born in Split, Dalmatia. Marulić's epic, *Istorija Svete Udovice Judit* (The History of the Holy Widow Judith; Vinegia, 1521), is the oldest Croatian epic and the first printed Croatian literary work. Like all of Marulić's poetry, it is both epic and didactic. Marulić's philosophical works were written in Latin and translated into German, French, Italian, Portuguese, and other languages. His *De Institutione Bene Beateque Vivendi per Exempla Sanctorum*, first published in Venice in 1506, was reprinted, in the original or in translation, fifteen times in the sixteenth and seventeenth centuries. His *Evangelistarium* (Venice, 1516) was printed nine times.

Marulić was influenced by the Renaissance humanists and was also a student of the classical Greek philosophers, but he was at the same time an outstanding representative of then-modern Christian philosophical thought. He enriched Christian moral teaching with the abundant wealth of Stoic-Platonic moral thought and revived traditional philosophy in the spirit of humanism. Marulić regarded Epicurean and Stoic ethics as antithetically opposed and Stoic ethics as superior to Epicurean. In general, he rejected all forms of hedonism and utilitarianism, and with them ethical subjectivism and relativism.

Marulić's exposition of a Christian ethics combined with elements of Stoicism and Platonism was enlivened by examples from life. This original synthesis of ancient elements, rejuvenated by humanism, was greatly appreciated in its day, especially for its service in the Catholic fight against the Reformation. Although ethical problems were Marulić's main concern, he also considered the fundamental problems of philosophy.

See also Epicureanism and the Epicurean School; Ethical Subjectivism; Ethics, History of; Hedonism; Humanism; Platonism and the Platonic Tradition; Reformation; Renaissance; Stoicism; Utilitarianism.

Bibliography

For additional philosophical works by Marulić, see *Quinquaginta Parabolae* (Venice, 1510); *De Humilitate et Gloria Christi* (Venice, 1519); and *Dialogus de Laudibus Herculis a Christianis Superacto* (Venice, 1524).

For works on Marulić, see *Zbornik Marka Marulića 1450–1950* (Zagreb, 1950), a commemorative volume honoring Marulić, published by the Yugoslav Academy of Arts and Sciences, with a complete bibliography of Marulić's works and of works about his life and writings.

Vladimir Filipović (1967)

MARX, KARL

(1818–1883)

Karl Marx was born in 1818 in the small German city of Trier in the Rhineland, then part of Prussia. He died in 1883 in London. His life thus spanned the better part of the nineteenth century, a time of rapid and profound economic, social, and political change in Western Europe and America. Philosophically, Marx can be seen as both the culmination of the tradition of German Idealism and its end. In this latter sense, and because most of his work consists of political, economic, and historical analysis, Marx has been taken as having moved beyond purely philosophical interests and investigations into the empirical realms of the social and historical sciences.

The primary goal of Marx's life and work, of course, was to facilitate the revolutionary overthrow of the capitalist system and to help give birth to the socialist society that he believed would inevitably follow the demise of capitalism. In the broadest sense, the project was to achieve the promise of human emancipation, a theme Marx inherited from Kant and Rousseau through German Idealism. Essential to this project was the understanding of the nature and limits of human reason, particularly as embodied in social institutions, a theme of critique also derived from Kant. Marx did not truly leave philosophy behind; he remained a philosopher whose project of liberation led him to increasingly empirical analyses of capitalist society and history. His central con-

cerns are freedom, alienation, and critique, themes at the center of the tradition of German Idealism.

LIFE

Marx came from a Jewish family with rabbinical roots on both his paternal and maternal sides. His father, however, broke with his family and converted to Lutheranism. Karl, his eldest son, was baptized in 1824. After a year studying law at the university in Bonn, Marx transferred to the university in Berlin to study philosophy. He received his doctorate from the University of Jena in 1841, but because of his close association with the radical Young Hegelians, he was unable to secure an academic appointment. Instead of pursuing a career in philosophy, he began to work as a journalist, the only career in which he ever earned any income. Increasingly engaged in the radical politics of the day, in 1843 he moved to Paris, the political heart of Europe, where he did his first serious work in the relatively new field of political economy as well as continuing his critical work on Hegel. This early work, *Economic and Philosophic Manuscripts*, unfinished and not published until 1932, is important to understanding the transformation of Marx the Young Hegelian philosopher into Marx the historical materialist. These manuscripts contain his most extended discussion of alienation, a discussion that helps shed light on how this concept was developed in his later writings, including *Capital*. It was also at this time that Marx established his lifelong friendship and collaboration with Frederick Engels.

While living in Brussels from 1845 to 1848, Marx made his final break with Hegel and the Young Hegelians, including Feuerbach. The two most important pieces of work from this period were the "Theses on Feuerbach" and *The German Ideology* (in collaboration with Engels). Neither was published in Marx's lifetime. These works are often regarded as the first statements of historical materialism and related ideas that would be further developed in Marx's mature thought. What is perhaps Marx's most famous writing, *The Communist Manifesto*, was written with Engels in 1848 at the request the Communist League, an association of revolutionary German workers headquartered in London. Soon after its publication, revolutionary activity burst out across Europe. Eager to participate, Marx went first to Paris and then Cologne, but within a year, as it became clear that the revolution would not succeed, he settled in London. He lived there for the rest of his life.

While not absenting himself entirely from politics, Marx spent the better part of the next fifteen years immersed in economic theory and history. In an effort to come to terms with recent events in France, he wrote *The Eighteenth Brumaire of Louis Bonaparte* in 1851–1852. Little else of note was published until the end of the decade, when he published *A Contribution to the Critique of Political Economy*. The preface to this work, often referred to as the "1859 Preface," contains his most famous succinct statement of historical materialism. Also during this period, he worked on manuscripts never published during his lifetime that have come to be known as the *Grundrisse*. These notebooks, which did not come to light until the middle of the twentieth century, are important for a number of reasons. They include what is the broadest outline of Marx's theoretical project, an early statement of the themes that became the focus of *Capital*, important points about Marx's method of working on texts, and insights into how Hegelian concepts such as alienation continued to be part of Marx's thinking.

In 1862 and 1863 Marx worked closely on the theories of political economists, Adam Smith and David Ricardo in particular, writing manuscripts later published as *Theories of Surplus Value*. This work culminated in 1867 with the publication of the first volume of his magnum opus, *Capital*. Marx continued to work on the remaining parts of this manuscript, never finishing them to his satisfaction. Engels published them only after Marx's death: Volume 2 in 1885 and Volume 3 in 1894.

Marx returned to more active political involvements in the 1860s, becoming one of the leaders in the The International Working Men's Association, formed in 1864. He remained politically active for the rest of his life, becoming recognized as the leading theoretician of the European working-class movement. Among his later notable writings are *The Civil War in France*, written as an address to mark the demise of the Paris Commune in 1871, and "Marginal Notes on the Program of the German Workers' Party," popularly known as "Critique of the Gotha Program," written in 1875 in an attempt to help unify the two major factions of the German working-class movement. These two later works are important for comments on the nature of society and the state in postrevolutionary, socialist society, a topic about which Marx wrote very little.

FREEDOM, ALIENATION AND CRITIQUE

Marx's philosophical views can be understood in terms of a series of central concepts: freedom, alienation and critique; historical materialism as a dialectical theory; the production of value and the problem of exploitation; and communism and the nature of a free society.

The chief good for Marx, as it was for Hegel, was freedom. For both, a fully free individual was autonomous, and this required rational understanding of and control over one's actions. Both Hegel and Marx appreciated that human emancipation, understood as autonomy, was a collective project. Individuals could be autonomous in the full sense only in a rational and free society. They differed concerning the conditions of a rational society and, in particular, whether the emerging commercial bourgeois society was rational and therefore yielded the conditions for human emancipation.

Marx followed Hegel in arguing that one major impediment to autonomy was a lack of understanding of one's self in relation to one's social world. Such a lack of understanding results in conditions of alienation wherein the individual is dominated to her detriment by states of affairs or objects that she has helped to produce but, in her misunderstanding, treats as independent of her. Conditions of alienation, the young Marx realized, undermined not only the possibility of freedom but created human misery and a sense of meaninglessness. Whereas Hegel analyzed alienation largely as a phenomenon of consciousness, Marx stressed the objective and social roots of alienation, locating its origins in the conditions of production and the nature of labor.

Part of the project of overcoming alienation, Marx realized, involved critique—philosophical analysis that reveals the nature and sources of the alienation and that allows the individual to break through the veils of misunderstanding. Importantly, since the young Marx also realized that alienation was produced by the conditions of social existence, he grasped that until these conditions were understood and overcome, critique alone could not free the world of the destructive consequences of alienation. If the project of emancipation were to be carried to success, Marx recognized that he would have to understand the conditions that give rise to alienation and how those conditions could be changed.

HISTORICAL MATERIALISM

Historical materialism is the theory Marx produced to explain the nature and sources of human alienation, oppression, and suffering and the possibility of attaining emancipation. In its fullest scope, historical materialism supplies an explanation of the central developments of human history, the series of stages of social development through which human societies have passed, and an account of the key dynamics determining the development of any given social formation. Marx's theory of capitalism is the most crucial and developed part of the overall theory of historical materialism.

The starting point of historical materialism is the claim that the central project of human history is the production and reproduction of material life. Humans exist within nature as creatures of needs that can only be satisfied through interaction with nature, that is, through labor. The necessity of labor is a manifestation of the fact that the human condition has been one of scarcity. While all animals are in a similar circumstance and must interact with nature to satisfy their needs, humans are distinguished because they have the capacity to develop tools, technology in the broad sense, that allow them to better satisfy their needs. With the development of technology, new needs were created as were the possibility of satisfying them. The production of ever more powerful technology and ways of putting it to use to satisfy an ever greater array of needs and wants, that is, the growth of human productive power, is for Marx the main theme of human history.

Human productive activity involves three elements: raw materials from nature, technology, and human labor. Marx referred to the first two factors, the natural resources and technology, as the means of production. Combined together, the three elements provide the productive power or, as it is more often called, the forces of production. The forces of production, to be put to use, must be organized in terms of some set or other of social relations that determines who has access to and control over the technology, the activity of labor and the product of the labor. Marx refers to these social relations of power as the relations of production. Typically, those who dominate the relations of production appropriate a disproportionate share of the product and dominate society. Two groups of people can be designated: those who dominate the relations of production and have power over the conditions of labor and the product and those who lack control. This division is the basis of Marx's theory of class and the inherently antagonistic class relations of the dominant ruling class and the subordinate workers class.

Historical materialism claims that the forces of production tend to develop in power over time. For any given level of the forces of production, there will be a set of relations of production in terms of which the existing forces can be best utilized and developed. That is, the relations of production that exist at any give point in history will tend to be those that are best suited to the further use and development of the existing forces of production. The existing forces of production together with the set of rela-

tions of production in terms of which they are organized form an economic structure that Marx calls a mode of production. Historical development proceeds through determinant stages characterized by the prevailing mode of production. According to Marx, there have been three modes of production prior to capitalism: the ancient slave mode of production characteristic of Greece and Rome, the feudal mode of production, and the Asiatic mode of production that is found in ancient India and China and that, unlike the modes of production found in Europe, does not develop beyond itself.

Within a mode of production, the forces of production continue to develop within the constraints of the existing relations of production. At some point in the development of the forces, the existing relations are no longer optimal to the continued use and development of the forces and the relations break down, allowing a new set of relations to emerge. These points of transition between old and new relations of production are considered revolutionary periods; such periods need not be violent and swift. Marx well understood that the transition from feudalism to capitalism took several centuries. With the emergence of a new mode of production and new relations of production, the nature of power relations within the economic order changes, and a new ruling class comes into being.

All modes of production, then, are made up of a dominant and a subservient class, with the members in the latter class far out numbering those in the former. Given the obvious disparities in power and freedom class society involves, one may ask why have they been as stable for as long as they have? According to historical materialism, the economic or class relations of a society form the basic institution of that society. The other principal institutions, including the political, legal, religious, and cultural, constitute what Marx calls the superstructure of society and justify and reinforce the economic relations. The superstructural institutions that tend to exist at any given point are those that help to stabilize the base. For Marx, just as the level of development of the forces of production determines and explains the nature of the existing relations of production, so the existing relations of production determine and explain the nature of the superstructural institutions.

Part of the superstructure of a society consists of what Marx terms the realm of consciousness; that is, the prevalent ideas and values in a society. As with other aspects of the superstructure, these ideas and values are explained in terms of their role in stabilizing class relations and the base. When such beliefs and values are produced and propagated by professionals (academics, religious authorities, cultural critics, and the like), Marx refers to them as the ideology of the society. As Marx famously states it: the ruling ideas of an age are the ideas of the ruling class, and they serve the interests of that class. Morality and religion are part of the ideological superstructure, according to Marx. Hence his well-known disdain for them.

Ideological beliefs are not necessarily false, although typically they are. But even when not false, they serve to limit or mislead understanding—for instance, by suggesting that a certain condition is natural and not socially constructed. Thus ideology creates false consciousness. Insofar as the members of the subordinate class accept the ideology of their society, they are misled about the nature of their actions, their society, and the role they play in creating it. In this way, ideological mystification is a major factor in the creation of the experience of alienation and the subsequent loss of freedom. Alienated conditions of existence, conditions that involve the domination of people by the reality they have produced but do not understand, are built into the nature of class society.

THEORY OF EXPLOITATION

In all class societies, the ruling class dominates and exploits the labor of the subordinate class. Such exploitation is fairly evident in slave societies and in feudalism. Capitalism, however, presents a far more complex case. The wage laborer (to use Marx's terms, the proletarian who is a member of the proletariat, the class of wage laborers in capitalism) appears to voluntarily accept work and to be paid for each unit of labor (typically, the hourly wage). The focus of Marx's most sustained work was to unmask this ideological appearance and expose how and why the proletarian was exploited in a way at least as bad, and perhaps worse, than was the slave or serf. By explaining the nature of capitalist exploitation, Marx believed, he could explain the nature and limits of the capitalist mode of production and why it was doomed to be replaced by a socialist society.

Marx's theory of capitalist exploitation is complex; it is grounded on the crucial distinction between labor and labor power. The proletarian, hired by the capitalist, is paid for every hour of labor he performs. What he sells to the capitalist and what the capitalist buys is the capacity of the worker to labor for an agreed upon period of time, say, a ten hour day. During that period, the capitalist owns the worker's capacity to produce goods and can use that capacity in any way he wants. He can use it effi-

ciently, making the worker work harder and produce more, or he can use it less efficiently. Since the capitalist already owns the other factors of production, the raw materials and machines and other technology, and now owns the labor that goes into producing the product, he owns all the factors of production and thus the entire product produced, which he then takes to the market to sell, hoping to return with profit.

Where does this profit come from? Marx asked. The answer resides in determining how commodities, goods produced to be sold in the market, get their prices. Marx used the labor theory of value, taken from Smith and Ricardo, to explain the nature of prices in terms of the labor necessary to produce the commodity. He extended the theory by treating labor power as a commodity that received a price, in this case called the wage, in the same way as other commodities. It is important to note here that human beings can produce under most circumstances more than they need to survive; they can produce a surplus. According to Marx's analysis, the wage (the price of labor power as a commodity) is determined by the value of what is necessary to keep the worker alive and able to work from day to day. The wage does not reflect the value of what the worker is able to produce, which includes both what is necessary and the surplus. Since in virtue of purchasing the worker's labor power and putting it to use as he wishes, the capitalist owns the entire product produced. The capitalist, that is, gets both the value of what is necessary for the worker to have in order to live and the surplus. The capitalist returns to the worker in the form of a wage, however, only the necessary value. He keeps the surplus, and it is this surplus that forms the basis of profit.

Marx noted that, according to the dominant values of capitalism, this exchange between capitalist and proletarian was neither unfair nor coercive. It is as fair and free as any other market exchange. Understanding morality as he did largely in its ideological function, Marx disdained moral critique and did not consider it important to morally condemn the exchange. What was important was to realize that through the process of exploitation, the worker produced, on the one hand, the wealth, privilege and power of the ruling class and, on the other, his own subordination, alienation and misery.

This analysis of the wage and profit is, one might say, Marx's microeconomics with a philosophical intent. His macroeconomic theory attempted to show how capitalism would, with increasing frequency, fall into various crises as the capitalists competing within the essentially anarchistic market struggled to maintain their profit. As this process continued, the misery of the workers would only increase as well. As the proletariat struggled against worsening misery, their political consciousness would be awakened by the ideologues of their class perspective, political activists and theorists like Marx and Engels. The dual movements, of the capitalists struggling to keep the system going and the workers struggling with increased understanding to overcome it, would eventually culminate in a revolution, ending capitalism and instituting a socialist society. In accordance with the general theory of historical materialism, a successful revolution would happen at or after the point when capitalism was no longer the mode of production best suited to allow optimal use and further development of the forces of production. At that point, socialism would be the best mode.

The dialectical nature of historical materialism is illustrated in the internal dynamics of capitalism and how they are claimed to lead to the overcoming of capitalism. As Marx used the concept, appropriated from Hegel, a theory is dialectical insofar as it reflects and captures a dialectical process in the world. Dialectical processes, typically organic processes, unfold according to a logic of internal development until the present stage of the object or being is fully realized, at which point, again according to the internal logic of development of the object or being, a new stage emerges from the crises and failures of the previous stage. The conditions for the appearance of a successor stage develop in and as a result of the internal developments of the previous stage. Thus the developing nature and struggles of capitalism give rise to a unified and self-conscious proletariat able to forge a new mode of production in its class interests, which happen to be, according to Marx, universal interests.

COMMUNISM

Marx wrote very little about the nature of the mode of production he predicted would displace capitalism. It is clear, though, that he thought human emancipation would be fully realized only in communism, the second stage of postcapitalist society. The first stage following the socialist revolution, referred to at times as socialism, would be dominated by the proletariat—hence the well known phrase, "the dictatorship of the proletariat." Socialism would eliminate the private ownership of the means of production and the exploitation that accompanies private ownership. Technological progress would promote the accelerated development of the forces of production. At some future point, a level of productive forces would be attained that allowed humans to transcend scarcity and enter "the realm of abundance." Abun-

dance refers to a condition in which all can satisfy their needs without depriving others of the satisfaction of needs and without having to spend the greater part of their time in undesirable, unfulfilling labor.

At this stage of human development, communism, all would be free to pursue truly human and creative activities that allowed each individual to fully realize himself or herself. Because all people would have equal access to the means of production, communism would be a classless society. Alienation and exploitation would be abolished. With conflicts over the distribution and fruits of labor eliminated or at least minimized, the primary source of social conflicts would likewise be eliminated, and there would be no need for state authority or for the distorting effects of ideology. There would be no further struggles of the sort that propelled the dialectic of history. Having provided the conditions for full human emancipation, communism would continue to allow optimal development of the forces of production. Hence, no mode of production beyond communism would be necessary or conceivable. Human life as a collective enterprise would gain a self-transparency that would allow humans for the first time to create with knowledge and intention their social fate. In this sense, Marx held that communism would be the end of history, or better perhaps, the beginning of truly human history.

See also Cosmopolitanism; Marxist Philosophy; Postcolonialism; Republicanism.

Bibliography

Avineri, Shlomo. *The Social and Political Thought of Karl Marx.* Cambridge, U.K.: Cambridge University Press, 1968.

Ball, T. and J. Farr, eds. *After Marx.* Cambridge, U.K.: Cambridge University Press, 1984.

Berlin, Sir Isaiah. *Karl Marx: His Life and Environment.* 4th ed. Oxford: Oxford University Press, 1978.

Brundey, Daniel. *Marx's Attempt to Leave Philosophy.* Cambridge, MA: Harvard University Press, 1998.

Buchanan, Allen. *Marx and Justice.* Totowa: Rowman and Littlefield, 1982.

Callinicos, Alex, ed. *Marxist Theory.* Oxford: Oxford University Press, 1989.

Callinicos, Alex. *The Revolutionary Ideas of Karl Marx.* London: Bookmarks, 1983.

Carver, Terrell, ed. *The Cambridge Companion to Marx.* Cambridge, U.K.: Cambridge University Press, 1991.

Carver, Terrell. *Marx's Social Theory.* Oxford: Oxford University Press, 1982.

Cohen, G. A. *History, Labour and Freedom: Themes from Marx.* Oxford: Clarendon Press, 1988.

Cohen, G. A. *Karl Marx's Theory of History: A Defence.* Princeton, NJ: Princeton University Press, 1978.

Cohen, M., T. Nagel, and T. Scanlon, eds. *Marx, Justice and History*. Princeton, NJ: Princeton University Press, 1981.

Draper, Hal. *Karl Marx's Theory of Revolution*. 2 vols. New York: Monthly Review Press, 1977–1978.

Elster, Jon. *Making Sense of Marx*. Cambridge, U.K.: Cambridge University Press, 1985.

Geras, Norman. *Marx and Human Nature*. London: New Left Books, 1983.

Giddens, Anthony. *A Contemporary Critique of Historical Materialism*. Berkeley: University of California Press, 1981.

Kolakowski, Leszek. *Main Currents of Marxism*. 3 vols. Oxford: Oxford University Press, 1978.

Little, Daniel. *The Scientific Marx*. Minneapolis: University of Minneapolis Press, 1986.

Lukes, Steven. *Marxism and Morality*. Oxford: Clarendon Press, 1984.

Marx, Karl. *Capital*. Vol. 1. Translated by Ben Fowkes. Pelican Marx Library. New York: Random House, 1977.

Marx, Karl. *Capital*. Vol. 2. Translated by David Fernbach. Pelican Marx Library. New York: Random House, 1981.

Marx, Karl. *Capital*. Vol. 3. Translated by David Fernbach. Pelican Marx Library. New York: Random House, 1981.

Marx, Karl. *Grundrisse: Foundations of the Critique of Political Economy*. Translated by Martin Nicolaus. Harmondsworth: Penguin Books, 1974.

Marx, Karl. *Marx Engels Collected Works*. New York: International Publishers, 1975–.

Marx, Karl. *Writings of the Young Marx on Philosophy and Society*. Edited and translated by Loyd D. Easton and Kurt H. Guddat. Garden City: Doubleday Anchor Books, 1967.

McLellan, David. *Karl Marx: His Life and Thought*. New York: Harper & Row, 1973.

Miller, Richard. *Analyzing Marx: Morality, Power and History*. Princeton, NJ: Princeton University Press, 1984.

Nielsen, Kai. *Marxism and the Moral Point of View*. Boulder, CO: Westview Press, 1989.

Peffer, R. G. *Marxism, Morality, and Social Justice*. Princeton, NJ: Princeton University Press, 1990.

Roemer, John, ed. *Analytical Marxism*. Cambridge, U.K.: Cambridge University Press, 1986.

Schmidt, Alfred. *The Concept of Nature in Marx*. London: New Left Books, 1971.

Schmitt, Richard. *Alienation and Freedom*. Boulder, CO: Westview Press, 2002.

Wheen, Francis. *Karl Marx*. London: Fourth Estate, 1999.

Wolff, Jonathan. *Why Read Marx Today?* Oxford: Oxford University Press, 2002.

Wood, Allen W. *Karl Marx*. 2nd ed. New York and London: Routledge, 2004.

Wright, Eric Olin, Andrew Levine and Elliot Sober, *Reconstructing Marxism: Essays on Explanation and the Theory of History*. London: Verso, 1992.

Lawrence H. Simon (2005)

MARXISM

Marxist theories, insofar as they are of philosophical interest, are discussed in detail in the entries *Dialectical Materialism*; *Historical Materialism;* and *Marxist Philosophy*. Various Marxist ideas are also discussed in the articles *Alienation*; *Communism*; *Dialectic*; *Ideology*; and *Socialism*. See "Marxism" in the index for thinkers who are usually regarded as Marxists.

MARXIST PHILOSOPHY

Marxist philosophy is the aggregation of philosophical ideas developed from various aspects of Karl Marx's social theory by later thinkers. Marx did not intend to write a philosophy and would have regarded "Marxist philosophy" as a contradiction in terms. He considered his work to be scientific, historical, and sociological, as opposed to "philosophical" divagations on social affairs, which he rejected as class-biased ideology. Moreover, he held that his social theory showed that philosophy was about to end. Philosophy, he said, was a symptom of social malaise and would disappear when revolution put society on a healthier foundation. The young Marx thought that this would happen because revolution would "realize" philosophy, would give solid reality to the ideal phantoms of reason, justice, and liberty that philosophers in sick societies consoled themselves with. The older Marx thought that revolution would destroy philosophy, would simply make it unnecessary, by bringing men back to the study of "the real world." Study of that world is to philosophy "what sexual love is to onanism." In either case Marx never varied in the opinion that the reign of philosophy over men's minds was drawing to a close. Thus, he naturally would not have contributed to its survival by writing a "Marxist philosophy."

MARXISM AND TRADITIONAL PHILOSOPHIES

Within a few years of Marx's death, however, there were attempts to turn Marxism into philosophy. These have continued ever since and, indeed, have gathered force since the discovery of Marx's earliest writings. There are two explanations for this posthumous transformation. First, there is the familiar paradox that efforts to get rid of philosophy by argument are themselves philosophical. Thus, Marx's antiphilosophy and the theory of historical materialism on which it is based blossomed into a veritable philosophical doctrine, to which Georg Lukács gave consummate form. Second, after the empirical social sciences had taken from Marx's work all that was useful to them (and it was a great deal), there remained much dross—disproven prophecy, hasty generalization, and plain error. Instead of being discarded, as the errors and absurdities of Isaac Newton and Louis Pasteur were discarded in the physical and biological sciences, this non-empirical material was kept alive by a social movement committed to preserving intact the whole of Marx's legacy. It has been called Marxist philosophy.

Because Marxism is not explicitly a philosophy, those who have treated it philosophically have largely sought to find the philosophy to which it "corresponds," from which it "derives," or which it "implies." Solutions have been extremely varied and incompatible. Enrico Ferri put Marxism into the Spencerian system, and Karl Kautsky connected it with Darwinism. Eduard Bernstein and Max Adler found its philosophical complement in Immanuel Kant, and "Back to Kant!" became the slogan of the revisionists. Georgii Valentinovich Plekhanov noted Marx's Hegelian origins but preferred to ally Marxism with materialism, notably that of Ludwig Feuerbach. This opinion was widely accepted by Marxian political activists but was ardently combated by intellectuals. Otto Bauer said that Marxism could not be annexed by materialism because it was compatible with any philosophical doctrine, "including Thomism." Henri de Man essayed a combination of Marx and Freud, whereas the Marburg school of neo-Kantians made a synthesis of Kant's ethics and Marx's socialism. The Russians whom V. I. Lenin attacked in *Materialism and Empirio-Criticism* had married Marxism to the positivism of Ernst Mach and Richard Avenarius. Lenin himself followed Plekhanov in putting Marxism in the tradition of mechanist materialism, later adding a dialectical theory of development to distinguish it from classic materialism. Georges Sorel, René Berthelot, and various Italian writers found the extension of Marxism in pragmatism, and this view became influential in the United States through the writings of Sidney Hook. Antonio Gramsci and Giovanni Gentile, in their different ways, reacted against the "materialist debasement" of Marxism by coupling it with Italian neoidealism. The search for new philosophic settings for Marxism, such as existentialism, continues and is necessarily inconclusive.

The variety of opinions confirms that there is no Marxist philosophy. Nevertheless, some efforts to incorporate Marxism into philosophy are less successful than others, for Marxism is not philosophically neutral even if it does fail to define its position in respect to the major philosophical traditions. Least successful are alliances of Marxism with materialism, from Baron d'Holbach to L. Büchner, or with positivism, whether Mach's or Herbert Spencer's. The tendency of decades of criticism has been to show that the idealist content of Marx's thought is too dominant to allow those confusions. Conversely, the alliance that has proven most fruitful and that has grown in authority over the years is that between Marxism and the Hegelian dialectic. Though Antonio Labriola had noted this, it was ignored for more than a generation until Lukács insisted that Marx belonged in the Hegelian tradition. In this Lukács has been followed by Karl Mannheim, Herbert Marcuse, Lucien Goldmann, Jean-Paul Sartre, and Maurice Merleau-Ponty. Everywhere, Marxism's principal philosophical consequence has been to stimulate the study of G. W. F. Hegel. Otherwise, it has had singularly little effect on philosophy, even on pragmatism, with which it has evident affinities.

ORTHODOX MARXISM

The distinction between a materialist and an idealist reading of Marx does not exactly coincide with the division between the orthodoxy of the Communist parties and the independent criticism of the so-called Western Marxists, but the history of the subject must be told in terms of the latter division. The orthodox tradition begins with Friedrich Engels, not with Marx. It uses two principal texts, Engels's *Anti-Dühring* and Lenin's *Materialism and Empirio-Criticism*. The name of Marx is very seldom mentioned in these discussions, for Marx never explicitly stated the doctrines set out by Engels, taken over and interpreted by Lenin, and then dogmatically systematized by Joseph Stalin. He sometimes appeared to hold opinions resembling those they expressed—for example, the representationist theory of knowledge—yet his early manuscripts seem far removed in spirit from the materialism of these works. That is why the early works, which are the basis of most Marxist philosophy in the West, were dismissed by Soviet writers as juvenile hangovers from Hegelianism that the mature Marx disowned.

EPISTEMOLOGY. Orthodox Marxist philosophy has developed very little over the years, being accepted as much by Rosa Luxemburg as by Lenin, as much by Leon Trotsky as by Stalin, as much by Mao Zedong as by Nikita Khrushchev. Its epistemology is naive representationism: The "concepts in our heads" are images, reflections, or copies of "real things." Objections to that view have been familiar since Bishop Berkeley, but they are held by orthodox Marxists to be answered by a reference to practice. We can compare mental images and the things they copy by noting our success or failure in manipulating those things. This manipulation is primarily economic activity or is affected by it, so it must differ for each technological age and each class. There is therefore no non-partisan science. There is a contradiction here, for it is contended that the mind has exact copies of reality and yet its knowledge is historically relative. This is admitted but is circumvented by asserting that absolute knowledge is the historical goal but relative knowledge is the present plight.

METAPHYSICS. In metaphysics the orthodox doctrine distinguishes itself from classic materialism by insisting on dialectic process, as opposed to mechanism, in the development of things. Matter is subject to laws that are causal and determinist but not mechanist. It evolves toward the better and more complex, and it does so in a series of revolutionary jumps, in which accumulations of quantitative difference produce sudden qualitative changes after a period of tension and conflict. Matter is the unique reality. Chance does not exist, and there is no breach in this absolute monism. Mind is an epiphenomenon producing, in consciousness, reflections of matter. Matter does not determine mind directly, as the medical materialists said, but indirectly, by way of society. Society, too, develops dialectically, in revolutionary jumps that resolve its recurrent self-contradictions or internal conflicts. Human liberty consists in awareness of the necessity of social process.

RELIGION, ETHICS, AND AESTHETICS. Religion is doomed to disappear, being a symptom of unjust and self-negating social conditions. Ethics and aesthetics evolve as society changes, for there are no eternal, nonhistorical laws in either. Beauty is objective but appreciation is relative to class, so art is implicated in the class struggle.

In ethics the situation is more complex. At first the exclusion of eternal, suprahistorical laws was held to warrant amoralism, ethical indifference, or at least some experimentation in new ways of living. Soviet authorities found that attitude socially inconvenient, and eventually Stalin formally condemned all applications of historical relativism that suggested that the new polity could have a new ethics (or a special new logic). Since then the position has been that Marxist philosophy substantially accepts the ethical ideals preached in other contemporary societies but adds that only a communist nation can escape hypocrisy by living up to those ideals, by practicing what it preaches. Thus, not only is ethical innovation discouraged in communist countries, but ethical criticism in noncommunist countries—for instance, by existentialists—is strongly deplored as a diversion from the work of creating the social conditions for the application of the uncriticized ethical code common to all modern societies.

WESTERN MARXISM

The Western Marxists, whose first generation, in the 1920s, comprised Lukács, Karl Korsch, Bela Fogarasi, and Josef Revai, rejected the representationist theory of knowledge, but their quarrel with orthodoxy centered on the dialectic. On this issue the orthodox followed Engels, the Westerners the young Hegelian Marx.

Engels had posited the triadic dialectic of thesis, antithesis, and synthesis as an eternal law of cosmic development, applying as much to nature as to mind and society. Everywhere, one would find constant progress from lower to higher by way of objective tensions. The tensions are caused when something engenders its own opposite or negation and are resolved when the opposites merge in a synthesis (the negation of the negation). Engels's immediate successors, whether social democrats, revisionists, Austro-Marxists, or independent students such as Benedetto Croce and Sorel, could make nothing of these ideas and simply ignored the dialectic. At first Lenin did the same, in 1894 dismissing it as a "vestige of Hegelianism." However, he later adopted Engels's dialectic as the badge that distinguished Marxist materialism from classic or vulgar materialism. This dialectic embellishment of materialism has remained a point of honor with subsequent Marxist philosophers even when the dialectic is seldom applied or evoked. The law of the negation of the negation has found little use, and the examples of it offered by Engels, August Thalheimer, and Paul Sandor have been generally rejected by philosophers and scientists. Stalin formally declared that the other law of dialectic, the law of the transformation of quantity into quality, did not have universal scope but applied only to class-divided societies. With the two laws in effect discarded, orthodox Marxist materialism no longer has a characteristic theory of development. There remains only the law of the union of opposites, which serves to reconcile contradictions (and to justify inconsistencies).

The role of the dialectic in Western Marxism is very different. It does not operate in physical nature and is not a law at all. It concerns the relation between mind and social history. That relation comes to the fore because of an evident difficulty encountered by the historical relativism of Marx. If all knowledge is partial, provisional, relative, class-biased, and historically limited, then is this not true of Marxism itself? The answer of Engels and Lenin was that everything was relative except a small number of absolutely true propositions that included logic and Marxist theory. Seeing the impossibility of maintaining this dualism of relative and absolute knowledge, Lukács abandoned absolute (or unconditionally true) knowledge and accepted the relative and partial character of all knowledge. The relation between our knowledge and all other worldviews that constitute cultural history is a dialectical one, meaning that none is completely true or completely false. More generally, all relations between subject and history are dialectical in the sense of being ambiguous, reciprocal relations that leave room for "contrary and inseparable truths." This is true because, on the one hand, the subject is a social and historical product and, on the other hand, because historical forces are alienated spirit, reified personality. There is conflict and tension between the two terms of that relation, and they will be removed by revolution, which will effect the synthesis of the two and will represent the triumph of the human spirit over the alienation or reification of its products. In this view the crux of historical materialism is the relation between mind and history, the dialectic relation between the personal subject and the apparently impersonal, material forces of society. In showing that those forces are really alienated personality, the theory denounces the objectification of spirit in inhuman institutions. It foresees the victory of spirit over that dehumanization.

Marxist historical materialism, said Lukács, thus criticizes itself according to its own principles. It comes to hold itself as provisional, as, at most, a progress toward a truth that is yet to be attained. Because this relativization seemed to lower Marxism from the status of a dogma to that of one ideology among others, it was no doubt the main reason for the condemnation of Western Marxist philosophy by the orthodox. Yet even the relativism of Lukács (and also of Karl Mannheim) still claims to have dogmatic knowledge of the whole of history, which is the total process into which all partial ideologies fit dialectically and which they all reflect more or less faithfully. With this notion of totality the relativists have brought back the Absolute that they first threw out in favor of the historically relative.

COMMON FEATURES

Because of a dualism in Marx's own thinking, which he never cared to resolve, Marxist philosophy has thus divided into two broad streams. On the one side, there is emphasis on the determinist, evolutionist, materialist, and sociological themes. On the other side, there is the idealist strain that looks forward to the deliverance of humanity from economic determinism. This idealist strain, stressing the primacy of present human activity over the solidified, alienated products of past human activity, has aptly been called titanism by Nikolai Berdyaev. It is a powerful factor in all modern Marxist thought—not only in Western Marxism, where it is explicit, but also in orthodox Soviet Marxism. After a profession of materialist faith, orthodox Marxism introduces the idealist element by attributing to matter a readiness to cooperate with progressive causes. (In other contexts such an attribution of spiritual purposes to matter is called magic.)

The two varieties of Marxist philosophy retain other common features. Both abandon the distinction between truth and falsity in favor of a relativist notion that sees truth as a historical goal and knowledge as never more than progress toward absolute truth. This relativist concept appears in all philosophical developments of Marxism, from Engels to Gramsci and Lukács. Moreover, both sorts of Marxist philosophy cling to the idea of an ultimate reality. Though this is called matter in one case and history in the other, the difference is not great wherever matter has tacitly been endowed with a purposefulness and spirituality (by evolving dialectically) that make it resemble history. Marxism started with the recognition of all things as events or processes that interact, and it emphasized, in the theory of historical materialism, some sorts of interaction that had been overlooked. In its philosophical extensions it has gone on from there to the concept of a moving totality of things to which single things are relative and within which single things have ambiguous, dialectical relations with one another. This view is as familiar to philosophers as the representationist theory of knowledge that Lenin revived and has been as thoroughly criticized. For this reason, among others, Marxist philosophy has seldom secured consideration or academic influence outside of countries where it is politically privileged.

See also Aesthetics, History of; Avenarius, Richard; Berkeley, George; Büchner, Ludwig; Darwinism; Engels, Friedrich; Existentialism; Feuerbach, Ludwig Andreas; Freud, Sigmund; Gentile, Giovanni; Gramsci, Antonio; Hegel, Georg Wilhelm Friedrich; Hegelianism; Holbach, Paul-Henri Thiry, Baron d'; Kant, Immanuel; Kautsky, Karl; Labriola, Antonio; Lenin, Vladimir Il'ich; Lukács, Georg; Mach, Ernst; Mannheim, Karl; Marx, Karl; Materialism; Merleau-Ponty, Maurice; Metaphysics; Neo-Kantianism; Newton, Isaac; Plekhanov,

Georgii Valentinovich; Positivism; Religion; Sartre, Jean-Paul; Sorel, Georges; Thomism.

Bibliography

WORKS BY MARX AND ENGELS

Engels, Friedrich. *Dialektik der Natur.* Berlin, 1927. Translated by Clemens Dutt as *Dialectics of Nature.* New York: International Publishers, 1940. This work was first written in 1872–1873.

Engels, Friedrich. *Herr Eugen Dührings Umwälzung der Wissenschaft.* Leipzig, 1878. Translated by E. Burns as *Herr Eugen Dühring's Revolution in Science.* London, 1935. The *AntiDühring.*

Engels, Friedrich. *Herr Eugen Dühring's der klassischen deutschen Philosophic.* Stuttgart, 1888. Translated as *Ludwig Feuerbach and the Outcome of Classical German Philosophy.* New York: International Publishers, 1934.

Marx, Karl. *Oekonomische-philosophische Ausgabe.* Frankfurt, 1932. Translated by Martin Milligan as *Economic and Philosophical Manuscripts of 1844.* Moscow and London, 1959.

Marx, Karl, and Friedrich Engels. *Die deutsche Ideologic.* Berlin, 1932. Translated anonymously as *The German Ideology.* Edited by S. Ryazanskaya. Moscow, 1964.

MARXIST WRITINGS

Gramsci, Antonio. *Il materialismo storico e la filosofia di Benedetto Croce.* Turin: Einaudi, 1940.

Lenin, N. *Materializm i Empirio-Krititsizm.* Moscow, 1908. Translated by David Kvitko and Sidney Hook as *Materialism and Empirio-Criticism.* New York, 1927.

Lukács, Georg. *Geschichte und Klassenbewusstsein.* Berlin: Malik, 1923. Translated as *Histoire et conscience de classe.* Paris, 1960.

Mannheim, Karl. *Ideologie und Utopie.* Bonn: Cohen, 1929. Translated by Louis Wirth and Edward A. Shils as *Ideology and Utopia.* London: Routledge, 1936.

Mao Zedong. *On Contradiction.* New York: International Publishers, 1953.

Mao Zedong. *On Practice.* New York, 1953.

Mao Zedong. *Selected Works,* 4 vols. New York: International Publishers, 1954–1956.

Plekhanov, Georgi. *Izbranniye Filosofskie Proizvedenia v Piati Tomakh.* Moscow, n.d. Translated as *Selected Philosophical Works.* London, 1961.

Plekhanov, Georgi. *Osnovnie Voprosi Marksizma.* 1910. Translated by Eden and Cedar Paul as *Fundamental Problems of Marxism.* London: M. Lawrence, 1929.

Stalin. *Concerning Marxism and Linguistics.* Moscow, 1950.

Stalin. *Leninism, Selected Writings.* New York, 1938. Contains the essay "Dialectical and Historical Materialism."

WORKS ON MARXISM

Berdyaev, Nikolai. *The Origin of Russian Communism.* Translated by R. French. London: Centenary Press, 1937. This work has never been published in Russian.

Bocheński, I. M. *Der sowjetrussische dialektische Materialismus (Diamat).* Bern and Munich, 1950. Translated by Nicholas Solluhub as *Dialectical Materialism.* Dordrecht, Netherlands, 1963.

Carew Hunt, R. N. *Marxism Past and Present.* New York: Macmillan, 1954.

Fetscher, I. *Der Marxismus: Seine Geschichte in Dokumenten, Vol. I, Philosophic, Ideologic.* Munich: R. Piper, 1963.

Hook, Sidney. *From Hegel to Marx.* London, 1936.

Hook, Sidney. *Towards the Understanding of Karl Marx.* New York: John Day, 1933.

Korsch, Karl. *Marxismus und Philosophie.* Leipzig, 1923; 2nd ed., 1930.

Leningrad Institute of Philosophy. *Textbook of Marxist Philosophy.* Translated by A. Moseley. London, 1937.

Lichtheim, George. *Marxism: An Historical and Critical Study.* London, 1961.

Marcuse, Herbert. *Soviet Marxism: A Critical Analysis.* New York: Columbia University Press, 1958.

Merleau-Ponty, Maurice. *Les aventures de la dialectique.* Paris: Gallimard, 1955.

Vranicki, P. *Historija marksizma.* Zagreb, 1961.

Wetter, Gustav. *Der dialektische Materialismus.* Vienna, 1952. Translated by Peter Heath as *Dialectical Materialism: A Historical and Systematic Survey of Philosophy in the Soviet Union.* New York: Praeger, 1958.

Neil McInnes (1967)

MARXIST PHILOSOPHY [ADDENDUM]

Post–World War II Marxist theory has been decisively shaped by historical changes: the growing irrelevance of orthodox Marxist political movements and the moral and economic decline (and eventual collapse) of the Soviet empire; the emergence of politically radical social movements based in nationalism, gender, and race rather than economic class; changes in the world capitalist economy including the emergence of globalization; and increasing environmental degradation. These developments are reflected in divergent formulations of historical materialism; the adaptation and transformation of Marxism by the new social movements and by seemingly culturally radical postmodern theories; neo-Marxist theories of contemporary capitalism; the cross-fertilization of religion and Marxism in Liberation Theology and its variants; and "eco-Marxism."

Western Marxists such as Herbert Marcuse, the early Jürgen Habermas, and Jean-Paul Sartre resisted the dogmatic and positivist versions of historical materialism found in Marx and in the Second and Third Internationals. These writers denied that a theoretical analysis of capitalist society could provide laws of historical development. Rather, they believed that, at best, economic theory could describe certain continuing contradictions in the social order, the resolutions of which necessarily depended on the self-awareness and political organization of contending social groups. Given the rise of fascism out of the depression and the triumph of capitalist hegemony over the industrial working classes after World War II, political revolution could no longer be thought of as a direct consequence of predictable economic collapse. It was necessary to investigate social forces that seemed to make the working class not only politically passive but also psychically attached to bourgeois authority.

These forces included not just conscious beliefs, but unconscious personality structures; not just the experience of work, but the experiences of sexuality and family life as well. Consequently, Marxist theory had to encompass psychology and cultural theory as well as economics and politics. It was further claimed that any assimilation of Marxism into a natural-science model was itself an element in political totalitarianism. Habermas (1970) developed this position into a critique of "science and technology as ideology." When we identify social theory with natural science, he argued, we fail to distinguish between science's goal of controlling nature and social theory's goal of understanding and liberating human beings. As a result we end up treating people like things.

French Marxist Louis Althusser posed an influential counterview in 1969 arguing that, while different aspects of society did possess a "relative autonomy" from the economy, it was class structure that always determined historical outcomes "in the last instance." Claiming to present the scientific view of Marxism, and in a move that anticipated later developments of postmodern thought, Althusser asserted that subjectivity was an effect of social structures and not a primary constituent of them.

There have been many subsequent attempts to connect postmodernism and Marxism, including debates about the validity of the former's criticism of totalizing theories and grand historical narratives, about the compatibility of the two perspectives, and about the claim that postmodernism is itself simply "the cultural logic of late capitalism" (Jameson 1991).

Anglo-American philosophy has seen a sophisticated reformulation of some of Marx's original claims about the social primacy of technological development. Analytical Marxist G. A. Cohen developed a "functional" analysis in which a universal human drive to develop forces of production conditioned social relations to change to support such development. Other analytic Marxist philosophers attempted to articulate a distinct moral perspective in Marx to ground claims about the immorality of capitalist exploitation and to critique the individualism of the

dominant liberal paradigms of writers such as John Rawls. This discussion has paralleled a rethinking of Marx's relationship to Georg Wilhelm Friedrich Hegel, and of the place of the concept of dialectic in Marxist philosophical and economic theory.

Because of the rise of radical social movements of racial minorities and women, Marxist theory was challenged to integrate accounts of patriarchy and racism with its traditional focus on class exploitation and technological development. Theorists argued that racism and sexism were not reducible to or simple consequences of class power. They were embedded in European culture and conferred certain limited privileges on the white and/or male working class itself. Rather than depending solely on the concept of economic exploitation, or on the traditional Marxist notion that the liberation of the working class would liberate all other subject groups, socialist or Marxist-feminist theorists and black liberationists analyzed the mutually supportive, conflicting, and at times disparate elements of class, racial, and gender domination.

From the 1960s to the 1990s the structural evolution of capitalism led to new versions of Marxist economic and sociological theory. Baran and Sweezy's analysis (1966) revealed how dominant sectors of the economy had become controlled by a small number of firms and that the classic price competition and overproduction oscillations of the nineteenth and early twentieth centuries had consequently given way to stagnation as a result of an unutilizable surplus. Other theorists (e.g., Wallerstein 1974–1980, furthered by Arrighi 1994) redefined capitalism as a capitalist "world-system" constituted by exploitative trade relations between a developed Euro-American core and an underdeveloped periphery.

Many writers claimed that the increased role of the state in the national economy mitigated the business cycle and redirected class struggles to competition over state resources. James O'Connor (1973) foresaw that contradictions between state support of capitalist accumulation and democratic legitimation would eventually cause a "fiscal crisis of the state." Habermas (1975), writing under the shadow of the political uprisings of the 1960s and 1970s, described conflict between ideals of democracy and equality and state support of capitalist accumulation as causing a "legitimation crisis."

Responding to the continued dominance of capitalism and the failure of almost all state-controlled communism, theorists of socialism have also raised the possibility of alternative forms of a socialist economy, especially a socialism in which consumer demand is allocated by markets but is not at the same time controlled by private ownership of the forces of production. For a number of writers, the key issue is no longer the traditional idea of "socialization of the means of production," which to some extent left open the question of the structure of that socialization, but rather that of "economic democracy," which identifies the structure of socialization with certain fundamental political, as well as economic, changes (Schweickart 2002).

One defining aspect of contemporary society is the worsening environmental crisis, which Marxist theoreticians have responded to not only by using familiar Marxist concepts to explain it, but by positing, as did O'Connor in 1988, an "eco-Marxist" analysis in which capitalist destruction of the environment becomes the "Second Contradiction of Capital." In this view capitalism's tendency to destroy its own physical basis of production (through ecological devastation) now coexists with the resistance it generates from the labor force as a major source of its own undoing. While some authors, such as Andrew McLaughlin (1993) accuse Marxism of an industrialism that is a major source our environmental problems, Jonathan Hughes (2000) and others argue that Marxism is crucial to understanding how to solve them.

On a much different front, several Latin American theorists—inspired by the renewed emphasis on social justice of Vatican II (1964–1965), the spread of communist movements, and the appalling degree of poverty and repression surrounding them—created what they called "liberation theology" (Gutiérrez 1988). This was an attempt to join Christian social ethics (most importantly the "preferential option for the poor") with Marxist social theory. Essential to liberation theology was the belief that "the poor" could only enter history as fully human beings if a fundamental social transformation—virtually a social revolution (preferably without violence)—were to occur. While the development of liberation theology would certainly have surprised Marx—and eventually prompted stiff resistance from the church hierarchy—it provided a model for the cross-fertilization of politically left ideas with religious moral concerns. The use of a quasi-Marxist vocabulary was found in Martin Luther King, who both criticized imperialism and called for a "beloved community," and in the appearance of politically radical forms of theology focusing on women, race, gay and lesbian issues, poverty and war (see Gottlieb 2003). In the 1990s theologians' and institutionalized religion's dramatically sharpening response to the environmental crisis led to positions increasingly resonant with Marxism.

Frequently their criticisms of the market, capitalism, and the global economy would not be out of place in a professedly Marxist journal or socialist party. Conversely, some (e.g., Gottlieb 2002) have argued that a sustained engagement with religious values of nonviolence, universal respect, self-examination, and humility would help compensate for widely shared limitations found in politically radical, including Marxist, perspectives.

Since the last decade of the twentieth century, all of these discussions have been shaped by globalization—an economic, social, and cultural phenomenon the very definition of which is the subject of intense debate. Early on, both the monopoly capital and the world-system models were challenged by the "global capitalism" perspective (Ross and Trachte 1990), which diagnosed an international economy dominated by multinational firms, intranational competition rather than a dominant Euro-American core, and increased power for capitalists as international mobility allows them to evade local labor movements, governments, and environmental regulations. In the twenty-first century, different accounts within a broadly Marxist paradigm include Hardt and Negri's analysis (2001) of globalization as a new form of imperialism or "empire" and Manuel Castells's discussion of globalization as a "network society." For Castells traditional forms of national sovereignty have become increasingly less relevant, and the separation of decisive social power from even remotely local control causes a dramatic resurgence in the importance of ascribed social identities, especially fundamentalist religion. The importance of globalizing economic structures has also led to increased interest in multidimensional global political resistance movements, which typically involve the working class, but also include peasants, community organizations, environmentalists, students, and progressive middle class. The possibility of an alternative to globalization, and the possible forms of that alternative, are perhaps the most critical questions for contemporary Marxism.

Despite the enormous variety of Marxist and Marxist-related writings since the middle of the twentieth century, there are significant areas that remain relatively unexplored. These include the relation of disability to other forms of social marginalization; sustained and honest examination of the subjective or psychological sources of leftist political failures (for example, how the character structure or ethical orientation of activists has caused destructive intragroup conflict and unnecessary antagonism of social groups outside the left); and a willingness to question the Marxist premise that human beings are essentially rational.

In sum, Marxism continues to evolve and mutate, with many of its basic concepts (the critique of ideology, the analysis of capitalism) still essential to socially critical perspectives such as postmodernism and feminism. If it is now virtually impossible to delineate any simple Marxist orthodoxy, or to say where Marxism ends and other left perspectives begin, one can (as in other intellectual traditions) trace the historical roots of philosophical perspective and revolutionary social intent from Marx, through enormous historical change, to the Marxisms of the present.

See also Civil Disobedience; Communism; Cosmopolitanism; Fascism; Feminist Social and Political Philosophy; Habermas, Jürgen; Historical Materialism; Liberation Theology; Marx, Karl; Modernism and Postmodernism; Multiculturalsim; Postcolonialism; Racism; Rawls, John; Republicanism; Sartre, Jean-Paul; Socialism.

Bibliography

Althusser, Louis. *For Marx.* Translated by Ben Brewster. New York: Random House, 1969.

Arrighi Giovanni. *The Long Twentieth Century: Money, Power, and the Origins of Our Times.* London: Verso Books, 1994.

Baran, Paul A., and Paul M. Sweezy. *Monopoly Capital.* New York: Monthly Review Press, 1966.

Buchanan, Allen E. *Marx and Justice: The Radical Critique of Liberalism.* Totowa, NJ: Rowman & Littlefield, 1984.

Castells, Manuel. *The Information Age.* 3 vols. Cambridge, MA: Blackwell Publishers, 1996–2001.

Cohen, G. A. *Karl Marx's Theory of History: A Defence.* Princeton, NJ: Princeton University Press, 1978.

Eisenstein, Z., ed. *Capitalist Patriarchy and the Case for Socialist Feminism.* New York: Monthly Review Press 1979.

Gottlieb, Roger. S. *Joining Hands: Politics and Religion Together for Social Change.* Cambridge, MA: Westview, 2002.

Gottlieb, Roger S., ed. *Liberating Faith: Religious Voices for Justice, Peace and Ecological Wisdom.* Lanham, MD: Rowman & Littlefield, 2003.

Gutiérrez, Gustavo. *A Theology of Liberation: History, Politics, and Salvation.* Rev. ed. Maryknoll, NY: Orbis Books, 1988.

Habermas, Jürgen. *Legitimation Crisis.* Translated by Thomas McCarthy. Boston: Beacon Press, 1975.

Habermas, Jürgen. *Towards a Rational Society.* Translated by Jeremy J. Shapiro. Boston: Beacon Press, 1970.

Hardt, Michael, and Antonio Negri. *Empire.* Cambridge, MA: Harvard University Press, 2000.

Harvey, David. *The Condition of Postmodernity: An Enquiry into the Origins of Cultural Change.* London: Blackwell Publishers, 1990.

Hughes, Jonathan. *Ecology and Historical Materialism.* New York: Cambridge University Press, 2000.

Jameson, Fredric. *Postmodernism, or the Cultural Logic of Late Capitalism.* Duke University Press, 1991.

Kuhn, Annette, and Ann Marie Wolpe, eds. *Feminism and Materialism: Women and Modes of Production.* London: Routledge and Kegan Paul, 1978.

Le Grand, Julian, and Saul Estrin, eds. *Market Socialism.* Oxford: Oxford University Press 1989.

Marcuse, Herbert. *Eros and Civilization: A Philosophical Inquiry into Freud.* New York: Vintage 1962.

Marcuse, Herbert. *One-Dimensional Man: Studies in the Ideology of Advanced Industrial Society.* Boston: Beacon 1964.

McLaughlin, Andrew. *Regarding Nature: Industrialism and Deep Ecology.* Albany: State University of New York Press, 1993.

O'Connor, James. "Capitalism, Nature, Socialism: A Theoretical Introduction." *Capitalism, Nature, Socialism* 1 (1988).

O'Connor, James. *The Fiscal Crisis of the State.* New York: St. Martins, 1973.

Ollman, Bertell. *Dialectical Investigations.* New York: Routledge, 1993.

Reich, Michael. *Racial Inequality: A Political-Economic Analysis.* Princeton, NJ: Princeton University Press 1981.

Ross, Robert J. S., and Kent C. Trachte. *Global Capitalism: The New Leviathan.* Albany: State University of New York Press, 1990.

Ryan Michael. *Marxism and Deconstruction: A Critical Articulation.* Baltimore, MD: Johns Hopkins University Press, 1982.

Sergent, Lydia, ed. *Women and Revolution.* Boston: South End Press 1981.

Sartre, Jean-Paul. *Critique of Dialectical Reason.* Translated by Alan Sheridan-Smith; edited by Jonathan Rée. London: New Left Books, 1976.

Schweickart, David. *After Capitalism.* Lanham, MD: Rowman & Littlefield, 2002.

Smith, Tony. *The Logic of Marx's Capital: Replies to Hegelian Criticisms.* Albany: State University of New York Press, 1990.

Wallerstein, Immanuel. *The Modern World-System.* 2 vols. New York: Academic Press 1974–1980.

Roger S. Gottlieb (1996, 2005)